The Structure of Political Geography

The *Structure* of *Political Geography*

Roger E. Kasperson
Julian V. Minghi
editors

Routledge
Taylor & Francis Group
LONDON AND NEW YORK

First published 1969 by Transaction Publishers

Published 2017 by Routledge
2 Park Square, Milton Park, Abingdon, Oxon OX14 4RN
711 Third Avenue, New York, NY 10017, USA

Routledge is an imprint of the Taylor & Francis Group, an informa business

Copyright © 1969 by Roger E. Kasperson and Julian V. Minghi.

All rights reserved. No part of this book may be reprinted or reproduced or utilised in any form or by any electronic, mechanical, or other means, now known or hereafter invented, including photocopying and recording, or in any information storage or retrieval system, without permission in writing from the publishers.

Notice:
Product or corporate names may be trademarks or registered trademarks, and are used only for identification and explanation without intent to infringe.

Library of Congress Catalog Number: 2011003509

Library of Congress Cataloging-in-Publication Data

The structure of political geography / Roger E. Kasperson and Julian V. Minghi, editors.
  p. cm.
ISBN 978-1-4128-1854-4
 1. Political geography. I. Kasperson, Roger E. II. Minghi, Julian V. (Julian Vincent), 1933-

JC319.K34 2011
320.1'2--dc22

2011003509

ISBN 13: 978-1-4128-1854-4 (pbk)

Contents

Preface   ix

Introduction   xi

Part I. Heritage

    Introduction   1

Heritage

    1. The Ideal State, *Aristotle*   13

    2. The Laws of the Spatial Growth of States, *Friedrich Ratzel*, translated by Ronald L. Bolin   17

    3. Earmarks of Political Geography, *Derwent S. Whittlesey*   29

    4. The Functional Approach in Political Geography, *Richard Hartshorne*   34

    5. A Unified Field Theory of Political Geography, *Stephen B. Jones*   50

    6. Studies in Political Geography, *Ad Hoc* Committee on Geography   57

    Annotated Bibliography   66

Part II. Structure

    Introduction   69

Territoriality and Hierarchy   89

    7. Rank and Territory, *Philip Wagner*   89

    8. Symmetry and Asymmetry as Elements of Federalism: A Theoretical Speculation, *Charles D. Tarlton*   94

Centrality and Nodes   99

    9. The Territorial Evolution of France, *Derwent S. Whittlesey*   99

    10. The City as a Center of Change: Western Europe and China, *Rhoads Murphey*   117

Contents

Boundaries and Frontiers 126

11. The Nature of Frontiers and Boundaries, *Ladis K. D. Kristof* 126
12. The Significance of the Frontier in American History, *Frederick Jackson Turner* 132
13. Boundary Studies in Political Geography, *Julian V. Minghi* 140

Global Structure 161

14. The Geographical Pivot of History, *Sir Halford J. Mackinder* 161
15. Heartland and Rimland, *Nicholas Spykman* 170
16. Geostrategic and Geopolitical Regions, *Saul B. Cohen* 178

Annotated Bibliography 187

PART III. Process

Introduction 195

Integration and Disintegration 211

17. The Growth of Nations: Some Recurrent Patterns of Political and Social Integration, *Karl W. Deutsch* 211
18. A Paradigm for the Study of Political Unification, *Amitai Etzioni* 221
19. Communications and Territorial Integration in East Africa: An Introduction to Transaction Flow Analysis, *Edward W. Soja* 231
20. Systems and the Disintegration of Empires, *Richard L. Merritt* 243

Transfer of Sovereignty 258

21. The Franco-Italian Boundary in the Alpes Maritimes, *J. W. House* 258
22. Independence and After, *Immanuel Wallerstein* 273

Growth and Development 281

23. Building the Newest Nations, *William J. Foltz* 281
24. Metropolitan Growth and Future Political Problems, *Anthony Downs* 286

Annotated Bibliography 293

PART IV. Behavior

Introduction 299

Territorial Behavior 319

25. The Noyau, *Robert Ardrey* 319
26. Space, Territory, and Human Movements, *David Stea* 323

Spatial Perception 328

27. Two Cognitive Maps:
    (a) A New Yorker's Idea of the United States of America 328
    (b) A Map of Derogatory Images 329
28. On the Chinese Perception of a World Order, *Norton S. Ginsburg* 330

29. National Images and International Systems,
    Kenneth Boulding 341

Decision Making 350

30. The West Indies Chooses a Capital, *David Lowenthal* 350

31. Toward a Geography of Urban Politics: Chicago, a Case Study,
    Roger E. Kasperson 366

Voting 376

32. Electoral Studies in Political Geography, *J. R. V. Prescott* 376

33. Impact of Negro Migration on the Electoral Geography of Flint, Michigan, 1932–1962: A Cartographic Analysis,
    Peirce F. Lewis 384

34. Discovering Voting Groups in the United Nations,
    Bruce Russett 407

Annotated Bibliography 419

PART V. Environment

Introduction 423

Environmental Impress upon Politics 436

35. The Challenge of the Environment, *Arnold J. Toynbee* 436

36. The Hydraulic Civilizations, *Karl A. Wittfogel* 442

Political Impress upon the Environment 450

37. The Impress of Effective Central Authority upon the Landscape,
    Derwent S. Whittlesey 450

38. The Political Influence in Australian Geography,
    K. W. Robinson 458

The Public Management of the Environment 464

39. The Conflict of Salmon Fishing Policies in the North Pacific,
    Julian V. Minghi 464

40. Environmental Stress and the Municipal Political System: The Brockton Water Crisis of 1961–1966, *Roger E. Kasperson* 481

Annotated Bibliography 497

APPENDIX: Aids to Research in Political Geography,
    Jeanne X. Kasperson 501

NAME INDEX 513

SUBJECT INDEX 521

Preface

The original idea for this project arose in late 1966. While the editors were both involved in an NDEA Institute in Advanced Political Geography at Clark University in the Summer of 1967, the volume was given concrete form, although work was not begun in earnest until the latter part of 1967. From the start, the editors had some basic goals in mind. There was a need for a volume to assess the field of political geography, to provide a clear sense of focus and purpose, to suggest a coherent conceptual structure for the field, and to attempt to integrate political geography with the development of the discipline of geography as a whole and with the social sciences generally.

The introductory essays and the selections which follow them will serve to indicate the editors' philosophy concerning the nature of this development and innovation. The interdisciplinary nature of political geography is underscored in that sixteen of the forty selections are by non-geographers. Some balance between theoretical and substantive works has been attempted. Selections are drawn from a wide range of related fields, including animal sociology, history, international relations, political economy, political science, social psychology, and sociology. The editors made their selections only after they had firmly established the conceptual structure of the volume. The classics in the field, although several are reproduced elsewhere, are, of course, an essential inclusion since the book would be incomplete without them. On the other hand, the editors have given preference to contributions never before printed, difficult to find, or not generally known or included in courses. In the same vein, given two equally valuable items, the one more readily available in other sources (e.g. Bobbs-Merrill Reprints, other readers) has been de-emphasized. Inevitably, length restrictions caused many useful items to be omitted. The selections included here have sometimes been edited both in text and in footnotes, and the reader might therefore wish to refer to the original publication for fuller treatment. While one can always debate the particular mix of inclusions and omissions, surely the selections in the present volume will be useful and pertinent to political geographers of diverse persuasion and to other social scientists interested in geographical approaches.

The editors wish to make the following acknowledgments: For initial and constant encouragement and advice, Alexander J. Morin and Norton Ginsburg; for generous help in suggesting improvements in the essays, Richard Copley, Peter Goheen, Roger Leigh, Judy Mehan, Gerard Rushton, and James Simmons; for help in organization and research, Rod Logan and Linda McKim; for typing assistance, Timmie Gayton, Janet Lawson, Erna Lay, and Petra LeBrón. The editors are particularly indebted to many of the contributors in this volume for their fine cooperation in writing translations, in updating articles by the addition of postscripts, or even by writing entirely new manuscripts without benefits other than those of a purely scholarly nature. In particular, thanks are due to Ronald Bolin for his translation of Ratzel, to J. R. V. Prescott for his original article on electoral geography, and to David Lowenthal for the addition of a postscript.

Last but not least the editors thank their wives for their help and patience during the rather short but often hectic period which marked the assembly of this volume.

R.E.K.
J.V.M.

Introduction

With characteristic candor, Carl Sauer once branded political geography as the "wayward child" of the geographical sciences.[1] Whatever its filial status, this subfield has in the past boasted some of the most renowned of academic geographers and has contributed notably to the emergence of scientific geography during the past century. Even four decades later, however, Sauer's assessment does suggest the often peripheral position of contemporary political geography in research and pedagogy both in geography and in the social sciences generally. A number of factors have contributed to the decline of political geography. Certainly geopolitics, environmentalism, loose speculation on world power distributions, and synoptic and descriptive studies of the form of states have all taken their toll. A corresponding concern with theory, rigorous hypothesis formulation and testing, and comparative analysis has always been present but is only now emerging strongly. Considerable confusion still exists as to the objectives, conceptual structure, and scope of political geography. Clearly the time is ripe for rethinking the basic issues and formulating a clear focus and organization for the field.

The task of reconsideration may begin with a look at the changing definition of political geography. Reviewing the development of the field in 1935, Richard Hartshorne defined political geography as "the study of the state as a characteristic of areas in relation to the other characteristics of areas."[2] Nearly twenty years later, his 1954 definition as "the study of areal differences and similarities in political character as an interrelated part of the total complex of areal differences and similarities"[3] showed relatively little change. This view of political geography as part and parcel of regional geography predominated until recently, when the growth of systematic and theoretical geography indicated the need for a new interpretation. In 1964 W. A. Douglas Jackson shifted the emphasis of political geography with his definition of it as "the study of political phenomena in their areal context."[4] The *Ad Hoc* Committee on Geography reconciled differences in these views by its 1965 definition: "the study of the interaction of geographical area and political process."[5]

The definition proposed in this volume is the *study of the spatial and areal structures and interactions between political processes and systems,* or simply, *the spatial analysis of political phenomena.* This definition is sufficiently broad to comprehend the pluralistic nature of the field and to involve political geography in the mainstream of current social science theory and research. The emphasis on inclusiveness

---

1. Carl O. Sauer, "Recent Developments in Cultural Geography," in Charles A. Ellwood *et al., Recent Developments in the Social Sciences* (Philadelphia: J. B. Lippincott and Co., 1927), p. 207.
2. Richard Hartshorne, "Recent Developments in Political Geography," *American Political Science Review,* XXIX (December 1935), p. 957.
3. Richard Hartshorne, "Political Geography," in Preston James and Clarence Jones (eds.), *American Geography: Inventory and Prospect* (Syracuse: Syracuse University Press, 1954), p. 178.
4. W. A. Douglas Jackson (ed.), *Politics and Geographic Relationships* (Englewood Cliffs, N.J.: Prentice-Hall, 1964), p. 1.
5. National Academy of Sciences—National Research Council. *The Science of Geography* (Washington: NAS–NRC, 1965), p. 32.

rather than exclusiveness draws attention to the important interdisciplinary contributions originating at the peripheries of the field or even outside the discipline completely.

The present volume has several aims. First, it seeks to provide a sense of purpose and order to the study of political geography. The editors directed much effort to devising a conceptual structure for the field so that an important aspect of the book resides there. Both the organization of and lengthy introductions to each part hopefully will contribute to this end. Second, the volume attempts to bring political geography more into line with trends in contemporary geography as a whole and with the other social sciences. Not only do the selections contain a wide variety of contributions from other fields, but the introductory essays and annotated bibliographies suggest other closely related research, the study of which is a prerequisite for competence in political geography. Moreover, the organizing structure of the book enjoys close parallels in the other social sciences. Third, the editors have tried to produce a balanced book. While the emphasis is on theoretical contributions, substantive works to illustrate the applications of theory are also included. The volume also aspires to be a "stocktaking" as of 1969, emphasizing particularly valuable past contributions, related interdisciplinary efforts, and profitable new approaches and lines of inquiry. In this respect, the editors have included lengthy annotated bibliographies and a special appendix reviewing research aids in the field, which should help meet the requirements both of undergraduate and graduate students, and which may also be of assistance to their peers.

The organization of the volume reflects the editors' definition and structuring of political geography. Part I, Heritage, includes works which have contributed significantly to the theoretical development of the field. It encourages the reader to bear in mind the intellectual context in which the selections were written and to stress their positive, not their dated, features. Heritage is a major section because of an editorial concern that the past is often neglected in courses in political geography. Despite the rather fashionable preference to read only contemporary writers and current works, an awareness and appreciation of intellectual heritage is valuable not only for avoiding mistakes and duplications but also for assessing the relevance of one's own work. In emphasizing the new and the interdisciplinary, let us not neglect the best of the past.

Part II, Structure, comprises the concern to which political geographers have devoted most of their past attention. The record of achievement is notable, especially in such topics as boundaries and frontiers. At the same time, many efforts have emphasized form at the expense of function, and the interplay between spatial structure on the one hand and process and behavior on the other has often remained obscure. The editors attempt to integrate this field with the rest of geography and with structural-functional analysis in the other social sciences.

Taken together, Parts III and IV, Process and Behavior, form the subject where much future theoretical and practical effort is needed. In fact, a deeper understanding of spatial processes and behavior will undoubtedly advance substantially our knowledge of spatial-political structure and environmental problems. Increased attention to this topic in recent and current research by political geographers reflects a development which is consistent with progress in geography as a whole.

Part V, Environment, provides the context in which spatial structure, process, and behavior occur. It represents a topic of traditional concern in political geography and also an interest in geography generally where exciting developments are now taking place. An examination of issues in the light of provocative past and contemporary interdisciplinary theory indicates possibilities for both teaching and research.

The most noteworthy organizational characteristic of the present volume is the interdependence of concepts, issues, and structure. The fact that there is a clear focus, a cluster of related problems, and conceptual interdependence in political geography is perhaps the greatest point of emphasis in this book.

The Structure of Political Geography

Part I: HERITAGE

Introduction

Every social science attempts to trace its roots back into the past. Such roots give a discipline tradition and prestige as well as a perspective from which to view current developments and to draw a thematic continuity over the span of time. Geography is no exception to this rule, and its branch of political geography is able to draw upon a particularly rich "heritage" covering many centuries of ideas concerned with the spatial structure of political organization and process. The readings and essays in this part contain a sampling of this heritage over a period of about 2200 years, from Aristotle to the present generation.

Rather than being content merely to reiterate the "greats" of the past in review form, we have decided to include wherever possible a representative sample of the authors' own writings. These are presented in chronological order, and, although there is not necessarily any logical and easily identifiable progression of thought from one selection to the next, it is hoped that the reader will be able to see the growth of a wide range of political-geographic notions in some kind of sequential order, and to evaluate for himself the relevance of these writings to the present status of the field as reflected in the remainder of this volume. Many of these concepts developed and utilized by authors in the selections on structure, process, behavior, and environment will have their direct antecedents in the notions introduced in the selections of this part.

It must be remembered that each writer discussed here was circumscribed in his thought patterns by the conventional wisdom of his own age and by the imperfect state of knowledge of much of the world outside his immediate environment. Furthermore, as most of the works were originally written in languages other than English (all but the last three selections fall into this category), we must assume that something has been lost in translation, certainly in style, and probably also in meaning.

Considering these restraints, it is remarkable how much of this heritage is directly relevant to political-geographic thought today. It will be seen that far from being a mere introductory and scene-setting exercise, this group of selections is an initial and essential element in any thorough consideration of the theory and practice of political geography.

INTRODUCTION TO THE SELECTIONS

We may usefully divide the discussion of the heritage of political geography into three basic parts or periods:

Environmental-Political Relationships
The Organic State and Geopolitics
Studies of Political Areas

Although there is some overlap, these three divisions represent basically distinct periods during each of which the contributions to the field have been molded by the dominant theme of the period. Of the six selections, the first—*Aristotle*—falls into the period of environmental-political relationships; the next—*Ratzel*—is a central figure in the Organic State and Geopolitics period; three—*Whittlesey, Hartshorne,* and *Jones*—serve best to illustrate the immediate background to the

Political Areas period of this generation. The last reading is taken from an assessment of the field in the mid-1960's by a committee of distinguished American geographers.

Normally included in any discussion of the heritage of political geography are the group of works which fall under the umbrella of "global strategic views" or "world equilibrium models." Such well known theories as Mackinder's Heartland, Haushofer's Pan-regions, and Spykman's Rimland all belong in this particular category. Although it is not in any way contested that such works are an integral and important part of past political-geographic literature, we have chosen in this volume to include a discussion of them with a few selections in the part on structure where they can be more meaningfully introduced within a general consideration of the structure of political geography as attempts at conceptualizing structures at the global scale.

Environmental-Political Relationships

In political geography there is a long-standing interest in the relationship between the environment, both in its natural state and as modified by man, and man's political activity, including all aspects of political structure, process, and behavior. This ecological tradition is still strong today, although in much different form, as evidenced by the cluster of research in resource management studies discussed in the final part, Environment.

The earliest writings in political geography are in the ecological tradition and usually have a particularly deterministic or environmentalistic bent. The relationship is seen mainly in terms of a one-way cause and effect, with the political activity of man assumed, in large measure, to be strongly influenced by aspects of the physical environment, especially climate and topography. This particular viewpoint is known as *environmental determinism*, a form of determinism that dominated geographical thought until the close of the nineteenth century.

Two points should be kept in mind. Whereas all the writings discussed in this section on environmental-political relationships demonstrate various degrees and varieties of deterministic thinking, they also provide valuable exposure of a mass of ideas pertinent to political geography. By the same token, although we recognize a new period starting with Ratzel, many of the deterministic notions about the role of the environment in influencing politics continued to enjoy unquestioned popularity among political geographers well into this century.

Aristotle (383-322 B.C.), a citizen of Athens, wrote within the political environment of the city-state world of Ancient Greece situated on the northern littoral of the Eastern Mediterranean. In his volume on *Politics*[1] he presented a model of the "ideal" or perfect state. He fully recognized the theoretical limitations involved in this, and thus spoke in terms of an "approximation" of the ideal state. For Aristotle, the two major ingredients of this state were the size of population and the endowments of territory. In respect to population characteristics, he was well aware that absolute size meant little, and he discussed the political implications of size variation. For instance, he found that too many can be "ungovernable" and too few can create a liability for defense. Aristotle implied that a political consideration might set the ideal size of a population in that, for the "good life" in the political community, electors must be known to all, and hence "the largest number that can be taken in at a single view" is the optimum size. This is a somewhat literal translation (the "largest surveyable population" has also been used), and the concern is essentially with the requirement of shared values in political integration. In the modern industrial state, when one considers the innovations in mass communication, such as television, open to electors, this aspect of accessibility does not seem too critical, yet it remains a crucial variable in the political integration of many new states in the underdeveloped world which more often than not possess poor communication networks.

The key to success in terms of territorial endowment, Aristotle felt, was the correct use of property and wealth with an aim toward achieving self-sufficiency, which sounds like an early call for state planning tending toward autarchy.

On the question of siting the capital city within the state, he was aware of the need for compromise between strategic considerations of defense from outside attack, and those of

1. *The Works of Aristotle, Vol. X, Politica* (Oxford: Clarendon Press, 1921), pp. 1325-1331.

nodality for successful hinterland relationships.

Also included is an interesting observation on the notion of territoriality. Aristotle insisted that all members of the army must be citizens in that they are to fight on and to defend their own state's territory, while the navy, operating outside the state's territory, can be made up of non-citizens.

Aristotle's ethnocentrism is manifest in his deterministic explanation of the ideal balance between what he called "spirit" and intelligence resulting from the climatic regime of the Hellenic states, and, by the same token, the imbalances which occurred in other parts of the then-known world due to climates' being too hot (not enough spirit) or too cold (a lack of intelligence). These notions were generally put forward two generations earlier by the physician Hippocrates (460–376 B.C.) (see Part V, Environment), which lends further proof that they formed part of the conventional wisdom of scientific research in ancient Greece. It will be seen that environmental determinism and ethnocentrism are persistently interrelated throughout this period.

Aristotle considered the various functions of the state with discussions of the location and morphology of capital cities, and concluded with an assessment of fortified as opposed to unfortified boundaries.

In short, Aristotle introduced many of the ideas that we shall later find have become important concepts in the field of political geography. These include notions of ideal sizes of populations and area for political viability and their relationship to changing technology, the distributional characteristics of the resident population, the locational and morphological problems of the capital city, including strategic and economic considerations, boundaries-versus-frontiers as limits of national space, problems related to the spatial integration of the state, and also notions of coexistence and interdependence within a larger system, both in the Hellenic sphere, and, under the assumptions about the impact of temperature on political behavior, in a "global" pattern.

Strabo (63 B.C.–24 A.D.), a Greek scholar and traveler writing at the height of the Roman Empire, was strongly influenced, as was Aristotle, by his own environment and times. In his work entitled *Geography*[2] he examined the prerequisites for the successful functioning of a large political unit. He came to the conclusion that a strong central government and a single ruling head of state were essential ingredients for success. Given the political environment of the times, it is not surprising that Strabo should conclude that Italy, the core of the Roman Empire, with its central location in the then-known world in the Mediterranean, its "ideal" climatic regime, and its balance of mixed resources, was best suited to fill this role. Again, ethnocentrism coupled with inherited deterministic notions concerning environmental-political relationships account for these conclusions.

Ibn-Khaldūn (writing between 1382–1405) was an Arab philosopher and historian. His *Muqaddimah* (or *Introduction to History*)[3] is the most detailed autobiography available in medieval Muslim history and reflects among other things the political-geographic thinking of the late fourteenth-century Arab world.

As with Aristotle's emphasis on city-states, Ibn-Khaldūn concentrated on the most powerful units in the political hierarchy of his own times—the tribe and the city—which were epitomized in the struggle between nomadic and sedentary states. Both Bedouins (nomadic or savage) and urban (sedentary) peoples were considered "natural" and interrelated groups. Ibn-Khaldūn explained their differences deterministically in terms of choice of livelihood: agriculture and animal husbandry necessitate desert life, while commerce and industry demand an urban location. Both groups, however, were held to be related on the evolutionary scale, with the Bedouins of the desert preceding the urban folk. The latter, descendants of immigrant nomads, had reached the last stage of civilization in their cities and hence were at the point where decay sets in.

Although cultural geographers may argue about the strict accuracy of this evolutionary idea, it was, at least, an attempt to link the Bedouin and urban dweller in time and space.

Ibn-Khaldūn also discussed the group's functioning in space, and it is here that the notions of environmental-political relations and of territoriality come into play. The

---

2. Strabo, *Geography* (London: Heinemann, 1917).

3. Ibn-Khaldūn, *The Muqaddimah; An Introduction to History*, Franz Rosenthal, trans. (New York: Pantheon Books, 1958). For his discussion of nomadic and sedentary states, see especially Volume I, pp. 249–253.

nomad, because of his desert environment, operated in small, mobile groups, giving him the qualities of courage and alertness, and also imposing the necessity of maintaining loyalties in a closely knit group of common descent. There were few territorial restrictions as a "savage" nation extended over territory at will, for there was no homeland, core of agricultural fertility, or capital city around which to cluster or with which to identify.

Sedentary states by contrast represented immobile concentrations of wealth and population and, lacking common lineage, were without tribal cohesion. Hence they had to devise new and complex systems of political organization for security against attack and for their own self-government. This concern with "group spirit" continued the tradition of interest in political integration earlier shown by Aristotle.

Where contiguous, the two types of states were interdependent not only in an evolutionary sense, but also functionally. The sedentary state dominated in this functional relationship both economically and politically by manipulation of factional disputes among tribal states, imposition of head taxes, the introduction of a money economy, and by restrictions on free migration. This trend, seen six centuries ago, is still prevalent in many areas of the Saharan edge and in South Central Asia.

The major notions arising from Ibn-Khaldūn's discussion relate, then, to the contrast among interdependent, contiguous, and genetically interrelated states in terms of their distinctive environmental-political relationships. These in turn lead to a major concern with political integration and disintegration. Furthermore, one of the first "life cycles of the state" formulated can be attributed to Ibn-Khaldūn.

Both Bodin (1530–1596) and Montesquieu (1689–1755) had a primary interest in the nation-state. Bodin was writing in a Europe that was slowly emerging from the restrictions on political thought imposed by religious domination throughout the Dark Ages. In his *Six livres de la République*[4] he expressed ideas not unlike those of Aristotle and Ibn-Khaldūn. He held that climate and topography are the chief determinants of national character, and that, in turn, the laws of states vary according to differences in national character. Thus a causal relationship was drawn between the physical environment and the political system. Refinement of the earlier theories, through greater knowledge about the rest of the world which was being rapidly "discovered" by Europeans at this time, enabled Bodin, and later Montesquieu, to generalize from more cases and also provided a basis for comparative analysis of differences both in aspects of the physical environment and in political systems from region to region.

The basic assumption about the crucial role of the physical environment led to the deterministic conclusion that, while man has certain choices available to him and can thus operate and reason independently to some degree, nature dominates man's will in terms of his political behavior, character, and works.

Montesquieu's ideas[5] were, as one would expect, based upon much more detailed and widely drawn scientific evidence of climatic effects than those of earlier writers. His assumptions about the role of climate in influencing human characteristics and behavior were based upon theories of human physiology prevalent at the time. Simply stated, these theories led to the conclusion that warm climates tend to favor despotism and slavery, and colder climates encourage democracy and liberty. This led to a "global" view which held that "freedom" tends to increase with distance from the Equator, and helped Montesquieu to expound a theory of Asian conquest and despotism through history. Unlike Europe, Asia is a continent without a temperate zone, and whereas Europe's strength lay in its freedom, Asia's weakness was its chronic slavery. This fact, coupled with the nature of Asia's terrain, more open with fewer natural barriers than in Europe, determined that power in Asia would always be despotic, for it was through slavery that political fragmentation was avoided, and fragmentation would be inconsistent with the nature of the country, i.e.

---

4. Jean Bodin, *The Six Books of the Commonweale* (Cambridge: Harvard University Press, 1962).

5. Charles Baron de Montesquieu, *The Spirit of the Laws*, Thomas Nugent, trans. (New York: Hafner Publishing Co., 1949). For his discussion on climate, subsistence, and laws, see Book XIV, pp. 221–227 and Book XVIII, pp. 271–281. For an in-depth evaluation of Montesquieu's political-geographic views see Karl Marcus Kriesel, "Montesquieu: Possibilistic Political Geographer," *Annals of the Association of American Geographers*, LVIII (September 1968), pp. 557–574.

unnatural. Africa and America, from Montesquieu's mid-eighteenth century viewpoint, were in the same category as Asia, while Europe alone, divided into free nations consistent with its natural divisions, was symbolized by its ability to maintain free states.

Montesquieu, however, was, as Kriesel has indicated, no simple determinist, and he examined at length the processes involved in the relationship among climate, agriculture, and political systems. Man, he felt, can manipulate given relationships in order to obtain desired results. For instance, he felt that laws could be used to counterbalance the undesired effects of climate on agricultural productivity by encouraging other existing human qualities. In other words, the political system could be fashioned to emphasize hitherto inert qualities which in turn could modify some of the effects of the physical environment.

He also observed that a relationship existed between agricultural productivity and the political system. Agricultural wealth tends to be located on flat, fertile plains open to invasion and conquest by stronger powers and hence is most often associated with the monarchical system. Agricultural infertility, on the other hand, tends to occur in less accessible mountain areas unattractive to outside conquest and hence tends to be correlated with democracy. In that democracy was the only wealth of such regions, it was stubbornly and usually successfully defended.

An associated and important statement held that the degree of cultivation in any region is a function of liberty, *not* simply of soil fertility. That is, the role of the political process, not that of a particular quality of the physical environment, is crucial. The aspect of accessibility, as mentioned above, was also given prominence, as Montesquieu points out the advantages of insularity in defence against tyranny. Furthermore, he saw a direct relationship between the complexity of a political system (law codes) and that of man's subsistence activities and the spatial extent of the nation. For example, he was particularly interested in the political organization of areas of subsistence agricultural systems and sparse population distribution and their resultant problems for integration.

These observations about the complex relationships among the physical environment, man's subsistence activity, and political systems were to have a major impact on political-geographic thought for the next 150 years.

By the mid-nineteenth century this philosophy of environmentalism had reached its peak. The influence of the "new" science, especially research breakthroughs in the biological sciences, was growing in the social sciences, geography included, resulting in a trend toward more rigorous and systematic study. In political geography this led to attempts at more precise measurement of the influence of the environment on political organization and behavior.

Karl Ritter (1779–1859), professor of geography at Berlin University, was far and away the most important writer of this period. His *Comparative Geography* was published in English[6] after his death although his major impact was to be felt in Germany a generation later. Ritter developed, by analogy with physical organisms, a cycle theory of state growth. Human cultures and political units were natural organic entities, each going through a natural cycle of birth, maturity, and death. This idea of a developmental stage of a culture gave Ritter a new independent variable for more sophisticated analysis and theory-building when coupled with the other variable, the physical environment, about which far more was then known than in the times of the writers discussed above. Furthermore, armed with a clearer understanding of the role of nature that this developmental stage idea provided, Ritter went on to suggest that prediction was now possible.

At the global scale, cultures were seen in continental proportions, each continent representing an organ in the "living world." In this scheme, Ritter, as Montesquieu before him, saw Europe as naturally gaining precedence over all the other "organs." Its comparatively compact size and shape, its location in the temperate zone, and its complexity of national entities equipped the continent for the most successful growth by immigration and cultural development, for Ritter believed that, given favorable environmental circumstances, "strong cultures" had the ability to "guide" their own destinies.

These notions about the workings of nature on the evolution of cultures, their implications for prediction and for global structure

6. Karl Ritter, *Comparative Geography* (Philadelphia: J. B. Lippincott Co., 1864).

models, and their applications to statecraft, were to lead, a generation later, to the theory of the organic state.

The Organic State and Geopolitics

Friedrich Ratzel (1844–1904) has been called the "founder" of political geography and is certainly recognized as the "father" of modern political geography. Yet he has also been viewed by many as a thoroughly deterministic meddler whose ideas helped found the Third Reich through their influence in the growth of a pseudo-scientific applied political geography in Germany between the Wars, a field that became known as *Geopolitik*. Without doubt Ratzel brought a radical change in political-geographic thinking in that, although following logically after Ritter, he represents a break with the largely impressionistic writings of the past by concentrating on the growth of political entities as living organisms, and by evolving through an organic analogue model a set of "laws" by which he attempted to explain the processes of the spatial growth of states.

In his famous landmark article of 1896 entitled "The Laws of the Spatial Growth of States," the subtitle—"A Contribution to Scientific Political Geography"—in a real sense epitomizes this break with the past.[7] This article, translated from the original German by Ronald L. Bolin,[8] appears for the first time in English in Part I.[9]

Ratzel has, in various ways, had a tremendous influence on political geography in virtually every nation where that subject is found, none the less so in the United States where the literature in the field often fairly bristles with shadowy references to this man. His contribution to the heritage of political geography is, however, still open to debate. The argument has often continued unabated amidst generations of American geographers who are too often either unequipped or unwilling to apply themselves to the none-too-easy task of a direct examination of Ratzel's work. Our purpose, in some small manner, is to bring the argument a little closer to ground by an examination of what Ratzel himself had to say regarding his ideas in a full translation of one of his shorter pieces often cited as being most representative of his thought.

It is hardly surprising that Ratzel should be seen in so many lights. The language barrier has already been mentioned, but there are yet other difficulties beyond this. Ratzel was a very prolific writer, leaving behind him a bibliography of some 1240 items, including 24 books, over 540 articles, more than 600 book reviews, and some 146 short biographies. Just as astounding is the number of subjects on which he wrote, extending from his well-known works such as the two-volume *Anthropogeographie* in 1882[10] and *Politische Geographie* in 1897[11] to such items as "On the History and Development of Earthworms," "New Investigations about Birds' Nests," "On the Statistics of British Burma," "Concerning the Formation of Fjords on Inland Seas," and "The Deterioration of Necrology." Ratzel was not only a writer, but was in his own right a stylist whose pen was honed by years of work as a travelling newspaper correspondent. Indeed, many have felt, and perhaps not entirely incorrectly, that he often forewent clarity for the achievement of style. All of these factors have combined to make of this man perhaps the least understood and most frequently criticized of the major geographical writers of the past century.

Ratzel's early training was in pharmacy. He studied zoology at Heidelberg, Jena, and Berlin. After much travel as a journalist he eventually took the Chair of Geography at the University of Leipzig in 1886, where he remained until his death.[12]

What is one to think of this man who is so much talked about and so little read? Our

---

7. Friedrich Ratzel, "Die Gesetze des räumlichen Wachstums der Staaten," *Petermanns Mitteilungen*, XLII (1896), pp. 97–107.

8. This discussion of Ratzel is based in part on an introductory note provided by Bolin to his translation. A full translation and annotation by Bolin of the first half ("General Geography") of Immanuel Kant's *Physical Geography* is shortly to be published by Indiana University.

9. An abstract in translation did appear in the *Scottish Geographical Magazine*, XII (1896), pp. 351–361. This is included in the annotated bibliography.

10. Friedrich Ratzel, *Anthropogeographie oder Grundzüge der Anwendung der Erdkunde auf die Geschichte* (Stuttgart: J. Engelhorn, 1882).

11. Friedrich Ratzel, *Politische Geographie*, 3rd ed. (Munich: R. Oldenbourg, 1923).

12. For more biographical detail see: Kurt Hassert, "Friedrich Ratzel: Sein Leben und Wirken," *Geographische Zeitschrift*, XI (1905), pp. 305–325, 361–380, and Harriet Wanklyn, *Friedrich Ratzel: A Biographical Memoir and Bibliography* (Cambridge: Cambridge University Press, 1961).

judgments seem to be colored primarily by various evaluative references to him and by Ellen Churchill Semple's *Influences of Geographic Environment*,[13] which was published as an interpretation for Americans of the essence of *Anthropogeographie*. Her volume appeared in 1911, twenty years after she had studied under Ratzel at Leipzig. From the standpoint of the time elapsed until her work was published, as well as from the simple criterion of good scholarship, it is hardly fair to Ratzel to judge his work by Miss Semple's interpretation.

One must examine Ratzel's work with caution, as he often wrote in an aggressive style and did not pause to put in the qualifiers. It is easy to attack such terms as "law" and "organism" on semantic grounds. We will run into these terms often in the translated article and it is interesting to look at the meanings which Ratzel imparted to them.

Briefly stated, Ratzel's seven laws of the spatial growth of states are:

1. The size of the state grows with its culture.

2. The growth of states follows other manifestations of the growth of peoples which must necessarily precede the growth of the state.

3. The growth of the state proceeds by the annexation of smaller members into the agglomerate. At the same time the relationship of the population to the earth becomes continuously closer.

4. The boundary is the peripheral organ of the state, the bearer of its growth as well as its fortification, and takes part in all the transformations of the organism of the state.

5. In its growth the State strives toward the envelopment of politically valuable positions.

6. The first stimuli to the spatial growth of states come to them from the outside.

7. The general tendency toward territorial annexation and amalgamation is transmitted from state to state and continually increases in intensity.

Let us first examine what he meant by the word "law":

But is it, one may ask, the primary goal of all sciences to find only that which the scientist calls a law? Geography in that case is not a science in the usual sense. Does not statistics deal with the same incalculability, with the many-faceted disposition of man, and which is, in this case, more expressive than strictly true? But the high probabilities which statistics derive from the comparison of many cases, what are they other than laws—we almost wish to say oscillating laws—in which strongly outstanding disturbances disappear in the totality. We too may attain to such probabilities though we must of course also deal with the further difficulty that history does not often offer us the many examples wanted for the statistical method.[14]

We can see then that the laws of spatial growth of which Ratzel spoke are not, as they have so often been interpreted, laws of "necessity" at all.

In speaking of the state as an "organism," Ratzel concentrated his comparison on the relation of man in the collective sense, i.e., the state and the land. His thinking here is difficult to follow, but it is apparent that his comparison was not of the strict dog-eat-dog nature so often attributed to him. He was referring to the relationship which develops between a people and the land which nourishes them, and the reciprocity which develops between them. Here again we must keep in mind what it was that Ratzel meant by the term "law." He referred to tendencies rather than absolutes, as is clear from the following passages:

Thus there arises a political organization of the land through which the state becomes an organism in that a fixed portion of the surface of the earth enters in to such a degree that the properties of the state are a combination of those of the people and of the land.

The state is not an organism merely because it forms a connection between a living population and the fixed earth, but rather because this connection is so strengthened by reciprocity that the two become one and can no longer be thought of as separate.[15]

The organism is most highly developed among animals and plants in that the members must make the greatest sacrifices of individuality in the service of the whole. Measured by this standard the "state" of man is an exceptionally undeveloped organism, for its members preserve an independence which no longer occurs even in the lower plants and animals.[16]

The comparison of the state with highly developed organisms is unfruitful. And if so many scientific attempts to approach the state as an organism have borne so little fruit it is primarily because of the limitation of such considerations to

13. Ellen Churchill Semple, *Influences of Geographic Environment* (New York: Henry Holt & Co., 1911).
14. Ratzel, *Anthropogeographie*, p. 49.
15. Ratzel, *Politische Geographie*, p. 4.
16. *Ibid.*, p. 8.

the analogy between an aggregate of men and the structure of an organic creature.[17]

These are hardly the words of one who sees the "biological *necessity* of growing by securing essential *missing organs*, if necessary, by *force*."[18] Thus it is obvious that Ratzel, a zoologist by training, was only too well aware of the limits of scientific biological analogy.

Ratzel, then, viewed the state as a living organism ("an organic entity increasingly attached to the land on which it lives") with no rigid limits, the key to successful growth being in the development of its civilization, as he tried to prove with an analysis of the growth of past empires. He adopted Ritter's notion of evolution from youth to maturity with a correlation between growing old age and diminishing size.

He included the idea of "community" as a prerequisite for political union and for the development of nationalism with the diffusion of ideas. The processes of integration and disintegration, he felt, formed a major portion of historical movements, depicted geographically as an interchange between larger and smaller political surfaces. He also recognized the relationship between cultural levels and areal scale of territoriality. The concept of the boundary of a state as a peripheral skin or organ, rather than a *de jure* line, has ramifications for the boundary-versus-frontier discussion which will be included in Part II.

These valuable insights are all too often overlooked because Ratzel's major impact in the two generations that followed was to be on the German school of geopolitics which "was doomed to extinction because [its] followers . . . departed from scholarly methods."[19]

The first and major post-Ratzelian disciple was the Swedish political scientist Rudolf Kjellén (1864-1922) of the universities of Goteborg and Uppsala, who wrote most of his important works in Swedish and whose contribution to political geography has been judged principally on the basis of one major book translated into German by M. Langfeldt.[20] However, as in the case of Ratzel, a doctrine or theory identified with one man cannot always be understood adequately without reference to a group of his works covering the evolution of his ideas over a given period. Edvard Thermaenius' review[21] of his works and ideas provides this necessary perspective on Kjellén. Kjellén's thoughts are systematically traced in chronological order from 1900 to 1919 through the examination of nine of his major works. Thermaenius is able to pick out a three-stage development from "experimental" through "theory" to a "complete system."

Kjellén is credited with creating the "science of geopolitics" and, although his doctrine had little or no impact whatsoever in Sweden, it fell on fertile ground in post-World War I Germany where a new school of political geographers, established formally in the early 1930's in the Institute for Geopolitics in Munich under Karl Haushofer (1869-1946), based much of its work on Kjellén's system.

Kjellén added the dimension of moral and intellectual capacities to Ratzel's state as a living organism. He defined geopolitics as "the theory of the state as a geographic organism or phenomenon in space, i.e. as land, territory, area, or, most especially, as country." Hence states were regarded not so much as legal bodies but as competing powers. The logical conclusion of this competition for power was, for Kjellén, the inevitable emergence of a small number of very large and powerful states in the world.

He was particularly interested in the *process* involved in the transformation of a territory from a natural area to a cultural-political region. He viewed this process as a perpetual interchange among "country, people, and government." This process of human occupation of a region gave it, in causal sequence, continuity, solidarity, interaction, loyalty, and nationality; that is, the creation of a nation with what Kjellén called a "geopolitical instinct."

It is not difficult to understand how these ideas, coupled with the Ratzelian tradition, caught the imagination of many geographers

17. *Ibid.*, pp. 9-11.
18. Russell H. Fifield and G. Etzel Pearcy, *Geopolitics in Principle and Practice* (Boston: Atheneum Press, 1944), p. 11. [Emphasis added.]
19. "Studies in Political Geography," in *The Science of Geography* (Washington: National Academy of Sciences-National Research Council, 1965), p. 34.

20. Rudolf Kjellén, *Der Staat als Lebensform*, M. Langfeldt trans. (Leipzig: S. Hirzel Verlag, 1917).
21. Edvard Thermaenius, "Geopolitics and Political Geography," *Baltic and Scandinavian Countries*, IV (May 1938), pp. 165-177.

in inter-war Germany.[22] This group, under the leadership of Haushofer as already mentioned, formed the so-called school of German geopolitics which dominated that country's geography from 1920 to 1945. Although we do not regard this epoch as a particularly auspicious part of the heritage of political geography, limited as it was in time and place, tainted with Naziism, and with little or no influence on theory formulation since, the era of *Geopolitik* does deserve some, if rather brief, consideration because it was an interesting offshoot from political geography and also because of its effect during its flourishing and immediately after in preventing any real advances in the field of political geography.[23]

Basic to *Geopolitik*'s ideas were Ratzel's organic state theory, its refinements by Kjellén, and the global strategic views principally of Sir Halford Mackinder.[24] Mackinder's prognostications were tied to the notion that in a world of declining sea power relative to land power, the core of Eurasia (at first called the "Pivot Area" and later, in 1919, renamed the "Heartland"), on the basis of its inaccessibility to sea-borne power and its vast resources, was the key to global power. Hence, it followed logically that any political power that could effectively occupy and control this Heartland could by definition achieve a dominant world position.[25]

To Haushofer and his group the ideas of Ratzel and Kjellén on the one hand, and of Mackinder on the other, formed a symbiosis which seemed to have especial relevance to Germany's post-World War I position, indicating, as they thought, Germany's geopolitical realities and dictating her "correct" policy in the world, particularly in relation to the form, direction, and chronology of her territorial expansion. Ratzel's laws about the state as an expanding organism were quoted, often without his many qualifications, to justify as scientifically natural and amoral such matters as the need of populous states for living space (*Lebensraum*), and hence the growth of some states, such as Germany, at the expense of less virile neighboring organs, such as Czechoslovakia and Poland. By the same token, the territorial and other restrictions placed on Germany at the Peace of Paris after World War I were regarded as "unnatural."

Such notions, of course, were hardly without precedence or restricted to German origin. Dominian wrote in 1917 that "Germany's expansion is a natural phenomenon. The country is overpopulated. It must expand." He went on to note that the only direction possible for this expansion was eastwards— "the line of least resistance"—making a drive toward the East (*Drang nach Osten*) "inevitable."[26]

Mackinder's Heartland idea seemed to indicate to the geopoliticians the necessity for a détente or even an alliance between Nazi Germany and the chief occupant of the Heartland, Soviet Russia.

Although there is some debate as to just how persuasive the voluminous literature turned out by the German geopoliticians was in influencing German policy,[27] there is no doubt that the rise to power of National Socialism gave the pseudo-science of Geopolitik much more prestige than it had previously enjoyed in Germany and also a greater circulation of its central ideas of the need for German expansion among not only the decision-making élite but the public at large. Although *Geopolitik* collapsed with the fall of the Third Reich, many of its associated notions such as the application of political-geographic concepts to problems of national policy, have, despite the inauspicious experience in Germany, survived in the general field of geopolitics or applied political geography, as we shall see in the section on "Global Structure" in the next part.

22. For an excellent review of this development see Richard Hartshorne, "Recent Developments in Political Geography, II," *American Political Science Review*, XXIX (December 1935), pp. 960–965.

23. There have been many analyses of the phenomenon of Geopolitik, some of which are included in the annotated bibliography.

24. Halford J. Mackinder, "The Geographical Pivot of History," *Geographical Journal*, XXIII (1904), pp. 421–437, and *Democratic Ideals and Reality* (New York: Henry Holt & Co., 1919, 2nd ed., 1942). The former work is among the selections in Part II (Structure).

25. Mackinder's ideas will be discussed in somewhat greater detail in the introductory essay to the following section.

26. Leon Dominian, *The Frontiers of Language and Nationality in Europe* (New York: Henry Holt & Co., 1917), p. 331.

27. William L. Shirer expressed the opinion that their influence was negligible in his *Rise and Fall of the Third Reich: A History of Nazi Germany* (New York: Simon and Schuster, 1960), pp. 48 and 837.

Political Area Studies

Overlapping with the two periods described above and evolving into the current generation of political-geographic thought is an era which we can characterize as being dominated by the focus of study on political areas with almost exclusive emphasis on the nation state, the most powerful territorial unit in the political hierarchy. Whereas interdependence and growth were the two chief conceptual contributions of Ratzel's and Kjellén's organic models, political geography has tended toward a period dominated by interest in the structure of a state's territory. Using the biological organism chiefly for analogy, Ratzel distinguished the territorial components as including the "kernel" area, the capital, the uninhabited zones, and the political boundaries. He also included as pertinent to any structural analysis such factors as location, size, shape, climate, soil types, etc.; factors which, as we have already seen, were included one way or another in the discussions of Aristotle and of the other contributors to the heritage of political geography. Ratzel's contribution was primarily one of more accurate and orderly identification, analysis, and correlation of these factors.

The approaches to which these influences have given rise can be classified, in rough order of importance, by the terms *inventory*, *morphological* (structural), *historical* (genetic or evolutionary), and *functional*. As these various approaches are discussed in considerable detail with numerous references to exponent works in the last selection in this section—the extract on political geography from *The Science of Geography*—we will here only briefly trace the relevant concepts of the major figures of this period.

Isaiah Bowman (1878–1950) was a distinguished geographer, President of Johns Hopkins University, Director of The American Geographical Society, and chief territorial adviser on the American Commission to the Paris Peace Conference in 1919. In 1921 he published *The New World: Problems in Political Geography*.[28] It is, as the subtitle suggests, a "problem-oriented" book addressing itself exclusively to the analysis of the political-geographic problems created by the many changes, territorial and other, wrought by the Great War. Although written very much from the American viewpoint and with the intention of providing a basis for United States government decision makers,[29] it remains today a classic in the field as the first modern work in English to analyze individual state and regional problems and to relate them to the global framework of which each state forms a part.

Although this structural-problems approach seemed apt for studying the impact of great change, another approach to the study of political areas was developed. This theme centered on the analysis of the distributional manifestations of political processes, especially those clearly observable in the landscape, and was typified by the historical approach which viewed the state in its genetic context. Derwent S. Whittlesey (1890–1956), who was Professor of Geography at Harvard University, is most directly identified with this approach. He published numerous works in historical as well as political geography and is best known for his monumental book published in 1939, *The Earth and the State: A Study of Political Geography*.[30]

In effect, to think of political geography as the analysis of the impress of central authority upon the landscape[31] is to reverse the viewpoint of Montesquieu. Emphasis on the influence of the political system—"the summation of laws which people make in order to extract a livelihood from their habitat"[32]—on the landscape is in marked contrast with the approach that views the laws of a political system in large measure as products of the natural environment. In Part V (Environment), both of these themes are discussed at length in separate sections.

Whittlesey felt that over time the laws of a political region become roughly suited to the "few compulsive conditions" laid down by nature. However, this mild environmentalism was tempered with his observation that different laws certainly produce contrasts in man's use of identical environments, with the

28. Isaiah Bowman, *The New World: Problems in Political Geography* (Chicago: World Book Co., 1921, 4th ed., 1928).

29. *Ibid.*, (1928), p. iii.

30. Derwent S. Whittlesey, *The Earth and the State: A Study of Political Geography* (New York: Henry Holt & Co., 1939).

31. Derwent S. Whittlesey, "The Impress of Effective Central Authority upon the Landscape," *Annals of the Association of American Geographers*, XXV (June 1935), pp. 85–97. [Reprinted in Part V, Environment.]

32. Whittlesey, *The Earth and the State*, p. 557.

suggestion that this can best be seen in contrasts in a borderland on either side of a political boundary.[33] We can thus describe this approach as the "law-landscape" theme. We will deal with it in more detail in Part V in the section "Political Impress on the Environment."

The selection from Whittlesey included in this section[34] serves as an example of this historical-morphological viewpoint. The kernel of political geography is seen as the political area made up of the nuclear core, constituent parts, problem areas, vulnerable zones, capitals, strategic spots, and boundaries—each of which takes form over time with respect to the specific conditions of the natural environment. As these elements of the spatial political structure are often maladjusted to their natural setting, constant rectification is needed in order to keep up with the changing times if the political area is to maintain its viability.

The importance of the perspective of the past is given special emphasis by Whittlesey as the following statement well indicates: "The present can be set in its perspective only by reconstruction of the fragmentary records of history, and in some places the still more meager remains of archeology."[35] In the section on structure we have included among the selections on "Centrality and Nodes" an abridged version of Whittlesey's analysis of the territorial evolution of France in order to give a direct illustration of the historical approach.

There remain two contributions to round out this discussion of the heritage of political geography. One is by Richard Hartshorne (1899–) in 1950[36] and the other by Stephen B. Jones (1903–) in 1954,[37] both of which appear in this section. Together these theoretical contributions, while maintaining political area as their focus, helped to change the general approach in political geography from some combination of inventorial, morphological, and genetic, to a more "functional" one.

Hartshorne, of The University of Wisconsin, has been prominent for well over a generation in general geographical theory and in political geography, both in specific case studies and in overviews and theoretical contributions.[38] In his presidential address to the Association of American Geographers in 1950, he suggested a view of political area differentiation in terms of functional organization in what he termed "The Functional Approach." The focus of interest became the spatial consequences of political process. Hartshorne felt that the major initial questions to be asked about the political geography of any region should be concerned with its *raison d'être* (in the case of a state, known as the *state-idea*), and with the viability of the region, i.e., its ability to function successfully as politically organized space. The principal component of this analysis is the balance between centripetal and centrifugal forces, the former set of forces being those that tend to integrate a political region, whereas the latter set provide disruptive elements. No one traditional approach is necessarily ruled out completely. The acid test as to the applicability of one or other of these is contained in the question, "Does it contribute to the understanding of the present-day functioning of the political unit in question?"

Hartshorne brought into more definitive focus the distinctive yet related roles of internal and external elements in his functional approach. He also gave, at least implicitly, a more central role to process in political geography in that his conceptual statement is not only an analysis of "functions" but also a geographical approach to the study of political integration, a theme discussed in Part III.

While Hartshorne was making an appeal for a more functional approach, he also recognized that many answers to the questions he raised were to be found in the past, and hence many aspects in the evolution of a political region could not be ignored. The main problem was to find an approach that assured relevance of material in tracing past events and processes. Stephen Jones of Yale University was to fill this need four years later with his paper suggesting a "unified field theory" for political geography. This

33. *Ibid.*, p. 588.
34. *Ibid.*, "Earmarks of Political Geography," pp. 585–593.
35. *Ibid.*, p. 586.
36. Richard Hartshorne, "The Functional Approach in Political Geography," *Annals of the Association of American Geographers*, XL (1950), pp. 95–130.
37. Stephen B. Jones, "A Unified Field Theory of Political Geography," *Annals of the Association of American Geographers*, XLIV (1954), pp. 111–123.

38. Several of Hartshorne's works appear in the annotated bibliographies.

theory (or "mental gadget," as Jones modestly called it) is concerned with the evolution of politically organized space and is built upon the ideas of Whittlesey and Hartshorne, on several intervening conceptual statements by Jean Gottmann concerning the evolution of political partitioning based on accessibility, and by Karl Deutsch.[39]

Jones suggests an idea-area chain expanding on Hartshorne's state-idea by splitting it as two ends of a chain and adding in between a logical progression of conceptual links making for a five-link chain: political idea-decision-movement-field-political area. An essential difference, as Jones points out, from the state-idea is that any political idea having an impact at any level in the political hierarchy can be included. Implicit then is the notion that a political system and a political process do not necessarily cover the same geographical area.

The advantages of Jones' "gadget" are many. Flexibility is obtained in that one may enter the chain at any link and go either way, or start at either end of the chain. By explicitly stating the theory in process terms, emphasis is given to the importance of political phenomena such as ideas and decisions not in themselves geographical in nature but placed in a paradigm with a spatial (movement) and areal (field and area) orientation.

Political geographers, it was now obvious, would have to go against their own earlier advice to themselves by paying increased attention to the concepts, techniques, and even jargon, of other related social science fields such as political science, sociology, and social psychology. Only then could advances be made in the understanding of the spatial structure and interactions of political organization and processes. Jones had pointed the way by his attempt to apply general systems theory to political geography. His unified field theory lacks only the feedback mechanism to be contemporary.

Virtually all the selections in Parts II through V were written in the two decades that have followed these last two conceptual statements. Some are by geographers, some by other social scientists. Many must be seen, at least in part, as tracing back their conceptual roots to the works discussed above.

THE INHERITANCE

Several general points should be made briefly in conclusion.

The constant preoccupation with the top unit in the hierarchy, in modern times the nation-state, and with the morphological description of political areas, has tended to impede the development of theory, and this legacy has been slow in fading.

On the positive side, political geography has inherited from its rich past several notions of stimulating utility. Deductions and extrapolations from the organic analogue model, particularly as related to the territorial growth and "life cycles" of states, have served to stimulate more scientific approaches. Much of what is now assumed grew out of this early conceptualizing. Moreover, this work has drawn attention to the relevance of studying behavior.

Hypotheses of political-environmental relationships have been common from the very beginning of the field and, although often strongly deterministic, they form a link with the new approaches now being developed toward these relationships.

Lastly, the formulation of spatial models of world power distribution also cover a long period and, although such models developed in more recent times were only briefly alluded to in this section, their relevance will be shown later in this volume.

This short discussion of the past will serve as a backdrop against which the variety of ideas presented in the essays and readings on structure, process, behavior, and environment can be seen in the perspective of their heritage.

---

39. Jean Gottmann, *La Politique des états et leur géographie* (Paris: Armand Colin, 1952); "Geography and International Relations," *World Politics*, III (January 1951), pp. 153-173; and "The Political Partitioning of Our World," *World Politics*, IV (July 1952), pp. 512-519. Karl W. Deutsch, *Nationalism and Social Communication: An Inquiry into the Foundations of Nationality* (Cambridge: Massachusetts Institute of Technology, 1953). A selection from Deutsch is included in a later section of this volume.

Heritage

1

The Ideal State

ARISTOTLE*

... The first point to be considered is what should be the conditions of the ideal or perfect state, for the perfect state cannot exist without a due supply of the means of life. And therefore we must presuppose many purely imaginary conditions, but nothing impossible. There will be a certain number of citizens, a country in which to place them, and the like. As the weaver or shipbuilder or any other artisan must have the material proper for his work ... so the statesman or legislator must also have the materials suited to him.

POPULATION SIZE

First among the materials required by the statesman is population: he will consider what should be the number and character of the citizens, and then what should be the size and character of the country. Most persons think that a state in order to be happy ought to be large; but even if they are right, they have no idea what is a large and what a small state. For they judge the size of the city by the number of the inhabitants, whereas they ought to regard, not their number, but their power. A city too, like an individual, has a work to do, and that city which is best adapted to the fulfilment of its work is to be deemed greatest, in the same sense of the word great in which Hippocrates might be called greater, not as a man, but as a physician, than some one else who was taller. And even if we reckon greatness by numbers, we ought not to include everybody, for there must always be in cities a multitude of slaves and sojourners and foreigners, but we should include those only who are members of the state, and who form an essential part of it. The number of the latter is a proof of the greatness of a city, but a city which produces numerous artisans and comparatively few soldiers cannot be great, for a great city is not to be confounded with a populous one. Moreover, experience shows that a very populous city can rarely, if ever, be well governed, since all cities which have a reputation for good government have a limit of population. We may argue on grounds of reason, and the same result will follow. For law is order, and good law is good order; but a very great multitude cannot be orderly. To introduce order into the unlimited is the work of a divine power—of such a power as holds together the universe. Beauty is realized in number and magnitude, and the state which combines magnitude with good order must necessarily be the most beautiful. To the size of states there is a limit, as there is to other things, plants, animals, implements, for none of these retain their natural power when they are too large or too small, but they either wholly lose their nature, or are spoiled. ... A state when composed of too few is not, as a

---

Reprinted by permission of the Clarendon Press, Oxford, from *The Works of Aristotle*, 1921.

* Aristotle (384-322 B. C.) was a Greek philosopher and political thinker.

state ought to be, self-sufficing; when of too many, though self-sufficing in all mere necessaries, as a nation may be, it is not a state, being almost incapable of constitutional government....

A state, then, only begins to exist when it has attained a population sufficient for a good life in the political community. It may indeed, if it somewhat exceed this number, be a greater state. But there must be a limit. What should be the limit will be easily ascertained by experience. For both governors and governed have duties to perform. The special functions of a governor are to command and to judge. But if the citizens of a state are to judge and to distribute offices according to merit, then they must know each other's characters; where they do not possess this knowledge, both the election to offices and the decision of lawsuits will go wrong. When the population is very large they are manifestly settled at haphazard, which clearly ought not to be. Besides, in an over-populous state foreigners will readily acquire the rights of citizens, for who will find them out? Clearly then the best limit of the population of a state is the largest number which suffices for the purposes of life, and can be taken in at a single view....

Territory

Much the same principle will apply to the territory of the state: every one would agree in praising the territory which is most entirely self-sufficing; and that must be the territory which is all-producing, for to have all things and to want nothing is sufficiency. In size and extent it should be such as may enable the inhabitants to live at once temperately and liberally in the enjoyment of leisure.

It is not difficult to determine the general character of the territory which is required (there are, however, some points on which military authorities should be heard); it should be difficult of access to the enemy, and easy of egress to the inhabitants. Further, we require that the land as well as the inhabitants ... should be taken in at a single view, for a country which is easily seen can be easily protected. As to the position of the city, if we could have what we wish, it should be well situated in regard both to sea and land. This then is one principle, that it should be a convenient centre for the protection of the whole country: the other is, that it should be suitable for receiving the fruits of the soil, and also for the bringing in of timber and any other products that are easily transported.

External Relations

Whether a communication with the sea is beneficial to a well-ordered state or not is a question which has often been asked. It is argued that the introduction of strangers brought up under other laws, and the increase of population, will be adverse to good order; the increase arises from their using the sea and having a crowd of merchants coming and going, and is inimical to good government. Apart from these considerations, it would be undoubtedly better, both with a view to safety and to the provision of necessaries, that the city and territory should be connected with the sea. The defenders of a country, if they are to maintain themselves against an enemy, should be easily relieved both by land and by sea; and even if they are not able to attack by sea and land at once, they will have less difficulty in doing mischief to their assailants on one element, if they themselves can use both. Moreover, it is necessary that they should import from abroad what is not found in their own country, and that they should export what they have in excess; for a city ought to be a market, not indeed for others, but for herself.

Those who make themselves a market for the world only do so for the sake of revenue, and if a state ought not to desire profit of this kind it ought not to have such an emporium. Nowadays we often see in countries and cities dockyards and harbours very conveniently placed outside the city, but not too far off; and they are kept in dependence by walls and similar fortifications. Cities thus situated manifestly reap the benefit of intercourse with their ports; and any harm which is likely to accrue may be easily guarded against by the laws, which will pronounce and determine who may hold communication with one another, and who may not.

There can be no doubt that the possession of a moderate naval force is advantageous to a city. The city should be formidable not only to its own citizens but to some of its neighbours, or, if necessary, able to assist them by sea as well as by land. The proper number or magnitude of this naval force is relative to the character of the state; for if her function is to take a leading part in politics, her naval power should be commensurate with the scale of her enterprises. The population of the state need not be much increased, since there is no necessity that the sailors should be citizens. The marines who have the control and command will be freemen, and belong also to the infantry, and wherever there is a dense population of farmers there will always be more than enough [sailors]. Of this we see instances at the present day. The city of Heraclea, for example, although small in comparison with many others, can man a considerable fleet. Such are our conclusions respecting the territory of the state, its harbours, its towns, its relations to the sea, and its maritime power.

Population Characteristics

Having spoken of the number of the citizens, we will proceed to speak of what should be their character. This is a subject which can be easily understood by anyone who casts his eye on the more celebrated [Greek] states, and generally on the distribution of races in the habitable world. Those who live in a cold climate and in Europe are full of spirit, but wanting in intelligence and skill; and therefore they retain comparative freedom, but have no political organization, and are incapable of ruling over others. Whereas the natives of Asia are intelligent and inventive, but they are wanting in spirit, and therefore they are always in a state of subjection and slavery. But the Hellenic race, which is situated between them, is likewise intermediate in character, being high-spirited and also intelligent. Hence it continues free, and is the best-governed of any nation, and, if it could be formed into one state, would be able to rule the world. There are also similar differences in the different tribes of [Greece]; for some of them are of a one-sided nature, and are intelligent or courageous only, while in others there is a happy combination of both qualities. And clearly those whom the legislator will most easily lead to virtue may be expected to be both intelligent and courageous. Some say that the guardians should be friendly towards those whom they know, fierce towards those whom they do not know. Now, passion is the quality of the soul which begets friendship and enables us to love; notably the spirit within us is more stirred against our friends and acquaintances than against those who are unknown to us, when we think that we are despised by them. . . .

The power of command and the love of freedom are in all men based upon this quality, for passion is commanding and invincible. Nor is it right to say that the guardians should be fierce towards those whom they do not know, for we ought not to be out of temper with any one; and a lofty spirit is not fierce by nature, but only when excited against evil-doers. And this, as I was saying before, is a feeling which men show most strongly towards their friends if they think they have received a wrong at their hands: as indeed is reasonable; for, besides the actual injury, they seem to be deprived of a benefit by those who owe them one.

. . . .

Thus we have nearly determined the number and character of the citizens of our state, and also the size and nature of their territory. I say "nearly," for we ought not to require the same minuteness in theory as in the facts given by perception.

Internal Structure

We have already said that the city should be open to the land and to the sea, and to the whole country as far as possible. In respect of the place itself our wish would be that its situation should be fortunate in four things. The first, health—this is a necessity: cities which lie towards the east, and are blown upon by winds coming from the east, are the healthiest; next in healthfulness are those which are sheltered from the north wind, for they have a milder winter. The site of the city should likewise be convenient both for political administration and for war. With a view to the latter it should afford easy egress to the citizens, and at the same time be inaccessible and difficult of capture to enemies. There should be a natural abundance of springs and fountains in the town, or, if there is a deficiency of them, great reservoirs may be established for the collection of rain-water, such as will not fail when the inhabitants are cut off from the country by war. Special care should be taken of the health of the inhabitants, which will depend chiefly on the healthiness of the locality and of the quarter to which they are exposed, and secondly, on the use of pure water. This latter point is by no means a secondary consideration. For the elements which we use most and oftenest for the support of the body contribute most to health, and among these are water and air. Wherefore, in all wise states, if there is a [lack] of pure water, and the supply is not all equally good, the drinking water ought to be separated from that which is used for other purposes.

As to strongholds, what is suitable to different forms of government varies: thus an acropolis is suited to an oligarchy or a monarchy, but a plain to a democracy; neither to an aristocracy, but rather a number of strong places. The arrangement of private houses is considered to be more agreeable and generally more convenient, if the streets are regularly laid out after the modern fashion which Hippodamus introduced, but for security in war the antiquated mode of building, which made it difficult for strangers to get out of a town and for assailants to find their way in, is preferable. A city should therefore adopt both plans of building. It is possible to arrange the houses irregularly, as [farmers] plan their vines in what are called "clumps." The whole town should not be laid out in straight lines, but only certain quarters and regions; thus security and beauty will be combined.

As to walls, those who say that cities making any pretension to military virtue should not have them, are quite out of date in their notions, and they may see the cities which prided themselves on this fancy confuted by facts. True, there is little courage shown in seeking for safety behind a rampart when an enemy is similar in character and not much superior in number; but the superiority of the besiegers may be and often is too much both for ordinary human valour and for that which is found only in a few; and if they are to be saved and to escape defeat and outrage, the strongest wall will be the truest soldierly precaution, more especially now that missiles and siege engines have been brought to such perfection. To have no walls would be as foolish as to choose a site for a town in an exposed country, and to level the heights; or as if an individual were to leave his house unwalled, lest the inmates should become cowards. Nor must we forget that those who have their cities surrounded by walls may either take advantage of them or not, but cities which are unwalled have no choice.

If our conclusions are just, not only should cities have walls, but care should be taken to make them ornamental, as well as useful for warlike purposes, and adapted to resist modern inventions. For as the assailants of a city do all they can to gain an advantage, so the defenders should make use of any means of defence which have been already discovered, and should devise and invent others, for when men are well prepared no enemy even thinks of attacking them.

2

The Laws of the Spatial Growth of States

FRIEDRICH RATZEL*

International law defines as the province of a state that part of the earth which is subject to the government of the state. Political geography as well is rooted in this definition, but has nothing to do with the clauses and provisos through which international law expands the domain of the state into either the sky or the earth to an indeterminate distance or extends that domain to all ships—particularly warships—which it interprets as a floating part of that state whose flag it flies. For political geography, on the other hand, all of those data are important which concern the extension of the jurisdiction of the state over adjacent seas and those various obligations which, in favoring one state, penetrate and violate the territory of another. Thus those Russo-Persian treaties of 1813 and 1828 through which the Caspian Sea became a "Russian Lake," which Russia "exclusively as hitherto" sails, should not go unnoticed. On maps the Russian boundary must be moved to before the roadsteads of Babol and Rascht as this Russian area of the Caspian Sea actually divides the Persian provinces of Khurasan and Azerbaijan as well as if a Russian province lay between them. The spread of the customs district of the German Empire over Luxembourg should also be pointed out in maps. The exercises of the Sea and Health Police of Austria-Hungary on the coasts of Montenegro cannot be represented on the map, but are greatly emphasized in every geographical description of these countries. Political geography in particular should emphasize the many such cases, for they fix more precisely that in the state which is related to the surface of the earth and is therefore the proper domain of geography, i.e., the region in its geographic sense. Moreover, such conditions are closely related to the spatial growth of states for two reasons: first because they appear at the periphery where such growth usually takes place and for which they pave the way, and second because they are the sign either of preparations for, or the remnants of, a growth process. Inventories of states which depict the territory of the state as a stable, fully fixed object come to this dogmatic and sterile conception primarily through disregard of such ruptures. Consideration of them can only strengthen the single correct conclusion: that in the state we are dealing with an organic nature. And nothing contradicts the nature of the organic more than does rigid circumscription. This is also true for political geography which, to be sure, deals primarily with the fixed bases of popula-

Translated by Ronald Bolin (1939–), who is a doctoral candidate in the Department of Geography at Indiana University.

* Friedrich Ratzel (1844–1904), a German geographer, was Professor of Geography at Leipzig University.

tion movements, but which must never lose sight of the fact that states are dependent both in their size and their form upon their inhabitants, i.e., they take on the mobility of their populations, as is particularly expressed in the phenomena of their growth and decline. Some number of people are joined to the area of the state. These live on its soil, draw their sustenance from it, and are otherwise attached to it by spiritual relationships. Together with this piece of earth they form the state. For political geography each people, located on its essentially fixed area, represents a living body which has extended itself over a part of the earth and has differentiated itself either from other bodies which have similarly expanded by boundaries or by empty space. Populations are in continuous internal motion. This is transformed into external movement, either forward or backward, whenever a fragment of land is newly occupied or an earlier possession is relinquished. We get, then, the impression that a population moves forward or backward as a slowly flowing mass.[1] Seldom in known history has it been the case that such movements spread over an unpossessed territory. Usually they lead to penetrations or displacements; or small areas, together with their populations, are combined into larger units without changing their location. In the same manner these larger states disintegrate again, and this process of union and disintegration, of growth and diminution, represents a major portion of the historical movements which are geographically depicted as an interchange of smaller and larger surfaces. Each spatial transformation has unavoidable consequences on all neighboring areas in Europe, as in any part of the globe, and its transmission from one area to another is one of the most potent motifs of historical development. Within this "spatial motif" there are two tendencies: *enlargement* and *reproduction*, both of which operate continuously as incitements to mobility. All philosophic theories of historical development are particularly defective in that they have overlooked these immediate conditions of the development of the state. In this respect the so-called developmental theories in particular are incorrect, whether they propose linear, spiral, or other developmental progression. To the aforesaid is added a third motif, *establishment*, or the nature of the relationship of the state to the land which determines the rate of the growth and in particular, the permanence of its result.

1. *The size of the state grows with its culture.* The expansion of geographical horizons, a product of the physical and intellectual exertions of countless generations, continually presents new areas for the spatial expansion of populations. To master these areas politically, to amalgamate them and to hold them together requires still more energy. Such energy can be developed only slowly by and through culture. Culture increasingly produces the bases and means for the cohesion of the members of a population and continually extends the circle of those who, through recognition of their homogeneity, are joined together.

Ideas and material possessions disperse from select originating and exit points, find new dispersal routes, and extend their area. In this manner they become the forerunners of the growth of the state, which then utilizes the same routes and fills the same areas. Above all we see a close relationship between political and religious expansion. But even these are surpassed by the enormous influence of commerce which yet today acts as a powerful impetus on all drives toward expansion. Lending support to all of these impulses are population pressures which increase with culture and which, having in their turn promoted culture, lead to expansion due to the pressures of space.

Though the greatest cultures have not always been the greatest state-builders—the formation of states is only one of many manners in which cultural powers may be utilized—all of the great states of the past and of the present belong to the civilized peoples. This is clearly shown by the contemporary distribution of the large states: they are situated in Europe and in the European colonial areas. China is the only state of continental dimensions which belongs to a cultural sphere other than European; at

---

1. The fluid nature of populations has often been used as an illustration. "La population des Etats Unis, comme un liquide que rien ne retient, s'est toujours étendue sur des nouveaux espaces," we read in the Count of Paris' *Guerre Civile* I, p. 362; the Russians were depicted by Leroy-Beaulieu as a slowly increasing sea which will soon have overflown its embankments. For political geography, however, it is more than this, for it lends to that subject, in its correlation between fixed land and mobile populations, the only correct interpretation of people and state, i.e., the organic regions in all of their variation.

the same time, however, of all non-European cultural regions, East Asia is the most highly developed.

If we go back to the beginnings of our own culture we find the spheres of the relatively largest states around the Mediterranean, which lands could not, however, build states of continental proportions due to their form and their location in a steppe zone. The amalgamation of several of them into the Persian Empire first brought to life a state the size of which, at about 5,000,000 sq. km., could be compared to European Russia. Egypt, together with its desert areas, was not larger than 400,000 sq. km., and the inhabited areas of Assyria and Babylonia not over 130,000 sq. km. Assyria's greatest, though uncommonly short-lived, expansion covered an area of about three times the size of present-day Germany.[2] Of all the former "World Empires" only the Persian corresponded to this grandiloquent name in that it drew upon the fullness of the Asian continent, particularly Iran, which is five times larger than Asia Minor. Neither the empire of Alexander (4,500,000 sq. km.) nor the Roman Empire (3,300,000 sq. km. at the death of Augustus) achieved this truly Asiatic dimension. The empires of the middle ages, particularly that of Charlemagne and the Roman Empire of the Hohenstaufens, were only fragments of the old Roman Empire, and constituted only a fourth of its area. The feudal system favored the formation of small states in that it divided and subdivided the land like a private estate causing, in the transition to more modern times, a general decay of states. What was left of old Roman spatial concepts died out after two of its presuppositions, learning and commerce, had already expired. From the ruins new formations arose which spread in Europe under the aegis of the equilibrium imposed by the wars. This system aimed at each having essentially the same area, whereas real power was unequally divided. In the lands outside Europe, first in America and Asia, political power spread with the trade, the beliefs, and the culture of Europe. The larger areas of these places formed the basis for states of two or three times the size of the largest which had previously existed. The speeded progress of geographical discoveries and knowledge of peoples permitted the growth of this new world empire over North America, north and south Asia, and Australia in less than 300 years. The relatively uninterrupted increase in population in Europe over the preceding 200 years and the invention of new means of transportation led them continuously to new means and motives for expansion and gave them a cohesion and permanence unheard of in history to that time. The British Empire (and within it Canada and Australia in their own right), the Asiatic-European empire of Russia, the United States of America, China, and Brazil, are states of a heretofore unprecedented size.

Just as the area of the state grows with its culture, so too do we find that at lower stages of civilization peoples are organized in small states. In fact, the further we descend in levels of civilization, the smaller become the states. Thus the size of a state also becomes one of the measures of its cultural level. No primitive state has produced a large state; none even one of the size of a German secondary state. Even among the larger and older powers we find, as in the interior of Indochina, village states of 100 inhabitants. Before the Egyptian occupation, in the nearly 138,000 sq. km. of the Azande territories assessed, Schweinfurth counted—probably not exhaustively—35 states, some of which did not extend beyond village boundaries. A large Azande state such as existed in the middle of the region even in Junker times, was scarcely as large as a third of Baden. Secondary states there were about the size of Waldeck or Lippe. Most, however, were from 3–12 sq. km. and were, in reality, sovereign villages. This was the case prior to that invasion of the entirety of the upper Nile between Nubia and Nyoro and between Darfur and Sennar. As the descriptions of Stuhlmann and Baumann show, it is still the same today in the whole of the north of German East Africa. Even in territories such as Usinje and Ukundi, inhabited by the Wakuma or Watusi who are renowned as the founders of states, the "village beadle" governs over small independent states of village district size with rustic shortsightedness and impotency. The fragments in which the Romans found the lands of the Rhaetians, the Illyrians, the Gauls and the Teutons, and the Germans those of the old Prussians, the Lithuanians, the Estonians, and the Livonians, were not much above such conditions.

---

2. Editors' note: This refers to the Germany of the 1890's.

Those peoples of powerful organization whose swarming, locust-like appearance often dealt terror to the young colonies in South Africa and North America also built only small states. Even though they devastated large areas, they lacked the capacity to hold and unite them. At annexation Basutoland comprised 30,000 sq. km., and Zululand 22,000 sq. km. Even these regions would have been reduced still further without the intervention of the whites. The league of the five, later (in 1712) six, tribes of the Allegheny region of North America were the most dangerous enemies of the young Atlantic settlements for more than a hundred years. Their territory occupied perhaps some 50,000 sq. km., though only spottily inhabited, and in 1712 they put 2150 warriors in the field. One need not accept the disparaging deductions of Lewis Morgan to conclude that the empire of Montezuma and the Inca empire were neither large states in the spatial sense, nor were they well integrated states. When we say that the Inca empire at the height of its militant expansion—which it had reached by the time of the arrival of Pizarro—comprised nearly the area of the Roman Empire at the time of Augustus, we must also add: it was nothing more than a loose bundle of conquered tributary states without stable or temporal cohesion, scarcely a generation old and already in disintegration even before the Spaniards overthrew it like a house of cards. Before the Europeans and Arabs had cultivated large states in America, Australia, north Asia, and inner Africa by conquest and colonization, these vast areas were not politically utilized. The political value of their earth lay fallow. Politics as well as agriculture led to a gradual knowledge of the powers that lie dormant in the earth, and the history of every country is that of the progressive development of its geographic conditions. The creation of political power by uniting smaller areas into larger is transmitted as an innovation into the "small-state" lands of the primitive peoples. In the struggles between smaller and larger state orientations which necessarily accompany this phenomenon, and in its disruptive effects, lies one of the main causes of the retrogression of these peoples since their more intimate contact with the cultured populations. That that race which has developed into a state has ended its political minority is called by Mommsen (*Röm. Gesch.* III, p. 220) a law, "as generally valid and as much a natural law as that of gravity." The precise expression of this, however, is to be found in the comparison of political areas. What a difference: North America, which today contains two of the largest states on earth, had, at the end of the 16th century, no single state of even secondary size. And what is it to the Papuans of New Guinea that they inhabit the largest habitable island in the world? They have not raised themselves in the least above the rest of the Melanesians, whose lands together do not make up a sixth part of New Guinea. Indeed, without the intervention of the Europeans they would have become increasingly tributary to dwarf-like Tidore (78 sq. km.).

States show then a gradation of size in accordance with their historical age. Among present-day states of continental size only China can be described as being old, and even it acquired the larger portion of its present area (Mongolia and Manchuria, Tibet, Yünnan, western Szechuan, and Formosa) only in the last century. All of the others on the other hand, the Russian Empire, Brazil, the United States, British North America and Australia, arose within the last two and a half centuries, and all of them on land which had formerly been made up of the small states of primitive peoples. The most remarkable trait in the present-day division of the earth—the powerful size of some few states—is a characteristic which has arisen in the last centuries and has been further developed and strengthened in our own time. Andorra is over a thousand years old, and Lichtenstein, as are several minor German states, is one of the oldest in its region. Compared to these, Prussia and Italy are in their first youth.

2. *The growth of states follows other manifestations of the growth of peoples, which must necessarily precede the growth of the state.* We have referred to diffusions which advance faster than the state; which precede and prepare the ground for it. Without political purpose of their own they come into the closest relationship with the life of states and do not stop at national boundaries. Ranke once said, "Over and above the history of single races I assert that general history has its own principle: it is the principle of the mutual interest of the human race which binds nations together and which dominates them, yet without being involved

in them" (*Weltgeschichte*, VIII, p. 4). This mutual interest in life lies in the ideas and goods which tend toward trade between peoples. It has seldom been possible for a state to set barriers on either the one or the other. More often the rule has been that these attract states along the same paths which they have already forged. Due to similar drives toward expansion and traveling similar paths, ideas and wares, missionaries and tradesmen often find themselves together. Both bring people closer together, create similarities among them, and thereby prepare the ground for political advancement and unification. Thus we find a coincidence to the point of mutuality in religion, weapons, cottages, domesticated plants, and animals in the states of the Azande even though they are sharply divided by wilderness boundaries. And commonality is still great even among the most distant tribes of North or South America though they give the impression of absolute political foreignness.

All of the ancient states and all states on lower cultural levels are theocracies. In them the spirit world not only dominates individuals, but conditions the state as well. There is no chief without priestly functions, no tribe without its tribal totem, no dynasty which does not boast of its divine origin. The theory of the divine right of kings and of the regional bishoprics is but a dim twilight of this condition. It is not in medieval Islam and Christianity alone that states were founded under the sign of the half-moon and the cross. In modern Africa, over and above state differences, the sphere of Islam looms opposite that of Christendom, and heathendom lies between; the latter consisting of small states as opposed to the large and secondary states of the former. In Europe the church hovered over a general political decay in which "all peoples turned their dissimilarities against one another," preparing new and greater state formations, while in west Asia and north Africa Islam assumed these tasks. The fantastically vast spatial notions of the Church at that time indicated a great superiority which, of course, retreated in the same measure as the worldly powers enlarged their scope. With science and trade, the Christian mission had prepared the way for the organization of new states in Africa, etc. by the Europeans. In Germany the lands of the Prussian order show vestiges of the broader purpose with which the church pursued the organization of states, while at the same time disintegration continued unabated in our country.

Primitive states are national in the narrowest sense. Their development is directed at the eradication of this limitation, and then returns to the national in a spatially broader sense. The states of the primitive peoples are family states. But the beginnings of their growth are greatly stimulated by their interaction with foreigners. Kinship groups can be a unifying force as far as the distributional area of the tribe extends; but this does not make a nation, even though common language and manners, engendered by apolitical commerce, make political unification easier. In times of advanced intellectual development this commonality comes to consciousness as a feeling for one's country and then operates toward integration and unification. Since, however, by its nature, this requires greater cultural development than is the case under conditions of rapid religious or mercantile expansion, this commonality comes into earlier conflict with the territorial expansion of the state which, since the Roman Empire for the first time aspired to a cosmopolitan character, has always ultimately triumphed over tribal distinctions. The state, however, recognizes the agglomerative value of national consciousness and seeks to reformulate it as a state consciousness by an artificial amalgamation of peoples in order that they may use it for their own purposes: Pan-Slavism. The Latin family of peoples shows how deeply and how broadly such a process may operate. It must set all cultural powers into operation and is therefore most successful in states which are, at the same time, large cultural regions. The modern, areally large yet fundamentally national state is its most characteristic offspring. Lying between these and the true confined tribal state are the numerous states of the past and the present, the cultural powers of which have been insufficient to unify their mixed ethnographic bases.

Commerce and communication far precede politics which follows in their path and can never be sharply separated from them. Peaceful intercourse is the preliminary condition of the growth of the state. A primitive network of routes must have previously been formed. The idea of uniting neighboring areas must be preceded by apolitical information. If the state has entered its growth period then it shares, with commerce, an interest in route connections. Indeed, it takes a lead in their systematic formation. The ingenious roads of both the Iranian and the ancient American states are better comprehended in terms of political than of economic geography. Highway and canal systems have, from the time of the mythical rulers of China to the present, had to serve the unification of the state, and every great ruler strove to be a builder of roads. Every commercial route paves the way for political influences, every network of rivers provides a natural organization for state development, every federal state allots commercial policy to the central government, every Negro chief is the primary, and if possible the only, tradesman in his territory. Colonization usually follows the "flag of commerce." The role of the trading post is prominent in the history of the North American states, as in the case of Nebraska with a post of the American Fur Company. The advancement of political boundaries is preceded by that of the customs frontier: the German Customs Union was the precursor of the German Empire.

The broadening of the geographical horizon by all of these apolitical expansions must precede political growth which, first borne by them, is later carried out independently as a goal of formulated policy. This is most clearly shown in that the sensible horizon of many a small Negro state is not as large as the area of a German secondary state, and that of the Greeks at the time of Herodotus had, at most, attained a magnitude comparable to the area of Brazil. The close relationship between geographic discovery and the growth of the state has long been recognized and is exhibited in the accomplishments of those who did both, such as Alexander, Caesar, Vasco da Gama, Columbus and Cook. To the present the greatest successes of expansive politics have been prepared under the guardianship of geography. The best contemporary example of this is that of the Russians in central Asia.

3. *The growth of the state proceeds by the annexation of smaller members into the aggregate. At the same time the relationship of the population to the land becomes continuously closer.* From the mechanical integration of areas of the most varied sizes, populations, and cultural levels there arises, through proximity, communication and the intermixture of their inhabitants, an organic growth. The growth of states which do not transcend mere annexation makes only loose, easily sundered conglomerates which can only be temporarily held together by the will of one whose intellect realizes a larger conception of space. The Roman Empire up to the first century before Christ was constantly threatened with disintegration until it created the military organization necessary to hold it together and had won for Italy the economic superiority which made of this most fortunately situated peninsula in the middle of the Mediterranean the focal point of a commercial sphere crossed by first-rate roads. Similarly we later see how, through the looseness of the "Gallic provincial alliance, continually vacillating between alliance and hegemony," the Roman merchant traced the path which the colonist, and after him the soldier, followed, and how all this worked toward the welding together of these adjacent, nearly inert elements into a mighty empire.

This process of the amalgamation of regional districts similarly enjoins the closer relationship of the people with their land. The growth of the state over the surface of the earth can be compared to the downward growth which leads to an attachment to the soil. It is more than a metaphor when one speaks of a people as taking root. The nation is an organic entity which, in the course of history, becomes increasingly attached to the land on which it exists. Just as an individual struggles with virgin land until he has forced it into cultivable fields, so too does a nation struggle with its land making it, through blood and sweat, increasingly its own until it is impossible to think of the two separately. Who can think of the French without France, or of the Germans without Germany? But this relationship was not always so firm and there are, even today, many states in which the people are not so intimately related to their land. As is true with regard to the size of the state, so also is there a historical series of stages in the relationship of the state and its land. Nowhere in the world do we encounter that detachment from the land which, according to many theoreticians, is supposed to be characteristic of more ancient conditions. However, the further we go back to primitive conditions, the looser this connection becomes. Men settle less densely and are more scattered; their cultivation is poorer and is readily moved from one field to another. Their social relations, particularly their system of moral organization, bind them so closely together that their relationship to the land is weak. And since small states at this stage isolated themselves from one another by wilderness boundaries and the like, not only is much space—often more than one half of a larger area—politically wasted, but competition for that which is politically most valuable in the land is also missing. Thus even the largest streams were often used neither as boundaries nor as trade routes by the Indians or the Negroes, but immediately became of inestimable value when the Europeans used them in their advance.

There is then a reduction in the political value of the land as we regress from the newer to the older states. This is closely related to the reduction of political areas. Even ancient observers of African life have alluded to the fact that in the innumerable small wars there it was not the acquisition of land, but rather the spoils of prisoners and slaves that was important. This fact is of great consequence for the history of Black Africa: slave hunts decimated the population and at the same time hindered the development of states, i.e., a double negative. The essential point is that the state is never at rest. A continuous outflow over its boundaries makes of it an exit point for expeditions of conquest which is surrounded by a belt of depopulated and desolate lands. Insecurity dominates its boundaries. They are dependent solely upon the energy with which these forward pushes are made, and as soon as these diminish the region shrivels up. No time is given for it to become stable on a particular piece of land. For this reason the duration of these powers, of which there are many examples in southeast Africa, from the Zulu to the Wahehe, is usually short. In the more advanced states of the Sudan this zone of conquest, or better, sphere of predatory incursion, is only a part of the state. The location and size of the Fulbe states, Bornu, Baghirmi, Waday, Darfur, etc. remain stable for long periods of time, but waver continuously at the point where they meet the unsubjugated "heathen lands," i.e., usually on the south side. Nachtigal in the north and Crampel and Dybowski in the south have shown in those areas how indefinite the location and extent of Waday is. But uncertainty regarding the political value of the land is still greater. The renowned "land-greed" of the conquering states of antiquity, particularly the Romans, is a notion which is not yet entirely settled. The acquisition of land was only an accompanying phenomenon in the great political revolutions of antiquity. Power, slaves and treasure were the prizes of battle, particularly in Asiatic wars, and hence the fleeting effects of their growth. In Rome from the time of the Pyrrhic wars a true struggle with the necessity of the acquisition of land may be observed. Desiring empire, a system of alliances and the checking of one power by another formed the base there. The expression of Mommsen regarding the Rome of the eighth century as "a dissolute block of lands without intensive occupance and suitable boundaries," is characteristic of this condition. The comparison with the Holy Roman Empire with its confusion of feudal kings, vassals, priests, exalted to the rank of princes, and independent cities is obvious. Caesar's greatness lay in the fact that he gave to the more stable body a definite, secure boundary as well as spatial expansion.

4. *The boundary is the peripheral organ of the state, the bearer of its growth as well as its fortification, and takes part in all of the transformations of the organism of the state.* Spatial growth manifests itself as a peripheral phenomenon in pushing outward the frontier which must be crossed by the carriers of growth. The closer these carriers live to the boundary, the more intimately do they share an interest in this process; and the larger the frontier, the more pronouncedly peripheral will the growth be. A state which stretches out toward a desired district sends out at the same time growth nodes which exhibit more activity than does the rest of the periphery. This is discernable in the shape of countries and in the distribution of their inhabitants and other power media. The outcrops of Peshawar and Little Tibet, and those from Merv and Kokand permit immediate recognition of that which even their history does not show; that in their direction British India and Russia grow together, determined to envelop all the benefits of the lands which lie between them, just as Rome through conquering Gaul grew counter to the advancing Teutons. On its German and Italian boundaries which for

centuries were positions of particularly strong growth, France concentrates its power media in striving to resume repressed growth. It is characteristic of such segments that they attract a major portion of the activity of the state. The marches of eastwardly expanding Germany which, as they were conquered piece by piece, were fortified and colonized, are repeated along the growing edges of America in the west and in Argentina in the south. There, in a few years large cities have arisen from the primitive log cabins of the fortified frontier. Given the crowded conditions of states in Europe such excellent portions of the periphery are at once among the most dangerous and the most fortified: the wounds which they can receive are to be feared above all others.

Other portions of the periphery of a state are given a special character because they are made up of the outwardly oriented peripheral segments of once independent regions which have grown together with that state. In every large frontier area we find such fragments of former national, provincial, or municipal boundaries which are the less altered the less they are adjusted to the forward and backward pushes of historical movements and the more practically they are created, i.e. have been adjusted and adapted to the terrain. There is a difference as between the worn outer banks and the highly indented inner shore of a spit, between a centuries old and a continuously developing boundary. The western and southern boundaries of Saxony can be offered as examples of this.

The frontier undergoes the same development as does the area, the consolidation, and the continuity of the state. If we go back to the first states on earth we find an indeterminacy of boundaries to the point of effacement. Where the area is uncertain, its periphery cannot possibly be distinct. The mania for transferring our conception of the boundary as a precisely determined line to conditions where the state comprises only an ill-defined spot on the earth has led, in the Indian policy of the American powers as well as in Africa, to the most arrant misunderstandings. As Lichtenstein[3] has said of the Kaffir boundary, the attempt was often made to fix a stable boundary which neither of the two parties should overstep without special permission from the sovereign; "in this, however, there has never been mutual consent." Not lines, but tiers are the important thing in this concept. In so far as a state is surrounded by politically empty space, the chances of encounter, of broad collision, are reduced and the state is drawn together. If its peoples, however, push beyond these limits, then it becomes more a matter of integration than of displacement: "The rights of property of the chiefs among the primitive peoples generally overlap."[4] If the untangling of such rights of property has presented the greatest of difficulties for the colonial authorities—is in actuality impossible—, there lies in this from the very first a powerful facility for every seizure and shift for the conquering and colonizing advance of the powerful states. Coupled with the primarily ruinous disparity in the political evaluation of the land, this has greatly speeded the dispossession of these peoples. Their political affairs were like their commerce in that they easily surrendered that which was most valuable as they didn't realize its worth. Long previously the cultural disadvantage of the closing off of one small state from another, one of the main causes of stagnation, was recognized. With the advent of the Europeans this concept went into decline. At a higher level, in the Sudan or in Indo-China, the boundary is fixed at many points on the periphery along mountains and watersheds. The system of the empty boundary zone is, however, also retained. One finds excellent examples of this in the Sudan in the works of Barth, Rohlfs, and Nachtigal. In contrast to cases in Africa and Indo-China, China a few years ago separated itself from Korea by a boundary line which was precisely determined. With regard to the further development of scientific boundaries, which are geodetically fixed, immovable, protected by fortifications and everywhere closely guarded—and which have not as yet been realized even in Europe—see my essay, "Über allgemeine Eigenschaften der geographischen Grenzen &c," in the reports on the conference of the K.S. Gesellschaft der Wissenschaften 1892.

5. *In its growth the state strives toward the envelopment of politically valuable positions.* In its growth and evolution the state practices selection of geographical benefits in that it occupies the good locations of a district before

---

3. *Reisen in Südafrika*, vol. I (1810) p. 353.

4. General Warren in *Blaubuch über Transvaal* (February 1885), p. 46.

the poor. If its growth is related to the dispossession of other states, it victoriously captures the good areas and the dispossessed continue in the bad. Therefore in the younger lands (colonies) whose entire history is known to us, the new political structures lie pronouncedly tiered along the sea, on the rivers and lakes, and in the fertile plains, while the older political forms are driven into the initially less accessible and less desired interior, into the steppes and deserts, the mountains, and the swamps. The same has happened in North America, in Siberia, in Australia and in South Africa. By the advantages which such locations offer to the first colonists they early determine the fate of large lands for a long time to come. Even if political possession is changed the earlier coming population remains at a cultural advantage, and the cultural miscarriage of many politically successful invasions can be explained in this manner. Carriers of the same culture have, all in all, the same concept of the value of the land, and for this reason all European colonies of the last centuries have undergone corresponding spatial development. At other times other assessments predominated. The ancient Peruvians did not go down the Amazon, but rather extended their domination in the plateau along a slender strip nearly 4000 km. long. The ancient Greeks did not seek large fertile interiors, but rather, following in this regard the Phoenecians, sought islands and peninsulas between inlets. The Turks, on the other hand, occupied the high steppes of Asia Minor which the Greeks disdained, and the Magyars the puszta of the Danube lowland. Custom as well as the level of culture are reflected in this and it is for this reason that political growth continues as long as possible in regions where there are similar living and working conditions. The Phoenicians settled on the coasts, the Dutch on islands, and the Russians on rivers. How greatly the expansion of the Roman Empire was benefited by the closed natural character of the Mediterranean lands was well known to the ancients. For Greece as well as for Rome these lands therefore presented the most fortunate of colonial regions where they could feel almost everywhere even more at home than does a central European in North America between 35° and 45° north latitude.

The envelopment of politically valuable locations is also expressed in the shape of the state. This we take to be a transitional stage of rest for the fundamentally mobile organism. Germany's expansion along the North and Baltic Seas, France's enclosure of the Meuse north of Sedan, Austria's encroachment over the ridge of the Erzgebirge along almost the total course of the Saxon-Bohemian border and her southern-most point which encloses the Boka Kotorska, and England's enclosure of the Channel Islands are some examples of this. Chile's northern boundary, drawn at 24° in the apparently useless Atacama desert, pushed up to 23° as soon as the guano deposits were discovered in the Bay of Mejillones. The discovery of diamonds on the Vaal River since 1867 followed the expansion of England across the Orange into an area which belonged to the Orange Free State; this is the direction in which Bechuanaland later grew further to the north. At lower stages states have a predilection for situating themselves on or near trade routes as is easily seen in the Sudan and in the interior of Africa. It is for this reason that Waday so seldom expanded toward Fezzan.

A major portion of the often long arrested growth tendency of states follows from the enclosure of politically advantageous locations, for since political growth consists of motion, or more the joining of countless movements, the state sees advantage in annexing those natural regions which favor movement. Thus we see it striving to attain the coasts, moving along the rivers, and spreading out over the plains. Another segment of the state pushes on through the barriers to those regions which are accessible to man. In this one must not think only of restraints but of the claims toward the filling out of naturally bounded regions as well. Rome grew along the desert in North Africa and West Asia. It had reached the southern foot of the Alps in 222 B.C. but first crossed them as a state some 200 years later after it had grown far beyond the Alps to the east and west. Bohemia filled its basin before any of the neighboring states had established fixed boundaries and as it grew beyond this basin its growth extended to the south east toward Moravia and the opening of the basin. Also of this same type is growth which takes place in the direction of least resistance. The growth of the central European powers to the east instigated at the first partition of Poland appears as an eastern backwash of the long frustrated western orientation of political energies. It is thus that the states of the Sudan grow uniformly, as has been said, from the Atlantic to the Indian Ocean in the direction of the weaker Negro states. Likewise the development of British dominion in India takes the form of an enclosing of the more powerful native states from the base of the more easily overpowered and weaker districts.

6. *The first stimuli to the spatial growth of states come to them from the outside.* Natural increase renews a simple political body and continuously reproduces it, but does not of itself produce any other form. The family renews itself in its offspring and begets new families and these remain together in the form of a family. Where exogamy dominates, two families follow precisely the same pattern. The tribe or family branches off to form another tribe, etc. All such bodies become, through their attachment to the land, a state. As they increase, larger states do not arise from the smaller, but rather a multitude of states of the same size. In order that an accustomed size not be exceeded, the size of the population is limited by all possible means, among which are the most cruel practices, and in this manner the growth of the state is limited. Growth is still further hindered by the enclosure of the state within a depopulated boundary area. The state is supposed to remain easily surveyable and within grasp. As far as our knowledge of primitive states extends their growth has never advanced without foreign influence. The origin of such growth is colonization in the broader sense. Men from regions of larger spatial conceptions carry the idea of larger states into districts of lesser spatial concepts. The native who is aware only of his own state is always at a disadvantage to him who knows at least two. Geographic location pointedly shows how the larger states in areas of small statism have grown inward from the most accessible outer side, i.e., from the coasts or the edges of the deserts. If we look at Africa prior to the time of the establishment of the European colonies we find large states along the line where Negroes, Hamites, and Semites are contiguous, and almost none where the Negroes are bounded either by each other or by the sea. Where, however, we find Negro states in the interior, there are also usually found sagas with regard to their founding concerning the foreign origin of their founders. Such tales are widespread over the earth. Often wandering hunters lay claim to this role which is reminiscent of the historical role of the slowly immigrating and infiltrating Kioko in the more recent transformation of the Lunda empire.

All of the states of Africa are conquered or colonial states. History shows a hundred times over this silent in-migration and expansion of a people which, first tolerated, suddenly comes to the fore in possession of power. Such has been the course of almost every European colonization. Thus the Chinese established their empire in Borneo. At the beginning of the Roman Empire, though cloaked in a mythical haze, we find the foreigners whose in-migration led to the ascendancy of Rome which was already better situated for trade and sea commerce than were other Latin cities. The first modern large state formation on Borneo since the empire of the Chinese gold miners, that of Rajah Brooke, is, in detail, the exemplification of such sagas of origin. At the advent of the Europeans there was in the entirety of Melanesia only one state structure, that of the immigrant Malayans on the northwest coast of New Guinea. The historical core of the wander sagas of the ancient American cultures cannot, it is true, be sorted out. But it cannot be by chance that the foundation of all states is assigned to foreigners. All other states of any size worth mentioning in America have, from European foundations, expanded inland into the small state regions of the Indians which are scattered throughout. America, Australia, and Africa south of the equator, which prior to the coming of the Europeans were left to their inhabitants and were the least stimulated areas of the earth, also exhibit the poorest development of states.

Whence comes the concept of a large state which is carried into these small state areas. Where they have not been carried by Europeans, sea, desert and steppe peoples; Hamites, Semites, Mongols and Turks, have been their bearers. If we further ask where the investigation of the origin of this concept leads in regard to the Europeans, we arrive at the shores of the eastern Mediterranean where fertile lands are situated in the midst of broad steppe areas. Egypt and Mesopotamia, Syria and Persia are large oasis lands which encourage the condensing of their populations into narrow areas and which are surrounded by districts which invite their inhabitants to spread out. From this distinction there springs a rich source of historical life. Just as Lower Egypt grew in the direction of Upper Egypt, as China grew in all directions from its loesslands, all such regions have furnished masses of men for martial inundation and slow colonial conquest. The political organization of these masses, however, and the great mastery of space which welded their single lands together, came from the steppes. From such lands have descended the founders of the great states in Egypt and Mesopotamia, Persia, India, China and also in the African Sudan. Because pre-Columbian America was without pastoral peoples—which peoples once dominated the greatest part of the old world—it was without continuous political ferment. This also provides a partial explanation for poor state development there.

The effects of wandering pastoralists on settled agriculturalists and tradesmen show, however, only one side of a more fundamental contrast. This same contrast underlies the bases of the state foundations of the sea-going peoples, the Phoenecians, the Normans, the Malayans, and again in the newest European colonies. We also encounter this in the worldwide tendency of the settled peoples, and particularly of the agriculturalists, to either retreat politically or to come to terms. All purely agricultural colonizations, that of the Achaeans in greater Greece, as well as those of the Germans in Transylvania and the Boers in South Africa, tend towards torpidity and are tainted by political clumsiness. The great success of Rome lay in the cross-fertilization of a robust peasantry and a more mobile, worldly element.

There is a difference in historical movements which is present throughout humanity. Some remain fast, others press forward, and both are encouraged in this by the nature of their dwelling places. For this reason the formation of states pushes forward from seas and steppes (regions of movement) into forest and arable lands (regions of persistence). Permanent settlement leads toward weakening and decay, whereas mobility, on the other hand, promotes the organization of populations. Such, in the Tartar hordes, the Vikings, and the Malay seamen, united lesser powers to greater effects. The most extreme cases of either can be found in Africa, as in the case of the Zulu, a warlike people organized to the point of the nullification of the family, and the Mashona, a people degenerated to slavery by generations of self-inflicted fragmentation. The two belong together since the former live from the latter. It is not necessary that a people in the process of the formation of a state force its nationality upon the politically passive as Babylon was Semiticised, because the laws of the growth of peoples and of states differ.

7. The general tendency toward territorial annexation and amalgamation is transmitted from state to state and continually increases in intensity. With an increasing estimation of its political value, the land has become of increasingly greater influence as a measure of political power and as a spoil in state struggles. As long as there is political competition the weaker states attempt to equal the more powerful. Carried over to the land there arises from this a struggle for spatial annexation and amalgamation. That the areas of Austria-Hungary, Germany, France and Spain can be expressed as 100, 86, 84 and 80; those of the Netherlands and Belgium as 100 and 90; and those of the United States of America and of British North America (with Newfoundland) as 100 and 96, and Ontario and Quebec as 100 and 97; and that throughout their history similar relationships have existed at the various levels of size and position, is the result of slow development and of annexation and amalgamation brought about by numerous struggles. Long before the sixteenth century which, in view of the struggles of Spain, Austria, and France for dominance in Europe had forged the concept of European equilibrium—the embryo of which however had already appeared at the end of the 15th century in Burgundian, Swiss, and Italian developments—this drive has been a law of the spatial development of states. At lower stages of development the same limited capacity for spatial domination may be active, as in the regional cluster of Uganda, Wanyoro, Ruanda or Bornu, Baghirmi, Waday and Darfur. Still lower we already see the joining together of smaller tribes following an attack by a stronger neighbor which operates as do the blows of a hammer in hardening political cohesion.

From the smallest beginnings of growth to the giant states of the present we see, then, the same tendency toward the emulation of the large on the part of the small and toward the largest by those which are already large and wish to equal the largest. This tendency is vital and, like a balance wheel, operates above variations and reverses to hold aloof the individual growth exertions together. It has shown itself to be as effective in the village states of the Azandeh territories as in the giant, continent-dividing states. And thus the drive toward the building of continually larger states continues throughout the entirety of history. We see it active in the present where, in continental Europe, the conviction of the necessity of joining together, at least economically, against the giants of Russia, North America, and the British Empire is awakening. Nor have the most recent colonial developments proven this law the less. In Africa it has called forth a veritable race of the powers for land, and England and Germany have made a division in a ratio of 125 to 100 of the remainder of New Guinea.

This goal is reached by very different means. A small state takes from its neighbor states enough land to become equal or similar to the greater among them: Prussia, later Germany, between France and Austria. States develop near and succeed one another in a common area of the earth, whereby the later ones approximate the dimensions taken by the earlier: Spanish America, French North America, the United States of America, and British North America. If a state is divided into two, they should not differ greatly in size: the kingdoms of the Netherlands and Belgium. A state which has been reduced in size takes at another side as much as is necessary in order to remain on that size level which it shares with its neighbors: Austria, which for a loss of 44,310 sq. km. on the Apennine peninsula then took 51,110 sq. km. in the Balkan peninsula. A fragmented partnership such as that of the Hansa operated according to the plan that the lands of the north not be allowed to join, i.e., that these lands remain in a situation similar to their own. Carthaginians and Greeks held each other in check so that Rome in central Italy was able to raise itself to the might of either of them. With reference to one broad area toward which one cannot remain passive, Russia and China are becoming the masters of Central Asia in that, according to an opinion of Wenjukow, the former have similar problems to solve as regards the Turkic peoples as have the latter with regard to the Mongols.

Naturally such emulation is not restricted to spatial size. Neighboring states differ as to advantages of position or natural endowment from which arise far-reaching commonalities of interests and functions. In the end even large states are concerned with selected areas. Canada, with its Canadian Pacific rivaled the Pacific-Atlantic connections of the United States, and shipping on the Great Lakes uses separate canals on both sides. Throughout the entirety of America there runs an imitation in organization and style of the political life of the North American free states, just as in the Sudan a pattern shines through all of the Islamic states whether their founder was a Fulbe or an Arabicized Nubian. So, too, the Persian and Roman Empires were patterns for a series of the states of antiquity and even throughout the old American plateau states there is a distant similarity which is strikingly apparent in the ingenious construction of roads.

In peaceful competition as in martial dispute the rule holds that those advancing must meet their opponents on their own ground. Insofar as they are victorious they become similar to them. States bordering on the steppes and in battle with steppe peoples must themselves become enough steppe states that they can master the advantages of the steppes; Russia and France show this in Central Asia and Algeria.

3

Earmarks of Political Geography

DERWENT S. WHITTLESEY[*]

THE POLITICAL AREA

The kernel of political geography is the political area. Every political unit describes an areal pattern of nuclear core, constituent or administrative regions, problem areas, vulnerable zones, capitals, strategic spots, and boundaries—all affecting its success even if not vital to its persistence. These features take form with respect to specific conditions of the natural environment. Commonly they harmonize with the earth conditions and the peopling of the place at the time of their origin. Once established they tend strongly to perpetuate themselves. It is a truism that maladjustment between a political feature and its natural setting may gradually increase for generations before it is rectified. The political areas which endure longest are noted for making frequent alterations by law in order to keep their institutions abreast of changing times. Where maladjustment is permitted to go on, it may have to be corrected by the dire expedients of revolution, disintegration, or conquest. In the meantime failure of the political pattern to fit the natural features which condition human existence causes friction. Indeed, the vise of crystallized political forms may distort the normal geographic design.

This is not to say that political areas are predestined subdivisions of the earth's surface. They may expand or shrink with the passage of time. Military conquests, folk migrations, discoveries of new lands, and changes in material technology have more than once altered the size, shape, and character of political areas. They may even lose their identity, although regions which have once stood out as leaders in political affairs are likely to reappear after longer or shorter eclipse. In the long view it must be conceded that the political significance of any area bears a well-defined relation to its climate, landforms, and natural resources. This relation remains unchanged, with the momentous exception that human ability to utilize and cope with nature advances or recedes and by so much alters it.

A factor in the persistence of those political areas which retain their identity is the pertinacity of the past in the realm of government. Political feeling is one of the strongest of all human emotions. Political attachments are correspondingly tenacious, and some part of the heritage of environmental conditions long vanished remains in the political order of every period. The political geography of few, if any, areas can be understood without recourse to their past. Study of the present-day political landscape must be supplemented by a review in their original setting of such relics of past

From *The Earth and the State: A Study of Political Geography* by Derwent S. Whittlesey. Copyright 1939 by Holt, Rinehart and Winston, Inc. Reprinted by permission of Holt, Rinehart, and Winston, Inc.

[*] Derwent S. Whittlesey (1890–1956) was Professor of Geography at Harvard University.

landscapes as survive in the patterns of today. The present can be set in its perspective only by reconstruction of the fragmentary records of history, and in some places the still more meager remains of archeology.

It seems likely that when a thorough canvass of the earth's political areas has been made, it will be possible to group them into well-defined categories, each characterized by specific inherent traits. This has been the line of advance in the study of natural regions and of economic regions. No such thorough canvass has as yet been made. Hence no satisfactory statement of the inherent traits of political areas is in the purview of the writer. It does seem possible to submit a crude catalog of major geopolitical designs.

1. Political areas tend to cohere about easily defended highlands, often folk-fortresses.
2. Conversely, others focus on fertile lowlands, particularly a natural nexus of rivers or other easy routes.
3. Margins of an inland sea may be rivals if they are alike in natural environment, or allies if they are reciprocal by nature. In any case they strive among themselves for political power.
4. Coastal footholds with penetration to the hinterland is a pattern commonly found in backward areas.
5. Jointure of strongly contrasted and reciprocal resources is urgent where the cleavage is sharp and no major barrier exists. The combination of a lowland with an adjacent highland is a common form. Another is the union of contrasted climatic regions.
6. Expansion over the whole of a unit area of climate is possible where desert or grassy vegetation predominates.
7. Transit lands find it difficult to remain independent and even to cohere, but they strive to achieve both objectives.

A crude outline of the elements in the study of a political area is suggested below.

1. Ecumene (often also the nuclear core).
    a. Natural environment, including size and shape, climate, landforms, and natural resources.
    b. Cultural structure—people, language, economic and social life.
2. Components—accretions to the ecumene or relics of territory once held.
    a. Relation of natural environment of each to that of the ecumene.
    b. Subordination of peripheral cultural structures.
    c. Unitary or federal character of the aggregate components.
3. Problem areas and friction zones.
    a. Natural and cultural items in the problem or friction.
    b. Relation of each district to the ecumene and to its immediate neighbors.
4. Capitals.
    a. Central—related to the whole area or to the ecumene.
    b. Peripheral—related to a defensive or offensive frontier, or to relict position.
    c. Subcapitals—of constituent members of a federation, and of administrative districts.
5. Boundaries.
    a. Naturally marked or otherwise.
    b. Antecedent or subsequent to current occupance of the area.
    c. Density of settlement and degree of interpenetration along each distinct segment of the boundary.
    d. Strategic reaches and points.
6. Allied areas and dependencies.
    a. Contiguous or separated.
    b. Character of separation—land or water.
    c. Cultural structure and the degree of subordination to the dominant area.

The Law and Regions

The agent whereby the political structure of any area is constructed is the law. Like any other human concept, the law freely flits from one region to another. Laws are frequently enacted which are so at variance with nature in the political area affected that they have to be rescinded or they remain among the statutes as dead letters. Others, while somewhat inharmonious, manage to operate; to some extent they modify utilization of earth resources. In time the fundamental law in each political area becomes roughly suited to the few compulsive conditions laid down by nature. A large body of law, even when introduced from outside, falls within the range of tolerance established by earth conditions. The legal forms which guide most human activities may vary considerably without doing violence to human living. At the same time they may produce contrasts in man's use of identical environments. Variations in culture patterns in uniform environments on opposite sides of a political boundary are common, and prove the possibility of modifying the landscape by political means. The operation of law can be traced only through patient study of the incidence of individual laws. Few such studies have been made.

The legal structure of only a few political areas today is wholly consequent upon local natural environment. Four basic legal structures may be recognized:

1. Migrant. Personal law inhering in the unfixed tribal group.
2. Sedentary. Territorial law adhering to fixed areas.
3. Transhumant. Territorial law extended over seasonally vacant spaces, in many cases by special agreement among groups concerned.
4. Commensal. Government by agreement or by domination divided between a sedentary and a migrant group.

. . . .

Most of the great legal systems of the earth are so flexible and adaptable that they operate in a considerable variety of regions. In some cases they have been transferred from their original homeland by colonization. Or they have been superposed on an existing regional society. In either case the adaptability of any broad system saves it by permitting necessary modifications. Even in the region of its origin every legal system is subject to continuous alteration to conform to changes in density of population, new material technology, and the cyclic changes in the character of human occupance of a region which occur as a result of the occupance itself. The interplay of law and regions is incessant. Each affects the other and in the process is itself modified. As in every other aspect of geography, earth conditions permit a wise range of laws in most regions, and at the same time set limits that nullify laws which stand outside the permitted range.

GEOPOLITICAL FORCES

The forces which give to earth conditions their expression in the law have been much discussed but are imperfectly understood. Doubtless some of them remain to be discovered. The tables of contents of most works on political geography abound in touchwords with which the authors endeavor to give tongue to these intangible forces; e.g., space, the ground, situation, natural domain. How many of them designate valid concepts is not known, because most of them have been deduced from theories of the state and of its relations to the earth.

An alternative approach to the veiled subject of geopolitical forces suggests itself, in the processes which entail interplay of regions and law. One of these is the functioning of political parties. Parties appear to be fundamental to any government, although they obtain free play only in democratic societies. One function of a political party is to give voice to regional interests; another is to exert its influence on lawmaking. Another pertinent process is administrative. Executive officers of government work within a legal framework, but their acts frequently exceed the specific instructions of laws. One of the reasons for this is the eternal divergence between law, which once passed is static until revised, and nature, unceasingly dynamic. A third process adheres to the third branch of government, the judicial. Laws are subject to interpretation by judges, although the freedom of action of judicial officers is narrower in most countries than in the United States.

To obtain a clear view of the geopolitical forces the earth processes must also be studied. Chief among these is the earth's inexorable march from causes to consequences. Laws flagrantly unsuited to regions where they operate ultimately destroy the resource which they govern; e.g., the state which taxes timberland annually soon finds on its hands denuded and worthless tracts which have reverted to the state because of non-payment of taxes. There is more than a little reason to believe that the current insistence in some states on national self-sufficiency at the level of world interdependence is depleting soil, upsetting the balance between nature and society, and undermining the state itself. Scarcely any considerable alteration can be performed upon the face of nature without unexpected repercussions. Most such operations are possible only to governments. The dams built in Egypt since 1900 have already made it necessary for Egyptian farmers to import fertilizer for fields which had got on very well without it for at least 7000 years.

Observation in Political Geography

Doubtless political areas, the interplay of law and region, and the underlying geopolitical forces can and should be studied from every conceivable angle of view. The utility of multiple working hypotheses in arriving at sound conclusions is well understood and needs no restatement here. Unfortunately the growth of modern geography has been retarded by a tendency of its sponsors to generalize on the basis of insufficient evidence. This has perhaps been true of the youth of all sciences, but human geography is so young that it still suffers from overzealous devotees, who claim for it a body of "laws" in advance of their proved validity.

In no sphere of geography has the disproportion between observation and speculation been so great as in political geography. This is natural. Political theory has been a favorite intellectual calesthenic from early times. Its application in the realm of geography is enticing, and the painstaking testing of its validity is hampered by three major difficulties.

The chief of these is observation of the facts *in situ*. It is axiomatic in geography that its data must be gathered from the field. Techniques for the study of physical geography are well established, and economic geography is becoming equipped with facilities for effective field observation. As yet the remaining branches of systematic human geography—social and political—almost totally lack recognized field techniques. Political forces generally etch the landscape but lightly, and still oftener their effects are inextricably entwined with phenomena of economic geography. The patent observable features of political geography are boundaries, capitals, administrative components, and a few areas of political friction or unquestioned strategic importance—no others. Its many further ramifications must be sought in the economic and social impress of laws upon the landscape, in the vestiges of political and military contests, and in the ephemeral man-made structures whereby government is facilitated. The observer in the field, confused by the complex intertwining of political, social, and economic patterns in the landscape, and perhaps thwarted in his efforts to trace any evidence whatever of political forces, can show only meager and piecemeal results of his efforts. These compare poorly with the splendid façade built up of theory spun from a few well established facts.

Political geography also thrusts strong and deep roots into the past. The emotional character of political thought holds communities and states to traditional patterns and practices long after their original connection with the natural environment has been forgotten. Sound political geography therefore must trace these relict forms and procedures to their source, by means of observation in the field, a duty which has too often been neglected. Even when undertaken, the quest in historical and archeological records may prove barren, for lack of adequate historical or archeological data or because the circumstances are recorded without reference to their environmental setting. Without the exact knowledge of place which comes only from observations on the spot, the most carefully gathered records of the past are likely to be geographically meaningless.

A further difficulty faces the political geographer, i.e., his political fealty. Nowadays every occidental person is born into a national state, the validity of which is accepted without question. It is easy to lose sight of equally valid rival claims of other states, especially if they conflict with axiomatic loyalties, accepted from earliest recollection. The shaping of political geography to serve the ends of statecraft is a natural human tendency. It inevitably vitiates any claim to scholarship. Unfortunately it has found such widespread expression in the years since the World War that a whole literature of books and papers has been published in support of the environmental rightness of political claims. Many of these biased statements can be distinguished from unprejudiced studies in political geography by the designation "geopolitics," commonly used by German proponents of the earth-based claims of their nation. They are not, however, confined to German writers, but may be found in chauvinistic work appearing in every country. Here again, the chief check against mistaking national aspirations for geographic truths is rigorous observation in the field. The field alone is uncolored by the prejudices, conscious or unconscious, of human minds.

In an effort to escape the dilemmas inherent in the present status of the subject (or perhaps because they are unaware of its central problems), some students have attached the name "political geography" to discussions of the economic or regional geography of political areas. This is nothing but reversion to the "general geography" current in the 19th century, and abandoned with the growing recognition of the paramount significance of economic phenomena and regional associations as compared to the mere outlines of states, as frames for assembling geographic data. The relapse to an outworn procedure is the more lamentable because it diverts the term "political geography" from its accepted sense. The mere fact that most compiled data needed by geographers are arranged by political units is no palliation of the sin of debasing a recognized and useful appellation. It should be noted that observation in the field promptly discloses the unreality of political lines as the fundamental subdividers of the earth.

4

The Functional Approach in Political Geography

RICHARD HARTSHORNE*

... I suggest that we start with the functions of politically organized areas, and that we maintain this procedure throughout.

In confining our attention to politically organized areas, I do not mean to assert by implication that there are not other political phenomena of concern to the geographer.... Suffice it to say that a distinct type of problem is presented us in the study of the geography of politically organized areas and I will therefore confine myself to that type of problem.

There are of course many varieties and different levels of politically-organized areas. If one were studying certain areas of Africa or Asia at an earlier period of history, one would be primarily concerned with the very loose form of territorial organization effected by tribal units. In a future, we trust better, world, the geographer may be concerned with the political organization of large international territories—ultimately, one hopes, of the whole world. In the present world, however, there are but two types of politically-organized territories, which together cover theoretically the entire inhabited world and are of transcendent importance—namely, the areas of the independent, sovereign states and those of dependent countries, whether called colonies, protectorates, or possessions, which are organized in greater or less degree by members of the first group, the imperial states.... The uninhabited oceans, together with Antarctica, do not constitute units for study under our major heading because they are not politically organized. Their use and control, however, will present us with problems in considering the relations among the politically organized areas.

There is of course a place for the geographic study of politically organized areas of lower levels—the subdivisions of states. The relationship between the units at different levels is not, however, comparable to that in non-political regional geography. A sub-region of the Corn Belt may include all the functions found in the Corn Belt, and its validity as a region is independent of the larger region. In contrast, the subdivisions of states—whether provinces, departments, counties, or townships—are generally created by the state and are specifically excluded from certain political functions performed for them by the state of which they are a part. This statement must be qualified in significant, but on the whole minor, degree in respect to the autonomous units of federal states—the States of the United States, or Australia, or the Provinces of Canada.

Units of political organization at a higher

Reproduced from the *Annals* of the Association of American Geographers, Volume XL, 1950, by permission of the author and publisher.

* Richard Hartshorne (1899–) is Professor of Geography at The University of Wisconsin.

level than the sovereign states include the empires that have been organized individually by certain of those states. Organizations of territory including more than one sovereign state have hitherto been represented only by the British Commonwealth, but both France and the Netherlands are now attempting to construct similar organizations. Finally students are not limited to what exists; we are free to use our imagination to study the potential basis for other larger units—whether an Arab union, a Western European Federation, a North Atlantic Union, or a world union.

For the purposes of this paper, I wish to focus attention solely on one type of political area—the sovereign state, even though that ignores the large part of the world that is organized in units dependent on outside sovereign states....

ANALYSIS OF THE POLITICAL GEOGRAPHY OF A STATE: INTERNAL

I propose [then], to consider the central problems of political geography in terms of the functions of state-areas. What comes first? The fundamental purpose of any state, as an organization of a section of land and a section of people, as Ratzel first put it, is to bring all the varied territorial parts, the diverse regions of the state-area, into a single organized unit.

What does the state attempt to organize, in all regions of the state-area?

In all cases, it attempts to establish complete and exclusive control over internal political relations—in simplest terms, the creation and maintainance of law and order. Local political institutions must conform with the concepts and institutions of the central, overall, political organization.

In many social aspects—class structure, family organization, religion, and education—a state may tolerate considerable variation in its different regions. But because of the significance of these factors to political life, there is a tendency—in some states a very marked effort—to exert unifying control even over these institutions.

In the economic field, every modern state tends to develop some degree of unity of economic organization. At the minimum, it establishes uniform currency, some uniformity in economic institutions, and some degree of control over external economic relations. Beyond that, states of course vary greatly in the degree to which all aspects of production and trade—price and wages levels, etc.—are placed under uniform control.

Finally, and most importantly, because we live in a world in which the continued existence of every state-unit is subject to the threat of destruction by other states, every state must strive to secure the supreme loyalty of the people in all its regions, in competition with any local or provincial loyalties, and in definite opposition to loyalty to any outside state-unit.

Throughout this statement of the organization of the state-area as a unit, the geographer is primarily concerned with emphasis on *regional* differences. The state of course is no less concerned to establish unity of control over all classes of population at a single place. In political geography, our interest is in the problem of unification of diverse regions into a single whole; the degree of vertical unification within any horizontal segment concerns us only as a factor aiding or handicapping regional unification.

Parenthetically, we may also note the ways in which this primary function of the state affects the general field of geography. Land-use, industrial development, trade, and a countless list of social aspects of human geography in any region will differ in greater or less degree as a result of the efforts of the state in which it is included to control its development as part of a single whole. Only the peculiarity of geographic study in such a large country as the United States, where we are usually forced to do most of our work within the territory of our single state, has permitted us to study geography as though we could ignore political geography.

Our analysis of the primary function of any state leads directly to the primary problem of political geography. For no state-area constitutes by the nature of its land and people, a natural unit for a state, in which one merely needs to create a government which shall proceed to operate it as a unit. The primary and continuing problem of every state is how to bind together more or less separate and diverse areas into an effective whole.

For the political geographer, this presents a wide range of specific problems for analysis. In every state area, larger than such anomalies as Andorra or Liechtenstein, the geographer finds: (1) regions that are more or less separated from each other by physical or human barriers; (2) regions that in greater or lesser degree diverge in their relations with outside states; and (3) regions that differ among themselves in character of population, economic interests, and political attitudes. Let us look briefly at each of these types of problems.

Centrifugal Forces

Geographers are familiar with the effect of particular types of physical features in handicapping communication between regions. Semple and others have described for our own early history the political consequences of the forested Appalachians and later of the mountain and desert barrier of the west. Whittlesey's study of the Val d'Aran depicts in detail the problem in that bit of Spain north of the Pyrenees.[1] In most modern states, however, these problems have largely been overcome by the development of the telegraph and the railroad. They continue of importance, however, in parts of the Balkans, in the highland states of Latin America, and in China.

Since state-organization requires communication not only from one region to the next, but from a central point to each peripheral region, distance itself is a centrifugal factor. Obviously distance within a state depends on its size and shape. Size and shape are significant to the state in other, quite different respects, but I suggest we wait until we have determined that in our analysis, rather than attempt to proceed deductively from size and shape to consequences.

Of human barriers, the most common is the absence of humans. Uninhabited or sparsely inhabited areas were, until recently, difficult and dangerous to cross. It was primarily on this account that relatively low mountains, in central Europe or the Appalachians, long functioned as dividing zones. Even in the Alps, the problem of surmounting high elevations was less serious, in the Middle Ages, than the difficulty of securing supplies along the way and the ever-present danger of attack from "robber barons."

Further, the presence of such relatively empty areas created, and still creates, a feeling of separation in the regions on either side. Both on this account and because of distance, oceans continue to function as the strongest separating factors, other than the Arctic ice, even though they have long been crossed with relative ease.

France has first inaugurated the interesting experiment of incorporating trans-oceanic areas into the organization of its state. Its West Indian islands and the island of Réunion in the Indian Ocean are now départements of metropolitan France, sending delegates to its national assembly. We may be about to do the same with Hawaii.

Perhaps the most difficult barrier to overcome is separation by a zone populated by a different people, especially an unfriendly people. The Germans have apparently convinced the world that the separation of East Prussia by the Polish Corridor was an experiment that is never to be repeated. (They overlooked the fact that there were not one but two alternatives to that device.)[2]

Serious difficulties may arise for a state if any of its regions have closer relations with regions of outside states than with those within the state. This is commonly the case where a boundary has been changed so that it now cuts across an area formerly within a single state. The partition of Upper Silesia, in 1922, presented a particularly intense case.[3] But there are many cases, not dependent on boundary changes, in which a region has closer connections, particularly economic connections, with regions of other countries than with other regions of its own state. We are familiar with the political importance of this factor in each of the major regions of Canada, each more closely related in certain respects with the adjacent areas of the United States than with the other regions within the Dominion. In some cases mutual interdependence among the regions of the state-area is less than the dependence of individual regions on remote, overseas countries. This is a major problem of the Australian Commonwealth, in which each state unit is primarily dependent on separate trade with Great Britain. In Western Australia, this factor,

---

1. Derwent Whittlesey, "Trans-Pyrenean Spain: The Val d'Aran," *Scottish Geographical Magazine* (1933), pp. 217–228.

2. Richard Hartshorne, "The Polish Corridor," *Journal of Geography*, XXXVI (1937), pp. 161–176.

3. Richard Hartshorne, "Geographic and Political Boundaries in Upper Silesia," *Annals* of the American Association of Geographers, XXIII (1933), pp. 195–228.

together with notable physical and human separation has led at times to demand for secession from the Commonwealth. Northeastern Brazil offers a somewhat similar problem for study.

The geographer, however, must beware of drawing conclusions from the physical map, or, on the other hand, of assuming that an economic situation to which we are accustomed represents a "normal" development in economic geography independent of a particular political framework. Consider southern California, separated by thousands of miles of desert and mountain from the main body of the United States, facing the Pacific highway to densely populated lands of the Orient. And yet which region of the United States is more completely bound into the economy of the country as a whole?

All the previous examples are relatively extreme cases. In most instances the potentialities are highly flexible. The plain of Alsace, separated from the rest of France by the rugged heights of the Vosges, facing southern Germany across the narrow band of the Rhine flood-plain and easily connected with northern Germany by that navigable river—with which state does it fit in terms of economic geography? Surely the answer must be that in terms of modern technology all these features are of minor importance and in terms of the economic potentialities of the area it can be associated almost equally well in either the French or the German economic unit.

Separation of regions by barriers or by divergence of outside connections are commonly less important than the centrifugal forces that result from diversity of character of the population. To secure voluntary acceptance of a single common organization requires some degree of mutual understanding; obviously this is easier in a population homogeneous in character. Further, where regions differ in social character, the tendency of the state to force some degree of uniformity of social life meets with resistance. Thus the very attempt to produce unity may intensify disunity. Hungary, before 1918, was the classic example; since then Yugoslavia has been perhaps the leading, among several, successors.

What particular social characteristics may be important depends on the particular state. Everyone thinks of language and religion. I suggest, also, education and standards of living, types of economic attitudes and institutions, attitudes toward class and racial distinctions, and, especially, political philosophy.

For materials on these topics we look to that branch of geography that has been least developed—social geography. In most cases what materials we have provide only the raw data, the facts about the distribution of, say, religions or races, rather than the regional differences in social attitudes towards these facts; it is the latter that we need.

Thus, the fact that Alsace was predominantly Roman Catholic, like France but unlike most of Germany, was less important than the the fact that its attitude toward the relation of church and state was similar to that in the German Empire of 1871–1918, and was in conflict with the anti-clerical attitude of the French Republic.

Racial differences, in the terms studied by the physical anthropologist, may be of no relevance to our problem. The distribution, percentage-wise, in the different countries of Europe, of blondes and brunettes, dolichocephalic versus brachycephalic—what does it matter? These facts have no reflection in social or political attitudes in those countries. Though standard material in most geographies of Europe, I submit that they have no significance to political geography, or for that matter, to geography in general.

In contrast, the United States is a country in which regional differences in attitudes of people toward the racial components of the regional group—as indicated by skin color—are of tremendous importance in social, economic, and political life. We have mapped and studied the underlying differences in racial composition, but we have not studied the phenomenon itself—namely the differences in attitudes. We need a map, a series of maps, portraying different kinds and degrees of Jim Crowism in the United States. These I would rate as a first requirement for an understanding of the internal political geography of the United States, for in no other factor do we find such marked regional cleavages, such disruption to the national unity of our state. For geography in general, in one quarter of our country, these attitudes are fundamental factors in every aspect of the human geography, and are significantly related to its physical geography.

Geographers are more familiar with differences in economic interests, since these are more closely bound to the land. But these are seldom seriously disrupting to national unity. It is true that almost every modern state has experienced marked political tension between the divergent interests of highly industrial regions and those of still primarily agricultural areas. But these very differences tend to lead to interlocking, rather than competing, interests. Even when competing, economic differences, Marx to the contrary notwithstanding, are easier to compromise than differences in social and political attitudes.

Furthermore, the state is only in partial degree an economic unit. Since it is basically a political unit, the state necessarily imposes the greatest degree of uniformity in political life. Political attitudes are peculiarly inflexible. If a region is accustomed to one set of political concepts, ideals and institutions—most especially if its people feel that they have fought in the past to establish those political values—it may be extremely difficult to bring them under the common cloak of a quite different system. Even where regions formerly in separate states have voluntarily joined together to form a state, on the basis of common ethnic character—for example the three Polish areas in 1918, or the Czech and Slovak areas—the marked difference in past political education led to difficult problems.

In times and areas of relatively primitive political development such factors were no doubt of minor importance. In long-settled areas of relatively mature political development they may be of first importance. The classic example is, again, Alsace. Thanks particularly to the French Revolution, the people of that province had become strong supporters of political concepts, ideals, and institutions that could not be harmonized within the semi-feudal, authoritarian monarchy of Hohenzollern Germany.

Conversely, one may understand, on this basis, the negative reaction of the Swiss in 1919, to the proposal that the adjacent Austrian province of Vorarlberg should be added to their state.

Centripetal Forces

The preceding discussion of political attitudes points to an essential ingredient that has been lacking in the discussion up to this point. We have been considering a variety of centrifugal factors in the regional geography of a state-area which make it difficult to bind those regions together into an effective unit. In considering how such difficulties may be overcome, we have not asked whether there was any force working to overcome the difficulties, anything tending to pull these regions together into a state.

This omission, I suggest, has been the single greatest weakness in our thinking in political geography. If we see an area marked clearly on both physical and ethnic maps as suitable for a state, but which for many centuries was not integrated as a state—as in the Spanish peninsula, the Italian peninsula, or the German area—we cudgel our heads to find factors in its internal geography that will explain the failure. We forget that before we speak of failure, we must ask what was attempted.

The Italian peninsula, together with the northern plain attached to the mainland but isolated by the Alps, with a settled population speaking approximately a common tongue since the Middle Ages, has offered one of the most obvious geographic units of Europe for the development of a state. Yet Italy, as an Austrian minister jeered, was only a geographic expression; there was nothing that could be called even the beginnings of a state of Italy. For no one of importance had any idea of producing an Italian state and had anyone tried, his purpose would have shattered in conflict with two opposing ideas: one, the concept of the Papal States, the secular control of mid-Italy by the Pope in order to secure his undivided domination of Rome as the spiritual capital of Western Christendom; the other, the concept of a single great empire in the heart of Europe, extending from northern Germany to northern Italy. Only after the power of these centuries-old ideas had been irrevocably destroyed by the ferment of the French Revolution was it possible for any Italian leader to consider seriously the unification of Italy.

One of the concepts that prevented integration in Italy is likewise the key to the failure of medieval Germany to develop a unified state, at the time when the kingdoms of France and England were being effectively established. For centuries the persons holding the title of King of Germany, and whatever opportunity that might give, were far more affected by the higher title of Emperor. Inspired by the grander idea of reincarnating the empire of Rome, they fought to build a state straddling the Alps, uniting many different peoples. The sacrifices made in the vain attempt to accomplish the greater idea destroyed the possibility of achieving the lesser when later emperors finally were reduced to considering German unity.

The fact that a country has a name and a government, that an international treaty recognizes its existence as a state and defines its territorial limits—all that does not produce a state. To accomplish that, it is necessary to establish centripetal forces that will bind together the regions of that state, in spite of centrifugal forces that are always present.

The State-Idea

The basic centripetal force must be some concept or idea justifying the existence of this particular state incorporating these particular regions; the state must have a *raison d'être*—reason for existing.

Although ignored in much of the literature of political geography, this is not a new thought. Ratzel defined the state as a section of land and a section of humanity organized as a single unit in terms of a particular, distinctive idea.[4] Maull, among other German geographers, has discussed the concept at some length.[5] It was presented to this Association a decade ago.[6]

At the primitive level, Ratzel explained, this idea may be no more than the will of a ruler to which, for whatever reasons, all the regional parts through their local leaders grant their loyalty. In such a case, as in the empire of Charlemagne or that of Ghengis Khan, the state may endure hardly longer than the lifetime of the individual ruler. In the attempt to perpetuate the binding idea of loyalty to a personal ruler, there evolved the concept of hereditary monarchy. Where that succeeded, however, we find there was always something more—politically-minded people in the various parts of the kingdom came to regard the state, for reasons independent of the monarch, as representing something of value to them. Today the monarchical institution is safe only in those states in which the monarch has exchanged the active power to rule for the passive role of personification of the national heritage.

To be sure, a state in which the original idea has lost its validity will not fall apart at once. The forces of inertia, vested interests, and fear of the consequences of change may keep it going more or less effectively for some time. But inevitably a structure that has lost its original *raison d'être*, without evolving a new one, cannot hope to stand the storms of external strife or internal revolt that sooner or later will attack it. For when that day comes, the state, to survive, must be able to count upon the loyalty, even to the death, of the population of all its regions.

It is not mere coincidence that the terms I have been using came to me from a Viennese geographer, in his analysis of the failure of the Habsburg monarchy. Unless Austria-Hungary, Hassinger wrote after the First World War, had been able to discover and establish a *raison d'être*, a justification for existence, even without the calamity of the war, it could not long have continued to exist.[7]

Those states are strongest, Ratzel had concluded, "in which the political idea of the state fills the entire body of the state, extends to all its parts."[8]

What does this mean for our study of the political geography of a state? It means, I am convinced, that before we can begin to study the problems presented by the centrifugal forces I have previously outlined, we must first discover the motivating centripetal force, the basic political idea of the state. Under what concept, for what purposes, are these particular regions to be bound together into one political unit, absolutely separated from every other political territory?

Does this seem too remote from geography? Too much like political science? The student of geography of climates must understand the nature of air-masses, as analyzed by the meteorologist. We cannot intelligently study

4. Friedrich Ratzel, *Politische Geographie*, 3rd ed., (Munich and Berlin: R. Oldenbourg, 1923), pp. 2–6.
5. Otto Maull, *Politische Geographie*, (Berlin, 1925), pp. 112–115.
6. Richard Hartshorne, "The Concepts of 'Raison d'Être' and 'Maturity of States,'" (abstract), *Annals of the Association of American Geographers*, XXX (March 1940), pp. 59–60.

7. Hugo Hassinger, in R. Kjellén and K. Haushofer, *Die Grossmächte vor und nach dem Weltkriege*, (Berlin and Leipzig, 1930), p. 34.
8. Ratzel, *op. cit.*, p. 6.

the geography of soils until we have grasped the soil scientist's analysis of soil types. In agricultural geography it is not sufficient, we now know, to study crops and animals; we are concerned with the farm unit of organization of crops from fields, livestock in barns and pasture, all directed toward ultimate production of food for the farmer and products to be sold from his farms. We are not ready to begin the study of farm geography until we have analyzed the farmer's purpose—the idea under which his piece of land is organized.

Geographers usually know quite a bit about farming, so they may know beforehand what is in the farmer's mind, or perhaps they can infer that from observation of the visible facts —the fields, silo, corncrib, or cow-barn. But to know for certain, you must ask the farmer.

Whom shall we ask concerning the idea of the particular state? Obviously one must go to those who actually operate the state in question. This is not so easy as in the case of the farm or factory. A modern state is an organization operated, in greater or less degree, by all of the politically-minded people included in it—ideally its entire adult population.

One might logically suppose that geographers should be able to find the answer to this question in studies in political science. Unfortunately, from our point of view, political scientists seem to have concerned themselves solely with the idea and purpose of the generic state—the purposes, that is, that are common to all states. This ignores the very thing that is of direct concern to the geographer—namely the idea that is distinct for the particular state in contrast with that of other states, that which makes for significant differences from country to country. Perhaps that means that it is logically a problem for the geographer.

In any case, unless we can find the answer to this fundamental question in the works of other students—perhaps of the historians if not the political scientists—we are apparently forced to work it out for ourselves. We must discover and establish the unique distinctive idea under which a particular section of area and of humanity is organized into a unit state.

I realize that the problem is remote from the geographer's training and knowledge. But years of stumbling effort have convinced me that there is no circumventing it. Until we can determine for any particular state the idea under which it is organized, we shall have no basis on which to analyze its political geography; we shall not have started on the significant contribution that geography can make to the study of states.

Perhaps we exaggerate the difficulty of the problem because it is unfamiliar. To pin down precisely the particular idea on which any state is based is certainly very difficult, but study of the essential historical documents may enable one to come fairly quickly to a rough statement sufficiently close to the mark to be usable.

Let me give you a case in which one of my advanced graduate students had particular difficulty—the state of Iraq. He finally arrived at something like this: The idea of an Iraqi state sprang from two factors: (1) the recognition by the Great Powers of the special strategic and economic significance of the Mesopotamian region, and (2) the need to provide a *pied à terre* for Arab nationalism banished from Syria. On the basis of these two considerations there was established a territory embracing the settled Arab region of the Tigris-Euphrates plain, together with adjacent but dissimilar regions of mountain and desert tribes, the whole to be developed as a separate Arab state.

You note that the idea of this state was a compound of purposes and those, external: foreign diplomacy and transported nationalist fire. That was the case in 1919. One would need to determine whether the Iraqi have since evolved a truly native concept.

In much older states, we may expect to find that an indigenous *raison d'être* has evolved that may have little or no relation to the original genesis. To determine the distinctive idea of such a state, therefore, we must study the current situation, rather than the remote past. In the well-developed modern state politically-minded people in all regions of the state-area are conscious of their loyalty to the state and have some common understanding, even though not clearly phrased, of what that state means to them. In such a case, we may recognize, I think, the existence of a *nation*— as something distinct from the state itself.

The Concept of Nation

At what I choose to call the more primitive level, the concept of nation represents simply a feeling of kinship, of belonging together, an extension of the concept of family, more properly an extension of the concept of the in-group versus outsiders. While usually expressed in terms derived from the language of the family—terms like "blood," "breed," "race," etc.,—it is in reality less of *kin* and more of *kind*—similarity of cultural, rather than of biological characteristics.

The direct significance of this elementary concept of nationality to the state lies first in the fact that all peoples tend to prefer government by those of their own kind, even if inefficient or unjust, rather than any government over them by foreigners, however beneficent. The second reason is that the individual seeks to identify himself with his state; nationality, someone said, is "pooled self-esteem." Indeed the state is sure of the loyalty of the people only if there is such identification. Each citizen must feel that the state is "his" state, its leaders, "his" leaders. For this to be possible he must feel that those who operate his state, who govern him, are people like himself.

The main purpose of a state, however, is not the furtherance of a particular language or culture. Its main purposes are political. The values over which it has complete control are political values. As the people in a state mature in positive political experience, their feeling of belonging together becomes less dependent on the such obvious similarities as common language, and more dependent on common adherence to particular political concepts, ideals, and institutions. It is for the sake of these that they are ready to devote their ultimate loyalty to their state.

It is in terms of these concepts, more specifically defined to fit the particular case, that we can explain the evolution of a Swiss nation out of a collection of many small regions, using four different languages, separated by imposing physical barriers, with sharply diverging outside connections, and originally brought together by a series of historical accidents, including force of arms.

In sharp contrast to Switzerland, and the other small states of long historic evolution in western Europe, is the situation in most of the small states of Eastern Europe. These owe their existence primarily to the opposition of individual nationalities, based on cultural kinship, to alien rule, but the geographic distribution of the nationalities made impossible a system of states each confined to the single nationality. In the relatively short period of their independent existence as states, none have been able to evolve political values and institutions commanding national loyalty on a higher level than that of cultural kinship —i.e., they have not been able to bring the national minorities, present in almost every case, into membership in the nation.

It is difficult to summarize the analysis of the concept of nation into a single statement, but, for those readers who wish a definition, I would suggest that a "nation" may be defined as a group of people occupying a particular area who feel themselves held together in terms of common acceptance of particular values that are of such prime importance to them that they demand that their area and people should be organized in a distinct state, as the political agency by which those values may be preserved and furthered.

. . . .

. . . Once the concept of a nation has been well established within an area, its spread outward is not necessarily limited by the frontier of the state-area. Thus, when the French national army in 1792 entered the French-speaking regions of Savoy, a region that had never been a part of the French kingdom, they found that the national concepts of revolutionary France had preceded them. The Savoyards, who had never belonged to a nation, but had merely been subject to a feudal state lacking in political ideals, were prepared to regard themselves as part of the nation of France. It would be interesting to compare their attitude with that of the French-speaking areas of Switzerland and Belgium which were likewise conquered at that time by the French armies.

The Concept of the "Core Area"

These considerations should enable us to look more critically than has hitherto been done, I believe, at the concept of the core area of a state. Commonly we look at France, England, Scotland, or Sweden—the classic cases in which the core area appears so important, whether in the history of development of the state-area or that of the evolution of national unity. Or we contrast the situation in those countries with that in Spain, where the central area, the Meseta, is relatively weak. But consider the territory of the old kingdom of Hungary, where the core-area of Magyar population in the rich plain of the Mid-Danube would appear to provide the natural focus for surrounding smaller lowlands and mountain highlands. While this situation no doubt facilitated conquest and organization of the large area included in the kingdom, national unity was never achieved.

In contrast the many scattered nuclei of the Norwegian people, connected only by sea, provided the basis for national unity and a modern state. In the United States, no one area ever functioned as a single core, but rather the association of a large number of regions, closely interrelated in an ever-shifting balance, forms the basis for effective unity.

Clearly we must draw negative as well as positive conclusions. A core area is neither sufficient nor essential to the evolution of a nation or state. What is essential is a common idea that convinces the people in all the regions that they belong together. Historically in certain states a core area *may* have played a major role in spreading that idea to other regions and it *may* continue today as in France, Argentina, or Mexico, to focus the interest of the regions on itself as the center of what has become a functioning unit; but the common idea for a state may develop where no core area exists.

The Application of the State-Idea in Political Geography

Whatever is found to be the *raison d'être*, the underlying idea of the state, it is with this concept, I submit, that the geographer should start in his analysis of the state-area. What use is he then to make of it?

His first concern is to determine the area to which the idea applies, then, the degree to which it operates in the different regions, and finally the extent of correspondence of those regions to the territory actually included within the state.

On this basis we may approach the most elementary problem in political geography—namely that of distinguishing within the legal confines of its territory, those regions that form integral parts of the state-area in terms of its basic idea, and those parts that must be recognized as held under control in the face of either indifference or of opposition on the part of the regional population.

The vast areas of the subarctic lands, whether in Alaska, Canada, Sweden, or the Soviet Union, sparsely populated by primitive tribes, with a few scattered settlements of civilized peoples, are organized politically as though they were colonies of an outside state, even where there is no break in the extent of territory under the same flag. The same is true of tropical lowland areas, in almost all the Latin American countries. In most of the latter, these essentially unorganized territories constitute over half the total area officially credited to the country.

A more difficult question for definition is raised in examining the areas of long-settled Indian population in the highlands of tropical America—both in Central American states and in the Andes. Are these areas of native language and culture to be considered as integral parts of states or are they not still colonial areas subject to outside control, even though the center of control is not in Spain but in the neighboring districts of Spanish-American culture?

A similar situation may be found in more highly developed countries. Thus during the centuries in which all of Ireland was recognized in international law as part of the United Kingdom, its greater part was certainly operated in fact as a subject area, distinct from the controlling state. Much the same may be true today of certain portions of the Soviet Union, notably the so-called republics of Central Asia—but the difficulty of determining the actual operations of the Soviet government make definite statement impossible. On the other hand, we have in the United States clear-cut though tiny relics of internal colonialism in the Indian reservations.

If the idea of the state is based on the recognition of the existence of a nation, then the major geographic question to consider is whether there is close correspondence between the area of the nation and that of the state. Are there regions within the state whose populations do not feel themselves part of the nation? Are there regions of the nation that are not included within the state—the issue of irridentism?

It is not easy to measure the area to be included in a particular national group. In many cases we must approach the question indirectly. If we can determine the essential factors involved in the particular nationality, we may be able to measure the area over which each of these factors exists. On this basis we may establish certain areas that are clearly included in the given nation, and other areas that adhere in terms of some factors, but not in terms of others.

The entire area over which the nation extends, but in varying degrees of intensity, may then be compared with the area presently included in the state. We have thus determined not only the areal correspondence of state and nation, but also the regions in which the national character is partial rather than complete. We shall thereby have presented, in part in map form, the basic factors and relationships involved in the primary problem of political geography—the analysis of the degree to which the diverse regions of the state constitute a unity.

Internal Organization

At this point we reach one other problem for analysis—the relation of the internal territorial organization of the state-area to the regional diversities we have analyzed. Though all the regions of a state are clearly included under the state-idea, have complete loyalty to the overall concepts of the national unit, regional differences inevitably cause some differences in interpretation and implementation of those concepts.

If these differences are relatively minor, as in most of France or, I presume, in Uruguay, the regions may accept unitary government from a single central authority. If the differences are great, the attempt to impose such a uniform system may provoke opposition endangering the national unity. Since such regional differences are important in most countries, but most states attempt to operate under a uniform, centralized government, the number of examples of this type of problem is very large. Spain, at the moment, provides one of the most striking.

Certain states recognize openly the need to permit diverging interpretations of the overall concepts of that state and hence significant differences in the institutions and laws thereunder. This is the system of the federal state, of which Switzerland provides the oldest example, the United States the largest. In both cases, a notable degree of regional heterogeneity is guaranteed by the constitutional division of powers.

. . . .

The possible ways of organizing the state-area are not limited to the unitary and the federal systems. The United Kingdom, for example, has evolved in the course of its long history a most complicated system under which Wales, Scotland, Northern Ireland, the Isle of Man, and the Channel Islands—each has a different degree of autonomy adjusted to its particular linguistic, religious, economic, and political geography.

In determining the method of state-organization of a country, the student must study the actual method of government, not merely the words written into a constitution. He will recognize that while the constitution of the Soviet Union grants on paper more independence to its member republics than is true of the individual States of this country, and even though it encourages and exploits a great variety of languages and folk cultures, in every other aspect of economic and political life it operates its vast area of radically different regions as a highly centralized, monolithic state.

ANALYSIS OF EXTERNAL FUNCTIONS

In a functional approach to the analysis of the political geography of a state, our first half was concerned with the internal problems of the state-area. The second half is concerned with the external relations of the state-area to the other areas of the world, whether those are also organized as states, controlled by outside states, or unorganized. For convenience we may group these relations as territorial, economic, political, and strategic.

Territorial Relations

Under territorial relations we are of course concerned in the first instance with the degree to which adjacent states are in agreement concerning the extent of territory which each includes. Whether the area in question is large or small, agreement ultimately requires the determination of a precise boundary.

Of all the problems of international relations, these concerning the allocation of territories and hence the determination of boundaries are the most obviously geographic. It is no doubt for that reason that they have been the most common object of study by geographers....

In much of this work however, we still tend to start on the wrong foot. In the initial classification of internal boundaries we have, as geographers, looked first at the physical character of the zones in which the boundary lines are drawn. This is not a classification of international boundaries, but rather of the features with which such boundaries are associated.

If we start with what we are studying—the state-areas—we can recognize the essential function of the boundary from its name: it is that line which is to be accepted by all concerned as *bounding* the area in which everything is under the jurisdiction of one state as against areas under different jurisdiction. In well-developed regions of the world it must be determined to the exact foot. (Consideration of the functions of a boundary zone, as an element of military defense, for example, is a separate question to be considered elsewhere.)

The first thing to know about an international boundary therefore is the degree to which it is accepted by all the parties concerned—i.e., the adjacent states and the population whose statehood is determined by the location of the boundary.[9]

Consider the following cases of international boundaries; the boundary between Great Britain and France (including the Channel Islands with Great Britain); that between France and Spain; that between Switzerland and Italy (including the Ticino boundary that reaches far down the Alpine slopes almost to the Po Plain); and, finally, the boundary between the United States and Mexico both east and west of El Paso. These run through radically different types of physical zones. Some correspond closely with ethnic divisions, others do not. But from the point of view of the primary function of an international boundary, all are in the same category, namely that of boundaries completely accepted as final by the states themselves and the people of the border areas.

In a different category is the Franco-German boundary (considered as of 1930). Though this was fully accepted by France and officially so by Germany in the Treaty of Locarno, one could not assume that the German leaders intended that acceptance to be final and by imprisoning certain of the local leaders in Alsace the French government demonstrated its lack of faith in the complete acceptance by the Alsatian people of their inclusion in the French state.

Still different is the case of the German-Polish boundary of the inter-war period, which neither state accepted as more than a temporary division of territory claimed by both sides.

Where boundaries run through primitive, essentially colonial, regions which at present have very slight productive value but offer possibilities for future importance, we may need to recognize a different set of categories. Thus we may find cases in which for a time the states concerned, while not committing themselves to an ultimate boundary, raise no question concerning the line lost in the wilderness, but may at any moment challenge, with the force of arms, the line that had apparently been accepted.[10]

If we first establish such a system of classification, based on the primary function of boundaries, and only then seek to determine to what extent those of particular categories are based on different types of features—e.g., on natural divides of population, on ethnic divisions, or on boundaries antecedent to state development—we may hope to avoid one of our more common forms of geographic determinism.

The second question concerning any international boundary (whether or not it is fully accepted) is the degree to which its bounding function is maintained by the bordering states, the degree, that is, to which all movements of goods and persons across the line are effectively controlled by the boundary officials. In examining that, the geographer will of course observe the ways in which the control is made easier or more difficult by the character of the

---

9. A consideration of a large number of international boundaries from this approach is given in Richard Hartshorne, "A Survey of the Boundary Problems of Europe," *Geographic Aspects of International Relations*, C. C. Colby, ed., Chicago: The University of Chicago Press (1938), pp. 163–213.

10. Robert S. Platt, "Conflicting Territorial Claims in the Upper Amazon," *Geographic Aspects of International Relations*, C. C. Colby, ed., Chicago: The University of Chicago Press (1938), pp. 243–273.

zone through which the boundary line is drawn.

A special aspect of boundary problems emerges where the territory of a state reaches to the sea. Though open to use by all, the seas are in fact little used by anyone. Hence, it is sufficient for most purposes to define the boundary simply as following the coast, as most treaties do. But for certain purposes, notably fishing, border control, and naval warfare, the exact determination of the line in the waters may be critical. There is no overall agreement in international law either as to the width of territorial waters—the zone of sea included as part of the possession of the bordering state—or as to the manner in which the off-shore line bounding those waters follows the indentations of the coast....

The use of territorial waters by merchant ships of a foreign state, commonly for the purpose of entering the ports of the country concerned, represents the most common occurrence of use of territory of one state for the purposes of another state. In this case the purpose is mutual. In other, more special cases, problems arise from the desire or need of the people of one state to utilize the territory of a foreign country in order to have access to still other countries, or in some cases to a different part of their own state. Both Canada and the United States have permitted the construction of railroads across portions of their territories whose major purpose was to connect regions of the other country—e.g., the Michigan Central across Ontario from Detroit to Buffalo, or the Canadian Pacific across the State of Maine from Montreal to St. John, New Brunswick. European countries commonly will not tolerate foreign railroads across their territories, but the Polish railroads in the inter-war period operated, for Germany, through trains between East Prussia and the main part of Germany.

Nearly all states recognize the need of providing transit service for trade across their territories between states on either side, though this involves a multiplicity of minor problems of control. Most important are provisions for transit from an inland state to the seacoast in order to have access to the countries of the world accessible by sea routes. The Grand Trunk Railroad of Canada, now a part of the Canadian National Railways, not only crosses New Hampshire and Maine to reach the sea, but, when the winter ice closes the St. Lawrence, uses the harbor of Portland, Maine as its port of shipment for foreign trade of interior Canada, which constitutes most of the total traffic of that American port. In certain European cases more specific arrangements seem necessary: a section of a port, as at Trieste or Hamburg, may be allocated exclusively to handle the transit trade of a foreign country.

Economic Relations

Trade in commodities among states is an essential part of the field of economic geography, treated usually as simply a form of interregional trade for which definite statistics happen to be available. Other forms of international economic relations, as in services, investments, etc., might no less logically be studied in economic geography, but as yet few geographers have attempted to do this. While it is obvious that these economic relations between individuals or corporations in one state and those in others are somehow significant to the states concerned, it is by no means easy to determine what that significance is. In consequence many writers in political geography see no alternative but to throw in a section treating the international trade of the country in standard economic-geographic fashion.

In the analysis of a state-area the need to consider its economic relations with outside areas arises from the fact that in many respects a state operates, must operate, as a unit economy in relation with other unit economies in the world. The difficulties arise because, while it must operate completely as a political unit, a state-area operates only partially as an economic unit.

The first problem is to determine to what extent the economy of one state-area is dependent on that of others, though the mere analysis of self-sufficiency is only a beginning. If one says that the United States produces a surplus of coal and iron, but is dependent on foreign countries for much of its supply of tin, nickel, and manganese, of sugar and rubber—such a statement, even in precise percentage figures, tell us directly little of importance. If a country has plenty of coal and iron it can normally secure the other metals mentioned from wherever in the world they are produced. Under abnormal conditions of war, or threat of war, it is essential to know that the manganese normally comes from the Transcaucasus in the Soviet Union, the tin from British Malaya (but can be obtained in Bolivia), whereas the nickel comes from adjacent Canada. Natural rubber supplies are available in adequate amounts only in one remote region—Malaya-East Indies—but nearby Cuba can supply most of our sugar needs.

In general, the geographer will analyze the economic dependence of one state-area on others in terms of the specific countries concerned and their location and political association in relation to the state he is studying.

Since all sound trading is of mutual advantage to both parties, to say that one state is economically dependent on any other necessarily implies also the converse. But the degree to which any particular commodity trade, shipping service, or investment is critically important varies in terms of the total economy of each of the two states concerned. It is only in this sense that the common question "Is a particular state economically viable?" has any validity, since every state above the most primitive level is in some respects critically dependent on others.

The problem is far from simple, but perhaps we can suggest two generalizations. As between two countries that differ greatly in the size of their total national economy, the economic relationships between them are more critically important for the lesser country (though this might not be true under war conditions). This is true because these economic relationships, which may be taken as equalized through international balance of payments, will form a larger proportion of the total national economy of the lesser state. An obvious example is found in the relation of Eire to Great Britain, of Cuba to the United States.

The second generalization rests on the fact that the critical significance of the trade depends on the possibility of alternatives, of finding other sources for needed supplies or other markets for products which must be sold to maintain the national economy. Most popular discussions tend to think only of the former, whereas under the capitalist profit-system under which most international trade operates, it is the latter that is more significant. The reason is that for most commodities of world production there are alternative sources of supply at moderate increase in cost; there may not be alternative markets even at greatly reduced selling prices.

Finally we may note that relatively few areas of the world now produce a surplus of manufactured goods requiring a high degree of technological development and these constitute therefore a relatively limited market for the surplus of primary products of farm, forest, and mine which can be produced widely over the world. Consequently the countries producing primary products, even the very necessities of life, may find it more difficult to find alternative markets for their products than the industrial countries producing articles less essential to life. With wider spread of industrialization over the world, this situation would of course be altered, conceivably reversed.

It should not be assumed, however, that these rough generalizations will provide the answer in any given case. Consider the problem posed by the independence of Austria after the dissolution of the Habsburg empire—a problem which Austria still faces. To survive as a viable economic unit, Austria needed to maintain with the adjacent regions, re-organized as independent states, a high degree of economic relationship. Its position in competition with otherwise more favored regions of industrial Europe, made it peculiarly dependent on markets immediately to the east. For these eastern neighbors such relationships were also necessary for the maximum economic progress, but were not vitally necessary to economic life. If, for political reasons, and to develop their own industries at greater cost, they preferred not to trade freely with Austria, they had the choice of the less profitable plan, whereas for Austria the alternative was economic collapse.

In the nineteenth century, international economic relations, though both supported and retarded by state action, were generally operated as the private business of individuals and corporations. With the depression of the 1930's, the rise of totalitarian states, and the last war, there has been an increasing tendency for the state itself to direct the operations of international trade and investment. In these respects states function increasingly as economic units so that the economic relations among them become increasingly important in the politico-geographic analysis of the state.

Political Relations

The most obvious form of political relation of a state to any outside territory is that of effective political control—as a colony, possession, dependency, or "protectorate." Commonly we recognize only a small number of states as colonial, or imperial, powers: eight or nine in western Europe, together with the United States, Japan, Australia, and New Zealand (the two latter functioning in islands of the Southwest Pacific). Germany was eliminated from the list by the First World War, Japan by the Second. If, however, we recognize the colonial reality of areas adjacent to a state and legally included in its territory but actually not forming an integral part of that state (as discussed earlier in this paper), the list is far longer—including Canada, Norway, Sweden, the Soviet Union, China, the Union of South Africa, and most of the Latin American states. A new-comer to this list is the Indonesian Republic, with large territories subject to it in the primitive areas of Borneo, Celebes, etc.

The legal forms of colonial relationship vary widely—even within a single empire, such as that of Great Britain. Further, these legal forms may or may not express the reality of the relationship, the degree to which political organization is imposed and operated by the outside state. It is the latter, I presume, that is our concern in political geography.

One characteristic of colonial areas that is of particular concern from our present point of view is the degree to which the governmental system of the home state is extended over the colonial territory. France is in the process of fully incorporating certain formerly colonial areas into metropolitan France, but others only partially. Many imperial powers have always extended their legal systems into colonial areas so far as citizens from the home country are concerned, so that within any colonial area there may be an overlapping of two authorities—one having jurisdiction over citizens of the home state, the other over native people.

Many countries recognized by treaty as independent states, and functioning in large degree as such, are nonetheless under some particular degree of political control by an outside power. This may be limited to utilization of small fractions of the territory of one state by the government, usually the armed services, of the other—e.g., Great Britain in military control of the Canal Zone of Egypt, the United States Navy at Guantanamo Bay. The most important, relatively, is the American control for essentially an indefinite period, of the Panama Canal Zone, across the most populous part of the Republic of Panama. In other cases, the outside country may control directly no part of the territory, but rather exercise limited control, as through an adviser, over major aspects of government, especially foreign relations, customs, or the national budget. The United States has in the past exercised such control for limited periods over small states in the Caribbean area; a group of outside powers for years operated the tariff customs of China to raise money to pay the Chinese foreign debts. The clearest case of political domination of supposedly independent states by an outside state today is found in the obvious control by the Soviet Union over the internal policies as well as foreign policy of the "satellite" states on its west, from Poland to Bulgaria, even though this relationship is expressed in no formal treaties.

Generally speaking, recognition of independent sovereignty of a state by the other states of the world presumes that that state will maintain similar political relations with all friendly states and will not be bound by special political associations with any particular states. Numerous exceptions, however, are widely recognized. Thus the dominions of the British Commonwealth are recognized as having emerged from colonial to independent status, even though they continue to be held together in continuously voluntary confederation with the United Kingdom, extending to each other numerous political and economic privileges not extended to other states. Likewise outside states have long recognized the special political concern of the United States for the Latin American republics, a concern now finally expressed in treaty as a mutual policy of association. Likewise they have recognized the long-standing political interest of the United States in the Negro state of Liberia. The recent North Atlantic Pact, though intended primarily for military purposes, contains political clauses which, if implemented, would tend to create a special political association of the United States, Canada and the states of western Europe.

Finally, of course, nearly all the states of the world have accepted certain political

Strategic Relations

Every state-area in the world lives in a strategic situation with other states, a situation that may be in part created by its own actions and policies, but in major part is determined for it by those other states.

Thus Switzerland in modern times has been a unit area of relatively small offensive power, though not inconsiderable defensive power, situated in the midst of a group of larger neighbors, each fearful of expansion of power by the others. In this situation Switzerland has found its best hope for security in a policy of armed neutrality because such a neutralized area was in the mutual interest, defensively, of the neighboring powers. In a much earlier period, in the sixteenth and seventeenth centuries, when Austria was the only major power bordering Switzerland, and many of its neighbors were small states, the Swiss Confederation followed a very different policy of strategic relations, frequently allying itself with any of various neighbors in conflict with the others.

The strategic relations of a state, in other words, must be adjusted to the particular strategic situation in which it finds itself at any time. With the unification of Germany in 1871, the strategic map of Europe was changed no less than the political map. Because that new unit increased in economic production, population, and power faster than any of its neighbors, and was able to establish close strategic relations with Austria-Hungary, forming a solid block of power across Central Europe, all the other states of Europe including Great Britain, were forced to change their strategic relations with each other.

. . . .

Summary and Conclusion

Political geography, as a distinct unit branch of geography, is to be justified neither in terms of political aspects of geography nor in terms of geographic foundations of politics, since each of those constitutes but a collection of partial solutions separated from the problems involved. The core of political geography is the study of one distinctive phenomenon in the total differentiation of areas, namely the sections of area organized as political units. Areal differentiation is both most marked and most important in respect to units of land at the level of state-areas.

The state-area, like a farm or an industrial plant, but unlike these sections of area that we ordinarily study as "regions," is an organized unit of land and people, organized by man according to a particular idea or purpose. Though in no proper sense an organism, the state-area is an organization that has genesis, structure, and function. Logically, therefore, the analysis of a state-area may be approached from any or all of these three viewpoints. In contrast to genuine organisms, there is no close mutual relationship between genesis on the one hand and structure and function on the other; on the contrary, states have tended to add pieces of territory whenever it was possible to do so, regardless of need, and then to adapt function to the automatically resulting structure. Hence the study of the genesis of state areas tends to be largely historical in interest, throwing little light on structure and function.

Likewise, in contrast with such areal units as farms or industrial plants, the state is not able to plan or evolve its regional structure, but must simply operate in whatever structure its history and geography have happened to produce. Since these vary for every state, not in minor degree, but fundamentally, the attempt to find a general principle of regional structure of state-areas is futile. Further, the state-area, though a genuine geographic phenomenon, is not a concrete object exciting direct interest in its morphology for its own sake. Hence the morphological approach to the study of the state-area is either a dull and lifeless description of something that appears real only on a map, or, if used as a method of approach to the understanding of function, tempts the student to naive forms of geographic determinism.

State-areas are important, both in the practical and in the academic sense, primarily in terms of their functions: namely what the state-area as a whole means to its parts and its relations as a whole with outside areas. These functions, determined by the human forces that operate the state-area as a unit, are greatly affected by the structure of the state-area, which of course is the current product of its past development. In a sequence of cause-and-effect relationships, science can safely proceed from cause to effect only in those situations in which the relatively small number of factors and a multiplicity of similar cases makes possible the establishment of reliable scientific laws or general principles. These requirements are lacking in political geography.

Consequently we conclude that the rational, scientifically reliable, and realistic approach to the study of state-areas is to start with the phenomena with which we are most concerned—the functions of the state-area—to determine how these have been affected by the character of the area itself, its structure and contents, and to utilize historic facts of genesis insofar as those aid us in understanding structural features previously determined to be significant.

There is however a practical situation in which we may be forced to reverse this procedure. If plans are being made for the construction of an entirely new state-area, or for major territorial alterations in an existing one, one is forced to attempt some prediction of the capacity of such a projected organization to function effectively as a unit. Political geographers will be able to claim superior competence in attempting predictions in such cases only if they have established a high degree of understanding of the reasons why present or past state-areas have or have not functioned effectively.

5

A Unified Field Theory of Political Geography

STEPHEN B. JONES*

... The current search for theory may not revolutionize geography or make it any more scientific, but a valid theory, however minor, is at least three things: a compact description, a clue to explanation, and a tool for better work. ...

... The most magnificent thing about the present theory is its name. You are likely to be disappointed in the content. I am not sure the theory is able to stand on its own feet in a critical world. It may, however, have its uses and the way to find out is to push it out before the public. ...

Although its name is a vainglorious imitation of theoretical physics, the unified field theory is not based on a physical analogy. Its intellectual base includes substantial borrowings from three eminent political geographers —Derwent Whittlesey, Richard Hartshorne, and Jean Gottmann. In fact, the adjective "unified" in the title stems from the belief that the concept of "field" unifies the ideas of these three men, as well as unites them with political science.

There are similarities and differences between the ideas of Hartshorne and Gottmann. Hartshorne recognized that circulation was a means of overcoming the physical barriers to state integration, but he did not list it as a centripetal force nor discuss its possible role in the development of a state-idea. He appears to consider circulation an expression of economic and political forces, rather than a primary force. Certainly an established state-area conditions the pattern of circulation to an astonishing degree, even though circulation originally helped shape the state-area. Iconography also can be recognized in Hartshorne's theory, both as the third of his centrifugal forces—"regions that differ among themselves in character of population, economic interests, and political attitudes"—and as the master centripetal force itself, the state-idea. Circulation, according to Hartshorne, does not necessarily make for instability and change. It may help stabilize a state, as railroads have done for Canada. Iconography does not always make for stability. There can be conflicts of lesser and greater iconographies, of sectionalism and nationalism, of national and international iconographies. Another of Hartshorne's ideas, that of the maturity of states, expresses a state-area co-extensive with the national iconography.[1]

Reproduced from the *Annals* of the Association of American Geographers, Volume XLIV, 1954, by permission of the author and publisher.

* Stephen B. Jones (1903–) is Professor of Geography at Yale University.

1. Richard Hartshorne, "The Concepts of 'Raison d'Être' and 'Maturity of States,' " (abstract), *Annals* of the Association of American Geographers, XXX (March 1940), p. 59.

The Idea-Area Chain

Let us proceed to our unified field theory of political geography. The theory simply states that "idea" and "state" are two ends of a chain. The hyphen with which Hartshorne connects them represents the three other links of the chain. One of the links is Gottmann's circulation, which I shall call movement.[2]

The chain is as follows: Political Idea—Decision—Movement—Field—Political Area. This "chain" should be visualized as a chain of lakes or basins, not an iron chain of separate links. The basins interconnect at one level, so that whatever enters one will spread to all the others.

Political idea, in this sequence, means more than just the state-idea. It means any political idea. It might be the idea of the state or it might be the idea of a speed limit on a country road. It might merely be a gregarious instinct, not consciously expressed. "War begins in the minds of men" and so does all other politics. But there are many political ideas that never reach the stage of action. They die aborning, remain in the realm of pure thought, or are rejected by the powers-that-be. A favorable decision is a necessary prerequisite to action. A formal, parliamentary decision is not necessarily meant. Much current research in political science is focussed on the informal or unconscious aspects of the idea-decision end of the chain, through studies of political behavior. Though most of the fishermen in the basins of idea and decision are political scientists, Gottmann and Hartshorne, both geographers, enter them when they speak of iconography and the idea of state.

Both political scientists and geographers have studied the phenomena at the other end of the chain—political areas. This term is used very inclusively to mean any politically organized area, whether a national state, a dependent area, a sub-division of a state, or an administrative region or district. It includes all three categories of areas listed by Fesler:[3] general governmental areas, special or limited-purpose governmental areas, and field service areas. The one common characteristic of all political areas is that they have recognized limits, though not necessarily linear or permanent. An administrative center within the area is common, but not universal.

Movement, I have said, is essentially Gottmann's circulation. What new twist it is given comes from placing it in a chain of concepts relating it to decisions. Every political decision involves movement in one way or another. There may be exceptions, but I have been unable to think of any. Some decisions create movement, some change it, some restrict it. Some create a new kind of movement to replace or to control the old. The movement may not involve great numbers of men or great quantities of matter—it may consist only of radio waves—but usually persons and things move as a result of political decisions. These politically-induced movements may be thought of as "circulation fields." The movements of state highway patrolmen produce a field, shipments of military-aid materials produce a field, the despatch and delivery of farm-subsidy checks produce a field.

A concrete example may clarify the thought behind this chain of terms. National prohibition had a long history as an idea. The Eighteenth Amendment and the Volstead Act were the final decisions that took national prohibition from the realm of ideas to that of action, though, to be sure, many smaller decisions had preceded these or were necessary later to implement them. The prompt effect of the Volstead Act was to inaugurate sweeping changes in movement. Legal shipment of liquor ceased, raw materials no longer flowed to distilleries, illicit movements were organized along new lines, enforcement officers went patrolling and prowling. The fields of these movements were not of uniform density nor did they exactly coincide with the boundaries of the United States. City slums and Appalachian valleys became centers of activity. Zones near the international frontiers were heavily policed. Enforcement reached twelve miles to sea. The effect on movement was felt overseas. No change in national territory resulted, but new administrative areas were set up. Had the law remained and been rigidly enforced, it is conceivable that our concept of the marginal sea might have changed, as later it was changed by the expanding field of activity of oil exploration.

---

2. Gottmann himself thinks "movement" an inadequate translation and suggests "movement factor." The present writer has adopted "movement" as more compact and commonplace than either "movement factor" or "circulation."

3. James W. Fesler, *Area and Administration*. University of Alabama, 1949, p. 6.

An earlier and more successful attempt at compulsory reform—the suppression of the slave trade—produced a field of enforcement on the high seas and led to the establishment of colonial areas in West Africa. Similarly, the idea-to-area chain is beautifully illustrated by the founding of Liberia.

In the case of prohibition, the existence of the political area of the United States gave general shape to the major fields produced by the Volstead Act, for obvious reasons. A political area in being is a condition of political ideas, decisions, and movements. Our linked basins, I have said, lie at one level. Add something to one, and it spreads to others. There is a general distinction, however, between flow from idea towards area and in the reverse direction. The former is essentially a process of controlling or creating. The prohibition law controlled some movements and created others. The idea of colonizing free Negroes created a migration to Liberia. The reverse spread is more correctly described as conditioning. The existence of a political area, field, movement, or decision conditions what may take place in the basins lying idea-ward. Eric Fischer's paper, "On Boundaries," is full of good examples of such conditioning.[4] Benjamin Thomas has shown how the political area of Idaho, created upon a flimsy and essentially negative idea in the first place, conditioned further political thoughts and decisions until the present Idaho-idea is as firm as any.[5]

The essential characteristic of a field, in physics, is not movement, but spatial variation in force. The gravitational field exists even when no apples fall. Since we are not bound to a physical analogy, this distinction need not greatly concern us. However, it may sometimes be important to keep in mind that movements and fields are not necessarily identical. A higher percentage of Democrats goes to the polls where the party is neck-and-neck with the Republicans than where the party is overwhelmingly strong. Movement to polls creates a field, but it is not identical with the field of party power.

... Karl Deutsch has suggested a "field" approach to the study of political community.[6] "According to this view, every individual is conceived as a point in a field consisting of his communications or other interactions with all other individuals." Deutsch suggests that this concept may be applied to both small and large "clusters," including families, villages, towns, countries, regions, peoples, nations, and federations. Some clusters are political areas, some are geographical but not political areas, others, like families and peoples, are not necessarily found in definable areas. Thus Deutsch's "interaction field" may be the general case of which the present writer's concept may be the politico-geographical subtype. On later pages of the same publication,[7] Deutsch gives fourteen tests of integration and a check-list of thirty-two possible indicators of social or political community, which should prove of value to the geographer as well as the political scientist.

A field exists in time as well as in space. Applying the ideas of Whittlesey,[8] we may say it has a time dimension as well as space dimensions and that the time dimension has three derivatives: velocity, pace, and timing. Highway patrols produce a field, as was mentioned above, but obviously it is important for both law-breaker and law-enforcer to know when the patrolmen operate as well as where. The effective scheduling of their patrols is a problem of timing. The whole of traffic and of traffic regulation can be considered a space-time field. Warfare and traffic are alike in this respect as in some others.

APPLICATION TO POLITICAL AREAS

Application of this theory to a case of one new national state is fairly simple: Zionism is the idea, the Balfour Declaration the conspicuous decision, permitting migration and other movements. A field of settlement, governmental activity, and war leads to the state of Israel. Such telegraphic brevity oversimplifies history, but the theory seems to fit. For a state

---

4. Eric Fischer, "On Boundaries," *World Politics*, I (Jan. 1949), pp. 196–222. The final paragraph on page 197 is a good description of the conditioning process.

5. Benjamin E. Thomas, "Boundaries and Internal Problems of Idaho," *The Geographical Review*, XXXIX (Jan. 1949), pp. 99–100.

6. Karl W. Deutsch, *Political Community at the International Level: Problems of Definition and Measurement*. Organizational Behaviour Section, Foreign Policy Analysis Project, Foreign Policy Analysis Series No. 2, Princeton University, September 1953, pp. 30–31.

7. Deutsch, *op. cit.*, pp. 37–62 and 70–71.

8. Derwent Whittlesey, "The Horizon of Geography," *Annals of the Association of American Geographers*, XXXV (March 1945), pp. 1–36.

with a longer and more complicated evolution, history could not be so readily compressed. The theory provides a path between geographical and political study, but not necessarily a short-cut. It does not reduce political geography to five easy steps. It does not permit world politics to be shown on a chart in five columns headed "idea," "decision," and so forth. It may, however, provide some intellectual clarification and it may prove a handy way of working back and forth among historical, political, and geographical ideas and data.

Karl Deutsch has recognized eight uniformities in the growth of nations from other political forms of organization.[9] Five of these are clearly "field" phenomena: the change from subsistence to exchange economy, the growth of core areas, towns, and communication grids, and the concentration of capital and its effect on other areas. The seventh and eighth are "iconographical," but have "field" connotations: the growth of ethnic awareness and its relation to national symbols and to political compulsion. The sixth item, the rise of individual self-awareness, is more difficult to relate directly to a field though decisions made in a framework of an increasingly individualistic philosophy would lead to changes in established fields. In short, the process of national integration, whether looked at by geographers, like Hartshorne or Gottmann, or by a political scientist, like Deutsch, can be interpreted as a process of changing fields. Conceivably the outlines of the political area may not change. The former colony of Burma is perhaps en route to becoming a true national state without change of boundaries or capital, but a study of the political fields would show changes.

One virtue of the field theory is that it is not confined to politically organized areas. It is applicable without difficulty to an unorganized area like the Mediterranean, which is undoubtedly a political field. As William Reitzel showed, decisions may affect the Mediterranean as a whole and may create or control movement over the entire sea.[10] The ideas may vary: Mussolini's dream of a new Roman Empire, Britain's concern with sea command, the American strategy of the containment of communism. Reitzel showed how American policy in the Mediterranean evolved as the cumulative result of small decisions taken first with the idea of winning specific military campaigns. These decisions, and the successful military movements that resulted, involved the United States in political and economic administration. The Soviet Union replaced the Axis as the rival Mediterranean power, Britain slumped down the power scale, and the United States found itself deeply embedded in Mediterranean politics. The Truman Doctrine of support to Greece and Turkey was an outcome, indicating the unity of the Mediterranean sea-power field. The accumulation of decisions created a field, the sea conditioned it.

In the case of administrative areas, a political area may arise from a decision with little or possibly no intervening movement. A new governmental agency may lay out its field service areas before it actually engages in any actions. In some cases, analysis will show that these field service areas reflect pre-existing fields, such as the areas used by other branches of government or known fields of economic activity, and in many cases existing boundaries will be followed. It is possible, however, that an administrative area might spring directly from a decision and reflect no existing field. T.V.A. may be an example, unless we say a field had been created by river boatmen, hillside farmers, hydrographic surveyors, and so forth. This seems far-fetched; rather it seems that the Tennessee Valley was proclaimed a political area and that a field of activity resulted. It should be noted, however, that the field spread beyond the limits of the drainage basin, once electricity began to circulate.

There is nothing deterministic about the idea-area chain. A given idea might lead to a variety of areas, a given area might condition a variety of ideas. Pelzer's study of Micronesia under four rulers demonstrates this point.[11] Although the area ruled was not identical in all four eras, it was basically the same. The number of possible uses for these small islands was limited. Nevertheless, the four rulers—Spain, Germany, Japan, and the United States—made different choices. Their fields were different in kind and intensity. If one

9. Karl W. Deutsch, "The Growth of Nations: Some Recurrent Patterns of Political and Social Integration," *World Politics*, V (Jan. 1953), pp. 168–195.

10. William Reitzel, *The Mediterranean: Its Role in America's Foreign Policy*. New York, 1948.

11. Karl J. Pelzer, "Micronesia—A Changing Frontier," *World Politics*, II (Jan. 1950), pp. 251–266.

insists (which the dictionary does not) that a theory must be able to predict specific behavior, then the field theory may not deserve its name.[12] With no theory whatsoever, a well-informed person with some map-sense could have predicted many American problems and decisions in Micronesia. As a guide to study, however, the field theory is applicable to such cases.

STUDIES OF NATIONAL POWER

Studies of national power may also be fitted into the field theory. Lasswell and Kaplan define power as "participation in the making of decisions."[13] If power is participation in the making of decisions, if power is necessary before an idea can produce movement, then we can easily fit power into our theory. Hartshorne distinguished between political geography and the study of power.[14] He felt a geographer might sometimes tackle the question of "how strong is a state?" if no one else had done so, but that in so doing he was "migrating into a field whose core and purpose is not geography, but military and political strategy." That power is linked with decision supports Hartshorne to the extent that geography has been more closely associated with the other end of the chain, but our aim is to pull political science and geography together, not to separate them. If power is more concentrated in the basin of decision, it is by no means absent in the others.

BOUNDARIES, CAPITALS, CITIES

The unified field theory fits boundary studies into the general pattern of political geography. A boundary is of course a line between two political areas, but it is also a line in a region, as was emphasized in Hartshorne's Upper Silesia study and in the present writer's book.[15] The boundary region is truly a field in which the line between the political areas conditions much of the circulation.[16] A boundary field may even be or become a political area as in the case of buffer states and frontier provinces.

Studies of capital cities also may be expressed in field-theory terms. Cornish listed the crossways, the stronghold, the storehouse, and the forward headquarters as characteristic situations for capital cities.[17] To these Spate added the cultural head-link.[18] There are other possibilities, such as compromise sites and geometric centrality. All of these words have meaning in terms of movement and field either explicitly (as in the case of crossways, forward headquarters, and cultural headlink) or implicitly (as in the case of storehouse). The idea of, or need for, central administration leads to a decision on the site of the capital. The choice is conditioned by the field and in turn distorts or recreates the field. Once the capital is chosen and the field about it established, many further decisions and movements are conditioned, leading in most cases to the creation of a primate city much larger than any other in the country.[19]

Not only capitals, but other cities, may be brought into the scope of the theory. In Gottmann's terminology, many of the problems of a growing city arise from the fact that its circulation expands faster than its iconography. The metropolitan district outgrows the political limits, and vested local interests and loyalties make political expansion difficult. A sort of "metropolitan-idea" may develop, leading usually to functional authorities rather than to political integration. In a few words, the urban problem is to make the political area fit the field.[20] There are a

12. The definition of "theory" most appropriate to the present paper is: "The analysis of a set of facts in their ideal relations to one another." Webster's Collegiate Dictionary, fifth edition, 1947.
13. Harold D. Lasswell and Abraham Kaplan, *Power and Society: A Framework for Political Inquiry*. New Haven, 1950, p. 75.
14. Richard Hartshorne, "The Functional Approach in Political Geography," *Annals* of the Association of American Geographers, XL (June 1950), pp. 125–127.
15. Richard Hartshorne, "Geographic and Political Boundaries in Upper Silesia," *Annals* of the Association of American Geographers, XXIII (1933), pp. 195–228. Stephen B. Jones, *Boundary-Making: A Handbook for Statesmen, Treaty Editors and Boundary Commissioners*. Washington, 1945. Especially Part I.
16. The pertinence of Eric Fischer's work on historical boundaries has already been mentioned.
17. Vaughan Cornish, *The Great Capitals, an Historical Geography*. London, 1923.
18. O. H. K. Spate, "Factors in the Development of Capital Cities," *The Geographical Review*, XXXII (Oct. 1942), pp. 622–631.
19. Mark Jefferson, "The Law of Primate Cities," *The Geographical Review*, XXIX (April 1939), pp. 226–232.
20. E. Smailes, *The Geography of Towns*. London, 1953, pp. 153–156.

number of choices possible such as annexation of suburbs, city-county consolidation, metropolitan districts, functional authorities, state assumption of local functions.

Kinetic and Dynamic Fields

Since politics consists of conflicts and the resolution of conflicts (though neither conflict nor resolution need be accompanied by violence), these fundamental activities must be expressible in field terms. There are conflicts of ideas, but they do not amount to much until they are embodied in decisions that create or obstruct movement. (It may be wise to re-emphasize that "movement" includes such things of little bulk as messages and money. A restriction on foreign exchange is a restriction on movement.) Fields may be in contact, but not in conflict, may indeed overlap but not conflict, if the movement is merely kinetic. But if there is a dynamic aspect, conflict often will arise. For example, New York City's growing need for water forces its activity in this respect to be dynamic, bringing conflict with other claimants to Delaware River supplies. The international oil industry is inherently dynamic, since new sources must be discovered. The result is potential conflict, sometimes anticipated and resolved at least *pro tempore*. The relations of political dynamics to such fundamentals as resource needs and population pressures have of course been repeatedly studied,[21] and the present theory does little more than incorporate them into the concept of the field.

The general attitude of Americans toward world politics is that dynamic problems should if possible be reduced to kinetic situations by agreement, or in other words that dynamic fields should be converted to kinetic fields. The philosophy of communism, however, is in many respects the opposite, except for temporary tactical purposes. In its grand strategy, communism would like to convert kinetic fields to dynamic fields, with the pressure from the communist side, of course. (The Nazis held a similar philosophy.) The failure of the United States to understand this difference accounts for a number of American blunders in diplomacy. The notion of peaceful co-existence of capitalism and communism, sincerely held by millions outside the Iron Curtain and occasionally uttered, with what sincerity is not known, by major figures within the Curtain, expresses the belief that the fields of the two ideologies can be merely kinetic in their relations, a belief that so far has little to support it.

There are no upper or lower limits on the magnitude of an idea. Man thinks easily of world government and can dream of spaceships and planetary empires. There are upper limits on decisions, movements, fields, and political areas, though these limits change with events (often, but not necessarily, upwards). Such ideas as the great religions, nationalism, liberalism, and communism have, in so far as they could produce decisions and movements, created fields. Whittlesey has shown how man's ideas of space have changed through primal and regional to worldwide conceptions, and how the third and fourth dimensions of the human habitat have been explored and put to use.[22] Ideas, fields of exploration, and in some cases political areas have expanded, reached above and below the earth's surface, and made better use of time. The idea of a Columbus, the decision of an Isabella, a voyage of discovery, a new field, a new empire—this progression might figuratively be compared to the idea of a chemist, the decision of an entrepreneur, an experiment, a new field of production, an economic domain.

Many of the most influential of ideas have been composite, or "culture-ideas." Western culture, for example, is more than just capitalism or democracy or Christianity—it is a composite of these and other factors. Toynbee holds that every culture tends to evolve its "universal state," a domain roughly co-extensive with the culture.[23] If this is true, then we have another example of the chain from idea through a vast number of decisions (not necessarily consciously derived from the general culture-idea) and movements, creating a field and tending towards a political area which would be the universal state of that culture.

---

21. For examples, by Frederick S. Dunn, in his *Peaceful Change*. New York, 1937, and by Brooks Emeny, in *The Strategy of Raw Materials*. New York, 1934.

22. "The Horizon of Geography."

23. Arnold Toynbee, *A Study of History*. London, 1939, Vol. 4, pp. 2–3.

Utility of the Theory

... Earlier, [I] said that a valid theory, however minor, is at least three things: a compact description, a clue to explanation, and a tool for better work. If this theory merely provides nomenclature it satisfies the first requirement. Perhaps it goes farther than merely supplying words. It may reduce the apparent diversity of aims and methods in political geography, found by Hartshorne and his students.[24] It may help to unify not only the theories of political geography, but political theories in general. It may help complete the tie between morphology and function, between region and process. It may show a relationship between "grand ideas" and the earth's surface.

This unified field theory can provide no more than a clue to explanation, if it even attains that success. It can hardly provide an ultimate answer to any question. But to relate several disciplines, to show connections, may give hints. The user of this theory is at least sure to be warned against single-factor explanations and be led to seek contributions from sister sciences.

It is as a tool for better work that I have the most hopes for this mental gadget. The chain of words in which the theory is expressed constitutes a sort of check-list ("check-system" might be better), by means of which one can orient oneself and tell where one should explore further. To return to the analogy of a chain of basins, one knows through which basin one has entered and where one can travel back and forth. If one begins with the study of a political area, ideas lie at the other end. If a study begins with movement, the scholar knows he should explore in both directions. For some of the basins one may need pilots from other disciplines, but at least one has a map of the chain. The theory tells students of geography and politics what (in very general terms) they need to learn

[24]. "The Functional Approach...", pp. 96–97.

from each other, what each has to add, but not how each fences himself off.

Another possible effect of this theory upon geographical work is that it may inspire the making of new types of studies and the compiling of new kinds of maps. Many maps either show or imply a field, but with the idea-area chain in mind, new sources of data suggest themselves: public-opinion polls, content analysis of publications, shipments of significant materials, movements of governmental officers, monetary transactions and so forth. The theory is "geographical" in that it makes mappable, through the concept of the field, the results of ideas and decisions that are themselves not mappable.

Conceivably the general plan of this theory can be extended to other than political studies. In fact, recent work in economic geography suggests a similar theory for that branch of our science. The idea-area chain may unite in one concept two main parts of geographical theory, the possibilist and regionalist views. Possibilism focusses on man's choices among environmental possibilities. Choices are decisions. They imply ideas and must lead to movements. The regional or chorological approach, beginning with the study of areas, can lead through movement to decisions and ideas.

Finally, the unified field theory may have utility outside academic circles. It seems possible that the concept can be used as an aid in evaluating diplomatic and strategic ideas and plans. This is an ambitious thought and may prove illusory. However, diplomacy and strategy begin with ideas, lead to decisions, result in movement, and therefore produce fields. In reverse, diplomacy and strategy are conditioned by the political areas and fields of the earth, which limit the possible decisions and practical ideas. No doubt such thinking goes on in high places unaided by our theory, but perhaps this bit of intellectual guidance will clarify some cases.

6

Studies in Political Geography

REPORT OF THE *Ad Hoc* COMMITTEE ON GEOGRAPHY

The spatial organization of political systems is so distinct and so conspicuous in the spatial pattern of world society that it demands study by special techniques. This has been recognized in geographical research for three-quarters of a century. Political geography's consistent concern with the expression of the sense of territoriality in man makes it one of the foremost keys to the spatial behavior of human society.

POLITICAL SYSTEMS AND POLITICAL SPACE

Every human being lives under, or in contact with, a political system. A majority, perhaps a vast majority, are in touch not only with their own system and its subsystems, but also with one or more outside systems. In an economically advanced section of the world such direct contact commonly concerns several political subsystems, some of them in a hierarchical arrangement. Consider a citizen of certain sections of southern or central California. He may be, and likely is, actively concerned with a school district, an irrigation district, a county, the California state government, and the federal government of the United States. Because he is a citizen of the United States, many political systems impinge upon his life indirectly in alliances like NATO, SEATO and CENTO, the United Nations, or the governments of individual foreign nations, like India, Taiwan, South Vietnam, or South Africa.

Every political system is prominently, if not preeminently, characterized by geographical area. Indeed, the concept of a nation, and by extension, the concept of any other political system, is almost unthinkable apart from association with specific territory.[1] The case of the Israeli people through the centuries vividly illustrates this point.

There are thus two inescapable general characteristics of a political system: the political process by or with which it functions, and the territory to which it is bound. Every political process has a geographical area uniquely associated with it and no geographical area escapes some relation with a political process. It is obvious that we are here concerned with one of the most important great subsystems on the face of the planet and one that never can be understood properly without the keenest observation and interpretation of its geographical dimension. It is no accident that the earliest geographical descriptions known referred to political units and that geography throughout most of its long history has rarely been without scholarly attention to the territorial units of political systems.

The Science of Geography, Publication 1277, Division of Earth Sciences, National Academy of Sciences–National Research Council, Washington, D.C., 1965. Reprinted by permission.

1. Cf. Friedrich Ratzel. "Every state is one part humanity and one part land." *Politische Geographie*, Munich, 1897.

The modern study of political systems is shared by several subjects. On one hand are political science, sociology, and anthropology, which center their attention upon the social attributes of people and the nature of political process. On the other is political geography, which centers its attention on the part of the earth occupied by a given political system, subsystem, or systems.

Political geography is the study of the interaction of geographical area and political process, or the study of the spatial distribution and space relations of political processes. *Political processes* are defined as the succession of actions or operations which man conducts to establish or to maintain a political system. Most of these processes operate through political institutions, although some are personal or man-institutional group actions.

Although bounded political units are the major focus of area interest, the variable impact of political processes within and beyond the boundaries of a specific political territory also fall within the scope of political geography.

A primary characteristic of political space is its "closed" quality. The territory associated with a political system is not only finite, it is highly specific. The common hunting grounds, the land condominia, and no-man's-land that characterized thousands of years of history on land have been replaced by the border problems of the modern world. These territorial border problems are by no means limited to international boundaries. Indeed, they are probably more numerous for subnational political systems, as exemplified by the problems of the average metropolitan area in the United States today.

Following the concept of Stephen Jones,[2] the "field" of a political system is normally the territory associated with it. In some cases, however, such "fields" extend beyond the territory of the system from which they originate or where they are sustained (e.g., the urbanizing influence of a large industrial and commercial center on surrounding political jurisdictions, or subversive activities inspired by political systems beyond its own borders, etc.). The fields that impinge upon one political system or another are created not only by political processes (expressed in diplomacy or military movement) but also by cultural, economic, and technological phenomena.[3]

The "closed" characteristic of political space is especially significant because some important economic functions, ideological and other social forces, and technological forces have space relations that are quite different from those of political processes. It may be said that these forces recognize no political boundaries. Yet they are mobile, sometimes rapid, and penetrating. Their space is a more "open" entity, whose boundaries can advance with astonishing rapidity but also can regress. Indeed, in the demands that the originally non-political processes make upon the internal structure of a given political system or subsystem, one discovers some of the most important problems in political geography.

The territorial phenomena of political systems include the: (a) supra-national, (b) national state, (c) domestic-regional political (provinces, states, counties), (d) urban-community or other organized densely settled area, and (e) local or regional special-purpose districts. Each of these territorial entities is associated with a specific political process; together, territory and specific process comprise a political system. The unitary element in the modern world is the political system known as a national state. It is the only entity capable of exercising all the possible political powers or of carrying out all the theoretically possible political processes which bear upon the life of one man or one specific group of men. All the other entities are subsystems, either in the sense of being regional units within the nation-state, special-purpose subsystems within the nation-state, or a regional division thereof (school districts, port authorities, soil conservation districts, development authorities, etc.),[4] or special purpose groupings of national states (military alliances, diplomatic catalyzing organizations like the United Nations, underground organizations for subversion, etc.).

There is one notable part of the earth's surface which is outside all political systems.

---

2. A Unified Field Theory of Political Geography, *Annals* of the Association of American Geographers, 44, 2, 1954, pp. 111–123.

3. N. Ginsburg, *Atlas of Economic Development*, Chicago: The University of Chicago Press, 1961.

4. 18,323 were enumerated by the Census of Governments—1962, in the United States. (Urban Survey Corporation, Boston, Massachusetts, 1964.)

This is the high seas, which ironically comprise the greater part of the surface of the planet. Viewed somewhat loosely they might be considered a condominium of all nations so situated as to be engaged in either marine or air traffic over them. Considered more carefully the seas have few of the attributes of political space. But the seas are of increasing interest to the nations who use them, and national states are encroaching upon this modern no-man's-land, extending territorial waters for economic and security purposes. On the other hand, air space control has undergone a change in the opposite direction. Orbiting satellites and manned high-altitude flights have changed territorial air space, once responsive to individual political systems, into a new "no man's land."

The earliest of the modern works on political geography were most concerned with the basic unit, the nation-state, or phenomena associated with it. Political geographers indeed were among the first scholars to think of the system they were studying in its relation to the total man-natural environment system of the entire earth. They were actively concerned with the dictum stated by Hartshorne that "geography has . . . one, individual, unitary, concrete object of study, namely the whole world."[5]

Because the world does not have a single political organization, and no comprehensively significant body of international law, the earliest memorable studies antecedent to the modern group treat the form and external relations of sovereign states. Thus came the first concerted attention to the subject-theme of political geography: the interaction between a political system in its closed space and political or economic processes kinetically or dynamically associated but not necessarily compatible with the system. Viewed in another way it is the study of the conditions of equilibrium in a political system as they relate to or derive from (a) spatial elements in the system, or (b) the spatial attributes of processes related to the system. The intellectual antecedents of the present cluster in political geography were concerned with the territorial endowments given to existing political systems as they expressed national power.

5. R. Hartshorne, *The Nature of Geography*, Association of American Geographers, Lancaster, Pa., 1939.

POLITICAL AREA STUDIES

a. The National State

From these beginnings in the United States two principal problem areas were cultivated. One was a traditional area, that of analyzing the evolution of political units, especially the national state in its historical setting. The state was treated in terms of both its internal and international structure. This approach perhaps reached its best expression in Derwent Whittlesey's *The Earth and the State*[6]. The other major problem area was that of natural resource management.

Because the prevailing methodological concepts of the time denied the possibility of extensive generalization in geography, many of the political area studies are regional descriptions in a historical context. This was true of the main body of Whittlesey's book. In it, however, he speaks of political systems.[7] and "geopolitcal forces." Political parties and political movements and "other processes in which laws and regions figure as protagonist and antagonist" are also mentioned by Whittlesey[8].

The hints given by Whittlesey about the importance of studying political processes were examined much more concertedly by Hartshorne[9], who set a keynote for modern political geography in treating political area differentiation in terms of functional organization. This approach focuses on the politically organized area as a spatial consequence of political process. Refinements were suggested by Gottmann[10] and Stephen Jones.[11] One essential difference between the older political geography studies and the recent point of view is more complete recognition that political system (political unit) as defined herein and political process do not necessarily cover

6. D. Whittlesey, *The Earth and the State*, Henry Holt & Co., New York, 1939.

7. *Ibid.*, "Every political system is the summation of laws which people make in order to extract a livelihood from their habitat" p. 557.

8. *Ibid.*, pp. 589–590.

9. R. Hartshorne, The Functional Approach in Political Geography, *Annals* of the Association of American Geographers, 40, 2, 1950. pp. 95–130.

10. J. Gottmann, Geography and International Relations. *World Politics*, III, 2, 1951–1952, pp. 153–173.

11. A Unified Field Theory of Political Geography, *Annals* of the Association of American Geographers, 44, 2, 1954, pp. 111–123.

the same geographical areas. Another difference is emphasis given in more recent studies to the historical and psychological perspectives from which national power is exercised and political behavior explained.

A recent study analyzing blocs of national states from a geographical point of view[12] stresses the dynamics of geopolitical equilibrium and the complexity of the processes associated with it. The study emphasizes distributional patterns and spatial interactions of peoples and materials who occupy unique political settings and are oriented to certain channels of movement.

Thus there emerges in recent work of this branch of the field a clear view of significant geographical patterns that are not obscured by focusing exclusively on the political system that is the national state.

b. Boundaries

Political area studies have included a number of microgeographical studies, mainly of a systematic nature. A large number of these have treated sections of national boundaries that in some way provide a "window" on the political system that they delimit or the interaction of two or more political systems of which they are an interface. Indeed, boundary study has been one of the most intensively cultivated problem areas of all geography. This is partly because boundaries, like islands, often have a discreteness attractive to the scholar seeking a foothold in a multivariate situation. To identify the frontier zone and its boundary is often easier than to identify the core. Boundary study has also been stimulated by the boundary problems following two world wars and the consequent interest of the United States Department of State. Hartshorne's studies of the Upper Silesian border[13] and the Polish Corridor,[14] Mackay's[15] and Minghi's[16] studies of the Canada-United States border, and Boggs'[17] and Pearcy's[18] studies of maritime boundaries, are illustrative of a great variety of boundary studies on many national areas. Several books that may be considered primary sources of boundary analysis have resulted, including Boggs' study of boundary functions,[19] Jones' handbook,[20] and Alexander's study of northwestern European offshore areas.[21]

c. Subnational Units

Boundary studies have in turn led to the study of political systems below the national level of organization, subjects otherwise treated only sparsely in political geography. These include both the domestic-regional and the urban-community. Thus studies by Jones of the Oregon counties,[22] by Ullman of the Rhode Island-Massachusetts boundary,[23] and Nelson on a section of Los Angeles County,[24] again are illustrative. However, such studies have been far fewer than the favored national-international boundary problems, even though a variety of interesting and significant internal boundary problems exist in the United States. Other topics such as electoral geography and the relation between internal physical diversity and political unity have been lightly touched. First treated in terms of counties[25] and provinces,[26] this area of research is now turning its attention

12. S. B. Cohen, *Geography and Politics in a World Divided*, Random House, New York, 1963.
13. Geographic and Political Boundaries in Upper Silesia, Annals of the Association of American Geographers, 23, 4, 1933, pp. 145-228.
14. Polish Corridor, *Journal of Geography*, XXXVI (1937), pp. 161-176.
15. The Interactance Hypothesis and Boundaries in Canada, *Canadian Geographer*, 11, 1958, pp. 1-8.
16. Television Preference and Nationality in a Boundary Region, *Sociological Inquiry*, 33, 1963, Spring, pp. 65-79.

17. Delimitation of the Territorial Sea, *American Journal of International Law*, 24, 1930, pp. 541-555.
18. Geographical Aspects of the Law of the Sea, Annals of the Association of American Geographers, 49, 1, 1959, pp. 1-23.
19. *International Boundaries: A Study of Boundary Functions and Problems*, Columbia University Press, New York, 1940.
20. *Boundary-Making: A Handbook for Statesmen, Treaty Editors, and Boundary Commissioners*, Columbia University Press, New York, 1940.
21. Offshore Geography of Northwestern Europe, Association of American Geographers Monograph Series 3, Rand McNally, Chicago, 1963.
22. Intra-State Boundaries in Oregon, *The Commonwealth Review*, 16, 3, 1934, pp. 105-126.
23. The Eastern Rhode Island-Massachusetts Boundary Zone, *Geography Review*, 29, 2, 1939, pp. 291-302.
24. The Vernon Area, California: A Study of the Political Factor in Urban Geography, Annals of the Association of American Geographers, 42, 2, 1952, pp. 117-191.
25. J. K. Wright, Voting Habits of the United States, *Geography Review*, 4, 1932, pp. 666-672.
26. Siegfried, A., *Switzerland*, Duell, Sloane, and Pearce, New York, 1950.

to the interfaces of urban units and political group behavior therein.[27]

RESOURCE MANAGEMENT STUDIES

The second major problem area in political geography in the United States has rarely been labeled as such, but its origins, content, and conceptual affiliation are nonetheless clear. It is concerned with resource management and land planning in various forms. In contrast with studies of the evolution of political units and the interaction of political area and process, resource management studies have been much more concerned with problems internal to the United States, although a few studies have treated the internal problems of other countries.[28, 29] One study of economic development covering the world also gives valuable information for resource management investigation.[30]

The generalized problem of these studies has been the disequilibrium in a political system caused by nonconformities between land occupance and the existing legal system. Their objective has been the application of spatial analysis to the problems of the *developing* state or political system and to point the way toward equilibria. As Whittlesey noted,

To obtain a clear view of the geopolitical forces the earth processes must . . . be studied. Chief among these is the earth's inexorable march from causes to consequences. Laws flagrantly unsuited to regions where they operate ultimately destroy the resource which they govern . . . scarcely any considerable alteration can be performed upon the face of nature without repercussions. Most such operations are possible only to governments.[31]

The impact of political decisions upon the use of land, be it land occupance for quasi-military purposes as in Israel's frontier areas, or the political organization of Canada's northern territories, this field supplies an almost unending series of problems.

27. P. Lewis, Geography in the Politics of Flint, Ph. D. dissertation, University of Michigan, Ann Arbor, 1958.
28. G. F. White, *Economic and Social Aspects of Lower Mekong Development*, Committee for Co-ordination of Investigations of Lower Mekong Basin, Bangkok, Thailand, 1962.
29. Ackerman, *Loc. cit.*
30. Ginsburg, *Loc. cit.*
31. Whittlesey, *Loc. cit.*, pp. 589–590.

The origins of attention to these studies are easily traced to the early twin interests of Professor Barrows in physical geography and in historical-political geography. He soon developed a conceptual framework for conservation that easily led into the studies of land and water resource planning that Barrows, Colby, White, and others spearheaded in the days of the National Resources Planning Board in the 1930's and early 1940's and that Barrows supervised at the United States Bureau of Reclamation. The peak commitment of geographers to work of this type probably took place in the late 1930's and early 1940's, although a modest flow of geographers into resource planning analysis has continued ever since. A large share of these studies has not been published, but they have contributed to the flow of data and insights that have helped legal and administrative systems in the United States to achieve adjustments to land and other resources. Records of typical activities in the 1930's and 1940's have been left in the publications of the land and water committees of the National Resources Planning Board.

Studies in this problem area have continued since the end of the Second World War consistently on a similar course. They often have been in response to a public need, such as studies for the Natural Resources Task Force of the Commission on the Organization of the Executive Branch (1948), or the President's Water Resources Policy Commission (1950), and the Senate Select Committee on National Water Resources report (1960). In all these examples an attempt was made to analyze discontinuities between the administrative machinery of the federal political system of the United States and the spatial phenomena to which they are related. An attempt was made to codify the "normal" situation for these relations in the light of modern technology by Ackerman and Löf.[32] Interesting social and psychological elements in resource management were brought out by White and his colleagues in their flood plain studies.[33]

An example of the study undertaken on a state level is that by the Maryland State

32. *Technology in American Water Development*, The Johns Hopkins University Press, Baltimore, 1959.
33. Changes in Urban Occupance of Flood Plains in the United States, *Department of Geography, The University of Chicago. Research Paper 57*, 1958.

Department of Planning.[34] That study caused a reorganization of Maryland state resource development agencies to a structure more responsive to regional problems than it had been (e.g., management of the tidewater areas). As before the war, study not leading to formal publication again has formed an important part of scholarly activity in this area. An example was the formulation of concepts which led eventually to the establishment of the Delaware River Basin Commission in Eastern United States, an experiment in combined federal-state management of an important resource in a heavily settled region.

The principal research on political geography . . . in recent years therefore has been divided into two main problem areas: the study of political areas, and especially their interfaces, and the study of domestic resource management and land planning problems. Both of these are special cases within the subject theme described earlier: study of the conditions of equilibrium in a political system as they relate to or derive from spatial elements in the system, or the spatial attributes of processes related to the system. The study of boundaries is essentially the study of interfaces between political systems. The study of resource management and planning essentially has been the study of spatial organization in the giant state. Viewed thus, we shall see that these research interests have a high degree of significance for future work in political geography.

Relations with Other Fields

Political geography can make a valid contribution to geography only by dealing with political process. This involves a working relation with other fields, particularly political science and history. Historically, political geography has had its closest contact with political science through the study of international relations. Indeed, the late 19th and early 20th century inquiry into the relationship between the political power of nations and the earth-man environment by geographers like Ritter, Guyot, Ratzel, Mackinder, was grasped by political scientists as a new realistic basis for analyzing the relation among states.

International Relations—essentially a series of approaches to interpret and systematize the various forces and factors that have characterized the relations among states . . . owes its emergence to the down-to-earth realism of 19th century geographers.[35]

Interdisciplinary communication in recent years, however, has been sporadic at best. Because of this and early emphasis on the foundations of national power by geographers, many political scientists misconceive geography as consisting of a number of variables of the physical environment.[36] Singer[37] speaks of "geographical variables which are only partially, if at all, subject to human modification." In the several articles contributed by political scientists to a survey of geography and international conflict[38] there is almost no reference to or recognition of contemporary geographical literature or thought. Yet some subjects of great significance to politics, like voting behavior and legislative redistricting, can be examined completely only with the aid of modern geographic techniques.

On the other hand, new methods and concepts in political scientist's study of political process are useful and should be attractive to geographers concerned with the study of boundaries and other spatial phenomena on the interfaces of political systems. Kirk[39] and the Sprouts[40] were among the first to introduce behaviorism and decision-making theories to geographers. Works such as those of Deutsch on social complementarity[41] and measuring the political community,[42] German's study of the application of national power, using national psychological and sociological intangibles to weigh and modify natural and human resources,[43] Koch's

---

34. *Future Administration of State of Maryland Water Resources Activities*, (2 vols.) Baltimore, 1961.

35. A. Gyorgy, in Cohen, *op. cit.*, 1963. [paraphrased]
36. T. Fritzsimmons, ed., Country Survey Series *Human Relations Area Files*, New Haven, 1959.
37. The Geography of Conflict: Introduction, *Journal of Conflict Resolution*, IV, 1, 1960, pp. 1–3.
38. *Ibid.*
39. Historical Geography and the Concept of the Behavioral Environment, *Indian Geography*, XXVI, Silver Jubilee Vol., 1951, pp. 152–160.
40. Man-Milieu Relationship Hypothesis in the Context of International Politics, *Center for International Studies*, Princeton University, Princeton, N.J., 1956.
41. *Nationalism and Social Communication*, Technology Press of M.I.T., Cambridge, Mass., 1953.
42. *Political Community at the International Level*, Garden City, New York, Doubleday, 1954.
43. A Tentative Evaluation of World Power, *Journal of Conflict Resolution*, 4, 1, 1960, pp. 138–144.

matrix analysis to indicate interaction between geographical variables and institutions and motivations,[44] and Schelling's application of game theory to political process[45] are worth exploring as avenues of joint research for geographers and political scientists. At the same time, game theory and decision-making studies of state behavior are being made with inadequate reference to global geopolitical equilibrium theories.

For those students of political geography who have been most concerned with resource management and other aspects of spatial organization in a giant state, decision-making in both its economic and political aspects also is an important related field of study, particularly the slowly reviving field of political economy. Hirshman's[46] research in political economics, such as his discussion of the role that political motivation played in leading to the multipurpose São Francisco development project, is an example of a study of process that has significance for geographical research. Study of the role of public policy and of personal motivation in the management and use of land resources[47] illustrates another closely related approach. The outmoding of county units, the consequences of the establishment of new administrative districts, and the retention of regional myths in national politics are other examples of topics dealt with by related fields that are pertinent to political geography. Jones[48] suggested that the study of administrative areas could be an attractive meeting ground for political scientists and political geographers.

There would seem to be a particularly rich source of collaborative interest with other social scientists now studying urban affairs, including sociologists, economists, and political scientists. Urban political and social motivational studies[49] and urban economics[50]—including public expenditures policies, manpower-budget, cost-benefit analyses and highway-impact studies—all contribute data that are extremely useful, if not vital, to the student of political spatial organization on a local scale. They are as yet very incompletely exploited by geographers. The interfaces between local political systems offer some of the most interesting materials for the future because of the rapidity of urbanization in the United States and many other countries. The clash between closed urban political space and the total earth-man urbanized system closely parallels the clash on the national-state-international level, warranting much more cross-field investigation than has been applied to date.

UNFULFILLED OPPORTUNITIES

With only a handful of practitioners in a field of vast potential scope, and they, sharply divided into two groups with only a moderate frequency of communication obviously cultivating a field which calls for close interdisciplinary attention and not yet having fully developed it, the problems of research in political geography are many. But the opportunities are many also and of the highest social significance.

In a world where high policy from politically sophisticated powerful nations can produce political-geographic monstrosities like the boundary between North and South Korea, the Berlin exclave, and the quadripartite division of former French Indochina, the need for professional study of political geography of international interfaces by students of the highest competence can only be described as urgent.

A need for studying the territorial viability of small states is also urgent. The break-up of the colonial system has seen the number of independent states grow from 71, on the eve of the Second World War, to 125 today. This proliferation of nations has created serious international complications by introducing many small, weak, and poor national states into the world system. More than 60 nations

44. J. Koch, R. North, D. Zinnes, Some Theoretical Notes on Geography and International Conflicts, *Journal of Conflict Resolution*, 4, 1, 1960, pp. 4–14.

45. *The Strategy of Conflict*, Harvard University Press, Cambridge, Mass., 1960.

46. *Journey Toward Progress—Studies in Policy-Making in Latin America*, The Twentieth Century Fund, New York, 1963.

47. M. B. Clawson, Held, and Stoddard, *Land for the Future*, The Johns Hopkins University Press, Baltimore, 1960.

48. Jones, Unpublished notes, 1961.

49. M. Levin and G. Blackwood, *Compleat Politician: Political Strategy in Massachusetts*, Bobbs-Merrill Co., Indianapolis, Ind., 1962.

50. H. Perloff, L. Wingo, et al., *Natural Resources and Economic Growth*, Conference on Natural Resources and Economic Growth, sponsored jointly by Resources for the Future, Inc., and the Social Science Research Council, through their Committee on Economic Growth, 1961.

have less than 5 million inhabitants each and 31 less than 2 million each. These small countries make every effort to maintain their economic and political postures as equals within the international community. Yet the role that such states can realistically hope to play in world affairs is a function of their territorial viability. It is a problem area that very seriously merits the attention of political geographers.

The need for equally competent study of political geography on an intranational scale, while not equally urgent, must also be considered pressing. Nations' populations are growing in total numbers with a rapidity never before equaled in history, concentrating those numbers in limited areas with unprecedentedly high densities, superimposing those masses of people on spatially organized political systems devised for relatively sparse or uniformly spread settlement, and at the same time coping with new and revolutionary technology. It is not surprising that disequilibria within the large national states, and particularly the United States, are the rule rather than the exception. The racial and urban-rural frictions today threatening the society of the United States undoubtedly have some of their causes in these spatial disequilibria, now poorly understood and little mentioned.

In the face of the formidable array of problems which the two clusters in political geography can treat, the important questions would seem to be those of future training of students of political area or resource management, enhanced communication both within geography and between geography and other fields, and the most strategic deployment of the limited research potential likely to be available. Stated in another manner, how can past tradition in these studies and present capacities of research workers in the two clusters of interest be capitalized on, and how are the research frontiers of the field to be developed?

To reach some conclusions as to how political geography may contribute with increasing effectiveness to research on political systems in the world, several background observations seem pertinent.

(1) Political geography problems are essentially interdisciplinary. That is, the most effective research and most meaningful answers result when methods and data from two or more traditional scholarly fields, including geography, are applied in research. In studying political area organization as the spatial consequence of political process, there are important questions on ideological concepts, individual and group behavior, rates of political maturation, degree of applicability or resistance to political laws, and diffusion of ideas that go far beyond the accustomed competence of the individual geographer. International relations, economics, sociology and social psychology, may in turn be absolutely essential to the understanding of specific problems in political geography. Determination of a research problem within its full system context is an essential step.

(2) Communication between geographers and political scientists and other social scientists has been sporadic and largely *ad hoc*, related to a specific and temporary research interest. The cultivation of an effective jointly based discipline, like biophysics or biochemistry, which could and should be a goal, thus has had little stimulus. If there is to be such a joint effort, the unit area framework used by political geographers is a window that can be valuable to political and social scientists in their concern with intra-state processes.

(3) Political geographers have been accustomed to thinking in terms of systems and system relationships almost from the beginning of their field (cf. Ratzel). Thus a system framework . . . will be easily understood by the political geographer, and his work easily adapted to it. Indeed, at least a few efforts toward treating the specific problems on a systems scale have appeared in the recent past.[51] However, nearly all political geography thought has been empirically oriented. Thus far it has had little relation to formal systems theory. The dialogue between the empirical and the theoretical has not been habitual. At the same time it is now obvious that at least some aspects of systems theory, like theories of diffusion, are fundamental to the study of political geography problems.

(4) No single group of political geography research workers exists at the present time. Instead there are the two clusters described above. One is the group which has studied political areas, especially their interface

---

51. E. A. Ackerman, G. Löf, *Technology in American Water Development*, The Johns Hopkins University Press, Baltimore, 1959.

problems within political systems, most often on an international plane—the successors to the older geographers interested in the evolution of the national state. The second is the group which has paid particular attention to the spatial organization of resource management in our political system. The general problem that this latter group is concerned with is the internal spatial organization of the giant state, whether it is federal or other.

. . . Students of political geography, in spite of their small number, have contributed effectively and consistently in the recent past to two research frontiers. These are in boundary studies, and in the spatial organization of resource management and planning. It is now reasonable to inquire as to whether either one or both of these does constitute a reasearch frontier. They should be judged both from the point of view of social significance and from the point of view of intellectual significance.

. . . Every reader of a newspaper, from his repeated exposure to Berlin and Korea, and more recently to Southeast Asia, knows that there are international boundary problems even though he may not reorganize them under such a classification. The sensitive interfaces between the two great international political systems are in themselves sufficient reason for competent professional study in this area. However, study of the interfaces between political systems should anticipate boundary and other problems; they should anticipate spatial causes of friction and barriers to interchange. The creation of more than 50 new nations within the last 20 years, many having boundaries that are relicts of colonial times, suggests that boundary tensions in Africa and Asia are very likely to remain as breeders of local wars for decades to come. Furthermore, the appearance of a totally new type of boundary, the Iron Curtain type, is a further challenge to study.

Studies of internal boundaries and the studies of the spatial organization of resource management and planning also . . . have a high degree of social significance. Both of the giant national states of today, the United States and the Soviet Union, have shown increasingly visible stresses in the last 10 years because of the internal spatial organization of their political systems, different as they are. The European Common Market grouping is just reaching a stage where these internal stresses may be even more sharply outlined. Geographic studies are needed to complement the new interest in study of political economy that has developed since 1945. International river basins, like the Mekong, the Jordan, the Indus, the Nile, and others, are also centers of stress, although they also can be viewed as potential bases for international accord.

It would thus seem difficult to choose two problem areas which have a higher social significance than these at the present time.

There remains a need to comment briefly on the intellectual significance of these two general subjects. Here again they appear to answer the tests for significance. They offer relatively discrete subjects; local problems may be chosen so as to give insights on the larger national political system or the interactions thereof with another system; both would seem to be attractive to an experimenter with the application of formal systems analysis; and both unquestionably have the study of geographical space prominent in needs for solution and understanding.

Lying beyond these immediately approachable subjects are others of great significance which may be susceptible to geographic analysis. For example, what is a small state and what is state viability? Must the geopolitical structure of the recently emerged small state conform to that of the larger traditional national state to afford viability? How does the proliferation of small states affect the geopolitical foundations of the United Nations, which was not structured to cope with such numbers?

In another vein, how are the attitudes of people toward the great ideologies (communism, socialism, nationalism, economic *laissez-faire*, etc.) spatially distributed and diffused in particular countries, and over the earth? What are the spatial parameters of different attitudes toward a minority group, and what are their dynamics? Voting behavior, a subject that is being examined in increasingly fine detail, has geographical components. What are they; and how significant are they? What is the geography of demagogic control?

We believe that these and other serious problems facing the world could receive helpful illumination by competent geographic study.

Annotated Bibliography

Bowman, Isaiah
"Geography vs. Geopolitics," *Geographical Review*, XXXII (October 1942), pp. 646–658.
    A biting critique of German geopolitics with the burden of documentation and argument supporting the author's conclusion that geopolitik is an illusion, mummery, and an apology for theft.

Bowman, Isaiah
The New World: Problems in Political Geography, 4th ed. (Chicago: World Book Co., 1928).
    As the subtitle suggests, this pioneering volume, first published in 1921, is a thorough analysis of the problems arising from the territorial and other changes in the political structure of Europe following World War I. Although Europe is the main focus, ramifications for other world areas are discussed at length.

Cohen, Saul B.
Geography and Politics in a World Divided (New York: Random House, 1963). Also published in London by Methuen, 1964.
    The first lengthy geographical work on global power structure to appear since Spykman. The world is divided into major geostrategic regions and these, in turn, into geopolitical regions. Two shatterbelts remain to complete the global system. Chapter 1 is of particular relevance to this section on heritage. The Methuen edition has the better maps.

Colby, Charles C., ed.
Geographic Aspects of International Relations (Chicago: The University of Chicago Press, 1938).
    A collection of lectures by a group of distinguished geographers, including Bowman, Hartshorne, and Whittlesey on a variety of political-geographic problems. Included are such aspects as migration, water resources, colonialism, and boundary disputes. Hartshorne's survey of European boundary problems, while now out of date, traces several interesting methods for measuring the geographical basis of the relative merits of the disputants in fifty-six disputed areas.

Fifield, Russell H., and G. Etzel Pearcy
Geopolitics in Principle and Practice (Boston: Ginn and Co., 1944).
    As the title suggests, an analysis of the principles (definition, scope, evolution, and prime factors) of geopolitics, which is defined as the geographic study of the state from the viewpoint of foreign policy. Geopolitical practice is examined in Germany, the United States, Japan, the Soviet Union, and the British Commonwealth. Chapter 2, "Evolution," is particularly useful as is the authors' summary of the major contributions of geopolitics.

Hartshorne, Richard
"The Concepts of 'Raison d'Être' and 'Maturity of States,' " (abstract) *Annals* of the Association of American Geographers, XXX (March 1940), pp. 59–60.
    An abstract of a paper given at the 1939 meeting of the Association of American Geographers. The author rejects the idea that the process of maturity of states is analogous to the life-cycle of a biological organism, or to any physiographic cycle. The state is geopolitically mature when it has established a *raison d'être*.

Hartshorne, Richard
"Political Geography", in P. E. James and C. F. Jones, eds., *American Geography: Inventory and Prospect* (Syracuse N.Y.: Syracuse University Press, 1954).
    The section on political geography put together by a committee of which Hartshorne was chairman in a volume assessing the status and future of American geography. The author essentially reviews the field's development and elaborates on his own ideas introduced four years earlier in his "Functional Approach."

Hartshorne, Richard
"Political Geography in the Modern World," *Journal of Conflict Resolution*, IV (March 1960), pp. 52–66.

A fairly short synopsis of Hartshorne's most recent ideas on political geography including a discussion of its scope. The author concentrates on the conditions and consequences of organizing political areas, under such headings as determination of territorial extent, internal sub-divisions, homogeneity, and coherence in organizing areas into functional units and viability.

HARTSHORNE, RICHARD
"Recent Developments in Political Geography," *American Political Science Review*, XXXIX (October and December 1935), pp. 785–804, 943–966.

A long, scholarly review of political-geographic literature as of the mid-1930's, with particular emphasis on the contributions of German writers hitherto not reviewed in English. The author covers the field's development prior to and after World War I under such headings as geographic analysis, interpretation, and appraisal of the state, and includes a discussion on the place of geopolitik. Full bibliographical citations are included.

JACKSON, W. A. DOUGLAS
Politics and Geographic Relationships (Englewood Cliffs, New Jersey: Prentice-Hall Inc., 1964).

A volume of some thirty-four edited selections under eighteen different sections and a brief introductory statement by Jackson in which he defines political geography as the study of political phenomena in their areal context.

JACKSON, W. A. DOUGLAS
"Whither Political Geography?" *Annals* of the Association of American Geographers, XLVII (June 1958) pp. 178–183.

An excellent and provocative review of the literature with special emphasis on integrating the work of Hartshorne and Jones with some ideas from non-geographers that had appeared more recently.

KRIESEL, KARL MARCUS
"Montesquieu: Possibilistic Political Geographer," *Annals* of the Association of American Geographers, LVIII (September 1968), pp. 557–574.

An examination of the portions of Montesquieu's work which treat the roles played by the physical environment and the non-physical societal attributes which together produce a particular political system. The author advances the notion that Montesquieu's political-geographic views were more possibilistic than environmentalistic or deterministic.

KRISTOF, LADIS K. D.
"The Origins and Evolution of Geopolitics," *Journal of Conflict Resolution*, IV (March 1960), pp. 15–51.

As the title suggests, a thorough and rather lengthy analysis of the basic notions behind the origins of geopolitics and a commentary on its growth. A very valuable work, especially for its wealth of bibliographical notes.

RATZEL, FRIEDRICH
"The Territorial Growth of States," *Scottish Geographical Magazine*, XII (1896), pp. 351–361.

An abstract in translation of Ratzel's longer article in German in *Petermanns Mitteilungen* of 1896. A useful summary of Ratzel's main ideas on the process of growth.

SPROUT, HAROLD
"Geopolitical Hypotheses in Technological Perspective," *Journal of Conflict Resolution*, XV (January 1963), pp. 187–212.

A critical examination of seventy-five years of geopolitical hypothesis-building, with special reference to aspects of scientific and technological change. Geopolitical hypotheses are categorized as: (a) derived from the layout and configuration of lands and seas, (b) based upon variations of climate in space and time, (c) built upon the uneven distribution of natural resources, (d) centered upon the uneven distribution of population, and (e) dependent upon science and its practical applications in engineering projects. The author concludes that the last-named approach is the most useful but also the most ignored.

THERMAENIUS, EDVARD
"Geopolitics and Political Geography," *Baltic and Scandinavian Countries*, IV (May 1938), pp. 165–177.

The best review of Rudolf Kjellén's ideas on geopolitics available in English. Appearing in an obscure and now defunct Polish journal sixteen years after Kjellén's death, the article attempts to place the "science of geopolitics" as one of the five branches in Kjellén's "System of Politics," and also to contrast it with the field of political geography as exemplified by the writings of Supan, Bowman, Vogel, Maull, and Numelin.

WEIGERT, HANS W.
Generals and Geographers: The Twilight of Geopolitics (New York: Oxford University Press, 1942).

An excellent if somewhat dialectical summary of the growth of German geopolitics and its development including a valuable analysis of, as the title suggests, Haushofer's own thinking.

WHITTLESEY, DERWENT
The Earth and the State: A Study in Political Geography (New York: Henry Holt & Co., 1939).

As with Bowman's *New World*, a classic and lasting work as the first real textbook in English in political geography. The author applies his well-known historical approach to the regional discussions with remarkable effect. He also includes some systematic treatment of political-geographic problems relating to communications, natural resources, international seaspace, and environmental relations.

WRIGHT, JOHN K.

"Training for Research in Political Geography," *Annals* of the Association of American Geographers, XXXIV (December 1944), pp. 190–201.

Part of a symposium on training for geographic research. The author discusses the scope of political geography including the nature of political groups and of their actions, and geographic aspects of political conflict. In the training for research in the subject, the author emphasizes the need for familiarity with the literature in political science, for a historic-mindedness, and for objectivity.

Part II: STRUCTURE

Introduction

As we have seen in the introductory essay and selections in "Heritage," political geography has naturally tended to be structure-oriented throughout its long existence as a field of study. The morphology of political regions has provided the focus of study, although the emphasis has shifted somewhat over the past few decades. Increasingly, the aspects of structure have been studied less from the point of view of inventory or evolution and more from a functional cast.

Structural-functional analysis in political geography has a well-developed tradition in the social sciences where the trend has long been dominant. A monograph published under the editorship of Don Martindale in 1965 gives an excellent overview of the functionalistic approach in the social sciences.[1]

Theoretically, functionalism is the analysis of social and cultural life from the standpoint of the primacy of systems, and methodologically it is the analysis of social events by methods thought peculiarly adapted to the integration of these events into systems.[2] In short, structural-functionalism attempts to provide a scientific theory of the system under study. The framework for such theory-building has been provided by Parsons and Levi, whose works have indicated that any social system has four functional prerequisites: pattern maintenance and tension management, goal attainment, adaptation, and integration.[3]

Although many other social scientists have made valuable contributions to structural-functional theory,[4] in political science a major advance has been made by Almond.[5] He distinguishes two categories of functions, political and governmental. The former includes political socialization, political recruitment, interest articulation, interest aggregation, and political communication, while governmental functions are rule making, rule application, and rule adjudication. Yet even in such a short list it is difficult to keep the incongruent elements of structure and process apart. Almond's political communication, as Flanigan and Fogelman have pointed out, is more

---

1. Don Martindale, ed., *Functionalism in the Social Sciences*, Monograph S (Philadelphia: The American Academy of Political and Social Science, 1965).

2. Don Martindale, "Foreward," *op. cit.*, pp. viii–ix.

3. Talcott Parsons, *The Social System* (Glencoe, Ill.: Free Press, 1951); Marion Levi, *The Structure of Society* (Princeton, N.J.: Princeton University Press, 1951); and Talcott Parsons and Neil Smelser, *Economy and Society* (Glencoe, Ill.: Free Press, 1956). The relevance of these ideas to the field of politics is discussed at length in Robert T. Holt, "A Proposed Structural-Functional Framework for Political Science," in Martindale, *op. cit.*, pp. 92ff.

4. For example, Robert Merton, *Social Theory and Social Structure* (Glencoe, Ill.: Free Press, 1957); George P. Murdoch, *Social Structure* (New York: Macmillan, 1949); Claude Lévy-Strauss, *Structural Anthropology*, C. Jacobson and B. C. Schoepf, trans. (New York: Basic Books, 1963); and A. R. Radcliffe-Brown, *Structure and Function in a Primitive Society* (London: Cohen and West, 1952), especially Ch. IX "On the Concept of Function in Social Science," pp. 178–187 (also published by The Free Press).

5. Gabriel A. Almond, "Introduction: A Functional Approach to Comparative Politics," in Gabriel A. Almond and James S. Coleman, eds., *The Politics of the Developing Areas* (Princeton, N.J.: Princeton University Press, 1960), pp. 3–64.

a process—a means of performing functions—rather than a function in itself.[6]

The promise of structural-functionalism in the field of politics is nothing less than to provide a consistent and integrated theory from which can be derived explanatory hypotheses relevant to all aspects of a political system. The premise is that if a given system is to be maintained adequately under a given condition certain requisite functions must be performed. Yet, unresolved problems abound. Objective criteria for determining when a system is being adequately maintained are not yet available. Changes in a structure involve changes in how a function is performed, and the nature of the interdependence of particular structures is not yet fully understood. Attempts to spell out functional requisites run into a mire of amorphous concepts.[7]

In their review, political scientists Flanigan and Fogelman conclude that, although the promise of structural-functionalism has not yet been fulfilled, the approach has contributed to political analysis by increasing sensitivity to the complexity of interrelationships among social and political phenomena, and by drawing attention to a *whole social system* as a setting for political phenomena.[8] These findings point up the interdisciplinary tradition of structural-functional analysis.

This trend in political geography, despite the emphasis given by such writers as Hartshorne, Gottmann, and Jones to the functional side of structure in the early 1950's, has been slow in gaining influence.[9] Description, classification, and areal comparisons of formal spatial evidences of political structure have formed the core of political geography. Study consequently has been organized around such phenomena as boundaries, capitals, political subdivisions, and concepts derived from these phenomena such as core areas, borderlands, problem areas, frontiers, buffer zones, and the like.

A glance over the contents pages of almost any textbook in political geography will reflect this largely formal-structural approach based on these organizing phenomena and associated concepts. Whittlesey's outline of elements of political area,[10] reproduced in Part I, bears a strong resemblance to the chapter headings of many topically organized textbooks published in the three intervening decades. Some of the internal emphases may have changed, with perhaps less attention given to the role of the natural environment, but the overall organizational framework based on structural elements has not. It is after all a logical starting point, as these elements are the only really palpable landscape features of political organization in space.

We do not intend to belittle this structural approach here. We wish, rather, to emphasize its place within the development of political geographic thought and its relationship to aspects of process and behavior discussed in Parts III and IV of this volume.

Aspects of structure are, of course, basic in that as with Jones' last two links in his unified field theory chain, "field" and "area,"[11] they provide the spatial manifestations of political process and behavior as well as the framework within which these processes operate. Thus they form an essential part of the spatial system of political organization.

Our claim is that the approach to political geography through structure has tended to emphasize the purely formal aspects of landscape features resultant from political activity in a fairly static manner with more interest in their origins, typologies, areal variations, distributional characteristics of size, shape, and so forth, than in their treatment as spatial functions of a political system incorporating a complex set of relationships of behavior, process, and structure. Furthermore, even in its more functional cast, structure has been overemphasized as a way into political geographic problems, thereby tending to divert attention away from these other aspects of the system such as political process and behavior without due consideration of which the functional aspects of structure cannot, in the final analysis, be fully understood.

---

6. William Flanigan and Edwin Fogelman, "Functionalism in Political Science," in Martindale, *op. cit.*, p. 117.

7. For a fuller discussion of these unresolved problems see Flanigan and Fogelman, *op. cit.*, pp. 120–122.

8. *Ibid.*, p. 125.

9. Martindale includes geography with demography and linguistics as the social sciences where theory in functionalism is least developed (Martindale, *op. cit.*, p. ix).

10. Derwent Whittlesey, *The Earth and the State* (New York: Henry Holt, 1939), p. 587.

11. Stephen B. Jones, "A Unified Field Theory of Political Geography," *Annals* of the Association of American Geographers, XLIV (1954), p. 115. (Reproduced in Part I.)

Nevertheless, because of its strong traditional ties and its many fruitful theoretical contributions, we regard a consideration of structure in political geography as a logical followup to the "Heritage" section and also as an essential forerunner to the discussions of process and behavior.

We have chosen to divide the selections on the spatial structure of political organization into four parts, each of which has traditionally enjoyed a degree of separate attention in the literature. Rather than focussing on formal phenomena, these divisions attempt to give emphasis to the functional aspects of structure. They are territoriality and hierarchy, centrality and nodes, boundaries and frontiers, and global structures.

All but the last division apply at all scales of political territory and incorporate the major structural elements associated with man's political organization of space. The last section includes attempts at analyzing the spatial structure of political organization at the world scale by the use of various global equilibrium models.

In the following discussions on each section, some general comments will precede a review of the major ideas pertaining to that particular section.

Territoriality and Hierarchy

We can begin this section by stating two basic concepts about the relationship between territory and political organization.

1. Any politically organized group operates within a well-defined area—its political territory. Within this territory there is a political hierarchy which is reflected in a territorial framework.
2. Within and among political units, there is a spatial structure to political organization and process.

These concepts relate directly to two fundamental notions in political geography, "territoriality" and "hierarchy." Territoriality can be defined as the ... propensity to possess, occupy, and defend a particular portion of space (see the introductory essay, Part IV), while hierarchy refers to a group of phenomena arranged in order of rank, grade, or class, which in a political sense implies different levels of authority within a politically defined territory.

Any person located at a given point will usually come under a complex hierarchical system of political activity, the various levels of which have an imprint on his daily existence through such things as taxation and a host of restraints on behavior. These overlapping and coexisting levels of a political hierarchy (for example, ward–city–metropolitan area–state–federal) create corresponding levels of territoriality so that feelings of territoriality of an individual or group will reflect some balance of reactions to the demands and rewards of each level in the hierarchy.

In this respect, Robert Brown developed the idea of "nested hierarchy" in his 1957 analysis of St. Cloud, Minnesota. In the United States, the Constitution provides for certain political functions to be reserved for the national government, while the states have responsibility for the other functions. The states in turn have subdivided their own areas and hence each subdivision has certain powers and functions. The overall result of this areal division of political functions has resulted in the evolution of a complex nested hierarchy of functions and areas.[12]

An important element of territoriality is, of course, the behavioral aspect. In Part IV, territorial behavior will be discussed and illustrated in the introductory essay and some of the selections, hence little attention will be devoted to it here. One can recognize a behavioral territorial hierarchy formulation in the selection on "Space, Territory and Human Movements" by David Stea in Part IV, Behavior. Neighborhoods and the "turf" of gangs are examples used by Stea.

The structural aspects of territoriality are obviously those pertaining to the interrelationships of the qualities of political territory and those of the population within it. As we have already seen, many writers, from Aristotle onwards, have devised ways of coming to grips with these relationships, working almost exclusively at the nation-state level.[13]

12. Robert Brown, *Political Areal-Functional Organization of St. Cloud, Minnesota* (Chicago: The University of Chicago, Department of Geography Research Paper No. 51, December 1957), pp. 4–5.
13. For example, in a recent textbook elements of the state, including territory, population, organization, and power, are discussed in early chapters. Harm J. de Blij, *Systematic Political Geography* (New York: Wiley, 1967), Chapters II and III.

Territorial Size and Shape

Invariably aspects of size and shape of political territory are first isolated and examined in terms of the area's viability. Typologies associated with these territorial qualities abound. In the matter of simple areal size of states one can talk about ranging on a scale from mini or micro through to giant, and in combination with population size, from sparsely populated to very densely populated on a crude density factor for the area in question. With the added qualities of resource endowment, stage of technology, and other pertinent variables, typologies on the basis of an underpopulated to overpopulated continuum have also been formulated.

Areal size in relation to population distribution gives another dimension to the last-named typology, and adds sophistication to notions of density which often have a direct bearing on problems of political organization. Political decisions originate, decisions are made, and policies are implemented on the basis of how population problems are perceived so that immigration laws, settler subsidies, tax exemptions, different political status within a system, and the like are based on this perception, and in turn have an impact in spatially differentiating parts of any politically organized territory.

Whereas externalities are kept to a minimum in attempts to isolate factors of size in both area and population, these same factors as they apply to external units, especially neighbors, often play a role in the internal situation in as much as they can influence political organization and viability. Canada's string-like population distribution, concentrated in a discontinuous strip along its southern border with the tenfold more populous United States, is an important factor in Canada's polity. For example, the dominance of mass communication media of American origin such as television transmission from border "pirate" stations located in the United States over Canada's major metropolitan areas tends to deny the Canadian public network (The Canadian Broadcasting Corporation) access to most of its own residents.[14] It has been argued, however, that because of the relatively "empty" areas on the United States side of the border, it is in fact the Canadians who have a natural advantage in this type of competition.[15]

These externalities become more important when aspects of shape are also considered. Usually typologies of shape include such labels as elongated, prorupt, compact, perforated, and fragmented. The last-named type calls attention to a fairly common aspect of shape which is characterized by the terms "exclave" and "enclave" used to describe situations where relatively small pockets of territory are located outside, but are politically part of, the main territorial unit. Typologies of this shape characteristic, known as noncontiguity, are associated with the factor of relative location especially with reference to neighbor territories. Pockets completely surrounded by neighboring territories are known as "normal" exclaves, while other terms such as "pene" and "quasi" are used to describe situations where physical contiguity is present but where accessibility between the pocket and the "mother" territory must still involve the neighbor.[16]

Relative Location

External aspects of political units as discussed in Hartshorne's functional system are included under territorial, economic, political, and strategic relations. All of these involve consideration of the factor of relative location. Generic terms derived from this consideration such as coastal states, island states, landlocked states,[17] riverine states, buffer states, pass states, and so forth, indicate the importance of relative location in both its physical and political context.

14. For a study of parts of the Vancouver metropolitan area see, Julian V. Minghi, "Television Preference and Nationality in a Boundary Region," *Sociological Inquiry*, XXXIII (Spring 1963), pp. 165–179.

15. Andrew Burghardt, "Canada and the World," in John Warkentin, ed., *Canada: A Geographical Interpretation* (Toronto: Methuen, 1968), pp. 575 and 581.

16. For a thorough discussion of noncontiguity, see G. W. S. Robinson, "Exclaves," *Annals* of the Association of American Geographers, XLIX (September 1959), pp. 283–295.

17. For a discussion of the geographic characteristics of land-lockedness, see W. Gordon East, "The Geography of Land-locked States," *Institute of British Geographers, Transactions and Papers*, XXVIII (1960), pp. 1–22, and Edmund H. Dale, "Some Geographical Aspects of African Land-locked States," *Annals of the Association of American Geographers*, LVIII (September 1968), pp. 485–505.

Population Quality

Thus far, the quality of the population as a factor in territoriality has been discussed only in terms of its relationship with aspects of territory in such matters as density and distribution. More specific consideration of these relationships has produced concepts such as "empty" areas and areas of "overconcentration," which in turn lead to notions about "problem" areas. Policy toward these areas and their political behavior often differs from the norm for the political region and hence creates spatial differentiations, a process discussed at greater length in Part V (Environment).

Internal variations in the feeling of territoriality among a population of a political region are related to demographic and other factors, and have important ramifications for the spatial structure of that region. In other words, the political system's hierarchy may undergo change which in turn will be reflected in the territorial framework.

Institutional political scientists have long used classifications of political systems based upon the degree to which internal powers are divided hierarchically and upon the character of the government in control. The former classification includes types on a continuum from loose federation to highly centralized (unitary system), and the latter classification involves variations on a democracy—dictatorship axis. Both classifications have obviously very basic ramifications for questions of hierarchy in its territorial setting.[18]

John Herz has challenged the whole question of territoriality as it applies today at the nation-state level. Although he wrote his "Rise and Demise of the Territorial State"[19] prior to what has become known as the decade of independence from colonialism, his study remains a classic analysis of the contemporary territoriality of states. He uses a time-scale analog in which the historic growth of ordered centralism from feudal anarchy at the nation-state level is compared with what Herz sees as a similar trend now at the global level. The underlying factor of uniqueness of a modern nation-state is, in Herz's words, "its physical corporeal capacity."[20] This bounded territory gives the state a territoriality which has been recognized through the protection and security that its "hard-shell" affords. However, just as the knights in their medieval castles eventually lost their "hard-shell" impermeability when challenged by technical, economic and military revolution, the modern state is threatened by increasing permeability because, among other factors, the power of destruction now can flow from center to center which is fundamentally in contrast with past eras when power flowed from a core outwards and decayed with distance, with the political boundary acting as a line of equilibrium with other "geographically anchored" units. With the scale of security now global, the nation-state "hard shell" is obsolete. Herz indicates clearly how change can challenge the traditional political structures associated with territory and hierarchy.

CENTRALITY AND NODES

Although boundaries, as we shall see, have been the structural element commanding greatest attention in political geography, capital cities and core areas at the nation-state level have also been objects of study. The capital city is more than an urban center—it is "the place wherein the political authority of a territorial unit is concentrated."[21] In the broader sense, the concept as such is valid at all levels in the political-territorial hierarchy, from a townhall within a township to a specially designated federal district in a federation of states.

The concept of core area is less easily defined, as it lacks the concreteness and the universal applicability of the "capital" idea. It is an abstraction by no means widely accepted as a useful analytical tool, and it has been developed and tested as a working concept only at the nation-state level. "Core area" is not easily defined and in a real sense has two meanings, which often become inextricably

---

18. For a thorough discussion of various forms of areal division of powers, see Arthur Maass, "Division of Powers: An Areal Analysis," and Paul Yivisaker, "Some Criteria for a 'Proper' Areal Division of Governmental Powers," in Arthur Maass, ed., *Area and Power: A Theory of Local Government* (Glencoe: Free Press, 1959), pp. 9-49.

19. John H. Herz, "The Rise and Demise of the Territorial State," *World Politics*, IX (1957), pp. 473-493.

20. *Ibid.*, p. 474.

21. O. H. K. Spate, "Factors in the Development of Capital Cities," *Geographical Review*, XXXII (1942), p. 622.

74 Structure

mixed and confused in any discussion.[22] On the one hand, it can be seen in a contemporary context as that region within the political area where there is a concentration of population, transportation, resources and so on. As such, a core area is often referred to as the "heart" of the state. Another definition, more original but with less utility, is framed in historical terms and describes the core area as the nuclear area in or about which the state originated and from which the state-idea spread. By this latter definition, its prerequisites for success as a core are made up of some workable combination of features at the time of germination including unusual fertility to support a nonagricultural development, physical features to facilitate defense, and a nodal position in respect to the transportation and communication network.

The essence of both the capital city and the core area is their centrality within the political unit functionally if not necessarily geometrically. They form the central focus of a political region defined in terms of nodality. In many cases there is a high degree of areal coincidence between the capital and the core by either definition, although this is by no means the rule. Pounds, de Blij, and Etzioni all stress the function of core area for political integration, although only Etzioni really demonstrates this.

Capital Cities

The location of a capital is the result of political choice at some point in time. In this respect the discussion in Part IV (Behavior) on decision making as a spatial process is pertinent.

Classifications of capitals on the bases of origin, relative location, and function have been constructed.

A common distinction made on the basis of origin is that between "natural" and "artificial" capitals, the former having evolved within a core, gaining in primacy as the state grew, while the latter are cities actually created "at a blow" at a new site. As with a similar simplistic division for boundaries, this distinction is not really a valid one.[23] A classification by position in which the capital is characterized as "central" or "peripheral" (eccentric) is not particularly helpful. There is the question of whether this refers strictly to shape or also to the relationship with population distribution. Spate has suggested a refinement of the eccentric type by adopting Cornish's "forward capital" idea.[24] Such a capital is located near and oriented to the frontier of the state expanding most rapidly, and by its location, is also open to external influences.

Capitals perform a wide variety of functions. Spate coins the term "head-link" to describe the dual function of a capital that is both a leader in organizing the state and a receiving chamber for external influences, translating them into stimuli of the local culture.[25] Spate concludes that on the basis of historical inertia and historical imitation, capitals can be classified by function into those that are *keystones* of a federation or complex state, those that are *forward* as frontier organizers of victory and union, and those that are *head-links*.

The primary difference between capitals and other urban places in a political system is their added function as a seat of power which creates a government industry with a host of ancillary activities associated with power concentration. The character of the capital contrasts with other cities. As the focus of national attention there is an attempt to make it a showplace for citizens and foreigners alike. (In Part V, we suggest that this activity may be referred to as "Symbolization.") Regulations may limit such things as "dirty" industries, building styles and heights, and so on, with emphasis on maintaining a clean city to make the best possible impression. The cosmopolitan and bureaucratic nature of such a center will often lead to a concentration of amenities which in turn may encourage such industries as "retirement" and "entertainment."

In both unitary and federal states a capital often enjoys a special political status in the state's own hierarchy. The General London

22. Norman J. G. Pounds, *Political Geography* (New York: McGraw-Hill, 1963), especially Ch. 7, "Core Areas and Capitals," pp. 171-192; Harm J. de Blij, *op. cit.*, Ch. XIII, "The Heart of the State: The Core Area," pp. 371-373 and pp. 391-405; and Amitai Etzioni, *Political Unification: A Comparative Study of Leaders and Forces* (New York: Holt, Rinehart and Winston, 1965).

23. Spate argues cogently against such a distinction (*op. cit.*, pp. 622-624).
24. Vaughan Cornish, *The Great Capitals: An Historical Geography* (London, 1923).
25. Spate, *op. cit.*, p. 628.

Council superseded the old London County Council by Act of Parliament in 1963. Reform of the metropolitan government of the capital was not left to local initiative.

As with many other federations, the United States has created a federal district to house the capital. Established in 1792 from land ceded by Virginia and Maryland, the District of Columbia was cut down to its present size of sixty-two square miles when the section on the south side of the Potomac was retroceded to Virginia in 1846. The great growth of the United States and its federal government has led to a process of necessary decentralization to the point where an ever-increasing number of government agencies are now located outside the District, making somewhat anachronistic the notion that as they happen to reside within the seat of national government, the almost one million people in the District of Columbia should not be represented directly in the Congress and should not have "home rule" in electing their own city government.[26] These are some of the problems at the local level created by the uniqueness of capitals.

Over the past decade or so, renewed attention has fallen on capital cities in the ex-colonial world. The new states, inheriting systems of extreme centralization from their colonial overlords, have demonstrated the importance of the capital city to the viability of the state by its manipulation in function and location.

Hamdan has attempted a classification of such cities in Africa on the basis of origins and historical evolution with four distinguishable types: historic, native, colonial, and post-colonial.[27] Historic capitals are found only in Arab Africa, because the political capital, like the nation-state, is a recent innovation in the rest of Africa. Native capitals, such as Kano, are seen as transitional between the historic and colonial types. The colonial capitals were created by the European administrations and dominate today over other types. The post-colonial capitals reflect closely the colonial variety but in an increasing number of cases there are shifts to new locations for varied reasons—in response to changing spatial patterns of centrality and accessibility, of necessity through processes of political integration or disintegration, or simply as part of a policy to eradicate relics considered to be neocolonialist.

Core Areas

As we have mentioned above, the core area idea is somewhat confusing and has not proven to be of general applicability in the study of the structure of political regions. The selection from Whittlesey demonstrates its utility within the evolutionary approach to France, where the notion of core area is perhaps best suited.

In one specific examination of the idea, Norman Pounds and Sue Ball review the territorial growth of twenty-five European states in testing the core area thesis.[28] They conclude that in the continent of its origin, the thesis fitted the majority of states in that fully fifteen have grown through a process of accretion around a core. The others, however, were found to have grown from a now peripheral core or from cores presently outside the state's area completely, while still others were created "at a blow." Pounds and Ball's conclusion that core growth states enjoy a greater degree of coherence and viability than the rest is somewhat doubtful. The complications of boundary changes and ethnic group migration cannot be properly included in the thesis, and this is an important drawback in such a partitioned and repartitioned continent as Europe.

The root of this trouble with the core area concept lies in the fact that the delimitation of core areas has been based largely on intuition which in turn has created problems for their scientific study. Furthermore, attempts at multidimensional definition of a core area produce the problem of a complex set of overlapping districts. One rather successful measure of core area is obtained from a study of group values held toward the national space as Herman demonstrates in a study which looks at this problem in reference to China.[29]

There is little doubt that the genetic idea of a core area is helpful in understanding the

---

26. Residents of the District of Columbia were allowed to vote for the first time in the presidential election of 1964.
27. G. Hamdan, "Capitals of the New Africa," *Economic Geography*, XL (1964), p. 239.
28. Norman J. G. Pounds and Sue Simmons Ball, "Core Areas and the Development of the European States System," *Annals* of the Association of American Geographers, LIV (1964), pp. 24–40.
29. Theodore Herman, "Group Values Toward National Space: The Case of China," *Geographical Review*, XLIX (April 1959), pp. 164–182.

origin and the processes of early territorial growth of many states, either from a nucleus endowed with centrality or, as in the case of many colonial and new world states, from an area with access from the outside and with increasing primacy in its nodality internally. As a device, however, to give insights into the contemporary structure of the political geography of political regions, it is limited in its utility to the extent that not all states possess an identifiable core, many have or have had two or more cores in their evolution, and even for others with definable cores, the core area seems largely irrelevant to the functioning of the state.

Nodes

The impact of twentieth century urbanization on political-territorial organization has given rise to several problems of spatial structure and functions. The rapid growth of cities and their nodal dominance in the evolving transportation network have eroded the traditional rural functions performed at the county level in many areas. For example, because of its anachronistic nature, the old county system in Connecticut has been abolished.

Largely due to their nodal regional qualities and to their growing population size, urban areas have emerged as critical new political territory in American federalism.[30] A consequence of this urban growth has been the disequilibria created in the spatial structure within the metropolis. This phenomenon has given rise to much discussion in the social sciences and it is a fascinating problem of growing complexity in territorial organization.[31] In Part V (Environment) we suggest problems (such as air pollution in urban areas) raised by structural aspects in the public management of natural resources.

One further aspect can be included in this discussion of the structural aspects of nodes. Recently there has been a dramatic increase in the attention given to revolutionary or guerrilla warfare.[32] The spatial aspects of the various theories propounded are of interest and growing significance to political geography.

The writings of Lenin, Mao Tsetung, Lin Piao, Vo Nguyen Giap, Régis Debray, and Ernesto (Ché) Guevara and the policies propounded to counter the actions resulting from the practical application of their ideas are all related, in part, to a structural base in space. Hence such terms as strategic hamlet policy, enclave theory, revolutionary base areas, pacification and relocation, secured areas, and so forth all directly involve spatial problems.

Robert McColl has made a start in this direction by examining the spatial aspects of revolutionary rural base areas in China during the civil war and their role leading to the Communist take-over in 1949.[33] McColl, quoting from Mao Tsetung, lists a set of "guiding principles" for the effective location and application of guerrilla base operations. Base areas should have experienced previous revolutionary activity, be politically unstable, have access to major political targets, be located in zones of weak or confused political control, be in terrain favorable for military operations, be economically self-sufficient, and be abandoned only under the most critical circumstances. From these principles, McColl suggests a "Communist model" of rural base areas which he applies to the ongoing situation in South Vietnam and also to the potential case of Thailand ("Thailand—Next?"), where there is growing revolutionary activity. By this application, McColl is able to conclude that revolutionary activity is not randomly distributed and that base area locations are *determined* primarily by political considerations and also can be generally predicted.[34]

Although any attempt to study the political geography of revolution is to be encouraged, McColl's analysis rests on the conspiratorial theory of Communist activity in Southeast Asia and thus tends to ignore such elements in influencing the location of antigovernment activities as chance events, reaction to oppres-

---

30. For a discussion of the growing political role of cities in the American polity, see Roscoe Martin, *The Cities and the Federal System* (New York: Atherton Press, 1965).

31. Wood's analysis of the political structure in the New York urban region exemplifies this problem, Robert Wood, *1400 Governments: The Political Economy of the New York Metropolitan Region* (Cambridge, Mass.: Harvard University Press, 1961).

32. For a discussion of evolutionary changes in the theory of guerrilla warfare, see Chalmers Johnson, "The Third Generation of Guerrilla Warfare," *Asian Survey*, VIII (June 1968), pp. 435–447.

33. Robert W. McColl, "A Political Geography of Revolution: China, Vietnam, and Thailand," *Journal of Conflict Resolution*, XXI (June 1967), pp. 153–167.

34. *Ibid.*, p. 166. Emphasis added.

sion and atrocities by central governments, and spontaneous uprisings independent of organized revolutionary "plans."[35] For more sophisticated models of revolutionary activity we must go beyond shop-soiled theories and the memoirs of ageing revolutionary leaders who have a vested interest in demonstrating that the success of their causes was due not to events largely beyond their control, but on careful planning based on their own Communist theories.

The French academic Régis Debray, who as a journalist joined Ché Guevara in Bolivia and was later imprisoned by the Bolivian authorities, has written a book on revolution in Latin America in which he shows a keen appreciation of the environmental as well as ideological factors affecting revolutionary activity through guerrilla warfare in the varied regional settings of Latin America.[36] He discusses aspects of worker and peasant "self-defense systems" in establishing "nuclei of subversion" and, in reference to the urban revolution, he emphasizes the pragmatic approach over the ideological when he states that "one may well consider it a stroke of good luck that Fidel had not read the military writings of Mao Tsetung before disembarking on the coast of Oriente: he could thus invent, on the spot and out of his own experience, principles of a military doctrine *in conformity with the terrain.*"[37]

Debray suggests three time stages for guerrilla warfare: establishment, development, and revolutionary offensive. Each phase is characterized by distinctive spatial patterns and influenced by specific environmental conditions. Two failures at revolution are analyzed in terms of these time stages. In the case of the peasant revolt of Marquetalia in southern Colombia in 1964, the end of the first stage did not result in the necessary political integration of revolutionary-held territory, and hence the guerrilla bands had to return to the nomadic phase of establishment extending the period of rural disruption and increasing the ability of the Colombian army to destroy them. In the case of the tin miners' revolt in Bolivia in 1965, a crucial factor in its failure turned out to be the spatial concentration of the Altiplano tin mines in a sixty square mile area, enabling the Bolivian government to crush and to isolate the rebellion with air and ground forces. Debray identifies other environmental factors: the ease with which food supplies could be cut to the food-deficit and isolated mining region; the concentration of the miners' homes in nucleated settlements, and the underground location of most of the mining operations allowing bombardments to threaten the population at minimum cost to production facilities; and the dispersion of the mining settlements, each several miles apart, allowing for ease in army encirclement and difficulty in coordinating resistance.

It would seem that models of revolution based more on spatial and environmental considerations as those suggested by Debray show more promise of relevant application in political geography than do those based on ideological dogma.

BOUNDARIES

Boundaries as spatial expressions of man's political organization and territorial partitioning have always been recognized to be of prime importance as structural features in political geography. It is therefore understandable that perhaps too much emphasis has been given to boundaries as a focus of political geographic study at the expense of other lines of approach and inquiry.

Both boundaries and frontiers are by definition peripheral features of politically organized space, and all too often in the literature their relevance to the problems of the political system they delimit has not been clearly made. This in turn has led to a series of single and unrelated studies with a preoccupation for *form* rather than *function* which has earned boundary studies a reputation, not entirely undeserved, of being themselves peripheral.

As an easily distinguishable landscape feature, however, a boundary does provide a useful focus for studying the function of the limits of political space as a "window" on a system, as a divider of political units (an

---

35. In his conclusion, McColl himself acknowledges the significance of the home districts of leaders and traditional centers of rebellion as location factors (*Ibid.*, p. 167).

36. Régis Debray, *Revolution in the Revolution? Armed Struggle and Political Struggle in Latin America*, Bobby-e Ortiz, trans. (New York: Grove Press, 1967). This is an English translation from the original versions in French and Spanish.

37. *Ibid.*, p. 20. Emphasis added.

"interface" between systems) and also as a role player in shaping the border landscape on either or both its sides. Consequently studies with such a focus have over the years contributed more theory to political geography than any other branch of the subject.

Political boundaries possess several other advantages as avenues of study. They reflect directly in a spatial sense the political hierarchy within a region. The complex pattern of boundaries, from those delimiting areas at the lowest level of the hierarchy all the way through to the international level, lends itself to a wide range of analytical techniques. It follows that international boundaries are also boundaries between regions at lower levels in the hierarchy and hence must be considered as such when analyzed. The implications of such coincidences of lines representing different hierarchical levels are too often overlooked. Many problems that occur along international boundaries such as pollution of waterways and conflicting land uses usually have their root not in any contrasts at the nation-state level, but in the contrasts between adjoining local political units at the municipal or county level.

As common generic features, boundaries can provide bases for generalizations in applying what is learned in one case to other cases at the same hierarchical level, and also, to some degree, to cases at different levels.

Furthermore, interest in boundaries is by no means restricted to political geographers. As common features in the delineation of all types of regions, boundaries have provided a focus of study for many types of geographers. For example, economic geographers are interested in the boundary properties of retail areas between competing centers and biogeographers in forest-grassland contact.[38] This general interest in boundaries as regional divides has provided concepts often applicable to political geography, as we shall see below.

The utility of boundaries in studying problems of political integration and disintegration and of transfer of sovereignty will be discussed in the following Part (Process).

38. Examples of this interest in boundaries in other fields are provided by: Ravi Kapil, "On the Conflict Potential of Inherited Boundaries in Africa," *World Politics*, XVIII (July 1966), pp. 656–673; and Bruce Russett, "Delimiting International Regions," in J. David Singer, ed., *Quantitative International Politics* (New York: Free Press, 1967), pp. 317–374.

Some Misleading Notions

The "natural-is-good" and "artificial-is-bad" concepts are based on the assumption that the degree to which a political boundary conforms to a natural feature is the measure of its success as a political divide. In other words, boundaries "established in an unrealistic manner tend to create problems commensurate to the degree with which they *defy* the *forces of nature*."[39] Although many political boundaries are based on physical landscape features, they are all by definition political and therefore, whether naturally based or not, are man-made, hence artificial. It follows that a boundary's "goodness" or degree of success is more a function of its role as perceived by members of the political systems it divides rather than of the environmental character of the line itself.

Another widely held notion, somewhat associated with the above idea, still enjoys currency and even official authenticity. This holds that boundaries are the "enemies" of geography because they "conflict" with the operation of "geographical principles," and hence social patterns are "compartmentalized" by these "unnatural" restrictions.[40] The notion that "it is unfortunate when society must accommodate itself to boundaries rather than boundaries to society" is a logical corollary to this line of thought.[41]

These ideas tend to put exclusive emphasis on the negative or barrier effect of boundaries without giving an indication of their many attractive functions toward movement and activities. More seriously, they ignore the fact that boundaries, as we have mentioned above, are *themselves* an integral part and a creation of society, and that social groups are often inextricably mixed in space anyway.

Form

Boundaries are found in a variety of landscape settings and their form in reality hardly ever resembles the red or stippled line which is traditionally used to show their location on a map. Normally, boundaries have no thickness and are often virtually invisible. Hence

39. G. Etzel Pearcy, "Boundary Types," *Journal of Geography*, LXIV (October 1965), p. 303. Italics added.
40. *Ibid.*, p. 300. Italics added.
41. *Ibid.*, p. 302.

the map, especially a small-scale or wall map will show the line (according to the map scale) to be several miles thick. This is of course a necessary but unfortunate feature of maps.

Linear boundaries separating political systems are of fairly recent origin. Many of the lines seen today are in the middle of what were once frontier zones, and have evolved to lines only as the desire and technical feasibility to extend the processes of a political system became irresistible on both sides.

Any classification based on form must take into account a most obvious formal difference already mentioned above—boundaries that are based on a physical feature predating political partitioning and those that are otherwise based.

1. Physically based boundaries have the great advantage of precise alignment. If the maps used at the time of allocation and delimitation were accurate, then the actual demarcation by the boundary commission will be a fairly simple matter in that the location of the line will coincide with a physical feature, usually of some importance (but not always) to the local population, and easily recognizable. This type of boundary falls into several subtypes:

a. *Relief.* Examples of this subtype include various aspects of mountain ranges such as crest-lines, watersheds, or some critical slope features.

b. *Hydrography.* Such phenomena as rivers, lakes, swamps, and coastland features are often used for boundaries. While these are obvious features in the landscape, many problems can develop from their adoption. For example, with rivers and lakes there can be problems of navigation, water use for a variety of (often conflicting) purposes, flood control, etc.

c. *Pseudo-Physical Features.* This subtype includes such boundaries as those based on physical differences, although largely culturally created, of real significance at the time of political partitioning. A boundary of this form is usually difficult to type as physical or nonphysical at present because of the different stages of evolution the border landscape has passed through since the boundary's inception.

2. Culturally based boundaries relate to the distribution of certain cultural features at some point or period in time thought to be of major political importance. If a current boundary is based directly upon a cultural feature such as language, religion, nationality, race, or tribe, we can call it an *ethnic boundary.* If, however, it is based on an old division of political systems since defunct, whose boundaries in turn might have been either culturally or physically based in the first place, the term used is *historical boundary.* It is not unusual for ethnic lines to change their location or even to disappear over time. In that cultural patterns and man's evaluation of them constantly change, pressures along an ethnic boundary are usually present in some form or other.

3. Mathematical boundaries are most easily delimited, but they are often very difficult to demarcate because of survey problems. Also, in many cases the original allocation and delimitation were based upon inaccurate maps and imperfect knowledge of the region, and hence upon erroneous assumptions.

In that sometimes the form of any one boundary can be classified equally well under two or more of the above types (i.e., a river can be a cultural divide), it is necessary to have an open-ended type known as *complex.* Furthermore, any given boundary between two states, especially if it be a long one, will usually vary in its form from place to place, and hence become a mix of several of the above forms. This is known as a "compound" boundary. In 1936, Hartshorne suggested a new classification based on association with cultural features existing in the region at the time the boundary is established.[42] The types in this classification—*antecedent, relic, subsequent,* and *superimposed*—are self-explanatory and have since come into common usage in boundary literature.

Function

As mentioned previously, the function of a boundary is more a product of the nature of

---

42. Richard Hartshorne, "Suggestions on the Terminology of Political Boundaries," *Mitteilungen des Vereins der Geographen an der Universität Leipzig,* XIV–XV (1936), pp. 180–192. As this work appeared in such an obscure and now virtually unobtainable German journal, the reader is referred to a brief presentation of the classification which appeared as an abstract in the *Annals of the Association of American Geographers,* XXVI (March 1936), pp. 56–57.

the states it separates and of the relationship between these states, than of its form. Hence, although boundaries function in general as barriers to movement (the circulation of people, goods, and ideas), there is no standard set of functions that fit a given form, despite the fact that, with certain kinds of form one can usually expect similar problems to arise (e.g., river boundaries may be associated with conflicts over use of the common water resource).

Boundaries also act as separators of territorial sovereignty (regional limits). In this role they can function, in a limited sense, as attractors. Crossing points become location factors on either side for border towns whose support comes directly and indirectly from administering and servicing the movement across the boundary. In this context, the concept (mentioned above) of a border landscape or borderland can be elaborated into a notion of a limited mirror-image effect, i.e., a great similarity between the opposite borderlands in the spatial arrangement and function of certain phenomena, reflecting the impact of the same regional focus, the boundary. Furthermore, the conscious creation of official border zones by a state on the one side,[43] or by agreement or coincidence of adjoining states on either side, will tend to emphasize this marked effect on the landscape.

National boundaries also function as filters or screens; they are seldom completely impenetrable barriers, nor are they normally passed with so much ease as to be no barrier at all, but rather have a filtering (quality) or screening (quantity) effect on movement. Problems arise in the measurement of this impact. Various attempts at measurement are reviewed by Minghi in Reading 13. One can equate the barrier function for any given movement to the friction of distance in terms of time, cost, or some other index.[44] The measuring in this manner of any two movements across the same boundary will serve to indicate the individuality in the boundary's function according to the particular movement measured. It might, for instance, seem to be a very minor filter for a certain commodity, while at the same time it could act as a major barrier to permanent immigration. Some kinds of movements, such as air waves carrying television signals, can in no way be effectively controlled at the boundary, so any measure of the function of the boundary in respect to this flow (aside from the location and size of the transmitter) must be made at the points of reception of the information.

This variety of barrier effects of any given boundary explains the difficulty in devising a classification in terms of function of any generic value.

More recently, however, John Nystuen has suggested a new classification for boundaries in terms of their impact on activities.[45] While not specifically formulated for political boundaries, this classification adds to our understanding of these phenomena. *Absorbing* boundaries tend to absorb energy touching them and hence are characterized by a reduction in the density of activities they "contain" within the domain. *Reflecting* boundaries contain activities by turning them back into the domain. The direction of movement is changed but the energy is not diminished. *Permeable* boundaries contrast with the impermeability of the first two types in that part of the energy reaching them passes through in some filtered and/or screened manner. The remainder is either absorbed or reflected.

By this classification, Nystuen is able to define three types of processes involved with boundary interaction: crossing, contained, and boundary-dwelling. He is able to discuss theoretically a boundary's "transfer potential" and "unit permeability."

Although there are obvious limitations in the applicability of this classification to political boundaries, some implications suggest themselves. Almost all political boundaries are a mixture of the permeable variety and one or other of the absorbing and reflecting types in their impact on a given activity. It is very difficult, however, to characterize a particular boundary as one type or another according to its impact on

---

43. For an example, see John P. Augelli, "The Nationalization of Frontiers: The Dominican Borderlands under Trujillo," read before the Annual Meeting of the Association of American Geographers at Toronto, August, 1966, Abstract in *Annals* of the Association of American Geographers, LVII (March 1967), p. 166.

44. J. Ross Mackay, "The Interactance Hypothesis and Boundaries in Canada," *Canadian Geographer*, No. 11 (1958), pp. 1-8.

45. John D. Nystuen, "Boundary Shapes and Boundary Problems," read before the Fourth North American Peace Research Conference, Chicago, November, 1966.

the sum of activities with which it is associated. The notion of boundary-dwelling activities is particularly attractive in the consideration of a borderland region.

Changes in Function

Any political system is constantly changing, setting into motion processes which often will express themselves in changing external relations, and hence will show at the boundary as a change in function. The elimination of a tariff on a good or the tightening up of immigration laws will have such an impact. Technical changes, such as the great increase in air travel, have transferred many processes, normally thought of as boundary functions, to more centrally located, larger cities away from the line itself.

The independence revolution of the last decade (the transfer of sovereignty from colonial to indigenous control) has led to the complete substitution of one system for another. This in turn has given rise to a new set of processes, in many cases radically changing the preexisting boundary functions.[46] Among any group of neighboring new states such variables as the chronology of transfer, the "colonial mix" of the group, and the evolution in the political systems after independence must all be considered in combination. For instance, the changes in boundary functions between two neighbors of different colonial backgrounds (say one French, the other British) after gaining independence simultaneously will differ from boundary-function changes evolving between two countries of the same colonial background or between nations which gained independence at substantially different times. The same ideas apply to changes at the local level—city incorporation, resistance to incorporation, and the chronology of metropolitan growth.

Boundary Perception and Behavior

Brief mention should be made of the influence of the way boundaries are perceived and the impact of the consequent behavior on spatial patterns. Robert Ardrey (see his selection "The Noyau" in Part IV) has detailed many cases of animal behavior at the boundaries to their domains.[47] Although care must be taken in transferring the notions of animal boundary behavior to the human political level, some interesting observations can be made from random cases.

Some animals will defend borders but not cross them. Border engagements, while stimulating, often lack real danger and are more of a mutually acceptable ritual.[48] Other animals pay great attention to boundary demarcation in order to reduce the likelihood of lethal conflicts over property rights.[49] Violation of boundaries, often with severe penalties, is common among the young, but on reaching maturity avoidance becomes the rule.[50]

Boundaries are also perceived as social contact zones. The three basic needs of security, stimulation, and identity are satisfied by this different feeling of territoriality in the peripheral zone where breeding takes place.[51]

There is a relationship between density and the desire for boundary delimitation. Under severe territorial pressure-cooker conditions boundaries are sharply defined and mutually accepted, while in areas of light density where properties are larger the boundaries are often poorly defined.[52]

These observations from the animal world suggest analogies with man's perception and behavior in relation to political boundaries. Some work has been done on spatial behavior and boundaries by Reynolds and McNulty.[53] They found, for instance, that the spacing of crossing points along a boundary has important consequences upon the subjective environments of boundary-zone residents

---

46. Vincent K. Shaudys, "Geographic Consequences of Establishing Sovereign Political Units," *Professional Geographer*, XIV (March 1962), p. 18.

47. Robert Ardrey, *The Territorial Imperative: A Personal Inquiry into the Animal Origins of Property and Nations* (New York: Atheneum, 1966).
48. "The lemur of Madagascar," *Ibid.*, pp. 196–198.
49. "The arctic wolf using a squirt of urine," *Ibid.*, pp. 9–10.
50. "The Eskimo dog of Eastern Greenland," *Ibid.*, p. 25.
51. "The darling," *Ibid.*, p. 170.
52. "The callicebus," *Ibid.*, p. 180.
53. David R. Reynolds and Michael McNulty, "On the Analysis of Political Boundaries as Barriers: A Perceptual Approach," *The East Lakes Geographer*, IV (December 1968), pp. 21–38.

which are manifested in spatial behavior patterns. People living most distant from crossing points regard the boundary as impassable while those near these points think it only troublesome. These attitudes in turn give rise to behavior patterns that contrast the relative mobility of the latter group in their boundary crossing activities with the immobility of the former out of all proportion to the *actual* accessibility factor of time- or cost-distance.

Another interesting notion advanced by Reynolds and McNulty concerns the impact of boundary restrictions on linked patterns of behavior that involve transboundary interaction. Restrictions on labor, for example, give the boundary a barrier effect on journey-to-work patterns, but *also* have an impact on other activities commonly associated with these patterns, such as the purchase of gasoline and convenience goods. Hence consumer or other types of behavior patterns must become *unlinked* if transboundary interaction is to take place.

In a study for the U.S. Bureau of the Census undertaken at The University of Chicago, Berry discovered an interesting example of boundary behavior in his examination of the journey-to-work evidence collected in the 1960 Census.[54] When commuting fields in SMSA's were mapped, a "bunching" of contours along city limits seemed to indicate a sharp discontinuity (as much as forty percentage points) in the proportion of residents of adjacent census tracts on either side of the city limits actually working in the city. The explanation for these discontinuities lies in systematic errors in the data due to some enumerators working in counties containing central cities of SMSAs, but outside the cities themselves, who failed to identify correctly these central cities as places of work.

The problem was possibly compounded by another source of error because of a systematic bias of the enumerator in completing the question regarding place of work, "inside the city limits." A consistent bias one way or the other, when the respondent did not really know, would also show a "boundary effect."

Berry's discovery suggests both a warning and an opportunity for political geographers. Data regarding human behavior collected in the field through enumerators (who may be biased and insensitive) from respondents (who may be ignorant of the realities of political space) should be questioned very carefully before any conclusions are drawn. The discovery, however, does indicate, when considered with the findings of Reynolds and McNulty and the notions discussed in Part IV (Behavior), that political geographers have much work to do. Even if we do not fully understand the motivation for such attitudes and behavior, we should pay more attention to the basis and impact of spatial behavior.

Frontiers

For several reasons very little space need be given here to the discussion of frontiers. The selection from Ladis Kristof serves as a review of the nature of frontiers by comparing frontiers with boundaries. Furthermore, the illustrative selection on frontiers from Turner is an established classic and speaks for itself.

In a recent book, J. R. V. Prescott deals with the question of political frontiers in a most comprehensive manner. He reviews the major literature on frontiers showing the influence of a frontier on the subsequent development of the cultural landscape.[55]

In that frontier zones have progressively given way to linear boundaries as man has desired ever-increasing rigidity in politically partitioning space, the land frontier has virtually become an historical phenomenon.

Apart from the Antarctic,[56] politically undifferentiated earth space has disappeared. The vast area of the high seas beyond the various zones of control associated with coastal states remains truly the last frontier of this planet, and it is progressively taking on the character, despite its three-dimensionality, normally associated with land frontiers. More intensive uses of its known resources and ever-increasing interest in further exploration have been made possible by technological develop-

54. Brian J. L. Berry, *Metropolitan Area Definition: A Re-Evaluation of Concept and Statistical Practice*, Bureau of the Census, Working Paper No. 28 (Washington: U.S. Department of Commerce, 1968), pp. 12–16.

55. J. R. V. Prescott, *The Geography of Frontiers and Boundaries* (Chicago: Aldine, 1965), pp. 40–49.

56. The Antarctic Treaty, effective in June, 1961, is an agreement among fifteen interested nations to renounce territorial claims and any military activity in the Antarctic continent. It has been held as a model for the moon in order to avoid conflict over lunar territorial sovereignty.

ments in fishing, mining, environmental control and so forth. The political implications of this growing frontier are beginning to be felt as, for example, in the case of the partitioning of the North Pacific to limit Japanese salmon fishing (which is discussed in a selection in Part V, Environment), and in the partitioning of the North Sea between Northwest European states for exploration and extraction of natural gas and petroleum.

Recently Lewis Alexander's review of the literature on geography and the law of the sea has drawn attention to this rather ignored frontier.[57]

GLOBAL STRUCTURE

As we have seen in the "Heritage" of political geography, there has been a consistent preoccupation with the world as a political system. An outcome of these preoccupations has been a series of "global views," each an attempt to describe the world political structure with an equilibrium model on some principal causal basis. With Aristotle and several others the pattern of global political structure was explained by the areal differentiation in environmental conditions. Over the last century there have been several spatial models of world power suggested based on a mix of such factors as historical continuity, shifting balances of power in world regions, changing ideological structures, and technological innovations in communications and weaponry.[58] Such models are ethnocentric in focus and open to rapid obsolescence, especially in terms of the prescriptions they implicitly contain.

The first really global view is commonly attributed to Alfred T. Mahan, a United States naval officer who emphasized the land-based importance of sea power by listing as the six fundamental factors affecting the development of the sea power of a state: geographical position, physical conformation, territorial extent, population size, national character, and governmental character.[59] Mahan's influence was felt in American expansionist policies in the Pacific and Caribbean.

Mahan also recognized the potentialities of the vast Asian land mass as a power core and Russia's role within it. In a sense, he anticipated Mackinder in his analysis.[60]

Mackinder read his paper (reproduced in the selections) to The Royal Geographical Society in London in 1904. As with Turner and the American Frontier a decade earlier, Mackinder sensed that an era was over. With the new century the "post-Columbian" era had begun. The long period of discovery and territorial expansion had ended and he felt that it was time to make a correlation between larger geographical and historical generalizations, with an aim of seeing human history as part of the life of the "world organism," i.e., on a global scale.

As Eurasia (the "World Island") was seen to dominate world history and geography, it became the focus of Mackinder's study. The lesson from history was that Asia had consistently dominated Europe and that, despite Europe's great era of sea power since the sixteenth century, the vast area of Central Asia, safe from maritime power and with good conditions for internal mobility, was the potential source of world power. This region Mackinder termed "the Pivot Area" and in 1904, as today, it fell largely within the Russian state. Later, in 1919, an enlarged pivot area was renamed the "Heartland."[61] Around this pivot area were arranged two regions, an "inner crescent" of partly continental, partly maritime lands, and an "outer crescent" of oceanic powers.

While Mackinder thought the peripheral states too strong for Russia, he did hypothesize that an alliance between the pivotal state (Russia) and one or more inner crescent states (such as Germany) would make an unbeatable combination of land and sea power and could mean that the "empire of the world" would be in sight. As we have seen in the "Heritage" part of this volume, it was this possibility that inspired the German geopoliticians.

By 1919 Mackinder viewed Eastern Europe as the key and he was able to make his famous dictum:

---

57. Lewis M. Alexander, "Geography and the Law of the Sea," *Annals of the Association of American Geographers*, LVIII (March 1968), pp. 177–197.

58. For a review of the major global views see, Stephen B. Jones, "Global Strategic Views," *Geographical Review*, XLV (October 1955), pp. 492–508.

59. A. T. Mahan, *The Influence of Sea Power Upon History 1660–1783* (Boston, 1890), Chapter 1.

60. A. T. Mahan, *The Problem of Asia* (Boston, 1900), pp. 24 ff.

61. Halford J. Mackinder, *Democratic Ideals and Reality* (New York, 1919 and 1942).

Who rules in Eastern Europe commands the Heartland,
Who rules the Heartland commands the World-Island,
Who rules the World-Island commands the World.

The reproduction of Mackinder's 1919 book verbatim in 1942 inspired a response by Nicholas Spykman which was published posthumously in 1944.[62] In an extract reproduced in the selection which we have entitled "Heartland and Rimland," Spykman challenged Mackinder's thesis. He felt that too much emphasis had been put on the Heartland. Its great problem of internal transportation and access through the barriers that surrounded it tended to lessen its importance. Spykman called attention to the critical inner crescent which he called the "rimland." Intermediate between the heartland and the marginal seas, the rimland forms a vast buffer zone of conflict between sea and land power, and hence has to function amphibiously, a fact which accounts for its security problems. Historical alignments have always been made in terms of the rimland. This led Spykman to enunciate his own thesis:

Who controls the Rimland rules Eurasia;
Who rules Eurasia controls the destinies of the World.

During the Second World War Spykman felt that the Allies should base their future policy on preventing any consolidation of the Rimland. In the cold war era that was to follow, this prescription became part of the American "containment" policy aimed at preventing the Soviet Union, and later China, from spreading their influence into new areas *anywhere* within the Rimland.

The technological innovation afforded by airpower in many minds revolutionized global power structure. Alexander P. de Seversky felt that complete global superiority in air power was possible.[63] Because of the intercontinental mobility of air power and the juxtaposition of the United States and Russia as cold war antagonists, this notion of absolute supremacy tended to encourage an "air isolationism" oriented to the Western Hemisphere.[64] The polar map projection employed by de Seversky showed that both the United States and Russia each held complete air dominance over vast areas within their orbit and that the critical area is that of overlap between them over the pole, de Seversky's so-called area of decision. This over-simplistic view of global power has not survived the test of time. In an era of intercontinental missiles, nuclear submarines and earth satellites, such events as the Vietnam War have made it abundantly clear that global strategic patterns do not depend upon potential military dominance in one sector.

Cohen represents a more recent all-inclusive academic global view,[65] basing it on the premise that power regions cannot be easily defined, are divisible, and are not necessarily dominant strategically over themselves. He questions the validity of Mackinder and Spykman[66] in the world of the 1960's in that we dare not rely on the concepts of the past. Basically, Cohen feels geostrategic dominance can be maintained in a region without total military and political control.

In an extract included in the selections, Cohen suggests that we think in terms of two major geostrategic regions, the Trade-Dependent Maritime World and the Eurasian Continental World, with the possibility of a third (second rank) region developing among the newly independent nations of the Indian Ocean Plateau Realm. Each of these is subdivided into geopolitical subregions. Two modern-day shatter belts remain, the Middle East and Southeast Asia. Certainly, in the years since Cohen wrote, these two belts of internal instability and weakness and external pressures have deserved their classification.

Bruce Russett suggests a global structure that groups countries into clusters by reason of their nearness to one another.[67] Straight line mileage between capitals of any two countries was used as a measure of distance. Thus a square, symmetrical matrix was constructed. The data are reduced by factor analysis in such a way that four factors are able to depict the configuration of political units. The four clusters so produced are

---

62. Nicholas J. Spykman, *The Geography of the Peace* (New York: Harcourt, Brace and Co., 1944).
63. A. P. de Seversky, *Air Power: Key to Survival* (New York: Simon and Schuster, 1950).
64. Jones, *op. cit.*, p. 503.
65. Saul B. Cohen, *Geography and Politics in a World Divided* (New York: Random House, 1963).
66. As have many others including Hall, Jackson, Meinig. These critiques are listed in the bibliography.
67. Bruce M. Russett, *International Regions and the International System: A Study in Political Ecology* (Chicago: Rand McNally, 1967), especially Chapters 10, 11, and 14.

Europe, the Western Hemisphere, Asia, and Africa.

As well as that for proximity, factor analyses are made for cultural homogeneity, similar political behavior, institutional ties, and trade transactions. Each is compared with the others to test the validity of such regional groupings as Communist Eastern Europe and Latin America. Furthermore, in his global divisions based upon behavior in the United Nations (see Reading 34 in Part IV), Russett divides the world into Western Community, Communist, Afro-Asian, Brazzaville Group, and Latin America.[68] While his findings are rather inconclusive, Russett does demonstrate the utility of factor analysis in the dynamic study of global structures.

One further aspect of global structure should be mentioned. Implicit and published views of statesmen regarding global structure are significant in that they provide the perceived environment in which these decision makers operate, and in that they form provocative hypotheses for pedagogic and research examination.

The present conflict in Southeast Asia has generated the so-called domino theory, essentially a spatial equilibrium model. Reminiscent of the speculative hypotheses of Mackinder and the "balance of power" view of Europe, this model, despite problematic assumptions, seemingly forms an important strain in American thinking. Yet geographers have said very little about this theory. In his selection (Reading 16) Cohen discusses the functions of the "shatterbelt" of Southeast Asia and concludes that complete control of the area by a single world power is neither possible nor desirable. Elsewhere in the book from which this reading is taken, Cohen does give critical attention to the "falling domino" game.[69] He feels that the Maritime World should select its allies in the Rimland with more discrimination on a basis of ideological as well as territorial significance, and that the internal structure of the states in Southeast Asia is more important than their relative location in terms of their resistance to Communist-inspired revolution.

More recently, Rhoads Murphey has published a very critical analysis of the domino theory.[70] He examines the theory's two underlying assumptions—that China is insatiably expansionist and that each state in Southeast Asia lacks only the impulse provided by a fallen neighbor to fall itself—and finds both with little or no foundation in fact. This leads Murphey to conclude that the domino theory is based on an inappropriate analogy and runs counter to rational inquiry.

Logically, an American theory that sees states lined up as a string of dominoes, spatially ordered and interdependent, seemingly makes the United States a policeman for every territory extending beyond her borders. Such automatic linkages among a group of units of course do not exist.[71] Adjacency does present opportunities for infiltration of men and arms and for ease in spreading propaganda, but the all-important variable of the internal structure of political units serves to undermine the domino theory, which is simply a narrowly deterministic notion based only on relative location and adjacency.

Perhaps still more interesting is the strategy of world revolution enunciated in 1965 by China's Defense Minister, Lin Piao.[72] Extrapolating on the traditional model of guerrilla warfare based on the successful Chinese experience in which rural areas are pitted against urban centers and nodes, Lin Piao sees a spatial pattern of world revolution in which underdeveloped areas (the "rural" areas of the world) will increasingly be converted to Communism and pitted against the western industrialized states (the "urban" areas). Recalling Harrison Brown's dire warnings in his *The Challenge of Man's Future*,[73] this hypothesis is both an interesting geographical outlook on world political conflict and a vivid reminder of the importance of spatial perception to policy-formulation.

---

68. Another interesting global grouping is suggested by Phillip M. Gregg and Arthur S. Banks, "Grouping Political Systems: Q-Factor Analysis of a *Cross-Polity Survey*," *American Political Science Review*, LIX (1965), pp. 602–614.

69. Saul B. Cohen, *op. cit.*, p. 59.

70. Rhoads Murphey, "China and the Dominoes," *Asian Survey*, VI (September 1966), pp. 510–515.

71. The successful establishment of a revolutionary régime by Fidel Castro in Cuba in 1960 gave rise to a Latin American "falling domino" theory. Thus far, the other "dominoes" of the Hemisphere have shown an amazing ability to stay upright.

72. Lin Piao, *Long Live the Victory of People's War!* (Peking: Foreign Language Press, 1965), pp. 22–31.

73. Harrison Brown, *The Challenge of Man's Future: An Inquiry Concerning the Condition of Man During the Years that Lie Ahead* (New York: Viking Press, 1954).

86 Structure

Nevertheless, the collapse of Ché Guevara's guerrilla movement in Bolivia in 1967 does indicate the flaws in hypotheses which underestimate the technological resources and independence of the developing nations.

Future Research Needs

A general need is for a greater degree of emphasis on the functional attributes of structure. Too many assumptions are made without verification concerning such problems as land-lockedness, smallness, emptiness, and other aspects of territoriality. We need to know much more about how the relationships between territoriality and the various levels of hierarchy are perceived. A more behavioral and perceptual approach to the study of capital cities and boundaries is also indicated. This would involve a greater emphasis upon comparative study of structural elements as a means of increasing our capability for generalizing and model building.

The traditional area of global structure model building will develop further by greater use of comparative political and social data and such methods as factor analysis and perhaps also by examination of statesmen's cognitive spatial models such as those of Nasser and Lin Piao. Basically, three approaches are involved: (a) largely intuitive statements of functional and strategical roles and relationships of various zones and regions (for example, Mackinder, Spykman, and Cohen); (b) views based on ideological and policy orientation of elites (for example, Lin Piao, Nasser, De Gaulle, and the notions behind Manifest Destiny, containment, and the domino theory); and (c) structural and behavioral analyses of cross-cultural data by techniques such as cluster and factor analysis (for example, Russett, and Gregg and Banks).

INTRODUCTIONS TO THE SELECTIONS

The two selections in the section on "territory and hierarchy" are fairly diverse in approach and content but serve to illustrate the wide-ranging interest in analysis and explanation of the association between man's political ranking and territory.

In the short extract on "Rank and Territory" from *The Human Use of the Earth*, Philip Wagner investigates the connection between social and spatial arrangements. Following a brief review of this connection in the animal world, Wagner introduces man into the picture with his political ranking, and examines the political partitioning of earth space as the geographical expression of human territoriality and hierarchy. On this basis, he defines a three-part classification of politically organized territories at the highest rank: the national state, alien dependencies, and politically ambiguous territories. It is significant that in an introductory text in cultural geography, Wagner should give prominence to this relationship between social and spatial aspects of rank.

In his "Symmetry and Asymmetry as Elements of Federalism," Charles Tarlton reviews and finds wanting in current application the major theories associated with federalism. This selection is included because Tarlton's theoretical speculations have direct relevance to our discussion on territory and hierarchy. He gives emphasis, hitherto avoided, to the diverse ways in which each unit of a federal system relates to the system as a whole, to the central authority, and to other member units. This functional-structural model is based on two concepts at either end of a symmetry-asymmetry continuum, the former describing the extent to which the sharing of conditions is common and the latter, the opposite.

This challenges previous approaches to federalism which assumed internal unification. By giving emphasis to the elements of internal contrast among units Tarlton encourages an approach which political geographers have used in their studies of federal states.[74] He describes the extreme of each model and goes on to suggest the development of a system of analytical categories which take into account the level, nature, and distribution of the federal system's symmetry, and would indicate the relative desirability between a unitary or federal system.

In the section on centrality and nodes, Whittlesey's chapter, "France, Archetype of the Occidental National State" is reproduced

---

74. See, for example, Edmund H. Dale, "The State-Idea: Missing Prop of the West Indies Federation," *Scottish Geographical Magazine*, LXXVIII (December 1962), pp. 166–176, and K. W. Robinson, "Sixty Years of Federation in Australia," *Geographical Review*, LI (January 1961), pp. 2–20.

in shortened form as "The Territorial Evolution of France." As it was written over thirty years ago, the data on the population, area, and boundaries of France are obviously anachronistic, but the piece remains essentially a timeless classic as the epitome of the evolutionary approach to the study of the growth of a state from a core area. The focus for France is provided by the concurrence of two areal forces, division and union, occurring in three alternations through time. Thus division in early Roman times was followed by the unity of the Roman Empire, division in the tribal period following the collapse of Rome by unity under Charlemagne, and division during feudal times by unity under the kings. The associated territorial pattern is traced and thus substance is given to this model of France's political geographic evolution.

In a cross-cultural study, Rhoads Murphey contrasts cities in the western world with those of the Orient in terms of their role as centers of political innovation. His "The City as a Center of Change: Western Europe and China" examines the assumption that in most societies the function of economic exchange and political organization is concentrated in cities to take advantage of the centrality they afford. He finds, however, that in their particular function as centers of radical change, Chinese cities, unlike their European counterparts, have tended to remain strong centers of the *status quo* within their administrative areas. Murphey suggests the explanation lies at least in good part in contrasting aspects of their political systems.

European cities have since the Middle Ages been centers of intellectual ferment and economic change. With the arrival of political integration and the urban-monarchical alliance, the city became automatically a center for political change. In China, environmental factors tended to encourage isolation. Given China's lack of interconnections between river systems, the cities remained traditional administrative centers of a unitary state, the epitome of the *status quo*. Wittfogel, Murphey notes, has suggested an organic connection between the need for man's water control (irrigation) and the growth of a monolithic structure (This notion is discussed in Part V, Environment). Because of the scarcity of land, investment was in agriculture with little urban commercial development. Furthermore, the nonagricultural sector was dominated by government monopolies. Thus the weight of bureaucracy stifled any European-style city growth as centers of change.

Because of the mass of literature available on boundaries and frontiers the three selections in this section are but a minute sample. Ladis Kristof's article on "The Nature of Frontiers and Boundaries" remains the best available work that clarifies the differences between the two phenomena in question. Basically he draws the contrast in that a frontier is not a legal or political entity but rather a fact of life defined by its external functions where centrifugal forces are manifested and where there is an ongoing attempt to integrate a transitional zone, whereas a boundary is the limit of a political unit with an internal function, a centripetal force, and a separator of space.

"The Significance of the Frontier in American History," given by Frederick Jackson Turner at the 1893 meeting of the American Historical Association, while famous among historians, has not been given the attention it deserves by political geographers, and hence we have reproduced parts of it in this section on frontiers.[75] Written at a point in time when the American frontier era had just ended, Turner's thesis states simply that the existence of an area of free land, its continuous recession, and the advance of American settlement westwards, *explains* American development. The frontier, he felt, developed vital forces that *compelled* American political institutions to adapt themselves to the changes in the frontier. This repudiation of the European "germ" theory of national growth was based upon an environmental factor, the existence of open space. In tracing the development of the frontier as a field for comparative study of social development, Turner picks out several types of frontier including Indian trading, ranching, farming, military, and mining, each having in turn an impact in American society. In this context, Turner calls on historians to study sequent occupance, a call since heeded by historical and cultural geographers. Turner also held that the frontier had influenced the national polity by being a basic ingredient in the

75. Some of Turner's works, including the "Frontier" essay, have appeared in a paperback book, *Frontiers and Section: Selected Essays of Frederick Jackson Turner* (Englewood Cliffs, N.J.: Prentice-Hall, 1961).

formulation of an American nationality, by decreasing America's dependence on the outside, and by "conditioning" legislation effecting improvements in transport facilities, protective tariffs, and disposition of public lands.

In his "Boundary Studies in Political Geography," Julian Minghi reviews and classifies boundary studies up to the early 1960's, and concludes with suggestions for future research.

The selections in the "global structure" section are extracts representing three major statements about world power equilibrium, already discussed in this essay: Sir Halford Mackinder's "Geographical Pivot" of 1904, Nicholas Spykman's "Rimland" of 1944, and Saul Cohen's "Geostrategic and Geopolitical Regions" of 1963.

7

Rank and Territory

PHILIP WAGNER*

It is significant that we use such originally spatial terms as "social position," "social distance," and "mobility," in talking about societies, for the social order is always closely correlated with particular spatial arrangements. This is true of many animals besides man. The close connection between social and spatial arrangements among men may become more easily intelligible if we consider first the general relationships of rank and territory among animals.

The Animal World

The territory within which an animal lives is almost always shared with animals of other species and with other members of its own species. There is, therefore, some considerable overlap in the demands placed upon the territory and its resources by the various creatures inhabiting it, and some competition in the use of sites and substances of the habitat. The conflicts of this kind that occur between individuals in a given habitat are not typically resolved by violent encounters; more commonly one individual acquiesces, giving up priority in the use of places and resources. There is much more deference and surrender than open warfare among animals, though

Philip Wagner, *The Human Use of the Earth* (New York: Free Press, 1960), pp. 51–58. Reprinted by permission of the author and publisher.
* Philip Wagner (1921–) is Professor of Geography at Simon Fraser University, Burnaby, British Columbia.

the order or precedence among species, and among individuals within species, rests ultimately upon the actual or potential use of force. These relationships that allocate prerogatives in a regular order among species and within species are known as *rank*.

Biological rank is the name given to the order of precedence among different species that governs the respective roles of their members in an encounter. The hyena cedes place to the lion, the deer shrinks away from the elk, the crow withdraws before the vulture, and almost all beasts flee the presence of man. This order of deference is not a matter of the predator-prey relationship as such, but rather of a recognition of the power of the individual of the dominant species to impose its will and to secure its claim upon any privilege that both desire. Biological rank appears to depend rather closely upon relative fighting ability, but few cases are reported of violent encounters between members of different wild species over booty; a snarl, a look, even the mere presence of the dominant animal is enough to provoke the prudent withdrawal of the weaker one.

Biological rank grades into the violent relationships of predation, on the one side, and on the other approximates a social relation, which provides stability and order in the community with a minimum of outright violence among species. Man is almost always the most feared and privileged member of the company.

Within a single-species population there

are two kinds of territorial arrangements: (1) the separate and exclusive occupation of contiguous territories by single animals or by mating pairs and their young, and (2) the joint occupation by a group composed of many individuals of various descent. These two possible arrangements are not necessarily mutually exclusive in a given species. The assignment of territories to individual males may occur, as among some birds, only for the duration of the courtship and mating period, after which the group harmoniously shares a single undivided territory. Exclusive territorial rights may be maintained, also, for only a small part of the territory used by an individual, and the rest may be shared; many animals defend their exclusive individual claims to the "home range" where the dwelling is, but forage in the company of their fellows in a common feeding territory.

Within a species, there is commonly a regular order of precedence similar to that among different species, known as *social rank*. The most striking demonstration of this system is the "peck-order" existing among chickens and other birds. There is normally a gradation of privilege and what might be called prestige, based upon combative success and enforced by threats where necessary, among a great many kinds of animals and also among men. Social rank is not always a straight line relationship: individual "A" may dominate "B," and "B" dominate "C," but on occassion "C" may dominate "A." This does not detract from the effect of social rank as a regulator of behavior in individual encounters, however.

Social rank is linked with territory. Almost any individual, in many species, is dominant within its own home territory, though he may be "at the bottom of the heap" outside it. Each particular hierarchy of ranked individuals, too, corresponds to a given specific population in a definite common territory, and any individual of the species introduced from outside must fight his way into the social order or be cast out or killed.

Biological and social rank and territorial behavior are as characteristic of man as of other vertebrate animals. Social rank is another of the powerful integrating mechanisms of human groups. Kinship position itself confers rank, tradition reinforces it, language expresses it. Among most adult humans within a ranked group there are seldom direct physical encounters to decide precedence of rank, but conflicts of interest are resolved among both men and animals by invoking rank and implied power.

Man and Political Action

Human societies are ranked systems in which not only individuals but large groups are assigned places in the order of precedence. These groups are often internally arranged by rank. Human societies, in other words, are often stratified into classes, castes, estates and other divisions. The assignment of rank to an individual within a social stratum, or to one stratum relative to another, does not normally depend upon the open use of force. There are other and subtler means of advancing claims to rank through what is called *political action*.

Political relations, as the term is intended here, are established in encounters where the direct exercise of force is held in abeyance, usually because some social agency monopolizes the predominant means of forcible action. *Politics* consists of the mutual assessment by interested parties of one another's ability to muster support for their respective opinions, and of the making of joint decisions in accordance with these judgments. The shadow of power always lurks behind political decision and the compliance it demands.

The *social order* is the ranking of social groups; it is enforced not only by kinship and tradition, but often by a legal structure that is the result of past political action. Social stratification is often changed gradually by means of legislative action. When ordinary political devices are abandoned in favor of the use of force to change the social order, we speak of *revolution*. Normally, though, the legislative political functions in a society assign rank and role to individuals and groups. The daily behavior of the individual and groups is regulated by the legal and the administrative structure, respectively. The legal establishes patterns for the solution of conflicts among individuals and groups. The administrative structures direct their cooperation. The political order usually embraces the whole society, whether the political functions reside in particular formal institutions or are embedded informally in other units of organization.

Besides the explicitly political order that

permeates the whole society, there are countless other ways in which political action substitutes for forcible action in regulating the relations among individuals and groups. "Politicking" is a form of behavior almost universal in its scope, an indispensable regulatory device. Political relations, having for their object the non-violent adjudication of differences, the establishment of ranking, and the making and enforcement of decisions in a group, are an extension of relations determined by tradition and by the emotions attaching to kinsfolk and familiar associates. In relations among individuals there are positive incentives, as well as negative sanctions that enter into political and other decisions; kindness, empathy, compassion, loyalty and solidarity are at least as characteristic determinants of human action as is the implication of force. Likewise, the relations of individuals to larger groups are governed by such motives as the sense of altruism, fair-play, honesty, dedication and patriotism as well as by power.

Political functions are essential to a society. Many societies otherwise united by language, tradition and sometimes by kinship also depend upon specific political institutions for their integration; in all, there reside some political functions. Political organization may either coincide with these other features of societal organization or go beyond them.

Politics and Territory

Political organization and political action have always a territorial basis. The group participating in and governed by decisions under a particular institution is defined by territorial limits. The interaction between groups and individuals inhabiting different territories where different political systems hold sway may also be regulated by political action. However, between the folk of different political and territorial units force is often employed in settlement of conflicts over material interests or over intergroup rank. "War is the extension of politics" between groups. Where no permanent accepted organs of political procedure are available to regulate relations among several different territorial, social, and political entities, war becomes a means of arriving at decisions. In some parts of the world intergroup relations are still almost entirely on a basis of permanent enmity. Even in the so-called advanced countries, the techniques of warfare have progressed farther and faster than have the techniques of peaceful political interaction among nations, so that war is a still greater threat to humanity in powerful industrial countries in close, mistrustful contact with each other.

Political Partitioning as an Expression of Territoriality and Ranking

The geographical expression of human territoriality and ranking is most striking in the division of the world into units of political organization, each sovereign and capable both of peaceable and of warlike interaction. All of the territories of the earth are under some form of state sovereignty. We may recognize among politically organized territories the following kinds.

1. First there are the *national states*. These are territories having populations of common tradition and language. Often the national states embrace within their borders seven minorities that have a tradition of their own rooted in distinct language, religion, or history. The prototypal and still most typical of national states, like France and England, possess substantial national minorities. In the Soviet Union, the national minorities have been accorded the status of autonomous nationalities within the all-embracing Soviet nationality. They are allowed to maintain their languages and some other elements of cultural distinctiveness, while being incorporated firmly into the political and social framework of the Communist state.

2. A second category of politically organized territories is the *alien dependency*. These entities are very diverse, falling into three different classes.

a. First are the areas pre-empted from their earlier inhabitants and settled predominantly by immigrants. These are perhaps best called true "colonies." They are exemplified by French Canada, the United States, Australia and New Zealand, Argentina, Manchuria, Siberia proper, Canada and Israel. All of these have been colonized by one or more "metropolitan countries." Often the colonies have in time chosen to sever their formal ties with the motherlands, and have opened their borders to the immigration of peoples other than the original settler group. They usually manifest a continuing unity of tradition with the countries of their origin.

b. A second class of alien dependencies is the territory seized and ruled, but little settled by the people of the controlling power. Some of these countries are used for the specialized production of certain goods, and may be thought of as primarily investment areas. Such are the tropical lands in which few people from European mother countries settle, but where valuable commodities like sugar, coffee, tea, spices, vegetable oils, fibres, and minerals are produced for market under enterprises managed by the outsiders, and often operated mainly by imported laborers. The tropical plantation dependencies of Western European countries were the scene of early forms of true capitalist production, dependent upon metropolitan investors for supervision and supply, and on coolies for labor. Such places as the West Indies, Ceylon, Java, the Philippines, Mauritius, and Réunion are or have been dependencies in this sense. In some such places the original population has disappeared, as in the West Indies; or unpopulated islands have been settled by folk imported to labor on them, like Mauritius; or both things have occurred, and mixed populations from everywhere like those of Trinidad, Hawaii, Tahiti, or Natal occur. Some of the tropical investment dependencies have been marginal to large areas, still inhabited by thriving native populations, and not used by the outsiders. These occur in the Philippines, West Africa, and Indonesia. Another sort of investment area is the mining country, which in earlier times was often a nucleus of foreign settlement and of labor immigration. Mexico and Peru are heritors of this kind of dependent regime blended with other types.

Of course investment is not always dependent upon political control, and foreign enterprise often continues to function when the political ties with the dependencies are severed. This frequently happens now. The turnover of power by a colonial power to a local regime often means that a new national state becomes established around one tribe or nation within a former dependent territory inhabited by many very unlike and inimical groups. The half-Westernized local intelligentsia, usually drawn from only a few favored peoples and strata of the population, comes to power over large territories in which the former colonial rule held sway, without necessarily representing more than a minute fraction of the populace. After colonial rule conditions never seem to return to the *status quo ante*.

c. A third kind of dependency is the purely *commercial* one, where a foreign power has stepped in to promote order and to enhance the attractiveness of a territory as an investment area or market for the goods and services of the metropolitan country. India was the best example of such a dependency. Nicaragua and Haiti were so occupied, temporarily, by the United States. In the long run, all three types of dependency relations are likely to occur together in different proportions within a territory, and the conditions introduced by colonial rule continue beyond independence. The link with a more cosmopolitan cultural tradition subsists, and Pakistanis go on speaking English, wearing plaid kilts, and wheezing bagpipes; elite Tunisians continue speaking French and sipping apperitifs after they are free. So also do the established commercial and investment activities continue under almost the same arrangements in some cases. And so does the skeleton of territorial jurisdiction remain, the same territories being under new rulers who are sometimes still practically alien to most of the population. The outlines of colonial territories, established without much regard for the ethnic complexities of the country, remain after the overlords are gone, so that there is a Ghana or a Nigeria with little true national foundation. Sometimes the administrative divisions of former great empires have persisted as separate countries, as in Hispanic America, where old provinces became independent states. Dependencies may also split up at independence, as did India and Indo-China.

3. A third category of political units is the type of closed and autonomous communities based on kinship, common language and tradition that lie within the spheres claimed by various national states. Of this kind are a multitude of local polities in New Guinea, Indonesia, Peru, Bolivia, Brazil, Mexico, Guatemala, Laos, India, Ethiopia, the Sudan, and so on.

The internal spatial structure as well as the extent and position of these three kinds of political units are significant. Most such units are built around what Mark Jefferson and Derwent Whittlesey called an "ecumene," that is, a core of densest settlement and most abundant transportation facilities. This feature is especially well marked in some places in Latin America, where a populous central zone is sometimes joined within a state to a great, almost empty hinterland. The concentration of formal political institutions in particular spots is also both a practical necessity and an important influence in the life of a political unit. Centers of power of this sort are most often in the largest cities of a modern country, where a variety of services and amenities is available to the political leadership, and where growth is probably much stimulated by their political functions. Cities have, since their earliest appearance, been associated with extended political relations in a dependent countryside.

One of the chief features of political organization of territory is its hierarchical nature. Political entities are grouped on the basis of territorial proximity into larger unions subject to the authority of superior agencies, with a regular increase in degree of authority and scope of territorial jurisdiction up to the supreme national authority. The nature of the association may be either central, in which the highest agency reserves all power and delegates it to subsidiary political units of lesser territorial jurisdiction; or federal, in which entities with sovereign powers delegate some of these powers for common purposes to a central agency.

8

Symmetry and Asymmetry as Elements of Federalism:
A Theoretical Speculation

CHARLES D. TARLTON*

... In studies of federalism the prevailing emphases avoid sufficient consideration of the diverse ways in which each member state in a federal system is able to relate to the system as a whole, the central authority, and each other member state. The federal relationship, in any realistic sense, means something very much different to nearly every participant unit in the system. Among the several states in a federal union, cultural, economic, social, and political factors combine to produce variations in the symbiotic connection between those states and the system.

Two concepts ... can be introduced and their general content suggested here. The first, the notion of *symmetry* refers to the extent to which component states share in the conditions and thereby the concerns more or less common to the federal system as a whole. By the same token, the second term, the concept of *asymmetry* expresses the extent to which component states do not share in these common features. Whether the relationship of a state is symmetrical or asymmetrical is a question of its participation in the pattern of social, cultural, economic, and political characteristics of the federal system of which it is part. This relation, in turn, is a significant factor in shaping its relations with other component states and with the national authority.

. . . .

In traditional approaches to the concept of federalism, the perspective from which the federal relationship is viewed leads to an important distortion. Federalism is almost universally defined implicitly in terms of component political and legal units sharing equally the federal relationship among themselves and with the general government. The federal relationship is usually visualized as that between the Federal Government and the State (or all of the States collectively). Regardless of the criteria by means of which federalism is delineated, a federal system is or is not deemed *federal as a whole*. This results in an important distortion because of the obvious fact that a federal system may be more or less federal throughout its parts. That is, the quality and levels of federalism present

Charles D. Tarlton, "Symmetry and Asymmetry as Elements of Federalism," *The Journal of Politics*, Vol. 27, No. 4, November 1965. Reprinted by permission of the author and publisher.

* Charles Tarlton (1937–) is in the Department of Political Science, Graduate School of Public Affairs, State University of New York, Albany.

in the relationship between the central government and each component government considered separately may vary in significant ways throughout the system. The "federalism" of the system is likely to be variegated and disparate among all the essential units.

A principal element in federal relationships, both essential to understanding federalism and too often not carefully distinguished and recognized, is the symmetry of the federal system. What I mean by symmetry is the level of conformity and commonality in the relations of each separate political unit of the system to both the system as a whole and to the other component units. The overall extent to which the federal system is characterized by a harmonious pattern of states partaking of the general features of the federal nation is at the core of the symmetry of federalism. The specific elements and the degree of symmetry in the relations of a single member state to the system and to other states and in the total pattern of federalism throughout the system are equally important in assessing the quality of federalism.

The Symmetrical Model

An ideal symmetrical federal system would be one composed of political units comprised of equal territory and population, similar economic features, climatic conditions, cultural patterns, social groupings, and political institutions. In the model symmetrical system each of the separate political units would in effect be miniature reflections of the important aspects of the whole federal system.

Each state would, because of this basic similarity, be concerned with the solution of the same sorts of problems and with the development of the same sorts of potential. There would be no significant differences from one state to another in terms of the major issues about which the political organization of a state might be concerned. Nor would there be significant differences in terms of the political machinery and resources with which the state would approach those major issues.

In the model symmetrical federal system each state would maintain essentially the same relationship to the central authority. The division of power between central and state governments would be nearly the same in every case. Representation in the central government would be equal for each component polity, and support of the activities of that central government would also be equally distributed.

In the symmetrical model no significant social, economic, or political peculiarities would exist which might demand special forms of representation or protection. The basic justification for having a federal constitutional arrangement rather than a unitary one would be found in the completeness and integral character of the various political sub-systems. Separate political existence rapidly becomes a self-justifying arrangement as political loyalties granted to local governments become permanent features of the prevailing political ideology. Each member state, while similar in most important features to every other member state and to the overall character of the federal society, would be a separate unit possessing general problems of its own in the solution of which local authority would be thought to be best suited. The federal authority would, in the main, be limited to concerning itself with those problems either common to the federal system *qua* system (e.g., problems of international relations), or requiring system-wide attention and resources for solution.

The Asymmetrical Model

The ideal asymmetrical federal system would be one composed of political units corresponding to differences of interest, character, and makeup that exist within the whole society. The asymmetrical federal system would be one in which ... the diversities in the larger society find political expression through local governments possessed of varying degrees of autonomy and power. ... An asymmetrical federal government is one in which political institutions correspond to the real social "federalism" beneath them.

In the model asymmetrical federal system each component unit would have about it a unique feature or set of features which would separate in important ways, its interests from those of any other state or the system considered as a whole. Clear lines of division would be necessary and jealously guarded insofar as these unique interests were concerned. In the asymmetrical system it would be difficult (if not impossible) to discern interests that could be clearly considered mutual or national in scope (short of those pertaining to national existence *per se*).

THE CHARACTER OF FEDERAL GOVERNMENTS

William S. Livingston, after developing his theory of socio-cultural federalism in 1952, argued that with it he was able to arrange societies in order according to the degree to which they were really federal or unitary. He came a step further than the formal-legal treatments of federalism which allowed really only for determining whether a state was constitutionally federal or unitary and whether that form was being purely applied or not. But both Livingston's categories and criteria and those of the formal-legal approach are only capable of leading to such judgments with respect to an entire political system. That is, they can classify whole nations as being federal or unitary or (in Livingston's case) some degree of either. They are unable, however, to provide a theoretical framework suitable for discerning areas of "federalism" or "non-federalism" within a single system. The upshot of this is that they cannot say to what extent parts of the system might be more or less "federal" than others. In assessing and evaluating whole federal governments the ability to discern the pattern of federalization throughout the whole system is crucial.

Thus ordinarily discussions of federalism in the United States have been more or less limited to (1) attention to the particular areas in which state-federal relationships are concentrated, e.g., education, highway construction, the grant-in-aid programs, criminal and civil law, and interstate commerce problems, (2) concern over the growing "octopus" of federal authority and the erosion of "states' rights," and (3) the origins and meanings of federalism in American political history. The general concern seems to have been with the condition of federalism in the United States at large. Now, certainly there is good reason to be concerned with the ways in which federalism has developed, just as there is good reason, in the broader theoretical sense, to pursue the kind of social/functional analyses that Livingston has suggested. But, while these are useful concerns, they go only part of the way.

No federal arrangement is likely to be made up of states, each of which stands in exactly the same relationship to the whole system. In actual cases each component unit will tend to reflect (or not to reflect) the overall national character to a greater or lesser extent. A federal system which resembled the symmetrical model would be a very different one and would involve very different legal, political, and economic problems than one which resembled the asymmetrical model. In this connection many important characteristics of the federal relationship can best be explained by a system of analytical categories which take account of the level, nature, and distribution of the system's symmetry. One basic characteristic that can adequately be explained only in this way is federal-state conflict, what might be termed the "secession-potential" of the federal system.

The question of federal-state conflict must be approached in terms of the shared goals, aspirations, and expectations of the elements constituting the federal union. When, through a particular asymmetry in the relationship between a state and the federal authority in consideration of basic processes and needs, the policies pursued and the conditions demanded by a single component state are importantly foreign to those of the overall system, then federal-state conflict is likely to be the result. It should be stressed at this point that where state-federal conflict occurs it is most likely to stem from complaints limited to one or just a few of the member states. It is rare for conflict to occur between the central government and *all* the states simultaneously.

Therefore federal-state conflict is a likelihood where the relationship between local and central authorities corresponds to the image of the asymmetrical situation, and where that asymmetry is characteristic only of a few of the states in their relation to the whole. To a real extent, then, the degree of harmony or conflict within a federal system can be thought of as a function of the symmetrical or asymmetrical pattern prevailing within the system. Most real federal states, however, would be somewhere between the complete harmony of the symmetrical model and the complete conflict potential of the asymmetrical model.

For example, the levels of conflict or harmony between California and Washington, D.C., or Mississippi and Washington, D.C., can be viewed in relation to the symmetry of each state's relation to the whole of the United States. The character of society in California is much closer to the pattern of society in the nation at large. Mississippi (or the hard core Southern states generally) differs in a variety of important ways from the social, economic, cultural, and ideological configurations of the nation. Conflict between California and the Federal Government is likely to be less frequent and less intense than in the case of Mississippi. The prevailing attitude of public officials toward the legal and political details of the federal-state relationship is also likely to vary greatly between California and Mississippi. The most basic factor involved and leading in the direction of explaining this difference is the symmetry of the underlying social-political relationship each state has to the nation at large.

I am compelled, at this point, to engage in some unorthodox speculations regarding the relation between the symmetry of a political society and its suitability for federal or unitary political organization. Concern for logical neatness has led, in writings on federalism, to the conclusion that the more diverse the elements within a political system, the better it is suited for federalism, and that the more homogeneous the political society, the clearer the need for unitary forms. There is a limit, however, in that the diversity can in some cases be so great that not even "federalism" can provide adequate bases for unification under a single political authority. These propositions appear to be pure common sense, but I am suggesting that this is deceiving, that they are not as true in all cases as they are assumed to be, and that they are often downright false and misleading.

A viable federal system can be examined from at least two points of view. One can concentrate on the question of the desirability of adopting a federal system in a particular set of social and political circumstances, or one can inquire into the workings of a particular extant federal system with a view to unearthing the factors contributory to its success. Depending upon the emphasis, the questions asked and the answers accepted must be very different.

Whether a particular country or collection of countries should adopt a federal structure is intimately bound up with the question of the symmetry of the whole. If, in the underlying structure, diversity is overwhelmingly predominant (approximating the asymmetrical model), then (according to the logic of the orthodox view of federalism's requisites) there exists a presumption of the applicability of some utilization of the federal principle, assuming, of course, that the diversity is not such as to preclude even federal forms. The argument would entail something to the effect that the various significant diversities ought to find political expression and protection within the system as a whole. Federalism, it is maintained, provides the necessary expression and protection.

The question, of course, really involves setting a hierarchy of values by means of which to judge the overall desirability of federalism. It can not turn simply on the logical formula "diversity, then federalism." The question of the workability of the system comes energetically to mind. Whether a state can function harmoniously with a federal constitution will, I argue, be a result of the level of symmetry within it. The higher the level of symmetry, that is, the more each particular section, state, or region partakes of a character general and common to the whole, the greater the likelihood that federalism would be a suitable form of governmental organization. On the other hand, if the system is highly asymmetrical in its components, then a harmonious federal system is unlikely to develop. If a formula were to be extracted from this, it would read: *The elements of similarity among component units of a federal system must, if that system is to function at an optimum level of harmony, predominate over existing elements of diversity.* Where diversity of elements is the rule, then it follows (presuming that sufficient political power and motivation exist to achieve unity *at all*) that a unitary and centralized system would be better. When diversity predominates, the "secession-potential" of the system is high and unity would require controls to overcome disruptive, centrifugal tendencies and forces.

Following this reasoning and applying it to a brief discussion of the quality of federalism in the United States, certain interesting conclusions are reached. *First*, the functioning of federalism in the United States has fluctuated with changes occurring in the underlying makeup of its basic components. Periods of greatest harmony in the relations between states and the federal authorities and among states themselves have paralleled periods in which the differences among the states have been overshadowed by the factors compelling to symmetry. *Second*, the periods of conflict and tension within the American federal system have been at times when particular interests and problems in some of the component states have developed independently to such proportions that their protection and expression overrode considerations of the common interest. In order for the political parcelling-out of authority basic to any definition of federalism to be part of a working system it is essential that the component units have shared characteristics to such an extent that the common pursuits are never lost sight of. *Third*, regions of the country where federalism is most hotly questioned, its constitutional features most frequently argued, and the propensity for subverting national interest the highest are just those areas in which certain problems have taken such deep hold of political life that they destroy the symmetry of the federal relationship. If the entire United States reflected relationships like those typical of the states of the Deep South, then federalism in the United States would long since have perished. Areas within the nation whose relationship to the whole is generally asymmetrical are just those areas in which federal presence is most keenly felt and in which meaningful participation in national affairs most often necessitates compulsion.

The concept of federalism has been a major panacea in Western political thought for an incredible range of problems—from the creation of new nation-states, the provision of government in metropolitan areas, to the creation of organizations designed to prevent international war. Federalism has been a kind of universal answer to the question of overcoming problems of diversity and disparity in the interests of harmony and unity. Whenever events have seemed to demand cooperation and coordination, while interests and anxieties have held out for the preservation of difference and diversity, the answer has almost unfailingly been some form of federalism. It is in this connection, then, that a clear understanding of the strengths and weaknesses, the benefits and liabilities, the predictability and the surprises of federalism is particularly important.

If there is anything of merit in the speculations which comprise the bulk of this essay, it seems clear that much of the ordinary optimism regarding the near magical qualities of federalism can profitably be re-examined. The most basic question that must be asked, then, is: To what extent can "federalism" be expected to sustain the stimulus to and the need for unity in the face of the pressures of separatism? The answer, plainly, is: To the extent that the forces of unity are dominant. Unless there is some factor or set of factors which clearly and inexorably push in the direction of commonality, then the pressures of asymmetry will increasingly present themselves, making continued federal existence nearly impossible.

This is a discomforting way of thinking about federal principles of governmental organization, because among the implications that derive from it is the idea that diversity, a factor so often raised by proponents of increased local autonomy in federal systems, tends really to necessitate increased central authority if the system is to continue operating as a system. Relieving the tensions and discord often attendant upon asymmetrical systems requires not further recognition of the elements of diversity and their protection in the complicated processes of ever-increasing federalization, but rather increased coordination and coercion from the centralizing authorities in the system. The implications of this kind of thinking about the federal process may entail serious skepticism regarding the feasibility of using federalism as a means of politically organizing local, regional, national, and international communities.

9

The Territorial Evolution of France

DERWENT S. WHITTLESEY*

No two states, even those which share in common a peripheral location on the western margin of Europe, are alike in all aspects of their natural environment. Partly for this reason the details of their political pattern and structure differ also. Of the nations of Western Europe, France is most representative, and may be considered the archetype of the group. Each of the three broad physical divisions of Europe—northern plain, central mountains, and Mediterranean coastland—extends into France. This entanglement with its landward neighbors makes its strong national unity more significant than that of countries more effectively insulated from Central and Eastern Europe. Its area ranks it first among the peripheral states (Germany and Poland being larger), but its population sets it below Britain, Germany, and Italy. Nevertheless, its ecumene is virtually coextensive with its area, so that it lacks the empty districts that so often mislead the earnest student of the political map. As one of the Great Powers, it is a political unit of first magnitude, and it incorporates a fair sampling of components of both the second and third magnitude. Alone among European states it includes large areas of both Mediterranean and North European landscape.

From *The Earth and the State: A Study of Political Geography* by Derwent S. Whittlesey. Copyright 1939 by Holt, Rinehart and Winston, Inc. Reprinted by permission of Holt, Rinehart and Winston, Inc.

* Derwent S. Whittlesey (1890–1956) was Professor of Geography at Harvard University.

No other, except Spain, occupies frontage on both the Atlantic Ocean and the Mediterranean Sea.

THE ALTERNATION OF DIVISION AND UNION

Two opposed areal forces have been constantly at work in shaping the French state, and their concurrence is the key to its political geography. The compact territory north of the Pyrenees and west of the Alps-Jura-Vosges-Ardennes tends to become politically unified (Map 9.1). No less does each of the major river basins—Rhône, Garonne, Loire, Seine, and Moselle-Meuse—tend to assert its independence. The degree of unity varies with the strength of the political organization current at any period. There have been in historic times three alternations between schism and union.

Division

One of the first Roman annexations outside the Italian Peninsula was the Mediterranean seacoast between the Maritime Alps and the Pyrenees, including the inseparable valley of the Lower Rhône. Known as "The Province," this territory was the prototype of Roman administration outside Italy. Seventy-five years later Caesar found non-Mediterranean

100 Derwent S. Whittlesey

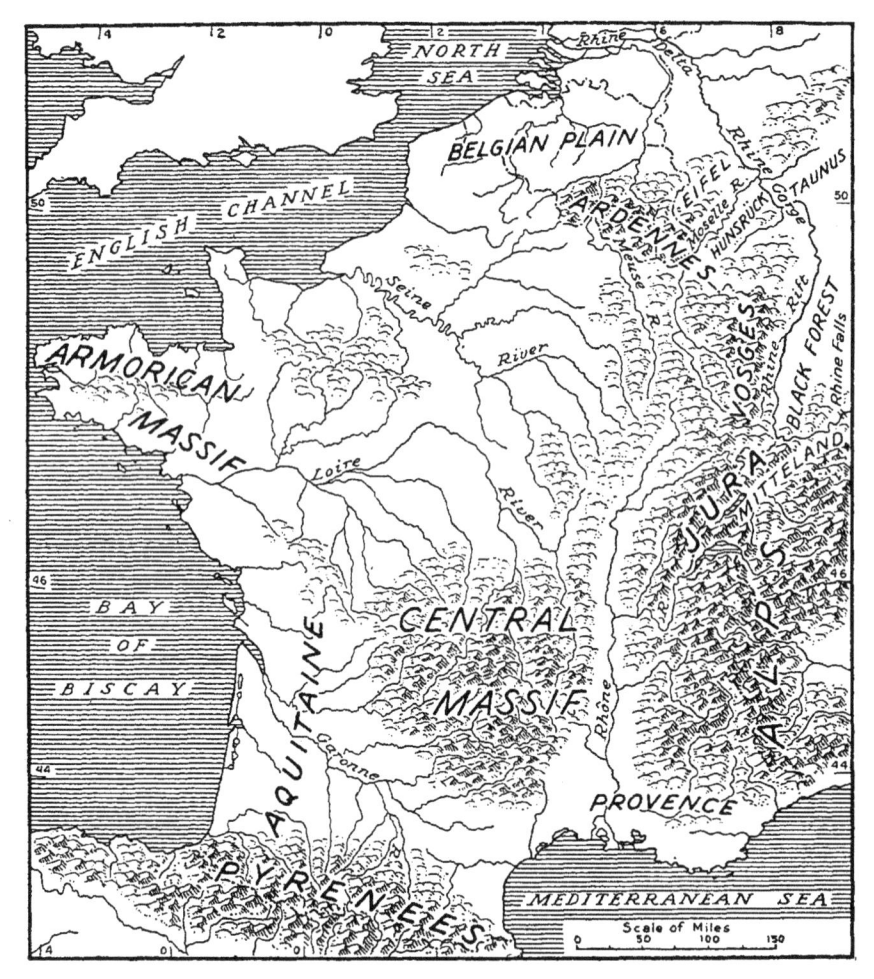

Map 9.1 THE PHYSICAL COMPONENTS OF FRANCE
Each type of country continues across the eastern boundary.

Gaul divided into three parts: Aquitaine (the basin of the Garonne), the Seine-Loire Basin, and the Belgian Plain (physically partly in the Rhine drainage, but politically often linked to France).

Union

As Roman territory Gaul continued to be administered in three units, with varying boundaries but with unchanging cores. In time the line between the new acquisition and The Province faded to the status of interprovincial boundary. The eastern border of the unified Gaul followed the crescent of the Western Alps all the way to the Falls of the Rhine, and included the Swiss Mittelland and the Jura Mountains, with all the passageways opening off to the eastward. From the Rhine Falls the stream itself was made the eastern boundary of the Empire. It was in no sense a barrier, but simply the most patent north-south marker in the low and easily traversable hill-land between the Alps and the North Sea. It could easily be announced and maintained as the military frontier against tribes disseminated through the German forests. At times the land along the left bank was organized into military provinces, at times it was incorporated into Gaul. Several fortress towns were constructed on the left bank, and two of them, Mainz and Cologne, were sites of permanent bridges, each with a fortified garrison at its eastern end. The weakest part of this line is a steep-sided and flat-floored valley between the great bend of the river near Basel and the gorge where it breaks through the Taunus, just below Mainz. This fertile Rift Valley, formed by the foundering of a strip of the earth's crust, is the western border of a deep reentrant between Upper Rhine and Upper Danube, the rest of which is rugged country that in enemy hands threatened the Roman frontiers. The conquest of Gaul had been followed by seizure of the Alps and their foreland as far as the Danube. Less than a century later the Romans built a series of walls and trenches from the great bend of the Danube to the Rhine below the confluence of the Moselle. Besides eliminating the dangerous reentrant this move incorporated the Black Forest which dominates the eastern side of the Rift Valley, and the fertile Neckar and Lower Main valleys. Although intended to be an advance base for further military operations, this proved to be the last outpost of Roman power toward Germany. After two hundred years it was abandoned; traces of the earthworks can still be seen.

Division

As the legions were withdrawn from the Rhine boundary by a relaxing Roman power, successive tribes of Germans penetrated Gaul. Major concentrations of power conformed roughly to the major river basins. Visigoths occupied Aquitaine, Burgundians the Rhône Basin, Alamanni pushed into the Rhine Rift Valley (without deserting their center in the hill country to the eastward), and Franks controlled the Seine Basin from a triple base along the Rhine—in the Main-Rhine confluence, on the North European Plain between the Rhine gorge and its delta, and on the fertile spots (limon soils) amid the marshes and sandy heaths of the Rhine delta itself. The Loire Basin lay divided between Visigothic and Frankish power. Caesar had noted some such division lines between Gaulish tribes as those of the Germanic invaders, and it was to reappear chronically for a thousand years after Roman unity broke down.

Union

Charlemagne, a Frankish ruler, welded the units together, along with much German and Italian territory. For decades after his death, the western triad of basins remained unified, but the Rhône-Rhine Depression was severed from the Frankish (i.e., French) territories.

Division

While in theory the unity of the western basins has never since Charlemagne been abandoned, in practice the country fell into feudalization so complete that effective political units were of the second or even the third order of magnitude, rather than the first. Only slowly did Aquitaine reassert its coherence. It was some centuries before the Inner Paris Basin was able to harmonize political and natural unity by conquering Normandy from the Norman dukes, and thus occupying the whole of the Seine Basin. The unity of the lands along the Loire is largely nullified by passage of the stream through three major landform regions, the middle one being the politically powerful "Paris Basin." The Loire Basin remained divided among a number of counties until each bit was absorbed by the French monarchy. (This dissection is visible in the map of French administrative provinces until the Revolution of 1789.)

Union

Slowly, under the French kings centered in the Paris Basin, nearly all Roman Gaul, including The Province, now known as Provence, was knit into the French state of today. The exception is the eastern borderland north of the Alps, where the river boundary failed to hold, once military force on opposite banks became equal.

INTERNAL PATTERN

France presents an irregular checkerboard of high and low land (Map 9.1). The Central, Armorican, and Vosges-Ardennes massifs, all hill lands rather than mountain lands, interspace with the lowland river basins. The lowlands, fertile farmed areas and foci of trade, have been the traditional centers of political integration, especially those with a single nuclear core. The lower and wider

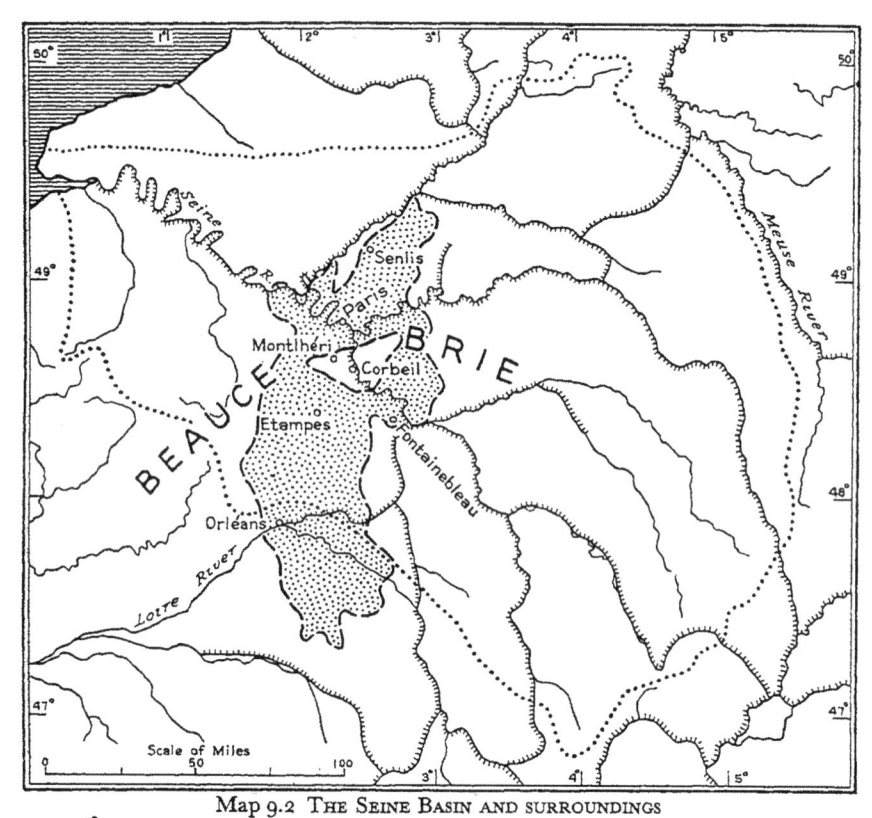

Map 9.2 THE SEINE BASIN AND SURROUNDINGS
The Île de France is stippled. The Seine Basin is outlined with dots. Feathered streams are navigable.

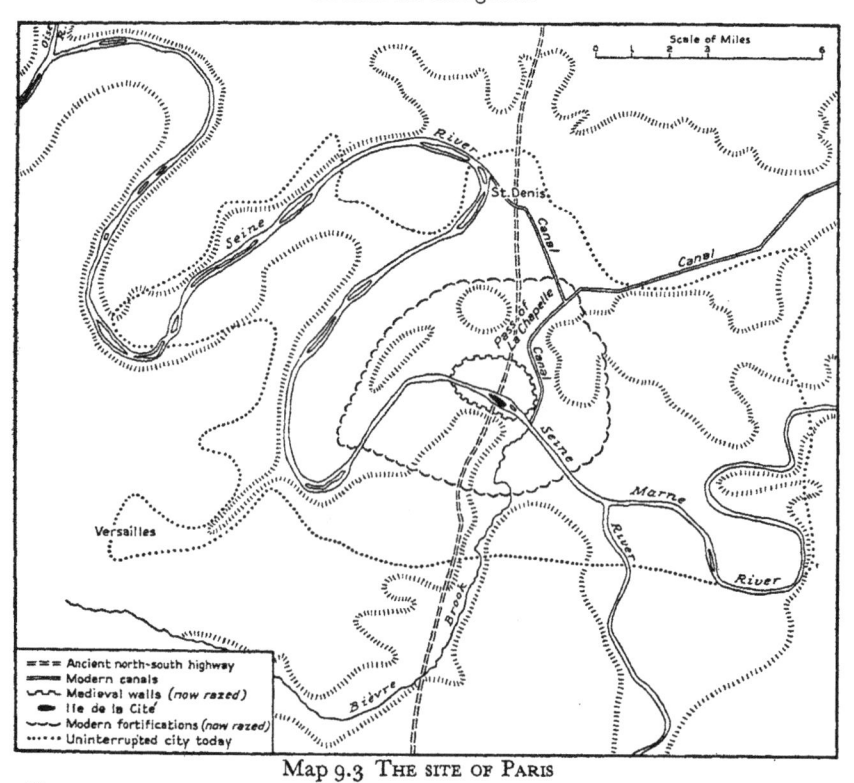

Map 9.3 THE SITE OF PARIS
The high ground immediately south and west of the city rises gently, whereas that to the north and east is precipitous and loftier.

Map 9.4 THE EASTERLY SIDE OF THE PARIS BASIN

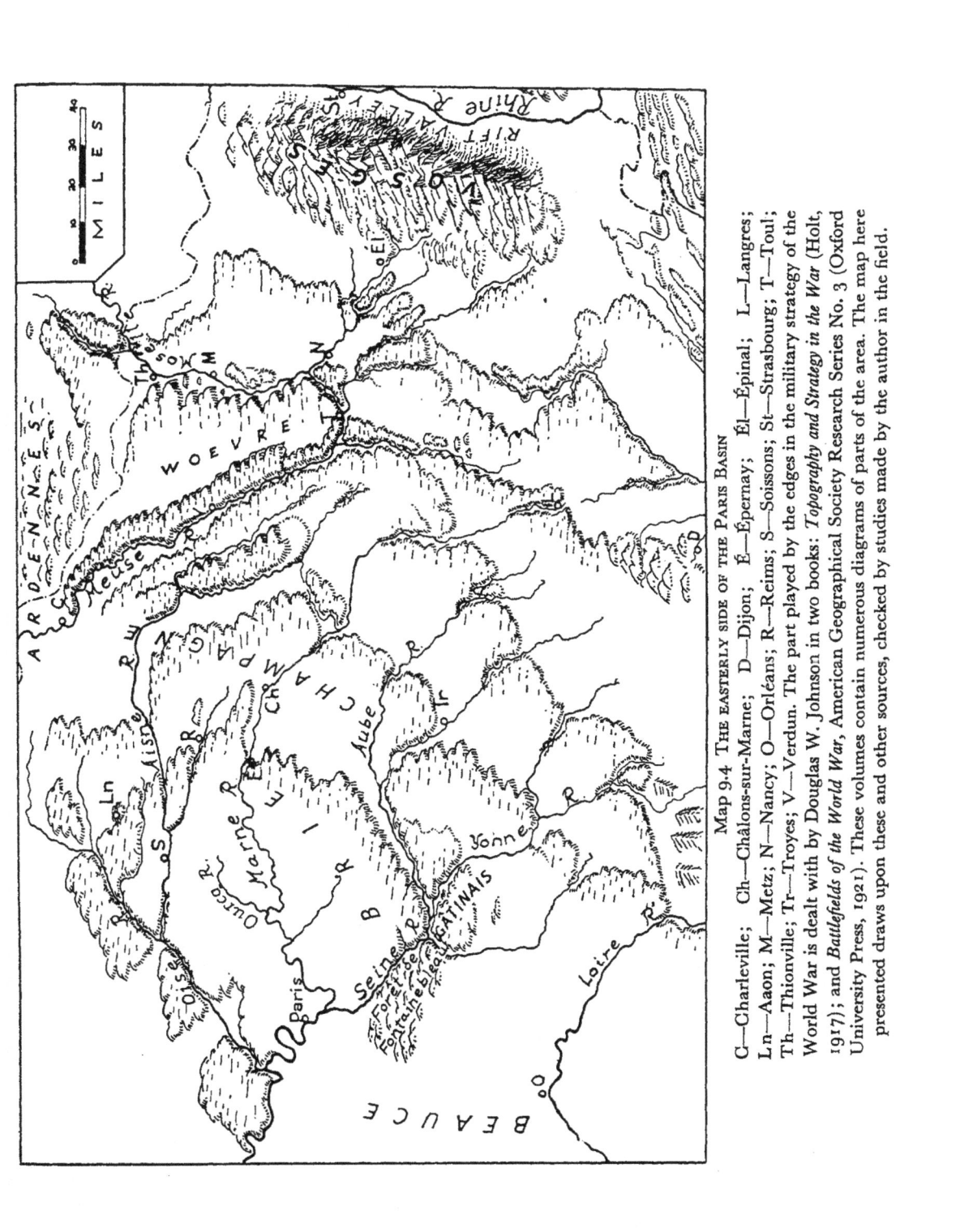

C—Charleville; Ch.—Châlons-sur-Marne; D—Dijon; É—Épernay; El—Épinal; L—Langres; Ln—Aaon; M—Metz; N—Nancy; O—Orléans; R—Reims; S—Soissons; St—Strasbourg; T—Toul; Th—Thionville; Tr—Troyes; V—Verdun. The part played by the edges in the military strategy of the World War is dealt with by Douglas W. Johnson in two books: *Topography and Strategy in the War* (Holt, 1917); and *Battlefields of the World War*, American Geographical Society Research Series No. 3 (Oxford University Press, 1921). These volumes contain numerous diagrams of parts of the area. The map here presented draws upon these and other sources, checked by studies made by the author in the field.

basins face different seas, and provide a diversity of outlook for their inhabitants. The Rhône, debouching into the calm Mediterranean with its connections to the Orient, belongs to a world very unlike that of the Garonne and Loire, leading to the tempestuous Bay of Biscay and the open Atlantic, or that of the Seine and Rhine, turned toward the semi-enclosed waters of north Europe. But if each basin faces outward, it has postern doors leading to its neighbors. Exchange of surplus between the moderately contrasting products of the several lowlands, and transfer of goods from overseas, have always maintained trade tracks across the intervening highlands along the lines most easily traversed. The highlands, beyond the sphere of these trade routes, have ever been refuge areas in times of stress. Armorica is the last stand of the Celts; the Central Massif is the home of the Albigensian protest against the Roman Church. As usual in highlands, these rugged and infertile hills produce more children than food, and the outflow of surplus population sometimes jeopardizes the political balance of the lowlands to which they move.

THE SEINE BASIN AND UNIFICATION

The Seine and its tributaries provide the most useful system of waterways in France. Except in their extreme headwaters, their gradients are gentle. Fed mainly by the uniform and moderate rains of the North, they carry enough water at all seasons to support laden boats. High water interferes with navigation once every few years for a short time in spring. Nearly every one of the larger tributaries makes easy and close contact with one of the other major river systems of the country (Map 9.1). Only the Garonne lies too remote. In time half a dozen canals were dug across the low watersheds, and the traffic in the masterstream and its connections toward the northeast remains large—one of the few active inland waterways in these days of rail- and motor-roads.

The river basin is elliptical, but all the principal tributaries lie in its eastern hemicycle (Map 9.2). More striking still, a crow flight of less than one hundred miles over the middle course of the river passes the confluence of every one of these larger streams. In the midst of this convergence of waterways islands half fill the stream. Partially protected by their natural moat, the islands provide defensible ground for any people forced to take refuge there. As they need to expand, rough terrain close to the river on the left bank provides a more vulnerable, but still defensible site. The marshy plain on the right bank promises much room for further extension of city. In addition to the river highway, an overland route crossing dry plateaus north and south of the Seine, descends to the river at this point by way of the Bièvre Valley and the Pass of La Chapelle. The river crossing is facilitated by the islands, which simplify the problem of bridge building, as soon as bridges might be desired, by dividing the wide stream into two narrow ones. This central location is, of course, the site of Paris (Map 9.3). Caesar found a Gallic tribe entrenched upon the fortress island. The peace which he and his successors enforced permitted the Roman town to expand to the hill of the left bank. The age of turbulence which followed saw the city reduced to the confines of its easily defended nucleus, the Île de la Cité. From this nucleus began the political expansion which created France. The Cité provided protection in times of stress for the surrounding farmlands, which in turn supported it by their husbandry. It served also as capital for a still wider area of surrounding plain.

The region intimately affiliated with Paris during the middle ages was known as the Île de France. Not of course an island surrounded by water, but a political island, surrounded by Norman, Burgundian, English, and other unfriendly powers. Yet in some sense it was and still is a physical island as well. The Seine Basin derives its circular shape from a series of underlying rock strata which dip gently toward a center at the site of Paris (Map 9.4). Where edges of these strata are exposed at the surface they have been worn away unevenly. Each stratum of resistant rock, protecting softer layers beneath, has thus come to form a concentric, although not continuous, ring of hills, sloping gently toward the Paris center, but presenting a steep and broken declivity on the out-facing flank. From the *edge*, as the English descriptively call the crest of this sort of ridge, the gentle slope behind hardly appears to be a hill, whereas the lowland in front lies spread out at the feet like a map. Where there are several resistant strata, as in the case of the country surrounding Paris, an outspread lowland such as this represents the surface of the next lower resistant member of the series, and in turn rises gently to an edge overlooking another lowland. It may be compared to a nest of saucers of very thick china. In the Paris Basin the concentric rings of hills disappear altogether at the south, and they are not clearcut at the west. In contrast, the easterly hemicycle is marked off at intervals by no less than seven conspicuous *edges*. Repeating them once more the Vosges Mountains, although quite different in structure, present a pseudoform, in that the slope toward Paris is relatively gentle, whereas the east face is a steep fault-scarp, at the base of which the Rhine Rift Valley, some 1500 feet below, appears as another flat.

The Inner Paris Basin came into its own with the reconstitution of Europe which is associated with the folk migrations of Germanic tribes. For the Romans it had always lain a little offside. When the Franks, after making their way along the narrows of the North European Plain, reached the northern tabular uplands of the Paris Basin, they destroyed the last vestiges of Roman power near Soissons. In a few years they had traversed the inviting overland route which crosses the Seine at Paris, and had defeated the Visigoths near Tours (*i.e.*, on the Threshold of Poitou). Whereupon the natural focus of the newly won region, Paris, was made the official capital. Its functions must have been few, since the court moved with the king, and the Frankish kings lived a migratory life. Later, this land fell to vassals of the king, who removed his capital to Laon, superb defense point at the northern apex of the Inner Paris Basin.

THE ANCIENT ÎLE DE FRANCE

The Île de France in its beginnings was merely a group of feudal units which owed allegiance to the Frankish Emperors, and later to their successors, the French kings. Several of its rivals were larger and some were wealthier. But its focal position helped its rulers to obtain for themselves the royal crown, at first intermittently, alternating with the line of Charlemagne, afterwards by right of inheritance. This honor, although an asset in the end, was often a handicap in days of feudal ascendancy, since it awakened the jealousy of powerful vassals who were equals, sometimes superiors, of their master in every material power, and incited them to pit their combined strength against their hapless sovereign.

The territory of the Île fluctuated in the manner of feudal units, which had notoriously fluid boundaries, but throughout its early period its strategic axis was the hundred-mile course of the Seine within which that river receives the waters of all its chief tributaries. Downstream, the Oise marked the political boundary. The heart of political France is the pair of limestone uplands which flank the Seine.

On the left bank, *i.e.*, mainly to the southward of Paris, Beauce reaches a long arm toward Orléans. Beauce is high, dry, and treeless. Its few streams are sharply trenched, and the ground-water table lies well below the surface of the level upland. Fortunately the previous limestone is mantled with limon soil, retentive of moisture. This soil, absorbing a fair share of the well distributed rains, somewhat reduces the rapidity of runoff and makes the district just moist enough for wheat. The most extensive area of high physical uniformity in all the country west of the Rhine and the Alps, it has been occupied by farmers ever since neolithic man began to practice crude agriculture. East and west it is flanked by country more broken, dotted with lakelets, largely wooded, and progressively infertile, a sort of terrain which the French designate as *gâtine*, *i.e.*, waste. So characteristic is this of the land immediately east of Beauce that it goes by the name of Gâtinais. To the west, the fertile plain gradually gives way to spots of *gâtine*, and finally to the Hills of Perche. These constitute the inmost *edge* of the Paris Basin on this side, but an ill-marked one. Moreover, the alignment is concave outward, and so spoils the circular form which elsewhere characterizes the rims of the saucers. Between these less favoured lands, the smooth Beauce runs unbroken except by minor, narrow valleys to the Loire, where that river encroaches upon the Paris Basin. Without interruption from the beginning of the 7th century, Paris controlled the eastern half of Beauce. For good measure, it incorporated the Loire valley itself in the vicinity of Orléans, a strategic town both because it lies on the outside of the great bend of the river, and because there an island facilitates bridging the unruly current. The Île de France found a suitable southern boundary in the lake-dotted Sologne, immediately south of the Loire. There, wet clay soils, useless for fields, kept the population sparse and poor, and so provided a reasonably satisfactory zone for a stable boundary.

In the heart of Beauce lay the strength of the Dukes of France in the first century of their rule as kings. They lived mainly at Orléans, sometimes at Étampes, halfway between Orléans and Paris, more rarely at Senlis to the north of Paris (Map 9.2). The first of the long line of French kings bestowed the County of Paris upon a vassal, and soon after it fell into the hands of the Bishop of Paris, already well entrenched on the eastern half of the Île de la Cité (Map 9.3). For a long time the mainland bridgeheads were controlled by vassals, and the king rarely risked himself to these dangerous subordinates. More awkward still, a block of territory in unfriendly hands lay immediately south of Paris. In it Corbeil on the Seine, and Montlhéri, the strongest defense point on the road to Étampes, interrupted communication between the two major parts of the king's demesne and reduced the commercial value of both his major trade routes.

When once this seat of disaffection was incorporated into the king's lands, the holdings of the Count of Blois threatened France from the west. Blois, a little below Orléans on the Loire, is in fertile country, extending northward the full length and half the width of Beauce, which the king was compelled to share with his powerful vassal.

East and southeast of Paris lies Brie (Map 9.4), to a degree a smaller counterpart of Beauce. Its cavernous limestone is underlain at no great depth by less pervious strata. Hence the ground-water table is near enough the surface to permit meadows and pastures, as well as wheat. Western Brie bears the treasured limon soil, and has been farmed *ab origine*. The eastern half is a wet country, not unlike Western Beauce, abounding in lakes and forests, and nearly everywhere mantled with cold clay soil. Besides, much of it is hilly.

Just as Paris disputed with Blois over Beauce, so it disputed with Champagne for Brie. The ancient boundary corresponded closely with the line separating arable from forested Brie. In rainy medieval North Europe, before tile drainage and fertilizer were known, wet lands were superabundant. Hence the distinction between the two parts was even more pronounced than it seems today. This appears in the derogatory term implying a miserable country, which was used to designate the east—La Brie Pouilleuse. But had it not been for the feebleness of the early French kings and the potency of their great vassals of Champagne, the boundary might easily have been pushed out to include both halves of Brie, which is encircled on the south and east by a stiff military barrier: none other than the innermost of the concentric *edges* of the Paris Basin. This, sometimes known as the Cliff of the Isle of France, stands on an average more than 300 feet above the Champagne lowland, and has figured critically in every military campaign of the region's history, usually to the advantage of the power centered at Paris. Champagne of the middle ages ranked among the wealthiest countries of north Europe—not from its sparkling wine, which was not invented until the 18th century, but from trans-European trade which, after leaving the Saône Plain, followed the wide and easily traversed lowland east of the *edge*, before forking, in Champagne, westward toward Paris and the Lower Seine and northward toward the corridor of the Belgian lowland. On these lines the Romans had maintained their chief roads in the region, and medieval trade followed the same routes. So long as the master of this lucrative and growing but vulnerable resource (trade) was able, he would prefer to keep his overlord at the safe distance of western Brie, rather than to have his hostile castles overlooking the main trade route itself.

The remaining bit of immemorial French royal domain lies to the north of Paris, between the Marne and Oise tributaries of the Seine. This region is reminiscent of Brie, although the range of its relief is greater and dissection is more pronounced. It is divided into a drier and more arable west and a wetter, more rugged, and more wooded east. And the political boundary remained for a long period to accentuate this contrast in the terrain. The principal streams, beginning with the Marne, have carved flat and marshy valleys scores of feet below the upland levels. Because most of them flow west, each forms a military barrier of a sort, available equally to an invader of the Basin and to its defender. Between the Ourcq and the Oise rivers a ridge of sandstone, deeply wooded as such ridges almost invariably are, parallels these river defenses more than 300 feet above the plain, and helps to outline the ancient confines of the Île de France.

THE NUCLEUS OF THE LARGER FRANCE

Even in its earliest period the kingdom of France foreshadowed its nuclear quality. The location of Paris, although by no means central in the France of today, combines two of the salient characters of a capital. First, it is focal. Its site is a crossing of land and water routes. Its location is near the foregathering of a wide circle of navigable streams with their easy portage connections. Its arable surroundings, the region most easily incorporated and defended as well as most necessary to its livelihood, reached modestly outward to west, north, and east, but extended far to the south, in the direction of the bulk of the territory which it was one day to fashion into France. Besides being focal, it stands as near as a focal capital may to the weak eastern frontier. More specifically, it looks northeast down the broad corridor north of the Ardennes, where, between tumbled hills and boggy plain, the roads from the continental interior of Eurasia lie open.

Although the early Île de France fell short of the first prime military barrier provided by nature, and its later territorial growth has only crudely conformed to the several concentric rims of the Basin, yet the terrain furnished a succession of domiciles for the growing state. Each one could serve for a habitation until it was outgrown—until the concepts and methods of governance had become powerful and flexible enough to embrace successfully the next adjacent terrain and its inhabitants.

In this territorial and national expansion there was no sharp break in principle from the simple procedure current in the darkest ages, of joining three or four manors into a single unit. Because of its natural grouping of tiny environmental units into clusters, and the equally natural assemblage of those clusters into regions, and of the regions into combinations having reciprocal resources, Western Europe is the best conceivable incubator for the national state. And nowhere else in Western Europe is regionalism at once so diverse and so neat, as at the convergence of all the great avenues of Eurasian culture, in the blend of highland and lowland, of North Europe and South, which goes by the name of France. The instrument of political union in that area, the Île de France, is not an accident, but the favored core of the Paris Basin and of concentrically larger zones which it was able gradually to dominate.

The Paris Basin possesses the virtue of moderation. It is neither tiny nor huge; its soil varies from moderately fertile to moderately infertile; its mineral wealth consists of the commonplace rocks, sands and clays; its streams, although navigable, cannot float large boats; it lies adjacent to, but not squarely athwart the major routes of commerce, either by land or by sea. Above all, its successive naturally marked military barriers give repeated pause to the enemy, but must be defended if he is to be repulsed; and the successive naturally marked political boundaries serve only to give an expanding state necessary breathing spells, because beyond each one lies the enticing vision of the next promised land.

The most natural direction of French expansion would appear to be downstream. Disregarding meanders it is only about 150 miles by way of the Seine Valley from the ancient boundary of the Île de France at the confluence of the Oise, to the open sea; the navigable Seine invites trade, and trade is a powerful incentive to political union. The configuration of the land along the lower river is much the same as in the Île de France. Scattered along the upland on both sides of the Seine, and bordering the Norman coast, are notable districts of limon soil. For a time the coastal zone, penetrated by navigable valleys, traced by sea-roving Saxons and Northmen, was more strongly Germanized than the Île de France, and always the proximity of the sea gave to Normans an interest in fishing and seaborne trade not shared by its inland neighbor. When the duke of Normandy, vassal of France, became king of England and so peer of France, latent enmity flared up. For a time Normandy was a pawn between the two realms; then adjacence, increasing trade, and a common language, all brought to popular attention by intermittent, enforced union with France, laid the kindling of national union which was ignited by the flaming patriotism of Joan of Arc. Once Normans had come to feel themselves compatriots of the French, these two major components of the Seine Basin welded themselves into a firm political union.

To bring under the aegis of the Île de France the farspread territories of Aquitaine was a task more slowly accomplished. The separate and often hostile feudal units in the Middle Loire Basin had first to be linked permanently to France. Then came the long struggle with the south (the Midi)—less Germanized, speaking Provençal (almost another language), remote in thought and feeling from Paris, and ardently supporting its allegiance to its local lords, one of whom was also king of England. The religious protest, precursor of the Protestant Reformation, which broke out in the County of Toulouse, was at the same time a symbol of the Midi's resistance to domination from the North, and the excuse for the king to prosecute to bitter success his conquest of that hotbed of heresy. When the Protestant Reformation did at last irrepressibly embroil Europe, it was in the Midi that the Huguenots were powerful, and gave to the local leaders encouragement to rebel against their Parisian king.

Incorporation of the Midi within the French state means much more than conquest of territory and the elimination of dangerous rival overlords. Until the levelling Revolution of 1789, the Midi retained many of its individual customs and laws—vestiges of its longstanding independence. It can scarcely be doubted that if the French state had not recognized and compromised with these regional traditions, there would have been incessant friction and frequent revolts. During the centuries between the conquest of the Midi and the regimentation of France by the Revolutionary and Napoleonic governments, many of the sharp distinctions between the regions blurred, although lesser ones, traditions and practices which do no violence to national unity, persist even today.

The Rhône-Saône Basin was attached to France bit by bit, some of it at about the time of the conquest of Aquitaine, the rest much later. As a major line of trans-European trade, with branches leading both northeast down the Rhine and northwest into the Paris Basin, its control vitally concerned the rising powers of the north—increasingly so as trade multiplied. Its lowland arable core is small, and its disproportionate length lies broken into separate basins, connected but tenuously by the waterway. Numerous easy routes east and west emphasize its character as a corridor with many doors. Little wonder that it has rarely been politically unified, and never for long until the last fragment was incorporated into the French national state near the end of its era of territorial expansion.

THE PARIS BASIN AND EASTWARD

The expansion of the Île de France toward the northwest, west, and south was delayed long enough to permit the necessary ingestion of each "country" before a new advance was made. In this way, the regions inhabited by peoples closest akin in origin, traditions, and language to the denizens of the Inner Paris Basin, and therefore most easily assimilated, became integral parts of France. The distinctions which they retained were relict expressions of their regionality, and those which they lost were sacrificed in the interests of prosperity engendered by political union—wealth based on reciprocal use of diverse regional resources. Despite interruptions and repulses, the nuclear Île de France had multiplied its area manyfold by the time English rule in Normandy and Aquitaine collapsed. With exclusion of the English, it incorporated most of the lands southwest of a line projected from the Mediterranean base of the Maritime Alps through Paris to the Channel. The only recalcitrant exception was the peninsula of Brittany, where infertile crystalline hills had provided a refuge for harassed Celts ever since, a thousand years before, they had been rammed into this bit of farthest western Europe by Germanic tribes.[1]

Northeastward from this line the Île de France protruded, but still the boundary stood little more than 100 miles from the gates of Paris in its maximum reach northeast, and well under 200 miles to the southeast. So slight an advance in this quarter relative to

1. Even in the 20th century the people of Lower Brittany are not fully reconciled to France, and demand a measure of autonomy. Thus do culture and environment join in separatism.

the large increments of territory west and southward suggests either lack of incentive to conquest or powerful opposing forces. The shape of the bulge, when applied to a physical map, is seen to correspond closely to the drainage pattern of the Seine system and the concentric *edges* of the Paris Basin (Map 4.9).

The first severe tussle of the lords of Paris with their antean enemies to the eastward, who appear to derive inexhaustible energy from contact with central Europe, centered upon Champagne.

Some 60 miles south of the city the Inner Paris Basin is separated from fertile Beauce and sodden Gâtinais by an expanse of sandy plain which has been deeply wooded from time immemorial and today goes by the name, Forest of Fontainebleau. There the Seine breaks through the innermost edge on its way to Paris. Inconspicuous to the west where it fades into the level Beauce, the Cliff of the Isle of France begins immediately east of the Seine whence it sweeps in an almost perfect semicircle 220 miles to La Fère, northwest to Laon. Below the edge lies a plain so lightly etched by the few rivers which cross it, so nearly unbroken by remnants of superior strata, and so uniformly underlain by porous limestone that its dry, featureless surface makes it by turns the favored highway for commerce and the inevitable theater for clashing armies. This is the Champagne Pouilleuse, the "miserable openland," sparsely peopled and good only for grazing sheep and growing pinewood.

The least unproductive section lies immediately southeast of Brie. For about 75 miles the Seine flows at the base of the *edge* which limits Brie, and which there stands 330 feet above the river valley, its even crest only slightly nicked here and there by a short tributary or by unequal erosion. The gently sloping surface of the lowland rises 800 feet in 50 miles to the next *edge*, which, like its neighbor to the north, stands about 300 feet above the succeeding lowland. Between the peat-covered valley of the Seine and the sandy, wooded crest of the second *edge*, plain is succeeded by gentle hills. Trenching the height and crossing the whole width of the backslope, the Yonne River makes an easy route from the hills overlooking the Saône plain all the way to its confluence with the Seine, not far above Fontainebleau. This route the Romans knew and utilized, and today it is traversed by the main line of railway between Paris and the Rhône Basin. Firmly entrenched in western Brie on the Cliff of the Isle, and commanding the easy sortie made by the Seine, the French kings won this part of the Champagne as the first of their possessions eastward of the nuclear Île de France.

Control of the remaining Champagne Pouilleuse was long delayed. The 125 miles of the east-facing innermost escarpment between the Aube-Seine confluence and the Aisne River, although appearing little broken when viewed from below, is cut through to the level of the Champagne by four streams and rather deeply notched by another, now vanished. He who can defend these passes can dominate the Champagne; and conversely, he who can take the passes holds the key to Paris. Although transected by valleys, this segment of the escarpment is higher on the average than the sections to the south and the north of it. It culminates dramatically in the massive bastion which pushed out into the plain between the Marne and the Vesle rivers—the Mountain of Reims. Near its outer end this promontory rises 550 feet above the adjacent plain. In the reentrant to the south, Épernay crowds into a cranny of the escarpment, safely above the marshy floodplain of the Marne. At the northern foot of its mountain, Reims spreads out beside the Vesle, in a vestibule of lowland screened from the open plain by a unique group of outlying hills.

Forty or fifty miles to the eastward the porous limestone of the Champagne Pouilleuse rises to form the second concentric *edge*, but, north of the Seine, reaching only about 150 feet above the narrow lowland beyond. This plain, in sharp contrast to its western neighbor, is mantled with clay holding numerous lakes and marshes and insuring the greenest of summer landscapes. Thus it has earned the sobriquet La Champagne Humide, the "wet openland." In spite of low relief, its marshy surface interferes with movement, and its only fertile parts are the alluvial valleys. Each principal stream, where it crosses the *edge*, has given rise to a combined market and defense town—Rethel on the Aisne, Vitry-le François on the Marne, Troyes on the Seine, and Joigny on the Yonne.

East of Champagne the country becomes

increasingly difficult for north-south movement until the Rhine Valley is reached. Hence the significance of the terrain of the Counts of Champagne lay in its utility as a highway of trade.

Where the Seine cuts through the second *edge*, Troyes gathers into a node all the highways from the east and south. No less than three separate routes to the Saône Plain meet there, and the easiest, although not the most direct, road between Paris and the upper Rhine and its western tributaries leaves the Seine Valley at Troyes. On this road grew up a chain of fairs which shifted about but together maintained a year round emporium patronized by merchants from all Europe. Two of these were in Troyes itself. Two others held at Provins, the metropolis of Eastern Brie, and on the route which led almost to the gates of Paris before leaving the territory of Champagne. The remaining two were at the confines of the country—one at Lagny, on the threshold of the Île de France, located at a narrows favorable for crossing the marshy Marne Valley on the way from Champagne to Paris; the other at Bar-sur-Aube, which guards a principal water-gate through the fourth *edge*, in the eastern precincts of the count's holdings.

Northward from Troyes the great trade route to the North European Plain and England takes its way obliquely across the dry Champagne by way of Arcis-sur-Aube, Châlons-sur-Marne, and Reims. From Reims roads fork to the narrows of the Channel, to the lower Rhine, and to the Lower Seine. From Châlons the Marne Valley leads to Épernay and Paris. Fairs less famous and prolonged, but well attended, were held at the four principal nodal sites on this route—Arcis, Châlons, Épernay, and Reims. All the Champagne fairs were protected by special legislation, administered by a corps of magistrates whose sole business it was. Roads were protected so far as possible from bandits, and canal building was undertaken to improve navigation on the Seine.

Waxing wealthy on trade in a land mostly too dry or too wet to farm, the lords of Champagne held territory outside Champagne and Brie from which they derived their title. Eastward these holdings reached into the Meuse Valley and crossed the line between the Kingdom of France and the Empire of the Germans. In the west for a time they included Blois, with half of Beauce, and Touraine, thus controlling the route to Aquitaine. Faced on the east with wealth flowing along busy trade routes, and on the west with wealth skimmed from fertile fields, the kings of France appeared to be no match for their powerful vassals of Champagne. In the long run the weakness of scattered holdings appeared, when the western fiefs were lost to Champagne. Seventy years later a lucky marriage brought to the French king Champagne itself, together with the eastern part of the Inner Paris Basin.

Either from a desire to deflect the trade to Paris, or because any agrarian state notoriously misunderstands the requirements of commerce, the new ruler forbade Flemish merchants to attend the fairs of Champagne. Although this was a staggering blow, the fairs continued to function for more than three centuries. A part of what the Champagne lost, the Île de France gained, and in time it came to foster trade as sedulously as its rival had done. By adding commerce to agriculture as a second mainstay of its people, the constitution of the French monarchy proved itself supple enough to continue to grow and to thrive in a radically changing political atmosphere.

It is oddly perverse that the vital addition to France of Champagne and its bordering *edges* was accomplished without battles, for the Dry Champagne is the age-old theater of war no less than of trade. For the Romans it served a triple purpose: highway to the Channel at its narrowest crossing; base line for the frontier garrisons along the Rhine; and main trade route between the Mediterranean and the north. When Roman Gaul was being shattered by armed populations wedging in from the east, many of the sledge-hammer blows fell in this critical zone. On its open, dry flat Attila deployed his horde of horsemen from the grassland of eastern Europe in making his final bid for control of western Europe, and was defeated.

Toward the end of the middle ages, in the long continued assaults upon France that awoke in the French a sense of nationality, and thus transformed a feudal territory into a national state, the Champagne battleground was again chosen, first by the English, then by the Burgundians and their successor, the Hapsburg Emperor. Three centuries more and Napoleon lost his imperial crown on these same fields. The latest chapter was written only the other day, in repeated battles between August 1914 and October 1918, the first and last of which were the two most decisive on the western front and therefore the turning points of the whole World War.

In all these battles the strategy has been similar. To enter Paris from the east, an army must control the escarpment of the Inner Basin. To obtain this control has always involved fighting on the Champagne lowland. Although Paris often has been threatened and occasionally taken, its possession of the strategic interior position coupled with its admirable natural defenses, have given it an advantage which in the long run of history has made it repeatedly the political core of the western apex of the Eurasian triangle.

Physically and historically the north-facing segment of the Inner Edge and its apron of dry lowland is intimately linked with that part which looks eastward. Politically it has a special niche which requires separate treatment.

Barely 50 miles of high ground marks the last stand of the *edge* between the Aisne and the Oise. All the north part of the Inner Basin is carved into blocks by the several right-bank branches of the Oise. Each block maintains its standard elevation of about 300 feet above the valleys. To dislodge an army posted above these marshy river trenches is a herculean task. As the World War proved, possession of one or more of these outlying military barriers does not necessarily devolve control of the Inner Basin, because either the south or the north margin of each block may be fortified for defense. At the salient where the trend of the *edge* alters from north-south to east-west, stands the Chemin des Dames, a ridge 15 miles long and half as broad. To the west is the larger and less steeply cliffed Forêt de St. Gobain. In the stream-carved depression between them stand two eminences, small and flat-topped—true mesas. The one in advance, a long sentinel on the plain, is crowned by the most conspicuous defense-point city in the whole Paris Basin. This is Laon, fortress and capital of the Frankish kings when Paris was vassal territory. From Laon they directed the struggle for supremacy which was at last won by the upstart island in the Seine with its nodal location. Physical outliers of the Inner Paris Basin, Laon and its neighbouring heights became part of the royal domain—political and defensive outposts of the Île de France. Between the two lay fiefs of independent vassals, entrenched in the hilliest part of the Inner Basin. Long before they were added to the royal domain, the French kings had pushed their holdings northward along the less broken sandy lowland bordering the Oise River, as far as Noyon and its protective screen of mesas. From them—most northwesterly outposts of the Cliff of the Isle of France—and from the disjoined heights of Laon, lies spread the plain of North Europe, a lowland generally below 600 feet elevation which from the Pyrenees sweeps unbroken and ever broadening until it becomes the vast expanse of Russia.

The Rhine Basin and Buffer Politics

Eastward along this narrow part of the plain the Romans pressed their advantage over the Gauls (Map 9.5). From the northeast came the Franks, pushing outward from the Rhineland of their origin without losing contact with it, thereby assimilating the Latin culture to their own without destroying either. Wars fought on this plain, rather than in the American or Asiatic colonies, determined the allocation of the 18th century colonial empire among the maritime states of Western Europe. A little south of Brussels, in the transition zone between Germanic and Romanic speech, is Waterloo, where the French ambition to dominate the Lower Rhine was abruptly checked in a single battle. A hundred years later, a hundred miles to westward, in the same transition belt, the German ambition to destroy French power was slowly mired in four years of muddy trench warfare which pivoted on the low ridge of Messines. No wonder this part of the Plain between the low limestone hills northwest of Laon and the Rhine Valley where it is flattest and where it narrows to a corridor 125 miles wide, has been called "the cockpit of Europe." It has been a battleground throughout history, at times for years without interruption.

It is not only in the strategy of battles that the region has been significant to a degree unwarranted by its size. Much of it is closely dotted with farm villages, among which sprawl numerous large cities. The population

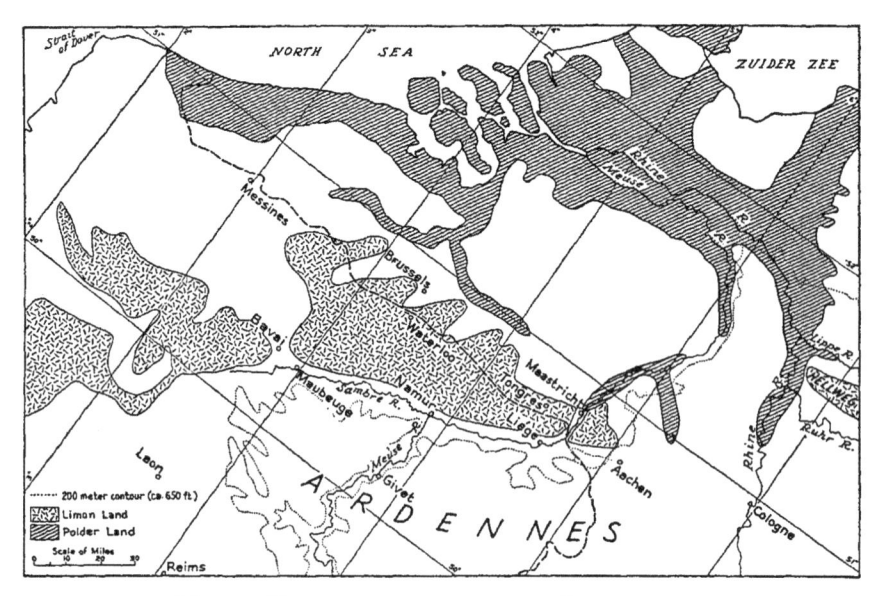

Map 9.5 THE NARROWS OF THE NORTH EUROPEAN PLAIN
The zone of coastal sand dunes is too narrow to be shown on this scale.

for some 800 years has been the densest in Europe, persisting in its lead throughout all the changes of agricultural, commercial, and industrial revolutions. This points to a unique combination of favoring circumstances—arable soil, a major crossroads for trade, and raw materials for manufacturing.

The coast is fringed by a band of sand dunes, rarely more than three miles wide, and averaging no more than one. Because the surface soil is dry, while potable water may be had anywhere by digging a shallow hole, this line can be used as a routeway. Because the surface is pitted and the sand makes heavy going, it is rarely so used. The dunes fend the sea from a considerable expanse of river-borne alluvium and clay soil which lies below or not far above high tide. With the aid of dikes along the rivers and innumerable drainage canals which crisscross the almost literally flat plain, this wet land has been converted into farms intensively worked and highly productive. This Flemish region was the first district of Europe to emerge from the crude farm system of the middle ages, and ever since it has been a rich larder for townsfolk of the vicinity and for invading armies. As a passway, however, it is handicapped by muddy roads, numerous bridges across the lesser waterways, and unbridged main streams.

South of the polders which have been reclaimed from the outer delta of the Meuse and Rhine, stretch sandy heaths, largely wooded even today and scantily settled. Near the western tip of the Ardennes, such a forest touched the hill country until the later middle ages. Elsewhere a belt of fertile limon soil lies between this heathland and the rugged, forested Ardennes. Almost straight, gentle in gradients, free from heavy forest and sodden marsh, this has been the traditional passway along this narrows in the plain of North Europe. At its eastern end it focuses on Cologne, the major crossing of the Rhine between the gorge and the delta of that stream. In the west it branches to the Strait of Dover, to the Lower Seine Valley, and to the Paris Basin. A main Roman road traversed the woodland about Bavai, in order to follow the open belt via Tongres, crossing the Meuse at Maastricht, and passing through Aachen. This broad highway is supplemented by an alternative route, the narrow but smooth road of the valleys of the Sambre and its master-stream the Meuse, a nearly straight trench cut into the Ardennes near their northern margin, past the fortress towns Maubeuge and Namur, to Liége, and thence across a spur of hills to Cologne.

As farms replaced forest and marsh, the region traversed by these routes was breathed

The Territorial Evolution of France

upon by all the currents of trade and politics stirring in Western Europe, and it became the first seat of manufacturing north of the Mediterranean coastlands. A list of the towns of Flanders is a catalog of textiles—named from the place of their origin. Manufactures, besides creating new wealth, increased trade and stirred the farmers to make their acres yield more abundantly. Grown rich, the cities excited the cupidity of all the princes of Europe. When the Industrial Revolution altered the meaning of *manu*facturing, the district was found to lie upon excellent coal. Thereby it kept its lead among manufacturing regions of the world. Long bandied about by vicissitudes of war and politics, the Low Countries have occasionally been united, more usually divided. Profiting from their border location, they have been able to establish independence of their larger neighbors.

For the past hundred years most of the strategic corridor has belonged to the Belgian monarchy, leaving the ends in the hands of two major powers. Independence in the Low Countries, and particularly Belgium, rests upon a stalemate between their powerful neighbors—a stalemate which has been maintained by the third interested power, England, whenever either of the belligerents domiciled at the ends of the Flemish corridor threatens to overthrow the balance.

The complementary nature of the Inner Paris Basin and the concentric Champagne has been established. East of the West Champagne the serried belts of lowland rising to an *edge* overlooking the next lowland are repeated. They are, however, less neatly arranged than their counterparts to the west, partly because they are less continuous and less uniform, partly because among them lies the watershed between the Seine and the Rhine basins. All this country has traditionally been quasi-independent of either the Paris Basin or the German lowlands. Frequently during the feudal age a local lord effectively unified a territory part of which he held (according to feudal law) from the king of France and part from the emperor of Germany. An irrepressible urge to create a long narrow country covering the Rhône-Rhine trade route, with this hill-land as its core, has repeatedly been quenched by the rival claims of the Rhône-Champagne route, supported by the well-manned natural defenses of the Paris Basin. It has been easier to shatter the longitudinal trading state, sprawling along its highway of commerce and open to attack on both sides, than to bring the many bits into which it breaks into cohesive union with either neighbor. Most of the area is now grafted into France, but scars of the prolonged struggle still appear in autonomous Luxemburg and in the repeated transfer of Alsace and Lorraine between France and Germany, to say nothing of the Low Countries and Switzerland.

At the north, four of the *edges* (Argonne to Côtes de Moselle) converge in the vicinity of the Charleville just south of the Ardennes Massif (Map 9.4). Between the two uplands lies a hilly east-west route which traverses Luxemburg and extreme southern Belgium, and enters the valley of the Meuse near Sedan, where that stream flows along the north face of the clustered escarpments. From the Champagne to the Rhine the Romans maintained a main road along this passageway, and routes follow it today, somewhat interrupted by its division among four nations. Southwards from this convergence the Argonne, less than 70 miles long, extends its narrow but forbidding, sandy, and forested bulk. In that distance it is trenched to the level of the adjacent plain in several places. The great route from northern Lorraine to Paris proceeds through one of these notches rather than digressing about the south end of the range only 10 miles away. No bar to passage in peacetime, the Argonne can become a formidable barrier to armies if only the notches are adequately guarded. The next *edge* (the fourth, counting from Paris) is low and the adjacent lowland is inconspicuously set off from it. Unlike the Argonne, it extends well round into the southeast quadrant of the Basin. Because of its insignificance as a surface feature, no first-flight trading towns have grown up along it, although it has served the exigencies of military commanders more than once. In its northern half, it forms the watershed between the Seine and Rhine basins. Its southerly extension is crossed by several tributaries of the Seine.

If this *edge* is the least noteworthy of the series, the next one to the east (the fifth from Paris), ranks with the Cliff of the Isle of France. From the north, where it leaves its easterly neighbors, it swings in a wide semicircle and transgresses into the basin of the

Loire River. To the south it forms no notable feature of the landscape, but to the north it rises to a great rampart. The Meuse, tributary to the Rhine, crosses it twice in a deeply entrenched valley, and eastward of the river the *edge*, called here the Côtes de Meuse, stands 500 feet above the Woevre, a plain as flat and as wide as the Champagne Pouilleuse, but mantled with clay, and therefore lake-studded, marshy, and verdant. Midway the *edge* is traversed by the main east-west route. Below, where this route crosses the Meuse, lies Verdun. Southwestward from the trench through which the Meuse passes behind its Côtes, the elevation of the *edge* diminishes to 300 feet or less, its eminence not always clearly distinguishable from the other hills in that generally rather rugged region.

The next (sixth) *edge* closely duplicates its neighbor. Swinging sharply southward, 800 feet high at the bend near Thionville, it likewise becomes entangled with a river, the Moselle, which flows at its base, now east and now west of the ridge, for nearly 100 miles. There the heights rise 500 feet above the lowland, which, about as wide as the Woevre, is rolling country and easy to traverse. Where the Moselle first crosses the *edge*, the city of Nancy guards a double door made by the Moselle and Meurthe. Inside, on the sharp bend, and screened by outliers of the Côtes de Meuse, lies Toul on the road between Strasbourg and the Seine Valley. Fifty miles north, where the Moselle again cuts the Côtes, Metz is guardian city. Verdun, Toul, Nancy, Metz—these strategic sites on the complex pattern of ridge and river are leads in the drama of life as played in this borderland between Western and Central Europe.

Southward the *edge* continues its well-marked course. Langres, standing squarely on a conspicuously abrupt crest, is close to the headwaters of the Marne and its route from Paris. Dijon, ancient capital of Burgundy, lies on the Saône Plain at the base of the bluff, where a stream has cut an easy route through the *edge*, here called the Côte d'Or, to the headwaters of the Yonne. Farther south the *edge* merges into the steep eastern face of the Central Massif.

Eastward from the Côtes de Moselle, beyond Metz and Nancy, lies a vale a few miles wide, crossed by the Moselle and its tributaries and largely in fields, although patched with forest where the soils are wet and heavy. This dip slope rises to a seventh *edge*, more irregular than any of those farther west, and cut by the streams into segments known by different names. Tongues and outliers of the heights project eastward between the valleys, forming natural bastions for mounting defenses, and permitting their defenders to rake the intervening vales along which the routes pass. One mass, the Côtes de Delme halfway between Metz and Nancy, is higher than the rest because it retains a cap of the strata which crown the Moselle *edge*. It rises steeply on both east and west flanks. In 1871 the German boundary was drawn to include this height, to serve as a defensive screen for Metz.

Beyond the seventh *edge* the country is rolling, characterized by minor ridges and deeply entrenched streams, and covered with clay and sand soils. This is the Plain of Lorraine, rising not too steeply to the Vosges Mountains, a mass of crystalline rocks, deeply dissected and covered with dense spruce forest. The eastern face of the Vosges marks a fault line, which from the east appears as a formidable mountain wall, reaching a maximum of 2100 feet elevation above the flat floor of the Rhine Valley. Toward the north end a defile permits road, canal, and main railroad to cross to Strasbourg. Still farther north the Gate of Lorraine, a rolling upland between the Vosges and the Ardennes, opens into the fertile heart of Germany, where the lower end of the Rhine Rift Valley spreads eastward into the confluence area of the Main and Rhine. By this broad, open way German armies invaded France in 1870 and 1914. At the south, the Vosges drop abruptly to the Burgundian Gate, an almost level passway between the upper end of the Rhine Rift Valley and the Saône Plain. It is the natural highway of trade from the Mediterranean to Central Europe. It was the inviting door which led the Romans to the country of the Germans, and which a few centuries later led the first German invaders into Roman Gaul —the Alemanni, a tribe which in the French tongue designates all Germans today.

From this corner of the Saône Plain Lorraine can be reached by way of alternative routes through the rugged Monts Faucilles. These routes converge upon Épinal, where the Moselle enters the Lorraine Plain.

The Eastern Boundary of France Today[2]

The Vosges constitute the last outpost of France on the east. Across the Rift Valley of the Rhine their counterpart, the Black Forest, presents a forbidding face to the west. For a short time the Romans controlled the whole Rift Valley and the mountains between which it lies, and the several "middle kingdoms" of the Rhône-Rhine trade route have forged but never permanently welded the two highlands into political unity. Today, with France and Germany centered well to the west and east, the Rift Valley is a borderland, not a coreland. It is untenable so long as an unfriendly power controls the heights immediately above. Alsace therefore goes with the Vosges and Baden with the Black Forest. The outlines of those two historic units faithfully portray their military strategy, and the marshy banks of the Rhine constitute the most clearly marked boundary in the whole zone. Contrarily, the river itself is a bond to those who occupy the adjacent lowlands and use its easily navigated current. Here, as nearly everywhere east of Paris, trade and war function in opposition on the same terrain.

The eastern boundary of France is unstable. It has always marked the zone in which concurrent forces have at the moment reached stalemate. During the feudal period the minute subdivision of landholdings, and the complex and often shadowy political connection between vassal territory and the king's domain, made a zonal boundary fitting and functional. For centuries the border was in constant flux. As communication became swifter and more regular, a linear and permament boundary became the goal. Traders desired it to guarantee minimum cost and annoyance in crossing from country to country. Kings in remote Paris no longer had to depend on the initiative of competent and often disloyal vassals to protect their borders, but could dispatch and maintain armies of their own along the frontier. Civil administration was extended to include the whole state, and became more and more centralized. Feudal quasi-sovereignties were suppressed into provinces. Improvements in geodesy made it possible to survey linear boundaries accurately, demarcation along the east side of France being the first line completed pursuant to the general readjustment of boundaries after Napoleon's downfall in 1815. (The linear boundary had been accepted in principle a century earlier.)

While the political *line* has succeeded the political *zone*, permanency has not supplanted flux. In the whole broad band of the boundary zone there is no belt so inhospitable as to be unpeopled. Even the mountains and hills modify the distribution of population surprisingly little. Rather, they are features significant primarily in military maneuvers, secondarily in the pattern of routes. The unprejudiced foreigner cannot point to a place where nature has unmistakably marked a boundary, and the gateways between the principal mountain masses are zones of such gradual human transition that the boundary arbitrarily cleaves linguistic units, cuts towns off from their trade territory, and describes lines most of which are historical accidents. At the south base of the Alps, along the Mediterranean coast, France has pushed eastward into Italian-speaking settlements. North of the Alps, where the Rhône Vale marks the transition between Alps and Jura, a long tongue of French speech belongs to Switzerland. The political boundary near the west end of Lake Geneva, severs the city Geneva from much of its natural trade territory. An attempt to solve the problem has created free zones for trade, but the solution is only partial and attempts are frequently made to move the economic boundary eastward to coincide with the political line. Between the Jura and the Vosges the Burgundian Gate marks the border between French and German speech, and all of lowland Alsace, alternately French and German in government, has remained for centuries Germanic in language. Between Vosges and Ardennes jumbled terrain goes hand-in-hand with mingled languages. The Saar Basin lies squarely in the Lorraine Gate. A plebiscite in 1935 ranged that district conclusively with Germany, after a decade and a half of special administration for the economic benefit of France. In general the German language overlaps the present political border, just as French overlapped the border between 1871 and 1918. The hilly lane which leads westward from the Lorraine Gate between the converging *edges* of the Paris Basin and the crystalline Ardennes Massif, is occupied by French-speaking people

---

2. [Editors' Note: This refers to France's pre-World War II boundary.]

except in its eastern end. From this point to the North Sea the interlacing of linguistic borders (German, French, and Flemish) with political boundaries (Luxembourg, Belgium, and France) traces an intricate pattern. Over an airline distance of 60 miles the Franco-Belgian boundary cuts through the midst of French-speaking people in order to follow high ground along the southern margin of the Ardennes. Where the Meuse furrows its deep trench through the massif, the Wedge of Givet pierces the side of Belgium, its point resting on an abrupt hill, military guardian of French interests. The length of the wedge crudely measures the age-old flux of political and ecclesiastical suzerainty along the whole front in dispute between the powers of the *edges* and those of the coastal lowland. The Plain between the Ardennes and the sea, least defined of all the eastern gates of France, is crossed by a political line which enters Flemish country near the coast.

The Unity of France

National unity burns as vigorously in France as in any other country, thanks to the long continued effort necessary to combine a number of distinct regions and to achieve and maintain an eastern boundary which the terrain made possible but never inevitable. The unitary form of government and the highly centralized administration of the state are concomitants of this tireless striving for territorial cohesion. Only in outer Celtic Brittany and in borderland Germanic Alsace are there groups which demand autonomy.

The part played by the nuclear Paris Basin in the long struggle to weld the lowlands into a single state has been crowned by a radial pattern of communication lines which is both the expression and the symbol of Paris as the hub of France.

It would be flying in the face of the long view of history to assert that French solidarity, forged of diverse regions, is invincible. It may be safe to expect that it will endure so long as the emotion of patriotism is identified with that group of physical units which we call France, and so long as the area wields the power to maintain its independence of potential enemies.

10

The City as a Center of Change: Western Europe and China

RHOADS MURPHEY[*]

Every sedentary society has built cities, for even in a subsistence economy essential functions of exchange and of organization (both functions dealing with minds and ideas as much as with goods or with institutions) are most conveniently performed in a central location on behalf of a wider countryside. The industrial revolution has emphasized the economic advantages of concentration and centrality. But is it true to say that change, revolutionary change, has found an advantage in urbanization; in concentration and in numbers? The city has instigated or led most of the great changes in Western society, and has been the center of its violent and non-violent revolutions. In western Europe the city has been the base of an independent entrepreneur group which has successfully challenged and broken the authority of the traditional order. In China, while cities with the same universal economic functions arose, they tended until recently to have the opposite effect on the pattern of change. China has consistently reasserted itself as a single political unit, but it is otherwise the appropriate qualitative and quantitative counterpart of Europe, and provides a reasonable basis for comparison. China and Europe have been the two great poles of world civilization, and an examination of the different roles which their cities played may help to elucidate other differences between them.

The following generalized and capsulized discussion aims only to suggest this difference, as an example of what might be made of an approach to the study of society through an analysis of the city's role in the process of change.[1] By cutting a familiar pie in another way we may arrive at useful insights. . . . In distinguishing between European and Chinese civilization, we must of course assume a complex multiplicity of causes, many of which may elude us, and many of which may have little or nothing to do with geography. The distinctions and the arguments which follow do not imply that this basic fact is disregarded, but they pursue the matter from a point of view which has frequently been neglected and which may be suggestive of important factors.

European Cities

The cities of western Europe have been, at

Reprinted from the *Annals* of the Association of American Geographers, Volume XLIV, December 1954, by permission of the author and publisher.

[*] Rhoads Murphey (1919–) is Professor of Geography and in the Center for Chinese Studies at The University of Michigan.

[1]. This is not a new idea. There are many other and older applications of it.

least since the high middle ages, centers of intellectual ferment; of economic change; and thus, in time, of opposition to the central authority. They became rebels in nearly every aspect of their institutional life. It was trade (and to a somewhat lesser extent specialized manufacturing) which made them strong enough to maintain their challenge to the established order. Their spirit of ferment was the spirit of a new group, urban merchant-manufacturers, which could operate from a base large and rich enough to establish increasingly its own rules. This setting tended to ensure that the universities, which grew up in cities originally for convenience and centrality, would frequently nourish skepticism, heresy, and freedom of enquiry.[2] Even where they did not overtly do so, the concentration of literacy and learning in the cities was a stimulus to dissent.

Most of the cities which rose out of the cultural and social chaos following the destruction of Roman unity and preceding the development of a new national unity grew in answer to new conditions, for northwest Europe was ideally situated for trade. Most of them were in their origins much older than this, and had begun as administrative, military, or ecclesiastical centers. But a score of major rivers, navigable and free from floods, silting, or ice throughout the year in this mild maritime climate, led across the great European plain to the open sea; the peninsular, indented nature of the coast critically heightened mobility. The invitation which this presented to inter-European trade furthered the ascendancy of the commercial function. The shift of commerce and associated urbanism from the Mediterranean to northwest Europe seems to have begun before the Age of the Discoveries, notably in the Hansa towns and in Flanders. This may be in part a reflection of the mobility inherent in the lands around the Baltic and North Seas, once they had learned from the Mediterranean the lessons of commerce and absorbed the civilizing influences of this earlier developed area. In any case, these northern cities came to be dominated by trader-manufacturers.

[2]. Oxford and Cambridge, as rural universities, help to enforce this point. They were proverbially conservative, their most important job the training of students for the ministry. Spain's distinction from western Europe on this and nearly every other point raised is merely a reminder of the old aphorism "Africa begins at the Pyrenees."

Trade was a heady diet, and enabled urban merchants to command cities which had originally been administrative creations. While the cities did not alone destroy feudalism, they owed much of their prosperity and independence to its decline: freer trade, wider exchange, and failing power of the landed mobility. And their very growth as rival power bases accelerated the collapse of the old feudal order.

As the growth of national unity progressed, under the institutional and emotional leadership of monarchy, an alliance of convenience between king and city arose which met the crown's demands for funds and the city's demand for representation. Urban merchants had the money to support the king in his foreign wars and in his struggle with the divisive domestic ambitions of the nobility and the church. In return the city received an increasing voice in the affairs of state, through representation in parliaments, and indirectly through the making of policy in which the throne was obliged to follow. But while this alliance of revenue in exchange for concessions was one of mutual interest, its ultimate result was the strengthening of the urban commercial sector until it overthrew or emasculated the monarchy, and with it the traditional order as a whole. Having helped the king to power over the nobility, the city achieved a *modus vivendi* with him which left it in control of the affairs vital to it. As a current reminder of the development of urban independence, "the city" of London retains its originally hard-won privilege of excluding the reigning monarch, who is also excluded from the House of Commons, in part the city's creation and in part its weapon. To a certain extent the king, and even the nobility, were willing to go along with the process of economic change instigated by the city since they profited from it as the principal source of wealth in which they were often investors as well as tax collectors. But the new values which the city emphasized, and their institutional expression, were in direct conflict with the traditional society based on land; the city repeatedly bred overt revolutionary movements designed to establish its new order as the national way of life.

As centers of trade, the cities were free of the land and of its social and political limitations embodied in the institutions of post-Roman society. They developed their own law which was in differing degrees independent of the traditional, rural law. Their institutions were self-made, and they were not beholden to the traditional system which they challenged. The companies and corporations which the merchants organized went far beyond the scope of guilds in their successful attempt to order most of the social and economic fabric (instead of being limited to a trade-union function, as the guilds of China predominantly were). Traditional guilds were overlaid with new merchant organizations, or were clothed with new functions and powers, although some of the older guilds remained as conservative or retarding influences. The economic institutions which arose concurrently were also new-made sources of strength: banking, letters of credit, private property, interest, speculation and investment, representing needs and ideas which were almost wholly foreign to the traditional society of the countryside, and which were the accompaniment of an ever-widening trade. For the invitation to commercial expansion overseas was as strong in Europe's geography as the earlier invitation to trade among the lands surrounding the Baltic, Mediterranean, and North Seas. A leading agent of this process was necessarily the city, where trade flowed through break-in-bulk points such as the mouths of the Rhine or the English ports facing the Channel. Merchant corporations for overseas trade became the strongest and most progressive, or revolutionary, of the city's agents. Interestingly, the original charter of the British East India Company stated that "gentlemen" (by which was meant the landed gentry) "shall be excluded" from membership.

The city was the natural center of political change as it had been of economic change. The growth of modern Europe may be regarded as the steady progress of a new class of urban traders and manufacturers toward a position of control in a society and economy which their own enterprise had largely created. It was they who had realized the potential of Europe's location for world trade, and they who had developed and applied the technological and economic tools which made Europe the center of the world. The destruction of the old pattern was implicit in this process, and also implicit was the revolutionary expression, by the cities, of their claim to political power. City-country alliances were formed, and the dissident groups from the country often bore the brunt of the effort, since they were the more numerous, as well as sharing in the spoils. But the city was in the van, and even diverted or perverted rural dissent and rural force to its own ends; leadership and money were frequently more decisive than numbers. It is of course true that at least in England this city-country alliance left and perhaps still leaves the landed gentry with prestige and thus with considerable power, while it left wealth with the urbanites. Characteristically this wealth was used to acquire land and gentry status. This balance of advantage was particularly pertinent in the matter of parliamentary representation.

Revolutionary changes are nearly always the work of an alliance of groups, but the history of modern Europe is suggestive of the city's key role, despite the recurrent blurring of city-country distinctions. The first great modern revolution, in seventeenth century England, was the work of a city-country alliance, but London was mainly Puritan, and the outcome might be regarded as the victory of urban merchants and their country confreres over the traditional authoritarian alliance of cavalier and peasant based on the land.[3] Two centuries later Manchester and Birmingham had joined London in the final stages of the contest between urban "radicalism" and country "conservatism," epitomized in the struggle over the Corn Laws, the Reform Bills, free trade, and the Manchester School. By this time cotton textiles had well supplanted woollen textiles as the chief manufacturing industry; since it came relatively late it was not greatly hampered by guild restrictions, as wool had been; it established itself in Manchester, which as a then unincorporated town lacked formalized controls. It may irritate many readers as a loose generalization, but still seems worth stating for argument, that representative government and the industrial revolution, perhaps modern Europe's two most significant products, were created by the city. The Low Countries provide as good an illustration of this as does England.

[3]. Generalization on matters such as this is particularly hazardous. A recent study has cast serious doubt on these commonly accepted alignments: see D. H. Pennington and Douglas Brunton, *Members of the Long Parliament* (London, 1953).

In France the picture was less clear since urban merchant-manufacturers were less prominent in the national economy. Even so, it was Paris which created and carried the revolution. Paris used peasant distress and rebellion, but was never dethroned by it. One may say that Paris later destroyed Charles X and Louis Philippe. By this time, however, the Napoleonic land reform had given the peasant a stake in the status quo and helped to keep him a conservative counter-influence to the city, after his revolutionary ardour of the 1790's had served its purpose and cooled. Thus, in part, is derived the country's role in the destruction of the Second Republic and the Paris Commune, "radical city movements." Across the Rhine these distinctions become increasingly blurred, as for example in the Peasant War in early Reformation Swabia and Franconia. In eastern Europe it is difficult to draw distinctions between city and country, or to find an independent urban-based group living on trade and challenging the existing order. Nevertheless even in twentieth century Russia, while the Soviet revolution was in part carried by peasant groups, leadership remained in the urban intellectual group which had instigated the change.

In northwest Europe, which is our concern here, the city has been a consistent seat of radicalism. This is not to overlook the recurrent Jacqueries which in every society have been the desperate recourse of an oppressed peasantry. But in the West these have often been closer to reaction than to revolution—the peasants were demanding the restoration of the status quo ante, not the establishment of a new order. Where they did attack the old order it was characteristically on specific points, such as Wat Tyler's demand in fourteenth-century England for the disendowment of the church. The same pattern is apparent in rural opposition in America, in uprisings like the Whiskey Rebellion or in political parties like the Populists. The removal of abuses does not necessarily mean revolutionary change, despite the violence or the "levelling" sentiments which usually characterized rural dissidence.

CHINESE CITIES

In China, while the peasant and the countryside were in some respects like the West, the city's role was fundamentally different. Chinese cities were administrative centers. With few exceptions this function dominated their lives whatever their other bases in trade or manufacturing. Their remarkably consistent, uniform plan, square or rectangular walls surrounding a great cross with gates at each of the four arms, suggests their common administrative creation and their continued expression of this function. Local defensive terrain, such as at Chungking, occasionally made this common plan unsuitable, but the stamp of governmental uniformity is nonetheless apparent. This was true for cities which had originally risen as trade centers, or which became more important commercially than they were administratively. It is possible to find a clear separation in many provinces between administrative and commercial cities, where the capital is not the most important commercial base, such as Chungking and Chengtu in Szechuan....[4] But despite this degree of functional specificity, little urban independence or urban-based revolutionary change appeared until the traditional fabric was rent by the growth of Western-inspired treaty-ports. Even in the exceptional cases where trade or manufacturing was the sole or predominant basis of the city: Chingtechen, the site of the Imperial Potteries, or Canton, the consistent focus of foreign trade, there never developed a merchant-controlled urban base free in any significant sense of the traditional state order.

. . . .

Large cities seem to have been proportionately more numerous in China than in Europe until the nineteenth century, and until the eighteenth century urbanism may have been higher. Perhaps a quarter or more of the population lived in towns and cities of more than 2500 population, and perhaps 10 or 15 per cent in cities over 10,000. The big cities of the East as a whole were huge by European standards; this was a consistent feature of what has been called "Oriental society."[5] In China most cities or towns of 5,000 or more had well-defined commercial

[4]. Compare for instance the original development of London as two cities separated by open country, Westminster as the administrative center, and "the city" as the center of business.

[5]. For example, ancient Alexandria had a population of about one million in a country (Egypt) with a total population of only seven million.

or manufacturing districts, and special areas for each important enterprise: banking, metal goods, food markets, textiles, woodwork, and so on. This pattern remains in most contemporary Chinese cities. But the cities were not decisive centers of change in a commercialized economy. They served as imperial or provincial capitals, seats for garrison troops, and residences for governors, viceroys, and the ubiquitous cloud of officials and quasi-officials with their "service-providers." Their business was administration, and exploitation, of the countryside. Marco Polo, in describing the magnificence of Peking, accounts for it as follows:

... and this happens because everyone from everywhere brings there for the lord who lives there and for his court and for the city which is so great and for the ladies and barons and knights of whom there are so many and for the great abundance of the multitude of the people of the armies of the lord, which stay round about as well for the court as for the city, and of other people who come there by reason of the court which the great lord holds there, and for one and for another ... and because the city is in too good a position and in the middle of many provinces.[6]

Here is a clear picture of a city based on administration from a central location, where trade flows in largely in response to the existing structure of officials, troops, court, hangers-on, and the host of people necessary to support them, from secretaries and servants to bakers and dancers. Six hundred years later at the end of the nineteenth century European travellers in China reported the same phenomenon, on a smaller regional scale: large cities whose sole function appeared to be administration, or important trading cities at key locations which were nevertheless dominated by officials and the magistrate's (office)....

The trade process appears to have lacked the dynamic quality by means of which Europe's cities rose to power. Pre-eighteenth century China had a trade as great as or greater than pre-eighteenth century Europe, but Europe's subsequent commercial expansion left China far behind. Why this happened, and why China never produced the revolutionary economic and political changes which re-made Europe into an arbiter for the rest of the world is a vital question. An analysis of the city's role may help to suggest some relevant factors. Why was the Chinese city not a European-style center of change?

EUROPE, U.S., CHINA

China is geographically isolated by a formidable assemblage of barriers. To landward lies the greatest mountain mass in the world, with its extensions from the Pamir Knot, reinforced on the south by rainforests and spectacular river gorges, on the north by the barren wastes of Siberia, and on the west and northwest by a vast sweep of desert. Seaward a coast deficient in harbours faces a huge and until recently commercially underdeveloped ocean, by European standards. Chinese trade with Japan was at several periods considerable, and with southeast Asia even larger, but it did not approach eighteenth or nineteenth century European levels. It tended to be characterized by luxury goods, strategic goods (such as copper for coinage), or specialties such as Chinese porcelain. With these exceptions, especially the highly developed and diversified trade between southeast coastal China,[7] and southeast Asia, China did not greatly extend herself commercially, and was for the most part content to send specialized goods, like silk, to the rest of the world through middlemen intermediaries: the Arabs by sea and the Turkish peoples of central Asia by land. Significantly, the largest concerted Chinese attempt in foreign trade was an imperial government project (the famous Ming expeditions of the fifteenth century), which lasted only some 30 years and apparently found no solid base in the Chinese economy or in its merchant group.

Internally, trade moved largely on the great river systems, running fortunately east and west, but there was no such close interconnection between these river basins as in Europe, by sea or across plains. Physically China is built on a grander scale, but the landscape presents no such invitation to

---

6. A. C. Moule and Paul Pelliot, *Marco Polo, the Description of the World*, (London, 1939), Vol. I, pp. 236–237.

7. Southeast China has many fine harbours and overseas trade has been prominent there for centuries. But it is effectively isolated from the main body of China by mountains, including those which help to make its harbours, and trade there has thus made much less impact on the rest of the country. The distinctiveness of the southeast is also clear in its many regional ethnic and linguistic elements.

exchange as has sparked the development of Europe. Europe is multi-peninsular, each peninsula tending toward economic distinctiveness and political independence, but joined by cheap sea and river routes. This plethora of complementary areas and their transport links magnified the basis and the means of exchange. Although its early trade development was not larger than China's, by the middle of the eighteenth century commercial expansion overseas had joined and accelerated commercialization at home, and Europe stood in a class by itself. The cities of western Europe were both the creators and inheritors of this development. But in China the cities remained centers of the unitary national state and of the traditional order rather than its attackers, epitomes of the status quo. As direct links in the official hierarchy, they were the props of the empire. The universities were urban, for convenience as in Europe, but they stimulated no dissent. Their accepted function was to train scholars who could staff the imperial civil service, and they fed their graduates into the imperial examination system. This, and the better economic and social position of scholars generally in China than in Europe, encouraged the universities and the literati to support the status quo; European intellectuals may have taken a vow of poverty, but they remained a dissident or discontented group.

Physically, China lacked Europe's outstanding advantages for trade, and on the other hand presented a base for highly productive agriculture, through irrigation. Wittfogel's revealing work on the organic connection between the need for mass organized water control and the growth of a monolithic bureaucratic state in China lends insight into the origins and pattern of the institutional structure.[8] With China's environmental advantages, water control made agriculture the massive core of the economy, and at the same time left the bureaucracy in a position of ramified command. It was not possible for urban merchants to win independence from this system. They had less economic leverage than the rising European merchants because, with the preponderant position of agriculture, they never occupied proportionately as large a place in the economy.

The state of course did its part to prevent the development of a rival group, and by taxation, requisition, and monopoly ensured that the merchants would be kept relatively impotent. This was a job which European states and monarchs, though equally determined, failed to accomplish; their merchants were in a stronger position, and the state was weaker: it was merely *primus inter pares*. Land hunger in China, as a reflection of a population too large for the available arable land (increasingly serious during the past 200 years, but even in Han times worse than in most other parts of the world, including Europe), also acted to restrict commercial development, since it meant high land rents. Capital could almost always be invested with greater profit and safety in land, or in rural loans, than in productive or capital-generating enterprises outside the agrarian sphere.

Where extra-agricultural opportunities for investment did exist, the individual entrepreneur was at the mercy of the bureaucratic state. Many of the major trade goods were government monopolies. Elsewhere the essentially Western concepts of private property and due process of law, in a word, of the entrepreneur, were lacking in a society dominated by agriculture and officials. Extortion, forced levies, confiscation, and simple financial failure as the result of arbitrary government policies were the daily risk of the merchant. Some individuals did indeed become very rich, for example the famous *hong* merchants of Canton, but their wealth came necessarily through official connection: by possession of gentry status, by office holding or official favour, or by trading as part of a government monopoly. . . .

In China merchant-capitalists did not use their money to establish their independence, as did the merchants of London or Antwerp, or to stimulate the growth of a new economic pattern. Unfortunately for the Chinese merchants, the imperial revenue was at most periods derived largely from the land tax and from the government trade monopolies.

---

8. K. A. Wittfogel, "Foundations and Stages of Chinese Economic History," *Zeitschrift für Sozialforschung*, IV (1935): 26–58. ibid., "Die Theorie der Orientalischen Gesellschaft," *loc. cit.*, VII (1938): 90–123. (This article clearly states the administrative basis of the Chinese city, and discusses the reasons and implications.) ibid., *Wirtschaft und Gesellschaft Chinas* (Leipsig, 1931). ibid., *Oriental Society and Oriental Despotism*, [1957]. [Editors' note: See the selection by Wittfogel reprinted in Part V of this volume.]

Agriculture was proportionately more productive than in Europe, and revenue from trade less necessary. Peking thus did not need the merchants as the king had needed them in Europe to finance the ascendancy of the national state, to pay for its wars with rival states, or to meet its normal bills. No concessions were necessary; the merchants could be squeezed dry, and were, with no harm to the state. The commanding position of the bureaucracy, and the fact of the bureaucratic state, are perhaps explainable by a similar process of default. Merchants were necessary or useful to perform essential (and, to the state, profitable) commercial functions; they were tolerated, but kept under strict control, and this was simpler and cheaper than for the state to manage all commercial dealings itself.[9]

But the merchants were also identified with the state as well as being stifled by it. Their numbers were recruited largely from the gentry class, who had the capital and the official connections essential to commercial success. Gentry merchants worked willingly with gentry officials in the management of the state monopolies, including foreign trade. Outside the monopolies, the same partnership operated, as a matter of mutual interest. In addition, most gentry members, whether or not they were engaged in trade, also performed other semi-official functions, comparable in some degree to the British landed gentry. These "services" represented a considerable part of their income; they were not likely to attack the system which nourished them. In a more general sense, the tradition of revolt in this hierarchical society did not include the re-ordering of social or economic groups, but concentrated on the removal of bad government. Individual or group improvement was not to be won by destroying the fabric, but by making optimum use of one's position within it.

Finally, China had maintained since Han times and with few breaks a remarkable degree of unity[10] and a central power which no single European state achieved until quite late in its modern development. In China even towns of the *chen* (market town) rank (population c. 3000–5000) were seats of garrison troops, whatever their prominence in trade. In Europe in the course of the crown's contest with the nobles, and of the international rivalries which also developed among the plethora of separate national states, urban merchants found an opportunity which contrasted sharply with the rooted monolithic nature of the Chinese state.

The cities of China were consequently microcosms of the empire, not deviants. They were not backwaters, for necessarily learning, art, and the trappings of cosmopolis were concentrated in them. Yet, each was a symbol of the imperial system, operating not only under the direct thumb of Peking, but according to its precepts. Obvious considerations of convenience made them central places, market towns, transport termini or break-in-bulk points, and exchange centers of varying degrees of sophistication. But these universal urban functions do not automatically bring with them the character of rebellion or innovation which we have rightly come to associate with cities in the West. The main distinction of the Chinese city was concentration, as the node of the traditional society and as its power base. Imperial authority filtered down more slowly into the countryside, becoming more dilute with every level. Every government with ambitions of central power attempted to control the peasant. In a largely pre-commercial and pre-industrial society of a basically molecular character, this could never be perfect control. China lacked not only the tools of control for its huge area, such as communications and literacy, but the bond of common interest and attitude which a completely commercialized economy tends to create, often by sublimating or suppressing conflicting interests. In the absence of such tools or conditions to implement rural control in China, the importance of the city as a center of political and military power on the side of authority was magnified.

CHANGE

Change in China, as elsewhere, has been the work of a city-country alliance, with the leadership coming usually from the gentry

---

9. K. A. Wittfogel in his *Oriental Society and Oriental Despotism* speaks of this arrangement as based on "the law of diminishing administrative returns."

10. The persistent unity of China despite wide regional diversity is something of a puzzle, but may be related to China's dramatic isolation and to the unitary rather than peninsular nature of her continental base.

based in cities or towns. But the origins of dissent and the main force of attacks on the status quo have been far less urban in China than in the West. While the rebellions were in many cases closer to the usually unsuccessful Jacqueries of the West than to the really revolutionary changes generated in Western cities, they were the predominant agents of what change did take place. They were successful where their Western analogues failed because there was no more potent agent of change, no other group (if we except the several nomadic invasions and conquests) and no other economic base by which change might even superficially be forced. The similarity with the Jacqueries lies in the fact that Chinese rebellions rarely challenged the basic nature of the existing order, but only its administration. The new dynasty which resulted might mean new blood, but seldom new institutions.

Given a largely closed, agrarian system, it is understandable that each dynasty, as it lost its momentum, lacked the means of maintaining a high productivity and effective distribution as population increased, and that it eventually declined into corruption. This was especially so in the rural sphere, easy prey to tax and rent manipulation (and the source of most of the national revenue and income), but marginal enough to be sensitive to oppression. At the same time, the lack of large extra-agricultural economic bases for an independent group prevented the growth of new ideas or new institutions to challenge the old, even while the old lay in ruins. The city-country alliance which in Europe made revolution made only a change of administration in China. The city was too dependent on the traditional order to attempt its destruction.

The accelerated impact of the West on China during the nineteenth century has by the twentieth century set in train profound changes, and it is natural to find that these are reflected also in the city's role. The Kuo Min Tang was a largely urban-based movement, and though its revolutionary aspects became less and less prominent under the more compelling problems of security against Communists and Japanese, it was far more than a change of administration. It was in fact the political vehicle of a new group, nurtured not only in Western thought, but in the essentially Western milieu of the treaty-ports. Negatively also the cities have made a new impression. The present Communist regime had prominent rural roots, and came to power with an announced resentment and distrust of cities, calling them the centers of reaction (and also of degeneracy, softness, and vice), though its venom was directed particularly against the foreign-created treaty-ports.

It was basically the impact of the West, including the Soviet Union, which ensured that this latest of rebellions would for the first time successfully destroy the existing fabric. In the treaty-ports themselves development had been too brief, and too much limited by the inertia of the agrarian economy, to produce an effective base for change to rival Communism in its originally rural base. Nevertheless these urban centers, many of them new as large cities dependent on trade, played much the same role as the cities of late medieval Europe. They were rebels against the traditional order because for the first time in the history of China they provided opportunity for the merchant. Money could not only be made, but invested, in trade or manufacturing, with safety, profit, and prestige. Private property, and all of the values of R. H. Tawney's "Acquisitive Society" had been enthroned in the treaty-ports by the West, and to the Chinese businessman Shanghai or Tientsin were all that traditional China was not. He was prepared to work for the establishment of a government and society which would make a respectable place for a commercial industrial bourgeoisie, based, as the term implies, in cities.

This new group, shaped by the West, largely created the Kuo Min Tang. They formed an alliance with some of the landed gentry, for example Chiang Kai-shek, who was both landed and bourgeois, but they were never in any sense a peasant party, and their ties with the land were feeble. While they answered, or promised to answer, many of the needs of the new class of treaty-port Chinese, and kept peace with the gentry, they did not seriously attempt to answer the questions and strivings of the Peking intellectuals, nor the more compelling needs of the peasants. Communism ultimately rode to power in part as a crusade against the "merchant capitalists" of Shanghai on the one hand and the Western-inspired intellectuals of Peking on the other.[11]

To be sure, the Chinese Communist Party and its leaders are urban-trained Marxists operating intellectually and practically in an urban framework, and dedicated to an industrialization program which necessarily centers in the cities. Their political control also depends substantially on their control of city populations and city enterprises. Insofar as they thus push the city toward the middle of the stage as a recognized base at least for economic and technological change, they continue the about-face in the city's role which the Western impact began in the treaty-ports. In any case, active urban agency for change is a recent phenomenon in China, perhaps one may say a direct transmittal from the West.

SUMMARY

This analysis, in attempting to particularize the city's role in the two great centers of world civilization, has necessarily dealt with institutions as much as with place. The urban differences were expressions of distinct societies. It was broadly speaking the bureaucratic state in China which stifled the growth of European-type cities despite the volume of trade or the regional specialization of commerce and manufacturing which existed. In Europe, too, wherever bureaucratic and/or persistently authoritarian governments ruled, commercialization and industrialization were late and/or little, and the urban-based entrepreneur usually exerted small influence. Some other common ground may exist between these bureaucracies, and the suggestion that physical conditions required or invited central control, and that geographic factors helped to minimize the opportunity of the merchant, are perhaps as applicable to eastern Europe, or to Spain, as to China. The imprint of Roman Law and of Mediterranean urban traditions may also help to account for the east-west distinction in Europe. In any case, maritime western Europe followed a course whose urban direction lay at the root of its wealth, its power, and its distinctiveness.

. . . .

The city has been a center of change in western Europe, while it has been the reverse in traditional China, despite the broad similarity in urban economic functions in both areas. Urban character and urban roles may be useful indicators of the nature and dynamics of the diverse entities of society.

---

11. As the capital and as the seat of the largest Western-founded universities, Peking was a center of intellectual ferment by the end of the nineteenth century since intellectual contact with the West was easiest there. Traditional, imperial China had by then lost enough prestige that dissension flourished in Peking itself. While many of the intellectuals rejected China's traditional civilization in whole or in part, their struggles in this scholar's community made little impact on the nation as a whole. The Chinese Communist Party was founded in Peking in 1921, but largely deserted it for a rural base. Student and intellectual ferment in Peking was revolutionary in thought, but ineffective in action. Both the treaty-ports and the countryside proved in the end to be much more effective bases for change or for rebellion.

11

The Nature of Frontiers and Boundaries

LADIS K. D. KRISTOF*

This study is concerned with the problem of clarifying, and disentangling for the purpose of theoretical understanding, the two elements which combine in what we commonly call frontiers and boundaries: the physical (or nonhuman geographical, or "natural") and the political, i.e., moral and legal, element.

THE ORIGINS AND EVOLUTION OF TERMS

In common speech we use the words "frontier" and "boundary" with the implication that these have not only a quite well-defined meaning but also that they are (or almost) interchangeable. However, it does not take much reading in pertinent literature to discover that the problem is not so simple.

Reproduced from the *Annals* of the Association of American Geographers, Volume XLIX, 1959, by permission of the author and publisher.
* Ladis Kristof (1918–) is a political scientist in The Institute of Political Studies at Stanford University.
The author, a political scientist and student of geopolitics, wishes to express gratitude to two geographers, Professors Norton S. Ginsburg (University of Chicago) and Stephen B. Jones (Yale University), for a very careful reading of the manuscript and critical remarks which helped to clarify certain points. All responsibility for the views expressed remains, of course, with the writer.

Frontier

Historically, the word "frontier" implied what it suggests etymologically, that is, that which is "in front." The frontier was not an abstract term or line; on the contrary, it designated an area which was part of a whole, specifically that part which was ahead of the hinterland. Hence it was often called the foreland, or borderland, or march. For the purpose of our discussion it must be stressed that in its historical origin the frontier was (1) not a legal concept, and (2) not, or at least not essentially, a political or intellectual concept. It was rather a phenomenon of "the facts of life"—a manifestation of the spontaneous tendency for growth of the ecumene. In antiquity, and later too, the frontier was on the margin of the inhabited world, but each particular ecumene, for instance, that of the agricultural society as opposed to the nomad society, also had a frontier. The *limes* of the Roman empire were those of the ecumene of Western civilization.

With the development of patterns of civilization above the level of mere subsistence strictly adapted to particular environmental conditions, the frontiers between ecumene became meeting places not merely of different ways of physical survival, but also of different concepts of the good life, and hence increasingly political in character.[1] But even at this stage the frontier was something very different from what a modern boundary is. It had not the connotation of an area or zone which marks a definite limit or end of a political unit. On the contrary, given the theory that there can (or should) be only one state—a universal state—the frontier meant quite literally "the front": the *frons* of the *imperium mundi* which expands to the only limits it can acknowledge, namely, the limits of the world. Thus the frontier was not the end ("tail") but rather the beginning ("forehead") of the state; it was the spearhead of light and knowledge expanding into the realm of darkness and of the unknown. The borderlands—the marches—were areas of dawn; they were frontiers in the sense of Turner's agricultural frontier: pioneer settlements of a forward-moving culture bent on occupying the whole area.

Boundary

The etymology of the word "boundary" immediately points to the primary function of the boundary: the boundary indicates certain well established limits (the bounds) of the given political unit, and all that which is within the boundary is bound together, that is, it is fastened by an internal bond.

"Boundary" is a term appropriate to the present-day concept of the state, that is, the state as a sovereign (or autonomous) spatial unit, one among many. Since the transition from tribal law to territorial law the essentials of statehood, both from the functional and legal point of view, are: territory, people, and a government in effective control internally, independent externally, and willing and able to assume obligations under international (or federal) law. Sovereignty is territorial; hence it must have a certain known extent: a territory under exclusive jurisdiction limited by state boundaries. The borderlands, the old marchlands, are defined more and more exactly until there is, in principle, an exact borderline. The modern sovereign state is bound within and confined to its legal limits. The boundaries bind together an area and a people which live under one sovereign government and law and are, at least presumably, integrated not only administratively and economically but also by means of a state idea or "crede."[2] At the same time "the state is marked off from its neighbors by political boundaries."[3] In an age in which we (with exceptions) do not think in terms of universal empires but accept the co-existence of many credes and states, it is important to have the spheres of the several centripetal, integrating forces legally delimited.

THE DIFFERENCES BETWEEN FRONTIERS AND BOUNDARIES

There are some difficulties in trying to distinguish between frontiers and boundaries. First, not all languages have separate words for the two.[4] Then, the historical transition from one to another in many regions tends to diminish the awareness of the essential differences. Still, this does not change the fact that frontiers and boundaries are in their very nature two different things.[5]

The *frontier* is *outer-oriented*. Its main attention is directed toward the outlying areas which are both a source of danger and a coveted prize. The hinterland—the motherland—is seldom the directing force behind the pulsations of frontier life. As history, American, Russian, or Chinese, well illustrates, the borderlands often develop their

---

1. (Paul de) Lapradelle distinguishes three types (or three stages of evolution) of the frontier: (1) the concept of the frontier in "pure geography" (i.e., "geography as a pure science applied to the study of the physical aspects of the earth") in which it designates zones under the influence of several physical phenomena; for instance, the estuary is subject to two different and contradictory forces, those of the river and those of the sea; (2) the concept of the "geographic frontier of the second degree," that is, the anthropo-geographical concept of the frontier between particular ecumene; and (3) the concept of the political frontier: *La Frontière: Étude de Droit International* (Paris: Les Editions Internationales, 1928), pp. 9–11.

2. Richard Hartshorne, "The Functional Approach in Political Geography," *Annals*, Association of American Geographers, Vol. XL, No. 2 (June, 1950), pp. 95–130; on pp. 110–12.

3. Derwent Whittlesey, *The Earth and the State* (New York: Henry Holt and Co., 1939), p. 5.

4. The French commonly use *frontière* both for frontier and boundary, but they could distinguish between *frontière* and *limite*. The Germans, however, have only one word: *Grenze*.

5. An interesting discussion of the differences between frontiers and boundaries can be found in Owen Lattimore, *Inner Asian Frontiers of China* (New York: American Geographical Society, 1940), pp. 233–242, 480–83, 495–510.

own interests quite different from those of the central government. They feel neither bound by the center nor binding its realm. Rather, they represent runaway elements and interests of the state's corporate body.

The *boundary*, on the contrary, is *inner-oriented*. It is created and maintained by the will of the central government. It has no life of its own, not even a material existence. Boundary stones are not the boundary itself. They are not coeval with it, only its visible symbols. Also, the boundary is not tied inextricably to people—people teeming, spontaneous, and unmediated in their daily activities on, along, or athwart the border. It is the mediated will of the people: abstracted and generalized in the national law, subjected to the tests of international law, it is far removed from the changing desires and aspirations of the inhabitants of the borderlands.

While the frontier is inconceivable without frontiersmen—an "empty frontier" would be merely a desert—the boundary seems often to be happiest, and have the best chances of long survival, when it is not bothered by border men. Yet, the boundary line is not merely an abstraction. Still less can it be a legal fiction. It must be reality, or, rather, reflect reality. In other words, it must be coordinated with an empirical force actually present and asserting itself in the terrain. The boundary is, in fact, the outer line of *effective* control exercised by the central government.

The *frontier* is a manifestation of *centrifugal forces*. On the other hand, the range and vigor of *centripetal forces* is indicated by the *boundary*. True, the frontier has, and always had, also a strategic meaning—the defensive line which keeps enemies out—and in this it depends on support from the hinterland. But precisely in order to be able to maximize its strategic forces the central government must mobilize and integrate all the available resources. All efforts and loyalties must be concentrated and coordinated under the banner of the state idea and interest. Consequently, the frontier lands, too, have to be controlled and bound to the state; they must be subordinated to the imperative and overriding demands of the sovereign *raison d'être* of the state as a whole. In other words, an effort is made to draw somewhere a line of effective control over both ingress and egress: not only the enemy has to be kept out but one's own citizens and resources have to be kept in. It is in the interest of the central government to substitute a boundary for the frontier.

The *frontier* is an *integrating factor*. Being a zone of transition from the sphere (ecumene) of one way of life to another, and representing forces which are neither fully assimilated to nor satisfied with either, it provides an excellent opportunity for mutual interpenetration and sway. Along the frontier life constantly manipulates the settled patterns of the pivotally organized socio-political and cultural structures. It is precisely this watering down of loyalties and blurring of differences that the central governments attempt to forestall by substituting the semi-autonomous frontiers with a controlled and exact borderline.

The *boundary* is, on the contrary, a *separating factor*. "[It is the] boundary [that] impinges on life.... Few natural obstacles restrict the movement of persons, things, and even ideas as completely as do the boundaries of some states."[6] The boundary separates the sovereign (or federal, or autonomous, or any other) political units from one another. However much physical–geographical, cultural, or certain political factors may tend to make it inconspicuous, it remains always a fixed obstacle; it impedes integration across the borderline. To propose, as one writer does,[7] the drawing of boundaries in such a way as to make them meeting places for people and thus rather an assimilative than a dissimilative factor is a misconception as to what a boundary is and what are its purposes and functions. Any assimilation, hence integration, cannot be stimulated by the drawing of a line which separates and delimits the spheres of the integrating forces, but, on the contrary, by the removal of such obstacles to interpenetration. Every confederation, federation, or merger of states must always begin with a (total, or at least partial) elimination of the limiting and separating factors inherent in the boundary, and thus a withering away of the boundary itself.

In general, discussing the differences between frontiers and boundaries, one faces a

6. Stephen B. Jones, *Boundary Making: A Handbook for Statesmen, Treaty Editors and Boundary Commissioners* (Washington, DC: Carnegie Endowment For International Peace, 1945), p. 11.

7. Lionel William Lyde, *Some Frontiers of Tomorrow: An Aspiration for Europe* (London: A. and C. Black, 1915), p. 2.

grave dilemma: to what degree is it possible to generalize about the frontier? The boundary is defined and regulated by law, national and international, and as such its status and characteristics are more uniform and can be defined with some precision. But the frontier is a phenomenon of history; like history it may repeat itself, but, again like history, it is always unique. It is difficult to pinpoint essential features of the frontier which are universally valid. For instance, the degree to which the frontier is an integrating factor depends on the attractiveness to the frontiersman of the way of life of his opposite number. This way of life usually seems attractive if the adoption of it promises better chances of survival in the given environment or if it appears generally "superior." On the American frontier both the white settler and the Indian were willing to learn from each other certain techniques, but on the broader cultural level each considered his way of life as definitely preferable ("superior"). Consequently, the integrating process along the American frontier touched only upon the externals—the internal lives of the two social groups remained incompatible, witness the fact that intermarriages were rather rare and almost no white American ever really "became" an Indian or vice versa. The Spanish and the native Mexican culture were relatively more compatible; hence much more integration occurred along the frontier in Mexico, and the result is a genuinely composite culture, especially outside the cities.

The importance of the relative compatibility of cultures which meet on a given frontier can be illustrated by comparing the advance of the Russian and the northern Chinese frontier. Both of these frontiers have been biting into the heritage of the Mongol Empire. But the Russian way of life, based on an extensive agriculture, was much less different from that of the pastoral nomad subjects of the Mongol khan than was the Chinese culture which was based on an intensive and irrigated agriculture. This helps to explain why the Russians succeeded in taking such a lion's bite of the Mongol Empire, and in integrating, even absorbing to a large extent, the natives, while the Chinese pushed their frontier only a few hundred miles or less into Extra-Mural China. Since the Russians did not, like the Americans, steam-roll the native cultures, or even the natives themselves, out of existence, the Russian expansion was not merely a *frontier of conquest* but also a *frontier of integration*: the new culture was the result of a fusion.[8] There are historians who think that the Russians paid a heavy price for integrating so many "barbarians": in the process they ceased to be Europeans and became Eur-Asiatics.

BOUNDARIES AS LEGAL–POLITICAL PHENOMENA *Par Excellence*

We have said that boundaries are fixed by law. There is, however, often confusion as to what a law is and what kind of laws determine the limits of states. The misunderstandings which arose from the use of the terms "natural boundaries" and "artificial boundaries" are at least partly due to this confusion. Thus, it will be helpful if we make the distinction between three types of law:

(1) *Law of nature, i.e., scientific law*, is a creature of facts. *Ex facto jus oritur*. It is ruled by the empirical world. We observe the natural phenomena (or reproduce them in a laboratory) and deduce from our observations certain generalizations about the behavior of elements and call them laws, e.g., the law of gravity. But these laws have no coercive power over nature. On the contrary, if facts do not conform to the laws, the latter are adjusted to conform to reality. The concordance between what *is* and the law must be absolute.

(2) *Natural law, i.e., moral law*, is as strict as the scientific law but in an exactly opposite sense. It is not the *is* but the *ought* which is sovereign. The status of the moral law is not affected by the facts. All Jews and Christians ought to obey the Ten Commandments, yet even if not a single one of them did, the Law would still be there; unchanged, categorical, and as binding as ever. The moral law exists in itself, that is, in the justice of "thou shalt" and not in the empirical world in which it

---

8. The American frontier was, of course, also an integrating factor—the proverbial "melting pot." It integrated *on* the frontier, it "melted" into a new nation all those Europeans who came into contact *with* the frontier, but it did not promote an *across-the-frontier* integration. In the writings of Frederick Jackson Turner the American frontier is not viewed as a borderland between two ecumene, between two different types of human societies. It is primarily a meeting place between man and nature.

may or may not be observed. While in the natural world a law which does not conform to facts is no law at all, in the moral world only that is a "fact," i.e., a moral fact, which conforms to the moral law.

(3) *Jural law* (*lex*) is a formal verbalization and particularization of the moral standards of a given socio-political order in respect to the practical (or at least observable) behavior of the members of the society. It is an attempt to bring the spiritual and empirical realms together, to make the moral standards "efficient." Three characteristics of jural law are important for our discussion: it is coercive, it may be violated, and its ultimate source is public opinion about values. Imperfect both in its moral substance and enforcing procedure, the jural law is, as all political phenomena are, the result of compromises reflecting the complexity of the social forces interacting on the given scene.

Boundaries are supported by jural laws. They are one of the spatial expressions of the given legal order. As distinguished from "boundaries" between phenomena of the physical geographical or natural history world, they are man-made geographical occurrences. A boundary does not exist in nature or by itself. It always owes its existence to man.

True, the "boundary" in the natural world, e.g., an orographic line, or the limit of the habitat of certain species of flora and fauna in the desert, steppe, or forest zone, also may occasionally be man-fixed, but it is not man created. It *is* in nature, and all man does is to shift and reshuffle it in space as he transforms the natural environment into a cultural environment.

The political nature of boundaries, and the nature of politics itself, is [well] understood by Haushofer. We may disagree with Haushofer's classification of boundaries and boundary problems, or with the solutions he envisages, but this is a political disagreement, one which has its roots in the values we cherish and the concepts of state we hold. It is not possible to deny the validity of his assertion that boundaries are zones of frictions.[9]

9. Karl Haushofer, *Grenzen in ihrer geographischen und politischen Bedeutung* (Berlin-Grünewald: Kurt Vowinckel Verlag, 1927), Chap. XV and II. Cf. Nicholas John Spykman, "Frontiers, Security, and International Organization," *Geographical Review*, Vol. XXXII, No. 3 (July, 1942), pp. 436–47, on p. 437.

The boundary is a meeting place of two socio-political bodies, each having its particular interests, structure, and ideology. Each generates loyalties and also imposes duties and constraints for the sake of internal harmony and compactness and of external separateness and individuality. Two neighboring states do not need to be engaged continuously, or at any time, in a struggle for life and death. They may compete peacefully and, in general, minimize their conflicts of interest. Still, the very existence of the boundary is proof that there are some differences in ideology and goals, if not of a virulent present-day character then at least imbedded in the historical heritage. . . .

CONCLUSION

The nature of frontiers differs greatly from the nature of boundaries. Frontiers are a characteristic of rudimentary socio-political relations; relations marked by rebelliousness, lawlessness, and/or absence of laws. The presence of boundaries is a sign that the political community has reached a relative degree of maturity and orderliness, the stage of law-abidance. The international society in a frontier era is like the American West during open-range ranching: limits, if any, are ill-defined and resented; there is little law and still less respect for law; and men afield do not always worry on whose territory or under whose jurisdiction they nominally are. Under a boundary regime the international society resembles rather fenced ranching: each rancher holds a legal title to his land, knows and guards its limits, and manages and surveys it with a view to some over-all end.

Both frontiers and boundaries are manifestations of socio-political forces, and as such are subjective, not objective. But while the former are the result of rather spontaneous, or at least *ad hoc* solutions and movements, the latter are fixed and enforced through a more rational and centrally coordinated effort after a conscious choice is made among the several preferences and opportunities at hand.

Boundaries are not boundaries of all political power. They are the limits of *internal* political power, that is, of the power which integrates the given political unit in the name of certain values and loyalties within the bounds of its territory as delimited under international law. *External* political power does not know territorial limits; it operates on the international scene. However, orderly international intercourse is possible only if it is, on the whole, a relation between legal governments: an encounter between the external governmental political powers. In other words, in order to have some stability in the political structure, both on the national and international level, a clear distinction between the spheres of foreign and domestic politics is necessary. The boundary helps to maintain this distinction.

It is a characteristic of contemporary, so-called ideological politics that it deliberately tends to blur the difference between foreign and domestic territory, and between internal and external politics, weakening thus the status and importance of boundaries. Governments, and nongovernmental organizations, bypass the legal channels in order to deal directly with peoples inhabiting territories under the jurisdiction of other governments. Supranational, non-national, and other loyalties and interests are promoted which integrate socio-political forces into unofficial or semi-official groupings and blocks transgressing upon the existing formal territorial arrangements.

These groupings and blocks are neither fully incadrated by, nor responsible for, the upholding of law. On their fringes—the edges of communities of thought and culture—there are borderlands, frontiers, and frontiersmen. On the fringes of the ideological ecumene of our divided world unintegrated elements occupy shifting frontier zones. These zones are not the cause of international instability; they reflect the unsettledness of the contemporary human society.

12

The Significance of the Frontier in American History

FREDERICK JACKSON TURNER[*]

In a bulletin of the Superintendent of the Census for 1890 appear these significant words: "Up to and including 1880 the country had a frontier of settlement, but at present the unsettled area has been so broken into by isolated bodies of settlement that there can hardly be said to be a frontier line. In the discussion of its extent, its westward movement, etc., it can not, therefore, any longer have a place in the census reports." This brief official statement marks the closing of a great historic movement. Up to our own day American history has been in a large degree the history of the colonization of the Great West. The existence of an area of free land, its continuous recession, and the advance of American settlement westward, explain American development.

Behind institutions, behind constitutional forms and modifications, lie the vital forces that call these organs into life and shape them to meet changing conditions. The peculiarity of American institutions is, the fact that they have been compelled to adapt themselves to the changes of an expanding people—to the changes involved in crossing a continent, in winning a wilderness, and in developing at each area of this progress out of the primitive economic and political conditions of the frontier into the complexity of city life. Said Calhoun in 1817, "We are great, and rapidly —I was about to say fearfully—growing!" So saying, he touched the distinguishing feature of American life. All peoples show development; the germ theory of politics has been sufficiently emphasized. In the case of most nations, however, the development has occurred in a limited area; and if the nation has expanded, it has met other growing peoples whom it has conquered. But in the case of the United States we have a different phenomenon. Limiting our attention to the Atlantic coast, we have the familiar phenomenon of the evolution of institutions in a limited area, such as the rise of representative government; the differentiation of simple colonial governments into complex organs; the progress from primitive industrial society, without division of labor, up to manufacturing civilization. But we have in addition to this a recurrence of the process of evolution in each western area reached in the process of expansion. Thus American development has exhibited not merely advance along a single line, but a return to primitive conditions on a continually advancing frontier line, and a new development for that area. American social

Reprinted from the *Annual Report of the American Historical Association* (Washington, 1894).

[*] Frederick Jackson Turner (1861–1932) was Professor of History at Harvard University and at The University of Wisconsin.

development has been continually beginning over again on the frontier. This perennial rebirth, this fluidity of American life, this expansion westward with its new opportunities, its continuous touch with the simplicity of primitive society, furnish the forces dominating American character. The true point of view in the history of this nation is not the Atlantic coast, it is the Great West. Even the slavery struggle . . . occupies its important place in American history because of its relation to westward expansion.

In this advance, the frontier is the outer edge of the wave—the meeting point between savagery and civilization. Much has been written about the frontier from the point of view of border warfare and the chase, but as a field for the serious study of the economist and the historian it has been neglected.

The American frontier is sharply distinguished from the European frontier—a fortified boundary line running through dense populations. The most significant thing about the American frontier is that it lies at the hither edge of free land. In the census reports it is treated as the margin of that settlement which has a density of two or more to the square mile. The term is an elastic one, and for our purposes does not need sharp definition. . . . This paper will make no attempt to treat the subject exhaustively; its aim is simply to call attention to the frontier as a fertile field for investigation, and to suggest some of the problems which arise in connection with it.

Stages of Frontier Advance

In the settlement of America we have to observe how European life entered the continent, and how America modified and developed that life and reacted on Europe. Our early history is the study of European germs developing in an American environment. Too exclusive attention has been paid by institutional students to the Germanic origins, too little to the American factors. The frontier is the line of most rapid and effective Americanization. The wilderness masters the colonist. It finds him a European in dress, industries, tools, modes of travel, and thought. It takes him from the railroad car and puts him in the birch canoe. It strips off the garments of civilization and arrays him in the hunting shirt and the moccasin. It puts him in the log cabin of the Cherokee and Iroquois and runs an Indian palisade around him. Before long he has gone to planting Indian corn and plowing with a sharp stick; he shouts the war cry and takes the scalp in orthodox Indian fashion. In short, at the frontier the environment is at first too strong for the man. He must accept the conditions which it furnishes, or perish, and so he fits himself into the Indian clearings and follows the Indian trails. Little by little he transforms the wilderness, but the outcome is not the old Europe, not simply the development of Germanic germs, any more than the first phenomenon was a case of reversion to the Germanic mark. The fact is, that here is a new product that is American. At first, the frontier was the Atlantic coast. It was the frontier of Europe in a very real sense. Moving westward, the frontier became more and more American. As successive terminal moraines result from successive glaciations, so each frontier leaves its traces behind it, and when it becomes a settled area the region still partakes of the frontier characteristics. Thus the advance of the frontier has meant a steady movement away from the influence of Europe, a steady growth of independence on American lines. And to study this advance, the men who grew up under these conditions, and the political, economic, and social results of it, is to study the really American part of our history.

In the course of the seventeenth century the frontier was advanced up the Atlantic river courses, just beyond the "fall line," and the tidewater region became the settled area. In the first half of the eighteenth century another advance occurred. Traders followed the Delaware and Shawnee Indians to the Ohio as early as the end of the first quarter of the century. Gov. Spotswood, of Virginia, made an expedition in 1714 across the Blue Ridge. The end of the first quarter of the century saw the advance of the Scotch-Irish and the Palatine Germans up the Shenandoah Valley into the western part of Virginia, and along the Piedmont region of the Carolinas. The Germans in New York pushed the frontier of settlement up the Mohawk to German Flats. In Pennsylvania the town of Bedford indicates the line of settlement. Settlements soon began on the New River, on the Great Kanawha, and on the sources of the Yadkin and French Broad. The King attempted to arrest the advance by his proclamation of 1763, forbidding settlements beyond the sources of the rivers flowing into the Atlantic; but in vain. In the period of the Revolution the frontier crossed the Alleghenies into Kentucky and Tennessee, and the upper waters of the Ohio were settled. When the first census was taken in 1790, the continuous settled area was bounded by a line which ran near the coast of Maine, and included New England except a portion of Vermont and New Hampshire, New York along the Hudson and up the Mohawk about Schenectady, eastern and southern Pennsylvania, Virginia well across the Shenandoah Valley, and the Carolinas and eastern Georgia. Beyond this region of continuous settlement were the small settled areas of Kentucky and Tennessee, and the Ohio, with the mountains intervening between them and the Atlantic area, thus giving a new and important character to the frontier. The isolation of the region increased its peculiarly American tendencies, and the need of transportation facilities to connect it with the East called out important schemes of internal improvement, which will be noted farther on. The "West," as a self-conscious section, began to evolve.

THE WEST

From decade to decade distinct advances of the frontier occurred. By the census of 1820 the settled area included Ohio, southern Indiana and Illinois, southeastern Missouri, and about one-half of Louisiana. This settled area had surrounded Indian areas, and the management of these tribes became an object of political concern. The frontier region of the time lay along the Great Lakes, where Astor's American Fur Company operated in the Indian trade, and beyond the Mississippi, where Indian traders extended their activity even to the Rocky Mountains; Florida also furnished frontier conditions. The Mississippi River region was the scene of typical frontier settlements.

The rising steam navigation on western waters, the opening of the Erie Canal, and the westward extension of cotton culture added five frontier states to the Union in this period. Grund, writing in 1836, declares: "It appears then that the universal disposition of Americans to emigrate to the western wilderness, in order to enlarge their dominion over inanimate nature, is the actual result of an expansive power which is inherent in them, and which by continually agitating all classes of society is constantly throwing a large portion of the whole population on the extreme confines of the State, in order to gain space for its development. Hardly is a new State or Territory formed before the same principle manifests itself again and gives rise to a further emigration; and so is it destined to go on until a physical barrier must finally obstruct its progress."[1]

In the middle of this century the line indicated by the present eastern boundary of Indian Territory, Nebraska, and Kansas marked the frontier of the Indian country. Minnesota and Wisconsin still exhibited frontier conditions, but the distinctive frontier of the period is found in California, to which the gold discoveries had sent a sudden tide of adventurous miners, and in Oregon, and the settlements in Utah. As the frontier had leaped over the Alleghenies, so now it skipped the Great Plains and the Rocky Mountains; and in the same way that the advance of the frontiersmen beyond the Alleghenies had caused the rise of important questions of transportation and internal improvement, so now the settlers beyond the Rocky Mountains needed means of communication with the East, and in the furnishing of these arose the settlement of the Great Plains and the development of still another kind of frontier life. Railroads, fostered by land grants, sent an increasing tide of immigrants into the Far West. The United States Army fought a series of Indian wars in Minnesota, Dakota, and the Indian Territory.

By 1880 the settled area had been pushed into northern Michigan, Wisconsin, and Minnesota, along Dakota rivers, and in the Black Hills region, and was ascending the rivers of Kansas and Nebraska. The development of mines in Colorado had drawn isolated frontier settlements into that region, and Montana and Idaho were receiving settlers. The frontier was found in these mining camps and the ranches of the Great Plains. The superintendent of the census for 1890 reports, as previously stated, that the settlements of the West lie so scattered over the region that there can no longer be said to be a frontier line.

1. Grund, *Americans*, 1836, II, p. 8.

Frontier Succession

In these successive frontiers we find natural boundary lines which have served to mark and to effect the characteristics of the frontiers, namely: the "fall line," the Allegheny Mountains; the Mississippi; the Missouri where its direction approximates north and south; the line of the arid lands, approximately the ninety-ninth meridian; and the Rocky Mountains. The fall line marked the frontier of the seventeenth century; the Alleghenies that of the eighteenth; the Mississippi that of the first quarter of the nineteenth; the Missouri that of the middle of this century (omitting the California movement); and the belt of the Rocky Mountains and the arid tract, the present frontier. Each was won by a series of Indian wars.

At the Atlantic frontier one can study the germs of processes repeated at each successive frontier. We have the complex European life sharply precipitated by the wilderness into the simplicity of primitive conditions. The first frontier had to meet its Indian question, its question of the disposition of the public domain, of the means of intercourse with older settlements, of the extension of political organization, of religious and educational activity. And the settlement of these and similar questions for one frontier served as a guide for the next. The American student needs not to go to the "prim little townships of Sleswick" for illustrations of the law of continuity and development. For example, he may study the origin of our land policies in the colonial land policy; he may see how the system grew by adapting the statutes to the customs of the successive frontiers. He may see how the mining experience in the lead regions of Wisconsin, Illinois, and Iowa was applied to the mining laws of the Sierras, and how our Indian policy has been a series of experimentations on successive frontiers. Each tier of new States has found in the older ones material for its constitutions. Each frontier has made similar contributions to American character....

Influences of the Frontier

1. Composite Nationality

... We may next inquire what were the influences on the East and on the Old World....

First, we note that the frontier promoted the formation of a composite nationality for the American people. The coast was preponderantly English, but the later tides of continental immigration flowed across to the free lands. This was the case from the early colonial days. The Scotch-Irish and the Palatine Germans, or "Pennsylvania Dutch," furnished the dominant element in the stock of the colonial frontier. With these peoples were also the freed indented servants, or redemptioners, who at the expiration of their time of service passed to the frontier. Governor Spotswood of Virginia writes in 1717, "The inhabitants of our frontiers are composed generally of such as have been transported hither as servants, and, being out of their time, settle themselves where land is to be taken up and that will produce the necessarys of life with little labour."[2] Very generally these redemptioners were of non-English stock. In the crucible of the frontier the immigrants were Americanized, liberated, and fused into a mixed race, English in neither nationality nor characteristics. The process has gone on from the early days to our own....

2. Industrial Interdependence

In another way the advance of the frontier decreased our dependence on England. The coast, particularly of the South, lacked diversified industries, and was dependent on England for the bulk of its supplies. In the South there was even a dependence on the Northern colonies for articles of food. Governor Glenn, of South Carolina, writes in the middle of the eighteenth century: "Our trade with New York and Philadelphia was of this sort, draining us of all the little money and bills we could gather from other places for their bread, flour, beer, hams, bacon, and other things of their produce, all which, except beer, our new townships begin to supply us with, which are settled with very industrious and thriving Germans. This no doubt diminishes the number of shipping and the appearance of our trade, but it is far from being a detriment to us." Before long the frontier created a demand for merchants. As it retreated from the coast it became less and less possible for England to bring her supplies

---

2. "Spottswood Papers," in the Collections of the Virginia Historical Society, I, II.

directly to the consumer's wharfs, and carry away staple crops, and staple crops began to give way to diversified agriculture for a time. The effect of this phase of the frontier action upon the northern section is perceived when we realize how the advance of the frontier aroused seaboard cities like Boston, New York, and Baltimore, to engage in rivalry for what Washington called "the extensive and valuable trade of a rising empire."[3]

3. National Legislation

The legislation which most developed the powers of the national government, and played the largest part in its activity, was conditioned on the frontier. Writers have discussed the subjects of tariff, land, and internal improvement, as subsidiary to the slavery question. But when American history comes to be rightly viewed it will be seen that the slavery question is an incident. In the period from the end of the first half of the present century to the close of the Civil War slavery rose to primary, but far from exclusive, importance. ... The growth of nationalism and the evolution of American political institutions were dependent on the advance of the frontier....

... The pioneer needed the goods of the coast, and so the grand series of internal improvement and railroad legislation began, with potent nationalizing effects. Over internal improvements occurred great debates, in which grave constitutional questions were discussed. Sectional groupings appear in the votes, profoundly significant for the historian. Loose construction increased as the nation marched westward. But the West was not content with bringing the farm to the factory. Under the lead of Clay—"Harry of the West" —protective tariffs were passed, with the cry of bringing the factory to the farm. The disposition of the public lands was a third important subject of national legislation influenced by the frontier.

4. The Public Domain

The public domain has been a force of profound importance in the nationalization and development of the government. The effects of the struggle of the landed and the landless States, and of the Ordinance of 1787, need no discussion. Administratively the frontier called out some of the highest and most vitalizing activities of the general government. The purchase of Louisiana was perhaps the constitutional turning point in the history of the Republic, inasmuch as it afforded both a new area for national legislation and the occasion of the downfall of the policy of strict construction. But the purchase of Louisiana was called out by frontier needs and demands. As frontier States accrued to the Union the national power grew. In a speech on the dedication of the Calhoun monument Mr. Lamar explained: "In 1789 the States were the creators of the Federal Government; in 1861 the Federal Government was the creator of a large majority of the States."

When we consider the public domain from the point of view of the sale and disposal of the public lands we are again brought face to face with the frontier. The policy of the United States in dealing with its lands is in sharp contrast with the European system of scientific administration. Efforts to make this domain a source of revenue, and to withhold it from emigrants in order that settlement might be compact, were in vain. The jealousy and the fears of the East were powerless in the face of the demands of the frontiersmen. John Quincy Adams was obliged to confess: "My own system of administration, which was to make the national domain the inexhaustible fund for progressive and unceasing internal improvement, has failed." The reason is obvious; a system of administration was not what the West demanded; it wanted land. Adams states the situation as follows: "The slaveholders of the South have bought the cooperation of the western country by the bribe of the western lands, abandoning to the new Western States their own proportion of the public property and aiding them in the design of grasping all the lands into their own hands. Thomas H. Benton was the author of this system, which he brought forward as a substitute for the American system of Mr. Clay, and to supplant him as the leading statesman of the West. Mr. Clay, by his tariff compromise with Mr. Calhoun, abandoned his own American system. At the same time he brought forward a plan for distributing among all the States of the Union the proceeds of the sales of the public lands. His bill for that purpose passed

---

3. Weston, Documents connected with History of South Carolina, p. 61.

both Houses of Congress, but was vetoed by President Jackson, who, in his annual message of December, 1832, formally recommended that all public lands should be gratuitously given away to individual adventurers and to the States in which the lands are situated."

"No subject," said Henry Clay, "which has presented itself to the present, or perhaps any preceding, Congress, is of greater magnitude than that of the public lands." When we consider the far-reaching effects of the government's land policy upon political, economic, and social aspects of American life, we are disposed to agree with him. But this legislation was framed under frontier influences, and under the lead of Western statesmen like Benton and Jackson. Said Senator Scott of Indiana in 1841: "I consider the preemption law merely declaratory of the custom or common law of the settlers."

NATIONAL TENDENCIES OF THE FRONTIER

It is safe to say that the legislation with regard to land, tariff, and internal improvements—the American system of the nationalizing Whig party—was conditioned on frontier ideas and needs. But it was not merely in legislative action that the frontier worked against the sectionalism of the coast. The economic and social characteristics of the frontier worked against sectionalism. The men of the frontier had closer resemblances to the Middle region than to either of the other sections. Pennsylvania had been the seed-plot of frontier emigration, and, although she passed on her settlers along the Great Valley into the west of Virginia and the Carolinas, yet the industrial society of these Southern frontiersmen was always more like that of the Middle region than like that of the tide-water portion of the South, which later came to spread its industrial type throughout the South.

The Middle region, entered by New York harbor, was an open door to all Europe. The tide-water part of the South represented typical Englishmen, modified by a warm climate and servile labor, and living in baronial fashion on great plantations; New England stood for a special English movement—Puritanism. The Middle region was less English than the other sections. It had a wide mixture of nationalities, a varied society, the mixed town and county system of local government, a varied economic life, many religious sects. In short, it was a region mediating between New England and the South, and the East and the West.

. . . .

The spread of cotton culture into the interior of the South finally broke down the contrast between the "tide-water" region and the rest of the State, and based Southern interests on slavery.

. . . .

It was the nationalizing tendency of the West that transformed the democracy of Jefferson into the national republicanism of Monroe and the democracy of Andrew Jackson. The West of the War of 1812, the West of Clay, and Benton and Harrison, and Andrew Jackson, shut off by the Middle States and the mountains from the coast sections, had a solidarity of its own with national tendencies. On the tide of the Father of Waters, North and South met and mingled into a nation. Interstate migration went steadily on—a process of cross-fertilization of ideas and institutions. The fierce struggle of the sections over slavery on the western frontier does not diminish the truth of this statement; it proves the truth of it. Slavery was a sectional trait that would not down, but in the West it could not remain sectional. It was the greatest of frontiersmen who declared: "I believe this Government can not endure permanently half slave and half free. It will become all of one thing or all of the other." Nothing works for nationalism like intercourse within the nation. Mobility of population is death to localism, and the western frontier worked irresistibly in unsettling population. The effect reached back from the frontier and affected profoundly the Atlantic coast and even the Old World.

But the most important effect of the frontier has been in the promotion of democracy here and in Europe. As has been indicated, the frontier is productive of individualism. Complex society is precipitated by the wilderness into a kind of primitive organization based on the family. The tendency is anti-social. It produces antipathy to control, and particularly to any direct control. The tax-gatherer is viewed as a representative of oppression. Prof. Osgood, in an able article, has pointed out that the frontier conditions prevalent in the colonies are important factors in the explanation of the American Revolution, where individual liberty was sometimes confused with absence of all effective government. The same conditions aid in explaining the difficulty of instituting a strong government in the period of the confederacy. The frontier individualism has from the beginning promoted democracy.

. . . .

So long as free land exists, the opportunity for a competency exists, and economic power secures political power. But the democracy born of free land, strong in selfishness and individualism, intolerant of administrative experience and education, and pressing individual liberty beyond its proper bounds, has its dangers as well as its benefits. Individualism in America has allowed a laxity in regard to governmental affairs which has rendered possible the spoils system and all the manifest evils that follow from the lack of a highly developed civic spirit. In this connection may be noted also the influence of frontier conditions in permitting lax business honor, inflated paper currency and wild-cat banking. The colonial and revolutionary frontier was the region whence emanated many of the worst forms of an evil currency. The West in the War of 1812 repeated the phenomenon on the frontier of that day, while the speculation and wild-cat banking of the period of the crisis of 1837 occurred on the new frontier belt of the next tier of States. Thus each one of the periods of lax financial integrity coincides with periods when a new set of frontier communities had arisen, and coincides in area with these successive frontiers, for the most part.

. . . .

ATTEMPTS TO CHECK AND REGULATE THE FRONTIER

The East has always feared the result of an unregulated advance of the frontier, and has tried to check and guide it. The English authorities would have checked settlement at the headwaters of the Atlantic tributaries and allowed the "savages to enjoy their deserts in quiet lest the peltry trade should decrease."

. . . .

But the English Government was not alone in its desire to limit the advance of the frontier and guide its destinies. Tide-water Virginia and South Carolina gerrymandered those colonies to insure the dominance of the coast in their legislatures. Washington desired to settle a State at a time in the Northwest; Jefferson would reserve from settlement the territory of his Louisiana Purchase north of the thirty-second parallel, in order to offer it to the Indians in exchange for their settlements east of the Mississippi. "When we shall be full on this side," he writes, "we may lay off a range of States on the western bank from the head of the mouth, and so range after range, advancing compactly as we multiply." Madison went so far as to argue to the French minister that the United States had no interest in seeing population extend itself on the right bank of the Mississippi, but should rather fear it. When the Oregon question was under debate, in 1824, Smyth, of Virginia, would draw an unchangeable line for the limits of the United States at the outer limit of two tiers of States beyond the Mississippi, complaining that the seaboard States were being drained of the flower of their population by the bringing of too much land into market. Even Thomas Benton, the man of widest views of the destiny of the West, at this stage of his career declared that along the ridge of the Rocky mountains "the western limits of the Republic should be drawn, and the statue of the fabled god Terminus should be raised upon its highest peak, never to be thrown down.[4] But the attempts to limit the boundaries, to restrict land sales and settlement, and to deprive the West of its share of political power were all in vain. Steadily the frontier of settlement advanced and carried with it individualism, democracy, and nationalism, and powerfully affected the East and the Old World.

The most effective efforts of the East to regulate the frontier came through its educational and religious activity, exerted by interstate migration and by organized societies. Speaking in 1835, Dr. Lyman Beecher declared: "It is equally plain that the religious and political destiny of our nation is to be decided in the West," and he pointed out that the population of the West "is assembled from all the States of the Union and from all the

---

4. Speech in the Senate, March 1, 1825; Register of Debates, I, 721.

nations of Europe, and is rushing in like the waters of the flood, demanding for its moral preservation the immediate and universal action of those institutions which discipline the mind and arm the conscience and the heart. And so various are the opinions and habits, and so recent and imperfect is the acquaintance, and so sparse are the settlements of the West, that no homogeneous public sentiment can be formed to legislate immediately into being the requisite institutions. And yet they are all needed immediately in their utmost perfection and power. A nation is being 'born in a day.' ... But what will become of the West if her prosperity rushes up to such a majesty of power, while those great institutions linger which are necessary to form the mind and the conscience and the heart of that vast world. It must not be permitted.... Let no man at the East quiet himself and dream of liberty, whatever may become of the West.... Her destiny is our destiny.[5]

With the appeal to the conscience of New England, he adds appeals to her fears lest other religious sects anticipate her own. The New England preacher and school-teacher left their mark on the West. The dread of Western emancipation from New England's political and economic control was paralleled by her fears lest the West cut loose from her religion....

As seaboard cities like Philadelphia, New York, and Baltimore strove for the mastery of Western trade, so the various denominations strove for the possession of the West. Thus an intellectual stream from New England sources fertilized the West. Other sections sent their missionaries; but the real struggle was between sects. The contest for power and the expansive tendency furnished to the various sects by the existence of a moving frontier must have had important results on the character of religious organization in the United States. The multiplication of rival churches in the little frontier towns had deep and lasting social effects. The religious aspects of the frontier make a chapter in our history which needs study.

From the conditions of frontier life came intellectual traits of profound importance. The works of travelers along each frontier from colonial days onward describe certain common traits, and these traits have, while softening down, still persisted as survivals in

5. *Plea for the West* (Cincinnati, 1835) pp. 11 ff.

the place of their origin, even when a higher social organization succeeded. The result is that to the frontier the American intellect owes its striking characteristics. That coarseness and strength combined with acuteness and inquisitiveness; that practical, inventive turn of mind, quick to find expedients; that masterful grasp of material things, lacking in the artistic but powerful to effect great ends; that restless, nervous energy; that dominant individualism, working for good and for evil, and withal that buoyancy and exuberance which comes with freedom—these are traits of the frontier, or traits called out elsewhere because of the existence of the frontier. Since the days when the fleet of Columbus sailed into the waters of the New World, America has been another name for opportunity, and the people of the United States have taken their tone from the incessant expansion which has not only been open but has even been forced upon them. He would be a rash prophet who should assert that the expansive character of American life has now entirely ceased. Movement has been its dominant fact, and, unless this training has no effect upon a people, the American energy will continually demand a wider field for its exercise. But never again will such gifts of free land offer themselves. For a moment, at the frontier, the bonds of custom are broken and unrestraint is triumphant. There is not *tabula rasa*. The stubborn American environment is there with its imperious summons to accept its conditions; the inherited ways of doing things are also there; and yet, in spite of environment, and in spite of custom, each frontier did indeed furnish a new field of opportunity, a gate of escape from the bondage of the past; and freshness, and confidence, and scorn of older society, impatience of its restraints and its ideas, and indifference to its lessons, have accompanied the frontier. What the Mediterranean Sea was to the Greeks, breaking the bond of custom, offering new experiences, calling out new institutions and activities, that, and more, the ever retreating frontier has been to the United States directly, and to the nations of Europe more remotely. And now, four centuries from the discovery of America, at the end of a hundred years of life under the Constitution, the frontier has gone, and with its going has closed the first period of American history.

13

Boundary Studies in Political Geography

JULIAN V. MINGHI*

A substantial part of the literature in political geography is centered on the study of boundaries and their associated regions. Because political boundaries form the areal expression of the limits of jurisdiction and power of the system to which they belong, they are perhaps the most palpable political geographic phenomena, and thus have held a strong attraction for students of political geography. Approaches to the study of the nature and role of boundaries as spatial factors have been varied, and ideas regarding boundaries have been related closely to their historical and geographical milieu.[1] The resultant methodological variety has produced a substantial set of findings that often are in conflict with each other. This review article attempts to take critical stock of the body of knowledge that has emerged.

We shall see how boundary classifications have evolved, from the simple artificial-vs.-natural division, through classifications describing the basis of the boundary, as physical, anthropogeographical, and so forth, to a classification which relates the boundary to the cultural landscape at the time of establishment. There has also been a shift in interest away from the nature of the boundary's location and history, to its function as it has changed over time. There has been a growing realization that it is the significant similarities and differences between the sociopolitical communities the boundary divides that are reflected in its functions. The importance of circulation zones describing intensity of movement in frontier regions has been increasingly noted, as has the close relationship of distance and the boundary in the spatial form of this circulation.

In order to define some of the basic concepts underlying the nature and role of boundaries, boundary studies in a general context will be treated first. On the basis of a classification according to content and aims, a number of selected case studies will be considered. If generalizations are to have any validity, they must be drawn from and tested by significant case studies that fulfill the requirements of objective research. Many of the boundary studies found in the literature do not meet such qualifications and thus conclusions from these studies have little value in the body of knowledge on the geography of boundaries.

BOUNDARIES IN GENERAL

One of the earliest systematic studies of boundaries is to be found in Semple's famous work, *Influences of Geographic Environment*, in her chapter on "Geographic Boundaries."[2]

Reproduced from the *Annals* of the Association of American Geographers, Volume LIII, 1963, by permission of the author and publisher.

* Julian Minghi is a co-editor of this volume.

1. Stephen B. Jones, "Boundary Concepts in the Setting of Place and Time," *Annals*, Association of American Geographers, Vol. 49 (September, 1959), pp. 241–55.

2. Ellen Churchill Semple, *Influences of Geographic Environment* (New York: Holt, 1911), pp. 204 ff.

Her thesis was that "nature abhors fixed boundary lines," and that consequently boundaries rarely attained an established equilibrium, but were subject to constant fluctuation. She, in fact, equated boundaries with frontiers. Uninhabitable areas, according to Semple, formed the most "scientific" boundaries because they both partitioned and protected. In this context, Semple cited the conscious creation of march areas to form artificial border wastes.

Even when a boundary's location was fixed exactly, Semple observed that the customs divide did not always coincide with it. To support this assertion, she pointed to the example of the "zona libre" idea, as between Mexico and Texas in 1858, under which an attempt was made to establish a commercial equilibrium in the frontier zone. In such a situation both modification and assimilation pressures took effect on either side of the boundary within the zone. The longer the reach of the arm of authority in the frontier area, the weaker that authority, and the more likely the political defection of the area to the stronger side, as in the case of Texas from Mexico to the United States, and of Acre from Bolivia to Brazil.

This dynamic view of boundaries, not as artificial lines, but as variable zones open to pressures from both the physical and cultural environments, was in close keeping with the organismic state theory of Ratzel, whose ideas Semple espoused and developed.

Semple's generalizations have some relevance to the situation existing at different periods in the history of the Canada–United States boundary region in the Far West. During the period of joint occupancy prior to 1846, the frontier area was without any equilibrium between the contending forces, and even in the era during the first forty years after partition, the modification and assimilation pressures exerted over the border region by the growing dominance of the United States commerce all but caused the political defection of the entire region to the stronger side.

Much of the literature on boundaries in general was written during the two world wars or in their aftermath. These studies were concerned with the nature of boundaries in terms of their being "good" or "bad" from the military point of view. They were part of a search for the causes of friction between nations and for a means of avoiding it. Such studies, although in large measure "utilitarian," served to focus attention on the phenomenon of boundaries and to provide many valuable findings. The redrawing of boundaries based on a variety of considerations in the postwar periods attracted much interest and research activity. This periodic preoccupation, however, has tended to concentrate the research effort within times of change, while interest in boundaries during more "normal" times has not been so great.

Holdich[3] and Lyde,[4] writing during World War I, differed in opinion on the relative merits of boundaries as barriers or bonds. Holdich viewed boundaries as barriers and maintained that the "best" boundaries (i.e., those least likely to be causes of war) must be mountains, lakes, or deserts (suggested as analogous to sea frontiers), while lines of longitude and latitude made for inherently "bad" boundaries. Lyde, however, argued that boundaries should act positively, encouraging peaceful international intercourse, and consequently thought that rivers, as regional bonds, would make good boundaries. This defense-vs.-assimilation argument permeated most discussion on boundary functions at this time. Johnson[5] later criticized both views as oversimplifications, maintaining that the sequences of World War I had disproved Holdich, and that litigation over water rights and uses usually bedevils relations between the riparian states. He also recognized that strategic and linguistic considerations could not be reconciled in the attempt to establish a boundary.

Fawcett,[6] like Holdich, held little respect for straight-line boundaries, not from military considerations, but because of their artificiality in that they were not marked by evident features of the natural landscape. He thought the forty-ninth parallel, already in existence for a century east of the Rockies, and for over seventy years on the Pacific slope, "absurd"

3. Thomas H. Holdich, *Political Frontiers and Boundary Making* (London: Macmillan, 1916), and "Political Boundaries," *Scottish Geographical Magazine*, Vol. 32 (1916), pp. 497–507.
4. Lionel William Lyde, *Some Frontiers of Tomorrow: An Aspiration for Europe* (London: A. & C. Black, 1915).
5. Douglas Wilson Johnson, "The Role of Political Boundaries," *Geographical Review*, Vol. 4 (September, 1917), pp. 208–213.
6. Charles B. Fawcett, *Frontiers: A Study in Political Geography* (Oxford: Clarendon Press, 1918).

and "a source of jokes as prolific as the mother-in-law." He attacked it as "perhaps the least efficient and most costly boundary on earth." Certainly there was great cost involved in demarcating the boundary, although its efficiency has been determined more by the relationship between the societies it divides than by the actual nature of the line.

In his "Principles in the Determination of Boundaries," Brigham[7] introduced a new concept, largely as a criticism of an article by Patten[8] which appeared four years earlier and was based on the traditional distinction between "natural" boundaries as "good" and "artificial" boundaries as "bad." Brigham wrote of "boundaries of economic equilibrium." He saw a conflict between the forces of nationalism, which in their European context produced small states, and those seeking economies of scale which demanded big states. He reasoned that economically unnatural boundaries (those resisting economies of scale) rather than those boundaries not marked by definite physical phenomena were wrong. He cited the boundary between Germany and the Low Countries with special reference to its role as a generator of friction in 1915.

Following the disorganization of spatial relations in the areas affected by the many boundary changes of the Versailles Peace Treaty, the consequent development of new patterns of spatial interaction stimulated renewed interest in boundary research in Europe. A method akin to a "before and after" approach, based on sound and plentiful data, was often adopted in the study of the recent evolution of some of these European boundaries.[9] The importance of the "before and after" approach will be made clear below in the section on boundary change in the review of case studies.

A critical and provocative note by Boggs[10] in 1932 held that up to that point boundary studies had been confined to international boundaries, and that they had usually been carried out on the false assumption that the functions of the boundaries studied were both uniform and static. All "scientific" geographical study of boundaries, he asserted, should take into account all types of boundaries and all their functions. Without being specific, Boggs suggested that certain general principles could be drawn from the relationship between different types of boundaries and the different sets of boundary functions. A most valuable observation noted that for both international and internal boundaries, functions are not static but do change over time.

Hartshorne[11] further clarified the distinction of function by his suggestions contained in a short note in 1936 for classifying boundaries, not according to physical type, but according to their relationship with the cultural landscape at the time of their establishment. Hence an *antecedent* boundary precedes development of most of the features of the cultural landscape, a *pioneer* precedes all settlement, and its associated zone is in *virginal* form until the arrival of human settlement, and a *subsequent* boundary has a degree of *conformity* with major and minor natural and cultural divisions. In the absence of *conformity* the boundary is held to be *superimposed*. The basic property of a boundary which results in inertia was noted by Hartshorne. No matter what its relationships when established, he pointed out, over time it becomes *intrenched* in the cultural structure of its surrounding region.

One of the more valuable, yet largely ignored, pre-World War II contributions to the geography of boundaries was made by Lösch.[12] Quoting Ratzel as his political geographic

---

7. Albert Perry Brigham, "Principles in the Determination of Boundaries," *Geographical Review*, Vol. 7 (April, 1919), pp. 201–219.

8. Simon N. Patten, "Unnatural Boundaries of European States," *Survey*, Vol. 34 (1915), pp. 24–32.

9. See for example, P. de Lapradelle, *La Frontière: Etude de Droit International* (Paris: Les Editions Internationales, 1928); J. Ancel, *La Géographie des Frontières* (Paris, 1927); Karl Haushofer, *Grenzen in ihre geographischen und politischen Bedeutung* (Berlin-Grünewald: Kurt Vowinckel Verlag, 1927); J. Ancel, "Les frontières, étude de géographie politique," *Académie de Droit International, Recueil des Cours*, Vol. 55 (1936), pp. 207–210; and Otto Maull, *Politische Grenzen* (Weltpolitische Bucherei, Vol. 13) (Berlin: Zentral-Verlag, 1928).

10. S. Whittemore Boggs, "Boundary Functions and the Principles of Boundary Making," *Annals*, Association of American Geographers, Vol. 22 (March, 1932), pp. 48–49.

11. Richard Hartshorne, "Suggestions on the Terminology of Political Boundaries," abstract, *Annals*, Association of American Geographers, Vol. 26 (March, 1936), pp. 56–57.

12. August Lösch, *The Economics of Location*, trans. from 2nd rev. ed. by William B. Woglom, with the assistance of Wolfgang F. Stolper (New Haven: Yale University Press, 1954). The lack of a translation in English until 1954, and Lösch's reputation as a student of location economics rather than of political geography, are no doubt largely responsible for our ignorance of Lösch's contribution.

authority, Lösch found it useful to compare his described economic regions with political regions in terms of their similarities and dissimilarities. This led to a comparison of the frontiers of the two regional types. Lösch noted a wide range of areal coincidence between them, although he recognized that political frontiers were more rigid and more sharply defined, thus reinforcing Hartshorne's *intrenchment* factor with a premium on continuity, as opposed to the "maximum prosperity" force behind economic boundaries. Lösch also threw light on why, following a shift in the political boundary, the new border regions so often become depressed areas. They must transpose their traditional economic activity and often curtail it. Furthermore, the greater the population of these regions the more apparent the effect. Although the forces of comparative advantage may work to the contrary, Lösch's observations have been proven to be true generally.

Lösch further studied national boundaries as locational factors. In comparing per capita sales in Windsor and London, Ontario, in 1931, both cities being virtually the same size in population, he found that the retails sales of goods which were cheaper in Canada were far greater in Windsor on the international boundary than in London, some distance back from the boundary; but of goods cheaper in the United States, the opposite was true. The presence of the political boundary created a price differential in certain goods, which in turn became a factor in the location of retail outlets for these goods. This situation has since been documented many times.

Lösch's greatest contribution came with his insight into the impact of a boundary on the flow of a commodity and on its consequent spatial pattern of distribution. El Paso's financial sphere was established by mapping the location of the banking houses keeping accounts with banks in that Texas city in 1914.[13] The pattern produced by mapping the flow of capital was identical to that deduced theoretically by Lösch for the movement of a good (Map 13.1 and Fig. 13.1). In his model, Lösch had found that distance as well as tariffs affected capital transactions and trade in physical goods in the same way that the United States–Mexican boundary affected the flow of capital to and from El Paso. Hence,

13. Some years prior to the establishment of the Reserve Bank System.

for the first time by applying location theory to the study of the impact of a boundary, Lösch indicated how one could actually measure a boundary by giving it a *distance* value. Yet it was to be some years before further work would be done along these lines.

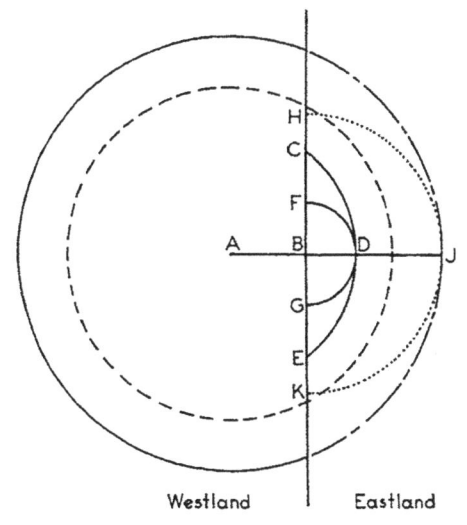

Fig. 13.1 REDUCTION OF MARKET AREAS BY A TARIFF

If Eastland collects duties of a height *DJ*, the market of *A* in Eastland would be bounded by *CDE* if deliveries can be made directly to every point, and by *FDG* if only through the customshouse *B*. If *HK* represents not a customs border but a river with only one bridge at *B*, the Eastland market area would be bounded by *HJK*. (After August Lösch, *The Economics of Location*.)

In his *International Boundaries*, Boggs took the view that boundary functions were "negative rather than positive,"[14] and repeatedly stressed their restrictive nature. He rejected Lyde's hypothesis, then a generation old, that boundaries acted as bonds. Boggs saw boundaries as barriers to economic intercourse with their "almost unimaginable multiplicity of restrictions." He spoke of this *interruptive* factor as a "nuisance effect."[15]

14. S. Whittemore Boggs, *International Boundaries: A Study of Boundary Functions and Problems* (New York: Columbia University Press, 1940), p. 11.

15. *Ibid.*, p. 16. Boggs devised an interruptive factor index for world regions based on boundary miles per 1,000 square miles of each state. This crude index showed the degree of political fragmentation in world areas while the international relationships of the political units therein, and their related boundary functions, were ignored.

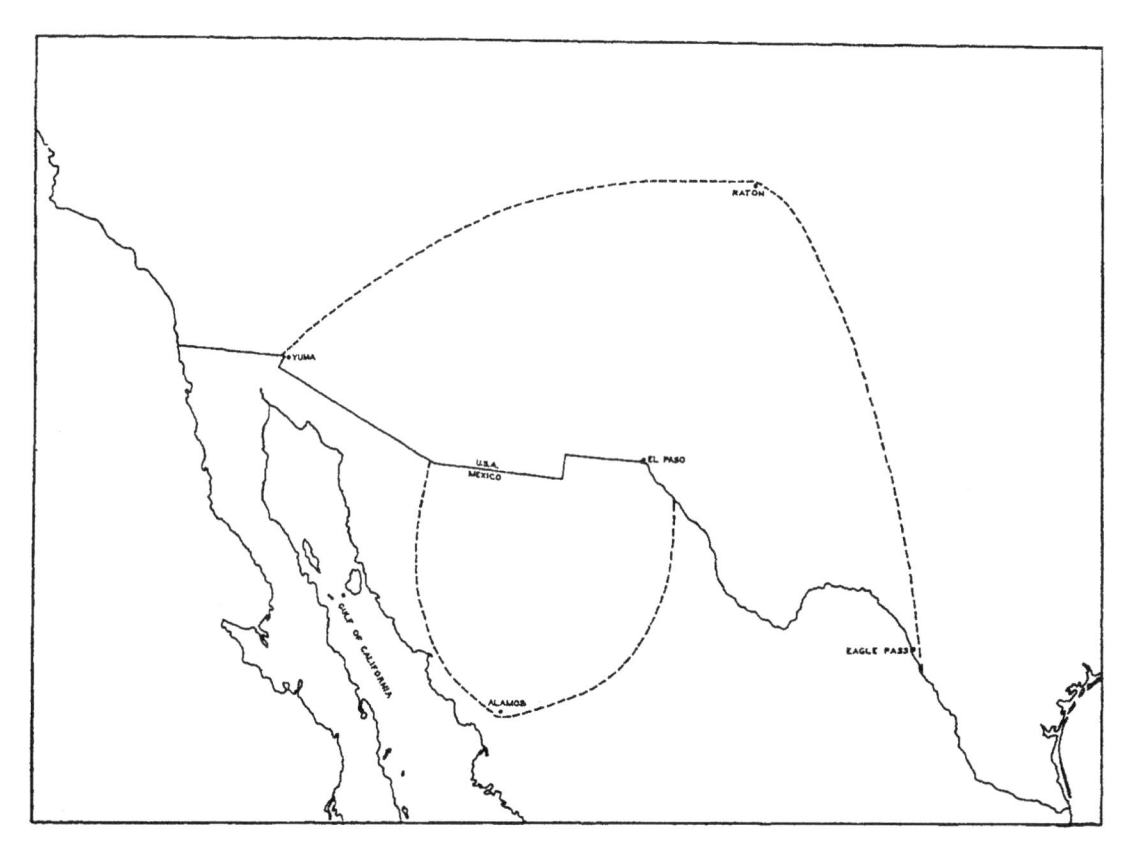

Map 13.1 EL PASO'S FINANCIAL SPHERE, 1914 (AFTER LÖSCH)
Dotted line marks limit of area within which banks kept accounts with El Paso banks.

Boggs' classification of boundaries into physical, geometrical, anthropogeographical, and complex, represented some advance in research techniques. He also presented a useful idea in metaphoric form when he asserted that any boundary is permeable and over time "a sort of osmosis takes place," the osmotic pressure increasing directly with institutional barriers to interactance.

In his 1940 lecture on "Natural Frontiers," Broek reiterated Lösch's observation concerning the difference between the sharp and definite political boundary on the one hand, and most other types of boundaries, which are "really merging zones of the areal distribution of different types of a phenomenon," on the other.[16] In addition, Broek proceeded to dispel the traditional idea of the inherent "goodness" of the "natural" boundary, emphasizing that boundaries were essentially man-made political phenomena, and even the "unbased" boundary, i.e., one not based on a physical criterion, created its own frontier region. This view served to reinforce Hartshorne's "intrenched boundary" concept. Broek further rejected the whole concept of natural boundaries by substituting the term "physiographic."

Under the influence of the increasing chaos in Europe, Boggs, in 1941, deplored the lack of good maps to show the relative effect of national boundaries.[17] He maintained that as the speed of travel and communication increases, and transport costs decrease, the factors producing fundamental change make

16. Jan O. M. Broek, "The Problem of 'Natural Frontiers,'" in *Frontiers of the Future*, Lectures, University of California, Los Angeles (Committee on International Relations), 1940 (Berkeley: University of California Press, 1941), pp. 3–20.

17. S. Whittemore Boggs, "Mapping the Changing World: Suggested Developments in Maps," *Annals*, Association of American Geographers, Vol. 31 (June, 1941), pp. 119–128.

possible the integration of a large single nation, and also make impractical the division of Europe along the highly nationalistic lines of numerous small states. He felt it important to show the distribution of, and regional contrasts in, such factors as travel-speed, communication-speed, and transport-cost, and how these are affected in regions with a multiplicity of international boundaries. This was the first attempt at a scientific approach in measuring the impact of a boundary on the normal flow of communication, and again there was the implication of the close relationship between the distance and the boundary factors.

In 1942 Spykman introduced for the first time in explicit terms, the study of boundaries as "points of contact of territorial power structures" as opposed to the more traditional approach which, he asserted, characterized boundaries as lines of demarcation between legal systems.[18] Viewed in this manner, the position of a boundary, when observed over time, could become an index to the power relations of the contending forces on either side.

Spykman dispelled the myth that boundaries could be "impassable barriers from nature," noting that the arrival of three-dimensional warfare had forced a change in frontier concepts.

Noting the tendency toward larger states, he suggested that the survival of smaller states was in part due to their strategic significance to the larger states. Furthermore, as the defensive value of a frontier decreased, so did the validity of the concept of buffer states, which were at best, according to Spykman, protective devices made obsolete by modern systems of communication.

Extending the "index of power potential" idea into the utilitarian sphere, Spykman suggested that when the time came to redraw international boundaries at the end of the then-current war, a premium should be put upon avoiding the creation of inequalities in power potential, because the major interest in frontiers should be no longer in terms of the strategic value of the border area but of the power potential of the territory it surrounds. Hence, for Spykman the ultimate objective was to have the new boundaries drawn in such a way as to create states of approximately equal strength.

Revolutionary as this concept was at the time, it left unanswered the problem of measuring the power potential of a given area at a point in time with the necessary accuracy, and, despite its dynamic nature, the concept assumed a static power potential for each geographic area contained within these "new" boundaries.

With the end of World War II in sight there appeared two books, by Peattie and Jones, on the problems of boundary making.[19] The thesis of Peattie's book was that boundaries with few functions were more serviceable to mankind than boundaries with many important functions; that is, the weaker the boundary the better. Although he had doubts about the feasibility of small states. Peattie advanced a type of resurrected buffer state idea which suggested encouraging regionalism in frontier areas, especially those that were traditionally sources of friction between adjoining states, such as Alsace between France and Germany.

In the other problem-solving work, Jones,[20] writing primarily as a guide to laymen who may be instrumental in decisions involving boundary changes of great importance, showed the deep influence of Boggs, under whom he had worked in the State Department. The book is generally considered a sequel to the latter's work of 1940.[21] Despite its utilitarian intent, there was, as Boggs stated in the foreword, "perhaps no better brief introduction . . . to the whole field of boundaries. . . ."[22] Jones hypothesized that, in the event of a period dominated by overripe nationalism, contrary to Peattie's belief, "the only good boundary will be the one that strengthens the power structure of one's own state."[23] Despite the recognized fact that governments are playing an inescapably increasing role in economic life, thus giving already anachronistic

---

18. Nicholas John Spykman, "Frontiers, Security and International Organization," *Geographical Review*, Vol. 32 (July, 1942), p. 437.

19. Roderick Peattie, *Look to the Frontiers: A Geography of the Peace Table* (New York: Harper, 1944); and Stephen B. Jones, *Boundary Making: A Handbook for Statesmen, Treaty Editors and Boundary Commissioners* (Washington, D.C.: Carnegie Endowment for International Peace, 1945).

20. Previewed earlier by Jones in "The Description of International Boundaries," *Annals*, Association of American Geographers, Vol. 33 (June, 1943), pp. 99–117.

21. Boggs, *International Boundaries*. . . .

22. Jones, *Boundary Making* . . . , p. vi.

23. *Ibid.*, p. 19.

boundaries even more ill-fitting functions, Jones saw little hope of solving problems by changing boundaries or by amalgamation because of the depth of national feeling over territorial claims. The solution, Jones thought, lay in changes in concepts of national sovereignty and in the evolution of some supranational control.

Thus during this period up to the end of World War II, the emphasis had been completely shifted from the criteria by which a boundary is drawn, to the functions which it performs. Jones emphasized the importance of understanding circulation patterns as one of the most significant organizing factors. By delimiting circulation regions one could, he suggested, determine places (or lines) of *minimum movement*, and thus avoid dividing a "region." In his context, Jones pointed out that, contrary to Lyde's belief, the division of a "region," such as Upper Silesia after World War I, did *not* have an assimilatory effect.

Although there have been no subsequent books on the general topic of boundaries, several political geography textbooks and a few articles have since contributed to our knowledge.

In his chapter on "Frontiers and Boundaries," Moodie reasoned that, as boundaries epitomized the growth of centralization of authority and power of the states they divided, the functions of a boundary were derived, not from the nature of the line, but from the nature of the communities it separated.[24] Yet Moodie later made the dangerous assumption that there was a direct relationship between the interruptive factor of Boggs' index and boundary friction. In support of his case, he contrasted the high index assigned to Europe with that of North America.

Fischer's article "On Boundaries"[25] appeared long enough after World War II to include consideration of the war's results in Europe. It was a call for more attention to "historical" boundaries. He observed that the criteria on which boundaries have been defined have varied over time. In 1919, language, as an indication of self-determination by cultural distinction, replaced the previous physical emphasis, and after World War II the emphasis shifted to economics coupled with the secondary consideration of population movement. Fischer argued that all boundaries left a lasting imprint, and that the longer a boundary functioned, the harder it was to alter. Hence, there existed concurrent persistence and obsolescence for many boundaries. After a boundary change, the preexisting line often became an internal boundary of secondary importance, yet could persist to be later resurrected. The *de facto* boundary dividing Hudson's Bay Company activity from areas of significant American settlement prior to 1846 in the Pacific Northwest was the Columbia River, which, in its lower course, has survived as an internal boundary dividing the states of Washington and Oregon.

The geopolitical idea regarding boundaries was rejected as representing but a "momentary and transitory expression of the power of adjacent countries," although Fischer did detect the "emergence of a new kind of boundary zone, a zone of economic and social penetration." Economic and various other changes could shift the secondary lines delimiting these zones of penetration, although the political boundary remained. According to him, it is imperative to view these zones in association with the historic importance of the boundary as a stabilizing factor and as a determinant of the distribution of phenomena.

In their textbook, *Principles of Political Geography*, Weigert et al. included two lengthy chapters covering the nature, functions, and impact of boundaries.[26] The barrier function of a boundary was dismissed as a fiction. It was viewed more in its selective role regarding movement across it. Borrowing from Boggs, the authors saw cross-boundary influences as osmotic pressure from the neighbor.

Kristof has written comprehensively on the nature of frontiers as opposed to that of boundaries.[27] Although the author was primarily occupied with the theoretical and philosophical aspects historically underlying this difference, some interesting comments were made concerning the nature of boundaries. The boundary was *inner-oriented*, the outer line of effective control of the central government,

---

24. A. E. Moodie, *The Geography Behind Politics* (London: Hutchinson's University Library, 1957), p. 83.
25. Eric Fischer, "On Boundaries," *World Politics*, Vol. 1 (January, 1949), pp. 196–222.
26. Hans W. Weigert et al., *Principles of Political Geography* (New York: Appleton-Century-Crofts, 1957), pp. 79–109 and 110–141.
27. Ladis D. Kristof, "The Nature of Frontiers and Boundaries," *Annals*, Association of American Geographers, Vol. 49 (September, 1959), pp. 269–282.

and indicated the range and vigor of centripetal forces. Contrary to the "frontier," the boundary was considered a *separating factor*. Jones, East, and Schöller were quoted to this effect, and Lyde, as so many times before, was taken to task for his "misconceived" assimilation concept.

Jones' 1959 presidential address to the Association of American Geographers traced boundary concepts over a breadth of time "from the age of the sling-shot to that of the sputnik...."[28] He concluded with the suggestion that nationalism was near its zenith, and that there was some evidence to support Boggs' belief that changes in boundary functions could lessen friction.

CASE STUDIES ON BOUNDARIES

There has been no previous attempt to categorize boundary studies in geographical literature. The following classification is based principally on the division of labor followed by students in particular studies. Eight categories were found to exist:

1. Studies of disputed areas.
2. Studies of the effect of boundary change.
3. Studies of the evolution of boundaries.
4. Studies of boundary delimitation and demarcation.
5. Studies of exclaves and tiny states.
6. Studies of offshore boundaries.
7. Studies of boundaries in disputes over natural resources.
8. Studies of internal boundaries.

Studies of Disputed Areas

Hartshorne introduced his article "The Polish Corridor" in 1937 with the comment that "the political geographer is interested in analyzing the areal facts and relationships involved in the problem of the Corridor."[29] These are the interests of the political geographer in any boundary study involving disputed areas. Hartshorne stated first the problem that the Corridor presented, and then filled in the political and geographical background of the disputed area. He reviewed the attempted solution by the Germans prior to World War I, during which period the inclusion of Polish territories in Prussia "constituted an indigestible element in the state, especially as nationalism developed." The problem after World War I was that the mixed population in the region (Poles in the rural areas and Prussians in the towns) made fair settlement on the ethnic principle impossible. The creation of the Corridor cut off East Prussia from the rest of Germany and thus established a permanent source of friction. A large German enclave remained within Polish territory. Hartshorne summarized that "there is NO geographical solution, i.e., by change of territory."

The time element, Hartshorne observed, is very important because the factual basis of a dispute is always shifting. Historical associations readily amend with time, and economic ties can easily be realigned, but the slowest to change is the cultural association. Hartshorne further made two interesting generalizations: (1) minorities on the "wrong side" of a boundary, with time, will tend to conform with their surroundings, and (2) local difficulties can be overcome by decreasing the importance of the boundary rather than by moving it.

In 1938, the same author, in a chapter entitled, "A Survey of the Boundary Problems of Europe,[30]" commented on the different conclusions geographers had come to with respect to European boundaries and questioned whether political geography may claim scientific validity, or is merely a vehicle for national prejudices. He found that there were too many unstated assumptions and consequently a lack of critical examination of these assumptions. Accordingly, Hartshorne stated four basic assumptions before his survey of boundary problems was begun. These were: (1) there is no distinction between "natural" and "artificial" boundaries, as all are man-made, (2) all boundaries in time can be disputed, so that the problems are relative, (3) the problems of a boundary are in human terms, and (4) the disputes are usually of minor importance to countries involved but of major importance to the people directly affected by the location of the boundary. Hartshorne then systematically considered

---

28. Stephen B. Jones, "Boundary Concepts in the Setting of Place and Time," p. 241.
29. Richard Hartshorne, "The Polish Corridor," *Journal of Geography*, Vol. 36 (May, 1937), pp. 161–176.

30. Richard Hartshorne, "A Survey of the Boundary Problems of Europe," in *Geographical Aspects of International Relations*, ed. C. C. Colby (Chicago: University of Chicago Press, 1938), pp. 161–213.

each European problem area under the headings: area, country now in, country claimed by, population, percentage who speak language of claimant state.[31] For each problem area he rated from A to E the area's geographical associations with the claimant state in terms of (1) nationality, (2) transport and trade, and (3) history. Despite its usefulness, this kind of approach lacks the dynamic factor of time, and hence it is impossible to see trends of changes over time. One must keep in mind the conclusions stressing the importance of the time element reached in the Polish Corridor study.[32]

Held's review of the Saarland[33] in 1951 began, as had Hartshorne's work on the Polish Corridor, with a brief history of the problem and with details of the evolution of the disputed area's boundary. Held distinguished between the Saar's *raison d'être* and *raison de création*. The former had its basis in the decision of 1919 to include and to keep intact the whole mining area within one state, while the latter was founded on the claims to the territory by France and Germany. However, the new boundaries of the Saarland of 1945 improved the area's economic integration. In contrast to the situation in 1919, it included all the manufacturing areas as well as the miners' homes, thus making it a more harmonious unit. The basic inconsonance or problem remained, in that the Saar and the Lorraine iron ore fields of France were economically linked, while ethnically the Saar was more closely related to Germany. Hence by geographical rearrangement of the boundaries, the *raison d'être* was brought to a closer spatial coincidence, but the problem of conflicting claims remained.

Two more recent studies[34] seem to reinforce Hartshorne's generalization that over time minorities tend to conform to their surroundings, if the period is long enough and if the state undertakes a concerted policy of assimilation. Both Wilkinson's study of the old Kosovo-Metohija region in Yugoslavia near the Albanian border, and Randall's work on the Klagenfurt Basin of Austria had similar ingredients and conclusions. Because of its ethnic mixture of Slavs and Albanians, Kosovo-Metohija was made an autonomous region in 1945, and renamed Kosmet. Albanian "irredentism" remained active, and the Albanian minority constituted a continuing problem, especially in terms of education. This centrifugal force within the Yugoslav state was being overcome by a campaign against illiteracy to pave the way for improved technology and closer economic union with the rest of the state.

Randall dealt with another part of the old Austro-Hungarian Empire which, like Kosmet, had been within the same state (in this case Austria) since 1919, and whose ownership had been disputed between Austria and Yugoslavia ever since. The area has a substantial Slavic minority (40 per cent by the 1919 plebiscite). The "geographic unit" upon whose "intactness" a premium was placed in 1919, was based upon the sphere of influence of the regional center of Klagenfurt, which, unlike the Saar, could be closely approximated by natural features. Again the problem was the assimilation of the population into the Austrian state, and again the solution was seen through education because of the linguistic, religious, and political differences of the Slavic minority.

There seems to be no standard methodology for studying disputed areas, although the backgrounds of the areas in terms of the bases of the conflicting claims are always deemed very important. There are built-in difficulties in measuring the ethnic content of a population of a given area. Both plebiscite and census data often lack reliability or are outdated. Mixed populations are seldom conveniently separated in distinct zones but more often than not are spatially distributed by their dominant socioeconomic roles, as for example on a rural/urban basis. Moreover, the premium put on maintaining the economic viability of a region often conflicts fundamentally with the concept of fair ethnic division. The *raison d'être* and *raison de création* should thus be sharply distinguished.

---

31. Not all inhabited disputed areas contain populations classifiable in terms of their cultural associations with the rival states. Platt found the native Aguarunas in the Upper Amazon "blissfully ignorant" that they could soon become Ecuadorans or Peruvians. Robert S. Platt, "Conflicting Territorial Claims in the Upper Amazon," in *Geographical Aspects of International Relations*, ed. C. C. Colby (Chicago: University of Chicago Press, 1938), pp. 241–276.

32. Hartshorne, "The Polish Corridor," p. 176.

33. Colbert C. Held, "The New Saarland," *Geographical Review*, Vol. 41 (October, 1951), pp. 590–605.

34. H. R. Wilkinson, "Yugoslav Kosmet: The Evolution of a Frontier Province and Its Landscape," *Institute of British Geographers, Transactions and Papers*, No. 21 (1955), pp. 171–193; and Richard R. Randall, "Political Geography of the Klagenfurt Basin," *Geographical Review*, Vol. 47 (July, 1957), pp. 405–419.

The economic orientation of a region seems easily changed, while changes in cultural tradition involve the longest time lag. The key to assimilation is usually education. It seems that the area directly involved is most often the most affected by a dispute, while this area is not usually of vital importance to the disputant states.

Studies of the Effect of Boundary Change

Although areas where shifts in boundaries have occurred are often also disputed areas, this section is concerned with a survey of those studies whose main theme is *not* the relative merits of claimants to the problem area.[35] It focuses instead on an analysis of the impact of the boundary shift on the preexisting spatial pattern of phenomena, and of its related role in the reorientation of economic, social, and political activities, both in the region which has undergone the change in sovereignty, and in the contiguous areas on either side.

The first truly systematic study of the impact of boundary change came in 1933 with Hartshorne's work on Upper Silesia.[36] Hartshorne himself complained that thus far boundary studies by geographers showed, among other things, "a lack of technique, no recognized terminology, and no means of measurement." The Upper Silesia study certainly added to our techniques, but it was rather limited in findings based on measurement, although many possible means to more accurate measurement were suggested and tentatively followed. Hartshorne first established the importance of the barrier effect of a boundary between states in their total social, economic, and political life, concluding that the primary concern of a proper study must center on associations "of all kinds" of different parts of the border area with each of the bordering states. Exactly what associations are most meaningful for study depends on the type of border area under consideration. In Upper Silesia, a rather densely populated, predominantly urban, industrial, and mining region, Hartshorne concentrated on such associations as accessibility to good roads, and road, rail, electric power, and water supply patterns. By mapping, in addition, such phenomena as industrial sites, and coal, zinc, and lead mines, some measurement of the interruptive nature of the political boundary across this established pattern was made. This was especially important for industrial operating linkages and home/work relationships in Upper Silesia because these had been bisected many times over by the new Polish–German boundary.

Also of interest have been Moodie's studies of the impact of boundary changes in the Julian March region of the Italo-Yugoslav borderlands. His first major work,[37] previewed by an article two years earlier,[38] was a classic in the before-and-after approach to the study of boundary change. Like the South Tyrol, the Julian March was, up to 1919, part of the Austro-Hungarian Empire. With the breakup of the Dual Monarchy, the Kingdom of the Serbs, Croats, and Slovenes (Yugoslavia) was formed bordering the Italian Kingdom. The boundary was set well to the east of what might be called a fair ethnic break between Slavic- and Italian-speaking peoples. Although well over half of Moodie's monograph was occupied by a full account of the physical geography and history of the region up to World War I, and a chronological account of the diplomacy surrounding the various claims prior to final settlement after the war, a clear idea of the impact of the boundary change was obtained by a comparison between the pre-World War I period, and the period of Italianization which followed. At the outset, Moodie admitted that the boundary zone of some 4,000 square miles had no ethnic, political, economic, nor even geological or morphological unity; yet, as an historic "zone of strain" it had developed a personality of its own, epitomized by its very nature as a region of shifting boundaries. An enlightening insight into the difficulty and dangers of attempting to compare ethnic data for the same area from different censuses taken under different sovereignties can be obtained

---

35. Such studies are best found in the field of international law and relations. For example, Norman Hill, *Claims to Territory in International Law and Relations* (New York: Oxford University Press, 1945).

36. Richard Hartshorne, "Geographic and Political Boundaries in Upper Silesia," *Annals*, Association of American Geographers, Vol. 23 (December, 1933), pp. 195–228.

37. A. E. Moodie, *The Italo-Yugoslav Boundary* (London: Philip, 1945).

38. A. E. Moodie, "The Italo-Yugoslav Boundary," *Geographical Journal*, Vol. 101 (February, 1943), pp. 49–65.

from the discussion following the presentation of the 1943 paper to the Royal Geographical Society. Census data since 1910, taken as they were during the era of Fascism, were held by Moodie to be unreliable for purposes of comparison with the 1910 base. The element of language was not enough for nationality definition. Furthermore, census questions on language, couched in phrases such as "usually spoken" or "spoken in the home," could hardly be truthfully answered by the Slovenes when there was official compulsion to speak Italian.

In his follow-up study three years after a further shift in the boundary, this time advantageous to Yugoslavia, Moodie was in the happy position of being able to draw from the "before" data of his own research.[39] In outlining the problems created by the 1947 change, he discussed the interruptive role of the new boundary with respect to such significant associations as the electricity and water supply, river use, the communication network, and the rural economic pattern of production and markets.

The first study[40] was preceded by a twenty-five-year span representing the "after" period, whereas the other study followed the change by barely three years. Obviously in the former case, it was possible not only to establish the disruptive effect of the change on the former pattern of spatial relations, but also to measure the long-run impact of the "new" sovereignty and associated policy in reshaping this pattern. In the latter case, however, only the short-run disruptive or negative effect could be measured, because a three-year period was too short to establish what the long term positive effect of the change would be.

Weigend, in his study of the South Tyrol,[41] was interested in the effects of the boundary changes in the area. He made quite clear, however, that *his* South Tyrol was the old province of Bolzano (Alto Adige) and not the entire autonomous region of Trentino–Alto Adige established by Italy in 1948. He judged the Italianization policy to have been a failure because of the singular lack of assimilation in both the social and political life of the German-speaking population, who even have their own political party at the national level, the Südtiroler Volkspartei (SVP). A needless assimilation move in the legal field brought a fundamental problem which had historically plagued the rural economy of other parts of Alpine Italy to an area hitherto free from it. In 1931 the primogeniture law was abolished, and in time this led to the fragmentation of land holdings. Industrialization, based on the Italian-developed sources of hydroelectric power in the region, and a sharp rise in tourism after 1933, were the activities most stimulated by the economic reorientation to the North Italian Plain. Again the importance of the time lag between change and research stands out. Weigend's research was done almost 30 years after the change, and yet if the study had been made at an earlier date, such important trends as the abolition of the primogeniture law, the uptrend in tourism, and the development of water resources, with all their consequent impact, would not at that time have been evident.

Alexander's study[42] of changes along the Benelux–German boundary is a good example of the extreme short-run type. He discussed the various implications of *possible* changes in an area where decisions concerning adjustments of the boundary were still to be made.

House's study on the impact of the boundary shifts in the Alpes Maritimes[43] came a decade or so after significant changes in 1947. The 1947 change which awarded France the upper valleys of the Roya, Vésubie, and Tinée, established the watershed boundary between France and Italy in the Alpes Maritimes. This contiguous area on the "French" side of the divide had been held by Italy since the time of Unification in 1861, when the Franco-Italian boundary was established through the defunct state of Savoy. Hence, House had two time periods to deal with: Italian control from 1861 to 1947, and French from 1947 onwards, although it was, of course, the latter change that received most attention. Two separate considerations of impact were made: (1) that on the state

39. A. E. Moodie, "Some New Boundary Problems in the Julian March," *Institute of British Geographers, Transactions and Papers*, (1950), pp. 81–93.
40. A. E. Moodie, *The Italo-Yugoslav Boundary*.
41. Guido G. Weigend, "Effects of Boundary Changes in the South Tyrol," *Geographical Review*, Vol. 40 (July 1950), pp. 364–375.

42. Lewis M. Alexander, "Recent Changes in the Benelux–German Boundary," *Geographical Review*, Vol. 43 (January, 1953), pp. 69–76.
43. John W. House, "The Franco-Italian Boundary in the Alpes Maritimes," *Institute of British Geographers, Transactions and Papers*, No. 26 (1959), pp. 107–131. [Reprinted in Part III of this volume.]

involved, and (2) that on the social and economic life of the actual frontier communities.

It is not easy to define the "frontier region," as one must include more than the area involved directly in the exchange. House considered its narrowest definition as the administrative boundaries of the communes immediately flanking the old and the new international boundaries. In a wider context it could be defined by the limits of such natural regions as those described by river valleys adjoining the boundary.

The major problem directly created by the boundary shift was the cutting of local communes by the new line. In an alpine pastoral economy there is a fine balance between private arable lands and public grazing lands. Furthermore, adequate lumber resources and water supply are essential to a commune's viability. This balance was upset in many areas, and disputes over grazing, forest, water, and local transit rights became common. The area became a key source of supply for the Riviera electrification scheme, and the *Electricité de France* had proceeded to develop the hydroelectric power potential to the full, thus further complicating the already dislocated rural economy by flooding grazing and arable land, settlements, and routeways. Consequently, depopulation, a phenomenon long common to the area, was given even greater impetus, rendering the region a truly depressed area.

Lösch's reasoning as to why areas directly affected by a shift in boundary often become depressed, seems to hold true in this case, although the situation is rather complicated. Because the borderland area was mountainous, it had hydroelectric potential. Furthermore, its relative proximity to the large and expanding population concentration along the Riviera made it feasible to develop this potential. The case might well have been no different had the area remained Italian, although in general since the war France has been far more active in the Western Alps than Italy in dam and reservoir construction.

During the last decade or so France and Italy have moved much closer together both economically and politically, thus relieving many of the tensions in the border region by diminishing the importance of the boundary function.

In the above studies much attention has been given to the difficulty of defining the "affected zone." All students are agreed that it must encompass at least the area transferred, as well as affected adjoining areas. There is certainly no need to employ the normal criterion of regional unity on political, cultural, or economic bases in order to establish the extent of this region. The vital factor is, instead, the effect of the new boundary.

Exactly what significant associations and circulation patterns need to be studied in order to measure the boundary effect depends on the character of the region in question. A clear picture of the preexisting complex of relationships in the area is essential to any study of the effect of change. The lapse of time between boundary change and study is also an important consideration. Many effects become evident in the long run that are not present to an observer in the early stages, while short-run results may disappear with the passage of time and hence be lost to the researcher working after a considerable period following the change. Perhaps we can learn something from the findings of the highway impact studies which show the necessity for at least two studies because of the difference, often basic, between short- and long-term trends: one study to be made soon after the innovation, and the second after a period sufficiently long for relationships to have become reoriented and normalized.[44]

Studies of the Evolution of Boundaries

Many geographers have been interested in the history of boundaries. For the most part, the emphasis in such studies has been placed on the methods used in the selection of the boundary, and the problems, mostly diplomatic, existing at that time concerning its establishment. Many of these studies also include a discussion of the problems of demarcation and an account of the evolution of the boundary area, especially in terms of boundary changes and disputes over territory.[45]

44. For example, William L. Garrison and Marion E. Marts, *The Geographic Impact of Highway Improvement* (Seattle: Highway Economic Studies, University of Washington, July, 1958). Many important long-run trends in business and land values in the bypassed settlement of Marysville, Washington, were not evident in the initial period after construction of the superhighway.

45. For example, John W. Davis, "The Unguarded Boundary," *Geographical Review*, Vol. 12 (October, 1922), pp. 586–601.

Jones' two articles[46] during the 1930's on the forty-ninth parallel marked a considerable advance in this type of study. Not only were problems of selection, of demarcation, and of disputes discussed, but Jones was also interested in the effect of the "almost totally antecedent boundary on subsequent settlement, transportation, and cultural patterns of the border zone." In his 1937 work, he set out to ascertain "the extent of interference with circulation" by the boundary since its establishment in 1846. The importance of changing modes of transportation is traced as a primary factor in regional development, and in the varying extent of interference attributable to that boundary.

Pounds' two papers[47] on the frontiers of France were of a somewhat different nature. In the first paper, Pounds examined the basis upon which the idea of the French natural boundaries was founded, and in the second, traced the changing role of this idea through different historical periods. The persistence of the idea that France had the "right and duty to attain" the natural boundaries of "the Ocean, Rhine, Alps and Pyrenees," was of prime importance in the historical political geography of the French state. Despite the different functions France has sought for these boundaries from one period to another, the basic idea has survived.

A recent book by Burghardt[48] adopts the historical approach to the study of the Austrian border province of Burgenland which adjoins Hungary. After presenting the region's physical setting and early history, Burghardt examines the development of the cultural landscape with special attention given to the evolution of boundaries. The visible present-day influence on spatial arrangements of a relict boundary within the region is noted. There is a before-and-after treatment of the 1922 boundary change, the most recent, which set Burgenland's eastern limit, and there is also an analysis of the delimitation and demarcation problems which resulted from these changes. The changes in function of this boundary over time are also discussed, with special emphasis on the most recent change following the unsuccessful 1956 uprising in Hungary when the barrier effect increased sharply. Burghardt touches on the "disputed area" character of Burgenland especially at the time of the 1922 change, noting that the very word "Burgenland" was Austrian-coined in 1918, while Hungary continued to call the region "West Hungary."

For the political geographer, the book's major drawback is the absence of any comparative analysis of similar borderland situations, and also the lack of general methodological statements and conclusions derived from the study of Burgenland regarding the nature of boundaries, borderland regions, and disputed areas.

This sense of history gives a critical perspective on a boundary's role through time to its present status. As one of the most inertia-prone features of the cultural landscape, the boundary lends itself well to this treatment.

Studies of Boundary Delimitation and Demarcation

A group of studies deals solely with the problems of delimiting and demarcating boundaries. Although many of these studies are merely day-to-day accounts of a boundary commission in the field,[49] some provide important insights into the problems of demarcation.

Dodge[50] described the difficulties of demarcating a linear boundary in unsurveyed tundra in 1921. Becuase of the extreme northerly latitude, an azimuth error of 100 meters had to be tolerated. Peake[51] came across a rather different set of problems in the tropics, where his commission took 7 years, from 1927 to

---

46. Stephen B. Jones, "The Forty-Ninth Parallel in the Great Plains: The Historical Geography of a Boundary," *Journal of Geography*, Vol. 31 (December, 1932), pp. 357–368, and "The Cordilleran Section of the Canadian-United States Borderland," *Geographical Journal*, Vol. 89 (May, 1937), pp. 439–450.

47. Norman J. G. Pounds, "The Origin of the Idea of Natural Frontiers in France," *Annals*, Association of American Geographers, Vol. 41 (June, 1951), pp. 146–157, and "France and 'Les Limites Naturelles' from the Seventeenth to the Twentieth Centuries," *Ibid.*, Vol. 44 (March, 1954), pp. 51–62.

48. Andrew F. Burghardt, *Borderland: A Historical and Geographical Study of Burgenland, Austria* (Madison: University of Wisconsin Press, 1962).

49. For example, E. H. M. Clifford, "The British Somaliland-Ethiopia Boundary," *Geographical Journal*, Vol. 87 (April, 1936), pp. 289–307.

50. Stanley D. Dodge, "The Finnish-Russian Boundary North of 68 Degrees," *Geographical Journal*, Vol. 72 (September, 1928), pp. 297–298.

51. E. R. L. Peake, "Northern Rhodesia-Belgian-Congo Boundary," *Geographical Journal*, Vol. 83 (April, 1934), pp. 263–280.

1933, to demarcate the Northern Rhodesia–Belgian Congo boundary. This was the third attempt at demarcation by Anglo-Belgian commissions. The watershed boundary was difficult to locate precisely because of the rather featureless character of the region. Consequently, where it crossed the copper-rich area, problems were continually arising, and in many cases the boundary demarcation had to be made several times. Hence, although the boundary was delimited prior to mineral exploitation in the region, it had almost a superimposed quality due to the time lag in establishing its exact location in the field.

The redrawing of boundaries on ethnic criteria in Europe after World War I stimulated several studies describing the difficulties encountered in this task. For example, Cree's study of the Yugoslav–Hungarian boundary demarcation reviewed the diplomatic history of the two countries involved, and then described the method which the boundary commission followed.[52] Of major significance in this study, was the account of the difficulties involved in interpreting a treaty whose boundary awards were based on outdated ethnic and economic data, and yet whose final settlement had to be based on an acceptable division on these cultural grounds.

Significantly, many of these studies are concerned with sparsely populated areas, most of them in the "colonial world" where the necessity to mark exact limits dividing spheres of influence of different colonizers arose only in relation to resource utilization, and even then, on a generally amicable basis without the passion of locally rooted nationalism. The above problems concerning boundary delimitation and demarcation are often at the root of present-day disputes over territory between contiguous newly independent states.

Studies of Exclaves and Tiny States

Studies of exclaves and tiny states are also by definition studies of the effects of boundaries, and hence have a place in this classification.

Whittlesey made studies[53] in the early 1930's of a Spanish quasi-exclave and a tiny state in the Pyrenees. In his study of the Val d'Aran, contiguous with Spain but on the north side of the drainage divide, Whittlesey traced the reasons for the origin and continued existence of this anomaly. The historical role of the Pyrenees as a political boundary is the key to this discussion. Whittlesey reasoned that when the lowland on either side of a mountain boundary was strong, the barrier-function became effective. When the opposite was the case, the barrier-function became ineffective, creating a complex cross-boundary pattern of togetherness among the people of mountain valleys. The actual content of any league of valleys depended to a great extent on the "chance events of history," such as marriage, inheritance, and war. The Val d'Aran was just such a valley left in league with valleys on the Spanish slope when the Pyrenees became more effective as a political barrier. Its origin and reasons for survival established, Whittlesey proceeded to describe the situation in the Val d'Aran as it existed in 1933. He found that Spanish and French influences were mixed.

The phenomenon of Andorra was treated in much the same way, being regarded as a "challenge to the political geographer to uncover the geographic roots of so exotic a plant." He rejected as a "weak environmental reed to lean upon," the popular explanation of Andorra's political separation as being based on isolation. The concept of "rugged individualism" was rejected on similar grounds, and Whittlesey only partly accepted mutual jealousy between Spain and France as a reason for Andorra's origin and survival. In the absence of any valuable resources, Andorrans protected their autonomy when they "learned the art of playing off their joint suzerains against each other." Whittlesey concluded that the *status quo* provided both France and Spain with sufficient advantages to encourage preservation.

On the basis that "uninterrupted territory was one of the principles for the smooth functioning of a political entity," Robinson[54] examined the case of West Germany and West Berlin. Again, the exclave's origin was established, after which its critical relationships with West Germany, East Germany,

---

52. D. Cree, "Yugoslav-Hungarian Boundary Commission," *Geographical Journal*, Vol. 55 (February, 1925), pp. 89 ff.

53. Derwent S. Whittlesey, "The Val d'Aran: Trans-Pyrenean Spain," *Scottish Geographical Magazine*, Vol. 49 (1933), pp. 217–228, and "Andorra's Autonomy," *Journal of Modern History*, Vol. 6 (June, 1934), pp. 147–155.

54. G. W. S. Robinson, "West Berlin: The Geography of an Exclave," *Geographical Review*, Vol. 43 (October, 1953), pp. 540–557.

and East Berlin were discussed. Lastly, in the light of these relationships, the internal functioning of the exclave itself was studied. Similarly, Pedreschi's study[55] of Campione d'Italia concentrated on origin, evolution, and linkages of the exclave with its homeland.

More recently, Robinson[56] suggested a classification for exclaves based on their degree of separation from the motherland. His divisions, *normal*, *pene*, *quasi*, *virtual*, and *temporary*, point up the fact that the very essence of an exclave, its separation, is a matter of degree and must include consideration of normal lines of communication as well as sheer physical aspects. In Robinson's systematic study, the reasons for origin and survival were again given a high place. He saw, too, a basic dichotomy in an exclave's external relations, those with its neighboring country and those with its mother country. The key relationships here were those involving communications, administration, and economics, for they all bore upon the conditions of life in the exclave itself.

The zonal dissection of Berlin after the war, and the growing barrier-function of the line separating the Soviet sector on the one hand, from the French, British, and American sectors on the other, has given geographers an opportunity of studying not only a city (West Berlin) as an exclave, but also a city (Berlin) as an entity divided. Hence, urban as well as political geographers have become interested in this postwar phenomenon.

Schöller[57] has examined the changes in Berlin's internal geographic structure as a consequence of the political division of the city, as well as of the isolation of West Berlin from its hinterland. By analyzing such phenomena as population shifts and changes in industrial location, Schöller determined that an "economic recrystallization" was taking place in the divided city. Further consequent to the division were changes he obesrved and measured in the communication pattern, urban foci, and distribution of urban services. Even dichotomies in architectural styles and sharp differences in the policies of urban renewal were found between the two halves of the city. However, at the time of writing in 1953, Schöller saw no changes as yet that would handicap future reunification.

More recently Schroeder[58] selected the public transport pattern, fundamentally affected by Berlin's division, as a criterion of the changes in the city's geographic structure. He made a before-and-after World War II study of the routes and frequencies of Berlin's public transport system. By this method he was able to find a high correlation between areas of lower density of transportation lines and the East-West sector boundary.

Minghi's paper on Point Roberts[59] examined the situation of an American exclave in north-western Washington to which land access from the United States proper is possible only through Canada. The Point's proximity to growing metropolitan Vancouver, British Columbia, its isolation from any equivalent population concentration in the United States, and its attraction as a summer resort, have, during the last decade, reoriented its economic and social links toward Canada. This process was furthered by an important improvement in highway access in 1959, which brought the Point within reasonable commuting distance of Vancouver. Some of the details of these changing economic and social linkages were examined, and were found to contrast ever more sharply with the political *status quo*.

Minghi discussed several research approaches which could be followed in studying such a paradoxical problem. These are suggested by concepts of political geographic theory, such as Gottmann's circulation and iconography, Harthsorne's centripetal and centrifugal forces, Deutsch's competing interaction fields, and Mackay's testing of the interactance hypothesis. Minghi believed that a valid approach to the study of exclaves lay in the quantitative analysis of interaction between the exclave and its contiguous state, and between it and its home state.

Exclaves, despite their uncommonness, their esoteric nature, and their primary

55. L. Pedreschi, "L'exclave italiano in Terra Svizzera di Campione d'Italia," *Rivista Geografica Italiana*, Vol. 64 (March, 1957), pp. 23-40.

56. G. W. Robinson, "Exclaves," *Annals*, Association of American Geographers, Vol. 49 (September, 1959), pp. 283-295.

57. Peter Schöller, "Stadtgeographische Probleme des geteilten Berlin," *Erdkunde*, Vol. 7 (March, 1953), pp. 1-11.

58. Klaus Schroeder, "Der Stadtverkehr als Kriterium der Strukturwandlungen Berlins," *Erdkunde*, Vol. 14 (March, 1960), pp. 29-35.

59. Julian V. Minghi, "Point Roberts, Washington: The Problem of an American Exclave," *Yearbook of the Association of Pacific Coast Geographers*, Vol. 24 (1962), pp. 29-34.

concern with *"raisons d'être"* and survival, are after all no more than a specialized type of boundary zone, characterized by an unusually high degree of cross-boundary circulatory pressure. Through this inextricable link with boundaries, they have provided geographers with a milieu for studies that have advanced knowledge in boundary science.

In the case of the west-coast region of the Canada–United States boundary, these exclave studies have a considerable significance. They provide convenient analytical tools for studying the impact of the boundary at various stages in the region's evolution. The boundary of 1846 left several Hudson's Bay Company exclaves south of the line; British Columbia itself was a virtual enclave of the United States between 1846 and 1885; and Point Roberts continues as a *bona fide* exclave today.

Studies of Offshore Boundaries

A maritime boundary, unlike a land boundary which directly affects only the two states it separates, marks the limits of the spatial encroachment of a state's sovereignty into the area of the high seas, and thus affects many states. There has been little agreement as to the width of the territorial sea. Studies in this category, consequently, have been largely legalistic in approach, and little attempt has been made to treat offshore boundaries as part of the general complex of political boundaries.

Most of these studies have concentrated on the problems and principles of delimitation, usually treating territorial sea boundaries as separate from other contiguous zone boundaries.

An early study by Boggs[60] centered on the delimitation proposals made by the American delegation to the Conference for the Codification of International Law at The Hague in 1930. Several years later, a more penetrating discussion by the same author[61] attacked the problem of giving a precise meaning to the term "median line," and of finding a type of boundary through territorial waters to the high seas that would be capable of general application. In a more recent article, Boggs[62] was concerned with the variety of territorial boundaries claimed by the states of the world. By map and comprehensive table, he classified states in terms of the boundaries claimed for territorial seas and for other contiguous zones. Boggs saw some order in this seeming chaos in the form of certain distinctive groupings. He noticed, for example, an indirect relationship between the width of the belt of sea claimed and the volume of a state's foreign commerce. Moodie,[63] several years later, actually showed this relationship cartographically for European maritime states.

As the title suggests, Pearcy's 1959 article on the "Geographical Aspects of the Law of the Sea"[64] was a geographer's analysis of the latest trends in maritime international law. In a section specifically on offshore boundaries, five distinct but overlapping zones were listed and discussed. These were: internal waters, territorial sea, contiguous zone, continental shelf, and high seas.[65] Pearcy concluded that there was an imbalance between the legal claims and physical realities in approaches to establishing satisfactory boundaries separating these zones.

Recently, two books have appeared on the subject of offshore boundaries, one by Shalowitz[66] on the technical–legal–physical problem of delimitation and demarcation, and the other by Alexander[67] on northwestern Europe's coastlands. The latter work, especially in a chapter entitled "Offshore Geography:

---

60. S. Whittemore Boggs, "Delimitation of the Territorial Sea," *American Journal of International Law*, Vol. 24 (1930), pp. 541–555.

61. S. Whittemore Boggs, "Problems of Water Boundary Definition," *Geographical Review*, Vol. 27 (July, 1937), pp. 445–456.

62. S. Whittemore Boggs, "National Claims in Adjacent Seas," *Geographical Review*, Vol. 41 (April, 1951), pp. 185–209.

63. A. E. Moodie, "Maritime Boundaries," in *The Changing World*, eds. W. Gordon East and A. E. Moodie (Yonkers-on-Hudson, N.Y.: World Book Co., 1956), p. 953.

64. G. Etzel Pearcy, "Geographical Aspects of the Law of the Sea," *Annals*, Association of American Geographers, Vol. 49 (March, 1959), pp. 1–23.

65. This zonal classification is now a standard approach to offshore areas in political geography texts. For example, Norman J. G. Pounds, *Political Geography* (New York: McGraw-Hill Book Co., 1963), pp. 112–113.

66. Aaron L. Shalowitz, *Shore and Sea Boundaries*, U.S. Dept. of Commerce, Coast and Geodetic Survey (Washington: Government Printing Office, 1962).

67. Lewis M. Alexander, *Offshore Geography of Northwestern Europe*, Association of American Geographers, Monograph Series, No. 3 (Chicago: Rand McNally, 1963).

Theoretical Considerations" and in the "Afterword," throws fresh light on our understanding of maritime boundaries. Alexander calls the various offshore zones, of which boundaries are an integral part, the "coastland complex." Boundaries are affected by the physical and cultural factors of a coastland, while they, in turn, have an impact on many nonpolitical aspects of the coastland complex.

Alexander notes further that studies of offshore boundaries have followed two principal methods of analysis: one, where theoretical principles of delimitation are applied to actual coastland conditions throughout the world, as in Pearcy's contribution; and the other, where generic principles of delimitation are evolved by generalizing from a wide range of specific cases, as in Boggs' 1937 study.

Alexander concludes that as offshore areas are in a state of continual change, both culturally and physically, the very nature of offshore boundaries is also changing. These boundaries are in general being extended seawards with increasingly vaguer definition as to their function and location. Thus Alexander suggests that we should think more in terms of "frontiers" than of boundaries. The section below discusses a study which reinforces this suggestion.

Studies of Boundaries in Disputes over Natural Resources

There are very few studies in this category. Although there is some similarity between boundary studies that are concerned with resource utilization and those that are concerned with disputed areas, the two fields are quite distinct. The latter centers on areas of dispute concerning the location of the boundary, whereas the former is concerned with a common resource whose mobility often remains unaffected by the boundary itself, but whose utilization by the states concerned is strictly determined by the boundary.

A common example has been the case of international rivers, concerning which a vast body of domestic and international law has evolved. A boundary crossing a river creates an upstream and a downstream state. The utilization of the water by one state can fundamentally affect its use by the other. Friction over the use of river water is especially important in dry-land regions, as Karan[68] pointed out. His comparative study of the problems growing out of conflicts over the use of the Colorado and Indus rivers is offered as a "starting point in research" involving the "seeking out" of new examples from "different and widely separated areas to illustrate difficult political geographic circumstances."

Recently a study by Minghi[69] on salmon fishing in the North Pacific served to draw attention to the oceans and the competition between states for the natural resources they contain. This competition has led, in the case of the North Pacific salmon, to a convention, the parties to which have agreed to recognize certain boundaries in the area as delimiting their fishing activities. Thus a kind of specialized oceanic division by "sphere of exploitation" has been created between Japan and the United States.[70] It seems certain that as pressure increases to use known resources more intensively and to discover new sources of food and energy, the oceans will come in for ever greater exploitation. This exploitation will tend, as it did in the continents of the New World, to demand a sharper definition of sovereignty as competition becomes fiercer. Given the continued existence of a world politically fragmented into nation-states, the areally defined boundary over the oceans, despite the inherent difficulties of demarcation, might be an answer. There seems to be a beginning in the trend concerning salmon in the North Pacific. Many important factors compounding the problem of any such evolutionary trend in oceanic sovereignty are present. Minghi's study showed that the two major factors were insufficient knowledge of the resource involved, especially concerning its spatial distribution, and the refusal over time by one or more interested but nonmember states, such as the U.S.S.R., to recognize any exclusive conventions formulated by interested states at one point in time. It might

68. Pradyumna P. Karan, "Dividing the Water: A Problem in Political Geography," *Professional Geographer*, Vol. 13 (January, 1961), pp. 6–10.

69. Julian Minghi, "The Conflict of Salmon Fishing Policies in the North Pacific," *Pacific Viewpoint*, Vol. 2 (March, 1961), pp. 59–84.

70. Japan has agreed not to fish east of the 175° West line of longitude, which at the time of the Convention (1952) was thought to separate Alaskan-spawned salmon from Asian-spawned. Such oceanic boundaries as 175° West must still be distinguished from boundaries in coastland areas which, despite their growing frontier nature, are merely direct extensions of land boundaries.

well be that with technological advance and population pressure shrinking space to an ever greater degree, the days of ambiguous oceanic sovereignty are numbered, and that the transfer to a system of partition will not be easy.

A study in historical political geography by Hartshorne some years earlier was concerned with control over mineral resources as a possible factor in a boundary change.[71] Specifically, Hartshorne examined the accepted explanation for the new boundary of 1871 in Alsace-Lorraine between France and Germany. This was that Germany wanted possession of the iron ore deposits of Lorraine for the iron and steel industry of the Ruhr. Upon scrutiny of the treaty and of the region's geographical associations at that time, Hartshorne concluded that German annexation was based on a combination of cultural and strategic factors rather than on any desire to gain the mineral wealth. The iron-rich area was, in fact, split between France and Germany by the new line. This study demonstrates the peculiar contribution which political geographers can make in the critical examination of accepted explanations concerning the motives behind boundary changes at specific points in time.

Studies of Internal Boundaries

Although most boundary studies in political geography have been concerned with international boundaries, lines separating internal divisions have also been the subject of research, both at the state and at the more local level. Despite the concentration of effort at the international level, it must be remembered that the pattern of spatial distribution of phenomena can be affected by boundaries separating political units at any level.

Jones' study[72] on Oregon's internal boundaries is one of the classic studies in this category. Essentially a "utilitarian" study designed to demonstrate how a realignment of Oregon's boundaries could effect greater economy and efficiency in government, it was based largely on the concept of nodal regions as defined by the state's circulatory system. Jones' work represented the first utilitarian study that suggested political boundaries be based on functional rather than physiographic regions.

Ullman's short note[73] four years later was partly a review of articles on boundaries in the Pacific Northwest and partly a suggestive paper on areas for further research. He recommended some guidelines to be followed if county consolidation ever became a reality in the Pacific Northwest. Besides the Cascade watershed, he suggested two other lines east of the Cascade Mountains that separate dissimilar regions. The first was a line about 50 miles east of the Cascades which would include the arid zone of the interior. This area, despite its climatic contrast with the Puget Sound lowlands, was in fact closely linked with the coast economically. The second was a potential boundary marked by the zone of minimum circulation, the "mid-desert traffic divide." After noting the strong resistance to change in the political milieu, Ullman was led to conclude that political divisions were equally if not more deeply entrenched psychologically than the physical environment itself.

Ullman's study[74] of the boundary region between two New England states was of a more systematic nature and explained many of the regional contrasts on either side in terms of the effect of the boundary. The historical evolution of the line was traced as background information. Comparative advantages as a result of the differential in tax structures between the two states were held to account for the particular location of many industrial sites. The spatial patterns of phenomena such as property lines, electrical transmission lines, and water mains were considerably modified by the state line, although elements of the communication network (such as roads and railroads) that antedate the establishment of the boundary in the study region were hardly affected by the line. The basic difference in religious attitude between puritan Massachusetts and liberal Rhode Island also had impact as a locational factor;

---

71. Richard Hartshorne, "The Franco-German Boundary of 1871," *World Politics*, Vol. 2 (December, 1949), pp. 209–250.

72. Stephen B. Jones, "Intra-State Boundaries in Oregon," *Commonwealth Review*, Vol. 16 (July, 1934), pp. 105–06.

73. Edward L. Ullman, "Political Geography of the Pacific Northwest," *Scottish Geographical Magazine*, Vol. 54 (July, 1938), pp. 236–39.

74. Edward L. Ullman, "The Eastern Rhode Island-Massachusetts Boundary Zone," *Geographical Review*, Vol. 29 (April, 1939), pp. 291–302.

Boston's nearest racecourse was forty miles away, just inside the Rhode Island state line. Although lacking any vigorous methodological approach, the study nevertheless marked a considerable advance in research on internal boundaries by observing the geography of the zone through the strict frame of reference of the political variable.

Two articles by Gilbert, one just prior to, and the other soon after World War II, pointed up the need, much as Jones' Oregon study did, for a reorganization of the internal political units of England and Wales.[75] In 1939, Gilbert found that current county boundaries had changed little in a thousand years and that new and larger administrative units were necessary to overcome the urban/rural split that had developed in many areas. He noticed that there was precedence for this in that only five provinces existed in Roman times, that during the Middle Ages several different kingdoms existed, and that in the Cromwellian era England and Wales were administered in only seven districts. The article was largely provoked by the intensive emergency defense planning going on at the time. Such planning involved the establishment of many varied functional regions, the boundaries of which seldom coincided. Gilbert found that radio broadcasting had become a great stimulant to regionalism and that the boundaries separating the listening areas of the various BBC regional stations might well form the basis for future administrative regions. This idea of basing internal divisions on regional consciousness expressed by circulatory zones of communication was most forward-looking and not without application at the international level.

Gilbert's postwar study again pleaded for changes in the anachronistic internal boundaries of Britain. After briefly describing the existing structure and explaining its anachronistic nature, he went on to suggest remedies. Boundaries should be drawn so as to create areas large enough for efficiency and for a measure of independence from the central government, while local sentiment and the feeling of neighborhood should be preserved at all costs. Furthermore, it was suggested that accessibility in terms of a time/cost factor could be used as an aid in redrawing the boundaries. The above two studies, along with Jones' contribution on Oregon and Ullman's on the Pacific Northwest, serve to demonstrate the political geographer's contribution in the realm of regional planning.

An examination of Idaho's peculiar problem of securing political unity in the face of serious intrastate barriers to circulation was made by Thomas in 1949.[76] This study may be considered a "boundary study" in that its findings would strongly suggest a good case for political division between North and South.

Mackay's work[77] on the measurement of the boundary's relative barrier-effect for various selected types of interaction marked a great advance in boundary research, in that for the first time the effect of a boundary was expressed in clear quantitative terms. A reasonably precise estimate of the effect of a boundary on such key types of cultural interaction as migration, intermarriage, telephone calls, etc., was held to be a powerful analytical tool for boundary studies. By using the non-linear form of the interactance model, Mackay was able to attribute a distance factor to a boundary as it affected certain types of human activity which crossed it. Mackay analyzed the frequency of long-distance telephone calls between cities within Quebec, and interprovincially between cities in Quebec and cities in Ontario with the same $PAPB/D$ value.[78] He found that the interactance between Quebec and Ontario varied between $\frac{1}{5}$ and $\frac{1}{10}$ of the norm between cities within Quebec. This, Mackay suggested, may be interpreted as a measure of the boundary. Extending this to include cities in the United States with the same $PAPB/D$ value, he obtained a distance factor between Quebec and the United States of some 50 times that between Quebec cities. Hence, the French-English language boundary, one may conclude, is small in its interruptive nature compared with the international boundary (Fig.

---

75. E. W. Gilbert, "Practical Regionalism in England and Wales," *Geographical Journal*, Vol. 94 (July, 1939), pp. 29–44, and "The Boundaries of Local Government Areas," *Geographical Journal*, Vol. 111 (April–June, 1948), pp. 172–206.

76. Benjamin E. Thomas, "Boundaries and Internal Problems of Idaho," *Geographical Review*, Vol. 39 (January, 1949), pp. 99–109.

77. J. Ross Mackay, "The Interactance Hypothesis and Boundaries in Canada," *Canadian Geographer*, No. 11 (1958), pp. 1–8.

78. PA and PB = the population of the two interacting cities, and D = the distance between them.

13.2). Mackay was, however, careful to point out that this use of the interactance hypothesis does not *interpret* the effect of the boundary, but simply states it in quantitative terms.[79]

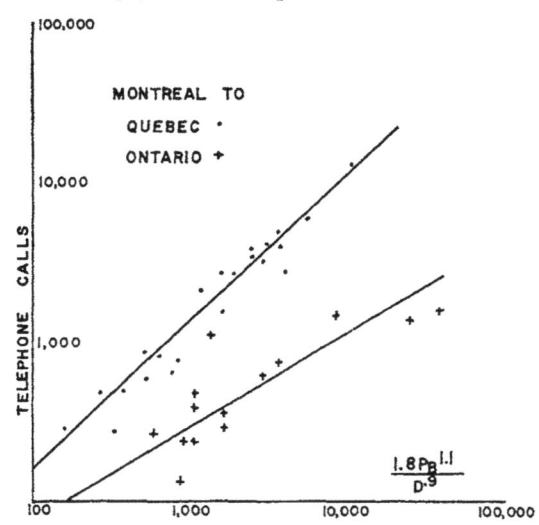

FIG. 13.2 LONG-DISTANCE TELEPHONE TRAFFIC ORIGINATING IN MONTREAL FOR A TEN-DAY PERIOD TO CITIES IN QUEBEC AND ONTARIO (after J. Ross Mackay, "The Interactance Hypothesis and Boundaries in Canada," *Canadian Geographer*, No. 11 [1958], p. 5).

Prescott's discussion[80] of Nigeria's boundary problems took the form of before-the-fact hypothesizing about potential frictions resulting from the poor demarcation of many of Nigeria's internal boundaries prior to independence and from their noncoincidence with the distribution of major ethnic groups. As in so many other parts of emergent Africa, the unmarked boundaries were "not meant to stand the strain of increasingly complex functions."[81] Prescott singled out several areas for study where there were serious degrees of nonalignment between the political boundary and lines separating economic or ethnic entities, and made recommendations for changes largely based on economic grounds.

Nelson's work[82] on the Vernon area of Los Angeles County concentrated on the political pattern, and is a contribution to the understanding of the areal distribution and functioning association of the numerous items in the urban landscape. Significantly, Nelson did not confine his study to Vernon itself, but included in the study area the "boundary zone" surrounding the city. Nelson found that the boundary was a significant factor in the transportation pattern and also in residential, commercial, and industrial land use. The evolution of the settlement, and its relationships over time with adjoining political units, proved to be important considerations in explaining the present-day impact of the boundary. In this respect, the inertia associated with industrial capital investment, and the importance of initial advantages became key factors.

Minghi has used the methods of the political geographer in analyzing the geography of a metropolitan area.[83] All metropolitan areas are characterized by some degree of political fragmentation, but the situation existing in the Washington, D.C. area involved not only fragmentation, but was peculiar in that parts of two states (Maryland and Virginia) and a federal district were included. Key functions with area-wide application such as water supply, sewage disposal, transportation, and planning were selected and their spatial pattern described in terms of the paradox of political fragmentation and economic integration in the metropolitan area. To provide controls, the situation in other metropolitan areas of similar size, such as St. Louis, was also considered. Minghi suggested that an estimate of the interruptive nature of the boundaries separating the political units in the Washington area could be obtained by comparing the actual pattern with an "ideal" pattern of circulation as indicated by the physiographic and demographic milieu. The author concluded that this interruptive effect on the circulation patterns of the key functions was considerable and in some respects would have most serious future consequences, unless

---

79. For a similar method of measuring the interruptive nature of a boundary, see Julian V. Minghi, "Television Preference and Nationality in a Boundary Region," *Sociological Inquiry*, Vol. 33 (Spring, 1963), pp. 65–79.

80. J. R. V. Prescott, "Nigeria's Boundary Problems," *Geographical Review*, Vol. 49 (October, 1959), pp. 485–505.

81. *Ibid.*, p. 486. This observation underscores the findings in the section on delimitation and demarcation.

82. Howard J. Nelson, "The Vernon Area, California: A Study of the Political Factor in Urban Geography," *Annals*, Association of American Geographers, Vol. 42 (June, 1952), pp. 177–191.

83. Julian Minghi, "The Spatial Pattern of Key Functions in the Washington Metropolitan Area," unpublished paper (Washington, D.C.: Washington Center for Metropolitan Studies, September, 1960).

the functions of the boundaries were to be drastically changed.

This type of utilitarian study demonstrated that the tools created for and moulded by studies of international boundaries could be further amended for use in analyzing the geography of urban regions.

SUMMARY AND CONCLUSIONS

In this review of boundary studies, one can see a trend away from the earlier thought-restricting boundary concepts, such as that based on the artificial-vs.-natural dichotomy, toward more function-oriented studies.

In disputed areas, the major problem arises from the intermingling of ethnic groups purported to represent the nationalities involved in the dispute. When the geographer steps from the scientific milieu of objective inquiry into the arena of biased international politics as, for example, in the case of the South Tyrol,[84] we have a glaring example of the misuse of political geography.

One of the most fruitful areas of research on boundaries was found to be the impact of boundary change. Before-and-after studies, if based on reliable data, and if made with full consideration of the length of time period between change and study, increase our knowledge about the two state systems in question by illustrating their differing organization of the same piece of territory.

A change in boundary location, however, is the exception rather than the rule, and although studies of changes have been of great significance in advancing boundary research, we cannot rely entirely on this method. Static boundaries have an impact on circulation patterns, and this impact varies according to the changing boundary functions. Furthermore, we can eliminate the variable of the changing function by measuring a selected form of interaction across the boundary at a certain point in time, as Mackay did in 1958.

More attention to the "normal" situation is needed in boundary research. Therefore, while the discussion in this paper has centered more on studies concerning boundary disputes and changes, the author believes that the studies falling in the other categories have served as important supplements to boundary science.

The significance of studies concerned with boundary evolution is that they provide an historical dimension which is frequently a critical factor in explaining present-day situations. Although studies of exclaves and tiny states are somewhat different in kind, they are essentially boundary studies and contribute a spatial dimension to boundary analysis.

The increased pressure for exploitation of natural resources leads us away from being land-bound in our thinking on boundaries. The oceans may well prove to be the last frontier in the spread of the national-state system, thus completing the political fragmentation of the globe.

Although internal boundaries have not enjoyed the same attention as those of the international variety, studies on this subject show that methodology evolved at the international level can be used successfully at all political levels.

In almost all studies, there has been a conspicuous reliance on secondary data. These data are often the best available and the most reliable in studying influence of the boundary on the flow of goods, services, and people. There is no question of the validity of such studies in political geography, provided that the data are the most appropriate secondary data. The study of international boundaries in political geography, however, must also take the view that boundaries, as political dividers, separate peoples of different nationalities and, therefore, presumably of different iconographic makeup. The political geographer must seek a measure of a boundary's viability as such a divider. For this we must concern ourselves with the role of the boundary in determining spatial patterns of selected behavioral activity which is itself an indicator of iconographic attitudes. Consequently, the political geographer must be prepared to collect data at the primary level. He must undertake investigations in the sociological field, as well as in the cultural and economic areas, for the spatial patterns of social behavior can be even more important than other patterns in determining the impact of a boundary and its viability as a national separator.

---

84. Julian V. Minghi, "Boundary Studies and National Prejudices: The Case of the South Tyrol," *Professional Geographer*, Vol. 15 (January, 1963), pp. 4–8.

14

The Geographical Pivot of History

SIR HALFORD J. MACKINDER*

When historians in the remote future come to look back on the group of centuries through which we are now passing, and see them foreshortened, as we today see the Egyptian dynasties, it may well be that they will describe the last 400 years as the Columbian epoch, and will say that it ended soon after the year 1900. Of late it has been a common-place to speak of geographical exploration as nearly over, and it is recognized that geography must be diverted to the purpose of intensive survey and philosophic synthesis. In 400 years the outline of the map of the world has been completed with approximate accuracy, and even in the polar regions the voyages of Nansen and Scott have very narrowly reduced the last possibility of dramatic discoveries. But the opening of the twentieth century is appropriate as the end of a great historic epoch, not merely on account of this achievement, great though it be. The missionary, the conqueror, the farmer, the miner, and, of late, the engineer, have followed so closely in the traveller's footsteps that the world, in its remoter borders, has hardly been revealed before we must chronicle its virtually complete political appropriation. In Europe, North America, South America, Africa, and Australasia there is scarcely a region left for the pegging out of a claim of ownership, unless as the result of a war between civilized or half-civilized powers. Even in Asia we are probably witnessing the last moves of the game first played by the horsemen of Yermak the Cossack and the shipmen of Vasco da Gama. Broadly speaking, we may contrast the Columbian epoch with the age which preceded it, by describing its essential characteristic as the expansion of Europe against almost negligible resistances, whereas mediaeval Christendom was pent into a narrow region and threatened by external barbarism. From the present time forth, in the post-Columbian age, we shall again have to deal with a closed political system, and none the less that it will be one of world-wide scope. Every explosion of social forces, instead of being dissipated in a surrounding circuit of unknown space and barbaric chaos, will be sharply re-echoed from the far side of the globe, and weak elements in the political and economic organism of the world will be shattered in consequence. There is a vast difference of effect in the fall of a shell into an earthwork and its fall amid the closed spaces and rigid structures of a great building or ship. Probably some half-consciousness of this fact is at last diverting much of the attention of statesmen in all parts of the world from territorial expansion to the struggle for relative efficiency.

It appears to me, therefore, that in the present decade we are for the first time in a position to attempt, with some degree of

Reproduced by permission from *The Geographical Journal*, Vol. XXIII, No. 4, 1904.
* Halford Mackinder (1861–1947) was Professor of Geography at Oxford University and Director of the London School of Economics.

completeness, a correlation between the larger geographical and the larger historical generalizations. For the first time we can perceive something of the real proportion of features and events on the stage of the whole world, and may seek a formula which shall express certain aspects, at any rate, of geographical causation in universal history. If we are fortunate, that formula should have a practical value as setting into perspective some of the competing forces in current international politics. The familiar phrase about the westward march of empire is an empirical and fragmentary attempt of the kind. I propose this evening describing those physical features of the world which I believe to have been most coercive of human action, and presenting some of the chief phases of history as organically connected with them, even in the ages when they were unknown to geography. My aim will not be to discuss the influence of this or that kind of feature, or yet to make a study in regional geography, but rather to exhibit human history as part of the life of the world organism. I ask you for a moment to look upon Europe and European history as subordinate to Asia and Asiatic history, for European civilization is, in a very real sense, the outcome of the secular struggle against Asiatic invasion.

European Civilization and Asiatic Invasion

The most remarkable contrast in the political map of modern Europe is that presented by the vast area of Russia occupying half the Continent and the group of smaller territories tenanted by the Western Powers. From a physical point of view, there is, of course, a like contrast between the unbroken lowland of the east and the rich complex of mountains and valleys, islands and peninsulas, which together form the remainder of this part of the world. At first sight it would appear that in these familiar facts we have a correlation between natural environment and political organization so obvious as hardly to be worthy of description, especially when we note that throughout the Russian plain a cold winter is opposed to a hot summer, and the conditions of human existence thus rendered additionally uniform. Yet a series of historical maps (Maps 14.1 and 14.2) will reveal the fact that not merely is the rough coincidence of European Russia with the Eastern Plain of Europe a matter of the last hundred years or so, but that in all earlier time there was persistent re-assertion of quite another tendency in the political grouping. Two groups of states usually divided the country into northern and southern political systems. The fact is that the orographical map does not express the particular physical contrast which has until very lately controlled human movement and settlement in Russia. When the screen of winter snow fades northward off the vast face of the plain, it is followed by rains whose maximum occurs in May and June beside the Black sea, but near the Baltic and White seas is deferred to July and August. In the south the later summer is a period of drought. As a consequence of this climatic *regime*, the north and north-west were forest broken only by marshes, whereas the south and south-east were a boundless grassy steppe, with trees only along the rivers. The line separating the two regions ran diagonally north-eastward from the northern end of the Carpathians to a point in the Ural range nearer to its southern than to its northern extremity. Moscow lies a little to the north of this line, or, in other words, on the forest side of it. Outside Russia the boundary of the great forest ran westward almost exactly through the centre of the European isthmus, which is 800 miles across between the Baltic and the Black seas. Beyond this, in Peninsular Europe, the woods spread on through the plains of Germany in the north, while the steppe lands in the south turned the great Transylvanian bastion of the Carpathians, and extended up the Danube, through what are now the cornfields of Roumania, to the Iron Gates. A detached area of steppes, known locally as Pusstas, now largely cultivated, occupied the plain of Hungary, ingirt by the forested rim of Carpathian and Alpine mountains. In all the west of Russia, save in the far north, the clearing of the forests, the drainage of the marshes, and the tillage of the steppes have recently averaged the character of the landscape, and in large measure obliterated a distinction which was formerly very coercive of humanity.

The earlier Russia and Poland were established wholly in the glades of the forest. Through the steppe on the other hand there came from the unknown recesses of Asia, by the gateway between the Ural mountains and

Map 14.1 Eastern Europe before the nineteenth century
(After Drude in *Berghaus' Atlas*)

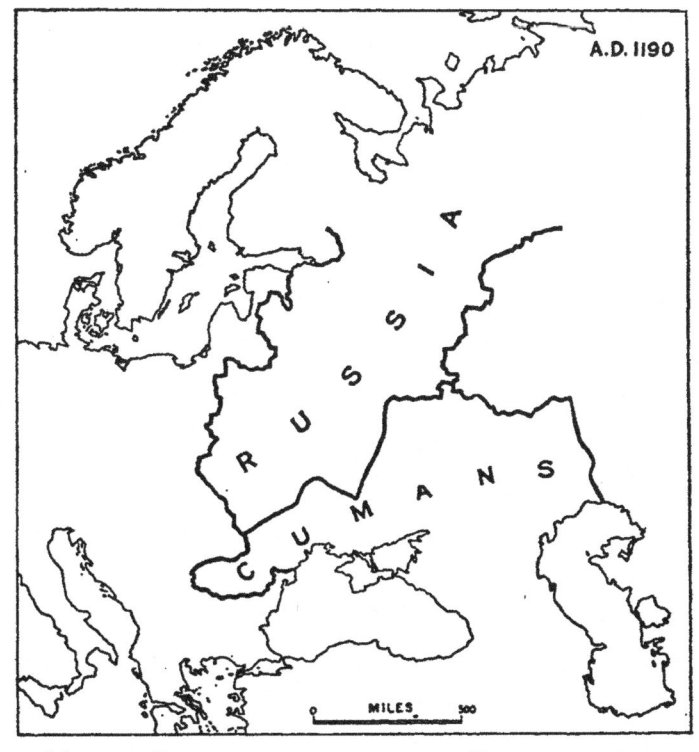

Map 14.2 Political divisions of eastern Europe at the time
of the Third Crusade
(After the *Oxford Historical Atlas*)

the Caspian sea, in all the centuries from the fifth to the sixteenth, a remarkable succession of Turanian nomadic peoples—Huns, Avars, Bulgarians, Magyars, Khazars, Patzinaks, Cumans, Mongols, Kalmuks. Under Attila the Huns established themselves in the midst of the Pusstas, in the uttermost Danubian outlier of the steppes, and thence dealt blows northward, westward, and southward against the settled peoples of Europe. A large part of modern history might be written as a commentary upon the changes directly or indirectly ensuing from these raids. . . .

The full meaning of Asiatic influence upon Europe is not, however, discernible until we come to the Mongol invasions of the fifteenth century; but before we analyze the essential facts concerning these, it is desirable to shift our geographical view-point from Europe, so that we may consider the Old World in its entirety. It is obvious that, since the rainfall is derived from the sea, the heart of the greatest land-mass is likely to be relatively dry. We are not, therefore, surprised to find that two-thirds of all the world's population is concentrated in relatively small areas along the margins of the great continent—in Europe, beside the Atlantic ocean; in the Indies and China, beside the Indian and Pacific oceans. A vast belt of almost uninhabited, because practically rainless, land extends as the Sahara completely across Northern Africa into Arabia. Central and Southern Africa were almost as completely severed from Europe and Asia throughout the greater part of history as were the Americas and Australia. In fact, the southern boundary of Europe was and is the Sahara rather than the Mediterranean, for it is the desert which divides the black man from the white. The continuous land-mass of Euro-Asia thus included between the ocean and the desert measures 21,000,000 square miles, or half of all the land on the globe, if we exclude from reckoning the deserts of Sahara and Arabia. There are many detached deserts scattered through Asia, from Syria and Persia north-eastward to Manchuria, but no such continuous vacancy as to be comparable with the Sahara. On the other hand, Euro-Asia is characterized by a very remarkable distribution of river drainage. Throughout an immense portion of the centre and north, the rivers have been practically useless for purposes of human communication with the outer world. The Volga, the Oxus, and the Jaxartes drain into salt lakes; the Obi, the Yenisei, and the Lena into the frozen ocean of the north. These are six of the greatest rivers in the world. There are many smaller but still considerable streams in the same area, such as the Tarim and the Helmund, which similarly fail to reach the ocean. Thus the core of Euro-Asia, although mottled with desert patches, is on the whole a steppe-land supplying a widespread if often scanty pasture and there are not a few river-fed oases in it,

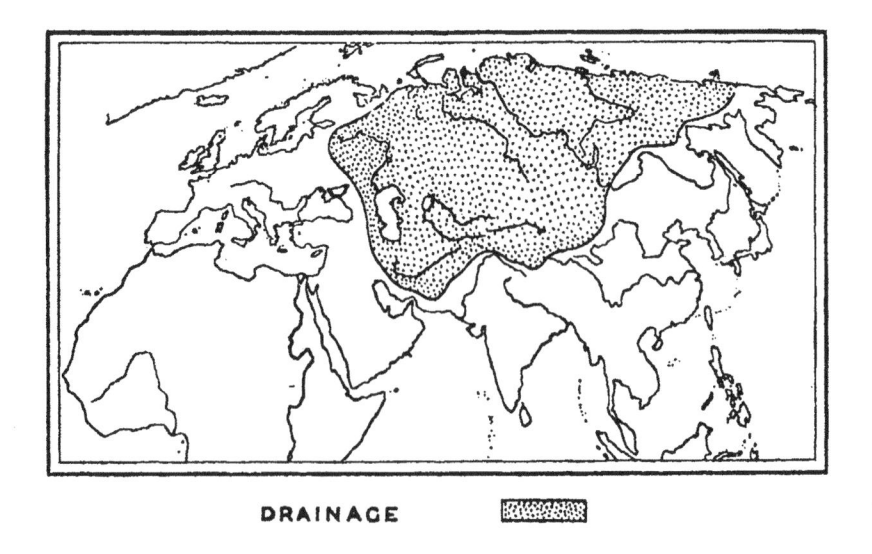

DRAINAGE

Map 14.3 CONTINENTAL AND ARCTIC DRAINAGE
(Equal area projection)

but it is wholly unpenetrated by waterways from the ocean. In other words, we have in this immense area all the conditions for the maintenance of a sparse, but in the aggregate considerable, population of horse-riding and camel-riding nomads. Their realm is limited northward by a broad belt of sub-arctic forest and marsh, wherein the climate is too rigorous, except at the eastern and western extremities, for the development of agricultural settlements. In the east the forests extend southward to the Pacific coast in the Amur land and Manchuria. Similarly in the west, in prehistoric Europe, forest was the predominant vegetation. Thus framed in to the north-east, north, and north-west, the steppes spread continuously for 4000 miles from the Pusstas of Hungary to the Little Gobi of Manchuria, and, except in their westernmost extremity, they are untraversed by rivers draining to an accessible ocean, for we may neglect the very recent efforts to trade to the mouths of the Obi and Yenisei. In Europe, Western Siberia, and Western Turkestan the steppe-lands lie low, in some places below the level of the sea. Further to the east, in Mongolia, they extend over plateaux; but the passage from the one level to the other, over the naked, unscarped lower ranges of the arid heartland, presents little difficulty.

The hordes which ultimately fell upon Europe in the middle of the fourteenth century gathered their first force 3000 miles away on the high steppes of Mongolia. The havoc wrought for a few years in Poland, Silesia, Moravia, Hungary, Croatia, and Servia was, however, but the remotest and the most transient result of the great stirring of the nomads of the East associated with the name of Ghenghiz Khan. While the Golden Horde occupied the steppe of Kipchak, from the Sea of Aral, through the interval between the Ural range and the Caspian, to the foot of the Carpathians, another horde, descending south-westward between the Caspian sea and the Hindu Kush into Persia, Mesopotamia, and even into Syria, founded the domain of the Ilkhan. A third subsequently struck into Northern China, conquering Cathay. India and Mangi, or Southern China, were for a time sheltered by the incomparable barrier of Tibet, to whose efficacy there is, perhaps, nothing similar in the world, unless it be the Sahara desert and the polar ice. But at a later time, in the days of Marco Polo in the case of Mangi, in those of Tamerlane in the case of India, the obstacle was circumvented. Thus it happened that in this typical and well-recorded instance, all the settled margins of the Old World sooner or later felt the expansive force of mobile power originating in the steppe. Russia, Persia, India, and China were either made tributary, or received Mongol dynasties. Even the incipient power of the Turks in Asia Minor was struck down for half a century.

EURO-ASIA AS A REGION

The conception of Euro-Asia to which we thus attain is that of a continuous land, ice-girt in the north, water-girt elsewhere, measuring twenty-one million square miles, or more than three times the area of North America, whose centre and north, measuring some nine million square miles, or more than twice the area of Europe, have no available water-ways to the ocean, but, on the other hand, except in the subarctic forest, are very generally favourable to the mobility of horsemen and camelmen. To east, south, and west of this heart-land are marginal regions, ranged in a vast crescent, accessible to shipmen. According to physical conformation, these regions are four in number, and it is not a little remarkable that in a general way they respectively coincide with the spheres of the four great religions—Buddhism, Brahminism, Mahometanism, and Christianity. The first two are the monsoon lands, one turned towards the Pacific, and the other towards the Indian ocean. The fourth is Europe, watered by the Atlantic rains from the west. These three together, measuring less than seven million square miles, have more than 1000 million people, or two-thirds of the world population. The third, coinciding with the land of the Five Seas, or, as it is more often described, the Nearer East, is in large measure deprived of moisture by the proximity of Africa, and, except in the oases, is therefore thinly peopled. In some degree it partakes of the characteristics both of the marginal belt of the central area of Euro-Asia. It is mainly devoid of forest, is patched with desert, and is therefore suitable for the operations of the nomad. Dominantly, however, it is marginal, for sea-gulfs and oceanic rivers lay it open to sea-power, and permit of the exercise of such power from it.

As a consequence, periodically throughout history, we have here had empires belonging essentially to the marginal series, based on the agricultural populations of the great oases of Babylonia and Egypt, and in free water-communication with the civilized worlds of the Mediterranean and the Indies. But, as we should expect, these empires have been subject to an unparalleled series of revolutions, some due to Scythian, Turkish, and Mongol raids from Central Asia, others to the effort of the Mediterranean peoples to conquer the overland ways from the western to the eastern ocean. Here is the weakest spot in the girdle of early civilizations, for the isthmus of Suez divided sea-power into Eastern and Western, and the arid wastes of Persia advancing from Central Asia to the Persian gulf gave constant opportunity for nomad-power to strike home to the ocean edge, dividing India and China, on the one hand, from the Mediterranean world on the other. Whenever the Babylonian, the Syrian, and the Egyptian oases were weakly held, the steppe-peoples could treat the open tablelands of Iran and Asia Minor as forward posts whence to strike through the Punjab into India, through Syria into Egypt, and over the broken bridge of the Bosphorus and Dardanelles into Hungary. Vienna stood in the gateway of Inner Europe, withstanding the nomadic raids, both those which came by the direct road through the Russian steppe, and those which came by the loop way to south of the Black and Caspian seas.

Here we have illustrated the essential difference between the Saracen and the Turkish controls of the Nearer East. The Saracens were a branch of the Semitic race, essentially peoples of the Euphrates and Nile and of the smaller oases of Lower Asia. They created a great empire by availing themselves of the two mobilities permitted by their land—that of the horse and camel on the one hand, that of the ship on the other. At different times their fleets controlled both the Mediterranean as far as Spain, and the Indian ocean to the Malay islands. From their strategically central position between the eastern and western oceans, they attempted the conquest of all the marginal lands of the Old World, imitating Alexander and anticipating Napoleon. They could even threaten the steppe-land. Wholly distinct from Arabia as from Europe, India, and China were the Turanian pagans from the closed heart of Asia, the Turks who destroyed the Saracen civilization.

Mobility upon the ocean is the natural rival of horse and camel mobility in the heart of the continent. It was upon navigation of oceanic rivers that was based the Potamic stage of civilization, that of China on the Yangtse, that of India on the Ganges, that of Babylonia on the Euphrates, that of Egypt on the Nile. It was essentially upon the navigation of the Mediterranean that was based what has been described as the Thalassic stage of civilization, that of the Greeks and Romans. The Saracens and the Vikings held sway by navigation of the oceanic coasts.

The all-important result of the discovery of the Cape road to the Indies was to connect the western and eastern coastal navigations of Euro-Asia, even though by a circuitous route, and thus in some measure to neutralize the strategical advantage of the central position of the steppe-nomads by pressing upon them in rear. The revolution commenced by the great mariners of the Columbian generation endowed Christendom with the widest possible mobility of power, short of a winged mobility. The one and continuous ocean enveloping the divided and insular lands is, of course, the geographical condition of ultimate unity in the command of the sea, and of the whole theory of modern naval strategy and policy as expounded by such writers as Captain Mahan and Mr. Spenser Wilkinson. The broad political effect was to reverse the relations of Europe and Asia, for whereas in the Middle Ages Europe was caged between an impassable desert to south, an unknown ocean to west, and icy or forested wastes to north and north-east, and in the east and south-east was constantly threatened by the superior mobility of the horsemen and camelmen, she now emerged upon the world, multiplying more than thirty-fold the sea surface and coastal lands to which she had access, and wrapping her influence round the Euro-Asiatic land-power which had hitherto threatened her very existence. New Europes were created in the vacant lands discovered in the midst of the waters, and what Britain and Scandinavia were to Europe in the earlier time, that have America and Australia, and in some measure even Trans-Saharan Africa, now become to Euro-Asia. Britain, Canada, the United States, South Africa, Australia, and Japan are now a ring of outer and insular bases for

Map 14.4 The Natural Seats of Power

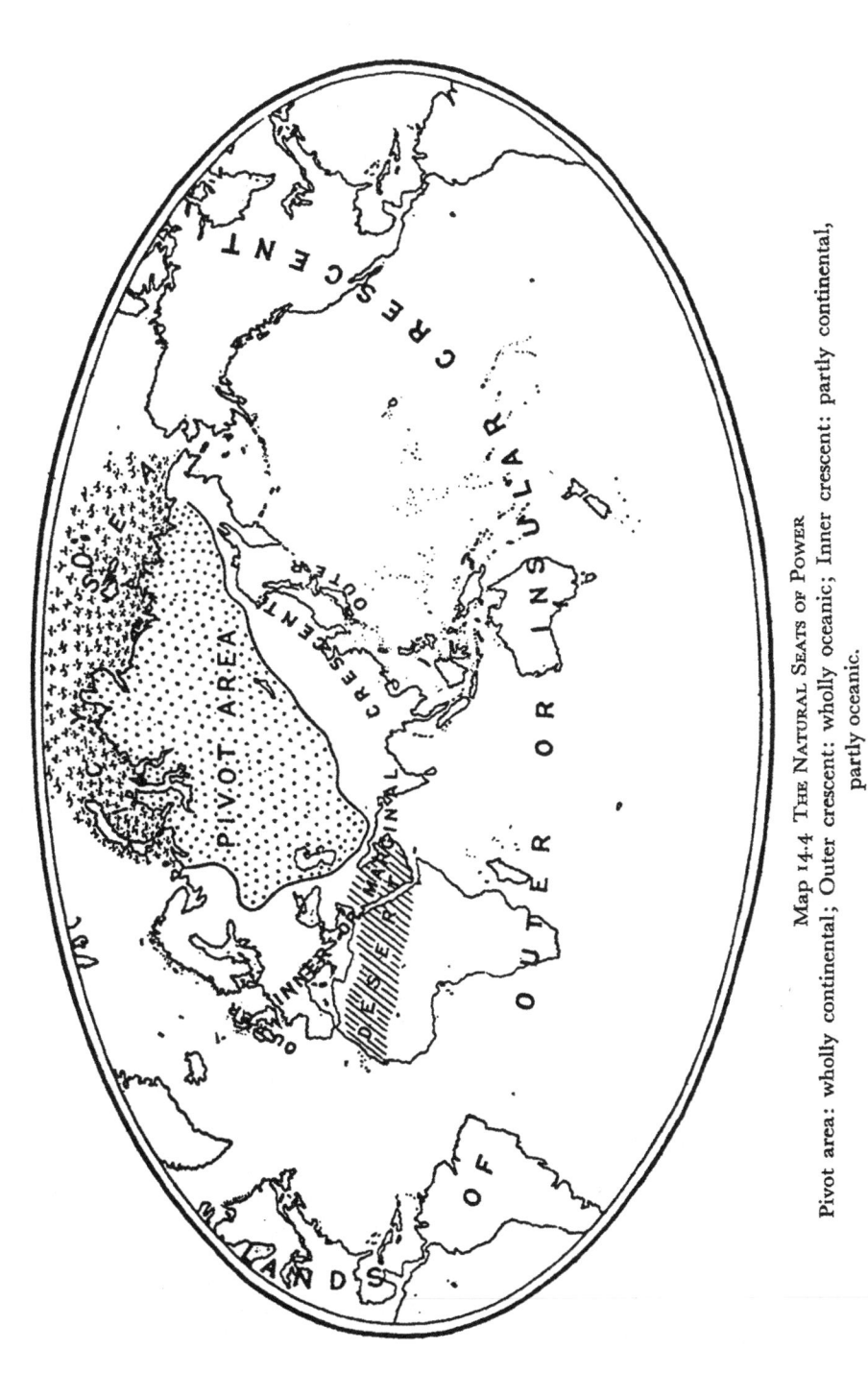

Pivot area: wholly continental; Outer crescent: wholly oceanic; Inner crescent: partly continental, partly oceanic.

sea-power and commerce, inaccessible to the land-power of Euro-Asia (Map 14.4).

But the land power still remains, and recent events have again increased its significance. While the maritime peoples of Western Europe have covered the ocean with their fleets, settled the outer continents, and in varying degree made tributary the oceanic margins of Asia, Russia has organized the Cossacks, and, emerging from her northern forests, has policed the steppe by setting her own nomads to meet the Tartar nomads. The Tudor century, which saw the expansion of Western Europe over the sea, also saw Russian power carried from Moscow through Siberia. The eastward swoop of the horsemen across Asia was an event almost as pregnant with political consequences as was the rounding of the Cape, although the two movements long remained apart.

It is probably one of the most striking coincidences of history that the seaward and the landward expansion of Europe should, in a sense, continue the ancient opposition between Roman and Greek. Few great failures have had more far-reaching consequences than the failure of Rome to Latinize the Greek. The Teuton was civilized and Christianized by the Roman, the Slav in the main by the Greek. It is the Romano-Teuton who in later times embarked upon the ocean; it was the Graeco-Slav who rode over the steppes, conquering the Turanian. Thus the modern land-power differs from the sea-power no less in the source of its ideals than in the material conditions of its mobility.[1]

In the wake of the Cossack, Russia has safely emerged from her former seclusion in the northern forests. Perhaps the change of greatest intrinsic importance which took place in Europe in the last century was the southward migration of the Russian peasants, so that, whereas agricultural settlements formerly ended at the forest boundary, the centre of the population of all European Russia now lies to south of that boundary, in the midst of the wheatfields which have replaced the more western steppes. Odessa has here risen to importance with the rapidity of an American city.

A generation ago steam and the Suez canal appeared to have increased the mobility of sea-power relatively to land-power. Railways acted chiefly as feeders to ocean-going commerce. But trans-continental railways are now transmuting the conditions of land-power, and nowhere can they have such effect as in the closed heart-land of Euro-Asia, in vast areas of which neither timber nor accessible stone was available for road-making. Railways work the greater wonders in the steppe, because they directly replace horse and camel mobility, the road stage of development having here been omitted.

The Russian railways have a clear run of 6000 miles from Wirballen in the west to Vladivostok in the east. The Russian army in Manchuria is as significant evidence of mobile land-power as the British army in South Africa was of sea-power. True, that the Trans-Siberian railway is still a single and precarious line of communication, but the century will not be old before all Asia is covered with railways. The spaces within the Russian Empire and Mongolia are so vast, and their potentialities in population, wheat, cotton, fuel, and metals so incalculably great, that it is inevitable that a vast economic world, more or less apart, will there develop inaccessible to oceanic commerce.

Euro-Asia—The Pivot Region

As we consider this rapid review of the broader currents of history, does not a certain persistence of geographical relationship become evident? Is not the pivot region of the world's politics that vast area of Euro-Asia which is inaccessible to ships, but in antiquity lay open to the horse-riding nomads, and is to-day about to be covered with a network of railways? There have been and are here the conditions of a mobility of military and economic power of a far-reaching and yet limited character. Russia replaces the Mongol Empire. Her pressure on Finland, on Scandinavia, on Poland, on Turkey, on Persia, on India, and on China replaces the centrifugal raids of the steppe-men. In the world at large she occupies the central strategical position held by Germany in Europe. She can strike on all sides and be struck from all sides, save the

---

1. This statement was criticized in the discussion which followed the reading of the paper. On reconsidering the paragraph, I still think it substantially correct. Even the Byzantine Greek would have been other than he was had Rome completed the subjugation of the ancient Greek. No doubt the ideals spoken of were Byzantine rather than Hellenic, but they were not Roman, which is the point.

north. The full development of her modern railway mobility is merely a matter of time. Nor is it likely that any possible social revolution will alter her essential relations to the great geographical limits of her existence. Wisely recognizing the fundamental limits of her power, her rulers have parted with Alaska; for it is as much a law of policy for Russia to own nothing over seas as for Britain to be supreme on the ocean.

Outside the pivot area, in a great inner crescent, are Germany, Austria, Turkey, India, and China, and in an outer crescent, Britain, South Africa, Australia, the United States, Canada, and Japan. In the present condition of the balance of power, the pivot state, Russia, is not equivalent to the peripheral states, and there is room for an equipoise in France. The United States has recently become an eastern power, affecting the European balance not directly, but through Russia, and she will construct the Panama canal to make her Mississippi and Atlantic resources available in the Pacific. From this point of view the real divide between east and west is to be found in the Atlantic ocean.

The oversetting of the balance of power in favour of the pivot state, resulting in its expansion over the marginal lands of Euro-Asia, would permit of the use of vast continental resources for fleet-building, and the empire of the world would then be in sight. This might happen if Germany were to ally herself with Russia. The threat of such an event should, therefore, throw France into alliance with the over-sea powers, and France, Italy, Egypt, India, and Korea would become so many bridge heads where the outside navies would support armies to compel the pivot allies to deploy land forces and prevent them from concentrating their whole strength on fleets. On a smaller scale that was what Wellington accomplished from his sea-base at Torres Vedras in the Peninsular War. May not this in the end prove to be the strategical function of India in the British Imperial system? Is not this the idea underlying Mr. Amery's conception that the British military front stretches from the Cape through India to Japan?

The development of the vast potentialities of South America might have a decisive influence upon the system. They might strengthen the United States, or, on the other hand, if Germany were to challenge the Monroe doctrine successfully, they might detach Berlin from what I may perhaps describe as a pivot policy. The particular combinations of power brought into balance are not material; my contention is that from a geographical point of view they are likely to rotate round the pivot state, which is always likely to be great, but with limited mobility as compared with the surrounding marginal and insular powers.

I have spoken as a geographer. The actual balance of political power at any given time is, of course, the product, on the one hand, of geographical conditions, both economic and strategic, and, on the other hand, of the relative number, virility, equipment, and organization of the competing peoples. In proportion as these quantities are accurately estimated are we likely to adjust differences without the crude resort to arms. And the geographical quantities in the calculation are more measurable and more nearly constant than the human. Hence we should expect to find our formula apply equally to past history and to present politics. The social movements of all times have played around essentially the same physical features, for I doubt whether the progressive desiccation of Asia and Africa, even if proved, has in historical times vitally altered the human environment. The westward march of empire appears to me to have been a short rotation of marginal power round the south-western and western edge of the pivotal area. The Nearer, Middle, and Far Eastern questions relate to the unstable equilibrium of inner and outer powers in those parts of the marginal crescent where local power is, at present, more or less negligible.

In conclusion, it may be well expressly to point out that the substitution of some new control of the inland area for that of Russia would not tend to reduce the geographical significance of the pivot position. Were the Chinese, for instance, organized by the Japanese, to overthrow the Russian Empire and conquer its territory, they might constitute the yellow peril to the world's freedom just because they would add an oceanic frontage to the resources of the great continent, an advantage as yet denied to the Russian tenant of the pivot region.

15

Heartland and Rimland

NICHOLAS SPYKMAN[*]

The fundamental fact which is responsible for the conditions of this age of world politics is the development of ocean navigation and the discovery of sea routes to India and America. Maritime mobility is the basis for a new type of geopolitical structure, the overseas empire. Formerly, history had given us the pattern of great land powers based on the control of contiguous land masses such as the Roman, Chinese, and Russian empires. Now the sea has become a great artery of communication and we have been given a new structure of great power and enormous extent. The British, French, and Japanese empires and the sea power of the United States have all contributed to the development of a modern world which is a single field for the interplay of political forces. It is sea power which has made it possible to conceive of the Eurasian Continent as a unit and it is sea power which governs the relationships between the Old and the New Worlds.

The German geopolitician, Haushofer, took over the interpretation of Mackinder and adapted it to his own peculiar needs. He has indicated the flow of rivers, a detail from which one accustomed to interpret maps can make some estimate of the location of mountain ranges. He has also sketched in certain areas of "political pressure" which illustrate the location of the centers of power Mackinder discussed but failed to locate on his map. Nevertheless, his chart fails also to afford a really adequate basis for discussion because it does not give the really important facts about topography which, in a geopolitical analysis, are indispensable.

We must, therefore, look at the topographical map and emphasize again the outlines of the land contours of the Eurasian Continent: the central lowland plain bounded by ice-covered waters to the north and by mountains in a great semicircle to the east, south, and west. Beyond the mountain belt lie the coastland regions consisting of plains separated by mountain spurs which stretch to the sea. In our further consideration of this picture of the earth, we shall have to refer again to these regions and it will be well to designate them by specific names (Map 15.1). The central continental plain can continue to be called the heartland but we may note that it is, in effect, to be equated with the political extent of the Union of Soviet Socialist Republics. Beyond the mountain barrier, the coastland region, which is called by Mackinder the inner crescent, may more effectively be referred to as the rimland, a name which defines its character accurately. The surrounding string of marginal and mediterranean seas which separates the continent from the oceans constitutes a circumferential

From *The Geography of the Peace* by Nicholas Spykman, Copyright, 1944, by Harcourt, Brace & World, Inc., and reprinted with their permission.

[*] Nicholas Spykman (1893–1943) was Professor of International Relations and Director of the Institute of International Studies at Yale University.

maritime highway which links the whole area together in terms of sea power. Beyond lie the off-shore islands and continents of Great Britain, Japan, Africa, and Australia which compose the outer crescent. The term "offshore" describes so well their essential relationship to the central land mass that we shall use this terminology rather than that of Mackinder. The oceanic belt and the transoceanic New World complete the picture in terms of purely geographical factors.

... We can now take up in detail the specific regions into which we have divided it and analyze their meaning in terms of power potential and the politics of global security. We must evaluate the role which each zone has in the past played in international society. ...

THE HEARTLAND

The importance of the heartland region was first suggested to Mackinder by his conception of the value of a central position with interior lines of communication made powerful and unified by the development of land transportation to a point where it could begin to compete with sea communication. He also envisaged the transformation of the steppe land from an area of low economic potential to one of high economic potential.

The actual facts of the Russian economy and geography make it not at all clear that the heartland is or will be in the very near future a world center of communication, mobility, and power potential. First of all, the distribution of climate in the world makes it certain that, in the absence of revolutionary developments in agricultural technique, the center of agrarian productivity will remain in western Russia rather than in the central Siberian region. A map plotting the cultivated land of the world emphasizes this fact (Map 15.2). Although the Russian state covers an area far larger than Canada, the United States, or Brazil, the actual extent of arable land is only a very small part of the total area. We must avoid the mistake of identifying all of Russia, or the heartland, as a region of great potential agrarian productivity.

Looking again at the geographic distribution of coal and iron deposits in the world as well as the oil fields and water power, we note that these essential elements of industrial power are located largely west of the Ural Mountains. It is true that there are reserves of coal and iron in Siberia, the exact extent of which are unknown but which undoubtedly constitute a sizeable quantity. Some reports say, also, that there are reserves of oil which can be important if developed. Certainly, the Soviet government has made and will continue to make constant and strenuous endeavors to shift the center of industrial production eastward. So far it has undoubtedly succeeded in developing factories and mines to an extent which has made it possible for Russia to provide herself with a large proportion of her vast war-time needs. The figures on the industrial production of the great area between the Urals and Novosibirsk remain vague and inaccurate and it is difficult to arrive at a complete estimate of the actual and potential importance of this region. It is, nevertheless, certain that it already supplements to an important extent the more fertile region to the west and southwest, although it must be remembered that it is not capable of supporting a large population from the produce of the land.

The railroad, the motor road, and the airplane have certainly created a new mobility in the center of the Eurasian land mass. It cannot, however, be ignored that this area is ringed to the north, east, south, and southwest by some of the greatest obstacles to transportation in the world. Ice and freezing temperatures for a large part of the year, and towering mountains pierced by only a few difficult passes, form its borders. A large part of the rimland areas which touch the heartland have even poorer transportation facilities. Afghanistan, Tibet, Sinkiang, and Mongolia are regions with no railroads, practically no motor roads, and only a few tortuous caravan routes of the most primitive sort. The law of the inverse ratio of power to distance remains valid within the same political unit as well as between political units. Within the immediate future, Central Asia will undoubtedly remain a region with a fairly low power potential.

The significance of this region was also defined by Mackinder in terms of position. The fact that the core of the heartland lies in the center of the Eurasian land mass gives it the advantage of interior communication with the lands of the inner crescent. It is obvious that the problems of an army which

Map 15.1 A Geopolitical Map of Eurasia

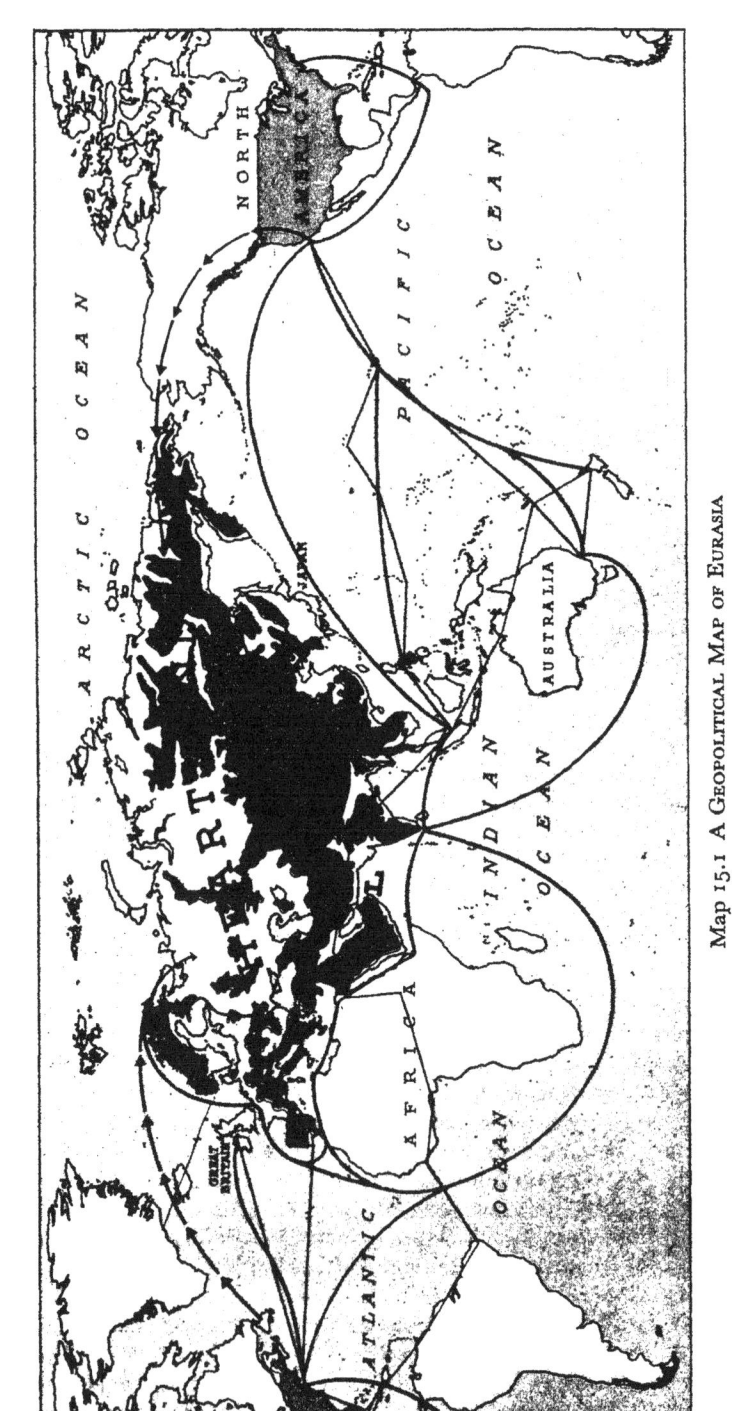

Map 15.2 The Cultivated Land of the World

is working along the diameters of a circle of territory will be less difficult than those of forces which have to function along the circumference of that same region. In comparison with the exterior lines of British naval power running from Great Britain through the circumferential highway around the Eurasian rimlands, Russia has interior lines of communication. The transportation lines between Russian Turkestan and Northwest India are certainly interior as compared with the sea route from Southampton to Karachi.

It must be pointed out, however, that interior lines function in terms of two points of reference rather than one. The relations between the center and the circumference may easily be changed if a point on the circumference becomes in turn the center of another circle of communication. Thus, the strategic implications of the position of the heartland in relation to the British Empire have meaning only if the military strength to be applied at the Indian frontier originates in Great Britain. The moment the defense of that frontier or the Persian frontier or the Chinese frontier rests on a locally developed war potential, the whole concept of interior and exterior lines is changed. What is true for India and China if they have to be defended by British sea power is no longer true if their military strength can be made a by-product of their own industrial development. In this case, unless the raw materials of power in the central Asiatic regions of Russia turn out to be great enough to balance those of the rimland regions, Soviet strength will remain west of the Urals and it will not be exerted overpoweringly against the coast lands to the east, south, and southwest.

The Rimland

In Mackinder's conception, the inner crescent of amphibian states surrounding the heartland consists of three sections: the European coast land, the Arabian-Middle Eastern desert land, and the Asiatic monsoon land. The first two regions are clearly defined as geographical areas but the third is a unit only from the special historical point of view represented by Great Britain. To the seaman, the Asiatic monsoon land looks like a single region. The similarities of climate and the easy accessibility of the area to sea power contribute to this impression. This territory is also well protected from the heartland by a string of barriers from the Himalayas and Tibet to the vast desert and mountain regions of Sinkiang and Mongolia. These mountains do not, however, make the monsoon lands behind them a single unit. The ranges of Burma and Indo-China extend down to the sea and interpose a great obstacle to contacts between the two great states. The fact that Buddhism reached China from India by way of Sinkiang and Thailand points to the difficulty of maintaining direct relations. Throughout their history, these two centers of oriental culture have remained fairly isolated from each other and their only contacts have been of a cultural and intellectual nature.

India and the Indian Ocean littoral, then, fall into a different geopolitical category from China, and it is scarcely accurate to classify them together as the Asiatic monsoon lands. The future will probably see the power of the two regions expressed as two distinct units connected only across the lower part of the Indo-China Peninsula by land or air power and around Singapore in terms of sea power. If this is true, then the Asiatic Mediterranean will continue to have great significance for the political strategy of the independent Asiatic world even as it has been of vital importance in the era of western sea power encirclement.

The rimland of the Eurasian land mass must be viewed as an intermediate region, situated as it is between the heartland and the marginal seas. It functions as a vast buffer zone of conflict between sea power and land power. Looking in both directions, it must function amphibiously and defend itself on land and sea. In the past, it has had to fight against the land power of the heartland and against the sea power of the off-shore islands of Great Britain and Japan. Its amphibious nature lies at the basis of its security problems.

The Off-Shore Continents

Off the southeastern and southwestern shores of the Old World lie the two mediterranean seas beyond which stretch the continents of Australia and Africa. The position of these two off-shore continents is determined largely by the state which controls the European and Asiatic Mediterranean Seas. The Mackinder analysis defines the great desert region of Africa as a continental area inaccessible to sea power and therefore a southern heartland comparable to the northern one. This concept was perhaps of some value in understanding the political history of Africa before the penetration of that continent by the white man. It also had a certain validity in terms of British-Russian opposition as long as the circumferential envelopment of the Old World went by way of the Cape of Good Hope.

Since the completion of the Suez Canal, this interpretation has lost all practical significance. There is no sense using a term which connotes that an area is impenetrable to sea power when that area has actually been transformed by sea power penetration. It must also be remembered that, notwithstanding any geographic similarity that can be suggested between the two regions, the southern heartland differs in one basic and fundamental respect from the northern heartland. It contains no political power and has no power potential of its own. It is not and never has been the seat of outward pressure toward the crescent. It does not, therefore, function in the total global picture in any manner similar to the northern heartland.

The significance of both these off-shore continents in world politics is limited by climatic conditions which restrict their productive capacity and, consequently, their power potential. The greatest proportion of Africa lies in the tropical zone and is either extremely dry or extremely humid. In either case the continent does not contain, except at the extreme southern tip, the resources necessary for the building up of political units capable of exerting an important influence on the rest of the world. In the same way, the desert regions of Australia are so extensive that the remaining territory is left without the size and resources required for the formation of a power of the first rank.

The Dynamic Pattern of Eurasian Politics

The general pattern of political action on the Eurasian Continent has been defined by Mackinder in terms of the pressure of nomadic peoples in the heartland outward against the states of the rimland. When the nomads who roamed the grasslands of the central lowland were replaced by the organized power of the Russian state, the same pattern was continued. The empire sought access to the sea and found its road blocked in the nineteenth century by British sea power which had expanded across the Eurasian littoral. The British imperial position rested on a maritime encirclement of the Eurasian land mass which was maintained by the predominance of her naval power along the circumferential maritime highway. This position could be threatened by the emergence of a competing sea power on the littoral of the continent, or by the penetration of Russian land power to the coast.

So convinced was Mackinder of the fact that any conflict in Europe must follow the pattern of land power-sea power opposition that he declared, in 1919, that the true character of the war which had just been concluded was not visible until after Russia had been defeated. British sea power could then be considered to be fighting against a land power which dominated the heartland. This interpretation would seem to be a little hard on the role of France as a land power, and it is strange to ignore the three years of Russian resistance on the eastern front.

Like all good geopolitical analyses, however, the Mackinder study represented a picture of the constellation of forces which existed at a particular time and within a particular frame of reference. It was first elaborated in 1904 before the conclusion of the British-Russian Entente of 1907 and was strongly influenced by the previous century of conflict between Russia and Great Britain. When, in 1919, his book *Democratic Ideals and Reality* was published, the conception of an inevitable historical opposition between Russian land power and British sea power was re-emphasized. The fallacy of this blanket application of a theory of history is seen when we realize that the opposition between these two states has never, in fact, been inevitable. Actually, in the three great world wars of the nineteenth and twentieth centuries, the Napoleonic Wars, the First World War, and the Second World War, the British and Russian empires have lined up together against an intervening rimland power as led by Napoleon, Wilhelm II, and Hitler.

In other words, there has never really been a simple land power-sea power opposition. The historical alignment has always been in

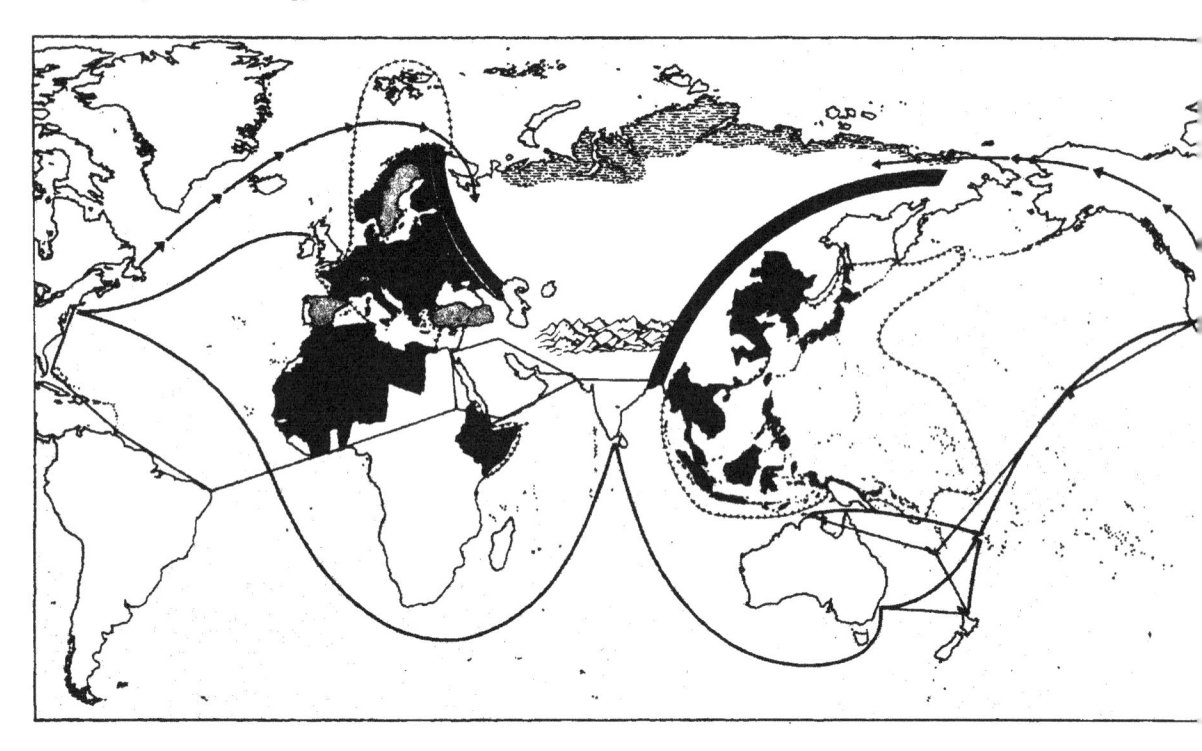

MAP 15.3 MAXIMUM EXPANSION OF GERMANY AND JAPAN, 1931-1942

terms of some members of the rimland with Great Britain against some members of the rimland with Russia, or Great Britain and Russia together against a dominating rimland power. The Mackinder dictum "Who controls eastern Europe rules the Heartland; who rules the Heartland rules the World Island; and who rules the World Island rules the World" is false. If there is to be a slogan for the power politics of the Old World, it must be "Who controls the rimland rules Eurasia; who rules Eurasia controls the destinies of the world."

Already the United States has gone to war twice within thirty years and the threat to our security each time has been the possibility that the rimland regions of the Eurasian land mass would be dominated by a single power. By the end of 1917, the success of the Germans in the east against Russia, which culminated in the Treaty of Brest-Litovsk of March 3, 1918, made it appear likely that the German bid for supremacy on the Atlantic littoral would be successful. At the same time, Japan, though ostensibly an ally of Great Britain and the United States, was also engaged in trying to achieve complete control over the Far East. In January of 1915 she began her campaign by pressing on China the Twenty-One Demands. Later, in 1918, she took part in the Allied invasion of Siberia and pushed her own interests there vigorously. Had she not been countered, she might have come out of the war with complete control over the Asiatic rimland.

The Washington Conference of 1921-22 achieved for us the partial withdrawal of Japan from the extreme claims of the Twenty-One Demands as well as a withdrawal from Siberia and from Shantung. Looking at the Washington treaties rather than the Treaty of Versailles as the end of the First World War we reduced our opponents to a relatively small area. It did not, however, take them long to resume their policies of expansion toward the control of the rimland and its vast power potential. The Second World War represents the continuation of that effort, begun in earnest by the Japanese in 1931 and by the Germans in 1936. At the point of maximum expansion this time, Germany reached indirectly to Dakar and Japan gained control as far as the Torres Strait between New Guinea and Australia (Map 15.3).

The course of the Second World War has emphasized in no uncertain terms the importance of a power equilibrium in Europe to the peace and well-being of the world. The most recent expression of the heartland concept by Mackinder[1] has recognized the predominant importance of the rimland and the necessity of British-Russian-United States collaboration to prevent the growth of German power in this area. He has modified his conception slightly by shifting the boundary of the heartland to the Yenisei River and lessening the emphasis on the Central Siberian grassland region. The focus of Soviet power is now located where its actual geographical concentration places it, west of the Urals. The heartland becomes less important than the rimland and it is the cooperation of British, Russian, and United States land and sea power that will control the European littoral and, thereby, the essential power relations of the world.

[1]. H. J. Mackinder, "The Round World," *Foreign Affairs*, July, 1943.

16

Geostrategic and Geopolitical Regions

SAUL B. COHEN[*]

In past global strategic views, emphasis has been placed upon the strategic unity of space, organized through a single arena of movement. Unity of the land-mass through the channel of railroads and highways is the basis of the Heartland concept. Unity of the sea through the channel of ships is the basis of the Rimland and North Atlantic Basin concepts. Unity of the air through bombers and missiles is the basis of the North Polar concept, and of the concept that brushes aside the variable significance of land and sea masses to say that the dominant airpower can command the world, regardless of the location of that power's land base.

A basic premise of these global strategic concepts is that the unity of one arena of movement is indivisible—that the dominant fleet can rule the entirety of the open seas; the dominant land army can rule all of the land space; the dominant airpower can rule all of the air.

But today's realities suggest otherwise. Unity of arenas of movement cannot be complete, and power within such avenues is therefore divisible. This is because complete dominance of one avenue of movement cannot be attained unless one power completely

Condensed from *Geography and Politics in a World Divided*, by Saul B. Cohen. © Copyright 1963 by Saul B. Cohen. Reprinted by permission of Random House, Inc., and the author.

[*] Saul Cohen (1925–) is Director of the Graduate School of Geography and Dean of Graduate Studies at Clark University.

destroys another through nuclear warfare. Sea-controlling powers cannot prevent the landpower from building up its air and sea forces and continuously attacking the sea lanes via the medium of aircraft, missiles, and nuclear-powered submarines. A landpower cannot be impervious to attack from the sea, because of the striking capability that sea-powers can exercise through aircraft, missiles, air-borne troops, and submarines. The basic advantages that these arenas offer to their prime users are, therefore, coming more and more to be shared by the secondary users.

GEOSTRATEGIC AND GEOPOLITICAL REGIONS

A framework for geopolitical analysis should distinguish between divisions that have global extent, and those that have regional extent. For this purpose, we shall employ the terms *geostrategic regions* and *geopolitical regions*.

The geostrategic region must be large enough to possess certain globe-influencing characteristics and functions, because today's strategy can only be expressed in global terms. The geostrategic region is the expression of the interrelationship of a large part of the world in terms of location, movement, trade orientation, and cultural or ideological bonds. While it is a single-feature region in the sense that its purpose is to embrace areas over which power can be applied, it is a multi-feature region in its composition. Control of strategic passageways on land and sea is frequently crucial to the unity of geostrategic regions.

The geopolitical region is a subdivision of the above. It expresses the unity of geographic features. Because it is derived directly from geographic regions, this unit can provide a framework for common political and economic actions. Contiguity of location and complementarity of resources are particularly distinguishing marks of the geopolitical region. Geopolitical regions are the basis for the emergence of multiple power nodes within a geostrategic region, as exemplified by the emergence of Mainland China as a second power center in the Communist world. Put another way, the geostrategic region has a strategic role to play and the geopolitical region has a tactical one.

It is important to keep clear the distinction between geostrategic and geopolitical units. Confusing their characteristics and functions may result in an overestimation of the capacity of geostrategic regions for political and economic unity, or in an underestimation of the capacity for unity within geopolitical regions. The attempt to convert the global Free World military alliances into a tightly knit political and economic unit, or the assumption that the political differences between Maritime Europe and the Maghreb, where basic geographic unity exists, cannot be reconciled, are examples resulting from such confusion.

The emerging concepts of geostrategic and geopolitical regions were a product of the rise of Europe's colonial empires and the drives to acquire key islands and coastal enclaves as a means of uniting ocean basins. The strategy of building the Portuguese, Spanish, French, Dutch, and British Empires, of carving out spheres of influence in the "exploitable" world, began to take on global or geostrategic connotations. And drives to expand the frontiers of the United States and Russia or to gain unified control over Maritime Europe and the Mediterranean sought to fulfill goals of political unity within and among geographical regions, and therefore took on geopolitical overtones.

Our scheme for the geostrategic partitioning of the earth rests essentially upon the yardsticks of *place* and *movement*. Place includes the location of regional population and economic cores and great barrier zones; movement includes trade orientation and ideological-cultural bonds.

There are, strictly speaking, only two geostrategic regions today: (1) The Trade-Dependent Maritime World, and (2) The Eurasian Continental World. Projecting our views into the future, we anticipate the eventual emergence of a third geostrategic region—the Indian Ocean Plateau realm. Such a region, likely to arise from the ashes of the British Commonwealth and other formerly European colonial areas, may not possess all of the qualifications for playing a truly global power role. Yet this former colonial intertropical world is likely to attain second-rank geostrategic status under certain eventualities that we will discuss in a later chapter.

The core of the Trade-Dependent Maritime World is the Maritime Ring of the United States; that of the Eurasian Continental World is the Russian Industrialized Triangle. Thus both regions can be described as "nodal." Maritime Europe and Mainland China have emerged as second power nodes within these geostrategic regions.

The United States is thrusting its development energies toward its coastal rims, intensifying connections with other parts of the Maritime World. The Soviet Union's development thrust is landward, with its major direction into the Eurasian Heartland. The secondary thrust along the western and eastern frontiers is spearheaded by pipeline and railroad construction.

Geostrategic regions can be subdivided into various geopolitical regions. The Trade-Dependent Maritime World includes: (*a*) Anglo-America and the Caribbean, (*b*) Maritime Europe and the Maghreb, (*c*) Offshore Asia and Oceania, and (*d*) South America. The Eurasian Continental World includes: (*a*) The Russian Heartland and Eastern Europe, and (*b*) The East Asian Mainland. Between these two geostrategic regions lie Shatterbelts—the Middle East and Southeast Asia. (Map 16.1).

Unaccounted for in this scheme are Africa south of the Sahara and South Asia. South Asia does possess qualities of geopolitical unity that make it likely to be recognized, in the near future, as a unit separate from both geostrategic regions. Africa, on the other hand, shows little sign of being able to attain

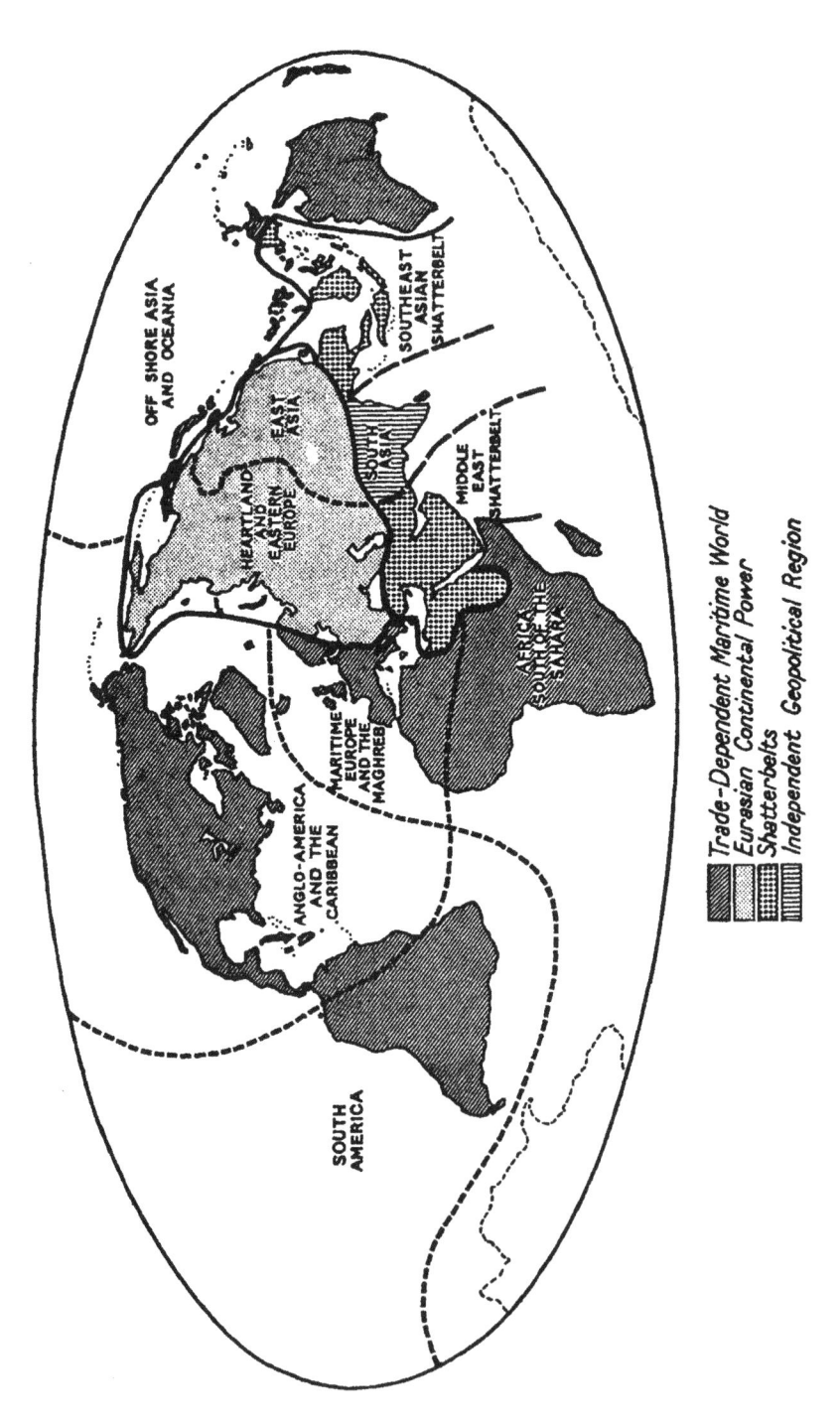

Map 16.1 THE WORLD'S GEOSTRATEGIC REGIONS AND THEIR GEOPOLITICAL SUBDIVISIONS

continental geopolitical unity. This does not mean that Africa is not important to the sphere of influence of the Trade-Dependent Maritime World, nor is it outside of it. What it does mean is that Africa south of the Sahara is not likely to find internal geopolitical unity within the framework that has been outlined. If, however, the European footholds in Central and South Africa should be lost, then the entire eastern half of the continent might gravitate geostrategically to South Asia.

Several criteria have been used to define the Trade-Dependent Maritime geostrategic region. These include: (1) orientation to the Atlantic and Pacific Ocean basins, (2) primacy of sea communications in interconnecting this region, (3) distribution of raw materials and people so as to call for regional specialization and interdependence, (4) a band of white settlement across the temperate lands of the southern hemisphere, (5) trade-dependence with the North Atlantic Basin, and (6) highest levels of technology. The major ecumene of this geostrategic region extends from the Northeastern United States through Northwestern Europe. This may soon grow to include the Southeastern United States and Cuba. The secondary ecumene extends from Los Angeles-San Francisco through Southern Japan. This is in the process of being extended to Taiwan and the Central Philippines. Although sea lanes tie these two ecumenes together, it is the combination of overland and coastal United States routes that directs these ties.[1]

Ideological bonds, complicated by present or recent aspects of colonialism, are not as strong within the Trade-Dependent Maritime World as they are within the Eurasian Continental Communist World. In part, these bonds will be strengthened as the "have" parts of the Maritime World share more of their wealth with the "have-nots." To help to describe this Trade-Dependent Maritime World, the dependence of nations upon sea trade has been mapped according to the ratio of imports to national income. This map (Map 16.2) reflects a variety of factors, such as limitations of land bases, underdevelopment or absence of resources for manufacturing, colonialism, and alliances.

If we look at the world as seen on Map 16.2, we note that certain parts of the so-called Maritime World are far less dependent upon sea lanes than other parts. What we see are groupings of trade-oriented "islands," which we have called *Ocean Trade-Dependent*. A second grouping is trade-oriented, but to a lesser extent. This we have called *Ocean Trade-Oriented*. Lastly, we have the *Inwardly Oriented* countries, mostly within the northern hemisphere. The economic and the strategic interests of these groupings vary, but the trade "islands," above all, must be free to trade with one another and with the rest of the world. The global nature of the American commitment is readily apparent from this map. As long as its important allies are so heavily dependent upon overseas trade, the United States has to help them maintain their sea contacts. When this map is related to global location, contiguity, unity of arenas of movement, strategic raw material trade, population distribution, and ideology, we arrive at the Trade-Dependent Maritime geostrategic region.

The major ecumene of the Trade-Dependent Maritime Region consists of the Northeastern United States and Western Europe. This ecumene's components in Anglo-America and Maritime Europe are the cores of the two most richly endowed and strongest geopolitical regions within the Free World. Co-ordinated action between these two geopolitical units is imperative if the strategic unity of the Maritime World is to be maintained. Such action must be on a global scale, because the Maritime World's extent is global.

To speak of the Eurasian Continental World as including Mainland East Asia may appear to some readers to be an over-weighting of ideology—Communism—as the criterion. Mackinder felt that the belt of deserts and mountains separating China from the Soviet Union would be a sufficient barrier to separate the Heartland from what he called Monsoonal Asia. And some contemporary observers, like George Kennan, hold that: "If time was against him [Stalin] in 1927, so was space. He faced the fact that he was 5,000 miles from the scene of action, and a foreigner, whereas Chiang and Mao were Chinese, and were right there... there are geographic

---

1. *Ecumene* is used to describe the area of densest population in coincidence with rail, highway, ship or air networks or any combination of these. Variability and low costs for sea lanes and variability and speed for air lanes make it unnecessary for the ecumene to require the contiguity on sea that it must show on land.

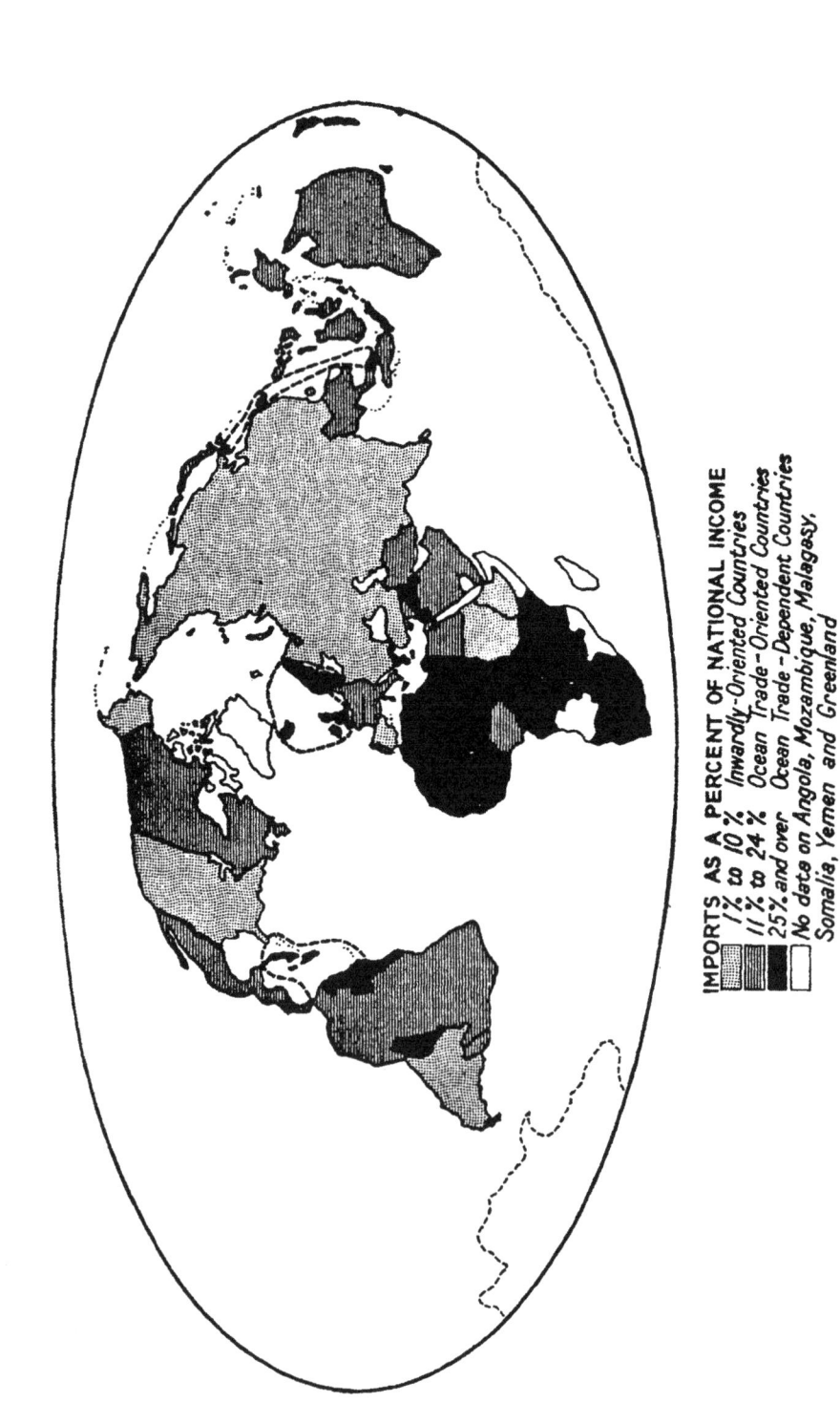

MAP 16.2 GEOPOLITICS AND TRADE

limits to the possibilities of military expansion"[2] (again with reference to Soviet relations with China). Kennan believes that the Sino-Soviet alliance is destined to break apart because of the cultural, racial, and physical differences that divide the two powers.

We may not be able to prove or to disprove the thesis that the gulf between a Westernized, Christianized Russia and Oriental China is too great to be bridged by Marxism. But we can challenge the thesis that China and the Soviet Union are too far apart to be able to operate within a unified geostrategic framework. While the distance from Canton to Riga is about 5,000 air miles, and that from Shanghai to Moscow is about 3,700 miles, the gap between Lanchow, China's "Chicago of the West," and Alma Ata, Kazakhstan's scientific university center, is only 1,500 miles. Paotou, the new steel city of North China, is but 900 miles from Irkutsk.

Admittedly, there are vast empty areas between the two states. Semipalatinsk, a site of Soviet nuclear testing, lies exactly midway between Peiping and Moscow and is surrounded by empty reaches. However, the true test of proximity in space is the distance that separates the two national ecumenes and the channels of movement that bind them together. Novosibirsk, a city of nearly one million people, and now the eastern edge of the Soviet ecumene, is 1,800 miles from Peiping, the focus of the North-Northeast Chinese ecumene. Moreover, Sinkiang, China's "New Frontier" of the Northwest for mineral and industrial development, adjoins one of the Soviet "New Frontiers," Kazakhstan.

Deep ideological rifts, such as those over Stalinism, coexistence, and the communes,

2. George F. Kennan, *Russia and the West under Lenin and Stalin* (Boston: Little, Brown, 1960), p. 276.

exist between the Soviet Union and China. Moreover, China has begun to challenge the position of preeminence hitherto held by the U.S.S.R. within the Communist bloc. The Chinese first issued this challenge in striving for regional hegemony over North Korean and Viet Minh Communist affairs. Then they broadened this challenge through support of Albania and a show of diplomatic strength in such countries as Cuba and Egypt. What is probably involved is not a permanent splitting of the Communist World, but rather the emergence of multiple power cores within it. Such a course is to be expected within any geostrategic region, because of the cohesion and uniqueness of its geopolitical subdivisions. As serious as Sino-Soviet divergencies are, they are no greater than, and in many ways resemble quite closely, the divisions that exist among the geopolitical regions of the Maritime World.

In viewing the ties of the East Asia Mainland geopolitical region to that of the Soviet Heartland-East European region, we can draw some useful parallels from the relations between two comparable units—Maritime Europe and the Maghreb, and Anglo-America and the Caribbean Basin.

First, the gap between the respective ecumenes is not substantially different. About 2,000 miles separate the Chinese and Soviet ecumenes, and 3,000 miles are needed to span the North Atlantic. In time-distance terms, the overland gap is shorter (three to four days as compared with five to six days). On the other hand, if we weight time-distance by cost of freight movement, we find that the advantage shifts to the North Atlantic sailing route and that, economically, the ecumenes that are the termini of this route are closer together. Sea routes also exist as links between China and the U.S.S.R. However, these (the 6,000-mile Northern Sea route and the

TABLE *Selected Data—Major Geopolitical Regions**

Geopolitical Region	Land Area (Sq. Mi.)	Population	Annual Gross National Product
East Asia Mainland	3,750,000	650,000,000	$35,000,000,000
Soviet Heartland and Eastern Europe	9,000,000	325,000,000	$190,000,000,000
Maritime Europe and the Maghreb	2,500,000	325,000,000	$215,000,000,000
Anglo-America and the Caribbean	8,000,000	260,000,000	$430,000,000,000

*North American lands north of the Arctic Circle are not considered here.

9,000-mile Indian Ocean route) are longer, slower, and less reliable, and should not enter this process of comparison.

Second, the mutual relations of these geopolitical regions are comparable in terms of size, population, and gross national product ... (see the Table).

The land area ratios are quite similar: 1 to 2.5 for China and its neighboring Heartland unit, and 1 to 3 for Maritime Europe and Anglo-America. The population ratios are somewhat wider apart, 2 to 1 and $1\frac{1}{4}$ to 1 respectively, but maintain the same order. Gross national product ratios, again in the same order, show a wider disparity, 1 to 5 as against 1 to 2. However, if we give combined weight to population and gross national product, we find China's ratio to the Soviet Heartland to be 1 to 2.5, while Maritime Europe's ratio to Anglo-America is 1 to 1.6.

Third, just as the North Atlantic regions have become increasingly interdependent strategically and economically, so have the two Eurasian Continental geopolitical units. Traditionally, the U.S.S.R. has feared the pressures upon its Siberian lands that might be exerted from Chinese Turkestan, Outer Mongolia, and Manchuria. In recent decades these pressures originated from Japan and more distant Pacific-held bases of the Western world. In the future, such pressures will emanate from Mainland Chinese areas that are within the strategic reach of Soviet landpower.

Shatterbelts

Two Shatterbelts divide the Trade-Dependent Maritime from the Eurasian Continental geostrategic regions. These are the Middle East and Southeast Asia. A Shatterbelt is here defined as a large, strategically located region that is occupied by a number of conflicting states and is caught between the conflicting interests of adjoining Great Powers.

In his volume *Geography and World Power*, James Fairgrieve called attention to a "Crush Zone" of small states that had gradually come into existence between the Eurasian Heartland and the seapowers (essentially European, such as Britain, France, Portugal, Spain, and Italy, but also Japan). He spoke of these states as "largely survivals from earlier time, when political and economic organizations were on a smaller scale ... each [with] characteristics partly acquired in that earlier time and partly natural ... [each] with sufficient individuality to withstand absorptions, but unable or unwilling to unite with others to form any larger whole."[3]

Fairgrieve viewed these states as buffers, "precariously independent politically, and more surely dependent economically." He listed within this "Crush Zone" such states as "Finland, Sweden, Norway, Denmark, Holland, Belgium, Luxemburg, Switzerland, Poland, the Balkans, Iran, Afghanistan, Siam, and Korea."[4] He conceded that in a certain sense Germany, China, and even India might be expected to belong to this belt. However, their uniqueness, Fairgrieve recognized, lay in size, resources, and historic relationship to the encircling land and sea worlds. Above all their uniqueness lay in their roles as possible centers from which the Heartland might be organized.

Much has happened to this "Crush Zone" in the military, political, and economic sense since Fairgrieve described it in 1915. In Central and Eastern Europe, the "Crush Zone" has disappeared, replaced by political and economic blocs, clearly allied with the contending geostrategic regions. Buffers like Finland, Austria, and Yugoslavia exist. However, they do not form part of a continuous zone and are in the process of strengthening economic ties with larger, neighboring units.

Reflecting the elimination of the European "Crush Zone" are World War II-inspired changes in boundary lines, political and economic consolidation of national states, integration of transportation along the North European and Danubian plains, and merging of economic core areas on a broad regional basis.

Mainland China is no longer even a possible part of the "Crush Zone" and Korea lies outside it. For Korea, as we have seen, is too small to provide elbowroom for bufferdom. Its partition serves as the line of contact between the two geostrategic regions. But elsewhere the zone described by Fairgrieve has retained its essential character. Indeed, the post-World War Two attainment of independence by many colonial peoples has tended to strengthen fragmentation in the "Crush Zone."

3. James Fairgrieve, *Geography and World Power*, (University of London Press, 1915), p. 329.
4. *Ibid.*, p. 330.

As we survey politically fragmentized areas of contact between the world's seaward-oriented powers and the Soviet bloc, we find, not a continuous zone, but two distinct belts. These are the *Shatterbelts* of the Middle East and Southeast Asia. Because they command strategic narrow seas and because of their specialized agricultural and mineral products, the political and economic fate of the Shatterbelts is of vital concern to the Trade-Dependent Maritime World. Because their land avenues project towards important parts of the Eurasian Continental World, their fate is of equal concern to this geostrategic region.

What is peculiar to the Shatterbelt is its fragmented political and economic character. Owing to physical, environmental, historical, cultural, and political differences, the Shatterbelt appears to be incapable of attaining political and/or economic unity of action. Parts of the Shatterbelts tend to seek neutrality and to lead the entire region into this path, but other portions are committed to external ties, either because of their self-interest or because of military and economic pressures from the external power centers.

Since the Second World War, both geostrategic regions have shown that they regard retention or establishment of spheres of influence within the two Shatterbelts to be strategically vital. In various discussions of the possibilities of reducing tensions within the Middle East and Southeast Asia through restriction of armament sales, the Great Powers have not been willing to restrict sale of arms to these regions in their entirety. Each of the Great Powers has allies which it insists upon strengthening.

A locational characteristic of these belts is that they do not adjoin the core areas of opposing Great Powers. Instead, they are physically removed and are not subject to the same rigid pressures that exist between the opposing sides in Central Europe or along Asia's inner seas. On the other hand, because these Shatterbelts are easily accessible to adjoining regions, they exhibit many extra-regional cultural and economic features.

Complete control of the Shatterbelts is no longer possible for either side, nor is it theoretically desirable, since this would mean an expenditure of energies in blanket fashion over an area of variable internal significance.

Each Shatterbelt offers footholds to the contending Great Powers. Footholds perform a variety of functions. First, these footholds can serve as bases in "cold" and "hot" war situations, checkmating adjoining areas which might be used as springboards for attack. Second, they maintain the buffer qualities of the Shatterbelt, ensuring that one force will not swallow it up. If, for example, the Middle East were to lose its current Shatterbelt characteristics and fall completely under Moscow domination, the arena of contention would shift directly to Africa, thereby placing Maritime Europe in mortal strategic danger. Third, the maintaining of Free World footholds within Shatterbelts clearly indicates, to Communist, neutral, and allied states alike, that we have no intention of withdrawing to positions that are so rigid and crucial as to leave no alternative but to wage nuclear wars. In other words, Shatterbelts offer the elbowroom for various forms of contention that other areas do not. Finally, footholds can better enable Great Powers to encourage "friendly" neutrals and to discourage "hostile" neutrals. But, for the Free World, these footholds would best be based upon stable alliances with internally popular governments. Otherwise, they become nothing but minority-controlled puppets and a constant source of weakness.

Conclusion

A policy of containment that views the world according to the Heartland-Rimland pattern draws us into grave strategic errors, for all parts of the Eurasian littoral are not of equal strategic significance to the Trade-Dependent Maritime World. Nor does a policy of complete disengagement from overseas areas meet the strategic needs of the United States and its major allies. We should, therefore, in our global approach distinguish between those parts of the world that: (1) warrant Free World support at the risk of total war; (2) warrant Free World support at the risk of limited wars, and therefore limited objectives; (3) warrant indirect military and diplomatic support; (4) warrant no Free World military involvement. The same applies to our economic activities in our economic war with the Soviet bloc. Only if we do this can we form alliances that will carry out the objectives of our strategy, rather than dictate our strategy.

Implicit in these observations is the fact that all geographic areas need not and should not be treated as strategic "wholes." In this respect, it is unsound to issue blanket invitations to countries of certain areas to enter defense pacts, or to ally ourselves with governments that are totally divorced from their people, when there is the possibility of our becoming committed to countries whose defense is not strategically vital to Free World survival.

These views are some of the results that we have obtained from relating our knowledge of geography to strategy. Since geography, in its broadest sense, is constantly changing, and since movement mirrors these changes, we dare not rely upon concepts of the past, but must be continuously on the alert to examine the changing geographic scene, and to interpret the impact of this change in the formulation of strategy. This is the approach through which we can genuinely understand geography's influences upon strategy—an influence that we may try to ignore, but that will not ignore us.

Annotated Bibliography

ALEXANDER, LEWIS M.
"Geography and the Law of the Sea," *Annals* of the Association of American Geographers, LVII (March 1968), pp. 177–197.
    A review of the pertinent literature on the geography of the sea. The author discusses the nature of the marine environment and various aspects of the international law of the sea in terms of control of access, resources, and specific objects. Valuable insights into future trends are contained in the author's conclusion on pages 196–197.

ALEXANDER, LEWIS M. ed.
The Law of the Sea: Offshore Boundaries and Zones (Columbus, Ohio: Ohio State University Press, 1967.)
    A study by a political geographer on the problems of sovereignty over sea space. It has superceded works on the law of the sea in the fields of international law and international relations as a source in political geography.

ALMOND, GABRIEL A. and JAMES S. COLEMAN, eds.
The Politics of the Developing Areas (Princeton, N.J.: Princeton University Press, 1960).
    A collection of essays on developing areas including Southeast Asia (Lucian W. Pye), South Asia (Myron Weiner), Sub-Saharan Africa (Coleman), the Near East (Dankwart A. Rustow), and Latin America (George I. Blanksten). The volume is a first effort to compare systematically political systems of developing areas according to a common set of categories. Although later criticized for its inadequate level of regional analysis by Flanigan and Fogelman in Martindale's *Functionalism in the Social Sciences*, the volume has a fine introduction by Almond which elaborates a functional approach to comparative politics.

BALL, GEORGE W.
"3¼ Super Powers," *Life Magazine*, March 19, 1968, pp. 74–89.
    An ex-Under Secretary of State predicts a post-Vietnam global structure made up of the U.S.A., the U.S.S.R., Western Europe, and Japan as superpowers. The author feels that these will operate with mutual interest in helping to solve the problems of the underdeveloped world within this reconstructed power equilibrium. A synthesis of the author's ideas contained in his *The Discipline of Power: Essentials of a Modern World Structure*, published by Atlantic-Little, Brown, in 1968.

BELOFF, MAX
"The Balance of Power," *Interplay of European/American Affairs*, I (August/September, 1967), pp. 14–18.
    A Europe-oriented global view through an updating of the balance of power model. In a world of a U.S.A.-U.S.S.R. rapprochement and of a united Europe, the author forsees a change in scale but no basic change in content of a bi-polar world balance. A synthesis of the author's ideas contained in his *Balance of Power*, published by McGill University Press in 1967.

BENEDICT, BURTON, ed.
Problems of Smaller Territories (London: The Athlone Press, 1967.)
    A collection of papers from a University of London seminar and published by the Institute of Commonwealth Studies. The authors through a variety of theoretical and case studies examine the impact of smallness of both population and area on the polity of territories. A valuable contribution to an increasingly significant yet rather ignored problem of territoriality.

BERNSTEIN, ROBERT A. and PETER D. WELDON
"A Structural Approach to the Analysis of International Relations," *Journal of Conflict Resolution*, XII (June 1968), pp. 159–181.
    A random sample of thirty-five nations from nine world regions is drawn and the units analyzed in terms of three variables: differentiation, articulation, and centrality. From the universe of possible interacting roles

coded for the three dimensions of diplomacy, trade, and military alliance, a scale attribute pool is formed for each. The scales are intercorrelated and a general scale of differentiation is developed which is compared with rankings by Berry, Staley and Caplow. A strong relationship is found between international differentiation and national development.

BLAIR, PATRICIA WOHLGEMUTH

The Ministate Dilemma (New York: Carnegie Endowment for International Peace, Occasional Paper No. 6, October, 1967).

An analysis of the problems of extreme smallness of territory for political viability. Although the main focus is the question of quality of membership in the United Nations, the author discusses problems of definition and function, and includes a wide variety of data on ministates in tabular form.

BUCHANAN, KEITH

"Profiles of the Third World," *Pacific Viewpoint*, V (September 1964), pp. 97–126.

An analysis of the "commonwealth of poverty" characterized in the title. The legacy of colonialism and exploitation of the third world is dramatically illustrated in world cartograms of various indices of poverty. The geopolitical position and search for identity of the third world is also discussed.

DALE, EDMUND H.

"Some Geographical Aspects of African Land-Locked States," *Annals* of the Association of American Geographers, LVIII (September 1968), pp. 485–505.

A logical sequel to East's paper on land-locked states in which the author attempts to generalize about the distinctive characteristics of Africa's land-locked states. He concludes that lack of access to the sea and to world markets are not the cause of the difficulties of these states as much as are their locational disabilities resulting from inadequate internal transport facilities. Their lack of homogeneity and cohesion does not serve to distinguish them from the newly independent coastal states of Africa.

DE SEVERSKY, ALEXANDER P.

Air Power: Key to Survival (New York: Simon and Schuster, 1950).

An "airman's" global view based upon the rejection of land-versus-sea power theories and the substitution of a concept of the possibility of total air dominance in a global scale.

EAST, W. GORDON

"The Geography of Land-Locked States," *Institute of British Geographers, Transactions and Papers*, XXVIII (1960), pp. 1–22.

Presented as a Presidential Address to the Institute of British Geographers, the paper discusses the general characteristics of land-locked states in a wide-ranging manner which covers all the world states without coastlands.

FISHER, CHARLES A., ed.

Essays in Political Geography (London: Methuen & Co. Ltd., 1968).

A collection of eighteen papers prepared for the Symposium on Political Geography at the 1964 International Geographical Congress. Following a brief introduction by the editor, the papers are arranged into three sections: Geographical Aspects of the Structure and Inter-relationships of States, Case Studies in Decolonization, and Aspects of Politico-Geographical Change in the Old World. Of particular significance are the papers by Hartshorne on "Morphology of the State Area," Cohen on "The Contemporary Geopolitical Setting," and House on "A Local Perspective on Boundaries and the Frontier Zone." The eleven case studies cover a wide variety of problems in decolonization.

FURNISS, EDGAR S.

"The Contribution of Nicholas John Spykman to the Study of International Politics," *World Politics*, IV (April 1952), pp. 382–401.

An appreciation of Spykman's contribution written a decade after his death. The best overall evaluation of this major figure in global structure analysis.

GOTTMANN, JEAN

"Geography and International Relations," *World Politics*, III (January 1951), pp. 153–173.

An examination into the relationship between environment and the behavior of states and its role in international relations. The author's work reproduced in the selections is a sequel to this article.

GOTTMANN, JEAN

"The Political Partitioning of Our World: An Attempt at Analysis," *World Politics*, IV (1952), pp. 512–519.

The author attempts to obtain a more theoretical explanation of man's partitioning of earth's space. On the basic assumption that space is limited, Gottman defines accessibility as the major variable in political partitioning giving emphasis to the uniqueness of position. Each political territory is under a distinctive iconography—a set of symbols in which people believe and with which they identify in contrast with those in neighbouring areas. While this iconography is the stable factor, *circulation*—the movement factor—is constantly acting as a dynamic force to change the existing iconography. As the impact of the movement factor changes the iconography, there is a corresponding change in the spatial pattern of political partitioning.

GOTTMANN, JEAN
    La politique des états et leur géographie (Paris: Armand Colin, 1952).
        Chapter 8, "Origin and Evolution of Regionalisms," is of particular significance to the notion of territoriality. The author's ideas of iconography and circulation are discussed at greater length than in his English language articles.

GREGG, PHILLIP M. and ARTHUR S. BANKS
    "Grouping Political Systems: Q-Factor Analysis of a Cross-Polity Survey," *American Behavioral Scientist*, IX (November 1965), pp. 3–6.
        Using data from 115 independent nations and covering 68 variables, the authors group nations according to such indices as areal groupings, type and stage of modernization, governmental and administrative structure, modes of articulation and party system, and political conflict. The analysis distinguishes five groupings of states: polyarchic, elitist, centrist, personalist, and traditional.

HAAS, ERNST B.
    "The Balance of Power: Prescription, Concept, or Propaganda?" *World Politics*, V (1953), pp. 442–477.
        As the title suggests, a lengthy examination of the various balance of power theories and their relevance to the bi-polar world of the Cold War.

HALL, ARTHUR R.
    "Mackinder and the Course of Events," *Annals* of the Association of American Geographers, XLV (June 1955), pp. 109–126.
        The most thorough and scholarly critique of Mackinder's thesis available. The author concludes that Mackinder has been largely right in his predictions but for different reasons than given.

HAMDAN, G.
    "Capitals of the New Africa," *Economic Geography*, XL (1964), pp. 239–253.
        An examination of the evolution of capital cities in Africa with special reference to their relevance to the post-independence period. Emphasis is given to locational (centrality and nodality) and size variables.

HARARY, FRANK
    "A Structural Analysis of the Situation in the Middle East in 1956," *Journal of Conflict Resolution*, V (June, 1961), pp. 167–178.
        An attempt at distinguishing between states of equilibrium and disequilibrium in the interrelationships between nations. The author bases his approach on the psychological theory of structural balance while the logical framework involves the mathematical theory of graphs. The corroborative material is provided by the rapid shifts in state behavior during the Middle East and Hungarian crises of 1956. Despite its limitations, this theory of structural balance offers a clear approach to the study of political geographic problems at the international level.

HARTSHORNE, RICHARD
    "The Franco-German Boundary of 1871," *World Politics*, II (1950), pp. 209–250.
        A classic historical study of the reasons behind the boundary changes following the Franco-Prussian War. The author is able to deduce from a variety of evidences that the usually accepted reasons behind the German demands for territorial gains are incorrect.

HARTSHORNE, RICHARD
    "Suggestions on the Terminology of Political Boundaries," *Mitteilungen des Vereins der Geographen an der Universität Leipzig*, XIV–XV (1936), pp. 180–192.
        Despite its unexciting title, a landmark work because it presented a new classification of boundaries based on their association when drawn with the cultural features of the boundary region. The types—antecedent, relic, subsequent, and superimposed—have since come into common usage in political geography. Besides an enlightening review of German boundary literature of the 1920's and 1930's, the article contains a thorough discussion of the old chestnut of "natural-versus-artificial" boundaries. The author assesses the degree of hindrance of natural divides as political boundaries in a very early attempt at quantification, illustrating the difficulties involved in making generalizations about the effect of "natural" boundaries.

HERZ, JOHN H.
    "Rise and Demise of the Territorial State," *World Politics*, IX (1957), pp. 473–493.
        The use of a time-scale analog to test the thesis that the modern nation state is losing its basic territoriality because modern developments are rendering obsolete the notion of "hard-shell" boundaries, just as technical innovations caused the collapse of the feudal system. Reprinted in the Bobbs-Merrill Reprint Series.

HESLINGA, M. W.
    The Irish Border as a Cultural Divide: A Contribution to the Study of Regionalism in the British Isles (Assen: Van Gorcum, 1962).
        As the subtitle indicates, not a simple study of the impact of Irish partition but a thorough examination of the present border as a cultural divider in the perspective of history. An excellent bibliography is included.

JACKSON, W. A. DOUGLAS
    "Mackinder and the Communist Orbit," *Canadian Geographer*, VI (1962), pp. 12–21.

JACKSON, W. A. DOUGLAS

The Russo-Chinese Borderlands: Zone of Peaceful Contact or Potential Conflict? (Princeton, N.J.: D. Van Nostrand Co., 1962).

A paperback in the Searchlight series. A modern study of an ancient political frontier. The author studies the borderland as a zone of contact, tension, and stabilization, and in the context of contemporary Russian-Chinese relations. The monograph contains a comprehensive bibliography.

JAMES, PRESTON E., and SPERIDIAO FAISSOL

"The Problem of Brazil's Capital City," *Geographical Review*, XLVI (July 1956), pp. 301–317.

Written prior to the selection of Brasilia as a capital, the article is concerned with the historical background of Brazil's quest for a new capital, with reasons pro and con a move, and with the political and environmental issues involved in the selection of a new site in the interior.

JEFFERSON, MARK

"The Law of the Primate City," *Geographical Review*, XXIX (1939), pp. 226–232.

Expounds the thesis that the largest city in a state will be supereminent in size and national influence which the author calls the Law of the Capitals. Exceptions are explained by the lack of nationalism.

JONES, STEPHEN B.

"Boundary Concepts in the Setting of Place and Time," *Annals* of the Association of American Geographers, XLIX (September 1959), pp. 241–255.

On the assumption that ideas about boundaries are related to their geographical and historical milieu, the author discusses the different and often conflicting boundary concepts in space and time. Reprinted in the Bobbs-Merrill Reprint Series.

JONES, STEPHEN B.

"Global Strategic Views," *Geographical Review*, XLV (October 1955), pp. 492–508.

A review of the global structure concepts of Mahan, Fairgrieve, Mackinder, Spykman, and de Seversky.

JONES, STEPHEN B.

"Power Inventory and National Strategy," *World Politics*, VI (1954), pp. 421–452.

An examination of the thesis that the conventional inventory of power factors *and* national strategy must be considered together on any estimate of national power. A classic study of power resources by a geographer.

KRISTOF, LADIS K. D.

"The State-Idea, the National Idea and the Image of the Fatherland," *Orbis*, XI (September 1967), pp. 238–255.

Focuses on the concepts of the state-idea, the national idea and the image of the fatherland in their political geographic context. Taking Russia as an example, the author examines the impact of policy on changing territoriality.

LATTIMORE, OWEN

"Inner Asian Frontiers," in *New Compass of the World*, Hans W. Weigert et al., eds. (New York: Macmillan, 1953), pp. 262–295.

The author examines the development of the frontier between Russia and China, and makes some comparisons with the American frontier. After tracing the origins of Steppe history and listing the characteristics of of the Steppe, he concludes that the combination of mobility, feudalism and warfare between the nomads and settled peoples, leads to a situation of chronic conflict between the mobility of the nomads as a whole, and the territoriality of a particular tribe. Furthermore, Lattimore sees a contrast in the processes of frontier integration, with the Chinese advancing by absorption and the Russians by incorporation. Most of his conclusions are still valid today.

LATTIMORE, OWEN

Inner Asian Frontiers of China (New York: American Geographical Society, 1940. 2nd ed., 1951).

A classic study of China's land frontiers. The author traces the evolution of the frontier regions of the Chinese state, from the earliest historical period into modern times. The continuity this evolutionary perspective provides is masterfully demonstrated by the author. Also published in paperback by the Beacon Press of Boston in 1962.

LEACH, E. R.

Political Systems of Highland Burma (Boston: Beacon Press, 1964).

A classical study of structural-functional analysis in political anthropology. The author recognizes three major political types in the societies of northeast Burma: *gumlao* (anarchistic and egalitarian), *shan* (aristocratic and authoritarian), and *gumsa* (intermediate). He then goes on to analyze the spatial, temporal, and functional dimensions among these types, and develops a model of "stable equilibrium" to describe the interrelationships.

LIN PIAO

Long Live the Victory of People's War! (Peking: Foreign Language Press, 1965).

In a speech commemorating the victory against Japan, the Chinese Defense Minister uses a time-scale analog to present his global view based on inevitable conflict between the rural areas (Asia, Africa, and Latin America) and the urban centers (North America and Europe). First propounded in 1963 by D. N. Aidit, secretary of the Indonesian Communist Party. Also reprinted in *Peking Review*, XXXVI (September 3, 1965), and excerpted in the *New York Times*, October 24, 1965, Part VI, p. 178.

MAASS, ARTHUR, ed.
Area and Power: A Theory of Local Government (Glencoe, Ill.: Free Press, 1959).

Theoretical essays on the spatial division of powers within the political system. The contributors analyze the diverse interests and needs within a metropolitan community, the indeterminate position of state governments, the example of Canadian federalism, and the French and American political heritage on this theme. The volume as a whole indicates directions for the development of a general theory of the areal division of governmental power. Of particular interest to political geographers is a discussion by Paul Ylvisaker of criteria for a "proper" areal division of governmental powers.

MACKINDER, HALFORD J.
Democratic Ideals and Reality (New York: Holt, Rinehart & Winston, 1942) and (New York: W. W. Norton & Co., 1962).

The classic statement of Mackinder's "Heartland Theory," first published in 1919. The 1962 paperback edition contains an Introduction by Anthony J. Pearce, and three additional papers by Mackinder: "The Scope and Methods of Geography" (1887), "The Geographical Pivot of History" (1904), and "The Round World and the Winning of the Peace" (1943).

MARTINDALE, DON, ed.
Functionalism in the Social Sciences (Philadelphia: The American Academy of Political and Social Science, Monograph 5, February 1965).

A symposium on the strengths and limits of functionalism in anthropology, economics, political science, and sociology. The extended treatment of structural-functional analysis in political science by William Flanigan and Edwin Fogelman is a particularly useful section for political geographers.

McCOLL, ROBERT W.
"A Political Geography of Revolution: China, Vietnam, and Thailand," *Journal of Conflict Resolution*, XI (June 1967), pp. 153–167.

An attempt to classify the location factors for successful revolutionary rural base areas on the basis of revolutionary war theory and of the actual Chinese and Vietnamese cases. The model is tentatively applied to Thailand for predictive purposes.

MEINIG, DONALD W.
"Heartland and Rimland in Eurasian History," *Western Political Quarterly* IX (September 1956), pp. 553–569.

On the assumption that both Mackinder and Spykman focused too much in their own geopolitical time context, the author attempts a re-evaluation of the Heartland and Rimland theories from functional criteria.

MIKESELL, MARVIN W.
"Comparative Studies in Frontier History," *Annals* of the Association of American Geographers, L (March 1960), pp. 62–74.

The author gives special attention to the Turner thesis as a theme in comparative colonization studies in this review article. Canada, Australia, and South Africa are tested against Turner's American Frontier thesis. Reprinted in condensed form in Richard Hofstadter and Seymour M. Lipset, eds., *Turner and the Sociology of the Frontier* (New York: Basic Books, 1968), pp. 152–171.

MINGHI, JULIAN V.
"Boundary Studies and National Prejudices: The Case of the South Tyrol," *Professional Geographer*, XV (January 1963), pp. 4–8.

A short article that demonstrates the subjectivity that can occur in studies of international boundaries adjacent to disputed areas. The author analyzes arguments between Italian and Austrian scholars over the South Tyrol region. Examples of cartographic misrepresentation and misinterpretation of data, biased selection of available source material, character assassination, and prejudice based on national stereotyping, are all found to exist.

MINGHI, JULIAN V.
"Point Roberts, Washington: The Problem of an American Exclave," *Yearbook* of the Association of Pacific Coast Geographers, XXIV (1962), pp. 29–34.

A brief study of a discontiguity problem using the criteria of size, access, and nationality to focus on Point Roberts, part of the state of Washington, but within the orbit of metropolitan Vancouver.

MURPHEY, RHOADS.
"New Capitals of Asia," *Economic Development and Cultural Change*, V (April 1957), pp. 216–243.

An analysis of the impact of independence on the capital cities of new states in Asia. Each capital's historical development as a colonial port is traced, and its changing function after independence is seen against this perspective.

NASSER, GAMAL ABDUL

Egypt's Liberation: The Philosophy of the Revolution (Washington, D.C.: Public Affairs Press, 1955).

In Part Three, "Geographic Limits," Nasser discusses the global strategic view of Arab nationalism in the early 1950's. An interesting discussion of territoriality in the Arab world.

PITTS, FORREST R.

"The Logic of the Seventeenth Parallel as a Boundary in Indochina," *Yearbook* of the Association of Pacific Coast Geographers, XVIII (1956), pp. 42–56.

An examination of the basis for the partition line dividing Vietnam drawn as part of the Geneva Accords of 1954. The author finds no precedence in the physical nor the historical-cultural milieu, underlining the disintegrative impact of the superimposed boundary.

POUNDS, NORMAN J. G.

"A Free and Secure Access to the Sea," *Annals* of the Association of American Geographers, XLIX (September 1959), pp. 256–268.

A discussion of the historical and international law aspects of land-lockedness as they pertain to access to sea outlets, with special attention paid to corridors and international waterways.

POUNDS, NORMAN J. G. and SUE SIMMONS BALL

"Core-Areas and the Development of the European States System," *Annals* of the Association of American Geographers, LIV (March 1964), pp. 24–40.

A test of the core area thesis by an analysis of the growth process of twenty-five European states. Core growth states outnumber those created "at a blow" but correlations with viability factors are inconclusive. Reprinted in the Bobbs-Merrill Reprint Series.

PRESCOTT, J. R. V.

The Geography of Frontiers and Boundaries (Chicago: Aldine Publishing Co., 1965).

A thorough examination of the nature of frontiers and boundaries updating Boggs (1940) and Jones (1945). The author discusses frontiers, the evolution of boundaries, border landscapes, boundary disputes, and geographical studies of intranational boundaries. Most case studies are taken from African areas with which the author is familiar.

RADCLIFFE-BROWN, A. R.

Structure and Function in Primitive Society (Glencoe, Ill.: Free Press, 1952).

A collection of essays and addresses by a distinguished social anthropologist. Of particular significance to political geographers are the chapters on the concept of function in social science and on social structure.

ROBINSON, G. W. S.

"Exclaves," *Annals* of the Association of American Geographers, XLIX (1959), pp. 283–296.

Formal analysis of the problem of discontiguity with a suggested classification for exclaves.

ROBINSON, K. W.

"Sixty Years of Federation in Australia," *Geographical Review*, LI (January 1961), pp. 1–20.

An assessment of six decades of political integration through federation on Australia's spatial patterns.

ROSE, A. James

Dilemmas Down Under (Princeton, N.J.: D. Van Nostrand Co., 1966).

A paperback in the Searchlight series which concentrates on the political geographic problems of Australia as an empty, isolated, federal state with a peripheral urban population concentration. Chapter 3, "Geography and Polity," and Chapter 5, "Empty Australia," are especially significant to political geography.

RUSSETT, BRUCE M.

"The Asia Rimland as a 'Region' for Containing China," *Public Policy*, XVI (1967), pp. 226–249.

Empirical data on economic transactions, international organizations, social-cultural homogeneity, and national political behavior are utilized to measure cohesiveness and potential integration in the Asia rimland. The author also considers the possibility of cohesiveness as a function of external threats. He pessimistically concludes that either the United States must indefinitely maintain an expensive presence in the rimlands or reconcile itself to living in a world where China has restored its traditional control over much of Southeast Asia.

RUSSETT, BRUCE M.

"Delineating International Regions," in J. David Singer, ed., *Quantitative International Politics* (New York: Free Press, 1967), pp. 317–374.

A thoughtful discussion of the role of regions in political theory which not only reviews the vast literature on this subject but also presents empirical data from the author's *World Handbook of Political and Social Indicators*. Particular attention is devoted to regions of homogeneity and regions of interdependence. The exhaustive bibliography will be useful for political geographers.

RUSSETT, BRUCE M.

International Regions and the International System: A Study in Political Ecology (Chicago: Rand McNally, 1967).

An exploration of the relations between political systems and their social and physical environment. Use of factor analysis in testing: (a) theories of political integration between two or more nation-states; (b) the operation and conditions of change in the international system; (c) the use of ecological data on national characteristics to test hypotheses and to describe national attributes and behavior.

RUSSETT, BRUCE M.
"Is there a Long-run Trend toward Concentration in the International System?," *Comparative Political Studies*, I (April 1958), pp. 103–122.

Emphasis is placed on the degree to which population and other power bases are concentrated in a few states of the global system. Four ways in which concentration can occur are: (a) more rapid growth rates in largest states; (b) death of small states by merger or annexation; (c) great increase in the number of small states; (d) emergence of giant states by regional union. After a series of statistical tests, the author concludes that there is no trend toward concentration in the global structure.

SOUSTELLE, JACQUES
"France and Europe: A Gaullist View," *Foreign Affairs*, XXX (July 1952), pp. 545–553.

A French view of European and global patterns prior to de Gaulle's rise to power by a supporter, later to fall out with his leader over the Algerian crises.

SPATE, O. H. K.
"Factors in the Development of Capital Cities," *Geographical Review*, XXXII (1942), pp. 622–631.

A systematic discussion of the nature of capital city growth in terms of historical inertia and historical imitation. The cases of London, Prague, and Belgrade are analyzed. Available in Bobbs-Merrill Reprint Series.

SPROUT, HAROLD and MARGARET SPROUT
"Geography and International Politics in an Era of Revolutionary Change," *Journal of Conflict Resolution*, IV (1960), pp. 145–161.

The authors explore the link between spatial distributions and arrangements, and international political behavior. Several geopolitical hypotheses are examined in the light of implications wrought by environmental change, both real and perceived.

SPYKMAN, NICHOLAS JOHN
"Frontiers, Security, and International Organization," *Geographical Review*, XXXII (July 1942), pp. 436–447.

The author considers the geographical aspects of security including a discussion on buffer states, collective security, and the environmental implications for national power potential.

STEPHENSON, GLENN V.
"Pakistan: Discontiguity and the Majority Problem," *Geographical Review*, LVIII (April 1968), pp. 195–213.

An examination of the Pakistani dilemma created by discontiguity, with the population majority in East Pakistan and yet the core area in West Pakistan. The "raison d'être" and centrifugal forces are studied with a review of the development of a national identity.

VANCE, JAMES E. Jr.
"Areal Political Structure and its Influence on Urban Patterns," *Yearbook* of the Association of Pacific Coast Geographers, XXII (1960), pp. 40–49.

The author observes that the nature and form of local civil divisions have been overlooked by political geographers. The processes of annexation and incorporation in California are examined in terms of their impact on urban spatial structure.

WOOD, ROBERT
1400 Governments: The Political Economy of the New York Metropolitan Region (Cambridge, Mass: Harvard University Press, 1961).

One of nine monographs making up the New York Metropolitan Study undertaken by the Harvard University Graduate School of Public Administration. The author examines the New York Metropolitan Area (with its 1467 distinct political entities in twenty-two counties in three states) in terms of the responses of the local governments to increasing pressures on the public sector, and of the current and future problems facing the metropolitan area as a whole. Of direct significance to political geographers interested in the impact of the fragmented spatial structure on metropolitan political integration.

ZAIDI, IQTIDAR H.
"Toward a Measure of the Functional Effectiveness of a State: The Case of West Pakistan," *Annals* of the Association of American Geographers, LVI (March 1966), pp. 52–67.

A case study attempting to apply Hartshorne's functional approach to test the viability of West Pakistan as a political region. Basic criteria of population density and transportation line density are used to define areas of varying functional effectiveness including extra-ecumenical, minimally effective, intensively effective, sub-core, and core area. A serious drawback is the ignoring of the fact that West Pakistan is *not* an independent unit but part of a discontiguous state.

Part III: PROCESS

Introduction

As we have seen in the Introduction and the last selection in Part I, Heritage, the *Ad Hoc Committee on Geography* defined political geography as "the study of the spatial interaction of geographical area and political process," or "the study of the spatial distribution and space relations of political processes." As stated at the outset, we would go a step further and propose a definition of political geography as the study of the spatial and areal structure and interactions of political processes and systems, or simply, the spatial analysis of political phenomena. From these definitions, a shift of focus away from regional analysis and typologies of structural elements toward a greater concern for process and behavior becomes obvious.

Of the ten selections that follow this introductory essay, six are by nongeographers. This reflects the dearth of published works in political geography that can be called "process-oriented." As we have seen in the first two parts, Heritage and Structure, much of the literature focuses on formal aspects and relationships. This is not to say that process is ignored, but rather that it is not directly involved in defining central problems to be solved. This is not surprising as, in traditional research, process is concerned with the arrangement of empirically observed units, flowing, moving, or interacting, where the whole complex of units constitutes the process. Hence the explanation of process often resides in the units chosen to describe the dynamic elements of process. In effect, most research in political geography has purposefully excluded political process for, in the words of Hartshorne (1935), it is "the concern of the student whose interest and training have been centered primarily on the state itself rather than upon areas."[1] American geographers at this time, with perhaps the notable exception of Whittlesey,[2] limited their analysis to the distributional manifestations of these processes, and particularly to those that were observable in the landscape.

Despite this orientation, as seen in Heritage and Structure, and in the last part on Environment, there have been several process-oriented attempts at model building. These include deductions and extrapolations from the organic analog model, particularly relating to territorial growth and the so-called life cycle of the state, the formulation of spatial models of world power distribution, and hypotheses of political-environmental relations.

Although originally fully developed by Ibn-Khaldūn centuries before, the theory of the "life cycle" of states was an offshoot of the organic analogy and the physiographic cycle. According to Van Valkenburg,[3] the state passes through youth, adolescence, maturity, and old age, each stage of which is associated with certain "personality" characteristics. In

1. Richard Hartshorne, "Recent Developments in Political Geography," *American Political Science Review*, XXIX (December 1935), p. 957.

2. While his entire historical treatment in *The Earth and the State* (New York: Henry Holt and Co., 1939) is implicitly concerned with process, see especially pp. 589–590 for his discussion on "geopolitical forces".

3. Samuel Van Valkenburg, *Elements of Political Geography* (New York: Prentice-Hall, 1939), First Edition, pp. 5–12. For a full discussion of this concept see Harm J. de Blij, *Systematic Political Geography* (New York: John Wiley & Sons, 1967), pp. 102–104.

1940 Hartshorne volunteered his concept of the "maturity" of states.[4]

These organic analogies persist in both popular and scholarly literature. Testing such hypotheses would reveal little correlation between the length of time a state has existed and characteristics of its political processes. The concept also oversimplifies the operation of politics at any given stage—obviously many states may be "mature" (however that may be defined) in one facet of domestic policy and equally "immature" in some aspects of foreign policy. Finally, there seems to be little empirical evidence that governments or states travel the progression of political stages hypothesized in this literature.

More useful and certainly more dramatic from the standpoint of geography were the spatial models of world power developed by Mackinder, Spykman, and de Seversky (see Global Structure in Part II). Despite the problems involved in assumptions, lack of supporting empirical data, and occasional weak reasoning in their hypotheses, they continue to be taught as integral parts of political geography, international politics, and military science courses. As Part V of this volume is devoted entirely to the important conceptual area dealing with environmental-political relationships, we will not dwell on the point here.

These process-oriented clusters have not proven to be of sufficient vitality to advance the field and hence, by borrowing from other social science disciplines, we hope to suggest useful areas of focus where political processes can be studied in terms of their spatial expressions and as products of the spatial structure within which they operate.

For a logical discussion of process in political geography we have chosen three major areas: integration and disintegration, transfer of sovereignty, and growth and development.

INTEGRATION

Basic to the discussion of functionalism in political geography is the concept of the viability of political territory—the question of the degree of success of, and problems inherent in, man's attempted political organization of a given territorial unit. In his "Functional Approach" Hartshorne hypothesized two dominant sets of forces—centrifugal and centripetal—which act upon the coherence of any political unit. Shortly thereafter, Gottmann enunciated a similar approach in which iconography acts as a force for cohesion and stability, whereas circulation (or the movement factor) leads to political change. In the light of the general introduction to this discussion of process, these conceptual statements are perhaps less a study of functions than an examination of political integration as a spatial process. Most of the factors considered important in the integration of political territory by Hartshorne, Gottmann, and Jones are included in greater depth in discussions about political integration by political scientists and others.

The tradition in geography, well illustrated by Hartshorne's "Functional Approach," has been to make processual inferences from structural elements, such as mountains, language complexity, and territorial discontiguity, which are centrifugal forces as they tend to impede political integration. Research into political integration over the past two decades has been such as to render much in these early efforts in geography more of historical than contemporary interest.

At the outset, it might well be helpful to review briefly the various definitions of political integration in current use. These definitions are usually in terms of both structure and behavior, suggesting the interdependence of process with spatial structure and behavior —a point which we have emphasized earlier in this volume.

More than a decade ago *Ernst Haas* characterized political integration as "the process whereby political actors in several distinct national settings are persuaded to shift their loyalties, expectations, and political activities toward a new center...."[5]

Three kinds of integration are stressed by *Amitai Etzioni*: (a) effective control over the use of the means of violence, (b) a center of decision making that is able to affect significantly the allocation of resources and rewards throughout the community, and (c) a dominant focus of political identification for

---

4. Richard Hartshorne, "The Concepts of 'Raison d'Être' and 'Maturity of States'," (abstract), *Annals of the Association of American Geographers*, XXX (1940) pp. 59–60.

5. Ernst Haas, *The Uniting of Europe* (Stanford: Stanford University Press, 1957), p. 16.

the large majority of politically aware citizens.[6]

Karl Deutsch et al. define "integration" (not necessarily political integration) as the relationship among units (countries) that no longer anticipate engaging in war with one another.[7]

Bruce Russett asserts that the higher the ratio of capabilities to loads or burdens in their relationships, the more states tend to integrate, because responsiveness is the behavioral consequence of that ratio.[8]

Despite the differences in emphasis displayed in these definitions, there is no basic disagreement on the scope of political integration. Etzioni's three-part definition and Russett's notion of responsiveness particularly suggest spatial connotations.

At this point it might be well to point out the difference between integration and interaction—a distinction often not made explicit in geographical studies. A group of states may well enjoy a high degree of interaction, but at the same time there may be little or no political integration taking place. All the definitions quoted above have strong behavioral (and most have structural) considerations which a study of interaction alone does not embrace. There is no doubt, however, that the analysis of interaction can be one tool for discovering how integration does grow as a process.[9]

Jacob and Teune have attempted to classify integrative factors in political communities at four levels: international, national, metropolitan, and local.[10] These include: geographical proximity, homogeneity, transactions and interactions, mutual knowledge, shared functional interests, the character pattern of a group, the structural framework of system of power and decision making, the sovereignty-dependency status, governmental effectiveness, and previous integration experience.

Four basic questions are posed regarding the interrelationships among these ten variables: (*a*) How much of any one factor has to be present for a community to cross the threshold, i.e., is there a critical mass necessary for integration? (*b*) Is there a formula or formulae of combination making up a necessary mix for an integration syndrome? (*c*) Depending on the level of integration, at what level in the political hierarchy does each factor become significant? and (*d*) Is there a sequence of ordering the variables as a condition for integration?

Jacob and Teune go on to suggest a costing model of integration based on cost–benefit principles. The cost of each variable is appraised. Those with political influence are the key variables. Where benefits exceed costs, the "price of merger" becomes clear. The spatial ramifications of this model of political integration are obvious. The internal distribution of the variables within the system is of critical importance, aside from the fact that the first factor listed is explicitly a spatial consideration.

A discussion of each of the variables distinguished by Jacob and Teune may well be useful. The proximity hypothesis holds that the closer communities are, the more likely integrative relationships will develop, and that, especially at the highest level—the international—contiguous states are likely to integrate as "a rough geopolitical calculation." It is a measure of the lack of attention given to political integration by geographers that Jacob and Teune can complain that "this assumption [of proximity] has not been subjected to rigorous testing."[11] It has been left to Russett and Merritt, both nongeographers, to develop ideas about the relevance of contiguity to integration.[12]

Proximity is, of course, related closely to the other variables of homogeneity, transactions, and mutual knowledge. Hartshorne's lengthy discussion of *homogeneity* in his "Functional Approach" is relevant here. Cohesiveness

---

6. Amitai Etzioni, *Political Unification* (New York: Holt, Rinehart and Winston, 1965), p. 4.
7. Karl W. Deutsch et al., *Political Community and the North Atlantic Area* (Princeton, N.J.: Princeton University Press, 1957), p. 31.
8. Bruce M. Russett, *International Regions and the International System: A Study in Political Ecology* (Chicago: Rand McNally, 1967), pp. 95–96.
9. Richard L. Merritt has provided a good example of this type of discovery in "Distance and Interaction among Political Communities," *General Systems*, IX (1964), pp. 255–263.
10. Philip E. Jacob and Henry Teune, "The Integrative Process," in Philip E. Jacob and James V. Toscano, eds., *The Integration of Political Communities* (Philadelphia: J. B. Lippincott Co., 1964), pp. 11 ff.

11. *Ibid.*, p. 17.
12. Bruce M. Russett, *International Regions and the International System: A Study in Political Ecology* (Chicago: Rand McNally, 1967), and Richard L. Merritt, "Noncontiguity and Political Integration," in James N. Rosenau, ed., *Linkage Politics: Essays on the Convergence of National and International Systems* (New York: The Free Press, 1969).

among communities can be measured by the extent of mutual relationships among them. One way to measure these relationships is by a focus on *transactions* that transpire.[13] Communications such as mail, telephone calls, and trade in goods and services are forms of transaction flow that often lend themselves to measurement as part of a process of political integration, as the selection from Soja will show.

It will be remembered from Part II, Structure, that a more functional stress in boundary studies has produced methods of measuring barrier effects of lines separating political systems. Distance or cost factors can be assigned to a line in relation to a given type of movement, and this method can serve to relate structural elements to the analysis of transaction flow.

The critical question in the case of *mutual knowledge* (or cognitive proximity) is how much and what kind of knowledge is needed to be significant for integration. The role of national images in international integration and conflict is discussed by Kenneth Boulding in a selection in Part IV. In a behavioral definition of political integration, as well as in communication theory, mutual knowledge plays a central role.[14]

The variable of *functional interests* in studies at the international level, such as of the European Common Market, has perhaps been given too much prominence by geographers.[15] The convergence of interests among groups evidenced by tariff lowering or defense treaties can often be taken as a sign of integration although dangerous assumptions can be made on a one-factor analysis based only on such functional interests.

The notion of communal character is based on the hypothesis that community behavior tends to run in set patterns and is strongly influenced by cultural inheritance and learning. Such behavior is reflected in symbols which can be studied through content analysis, as, for example, in the selection from Merritt on the integration of the early American colonies. In Part V, Environment, it will be seen that symbolization is one of the processes by which political goals are impressed upon the landscape.

The *structural framework* of the political system in question is a different class of variable from the first six. For the political geographer it provides the milieu within which the processes operate, particularly with its aspects of territoriality and hierarchy. In fact, most definitions which include structural considerations stress the need for centrality.[16]

Ake has hypothesized that a political system driving for integration maximizes its chances of achieving a high degree of integration and of remaining stable in spite of short-run destabilizing effects, if it is authoritarian, consensual, identificatory, or paternal.[17] Whereas in the absence of any of these four types of system there are destabilizing effects on the integration drive.

Related is the *sovereignty-dependency status*, which simply defines the degree to which the political unit departs from the classic status of sovereignty in which theoretically all members are subject to a supreme political authority (internal cohesion) and the political entity is completely independent from any outside control (external autonomy). This variable is particularly important in new states, and Jacob and Teune suggest that a convenient experiment to test the significance of political autonomy as a factor in integration is found in before-and-after independence studies where the sovereignty variable is pinpointed while the other variables are held fairly constant.[18]

As government inefficiency in managing economic and other problems that arise is a factor in creating pressures and possible disintegration, the *effectiveness of the government* is an important variable. Karl Deutsch, in his study of social communication in the metropolis, explains the growth of suburbs by the ineffectiveness of government in combating communication "overload."[19]

---

13. Relevant to this particular integration variable are the discussions by Deutsch in the same work, Karl W. Deutsch, "Communication Theory and Political Integration," and "Transaction Flows as Indicators of Political Cohesion," in Jacob and Toscano, eds., *op. cit.*, pp. 46–97.

14. Russett's notion of "responsiveness" and Etzioni's term "shared culture" are relevant here. Etzioni, *op. cit.*, pp. 34–37.

15. See, for example, J. Warren Nystrom and Peter Malof, *The Common Market: The European Community in Action* (Princeton, N.J.: D. Van Nostrand Co., 1962).

16. Both Deutsch and Etzioni elaborate on the role of core areas in integration, although Etzioni uses the term "elite unit" (Etzioni, *op. cit.*, p. 45).

17. Claude Ake, "Political Integration and Political Stability: A Hypothesis," *World Politics*, XIX (April 1967), pp. 486–499.

18. Jacobs and Teune *op. cit.*, p. 41.

19. Karl W. Deutsch, "On Social Communication and the Metropolis," *Daedalus*, XC (1961), pp. 101 ff.

The last-named variable takes into account the "spill-over" or "secondary priming" effect from *previous experience of political integration*, with the assumption of a geometric progression—the more experience, the more integration—although it might act mainly as a reinforcement to integration when rewards are expected, and to disintegration when experience indicates that penalties can result.

Following the discussion of variables, we may now attempt to distinguish major analytical approaches to the study of political integration. We suggest five: structural, communications theory, behavioral, systemic, and combination.

1. Structural

This type of approach falls into the "ideal" category as few adopt it because of the restrictions it imposes. Both Hartshorne and Gottmann tend to emphasize this approach although they do include some behavioral elements such as the "state idea" and "iconography." Generally, the inference is that structural elements or spatial configuration produces political integration (or disintegration).

2. Communications Theory

This approach rests heavily on the notion of "information" and the variable of "mutual knowledge" discussed above. The study of transaction flow and interaction rests upon the underlying validity of this theory, with the most critical notions being those of *salience* and *covariance*.[20] Transactions are the first step to salience and the study of quantitative densities of transactions is the first step toward estimating the degree to which people or nations are connected with each other. The study of covariance (joint rewards and penalties) is the second step in measuring the degree to which people are linked.

A basic problem here is that the link between transaction and interaction on the one hand and political integration on the other is still unclear, and hence possible inferences are very limited, although such inferences are undeniably a useful aid if seen in proper perspective. A difficulty faced by all researchers using the transaction flow approach lies in the selection of the transaction to be measured. Unfortunately, reliable data are often in short supply, especially in developing areas, and the type of transaction for which usable data are available is not always the most salient and hence not helpful in measuring political integration. Russett analyzes trade, voting in the United Nations, membership in international organizations, and contiguity, and yet is still properly *very* cautious in his inferences.[21] Similarly, Brams, after measuring diplomatic exchanges, trade, and shared membership in international organizations, refrains from the temptation to infer too much about political integration.[22]

The measurement of flows and the relevance of transaction to integration are two worthwhile research problems outstanding. For aid in solving the latter, some kind of multivariate analysis of flows to assess salience to political integration might be useful. Such help should not be long in coming as studies at almost all levels of the political hierarchy are now employing this approach.

3. Behavioral

There seems to be a general leaning toward this orientation. Important in this approach are such factors as nationalism and the presence or absence of violence in interunit relations.[23]

One interesting study by Inglehart within the general theory of socialization uses some of the same data as Deutsch and yet comes to an entirely different conclusion about European integration, at the same time pointing out some of the weaknesses of transaction flow analysis.[24]

---

20. The selection by Soja discusses these terms in some detail, as does Karl Deutsch, *op. cit.*, pp. 51-56.

21. See his Chapter 13, "Some Problems of Priority and Causation," Russett, *op. cit.*, pp. 206-217.

22. See his conclusion, Steven J. Brams, "Transaction Flows in the International System," *American Political Science Review*, LX (December 1966), p. 898.

23. We now have fairly good cross-cultural data on this problem, as indicated in the annotated bibliography for Part IV.

24. Contrary to Deutsch, Inglehart concludes that the rate of European integration has *increased* since 1958, Ronald Inglehart, "An End to European Integration?" *American Political Science Review*, LXI (March 1967), pp. 91-105.

4. Systemic

Although closely related to both the communications theory and structural approaches, it provides a systems framework to the study of the interdependence of units and various forms of message flow. In the selection by Merritt, data on trade and self-referent symbols in newspapers are used. The major problem involved in this approach lies in the difficulty in applying it empirically because of the comprehensive nature of the analysis required.[25]

5. Combination

Most studies now fall in this category, thus indicating the need for various perspectives rather than a reliance on a particular approach which too often proves to be restrictive or overcomprehensive.

Although there is increasing evidence that geographers are turning their attention to the problem of political integration at the national level, most interest thus far seems to have been in political union of groups of two or more states—that is, in changes in the world political pattern. Very often such interest has been manifested in studies of newly-forming or -formed federations of some kind.[26] The tendency has been to view such unions as "events" rather than processes, by a concentration on a comparison of the situation before and after the date of union. In this context, the selection from Etzioni should serve to illustrate the processual aspects of political unification.

It was mentioned above that studies at all levels of the political hierarchy are using the communications theory approach. This approach has been particularly rewarding at the urban level in studies of the integration of annexed areas and in studies assessing the degree of integration in metropolitan areas recently unified or open to potential unification.

In 1960, J. Vance noted that political geographers had overlooked the nature and form of local civil divisions.[27] While not particularly interested in the problem of integration, Vance does draw attention to the phenomena of annexation and incorporation, and the role they play in influencing urban growth. More recently, Dye has examined the link between annexation and political integration in a study based on changes in American urban areas between 1950 and 1960.[28] Dye is able to hypothesize that, whereas legal restraints or laxity and the size of urbanized area are not important variables in annexation activity, the form of government organization, the age of settlement, and the spatial distribution of persons of differing status attributes are all of critical significance.

In an outstanding contribution to theory on metropolitan integration, William Wheaton modifies and restates power-influence theories by stating a set of propositions and suggesting methods of testing them.[29] These propositions stress the distribution of political influence, both vertical and spatial, communications, linkages, and policy decisions. Metropolitan public policy decisions are treated as a separate class, and Wheaton has a very useful discussion on the theme of local integration and metropolitan fragmentation.

With the fairly successful establishment of metropolitan government systems, such as Toronto, Dade County (Miami), and Nashville, it seems certain that various forms of metropolitan unification will become prevalent in the next few decades and, consequently, interest in political unification at the urban level will continue to grow.

One very important point often overlooked, or at least not given due consideration, is the *time aspect* in studies of unification. The stage which the unification process has reached at the time of writing or of data collection, and

---

25. For example, see Morton A. Kaplan, *System and Process in International Politics* (New York: John Wiley and Sons, 1964).

26. For example, K. W. Robinson, "Sixty Years of Federation in Australia," *Geographical Review*, LI (January 1961), pp. 1–20; Charles A. Fisher, "The Geographical Setting of the Proposed Malaysian Federation," *Journal of Tropical Geography*, XVII (May 1963), pp. 99–115; and Edmund H. Dale, "The State-Idea: Missing Prop of the West Indies Federation," *Scottish Geographical Magazine*, LXXVIII (December 1962), pp. 166–176.

27. James E. Vance, Jr., "Areal Political Structure and its Influence on Urban Patterns," *Yearbook of the Association of Pacific Coast Geographers*, XXII (1960), p. 40.

28. Thomas R. Dye, "Urban Political Integration: Conditions Associated with Annexation in American Cities," *Midwest Journal of Political Science*, VIII (November 1964), pp. 430–446.

29. William L. C. Wheaton, "Integration at the Urban Level: Political Influence and the Decision Process," in Jacob and Toscano, eds., *op. cit.*, pp. 120–142.

the rate of the integration process, are both critical in any study.

DISINTEGRATION

Although the process of political disintegration is much the same as that of integration in reverse,[30] we will consider disintegration apart because much of the literature in geography treats this process separately under such descriptions as defederation, dissolution of empires, and partition. Basically, disintegration is the process by which integration and interdependence are disrupted and political systems break down and fall apart into two or more units—the successors to the disintegrated system. The political geographer is interested in the spatial aspects of disintegration and hence also, by definition, in the problems of integration of the newly created units.

Defederation

As federal systems have become commonplace only recently, there have been few cases of federal breakups. However, federations have been adopted as postcolonial systems in several instances. The United States, Canada, and Australia are early examples from temperate world settler regions. Since World War II several federations have been established including, among others, Nigeria, the Central African Federation, the West Indies Federation, the Malaysian Federation and the Federation of South Arabia. All these political-territorial arrangements have had difficulty in surviving because of internal problems. The federations in Central Africa, the West Indies, and South Arabia have collapsed with a variety of successor states in each region.

The basic aspect of defederation is that there is a reversion to the *status quo ante* inasmuch as the successor units are not new but at one time existed as separate units prior to federation. The two major variables involved in this reversion are time and sovereignty.

The duration of the federation's existence will at least give some indication as to the degree of integration that has taken place and hence will affect the process of defederation. The transfer of sovereignty from colonial to independent status may well come at, or soon after, the time of defederation, as in the case of some units in the defunct West Indies Federation (Jamaica, and Trinidad and Tobago) and the defunct Central African Federation (ex-Northern Rhodesia, now Zambia and ex-Nyasaland, now Malawi). In the cases of Malaysia and Nigeria, independence preceded federation and the partial defederation caused by the secession of Singapore and Biafra (Eastern Region of Nigeria) has taken place without third-party colonial involvement.

Two separate but interrelated elements involved in defederation are the actual event itself at a particular point in time, and the process involving the breakdown of the integrative forces which may be traced over a considerable period. Normally the former element is the culmination of the latter, but this is not always so.

In a study of defederation, Dale hypothesizes that the West Indies Federation collapsed because of the lack of a "state-idea."[31] The various units involved lacked cultural solidarity. Separatist views and tendencies predominated throughout, in that the federation was not a result of West Indian consciousness but was imposed from the outside by Britain. Despite certain constitutional features common to all islands because of British influence, there were many basic contrasts in the various constitutions and in the stage of self-government reached among the units involved. The nature of the federation itself was a contributary factor in the collapse because of its loose nature and weak center. The difficulties involved in finding a federal capital whose location would be acceptable to all units is symptomatic of internal lack of integrative forces within the islands, as Lowenthal has clearly shown.[32]

The symmetry-asymmetry of federalism suggested in the selection from Tarlton in Part II, Structure, might well be an aid to examining disintegrative forces in the relationships among units, and between units and the central authority, in a federation.

---

30. Both Deutsch and Etzioni draw attention to this two-way movement.

31. Dale, *op. cit.*

32. David Lowenthal, "The West Indies Chooses a Capital," *Geographical Review*, XLVIII (July 1958), pp. 336–364. Reproduced in Part IV, Behavior.

Dissolution of Empires

The breakup of formal structures such as the Ottoman and Austro-Hungarian empires usually occurs at the very end of a long period of political disintegration during which what little homogeny the political system ever shared as a whole has steadily decreased to the point of disappearance.

The selection by Merritt illustrates a systems analysis approach to the study of political disintegration of empires and provides a clear focus on disintegration as a process. His analysis of the interruption and diversion of various types of flows and the growing independence of the spatial subsystems should be suggestive to political geographers.

Merritt has also examined the link between political integration and territorial noncontiguity (the latter being a common feature of empires).[33] He is not satisfied with the commonly held but untested notion that noncontiguity has a deleterious effect upon the capabilities of a polity. Merritt cites Etzioni as stating that noncontiguity impedes the process of political integration because it hinders the transportation of goods and people, but he criticizes Etzioni for confusing the effects of noncontiguity with those of distance, in that the key variables in noncontiguity are the distinctiveness of the noncontiguous regions, the nature of the intervening space, and the distance (including cost, time, and other factors) between major components. The last two variables, of course, have an important impact on the *form* of the linkages among component parts of the polity.

After an analysis of, among other cases, Greece in the Golden Age and the Anglo-American Community of the eighteenth century, Merritt is able to make several generalizations. The most crucial effect of noncontiguity is its impact on the establishment and maintenance of effective patterns of communication, leading to discontinuities which in turn can cause political disintegration. Noncontiguity is but one of a large class of discontinuities within polities. The centrifugal effect of discontiguity is stronger than distance alone, and, over time, separated parts of a polity will drift apart and become more introspective. The more important the noncontiguous territory is perceived, the greater the compensation to counter the centrifugal effect by efforts toward the maintenance of unity, including the granting of preferred status and a stress on the threat of foreign intervention in the intervening space.

Although noncontiguity was discussed briefly in Part II, Structure, the interest here has been in its relevance to political disintegration.

Richard Hartshorne has written on the collapse at the time of World War I of the Dual Monarchy of Austro-Hungary.[34] He found that prior to dissolution, the political area of the Middle Danube lands constituted a fairly harmonious economic-geographic unit. Yet in this territorial empire that had grown more or less by accident, the principle of the nation-state was not only inapplicable but actually contrary to its cultural heterogeneity. Hartshorne felt that the one way to have avoided the disintegration of the empire could neither be perceived nor accepted by the leadership elite: a federation of largely autonomous cultural areas of free peoples. That is to say that a lowering of the scope of integration would have increased its level.

Partition

A more simple form of disintegration involves the phenomenon of partition, a solution used many times in this century. The dictionary provides us with a legal definition for partition: "The process of dividing property and giving separate title to those who previously had joint title."[35] While there is also justification in defining the word in a very general manner, in the context of this section we are referring to the narrow view of partition as "the action of dividing an area forming a single governmental unit into two or more areas under separate authorities," a definition used by Klieman in 1964 in the Editor's Foreword to an issue of the *Journal of International Affairs* devoted entirely to this

---

33. Richard L. Merritt, "Noncontiguity and Political Integration," in James N. Rosenau, ed., *op. cit.*

34. Richard Hartshorne, "The Tragedy of Austro-Hungary: A Post-Mortem in Political Geography," (abstract), *Annals* of the Association of American Geographers, XXVIII (March 1938), pp. 49–50.

35. *Webster's New World Dictionary* (New York: World Publishing Co., 1960).

problem.[36] Although we have an early biblical example of partition in the Land of Canaan divided between Abraham and Lot, it is in the twentieth century that we have seen partition reach an unprecedented degree of legitimacy. Diverse in form, scale, and motivation, and usually imposed from the outside, partition has had a momentous impact in both expediently solving immediate and seemingly irreconcilable problems, and creating a lasting effect upon the destinies of societies and cultures so divided with important long-term problems.

At first sight it would seem that disintegration, unlike the cases of defederation and dissolution of empires, is the creation of partition and that consequently the event sets off the process of political disintegration rather than being its end product. In many cases, however, disintegration has often already been under way prior to partition, as for example with Turkish-Greek partition in 1829 and in the partition of the Indian subcontinent between India and Pakistan in 1947.

All acts of partition can be dated, with the overnight creation of two or more new sovereign units leading to a process of disintegration which could probably have got its start prior to partition even on the basis of speculation about the fact of partition and the likely location of the new dividing line or lines.[37]

Partition, of course, can take place at the local, metropolitan, and state or provincial level, but it is best known and studied at the national level. In modern times there have been several cases, including Ireland, Germany, Korea, India (and Kashmir), Palestine, and Vietnam, and partition has often been seriously proposed as a solution to the communal conflict on Cyprus.[38] It is no coincidence that, perhaps with the exception of Ireland—partitioned fifty years ago—these areas, all partitioned on a "temporary" basis originally, are currently areas of world tension, divided by boundaries which have been superimposed on the cultural landscape but which have now become entrenched as relatively impermeable barriers between contrasting and hostile political systems.

Klieman complained that partition has been "virtually unacknowledged as a social-political concept worthy of theoretical study and comparative analysis."[39] In fact, partition, by definition a geographical concept, has long been studied by geographers, primarily from the standpoint of the impact of a superimposed boundary,[40] and the changing spatial relations of the newly created units.[41] True to the tradition found in the literature on boundaries, these studies have been largely one-shot affairs with little or no comparative analysis, and have not developed much theory about partition as a general political geographic process.

There are probably several reasons for this. Under the narrow definition used here, there

---

36. Aaron S. Klieman, Editor's Foreword to "The Politics of Partition," *Journal of International Affairs*, XVIII (1964), p. vii. In the same issue, Pounds uses a broader definition, part of which we would include under the dissolution of empires (Norman J. G. Pounds, "History and Geography: A Perspective on Partition," pp. 161–172).

37. For example, several years prior to the 1846 Oregon Treaty, which established the forty-ninth parallel as the boundary partitioning the jointly occupied Oregon Territory between Britain and the United States, the Hudson's Bay Company made no new investments south of the parallel. See Julian V. Minghi, "The Evolution of a Border Region: The Pacific Coast Section of the Canada-United States Boundary," *Scottish Geographical Magazine*, LXXX (April 1964), pp. 41–42.

38. Firstly in 1959 prior to independence, and again in 1966–67 after the outbreak of violence between the Greek and Turkish communities. For an interesting analysis of the potential impact of the British and Turkish proposals of 1959, see Alexander Melamid, "Partitioning Cyprus: A Class Exercise in Political Geography," *Journal of Geography*, LIX (March 1960), pp. 166–176.

39. Klieman, *op. cit.*, p. vii.

40. For example, Aloys A. Michel, *The Indus Rivers: A Study of the Effects of Partition* (New Haven, Conn.: Yale University Press, 1967); Melamid, *op. cit.*; O. H. K. Spate, "The Partition of the Punjab and Bengal," *Geographical Journal*, CX (October–December 1947), pp. 201–222; P. P. Karan, "The India-Pakistan Enclave Problem," *Professional Geographer*, XVIII (January 1966), pp. 23–25; and Forrest R. Pitts, "The Logic of the Seventeenth Parallel as a Boundary in Indochina," *Yearbook* of the Association of Pacific Coast Geographers, XVIII (1956), pp. 42–56.

41. For example, O. H. K. Spate, "The Partition of India and the Prospects for Pakistan," *Geographical Review*, XXXVIII (January 1948), pp. 5–30; A. Tayyeb, *Pakistan: A Political Geography* (London: Oxford University Press, 1966); M. W. Heslinga, *The Irish Border as a Cultural Divide* (Assen: Van Gorcum, 1962); Norman J. G. Pounds, *Divided Germany and Berlin* (Princeton, N.J.: D. Van Nostrand Co., 1962); James H. Johnson, "The Political Distinctiveness of Northern Ireland," *Geographical Review*, LII (January 1962), pp. 78–91; and Shannon McCune, "The Thirty-Eighth Parallel in Korea," *World Politics*, I (January 1949), pp. 223–232.

have not really been enough cases of partition to make many valid generalizations. Furthermore, the basis, manner, scale, and cultural background of partition have varied to such an extent that there are many unique aspects in each case.

In terms of methodology, probably because of the restraints cited above, studies of partition in political geography have tended to center around familiar structural concepts. For example, partition means a new boundary, usually with little or no precedence and superimposed on the cultural landscape. Studies of the impact of such a boundary especially at the local level, as in those by Spate and Melamid cited above, are in a strongly established tradition.

One final aspect of partition should be mentioned. Partition is usually considered a pejorative term associated with outrage, abuse, and arbitrariness. It is a remedy to a dispute which satisfies no one fully but which serves to give opposing factions a territorial base and thus minimizes direct conflict by enforced territorial separation. Because of these advantages, partition has been proposed in many disputes, even for problems in areas with no past experience of territorial political fragmentation.

Such proposals have led Pounds to make deterministic sounding statements such as "... there exist many discrete territorial entities, so distinctive and so separate from their neighbors that they *almost demand* to be administered as units."[42] Pounds, however, goes on to condemn the "natural unity" argument, so often raised in the case of partition, as "foolishness" in that physical units, such as islands and river basins, do not necessarily provide good frameworks for political units.[43]

TRANSFER OF SOVEREIGNTY

In this section we are concerned with similarities between the phenomenon of change in the location of political boundaries and that of independence of former colonial areas, especially in terms of the processes that these phenomena create—processes whose spatial consequences can be termed "the geography of sovereignty transfer." Both types of transfer involve a constant in one of the two essential characteristics of a political system—that of territory to which the system is bound—while the other characteristic, political process, is the variable.[44] In other words, a shift in a boundary location between states *or* the achievement of independent status by a new state creates in the transferred territory a new "succession of actions or operations" conducted to establish and to maintain the political system of the gainer. A new sovereignty is substituted for the old in the same territory in both cases, and hence we hypothesize that the processes so created will have similar spatial expressions.

Boundary Change

Geographers have long been interested in the effects of changes in political boundaries and a considerable literature exists on the subject.[45] It is a common occurrence and has been one way in which the world has rearranged its political partitioning of earth space. Prescott[46] has asserted that as political boundaries often influence the cultural landscape, interest in their changes in position is justified, and he refers to the problem of boundary change as "the evolution of boundaries in position." In a review of the literature on this subject reproduced in Part II, Structure, Minghi concluded that the major problems involved in such studies were associated with (a) the actual definition of the affected zone, (b) the distinction to be drawn between studies of the impact of boundary change and other boundary studies, (c) the need for a clear "before" picture with some temporal depth, and (d) the importance of the time lapse between the date of the change and that of the actual study.

Three further generalizations may be made at this point:

1. There cannot be a *definitive* study of the impact of a boundary change, but rather,

---

42. N. J. G. Pounds, "History and Geography: A Perspective on Partition," *Journal of International Affairs,* XVIII (1964), p. 169. Emphasis added.

43. *Ibid.,* p. 170.

44. *The Science of Geography,* Publication 1277 (National Academy of Sciences–National Research Council: Washington, D.C., 1965), p. 32. See Reading No. 6 in Part 1.

45. See the section on "Studies of the Effect of Boundary Change" in the selection from Minghi in Part II on Structure.

46. J. R. V. Prescott, *The Geography of Frontiers and Boundaries* (Chicago: Aldine Press, 1965), pp. 72–73.

because of the continuing processes that the change generates there are recordings of impacts at different points in time.

2. Prediction on the basis of a study carried out over a short-term period can be misleading as the longer-term effects will often depend upon the changing relations between the gainer and loser states and upon principally the former's perception of the role of the gained area in its political system.

3. Integration of the exchanged area with the system of the gainer state will not necessarily increase in direct relation to the passage of time.

Independence

There is little in the geographical literature that deals directly with this aspect of sovereignty transfer. Textbooks often include sections relating to this problem,[47] and there have been many writings emphasizing the disruptive implications of inherited and ethnically superimposed colonial boundaries of newly independent states, although on this latter point Kapil[48] has found that, as the major post-independence problem in Africa has been the integration of diverse groups into an emerging society, the question of external limits becomes more marginal. In an attempt at systematic analysis of the geography of independence in 1962, Shaudys[49] found that the internal consequences of sovereignty transfer, while not as impressive as the external ones, included administrative and territorial changes, the development of factionalism, counter-moves to combat growing regionalism, and assorted economic changes. He also emphasized, in the context of increased boundary problems, the importance of the chronology of independence. The boundary separating any two political regions of different colonial sovereignty will, unless independence is simultaneous for both, change its function at least twice from a colonial-colonial divider, to colonial-independent, to independent-independent.

Sovereignty Transfer

It is obvious that some basic contrasts exist between the two types of sovereignty transfer considered.

1. A change in boundary usually involves but a small part of the loser's and gainer's political territory, whereas independence encompasses the entire political region which is perhaps only a small part of the loser's colonial holdings but nevertheless is coterminous with the newly independent state.

2. Boundary changes are usually fairly sudden events, whereas independence normally has involved a transition period—period of diarchy—during which the system gradually changes and the impact of the new process thus generated becomes observable even before the official change, although this concept of "preparation for transfer" has been challenged recently by Schaffer.[50]

3. Unlike the case of boundary change, there is not necessarily any continued physical contiguity with the former sovereignty in the independence case, although sometimes an adjoining territory may remain a colony for a while under the former sovereignty, thus providing a similar basis for measurement of change impact as exists in regional comparisons across both relict and new boundaries in the boundary change case.

4. The transfer of sovereignty in the case of independence is normally a *permanent* arrangement (the events of 1960 in the ex-Belgian Congo notwithstanding) while a boundary change has often been simply part of an on-going process which leads to further dispute which, in turn, is followed by another boundary change.

5. The new sovereignty in the case of independence is by definition without precedence, whereas in the case of boundary change

---

47. For example, Lewis M. Alexander, *World Political Patterns*, 2nd ed. (Chicago: Rand McNally, 1963). Chapter 6, "The Decline of Western Colonialism." Harm J. de Blij, *A Geography of Subsaharan Africa* (Chicago: Rand McNally, 1964), Part 3, "Equatorial Africa," and Part 5, "West Africa." Norman J. G. Pounds, *Political Geography* (New York: McGraw-Hill, 1963), Chapter 13, "Colonies and Colonialism," and Chapter 14, "The Underdeveloped World." Harm J. de Blij, *Systematic Political Geography* (New York: Wiley, 1967), Chapter XVII, "Colonialism and Resurgent Nationalism."

48. Ravi L. Kapil, "On the Conflict Potential of Inherited Boundaries in Africa," *World Politics*, XVIII (1966), pp. 656–673.

49. Vincent K. Shaudys, "Geographic Consequences of Establishing Sovereign Political Units," *Professional Geographer*, XIV (1962), pp. 16–20.

50. B. B. Schaffer, "The Concept of Preparation: Some Questions about the Transfer of Systems of Government," *World Politics*, XVIII (1965), pp. 42–67.

the gainer state has usually been in existence for a long time prior to the change.

The similarities between the two types are, however, overwhelming, and an attempt at formulating them into general statements follows:

1. There is usually a conscious attempt at systematic elimination of landscape relics of the former sovereignty, and an urge to create visible evidences of the new sovereignty.

2. Different sets of priorities under the new sovereignty lead to changes in such features as agricultural land use, land tenure patterns, and transportation routes.

3. Forced or voluntary emigration of citizens of the former sovereignty "back" to areas under their own flag can cause changes in population distribution and at least short-term economic decline in areas most affected.

4. Immigration of "new" sovereignty population usually takes place especially in the administrative and economic sphere to replace the emigrants—both spatially and vertically in the boundary change case, and vertically in the independence case.

5. Internal reorganization of administrative regions is often carried out with the aim of increasing the role of the central government.

6. The success or failure of the new sovereignty should be measured in terms of the degree of stability and integration achieved rather than of its survival over time.

7. Rash promises made in the immediate pre-transfer period by the spokesmen for the prospective successor sovereignty can eventually cause popular dismay over the failure of the act of transfer to solve economic problems and can lead to violent reaction and growing instability.

8. Residual images are often inherited from the values of the former sovereignty in the perception of places such as, for example, the bright image of the Jos district in Nigeria which was a local vacation resort for the European population in colonial times,[51] and of Merano in the Italian South Tyrol which was, when part of Austria prior to 1919, a spa for the aristocracy of the Dual Monarchy.

These established similarities indicate that political-geographic research into independence may well benefit from the examination of concepts developed in the area of boundary change analysis, and that sovereignty transfer is a spatial process which merits more attention by geographers. The attempt here is to bridge the gap between the selection from House on the Franco-Italian boundary and that on African independence by Wallerstein.

Growth and Development

There is a body of literature that focuses on an examination of the political process in a particular territorial setting which analyzes past and future growth and development in terms of social and political theory. The selections on this topic represent such a focus at the international, national, and metropolitan levels, although it is at the national level particularly that most fruitful work has been done.

The theme of growth and development, especially when related to "nation-building," is far more multi-dimensional and comprehensive than political integration alone. Such notions, for example, as the "life cycle of the state" and Ratzel's laws of spatial growth discussed in Part I are related to general theories of development in the social sciences which for the last century have tried to explain the essential differences between social relations in a *traditional community* and those in a *modern society*.[52]

In general terms, nineteenth century theorists established the notion that societies are divided into these two groupings—traditional and modern, rural and urban, agricultural and industrial, and so on—and argued that the development of societies involved the transition from tradition-bound and status-oriented relationships to more contractual and territorially-based relationships. From this point of departure many other dichotomous schemes have been advanced.

Max Weber's thinking on social change[53] and nation-building[54] added a new dimension

---

51. Peter R. Gould, "On Mental Maps," *Michigan Inter-University Community of Mathematical Geographers*, Discussion Paper No. 9 (Ann Arbor: University of Michigan, September 1966), pp. 52–53.

52. For a concise discussion of the contribution of social theorists to political development, see Lucian W. Pye, *Aspects of Political Development* (Boston: Little, Brown and Co., 1966), pp. 58–62.

53. See Reinhard Bendix, *Max Weber: An Intellectual Portrait* (New York: Doubleday, 1960).

54. Max Weber, *The Theory of Social Organization*, A. M. Henderson and Talcott Parsons, trans. (Glencoe, Ill.: The Free Press, 1947).

to development theory with the concept of the *transitional society*, thus clarifying the process of growth and development. In turn this has led to the modern era in which the social, economic, and political realms are seen as different aspects of human behavior.

Ratzel's ideas, the "life-cycle of the state" theory, and even Toynbee's theories on the rise and fall of civilizations (discussed in Part V) all stress the spatial ramifications of growth, and provide a relevant link between social theory on growth and development, and political geography.

There is general agreement among those who have attempted to define approaches to political development that ambiguity and imprecision exist in the use of the term.[55] Pye detects ten definitions of, or points of view on, political development. These see the phenomenon, in turn, as (1) the political prerequisite of economic development, (2) the politics of industrial societies, (3) political modernization, (4) the operation of a nation-state, (5) administrative and legal development, (6) mass mobilization and participation, (7) the building of democracy, (8) stability and orderly change, (9) mobilization and power, and (10) one aspect of a multidimensional process of social change. Packenham's taxonomy of approaches includes five types: (1) legal-formal, (2) economic, (3) administrative, (4) social system, and (5) political culture.

The "social system" and "political culture" types of Packenham and Pye's notion of political development as the operation of the nation-state (4) and as one aspect of a multidimensional process of social change (10), seem particularly pertinent to process in political geography. The spatial co-ordinates of political development, if viewed primarily as a function of a social system, include variations in the hierarchical structure of participation in political processes, and distributional aspects of religious, caste, linguistic, tribal, and other cleavages. The relevance of this approach can best be seen in the study of the development of nationhood and the process of nation building, as already discussed above in the section on "Political Integration."

The lesson to be learned from research on political development in the social sciences is that assumptions suggesting national development to be unilinear, and Western countries to be the objective or "end product" of development—assumptions so often underlying the notions of past geographical contributions to the study of growth—are invalid, and thus must be rejected, as must also the notion of cultural relativism. On the other hand, the "nation-building" approach, within a framework of social change as a multidimensional process, views all forms of development within a historic context in which externalities, and internal aspects of change within the society, are all related and impinge on one another with both vertical and spatial ramifications.

This multidimensional emphasis suggests that geographers have a particular role to play in growth and development studies as their focus is traditionally on the integration and interrelation of phenomena in space, and hence the notion of a "spatial system" may be useful to emphasize the essential interdependence of dimensions in development problems.

Within this context, some spatial processes appear particularly important. For example, Pye emphasizes *diffusion* of the concept of the state over the last three hundred years by Europeans into the non-Western world because the modern nation-state idea, spread by this phenomenon of diffusion, is now the essence of contemporary political development.[56] Also, the notion of *imitation* is closely related and possesses obvious spatial components. Similarly, the idea of *take-off* in the process of development is associated with distinctive spatial patterns.

Despite the sizeable literature in political science which goes under the title of "theories of political development," it can be seen that much of the work, thus far, has been in establishing typologies and characterizing levels of states and of development. As Berry has pointed out, these efforts tend to yield static and cross-sectional rather than dynamic, sequential, and longitudinal models of growth and development.[57]

---

55. Two especially useful sources on classifying approaches are: Pye, *op. cit.*, pp. 33–45; and Robert A. Packenham, "Approaches to the Study of Political Development," *World Politics*, XVII (October 1964), pp. 108–120.

56. Pye, *op. cit.*, pp. 6–8.

57. Brian J. L. Berry, "By What Categories May a State be Characterized?," *Economic Development and Cultural Change*, XV (October 1966), p. 93.

Introduction to the Selections

As we have already seen, the writings of Karl W. Deutsch have had quite an impact on thought in political geography (for example, on Jones in Heritage), and particularly in this part on Process we will find that Deutsch's ideas have been influential both in theory testing and in providing analytical structures.[58] Although Deutsch has written much since, the selection reproduced here remains a classic as a paradigm of nation formulation and growth based upon the processes of social communication and mobilization.

Deutsch is interested in the uniformities in the general process of history which links the two-way developmental chain: peoples-tribes-nations-empires. The model suggested to describe these uniformities in the process of integration and disintegration includes spatial connotations at every step in its progression. (a) The shift to an exchange economy results from a growing concentration of population in more viable agricultural areas, then (b) through increased social mobility of rural peoples, core areas are formed, leading to (c) the development of urban places with ever-increasing social mobility internally, and between town and hinterland, (d) the evolution of a basic communication grid, followed by (e) the concentration of capital, (f) an increase in group interests, (g) ethnic awareness and national symbol development, and lastly (h) the emergence of political compulsion including organization by classes with its spatial aspects of territoriality and hierarchy.

The political system thus formed then begins to grow and integrate its territory by reproducing itself from generation to generation, by increased social and political divisions of labor, by the accumulation of "national" symbols, and by its ability to re-allocate its resources and thus to influence its own development.

Etzioni, on the other hand, is interested less in the growth and development of nations but more in the process of political unification among already formed political units, and so, in a way, carries on from where Deutsch leaves off. The selection from Etzioni is taken from his *Political Unification*[59] in which he goes on to apply his paradigm of political unification to several cases, including the European Economic Community, the United Arab Republic, the Federation of the West Indies, and the Nordic Association.

His paradigm has three major tiers: a beginning or initiation stage (the conditions for take-off), a middle process (the path unification takes), and an end or termination state of unification. He distinguishes throughout between the *level* of integration and the *scope* of integration in his attempt to outline, whatever the independent variables in any case, the dependent variables in each tier for both scope and level.

The utility of the analytical approach of transaction flow analysis as a measure of territorial integration is illustrated by Edward Soja. He measures changes in the pattern of telephone traffic in East Africa for illustrative purposes. His aim is to bring to the political geographer's attention an approach developed by other disciplines for the analysis of such multivariate processes as political integration. This approach has been developed primarily at the metropolitan level or in the study of well known efforts at political unification such as in Western Europe.

Soja reasons that as communication is vital to political integration, the density of transactions among groups and units should provide a useful indicator of mutual awareness, and that patterns of flows create systems of interaction and communication. Transactions that give positive salience effects are, Soja maintains somewhat optimistically, relevant measures of political integration.[60] Soja is thus able to conclude from his application of the origin-destination transaction flow model to telephone traffic in the region of Kenya, Tanzania, and Uganda that between 1961 and 1965 basic reorientations occurred generally, showing a decrease in regional integration and an increase in the nodality of the three national capitals within their political territory.

While we may raise questions about the significance of telephone traffic in an underdeveloped area, of its validity as a surrogate

---

58. For example, Roy I. Wolfe tests some of Deutsch's ideas in his "Transportation and Politics: The Example of Canada," *Annals* of the Association of American Geographers, LII (March 1962), pp. 176–190, and T. G. McGee applies Deutsch's model of nation growth in his "Aspects of the Political Geography of Southeast Asia," *Pacific Viewpoint*, I (March 1960), pp. 39–58.

59. Etzioni, *op. cit.*

60. There is no conclusive evidence that a direct relationship does in fact exist between transactions of positive salience and political integration.

for political integration, of possible qualitative and quantitative changes in the population distribution during the four-year period, and of basing conclusions on an analysis of contrasts in cartographic patterns, Soja has contributed by bringing this approach to the geographic literature.[61]

Seventeenth-century mercantile imperialism provides Merritt with an opportunity to apply a systems analysis approach to the study of political disintegration. He analyzes the variables governing the actors and their relationships, the structure, and the sources of internal disequilibria in the British imperial system. Britain, as the metropolitan country, is the dominant subsystem while the North American colonies form the dependent subsystems. The relationships between the dominant and dependent subsystems, and among the dependent subsystems are studied in terms of the directions of policy, communication and loyalties by means of techniques such as transaction flow and content analysis based on primary data drawn from trade figures, self-referent symbols in the colonial press, and political commentaries of the period. These relationships show major dysfunctions and point up the inherent instabilities of the imperial system. Merritt is thus able to trace the structural and spatial degeneration of the system into two separate systems despite attempts to maintain it by shifting to system dominance pluralism. This historical study of political disintegration has important ramifications for the problems of discontiguity, transfer of sovereignty, and the growth and development of new states. The unambiguous spatial structure of the units and flows indicate possible adoption of this approach by geographers.

In his study published in 1959, House assesses the impact of a change in boundary at the small scale level of the frontier communities for the decade following the shift. That is, he concentrates on the borderland itself—the region which has actually experienced the transfer of sovereignty, and the adjoining areas directly affected—rather than attempting to analyze the impact of the territorial loss or gain at the national level.

61. For more detailed analyses using this approach see Steven J. Brams, "Transaction Flows in the International System," *American Political Science Review*, LX (December 1966), pp. 880–898; the selections in Jacob and Teune, *op. cit.*; and in numerous works by Karl W. Deutsch.

House finds that in the Franco-Italian case he selects, the alpine environment as well as relations between rival sovereignties, have played a role in influencing past attempts at boundary making and that the impact of the most recent change in 1947 can be fully understood only by an analysis of the penultimate change in 1860, and of developments in the period from 1860 to 1947. Both external linkages (hydro-electric power and transportation reorientation) *and* internal economic and social structure (sovereignty substitution in and partition of local communes) are of central significance, as is also, in the longer-run context, the trend toward integration between the two loser and gainer states, France and Italy.

The short selection extracted from Wallerstein's book, *Africa: The Politics of Independence*, serves to illustrate the process of the transfer of sovereignty with the issue of independence in Africa. Wallerstein traces the change wrought by the impact of the European colonizers in Africa, the reaction in the colonies culminating in the rise of nationalism, and the role of the legacies left by the colonial sovereignties in the new states created by independence. He further suggests a close correlation between the strength of the processes of modernization and integration, and that of the party and hero in any state. Thus he draws attention to the interrelationships among the one-party system, its adjunct, the national hero, and the internal structure of new states in their short-run efforts at integration following independence.

Also included is a brief discussion of African regional unification in which Wallerstein lays emphasis on the legacy of colonial fragmentation and immediate pre-independence policies as largely negative factors in Pan-African development.

Of the two selections on "Growth and Development," one is a theoretical work concerned with new states, and the other focuses on problems at the metropolitan level.

Foltz considers the growth and development problems of new states in their post-independence era. He finds that the gap between their short-run strategies and their long-run problems is complicated by the inherited patterns of the colonial era and environmental restraints.

The success of the single, mass political parties in winning independence rested on four factors: (a) the appeal of the rallying cry of "Independence!", (b) the inclusion of virtually all the modern elite in the party, (c) the lack of competition, and (d) good organization. The winning of independence was, however, only a first step in nation-building and the factors making for success in this step, Foltz suggests, may be weakened by the day-to-day exercise of governing a new state. Hence new goals must be set to ensure continued growth. These can include attempts to transform the world outside the state (territorial claims on neighbors, Pan-Africanism, etc.), to unite its people by focusing animosities and frustrations on an external enemy, or to find a new rallying cry on an internal basis, such as the "battle for economic development."

In a prophetic paper published in 1961, Anthony Downs looks into the future problems of political integration at the metropolitan level. He states that in the "next few decades" in the United States, metropolitan problems will rival world politics in importance. Within a decade the truth of his prediction has been painfully illustrated with bitter racial and political antagonisms in urban areas.

Downs sees two forces in basic conflict: the dispersal of population in metropolitan areas with the consequent proliferation of political units, and the need for a more centralized power for decision-making as this growth gives rise to greater social and economic complexities.[62] He discusses as a consequence of this conflict six problems which we have characterized in sub-titles as follows: (a) central city access to resources, (b) suburban imbalance in resource access, (c) political fragmentation and functional coordination, (d) central city renewal and neighborhood autonomy, (e) residential choice and minority groups, and (f) economic growth and unemployment of central city populations. The spatial coordinates of these problems are self-evident, and the discussion and selections on urban problems in Part IV, Behavior, have direct relevance in this context.

FUTURE RESEARCH NEEDS

After a long period of concentrating on formal aspects of cohesion and homogeneity in the study of the viability of political units, geographers must now begin to apply and further develop some of the theory and techniques developed in other disciplines to analyze phenomena significant to the spatial integration of political territory.

The process of integration should be analyzed directly, by looking at the actual spatial integration of territorial units through the study of such processes as interaction (at the personal level as well as trade and communication), diffusion, and imitation. The departure from political science lies in our primary concern with spatial rather than vertical (class, group, institutional) integration.

The processes involved in the transfer of sovereignty must be researched more thoroughly in order to get a clearer understanding of the reorientation of spatial patterns in the new states. In the realm of growth and development, the greatest need is to integrate research in political geography with rigorous research being done in the field of political development.

---

62. Relevant to Downs' discussion of future problems is Dye's analysis of annexation, Thomas R. Dye, "Urban Political Integration: Conditions Associated with Annexation in American Cities," *op. cit.*

17

The Growth of Nations:
Some Recurrent Patterns of Political and Social Integration

KARL W. DEUTSCH*

At many places and times, tribes have merged to form peoples; and peoples have grown into nations. Some nations founded empires; and empires have broken up again into fragments whose populations later attempted again to form larger units. In certain respects, this sequence appears to describe a general process found in much of history. This process shows a number of patterns which seem to recur, and which to a limited extent seem to be comparable among different regions, periods, and cultures.

Such recurrent patterns of integration, like other relative uniformities in history, raise the problem of the comparability or uniqueness of historical events. Yet the search for such relative uniformities in politics and history is essential to the pursuit of knowledge in these fields. No historical or political analysis can be written without the use of general concepts in which some notions of uniformity are necessarily implied. Indeed, such recurrent patterns offer a background of similarities against which differences can stand out, and against which investigators can evaluate the specific and perhaps unique aspects of each particular case of national or supra-national integration.

Reprinted by permission of the author and publisher from *World Politics*, Vol. V, 1953.
* Karl Deutsch (1912–) is Professor of Government at Harvard University.

At the same time, the study of the growth of nations may reveal cumulative change. It may suggest that the present period is unique in respect to both the extent of nationalism and the potentialities for supra-national organization. To the student of contemporary politics, it may further suggest specific problems of research and policy in the ongoing process of social and political integration on the national as well as the international level.

Before discussing the recurrent problems of national integration, it may be well to note the use of a few terms. For the purposes of our discussion, a distinction is made between a *society*, which is defined as a group of persons who have learned to work together, and a *community*, which is defined as a group of persons who are able to communicate information to each other effectively over a wide range of topics.[1] A similar distinction is adopted between a *country*, which denotes a geographic area of greater economic interdependence and thus a multiple market for goods and services, and a *people*, which is a group of persons with complementary communications habits. A *nation* is then a people which has gained control over some institutions of social coercion, leading eventually to a full-fledged *nation-state*; and *nationalism* is the

1. Cf. K. W. Deutsch, *Nationalism and Social Communication*, Cambridge, Mass., and New York, 1953.

preference for the competitive interest of this nation and its members over those of all outsiders in a world of social mobility and economic competition, dominated by the values of wealth, power, and prestige, so that the goals of personal security and group identification appear bound up with the group's attainment of these values.[2]

While peoples are found at almost any period in history, nationalism and nations have occurred during only a few periods. A nation is the result of the transformation of a people, or of several ethnic elements, in the process of social mobilization.

The processes of partial social mobilization and of nation-building have been recurrent phenomena in history, at least in certain general characteristics. What uniformities can we find in this growth of nations in the past? And in what ways is our own age different in respect to the growth of nations from any age that has gone before?

SOME POSSIBLE SPECIFIC UNIFORMITIES

Uniformities which have been found in the growth of nations include the following:

1. The shift from subsistence agriculture to *exchange economies*.
2. The social mobilization of rural populations in *core areas* of denser settlement and more intensive exchange.
3. The growth of *towns*, and the growth of social mobility within them, and between town and country.
4. The growth of *basic communication grids*, linking important rivers, towns, and trade routes in a flow of transport, travel, and migration.
5. The differential accumulation and *concentration of capital* and skills, and sometimes of social institutions, and their *"lift-pump" effect* on other areas and populations, with the successive entry of different social strata into the nationalistic phase.
6. The rise of the concept of *"interest"* for both individuals and groups in unequal but fluid situations, and the growth of *individual self-awareness* and awareness of one's predispositions to join a particular group united by language and communication habits.
7. The awakening of *ethnic awareness* and the acceptance of *national symbols*, intentional or unintentional.
8. The merging of ethnic awareness with attempts at *political compulsion*, and in some cases the attempt to transform one's own people into a privileged class to which members of other peoples are subordinated.

(1) *The Shift to Exchange Economies*

The shift from subsistence agriculture to an exchange economy seems to have characterized all cases of wider national integration which I have been able to find. Where the exchange economy came to embrace the bulk of the population and to bring many of them into direct contact with each other in the interchange of a wider variety of goods and services, there we find a tendency to "national" or at least regional, linguistic, and cultural "awakening," provided only that sufficiently large numbers of individuals enter the exchange economy and its more intensive communication *faster* than they can be assimilated to another "alien" language or culture.

Where these shifts take place, the ethnic and in part the linguistic situation becomes, as it were, loosened or softened, and capable of settling again into new and different molds. . . .

(2) *Further Social Mobilization and Integration in Core Areas*

The shift to an economy and culture based on wider interchange takes place at different times and different rates of speed in different regions. The result is often the existence of more "advanced" regions side by side with more "undeveloped" ones. The former are then often in a position to function as centers of cultural and economic attraction for some of the populations of the latter, and thus to become nuclei of further integration. The "when" is thus often as important and sometimes more important than the "where," and the processes of social mobilization and partial integration are truly historical in the

---

2. Ibid.; and "Nationalism and the Social Scientists," in L. Bryson, et al., eds. *Foundations of World Organization: A Political and Cultural Appraisal*, New York, 1952, pp. 9–20, 447–468. On recent studies in this field, cf. K. W. Deutsch, *An Interdisciplinary Bibliography on Nationalism, 1935–1951*, Boston, 1953.

sense that each step depends to a significant extent on the outcome of the step that went before.

Political geographers have sought to identify *core areas* around which larger states were organized successfully in the course of history. Characteristic features of such core areas are unusual fertility of soil, permitting a dense agricultural population and providing a food surplus to maintain additional numbers in non-agricultural pursuits; geographic features facilitating military defense of the area; and a nodal position at an intersection of major transportation routes. Classic examples of such core areas are the Ile de France and the Paris basin, or the location of London.[3]

It should be noted that the density that makes a core area is one of traffic and communication rather than mere numbers of passive villagers densely settled on the soil. Thus the dense population of the Nile valley seems to have been less effective as a wider center of integration than the sparse population of the Arab territories beyond Mecca and Medina, who more than compensated for their smaller numbers by their proportionately far greater mobility, activity, and traffic.

The theory of core areas, however, cannot account for the persistence of some states and the failure of others. What counts for more may well be what happens within each core area, and perhaps particularly what happens in its towns.

(3) *The Growth of Towns, Mobility, and Ties Between Town and Country*

There is no developed nation, it appears, without towns which have or have had a period of considerable growth, of mobility within the towns, and of increasing ties of social mobility, communication, and multiple economic exchange between town and country.

There have been towns, of course, where one or more of these conditions did not exist, and to that extent national development has been incomplete, absent, halted, or retarded. On the other hand, to the extent that there was such growing mobility and communication within towns and between town and country, national development was accelerated.

(4) *The Growth of Basic Communication Grids*

Most nations do not seem to have grown from single centers. Many nations have had several capitals and have shifted their central regions several times in the course of their history. Even the classical example of growth around one center, France, has long had two capital cities, Paris and Orléans; and some significant phases of the unification of the French language took place at the Champagne fairs and along the trade routes leading through that region—not to mention the role of the North-South routes and connections in helping the North to consolidate its victory over separatist and Albigensian elements in the Midi during the religious wars of the thirteenth century.[4]

A more extreme case, Germany, has no single core that could be easily identified,[5] and it seems more helpful to think of Germany as essentially a grid of routes of traffic, communication, and migration.

The same notion of a basic grid seems to be applicable to the unification of China, Russia, Switzerland, Canada, and the United States. It would be interesting to investigate the relationship of such a grid to the incomplete unification and more recent separation of the areas that now comprise India and Pakistan.

It is not suggested that a grid in itself can make a nation. Also necessary, as a rule, are a minimum of cultural compatibility and, in many cases, sufficient similarity between spoken dialects to permit the emergence of a common language for large sections of the population. The cultural and linguistic data in themselves are given by history, of course, at each stage of the process. Yet we know how much of a difference in language or

---

3. For core areas and population clusters, see D. Whittlesey, *The Earth and the State*, New York, 1939, pp. 11–12, 142–152; and Preston James, *Latin America*, New York, 1942, pp. 4–8. For the nodal location of London, see Sir Halford Mackinder, *Britain and the British Seas*, New York, 1902.

4. Whittlesey, *op. cit.*, pp. 138–139, 151.

5. This is illustrated by the divergent views of such writers as Whittlesey, *op. cit.*, pp. 166–170; Josef Nadler, *Das stammhafte Gefüge des deutschen Volkes*, Munich, 1934, pp. 104–109; Theodor Frings, *et al.*, *Kulturräume und Kulturströmungen im mitteldeutschen Osten*, Halle, 1936, p. 312; etc.

culture has been bridged successfully in the emergence of such nations as the Swiss, the British, or the Canadians, provided that enough tangible and intangible rewards and opportunities were present, ranging from greater wealth, security, freedom, and prestige to the subtler attractions of new common symbols, dreams, and ways of life.

(5) *The Differential Concentration of Capital, Skills, and Social Institutions*

A major factor in national differences and national pride today are the differences in the general standard of living. To some extent such differences tend to cut across the differences between social classes; there is a social, moral, or traditional component in what is considered "bare subsistence" in a given community, or in what counts as "luxury", in another; and a significant part of what is considered the poor population in a relatively wealthy community may be appreciably better off in terms of physical goods and services than even many of the relatively well-off members of a poor or economically backward people. This difference between the generally prevailing standards of wealth, comfort, and opportunity among different regions or peoples has sometimes been called the *Kulturgefälle* ("the drop in the level of culture") by German writers who have employed this concept to bolster claims to German supremacy or exclusiveness vis-à-vis the populations of Eastern Europe and the Balkans.

Behind the differences in the standards of living lie differences in levels of productivity and in the supply of factors of production, that is, in the material means to pursue any one of a wide range of conceivable ends regardless of the difference in importance assigned to some of these ends relative to others in some particular culture. These differences in productivity may involve geographic factors such as soils, water supplies, forests, mineral deposits, and the absence of obstacles to transportation. All such geographic factors, however, depend on specific technologies to give them significance. Every concentration of natural resources requires, therefore, a concentration of productive skills and knowledge if men are even to know how to use them; and resources as well as skills require a concentration of invested *capital* if they are to be used in fact.

It should be clear that, as technology progresses, the relative importance of the man-made factors of production, such as capital and skills, has tended to increase relative to the importance of the few natural facilities which once were the only ones that more primitive technologies could exploit. There is reason to believe that present-day differences in living standards are due far less to differences in natural factors of production, and far more to differences in the supply of skilled labor, schools, housing, and machinery.

Particular peoples and nations may then tend to crystallize, as it were, around particular concentrations of capital and technology, or of particular social institutions which offer individuals greater opportunities for the pursuit of the goods or factors which they have learned to desire.

Thus we find in very different parts of the world the growth of peoples around specific social institutions or specific concentrations of economic opportunity.

The effects of differential standards of living and of productivity operated long before the Industrial Revolution, but they were increased by its coming. Where large economic or industrial developments have taken place, they have had a "lift-pump" effect on the underlying populations. They have induced migrations of populations to the regions of settlement, employment, and opportunity, and put these newcomers into intensive economic and political contact with the locally predominant peoples, and with each other. This physical, political, and economic contact had one of two cultural and linguistic consequences: either it led to national assimilation, or, if national assimilation to the dominant group could not keep pace with the growing need for some wider group membership for the newcomer, then the "lift-pump" effect would tend to lead eventually to a new growth of nationalism among the newly mobilized populations. Eventually, it might result in the assimilation of some previously separate groups, not to the still-dominant minority, but to the "awakening" bulk of the population.

This rebellious nationalism of the newly mobilized population rejects the language or culture of the dominant nationality. Yet it shares many of its values and it desires to share or acquire its wealth and opportunities. The motives for this secessionist nationalism are thus to a significant extent the same motives that would lead, under different circumstances, to national assimilation. Nationalism and assimilation are, therefore, ambivalent in the economic as well as in the psychological sense. The same wealth and prestige are pursued by either method: in national assimilation they are to be attained through sharing, while in national resistance they are to be attained by power.

Both national assimilation and national resurgence thus respond in a "lift-pump" situation to the power of the "pump." The intensity and appeal of nationalism in a world of sharply differentiated income and living standards perhaps may tend to be *inversely proportional to the barriers to mobility between regions and classes*, and *directly proportional to the barriers against cultural assimilation, and to the extent of the economic and prestige differences between classes, cultures, and regions*.

Seen in this light, the rise of nationalism and the growth of nations have some semiautomatic features, even though they have other features which are by no means automatic. As the distribution of scarce rewards is made unequal by economic or historic processes; as men learn to desire the same kinds of rewards; as they fail to be assimilated to the language and culture of the dominant group; and as they succeed in becoming assimilated with other men who possess cultural and language habits more compatible with their own—as all these processes go on, situations conducive to nationalism are created without anyone's deliberate intention.

(6) *The Concept of Self-interest and the Experience of Self-awareness*

The concept of a nation is bound up with that of a national interest. Already the nonnational or proto-national institutions of the city-state and the princely state imply the notion of group interests and interests of state, and all these notions of national, state, or city interests imply in turn the interests of individuals. But this concept of individuals with interests has itself gained its present importance only gradually in the course of certain developments of history.[6] Even today different regions and civilizations ascribe to it different degrees of significance, and it may lose again in the future much of its present importance.

At bottom the notion of interest perhaps implies a situation in which men are pitted against each other in a competitive situation in which some of them can improve or even maintain their positions only at the expense of others. The word "interest" denotes then the ensemble of an individual's chances for improving or maintaining his position against all competitors, and thus, indirectly, the amount and effectiveness of disposition of his resources applicable to the competitive situation in which he finds himself. Such competitive situations may be relatively vague and unpredictable, or they may be formalized and hence in part predictable to a more or less high degree. The more predictable they are, the more easily can they be recognized as competitive by the participants. Among the most highly formalized competitive situations are games.[7] Most real-life situations tend to differ from formalized games in their far greater range of possibilities for changes in the rules and even in the very units of the competition—a difference immortalized by Lewis Carroll in Alice's croquet game in Wonderland.

Nevertheless, there is perhaps one characteristic similarity between games and competitive social or economic situations, and that is the distinction between objectively "rational" behavior, i.e. behavior rewarded by the intrinsic rules of the game, or the "logic of the situation," as against subjectively convenient behavior, i.e. behavior that is most probable because of the previously acquired personal memories and habits of the players. Most individuals and groups learn only to a limited extent from playing games, regardless of experience; much of their behavior may remain an experience of their previously acquired and slow-changing personalities or habits, rather than of any strategy objectively conducive to winning.

Actual performance in a competitive situation is thus a series of compromises

6. Cf. Charles A. Beard, *The Idea of the National Interest*, New York, 1934, pp. 22–25. I am indebted to Professor Hans Kohn for valuable suggestions on this point.

7. Cf. John von Neumann and Oscar Morgenstern, *The Theory of Games and Economic Behavior*, Princeton, N.J., 1944.

between acting out one's character and "playing the game," but if one learns enough to be able to stay in the game at all, the continued experiences of the cues and rewards which the game offers may lead to cumulative learning of new habits and thus to modifications of character in the direction of the traits rewarded by the game.

Markets and power contests resemble such "games." They reward certain kinds of behavior on the part of the players; and they may teach them certain patterns of habits and values. The simplest result of this process has been stated vigorously by Ruth Benedict: a highly competitive culture, such as modern Western civilization, has often tended to elevate to positions of power and prestige individuals with such markedly aggressive and competitive behavior that other cultures might at times even doubt their sanity.[8]

The late Professor Joseph Schumpeter has suggested almost the opposite observation: according to his view, the competitive games of the free market and of laissez-faire industrialism have functioned very well in Western society, but in the course of the decades and generations since the Industrial Revolution these competitive economic institutions have inculcated something like a psychological revulsion from competition and insecurity among the people who grew up to live under them. Competitive institutions, according to Schumpeter, unwittingly have taught people a non-competitive and even anti-competitive set of desires and behavior norms which center on security: the continued operation of such institutions is gradually becoming impossible due to the state of mind which they have engendered, and which already has led to the widespread replacement of laissez-faire private enterprise by various institutions of socialism or the "welfare state."[9]

These seemingly contradictory observations perhaps illuminate two sides of the same reality. As men leave the relative security of villages and folk cultures for the mobility and uncertainty of travel, towns, and markets, and for the competition of wealth-getting, politics, and warfare, they may find greater opportunities and rewards for aggressiveness and self-assertion; and at the same time they may come to feel more poignantly the loneliness, the loss of security, and the loss of context and meaning in their lives which the transition to the new ways of life entails.

Nationalism is one peculiar response to this double challenge of opportunity and insecurity, of loneliness and power. Men discover sooner or later that they can advance their interests in the competitive game of politics and economics by forming coalitions, and that they stand to gain the firmer these coalitions can be made, provided only that they have been made with individuals and groups who have to offer in this game the largest amount of assets and the least amount of liabilities. To form the firmest possible connections with the most promising group of competitors would seem to be sound long-run strategy. With which group such firm connections can be formed is by no means arbitrary: in politics and economics such coalitions will depend to a significant degree on social communication and on the culture patterns, personality structures, and communications habits of the participants. Their chances of success will thus depend to some degree on the links that make a people, the ties of nationality.

Organization along ethnic or national lines is by no means the only type of alignment which may be tried in the competitive game. Yet of all these probable patterns of organization, ethnic or national alignments often combine the greatest strength and resilience with the greatest adaptability to a competitive world. So long as competitive institutions continue to prevail, nationalism can mobilize more people and organize them more firmly than can many competing types of organization. The potential rewards of nationalism then grow in proportion to the potential resources of wealth and power to which members of a particular people have, or can gain, access on preferred terms.

To develop thus the economic, intellectual, and military resources of a territory and a population, *and to knit them together in an ever tighter network of communication and complementarity based on the ever broader and more thorough participation of the masses of the populace*—all this is sound power politics; and those who carry out such policies tend to be rewarded by the long-run outcome of this contest.

What may fit the necessities of the competitive game may also fit some inner needs

---

8. Ruth Benedict, *Patterns of Culture*, New York, Penguin-Mentor Books, 1946, p. 256.

9. Joseph Schumpeter, *Capitalism, Socialism, and Democracy*, 2nd ed., New York, 1947.

of its participants. Ages of social mobilization, of rapid changes in the traditional social contexts, tend to be ages of increasing self-doubt and self-awareness for the individuals who live in them. The questions: Who am I? Whom do I resemble? In whom can I trust? —are asked with a new urgency, and need more than a traditional answer.

As a man seeks answers to these questions he must try to take stock of himself, of his memories, his preferences, and his habits, of the specific images and indeed of the specific words in which they were conveyed and in which they are now stored in his mind. As old cultural or religious patterns, beliefs, and ceremonies become questionable, self-searching must lead back to the childhood memories and the mother tongue, in terms of which so many experiences have been acquired, and out of which, in a sense, the individual's character and personality have been built up. When men seek for themselves, they thus may come to find their nationality; and when they seek the community of their fellows, they may discover once again the connection between ethnic nationality and the capacity for fellowship.

The phase of self-doubt and self-survey may end in conversion to a new religion or ideology, perhaps even one complete with a new language and traditions, such as was once the case in the matter of conversion to Islam, and sometimes to the Arab language; or in deliberate assimilation to a new nationality, as in many cases of emigration overseas, or in deliberate assimilation even in one's original country to the language and traditions one has now chosen to accept (e.g. Indians learning to speak Spanish and accepting Peruvian or Mexican national loyalties). In any case, the phase of self-doubt and self-appraisal tends to be followed by a phase of decision and of conscious or even deliberate identification with a group; and with the loosening of the ties of religion or status that group is likely to be a group delimited at least in part along national lines, in terms of habits of language and communication.

Our hypothesis finds some confirmation in a well-known pattern in the history of nationalism and the biographies of nationalist leaders. Many emotionally, culturally, and politically sensitive individuals react to a sojourn abroad, i.e. away from their native region or culture, with a far stronger assertion of nationalism and of allegiance to their own language, culture, and people. This precipitating crisis in the lives of many nationalists has been dubbed the *Fremdheitserlebnis* ("the experience of strangeness"). . . .

(7) *From Group Awareness to the Nation-State*

Individual awareness of one's language and people may appear to be a matter of personal psychology, even though there are social situations which make such awareness more probable. Group awareness, on the other hand, seems clearly a matter of social institutions. Some secondary symbols are attached to some aspects of group life and are repeated and disseminated over and over again by an organization or institution, often for a purpose that has nothing to do with nationality, or which might even be opposed to it. After a time, the institution may change or disappear, the organized repetition of the symbols may cease—but if there were enough of a primary reality capable of being symbolized, *and if there had been going on that basic process of social mobilization* which has been described earlier, then the results of the dissemination of those symbols may well prove irreversible. A stream of memories has been started that is partly self-regenerating, and so long as the foundations for the ethnic group exist, and social mobilization and communication continue to weld its members together, national group awareness may be there to stay. It can hardly be expected to give way to a wider supra-national allegiance until a basis for the appeal of wider symbols has again developed in the realm of objective fact, in experiences at least as real, as frequent in the daily life of individuals, and as relevant to their personal concerns, to their language, their communications, and their thoughts, as were those experiences which provided the basis for the awareness of nationality.

Given these underlying conditions, symbols and institutions of group awareness may be produced quite unintentionally. A process of social mobilization may even transform the function of existing symbols or institutions so as to turn them into agencies of group awareness, regardless of their original purposes. Thus nationalism was promoted sometimes by a supra-national church.

Similar nationalistic effects might follow upon dynastic accidents, passing combinations of territories by the fortunes of war, inheritance, or marriage, but these nationalistic effects themselves were by no means accidental. Almost every territory in Europe has been combined at some time or other with almost every one of its neighbors, but only certain of these combinations have endured and kindled the loyalties and imaginations of their peoples. The combinations which endured in fact or sentiment were those which were reinforced by other elements in the process of social mobilization and integration, and they would themselves in turn strengthen this process by adding to it political memories, symbols, grievances, and "historic rights."

The same considerations hold for the long-range effects of earlier administrative divisions in some empire or kingdom of the past. Even then, most administrators would pay some attention to population clusters, transport, and communication lines in laying out their districts. Yet many long-standing administrative divisions or provinces have disappeared without giving rise to corresponding peoples or nations....

Even symbols of insult may serve this organizing function, if the other conditions for national awakening are given. The term *les gueux*—"the beggars"—once applied to insurgent Netherlanders by their Spanish rulers, became a term of honor in Dutch history.

Reinforcing the impact of these symbols there appear the institutions of modern economic life and of the modern state, all of which require more direct communication with large numbers of peasants, artisans, taxpayers, or conscripts than was the case before.

. . . .

Once the process of group consciousness has started there appear also the deliberate pioneers and leaders of national awakening. There appear grammarians who reduce the popular speech to writing; purifiers of language; collectors of folk epics, tales, and songs; the first poets and writers in the revised vernacular; and the antiquarians and historians who discover ancient documents and literary treasures—some genuine, some forged, but all of them tokens of national greatness.

Side by side with the awakeners of national pride and fashioners of symbols appear the first organizers. There arise the first social circles and literary societies where the formerly despised native language is read or spoken. There follow the first benevolent societies, fraternal orders, credit cooperatives, and all the devices of mutual credit, support, or insurance, which now begin to collect the financial resources of the awakening nationality. There appear the organizers of the first schools, singing societies, athletic organizations, agricultural colleges, which herald the array of all the organizations for cultural, physical, and technological improvement which characterize every full-fledged modern nation.

Together with all this activity we find the gradual acceptance, or the deliberate proposal, of national symbols, of national colors, flags, animals, and flowers, of anthems, marches, and patriotic songs, from the "Rule Britannia" and the "Marseillaise" of the eighteenth century to the "*Nkosi sikelel i Africa*"—"God Save Africa"—of today's nationalist South African Negroes.[10] How all these symbols, maps, anthems, flags, and flag-salutes are then taught and impressed upon the populations and their children by informal group pressure and the media of mass communication as well as by all the coercive powers of the state and its system of compulsory public education....

(8) Political Compulsion

What does this process accomplish, and what does it aim at? When a nation has been built up, and when it has been reinforced finally by the full compulsive power of the state, then four things have been accomplished.

(1) A relatively large community of human beings has been brought into existence who can communicate effectively with each other, and who have command over sufficient economic resources to maintain themselves and to transmit this ability for mutual communication to their children as well. In other words, there has been brought into being a

---

10. Detailed documentation here would be unnecessary. For a novelist's description of the singing of the Negro anthem in South Africa, cf. Alan Paton, *Cry the Beloved Country: A Story of Comfort in Desolation*, New York, 1948.

large, comprehensive, and very stable human network of communication, capable of maintaining, reproducing, and further developing its channels.

(2) There has been both an effective accumulation of economic resources and a sufficient social mobilization of manpower to permit the social division of labor necessary for this process and to permit its continuation.

(3) There has been a social accumulation and integration of memories and symbols and of individual and social facilities for their preservation, transmission, and recombination, corresponding to the level of mobilization and integration of material and human resources, or even pointing beyond it.

(4) There has been at least some development of the capacity to redirect, re-allocate, or form a new combination of economic, social, and human resources as well as of symbols and items of knowledge, habit, or thought—that is to say, of the capacity to learn. Some of the social *learning capacity* is developed invisibly in the minds of individuals; some of it can be observed in the habits and patterns of culture prevailing among them; some of it finally is embodied in tangible facilities and specific institutions. Together, all these constitute the community's capacity to produce and accept new knowledge or new goals, and to take the corresponding action.

On all four counts, it should be evident, the nation represents a more effective organization than the supra-national but largely passive layer-cake society or the feudal or tribal localisms that preceded it.

On all these counts, there may be considerable contrasts between different nations. The social models accepted for imitation, the established institutions, the economic practices, and the methods of compulsion within each nation are all intimately connected with the cultural traditions and leading social classes currently prevailing there. Whether a leading class of businessmen or farmers or wage earners will prove more hospitable to accumulation of resources and to efficient dynamic innovation in their use may depend not merely on the general outlook to be found prevailing in each particular stratum, but also—and perhaps sometimes crucially—on the particular cultural goals and traditions which have become accepted by that particular class in that particular nation. Yet, the impression remains that even the worst-led nation represents, relative to its numbers of population, a greater amount of social communication facilities, of economic resources, and of social learning capacity than any pattern of ethnic or social organization preceding it.

Where does this process aim? The nation has been valued as a means of social advancement. In a world of extreme differences between living standards, men have tended to use the nation as an instrument to improve their own standards relative to those of their neighbors. The intrinsic bias of this process has been, where the opportunity offered itself, to produce in the temporarily most successful nation a sociological pattern reminiscent of a *mushroom cloud*. The stem of this social mushroom was formed by the "national solidarity" between the poorest and the lower-middle strata of the nation; the poorest strata, both rural and urban, however, tended to be somewhat less in relative numbers, and offered their members greater chances for "vertical mobility" than was the case in other less "successful" nations. The middle and upper strata, on the other hand, tended to form the crown of the mushroom; they tended to be somewhat larger in number than the corresponding group in other nations, with a greater propensity to spread out horizontally into new positions of privilege or control over new territories, populations, or capital resources, and correspondingly with at least somewhat greater opportunities to accept in their midst newcomers from the less favored strata of their own nation.

It is perhaps this sociological explosion into a mushroom cloud that has been at the heart of the transitory popularity of empire-building. Nationalism typically has led to attempts at empire or at least at establishing privileges over other peoples. The essence of this empire-building has been perhaps the attempt at ruling without sharing, just as the essence of nationalism has been the attempt at improving the position of one's "own" group without any sharing with "outsiders." To the extent that this process was successful it could only tend ultimately to transform the whole nation into a privileged class, a *Herrenvolk* lording it over servant peoples, as the Nazis dreamed of it, or a small, select population monopolizing vast natural resources or accumulations of technological equipment regardless of the fate of the rest of mankind. In reality, this state has probably never been achieved; and where it was even partially approximated, the results in the long-run were anything but lasting. Invariably, thus far, the same nation-building process which had permitted one nation to get temporarily on top of its neighbors subsequently raised up other nations to weaken or destroy it.

From this it might seem at first glance that the whole process of the rise and decline of nations has been cyclical, with only the names of the actors changing in an endlessly repeated drama. Closer scrutiny may show that this is not the case, and that some tentative inferences may be drawn from the events and processes surveyed.

The Uniqueness of the Present Period

Our survey offers no support for the belief of many nationalists that nations are the natural and universal form of social organization for mankind. But neither does it confirm entirely the opposite view held by many thoughtful and distinguished observers—the view that nations are exclusively the product of the modern period and of Western civilization. Perhaps the impression that remains might be summed up by saying that the West has gone much farther on a road which all the world's great civilizations have traveled to some extent.

What we call today Western civilization is in a very real sense a World civilization, not merely in what it brought to other countries, but also very significantly in what it received from them. Perhaps its "Western" peculiarities lie, then, not only in its ability to originate, but also in its ability to innovate, that is, to learn actively from others.

Traits of creativity and of the ability to learn are present in all great civilizations of the world, and the West here, too, has perhaps gone faster and farther on a road traveled to some extent by all. In a real sense, Western civilization is carrying on some—though certainly not all—of the traditions of all other civilizations, and its crisis in the world today is also their crisis, and not merely in externals.

It is this universal aspect that also characterizes the growth of nations in the present. During the last fifty years, there seems to have been growth in all the important regions of the world. Everywhere there has been growth in population, in gross economic wealth, and in national awareness. In no region has there been a decline to compensate for an advance elsewhere. Many of these advances in widely different areas have been the continuation of long-standing trends, which have been helped and speeded by the new resources and possibilities offered by the diffusion of science and technology during those last fifty years.

The result is that today all peoples are involved in the growth of national awareness, and that soon there will be no peoples left to play the role of submerged nationalities or underlying populations, or passive bystanders of history, or drawers of water and hewers of wood for their better organized neighbors.

The process has gone further. Within each people, all social strata have been mobilized, socially, economically, and politically, or are in the process of being so mobilized before our eyes. Wherever this social mobilization has progressed, it has undermined the patterns of authority and privilege inherited from an earlier day. The time can be envisioned now when the majority of all mankind will have shifted to non-agricultural occupations. There has never been a period like this in the history of the world.

18

A Paradigm for the Study of Political Unification

AMITAI ETZIONI*

Four major questions can be asked about every process: Under what conditions is it initiated? What forces direct its development? What path does it take? And what is the state of the system affected by the process once it is terminated? We use this paradigm of processes to construct one for the study of unification, especially for the study of the unification of nations. We ask, first, what is the state of the various units and the relations among them when the unification process is initiated and which factors enhance and which hinder this initiation. Once the process has been initiated, we ask what powers are applied to control unification and how these powers are distributed among the various participants. What pattern does unification itself follow? Do all societal sectors unify simultaneously or successively, and if successively, in what order, that is, which sector comes first and which later? Finally, we ask, once unification is interrupted or ceased, what level of integration has the system reached, how encompassing has its scope become, and what new function does it serve?

Whatever the independent variable—background conditions, integrating powers, retarding factors—we turn to the same dependent variables: the level and scope of integration; that is, we wish to outline the problems involved in determining the effect these various factors have on the success or failure of unification.[1]

More specifically, our paradigm includes the following dimensions:

(I) THE PREUNIFICATION STATE
  Unit Properties
    Individual Properties
    Analytical Properties
  Environment Properties
    Nonsocial (Ecological) Properties
    Social Properties
  System Properties
    Shared Properties (Other Than Integration)
    Preunification Integration

From Chapter Two of *Political Unification: A Comparative Study of Leaders and Forces* by Amitai Etzioni. Copyright © 1965 by Holt, Rinehart and Winston, Inc. Reprinted by permission of Holt, Rinehart and Winston, Inc. and the author.

* Amitai Etzioni (1929–) is in the Department of Sociology at Columbia University.

1. "Success" and "failure" [refer] to the accomplishments of a unification effort, as reflected in a later state of the system compared with an earlier point in time. No implication is made that unification is desirable, or de-unification undesirable.

(II) THE UNIFICATION PROCESS: A. INTEGRATING POWER
　Effective Compositions[2]
　　Differences in Kind
　　Differences in Quantities
　　The Communication Factor
　Effective Distributions
　　Degree of Elitism
　　Degree of Internalization
(III) THE UNIFICATION PROCESS: B. INTEGRATED SECTORS
　The First Stage: Take-off
　　Determinants of Take-Off
　　The Take-Off Sector
　Expansion of the Union's Scope
　　A Stable Scope
　　Sequences of Unification
(IV) THE TERMINATION STATE
　Level and Scope
　The Dominant Function

(I) THE PREUNIFICATION STATE

The question of the conditions under which the process of unification is initiated is considered from four viewpoints. First, what is the state of each societal unit that is to become a member of a particular union: is it likely to resist unification or to support it? Second, what is the nature of the aggregate of these units: are most or all units "ready" to unify or are only a few ready? Third, are environmental factors favorable for unification? Finally, to what degree was there interdependence and integration before a specific process of unification was initiated? Many specific questions have to be answered before these general questions can be fully considered.... Each of the basic four perspectives is illustrated by discussing one or two of the specific questions raised in the effort to establish the conditions which existed before unification began, or as a process of unification is initiated.

Unit Properties

Individual Properties: Integration and Resistance to Unification The unification process is one

2. "Effective" refers to a union's ability to maintain its level of integration and scope if it is in a termination state, or to increase its level of integration and scope if it in a unifying stage.

in which control of the means of violence, the capacity to allocate resources and rewards, and the locus of identification are transferred from member-units to the system in which they are members. This obviously involves at least some reduction of the integration of the member-units as they become increasingly incorporated into the system. It would appear, therefore, that the degree to which these units are initially internally integrated would greatly affect their potential resistance to unification and therefore the success of any specific unification effort. The question is, what level (or levels) of unit-integration are most conducive to the initiation and development of unification? One possibility is low level unit-integration. The integration of Malaya, for instance, is believed to have been enhanced by the fact that racial groups were so dispersed among ecological units that unit-identification was low. ...[3]

Another possibility is that low unit-integration impedes unifications. Countries that fall apart, like the Republic of the Congo in the early 1960s, can hardly form a union with other countries.... Thus, lack of unit integration might hinder system integration.

. . . .

The term international is used rather misleadingly to refer to relations among states that are not nations. In this way one possible value of a variable, namely a high degree of identification of politically conscious citizens with their states (which characterizes nation-states), is included in the mere definition of the system. Actually, many past *and* contemporary unions have been initiated among units whose politically active citizens either were expressing their nationalist sentiments by creating the union (for example, Germany and Italy) or took place before such sentiments significantly affected either the units or the system (for example, the federation of Canada).[4] In short, unification might be initiated in a prenationalist period, in a postnationalist one, or be, itself, an expression of nationalism....

3. Max Beloff, "The 'Federal' Solution in Its Application to Europe, Asia, and Africa," *Political Studies*, vol. 1 (1953), p. 118.
4. Similarly, the term, "supranational authorities" should be reserved to refer to centers whose decisions are binding on units that are nations, not merely states.

Analytical Properties: Heterogeneity and Unification Analytical properties are not properties of any single unit but are derived from a study of the distribution of unit-attributes.[5] Unlike unit-properties or relational properties, analytical properties cannot be observed. They are "second order" abstractions.

The most important analytical property for the study of the prerequisites of unification seems to be the degree of heterogeneity of the member units. On the one hand, it has been suggested that the less homogeneous a group, whether it is a small group, a community, or a nation, the less likely it is to be highly integrated.... On the other hand, there are reports of instances in which this relationship between homogeneity and integration did not hold....

It seems that not all background characteristics are of the same relevance to integration. Some may have great effect while others have very little or no effect; moreover, we shall see that the existence of some heterogeneity might enhance rather than undermine integration. The study of the effects of heterogeneity must hence proceed by examining the effects of the diversity of each major background characteristic on integration, in addition to examining the effects of this variable holistically....

In the economic sphere, the composition of the production of the merging units and their comparative wealth are of great interest. It is almost universally assumed that countries that *differ* in the composition of their economies will integrate more easily than those that have similar economies....

Two or more industrial countries might complement each other in the type of industries whose products they export, for example, light and heavy industries; lesser distinctions, such as trucks and passenger cars, long and short cotton grain, etc., may similarly serve as complements. Some differences are to be found in the products of any two units, even those in the same economy, if only in the name of the brand. Moreover, under a certain distribution of tastes, as found now in the EEC, some citizens of one country have a preference for certain products of another country, even if their own country produces a rather similar product.

But complementary becomes a meaningless concept if it is applied to products that can be readily substituted for each other. More important, we find significant reasons for countries to engage in economic unification when their products are similar and they have no taste for each others' bananas, coffee, cotton, oil, steel, etc. One reason is the desire of some important industries to form international cartels to protect prices and to allocate markets for their products. This is more easily done in integrated economies than in those separated by national boundaries. Similarly such integrations are believed to help small countries to improve their terms of trade when they purchase collectively rather than as individual countries. Thus, homogeneity in certain economic sectors provides a motive for integration. In fine, there are some reasons to believe that economic heterogeneity enhances unification and some evidence that similarity of economic production enhances it. Possibly both approaches are valid, though for different products or under different conditions. At this stage of our knowledge, it remains an open question as to whether this is indeed the case, and for what products and under what conditions homogeneity might be more predisposing to unification than heterogeneity, or vice versa.

The picture regarding differences in the national wealth or per capita income of integrating units is not much clearer. If we use an absolute scale, in which the integrating units are compared to all existing units, ranging from $10 per annum for Somalia to $2300 for the United States, we find that most unifications encompass countries that fall in the same general category of wealth....[6]

While there are cases in which a union exists or progresses despite large internal differences, there is also considerable evidence that such differences in per capita income have been among the factors that hindered or undermined unions....

Homogeneity of background in ethnic origin, cultural tradition, language, and religion were once deemed essential for stable political unity. Actually, however, a large number of nations, such as Switzerland and

---

5. Paul F. Lazarsfeld and Herbert Menzel, "On the Relation Between Individual and Collective Properties," in Amitai Etzioni (ed.), *Complex Organization: A Sociological Reader*. New York: Holt, Rinehart and Winston, Inc., 1961, pp. 422–440, esp. p. 427.

6. [These] figures are for the early 1960's.

Canada, are highly divergent on all these counts.... However, we find that quite a few successful unifications have been initiated, and political communities established, without cultural homogeneity. Moreover, one look at a map will suggest many instances in which cultural homogeneity existed for many generations in an area, and yet no political unification has taken place. Thus, cultural homogeneity is neither a prerequisite to unification nor a sufficient condition, though it might very well affect the probability that a union will evolve....

Of all the conditions prior to unification, the effects of homogeneity of political orientation and structure are least clear. With respect to foreign policy, we find unions that are homogeneous and unions that are quite diversified.

Regarding internal political structures, the variance is even greater. On the one hand, there are homogeneous unions; all the members of the East European union, for instance, are Communist countries though there are significant differences in degree of de-Stalinization. On the other hand, NATO includes both firmly established democracies and Portugal....

The extent to which heterogeneity stands in the way of initiation of a union has to be empirically determined. Some degree of political heterogeneity can obviously be tolerated; a large degree might be disintegrative in effect.

Heterogeneous units might initiate a union if the elites in power are "homogeneous." A unification drive might be initiated in several countries at an historical moment when "congenial" factions are in power simultaneously. But their domestic opponents may later come to power and undo the agreement or limit its expansion....

Thus several heterogeneous countries can initiate a union if congenial factions are in power simultaneously. And perhaps the political union would remain in effect if these factions remained in power permanently or regained power frequently. But even if heterogeneity were much lower, unification would be less likely to be initiated if it so happened that the "uncongenial" political and social factions were in power simultaneously in the various countries....[7]

In sum, the statement that heterogeneity

[7]. I am indebted for this point to William Glaser.

is inversely related to unification is much too simple to be tested, let alone to be held as valid. The effects of heterogeneity in each of the major social sectors (economic, cultural, political) are to be studied. Such a study will have to take into account differences in the scales used, and the stage of unification—initiation, termination, etc.—of the union under study. The role of homogeneity is to be examined in the preunification stage, to determine to what degree it is required as a *prerequisite*. A careful distinction is to be made between what is a necessary prerequisite and what is only an enhancing factor. Further, we would like to know if the need for homogeneity decreases or increases as unification progresses. The question is, therefore, not whether heterogeneity does or does not block unification, but what kinds and degrees of heterogeneity block or enhance unification—to what degree, at what stage of the process, and what effect one kind of heterogeneity has on the others.

The Environment: Ecological and Social Properties

Environmental properties include ecological factors, such as the physical environment in which the union is initiated and by which it is surrounded; and social factors, the properties of nonmember units that affect unification.

Nonsocial (Ecological) Properties: The Effect of Discontiguous Territories Many ecological factors affect the probability that a union will be initiated, including the morphology of the region, the distribution of natural resources within it, and the existence (or nonexistence) of a natural border that defines the area. In general, contiguous territory and a morphology that allows easy transportation and communication is believed to enhance unification. High mountain ranges, for example, are reported to have been an important barrier to unifications of Central America and South America; the recent development of a Pan American Highway is viewed as improving the chances that future unions will be more successful.[8]

Ecological unity has often been considered

[8]. See Norman J. Padelford, "Cooperation in the Central American Region," *International Organization*, vol. 11 (1957), p. 50.

so essential for political communities that there is a question as to whether a union of nonadjacent territories, that is, one in which the ecological base of the union is broken up by a "no-man's land" (such as seas) or by nonmember countries, can be successfully formed at all.

A discontiguous territory is an unsettling, tension-provoking factor even for national political communities. West Berlin and West Germany and West and East Pakistan are two well-known cases.[9] Another well-remembered instance was the separation of East Prussia from the rest of Germany by the Polish corridor....

It would be hasty, however, to conclude that political unification is impossible without territorial unity. Japan is well integrated. So seem to be the Philippines. While the Union of Britain with Ireland was dissolved in 1922, Britain maintained its ties with North Ireland. Similarly, Canada's union with Newfoundland is viable. And the United States seems to have no difficulties in bridging the 2000 miles that separate Hawaii from the mainland.

The study of the effect of territorial contiguity on unification will have to proceed by examining the underlying sociological and political variables that are affected by lack of adjacency in order to determine, first, their specific effects and, second, whether those effects are entirely or predominantly negative; and then by studying what compensating mechanisms, if any, are used to reduce or overcome the disintegrating effects of discontiguity. The most often cited effect is the hindrance of transportation of goods and people, which in turn obstructs the integration of the societal units and cultural interaction by curbing commercial and interpersonal relations.

A second hindering effect of discontiguity is the limitations it sets on movement of military units. Nasser might have suppressed the 1961 Syrian secession, or it might not have occurred, if the Egyptian army had been free to interfere from its home bases, unhindered by the interposed states of Jordan and Israel....

Third, because of the long association with statehood and nationalism, territorial unity has become a symbol of political unity, and its lack has therefore become an expression and symbol of division, as is the case in the West Indies, where the islands, rather than their federation, are the major frame of political identification.... To what degree the command over modern means of communication and transportation, which some of those countries are gradually acquiring, will allow them to facilitate the movement of troops and goods and to overcome differences in cultural tradition, language, and historical experiences created by the lack of such means in earlier generations is a question that has to be answered before the impact of the lack of adjacency on unification can be determined.

Finally, the fact that under some conditions geographical *dis*-contiguity reduces the need for integration is to be further explored. Separation of groups that adhere to incompatible values—at least until nationwide education can build up shared values—seems to help preserve whatever unity exists in many a new nation. Developing communication at a more rapid pace than education might well increase the level of tension in such societies.

Social Properties: Enemies, Partners, and Diffusion
The threat of a common enemy is probably the condition most often credited with initiating the union of countries. Wheare, for instance, listed "a sense of military insecurity and the consequent need for common defense" as one of six factors present in every case in which the desire for federation has arisen....[10] But Deutsch and his associates have pointed out that when a union is initiated to counter an enemy, it tends to disintegrate as the threat passes.[11] The question is why a defensive alliance sometimes does mature into a more encompassing and lasting union, while in other cases its life is as short, if not shorter, than that of the real or conceived threat.... The study of "initiation under threat" will have to take account of the predisposition toward unification of sectors *other* than the military, to determine the chances for such a union to succeed.

. . . .

A way in which a union may be affected

---

9. On the strain created by discontiguity in Pakistan see Charles Burton Marshall, "Reflections on a Revolution in Pakistan," *Foreign Affairs*, vol. 37 (1959), p. 253, and *New York Times*, February 18, 1962.

10. K. C. Wheare, *Federal Government*. London: Oxford University Press, 1946, p. 37.

11. Karl W. Deutsch *et al.*, *Political Community and the North Atlantic Area*. Princeton, N.J.: Princeton University Press, 1957, pp. 44-46.

by nonmember units is through diffusion or imitation, a process often studied by anthropologists but rarely by students of international relations. To put it more colloquially, there seems to be in international relations such a phenomenon as "fashion," which enhances the transfer of the institutions of one region to another. The Marshall Plan directly affected the formulation of the Molotov Plan; the formation of the Organization of European Economic Cooperation (OEEC), in Western Europe, under the initiative of the United States, affected the foundation of the Council for Mutual Economic Aid (CMEA) in Eastern Europe by the U.S.S.R.

. . . .
The question that arises whenever social patterns or political institutions (for example, the American Constitution) are transferred from one region to another, is: Are the conditions that allowed for the functioning of the pattern in one region available or reproducible in the second region? When this is not the case, one of two things is bound to happen: (a) The imitation fails to be grafted because of different conditions and the new institutions are rejected.... Or, (b) the imported institutions survive, maintaining more or less the same formal structure as in the original region, but actually fulfilling different functions....

System Properties

... The study of the preunification stage is not complete unless the relationships among the potential participants in a union are investigated, even if the finding is that no such relationships existed. Both the pre-unification level of integration and its scope have to be assessed, and other relevant properties of the system have to be determined.

Preunification Integration and Scope Unification is a process in which the integration of a system is increased, a process that tends to be accompanied by expansion of the scope of the system in terms of the sectors that are controlled on a system rather than a unit level....

Shared Properties: The Example of Culture[12]

. . . .
... Shared culture is not a *pre*requisite for unification but a requirement that has to be fulfilled before the process can be advanced. No union, one might suggest, is highly integrated unless a shared culture has evolved. This would also imply that while cultural exchange programs can hardly trigger a unification process when other factors are missing, once unification is progressing—let us say due to economic, military, or political factors—cultural interchange makes an independent contribution to unification in an "advanced" stage of the process (as compared to the initial). That is, the exchange acts as a *solidifier* rather than as a prerequisite or initating factor.

(II) THE UNIFICATION PROCESS:
A. INTEGRATING POWER

Sociopolitical processes such as unification do not proceed in a trial and error fashion. Once initiated they tend to follow one of a limited number of patterns (which will be discussed in the subsequent section). Which pattern they follow is in part determined by the *kind* of integrating power that various elites exercise and that the evolving union commands. This raises the question of what kinds of integrating power are applied in the unification process and who is applying them.

A Classification of Power: A Conceptual Digression

To study the effect of integrating power on the successful launching of unification endeavors requires a clear conception of the kinds of integrating powers that exist. The following threefold classification seems to be satisfactory; integrating power, we suggest, is either coercive (for example, military forces), or utilitarian (for example, economic sanctions), or identitive (for example, propaganda). The classification is exhaustive; each concrete power is either one of the three

12. Culture is viewed in the broadest sense of the term, including religion, secular ideologies, language, arts, etc.

or is composed of their various combinations.[13]

. . . .

Utilitarian assets include economic possessions, technical and administrative capabilities, manpower, etc. Utilitarian power is generated when these assets of a unit are allocated or exchanged in such a fashion as to allow it to bring another unit to comply with norms it upholds, or with the system it upholds for its members.

Coercive assets are the weapons, installations, and manpower that the military, the police, or similar agencies command.

The term *identitive* assets refers to the characteristics of a unit or units that might be used to build up an identitive power. These identitive potentials are usually values or symbols, built up by educational and religious institutions, national rituals, and other mechanisms.

International relations, in general, are characterized by the more frequent use of a coercion by one unit against another as compared to the interaction of other social units, and by the less frequent and less effective exercise of identitive power. Utilitarian power is frequently used in international as well as intranational relations. Unification processes are directed by all three kinds of power.

. . . .

Effective Compositions

Differences in Kind The question of which composition of power is most effective for unification has not been answered. It is quite evident that different kinds of unions (such as military only or economic only) develop effectively when different kinds of power are used. The transition from stage to stage of unification of the same kind of union might well also require a change in the power applied to maximize the development of the union.

. . . .

Differences in Quantities Unification processes require changes in member-units and in the relations among them. Such changes tend to be resisted at least by some subunits[14] or by outsiders whose utilitarian interests and identitive commitments motivate them to support the maintenance of the status quo.[15] Hence, a comparison of the amounts of power supporting unification with the amounts of power wielded by resisting subunits or outsiders—that is, the drawing up of "balance sheets" and power inventories—is an essential part of the study of unification.

It is widely understood that power cannot be abstracted from its use. Power is a relational concept; a country has a power advantage over some countries and not over others; it has power for some purposes but not for others. . . .

We are also helped in estimating the power potential of a country by having some knowledge of the universal scale (or total range) of assets there are and the rules for conversion of assets into actual power. . . .

Communication and Responsiveness The communication capacity of a unit, as Deutsch pointed out extensively, is a major determining element in the unification process.[16] The effectiveness of the communication network of a unit or system affects the degree to which its assets can be converted into actual power. . . .

Finally, Deutsch points to the need of the recipient of communication to be able to digest such information and respond properly.[17] Effective communication requires not only the transmission of information but also certain qualities and processes within the receiving units. Obviously if a decision-making unit is flooded (or "overloaded") with communications, is ideologically rigid, or for some other reason is not able to digest the communications received, the conversion of assets into powers, if not completely misdirected, will be as inadequate as if the unit had not received inadequate communication to begin with.

---

13. This classification is extensively discussed and applied in my *A Comparative Analysis of Complex Organizations*. New York: The Free Press of Glencoe, 1961, esp. chap. 1.

14. A subunit is a segment of a member-unit (such as the agricultural subunit of West Germany, which is a member of the EEC). The three-level distinction—of system, unit (or member), and subunit—is necessary for the following analysis.

15. On these "vested interests," see Talcott Parsons, *Essays in Sociological Theory*. New York: The Free Press of Glencoe, 1954, pp. 138–141 and pp. 315–318.

16. Deutsch *et al.*, *Political Community*, pp. 12ff. See also Karl W. Deutsch, *Nationalism and Social Communication*. New York: John Wiley & Sons, Inc., 1953.

17. *Nationalism and Social Communication*, pp. 96ff.

What is far from clear is the relative weight of the communication factor. Some authorities tend to see communication as a most central factor. Others stress much more the relative assets of a unit, viewing communication as one aspect of such assets, a condition that affects activization of the other assets but of little import in itself.[18] Moreover, the level of communication received and digested is itself largely affected by the power-backing a particular message has been given....

Effective Distributions

Whatever the kinds and amounts of power employed to initiate and bring about a union, the way this power is distributed among various units, that is, the relative power the units have, is of great consequence to the unification process. Two major dimensions have to be taken into account: (a) The degree of elitism, that is, the degree to which power is concentrated in the hands of one or a few units as against a more or less equal distribution among many, and (b) the nature of the unit (or units) that has more power than others (if any), in terms of membership in the emerging union. Is the elite-unit (the power holder) a member or does it impose unification from the outside?

(III) THE UNIFICATION PROCESS: B. INTEGRATED SECTORS

When the prerequisites are present and the integrating power is operative so that the level of integration of the system grows, its scope also tends to expand....

The First Stage: Take-off

... The concept of take-off, first used by students of aerodynamics, then economics, and recently introduced into political science by Deutsch and by Haas, calls attention to a second point in the "inauguration" of a process which is in many ways more important than its formal initiation.[19] Take-off occurs when a process has accumulated enough momentum to continue on its own, that is, without the support of nonmember units. This is not to suggest that the initiation point is irrelevant; the virtue of the concept of take-off is that it calls attention to the fact that for many processes the initiation stage and the take-off stage are not identical.

. . . .

Determinants of Take-off What actually happens when unification takes off is far from clear. At least two changes in the nature of the process seem to occur that might account, at least in part, for the take-off phenomenon. One change is that the flow of people, goods, and communications across the national boundaries increases. Some such changes, though by no means all of them, require an increase in the amount of interunit decision-making. Increased *shared* activities—such as holding a common defense line—seem to increase the need for common decision-making even more than increases in interunit flow. Since the intergovernmental procedures are cumbersome for a large volume of decisions, such increases in flow and shared actions generate pressure to form a system-unit for decision-making, such as a "supranational" bureaucracy.

. . . .

Another factor accounting in part for take-off is *secondary priming;* that is, unification in one sector tends to trigger unification in others.[20]

. . . .

The main point about this expansion of the original unification effort, or spill-over as Haas called it[21] is that it is based on secondary

---

18. The dispute about the relative weight of power versus communication is one of the central issues in the human relations versus structural-functional dispute. For presentations of both sides see Amitai Etzioni (ed.), *Complex Organizations: A Sociological Reader.* New York: Holt, Rinehart and Winston, Inc., 1961, pp. 99–130.

19. W. W. Rostow, *The Stages of Economic Growth.* Cambridge, Eng.: At the University Press, 1960, chap. 4. Deutsch *et al., Political Community*, pp. 83–85. Ernst B. Haas, "Challenge of Regionalism," *International Organization*, vol. 12 (1958), pp. 440–458.

20. See Rostow, *The Stages of Economic Growth*, p. 52, on "derived-growth sectors."

21. Haas provides an insightful analysis of this process in his *Uniting of Europe*, esp. chap. 8. The term secondary priming is preferred to spill-over as the latter term is used to refer to any secondary expansion including, for instance, an ecological one, while we seek to designate a specific kind of social expansion involved in unification, i.e., from one social sector to another, within one sector or from one subsector to another.

priming. Unification in one sector (or subsector) triggers a similar process in others, rather than a thrust by any external force—hence the significance of the study of secondary priming for take-off. Once secondary priming sets in, unification continues even if the external powers that initiated the process have ceased to support it or are now trying to hinder its advance. How far secondary priming carries unification before it is exhausted is a question whose answer is as yet largely unknown.

In sum, the foundation of supranational bureaucracies and secondary priming accounts, at least in part, for the take-off of unification. This raises two questions: what patterns does unification follow once it has taken off and what is the optimal sector in which to initiate unification with a view to maximizing the extent to which integration will progress before it comes to a standstill.

The Take-off Sector Unions may be initiated in many societal sectors including the military, economic, political, and educational sectors. . . .[22] The effort to establish which sector (or sectors) is the optimal take-off base will have to draw on an analysis of the internal structure of the societies which participate in the unification process. Various societal sectors seem to differ in the degree to which they are interrelated. The more interrelated they are, obviously the more spill-over will occur. . . .

Expansion of a Union's Scope

A Stable Scope

. . . .

The highest degree of stability is reached, we suggest, only when a full-fledged political community is established; that is, when integration on all three dimensions (monopoly of violence, center of decision-making, and focus for identification) is high, and unification has penetrated all major societal sectors. Unification might stop short of high integration and full scope, and the resulting union might exist for a considerable period of time; moreover, high integration and full scope might be more difficult to attain and, hence, more risky to aim at than some less integrated and less encompassing form of unification. All that we hypothetically suggest is that, once attained and in the long run, unions that have become highly integrated and have a broad scope are more stable than those that are not so well integrated or inclusive.

. . . We suggest that a full collectivity is one that solves autonomously its four basic functional problems: *adapts* to its ecological and social environment, *allocates* means and rewards among its subunits, *integrates* its subunits into one polity, and establishes as well as reinforces the *identitive* commitments of its members to a set of values. A union that has matured into a political community would tend to share and centrally regulate activities of all four types.

Sequences of Unification Naturally the next question is, in what order, if any, are the various sectors unified? Do they have to be "assembled" in a specific order? If one is skipped, will this disintegrate the union, just retard it, or allow it to continue in a limping way until the missing link is added (though in the "wrong" order)?

We should be open to the possibility that there is, in fact, no one optimal sequence for unification but that each kind of union is "assembled" best in a different fashion. This brings us to the question: what kinds of unions are there?

(IV) THE TERMINATION STATE

A union "takes off" and "spills over" following one sequence or another, until it reaches a *termination* state. That is, for a period of time—before additional unification or regression sets in—the union's scope and level of integration remain basically unchanged.[23] Unions differ greatly in the levels of unification at which they stabilize, that is, stop increasing their integration and expanding their scope. . . . Unions that differ in the state at which they stabilize might differ also in the conditions under which they are

22. Societal sector refers to all the social activities devoted to the service of one particular societal function. The adjective—economic, military, etc.—characterizes the function.

23. The length of the period is, like all such "cut-off" points, largely an arbitrary decision of the reasearcher, affected more by the scope of his study and the problem he is studying than by "reality."

initiated, in the forces that integrate them, in the sequence they develop, etc.

LEVEL AND SCOPE

The state at which unification is terminated (or interrupted) can be measured in terms of the similarity of such a state to that of a political community. The preceding discussion suggests the following criteria:

(*a*) *The level of integration, calculated on the basis of the degree of integration on each one of the three dimensions.* . . .

(*b*) *The number of sectors in which unification has taken place and their nature in terms of the secondary-priming potential of these sectors.* . . .

(*c*) *The degree of unification in each sector*, for example, the ratio of international versus international trade.

. . . The nature of the dominant function is an important variable for the study of unions and communities. For instance, we can already suggest that some functions—especially the political, social, and ideological ones —require higher integration and broader scope than others (for example, individual-oriented consumption). Hence, the level and scope at which the unification process is terminated and the nature of the function serviced collectively are crucial variables that both affect and are affected by the dominant function of the new unions and communities.[24]

The Dominant Function

Another major difference among various termination states is the dominant function that the new collectivity serves. This criterion not only differentiates unions (for example, military, economic, cultural unions), but also communities. It is true that a community encompasses all major societal sectors and in this sense serves all major functions; but communities can be characterized according to the function in which they invest more resources, manpower, energy, and which they value more highly as compared to other communities. While this predominant function changes over time, one can usually point to a particular function as dominating a given historical period.

24. For an outstanding examination of the European scene from this viewpoint see George Lichtheim, "Post-Bourgeois Europe," *Commentary*, vol. 35 (1963), pp. 1–9.

19

Communications and Territorial Integration in East Africa:

An Introduction to Transaction Flow Analysis

EDWARD W. SOJA*

In this paper, a technique known as transaction flow analysis is described and subsequently applied to the network of telecommunications in East Africa. The objectives of this exercise are to illustrate the potential contribution of a communications approach to the examination of the spatial aspects of territorial integration and to suggest an addition to the relatively bare quantitative tool kit of political geography.

Political geographers have long recognized that a primary function of any politically organized area is to integrate effectively its territorial components—to create a community of interests which accommodates innovation, sustains development, and promotes the general welfare of its adherents.[1] Nevertheless, there has been surprisingly little systematic research by geographers directly related to the analysis and measurement of political integration within a spatial context.

In recent years, however, a number of political scientists, borrowing from such relatively new and rapidly expanding fields as cybernetics, information theory, and systems analysis, have provided a fresh perspective on the fundamental processes which bind areas (and their populations) together.[2] This perspective revolves around the central

Reprinted from *The East Lakes Geographer*, Henry L. Hunker, Editor, Vol. 4 (December, 1968), pp. 39-57, with permission of the author and editor.

* Edward Soja (1940–) is in the Department of Geography, Northwestern University.

1. See, in particular, R. Hartshorne, "The Functional Approach in Political Geography," *Annals of the Association of American Geographers*, XL (1950), pp. 95-130; and "Political Geography in the Modern World," *Journal of Conflict Resolution*, Vol. 4 (1960), pp. 52-67.

2. An excellent introduction to the basic concepts of the three closely associated fields of cybernetics, information theory, and systems analysis can be found in W. Ross Ashby, *An Introduction to Cybernetics* (London: Methuen, 1956). Other standard works include Norbert Weiner, *Cybernetics: Communications and Control in the Animal, the Machine and Society* (Cambridge: MIT Press; and New York: Wiley and Sons, 1948) and *The Human Use of Human Beings* (Boston: Houghton Mifflin Co., 1950); Colin Cherry, *On Human Communication* (Cambridge: MIT Press; and New York: Wiley and Sons, 1957); Claude Shannon and Warren Weaver, *The Mathematical Theory of Communications* (Urbana: University of Illinois Press, 1949); L. von Bertalanffy, "An Outline of General System Theory," *British Journal of the Philosophy of Science*, I (1951), pp. 134-165; and J. G. Miller, "Living Systems: Structure and Process," *Behavioral Science*, Vol. 10 (1965). A brief review of the impact of these fields on political science is supplied by W. J. M. Mackenzie, *Politics and Social Science* (Harmondsworth: Penguin Books, 1967), pp. 96-120. References more specifically related to questions of political integration will be noted in later sections.

role of communications in human behavior and has introduced into the social science literature several valuable concepts of relevance not only to the present discussion but to the methodology and approach of political geography as a whole. This paper attempts to explore these developments, and particularly one of the analytical techniques they have generated, with the intention of stimulating greater interaction between political geography and political science. It is hoped that, through increased interdisciplinary communications, the distinctive points of view of each discipline can mesh more effectively together to the general benefit of both.

The use of transaction flow analysis in the study of territorial integration must be cone sidered within the broader context of what might be called a behavioral theory of communications. As previously mentioned, the growing acceptance of communications as a primary factor in human behavior has led to numerous attempts to extend the theoretical formulations of the related fields of cybernetics, information theory, and systems analysis into the various social sciences in the desire to provide new and more powerful interdisciplinary perspectives on problems of focal interest.[3] One of the leading figures in these developments has been Karl Deutsch, whose past works have proven of great interest to the political geographer and with whom the techniques of transaction flow analysis are most closely associated.[4]

Regarding the role of communications in the growth of integrated political communities, Deutsch has asserted that "The study of quantitative densities of transactions is the first step toward estimating the degree to which people are connected with one another."[5] A *transaction* may be defined as an exchange between units which always involves the communication of *information* and may represent a transfer of people, goods or services. R. L. Meier, in his stimulating volume, *A Communications Theory of Urban Growth*, describes a transaction in the network of human relations as involving "discrete interaction over space, an adjustment to recent events and new opportunities, and a joint experience which accommodates the participants to the changing socio-economic system."[6]

Before moving further, however, it is necessary to return briefly to the more basic concept of information. In the theories of cybernetics—the science of communications and control—information is used in a highly specialized way. In simplest terms, it can be defined as "amount of order" and refers to that which is not random and can therefore convey meaning. Information has also been associated with *negative entropy*, where entropy is defined as disorder or more broadly as a process in which order (i.e., information) is gained or lost due to energetic transactions between parts of a system.[7] But rather than plunging further into the complex terminology of information theory—a very worthwhile exercise but one which cannot effectively be undertaken here—perhaps greater clarity can be provided by a short discussion of how these concepts have been applied within social science research with particular reference to the integrative process.

Information, as used by Meier, refers to the capacity to select from a set of alternatives. It involves knowledge concerning the physical and human environment and is related to a potential for control or regulation. Wherever information is concentrated, behavior is more ordered and predictable. The choices available can be more clearly discerned and the probable outcomes of these choices more easily identified and evaluated—hence the potential for system regulation and control.[8]

---

3. Two illustrations of this development include David Easton: *A Systems Analysis of Political Life* (New York: Wiley and Sons, 1965) and Richard L. Meier, *A Communications Theory of Urban Growth* (Cambridge: MIT Press, 1962).

4. Deutsch develops his views on the role of communications theory and cybernetics in political theory building in *The Nerves of Government* (New York: The Free Press of Glencoe, 1963). More direct inquiries into the role of communications in political integration can be found in his several contributions to P. E. Jacob and J. V. Toscano (eds.), *The Integration of Political Communities* (New York: J. P. Lippincott Co., 1964). Other works by Deutsch of interest to the political geographer include *Nationalism and Social Communication* (Cambridge: The MIT Press, 1953 and 1966) and "The Growth of Nations: Some Recurrent Patterns of Political and Social Integration," *World Politics*, Vol. 4 (1953), pp. 168–195.

5. "Communications Theory and Political Integration," in Jacob and Toscano, p. 51.
6. *Op. cit.*, p. 66.
7. See J. G. Miller, *op. cit.*
8. *Op. cit.*, pp. 150–152.

The exchange and conservation of information within a network of social relations provides the integrative glue enabling the network to survive and grow as a cohesive, organized unit. Essential, therefore, to an understanding of the integrative processes at work in any territorial community is a knowledge of the pattern and intensity of information flow in space, for it is this dynamic exchange between the component parts of a system that creates the bonds of mutual awareness and interdependence which promote integrative behavior.[9]

This brings us back to the transaction, which is the basic unit of information flow. Transactions between areas can be viewed as indicators of the flow and concentration of information within a network of human relations in space, and consequently of mutual awareness and at least potentially integrative behavior. Charting the pattern and measuring the direction, intensity, and persistence of transaction flows in space thus offers an insightful window on the processes of territorial integration.[10]

There must be some threshold in the flow of transactions, however, beyond which two units become solidly locked together in a chain of inter-reactive behavior. Below this level, the flow of information from A to B, for example, may not be sufficient to sustain a close tie due to the flood of additional information being received by B from other parts of the system. One can easily accept the virtual inevitability of mutual awareness that would develop, once communications had been established and maintained, between two persons stranded on a small island, or to stretch the point somewhat further, between Adam and Eve. It would be difficult to imagine the behavior of one not being affected by that of the other. Add more people to the growing micro-community, however, and soon levels of mutual awareness become highly variable and the behavior of each individual may not necessarily involve a sensitivity to the presence and behavior of all others.

Identification of this important threshold has been operationalized in the concept of *salience*. Whereas transactions may be considered to convey images through the exchange of information, salience sustains these images through a significantly greater than normal flow of transactions. Salient units are not indifferent to each other's behavior for a significant level of interaction has been reached. Developing a measure of salience—the greater than expected flow of information used as an indicator of mutual awareness—is a primary aim of transaction flow analysis in the form discussed in this paper.

There remains, however, the problem of interpreting salience with respect to integrative behavior. Salience can lead to both positive and negative reaction, to community feeling as well as conflict, depending on the kinds of information being exchanged and consequently the nature of the images conveyed. Two noninteracting strangers are much less likely to do violence to one another than are a husband and wife!

In an attempt to solve this problem, one author has distinguished between those transactions which lead to positive reaction, or are "mutually-rewarding," and those which increase the chances of conflict, or are "mutually-depriving."[11] Before relating salience to the potentials for integration, therefore, the nature of the information being exchanged should be properly evaluated. Very often, however, the informational content of transactions cannot be clearly identified and interpreted with respect to this distinction and furthermore the two may be extremely difficult to distinguish even if this were possible. This is one of several areas where a certain unresolved "fuzziness" enters into the analysis of transaction flows. Hope-

---

9. Ackerman, in discussing the role of systems analysis as a fundamental integrating concept in geography, has stressed the great importance of studying spatial interaction and information flow: "... to choose a research problem without reference to the connectivity of the system is to risk triviality. What space relations tell us of connectivity in the system is significant to the science as a whole. Areal differences are significant *only* insofar as they help to describe and define the connectivity or 'information' flow." Edward A. Ackerman, "Where is a Research Frontier?" *Annals of the Association of American Geographers*, Vol. 53 (1963), p. 437.

10. It is interesting in this context to note the similar statement by Meier: "The use of an index of social communications representing the degree of interaction as *information* flow, and of knowledge as *information* storage, provides an important direct link to the other sciences. Advances in insight in any of them may now be translated quickly into implications for human organization, most particularly the culture of cities." *Op. cit.*, p. 152.

11. J. V. Toscano, "Transaction Flow Analysis in Metropolitan Areas," Jacob and Toscano, *op. cit.*, pp. 100–102.

fully, these problems are symptomatic of the early stages in the development of an important analytical technique and will resolve themselves with further application and elaboration.

In summary, therefore, the use of transaction flow analysis as a tool for studying territorial integration is based on the following assumptions: (1) the greater the level of transaction flow between areas, the greater become the chances for salience; (2) salience is an indicator of a high level of mutual awareness; (3) the greater the level of transaction flow of the mutually-rewarding kind, the greater the likelihood for cooperation and integration; (4) an integrated territorial community is maintained by a complex pattern of information exchange which hinges upon a connected network of salient transaction flows encompassing all its major areal components; (5) existing and potential levels of integration between areas will be reflected in a mapping of salient flows. This approach to the study of territorial integration shifts the focus from an examination of the degree to which certain key characteristics (e.g., language, religion, levels of development) are shared by the population in an area to the more fundamental analysis of *interaction patterns*.

There are many kinds of transaction flows one can examine and an equally large variety of methods to apply.[12] Of some value, for example, are preoccupation ratios, which use the relationship between internal and external transactions as a gauge of community insularity. Simple gravity models have also been suggested as tools for examining the impact of distance and social or political boundaries on the flow of transactions.[13] One such model has been applied with interesting results by a geographer to interaction patterns within Quebec and between Quebec and surrounding regions of Canada and the United States.[14]

The method used here, however, involves the application of an indifference, or null, model to obtain expected transaction flows (given a number of assumptions) from which salience is measured. This model, which will be referred to hereafter as the transaction flow model, has been used most frequently in the analysis of international trading patterns, but is equally applicable to other types of transactions and to the national, regional, and local levels as well.[15]

As developed by Deutsch and Savage,[16] the transaction flow model is based on an assumption of origin-destination independence—that is, assumption that the specific character of the origin of a transaction will not affect its destination, and vice versa. All possible destinations have an opportunity to receive the transactions in proportion to their relative sizes. Put in another way, the model presumes that the number of transactions from area A to area B will reflect only some measure of what might be called the relative attractive power of B within the entire system. The most commonly used yardstick for attractiveness, and the one that is used in the illustrations which follow, is the proportion of all transactions made in the system which are received at a particular point (e.g., B), although other measures such as population size or wealth can be used, as can the relative figures for outgoing transactions.

As an example, let us suppose that Great Britain is the destination for ten percent of all international trade. Under the assumptions of the transaction flow model, France, the United States, Madagascar, and all other trading states should send approximately ten percent of their exports to Great Britain.[17] In other words, Great Britain will expect to receive essentially the same percentage of trade transactions from all parts of the international trading system regardless of

---

12. See Karl Deutsch, "Transaction Flows as Indicators of Political Cohesion," *ibid.*, pp. 73–97.
13. Karl Deutsch and Walter Isard, "A Note on the Generalized Concept of Effective Distance," *Behavioral Science*, Vol. 6 (1961), pp. 308–311.
14. J. Ross Mackay, "The Interactance Hypothesis and Boundaries in Canada: A Preliminary Study," *The Canadian Geographer*, Vol. II (1958), pp. 1–8.

15. See, for example, the interesting applications to integration within metropolitan areas in J. V. Toscano, *op. cit.*, pp. 98–119, as well as illustrations from other chapters in this stimulating volume.
16. I. R. Savage and Karl Deutsch, "A Statistical Model of the Gross Analysis of Transaction Flows," *Econometrica*, Vol. 28 (1960), pp. 551–572.
17. Actually the expected percentage will be slightly higher than ten percent, since an area is not permitted in the model to have transactions with itself. The predicted percentage of A's transactions to be sent to B will therefore be equal to the number of transactions received at B divided by the total number of transactions within the system *minus* the amount received at A.

their actual state of origin. Hence the idea of origin-destination independence.

Interaction, therefore, is considered to be indifferent to all other influences within the system except the relative size or attractive power of its component parts.[18] The model does not identify the largest generators of transactions nor does it help in charting absolute flows. These, in fact are given. Instead, the model provides a statistical standard from which can be measured those flows which, for one reason or another, exceed what might normally be expected in a system with transactions reflecting only differences in size.[19]

In reality, of course, such forces as the friction of distance, political boundaries and cultural and economic influences affect very powerfully the patterns of communication flow. The model, however, by *not* initially incorporating these factors, provides a means for evaluating their relative impact within the system. It identifies those pairs of points or areas which are interacting at a higher than expected level and challenges the investigator to discover the relevant variables most closely associated with these deviations. A properly selected index of salience is thus susceptible to the techniques of regression analysis to assess quantitatively these spatial associations.

To illustrate its use, the transaction flow model was applied to telephone traffic between 24 exchange regions in East Africa in 1961 and 1965.[20] The computer program used was a modification of the Deutsch-Savage model in which the origin-destination assumption is applied to predict the expected flows only for those units which actually have exchanges.[21]

Federal institutional structures such as the former East African Common Services Organizations have existed for many years linking the three states of Kenya, Uganda, and Tanzania [22] and it was generally felt that the potentials for supra-national integration in East Africa were greater than those for any other cluster of African states. In the late 1950's and early 60's, Tanganyika and Kenya were in the forefront of the drive toward federation, and in 1960, the current President of Tanzania, Julius Nyerere, even stated his willingness to postpone Tanganyikan independence until Kenya and Uganda received theirs—on the condition that the three federate immediately. Nyerere apparently suspected that separate independence would foster national introversion and hinder the federal effort.

From 1961 to 1965, the three component territories of East Africa obtained their independence (Tanganyika in 1961, Uganda in 1962, and Kenya in 1963) and, as Nyerere had feared, the once bright prospects for their federation began to fade rapidly as each state turned increasingly toward problems of internal unity and nation building. During this period, Uganda appeared least in favor of federation and in the unsuccessful negotiations of 1963 was, as one author puts it, the "reluctant partner."[23] After these negotiations, however, Nyerere's Tanzania seemed

---

18. In some ways, the model describes a situation similar to the "steady-state" or "dynamic equilibrium" of open systems with an established pattern of hierarchical dominance.

19. For a more detailed discussion of transaction flow analysis, its terminology, major concepts, and applications within political science, see S. J. Brams, *Flow and Form in the International System*. Unpublished Ph.D. dissertation, Department of Political Science, Northwestern University (June, 1966); and, by the same author, "Transaction Flows in the International System," *The American Political Science Review*, Vol. 60 (1966), pp. 880–898.

20. The data were based on telephone trunk call censuses for East Africa which were made available to the author by the East African Posts and Telecommunications Administration, Nairobi. The 1961 census was recorded over a two-day period with a total recording time of nine hours, while the 1965 census involved a five-day period and thirty hours of recording time. In reference to the differences between the two censuses, see note 26.

21. This modification was suggested in L. A. Goodman, "Statistical Methods for the Preliminary Analysis of Transaction Flows," *Econometrica*, XXXI (1963), pp. 197–208. Goodman's modification was the basis for S. J. Brams, "A Generalized Computer Program for the Analysis of Transaction Flows," which was used in this study. A write-up and listing of the Brams program are available from the Vogelback Computing Center, Northwestern University. If nonexistent exchanges were not ignored in the present illustration, the smaller regions would be salient with nearly every other region to which they made more than the absolute minimum of calls.

22. Tanganyika and Zanzibar joined together in 1964 to form the United Republic of Tanzania. Although Zanzibar was not included in the telephone censuses, Tanzania rather than Tanganyika will be referred to in the text when the 1965 data are discussed.

23. J. S. Nye Jr., *Pan-Africanism and East African Integration* (Cambridge: Harvard University Press, 1965), p. 189.

236 *Edward W. Soja*

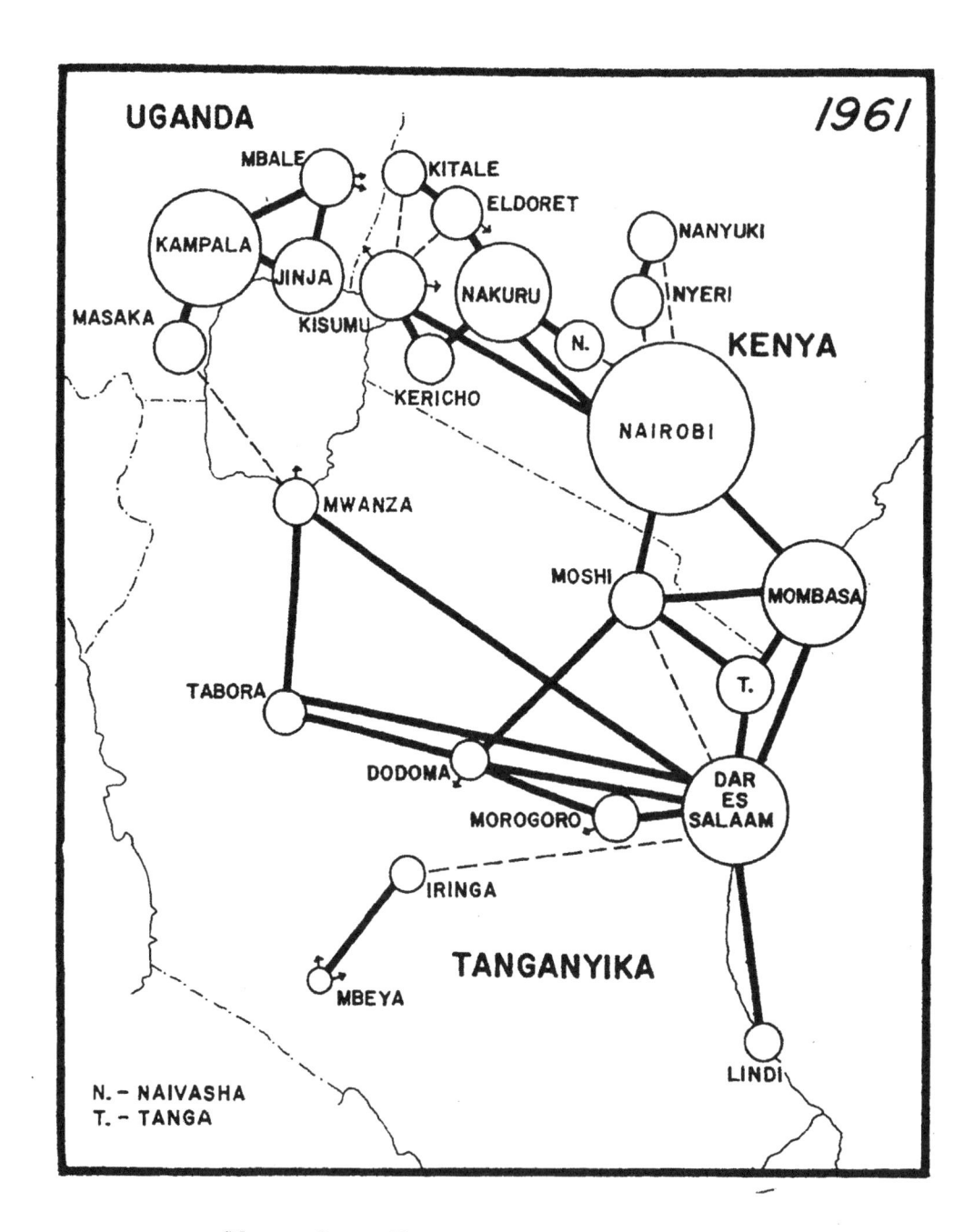

Map 19.1 Salient Transaction Flows in East Africa—1961
Solid lines = RA < .25 and D < 1 in both directions
Dashed lines = RA < 0 in both directions but > .25 at least one way
Arrows = RA < 0 in one direction only
Size of circles is in proportion to percentage of total trunk calls made between 24 exchange regions in East Africa.

to take the strongest steps toward nation building and weakening her contacts with her neighbors to the north. As a result, by the end of 1965, the issue of political federation had been pushed into the background.[24] It was expected that the critical events of this period would be reflected in the changing pattern of salient telecommunications linkages, thus providing a propitious testing-ground for transaction flow analysis.

The solid lines on Maps 19.1 and 19.2 represent the pattern of salience which existed in 1961 and 1965 respectively. The primary measure of salience used is the Relative Acceptance (*RA*) Index, equal to the actual number of transactions between two regions, minus that expected from the indifference model, divided by the expected value:

$$RA_{ij} = \frac{A_{ij} - E_{ij}}{E_{ij}}$$

A positive value for the *RA* Index was not automatically considered to indicate salience, but instead $RA = .25$ was arbitrarily selected as the critical threshold. Thus, for two regions to be salient, the flow of transactions *in both directions* must be at least 25 percent greater than expected from the model. Due to the arbitrariness of this threshold level, however, all positive *RA* values are shown on the maps, with dashed lines representing flows in which *RA* is greater than zero in both directions but less than .25 in at least one; positive flows in one direction only are indicated by arrows from the region of origin.

In addition, a minimum absolute deviation ($D_{ij} = A_{ij} - E_{ij}$), also set arbitrarily, was considered prerequisite to salience.[25] This absolute measure has been used in previous studies in the attempt to alleviate a sensitivity to above normal exchanges from small units which is inherent in the *RA* Index.[26] The *RA* Index alone would tend to "favor" very small regions in that a minor deviation from expected (e.g., $A_{ij} = 5$, $E_{ij} = 4$, $RA_{ij} = .25$) could produce a significant index. Thus, D_{ij} is used to achieve a balance by "favoring" larger regions.

As is evident, both indices have their built-in disadvantages and there is need for further refinement of the index of salience. But it should be stressed that any possible refinement must be made with full recognition of the conceptual connotations of salience within communications theory. In particular, this will require more extensive investigation of the comparative behavioral consequences of salience in large and small units.

It is difficult to draw many significant conclusions from an analysis of only one type of transaction flow, especially when it is not possible to evaluate the content of information

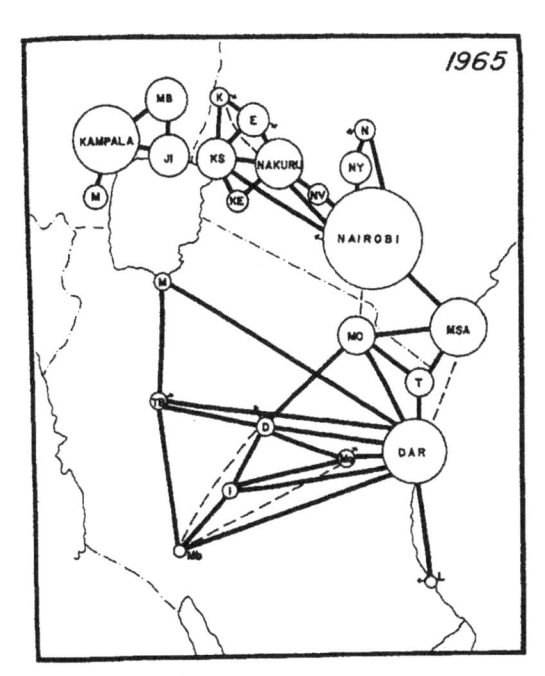

Map 19.2 SALIENT TRANSACTION FLOWS IN EAST AFRICA—1965
Symbols are the same as in Map 19.1. Size of circles is in proportion to percentage of total trunk calls made between 24 exchange regions in East Africa.

---

24. For a general geographical analysis of the potentials for integration in East Africa, see William A. Hance, "East Africa: A Study of Integration and Disintegration," Chap. 6 in Hance's *African Economic Development* (New York: Praeger, 1967). An excellent analysis of the political, economic, and historical background to this topic can be found in Nye, *ibid.*, and in Colin Leys and Peter Robson (eds.), *Federation in East Africa: Opportunities and Problems* (Nairobi: Oxford University Press, 1965).

25. The minimum *D* values in 1961 and 1965 were one and three respectively.
26. See the works of Brams, *op. cit.*

being transacted.[27] Several different patterns (trade, postal traffic, passenger movements, perhaps content analysis of newspapers or visits from government officials) and their interrelationship are more indicative of the realities of information flow through a communications network. Telecommunications offer only one window onto the larger picture.[28]

Furthermore, in a developing area such as East Africa, telephone calls are made almost entirely by a very small stratum of society and this restricts any attempt to extend interpretation beyond the economic and governmental elite. The confidence with which one can classify the flows as mutually rewarding or depriving is still another problem.

Nevertheless, telephone communications probably offers the best nexus within which to examine salience and its bearing on territorial integration in an area as large as East Africa. It is an extensive form of communications and consequently should provide more realistic patterns with respect to the assumptions of the indifference model than most other forms of information exchange. In addition, telephone traffic has been found elsewhere to be an excellent index of spatial interaction and social communications.[29] A more basic justification is that of all the types of detailed origin-destination data required for transaction flow analysis, at this scale, telephone traffic data is probably most easily available. All these reasons, however, do not eliminate the need to interpret the patterns revealed in the present illustration with appropriate caution.

Returning to the example at hand, an examination of Maps 19.1 and 19.2 clearly reveals that the most striking feature of salient transaction flows in East Africa is their marked degree of national clustering. Although distance and other variables are important, the impact of national boundaries seems to be the major factor causing divergence from the indifference model and producing the pattern of salient links.

The salient flows of the four Uganda regions, for example, form a network isolated from the rest of the East African system. No reciprocally significant links exist across its borders and moreover there appears to have been an increase in Ugandan isolation from 1961 to 1965. In the earlier year, there existed a reciprocally positive flow between Masaka and the Tanganyikan lake region around Mwanza, and positive one-way flows from Mwanza to Jinja; from Mbale to Kitale and Eldoret in Kenya; and from the Kenya lake region around Kisumu to Mbale. At this time, the seeds of an inter-state circulatory system in the Lake Victoria basin appeared to exist, with the potential perhaps to develop into a major centripetal force for an East African Federation.[30] In 1965, however, all these positive flows disappear and the Uganda network of positive linkages becomes totally isolated.

There is a similar national focus in Tanganyika (now Tanzania after the incorporation of Zanzibar in 1964) and Kenya, but several salient relationships did exist cross-nationally, the highest and most permanent of which—between Mombasa and Tanga—probably reflects the persistence of an important circulatory subsystem along the long-settled East African coast. But again, these cross-national flows are weakened significantly from 1961 to 1965, while the intra-

27. A difference in sample time for the 1961 (nine hours) and 1965 (thirty hours) censuses creates a potential source of distortion when comparing the two patterns of salience. Many regions had a larger number of partners in 1965 than in 1961 simply because of the longer time period sampled. This had the effect in some cases of reducing the expected flow predicted by the model for the 1961 partners, thus increasing the *RA* indices in 1965. This possible distortion was carefully considered when interpreting the changes in the salient flow pattern and no observations have been made which were not supported by trends identified in an analysis of the 1962 and 1963 censuses, which were also based on nine-hour samples but have not been included in this study.

28. An interesting review of the role of mass communications in the developing countries is given in Wilbur Schramm, *Mass Media and National Development* (Stanford: Stanford University Press, 1964).

29. For example, see Mackay, *op. cit.*; and J. D. Nystuen and M. F. Dacey, "A Graph Theory Interpretation of Nodal Regions," *Papers and Proceedings* of the Regional Science Association, Vol. 7 (1961), pp. 29–42. Telephone traffic has also been widely used in diffusion studies to estimate the local range of private communications. See T. Hägerstrand, "On Monte Carlo Simulation of Diffusion," in W. L. Garrison and D. F. Marble (eds.), *Quantitative Geography*, Part I: Economic and Cultural Topics (Evanston: Northwestern University Studies in Geography, Number 13, 1967), pp. 1–32.

30. An interesting discussion of the potential role of the Lake Victoria basin in the development of East Africa is found in T. J. D. Fair, "A Regional Approach to Economic Development in Kenya," *South African Geographical Journal*, Vol. 45 (1963), pp. 55–77.

national network becomes much more dense.

Two isolated cells which appeared in 1961, one north of Nairobi and the other in southwestern Tanganyika, establish salient links with their respective national networks in 1965. The new salience with Mbeya and Iringa is indicative of the greater attention being paid by the government of Tanzania in Dar es Salaam to its isolated and underdeveloped southwest and may be a precursor of more intimate relationships with neighboring Zambia.[31]

Another interesting intra-national change is the increase of salient links for the Kisumu region of Kenya. The new links are all with sections of the former White Highlands, most of which is now being turned over to African farmers in a large-scale resettlement program. This increase in salient mirrors the growing importance of the Kisumu region in independent Kenya.

The only salient international flows which remain in 1965 are between Mombasa and the Tanga and Moshi regions of Tanzania. But perhaps most revealing are the changes which occurred in the Moshi region itself, which includes the two important towns of Moshi and Arusha. While the average *RA* Index for Nairobi-Moshi dropped from .62 in 1961 to .26 in 1965, the figure for Moshi-Dar es Salaam increased dramatically from .26 to 1.42. A comparison of the Moshi-Mombasa and Moshi-Tanga links shows similar but much smaller changes, which in combination appear to signify a pronounced reorientation of this fertile and densely populated region on the slopes of Mt. Kilimanjaro, hitherto very closely tied to parts of Kenya, to the national communications grid of Tanzania.[32]

In late 1967, however, the town of Arusha —once considered as a site for the capital of an East African Federation—was selected as the administrative headquarters for the new East African Economic Community (E.A.E.C.) and a number of institutions for inter-territorial cooperation formerly housed in Nairobi, or, to a much lesser extent, Dar es Salaam and Kampala, are now being shifted to it. It will be most interesting to chart the changes in the communications pattern in East Africa that might be generated by these developments.

The patterns of salience represented in Maps 19.1 and 19.2 also appear to indicate that information flow in Tanzania is more heavily concentrated in its capital region than is true in Kenya. Dar es Salaam, for example, was salient to every other Tanzania region in 1965 and also had the largest number of salient linkages of any exchange region. Kenya, in contrast, had three major nodes of salience, Nairobi with six links and Kisumu and Nakuru with five. (The small number of exchange regions in Uganda makes a similar assessment much more difficult.)

It is tempting to interpret these patterns as reflecting the differences between Kenya and Tanzania with respect to their internal problems of national integration. Kenya, on the one hand, has been plagued by ethnic and regional rivalries both before and since independence, while Tanzania has faced far fewer problems of such a nature but has instead been more concerned with developing its much poorer system of transport and communication to avoid regional isolation.

But before extending this interpretation further, it should be noted that salience in the examples being examined is based on the sending and receiving totals of regions throughout East Africa. The pattern would be very different if the analysis were applied to only Kenya or Tanzania. Whereas the actual number of calls between Dar es Salaam and Dodoma, for example, may produce salience within the East African system, the same number may not do so when only inter-regional calls within Tanzania are being considered.[33]

To illustrate some of the modifications which occur when the East African system is

---

31. *The New York Times*, in its review of economic conditions in Africa (January 27, 1967), made the observation that Zambia was transformed in 1966 from the northernmost section of Southern Africa to the southernmost section of Eastern Africa! This referred particularly to the increased ties between Zambia and Tanzania created after the unilateral declaration of independence by Southern Rhodesia forced Zambia to seek new avenues for its imports and exports.

32. The Tanzanian government has fostered this reorientation in several ways. A toll, for example, was levied at the major border crossings, the two most important of which lead to Moshi and Arusha. In addition, the government has urged exporters based in the Moshi-Arusha region to use the Tanzanian port of Tanga rather than Mombasa, which is actually closer by rail.

33. This is because the relative attractive power of Dar es Salaam and Dodoma is much greater within the Tanzanian communications system than within that of all East Africa.

broken down into its component parts—essentially a reduction in the scale of examination—a separate analysis was run on the ten exchange regions of Tanzania and the ten for Kenya in 1965 (Maps 19.3 and 19.4). The most evident result is a large reduction in the number of salient flows due primarily to the reasons stated above. The role of distance becomes more important, with nearly all the regions in both Kenya and Tanzania being salient only with other nearby regions. These changes result in a marked reduction in the degree of focus on the two national capitals, both of which stand isolated from the remainder of their networks in terms of salient linkages.

Map 19.3 SALIENT TRANSACTION FLOWS IN KENYA—1965
Symbols are the same as in Map 19.1. Size of circles in proportion to percentage of total trunk calls made between ten exchange regions in Kenya.

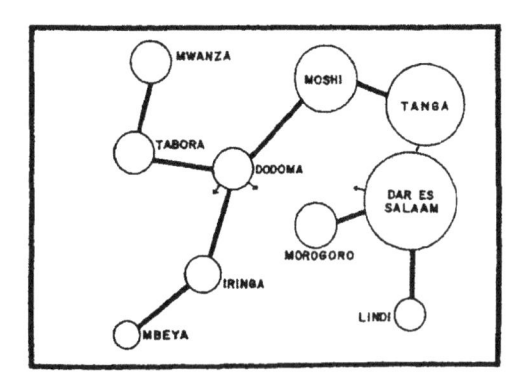

Map 19.4 SALIENT TRANSACTION FLOWS IN TANZANIA—1965
Symbols are the same as in Map 19.1. Size of circles in proportion to percentage of total trunk calls made between ten exchange regions in Tanzania (Zanzibar excluded).

Nairobi is now salient only with Mombasa, and Dar es Salaam only with Morogoro and Lindi. Except for the importance of Dodoma, the Tanzanian network of salience is rather simple and indicative of the relatively poor development of communications in the country and the absence of a dominant interregional focus. In Kenya, however, a distinct split into two subsystems is evident, one focusing on Nairobi and encompassing much of central Kenya and the coast, the other centered on Kisumu and Nakuru and showing signs of becoming very tightly interconnected.

In another work, the present author has discussed the potentially critical role of Nakuru in tying together the two major population clusters of Kenya (in the eastern highlands and the Lake Victoria basin) to prevent the growth of a disintegrative form of regionalism.[34] But in terms of the salient links existing in 1965, it appears that this has not been achieved and many of the events in Kenya since independence—particularly the emergence of a powerful opposition party with its primary support in the Kisumu area —reflect the problems of effectively integrating these two populous regions.

Summarizing briefly, transaction flow analysis of telephone calls in East Africa has shown that the primary factor shaping the patterns of salient relationship between regions was the existence of international boundaries which compartmentalize information flow within three distinct communications subsystems. This compartmentalization, moreover, appears to have increased from 1961 to 1965 paralleling the progressive introspection of the three newly independent states and dissipation of the potentials for effective political federation. If the behavioral implications of salience are accepted, one must conclude that interterritorial communications have not been sufficiently well-developed to support a tightly-knit East African Federation. In a behavioral sense, there are virtually no "East Africans," just Kenyans, Ugandans, and Tanzanians.

Most isolated within the framework of interterritorial communications has been

---

34. Edward W. Soja, *The Geography of Modernization in Kenya*, (Syracuse: Syracuse University Press, Geographical Research Series, No. 2, 1968), Chap. IX.

Uganda—the "reluctant partner." Despite the physical proximity of much of Uganda to parts of Tanzania and Kenya, its national boundaries have acted as formidable barriers to interaction. This barrier effect has prevented the growth of intensive interaction in the Lake Victoria basin, shared by all three states and located in or near the most densely populated and productive sections of East Africa. The success of the newly formed East African Economic Community will depend largely on its ability to stimulate increased transaction flow within this important focal area.

Closer relations exist between Tanzania and Kenya, particularly along the coast and between the coast and the interior regions of Moshi-Arusha and Nairobi. Although weakened between 1961 and 1965, this international network remains much stronger than that in the Lake Victoria region and will probably intensify further with the development of Arusha as headquarters for the EAEC.

Whereas the political subdivision of East Africa is the major factor structuring the patterns of salience at the international level, physical proximity becomes most important within the three states. This relationship was brought out most clearly in the separate transaction flow analyses for Tanzania and Kenya. These analyses, in addition, indicated that the networks of salience at the national level are not as dense as might be inferred from the East African maps. The Tanzanian network is almost at minimum connectivity, while that for Kenya is significantly split into two subnetworks reflecting internal ethnic and political divisions. These observations further emphasize the fact that the measurement and interpretation of salience is bound to the particular system under examination. Thus the associations between salience and the potentials for territorial integration at the East African level cannot be directly applied to the national situation.

In conclusion, therefore, the application of transaction flow analysis to telecommunications in East Africa, even on such a generalized and exploratory basis, has revealed a number of important patterns of interaction which are directly relevant to the study of territorial integration. The maps of salient relationships, for example, can be viewed as representing a set of behaviorally significant linkages within the communications system of East Africa, a subnetwork of intensive contacts indicative of the degree of mutual awareness existing between various sections of the larger region. As such, the measures of salience provide valuable estimates of the *behavioral distance* between subregions with respect to the potentials for territorial integration. In this study, only the most obvious factors affecting salience (i.e., political boundaries and physical proximity) have been mentioned, but the need has been recognized for more rigorous examination of these and other variables which influence the quantitative densities of transaction between areas.

There remain many additional problems and questions involving the use of transaction flow analysis in geography which have barely been touched upon here. For example, is the assumption of origin-destination independence a realistic one with respect to all forms of transaction flow? Should a measure of physical distance be incorporated into the method for predicting the expected flow between units? If so, how will this change the patterns of salience and how can these changes be interpreted? What does asymmetry—a "lopsided" flow between regions—indicate? Of what significance is a large number of salient links? An evenness of transaction flow (i.e., few if any very salient links)? How can the information content of transactions be evaluated and measured, particularly with respect to mutually-rewarding vs. mutually-depriving characteristics? Are reductions in the amount of deviation from the indifference model, as one author suggests, a sign of increasing integration?[35] What are the most revealing kinds of transactions to examine? Can measures of salience contribute more realistic frameworks for the use of diffusion models?

These questions point out the great need for further application and refinement of the technique, particularly in conjunction with studies of communications and behavior at the local level. It is hoped, however, that this

35. Brams, *Flow and Form in the International System*, p. 123. Divergence from the model involves the Percentage Discrepancy Statistic (P), which represents the percentage of transactions which would have to be moved from one cell to another to make the model fit the data perfectly. The P-values for East Africa were 43.8 in 1961 and 44.8 in 1965, a very small change but one towards weaker integration if one accepts the initial assumption.

study has not only suggested an interesting new tool, but has also opened up new avenues for research into the behavioral aspects of communications which can contribute to a more theoretical, quantitative, and spatial political geography.

20

Systems and the Disintegration of Empires

RICHARD L. MERRITT*

This paper, in a sense, represents an attempt to put some old wine into a new bottle. The old wine is that heady system of imperialism as it was known and practiced in the middle of the seventeenth century most immediately in the British version of imperialism. The new bottle is really a flask for fractionated distillation. By using the concepts and tools of systems analysis to re-examine mercantile imperialism, I hope to isolate some of its more important factors, and hence to add to our understanding of the more significant systems and processes in international politics [and political geography.]

THE SEVENTEENTH-CENTURY IMPERIAL SYSTEM

The environment of mercantile imperialism in the seventeenth century was the European state system. Europe in the 1650's, after the Peace of Westphalia, consisted of a number of more or less independent actors: absolute monarchies, monarchies with constitutional limitations, confederations, republics, principalities, and even duchies. The two actors

Reprinted by permission of the author and publisher from *General Systems*, Vol. VIII, 1963.
* Richard Merritt (1933–) is in the Department of Political Science at The University of Illinois, Urbana.

with claims to universal roles within the system—the Holy Roman Empire and the Catholic Church—had lost their effectiveness in more than half of the system. Only one non-European actor, the Ottoman Empire, played a role in the European state system. But even this actor was perceived as an outside threat to the system rather than as a full-fledged member, subject to the same rules of behavior and principles of treatment as were the European actors. The actual structure of the European state system need not concern us here. I might merely note that, although the system was in a state of flux, it tended toward what might loosely be termed a balance of power" instead of hegemony by a single actor. In large part it was system-dominant rather than subsystem-dominant.

As early as the fifteenth century a number of actors were going outside the European state system—trading, colonizing, exploiting —in efforts to enhance their position within the system. During the course of the next two centuries they created new systems, called "empires," with new actors and rules of conduct. In part the rules governing the behavior of actors within the European state system were transferred to the individual imperial systems. But, strictly speaking, each metropolitan country was able to determine its own relationship with its colonies, as well as the structure of its own imperial system. Hence these empires were subsystem-dominant rather than system-dominant.

If we analyze the individual imperial systems created by the European actors, we find a number of structural and behavioral regularities. Together these regularities—actors, variables governing the relationships of the actors, structures, and sources of instability—comprise the mercantile Imperial System.

The Actors in the Imperial System

The mercantile Imperial System comprises two subsystems—a Dominant Subsystem on the one hand and one or more Dependent Subsystems on the other. The Dominant Subsystem is the Metropolitan Country. We may consider the Metropolitan Country as a single actor, although clearly it, too, has subsystems. In the political field alone such subsystems include the chief executive officer of the government (for example, the monarch or the prime minister), a parliament or some other forum for the representation of the nobility and commoners, a cabinet or other advisory board, a board of trade or minister responsible for imperial matters, and enforcement and judicial officers. For the most part we shall ignore the subsystems of the Dominant Subsystem, concentrating upon the latter as a single actor in the Imperial System.

The Dependent Subsystems are the colonies founded or otherwise acquired by the Metropolitan Country. Geographically, the colonies may be contiguous to the Metropolitan Country (as the eastern provinces were to Germany in the twelfth century, or as the frontier settlements were to the American Republic in the nineteenth century) or—and this is the more likely possibility in the seventeenth century—they may be noncontiguous or overseas colonies. Like the Metropolitan Country, the Dependent Subsystems have their own social, political, economic, and other subsystems. Except in one important respect, however, we shall treat the Dependent Subsystems as single actors in the Imperial System. The exception to this general rule will be the occasional necessity to differentiate between two residential groups within the Dependent Subsystems: the colonists and the colonial administrators coming from the Metropolitan Country; and the indigenous or native population in the colonial territories.

The Variables Governing Relationships Among the Actors

The first variable to be considered is the direction of the flow of policy decisions among the actors. By the phrase "policy decisions" I mean control over the key values operative in the Imperial System: the distribution of power and income, the establishment of principles of legitimacy, the use of force, the allocation of scarce resources, the distribution of honors and other symbols of social status. In considering the relationship between two actors in the Imperial System, we shall essentially be asking the question: who influences whom, over what ranges of action, using what means, and with what effect?

The second variable is the direction of communication transaction flows among the actors. This variable includes patterns of attention and migration, a division of labor, the flow of trade, the flow of mail, and other means of interpersonal communication—in short, the entire set of facilities for and habits of communication. The important question here is the extent to which the individual actors in the Imperial System direct their attention to other actors within the System, as opposed to the extent to which they direct their attention to actors outside the System.

Third, what is the direction of loyalties and group identification within the Imperial System? In large part this is the question of a sense of community: is it System-wide, or does each actor have its own sense of community, not identifying psychologically with any other actor in the System? A sense of community comprises, first of all, an awareness—both by members of the group itself and by actors outside the group—that the group does in fact exist as a separate entity, distinct from other such groups, and that its members are in some ways interdependent. When a group awareness is present, members as well as outsiders will use specific collective terms in referring to the group. Second, there is an internalization of group interests: a recognition that certain events or processes are of common interest to the members of the group; a certain degree of probability that the members will be able to coordinate their behavior in a way that will promote their common interests (and even to coordinate their activities to extend beyond those of immediate necessity to the group); and the presence of certain structures or processes to perform certain functions in the group interest. What we are asking here is whether or not the Dependent Subsystems identify themselves, their interests, and their fates with those of the Dominant Subsystem. And, conversely, we want to find out whether the latter reciprocates this sense of community. In its use of collective symbols, for example, does the Metropolitan Country seek to differentiate itself from its colonies? Or does it seek to tighten the bonds of loyalty and community?

The Structure of the Imperial System (See Fig. 20.1)

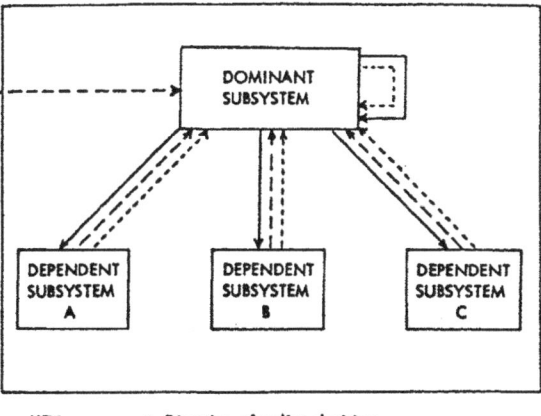

Fig. 20.1 THE MERCANTILE IMPERIAL SYSTEM

KEY: ⟶ Direction of policy decisions
— — → Direction of communication transactions and attention
······→ Direction of loyalties and identification

Since the Dominant Subsystem is in effect the creator of the Imperial System, that is, since it provided the impetus for the establishment of the Imperial System, the Dominant Subsystem determines what the Imperial System will be. The Metropolitan Country is primarily self-interested; its attention and communication patterns focus primarily upon itself, and little or no attention is paid to the Imperial System as a system. Nor does the Metropolitan Country pay much allegiance to or otherwise identify itself with the Imperial System. There is no perceived duty on the part of the Dominant Subsystem to maintain the stability of the Imperial System, except insofar as it is to the ultimate good of the Metropolitan Country to protect and foster its colonies.

The Relationship Between the Dominant Subsystem and the Dependent Subsystem

It is the goal of the Metropolitan Country to make its colonies totally dependent upon it for their social, psychological, political, and economic rewards as well as for their models of behavior and taste. At the same time, the Metropolitan Country attempts to use the colonies to enhance its own welfare (and, presumably, its own power position in the contemporary international system, that is, the European state system) without, however, becoming a prisoner of the colonies by being too dependent upon their resources or trade.

The primary means to make the Dependent Subsystems actually dependent upon the Dominant Subsystem come under the heading of "mercantilism." Among the more important mercantilist policies are: excluding foreign shipping from trade with the colonies; enumerating commodities which the colonies may obtain from or ship to the Metropolitan Country only; encouraging the colonies to produce commodities needed (whether for consumption, finishing, or re-export) by the Metropolitan Country; discouraging the colonies from producing commodities exported by the Metropolitan Country.

In such a relationship policy decisions flow from the Dominant Subsystem to the Dependent Subsystems. The latter must look to the Dominant Subsystem itself rather than appealing to some broader concept of imperialism in order to secure changes in the policies and attitudes of the Metropolitan Country. Although their communication patterns (and particularly trading patterns) bind the colonies individually to the Metropolitan Country, the reverse is not true. The Metropolitan Country not only has a larger number of opportunities to enter into communication and trade transactions with actors outside the Imperial System, but is likely to utilize these opportunities as a way of precluding too great a dependence upon the colonies. Finally, the colonies pay their primary allegiance to the Metropolitan Country, although it is by no means clear that the Metropolitan Country reciprocates this demonstration of affection and loyalty.

The Relationship Between a Dependent Subsystem and Another Dependent Subsystem

A mercantilist policy operates to keep the colonies isolated not only from the colonies of other metropolitan countries (as well as those countries themselves), but also from one another. It is, therefore, unlikely that there are any strictly intercolonial policy decisions to be made. Minimal intercolonial communication and trade ties force the individual colonies to look to the Metropolitan Country for their rewards and for models of behavior, fashions in clothing and table manners, linguistic conventions and styles of speaking, standards of excellence in literature and the arts, methods of agriculture and production, the art of government, and so forth. This being the case, colonial administrators and colonists alike are extremely apt to identify themselves psychologically with the Metropolitan Country, and to pay it their primary allegiance. Identification with and loyalty to the individual colony is only secondary.

Thus the relationship between the Dominant Subsystem and the Dependent Subsystems is *star-shaped*, that is, the lines of decision making, communication, and loyalty run between the Metropolitan Country and each individual colony, with very few lines running between the colonies themselves. In fact, the colonies may be mutually jealous, fearing that other colonies will receive preferential treatment from the Metropolitan Country.

Destabilizing Elements in the Imperial System

The star-shaped, subsystem-dominant Imperial System that I have just described pictures mercantile imperialism as being essentially in equilibrium with itself. In fact, however, several sources of instability are inherent in the Imperial System, producing what might be termed a dynamic rather than a static model of mercantile imperialism and, unless checked, may lead to the breakdown of the model.

One important dysfunctional element in the Imperial System lies in the opportunities available to the individual colonies to end their isolation by communication and trade with one another. Such opportunities are particularly visible when the colonies are contiguous or, at least, closer to one another than to the Metropolitan Country in an era when means of transportation and communication are slow and generally irregular. And it is not unreasonable to expect that, once the different Dependent Subsystems do communicate, they will find points of commonness in spite of their diversity, possibly even grievances against the Dominant Subsystem. Again, they might find that trade among themselves would serve their individual and joint interests better than trade patterns connecting them individually to the Metropolitan Country.

Similarly, in the absence of rigid controls by the Metropolitan Country over the activities of its colonies (especially in the area of commerce), the Dependent Subsystems may seek new relationships with actors outside the Imperial System. If the colonies are successful in their attempt to establish outside contacts, the effect is to give the colonies a measure of control over their own policy decisions. They may choose, for example, to trade with countries with whom their terms of trade are better rather than to send their produce dutifully to the Metropolitan Country. The cost of stopping such practices could place tremendous burdens upon the Dominant Subsystem. Efforts by the Metropolitan Country to place its colonies under more rigid controls would probably be met at the very least by resistance and evasion, and possibly even by rebellion.

The preoccupation of the Dominant Subsystem with its own affairs is another source of instability in the Imperial System. A lack of responsiveness to the needs and desires of the Dependent Subsystems, or a simple disinterest in their development, may lead to an unawareness of disaffection and the possibility of growing hostility. Such a policy of drift encourages the colonies to seek ties with one another and with actors outside the Imperial System. And, by the time that the Metropolitan Country does turn its attention to the colonies, it may already be too late to prevent the disintegration of the Imperial System as a whole. In overcompensating for its past self-preoccupation, the Dominant Subsystem may accomplish little more than to drive a wedge between itself and the Dependent Subsystems.

Turning to the colonists and the colonial administrators in the Dependent Subsystems, we find another possible source of instabilities. On the one hand, the mass of colonists often comprises the disaffected elements of the Metropolitan Country's population. If migration is entirely voluntary, the ranks of the colonists may be filled with communicants of persecuted minorities, politicians in disfavor, social and economic failures, criminals and revolutionaries escaping possible punishment. Then, too, there will be an abundance of fortune-seekers, spinners of dreams of glory that they hope to fulfill in a new world. If migration is not voluntary, the ships may well be filled with such social undesirables as debtors and convicted criminals. In neither case are the colonists likely to be bubbling with affection for the Metropolitan Country, imbued with the spirit of the Imperial System.

On the other hand, colonial administrators often contribute to the instability of the Imperial System. It is not uncommon for the Metropolitan Country to banish its unwanted or obstreperous politicians to the colonies, there to sulk or to build their own satrapies of power as they see fit. However shortsighted a policy it may be, retaining the best officials and politicians for service in the Metropolitan Country is understandable. But even worse for the stability of the Imperial System is the petty tyrant, the incompetent and bumbling member of the lesser nobility, perhaps, who sees the power and authority of a colonial governor as his chief goals in life. Instead of spending his time conspiring to regain his position in the political subsystem of the Metropolitan Country, thereby ignoring his administrative duties and subjecting the Imperial System to a policy of drift, he gratifies his own ego by the overexuberant and even despotic exercise of his authority, driving the colonists into a search for new patterns of communication and loyalty.

In focusing upon the colonists and colonial administrators as destabilizing elements, I do not mean to suggest that every one of them fits into the categories discussed in the previous paragraphs. Indeed, far from it, for most might well be loyal, conscientious, and dedicated to the service of the Metropolitan Country. What I am suggesting is that the Imperial System has an inherent bias in favor of instabilities of this sort. It would be the exceptional Metropolitan Country that would send its best citizens and administrators to the colonies. Such a conscious and alert policy was not prevalent in the seventeenth-century Imperial System.

Still another dysfunctional element is the relationship between the colonial administrators and the colonists on the one hand and the indigenous population of the colonies on the other. There are a number of approaches that the Dominant Subsystems (and, by implication, the colonial administrators and colonists) may take toward the native population: eliminating them; enslaving them; either outrightly or by forcing them to pay taxes with money that could be earned only by working as unskilled laborers for the colonial administrators; ignoring them or treating them as nuisances, meanwhile keeping them generally ignorant and uneducated in the ways of self-government; putting them on the path toward social mobilization and at least local self-government; treating them as equals with whom even inter-marriage is considered acceptable. But each of these approaches creates its own problems for the colonial and native populations of the colonies; and none contributes to the stability of the Imperial System over the long run.

THE COURSE OF EMPIRE

With such dysfunctional elements at work, it is not surprising that seventeenth-century imperialism—the state of reality most closely approximating the paradigm of the mercantile Imperial System that I have described—degenerated more or less rapidly into newer and generally more complex types of systems. It might be useful at this point to characterize briefly some of the ways in which these seventeenth-century empires changed.

Attempts to Maintain the Imperial System

In some cases metropolitan countries have sought to use every and any means at their disposal to prevent the disintegration of their own imperial systems. Such policies include: jealously-guarded dominance over the policy-making processes for the colonies; short tours of duty and rapid rotation for colonial administrators to prevent them from forming ties of community in the colonies; the encouragement of one-crop economies and other measures designed to make the colonies economically dependent upon the mother country; strict controls over internal migration in the colonies, particularly with respect to the indigenous population; conscriptive labor forces; the retention of low literacy and mobility rates for the native population, as well as a near-subsistence level of income; close supervision over the colonists migrating from the mother country.

Such an inflexible policy viewing imperial relationships as static rather than as dynamic, and holding that the stability of the relationships rests primarily upon the firm application of measures of control over the colonies, may be successful at certain times in some places. The history of Portuguese policies toward Angola and Mozambique provides the world with cases in point. But over the long run, I would suggest it is an attitude that seems most likely to produce the structural tensions that eventually break out into open rebellion and nights of the "long knife."

Shifts to System-Dominant Pluralism

It is possible that, as the Dependent Subsystems grow in population, levels of technology, and skills of government, they will become co-equal with the Dominant Subsystem in decision-making for the Imperial System as a whole. Carried to an extreme, as in the Commonwealth today, each of the actors within the Imperial System would have control over its own policy decisions, with none having the ability or right to impose its will upon the others. The communications net within the System would be more or less symmetrical, with each actor directing more of its attention to other actors within the Imperial System than to outside actors. With respect to trade and patterns of production, however, a symmetrical relationship need not predominate. Indeed, it might prove most advantageous to all if a system-wide division of labor were instituted. Whatever the structure of the relationship, the cardinal principle will be that each subsystem must benefit more by remaining a member of the Imperial System than it would if it dissociated itself from the System. As long as this were the case, each of the subsystems would place a high value on the maintenance of the System. In consequence, each actor would direct a fair share of its allegiance to the System, even though its primary loyalty might be self-directed. The formerly Dominant Subsystem might hold a position as *primus inter pares*, possibly even retaining the ties of affection previously linking it to the Dependent Subsystems, but it would no longer direct the decision-making processes of the Imperial System.

The Political Integration of the Imperial System

The structure of the Imperial System may degenerate from a dominance-dependence relationship among the actors to one amalgamating the actors upon the basis of equality into a single, integrated system (such as a federation or a confederation). In such a process we might anticipate that the political subsystem of the Metropolitan Country would undergo the least amount of structural change, and that the former colonies would adapt themselves to accommodate the structure of the Metropolitan Country. It is, of course, also possible that mutual structural changes will ensue. Or the value of a given colony may be so great—if, for example, large deposits of scarce resources are to be found in the colony —that the Metropolitan Country would be willing to pay a price in terms of structural changes or other concessions to entice the colony into a system-dominant union.

A number of conditions render it more or less difficult to form an amalgamated union between the Dominant Subsystem and one or more Dependent Subsystems. Political integration may be easier if the actors are contiguous to one another. Examples of such cases include twelfth-century Germany, which successfully absorbed the eastern provinces, and nineteenth-century America, which incorporated the newly-opened western territories into the Union as states. That the same process is conceivable for non-contiguous areas is demonstrated by the accession of Alaska and Hawaii to the American Union in 1959. Most imperial powers, however, have found it difficult if not completely impossible to integrate and assimilate their overseas colonies.

If there are sharp ethnic or racial differences between the native population of the colonies on the one hand and the population of the

Metropolitan Country on the other, the problems of assimilation might be quite complex. A successful effort on the part of the Metropolitan Country to inculcate a common group loyalty in the native population or, conversely, the success of the latter in infusing their own values into the societal system of the Metropolitan Country could facilitate the process of assimilation. Clearly, however, the assimilation of an ethnically- or racially-differentiated native population into that of the Dominant Subsystem depends upon the rate of social mobilization among the natives, and upon the efforts of the Metropolitan Country to accelerate the process of social mobilization.

The Disintegration of the Imperial System

A fourth type of structural degeneration is the outright disintegration of the System. This might result from any one of the three policies just mentioned, particularly if the policy were to be inflexibly or, perhaps, prematurely applied and implemented. But disintegration might also result from a policy of drift or any of the other dysfunctional elements in the System. It is even conceivable that the Dominant Subsystem is the actor most anxious to do away with the System. This might be the case if the Metropolitan Country valued the structural integrity and solvency of its own subsystems more highly than the maintenance of the System as a whole. President De Gaulle's ultimate disposition of the Algerian question seems to be an example of such an attitude.

Regardless of the cause, however, the disintegration of the Imperial System ends in the creation of new and separate systems. Each of the Dependent Subsystems may become a system in itself; a few of them may retain their ties of dependence to the Metropolitan Country; several of them may regroup themselves into a new system; others may align themselves with actors outside the Imperial System. The former colonies may establish friendly or hostile relations with the Metropolitan Country. They may retain their ties of trade and communication with the Metropolitan Country, or seek new markets for their produce and attention. In short, the aftermath of empire may be, and indeed has been, quite varied.

THE DISINTEGRATION OF EMPIRES: A CASE STUDY

I shall now examine in more detail a case study of the mercantile Imperial System—the relationship of the American colonies to Great Britain—and its disintegration into two separate and, for several decades at least, mutually antagonistic systems. The first question that must be answered is whether or not the realities of the seventeenth-century Anglo-American empire in fact match the most essential aspects of the paradigm that I have been discussing.

The Anglo-American Empire as an Imperial System

The seventeenth-century American colonies existed in a state of semi-isolation, separated from one another in many cases by stretches of uninhabited wilderness and more generally by inadequate means of intercolonial transportation and communication. Contacts with the mother country were often easier to maintain, and perhaps more fruitful, than those with neighboring colonies. To the extent that there was any coordinating among separate colonial administrations, it was the result, not of the colonists' cooperation, but of the efforts of His Majesty's Government in England. Even as late as the middle of the eighteenth century the colonists were unable to organize an effective intercolonial defense against marauding Indians on the western frontiers; and some voices expressed fears of armed conflict among certain colonies.

In the area of policy decisions, the seventeenth-century colonies underwent several changes. "All but a very few of the English colonies in America were begun as private enterprises. Some were started as joint-stock trading companies, others by feudal proprietors, and still others by groups of private individuals unauthorized by the king." Although decision making was diffused during their early years, "gradually private ownership gave way to royal control; charters were surrendered or annulled; unsanctioned settlements were absorbed by their duly constituted neighbors. Finally only a handful of colonies lay outside the direct administration of the crown."[1] The colonies generally retained control over

1. Leonard W. Labaree, *Royal Government in America: A Study of the British Colonial System Before 1783* (New Haven: Yale University Press, 1930), p. ix.

purely local matters, but the political subsystem of the mother country determined the most important policies distributing power and income, allocating resources, directing the use of force, establishing principles of legitimacy, distributing honors and other symbols of social status. The flow of decisions went from the mother country to the colonies, and not the other way around.

The nature of the communication ties between Great Britain and the colonies cannot be so sharply delineated. One reason for this is the unavailability of certain types of information, particularly quantitative political, social, and economic data. We do know some basic facts, however, from which we can extrapolate the patterns of communication transactions between Great Britain and her colonies in America.

In the first place, a very high percentage of the colonists were of English extraction. In 1790 about 61 per cent of the more than three million white Americans had family names that could be identified as English (and another 18 per cent had Scotch or Irish family names). If we accept these population estimates as accurate, and remember that European political struggles and shortages of food during the middle of the eighteenth century drove significant numbers of Scots, Irish, and Palatine Germans to American shores, then we might well assume that the colonial population of the previous century (estimated at 50,000 in 1650 and at 251,000 fifty years later[2]) was even more homogeneous and more predominantly English in origin.

English life and manners provided the colonists with a model of social behavior that they then sought to adapt to their existence in the wilderness. With their common English (or at least British) heritage, the seventeenth-century colonists looked to the Mother Country for their fashions and standards of excellence, their customs and language, their methods of agriculture, production, and local self-government. Wealthier colonial families sent their children to England to be schooled; and study at an English university was widely considered a *sine qua non* for would-be lawyers and medical practitioners, as well as for many men of the church. London—and not Boston or Philadelphia, New York or Williamsburg —was the bright star in the colonists' firmament. It was England that the American colonist wanted to visit once more before he died. So great was this sense of attachment in some instances that writers in South Carolina occasionally referred to England as home even in the early 1760s.[3]

Available data on the trade patterns of the seventeenth-century American colonies suggest a picture consistent with classic mercantile doctrine in its main lines if not in all of its details. Margaret Shove Morriss tells us, for example, that during the years from 1689 to 1701, an estimated 75 ships per year passed between England and Maryland (with about half of them going to or coming from London), that "the trade to foreign countries, on the whole, was extremely small," and that about 25 ships engaged in the intercolonial trade stopped at Maryland's ports each year.[4] And, regarding the last four decades of the seventeenth century, Bernard Bailyn writes that "the heart of New England's commerce was mercantilistically sound." Bailyn adds that, by the middle of the 1670s, the New England merchants recognized that their "economic activities were now at the mercy of diplomatic decisions made by European statesmen motivated by considerations utterly unrelated to New England or its merchants."[5] This is not to say that the mercantile relationship of the colonies to the mother country during this era was strictly regulated; for, due among other things to England's involvement in European wars, the mother country had neither the time nor the material resources needed to control every aspect of the colonist's trade. But, in the main, the imperial relationship suggested previously (Fig. 20.1) was ascendent in the seventeenth century.

Drift, Dynamic Ecology, and Shifting Colonial Perceptions

Lest it seem that the imperial relationship between Great Britain and the American

---

2. U.S. Bureau of the Census, *Historical Statistics of the United States, Colonial Times to 1957* (Washington, D.C.: U.S. Government Printing Office, 1960), Series Z 1–19, p. 756.

3. See *The South-Carolina Gazette*, 31 October 1761.

4. *Colonial Trade of Maryland, 1689–1715* (Baltimore: The Johns Hopkins Press, 1914), pp. 86–87, 108–109, 110–113. The last set of figures has been revised to exclude ships listed as sailing only between Maryland and England or the West Indies.

5. *The New England Merchants in the Seventeenth Century* (Cambridge, Massachusetts: Harvard University Press, 1955), pp. 127–128.

colonies was approaching a steady state of equilibrium by the beginning of the 1700s, several sources of instability must be noted.

The first of these was an English policy toward the colonies that can only be described as "drifting." By 1680 His Majesty's Government in London had decided upon its principles and policies of colonial rule, as well as upon the means of implementation and administration. In brief, the principle was government by instruction, with the colonial governor solely responsible for carrying out the instructions sent to him by the Board of Trade. There is much to commend such a relationship, perhaps, but it was also conducive to practicing an eighteenth-century version of the "law of least effort." After observing that "the commissions and instructions to the governors underwent no fundamental change" during the hundred years after 1680, Leonard W. Labaree points out that "at bottom the system was fixed, static, and unchanging, an expression of what the Board of Trade loved to call 'the true principles of a provincial constitution.' "[6] Such "true principles" did not, however, take into account changes in the colonies and the imperial relationship, and the changing needs, perceptions, and demands of the colonists.

Thus, with what they thought was a resolution of the colonial issue, the British went back to their own political problems and court intrigues, and to the complications of the power struggle in the European state system. As long as the colonial relationship continued to function adequately, they saw no need to concern themselves overmuch with colonial affairs; and they were loath, given the dearth of able administrators in the British Isles, to send good men out to the provinces.

While the Royal Government was following a policy of drift, the colonists were developing ways of life and patterns of self-government that began to vary widely from the English model. One such pattern was the increasing power of the colonial assemblies, stemming from their right to initiate legislation and their control of the purse. Although the Board of Trade sent fairly uniform instructions to the colonial governors, it left them to find their own means of implementing the instructions. Thus each governor had to fight his own battle with the assembly in his colony. He had to convince the legislators, first of all, that certain measures proposed by the Crown were necessary and, second, that the assembly should appropriate the requisite monies. As Morison and Commager have written:

Colonial politics are largely the story of struggles between the assemblies and the royal or proprietary governors. In such a conflict between colonists with a lively sense of their rights and interests, and the representatives of a central government with not so keen a sense of imperial needs or English interests, and which did not wish to be bothered, the colonists generally won. The system worked well enough, for the British Government by veto or disallowance was able to prevent things, such as abuse of paper money, that it did not like; but it was unable to get positive things done, such as full cooperation in time of war.[7]

The net result of these processes was the increasing power of the colonial assemblies to make policy decisions over an ever wider range of activities, and hence a diffusion of the decision-making function in the Imperial System.

Meanwhile the ecology of the colonists' perceptions of themselves, the mother country, and the Anglo-American empire as a whole—that is, the relationship of the perceptions to the environment in which they occurred—was undergoing gradual but vital changes. On the one hand, Great Britain was assuming a less important role in the lives of the colonists while, on the other, the number and scope of intercolonial communication transactions of all sorts were growing.

Illustrative of these developments is the shift in colonial trading patterns. The number of ships plying between the ports of New York, Philadelphia, Hampton, and Charleston in America and harbors in the British Isles doubled from 1734 to 1772 (increasing in number from 264 to 556); but the number of ships engaged in the coasting trade quadrupled (from 402 to 1750) during the same period. Comparable figures for the Port of Boston are even more dramatic: the number of ships sailing from Boston to the mother country rose from an average of 48 per year in the 1714–1717 period to 59 per year in the four years from 1769 to 1772 (an increase of

---

6. Labaree, *Royal Government in America, op. cit.*, pp. 422, 426–427.

7. Samuel Eliot Morison and Henry Steele Commager, *The Growth of the American Republic*, fourth edition (New York: Oxford University Press, 1950), vol. I, p. 116.

23 per cent): the number of coastal vessels jumped from 117 to 451 (an increase of 286 per cent!). In terms of the total annual tonnage shipped from Boston, 19 per cent (3,985 tons) went to Great Britain or Ireland in 1714–1717, while 16 per cent (6,171 tons) of the yearly tonnage did so in 1769–1772. The share of the total tonnage shipped each year from Boston to other colonial ports rose from 17 per cent (3,583 tons) in 1714–1717 to 43 per cent (16,766 tons) in 1769–1772.[8] In short, while the shipping facilities of the colonies expanded generally during the course of the eighteenth century, intercolonial trade grew at a much more rapid rate than did trade with the mother country.

Other indicators of colonial communication patterns during the first six decades of the eighteenth century point to a similar increase in intercolonial communication.[9] The expanding American population began to fill the gaps separating the urban clusters scattered along the Atlantic seaboard, establishing a fairly continuous line of settlement from Penobscot Bay in the north to Savannah in the south. And with the expansion of the population came the construction of postroads, ferries, and other means to facilitate intercolonial travel and communication. Intercolonial mobility, in turn, made increasingly possible the exchange of ideas among the colonists: religious organizations and movements (such as the "Great Awakening") spread throughout America; the newspapers increased in number, size, and scope of coverage, drawing to an ever greater extent upon intercolonial news sources; colonial printers, such as Benjamin Franklin, and other colonial merchants normally had extensive familial and business connections in several colonies; while lawyers, doctors, and men of science often traveled to or corresponded with their colleagues in other parts of America.

There were, to be sure, factors working against increased intercolonial cooperation and communication. Diverse and often unstable colonial currencies, as well as the virtual absence of intercolonial credit facilities, hampered trade and commercial relations. Conflicting territorial claims led to harsh words and occasionally even bloodshed. Religious factionalism and regional jealousies sowed the seeds of mutual antagonism. In spite of the importance of these divisive factors, however, they did not prevent the triumph of mutual interests among the colonists over their mutual hostilities when the time of decision arrived.

Significant shifts in the colonists' focus of attention and patterns of self-perception accompanied the political drift and changing ecology of the eighteenth century. Data derived from a quantitative analysis of place-name symbols (such as "London," "Williamsburg," or "Italy") appearing in the colonial press from 1735 to 1775 suggest several interesting trends.[10]

While maintaining a fairly constant interest in the mother country, the colonists shifted their attention from European wars and other events outside the Anglo-American empire toward an interest in American news. Although symbols of place names located in the British Isles generally occupied about one-fifth of the newspapers' symbol space throughout the entire 41 years, their share declined sharply relative to the space given over to American symbols. From 1735 to 1762 about one in seven symbols referred to place names in the American colonies: during the next thirteen years almost one in three symbols did so. The years 1774 and 1775 found the colonial printers devoting more than half their symbol space to news of America.

A more detailed analysis of American symbols in the colonial press[11] suggests a second

---

8. Computed from data given in U.S. Bureau of the Census, *Historical Statistics of the United States, op. cit.*, Series Z 56–75, pp. 759–760. The earlier figure for the port of Hampton is 1733 rather than 1734.

9. For a more complete discussion of eighteenth century communication patterns in the colonies, see Richard L. Merritt, "Nation-Building in America: The Colonial Years," in Karl W. Deutsch and William J. Foltz, editors, *Nation-Building* (New York: Atherton Press, 1963).

10. The entire contents of four issues per year of the *Massachusetts Gazette* (from 1735 to 1775), the *Boston Gazette and Country Journal* (from 1762 to 1775), the *New York Weekly Journal* (from 1735 to 1751), the *New York Mercury* (from 1752 to 1775), the *Pennsylvania Gazette* (from 1735 to 1775), and the *Virginia Gazette* (from 1736 to 1775) were systematically analyzed. For further details, see Richard L. Merritt, *Symbols of American Community, 1735–1775*.

11. In tabulating the distribution of American symbols only, both direct place-name symbols ("Virginia" or "Boston") as well as indirect references to such place names ("this colony" or "this city") were included. In the comparison of the total number of American place-name symbols with the number of British place-name symbols in the previous paragraph, such indirect symbols were not tabulated.

trend: a shift away from purely local interests to an awareness of events affecting the colonies as a whole, with attention paid by the newspapers to symbols of colonies other than their own remaining essentially unchanged over the long run. News of the home colony was important throughout the 41 years from 1735 to 1775. It declined in importance, however, relative to intercolonial news. The salience of a collective concept in the colonial press, that is, the use of symbols referring to all of the American colonies as a single unit, was low until 1763. After that date such collective symbols comprised about one-quarter of the total number of American symbols in the newspapers.

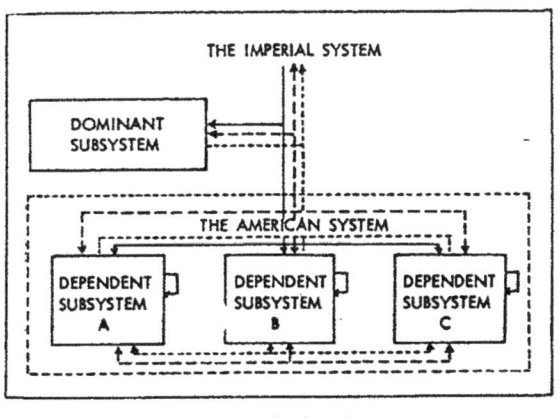

The Imperial System in Transition

Fig. 20.2 THE IMPERIAL SYSTEM IN TRANSITION

A changing perception of America's place in the Anglo-American empire—a change that had actually begun to develop in the late 1750s—assumed dramatic proportions in the early 1760s. I have already noted the increased emphasis in the press upon place-name symbols identifying all of the colonies as a single unit during these years. The question that we want to examine now is, what was the content of these symbols? In answering this question I shall consider only symbols in articles with American datelines and, for the sake of convenience, I shall divide the collective symbols into three groups: first, those specifically identifying the colonies as British or royal domain; second, symbols (such as "the colonies" or "the provinces") that emphasize the imperial relationship and omit any specific mention of the mother country; and, finally, those that implicitly or explicitly identify the area as American, separate from any British community.

By looking at the symbols linking the colonies to the empire as a ratio of symbols identifying the area as British, an interesting and, I believe, significant finding emerges. For every ten British-oriented symbols appearing in the press during the two decades from 1735 to 1754, there were nine empire-oriented symbols. This ratio almost reversed itself during the next five years. The number of empire-oriented symbols appearing for every ten British-oriented symbols during the remaining colonial years were: fifteen from 1755 to 1759; thirty-four from 1760 to 1764; forty-six from 1765 to 1769; and sixty-three from 1770 to 1775. Thus, over a twenty-year period, the ratio of empire-oriented to British-oriented symbols multiplied sevenfold. In effect, through their use of self-referent symbols, the colonists (or at least their newspapers) were substituting an allegiance to the Imperial System for their former ties of loyalty to the Dominant Subsystem, that is, Great Britain.

Such a finding accords well with what we already know about the changing political philosophy in the colonies during the 1760s. The colonists had begun to emphasize the heritage and rights that were common to both Englishmen in the British Isles and Englishmen in the American colonies; and they had begun to express their resentment toward perceived infringements of those "common" rights. The response to the Sugar Act of 1764 and the Stamp Act of 1765 are cases in point. As early as 1764 James Otis of Massachusetts referred to Harrington's assertion that "*Empire* follows the balance of property," and argued:

The Colonists being men, have a right to be considered as equally entitled to all the rights of nature with the Europeans [that is, the English], and they are not to be restrained in the exercise of any of these rights, but for the evident good of the *whole community*. . . .[12]

12. Cited in Samuel Eliot Morison, editor, *Sources and Documents Illustrating the American Revolution, 1764–1788, and the Formation of the Federal Constitution,* second edition (Oxford: Clarendon Press, 1929), pp. 4–5. Emphasis added.

There is more than just a statement of natural law in Otis' remarks. There is the implication that the "whole community" of the empire is somehow superior to the English in the mother country as well as to the colonists in America.

Within the next decade the idea of an Imperial System superior to its subsystem became common coin in the arguments of colonists. In 1774 James Wilson of Pennsylvania wrote of the doctrine of imperial equality that "the Commons of Great Britain have no dominion over their equals and fellow-subjects in America; they can confer no right to their delegates to bind those equals and fellow-subjects by laws." Was Wilson arguing in favor of the outright independence of America? To the contrary, he wrote of the Americans that "They are the subjects of the King of Great Britain. They own him allegiance." Of the "strict connection between the inhabitants of Great Britain and those of America," he wrote:

... They are fellow-subjects; they are under allegiance to the same prince; and this union of allegiance naturally produces a union of hearts. It is also productive of a union of measures through the whole British dominions. To the King is intrusted the direction and management of the great machine of government.... He has a negative on the different legislatures throughout his dominions, so that he can prevent any repugnancy in their different laws.[13]

The king, then, is representative of the Imperial System as a whole; and, while Parliament is the chief legislator for Great Britain, it is no more than the co-equal of the colonial assemblies within the Imperial System.

Concurrent with this changed attitude toward the structure of the Imperial System was an emerging group loyalty among the colonists themselves. We have already seen signs of this in their changing attention patterns. Throughout the 1760s and early 1770s the colonists found it increasingly possible to work together—in the Stamp Act Congress of 1765, in the committees of correspondence, and eventually in the Continental Congress—as well as to think of themselves as a community of fate. John Dickinson of Pennsylvania wrote in 1768, for example, that "every man amongst us who in any manner would encourage either dissension, diffidence, or indifference between these colonies is an enemy to himself and to his country."[14] And, by July of 1775, the delegates to the Continental Congress could assert: "our union is perfect."[15]

By the middle of the 1760s, then, the colonists have evolved a perception of the Imperial System differing considerably from that of the seventeenth-century mercantilist. The changing context of colonial society was in part responsible for the newer perceptions. First of all, the colonies were no longer isolated from one another, almost solely dependent upon the mother country for their sources of rewards and models of behavior. Decision-making for the system as a whole was diffused, with the colonial assemblies enjoying an ever greater measure of freedom to determine their own policies, and with mounting opposition to attempts by Parliament to legislate for the colonies. Second, the lines of communication were stronger among the colonies themselves than between the colonies and the mother country. Third—and this is perhaps the crucial point—the colonists were dividing their loyalties. To an increasing extent, on the one hand, they were redirecting their ties of allegiance, away from the Dominant Subsystem, that is, Great Britain, and toward the Imperial System itself. There was, to be sure, a continued recognition of the superior role of Great Britain in the Imperial System, but the relationship that the colonists perceived was one of *primus inter pares*, and not one of dominance and submission. On the other hand, however, there was growing group loyalty among the colonists themselves, pointing the way to identification with an exclusively American System.

In brief, the 1760s found the colonists consciously or unconsciously pushing the Imperial System toward degeneration into what I earlier termed "system-dominant pluralism," with the British monarch as the titular head of the system. If the British government had perceived the Anglo-American empire in the same light as did the colonists, the result might have been the emergence of a British Commonwealth in the eighteenth century. But the British did not concur in the Americans' perception of a

---

13. Cited in Morison, *Sources and Documents, op. cit.*, pp. 111, 114, 115.

14. *Ibid.*, p. 53.
15. *Ibid.*, p. 144.

dynamic Imperial System. It was the clash between the British perception of static imperialism and the American perception of dynamic imperialism that was to lead to the eventual breakdown of the Anglo-American empire.

Thus the Anglo-American Empire of the 1760s was in transition. A century before it had closely approximated the paradigm of the mercantile Imperial System. What it would become rested upon the attitudes and actions of both the British and the Americans.

The End of Empire: The Clash of the 1770s

As it turned out, the British persisted in maintaining their image of the mercantile Imperial System during the ensuing years. Overreacting, perhaps, to long decades of drift, Britain set about to bring its colonial relationships in order. The Townshend Acts of 1767 reorganized the customs service in the colonies, providing for more effective enforcement of existing regulations, and instituting new duties on colonial imports from Britain. The duties themselves were to be used for paying the salaries of the colonial governors, thereby relieving them from their dependence upon the assemblies. Instructions to colonial customs officers in 1769 revamped the existing trade regulations and sought to close some of the loopholes that had proved so advantageous to colonial merchants. The British response to the "Boston tea party" of 1773 was a policy of toughness: the Port of Boston was closed; extensive changes in Massachusetts' form of government were ordered; provision was made for transporting criminals to England for trial. But the policy of toughness backfired. Although it conceivably could have some effect in maintaining the system during an earlier era, it merely succeeded in pushing the colonists to greater extremes in the 1770s.

Nor were the Americans ready to retreat from their minimum demands for dynamic imperialism. Expressions of the idea of Anglo-American co-equality in decision making under the aegis of the Crown appeared regularly throughout the early 1770s. In what might be termed the last major colonial effort to save the Anglo-American empire from disintegration, Joseph Galloway of Pennsylvania sought to reconcile the differing British and American perceptions by institutionalizing the American idea of empire within the British framework. In September of 1774 Galloway boldly suggested to the delegates of the first Continental Congress "That a British and American Legislature, for regulating the administration of the general affairs of America, be proposed and established in America, including all the . . . colonies; within and under which government, each colony shall retain its present constitution and powers of regulating and governing its own internal police in all cases whatsoever."[16] But his efforts went for naught. By a majority of one vote the colonies rejected Galloway's plan of union, and in its place they drafted a series of far-reaching resolutions petitioning King George III and the English population to listen to the light of colonial reason and calling upon the colonists to refrain from trading with the mother country should the so-called "coercive acts" not be repealed.

By the end of 1774 the idea of complete independence from Great Britain seems to have taken hold of the colonists' thoughts. Anglo-American co-equality under an imperial monarch was no longer an acceptable solution for the Americans who wanted even greater freedom of action in policy making.

It is possible, I would suggest, to trace the trend toward thoughts of independence by looking at the colonists' changing perceptions of their country and themselves. The first of these changes, as indicated by the use of self-referent symbols in the colonial press, was a growing tendency to distinguish the American colonies from both Britain and the empire. For every ten British- or empire-oriented symbols appearing in American-datelined items during the twenty-five years from 1735 to 1759, less than six identified the colonies as "American." This ratio shifted sharply, however, after 1760. During the last sixteen years of the colonial era, sixteen symbols identifying the colonies as American were printed in the newspapers' columns for every ten symbols identifying them as part of Britain or the empire.

It is interesting to note that this wave of what might be called increasing American separatism followed closely upon an earlier wave that sought to dissociate the colonies

---

16. *Journals of the Continental Congress* (Ford edition), vol. I, pp. 49–51; cited in Morison, *Sources and Documents, op. cit.*, p. 117.

from Great Britain while associating them with the empire. In the usage of symbols at least, the transition from empire to independence took place in three steps: from alignment with the Dominant Subsystem to identification with the Imperial System itself to, finally, dissociation from both the Dominant Subsystem and the system. Let me again stress the fact that these transitional steps took place in a context of increasing emphasis upon terms symbolically uniting all of the American colonies into a single political unit.

The second major change in the colonists' perceptions during the late 1760s and early 1770s pertained to their views of themselves. Before 1763 the use of symbols identifying all of the colonists as a single group was rare indeed: they comprised about seven-tenths of one per cent of the total number of symbols referring to American place names. Moreover, the newspapers were virtually unanimous in associating the colonial population with Britain.

The turning point came in 1763. From that year until 1769 the average issue of a newspaper contained eight times as many symbols collectively identifying the colonists as did the average issue from 1735 to 1762; and the use of such symbols increased by another 50 per cent during the six years from 1770 to 1775.

Once the collective concept had become salient, however, the colonists were quick to use self-referent symbols differentiating themselves entirely from their brethren in the mother country. Collective symbols referring to the population did not follow the pattern previously set by collective symbols referring to the territory—shifting from British-oriented symbols to empire-oriented symbols and finally to symbols of American separation. The middle stage in this transitional process never materialized. Rather, the transition from perceptions of the colonists as British to perceptions of them as Americans took place in one step. For every ten British- and empire-oriented symbols appearing in the press from 1763 to 1769, there were four American-oriented symbols; and from 1770 to 1775 there were eleven American-oriented symbols.

What I am suggesting is that the recognition of American nationality came as a step-level function for the colonists. The years immediately after the conclusion of the French and Indian War saw the rapid acceleration of a number of processes under way in colonial America since the turn of the eighteenth century: a drifting British imperial policy broken by sporadic attempts to recapture Britain's position of dominance in the Anglo-American empire; colonial efforts to widen the decision-making powers of their assemblies; increasing intercolonial trade and communication transactions of all sorts, in a context of fairly constant or even diminishing contacts with the mother country; the development of an interest in American events as well as a growing perception of the colonies as a single unit. The 1760s were years of transition, years in which people who called themselves "British-Americans" or "colonists" sought to reconcile their own desire for a greater measure of freedom with a sense of loyalty demanding the maintenance of the Anglo-American empire. At this stage, substantial British concessions in the area of policy making might even have prevented or postponed the disintegration of this empire.

By about 1770, however, the inhabitants of the thirteen colonies no longer considered themselves to be "British-Americans" or even "colonists." They were Americans, living on American—not British or imperial—soil. They were no longer trying to reconcile two differing perceptions of the Imperial System so much as they were becoming aware of their basic opposition to that Imperial System.

The path that the Anglo-American empire followed during the 1770s is familiar to us all: the increasingly hostile postures of both the British and the Americans; the feverish activity of colonial patriots; the efforts of the British government to restore the dominance-submission relationship envisioned in the ideal Imperial System; the outbreak of fighting at Lexington and Concord; and, ultimately, the Declaration of Independence.

By 1776 the Anglo-American empire had disintegrated into two independent systems (see Fig. 20.3). Great Britain and the United Colonies had separate decision-making processes; trade and other communication transactions between the two countries had all but ceased; and the ties of loyalty and identification were self-contained in each system. Within the American System a confederal political structure was created—a structure with decentralized decision-making in some important areas, but nonetheless adequate enough to conduct and win the War of Independence.

It is particularly interesting that the colonies, having declared their independence from the Anglo-American empire, were willing to unite in an American political community. In large part, I would suggest, this willingness stemmed from a strong sense of community or group loyalty—a group loyalty resting upon decades of mutually beneficial transactions of all sorts as well as the development of mutually compatible perceptions and attitudes. It is

```
┌─────────────────────────────────┐
│          SYSTEM₁                │
│     THE BRITISH SYSTEM          │
└─────────────────────────────────┘
                ↑
                ↓
┌─────────────────────────────────┐
│          SYSTEM₂                │
│      THE AMERICAN SYSTEM        │
│  ┌────────┐ ┌────────┐ ┌────────┐│
│  │SUBSYSTEM│ │SUBSYSTEM│ │SUBSYSTEM││
│  │OR COLONY│ │OR COLONY│ │OR COLONY││
│  │    A    │ │    B    │ │    C    ││
│  └────────┘ └────────┘ └────────┘│
└─────────────────────────────────┘
```

KEY: ———→ Direction of policy decisions
— — — → Direction of communication transactions and attention
·········→ Direction of loyalties and identification

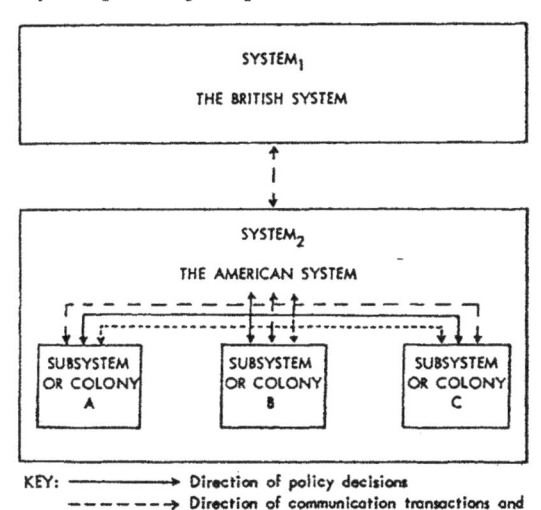

Fig. 20.3 THE AFTERMATH OF IMPERIAL DISINTEGRATION

of course true that the events of the 1760s and the 1770s played a role in making the colonists conscious of their mutual interests and problems. But it is also true that rapidly expanding facilities for and habits of intercolonial communication paved the way for a situation in which the colonists could perceive and react to these events in a mutually compatible manner. On top of this interplay of communication transactions and external developments was built a superstructure of formal governmental structures and processes that, in their own turn, contributed to the emerging sense of American nationality.

SYSTEMS AND EMPIRES

The chief value of a paradigm for students of international politics and political geography lies in its explanatory power, in its helpfulness in trying to understand the structure or process that it seeks to picture. Such an "understanding" may take place on several levels of analysis. We might, for example, merely be interested in finding a paradigm of some system (mercantile imperialism, perhaps, or the twentieth-century international system) that will give us an intuitively sound notion of its operation during a given period of history or under certain conditions. If this paradigm will help us to understand or at least to analyze specific examples of such systems in practice, and particularly if it will help us to explain deviant cases, that is, examples of the system that do not conform to the paradigm, then it will be of even more value. Finally, we might be interested primarily in finding a paradigm that will enable us to predict the future development of the system in question.

In seeking to understand such a system as modern or seventeenth-century imperialism, a main problem is finding means to make its key variables operational. How can we find (quantitative) measures of the flow of communications and attention within a system? Or, how can we find (quantitative) measures of patterns of identification? A start has been made in this direction, concentrating especially upon examples of modern empires and other state systems. To operationalize key variables in the Anglo-American empire of the seventeenth and eighteenth centuries, however, poses a different and more complex task. Many of the quantitative political and social data that we need for analyzing significant trends in colonial America are neither accurate nor complete enough to be of much value. In this respect, as I tried to point out, some of the newer research concepts and tools of the social sciences offer possibilities at once fruitful and exciting. We may hope that the application of these ideas and methods to such systems as imperialism will enhance our knowledge and understanding of their operation.

21

The Franco–Italian Boundary in the Alpes Maritimes

J. W. HOUSE*

Studies of the broad effects of boundary change upon the economies of the states concerned are more numerous[1] than those of localized results in the economy and social life of frontier communities.[2] Focus on the frontier communities means a review of political geography related, as it were, to the scale of the topographical map. With the enlarged view thus obtained the local problems may appear exaggerated, but successful solution or compromise at this level may have far-reaching beneficial effects upon inter-State relations. A peace treaty which changes the boundary between States may be expected to create or sharpen problems in the frontier areas, but within the west European community since 1945 the working of bilateral post-treaty arbitration and the closer co-operation of commercial and administrative interests in the borderlands have mitigated the effects of some of these problems. A review of such arbitration procedure and frontier cooperation between France and Italy yields results of geographical interest and indicates a further field for applied political geography.

The Alpine environment offers a distinctive setting for the study of the problems of frontier communities. The economy is relatively simple, often traditional, and broadly similar in its general traits over wide areas. It has long been founded on pastoralism, of sheep or cattle, with transhumant movements of stock and people, if on a diminished scale during the past few decades; the conflict of stock-rearing with afforestation in the upland grazing grounds is a common feature today on both flanks of the Alps. There has been some revaluation of Alpine resources during

---

Reprinted by permission of the author and the Council of the Institute from *Transactions of the Institute of British Geographers*, Number 26 (1959).

* John House (1919–) is Professor of Geography at The University of Newcastle upon Tyne.

1. H. R. Wilkinson, "Jugoslav Kosmet: the Evolution of a Frontier Province and its Landscape", *Transactions and Papers, 1955*, Institute of British Geographers, 21 (1955), pp. 171–193; R. Hartshorne, "Geographic and Political Boundaries in Upper Silesia", *Annals of the Association of American Geographers*, 23 (1933), pp. 195–228; A. E. Moodie, *The Italo-Yugoslav boundary* (1945), 241 pp.; N. L. Nicholson, *The Boundaries of Canada, its Provinces and Territories* (Canada, Department of Mines and Technical Surveys, Geographical Branch), memoir 2 (1954 and 1964).

2. H. Posselt, "Die Annektion von Dollart, Bourtanger Veen und Nieder Bentheim", *Mitteilungen der Geographischen Gesellschaft zu Wien* (1948), 145–149; M. Schwind, *Landschaft und Grenze. Geographische Betrachtungen zur deutsch-niederländischen Grenze*, Bielefeld (1950), 127 pp.; J. Sölch, "The Brenner Region," *Sociological Review*, 19 (1927), pp. 1–17; D. Whittlesey, "The Vall d'Aran: Trans-Pyrenean Spain," *Scottish Geographical Magazine*, 49 (1933), pp. 217–218.

this century, with the rise of tourism, the improvement of communications, and the generation of hydro-electric power. These newer developments have broken down in part the subsistence outlook of pastoralists and the parochial viewpoint of communities, and have promoted greater mobility of workers and freer contacts of people in adjacent valleys and across the Alpine watershed.

The traditional Alpine economy, with its poverty of local resources, was early allied with distinctive expressions of sovereignty. Society was organized in villages, often in the federal unity of a valley, owing allegiance to a local ruler, who in turn acknowledged a wider suzerain. Though the territorial expression of these wider allegiances changed much during the centuries, the local attachment was usually constant. The local ruler, in his well-sited and often almost inaccessible strongpoint, was in close touch with his pastoral retainers, and his wealth, in a region of limited resources, related to his partial control of important trans-Alpine trade routes. Sovereignty frequently flowed across the Alpine watershed and extended down both flanks, but the problems of boundary definition and demarcation were not seriously raised until the Western Alps became a frontier march between the evolving nation-states of France and, later, of Italy.

THE ALPES MARITIMES

The southern extremity of the Alpine arcs is an area of intricate relief and great structural complexity. The structural diversity is reinforced by the features of morphology and topography (Map 21.1). There are four roughly parallel north-south trending valleys, with steep and highly dissected courses transverse to the main geological trend-lines, except in the case of the Roya-Bévéra system on the east. The alternate succession of basins, gorges and strike-vale sections along each valley made for difficulty of transport. The turbulent, irregular régimes of the rivers in the natural state, flowing on short, steep courses from an Alpine to a Mediterranean environment, added to the difficulties of passage along these immature, ungraded valleys. In Roman and early medieval times the control of the defiles of "cluses" was important for the levying of tolls and, in the Western Alps, often marked the boundary of effective

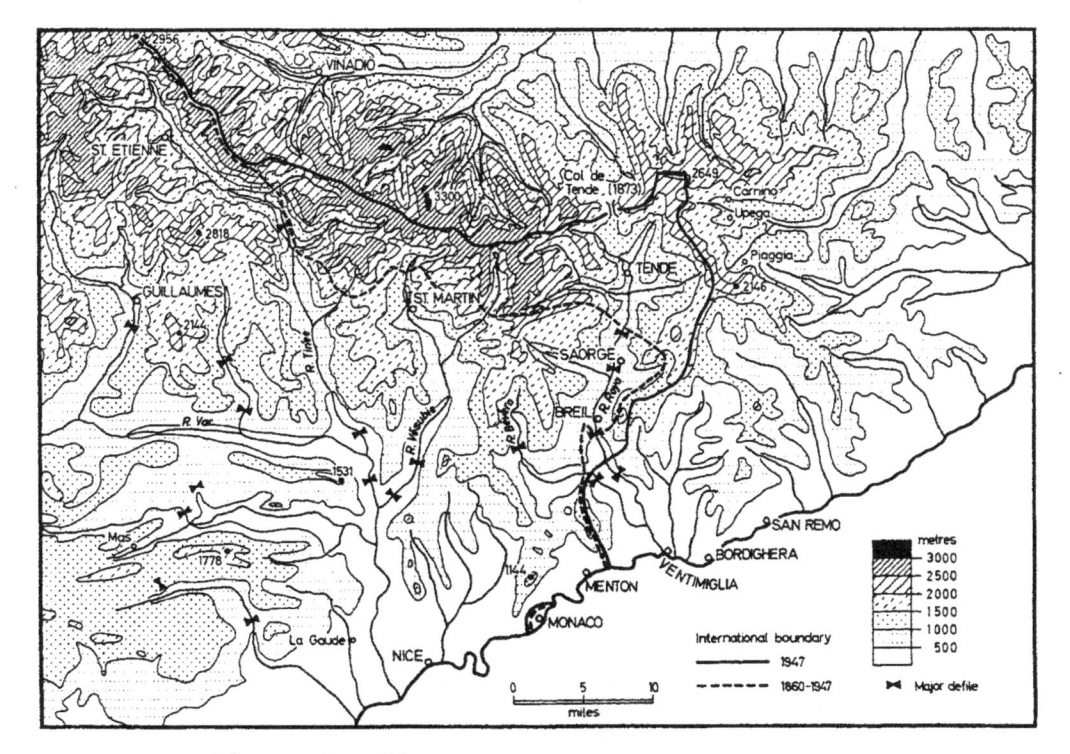

Map 21.1 ALPES MARITIMES: PHYSIOGRAPHY OF THE FRONTIER ZONE

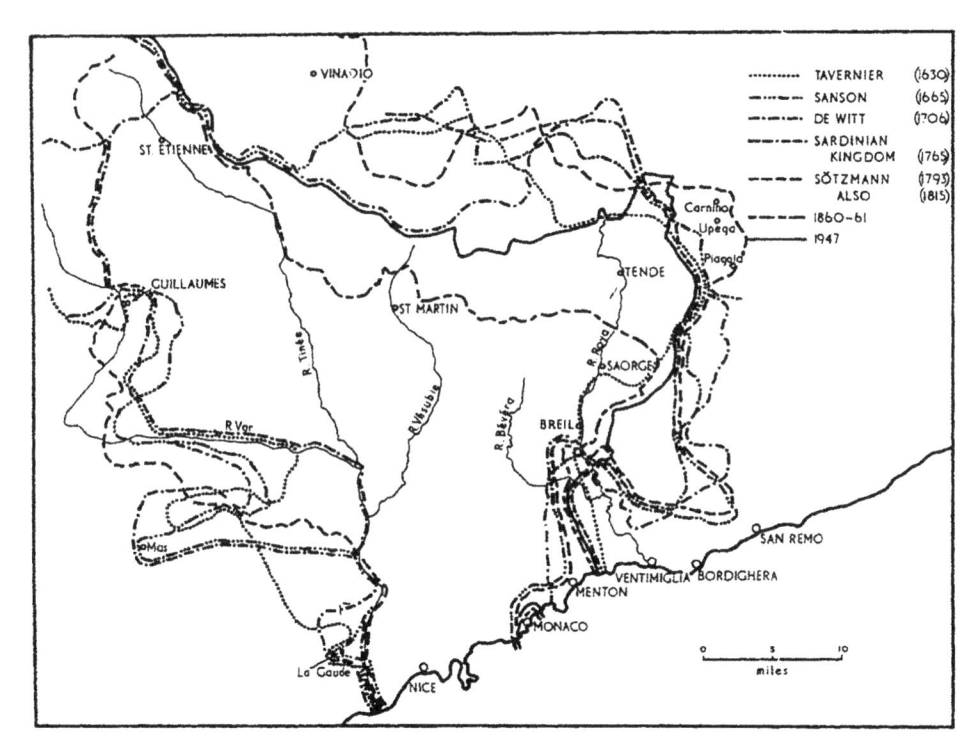

Map 21.2 HISTORICAL EVOLUTION OF BOUNDARIES IN THE ALPES MARITIMES (COMTÉ DE NICE) SINCE THE EARLY SEVENTEENTH CENTURY, BASED ON CONTEMPORARY MAPS

sovereignty against the mountain peoples. The local communities long remained isolated, underdeveloped and little disturbed, economically backward but with a strong sense of unity in a pastoral way of life.

The Alpes Maritimes bestride the route linking the Riviera-Provence with Piedmont and the North Italian plain, with the Col de Tende (natural col, 6258 feet; road and rail tunnel, mean height 4264 feet) one of only two all-weather passes across the Western Alps. ...

. . . .

The zenith of the Roya valley route was reached during the early nineteenth century; the population of Tende rose from about 1600 in 1815 to 8059 persons in 1823, an indication of its enhanced trading status. Yet until the mid-nineteenth century the upland pastoral economy was mostly for subsistence with little surplus and few routes for marketing it. The economy of almost every valley showed distinctive traits in pastoral organization and transhumance, whilst varied crafts and industries were only on the scale permitted by the limited size of the local market.

BOUNDARY EVOLUTION

The evolution of provincial and national boundaries in the Alpes Maritimes during the past three centuries (Map 21.2) shows the long-term struggle for:

(i) the Alpine watershed, or a forward position on the glacis, commonly on the Piedmontese slopes;

(ii) the mouth of the Roya valley, with the ports of Monaco and Ventimiglia. This has contained an inter-State boundary since the establishment of coastal sovereignty by the Republic of Genoa in the early Middle Ages;

(iii) the possession of bridge-heads on the river Var boundary, a natural demarcation

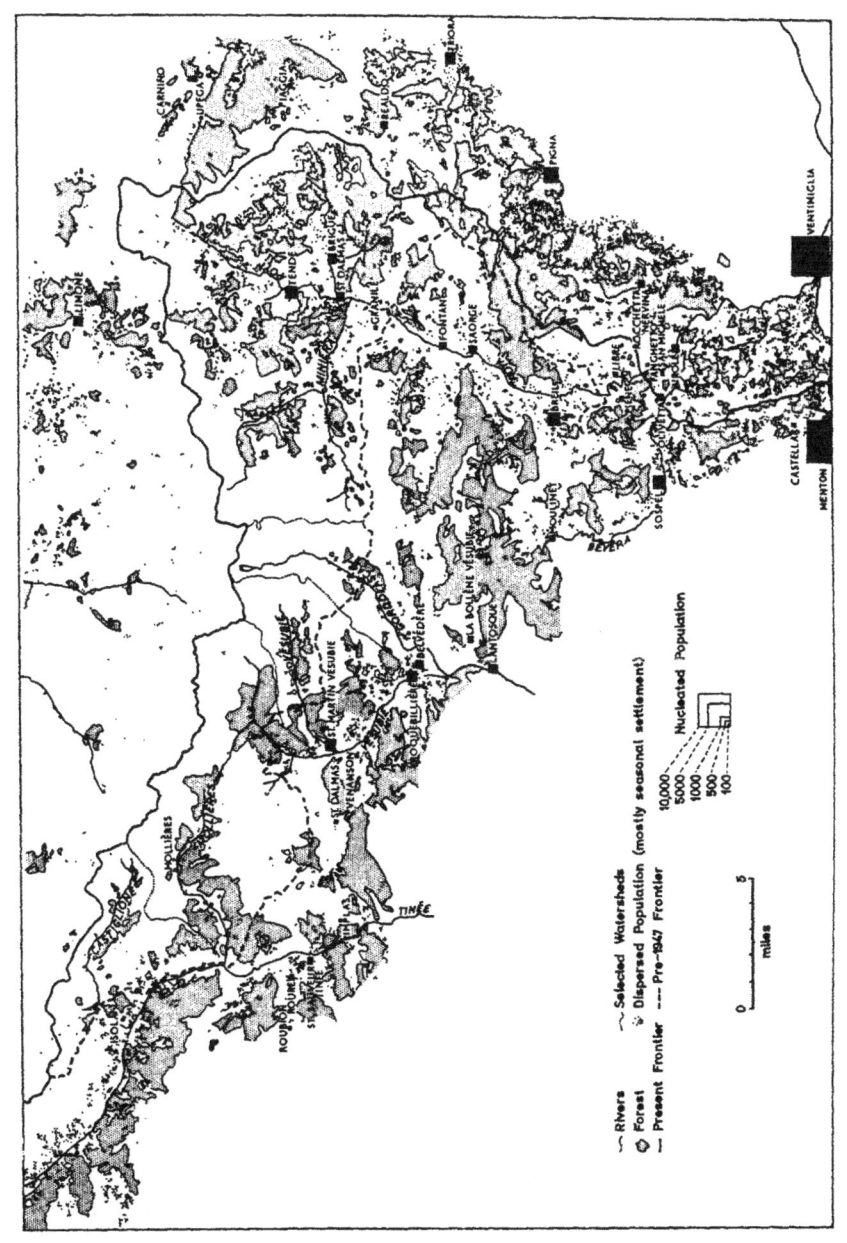

MAP 21.3 THE FRANCO-ITALIAN BOUNDARY IN THE ALPES MARITIMES, 1860–1947

line, utilized as early as Roman times, and the approximate international demarcation line, in its lower course, until the treaty of 1860.

THE INTERNATIONAL BOUNDARY: ESTABLISHMENT IN THE UPPER ALPINE VALLEYS, 1859–60

By the treaty of Turin (March 24th, 1860), the international boundary between the Piedmont territory of the House of Savoy (then called the Sardinian Kingdom) and France was established in the higher Alpine valleys and persisted unchanged until the Peace Treaty of 1947 (Map 21.3).

The 1860 boundary in the Alpes Maritimes was an important departure from the general contemporary principle of boundary delimitation in the Western Alps, that of the line of highest crests.[3] The boundary deviation to a course south of the Alpine crests, on the French glacis, was officially the result of agreement by Napoleon III to the preservation within the Sardinian kingdom of the royal hunting grounds of Victor Emmanuel II of Sardinia, though strategic arguments played an important role in Italian policy. The ancient Comté de Nice, a compact block of territory, including the Comté de Tende since 1576, was thus partitioned for the first time for centuries. The Treaty of Turin speaks of the cession of part of the arrondissement (circondario) of Nice, rather than of the Comté de Nice: the latter extended beyond the Alpine crest line; the former was defined by the Napoleonic watershed boundary. The arrondissement of Nice was too small to form a Département, but by Decree of October 24th, 1860, it was united with the arrondissement of Grasse, to form the Département of the Alpes Maritimes, the last step in the territorial formation of France.

3. The terms of reference of the Boundary Commission were sufficiently vague to allow departure from the general principle: "... A mixed Commission will determine, in a spirit of equity, the boundaries of the two States, taking account of the configuration of the mountains and the needs of defence" (*Article III, Treaty of Turin, 1860*). The earliest version read: "... taking account of mutual interests, as indicated by the configuration of the mountains". In this later stage of the negotiations the term "line of highest crests" came into common usage, as the most desirable boundary. The ultimate effect of the 1860 boundary was to create a strategic stalemate, since both France and Italy were able to dominate each other in different sections.

The human geography of the frontier zone was disturbed

(i) by the partition of communes and, in particular, the severance of upland grazing grounds and communal forests from their centres of permanent settlement and administration, though French owners, private and communal, continued to enjoy property rights in the lands passing to Italy.[4] The severed lands included the headwaters of five tributaries of the Vésubie and Tinée rivers (Fig. 5);

(ii) by the partition, in the east, of the Roya-Bévéra valleys. The Roya route gives access to the Col de Tende, passing through the feudal stronghold of Tende. The lower reaches of the valley historically had long been part of the Contea di Ventimiglia, until 1814 under Genoa, and remained within the Sardinian realm; the French gained the strategic salient across the middle Roya, around Saorge, while the old communes of Tenda (Tende) and Briga (La Brigue) remained in Sardinian hands, thus covering the southern approaches to the Col de Tende.

The principality of Monaco remained an independent city-state, as it had been for centuries. Its political existence dated from 1215, when the Grimaldi from Genoa founded a small trading station protected by a fortress; in 1488 the House of Savoy acquired the title, confirmed in 1506, to the adjacent settlements of Menton and Roquebrune. Monaco passed under French protection from 1641 to 1714, after the Prince again paid homage to the House of Savoy following the Treaty of Utrecht. In 1816 Monaco leased Menton and Roquebrune from Savoy, but in 1861 these were sold to France. The western boundary of Monaco, at La Turbie, marks a boundary delimitation reached already in the late fourth century, but one whose detailed demarcation has been a long-standing source of litigation.

THE INTERNATIONAL BOUNDARY, 1860–1947

The partition of local economic regions led in the first few years to widespread friction and the introduction of special economic

4. In Public International Law the boundary line is a limit of sovereignty but not of property, and customary law reinforced the rights of French border land owners.

benefits for the inhabitants of the zone between the 1860 boundary and the Alpine crest line. The main advantage lay in the duty-free movement of stock and farm produce either north into Piedmont or south into France, provided such commodities were the genuine produce of the zone, and in the natural unprocessed state. In spite of this legislation the zone on the French glacis was at an economic disadvantage in the region as a whole.

The Customs benefits were variously interpreted, according to the politics of the moment, and the general result was to keep the local economy solely on an agricultural basis, founded on an antiquated system of extensive pasturage, producing only the simplest and crudest forms of animal products (see Table 21.1).

[Since the 1880s] the economy of the Alpes Maritimes has been transformed, with important contrasts between the French and Italian flanks. The French Riviera, long the fashionable European winter coast, had by the inter-war years become an all-year resort area, attracting a growing multitude of tourists. Towns such as Nice and Cannes, and settlements between Nice and the Italian boundary, grew rapidly, in strong contrast to the then undeveloped state of the Italian Riviera coast. The demands for labour in the towns further denuded the inland areas of young workers, especially from the lower reaches of the French valleys. Coastal agriculture, for flowers, fruit and vegetables, received a tremendous impetus from the local urban demand but the interior valleys enjoyed no such benefits and in the late nineteenth century there was much abandonment of land and forest between the 1860 boundary and the Alpine crest line. The gradient in living standards between the coast and the Alpine crest was as striking as any natural change in altitude, structure or climate.

It is only within the last few decades that the improvement of roads, provision of rural transport, and increase of accommodation has led to economic betterment in the high valleys, mainly through the tourist trade. There has been State aid in the improvement of agriculture, yet without radically transforming traditional patterns. Likewise the installation of hydro-electric stations has benefited the local area little, in respect either of permanent employment or attraction of industry. Rural depopulation has continued to the present day.

The five tributary valleys of the Vésubie-Tinée system, in Italian control until 1947, continued to suffer from the partition of communes to which they belonged (Map 21.4). The valleys were reached with difficulty from the Italian flank and then for only a few months each year. Access by French pastoralists and foresters to French property within Italy was impeded during the years 1860–1947, especially in the 1930s when the Italian Government was transforming these pastoral valleys into a heavily fortified glacis, and the use of resources of the land, for timber and grazing stock, was seriously diminished. Revenues from timber and the leasing of pastures, vital to the economic stability of the French border communes, declined to negligible proportions.

The fortification of both flanks of the Alps

TABLE 21.1 *Middle Roya valley: Customs Data (1911)*
San Dalmazzo, to the north, and Piène, to the south of the Saorge salient (percentage figures, by value).

San Dalmazzo				Piène			
Imports		Exports		Imports		Exports	
Mules	40.8	Grapes	65.5	Fresh milk	27.0	Fresh fruit	37.8
Cattle	27.2	Fresh fruit	12.7	Firewood	13.5	Stone cubes	31.0
Horses	12.0	Cheese	10.8	Hay	13.9	Pot-herbs	7.3
Woollen cloth	9.4	Fowls	3.8	Sawn-wood	13.8	Cottoncloth	6.9
Soap	3.0	Butter	2.3	Potatoes	11.8	Charcoal	5.5
Skins	1.1	Chestnuts	1.8	Skins	7.9	Bricks	2.9
Firewood	0.7	Wine	0.5	Fresh fruit	7.8	Firewood	2.2
Others	5.8	Sheep/Goats	0.4	Charcoal	1.5	Others	6.4
		Others	2.2	Others	2.8		
	100		100		100		100

after the signing of the Triple Alliance in 1882 had progressively unfavourable effects on pastoralism and the social life of the frontier communities.

In the main Roya valley, in the early twentieth century, international agreement was necessary for the establishment of hydroelectric stations and a railway. The 1914 Agreement on the use of waters of the Roya[5] gave equal rights to the riparian powers: no works were to be started without prior agreement and no alteration was to be made by either party to the river flow. A chain of hydroelectric stations grew, mostly on Italian soil, but also in the French section, to utilize to the full the potential of the Roya. Electricity was exported from the area to the industrial establishments of Genoa and La Spezia, providing two-thirds of Ligurian needs and traction power for the coastal railways.

Negotiations for a railway from Nice to Piedmont, using the Roya valley and the Col de Tende, were long opposed by the French General Staff. The line was opened from Cuneo to Limone in 1889, the railway tunnel through the Col de Tende being pierced in 1898. The route was extremely difficult and costly to build and was not completed until 1928, being thus worked only twelve years before its destruction during the Second World War. An elaborate Agreement covered rights of operation and transit on the international section.[6]

. . . .

France continued to press for a crest-line boundary in the Alpes Maritimes but Italy would consider this only as part of a wider settlement of the international boundary. After wartime destruction in the area France prepared proposals for boundary revision in 1946, supporting them by holding a plebiscite in a part of the zone between the 1860 boundary and the Alpine crest line. The plebiscite secured a heavy majority in favour of union with France, even among some Italian-speaking villages.[7] Table 21.2 shows the results of somewhat a later, more reliable plebiscite, held on October 12th, 1947.

THE 1947 TREATY

By this treaty[8] the Alpine boundary was adjusted, wherever possible, to the line of highest peaks (Article 2). In the Alpes Maritimes

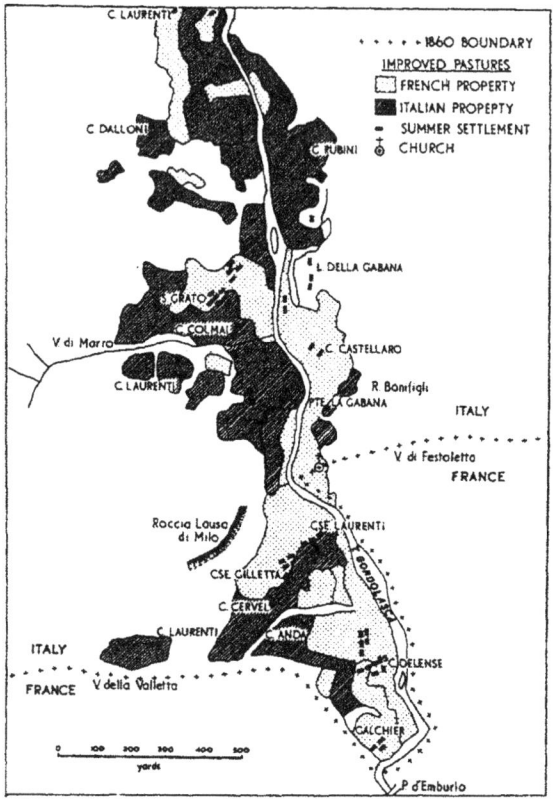

Map 21.4 GORDOLASCA VALLEY (VÉSUBIE) Distribution of French property in Italy after the 1860 boundary demarcation.

5. *Convention of 7th March, 1914*, governing the use of the river Roya and its tributaries. Articles I–IX. This was subsequently not ratified in important particulars and was a source of litigation up to 1940.

6. *Conventions of 6th June, 1904 (Articles I–XII) and 8th July, 1930*.

7. The Franco-Italian language boundary, as an indicator of national feeling, is not clearly defined in this area, viz.: A. Dauzat, "Le déplacement des frontières linguistiques du français de 1806 a nos jours", *La Nature* (1927), pp. 529–536; C. Guarnier, "Nobe sur la répartition des langues dans les Alpes Occidentales", *Révue de Géographie* (1897), pp. 6–12; O. Marinelli, "The Regions of Mixed Population in Northern Italy", *Geographical Review*, 7 (1919), 129–148.

The Roya valley has long been an area in which French is widely disseminated; Old Ligurian and Provençal type dialects have also been traditionally spoken. In the inter-war years Italian gained ground; during and since the war many Italian speakers left and have been replaced by Frenchmen.

8. Treaty Series No. 50 (1948). *Treaty of Peace with Italy*. Paris. February 10th, 1947. Cmd. 7481. 500 pp., with maps.

TABLE 21.2 *1947 Plebiscite, Tende and La Brigue*
Registered voters, 3027; voted for France, 2603 persons.

	Tende	La Brigue	Piène	Libre	Mollières (Upper Tinée)	Total
Registered	1661	831	148	218	169	3027
Voted	1521	790	140	209	168	2828
For France	1445	759	91	142	166	2603
For Italy	76	26	48	67	2	219
Invalid	—	5	1	—	—	6

the partition of the frontier administrative zone gave 160 square miles to France, with a 1946 plebiscite population of 2821, dividing all the frontier communes except that of Tende, which was transferred in totality. The headwaters of the Roya system and of the tributaries of the Vésubie and Tinée became French. In the lower Roya valley the boundary was moved slightly south to include the villages of Piène and Libre within France. Much of the area was sparsely settled and underdeveloped, and had suffered long-term and serious depopulation. The pattern of land tenure, by communes and individuals, was complex and disturbed once more by the new boundary. The rural economy of the frontier zone shows a transition from Mediterranean "polyculture" in the south to the sylvo-pastoral economy of the higher Alps.

Two problems, those of the hydro-electric stations and the international route along the Roya, have been satisfactorily settled, the latter included in the convention of January 29th, 1952, regulating boundary traffic. The more fundamental, if more localized, issues of grazing and forest ownership, water rights and freedom of transit for the local inhabitants, disregarding the new boundary, have proved more intractable and are not yet finally solved.

Hydro-electric Stations (Map 21.5)

In the 1947 Treaty (Article 9 and Annexe III, B) France accepted guarantees to Italy for the continuance of electricity supplies until 1961 from former Italian stations now under Electricité de France. Provision of technical information and pricing policies were also settled and have since been in force. The volume of current exported has risen in post-war years but demand in the Ligurian industrial centres and on the railways has outstripped the possibilities of local generation of power. The Roya power stations are now somewhat outdated and realize less power than a smaller number of more modern plants might achieve. The plants are peripheral to France which has ambitious developments elsewhere in the Alps; they are not likely to be rebuilt to serve the growing Italian market, even though general agreement was established in the 1947 Treaty that a co-ordinated plan for the exploitation of the Roya waters should be drawn up. A new transmission line, for the export of surplus electric power, has been constructed across the Col di Tanarello.

In the upper reaches of the Vésubie valley and in the Tinée large new hydro-electric power schemes are in course of construction, with feeder tunnels deriving water from areas in Italy before 1947.

The Roya Valley International Route

A Franco-Italian commission reported in 1953 that it would not be economic to repair the Nice/Ventimiglia–Piedmont railway, in spite of protests from the inhabitants of the Roya valley and continued pressure by the Joint Franco-Italian Frontier Chambers of Commerce. Immediately before the war this railway had carried substantial traffic in sand, stone and timber. Goods traffic is now carried by lorry, and passengers are served by national and international postal buses.

The post-war tourist traffic on the Roya route has increased considerably, some 100,500 cars passing over the Col de Tende in 1957, in each direction (cf. Montgenèvre pass,

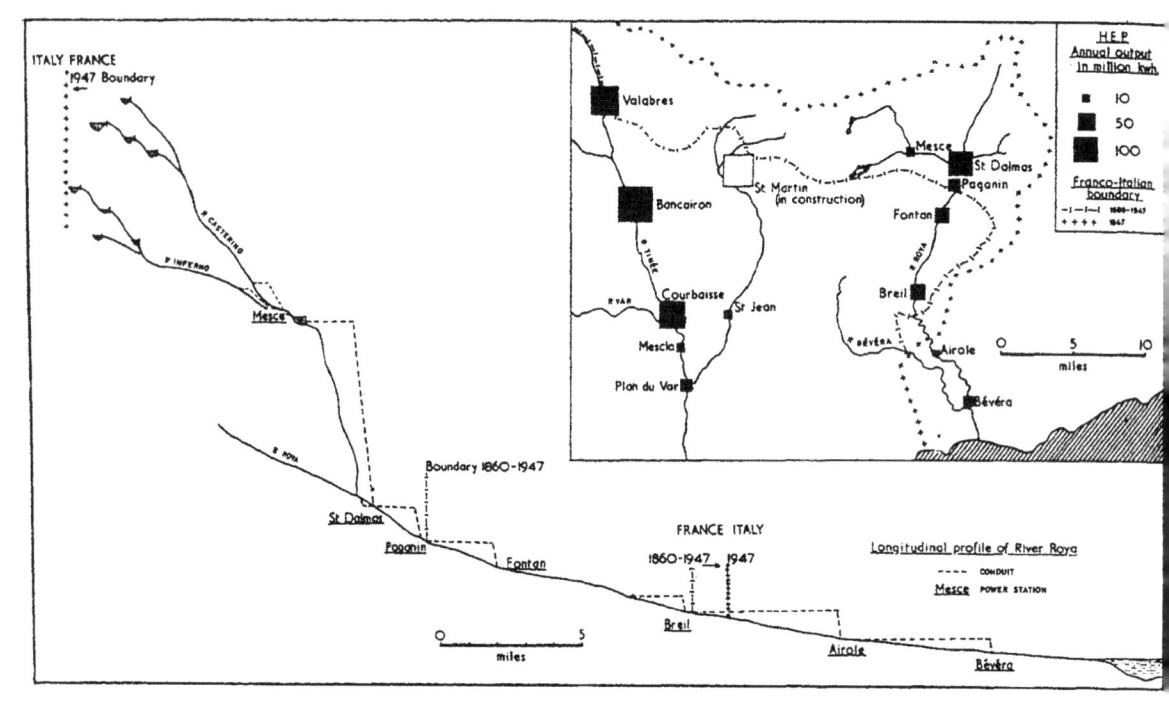

Map 21.5 ALPES MARITIMES
Hydro-electric power stations in the frontier zone.

52,500 cars). In the first few years transit rights on the Italian section were grudgingly granted but a bilateral negotiation in 1948 removed that difficulty, in return for French agreement, in principle, to territorial concessions at Piène. Timber traffic from the Tende area over the col into Piedmont is now the most important freight movement along the route.

The lower section of the Roya valley has long suffered in its local economy from the presence there of an international boundary, partitioning a small geographical region. For the past fifty years the local authorities have tried to interest the respective national governments in boundary reform; in 1946, a customs-free zone was proposed for the lower Roya valley and coastal Liguria.

Completion of the proposed Mont Blanc tunnels might revive interest in the re-establishment of the Nice–Piedmont railway as part of a shorter route from the Low Countries and eastern France to the Riviera coast.

THE FRANCO-ITALIAN CONCILIATION COMMISSION, 1948

This commission was established under Article 83 (Settlement of disputes) of the 1947 Treaty, for joint investigation of friction in the frontier area, particularly in relation to the complex problems of rural land use and access rights; at the outset France stipulated that concessions of land by her could relate only to uninhabited territory. On March 6th, 1954, the Commission reached agreement on the re-allotment of communal possessions partitioned by the 1947 Treaty. The geographical interest of the work may be shown by its treatment of two problems: near Olivetta San Michele and in the area east of La Brigue (Fig. 4).

Olivetta San Michele (Map 21.6)

Before 1947 the commune of Olivetta extended north-west in a salient including Mont Grazian. The French railway tunnel below that mountain thus lay technically in Italian territory, though in the 1904 Convention Italy waived her sovereign rights in this respect. The traditional economy of the commune, including the hill-village of Piène, was based on olive groves, almost as a form of monoculture. This economy had for some time been unprofitable, the villages were backward, and depopulation had been severe.

In the 1947 Treaty the new international boundary split the commune and passed immediately north of Olivetta village, Mont Grazian and Piène being incorporated in France, the former for military reasons.[9] The immediate effect was to prevent the villagers of Olivetta from entering the communal olive groves across the new boundary; at the same time control was lost over the sources of the

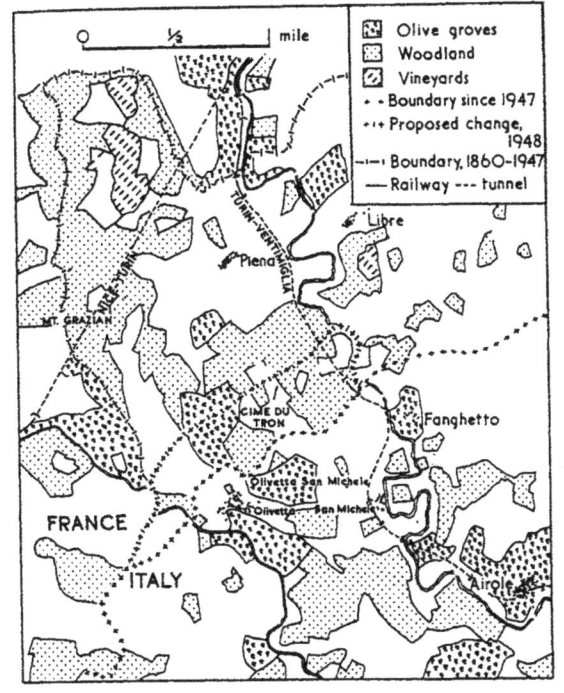

Map 21.6 OLIVETTA SAN MICHELE
Boundary changes, 1860–1947.

village water-supply, though special arrangements were later negotiated for water supply to Fanghetto and for the extraction of water from the Bévéra, for oil-pressing and irrigation. The severance of Piène represented no immediate loss as the olive economy was seriously depressed, access by mule-track was difficult, and the population had been depleted during the war. Any post-war rehabilitation there, however, depended on the

9. The partition of the Commune and communal property showed:
   To France: 6.1 sq. miles (1584 ha.), 53 per cent; 384 persons (44 per cent).
   In Italy: 5.4 sq. miles (1389 ha.), 47 per cent; 489 persons (56 per cent).
   Communal property:
   To France: 3.2 sq. miles (831 ha.), 61 per cent, pastures and woods. The woodland of Colle di Paola to be held in indivisible co-proprietry.

olive groves to provide the main surplus for exchange.

During 1948, the Italian Government proposed that the international boundary should be adjusted northward from Olivetta village, to return an uninhabited area of some 660 acres to Italy. This would have given the village access, on Italian soil, to part of the communal olive groves and control over its water supply, but Piène would thereby have lost almost 90 per cent of her post-war olive-growing area. Agreement in principle was reached (Quaglio-Bidault Agreement, July 8th, 1948) but the French parliament subsequently refused ratification, and no international arbitration appears to have been sought, as laid down in Article 83 of the 1947 Treaty.

The proposed territorial adjustment at Olivetta, in the Mediterranean zone of peasant agriculture, affects fixed resources of an olive-gathering and processing economy. Any partition of such resources, adjusted as they have been over many years to local conditions of supply and demand, must adversely affect one or other party, since the trees are fixed capital and there is insufficient land of the right quality on which to replant and necessarily a lengthy period must elapse before new trees would bear. A settlement may seem less urgent at a time when the olive economy is depressed, but the longer-term prospects of the hill village of Piène are closely tied to an eventual solution. In 1954 a division of communal properties of the former commune of Olivetta San Michele was agreed upon; additionally San Michele was to have rights to harvest hay on certain lands which had passed to France.

As part of the proposed 1948 boundary rectification in the same area a further 215 acres were to have been returned to Italy. This land included a water intake from the Roya for the Italian power station of Airole, some miles downstream, and part of the supply channel, both of which had been transferred to France in 1947. Ratification of this change also has been refused.

La Brigue (Briga) (Map 21.7)

This area formed part of the Tenda and Briga communes, the most substantial transfer of land from Italy to France under the 1947

Treaty. It included land which had benefited from customs-free movement of its products during the years 1860–1947. The economy is extensive rather than intensive, as at Olivetta, and pastoral, mainly for sheep, rather than agricultural. Communal forests play an important role in the revenues of local authorities. The area has traditionally been linked by transhumance with the French Riviera coast

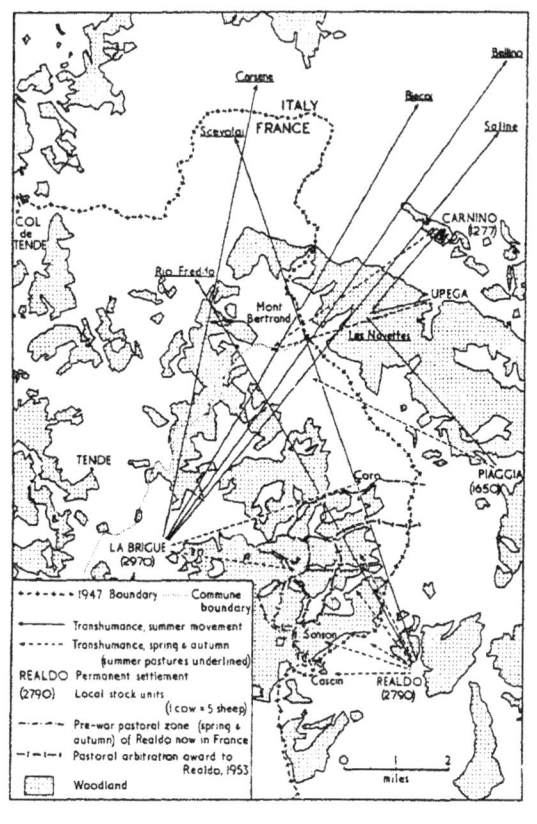

Map 21.7 LA BRIGUE (BRIGA) AND TENDE COMMUNES
Effects of the 1947 boundary upon transhumance and rural economy; 1953 pastoral arbitration award.

and coastal Liguria, the sheep spending the winter at the coast and the spring, summer and autumn on the Alpine pastures.

As frequently in an upland pastoral economy, rights of access to pasture and woodland are intricate and legally complicated. The commune and private owners have rights and the forestry authority exercises some control over pasturing, in terms both of its location and volume. The resultant problems must be viewed against a background of rural depopulation, decline of transhumance, and the reversion of land to semi-natural waste.

In the Briga area transhumant flocks returned from the coast to spring pastures in the first fortnight of June, went to the higher summer pastures on July 2nd, descended to autumn pastures (sometimes distinctive from those of spring) in early September, and left for the coast at the time of the first snows in late October. Part of the autumn might be spent grazing in woodland (pré-bois) specially rented for the purpose. The movement of flocks thus covered a wide area and each small part of the territory had its distinctive role in the system of transhumance.

By adopting the line of crests as a boundary in 1947, the Peace Treaty partitioned the former Briga commune, part of whose lands, as those of Tenda (Tende), lay on both flanks of the Alpes Maritimes. This disrupted the mechanism of transhumant movement and disturbed rights of access to, and possession of, pastures and woodland (Map 21.7).

For some months in 1946 the inhabitants on the Italian side of the crest line petitioned to be incorporated in France, as part of La Brigue commune. This could not be allowed without abandoning the principle of boundary delimitation along the line of highest crests. The partition of the commune became effective in the 1947 Treaty and presented the Conciliation Commission with its most thorny problem.

Territorial adjustment of the boundary was not permissible and some compromise was necessary on claims to the use of land across the demarcation line.

Determination of the size of local flocks and of the carrying capacity of pastures was a first essential, but the views of the Swiss pastoral arbitrator were contested on the facts of both these issues. By the partition the French part of La Brigue commune lacked sufficient summer pastures and, conversely, the Italian settlement of Realdo, for example, had insufficient spring and autumn pastures. The dearth of spring and autumn pastures in the frontier zone (for only 45 per cent of total sheep) has meant extensive pasturing in woodlands. Italian needs were the greater since transhumance on the French side had declined for some years, but the French local authority at La Brigue would not grant spring and

TABLE 21.3 *Partitioned Briga Commune (1952): Local Livestock and Ownership*

	Cattle	Proprietors	1940–50 Sheep (mean)	Proprietors (mean)	Stock units (1 cow = 5 sheep)
France					
La Brigue	74	17	1800*	11	2170 (2970)
Italy					
Piaggia	151	34	895	10	1650
Upega	36	13	540	4	720
Carnino	85	20	132	2	557
Realdo	34	30	2620	34	2790

* Later increased by 800, to include flocks of shepherds who had left pre-war but who might return.

Carrying Capacity of Pastures (in sheep per hectare)

Summer: improved 2.5   spring and autumn: lower levels 0.75
        unimproved 0.5   around 'mayens' 1.5

French side of 1947 boundary, in La Brigue commune, capacity for 2172 sheep in summer and 2400 sheep in spring and autumn.

Italian side of 1947 boundary, in Briga commune, capacity for 6312 sheep in summer and 630 sheep in spring and autumn.

autumn pasturages without compensation, claiming that local French transhumant flocks might increase in future. An alternative solution was that the Italian sheep flocks might pasture in spring and autumn on land on the Italian side of the boundary (Les Navettes) belonging to the adjacent French commune of Tende. The necessary compensation for such an exchange between the two French communes was not forthcoming, though an agreement in principle on the division of property rights was made in March 1954.

The Swiss arbitrator's recommendation was that:

(i) Italian flocks should have limited spring and autumn pasturage rights on French soil (Map 21.7), the pasturages to be held in communal ownership but not sovereign possession by the Italian village of Realdo, i.e. not as a part of the Italian State. The pastoral area to be transferred (5 square miles) was further reduced to 2.3 square miles, to take account of the general regional scarcity of spring and autumn pastures;

(ii) in return for this and for the extinction of surplus summer pasturage rights of France in Italy the French village of La Brigue was to have compensation in woodland, a resource which already provided one-third of the communal revenues. The basis of this compensation was the division of the total woodland area of the former Briga commune, according to the population numbers in the parts partitioned between France and Italy (France 850 inhabitants, Italy 650), the result then being corrected to offset the additional richness and volume of summer pastures remaining in Italy and thus cut off from the transhumant centre of La Brigue. Other woodland, particularly in the 1953 pastoral arbitration award area, was to be held in joint possession by the French and Italian communes. The volume of commercial timber available and the rate of its proposed extraction remain in dispute.

Such a finely balanced compromise, breaking across the traditions of centuries, has not proved a final answer to the complicated rights to the use of land, even though it was established on the basis of the needs of the partitioned local economy. It does, however, illustrate the need for and the value of a detailed human-geographical appreciation of the area, in wider terms than the specific and limited economic issues before the Swiss arbitrator in 1952–53.

THE FRONTIER ZONE AS A REGION

The boundary changes of the 1947 Peace Treaty have been in effect for rather more than ten years. The new sections of the boundary line for the most part lie in sparsely settled mountain terrain and the friction and conflict have been local, affecting the social

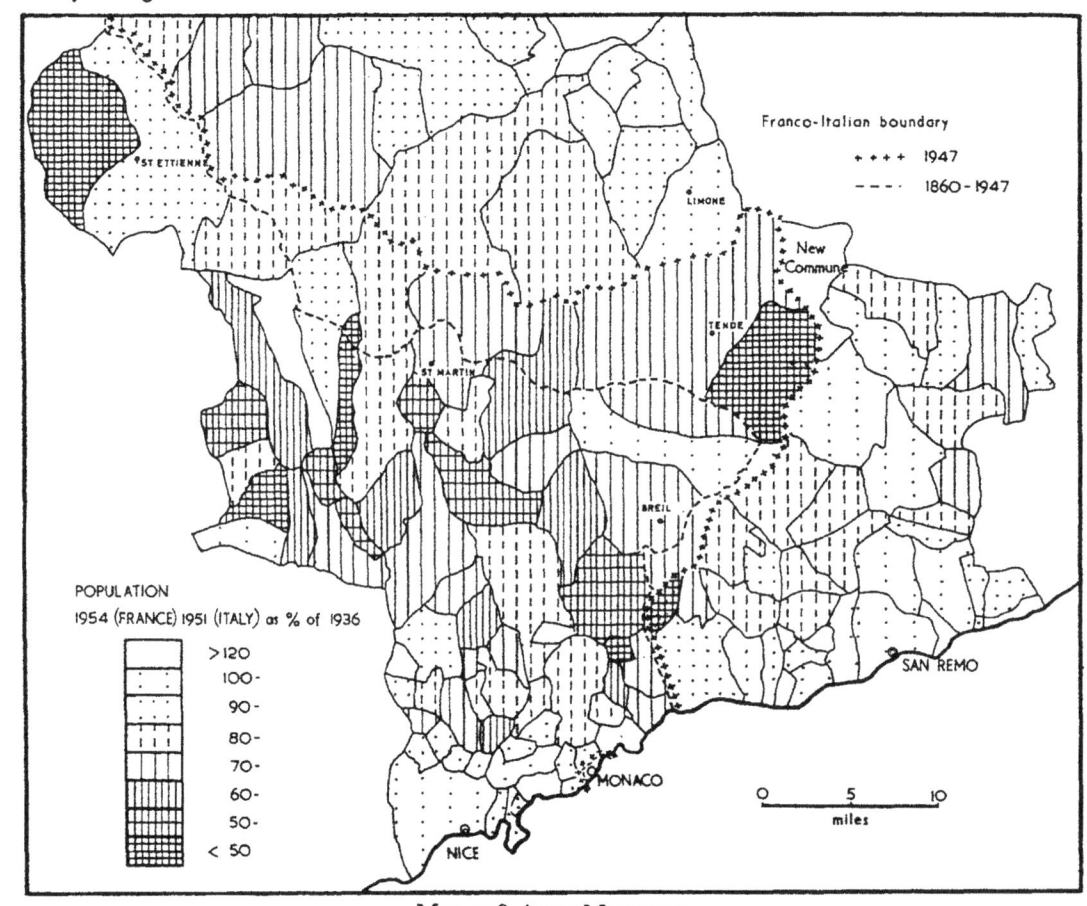

Map 21.8 ALPES MARITIMES
Recent population changes in the frontier zone.

and economic life of border communes rather than wider national interests.

In the economies of France and Italy the Alps have been defined as depressed rural areas, meriting Government assistance and preferential treatment.[10] Many of the problems of pastoralism, rural social structure, hydro-electric power development, industrialization and tourism are common on both flanks of the Alps but solutions have hitherto been approached on a national basis, looking upon the frontier tracts as peripheral and marginal to the national economy. Policies of France and Italy have varied in the treatment of these problems and before 1947 there were differences to be seen in the local frontier economy and cultural landscape as a result.

10. V. Pizzigallo, *La montagna italiana. I problemi e le leggi* (1955), 105 pp.; Comité Régional d'expansion économique, *Problèmes économiques communs à la région Centre-Sudest* (Lyon, 1957), 27 pp.

The differences may be summarized:

(i) *on the Italian side:* a greater density of rural population (Map 21.8), living at a generally lower standard, with a labour force surplus to local needs and a scarcity of improved land for development. Emigration is either abroad, especially to South America, or northward to the industrial cities rather than to the Riviera coast.

The Italian Government has the more severe rural problems, and resources are being developed under conditions of population pressure rather than the reverse, as in France. The more recent boom growth of Italian Riviera towns is, however, now adding the kind of attraction to labour enjoyed on the French flank of the Alps for several decades.

(ii) *on the French side:* there has been more severe rural depopulation, and resources and even land have lapsed from use. The Riviera has long proved the magnet attracting labour from the interior. It is only in recent years that tourism has begun effectively, if on a small scale, to penetrate the interior valleys, and attempts to vary and stimulate mountain farming are still on a restricted basis.

In pre-war years the boundary acted as a firm dividing line, between economies autarchic in policy, and circulation of both goods and people in the frontier zone was increasingly restricted. It is difficult to define a precise region on either flank of the boundary over which it exercised a detectable influence on the cultural landscape and local economy.

Boundary legislation as far back as the Treaty of Turin (1760) had recognized the special rights and difficulties of those living close to an international boundary. In the Protocol of 1861, following the Treaty of Turin (1860), elaborate arrangements had been made for the inhabitants of a zone up to 5 kilometres (demi-myriamètre) in depth flanking the new boundary. In the 1947 Treaty the demilitarization of a zone 20 kilometres in depth on the Italian side of the amended Alpine boundary was decreed and thereby one of the adventitious economic supports of border social and economic life was weakened. In the same treaty the special rights of frontier dwellers were again recognized and safeguarded.

The narrowest definition of the frontier zone is thus almost in terms of the administrative boundaries of the communes immediately flanking the boundary. In a wider context it is clear that the limits of the natural regions flanking the boundary have some significance in defining its effects on the cultural landscape and lives of the people. This frequently indicates the significance of the drainage basins of the Var tributaries, the Tinée, Vésubie and Roya-Bévéra in France, and the Stura-Gesso and Upper Tanaro valleys with their tributaries, in Italy. In a still more diffuse and yet detectable sense the administrative areas of the adjacent Département of Alpes Maritimes in France and the Provinces of Cuneo and Imperia in Italy have been affected by the presence and movement of the boundary and frontier policies are important at this level of regional governments.

Yet the significance of the trade across the boundary or of changing Government policies may not have the most substantial effects in the frontier zone, however defined. In the tariff war between France and Italy in 1886, for example, the area to suffer most severely was the wine-growing district of Puglia, at considerable distance. Similarly in the evolution of Franco-Italian contacts in the European Common Market, the frontier zone is not likely from its position alone to be more or less affected than other parts of the two States; the main elements lie in the comparison of local resources and means of interconnection.

In the period since the 1947 Peace Treaty there has developed a closer association between the two flanks in the frontier zone, broadly defined as the adjacent administrative divisions of Département or Provincia size. The liaison has been effected through a Standing Committee of French and Italian Chambers of Commerce of the frontier zone, with the policy of stimulating complementary exchange between frontier economic regions, reviving the economy of border communities and providing the improved through communications, by road and rail, between the two States, necessary to derive the greatest benefits from the Customs Union Treaty and the European Common Market.

In 1951 a Convention was signed between France and Italy, relating to frontier circulation.[11] This defined a frontier zone, approximately 10 kilometres in depth on either side of the boundary (Article I), within which freedom of circulation of persons and of movement of livestock, vehicles, seeds, tools and fertilizers was to be stimulated (Article III).

During the 1950s the effects of policies to promote the frontier economy have been slight in the short term. There is a traditional background to a local trans-boundary exchange of products, between the Mediterranean and Piedmont flanks of the Alps, habitats within which the blend of common Alpine resources is distinctively different. During the period 1892–1949, however, the decline of trade between France and Italy and the increase in barrier status of the boundary had been accompanied by depopulation and decay in the economy of the border communes. The re-activation of trans-boundary contacts between communes with many social and economic problems has thus been a difficult process.

The recognition of the common economic and social problems of the borderlands, and the making of joint representations to the

11. Decreto del Presidente della Repubblica, 2 luglio 1951 (1953).

respective national governments, have proved an effective first trial step towards the closer cooperation between the two States within a zone of frontier contact. This should help to reduce the social and economic significance of boundaries as intended by the Customs Union Treaty and the European Common Market. The zone of the Alps offers sister nations a series of meeting-places, easily controllable, as a base for the study of wider economic cooperation, in contrast to the function of separation which the existence of a watershed or crest-line boundary in the High Alps has hitherto generally performed.

22

Independence and After

IMMANUEL WALLERSTEIN[*]

INTERNAL UNITY: PARTIES AND HEROES

Independence, as the nationalists had always insisted, makes a lot of difference. It transfers much of the effective power to individuals and structures internal to the country. It gives the governing elite many levers to reclaim still more power from outside agencies. There are, however, many claimants to the exercise of this power, all internal to the country. Unless the power is effectively exercised by a central agency, and unless the rules of the power game are generally accepted by all the competitors, disintegration and secession become not merely possible but probable.

Most African nations do not have long histories as nationalities. Their nationhood has been created in the crucible of a revolutionary struggle against a colonial power. The unity of the nation was forged in the fight against the external enemy. . . . Colonial governments bred their own dissolution, and nationalism came about as a resolution of many of the basic strains of the colonial situation.

The government of a new nation, immediately after independence, is a very unstable thing. For one thing, the existence of an external enemy—the major motivation for unity in the nationalist movement—has largely disappeared. The political mobilization, the subordination of private and sectional claims to the needs of the whole, is inevitably diminished. The country's sense of tension, and of antagonism, is partly abated, partly turned inward. Moreover, there is a sense of disappointment at unfulfilled expectations.

In nationalist activity in Africa there was an implicit promise that the tension resulting from oppression and antagonism, from the restraints of the colonial ruler and from the discipline of the nationalist organization would be temporary. There was a touch of the utopian hope characteristic of every revolution, even when nationalist movements were peaceful and unmilitant, as they were in perhaps half the African states that gained independence. And there were many in all African states who thought that freedom meant the end of social control or the immediate radical redistribution of wealth. The cadres of the nationalist parties may not have had such naïve expectations, but it is understandable that among the peasants or uneducated urban dwellers such illusions existed. Even if these illusions were only momentary, unfulfillment meant a sense of disappointment. Independence was not magic. In country after country in Africa, during the first weeks of independence, the leaders felt the need to make speeches on the theme that independence means hard work and self-reliance.

Condensed from *Africa: The Politics of Independence*, by Immanuel Wallerstein. © Copyright 1961 by Immanuel Wallerstein. Reprinted by permission of Random House, Inc. and the author.

[*] Immanuel Wallerstein (1930–) is in the Department of Sociology at Columbia University.

Even leaving aside simplistic notions, the transfer of power inevitably involves some administrative confusion. In those countries where the transfer was abrupt, as in Guinea, the problem was much greater than in those where the transfer was meticulously planned, as in Ghana or Nigeria.

The removal of the prod to unity—that is, colonial rule—combined with the uncertainty, disillusion, and hence opposition, created by the new government, inevitably causes the ethnic, regional, and other particular interests which had temporarily held back their claims to reassert them. This, of course, is not startling. The assertion of the rights of private interests to their share of the community's assets is the daily business of all governments, not only those in Africa. What is different in new nations is that the government cannot assume a residual loyalty to the state among the majority of its citizens.

Loyalty to the state can be measured by the sense of restraint its citizens feel in pursuing their opposition to specific policies of the government. If they oppose the particular government in power but stop at a point short of destroying the state or seriously weakening it, they can be said to be loyal. This kind of legitimation of the state rather than of a particular government is something that is inculcated in the population over a period of time. Children are taught it in schools. But African nations have not yet had time for this. At present many Africans cannot determine the limits of opposition, do not understand the distinction between opposition and secession. This is what leaders of African governments mean when they argue that "our oppositions are not constructive." It is not that they tend to be destructive of the government in power; this is the purpose of an opposition. It is that they tend to destroy the state in the process of trying to depose the acting government.

This is particularly true because, in almost every African country, the opposition takes the form of a claim to regionalism—a demand for at least decentralization in a unitary state, federalism in a decentralized state, confederation, total dissolution of a confederation. Regionalism is understandable because ethnic loyalties can usually find expression in geographical terms. Inevitably, some regions will be richer (less poor) than others, and if the ethnic claim to power combines with relative wealth, the case for secession is strong. Ashanti in Ghana, the Ivory Coast in French West Africa, the Western Region in Nigeria, Gabon in French Equatorial Africa, Katanga in the Congo are well-known examples. But every African nation, large or small, federal or unitary, has its Katanga. Once the logic of secession is admitted, there is no end except in anarchy. And so every African government knows that its first problem is how to hold the country together when it is threatened by wide disintegration.

The integration of a country can be assured in the long run only if the majority of the citizens begin to accept the state as the legitimate holder of force and authority, the rightful locus of legislation and social decision....

... One problem of new African nations is that they are new. People are not used to them. People cannot tell themselves that the ways of the state are hallowed by tradition, justified by experience. Even a modern rational state depends in part on its tradition ... to reinforce its legal structure. But tradition is in any case, and anywhere, largely myth. It exists in the minds of men. And if it is not there already, tradition can be created or re-created, revived and installed. And so in countless ways, African nations are today reëmphasizing their links with the past, their historical roots and glories, their cultural achievements, their unique virtues. Thus, Nigeria will invest in archaeological research, Senegal will sponsor a Festival of African Culture, and Morocco will recall the glories of the Almoravid Empire. Every state will build museums and encourage its historians to review and revive its past.... One of the immediate results of such emphasis on tradition is that it leads to a greater legitimation of the state.

To build a nation, it is not enough to have a past. One must have a present. To the extent that the various parts of a country are economically interdependent, to the extent that specialization proceeds and division of labor occurs within national boundaries, it becomes difficult, or rather expensive, to "secede." It is no accident that immediately after independence, customs and immigration barriers suddenly become tighter, as for example between Ghana and Togo, or between Guinea and Sierra Leone. There are many reasons for such a development, but one is that it fosters the creation of a *national* economy, which among other things reinforces the sense of nationhood and hence the basic loyalty of the citizens.

Before an African colony achieves independence it is part of an imperial economy. The shift to a national economy after independence is sometimes only a partial one, though the new government may try to intensify it for political rather than economic reasons. The expansion of the road and rail network, the diversification of agriculture, the building of dams and the spread of light industries—all of which have such a high priority in the newly independent African countries—serve many economic functions. They serve as well, however, to make less likely, more difficult, any weakening of the political bonds. The desperate hurry of African leaders for economic development is due not only to the desire for a higher standard of living and the need to fulfill their promises on this front, but also to the sheer political need to hold a unit together. Economic development does this both by showing that the nation works, and by enlarging the penalties of disintegration of the state. The changes in the economy thus affect the psychological attitude of the population toward the state.

Greater functional interdependence, then, leads to greater integration, because as movements grow up which pull the state apart they come to see more and more the disadvantages of their own disruptive processes. The earlier they see this, the steadier will be the path of government. For functional interdependence leads to greater integration only if the citizens are aware of how interdependent they have become. The nation and its economic network must become "visible." And whether what is visible is reality or an inflated reality is rather irrelevant in terms of its effect in enhancing the loyalty of the citizens; hence, the very great importance of public relations—what is pejoratively known as propaganda. So everywhere in independent Africa we see an immediate creation or expansion of the government information service, of a radio station, of official newspapers. It is not merely for international prestige that Nigeria or Tunisia, Mali or Ghana puts loudspeakers in every village. It is for the sake of informing large numbers of people regularly that the nation is not merely an invention of remote intellectuals but something whose structure affects their lives and economic well-being intimately and increasingly. Perhaps even more than for the sake of informing people, it is for convincing them.

The legitimation of which we speak, the citizens' sense of loyalty to the nation, is best tested by the willingness of the average person, in the daily events of life, to promote the enforcement of the laws, customs and mores of the state. To some extent it is a question of their thinking of the state as "we" and not as "they." If the punishment for deviation must always await the presence of the policeman, the state will not function very well. To be sure, formal punishment is important, and every new African state is eager to ensure that it has at its disposal an adequate army and police force which will be entirely loyal to it. However, government control of the army and police force is not enough. The people must be willing to recognize the authority of the law enforcement agencies and the government controlling them.

In the colonial situation, African national movements had taught their followers to think of the (colonial) state as "they," not "we." Independence demands a rapid reversal in outlook from opposition to support of the state's authority. This transition is difficult even for the educated and trained cadres of the movement.

In speaking of the activities to enhance the integrity of the new African states we have referred somewhat loosely to the "nation" as undertaking these activities. But who exactly is it that does this "enhancing?" To some extent it is the government, and we have mentioned various governmental activities. But the government rests on weak ground because of the shallow loyalty of its citizens.

. . . .

Since the government cannot perform the functions necessary for increasing its own integrity, the modernizing elite, which is in control of most of the newly independent African nations, looks around for integrating institutions, mechanisms which are intermediate between the citizen and the state but national in orientation, mechanisms which can attract the necessary loyalty more rapidly and turn this loyalty to the service of the nation. There are, unfortunately, very few such institutions available in these new nations.

. . . .
These institutions must somehow make the citizens aware of the nation as an economic entity, of the impact of economic acts on various parts of the country, of the degree to which the peasant relies on the port worker. They have to continue to stimulate the movement of people from the villages to the towns and mines, and, for the individual, they have to serve as a tangible institution on which he can rely for help, for advice, for consolation. These are large tasks, and the party and the national hero do not do them alone. But as one surveys the African scene today, one observes that where the party and the hero are weak, so are the processes of modernization and integration of the nation.

. . . .
We speak of *the party*, but are there not *parties*? There are in some countries. Most African nations came to independence by organizing a nationalist movement which laid effective claim to power. The standard pattern was the existence of one major party which symbolized the struggle for independence, with some weak, often regionalist, opposition parties. Ghana, Togo, Sierra Leone, Somalia are examples of this. In some few cases, as a result of either absorption or suppression, the opposition totally ceased to exist before independence—notably in the Ivory Coast, the Republic of Mali, Tunisia; or it expired soon after independence—as in Guinea and Upper Volta. Where there was no one party which commanded overwhelming support—the Congo, Sudan, Nigeria—or where the nationalist party split after independence, as in Morocco, there often was considerable trouble. Where a major segment of the nationalist movement was systematically excluded from power, as in Cameroun, there was continued civil war. Almost everywhere, the trend after independence has been in one of two directions: toward a one-party state with consequent stability (if the resulting single party grouped the major elements) or toward a breakdown of the party system with consequent instability and a tendency for the army to play a growing role (Sudan, Morocco, Congo).

The choice has not been between one-party and multi-party states; it has been between one-party states and either anarchy or military regimes or various combinations of the two. The military regime, beset by internal troubles, finds it difficult to mobilize energies for economic development, to keep the intellectuals satisfied and in line, to allow for participation in government by any factions other than the small ruling group. On the contrary, the single-party state—at least the single-party state where the party structure is well articulated and really functioning—provides a mechanism whereby the majority of the population can have some regular, meaningful connection with, and influence upon, the governmental process, and vice versa.

Since "single-party systems" seem to be a standard feature of the new African nations, it is well to distinguish them from the "single-party systems" in Eastern Europe, for example. The party in Africa, heir of the nationalist movement, is first of all a mass party, at least in theory. It seeks to enroll all the citizenry in its branches, including its women's and youth sections. In those nations where the party is an effective and real one, the sections meet on a regular basis, often weekly, in every village and town ward. Because almost the whole population belongs to the party, these meetings resemble "town meetings." The function of the meetings is twofold. They are arenas whereby the government via the party cadres can transmit new ideas, new projects, new demands for sacrifices—that is, they function to educate the population, so that government decisions do not remain dead letters but are really carried out. But they also serve to communicate the ideas of the people to the government as well; they are a direct channel of complaint and suggestion through which the government can be made sensitive to the internal realities of the nation and flexible in the means it uses to achieve its goals. There seems to be considerable evidence that this two-way process is not a sham, or in any sense based on terror, but that it works fairly well. . . . Some party structures place less emphasis on participation, using more nebulous antennae to remain sensitive to popular will. In these cases, the pipe lines transmitting points of view—both upward and downward —sometimes get clogged. . . .

Along with such a structure goes an ideology which argues that the party incarnates the nation, not because it is in tune with historical destiny, but because of its past and present accomplishments. In the past, it fought for freedom and helped to create a national consciousness. And in the present, it is a mass, not a class, party. If it is not a class party, it is even less an elite party. (This is, of course, a fundamental theoretical difference between African parties and Communist parties in Eastern Europe.) It is a party to which everyone is encouraged to adhere, and to which the majority does adhere.

This ideology is the basis of justification for the theory of parallel authority—the matching of each governmental structure (national, regional, local) with a party structure, priority always being assigned to the political over the administrative structure. It is considered the essence of popular control over government in Ghana and the Ivory Coast, Niger and Tanganyika, that the Political Bureau of the party should take precedence over the Cabinet. The party should run the government, not vice versa, because the party, not the government, is the emanation of the people, that is, holds their loyalty and ties them to the state. The party integrates the nation and allows the integration to be accomplished by a method that maximizes the opportunity of every citizen to participate on a regular and meaningful basis in the decision-making process. In practice small elites may still run the show, but they do so to a lesser degree than if there were no party structure.

The party is not alone, however, in performing the integrating function. It shares the stage with its most important adjunct, the national hero. The hero, the leader, is not an isolated phenomenon. He is the leader of the party as well as of the nation. Should he break his ties with the party, he could find it difficult to survive, as we see from the decline of Messali Hadj in Algeria. Nevertheless, his power is not identical with that of the party; he has a drawing power of his own, as a potential arbiter, as a militant fighter, as one who has proved his mettle and will seek the nation's good.

The appearance of national heroes in Africa often makes outside observers uncomfortable, for the latter think of parallel strong men and "dictators" elsewhere. It is important, therefore, to see why the hero looms so large in the new African nations and what function he really fulfills.

The role of the hero is first of all to be a readily available, easily understood, symbol of the new nation, someone to incarnate in his person its values and aspirations. But the hero does more than symbolize the new nation. He legitimizes the state by ordaining obedience to its norms out of loyalty to his person. This is what people usually mean when they speak of the charismatic authority of these leaders.

The problem of integration is essentially one of getting people to shift loyalty from a structure based on tradition to a new artificial entity, the nation-state, whose only justification for authority lies in its constitution. This is a new basis for authority in Africa, and as we have seen, the majority is often reluctant to give it much credence, particularly if there is some immediate economic or prestige advantage for not doing so—thus "regionalism" based on "tribal," traditionalist loyalties. The charismatic justification for authority can be seen as a way of transition, an interim measure which gets people to observe the requirements of the nation out of loyalty to the leader while they (or their children) learn to do it for its own sake. In short, the hero helps to bridge the gap to a modern state. The citizens can feel an affection for the hero which they may not have at first for the nation. Insofar as the hero works in tandem with a party structure, he provides a very powerful mechanism for integration of the state. Those African nations which have not thrown up sufficiently "heroic" leaders clearly suffer by their absence. And since heroes are largely made, not born, most new African nations are doing their best to create or reinforce the image of their hero.

The problem is keeping the special, inflated status of the hero untarnished. The hero is a human being. He makes mistakes, antagonizes people. He often gets bad press at home as well as in other African countries and beyond Africa. He is particularly under attack by intellectuals, who resent his nonintellectual claims to authority and often his scorn for their pretensions. Actually, the hero himself may be a full-fledged intellectual (Senghor, President of Senegal and poet, Kenyatta of Kenya, an anthropologist), or at least a university graduate (Bourguiba, Nkrumah, Azikiwe, Nyerere). This does not mean that he will not find a majority of the intellectuals opposed to him or chafing under his authority. For as a national hero he represents a nonintellectual outlook. The hero must establish a national myth. The intellectual attacks national myths—though often in the name of other myths, some more local, some more universal.

Under this attack on the hero's status, the new African states have worked out a number of ways of preserving his image so that he may fulfill his function as a mediator between new citizen and new state. The most obvious way is the glorification of the hero. His name must be everywhere.... There is scarcely a country where the face of the hero does not appear on stamps, where the hero does not regularly conduct triumphal tours of his country in somewhat regal style.

But if in ceremonies the hero becomes more regularly apparent after independence, in actual fact he becomes more removed—both from foreigners and from his own people. He is shielded from soiling his reputation with the day-to-day harsh situations that governments face. He is surrounded by lieutenants and associates who bear the brunt of direct contact with the complainants, who serve as sources of information for the hero and scapegoats for blame. In moving about independent Africa, one can hear the same theme song again and again. "If only the hero knew, he would not permit it. He is good, but the men around him do not understand us."

If all these ways of preserving the leader's authority fail, the hero can resort to "religious" sanctification.... The hero often allows an aura of secrecy to build up and rumors to spread about his consulting the imam or the marabout or the fetish priest—any or all of them—without much regard for his own religious affiliation.

The hero and the party, then, work together to keep the nation unified, to hold it tightly together until the majority of the citizens begin to internalize a degree of loyalty to the state which will allow the government to take this loyalty for granted....

There is a correlation between the strength of party and hero and the degree of national integration and stability. And integration and stability make possible economic development and increase the ultimate prospects for a flexible democracy. Let us turn from the problem of how to achieve or maintain internal unity in the newly independent states to the problem of how to achieve larger unities among African states—the question of pan-Africanism.

LARGER UNITIES: PAN-AFRICANISM AND REGIONAL FEDERATIONS

The drive for larger African unity, pan-Africanism, is probably stronger than similar movements elsewhere in the world. It is not strong enough to assure immediate success, perhaps not even ultimate success. But pan-Africanism seems likely to loom large as an active issue in African politics in the near future.

. . . .

Ghana's independence and the first Conference of Independent African States, held in Accra in April 1958, changed the character of pan-Africanism. It was still a tool in the African colonial struggle, although now a complication arose. Who would direct and control this movement? Whether independent African nations had some greater right to wield this tool than the nationalist movements in countries not yet independent would become an issue. However, as more and more African countries gained their independence, the central question became rather the unification of sovereign states.

Pan-Africanism has had at least three political objectives, which to some extent can be seen as occurring in three successive periods. First, it has been a protest movement against racism, largely of American and West Indian Negroes. In this capacity, pan-Africanism still continues. It is an interesting and important story, but we shall not tell it here. Second, pan-Africanism has been a tool in the hands of African nationalist movements struggling for independence. It probably has not been the most important tool in this struggle. It has played some role, but one far less important than internal party organization and, as a rallying force, it has been no more important than territorial nationalism. At some points, it has even caused strains and hence, perhaps, setbacks for particular nationalist movements.

Third and most recently, pan-Africanism has been a movement to establish a supranational entity or entities encompassing various independent African states—at its most hopeful, the United States of Africa. In this last aspect, pan-Africanism has perforce had only a short life, much too short for us to be able to evaluate its achievements properly. Yet in its short history, the pan-African movement has had some important successes and suffered some serious setbacks....

The economic case for larger unities, to be sure, is strong. It was used for a long time by colonial governments to justify the establishment of federations of which they approved, such as the Federation of the Rhodesias and Nyasaland....

Basically, though, pan-Africanism is a political (and cultural) movement. Economic arguments have proved insufficient to accomplish anything positive. But in the political arena, the quarrels over the pace and method of decolonization since 1957 on the one hand have destroyed some old possibilities of unity and on the other hand have created some new and unexpected channels for unity. In fact, decolonization has caused major political realignments in Africa, largely around the issues of pan-Africanism.

Colonial governments created units larger than the individual territories. Units such as French West Africa or French North Africa, British West Africa or British East Africa existed as institutional structures or at least as well-defined regions with common problems.

. . . .

Decolonization in Africa, although occurring within a relatively short span of time, seldom occurred simultaneously in different territories, even those in the same area. Thus in British West Africa, Ghana became independent before Nigeria which became independent before Sierra Leone. In French West Africa, Guinea became independent before the Federation of Mali, which became independent before the four states of the Conseil de l'Entente (Ivory Coast, Upper Volta, Niger and Dahomey). Sometimes, as in French West Africa, the very pace of decolonization became a major issue *between* various African countries. The first ones to become independent in a group of territories were reluctant to remain in joint administrative structures with territories that were still colonies. Thus, in 1957, Ghana withdrew from such joint enterprises as the West African Airways Corporation. After Guinea's independence in 1958, she was excluded from the French West African interterritorial structures, which were to disintegrate completely by 1959. The administrative dismantling was sometimes matched by partial collapse of the interterritorial nationalist structures during this period....

The vagaries of the decolonization process, insofar as they have affected the possibilities of African unity, have not been entirely fortuitous. Colonial governments were not entirely indifferent to these questions. On the contrary, it can be argued that France was systematically, although not outspokenly, hostile, the British to a limited degree favorable, and the Belgians veered sharply between extremes.

Between 1956 and 1960, as French black African territories went from colonial status to autonomy to independence, the French seldom threw their support to elements favorable to larger political unities. The reason was very simple. Those who most strongly advocated unity were also those who most strongly pushed the advances toward independence. French repudiation of the goal of independence led to deep suspicion of the goal of unity....

The British position was less clear-cut. In the early colonial era, they too sought to divide and conquer. But once they came to terms with the nationalist movement in a particular area, they looked with favor on achieving larger unities, chiefly on the grounds that larger entities showed more potential for stability and economic development.... In Nigeria, the British bore much responsibility for the rise of regionalism. But once having decided to go forward to independence, the British, between 1956 and 1960, were one of the important forces working toward the establishment of the strongest possible federal state for an independent Nigeria. In the settler territories of East and Central Africa, the Colonial Office was historically a stalwart supporter of moves toward federation, imposing its point of view on the Africans and to some extent even on the settlers. Nevertheless, by 1960 British support had somewhat abated as a result of the persistent African opposition. At this stage, having once again decided to go forward to independence (with universal suffrage), the British sought means of preserving the federal link (tainted by its association with white-settler domination) between the future independent African states....

The factor that has made for the greatest difference between the British and the French attitudes toward larger unities in Africa has been the British willingness to acknowledge the legitimacy of the goal of independence. This has enabled the British, during the transition period, to look ahead to the post-independence period and plan their policy accordingly. They have thus always been able to take a more relaxed view of African unity than the French.

The Belgian policy has been quite different from both the French and the British. The Belgians had always ruled the Congo as a unitary state with some administrative decentralization. When they decided to grant the Congo its independence, they were eager to retain this unitary character. They feared that separatist movements would destroy the strong economy of the Congo in which they intended to remain involved.[1] Shortly after independence, when it appeared that Belgium's continuing political and economic relationship with the Congo was threatened by the strong supporters of the unitary state, the Belgian government veered to a strong support of separatist, indeed secessionist, elements.

The policies of the colonial powers in relation to larger African unities can be seen to reflect their views of their own interests. That Britain, France and Belgium analyzed these interests differently does not detract from the reality of this motivation. Even insofar as colonial powers were favorable to unity, it was a unity within the family, so to speak. When it came to moves for pan-African unity that cut across the traditional colonial divisions, even the more sanguine British hesitated occasionally. Yet, of course, African unity will have real meaning only in the degree to which the new entities will cut across divisions of European language and demarcations of European colonial spheres....

[1]. However, during this period, 1959–60, the *French* government, characteristically, gave tacit encouragement to the Bakongo separatists led by Joseph Kasavubu.

23

Building the Newest Nations

WILLIAM J. FOLTZ*

Most of the currently ruling political parties in the newest states grew up under the late colonial regimes as instruments for attaining national independence. Particularly in the British and French colonial empires, the single, mass parties were singularly successful in leading the way to independence and quickly consolidating control over the government and administrative apparatuses once independence was achieved. The strength and success of these parties have rested on four principal factors. First, in "Independence!" they had a rallying cry of universal appeal. Typically, in any competitive party situation, the party that first proclaimed, "Freedom now," "Uhuru," or "N'dépendence" ended up on top once it had made itself the recognized spokesman for the feelings of vague revolt and common identity that usually make up modern nationalism in the underdeveloped countries. Its espousal of national independence provided a focus around which both elite and mass could unite. Second, the single, mass party usually included virtually all the modern elite. These men were united by ties of personal friendship, frequently reinforced by common educational and agitational experiences and by dedication to the nationalist cause. . . . Third, because of the dominance of the nationalist issue and because of the general lack of other modern structures, the single political party had no serious competition from other modern associations as a focus for popular loyalties. Finally, the single, mass party was generally well organized. . . . It both embodied and promoted a preliminary sense of national unity and identity.

Short-run Strategies

But winning independence, although it may be a necessary condition, is only the first and perhaps easiest step in building a nation. The new state apparatus must then be solidly implanted and extended, and the loyalty of the people to a stable governing regime, not to an agitational opposition movement, must be assured. However, the very factors making the mass party such an effective tool in the struggle for independence and permitting it to take over governmental power may be weakened by the day-to-day exercise of governmental responsibilities and by the nation-building process itself. Once formal independence is won, the unifying slogan of "Independence" has lost its magic force, and it is unlikely that anything quite so dramatic and effective can be found to replace it. Defending a revolution is always a less exciting and more onerous task than making it. Frequently, newly independent states seize on a new derivative slogan or

Reprinted from *Nation-Building*, Karl W. Deutsch and William J. Foltz, Editors, by permission of the author and the Publishers, Atherton Press, Inc. Copyright © 1963, Atherton Press, New York. All rights reserved.

* William Foltz (1936–) is in the Department of Political Science at Yale University.

goal to replace "independence" as a means of unifying both elite and mass. These secondary goals have frequently involved transforming the world outside the state to bring it more into line with the desires and presumed advantages of the new state, thus symbolically continuing the movement of independence. Such movements have sometimes, but not always, sought to export a national revolution or, as in Africa recently, to continue the independence movement to areas not yet favored by an enlightened colonial master. Of the same sort are the many irredentist movements designed to annex a lost or related territory or region. . . .

Although turning to the outside world may provoke as strong an emotional yearning for unity as did the simpler search for national political unity and independence formerly, it may, in the short run, simply dilute or confuse more specific national sentiment. To the degree that it makes the success of the territorial nationalist movement dependent on that of a greater whole, it may in the long run succeed only in calling into question the worth of the national regime when the larger unity proves unrealizable.

The new state may try to unite its people by focusing animosities and frustrations on some external enemy, just as the nationalist movement focused its resentments on the colonial power or previous ruling class. To this end, the term "neo-colonialism" has recently been invented. . . .

Finally, the new state may choose some purely internal, non-symbolic goal to replace national independence as a national rallying cry. The "battle for economic development" is the most common and significant such goal today, as one would expect. However praiseworthy economic development may be as a national goal and however important it may be as a national goal and however important it may be for long-term nation-building, it is still not likely to have the political potency of "independence." . . .

As the mass party in the newly independent state is deprived of "independence" as a national rallying cry, so, too, its organization may suffer once it has passed from systematic opposition to coping with the demands of day-to-day administration. Talents that once were available for the crucial work of party organisation may now be preoccupied with running a ministry or government bureau. This will be particularly true where the conditions under which independence was obtained led to the withdrawal of European advisors and technicians and threw the whole technical and administrative burden on the shoulders of the young indigenous politicians. Unless new sources of loyal organizational and administrative talents can be found immediately, the party's organization—and, therefore, the major link between the regime and the masses—is likely to be weakened.

If, in the days of nationalist agitation for independence, the mass party provided the unique and inclusive instrument for popular political participation, this is not likely to be the case after independence is attained. Governing an independent country requires indigenous participation in a great variety of new, formally constituted units. A civil service and national army are only the minimal, though most essential, organizations that must be staffed. Although these, like the governmental apparatus, will formally be brought under the control of the mass party, they can be expected to become new focuses of loyalty and to develop new goals, priorities, and methods that are at variance with those of the mass party. With increased specialization of function, the elite will share fewer and fewer common perspectives and experiences and will develop personal and group interests that could well produce internal scissions that were absent when the mass political party was the single organ of political expression, participation, and planning.

Of course, in theory, the new organizations should complement the mass party as the means of bridging the gap between the elite and the masses. However, if a struggle for influence pitting army or administration against the party develops, the very contacts of the new organizations with the masses may serve to divide the people more deeply than they were when only the party undertook to link them with the realm of modern politics. This will be particularly the case in cultures where personal leadership is important, and an army general, top administrator, or cabinet minister may build a personal following among the population at large.

The dispersion of leadership talents and the competition of different decision-making units may be further accentuated if economic development is given top priority by the ruling elite. It is in part to prevent the creation of autonomous domestic decision-making units with a basis of economic power that many new states have refused to expand the private sector of the economy, even when such expansion would clearly contribute to economic development....

Even where economic planning and execution remain firmly in governmental hands one may expect to find a new center of power created in the planning ministry, allied or not allied with the civil service against the party and regime. This would seem almost inevitable if economic development is to be given serious priority. On almost every level, the demands of economic efficiency are sure to conflict at some point with the demands of political expediency or orthodoxy. Since their independence, Indonesia and Ghana have continually faced such conflicts.

In a somewhat broader perspective, the implementation of rapid economic and social change and, in particular, of educational development can open a whole range of new problems centered around controlling the burgeoning new elites. In part this is simply a qualitative problem. The promising young men who are trained after independence has been won will have quite different associations, perceptions, and preoccupations from those of their elders of the nationalist generation. Furthermore, since the nationalist generation is likely to come into power around age forty at the most, it is unlikely to fade from the scene so quickly as the new generation would like. On the other hand, the new generation is likely to have more formal education than its elders, particularly in technical domains. Also, since it will in all probability be trained abroad for the most part, it will escape the direct influence of the single-party regime during the crucial formative years of adolescence. It is not surprising that a recent survey of African students in France revealed that 63 per cent considered themselves in serious conflict with their governments.[1] After their return to home, one would naturally expect these young men to side with one of the alternative loci of power in the country, particularly if they are blocked, as they must be if the single-party regime's continuity is to be maintained, in their attempt to accede immediately to posts of high responsibility and power....

But the rapid creation of new elites has a quantitative dimension of equal importance. It is one thing to integrate smoothly ten, twenty, or fifty returning students a year into the single-party regime and to inculcate in them the established political values and perceptions, but it is quite another to integrate a hundred or five hundred, particularly if they cannot be given the positions of top leadership to which they aspire because their fathers or older brothers are reluctant to step down. Without the clear necessity of pulling together to achieve independence and with a wider range of choices than faced the nationalist generation, these young men are unlikely to melt quietly into the previously established single-party regime. Nor are they so likely as were their elders to make the attempt to bridge the gap separating them from the masses, since by doing so they may only diminish the distinctiveness of their personal elite position without necessarily gaining corresponding political advantage. With no provisions for a loyal open opposition, a disloyal covert opposition may seem the only choice.

The emphasis on rapid social and economic change also poses problems for the single-party state on the level of the masses. If, through economic and social planning, one increases the rate of popular mobilization,[2] one also increases the demands made on the government. Although this mobilization is essential for building national sentiment among the masses, it may also threaten the regime if the government cannot keep pace with the new demands. Although in most cases this social mobilization was begun under the colonial regime, the colonial power was seldom attentive to these demands, even if it had been capable of responding. The nationalist single-party movement learned to be attentive to the masses' demands and used the colonial regime's reluctance to respond as an argument for seizing power. The independent single-party regime may continue to be attentive, but it is unlikely to possess the resources for responding effectively if mobilization proceeds at too great a pace. Alternatively, it may emphasize building an effective response capability by giving the younger

[1] J. P. N'Diaye, *Enquête sur les étudiants noirs en France* (Paris: Réalités Africaines, 1962), p. 223.

[2] On the concept of mobilization, see Karl W. Deutsch, "Social Mobilization and Political Development," *American Political Science Review*, LV, No. 3 (1961), pp. 493-514.

technical elites their head and playing down the political party structure. But, in doing this, it may end by making the new regime less well attuned to the immediate wants of the mobilized and dissatisfied masses, thereby inadvertently re-creating a situation analogous to that of the colonial era. A rigid new bureaucracy, even if technically competent and filled with good intentions, may open the possibility of new popular revolts led, perhaps, by disaffected politicians of the older nationalist generation who have maintained their links with the masses. Such a conflict between a distant technical bureaucracy and politicians of the nationalist generation has been particularly acute in the new states where the military has seized power.[3]

LONG-RUN PROBLEMS

The new states will increasingly be obliged to make some hard long-range decisions for which the experience and habits acquired in the period of nationalist agitation will provide little guidance. Stated most baldly, the polar choices open to the new states hold terrors equal to those of Scylla and Charybdis. At one extreme, a state may choose to ride the tiger of exacerbated pluralism and possible internal strife and disintegration, and, at the other extreme, it may choose to restrain social and economic change to a level that can be handled by the existing political structures. Similarly, the new regimes face a choice between transforming themselves completely to the profit of the new post-nationalist elites, with the attendant danger of losing political attentiveness to popular demands and what remains of the prestige (and personnel) of the nationalist movement, and, on the other hand, constricting access to the political elite, with the possibilities of political stagnation and turning the younger generation of elites against the regime.

It is difficult to predict at what point a given regime will succeed in striking a balance between these extremes. In general, it would seem that the closer to either extreme a regime comes, the poorer its chance of maintaining political integrity and eventually building a nation. Long-run pressures, especially those of an economic sort, would seem to be on the side of a more pluralist political process permitting entry of at least some new elites into the legitimate political arena and associating at least some newly mobilized sectors of the population with these elites through structures more or less outside the existing single-party framework. If this increase in political and social pluralism does not seriously weaken central governmental authority and create focuses of loyalty that challenge the legitimacy of the nation itself, rather than just a particular group of leaders or a specific policy, the nation-building process should be considerably advanced. For such a dynamic compromise to be maintained over the long run, the existing regime in most of the newest states must first feel itself secure enough from disruptive internal and external pressures to permit it to accept the necessary loosening of direct political control. At least in the short run, most such regimes will require absolute loyalty from new elites and acquiescence from the population at large, if only as evidence that the state is firmly enough established to permit the nation to be built.

Ensuring the short-run stability of the new states has led many regimes into practices which appear particularly objectionable to most people with a liberal democratic tradition. The "cult of personality" built around the national hero, the mouthing of seemingly senseless revolutionary slogans after the apparent revolution has been won, and the suppression of opposition groups and leaders are among the practices most commonly noted in the Western press. Although the disadvantages of these practices are readily apparent—at least to the outside observer with no immediate policy responsibilities—they may also serve useful functions in permitting the regimes to survive the initial period of building the state and make a successful transition to building a nation. Popular identification with a national hero and commitment to a revolutionary program, whether or not confined purely to the verbal level, both have the advantage of dissociating the state from a particular group of individuals making up the nationalist regime and permitting the people at large or new elites to serve and identify with a specific leader or set of policies. The national hero can retain not

---

3. See Lucian W. Pye, "The Army in Burmese Politics," in John J. Johnson, ed., *The Role of the Military in Underdeveloped Countries* (Princeton: Princeton University Press, 1962), pp. 231–251.

only the loyalty of the mass of the people, who are perhaps annoyed at specific government agents for specific causes, but can also go against his own lieutenants and bring new elites into the regime. . . . Similarly, concentration on some sort of ideology, even if only symbolic, permits popular recognition of particular governmental functions above and beyond the specific individuals fulfilling those functions. At the same time, it holds up a national goal for younger elites to follow, and, by their acceptance of such a goal, they may more easily be brought into smoothly-functioning relationships with the incumbent elite.

Finally, the suppression of opposition leaders, and even of some of the new elites, may, with luck, permit the new states to get over the most trying period of postrevolutionary letdown without a collapse of the ruling regime, either through internal bickering or outside attacks. To the extent that the new state concentrates on building a more continuous educational system at home and to the extent that it has time to indoctrinate the younger elites in loyalty to the new political order, succeeding elites should pose fewer problems to the regime than does the immediate postrevolutionary generation.

The ability of the newest states to grow out of their initial periods of restrictive consolidation of power and into a more balanced society-wide pattern of national growth will depend in part on the willingness of the leaders to envisage fundamental revisions in the relations between the regime and its people and also on whether the adoption of less restrictive policies brings with it sufficient rewards to make the risk of pluralism worth taking. Certainly, if economic and social development seem impossible no matter what course of action is adopted or if the nations in the best position to assist a new state turn a deaf ear to a regime's initial pleas for assistance, the sterile pattern of repression, stagnation, and revolt will become the lot of most states. Instead of profiting from the West's arduous history of nation-building, the newest nations may then be condemned to repeat the long apprenticeship of "coups, conquests, revolutions, and wars" before they, too, evolve viable national societies.

24

Metropolitan Growth and Future Political Problems

ANTHONY DOWNS*

During the next few decades, political problems within American metropolitan areas will become so critical that their importance may well rival that of world politics in our national life. The force which will cause this realignment of political urgencies is the rapid growth of metropolitan population that can be expected to occur in the United States over the next 25 years.

In his book, *Metropolis 1985*, Professor Raymond Vernon estimates that the population of the United States will be 286 million by 1985—an increase over the 1960 population of approximately 106 million persons.[1] Since almost 100 per cent of this increase can be expected to occur in present and future metropolitan areas, Vernon's projection envisions almost a *doubling* of our 1960 metropolitan area population of 108 million within 25 years. Although I believe his projection is somewhat high, it nevertheless serves to illustrate the order of magnitude of the population growth which will occur.

Furthermore, the amount of land covered by metropolitan areas will grow much faster relative to their present size than will their total population relative to its present level. This is true because a high proportion of the new urban residents will live in suburbs which have a low density of about three families per acre or 7,000 people per square mile. At present, about half of the people in metropolitan areas live in central cities which have much higher densities—as high as 15,000 persons per square mile in Chicago and 24,000 in New York. Even if some recentralization occurs and many people move back into central cities, a major portion of the new population growth will take place on the periphery of present metropolitan areas. Thus it is realistic to suppose that the amount of land covered by these areas will triple or quadruple if their population doubles.

A basic political dilemma will arise out of this situation because of the conflict of two forces: (1) the continuing dispersal of population in space which results in the formation of more and more political units, particularly new cities and towns; and (2) the increasing complexity of metropolitan economic and social relations which requires more centralized power and decision-making if metropolitan areas are to function effectively. For several dozen years, urban analysts and plan-

Reprinted by permission of the author and publisher from *Land Economics*, Vol. XXXVII, 1961. Copyright © 1961 by the Regents of the University of Wisconsin.

* Anthony Downs (1930–) is Senior Vice President and Treasurer of the Real Estate Research Corporation of Chicago.

1. Raymond Vernon, *Metropolis 1985* (Cambridge, Massachusetts: Harvard University Press, 1960).

ners have been urging the adoption of metropolitan government as a way out of this dilemma. However, experience proves that neither voters nor politicians will accept metropolitan government since it reduces the amount of power in the hands of the average citizen and the average local politician. We can expect this same attitude to prevail in the future; therefore, new local political entities will spring up like mushrooms across the landscape as the area of residential settlement spreads out and power over metropolitan affairs will become ever more decentralized among thousands of governments.

The resulting tension between increased dispersion of political power on the one hand and increased need for central control and direction on the other hand will give rise to at least six major political problems. Most of them are already making themselves felt but they will soon become much more serious. In this article I will list these six problems, discuss each briefly, and then attempt to point out what fundamental trends can be expected to arise from them.

Central City Access to Resources

The first problem can be stated as follows: *Central cities will become increasingly isolated from political access to the resources they need to pay for the special costs generated by their function in the metropolitan area.* At the present time, central cities within our metropolitan areas contain a large portion of the industrial resources of the nation and a great many of its commercial assets.[2] ... In particular, central cities contain (1) our major cultural institutions, (2) the residences of most of the lower-income workers who form the underpinnings of metropolitan economies, (3) the transportation networks which move people from outlying residences to centralized places of work, and (4) the agglomerations of office buildings and other central-place-oriented structures in which many residents of outlying areas earn their living. All of these features generate special public costs not present (at least to the same extent) in outlying suburbs, whereas only the last feature contributes substantially to the tax rolls or even pays for its

2. Raymond Vernon, *The Changing Economic Function of the Central City* (New York, New York: Committee for Economic Development, 1959).

own needs. As metropolitan areas grow, more and more industry can be expected to locate outside of central cities.... Not only will fewer new industries locate in central cities but the construction of new highways and urban renewal projects may drive many existing businesses now located therein to new outlying sites. Thus we can expect financial problems within central cities to become steadily worse.

Even if these cities can attract suburban middle-income families back into redeveloped areas, financial problems will not diminish. In order to make residential neighbourhoods attractive to middle-income families, cities must provide high levels of social service (such as police protection, garbage collection, building code enforcement, and maintenance of school standards)—higher than the average levels now experienced in these cities. Therefore, the addition of such redeveloped areas to the tax base will not cause any substantial net gain in revenues over expenditures.

As this financial squeeze becomes tighter and tighter, we can expect central cities to adopt the following devices to ease the pressure: (1) They will increasingly turn to federal government programs for assistance. (2) They will make more use of local non-property taxes (such as earnings taxes) whenever such devices will not drive people or businesses out of town. (3) They will begin reassessing property on the basis of its income-earning power rather than its depreciated book value. (4) If the financial squeeze really gets tight, they will reduce welfare expenditures and lower the general level of city services.

Suburban Imbalance in Resource Access

The second political problem arising from metropolitan growth can be stated as follows: *In new suburban communities there will not be enough industrial and commercial property to "go around" to all the new political entities formed; therefore, in many of them home owners will have to bear tremendous tax burdens if they are to maintain adequate public services.* As indicated before, we can expect a high percentage of new industrial establishments and other production facilities to be located in outlying areas, either in suburbs or more rural environments. Therefore suburban and rural communities will receive increments to their tax bases that would seemingly ease the burden upon residential property owners. However, even if the overall tax base of those portions of a metropolitan area outside the central city rises rapidly because of new production facilities, these facilities will not be evenly distributed among the new cities and towns formed in suburbia. In high-density cities a very large number of people can be located within the same political boundaries as a large number of industrial and commercial establishments. But in our new suburban communities the average population within each political unit is much lower than in central cities, both because these units are small and because their population is spread thinly over the landscape. Hence, we can expect a given population to be divided into many more political entities in the suburbs than in central cities; so the taxable resources formed by industrial and commercial establishments must be split up among many more governments.

There is no *a priori* reason to suppose that these resources will be evenly distributed among the many new governmental territories so formed. The high mobility of auto-driving workers, customers, and shoppers in suburban areas allows industrial, office, retail, and other facilities to be located in a few concentrated clusters which serve very widespread areas. Such clustering is further encouraged by the specific factors like the convergence of highway systems in a few key spots, irregular geographic features such as rivers and hills, advantages of locating near existing railroad networks, and the creation of attractive industrial parks in well-located communities.

Consequently, some suburbs will find themselves endowed with non-residential additions to their tax base more than adequate for handling all their governmental expenses; others will be forced to pay for the heavy expenditures caused by growing populations with very few commercial or industrial properties on which to place some of their resulting tax burdens. Recently, some shrewd industrial firms have even managed to forestall almost all local property taxation by incorporating their plants along with a few acres of residential land as separate communities. Thus the political fragmentation of suburbia combined with geographically uneven distribution of productive facilities will place very heavy tax burdens on many suburban residents.

These burdens will be accentuated by the fact that the expenses of providing certain types of social service in low-density areas are relatively great and the standards of normal public service expected by suburban residents are much higher than those expected by the lower-income residents of central cities. Moreover, the resulting tax-rate disparity among suburbs cannot be eliminated by merger of "have" and "have-not" suburbs. The "have" suburbs will naturally oppose any dilution of their tax base by consolidation with "have-nots"; hence democracy will prevent equality.

For these reasons, many suburban residents will also feel a financial squeeze. Furthermore, they cannot use federal aid to escape from this squeeze as effectively as central cities can. Except in periods of substantial unemployment, federal aid programs are financed largely by income taxes. Since suburban residents have relatively high incomes, they contribute more-than-proportionally to such programs. Thus, in the long run, use of federal aid does not represent a significant net gain for suburban areas, although specific suburbs receiving large grants benefit at the expense of those which receive none. Essentially, those suburban residents caught in the squeeze described above can solve their local tax problems only by allocating more of their personal incomes to local government needs or by accepting lower levels of community service than have been considered adequate in suburban areas.

Political Fragmentation and Functional Coordination

The third political problem arising from metropolitan growth is closely related to the first two: *As metropolitan political power becomes more dispersed in many political units but the economic and social interrelations among these units become more complex, the need for coordinating specific functions will rise at the same time as the ability to coordinate them falls.* Examples of specific functions which must be coordinated among many political units are highways, sewerage systems, water systems, public utilities, public transit, port and airport operations, recreational facilities, and law-enforcement machinery. In addition, land-use planning and zoning in one section of the metropolitan area cannot be intelligently carried out unless developments in other sections are taken into account. Yet, as the number of governments multiplies, the possibility of effectively coordinating their efforts will steadily decline.

Since metropolitan government *per se* will not be adopted, substitutes for it concerning specific functions will be invented. These substitutes will consist either of programs run by the federal government (or in fewer cases, by state governments), or will be metropolitan-level "authorities" or other public bodies especially constructed to deal with specific functional problems. Many such quasi-independent bodies already have jurisdiction across local political boundaries and their number can be expected to increase.[3] Sooner or later, the problem of coordinating these coordinators will also become acute. It is conceivable that a super-authority will then be created to oversee all the specific authorities. Thus a new form of metropolitan government may eventually sneak in by the back door.

All these devices are essentially evasions of the need to obtain voter approval for creating metropolitan government. For reasons we shall discuss below, voters do not wish to sacrifice local autonomy in government but the hard facts of metropolitan life will force them to agree tacitly to the creation of metropolitan-wide authorities. As a result, we will experience an unplanned, rather chaotic growth of metropolitan authorities existing side by side with local governments although the latter will zealously retain certain prerogatives. The federal government will undoubtedly act as an instrument for creating such metropolitan-wide authorities by drafting programs which require that area-wide plans be drawn up before funds can be released. This has already occurred to some extent in the highway program and will occur in other areas. In any event, the solution to the coordination problem will not be based on adoption of one simple and logical mechanism like metropolitan government, but will instead spring from an increasingly bewildering proliferation of both local and area-wide governmental units.

Central City Renewal and Neighborhood Autonomy

The fourth political problem is confined largely to central cities and can be stated as follows: *In order to attract middle-income and high-income residents into redeveloped neighborhoods, central cities need to create devices for giving enough local autonomy to these neighborhoods so that different levels of social service can be provided in different parts of the city.* In our democratic society we dislike admitting that the desire for segregation—both racial and cultural—has been one of the major causes of our suburban growth. A great many people move to the suburbs seeking a cultural and social homogeneity which exists within each suburb but is absent in our larger cities. Such homogeneity appeals to young people rearing children because it creates the kind of atmosphere in which they can pass on their cultural values to their offspring without exposing them to conflicting viewpoints. Naturally, this homogeneity is not everywhere of the same character; there are markedly different cultural levels and outlooks in different suburbs with the differences often highly correlated with variations in the income-levels of the residents.[4]

However, all suburbs have one major advantage regarding cultural homogeneity that is not shared by larger cities: suburban residents can make use of legal machinery to maintain their homogeneity by excluding those who might change it. Of course, they cannot directly prevent any particular group from entering by passing discriminatory laws but they can set up and enforce specific standards regarding building quality, tax rates, the character of public services, and the nature of the school system. By raising these standards high enough, they can make it economically impossible for "disrupting" elements to enter the area and dilute the homogeneity they seek to establish.

Within central cities such legal differentiation between neighborhoods is not possible.

---

3. For a discussion of this development see Robert C. Wood, *1400 Governments* (Cambridge, Massachusetts: Harvard University Press, 1961), chapter 4.

4. For many of the ideas expressed in this section I am indebted to Professor Richard Meier of the University of Michigan.

Residents of one part of the city cannot legally prevent people from other parts of it from moving into their area by raising neighborhood building standards; therefore they cannot permanently maintain differential standards regarding schools and public services. True, in some urban renewal neighborhoods strict enforcement of existing laws creates *de facto* legal differentiation because the same laws are loosely enforced elsewhere. However, such maintenance of local standards requires the sustained efforts of a major local political force (such as a university), and forces of this caliber are few and far between.

Even if the residents of a particular central-city neighborhood were willing to pay higher taxes to give themselves better schools and public services *in their own area*, there are no mechanisms by which they can do so. This inability to establish and maintain local homogeneity has driven many thousands of families from central cities when their own neighborhoods were faced with radical changes in cultural and economic standards through in-migration. In fact, much of the flight from areas of racial transition is ultimately fear of social and cultural change rather than fear of ethnic change *per se*. It is not the color of the Negro doctor who first moves into an all-white neighborhood that "frightens" the whites away; it is their belief that he will be followed by a "horde" of Negroes with much lower cultural, economic, and moral standards.

In my opinion, middle-income and upper-income white families will not move into central cities in any large numbers unless cultural (not racial) homogeneity of local neighborhoods can somehow be reconstituted. At present, the only legal method of maintaining such homogeneity within central cities is through the market; that is, by driving the price of residences in a certain area up so high that only persons with high incomes—and therefore presumably high cultural standards also—can afford them. However, there are only a few areas within each central city which have natural locational features that will generate such high prices. Furthermore, these prices are too high to attract income groups which are numerous enough to cause any real revival in central cities.

These facts imply that any central city which seeks to foster a large-scale "return to the city" by middle-income groups must create devices for allowing local neighborhoods to have more control over governmental matters in their own areas.[5] In particular, there are four different aspects of government regarding which more local autonomy can be given: (1) schools, (2) the level of social services, (3) building code standards and enforcement, and (4) local taxes. In the past, local differentiation concerning some of these aspects of government has in fact been tacitly accomplished. A return to such differentiation is also implicit in the new urban renewal projects now being carried out in many cities. The level of government services within these renewal areas is often much higher than it is in nearby slum areas because otherwise no new residents of the requisite income levels could be attracted into the redeveloped area.

Theoretically, it would be possible to achieve the same results without differentiation among neighborhoods by raising the total percentage of all central-city personal incomes devoted to local government services. However, it is quite possible that lower-income citizens do not want the same services from their government as do their higher-income neighbors. Therefore, it may in fact be more democratic to introduce more local autonomy within central city government than to maintain our present theoretically-identical levels of service throughout the city. Without question we should still spread the tax income from major industrial and commercial establishments in the city over all citizens equally so as to provide everyone with a basic minimum level of service. We should also leave the central-city government with full powers to carry out overall planning functions and locate such community services as highways, sewers, parks, and transportation. But it would still be in the tradition of American self-government to allow residents of each local area within the city to add onto this basic minimum level—at their own expense—if they wanted to do so.

However, the political problems of creating the legal machinery for such local autonomy are enormous because of the tremendous complexity of forces operating within our cities. For example, greater local autonomy

5. This device was first suggested to me by Professor Norton Long of Northwestern University.

leading to higher building standards in some areas might create barriers to movement within central cities for lower-income citizens. Such barriers might aggravate the existing "ghetto" concentrations of low-income Negroes, especially since the constant stream of rural Negroes into central cities would tend to expand these "ghettos" until they ran into the barriers created by local autonomy.

Because of such difficulties it may in the long run prove more practical to increase local autonomy through private non-governmental organizations than by creating more legal independence in each neighborhood. Already, citizens committees within specific neighborhoods are acting as watchdogs, encouraging high standards of building repair, compliance with density regulations, and aesthetic appearance....

... The process of working out effective means of supplementing the market in maintaining high neighborhood standards will be extremely complex. For this reason it will probably take the citizens of central cities at least a decade to formulate the devices necessary to accomplish this goal. Therefore, for the next ten years, we can expect relatively little mass recentralization in central cities by middle-income families in the child-rearing age groups. The only way in which this long gestation period could be circumvented is creation of a truly massive urban renewal program supported by the federal government. Such a program would have to be so large that whole neighborhoods of high-school-district size would be demolished and replaced by newly-constructed developments occupied by middle-class residents who would initially establish high standards and maintain them henceforth. At present, urban renewal spending on such a scale seems improbable.

Residential Choice and Minority Groups

The fifth problem which is arising because of metropolitan growth can be expressed as follows: *Unless minority groups—particularly Negroes—are given wider residential choice and greater access to all other symbols of social status, there will be increasing social cleavage between ethnic groups and a serious possibility of disaffection from our governmental system by racial minorities.*

Although some cultural segregation can be regarded as an inescapable part of suburban growth in metropolitan areas, there is no real need for such segregation to be maintained along racial lines. However, it has been so maintained in our Northern and Western cities. Insofar as Negroes and other minority groups have been kept "bottled up" within specific areas—often overcrowded and less desirable in character—the aspiration of middle-income and upper-income Negroes to attain the same standards as their white counterparts has been seriously frustrated. These Negroes are just as anxious as whites to protect their own social and cultural standards by creating local homogeneity but they have rarely been able to create middle-class suburbs which already have the kind of cultural standards they seek. As metropolitan areas rapidly expand outward, either this blocking of legitimate aspirations by Negro citizens must be alleviated or we can expect them to become increasingly hostile towards our white-dominated society. It is certainly true that housing for Negroes has become more widely available because of the surplus in the housing market which has developed since 1957. As this surplus expands and vacancy rates rise we can expect some of this Negro frustration to be relieved. Nevertheless, the rapid growth of the Black Muslim separatist movement among urban Negroes is a disquieting sign of outright hostility to all white people. Yet we must expect such signs to become more numerous if we deny to Negroes and other minorities access to the status-paths along which whites move. This problem is most acute in the South regarding schools, but it will become considerably more significant in the North in spite of the diminished movement of lower-income Negroes to northern and western cities. Furthermore, the international ramifications of our domestic relations between whites and Negroes are becoming daily more significant. In the long run the ethnic tension connected with urban growth will be both the most serious and the most difficult of all our urban problems.

Economic Growth and Unemployment of Central City Populations

The last problem which I wish to point out as related to metropolitan growth is the following one: Since the basis for an expanding population is ultimately an expanding number of jobs, we must have reasonably rapid economic growth to sustain our living standards but *the particular kind of economic growth we are likely to experience may create a growing pool of unemployed and perhaps unemployable labor in central cities and mature suburbs.*

. . . .

... Unemployment rates among young members of the labor force are disproportionately high. This is particularly true of young Negroes since they are more likely to drop out of high school before graduation than whites and less likely to receive impartial consideration for whatever jobs are available. Hence, unemployment rates among Negroes aged 16 to 21 who are out of school range as high as 50 percent in some large cities. Especially in our larger Northern metropolitan areas, low-income Negroes and whites are concentrated in central cities and some older suburbs. Because of the much higher incidence of high school drop-outs among these groups than among the higher-income groups living in newer suburbs, problems like juvenile delinquency and high crime rates often occur primarily within the boundaries of central cities and older suburbs.[6] Thus the already-noted difficulties caused by the heavy social-service burdens borne by these cities will be further aggravated by the type of structural unemployment likely to occur in the near future. Moreover, the concentration of unemployment and related social maladies among Negroes is likely to further aggravate the potential disaffection of Negroes from our white-dominated society.

Although both these problems are much more acute in our larger Northern metropolitan areas than in other parts of the country, these particular areas contain a significant proportion of the nation's total population, both white and nonwhite. The only way to prevent the above-described dual aggravation of existing political problems in these areas is to maintain a high level of employment among *all* elements of our future population. This objective will require expanding aggregate demand, considerable retraining of presently-unemployed workers, and improved educational standards among young people in high school. All three of these goals will necessitate continued high levels of federal government spending, both in federal programs and in programs of assistance to state and metropolitan-area governments. For this reason we can expect increasing willingness on the part of the federal government to engage in programs of assistance to local and state governments. . . .

The six fundamental problems arising from metropolitan growth which are enumerated above are not new nor are all of them found to an equal extent in all parts of the country. However, their intensity is bound to increase as our metropolitan areas "explode" outward in space and upward in total population. From what has been said, it appears that the basic dilemma caused by increased dispersal of people and local government authority versus the need for greater centralization of power will be solved in two ways. First, more metropolitan-wide authorities will appear on the scene to fill the vacuum left by the unwillingness of existing entities to merge into metropolitan governments. Second, the federal government will increasingly act as an intermediary collecting funds from people throughout the metropolitan area via personal and corporate income taxes and disbursing those funds into the specialized areas where the need for them is greatest. Thus it will fulfill the economic function which unmerged local governments cannot undertake.

---

6. An excellent discussion of this problem is presented by James B. Conant in *Slums and Suburbs* (New York, New York: McGraw-Hill Book Company, Inc., 1961).

Annotated Bibliography

AKE, CLAUDE
"Political Integration and Political Stability: A Hypothesis," *World Politics*, XIX (April 1967), pp. 486–499.
 A research note that relates political stability, provided by systems that are authoritarian, consensual, identificatory, or paternal, and political integration. The hypothesis is that a system driving for integration maximizes its chances for success if it is one of these four varieties.

ALMOND, GABRIEL A.
"A Developmental Approach to Political Systems," *World Politics*, XVII (January 1965), pp. 183–215.
 A major statement suggesting an approach to political development in terms of systematic comparative history by means of the adaption of political systems theory to formulate a developmental concept. The author suggests that the performance of a political system, its conversion characteristics, the operations of its recruitment and socialization processes, are explainable in terms of a peculiar history of interaction between the political system and its social and international environments.

BANFIELD, EDWARD C.
"Managing Metropolis," *Interplay of European/American Affairs*, I (October 1967), pp. 20–22.
 A short article by a student of metropolitan government. The author compares the achievement of metropolitan government in London with the myriad of jurisdictions in the New York region. The contrast in approach to metropolitan integration is related to the different structure of and philosophy toward local government in Britain and the United States.

BRAMS, STEVEN J.
"Transaction Flows in the International System," *American Political Science Review*, LX (December 1966), pp. 880–898.
 An analysis of international transaction flows which indicate the coherence present in the totality of interaction. The author utilizes diplomatic exchanges, trade, and shared membership in intergovernmental organizations as the types of transactions. An excellent discussion of the transaction flow model then follows. Diagrammatic mapping illustrates both the discrepancy of flows and how the actual distribution structures the international system.

BRECHER, MICHAEL
The New States of Asia: A Political Analysis (New York: Oxford University Press, 1966).
 An analysis of the problems of integration in the newly independent states of Asia. Following one chapter on colonialism and the coming of independence, the author concentrates on internal and external aspects of these new states.

CUTRIGHT, PHILLIPS
"National Political Development: Measurement and Analysis," *American Sociological Review*, XXVIII (April 1963), pp. 253–264.
 An index of political development is applied to seventy-seven independent nations, and knowledge of the level of the development of the communications system of a nation accounts for sixty-five per cent of the variation in scores around the mean of the political development index. A matrix of high intercorrelations among a variety of indicators of specialization and level of development supports the idea of interdependence among the parts of the system. This concept of interdependence and the statistical method used lead the author to consider the existence of hypothetical equilibrium points toward which each nation is moving.

DALE, EDMUND H.

"The State-Idea: Missing Prop of the West Indies Federation," *Scottish Geographical Magazine*, LXXVIII (December 1962), pp. 166-176.

An examination into the disintegration of the British-proposed Federation of the West Indies. The author identifies the basic reason for disintegration as the absence of a state-idea. Aspects of the Islands' cultural heterogeneity and separatist views are examined.

DEUTSCH, KARL W.

Nationalism and Social Communication, 2nd ed. (Cambridge, Mass.: M.I.T. Press, 1966).

An important volume which develops a theory of nationalism as a community of social communication. Chapter 2, "Building Blocks of Nationality," and Chapter 4, "Peoples, Nations, and Communications," are especially useful. Available in paperback.

DEUTSCH, KARL W.

"On Social Communication and the Metropolis," *Daedalus*, XC (1961), pp. 99-109.

A theoretical speculation on the function of a metropolis in providing freedom and choice for its inhabitants. The author utilizes communications theory to analyze the effectiveness and efficiency of "contact choices" in the American metropolis. He then describes many of the contemporary problems of urban society in terms of communications overload at concentrations in space and time. Finally, a strategy is provided to solve these problems.

DEUTSCH, KARL W. et al.

International Political Communities (Garden City: Anchor Books, 1966).

This inexpensive paperback brings together many of the most important writings on political integration. In addition to theoretical statements by Karl Deutsch, Amitai Etzioni, and Ernst B. Haas, regional analyses of Switzerland, Europe, Latin America, COMECON, East Africa, and Pan Africanism are also provided.

DYE, THOMAS R.

"Urban Political Integration: Conditions Associated with Annexation in American cities," *Midwest Journal of Political Science*, VIII (November 1964), pp. 430-446.

The relationship between metropolitan political integration and annexation activity is examined quantitatively. Legal restraints, metropolitan area size, form of government, and the age of settlement are each analyzed in terms of incidence of annexation. The author also examines the relationship between annexation activity and the status characteristics of central cities and city-suburban social distance. A multivariate approach indicates that annexation is a likely integrative device in some but not in all cases.

ETZIONI, AMITAI

"European Unification: A Strategy of Change," *World Politics*, XVI (October 1963), pp. 32-51.

From the experience of the first five years of the Common Market, the author extrapolates a general statement about the process of European integration which includes notions of building up homogeneity, using a gradualistic approach, not reallocating resources prior to political integration, and providing cushioning mechanisms to solve regional problems.

FISHER, CHARLES A.

"The Geographical Setting of the Proposed Malaysian Federation: Some Preliminary Considerations," *Journal of Tropical Geography*, XVII (May 1963), pp. 99-115.

An analysis of the then-proposed Malaysian Federation. The author finds the proposal entirely in accord with historical and geographical realities. After a consideration of past attempts at political integration at different levels, the author concludes that the current divisions have outlived their usefulness and that integrative forces are sufficient to justify the new federation.

FISHER, CHARLES A.

"The Vietnamese Problem in its Geographical Context," *Geographical Journal*, CXXXI (December 1965), pp. 502-515.

An examination of the conflict in Vietnam from a political geographic viewpoint. The author traces the evolution of political-territorial organization, as well as the impact of French colonial rule and that of partition on spatial patterns. A very good select bibliography is included.

FLEMING, DOUGLAS K.

"The Common Market Today," *Journal of Geography*, LXVI (November 1967), pp. 449-453.

The author appraises the degree of regional cohesion in the Common Market by examining the forces for and against political integration. Special emphasis is put on the emergence of a spatial network resulting from the circulation of the idea of community, and on the feedback effect of this network.

HARTSHORNE, RICHARD

"The Role of the State in Economic Growth: Contents of the State Area," in Hugh G. J. Aitken, ed., *The State and Economic Growth* (New York: Social Science Research Council, 1959), pp. 287-325.

A rather long and now somewhat dated work which identifies and analyzes the factors within the area of the state. The author concerns himself with factors of diversification including transport facilities, capital goods, power resources, raw materials, entrepreneurship, money capital, labor, and markets, domestic and foreign.

HAZLEWOOD, ARTHUR, ed.
African Integration and Disintegration: Case Studies in Economic and Political Union (London: Oxford University Press, 1967).
 A collection of original essays on the problems of integration in Africa. An excellent introduction by the editor followed by seven case studies of economic and political unions with two final selections on wider economic and political unions with two final selections on wider groupings. A useful bibliography is included.

HUNKER, HENRY L., ed.
"Political Interaction," *The East Lakes Geographer*, IV (December 1968).
 This issue is devoted to the problems of political interaction in geography and, under the guest editorship of Kevin Cox, contains four papers presented to the 1967 Meetings of the Association of American Geographers. In addition to the study by Soja, reproduced in this book, are papers on "The Spatial integration of Uganda," by Burton O. Witthuhn; "The Analysis of Political Boundaries as Barriers," by David R. Reynolds and Michael L. McNulty; and "A Spatial Interactional Model for Political Geography," by Kevin R. Cox, who also contributes a "Guest Editorial." This collection is representative of the interest in the spatial dimensions of political interaction in political geography.

INGLEHART, RONALD
"An End to European Integration?," *American Political Science Review*, LXI (March 1967), pp. 91–105.
 An analysis of the scope and pace of European integration by means of political socialization. Two cross-national studies of adult attitudes and surveys of secondary school populations provide the data for the study. The author calls into question Karl Deutsch's study which contends that European integration has slowed down since the mid-1950's and has stopped or reached a plateau since 1957–58. Inglehart argues that integration may have moved into full gear only since 1958. This approach provides a noteworthy dimension to studies of political integration and illustrates some of the weaknesses in transaction flow analysis.

JACOB, PHILIP E. and JAMES V. TOSCANO, eds.
The Integration of Political Communities (Philadelphia: J. B. Lippincott Co., 1964).
 A collection of ten essays on political integration by, in various combinations, the editors, Henry Teune, Karl W. Deutsch, and William L. C. Wheaton. There are no case studies and the emphasis is on theory and techniques at the national and urban levels.

JOHNSON, JAMES H.
"The Political Distinctiveness of Northern Ireland," *Geographical Review*, LII (January 1962), pp. 78–91.
 Advances and documents the thesis that Ireland has two state-ideas, now epitomized by the line of partition. The author examines the historical background of this development, and uses cartographic analysis of electoral data to show this distinction.

KAPLAN, MORTON A.
System and Process in International Politics (N.Y.: John Wiley and Sons, 1964).
 An analysis of international politics in terms of systems theory. Chapter 5, "The Integrative and Disintegrative Processes," analyzes the conditions of stability in a system which permits it to respond adequately to environmental disturbances. Nine hypotheses are developed indicating those factors upon which stability and integration depend. Chapter 6, "Processes and the International System," applies regulatory, integrative, and disintegrative processes to the operation of the international political system, and indicates those conditions which produce one rather than another process.

LERNER, DANIEL
The Passing of Traditional Societies: Modernizing the Middle East (New York: Free Press, 1958).
 This work has become a classic among case studies of political development. Chapters II (Modernizing Styles of Life) and III (The Passing of Traditional Society: A Survey) contain the author's basic philosophy including a model of transition in which he suggests a typology of modernization (modern, transitional, and traditional) with each type tested against the indicies of literacy, urbanization, media participation, and empathy. The data for the case studies of Turkey, Lebanon, Egypt, Syria, Jordan, and Iran were collected largely from interviews in the field.

LUBASZ, HEINZ
The Development of the Modern State (New York: Macmillan, 1964).
 A collection of ten articles all appearing earlier in a variety of publications, tracing the development of the modern state from its origins to the problems of the present period.

MACKAY, J. ROSS
"The Interactance Hypothesis and Boundaries in Canada," *Canadian Geographer*, No. 11 (1958), pp. 1–8.
 A pioneering work which quantitatively assesses the role of political boundaries in interrupting spatial processes by the application of the interactance hypothesis on circulation patterns between centers either side of the Canadian-United States boundary and inter-provincially within Canada.

MCGEE, T. G.
"Aspects of the Political Geography of Southeast Asia: A Study of a Period of Nation Building," *Pacific Viewpoint*, I (March 1960), pp. 39–58.

The author examines the evolution of political integration in Southeast Asia. He applies Deutsch's model of growth of nations to nation-building in his region which enables him to define four historical phases of political organizations, each characterized by a different spatial pattern: tribal units, aristocratic kingdoms, European colonies, and new states. He adds to his historical analysis a consideration of the current status and likely development of the units in the fourth stage, both as individual political entities and as making up part of the same world region. The events in Southeast Asia during the past decade tend to date McGee's predictions.

MELAMID, ALEXANDER

"Partitioning Cyprus: A Class Exercise in Applied Political Geography," *Journal of Geography*, LIX (March 1960), pp. 166–176).

Written prior to Cyrpus' independence, an assessment of the probable impact if suggestions for partitioning Cyprus were adopted. Illustrates clearly the impact of disintegration at the small scale of the borderland as well as at the island level with disruption of city-hinterland relationships.

MERRITT, RICHARD L.

"Distance and Interaction among Political Communities," *General Systems*, IX (1964), pp. 255–263.

One measure of spatial interaction is that which postulates that interaction between two bodies varies directly with the product of their masses and inversely with the distance separating them. According to Zipf and others, interactions of all kinds between populations follow a similar pattern. Merritt modifies Zipf's formula so that he can deal with interactions both between and within communities. He tests Zipf's formula with reference to distance and interaction by analysis of data from American colonial newspapers. Specifically, he examines the attention that colonial America paid itself. He suggests that a dynamic element can be introduced into Zipf's model by computing attention distances between pairs of states.

MICHEL, ALOYS A.

The Indus Rivers: A Study of the Effects of Partition (New Haven, Conn.: Yale University Press, 1967).

A very thorough examination of the interplay between an irrigation system and political disintegration. The Indus River Basin partitioned between India and Pakistan in 1947 is the author's focus. The pre-partition situation is carefully illustrated, and the short- and long-run impact of partition are examined. An excellent bibliography and the text of the Indus Waters Treaty of 1960 are included.

MOODIE, A. E.

"Some New Boundary Problems in the Julian March," *Transactions and Papers, Institute of British Geographers*, No. (1950), pp. 81–93.

A good example of a study of the impact of boundary change in the short-run context. Three years after a substantial change in the Yugoslav-Italian boundary, the author describes the changes in detail, documents the disruptions to circulation of the new line, and hypothesizes about long-run impacts of the sovereignty change on the transferred area.

PACKENHAM, ROBERT A.

"Approaches to the Study of Political Development," *World Politics*, XVII (October 1964), pp. 108–120.

A research note which offers a taxonomy of five approaches to the study of political development based on traditional and contemporary sources on both developed and developing areas. The five approaches are (1) legal-formal, (2) economic, (3) administrative, (4) social system and (5) political culture. The author also suggests the possibility of a "geographical" approach citing Turner, Wittfogel, Mackinder, Mahan, and Spykman as practioners.

POUNDS, NORMAN J. G.

Divided Germany and Berlin (Princeton, N.J.: D. Van Nostrand Co., 1962).

The first book in the Searchlight Series. Following a brief discussion of German partition, the author traces the historical development of the German state and nation ("realm") through to the Second World War, and concludes with an assessment of the viability of the two new German states. The author's thesis that the present division was anticipated in the Middle Ages and in earlier modern times has been vigorously challenged by Schöller.

POUNDS, NORMAN J. G.

"History and Geography: A Perspective on Partition," *Journal of International Affairs*, XVIII (1964), pp. 161–172.

The lead article in an issue devoted entirely to "The Politics of Partition." As his title suggests, the author takes a broad view of partition with emphasis on the enduring role of boundaries and its use as a remedy for disputes. The issue also includes original articles on Vietnam by Bernard B. Fall, India and Pakistan by Wayne Wilcox, The Cameroons by Victor T. Le Vine, Jerusalem by Don Peretz, Korea by Chong-Sik Lee, North America by Mason Wade, and South Africa by Gill Evans.

PRESCOTT, J. R. V.

The Geography of State Policies (Chicago: Aldine Publishing Co., 1968.)

A multivariate approach to problems of polity and development and of territory and policy. The author discusses the political geography of states under such headings as Global Policies, Policies for the Defense of the State, Administrative Policies, and Policies for the Development of the State.

Pye, Lucian W.
Aspects of Political Development (Boston: Little, Brown and Co., 1966).

Part I (The General Issues of Political Development) is of special significance in this major work on the subject of political development. The author views political development in historical perspective and elaborates on the confusion arising out of the diversity of definitions for "political development." From this elaboration a development syndrome is identified and its components (equality, capacity, and differentiation) are discussed. A plea is made for more theory to analyze adequately the crises of identity, legitimacy, penetration, participation, integration, and distribution which a country faces in its political development.

Pye, Lucian W. ed.
Communications and Political Development (Princeton N.J.: Princeton University Press, 1963).

The volume explores the link between communications and political development. The eleven contributors cover a wide range of material including case studies of Thailand, China, and Turkey. The introduction by the editor (pp. 3-23) is of particular significance as Pye discusses the role of communications in public policy for development and modernization. An excellent selected bibliography prepared by Thelma Jean Grossholtz and Richard Hendrickson is included at the end of the volume.

Pye, Lucian W.
Politics, Personality, and Nation Building: Burma's Search for Identity (New Haven: Yale University Press, 1962).

An incisive analysis of political development in a transitional society at both the micro and macro levels and which gives particular emphasis to the human dimension of social change. Part I, "The Problem of Nation Building," explores the theoretical issues and formulates a general developmental model. The remainder of the volume applies the theory to Burma's particular experience.

Riggs, Fred W.
"The Theory of Political Development," Chapter 16 in *Contemporary Political Analysis*, James C. Charlesworth, ed. (N.Y.: Free Press, 1967), pp. 317-349.

This essay has three major parts: an examination of the primary impact of the interest in new states on the study of comparative politics, an assessment of the idea of "political development," and thoughts on a possible direction for the generation of relevant theory. An excellent review and critique, with extensive bibliographic citations, of the literature on this subject. The author concludes with an attempt to formulate a dialectical theory.

Rosenau, James N. ed.
Linkage Politics: Essays on the Convergence of National and International Systems (New York: The Free Press, 1969).

A collection of essays on political integration including selections on the confluence of systems, regional circumstances, systematic roles, geographic conditions, and transitional structures. Of special significance are essays by Robert T. Holt and John E. Turner on "Insular Politics" and by Richard L. Merritt on "Noncontiguity and Political Integration." Merritt suggests a classification of varieties of noncontiguity and, from four case studies, attempts generalizations about the relationship between integration and noncontiguity.

Rothchild, Donald S.
"The Politics of African Separatism," *Journal of International Affairs*, XV (1961), pp. 18-28.

The author lists and discusses the major obstacles in the way of interritorial consolidations in Africa. Among these disintegrative forces are racial and tribal diversities, wealth disequilibria, nationalism, personalized politics, external pressures, and competition for capital.

Sabbagh, M. Ernest
"Some Geographical Characteristics of a Plural Society: Apartheid in South Africa," *Geographical Review*, LVIII (January 1968), pp. 1-28.

In the plural society of South Africa, the spatial consequences of the Apartheid policy are at odds with the reality of urban concentration and industrialization. The author examines this conflict in considerable detail. The best source on the geography of apartheid.

Schöller, Peter
"The Division of Germany: Based on Historical Geography?," *Erdkunde*, XIX (June 1965), pp. 161-164.

A reply to Pounds' assertion that the present partition of Germany has historical precedence. In a biting review, the German author, citing earlier works by Pounds to support his own case, accuses Pounds of oversimplification and compression of historical data, and of connecting incomparable facts that lead to untenable constructions which do not stand up to critical examination.

Shaudys, Vincent K.
"Geographic Consequences of Establishing Sovereign Political Units," *Professional Geographer*, XIV (March 1962), pp. 16-20.

One of the few attempts at conceptualizing the spatial impact of independence. On the basis of the three dozen new states created by 1962 since World War II, the author discusses the internal and external consequences of the transfer of sovereignty.

SPATE, O. H. K.
"The Partition of India and the Prospects for Pakistan," *Geographical Review*, XXXVIII (January 1948), pp. 5-30.

On the partition of India that had just taken place with special reference to Pakistan. The author documents a good case for partition on an economic basis. Very good source material in maps and statistics used.

TAYYEB, A.
Pakistan: A Political Geography (London: Oxford University Press, 1966).

A very thorough analysis of Pakistan's political geography including the problems of its duality, boundaries, economic and political viability, and external relations. Of particular relevance are Chapters II and III on unity and disunity in the Indian subcontinent, and on the 1947 partition.

VON VORYS, KARL. ed.
"New Nations: The Problem of Political Development," *Annals of the Academy of Political and Social Sciences*, No. 358, (March 1965), pp. 1-179.

A volume devoted to the process of "political development" in which an attempt is made at defining the concept. An evaluation is made of the role of various leadership patterns, and case studies on Pakistan, India, Iran, Tanganyika, Venezuela, and Yugoslavia are included. Of prime importance are the introductory essays by Lucian W. Pye and the editor. Pye analyzes ten definitions of political development and concludes that the problems of political development revolve around the relationship between the political culture, the authoritative structure, and the general political process.

WALLERSTEIN, IMMANUEL
"Ethnicity and National Integration in West Africa," *Cahiers d'études Africanes*, I (1960), pp. 129-139.

The author examines the common assumption that ethnicity (tribalism) is dysfunctional for national integration. Defining ethnicity as the feeling of loyalty to the new ethnic group of the towns, he suggests that ethnicity aids national integration in four principal ways. First, ethnic groups tend to assume some of the functions of the extended family and hence diminish the importance of kinship roles; second, ethnic groups serve as a mechanism of resocialization; third, ethnic groups keep the caste structure fluid, and so prevent the emergence of castes; and fourth, ethnic groups serve as an outlet for political tensions.

WEIGEND, GUIDO G.
"Effects of Boundary Changes in the South Tyrol," *Geographical Review*, XL (July 1950), pp. 364-375.

With a perspective of three decades, one of the studies that best illustrates the long-term effects of boundary change. The author finds particularly relevant in this German-speaking area, which changed from Austrian to Italian territory in 1919, the changes in Italian policy regarding the region's integration, and Italy's changing relations with the neighboring sovereignty over the thirty-year period.

WOLFE, ROY I.
Transportation and Politics (Princeton, N.J.: D. Van Nostrand Co., 1963).

One of the Searchlight Series, a short and very readable volume on the role of transportation in political integration. Of particular relevance are Chapter 3, "Nation and Empire," and Chapter 5, "The Role of Government."

WOLFE, ROY I.
"Transportation and Politics: The Example of Canada," *Annals* of the Association of American Geographers, LII (June 1962), pp. 176-190.

The author focuses on the role of transportation in political integration. As an example, he selects Canada where transportation has been of particular political significance. Wolfe builds on Jones' unified field theory by identifying transportation with the "movement" link in the chain and adding Deutsch's ideas on nation formulation and Ullman's notions concerning the bases for interaction. Wolfe, however, finds that this is not enough to explain Canada's survival, and so suggests an "idiosyncratic" factor, the determination to have a country "from sea to sea" coupled with the improved technology of transportation which made such a vision feasible. Hence Wolfe's analysis is of the process of railroad development in Canadian territorial consolidation, including its role in changing the idea of Canada.

Part IV: BEHAVIOR

Introduction

"The behavioral approach... is rather like the Loch Ness monster; one can say with considerable confidence what it is not, but it is difficult to say what it *is*."[1] In the seven years since Robert Dahl's premature epitaph to behavioralism in political science, this observation continues to summarize rather well the confusion as to the ends, if not the means. of behavioral research. Despite a lack of general consensus even as to what behavior is, a burgeoning number of geographers and other social scientists think of themselves as behavioralists, share a common professional language and set of research preferences, and direct their efforts to the formulation of theory and the improvement of research methods. What then are the objectives of behavioral research in political geography? How does behavioral research differ from alternative concerns and approaches? What is its relevance to the field as a whole? Finally, how does behavioralism relate to structure, process, and environment as developed in the other sections?

Preliminary Definitions

Let it be clear at the outset that *behavioralism* refers to a different, though equally fickle, academic creature than *behaviorism*. The latter, a school of psychology developed during the 1920's, focuses on observable behavior resulting from various external stimuli—thus the behavioristic paradigm S—R (stimulus—response). Behaviorist psychologists stress the accurate measurement of stimuli and recording of observable responses, and sharply restrict their interest in the "mental" or "psychic" processes to some rather vague assumptions about ideas and feelings. To minimize variables in simplified situations, the rat rather than the human is the standard subject of research. Only observations obtained through the sense organs or mechanical equipment were used as study data. J. B. Watson and B. F. Skinner perhaps best represent this school of thought,[2] later labeled "empty organism psychology." Behavioralism, by contrast, is as concerned with what occurs in the "little black box" between stimulus and response—namely such processes as perception, valuation, motivation, and learning—as with the actual acts of man.

Behavior, the object of study, has proved to be an intellectual hairshirt, frustrating the efforts of legions of scholars with a penchant for precision to approach agreement even as to what they are studying.[3] In fact, the term

---

1. Robert A. Dahl, "The Behavioral Approach in Political Science: Epitaph for a Monument to a Successful Protest," *American Political Science Review*, LV (December 1961), p. 763.

2. John B. Watson, *Psychology from the Standpoint of a Behaviorist*, 3rd edition (Philadelphia: J. B. Lippincott Co., 1929); John B. Watson, *Behaviorism*, Revised edition (Chicago: The University of Chicago Press, 1930); B. F. Skinner, *Science and Human Behavior* (N.Y.: Macmillan Co., 1953). See also his ideas applied in fictional form to a modern utopia in B. F. Skinner, *Walden Two* (N.Y.: Macmillan Co., 1948). See also the useful general discussion of behaviorism in Charles E. Osgood, "Behavior Theory and the Social Science," *Behavioral Science*, I (1956), pp. 167–185.

3. An attempt by one distinguished practitioner to define political behavior led him ultimately to propose that the term be dropped. See Alfred de Grazia, "What is Political Behavior?" *PROD* (predecessor of the *American Behavioral Scientist*) (July 1958).

behavior is nearly meaningless in its generality; in a purely lexical sense it connotes simply the manner in which anything acts or operates, thereby encompassing the entire realm of animal and human activity. As used here the term *behavior* will refer to the sequence of interrelated biological and mental operations by which an organism responds to stimuli.

It is possible to distinguish among various forms of human behavior. *Individual behavior* is the most common subject of study, and many scholars feel that it is the only proper unit of analysis. They argue that any form of aggregate behavior is only a summation of individual actions, and, therefore, all behavior can be reduced to individual behavior. This leads some to conclude that psychology is the basis of all the social sciences and that all understandings of behavior must derive from this source. Such a thorough reductionism rests on the precarious assumption that people individually behave identically as do people in masses, groups, or institutions; that the removal of the social context would not alter behavioral characteristics. Any layman who has ever attended a political meeting, observed a riot, or participated in a mass audience would probably raise his eyebrows at such an assertion. The literature pertaining to the impact of masses and social groups upon individual behavior has established convincingly the impossibility of reducing entirely social facts to psychological facts.[4]

Units larger than individuals, then, are frequently the subject of study in behavioralism. This entire class, referred to as *aggregate behavior*, includes such types as mass, group, institutional, and international behavior. While there is great utility in the analysis of aggregate behavior, one cannot overlook the methodological difficulties inherent in such analysis. First, at what point does a leader in a group context cease to speak for the group and begin to speak for himself? Second, as W. S. Robinson pointed out in an early and influential article, what is true of an aggregate is not necessarily true of its individual members.[5] One cannot achieve explanation of the behavioral process by reference to aggregates in areal units. An unfortunate if common methodological weakness is to collect information about individuals and then to aggregate it for analysis. Such a procedure does not permit investigation into the behavioral process since the aggregate cannot perceive, think, learn, or decide; only its members can. It is more meaningful to analyze the data for each individual and then through interpersonal analysis to generalize about behavior. It is worth bearing in mind that inanimate objects cannot have animate characteristics—the physical environment or an organization cannot see or feel. This metaphorical reification is, as the Sprouts point out, common in geographical and political analysis.[6]

It may prove useful to make a final distinction between spatial behavior and behavior in space. *Spatial behavior* indicates cases where the various attributes of space enter into the behavioral process as salient and independent variables. Behavior which relates specifically to objects and points in space does have definite characteristics.[7] Route selection plans for a trip across the United States, for instance, might well take into account the perceived attractions of different recreational and entertainment sites. To take an example more relevant to political geography, as the introduction to Part II, Structure, shows, the perception of and attitudes toward foreign countries among political decision makers may well affect foreign policy. Certainly General DeGaulle's conception of Europe as a geographical and political entity extending from the Atlantic to the Urals conflicts with

---

4. See the excellent overview in Herbert Blumer, "Collective Behavior" in Joseph B. Gittler, *Review of Sociology* (N.Y.: John Wiley and Sons, 1957) and the sources cited therein.

5. W. S. Robinson, "Ecological Correlations and the Behavior of Individuals," *American Sociological Review*, XV (June 1950), pp. 351–357. One fallacy arising from this problem is examined in Warren E. Miller, "Presidential Coattails: A Study in Political Myth and Mythology," *Public Opinion Quarterly*, XIX (Winter 1955–1956), pp. 353–368. A full discussion of this subject is available in Austin Ranney, "The Utility and Limitation of Aggregate Data in the Study of Electoral Behavior," in Austin Ranney (editor), *Essays on the Behavioral Study of Politics* (Urbana: University of Illinois Press, 1962).

6. Harold and Margaret Sprout, *The Ecological Perspective on Human Affairs* (Princeton: Princeton University Press, 1965), pp. 34–39.

7. See the lengthy discussion in Clark L. Hull, *A Behavior System* (New Haven: Yale University Press, 1952), pp. 215–274.

the American notion of an "Atlantic Alliance." It is possible to view *territorial behavior* or *territoriality*—the propensity to possess, occupy, and defend a particular portion of space (the "territory")—as a form of spatial behavior. *Behavior in space*, by contrast, refers to spatial patterns of behavior, in which each occurrence can be located by geographical coordinates and the resulting patterns can be analyzed. Both types of behavioral research are common, although political geographers have leaned to the latter form of analysis.

OBJECTIVES AND CHARACTERISTICS OF BEHAVIORAL RESEARCH IN POLITICAL GEOGRAPHY

Objectives

Generally, behavioral research in political geography aims to relate political behavior to certain locations, and, under specific assumptions, to explain how and why this behavior occurred where it did and its significance to the spatial structure of political organization and processes. These explanations may then be useful for predicting how men will probably behave under similar assumptions and at like locations. Further, the research may also indicate locations or situations where certain types of political behavior are *not* likely to occur. Finally, it may link political behavior to the pattern of political organization, to such processes as political integration and development (see Part III), and to the functioning of political systems.

Is behavioral research simply the mod reappearance of traditional political-geographical inquiry in a new and fashionable garb? It is true that much behavioral study concerns long-standing questions in geography. On the other hand, the traditional viewpoint has tended to suggest that geography "... is a science that has nothing to do with individuals but only with human institutions or cultures."[8] Much of past geographical research has provided little understanding of the process of man's activities—why men engaged in certain behavior and made particular decisions rather than others. Geographers usually relegated such questions to the realm of assumption and speculation. The behavioralist has been instrumental in clearing away some of the confusing underbrush and in offering explanations for the behavioral process. In short, he has demonstrated that there are in human behavior regularities which he can express in generalizations and theories having explanatory and predictive qualities. His analysis of distributions and spatial relationships has acquired a new and useful depth, since he sees them as outcomes of the behavioral process operating through space.

Explanation

As an avowed objective of behavioral research, "explanation" merits closer examination. Initially, it is worth noting that there are many forms of explanation; only three types will be discussed here. *Causal explanation* is defined by Karl Popper: "To give a causal explanation of an event means to deduce a statement which describes it, using as premises of the deduction one or more universal laws, together with certain singular statements, the initial conditions."[9] This type of explanation involves then both the initial conditions and the universal law(s), and effectively answers the question "Why did a particular event occur?" by connecting the initial conditions with the event by means of a law. It explains all events of the class and is the type of explanation to which all social science research aspires. The political geographer is particularly interested in discovering whether political events are invariant through space.

Statistical explanation, by contrast, asserts that if specified conditions are met then a particular event will occur with such and such a probability. Like causal explanation, it assumes general laws, but in this case they are probabilistic rather than deterministic. This type of explanation tends to be more inductive and is less effective in answering the question "Why?" in explaining the causes of individual events and in providing justification?[10] It does have great utility, however,

8. Carl O. Sauer, "Forward to Historical Geography," *Annals of the Association of American Geographers*, XXXI (1942), p. 7.

9. Karl R. Popper, *The Logic of Scientific Discovery* (London: 1959), p. 59.
10. May Brodbeck, "Explanation, Prediction, and 'Imperfect Knowledge,'" in H. Feigl and G. Maxwell, eds., *Minnesota Studies in the Philosophy of Science*, III (Minnesota, 1962), p. 239.

in the analysis of mass events or occurrences and in theory formulation. The important thing to remember is that all explanation is only as good as the underlying theory, a fact too often overlooked by social scientists. As Leslie Curry noted in a recent review of quantitative geography, "the lack of formal theorizing is the major bottleneck to progress. . . ."[11]

Rational explanation enjoys wider use in history than in the social sciences. This form of explanation seeks to explain a particular event in terms of the underlying rationale of the actor.[12] What ends did the actor seek? What did he perceive as the alternative courses of action? What were the principles of conduct to which he adhered? Rational explanation, while requiring the same richness of empirical data as other forms, relies upon the researcher's empathetic reconstruction of the likely motivations producing certain behavior rather than determining causality by reference to universal or statistical laws. The limitations of rational explanation arise from the unreliability of intuition and its lack of predictive qualities.[13] It boasts, however, a long tradition of utility in historical analysis and can be a powerful explanatory tool in the hand of a skilled researcher. Nevertheless, most behavioral explanation will probably continue to be causal and statistical.

Approaches to Theory Formulation

It is possible to distinguish two major approaches to theory formulation in behavioral research. First, the researcher may hypothesize very simple situations in which most variables are controlled and then go on to develop rigorous, perhaps even deterministic, models. He may then try, by examining the distortions introduced and by adding components to the model, to explain the real world in all its complexity. In location theory, for example, one could postulate theory in Euclidean space and then through "space stretching" (map transformations) attempt to explain the greater complexity of multi-dimensional space. The problem is that, with a large area of *ceteris paribus*, gross oversimplifications of reality may severely restrict the utility of the research. If the assumptions are unrealistic at the start, the model will have little explanatory power.[14] Frequently, this research never bridges the gap between the theoretical and the real world except by something resembling a Kirkegaardian "leap of faith."

The second approach is more inductive, and individual studies have more modest objectives. The research begins with the real world complexity and attempts to formulate theory through the cumulative development of typologies, generalizations, partial theories, and finally general theories. The advantages of this approach lie in its direct relevance to reality and in its immediate utility for other researchers. Its disadvantage is that it lacks the rigor and predictive attributes of more formal models. Studies by Robert Kates and Julian Wolpert in geography and Lester Milbrath in political science exemplify its usefulness.[15]

Both approaches are necessary in behavioral research; they may well have a dialectic relationship to each other. Contributions will flow from studies all along the deductive-inductive continuum. What is needed is an appreciation of the strengths and weaknesses of the alternative approaches.

---

11. Leslie Curry, "Quantitative Geography, 1967," *Canadian Geographer*, XI, No. 4 (1967), 277.
12. For a full discussion of this type of explanation, see William Dray, *Laws and Explanation in History* (London: Oxford University Press, 1957), pp. 118–155; Carl G. Hemper, "Explanation in Science and History," in William H. Dray (ed.), *Philosophical Analysis and History* (N.Y.: Harper and Row, 1966), pp. 95-126.
13. Prediction is not, however, the only criterion of knowledge. See the interesting comparison of types of explanation in Anatol Rapoport, *Fights, Games, and Debates* (Ann Arbor: University of Michigan Press, 1960), pp. 101–103.
14. Allan Pred points out one such case. Peter Gould in his employment of game theory to explain real world patterns makes the unrealistic assumption that the environment presents to farmers only two strategies—wet years and dry years, thus casting doubt on the utility of the entire study. See Allan Pred, *Behavior and Location*, Lund Studies in Geography, Series B (Human Geography) No. 27, Part I, p. 15. For the study to which Pred refers, see Peter Gould, "Man Against his Environment: A Game Theoretic Framework," *Annals of the Association of American Geographers*, LIII (1963), pp. 290–297.
15. Robert W. Kates, *Hazard and Choice Perception in Flood Plain Management*, University of Chicago, Department of Geography Research Paper No. 78 (Chicago: 1962); Julian Wolpert, "The Decision Process in Spatial Context," *Annals* of the Association of American Geographers, LIV (1964), pp. 537–558; Lester Milbrath, *Political Participation* (Chicago: Rand McNally, 1965).

Characteristics of Behavioral Research

Behavioralism comprises a number of research characteristics which distinguish it from other forms of study. First, it requires that all generalizations and theories be verified against reality. Second, verification or verifiability in turn requires empiricism. Generalizations must undergo tests against observations of real events or occurrences rather than gain automatic acceptance as *a priori* truths. Geography has long been a strongly empirical science so that there is a well established tradition for this aspect of behavioral research. Third, studies should be such as to guarantee identical results to another scholar conducting the same research. Fourth, researchers place a premium upon research design and methodology, particularly in the definition of concepts, the articulation of assumptions, the clear selection of hypotheses, and the verification of all generalizations. Behavioral methodology also includes an attention to the specificity of variables and the analysis of variables in their various dimensions and meanings so that precision can be achieved. Fifth, research rigor necessitates precise measurement and quantification. Sixth, behavioral research often involves the development of models and theory, a relatively new emphasis in political geography. Finally, behavioralism involves a strong interdisciplinary orientation with the general objective of a comprehensive description and explanation of the entire realm of human behavior. Political geographers can shelter themselves in their disciplinary cocoons only at the peril of duplicating research and undermining the catholicity and utility of the results.

Pitfalls and Limitations

It is important to pinpoint the limitations of behavioral research in political geography in order to avoid its application to inappropriate problems and in order to avert certain types of errors. A first limitation involves the presumed regularities in behavior. The ability to identify regularities depends upon generic characteristics of events or occurrences, be they spatial, social, or temporal. William Bunge has shown that all events share certain characteristics of their class even though they may differ in other respects; they are therefore individual, not unique, cases.[16] The package may not be as neat as it initially appears, however. Properties of events or events themselves may combine in ways which thwart their explanation by existing theory or generalizations. Further, it may well be helpful to explain what did happen by the "nonevent," that conceivable event which did not happen.[17]

A second limitation involves the lack of readily available data on human behavior. Although there are important data archives with a great wealth of information available for use,[18] researchers often must accumulate their own data by interview, direct observation, simulation, content analysis, or psychological testing Each alternative has its problems and error components, so that accurate and reliable data are difficult to gather.

The presumed hedonistic or unipurposeful nature of man is another common assumption in behavioral study. In electoral behavior, for example, it is often assumed that men vote in ways which will achieve a particular goal or gratify a particular need. An important contribution of psychological research has been to demonstrate that man is a multi-goaled organism who may, at any time, pursue a variety of goals, several of which may actually be incompatible.

One of the aims of all study utilizing the scientific method is the objectivity of the research and the researcher. The problem is that the subject matter in political geography is not, to begin with, neutral in value. Political objects generally exist only in the realm of human opinion; most so-called political facts, which pass in innumerable quantities before us, can be identified only by reference

---

16. William Bunge, *Theoretical Geography*, Lund Studies in Geography, Series C (General and Mathematical Geography) No. 1 (Lund: 1962), pp. 18–23.

17. For interesting discussions of the utility of "nonevents," see K. W. Kim, "Limits of Behavioral Explanation in Politics," *Canadian Journal of Economics and Political Science*, XXXI (August 1965), pp. 322–324; Peter Bachrach and Morton S. Baratz, "Decisions and Nondecisions: An Analytic Framework," *American Political Science Review*, LVII (September 1963), pp. 632–642.

18. Council of Social Science Data Archives, *Social Science Data Archives in the United States*, 1967 (N.Y.: The Council, 1967); Ralph L. Bisco, "Social Science Data Archives: A Review of Developments," *American Political Science Review*, LX (1966), pp. 93–109.

to our value systems.[19] Even the determination of what problems are important involves the researcher's reference not to science itself but to goals which he associates with political society. A recent analysis of boundary studies illustrates the extent to which political values may permeate research in political geography.[20]

Generalization about political behavior without proper attention to its situational context is another danger. Experiments in laboratories and artificial settings, for example, betray a common flaw in sociological and psychological investigations. While such techniques as simulation and game theory can be powerful tools in generating hypotheses and developing theory, no proposition concerning the real world can ever be tested adequately in the laboratory or in an artificial setting. The occurrence of two similar actions may, for example, lead the researcher to deduce behavioral regularities when, in fact, it is the situation which has changed. Ivan London and Nikolai Poltoratzky illustrate this point by citing the change, within the span of a few months following the German invasion of Russia, from disloyal to loyal Soviet behavior.[21] The regularity of behavior (loyalty "potential") probably has not changed; rather the situation has. The Russians initially viewed the Germans as liberators and later as destroyers. Nor can the researcher simply treat situation as another variable in the equation since the situation changes the equation itself.

The application of generalizations and theories from one conceptual structure or class of phenomena to an unlike counterpart is another possible problem of behavioral research in political geography. The utility of such borrowing is clear; theoretical progress in any discipline is closely tied to the adoption and adaptation of ideas developed in other fields. At the same time, it should be realized that the transposed theories, developed for specific phenomena, based upon certain assumptions, and tested against a certain realm of reality, may lose their validity. As long as the researcher exercises due caution, however, such interdisciplinary borrowing can only enrich political geography.

THE BEHAVIORAL PROCESS

Since the spatial analysis of political behavior requires examination of its social and psychological roots, political geographers must devote attention to the behavioral process. While they may select different segments of the process for analysis, the general goal is the cumulative explanation of the entire process as it relates to space. As a process, both time and a sequence of interrelated events, actions, and relationships are the major dimensions. The importance of time lies in its effect upon the components of the process—levels of knowledge, motivation, personality, and the definition of alternatives. Time, however, is a complex dimension whose properties are not well understood. Because we do not experience time as though it were divided into equal intervals, it is useful to distinguish between physical and phenomenal time. Phenomenal time, like space, has its centers, distances, and peripheries which vary according to differences in culture, personality, and situation. Whereas Americans, for example, tend to limit their view of the future to that which is immediately forseeable, South Asians may well contemplate a future of centuries. Americans think of time as a road stretching into the future, along which man progresses and which is carefully divided into discrete segments.[22] Compare this with the South Asian conception: "Time is like a museum with endless corridors and alcoves. You, the viewer, are walking through the museum in the dark, holding a light to each scene as you pass it.... One lifetime represents one alcove."[23] Edward Hall elsewhere distinguishes between people who have monochronic

---

19. See Walter Berns, "The Behavioral Sciences and the Study of Political Things: The Case of Christian Bay's *The Structure of Freedom*," *American Political Science Review*, LV (September 1961), pp. 550–559; Henry V. Jaffa, "The Case Against Political Theory," *Journal of Politics*, XXII (May 1960), p. 259.
20. Julian V. Minghi, "Boundary Studies and National Prejudices: The Case of the South Tyrol," *Professional Geographer*, XV (January 1963), pp. 4–8. The two cognitive maps reprinted in James C. Davies, *Human Nature in Politics* (N.Y.: John Wiley and Sons, 1963), pp. 138–140 are an excellent illustration of this point.
21. Ivan D. London and Nikolai P. Poltoratzky, "The Problem of Contemporary Analysis in History and Psychology," *Behavioral Science*, III (July 1958), pp. 274–275.

22. Edward T. Hall, *The Silent Language* (Greenwich, Conn.: Fawcett Publications, 1959), p. 19.
23. *Ibid.*, pp. 20–21.

and polychronic ways of handling time.[24] An explanation of behavior requires increased attention to the functional meaning of time.

The second dimension involves the sequence of interrelated events, actions, and relationships which, together with time, results in the behavioral process. Within this integrated process, it is possible for research purposes to distinguish phases (or components) as analytical constructs, though they are in reality interdependent units in the sequence.

The environment in which man lives contains an almost innumerable quantity of stimuli, the selection and impression of which are known as *perception*. The entire universe (including man himself), as it is experienced by the individual at a given time, may be termed the "perceptual field." The individual classifies and organizes these percepts—these "pictures of the world"—into simple, manageable, and coherent entities. In this way, a distortion of reality serves to make his perceptions consistent with concepts and categories he may or may not have had before. In political issues, this process tends to lead men into simple categorical views of complicated policy questions,[25] and can be used for political advantage. Since man behaves in respect to his perceived world rather than to the objective world, behavior depends heavily upon an individual's perceptual field.

A number of factors affect perception. Systematic rewards and punishments shape recognition thresholds for stimuli. The needs of the individual are important; a hungry person, for example, will recognize and recall food more quickly than other stimuli. Cultural background, particularly in its effect on language, may also elicit differing perceptual selectivity. Perhaps the greatest impact, however, comes from variations in cultural and individual values.

Values refer to the preferred paths or strategies which direct specific acts, thus setting the goals and general directions of the individual's motive pattern. They tend to form in childhood and show remarkable persistence in adult years.[26] Values affect the rest of the behavioral process in diverse ways. Poor children, for example, tend to overestimate the size of coins.[27] Extremists in matters of ethnic and racial prejudice are more likely to recognize words and signs relating to minority groups.[28] Values apparently affect perception in three major ways: through selective sensitization, whereby values lower the recognition thresholds for acceptable stimulus objects; through perceptual defense, whereby values raise the thresholds for unacceptable stimulus objects, and through value resonance, whereby the perceiver favors presolution hypotheses which reflect his value orientation.[29] Values also intrude widely into the choice process. Yet, despite the central importance of goals and values, their analysis has been anathema to social scientists, perhaps because of the difficulties in conceptualization, identification, and measurement. As a result there has been a serious shortcoming in much social science research, for if a person's values and goals can be determined, it is often possible to predict with great accuracy how he may behave in given situations.[30] It is doubtful, as the notion of the "economic man" eloquently illustrates, that an isomorphic model of the behavioral process is probable when values and goals are assumed and not determined empirically.

Motivation refers to the psychological state of the actor in which he directs energy selectively toward aspects of the perceptual field. In other words, motivation is the disposition of an individual toward certain actions. Psychologists have distinguished two major types of motivation: *intrinsic*, that state which is a relatively enduring characteristic of the individual; and *induced*, the transitory state which the manipulation of incentives

---

24. Edward T. Hall, *The Hidden Dimension* (Garden City, N.Y.: Doubleday and Co., 1966), pp. 162-163.

25. Davies, *op. cit.*, pp. 112-113.

26. M. Kent Jennings and Richard G. Niemi, "The Transmission of Political Values from Parent to Child," *American Political Science Review*, LXII (March 1968), pp. 169-184.

27. Jerome S. Bruner and C. C. Goodman, "Value and Need as Organizing Factors in Perception," *Journal of Abnormal and Social Psychology*, XLII (1947), pp. 33-44.

28. L. Postman *et al.*, "Personal Values as Selective Factors in Perception," *Journal of Abnormal and Social Psychology*, XLIII (1948), pp. 148-153.

29. J. C. Gilchrist *et al.*, "Values as Determinants of Word-Recognition Thresholds," *Journal of Abnormal and Social Psychology*, XLIX (1954), pp. 423-426; P. F. Secord *et al.*, "The Negro Stereotype and Perceptual Accentuation," *Journal of Abnormal and Social Psychology*, LIII (1956), pp. 78-83.

30. Arthur W. Combs and Donald Snygg, *Individual Behavior: A Perceptual Approach to Behavior*, rev. ed. (N.Y.: Harper and Row, 1959), p. 105.

arouses.[31] In any case, crude assumption will detract from the strength of analysis.

An *attitude* is an individual's readiness to be motivated in certain directions. Since an attitude is always expressed toward some object, it reflects the "state of mind of the individual toward a value."[32] "Attitude formation" indicates the process by which individuals relate themselves psychologically to objects. One cannot directly observe an attitude—it is necessary to enter it—yet attitudes are more easily recognizable and measureable than values. As a result, social scientists have devoted much effort to attitude study, and polling agencies have accumulated a wealth of data about American political attitudes.[33] With the growth of communications and the activity of polling agencies, public attitudes are increasingly entering into political decision making in American society. Political geographers can profitably study both the spatial pattern of political attitudes and the role of space in attitude formation and change (behavior in space versus spatial behavior).

Prerequisites for rigorous attitude study include an assessment of the range of the subject's position vis-à-vis the object of the attitude, an assessment of the intensity of the attitude (degree of ego involvement), and safeguards so that the subject responds in terms of his attitude and not what he perceives as the interviewer's conception of a desirable response.[34] As in valuation research, measurement problems are a major difficulty in attitude study. Research often overlooks peoples' resistances to attitude change, their relative tolerance of opposing attitudes, and their intensities of commitment. For those investigating attitude change, there is a range of theories to consider.[35] Political geographers dealing with this complex topic will need conceptual and methodological precision.

Learning and attitude formation require *information*. Since the concept of information may be used in several ways and in different theoretical structures, it is necessary to cite some distinctions. Used within the context of cybernetics, information refers to the internal control mechanism correcting, largely through the process of feedback, fluctuations in the operation of a complex mechanism.[36] Within the context of learning behavior, information emerges out of search activity via hypothesis formulation and testing.[37] This stimulus-information takes the form of "cues" which broaden the range of hypotheses and confirm or reject specific hypotheses. If the hypothesis is weak or if there are many alternative hypotheses, confirmation or rejection requires a large amount of information, whereas the reverse is true of strong or lone hypotheses. The quantity and accuracy of information are often prime factors in the choice process of a decision maker.

Since Herbert Simon's demonstration of their remarkable effectiveness as a unit of analysis,[38] decisions have received much attention from social scientists. A *decision* may be defined as a choice among alternative courses of action to produce some future desired state of affairs. Such a choice may be habitual, unconscious, or conscious;[39] most research involves the latter class. The decision-making process integrates many other behavioral elements, and an understanding of the interrelationships among these elements is consequently necessary for decision analysis. This analysis, however, will require a number of considerations.

A first step is to identify the *locus of decision making*. While the locus is readily apparent in individual behavior, aggregates may create problems. In such cases, one may identify the decision unit as "the actors and the system of

---

31. W. Vogel, R. Baker, and R. Lazarus, "The Role of Motivation in Psychological Stress," *Journal of Abnormal and Social Psychology*, LVI, No. 1 (1958), pp. 105–112.

32. Gordon W. Allport, "Attitudes in the History of Social Psychology," in Marie Jahoda and Neil Warren (eds.), *Attitudes* (Baltimore: Penguin Books, 1966), p. 19.

33. No attempt is made here to distinguish between "opinion" and "attitude" because they both refer to the same predisposition. See M. B. Smith *et al.*, "On Understanding an Opinion," in *Opinions and Personality* (N.Y.: John Wiley and Sons, 1956), pp. 33–34.

34. See Carolyn W. Sherif *et al.*, *Attitude and Attitude Change* (Philadelphia: W. B. Saunders Co., 1965), pp. 20–21.

35. Chester A. Insko, *Theories of Attitude Change* (N.Y.: Appleton Century Crofts, 1967).

36. See the discussion of information in Karl W. Deutsch, *The Nerves of Government* (N.Y.: Free Press, 1966), pp. 82–91.

37. For a detailed application of learning theory to market area behavior, see R. G. Golledge, "Conceptualizing the Market Decision Process," *Journal of Regional Science*, VII, No. 2 (Supplement) (1967), pp. 239–258.

38. Herbert A. Simon, *Administrative Behavior* (N.Y.: Free Press, 1957).

39. Kates, *op. cit.*, p. 18.

activities which result in a decision."[40] Not only the locus but the *point of decision* requires investigation. One of the complexities pervading decision-making research is the identification of the point in time where choice among alternatives occurs. In fact, many political decisions tend to be incremental and cumulative. Choice is, of course, involved throughout the predecision stage, especially in perception and information gathering. In organizations, a decision often entails a system or chronological set of choices among both subordinates and superiors. In the present discussion, the point of decision is that stage in the behavioral process when an actor possessing authority for the decision chooses among alternatives and assumes responsibility for the choice.

Five additional dimensions of decision making merit discussion: decision objectives, rationality, and certainty–uncertainty continuum, the sense of efficacy scale, and the threat or stress level. *Decision objectives* refer to the goals for which an actor strives in his choice among alternatives. In economic behavior it is becoming increasingly clear that noneconomic utilities are intruding heavily upon the past inviolable domain of "efficiency."[41] Simon has demonstrated that individuals often do not systematically rank outcomes to achieve maximum utility but instead simply divide them into satisfactory and unsatisfactory classes; consequently behavior tends to be "satisficing" rather than optimizing or maximizing. In politics, the reward may arise from simply playing the game. If individuals do indeed tend to have multidimensional goals, then the recognition of simple categories of objectives may be more misleading than many social scientists realize or admit. In any case, objectives should be determined empirically rather than assumed whenever possible.

Rationality, the degree to which choice is consistent with underlying values and leads to the individual's goals, is another factor in decision-making analysis. The traditional model in economics, of course, has been the Economic Man of omniscient rationality. Anthony Downs has presented a similar view of the voter.[42] The concept of "intended" or "bounded" rationality states that an actor has a simplified model of reality, formed either through cognitive selection and organization or through incomplete or inefficient search behavior, and he behaves rationally with respect to this model. While the notion of "intended" rationality enjoys wide endorsement, it may have more utility for conceptual reference than for the demarcation of areas of irrational behavior. The margin of error involved in identifying and measuring the valuative and evaluative processes of the individual would render assessments of rationality levels hazardous.

The certainty-uncertainty continuum may refer either to the setting in which behavior occurs or to the outcomes associated with particular decisions. Outcomes with a known probability distribution entail *risk*; those with an unknown probability distribution *uncertainty*. Individuals vary in their aversion or acceptance of risk and uncertainty levels. A recent sociological study, for example, developed the theory that social stratification explains variations in risk taking.[43] Julian Wolpert, in his study of Swedish farmers, found that individuals attempted to reduce the uncertainty and risk associated with both setting and outcomes.[44] Robert Kates found that variation in uncertainty was the most distinguishing characteristic of six sites in his study of flood-plain management.[45] The decision-making dimension would appear to have great utility for research in political geography. Surely risk and uncertainty as to the future actions of Presidential candidates enter into voting and into such crisis decisions as the Korean intervention,[46] the Cuban

40. Richard C. Snyder, "A Decision-Making Approach to the Study of Political Phenomena," in Roland Young, ed., *Approaches to the Study of Politics* (Evanston, Illinois: Northwestern University Press, 1958), p. 20.

41. Herbert A. Simon, "Theories of Decision-Making in Economics and Behavioral Science," *American Economic Review*, XLIX (June 1959), pp. 253-274; Herbert A. Simon, "Economics and Psychology," in Sigmund Koch, ed., *Psychology: A Study of a Science* (N.Y.: McGraw-Hill, 1963).

42. Anthony Downs, *An Economic Theory of Democracy* (N.Y.: Harper and Row, 1957).

43. Frank Cancian, "Stratification and Risk-Taking: A Theory Tested on Agricultural Innovation," *American Sociological Review*, XXXII (1967), pp. 912-927.

44. Wolpert, *op. cit.*, pp. 547-553.

45. Kates, *op. cit.*, pp. 83-88.

46. See the interesting analysis of the Korean decision in Richard C. Snyder and Glenn D. Paige, "The United States Decision to Resist Aggression in Korea: The Application of an Analytical Scheme," *Administrative Science Quarterly*, III (December 1958), pp. 341-378.

blockade, and escalation in Vietnam. The preparation of "risk cartograms" for alternative policies in simulated conflicts for different areas throughout the world might be one interesting contribution to political geography.

A fourth dimension of decision making, largely ignored by geographers but widely used in political science, is the *sense of efficacy* scale. Sense of efficacy may be defined as the extent to which an individual feels himself capable of affecting the world about him.[47] Research shows that efficacy is an important decision-making variable in political participation generally and in voting behavior in particular. Moreover, it may be self-reinforcing since increased participation will probably contribute to a higher sense of efficacy.

The degree of *threat or stress* present in the decision-making environment is a final consideration. Decisions reached under considerable stress or urgency often are made in a short time, restricting the consideration of range and relative merits of alternative choices. In addition, the search for information may be abbreviated or inefficient, and the evaluation of uncertainty and risk limited. One political geographer has developed the notion of a "managerial matrix," incorporating types and intensity of stress, to analyze political behavior in the municipal political system.[48] Since the environment of political decisions often does contain threat and stress, its effects merit attention.

Because of the interdependence of stages in the behavioral process, most research focuses upon a complex of components. Scholars concentrate on the decision process since it integrates earlier stages. It may well prove profitable, however, to employ other frames or units of analysis. Kurt Lewin, for example, combined research in gestalt and field psychology with topological geometry and vector analysis to develop his concept of the *life space* of the individual.[49] The life space consists of the person and his psychological environment as it exists for him at the present time, as well as the unconscious states which have effects. A number of psychic regions, each with positive or negative valences, comprise the life space. Changes in region, valence, location, and strength of boundaries all contribute to personality differences.

Drawing upon psychological research, geographers have adapted some of the foregoing psychological concepts for their own study. William Kirk, for example, uses the term *behavioral environment* in discussing historical geography.[50] Wolpert's *decision environment* includes such notions as perception, information, uncertainty, rationality, and threat.[51] *Action space* he defines as the "immediate subjective environment" or "the set of place utilities which the individual perceives and to which he responds."[52] Given a fixity to a specific location, the degree to which man's action space conforms to the objective environment has a spatial bias. According to Wolpert, information and knowledge of alternatives arise from a combination of search effort and the number and intensity of contacts which convey information. These notions may prove useful in the analysis of the environment in which political behavior occurs.

INTRODUCTION TO THE SELECTIONS

Selections in the present volume are representative of four themes in behavioral research in political geography. Robert Ardrey examines findings from animal societies for possible generalizations concerning the territorial behavior of man. David Stea culls psychological theory for his treatment of spatial behavior. Selections by Norton Ginsburg, Kenneth Boulding, and two cognitive maps focus specifically upon spatial perception. David Lowenthal and Roger Kasperson then illustrate the relevance of cognitive spatial structure to political decision making. Finally, studies by J. R. V. Prescott,

---

47. See Angus Campbell *et al.*, *The Voter Decides* (Evanston, Illinois: Row, Peterson Co., 1954), pp. 187–194; Milbrath, *op. cit.*, pp. 56–60.
48. Roger E. Kasperson, "Environmental Stress and the Municipal Political System," Part V, Environment.
49. Kurt Lewin, *Field Theory in the Social Sciences* (N.Y.: Harper and Row, 1951).
50. William Kirk, "Historical Geography and the Concept of the Behavioral Environment," *Indian Geographical Journal*, Silver Jubilee Edition, George Kuriyan, ed., (Madras: Indian Geographical Society, 1952), pp. 152–160.
51. See Wolpert, *op. cit.*; Julian Wolpert, "Departures from the Usual Environment in Locational Analysis" (Paper Prepared for Delivery at the Center for Regional Studies, University of Kansas, October 31, 1967), mimeographed.
52. Julian Wolpert, "Behavioral Aspects of the Decision to Migrate," *Papers of the Regional Science Association*, XV (1965), p. 163.

Peirce Lewis, and Bruce Russett exemplify the utility of spatial analysis of voting behavior.

Spatial Behavior

Early studies in animal sociology, such as H. E. Howard's *Territory in Bird Life*,[53] stimulated interest in the territorial causes of behavioral regularities. Unfortunately, most research has dealt with the role of space in animal societies, both in laboratory and natural settings; there has been relatively little research devoted to human spatial behavior. Yet, there exist in the city spatial divisions delineating the "turfs" of different gangs[54] and the concentrations of ethnic and income groups. Location in one area rather than another may profoundly influence social status and "life-style." Salesmen mark out their territories which they defend and attempt to enlarge. In fact, all individuals and social groupings live and move in space. What is the relevance of space for human behavior?

In his stimulating and controversial *The Territorial Imperative*, Robert Ardrey discusses the functions of territory and conceptualizes two major types of territorial-political systems, each of which is associated with particular behavioral characteristics. He notes three major functions of territory. First, the "castle" or "heartland" provides security for the inhabitants. Second, the territory has a border or periphery where conflict is concentrated and stimulation provided.[55] Finally, Ardrey argues that territory provides identity, an important need of both animal and human members.

Several functions of territory or space not noted by Ardrey merit discussion. In animal societies, territory insures the propagation of the species by regulating spacing and providing population control. Crowding would soon exhaust a limited food supply, so that territorial conflict insures safety. Gang territories may similarly guarantee the spacing of crime so that its economic support will not be lost due to a police "crackdown." Territory also provides a spatial framework for animal and human activities, giving structure and cohesion to group and individual behavior. Furthermore, territory permits individuals to develop an inventory of reflex responses to terrain features and environmental cues, so that when danger strikes the individual or group may respond or seek safety instantaneously. The social ranking involved in the early "right" and "wrong" side of the tracks and the current hierarchy of social prestige distributed throughout the suburban rings surrounding central cities suggest a final long-standing function of territory—the definition of social status and patterning of interaction.

The conceptualization of the *biological nation* and the *noyau* as types of political-territorial systems is a second major contribution of Ardrey's volume. He defines the nation as "a society of most perfect outward antagonism which has achieved a most perfect inward enmity."[56] In this type, members direct aggressive energies toward foreign sources. A noyau, by contrast, is "a society of inward antagonism." Whereas the members of a nation work for compromise and inner peace, all forces in Ardrey's noyau work for division and emotional mayhem. Rent by internal antagonism, the noyau has no innate mechanism to command the loyalty of its members. Confronted by either internal or external threat, it must make deals with

---

53. H. E. Howard, *Territory in Bird Life* (London: Murray, 1920). Since Howard's classic study there has been a great number of individual studies of animal territorial behavior. For comprehensive summaries see C. R. Carpenter, "Territoriality: A Review of Concepts and Problems," in A. Roe and G. G. Simpson (eds.), *Behavior and Evolution* (New Haven: Yale University Press, 1958); I. Eibl-Eibesfeldt, "The Fighting Behavior of Animals," *Scientific American*, CCV (December 1961), pp. 112–122; H. Hediger, "The Evolution of Territorial Behavior," in S. L. Washburn, ed., *Social Life of Early Man* (N.Y.: Viking Fund Publications in Anthropology, No. 31, 1961); V. C. Wynne-Edwards, *Animal Dispersion in Relation to Social Behavior* (N.Y.: Hafner Publishing Co., 1962); John B. Calhoun, "The Role of Space in Animal Sociology," *Journal of Social Issues*, XXII (October 1966), pp. 46–58.

54. F. M. Thrasher, *The Gang: A Study of 1,313 Gangs in Chicago*, Abridged and edited by J. F. Short, Jr. (Chicago: The University of Chicago Press, 1963).

55. Kenneth Boulding qualifies this concept for international conflict by pointing out that there is a series of shells or boundaries of varying degrees of importance. The one closest to the home base of a nation is the "critical" boundary. See Kenneth E. Boulding, *Conflict and Defense: A General Theory* (N.Y.: Harper and Row, 1963), pp. 265–266.

56. Robert Ardrey, *The Territorial Imperative* (N.Y.: Atheneum, 1966), p. 214.

external foes and choose internally between despotism and disaster. Finally, Ardrey associated each type with certain human or personality characteristics: the noyau produces geniuses and artists, the nation heroes.

A profitable reading of Ardrey requires a critical eye. His observations of behavioral regularities are better founded for animal than human societies. His contention that territoriality is instinctual rather than learned has generated the chief controversy regarding the book. It is also doubtful, however, that antagonism centered upon territorial divisions adequately explains complex social interactions and the formation of nationalism. Edward Banfield, for example, observing the same phenomenon in Italy, explained the "inward antagonism" as a quest to maximize family social status for the short-run.[57] It may be more useful to think of the nation and noyau, each but one of many variables entering into political behavior, as ideal types at either end of a continuum of territorial-political systems.

Konrad Lorenz's *On Aggression* (not represented in this volume) examines the relationship between territory and aggression. He found that "in nearing the center of the territory the aggressive urge increases in geometric ratio to the decrease in distance from this center.[58] This view would seem to imply that there would exist in Ardrey's heartland a greater readiness and effectiveness in fighting as well as a higher intensity in other autonomous activities. Lorenz argues also that the territorial pattern of aggression is essential to survival value in that it produces a regular spacing of members, thereby insuring ecological balance. Finally, the balance of power and outcomes of conflict define exclusively the borders of the territory.

David Stea adopts the modern office building as his unit of analysis as, in his selection, he examines the reciprocity between behavior and the spatial structure of man's territory. His brief treatment is richly suggestive of the relevance of behavioral study to political geography. While political geographers have long been familiar with the concept of areal-functional organization,[59] Stea presents a hierarchy of areal-behavioral organization which recognizes "personal space," the "territorial cluster," and the "territorial complex." His major theme is, however, "that changing the defining characteristics of territory changes the behavior that occurs within it and, conversely, that changes in behavior lead to changes in territory."[60] His recognition of the alterations in behavior consequent upon territorial changes illustrate the central role which spatial organization exercises in authority, conflict, and social change, and suggests a whole realm of research possibilities as yet unexplored in political geography.

A number of other studies have expanded our understanding of spatial behavior. In a number of studies, psychologists have analyzed the relationship between spatial arrangements and human interaction. Humphrey Osmond has suggested that there are two dominant types of spatial arrangements in social environments: *sociopetal*, those which increase interaction; and *sociofugal*, those which inhibit interaction.[61] In a series of very stimulating studies, Robert Sommer has examined classrooms, cafeterias, bus stations, and libraries to learn "how the arrangement of people affects what goes on between them."[62] He has found that individuals assume positions in space which are related to territorial offense, defense, threat, privacy,

57. Edward Banfield, *The Moral Basis of a Backward Society* (Glencoe: Free Press, 1958).
58. Konrad Lorenz, *On Aggression* (N.Y.: Harcourt, Brace and World, 1963), p. 36.
59. Robert H. Brown, *Political Areal-Functional Organization, with Special Reference to St. Cloud, Minnesota* (Chicago: The University of Chicago, Department of Geography Research Paper No. 51, 1957).
60. David Stea, "Space, Territory and Human Movements," *Landscape*, XV (Autumn 1965), pp. 13–16.
61. Humphrey Osmond, "The Relationship Between Architect and Psychiatrist," in C. Goshen, ed., *Psychiatric Architecture* (Washington, D.C.: American Psychiatric Association, 1959).
62. Robert Sommer, "The Ecology of Privacy," *Library Quarterly*, XXXVI (1966), p. 234. See also Robert Sommer and H. Ross, "Social Interaction on a Geriatric Ward," *International Journal of Social Psychology*, IV (1958), pp. 128–133; Robert Sommer, "Studies in Personal Space," *Sociometry*, XXII (1959), pp. 247–260; Robert Sommer, "Leadership and Group Geography," *Sociometry*, XXIV (1961), pp. 99–109; Robert Sommer, "The Distance for Comfortable Conversation: A Further Study," *Sociometry*, XXV (1962), pp. 111–116; Robert Sommer, "Further Studies of Group Ecology," *Sociometry*, XXVIII (1965), pp. 337–348; Robert Sommer, "Man's Proximate Environment," *Journal of Social Issues*, XXII (October 1966), pp. 59–70.

etc. Finally, Edward Hall's fascinating *The Hidden Dimension* devotes an entire volume to proxemics—"the study of man's use of space as a specialized elaboration of culture."[63]

Spatial Perception

Walter Lippmann, in his early interpretation of public opinion,[64] distinguishes the objective environment from what he calls the "pseudo-environment," which would probably now be termed the perceptual field or the behavioral environment. Noting that there may be a substantial discrepancy between the two environments, he anticipates Simon's "intended rationality" by observing that although we have to act in the objective environment, we have to reconstruct it on a simpler model before we can manage it. To understand man's behavior, it is necessary to realize that man acts vis-à-vis his cognitive model rather than reality.

The first selection, the "A New Yorker's Idea of the United States of America," is a hypothetical mental map which exemplifies the imagery arising from the spatial structuring of cognition. It is not unreasonable to regard the map as the outcome of the interplay among four behavioral components—perception, information, values, and attitudes. The quantity of map information reflects the fixity of the individual and his values. The latter generate selective perception and information gathering. Information is not, however, solely a function of distance. The values and attitudes of the perceiver convert the spatial arrangements of the objective environment into a surface of utilities. While the map certainly owes its development to a tongue-in-cheek outlook, it nevertheless does articulate the potential significance of spatial perception for geographical knowledge.

Based upon local anecdotes, the map of derogatory attitudes in the Canton of Zurich[65] illustrates the spatial extent of a locality's reputation as a "Schilderbürgerorte"—literally, "stupid bourgeois place," a designation which no doubt loses some of its meaning in the translation. "Podunk" or "hick town" conveys perhaps the closest American equivalent. The map does depict graphically the prevailing feeling of superiority possessed by inhabitants of one locale in regard to the inhabitants of other places. People of Hegnau, for example, because of their local cuckoo bird, suffered the derisive taunt "cuckoo, cuckoo!" from delighted members of other communities for miles around. The cartographic correlation of attitude distribution and various religions is striking, although further research would be necessary to demonstrate the presence or absence of a third variable. Given careful field research, this type of attitudinal map could aid political geographers to analyze hostility or friendliness pairings rather than derogatory anecdotes. The technique might also serve to analyze interregional as well as interplace relationships.

Norton Ginsburg in "On the Chinese Perception of a World Order" examines the question "How do people see their place and that of others in political relations, and how does this perception enter into foreign policy?" That peoples differ in the ways in which they view each other has been well known since W. Buchanan and H. Cantril's *How Nations See Each Other*.[66] An important contribution of Ginsburg is his linking the national characteristics of space perception with the Sinocentric "space-polity," a model possessing a center of hegemony and concentric surrounding zones, and the Chinese notion of what an ideal world order ought to be. The zones reflect the operations and processes involved in political organization, and the values attached to each zone differ

---

63. Edward T. Hall, *The Hidden Dimension* (Garden City, N.Y.: Doubleday and Co., 1966).

64. Walter Lippmann, *Public Opinion* (N.Y.: Macmillan Co., 1949), Chapter 1.

65. The editors wish to acknowledge their indebtedness to Professor Alexander Melamid for drawing their attention to this map.

66. William Buchanan and Hadley Cantril, *How Nations See Each Other* (Urbana, Illinois: University of Illinois Press, 1953). See also Harold R. Isaacs, *Images of Asia: American Views of China and India* (New York: Capricorn Books, 1962); John Haddon, "A View of Foreign Lands," *Geography*, LXV (1960), pp. 286–289; Hans Weigert, "Asia Through Haushofer's Glasses," in Hans Weigert and Wilhjalmer Stefansson, eds., *Compass of the World: A Symposium in Political Geography* (New York: Macmillan Co., 1944), pp. 395–407; Richard H. Willis, "Finnish Images of the Northern Lands and Peoples," *Acta Sociologica*, VII, Fasc. 2 (1964), pp. 73–88; Wallace E. Lambert and Otto Klineberg, *Children's Views of Foreign Peoples: A Cross-National Study* (New York: Appleton-Century-Crofts, 1967).

with distance and accessibility from the center. Ginsburg further notes that China's relations with each of these contemporary, modified zones may well be expected to differ. The idea that foreign policy may be closely tailored to a perceptual and conceptual organization of space and to certain goals as to the country's place in this spatial-political order is a stimulating suggestion. The Chinese view that American presence in Asia can result only from aggressive and imperialistic ambitions on the part of the United States, may suggest an inability to appreciate the relativity of cognitive and valuational stance. Recently several revisionist interpretations of the cold war have suggested that conflict may be due in large part to differing perceptions, misunderstood motivations, and disagreement over underlying values.[67]

In "National Images and International Systems," Kenneth Boulding discusses the importance of spatial perception to the great issues of war, peace, and international tensions. By associating imagery with the political partitioning of space, he points out the problems arising from the exclusiveness of territorial occupation, political units, such as empires, where populations do not share a national image of map-shape upon foreign policy. Boulding also proposes an image matrix which can serve to analyze the dynamic properties of hostility in the international system. Geographical ignorance or stereotyping plays an important role in conflict since an individual or people may be able to view problems only through one perspective. Boulding's study is a persuasive statement on the role that "geographical socialization" can play in enabling individuals to see through the eyes of others and to develop a "systems attitude."

Decision Making

The earlier discussion has already established the major parameters of the decision-making process. The two selections included in this section demonstrate the applicability of this type of research in political geography.

Geographers have long examined the localization of various activities in particular places. Political geographers in particular have studied the location of capital cities and their relevance to the functioning of the political system. Yet there have been surprisingly few attempts to analyze decision making in relation to spatial conflict. Actually, prior studies have contributed little to explaining the process by which a capital came to be in one place rather than another. For this reason, David Lowenthal's "The West Indies Chooses A Capital" is particularly valuable, for it is an articulate demonstration of the utility of behavioral research.

Lowenthal's study focuses on the linkage between interisland images and attitudes on the one hand and the decision process on the other. As he demonstrates, men behave in accordance with their own images of themselves, of others, and of their surroundings. Drawing upon newspaper accounts, government reports, local literature, and an impressive first-hand knowledge, he evaluates widely-held West Indian beliefs about and attitudes toward the various islands, and he then reconstructs their probable role in the decision process. A significant feature of the research is the extensive use of quotation which imparts an awareness of the form and intensity of attitudes. There is a divergence not only between islanders' images of others and reality but also between self images and reality as well. This latter observation is a theme most other studies in spatial perception do not explore. Perhaps Lowenthal's primary contributions, however, are the interpretation of attitude formation, the sources of political imagery, the salience of imagery in the decision process, and the unambiguous spatial framework of the analysis.

The study by Kasperson, unlike the later selections, does not seek to explain voting behavior. Rather, it starts with a given spatial pattern of electoral results and then inquires as to its relevance in the operation of the urban political system. The contribution of the article is fourfold. First, the study emphasizes the dynamic properties of electoral spatial structure, especially in its flexibility and manipulative capabilities. Second, it relates this structure to the distribution of tangible and intangible rewards

---

67. Cf. Louis J. Halle, *The Cold War as History* (N.Y.: Harper and Row, 1967); Walter La Feber, *America, Russia and the Cold War, 1945-1966* (N.Y.: John Wiley and Sons, 1967); Richard H. Rovere, *Waist Deep in the Big Muddy: Personal Reflections of 1968* (Boston: Atlantic-Little, Brown & Co., 1968).

used in support maintenance and aggrandizement. Third, it emphasizes the spatial conflict in group values, attitudes, and policy demands. Finally, and perhaps most important, Kasperson analyzes the significance of spatial political structure to municipal decision making, especially as regards locational conflict. As an initial attempt to develop a general model of spatial structure in urban politics, the conceptualization suggests a number of research avenues.

Voting Behavior

Political geographers have devoted to voting behavior more attention than to any other form of political behavior. These studies exemplify pattern analysis of the "behavior in space" approach. Since E. Krebheil's early study of environmental influences on election results between 1885 and 1910,[68] geographers have concentrated on the temporal and spatial variations of voting aggregates and their association with environmental, social, and economic variables. With the maps of voting results in C. O. Paullin's *Atlas of the Historical Geography of the United States*[69] as a model, this research has generally stressed the construction of a series of electoral maps, depicting results over long periods of time. As early as 1932, for example, John K. Wright analyzed "average voting habits" from 1876 to 1928.[70]

Beginning with André Siegfried's classic study of the Ardiche region of France,[71] French geographers and sociologists since World War II have contributed a wealth of research in which they associate voting behavior with population characteristics and socio-economic activities. François Goguel, for one, has published an impressive number of electoral studies, the best-known of which is probably his *Géographie des élections françaises de 1890 à 1951*.[72] A series of lengthy, excellent regional studies have complemented the more general works of Siegfried and Goguel.[73] Canadian geographers, in a monograph on provincial elections in Quebec,[74] have continued this French contribution. For the most part, this stream of electoral research has utilized and analyzed areal voting data by means of areal association; nevertheless, the large number and generally high quality of these studies far overshadows the contributions by American geographers.

Unquestionably the most important developments in the interpretation of voting behavior emanate from political science, where relatively sophisticated analysis began at an early date. In one of the earliest studies, F. Stuart Chapin examined the trend of independent voting in presidential elections by using the standard deviation of state votes for a party as an index of temporal variability of party loyalty.[75] Stuart Rice, in his pioneering *Quantitative Methods in Politics*,[76] utilized

68. Edward Krebheil, "Geographic Influences in British Elections," *Geographical Review*, II (March 1916), pp. 419–432.
69. C. O. Paullin, *Atlas of the Historical Geography of the United States* (New York: Carnegie Institute of Washington in cooperation with The American Geographical Society, 1932).
70. John K. Wright, "Voting Habits in the United States, A Note on Two Maps," *Geographical Review*, XXII (October 1932), pp. 666–672.
71. André Siegfried, *Géographie électorale de l'Ardiche* (Paris: A. Colin, 1947).

72. For a small sample of his work, see François Goguel, *Géographie des élections françaises de 1890 à 1951* (Paris: A. Colin, 1951); "Géographie du référendum et des élections de mai–juin 1946," *Esprit*, XIV (July 1946), pp. 27–54; "Géographie des élections sociales de 1950–1951," *Revue française de science politique*, III (avril–juin 1953), 246–271; *Nouvelles études de sociologie électorale* (Paris: Colin, 1954); "Les élections françaises du 2 janvier 1956," *Revue française de science politique*, VI (janvier–mars 1956), 5–17; "Géographie du référendum du 8 janvier 1961," *Revue française de science politique*, XI (mars 1961), 5–28.
73. See, for example, Paul Guichonnet, "La géographie et le temperament politique dans les montagnes de la Haute-Savoie," *Revue de géographie alpine*, XXXI (1943), pp. 39–85; R. Arambourou, "Reflexions sur la géographie électorale: A propos d'une étude de l'arrondissement de la Reole (Gironde)," *Revue française de science politique*, II (July 1952), pp. 521–542; S. Hugonnier, "Temperament politique et géographie électorale des deux grands vallées des Alpes du Nord: Maurienne et Tarentaise," *Revue de géographie alpine*, XLII (January 1954), pp. 45–80; H. Billet, "L'expression politique en Gresivaudan et son interpretation géographique," *Revue de géographie alpine*, XLVI (1958), pp. 97–120; Jean Masseport, *Le comportement politique du massif du Diois: essai d'interpretation géographique* (Grenoble: Allier, 1960); Antoine Olivesi and Marcel Roncayolo, *Géographie électorale des Bouches-du-Rhone sous la IVme Republique* (Paris: A. Colin, 1961).
74. See the interesting cartographic analysis in Jean Hamelin, Jacques Letarte, and Marcel Hamelin, "Les élections provinciales dans le Quebec," *Cahiers de géographie de Québec*, IV (1959–1960), pp. 5–207.
75. F. Stuart Chapin, "The Variability of the Popular Vote at Presidential Elections," *American Journal of Sociology*, XVIII, No. 2 (1912), pp. 222–240.
76. Stuart Rice, *Quantitative Methods in Politics* (N.Y.: Alfred A. Knopf, 1928).

aggregate data to relate attitudes to election results and analyzed such topics as urban-rural and regional variations in voting behavior. Harold Gosnell employed both correlation and factor analysis in his study of the 1932 presidential vote in Chicago.[77] Throughout the 1930s, the statistical analysis of relationships between ecological and areal voting data remained that dominant approach.[78]

Because aggregate data imposes limits on valid interpretations of individual behavior, the appearance of *The People's Choice*,[79] a study of the 1940 presidential election by a team of sociologists, was a landmark in voting research, for the authors introduced both survey research and the "panel" method. The latter method requires voter interviews not once but at regular intervals during the campaign and after the election. This study and its successor, *Voting*,[80] emphasized the importance of the interaction between the individual and the group structure of his social life. Both studies concluded that the voting decision reflected the interrelationships among such diverse social variables as membership in organizations and primary groups, socio-economic status, and community environment.

The activities of the Survey Research Center at the University of Michigan with regard to political attitudes produced the next major stride forward in voting behavior research. *The Voter Decides*[81] focused on the voter rather than the vote by stressing psychological factors. It also employed a national, instead of local, probability sample. This approach mobilized the full power of survey research which is extremely well suited to socio-psychological analysis. The effort emphasized three major dimensions—party identification, issue orientation, and candidate orientation. The authors evaluated social environment largely in terms of its effects upon these "intervening" psychological variables. In *The American Voter*,[82] the Center extended its research by including other elements, such as the perception of candidates and issues, attitude and ideology structure, and the formation of partisan identification of the behavioral process. Still another innovation in electoral analysis characterizes those current attempts to develop a more systemic approach to voting, an approach stressing the mutual interdependence among general movements of political parties, candidates, and the electorate.[83]

On the basis of this evolution of research, it is possible to cite a number of concepts and general considerations pertinent to studies in electoral geography. First, there are numerous types of elections—presidential, congressional, mayoral, general elections, primaries, referenda, plebiscites, legislative, judicial, and committee to name but a few. Since the same areal unit often defines constituency for diverse elections, the determination of which election best reveals the political preferences of the electorate merits careful attention. The choice will depend, of course, upon the objectives of the research. Unless there is a specific interest in issues, there are advantages to studying the election which minimizes "short-run" factors and which most approximates the "normal" vote, that which reflects

77. Harold F. Gosnell and Norman N. Gill, "An Analysis of the Presidential Vote in Chicago," *American Political Science Review*, XXIX (December 1935), pp. 967–984 and Harold F. Gosnell, *Machine Politics: Chicago Style* (Chicago: The University of Chicago Press, 1937). For several other samples of Gosnell's extensive early writing on voting behavior, see Charles M. Merriam and Harold F. Gosnell, *Why Europe Votes* (Chicago: The University of Chicago Press, 1930); Harold F. Gosnell, *Grass Roots Politics: National Voting Behavior of Typical States* (Washington: American Council on Public Affairs, 1942).

78. See, for example, the interesting interpretations of economic determinants in Clark Tibbits, "Majority Votes and the Business Cycle," *American Journal of Sociology*, XXXVI (January 1931), pp. 596–608; William F. Ogburn and N. S. Talbot, "A Measurement of Factors in the Presidential Election of 1928," *Social Forces*, VIII (December 1929), pp. 175–183; William F. Ogburn and Abe J. Jaffe, "Independent Voting in Presidential Elections," *American Journal of Sociology*, XLII (September 1936), pp. 186–201.

79. Paul F. Lazarsfeld, Bernard R. Berelson, and William N. McPhee, *The People's Choice*, 2nd ed. (New York: Columbia University Press, 1948).

80. Bernard R. Berelson, Paul F. Lazarsfeld, and William N. McPhee, *Voting: A Study of Opinion Formation in a Presidential Campaign* (Chicago: The University of Chicago Press, 1954).

81. Angus Campbell, Gerald Gurin, and Warren E. Miller, *The Voter Decides* (New York: Harper Row and Co., 1954).

82. Angus Campbell et al., *The American Voter* (New York: John Wiley and Sons, 1960).

83. See Donald E. Stokes and Warren E. Miller, "Party Government and the Salience of Congress," *Public Opinion Quarterly*, XXVI (1962), pp. 531–546; Warren E. Miller and Donald E. Stokes, "Constituency Influence in Congress," *American Political Science Review*, LVII (1963), pp. 45–56; Ithiel de Sola Pool and Robert Abelson, "The Simulmatics Project," *Public Opinion Quarterly*, XXV (1961), pp. 167–183.

the stable partisan division of the electorate.[84]

A second consideration involves the meaning of a vote. Can the researcher assume that there is a direct link between the vote and underlying attitude? Such an assumption may be questionable because strategy often enters into electoral choice. It is well-known, for example, that voters frequently register protest to a particular program or personality by supporting opposition parties. In some cases, voters may cast ballots for candidates not of their preference in order to avoid "wasting" their votes. Reference groups may even alter the expression of underlying political attitudes. Further, since a vote often reflects a sharply-restricted range of choice, variation of attitude intensity may be greater within than between categories. In short, a vote is a complex decision which only imperfectly mirrors underlying political preference.

The mechanics of an election comprise a third set of variables to be taken into account. Malapportionment or gerrymandering may introduce bias into the results. Changes in election districts frequently plague attempts to analyze voting behavior over time and space. It is necessary to consider the universality of the franchise and the rules of the particular election system. J. R. V. Prescott, in the selection reprinted here, discusses these problems.

Variability in turnout is a fourth consideration in electoral analysis. What may initially appear to be a change in political attitudes within a particular district may in fact arise from a somewhat different segment of the electorate actually casting ballots. Angus Campbell has discussed the causes and effects of *surges* and *declines* in the turnout of the electorate.[85] Surge elections, for example, are characterized by an absence of great ideological issues, and circumstances and personalities tend to increase turnout. Such elections often upset the "normal" partisan division, because greater proportions of those voters with relatively weak party identification and little political information cast ballots. Further complication of the pattern of voter participation emanates from *cross-pressures* in an individual's attitudes which may lead otherwise highly motivated individuals to refrain from voting and to split their tickets.[86]

Although there is no general theory of voting behavior, an organizing concept known as the *funnel of causality* may be useful.[87] This metaphorical notion sees voting behavior as resulting from the convergence of a number of determinants—historical, institutional, sociological, and psychological. The stem of the funnel represents the voting decision, whereas psychological variables occupy an intervening position close to the stem, and institutional and social context are farther away. Because of the greater remoteness of the latter, they explain much less variance than the attitudinal and cognitive structures which are closer to the decision. The axis of the funnel represents the time dimension, and events follow each other in a converging sequence of causal chains from the mouth to the stem of the funnel. The major processes at work are communication and political translation.

A final concept which may prove relevant to the analysis of voting behavior by political geographers is a typology of elections. V. O. Key has theorized that there are a small number of *critical* or *realigning* elections which dramatically change long-standing partisan divisions.[88] These upheavals, which occur infrequently in American political history, bear a definite association with national crisis. The emergence of the Republican Party in the 1850s, for example, arose from the great conflict over slavery. The election of 1896 led to a sectional realignment whereby the industrial East gravitated toward the Republican Party and the West toward the Democratic Party. The depression of the 1930s profoundly changed patterns of party identification as urban workers and immigrants flocked to the Democratic Party whereas others, alienated by the New Deal, moved into the Republican Party. Despite the clear spatial dimensions of these realignments and their relevance for analyzing political regionalism, geographers have unfortunately neglected their

---

84. This important consideration is discussed in detail in Angus Campbell, Philip Converse, Warren Miller, and Donald Stokes, "The Concept of a 'Normal Vote'," Chapter 1 in *Elections and the Political Order* (New York: John Wiley and Sons, 1965).

85. Angus Campbell, "Surge and Decline," *Public Opinion Quarterly*, XXIV (1960), pp. 397–481.

86. See Campbell *et al.*, *The American Voter*, pp. 80–88.

87. *Ibid.*, pp. 24–37.

88. V. O. Key, Jr., "A Theory of Critical Elections," *Journal of Politics*, XVII (February 1955), pp. 3–18; V. O. Key, Jr., "Secular Realignment and the Party System," *Journal of Politics*, XXI (May 1959), pp. 198–210.

special importance.[89] The Survey Research Center has extended Key's notion of realignments by adding two types of elections.[90] *Maintaining* elections are those in which past patterns of partisan identification persist and influence the forces governing the election. *Deviating* elections are those in which basic partisan loyalties remain intact but short-run forces bring about the defeat of the majority party.

With the evolution of electoral research and an established foundation in concepts and considerations, it is possible to assess the status and prospects for the analysis of voting behavior in American political geography. Since World War II, there has been a rapid growth of interest in such research among geographers. In 1948 Robert Crisler analyzed voting patterns in his regional delimitation of Missouri's "little Dixie,"[91] and he later commented more generally on voting habits in the United States.[92] In 1949 Vera K. Dean examined the geographical characteristics of the Newfoundland referendum.[93] Howard R. Smith and John Fraser Hart have studied sectional differences on one specific political issue—tariffs.[94] By means of electoral analysis, predominantly cartographic, geographers have analyzed political regionalism within various states,[95] and, more recently, have employed both cartographic and statistical techniques in studies of voting patterns in urban areas.[96]

Studies of voting behavior by French and American geographers have focused almost exclusively on areal voting aggregates. This approach has performed useful functions in electoral research; indeed, much of what is known about voting behavior grew out of these early studies. As V. O. Key's *Southern Politics*[97] indicates, this approach has produced some very thoughtful research. Nevertheless, the limited cumulative progress in theory, the conceptual lag behind political science, and a frequent failure to demonstrate adequately the relevance of electoral studies to political geography as a whole raises questions about the contributions and useful future directions of such research.

The analysis of areal voting data will for a number of reasons continue to offer a highly useful dimension to electoral research. First, voting studies distinguish the general distribution of support for candidates and parties among major population groups within any study area. Second, such studies, delineating temporal continuity and fluctuations in turnout and partisan divisions, are rich in historical perspective. Third, since this approach focuses upon constituencies, results have immediate relevance to the distribution of other political phenomena and to the functioning of the political system. What is important is the selection of appropriate data and research design in conformance with the objectives of the study.

The selections indicate both the purpose and useful directions available for research in political geography. J. R. V. Prescott's

---

89. For one attempt by a geographer to analyze electoral realignment as a spatial process, see Roger E. Kasperson, "The Know-Nothing Movement in Massachusetts, 1853–1857: A Study in Historical-Political Geography" (Unpublished Thesis, The University of Chicago, Department of Geography, 1961).

90. Campbell, *et al.*, *The American Voter*, pp. 531–533.

91. Robert M. Crisler, "Missouri's Little Dixie," *Missouri Historical Review*, XLII (January 1948), pp. 130–140. See also Robert M. Crisler, "Republican Areas in Missouri, *Missouri Historical Review*, XLII (July 1948), pp. 299–310.

92. Robert M. Crisler, "Voting Habits in the United States," *Geographical Review*, XLII (April 1952), pp. 300–301.

93. Vera K. Dean, "Geographic Aspects of the Newfoundland Referendum," *Annals* of the Association of American Geographers, XXXIX (March 1949), p. 70.

94. Howard R. Smith and John Fraser Hart, "The American Tariff Map," *Geographical Review*, XLV (July 1955), pp. 327–346.

95. See Edward J. Miles, "New York Politics, 1860–1958," in R. J. Raybeck, ed., *Richards Atlas of New York State* (Phoenix, N.Y.: Richards, 1959); J. Trenton Kostbade, "Geography and Politics in Missouri" (unpublished Ph.D. thesis, University of Michigan, 1957); Lloyd H. Haring, "An Analysis of Spatial Aspects of Voting Behavior in Tennessee" (unpublished Ph.D. thesis, State University of Iowa, 1959); Andrew Burghardt, "The Bases of Support for Political Parties in Burgenland," *Annals* of the Association of American Geographers, LIV (September 1964), pp. 372–390.

96. Peirce F. Lewis, "The Impact of Negro Migration on the Electoral Geography of Flint, Michigan, 1932–1962: A Cartographic Analysis," *Annals* of the Association of American Geographers, LV (March 1965), pp. 1–25; Roger E. Kasperson, "Toward a Geography of Urban Politics: Chicago, A Case Study," *Economic Geography*, XLI (April 1965), pp. 95–107, Carolyn Ann Steidle, "Some Investigations of the Voting Patterns of Cincinnati, Ohio, 1928–1960" (unpublished M.A. thesis, Clark University, 1961); Edward F. Van Duzer, "An Analysis of the Difference in Republican Presidential Vote in Cities and Their Suburbs" (unpublished Ph.D. thesis, State University of Iowa, 1962); Kevin R. Cox, "Suburbia and Voting Behavior in the London Metropolitan Area," *Annals* of the Association of American Geographers, LVIII (March 1968), pp. 111–127.

97. V. O. Key, Jr., *Southern Politics* (New York: Vintage Books, 1949).

"Electoral Studies in Political Geography," published here for the first time, distinguishes three main aspects of voting behavior of interest to geographers: the geographical reasons for a particular electoral method and set of districts, the geographical factors contributing to an electoral pattern and the extent to which the electoral pattern reflects the summation of political-geographic variation throughout the state, and the alteration of electoral patterns by government. Prescott indicates that elections which offer real chance and whose electoral system is free of bias are worthy of spatial analysis. Elections involving the *raison d'être* of a state will be especially useful for identifying political regionalism. Where *raison d'être* is not involved, he suggests that study is most useful where deeply contrasting policies on numerous subjects or one central issue is involved in the election. In any case, temporal perspective and detailed information on election issues are prerequisites for careful analysis.

Prescott points out types of background knowledge necessary for electoral study in political geography. He discusses specifically the background information about political parties and the electoral system on which any research depends. Further, in a particularly valuable portion of the article, he indicates the underlying difficulties in statistical and cartographic analysis, illustrating his comments by references to recent contributions. The discussion of these data and methodological limitations should be especially useful to future researchers dealing with voting behavior.

The selections by Peirce Lewis and Bruce Russett indicate profitable directions for future voting research in political geography. In his excellent study of Flint, Michigan, Lewis analyzes both the impact of Negro migration on the distribution and composition of the electorate and the effect of Negro voting behavior on electoral geography. To deal with these problems, he employs both cartographic and graphic analysis. The development of an overlay technique relating voting isopleths to choropleths of population changes is a major methodological contribution. Lewis carefully notes the limitations as well as the utility of the technique. Through a thoughtful study of the problem, he both contributes to our knowledge of voting behavior and provides a useful technique for future research efforts.

Russett's "Discovering Voting Groups in the United Nations" is also an important contribution both because of its findings and the method employed. First, his electoral research effectively destroys the myth of an "East-West-Neutral" division of the world. In fact, Russett distinguishes six factors and seven voting groups—the Western community, Brazzaville Africans, Afro-Asians, Communist bloc, Conservative Arabs, Iberia, and Latin America. He also suggests that this multiple grouping of states is not a recent development in international relations. Further, the study demonstrates both one way of relating spatial political units to a larger political system and the utility of legislative voting patterns to the delineation of regional groupings, and discusses the particular advantage of Q-factor analysis, a device for producing both factors and groupings of observations.

Future Research Needs

Lack of manpower may be the most serious constraint on the development of behavioral research in political geography. Presently, there is probably no more than a handful of geographers studying political behavior. This is, of course, a cogent reason for a strong interdisciplinary orientation, for political geography could well lag behind behavioral research in sister disciplines. There is a pressing need for a greater volume of research on behavioral topics.

An enlargement of the scope of research effort is a second need. To date the bulk of behavioral studies has been sharply restricted to voting behavior, a complex type of behavior in which the spatial component may be less important than in other forms of behavior. It is questionable whether additional studies relating areal voting aggregates to social environment will have more than an informational contribution. Further electoral research might well move in the direction of spatial causation (e.g., interaction with sources of attitude formation), more sophisticated pattern analysis (e.g., the selection by Peirce Lewis), or the relation between voting behavior and the functioning of the spatial-political system and spatial processes (e.g., political cohesion). The utilization of the wealth of information in major data archives could provide a marked advantage for future research.

The need for greater balance in behavioral topics is more essential than further progress in voting research. Conflict behavior, which lends itself to study as either spatial behavior or behavior in space, is one of the most promising areas for geographical analysis. Lorenz has depicted the spatial structuring of conflict which is present in animal societies. Lewis Coser has stressed the role of social interaction in the occurrence and resolution of conflict.[98] Moreover, conflict involves a temporary tendency toward an interruption in various forms of spatial interaction. Since conflict often also involves an attempt to gain control over scarce resources, geographers can play an important role in examining the sources and intensity of conflict. Geographers can also work at a number of scales in the political hierarchy. Contemporary patterns of crime, racial conflict, and urban violence are certainly appropriate subjects for spatial analysis.[99] Studies in proxemics and topological psychology suggest a promising research avenue in territorial behavior and interpersonal conflict. At the national and international scale, spatial perception, geographically biased information, and breakdowns in spatial interaction may well contribute to conflict. Geographers might profitably study the distribution of coups, rebellions, and other forms of political instability.[100]

A consideration of forms of political participation other than voting might also be worthwhile. Membership in groups and associations, campaign activity, letter writing, civil disobedience—all represent possible types. There are some general notions available concerning the spatial parameters of participation. Stein Rokkan and Henry Valen, for example, have found that individuals who view themselves to be on the periphery of society tend to be passive and apathetic compared to those who see themselves at the center.[101] Intensive behavioral research might provide us with added understanding of the causes of spatial breakdowns in political integration.

Finally, as in all research, there is a need in political geography to select meaningful problems which will advance our knowledge in theoretical and methodological, as well as informational terms. Particularly pertinent will be those studies which demonstrate the interplay between behavior and spatial structure and processes. Much of the impetus for progress will derive from broadly based research in the social sciences. Although researchers should, of course, devote due attention to the traditions of the discipline and the fertility of past research, it is evident that geographers are long overdue in capitalizing upon training and research in the sister social sciences.

---

98. Lewis Coser, *The Functions of Social Conflict* (N.Y.: Free Press, 1956), especially Chapter 5.

99. For an excellent symposium on urban violence and disorder, see the *American Behavioral Scientist*, XI (March–April 1968).

100. There is an extensive literature on international conflict. For several general discussions, see Raymond W. Mack and Richard C. Snyder, "The Analysis of Social Conflict—Toward an Overview and Synthesis," *Journal of Conflict Resolution*, I (June 1957), pp. 212–248; R. J. Rummel, "Dimensions of Conflict Behavior Within and Between Nations," *General Systems Yearbook*, VIII (1963), pp. 1–50; Frank H. Denton, "Some Regularities in International Conflict, 1820–1949," *Background*, IX, No. 4 (1966), pp. 283–296.

101. Stein Rokkan and Henry Valen, "The Mobilization of the Periphery: Data on Turnout, Party Membership and Candidate Recruitment in Norway," *Acta Sociologica*, VI (fasc. 1-2), pp. 111–158.

25
The Noyau

ROBERT ARDREY*

I have taken from the French ethologist Jean-Jacques Petter the term *"noyau"* as a label for the society of inward antagonism. It is awkward—even bad taste, perhaps—to introduce a foreign word to a discussion in which we are afflicted by so many concepts foreign to our normal thinking. It has seemed to me wise, however, to get as far away as possible from all those English words like "community" or "society" which inevitably bear connotations of co-operation. *Noyau*—meaning, roughly, a nucleus—is correct in that it implies a primitive evolutionary step toward societies characterized by mutual aid. But more important to this inquiry than its precision is its lack of connotation for the English-thinking mind, and that is what we shall need if we are to build up an appreciation for those groups of individuals held together by mutual animosity, who could not survive had they no friends to hate.

. . . .

Now he [Darling] emphasized what had never been properly suggested by science before: "I would like to put forward the hypothesis that one of the important functions of territory is the provision of *periphery*—periphery being defined as that kind of edge where there is another bird of the same species occupying a territory. By pushing up against each other, rather than spreading themselves out, the birds are giving themselves peripheries. The breeding territory... is a place with two focal points, the nest site *and* the periphery."[1]

In other words, it is what I might call the castle-and-border interpretation of territory. There is the castle or nest or heartland or lair to provide security, and, just as important, the border region where the fun goes on. These are basic needs of a psychological order, for security and for stimulation, and under normal circumstances they would conflict. The territorial principle has, however, satisfied both without loss to either. And I believe that if we elaborate Darling's hypothesis with the addition of a third basic need, also satisfied by territory, we shall complete a psychological pattern common to all higher animals, and perhaps to many lower animals as well.

That third need I describe as one for identity. I find it useful to define the three needs in terms of their opposites: to think of security as the opposite of anxiety, of stimulation as the opposite of boredom, of identity as the opposite of anonymity. The bird seeks his invariable branch from which to advertise his presence; it is a portion of his identity. The immature Atlantic salmon seeks his unchanging pattern of pebbles on the bottom of

Reprinted from Robert Ardrey, *The Territorial Imperative* (New York: Atheneum, 1966), pp. 167–172, 179–188 by permission of the author and publisher.

* Robert Ardrey is a naturalist and writer.

1. [Editors' note: See Frank Fraser Darling, "Social Behavior and Survival," *Auk*, LXIX (1952), pp. 183–191.]

his swift-rushing stream: they make possible his identity. A flock of Canadian geese seeks that tract of marsh which is distinguishable only to the eyes of a goose, but which distinguishes the flock from all others; the lone Uganda kob will be found always near his rock, his tree, the cricket always in his particular niche; a family of viscachas, little non-territorial rodents in the Peruvian highlands, will have an unchanging, undisputed resting place in the midst of the colony; the non-territorial starling will have always its same perching place when the flock, though numbering tens of thousands, settles for the night's rest. Neither a need for stimulation nor a need for security can explain the motivation for such attachments, but I believe that the third need can.

. . . .

Like that small ape, the gibbon, the callicebus (monkey) operates a family-sized territory which father and mother defend with whole heart. Like the gibbon also, they are treetop creatures who normally descend to the ground only because they have missed their footing; and they are monogamous. Male and female evidently pair for life, but, unlike the gibbon, the exclusiveness of the arrangement, as we shall see, applies to everything except sex. It has been suggested to me that the chief social attribute of the primate has been his willingness to try anything. Nothing could be more true of the callicebus, the Parisian's delight. Or perhaps it is the *noyau* that encourages originality.

The principal area of the study is a twenty-acre grove containing nine family territories. Every family knows its boundaries to the last inch: a broken branch here, an isolated bush there, a slanted tree trunk across the way. Were the grove not so isolated and the territorial pressure-cooker not so severe, the properties might be larger and the boundaries less sharply defined. The callicebus, however, in the situation in which he finds himself, knows like a peasant every inch of his domain. And its periphery... represents his fun in life.

The little red-haired monkey wakes up in the morning with a sigh, a yawn, and a shudder of monkey regret that the night is gone.... One finds in these forests no sudden, splendid tropical dawn. Here the dawn comes along like gentle, insistent fingers scratching cautiously at the nape of one's neck. Slowly the callicebus family wakes. Mother and father sleep side by side, tails frequently intertwined. He, the good husband, does all the lugging about of children, and if they have an infant under four months he will be so burdened. The family shuffles about in its heartland, its castle, its sleeping tree, lapping dew off leaves, snipping a bit of fruit or a berry or two. Then about seven o'clock, suddenly galvanized, the family makes for the periphery.

I find that one of the most touching qualities in the callicebus monkey is its willingness to sacrifice a hearty breakfast for a hearty periphery. Not unless faced by extreme emergency should I make such sacrifice myself. The little family makes no compromise with principle, but bright and early is on duty at the border, only partly fed, hankering for action, waiting for the arrival of neighbors to be angry at. Shoulder to shoulder mother and father wait, tails intertwined, nursing their grudges, feeding on their animosities, impatient for the arrival of their beloved enemies. Not one foot will the family place on the neighbors' domain unless neighbors are present to make intrusion worthwhile. But let the neighbors appear, having had their dew and their scanty snack, and callicebus hell will break loose.

When I was a young man in Chicago we used to say that the secret of acknowledged Chicago vitality was the *Chicago Tribune*. We read it at breakfast, we hit the ceiling in rage either for or against it, we hit the street on a dead run, and we could not survive without it. The callicebus monkey has substituted the periphery for the *Chicago Tribune*. There is a deal of screeching to begin with. Then father intrudes. The opposing father chases him back and intrudes in turn. Now family is after family. Mothers put aside all grace and give themselves over to lifetime grudges. Juveniles learn the way of all flesh. Bedlam and bellicosity rule for half an hour or so, then someone recalls that there is another boundary undefended and unexploited. The family withdraws. The family across the way recalls that it too has another border, another enemy to become enraged at. No cards or apologies are exchanged, for the rules of the game are too well understood. Were the opponents medieval knights, haughtily bowing, spreading their mailed fists in a gesture of you-know-how-it-is, the callicebus monkey could no more perfectly execute the gallant code of chivalry. Here are Wynne-Edwards' conventional prizes competed for by conventional means.

On other boundaries the contestants will oppose other rivals. Vast must be the satisfactions of such engagements. Blood pressures rise, tissues expand, brains roil with conventional angers. Then just about nine o'clock in the morning, after a couple of hours of emotional daily dozens, it will occur to someone that somebody is hungry. That will be the end of the day's hostilities as all take their ravenous appetites to the breakfast trees.

. . . .

Italy is a *noyau*. It is not a nation. Shortly before he died, Cavour is reputed to have said, "We have created Italy, now we must create Italians." But a century has passed since the *risorgimento*, and no one has yet succeeded.

Italy was a *noyau* even in the time of the Empire. Rome with firm hand and clear eye ruled provinces at the end of the known world, disposed law, order, stability, and a measure of justice, established memories and purposes to endure the millennia. But it could not thus rule its own peninsula. Italy remained a patchwork of jealousies, feuds, ambitions, rivalries, and headless horsemen. Rome, a small city-state, was lucky to make Italian alliances lasting a generation.

A society founded on family territories, innumerable peripheries, and an unholy complexity of inner antagonisms is a society of remarkable staying power. It is flexible. Lacking heart or head, it is difficult to kill. It may lose a portion of its body this century and get it back the next; in the meantime the absence of an arm or leg goes virtually unnoticed. It is healthy. I have only one Italian within my acquaintance suffering from ulcers, and he spent too many years in America: although daily life borders on the apoplectic, few die of cerebral hemorrhage.

Noise, naturally is a prominent characteristic of a *noyau*. You can hear one from a long way off. There is not only the screeching, the yowling, and the hammered insults of the peripheries, but decibels rise like chimney smoke from the heartland too. As a bird must sing from his accustomed twig to announce his propertied existence, so the Italian must turn up his radio or his television set to maximum volume or quarrel with his wife in such tones as to leave no neighbor in doubt that the master is home and in charge of the situation. If an Italian drove his car quietly or failed to rev up his engine at four in the morning, it would be a public humiliation, an announcement that he did not own a car.

Life in a *noyau*, for all its din of battle, is markedly lacking in danger. There are the normal bloody rendezvous, of course, for Italians are not inhuman. But life, despite the corpses floating down the Tiber or Po, is dedicated to stimulation, not assassination. I have lived for five years in a part of Rome famed for its cutthroats; New York's upper East Side is more dangerous. I have windows overlooking one of the rowdiest piazzas in town, and no Elizabethan tavern ever supported discussions more passionate; I have yet to witness a bloodied nose. A successful *noyau*, like any successful gullery, has its rules and regulations which all understand. Should a society of inward antagonism produce nothing but decimation, little could be said for its survival value.

All forces in a true nation work for compromise and inner peace; all forces in a true *noyau* for division and emotional mayhem. If in Britain two drivers lightly touch their bumpers, both will say "So sorry" and drive on. In Italy there is no worse moment than when, late for an appointment, you hear a featherlike touch against your taxi's bumper. You are finished. Your drivers will stop, descend into the street, and explain their woes to heaven, to each other, and to whoever else will listen. Why else touch bumpers? But while you in your back seat explain your own woes to heaven, it will be wise to recall how infrequently you have observed a drunken Italian. It is the courteous American, Briton, Scandinavian who drinks up the world's hard liquor. The members of a *noyau*, for stimulation, need only drive across Rome.

Nations produce heroes, *noyaux* geniuses. The nation is fundamentally anti-genius, since survival rests on uniformity of response; the *noyau* is fundamentally anti-hero, since variation is its life's blood. The *noyau* must look skeptically on the hero and hope that he will not get anybody into too much trouble. The nation must look with suspicion on the genius and pray that common sense will somehow survive him.

   . . . .

Best of all from the viewpoint of the foreigner is that he need not commit himself to the *noyau's* hazards, immediate or ultimate. They are real, and he can always go home. The society of inward antagonism, confronted by crisis, contains no innate mechanisms to command the loyalty of its members. It is not for lack of personal courage that the Italian soldier has acquired a reputation of doubtful merit. It is for lack of inward motivation. To die for one's country is a dull way to end one's days if one has no country. The *noyau*, confronted by an aggressive power, must lose or make deals. Confronted by internal crisis, it must choose between disaster and the despot. Either, of course, it will outlive in a century or two.

It is an odd sort of comment, yet I should suspect that an African tribe called the Baganda, a valid nation with a million and a half members on the northern shore of Lake Victoria, has generated in the last three centuries more loyalty, more mutual aid, more self-sacrifice and dedication to the common good, than has Italy as a whole in the last three thousand years. But neither has the Baganda gallery, or the gallery of any other valid nation of greater privilege, mounted the portraits of a Michelangelo or a Machiavelli, a Leonardo da Vinci or a Lorenzo di Medici, a Dante, a Fermi, a Giotto, a Marconi, a Cristoforo Colombo or a Galileo, a Titian, a Raphael or a Modigliani, a Hadrian, a Marcus Aurelius, a Julius or Augustus Caesar, a Vergil, a Verdi, a John or a Gregory or a Thomas Aquinas, a Cicero, a Caruso, or, for that matter when you come down to think about it, an Al Capone or a Cesare Borgia.

The nation has its deficiencies. None can but bow before the legitimate splendor of the Italian *noyau*. The splendor has been bought, however, at heavy cost. There is not only the social vulnerability; there is individual vulnerability as well. Italy is the loneliest place on earth.

26

Space, Territory and Human Movements

DAVID STEA*

We tend to regard space, in the designed environment, as defined by physical barriers which are erected to restrict motion and the reception of visual and auditory stimuli. In fact, it is also defined by the behavior of organisms occupying the space. The characteristics of their spatial behavior are many, but several similar ones have been grouped under the general heading "territoriality."

In describing organisms lower than man, we speak of certain spatial volumes as individual and collective territories, and further define these in terms of the animal's inclination to defend them against intruders and to "aggress" against these intruders when they violate the boundaries of his territory. In civilized man, aggression is highly socialized, so we cannot always use this form of overt behavioral expression as an index. Nevertheless, we have reason to believe that "territorial behavior," the desire both to possess and occupy portions of space, is as pervasive among men as among their animal forebears —witness the attitude of slum-area street gangs toward their "turf." There is some suggestion, coming largely from the animal world, that territorial possession is not less fundamental than sexual possession, as had originally been supposed, but is equally or even more fundamental. Our legal code bears little resemblance to organic and behavioral evolution, but recent changes in certain statutes would seem to be in accord, to stretch a point, with the new behavioral view: for example, in most states you may still shoot a man with relative impunity if he attempts to run away with your household possessions but not if he runs away with your wife. It appears, too, that private property is likely to be the most tenacious sacred cow of western civilization. The reason certainly does not lie in utility *per se*, for there is no intrinsic reason why objects and spaces held as individual property have more utility than objects and spaces open to the use of many.

When space is held collectively by men, their behavior regarding it greatly resembles the behavior of animals defending their individual territories. Hostility is overt and socialized individual patterns of aggression in men are collectively released. When our own tribe engages in this behavior we call it patriotism; when another does the same, we call it nationalism or aggression. Often, we merely advertise our possession by means of an obvious *display*, not unlike the vocalizations of common song birds; in former centuries we rattled swords—now we rattle bombs.

Reproduced by permission of the author and publisher from *Landscape*, Vol. XV, 1965.

* David Stea (1936–) is Assistant Professor of Geography and Psychology at Clark University.

But, as previously indicated, territorial manifestations exist on smaller levels too, on levels more readily amenable to empirical investigation. And it is my contention that these smaller territories are in some way affected or shaped by the designed environment; if the designed environment changes, the territory may also change.

Suppose we take a fraction of the real world, of the existing environment, and subject it to examination. As an example rich with theoretical promise, let us look at a hypothetical large business concern. The firm, located in a major city, occupies several closely spaced tall buildings, each consisting of many offices. It employs a wide variety of people: there is a small executive pinnacle, inaccessible to almost everyone, and a broad base of managerial personnel, sales engineers, investment analysts, accountants, clerks, draftsmen, maintenance crews, etc. The company has provided an environment which takes care of most of the employees' diurnal needs: there are libraries, cafeterias, a restaurant, snack bars and areas for active and passive relaxation within its buildings.

The system of behavioral actions and interactions within this building constitutes a legitimate subculture, in anthropological terms, and the membership of this subculture is highly varied. For the purpose of the present discussion, I exclude the lowest echelons (janitors, messenger boys, etc.) and the highest echelons (president and vice-presidents). Among the working staff, the former have no permanent place within the design; the latter can frequently (but not always) alter the design to suit themselves. Most of these inhabitants occupy fixed places within the environment whose physical aspects they cannot markedly alter. In inhabiting a given portion of space, they necessarily identify with it; regardless of who, in a strictly legal sense, owns the furniture, the individual comes to regard that portion of space centering about his desk and working area as conceptually "his." He symbolizes the fact and degree of this possession by the number and arrangement of his personal effects, by the detailed nature of his image of the space and by the attitude he adopts, while occupying it, towards visitors.

Let me digress briefly, in order to suggest the beginnings of a conceptual framework. First, we shall call the element of space described above the *territorial unit*, and the individual who "dwells" within it the inhabitant. This is not his *only* territorial unit; he has one at home and also, perhaps, in his car, but it is the office with which we are now concerned. It should be noted that, however physically separated, all these territorial units are conceptually close to one another.

The inhabitant of such a unit must be distinguished from the *occupant* who is in (but does not possess) the territory of another, and the occasional *visitor*.

When the individual leaves his territorial unit, his behavior makes two other important behavioral characteristics of space evident.

○ *territorial unit*

⌬ *territorial cluster*

⌬ *territorial complex*

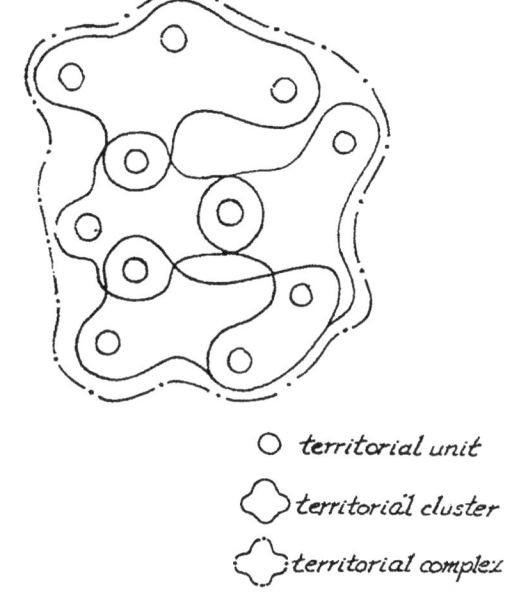

Fig. 26.1

The first is *personal space* (described by E. T. Hall and experimentally investigated by Robert Sommer and others), defined as a small circle in physical space, with the individual at its center and a culturally-determined radius. The second is the *territorial cluster*, enclosing those people (or other territorial units) frequently visited and the paths taken to reach them. Each of the individuals in this cluster has his own cluster, too, and the set consisting of the original cluster and these others is loosely termed a *territorial complex*. The three "stationary" territories just described are schematically summarized in the facing diagram: [Figure 26.1]. Some territorial clusters are simply clusters of territorial units; others are genuine collective territories, viewed as "ours" by their members.[1]

Our major interest is in territorial changes and their effects, but change cannot be asserted without defining the situation that existed before the change. A variety of techniques exists for asserting contributory aspects of behavior. In examining the office situation, sociometric choice and other inventories can be used to identify the personnel with whom an individual interacts, for example, thus determining the size, shape and boundedness of the cluster. The individual, it may be assumed, also possesses a mental map or environmental image of the space represented by the cluster; using techniques similar to those employed by Kevin Lynch in his investigation of the conceptual form of cities, we can determine the perceived nature of units, clusters and complexes, and of the paths connecting them.

The changes take two forms: behavior change and design change. Our hypothesis, in most general terms, is that changing the defining characteristics of territory changes the behavior that occurs within it and, conversely, that changes in behavior lead to changes in territory. We are less interested in the cause-and-effect aspects of this than simply in the relationship; we may even ask: "What change in behavior, with physical aspects of design held constant, is equivalent to a given change in design?"

Having theorized at length, let us consider some problems of the physical aspects of office design in particular and, later, of environmental design in general. The most commonplace example involves that ubiquitous piece of office furniture, the file cabinet. File cabinets are often quite tall, and it is sometimes impossible to see over them; they provide good visual and acoustical insulation. They are good social insulators too, and alteration in their positions, once territorial boundaries have become firmly established, often produces considerable confusion.

But the situations are often more complex. In the past few years German architects have developed a radical approach to the treatment of office spaces which they term *bürolandschaft* (office landscape). This system for office planning is distinguished by a lack of subspace-defining walls and barriers and an intentionally amorphous arrangement of furniture (actually determined from work flow and desired communication and circulation patterns). One of its claimed advantages is flexibility but this is nothing new in concept. To see flexibility in *practice* is something else again since studies of offices performed in the past indicate that many so-called "flexible" partitions remain fixed from the day of their installation. The psychological reluctance to change may be more precisely termed a reluctance to alter territorial boundaries.

The designers of *bürolandschaft* seem to recognize that there is a certain discomfort associated with sharing a large space with so many people for a large part of each day; and they have sought to alleviate the problem by providing floor coverings of domestic finish, by facing desks in different directions to afford a modicum of privacy, by removing patterned auditory stimulation and by adding extensive acoustical insulation to supplement the constant noise level of an air-conditioning system. This environmental manipulation is in line with findings that too-quiet open spaces can be disturbing after a period of time.

---

1. Both *stationary* and *moving* territory have been defined; similarly, with respect to either form of territory, the individual participant may be either stationary or moving. Moreover, the space may be either *individual* (personal space, territorial unit), or *collective* (some territorial clusters and territorial complexes), and *formal* (professional) or *informal* (social) on the collective level. Further, these spaces are held to possess certain properties which we can summarize as: shape, size, number of units, extensiveness and types of boundary, differentiation (detail), relatedness and so on.

If the little circles representing territorial units are thought of as the cross-sections of columns conceptually linking several of the same individual's territorial clusters (home, office, etc.), this reflects the similarity, mentioned earlier, among the territorial units in a variety of physical locations. The resulting three-dimensional diagram bears a marked resemblance to graphic descriptions of Kurt Lewin's behavioral "field theory" or "topological psychology," but there is an important difference: while the territorial hierarchy is behaviorally *defined*, it represents, for any given location, a set of physical entities. It is hypothesized that its shape and extensiveness are frequently determined by elements of the designed environment. To cite an extreme case from our office example, a minor supervisory accountant may be physically in closest proximity to an individual directly above him on the next floor, a person with whom, at most, he has few contacts and whom he may never even have met.

American designers have been more concerned with removing patterned visual stimulation than patterned auditory stimulation, through the use of opaque but unsubstantial partitions. The German *bürolandschaft* designers assumed on the other hand, that in a constantly varying visual environment, any individual event will be less disturbing (e.g., a fellow worker departing for a "coffee break"). Since German workers typically take breaks at will, this form of environmental variation is a recurring event in their surroundings; such is not the case in American offices, where work pauses are highly regimented.

But visual chaos is one of the less important potentially adverse consequences of open offices in America. If we assume that a more regimented system of control is also more threatening, and that the greater the supervisory pressure, the greater the need for physical territorial boundaries, then the possibility of acute "employee insecurity" must be faced. In this regard, the following example is outstanding:

Richards and Dobyns's article in *Human Organization* (1957)* describes a territorial cluster almost entirely dependent for its existence upon aspects of design. The cluster in this case was the Vouchercheck Filing Unit of a large insurance company. The Unit consisted of six fulltime and three parttime employees, all engaged in document filing and locating. The external territorial boundaries were clearly defined: one of the walls was enclosed in steel mesh, giving the unit its nickname "The Cage" and this frontier was further reinforced with a row of filing cabinets, their effective height increased with stacks of pasteboard boxes. One door gave access to the Audit Division, of which the Cage was a part, and another opened onto the outside corridor. Its "cluster" nature was indicated by the *esprit* and general effectiveness of the team and by their attitudes toward the various items of company property surrounding them (furniture, pencils, pads, rulers and so on) which the workers regarded as collectively theirs. Further, they possessed a privilege—a status symbol—denied to other workers in the division: one Cage-member would go out during the afternoon, when the mood struck the group, and bring back "snacks" for the remainder.

When the company relocated two divisions together on one floor, the Cage's topography was altered in several apparently small ways: (1) The territory was slightly reduced in size; (2) the protective file-cabinet barrier was removed, allowing an external supervisor visual access into the territorial interior; (3) access to the outside corridor was removed; (4) disposition of their territorial property was taken out of their control; and (5) arrangement of territorial units within the cluster was altered. The result of an increased opportunity for external regimentation was increased regimentation in fact, a loss of the primary status symbol and, inevitably, greatly decreased morale and a nearly catastrophic reduction in work efficiency. Thus, as the external boundaries of the territory became increasingly permeable, this miniature social system lost its autonomy; and, as autonomy was lost, psychological stress resulted from a reduction in the number of alternative behaviors available to the members, restrictions in freedom of movement and a loss of "overt behavior symbols of in-group uniqueness." In other words, with the alteration in the shape, size, boundedness and differentiation of the territorial cluster and of the territorial units came marked alteration in the behavior of the individual members.

A. E. Parr in his article in the Winter 1964–65 issue of *Landscape* stressed the importance of *variability* in the environment, the need for change, for variety in what might be termed the stimulus field.* The overall suggestion is that, unless forcibly restrained, most higher organisms engage in an active process of seeking this variability if it cannot be found in the immediate surroundings. Of course, many sources other than the designed environment may provide such stimuli. A man's work, if varied and interesting, may more than adequately compensate for an unvaried and uninteresting working space. Work is obviously so very important to so very many people that we might better ask the question (in light of Paul Goodman's identification of the apparent pointlessness

* [Editors' note: See Cara B. Richards and Henry F. Dobyns, "Topography and Culture: The Case of the Changing Cage," *Human Organization*, XV (Spring, 1957), pp. 16–20.]

* [Editors' note: See A. E. Parr, "Environmental Design and Psychology," *Landscape*, XIV (Winter, 1964–65), pp. 15–18.]

of the wage-earning tasks in which a large proportion of the population engage): "How does the environment compensate for the 'boredom' of the office job?" Our hypothesis is that the bored worker engages in active stimulus-seeking behavior and, in the terminology of the framework developed earlier, enlarges the boundaries of his territorial cluster without increasing the number of territorial units actively included. Perhaps he takes only more frequent and more farflung coffee breaks, but he may also take many prolonged and apparently purposeless trips to a library located in another of the company's buildings. He may pick up social acquaintances along the way and may even attempt to acquire professional contacts in this (to him) remote area of the organizational landscape to give further excuses for his ramblings. The result is often termed restlessness, under the assumption that if we attach a name to a phenomenon we can then file it away and forget it (which is what usually happens).

The territorial cluster in the office, as it has been described, seems a static thing. But the cluster cannot exist without *movement* within it, nor the complex without movement among clusters. Human movement within the cluster, the complex, the building and the city is closely related to the general problem of topographical orientation (location, navigation, pathfinding, etc.). When we ask whether an individual is well-oriented, we are in fact asking whether he is oriented at all, how long he took to become oriented, the process by which he became oriented and the techniques he uses to *maintain* this orientation.

This relates to what some architects may mean when they speak of space and sense of space, to the problem of the familiar path in the *Umwelt* (phenomenal world) described by Jakob von Uexküll three decades ago. Thirty years later, John Barlow suggested that von Uexküll's three sensory spatial cues could be reduced to two: sense of direction and sense of distance. From recent experiments with human and animal subjects, we know that humans are not the only ones who tend to alter their familiar paths in retracing a point-to-point route. But we do not really know very much about the variables controlling the *establishing* of familiar paths in designed environments. That no two human *Umwelten* are the same implies that even two *objectively identical* familiar paths are *subjectively* different. The difficulty one experiences in finding one's way about a city on the basis of directions given by a friend has its parallel in the confusion engendered by first contact with modern office environments. Architects deplore directional signs, but they seem unable or unwilling to design environments to which most participants orient with ease; in the end, signs must be provided anyway.

Both the uniqueness of the office environment and its communality with other spaces may be made clearer by comparing it with an environment whose function is quite distinct: the museum. The two broad behavioral classes we have mentioned— territoriality and topographical orientation— play very different roles in the office and the museum. The office is designed primarily for the worker, not the visitor, and to the worker both territory and orientation are important. The museum is designed for the visitor, not the worker, and to the visitor, as a very occasional inhabitant of the museum space, territory is of no importance, and orientation, unless he is in a hurry, is perhaps of much less pressing importance than in the office. In the office, paths and goals are usually quite distinct; thus corridors serve only as quick-communication channels between working areas for men and material. In the museum, both the path and the goal are important; indeed, they are often indistinguishable, and the designer's usual elimination of corridors in favor of a network of interconnected galleries is a recognition of this.

But the designer's desire to provide an "exciting experience" for the participant is often realized in the museum, often frustrated in the office, where the 40-hour-a-week worker rapidly becomes habituated to the design elements which excite the occasional visitor. This does not negate my original thesis; it simply reiterates that the intuitions of the designer are frequently inadequate to cope with the subtle contributions of the designed environment to behavior.

Spatial Perception

27

Two Cognitive Maps

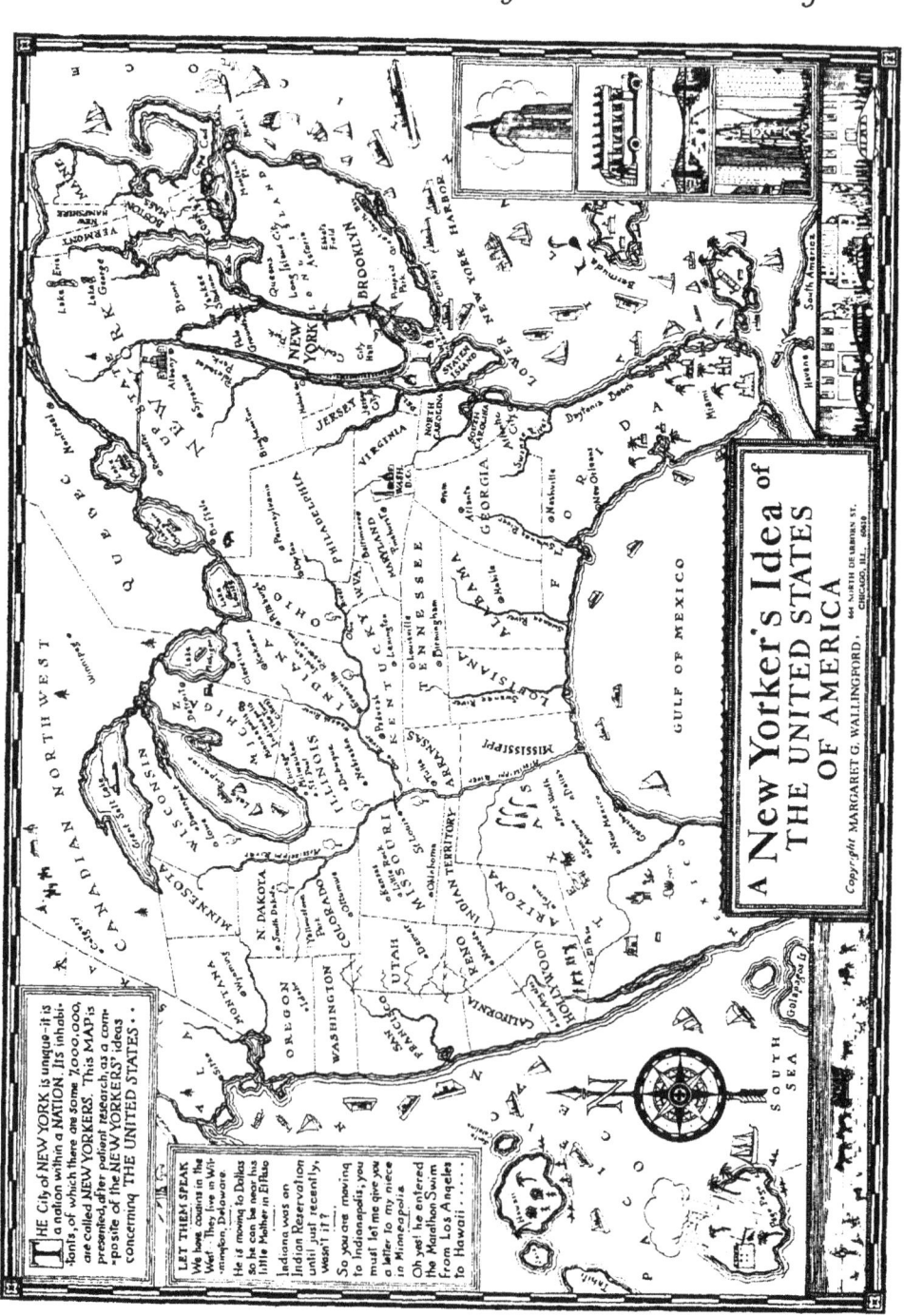

a. Map "A New Yorker's Idea of the United States of America"

b. Map of Derogatory Attitudes

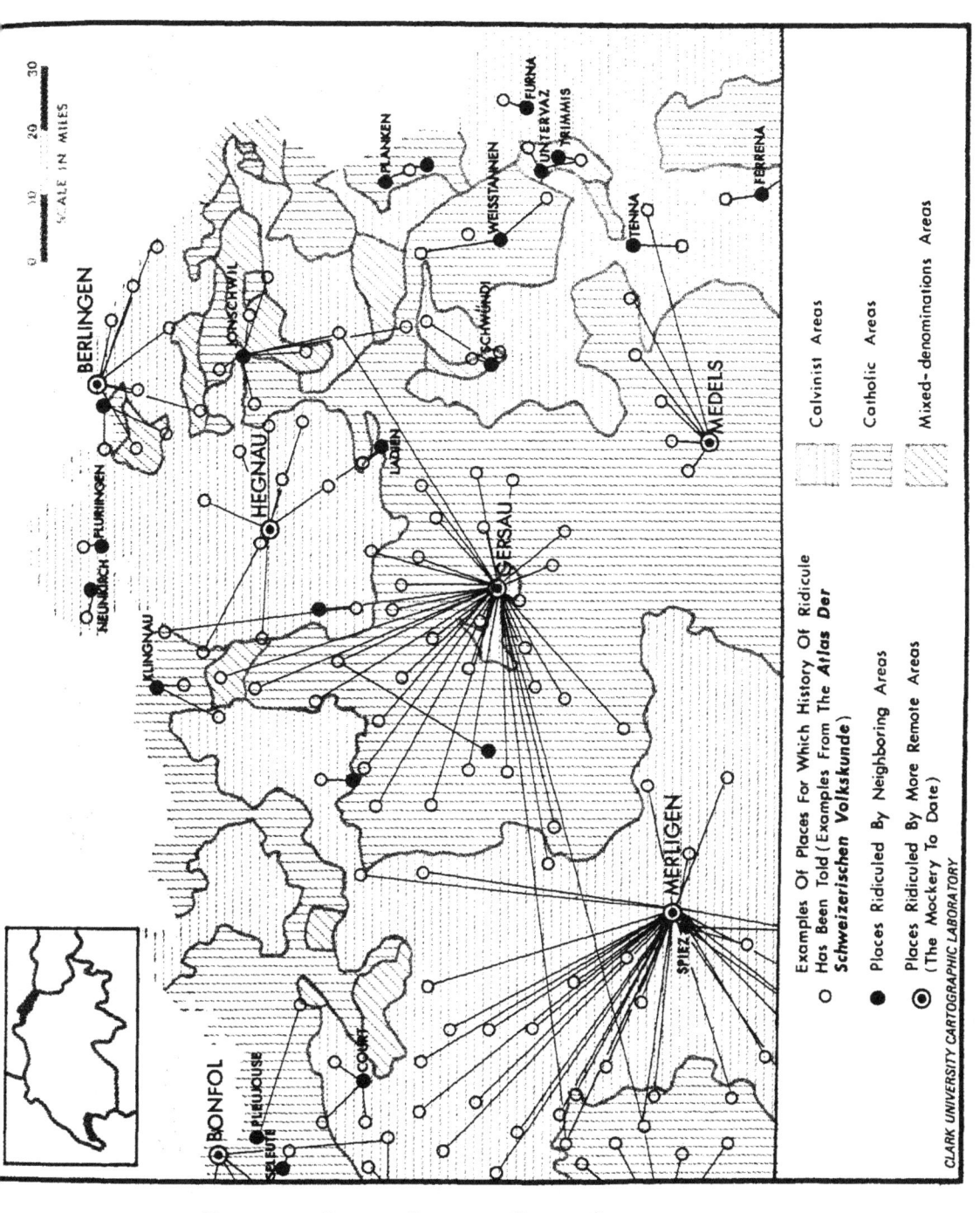

DEROGATORY IMAGES—CANTON OF ZURICH, SWITZERLAND
How extensive the reputation as a "stupid-bourgeois place"?

28

On the Chinese Perception of a World Order[1]

NORTON GINSBURG*

A careful observer must be struck by numerous apparent paradoxes and contradictions in China's recent foreign policy.[2] These contradictions relate, *inter alia*, to the differential attitudes displayed by the Chinese toward various Asian and other countries; to the contrast between China's pronouncements about "wars of national liberation" and her actions; to certain non-ideological bones of contention between China and the U.S.S.R.; to vacillations and peculiarities of China's relations with Japan; to the intensity of her concern with internal affairs in Korea and Vietnam and her relatively lesser involvement with them in other neighboring countries; to pronouncements about wars without boundaries; to China's behavior toward India and Pakistan, among others.

To some extent the questions raised by these seeming contradictions may be answered in terms of China's limited military capabilities, despite her possession of the "bomb," to act beyond her territorial confines. There is widespread consensus that China's military establishment, though admittedly formidable on its home ground, becomes less formidable with distance from the Chinese ecumene. Even more significant are ideological considerations. It would be both rash and incorrect to propose that major decisions about China's foreign policy are not grounded in ideology for, of course, they are; but even the careful study of ideological considerations, of Maoist doctrine and practice as they resemble or differ from other Communist philosophy and practice, fails to

---

Reprinted by permission of the author and publisher from *China's Policies in Asia and America's Alternatives*, Volume 2 by Tang Tsou (ed.). © 1968 by The University of Chicago Press.

* Norton Ginsburg (1921–) is Professor of Geography at The University of Chicago.

1. The concept of an idealized "world order" in Chinese culture has been discussed by Theodore Herman in his "Group Values toward the National Space: The Case of China," *Geographical Review*, April, 1959, pp. 164 ff.; and later, even more persuasively, by John K. Fairbank in "China's World Order," *Encounter*, December, 1966, pp. 1–7, although this article was not available to the author at the time this paper was drafted. Nevertheless, he has a clear intellectual debt to Professor Fairbank. See also the discussion in O. E. Clubb, *Twentieth Century China* (New York: Columbia University Press, 1964), especially pp. 413 ff., and in K. T. Young, "The Working Paper," in L. M. Tondel, Jr., ed., *The Southeast Asia Crisis* (Dobbs Ferry: Oceana Publications, 1966), especially pp. 18 ff. and 27–28.

2. In part, these contradictions may reflect lack of harmony between China's "ideological aspirations" and the perception of her national interests. See C. P. FitzGerald, "Chinese Foreign Policy," in Ruth Adams, ed., *Contemporary China* (New York: Pantheon, 1966), pp. 7 ff. See also his *The Chinese View of Their Place in the World* (London: Oxford University Press, 1964), pp. 68–72.

account for many of the paradoxes in that foreign policy, and in general much uncertainty remains.

To help resolve that uncertainty there is need to inquire into the Chinese perception of what a world order *ought* to be like, and about the role China would play in such an order. Admittedly, such an attempt is likely to be more speculation than scholarly inquiry, but this does not mean it should not be undertaken, given the importance of the issues at stake. How, then, might the Chinese see themselves, as a state among states, as a nation among nations, as the oldest, largest, longest-lived of all the countries of the world?

The fact that the Chinese state has been so long-lived and has a history of unprecedented longevity documented in voluminous records surely is relevant to the problem. Communist China's leaders, though in ideological disagreement on certain issues, including many aspects of foreign policy, are all middle-aged or elderly men. All have been educated in large if varying degree within the intellectual and historical framework of traditional Chinese society; all are nationalist; most appear to have a singularly limited knowledge of much of the outer world;[3] all appear to be conscious of their historical heritage. It would be incredible if their percepts of an ideal world order were not strongly influenced by these circumstances, subconsciously or otherwise. This is not to say that Marxist ideology is not of overrriding significance in understanding their political behavior. It simply allows for the fact that they are the brainwashers, not the brainwashed, and their intellectual roots lie deep within a cultural matrix different from, and not merely antecedent to, the one they are trying to build.

That there is a long history for China in which accomplishment looms large, as compared with other parts of the Communist world such as Russia, is not irrelevant for other reasons, let alone as it bears on Sino-Soviet rivalry itself. The Chinese classics, historical records, scholarship, and literature, all record the glories of the Chinese state at a time when other contemporary states were either not yet born or were struggling to acquire some identity. These documentary materials continue to be reproduced and circulated or commented upon within China, especially those which bear upon the power of China as an empire among empires on the one hand, or upon the aggression of China's enemies when China was divided and weak, especially in modern times, on the other. There is widespread consensus that one of the strong appeals of the Peking regime is to the Chinese sense of nationhood (qualitatively at least different from nationalism elsewhere) and national destiny. It would be beyond reason to assume that in some fashion this destiny does not assume a geographical pattern in the minds of Chinese, whether leaders or followers.

Furthermore, in the course of Chinese history there appear the broad outlines of a traditional view of the world political order. Although difficult to document, there is widespread agreement that such a view exists. There is reference to it in the ancient Yü Kung.[4] The territorial patterning of China's polity for over two millennia lends credence to it. The earlier relations of the Empire with the West, the lofty disregard for Western philosophy and achievement, though with notable exceptions, the assumption of autarchy, the seeming confusion between trade and tribute, all support the existence of an ideal construct, whether or not it has accorded at all times with political reality.

The traditional view of the world order was Sinocentric. This assertion is not merely a truism arising from a naïve interpretation of the term *Chung-kuo* (Central State). Most national views of the world order are to a greater or lesser degree centered upon the state concerned. This provincial, or national, view is true of modern France and to some extent of the United States of America; and it has been true of Britain, Germany, and at times of other Western powers. To this extent, then, China is by no means unique, but it is unique in that China possessed this view long before the modern European state

---

3. Chou En-lai, for example, would be an obvious exception. See H. L. Boorman, ed., *Biographical Dictionary of Republican China* (New York: Columbia University Press, 1967), pp. 392–393. Other exceptions are found among younger officials such as Hsiung Hsiang-hui, the former Chinese Chargé d'Affaires in London. See Donald W. Klein, "Men of the Moment (III)," *China Quarterly*, no. 26 (April–June, 1966), pp. 102–104.

4. James Legge, trans., *The Texts of Confucianism, Part I, The Shu King* ... (Oxford, 1879), p. 19. See also the summary in Herman, "Group Values toward the National Space," pp. 171–172.

had come into existence. This means that it was held long before it was assumed that state power extended to delimited and demarcated boundaries and that all the territories of a given state were equally well-controlled and were of equal political value. On the contrary, China's traditional view of her role in the world order did not place equal premium on all of her territory, and also placed different value on territories beyond her actual control.[5] In other words, some areas were more important than others. The localization of power and authority was greatest in a core area and tapered off in all directions, in some direct relation with distance and accessibility. Formal boundaries, with one partial exception, were of little moment.[6]

The spatial model that incorporates these conditions was composed of a series of overlapping, merging concentric zones; each associated in somewhat different ways with the core; each varying somewhat in their relations with the others as the power of the Chinese state waxed and waned. The notion of concentric zonation need not be regarded simply as formal and static. Just as Ernest Burgess' concentric zonal hypothesis of metropolitan organization in modern America reflected the processes of urbanization,[7] so did the traditional Chinese model of the world order reflect the kinesis of China's internal organization and the dynamics of her changing relations with territories in political relation with her.

The zonal model, then, had at the center of the system Zone I or *China Proper*, what commonly is identified as the Eighteen Provinces (*shih-pa sheng*), or what might be termed the hub of a Sinocentric universe; but even this assertion is too simple. China Proper itself could be divided into at least two types of areas: those over which control was virtually continuous from Han times to the present and those over which control was present but less effective. These might be called the "Core" (or cores) and the "Ecumene," respectively.[8]

Outside of China Proper lay an irregular concentric zone of territories over which China had exerted varying degrees of control or had been in intimate relation, and which we might term the *Inner Zone* (Zone II). As part of this Inner Zone and contiguous to the Eighteen Provinces (to which must be added the so-called "Chinese Pale" in Manchuria) were a number of extra-ecumenical areas over which China, at least in Ch'ing times if not before, exerted nominal if not genuine sovereignty and which included much of Manchuria, Mongolia, Chinese Turkestan, and both eastern Tibet and Tibet Proper. To these could be added the sometime dependencies of strong Sinitic cultural heritage—Korea and Annam. To this largely continuous but open ring of territory we might apply the term, the "Periphery." In addition and beyond these were various territories ranging from those actually held under Chinese suzerainty for relatively long periods, such as the Trans-Amur territories in eastern Siberia[9] or the eastern parts of Soviet Middle Asia to those which were tribute-bearing or otherwise subordinate states, extending from Afghanistan to the Ryukyus.[10] Whatever the particular relation of these territories to China, all were regarded as, and to a large degree actually behaved as though they were, subordinate areas or "client" states.

---

5. I am grateful for this idea to Mr. J. B. R. Whitney of Earlham College whose chapter on China's political geography in H. L. Boorman's forthcoming history of modern China has been drawn upon freely, but the idea also appears in various guises in a number of secondary sources.

6. This does not mean, however, that the Chinese were not concerned about their peripheral territories and how they were controlled. As Philip Kuhn has pointed out in a personal communication, one could even argue that "the farther from the ... center, the more elaborate the control mechanisms" developed and applied.

7. E. W. Burgess, "The Growth of the City," in R. E. Park, E. W. Burgess, and R. D. McKenzie, *The City* (Chicago: University of Chicago Press, 1925). pp. 47–62.

8. For a variant cartographic definition of the "Core," based on estimates of population and cultivated land, see Herman, "Group Values toward the National Space," p. 178.

9. These areas were not in fact part of China in terms of direct territorial control prior to the Manchu period when they were "brought" to China by its Manchu conquerors. See C. P. FitzGerald, "Chinese Expansion in Central Asia," *Royal Central Asian Journal*, July–October, 1963, pp. 292–93.

10. For a listing of areas which sent tribute embassies to the Ch'ing court, see J. K. Fairbank and S. Y. Teng, *Ch'ing Administration*, Harvard-Yenching Institute Studies, 19 (Cambridge: Harvard University Press, 1960): 193–198. For references to tribute-bearing missions from Afghanistan, not noted by Fairbank and Teng, see Dai Shen-yu, "China and Afghanistan," *China Quarterly*, January–March, 1966, pp. 213–215.

CHINA: The World Order
-Traditional Model-

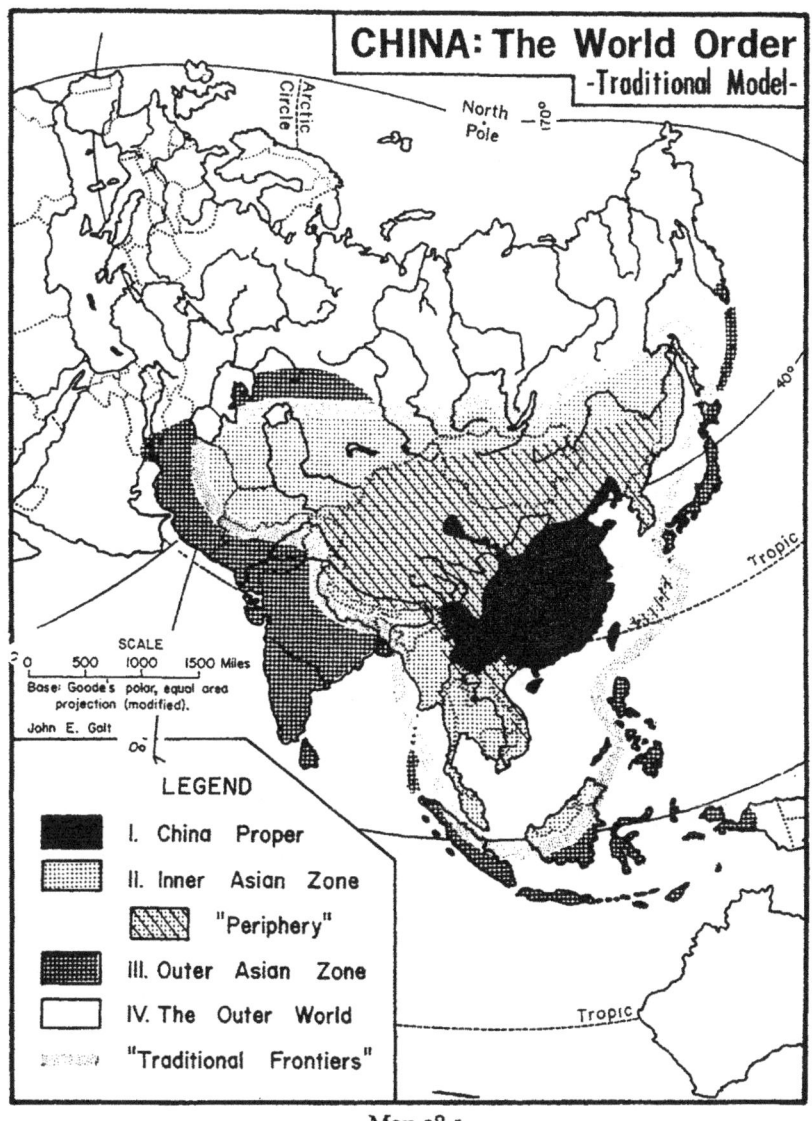

LEGEND
- I. China Proper
- II. Inner Asian Zone
- "Periphery"
- III. Outer Asian Zone
- IV. The Outer World
- "Traditional Frontiers"

Map 28.1

Although no delimited boundaries girdled Zones I and II, Chinese territorial claims during the Ming and especially the Ch'ing periods suggest a north-south trending maritime frontier running through the Sea of Japan and the Straits of Korea, through the Bashi Channel (between Taiwan and the Philippines), through the South China Sea but incorporating most of British Borneo and the Sulu Archipelago, and around the southern tip of the Malayan Peninsula until it recurved northward through the Andaman Sea (Map 28.1). The frontier enveloped all of mainland Southeast Asia and then recurved inland to include Assam, the Himalayan Kingdoms, and much of Soviet Middle Asia —at least the eastern portions of the contemporary six constituent republics of the U.S.S.R. there. Finally, to the north and northeast, it included all of Mongolia and the territories northward to the *taiga* in what is now the Soviet Union, and ran eastward to the Pacific, including Sakhalin Island.[11]

[11] These boundaries appear, with variations, in numerous atlases and reference works published in Republican China. See, for example, the middle-school atlas, *Hsien-tai pen-kuo ti-t'u* (Shanghai: World Geography Company, 1940), plate 45. A more refined presentation for the Ch'ing period appears in Albert Herrmann, *An Historical Atlas of China*, ed. Norton Ginsburg (Chicago: Aldine, 1966), plate 51.

Although the territories of Zone II were regarded in greater or lesser degree as "Chinese," they were held as being of lower value, except for certain commercial and strategic purposes, than those of Zone I.

Beyond Zone II lay an *Outer Asian Zone* (Zone III) composed of a number of territories, which was discontinuous and for the most part not contiguous to China, though parts of it lay very near to what was regarded as "Chinese" territory. All of this zone lay in Asia, and it ranged from Persia on the west through India, Indonesia, and most of the Philippines to, perhaps paradoxically, Japan on the east. With the partial exception of Japan, the states occupying these territories had never been in true tributary or client relationships with the Chinese Empire, but they were relatively well known to the Chinese and fell more in the category of *terrae cognitae* than otherwise. Indeed, the extent of Chinese trade and cultural relations with certain of these territories might suggest their more appropriate position in Zone II, of which more below.[12]

Beyond Zone III lay Zone IV. It is not inappropriate to suggest the name "The Great Beyond" for this *Foreign Zone*, which included only a small part of Asia (the eastern Mediterranean), but all of Europe, Africa, and the Americas. "All the Rest" would also not be inappropriate nomenclature, since it was in Chinese eyes largely undifferentiated.

In the traditional model, this concentric pattern reflected a political spatial system, a "space-polity" in short, within which China Proper might be likened to a sun and the areal constituents of Zones II and III to planets revolving about her, the whole blending off into other possible systems in the "Great Beyond," Zone IV. Over time, inventories of the members of this system would vary, however, as some most accessible would merge with the central sun as it flared across neighboring territories; others might be absorbed by *their* neighbors; still others might spin out of orbit; and yet others would become orbital (as in the case of European Russia during the early Mongol period) for limited periods of time. Nonetheless, these dynamics should not invalidate the basic premises or structure of the model.

For centuries upon centuries the perceived political spatial system remained Sinocentric, zonal, roughly concentric, without formal boundaries, characterized by a distance-intensity relationship between power and territorial control, almost exclusively Asian-oriented, and separated from the rest of the world by indifference or ignorance. Nowhere in those centuries of China's history for which the model appears to apply did China perceive of herself as a state of states, a neighbor among neighbors, a member of a family of nations.[13]

Although the model is geographically comprehensible as here proposed, certain constraints operated on it to make it geometrically asymmetrical and to distort its pattern, though such qualifications need not, again, diminish its utility. Concentricity was broken on the east by the sea and the offshore archipelagoes of eastern Asia to which, however, both maritime and trans-maritime Chinese claims were made. To the north, the Siberian *taiga* comes close enough to the Amur so that client states in the Trans-Amur territories were unlikely or short-lived; and even to the northwest the steppe and the northern forests which blended into it provided a distinctive ecological setting in marked contrast to those elsewhere and within which great nomad-controlled empires rose and fell. In the southwest, the Tibetan Highlands and the Himalayan ranges acted as formidable barriers to penetration and control and, in effect, greatly increased the effective distances from the Chinese Core and Ecumene (Zone I) to the southwestern frontiers. In the north, too, as Lattimore points out, is found the only clear expression of a boundary between China Proper and the

---

12. Fairbank, "China's World Order," pp. 1–4, also proposes four zones, but he restricts the second to "the closest and culturally-similar tributaries, Korea and Vietnam ... and also the Liu-ch'iu Islands and in certain brief periods, Japan." This he calls the "Sinic Zone." The next he calls the Inner Asian Zone and composed of "the tributary tribes and states of the nomadic or semi-nomadic peoples of northern Manchuria, Mongolia, Eastern or Chinese Turkestan, and Tibet. . . ." Oddly, except for Vietnam, his scheme contains no specific zonal niche for Southeast Asia, but it apparently is included in his Outer Zone, "consisting of the 'outer barbarians' generally, at a further distance over land or sea."

13. Fairbank, "China's World Order," pp. 2–3, succinctly notes the lengths to which traditional China's foreign relations were distorted so as to avoid implications of egalitarianism between China and other states.

rest of Asia, the Great Wall;[14] but even this extraordinary feature was less a political boundary in the modern sense than a somewhat arbitrary line marking an ecological transition from "sown" to steppe, across which Chinese and "barbarian" power has shifted from period to period.

In fact, the only direction in which the model operated with a minimum of such constraints (although they were there nonetheless) was the south, that is, along the frontier of expansion and "inclusion," to use Lattimore's term, leading toward and into Southeast Asia, in contrast with the frontier of "exclusion" in the north and northwest.[15] That the southerly frontier leads into Southeast Asia has relevance also to current events.

Finally, it should be understood that the various zones merged into one another and that their territorial composition varied from time to time. Thus, although Tibet has been included not only in Zone II, but also in that part of it functionally nearest China Proper, the so-called Periphery, in fact it did not clearly come within China's orbit until the Yüan, and for much of its later history, until the early eighteenth century, it would properly have fallen in the Outer Asian Zone (III). Conversely, Annam in its history has moved outward from Zone I to Zone II, and Japan, in Chinese eyes, apparently has fluctuated between Zones II and III.

Certain aspects of and problems in China's foreign policy become more nearly comprehensible, if one assumes that this spatial model still has relevance and that China's leaders perceive as one of the objectives of that policy a reconciliation of contemporary political geographical realities with the essence of that model. On the other hand, the course of history has resulted in certain substantial changes in the world map which makes a return to the traditional spatial system impossible. Empires and dependencies have come and gone; the technological revolution in transportation and communications has resulted perforce in major shifts in the relations among areas; and the balance of power in Asia has been transformed not only because of these developments, but also because what Mackinder has called the "closed world" also has come into being.

It is not unreasonable to propose, therefore, that a current acceptable model of the "proper" world order, as perceived by China's leaders, would differ from the traditional model in some respects, though the principles of merger and fluctuation would continue to hold (Map 28.2). The Core and Ecumene of Zone I and most of the Periphery of Zone II would be regarded as inseparable, since they are joined as one to form the modern Chinese state. Zone II, as a zone of presumed or possible dependent or client states, would now include Korea, Mongolia, Vietnam, Laos, Cambodia, Thailand, Burma, the Himalayan States, and possibly Afghanistan,[16] as well as the northern irredentist territories which lie within the Soviet Union. Zone III would encompass the rest of Southeast Asia, Japan, and perhaps the countries of South Asia. Some of these territories border China itself, though generally removed from its ecumenical areas; others are more distant, but in some cases might be assumed to possess a more intimate relationship with China either on ethnic grounds, as in the case of Malaya, or by shared Sinitic cultural traditions, as in the case of Japan. Zone IV continues to be recognized, but now it falls logically into two parts: that which is developed, metropolitan, capitalistic or retrograde socialist, and presumably imperialistic; and that which is underdeveloped, "colonial," "rural," and unstable, as well as non-Asian.

China's relations with the countries and territories in these modified zones logically can be expected to differ, and indeed there is reason to believe that China's foreign policy varies with the roles prescribed for countries in them. This proposition may be illustrated with reference to some of the historical events that have led to differences between the "current" as contrasted with the "traditional" model. Two related hypotheses worth considering here as well propose that China's foreign policy reflects both an ambivalence

---

14. Owen Lattimore, "Origins of the Great Wall of China," *Geographical Review*, XXVII (October, 1937).

15. Owen Lattimore, "The Frontier in History," *Studies in Frontier History* (The Hague: Mouton, 1962), p. 477.

16. Dai lends support here by stating: "If China is to restore the glory of the Sui-T'ang period along the Silk Road..., it will be in the recognition of China's moral or political suzerainty, particularly along the Pamir-Himalayan fringes" ("China and Afghanistan," pp. 221). As a step toward establishing a détente with Afghanistan, China agreed to the demarcation of the short (75 km.) border between the two countries in March, 1964.

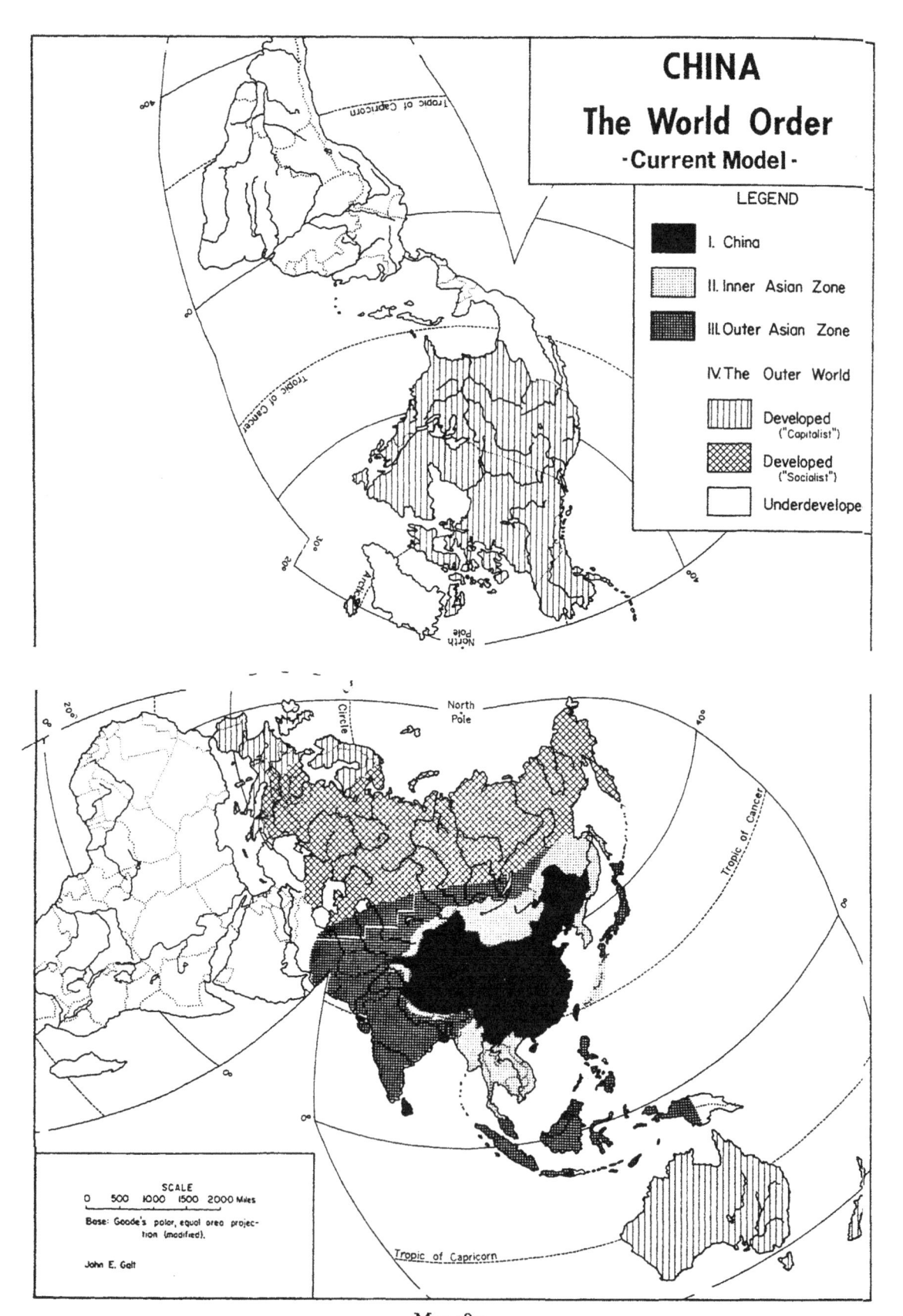

Map 28.2

between the two models and an attempt to adjust contemporary affairs to what the Chinese perceive as the "proper" ordering and distribution of power.

One of the crucial constraints on effecting a pattern based on the traditional model was the imposition of formal, delimited boundaries upon the Chinese state by foreign, chiefly European, powers, but also Japan.[17] The Chinese conception of a concentration of power in core and ecumenical China, gradually tapering off into unbounded and fluctuating frontier zones, was confronted in the seventeenth century by Imperial Russia's drive to the Pacific and by the establishment in the nineteenth century of boundaries in the north and west, which marked the formal limits of Chinese power. Similar boundary impositions occurred, also in the nineteenth century, along China's southern frontiers, although, as is well known, not all the boundaries were delimited, let alone demarcated. In any case, there is little evidence to suggest that the Chinese, whether Imperial, Republican, or Communist, have accepted the modern notion of the delimited boundary as a formal limit of the power of the state,[18] although for special reasons referred to below, the Chinese have come to terms on boundary delimitations. *It follows, therefore, that a continuing problem in China's foreign policy will be border disputes, whatever other relations may exist between China and contiguous countries.*

As a corollary, the Chinese unwillingness to accept the boundary as an integral quality of the modern state must lead to disputes over territories which she regards as *terrae irredentae*.[19] For the most part such territories lie within the USSR, into which have been absorbed huge areas, up to 600,000 square miles, of northern and western forest, steppe, and desert, all of which at various periods formed part of Inner Zone II. The Mongolian People's Republic also falls into this category. To a remarkable degree, however, *terrae irredentae* in this sense are not part of the contemporary pattern in the southern and southeastern marchlands, where *direct* Chinese control either has never existed or was relatively long past. *It follows, therefore, that another continuing force in China's foreign policy would derive from attempts to restore Chinese hegemony not over Southeast Asia, but over those territories of Outer Mongolia and the Soviet Union which formerly were part of traditional Zone II.* So long as China and the USSR were wedded through ideological harmony, these pressures were thrust into the background. Once harmony disappeared, they rose again to exacerbate ideological differences. Thus, in 1964 Mao himself spoke of China's not yet having "presented our account" for a list of Soviet-held areas including not only the Trans-Amur territories, but also the Soviet Maritime Province, the port of Vladivostok, and Sakhalin island.[20]

The issue of *terrae irredentae* appears in different guise but even more excruciating form in connection with Taiwan. Neither the traditional nor the current spatial model allows for a Taiwan other than as an integral part, not merely of a Chinese polity, but as part of ecumenical China. To be sure, Taiwan did not become convincingly Chinese until after the fall of the Ming, and it did not attain provincial status until 1886. However, unlike other contiguous or nearby territories over which the Chinese might claim suzerainty but do not, such as Vietnam and Korea, Taiwan has had only one incarnation, and that has been Chinese; the pre-Chinese aboriginal period was, in effect, prehistoric and therefore irrelevant. Thus, Taiwan, despite a half century of separation under Japan between 1895 and 1945, is perceived to be as much Chinese as is Hainan. It follows, then, that attempts to deal with Taiwan as an issue separate from China itself are confronted with a Chinese perception that blocks communication even before it can begin. *The restoration of Taiwan to China is an essential and particularly sensitive issue of China's*

---

17. For a classification of these impositions, see Herman, "Group Values toward the National Space," pp. 175–176.

18. A special instance of this point is the Chinese espousal of the principle of *jus sanguinas* rather than that of *jus solis*, as shown in the Nationality Law of 1929.

19. Shinkichi Eto correctly observes, however, that such claims and disputes need not mean "unlimited expansionism." See his "Some Underlying Principles of Peking's External Activities," *Japan's Future in Southeast Asia*, Symposium Series 2 (Kyoto: Center for Southeast Asian Studies, 1966), pp. 105 ff. For relevant maps other than those cited previously, see Clubb, *Twentieth Century China*, p. 415; and G. B. Cressey, *Land of the 500 Million* (New York: McGraw-Hill, 1955), p. 40.

20. For a fuller account see W. E. Griffith, "Sino-Soviet Relations 1964–65," *China Quarterly*, no. 25 (January–March), 1966, pp. 28–30.

foreign policy, but it is strategic-spatial in nature, not ideological.

During the nineteenth century, as the power of the Chinese Empire waned, many of the areas in both the Inner and Outer Asian Zones of the traditional model were drawn out of China's orbit and incorporated in varying degrees into European-based empires, even as boundary agreements were proposed and reluctantly accepted or quietly ignored by the Chinese. Most of these areas have now become independent, and their relationships with China have been unstable or uncertain.[21] *One of the major objectives of China's recent foreign policy appears to be a clarification of these relationships and the aligning of these countries in accordance with the Chinese perception of their place in a Sinocentric, Asian-oriented power system; thus the policy of establishing détentes with them wherever possible.* Those which had been dependent or tribute-bearing states in the pre-modern period are expected to be both friendly and subordinate; those farther removed would be expected to be at least friendly. Of course, ideological intimacy would be welcomed, but it does not appear to be a prerequisite to the establishment of détentes, either for former tribute-bearing states of Zone II, such as Burma,[22] or of states in Zone III, such as Pakistan. As Richard Lowenthal has pointed out,[23] the issue is not whether these states follow China's ideological bent. Conditions of their entry into the system are not whether or not they are Communist, but whether they accept, or seem to accept, the Chinese conception of

order. That concept involves, *inter alia*, no or minimal entangling alliances with non-Asian powers and the banning of foreign military forces.[24] In these terms, the presence of American troops in Thailand and Thailand's key role in SEATO present a particular embarrassment; but the terms of acceptance do not deny the possibility of a sub-dominant non-Communist Thailand, free from these involvements and willing to suppress its own interests in *terrae irredentae*, some of which lie within China herself.

Even more difficult as a problem in foreign relations is Japan, which occupies a peculiarly equivocal position within the model political-geographic systems. On the one hand, Japan's partially Sinitic heritage is associated with mutual sentiments about the relations between the two countries, as A. M. Halpern has noted.[25]

On the other hand, Japan has always played an ambivalent role in China's foreign relations. Never occupied by the Chinese, it paid tribute to China only during a short period in the fifteenth and sixteenth centuries.[26] Later, it competed with China for control of certain territories in Zone II, such as Korea, and, what is more important, controlled Manchuria and Taiwan in Zone I and eventually large portions of the Core of China. Moreover, Japan has moved economically into the world of the developed nations and has become one of the world's leading industrial powers. *Ceteris paribus*, one would have anticipated China's making use of Japan's expertise in developing the Chinese economy, and the Japanese certainly have been willing. However, the Chinese have chosen, despite recent rapid increases in Sino-Japanese trade, more to ignore than to accept Japan, as also was the case during most of Ch'ing times. *Rooted in historical relationships, the Japanese enigma continues to be a crucial problem in China's foreign policy*, exacerbated by what appears to be a remarkable ignorance in China of the potency of the Japanese

---

21. A useful analysis of these changing relationships since 1950 is given by V. P. Dutt, "China and Southeast Asia," *Japan's Future in Southeast Asia*, Symposium Series 2 (Kyoto: Center for Southeast Asian Studies, 1966), pp. 89–102, but his orientation is chiefly toward the relationship between ideology and policy.

22. Thus, in 1960 China and Burma concluded a boundary agreement, not unfavourable to the Burmese, which might be regarded as a symbol of the costs the Chinese are willing to bear in order to draw Burma into the system, reconstitute Zone II, and prevent their "encirclement" by foreign, that is, United States power. Nevertheless, Peking's recent fulminations against the Ne Win government indicate extreme sensitivity to possible shifts in Burma's position vis-à-vis the Chinese and demonstrate China's willingness to exert strong pressure on the states of Zone II to prevent their "drift" away from dependency or subordination. For a succinct summary of the Sino-Burma rift, see John Badgely, "Burma's China Crisis: The Choices Ahead," *Asian Survey*, 7 (November, 1967): 753–761.

23. In discussion at the China Conference, Chicago, February 8, 1967.

24. See Rhoads Murphey, "China and the Dominoes," *Asian Survey*, September, 1966, p. 512.

25. For a thoughtful appraisal of these views, see Sadako Ogata, "Japanese Attitudes toward China," *Asian Survey*, August, 1965, pp. 389–398, as well as A. M. Halpern's essay in this volume, chapter 15. [Editors' note: See the credit footnote for this article.]

26. See Yi-tung Wang, *Official Relations between China and Japan, 1368–1549* (Cambridge: Harvard University Press, 1953), in which these relations are documented.

economy and the relevance of the Japanese socioeconomic revolution to the viability of the Chinese perception of the world order. Long regarded by the Chinese as a client state but never unambiguously one, Japan continues on her own increasingly non-Asiatic way. Nevertheless, there is some justification for regarding China's policies toward Japan as part of an attempt to bring Japan "back" into Zone III and indeed into greater involvement with Asia.[27]

Vietnam presents, in the short run, far more difficult problems to China, and their nature is illuminated by reference to the postulated Chinese scheme of things. Unlike Japan, but like Korea, Vietnam was for several centuries, until the tenth century, part of China's Periphery and even longer a client state in tributary relation to China. The traditional spatial model suggests an involvement between China and Vietnam, therefore, significantly greater than that between, say, China and Thailand or Burma. Ideally, then, one might expect an ambivalence in China's policies toward Vietnam, as between reabsorbing it into the traditional Periphery on the one hand and drawing it back into orbit as part of a contemporary Inner Zone of client states on the other. Here, as in the somewhat similar case of Korea, one would expect ideological considerations to play a more significant role than elsewhere among the contiguous territories, but these have come to be subordinated to an even greater problem.

The presence of American and other foreign troops in South Vietnam effectively prevents the reconstitution of continuous Zone II dominated by China and free from foreign involvement, and therefore the restoration of either the traditional or current hypothetical spatial orders. It means also the interjection of Russian influence in what the Chinese regarded as their appropriate sphere of influence (*shih-li fanwei*). From the Chinese point of view a unified, Communist, satellite Vietnam would be ideal, but, again, that view does not place an equal value on all territory, and it places some territorial objectives over others. It can be argued that reunification ranks low on the Chinese scale of values, whereas a dependent and, ideologically intimate North Vietnam would rank higher; but highest of all would be a South Vietnam free of foreign troops which might become a threat to China itself, as escalation of the current war proceeds.

Under these circumstances, *the objectives of China's foreign policy might be attained, at least minimally, by a divided Vietnam in which the South need not be Communist but would be free from foreign troops and foreign interference in internal affairs.* Not only would the aspirations of the Democratic Republic of Vietnam toward a unified Communist state perpetuate a dangerous condition on the edge of ecumenical China, but they also would, if satisfied, create a potentially powerful element in the world Communist system, which might create further difficulties for China in her ideological conflict with the Soviet Union.

In this context one can begin to comprehend the agonies of irresolution which have wracked China's leaders with regard to the issue of more active and substantial support for North Vietnam and the Viet-cong. A greater commitment means not only the dangerous extension of Chinese supply lines in mainland Southeast Asia, far more difficult of access than northern Korea for example, but also the even greater danger of American reprisals on the Chinese mainland. Failure to support means severe loss of face in Asia. Either might require abandonment of a China-oriented constellation of subordinate States in Asia.

Consideration of these issues suggests justification for the Chinese attitude toward wars of national liberation—encourage them everywhere but in those Asian areas in which Chinese domination is desired! Encourage them by words, money, and arms in the Near East, in Africa, in Latin America, but keep them far enough away from the Asiatic mainland so that foreign troops do not constitute a threat to China itself! It might be heretical, but consistent, to propose that the Chinese would not have encouraged a war of national liberation in Vietnam had one not, in effect, already been under way. When Lin Piao emphasizes the importance of adhering to the policy of "self-reliance" in fighting "people's wars," he recognizes both China's inability to participate directly and actively in them and her unwillingness to have responsibility for them on her doorstep. When

---

27. Almost continually, China has expressed displeasure at Japan's ties with the United States and her failure to recognize the Peking government, but quasi-official relationships continue to exist.

Chen Yi speaks of "wars without boundaries," he serves notice that China does not necessarily recognize the system of territorial delimitation imposed on her.[28]

The underdeveloped, "rural" countries of the "Great Beyond," Zone IV, in contrast to the metropoles, provide superb milieus within which the ideologically hostile and physically threatening West might be distracted, diverted, and possibly weakened, even as China buys time for her internal economic development.[29] Such might well have been the policy adopted by China in late Ch'ing times had she had the technological and economic means to have done so, again with the objectives of distraction and diversion.

The metropoles, on the other hand, are little understood as compared with the poorer countries, and their motives, particularly those of the United States, barely comprehended. With a few exceptions, none of the senior Chinese leaders knows the United States firsthand. Their perception of the world order cannot explain the interests of the United States in Asia, except as a reflection of irrational aggression and the imperialistic ambitions associated with Admiral Mahan's views on Asia and the establishment of American power as far removed from the North American mainland as possible. Perhaps the Chinese understand Mahan, but they are apparently much less perceptive about the changes that have taken place in the United States since his death.

The purpose of this essay has been to suggest the need for considering alternative explanations to the ideological, in explaining, understanding, and forecasting Chinese behavior in the world political arena. Clearly that behavior is a function of four major ingredients: (1) ideological considerations, vis-à-vis both the capitalist powers and the U.S.S.R.; (2) domestic economic and other factors, including chance; (3) factors exogenous to China; and (4) strategic-political imagery and objectives, based in part on historical circumstances and tradition. For the most part the attention of analysts of China's foreign policy has been concentrated on the first and second of these and to some extent the third. The fourth has been relatively neglected. In approaching it, the models proposed should not be dismissed as mere exercises in spatial geometry. They relate to but are not identical with Professor Fairbank's exhortation to "look at the map" in seeking understanding of contemporary China. The important consideration is not symmetry or concentricity, but perception and imagery of the world as it ought to be, and the relations of these to the formulation of China's foreign policy. That partial concentricity and some symmetry may appear in that perception is a consequence of the processes that relate geography and history in contemporary China's polity and which feed back into the complex procedures by which China plays out her role in world affairs.

---

28. Ideological considerations appear here as well, since "all (working) men are brothers," or are said to be, within the framework of Marxist philosophy, and national boundaries must not separate them. On the other hand, Chen Yi has also accused the United States, rather than China, of failing to respect boundaries. See *Peking Review*, October 8, 1965, p. 14.

29. Charles Fisher would agree with this point as far as it goes, but would argue that the next step might be attempts at establishing hegemony over the Inner Zone countries. See his "The Chinese Threat to South-East Asia: Fact or Fiction," *Royal Central Asian Journal*, July-October, 1964, pp. 251–267.

29

National Images and International Systems

K. E. BOULDING*

An international system consists of a group of interacting behavior units called "nations" or "countries," to which may sometimes be added certain supra-national organizations, such as the United Nations.

Each of the behavior units in the system can be described in terms of a set of "relevant variables." Just what is relevant and what is not is a matter of judgment of the system-builder, but we think of such things as states of war or peace, degrees of hostility or friendliness, alliance or enmity, arms budgets, geographic extent, friendly or hostile communications, and so on. Having defined our variables, we can then proceed to postulate certain relationships between them, sufficient to define a path for all the variables through time. Thus we might suppose, with Lewis Richardson,[1] that the rate of change of hostility of one nation toward a second depends on the level of hostility in the second and that the rate of change of hostility of the second toward the first depends on the level of hostility of the first. Then, if we start from given levels of hostility in each nation, these equations are sufficient to spell out what happens to these levels in succeeding time periods. A system of this kind may (or may not) have an *equilibrium* position at which the variables of one period produce an identical set in the next period, and the system exhibits no change through time.

Mechanical systems of this kind, though they are frequently illuminating, can be regarded only as very rough first approximations to the immensely complex truth. At the next level of approximation we must recognize that the people whose decisions determine the policies and actions of nations do not respond to the "objective" facts of the situation, whatever they may mean, but to their "image" of the situation. It is what we think the world is like, not what it is really like, that determines our behavior. If our image of the world is in some sense "wrong," of course, we may be disappointed in our expectations, and we may therefore revise our image; if this revision is in the direction of the "truth" there is presumably a long-run tendency for the "image" and the "truth" to coincide. Whether this is so or not, it is always the image, not the truth, that immediately determines behavior. We act according to the way the world appears to us, not necessarily

---

Reprinted by permission of the author and publisher from *Journal of Conflict Resolution*, June 1959.

* K. E. Boulding (1910–) is Professor of Economics at the Institute of Behavioral Sciences, University of Colorado.

1. See Anatol Rapoport, "Lewis F. Richardson's Mathematical Theory of War," *Journal of Conflict Resolution*, I (September, 1957), 249, for an excellent exposition.

according to the way it "is." Thus in Richardson's models it is one nation's image of the hostility of another, not the "real" hostility, which determines its reaction. The "image," then, must be thought of as the total cognitive, affective, and evaluative structure of the behavior unit, or its internal view of itself and its universe.[2]

Generally speaking, the behavior of complex organizations can be regarded as determined by *decisions*, and a decision involves the selection of the most preferred position in a contemplated field of choice. Both the field of choice and the ordering of this field by which the preferred position is identified lie in the image of the decision-maker. Therefore, in a system in which decision-makers are an essential element, the study of the ways in which the image grows and changes, both of the field of choice and of the valuational ordering of this field, is of prime importance. The image is always in some sense a product of messages received in the past. It is not, however, a simple inventory or "pile" of such messages but a highly structured piece of information-capital, developed partly by its inputs and outputs of information and partly by internal messages and its own laws of growth and stability.

The images which are important in international systems are those which a nation has of itself and of those other bodies in the system which constitute its international environment. At once a major complication suggests itself. A nation is some complex of the images of the persons who contemplate it, and as there are many different persons, so there are many different images. The complexity is increased by the necessity for inclusion, in the image of each person or at least of many persons, his image of the image of others. This complexity, however, is a property of the real world, not to be evaded or glossed over. It can be reduced to simpler terms if we distinguish between two types of persons in a nation—the powerful, on the one hand, and the ordinary, on the other. This is not, of course, a sharp distinction. The power of a decision-maker may be measured roughly by the number of people which his decisions potentially affect, weighted by some measure of the effect itself. Thus the head of a state is powerful, meaning that his decisions affect the lives of millions of people; the ordinary person is not powerful, for his decisions affect only himself and the lives of a few people around him. There is usually a continuum of power among the persons of a society: thus in international relations there are usually a few very powerful individuals in a state—the chief executive, the prime minister, the secretary of state or minister of foreign affairs, the chiefs of staff of the armed forces. There will be some who are less powerful but still influential—members of the legislature, of the civil service, even journalists, newspaper owners, prominent business men, grading by imperceptible degrees down to the common soldier, who has no power of decision even over his own life. For purposes of the model, however, let us compress this continuum into two boxes, labeled the "powerful" and the "ordinary," and leave the refinements of power and influence for later studies.

We deal, therefore, with two representative images, (1) the image of the small group of powerful people who make the actual decisions which lead to war or peace, the making or breaking of treaties, the invasions or withdrawals, alliances, and enmities which make up the major events of international relations, and (2) the image of the mass of ordinary people who are deeply affected by these decisions but who take little or no direct part in making them. The tacit support of the mass, however, is of vital importance to the powerful. The powerful are always under some obligation to represent the mass, even under dictatorial regimes. In democratic societies the aggregate influence of the images of ordinary people is very great; the image of the powerful cannot diverge too greatly from the image of the mass without the powerful losing power. On the other hand, the powerful also have some ability to manipulate the images of the mass toward those of the powerful. This is an important object of instruments as diverse as the public education system, the public relations departments of the armed services, the Russian "agitprop," and the Nazi propaganda ministry.

THE FORMATION OF NATIONAL IMAGES

In the formation of the national images, however, it must be emphasized that impressions

---

2. See K. E. Boulding, *The Image* (Ann Arbor: University of Michigan Press, 1956), for an exposition of the theory on which this paper is based.

of nationality are formed mostly in childhood and usually in the family group. It would be quite fallacious to think of the images as being cleverly imposed on the mass by the powerful. If anything, the reverse is the case: the image is essentially a mass image, or what might be called a "folk image," transmitted through the family and the intimate face-to-face group, both in the case of the powerful and in the case of ordinary persons. Especially in the case of the old, long-established nations, the powerful share the mass image rather than impose it; it is passed on from the value systems of the parents to those of the children, and agencies of public instruction and propaganda merely reinforce the images which derived essentially from the family culture. This is much less true in new nations which are striving to achieve nationality, where the family culture frequently does not include strong elements of national allegiance but rather stresses allegience to religious ideals or to the family as such. Here the powerful are frequently inspired by a national image derived not from family tradition but from a desire to imitate other nations, and here they frequently try to impose their images on the mass of people. Imposed images, however, are fragile by comparison with those which are deeply internalized and transmitted through family and other intimate sources.

Whether transmitted orally and informally through the family or more formally through schooling and the written word, the national image is essentially a *historical* image—that is, an image which extends through time, backward into a supposedly recorded or perhaps mythological past and forward into an imagined future. The more conscious a people is of its history, the stronger the national image is likely to be. To be an Englishman is to be conscious of "1066 and All That" rather than of "Constantine and All That," or "1776 and All That." A nation is the creation of its historians, formal and informal. The written word and public education contribute enormously to the stability and persistence of the national images. The Jews, for instance, are a creation of the Bible and the Talmud, but every nation has its bible, whether formed into a canon or not—noble words like the Declaration of Independence and the Gettysburg Address—which crystallize the national image in a form that can be transmitted almost unchanged from generation to generation. It is no exaggeration to say that the function of the historian is to pervert the truth in directions favorable to the images of his readers or hearers. Both history and geography as taught in national schools are devised to give "perspective" rather than truth: that is to say, they present the world as seen from the vantage point of the nation. The national geography is learned in great detail, and the rest of the world is in fuzzy outline; the national history is emphasized and exalted; the history of the rest of the world is neglected or even falsified to the glory of the national image.

It is this fact that the national image is basically a lie, or at least a perspective distortion of the truth, which perhaps accounts for the ease with which it can be perverted to justify monstrous cruelties and wickednesses. There is much that is noble in the national image. It has lifted man out of the narrow cage of self-centeredness, or even family-centeredness, and has forced him to accept responsibility, in some sense, for people and events far beyond his face-to-face cognizance and immediate experience. It is a window of some sort on both space and time and extends a man's concern far beyond his own lifetime and petty interests. Nevertheless, it achieves these virtues usually only at the cost of untruth, and this fatal flaw constantly betrays it. Love of country is perverted into hatred of the foreigner, and peace, order, and justice at home are paid for by war, cruelty, and injustice abroad.

In the formation of the national image the consciousness of great *shared* events and experiences is of the utmost importance. A nation is a body of people who are conscious of having "gone through something" together. Without the shared experience, the national image itself would not be shared, and it is of vital importance that the national image be highly similar. The sharing may be quite vicarious; it may be an experience shared long ago but constantly renewed by the ritual observances and historical memory of the people, like the Passover and the Captivity in the case of the Jews. Without the sharing, however, there is no nation. It is for this reason that war has been such a tragically important element in the creation and sustenance of the national image. There is hardly a nation that has not been cradled in violence and nourished by further violence. This is not,

I think, a necessary property of war itself. It is rather that, especially in more primitive societies, war is the one experience which is dramatic, obviously important, and shared by everybody. We are now witnessing the almost unique phenomenon of a number of new nations arising without war in circumstances which are extremely rare in history, for example—India, Ghana, and the new West Indian Federation, though even here there are instances of severe violence, such as the disturbances which accompanied partition in India. It will be interesting to see the effect, if any, on their national images.

NATIONAL IMAGES AND INTERNATIONAL RELATIONS

1. *The Geographical Dimension*

We now come to the central problem of this paper, which is that of the impact of national images on the relations among states, that is, on the course of events in international relations. The relations among states can be described in terms of a number of different dimensions. There is, first of all, the dimension of simple geographical space. It is perhaps the most striking single characteristic of the national state as an organization, by contrast with organizations such as firms or churches, that it thinks of itself as occupying, in a "dense" and exclusive fashion, a certain area of the globe. The schoolroom maps which divide the world into colored shapes which are identified as nations have a profound effect on the national image. Apart from the very occasional condominium, it is impossible for a given plot of land on the globe to to be associated with two nations at the same time. The territories of nations are divided sharply by frontiers carefully surveyed and frequently delineated by a chain of customs houses, immigration stations, and military installations. We are so accustomed to this arrangement that we think of it as "natural" and take it completely for granted. It is by no means the only conceivable arrangement, however. In primitive societies the geographical image is not sharp enough to define clear frontiers; there may be a notion of the rough territory of a tribe, but, especially among nomadic peoples, there is no clear concept of a frontier and no notion of a nation as something that has a shape on a map. In our own society the shape on the map that symbolizes the nation is constantly drilled into the minds of both young and old, both through formal teaching in schools and through constant repetition in newspapers, advertisements, cartoons, and so on. A society is not inconceivable, however, and might even be desirable, in which nations governed people but not territories and claimed jurisdiction over a defined set of citizens, no matter where on the earth's surface they happened to live.

The territorial aspect of the national state is important in the dynamics of international relations because of the *exclusiveness* of territorial occupation. This means that one nation can generally expand only at the expense of another; an increase in the territory of one is achieved only at the expense of a decrease in the territory of another. This makes for a potential conflict situation. This characteristic of the nation does not make conflict inevitable, but it does make it likely and is at least one of the reasons why the history of international relations is a history of perpetual conflict.

The territorial aspect of international relations is complicated by the fact that in many cases the territories of nations are not homogeneous but are composed of "empires," in which the populations do not identify themselves with the national image of the dominant group. Thus when one nation conquers another and absorbs the conquered territory into an empire, it does not thereby automatically change the culture and allegiances of the conquered nation. The Poles remained Polish for a hundred and twenty-five years of partition between Germany, Austria, and Russia. The Finns retained their nationality through eight hundred years of foreign rule and the Jews, through nearly two thousand years of dispersion. If a nation loses territory occupied by disaffected people, this is much less damaging than the loss of territory inhabited by a well-disposed and loyal population. Thus Turkey, which was the "sick man of Europe" as long as it retained its heterogeneous empire, enjoyed a substantial renewal of national health when stripped of its empire and pushed back to the relatively homogeneous heartland of Anatolia. In this case the loss of a disaffected empire actually strengthened the national unit.

The image of the map-shape of the nations may be an important factor affecting the general frame of mind of the nation. There is a tendency for nations to be uneasy with strong irregularities, enclaves, detached portions, and protuberances or hollows. The ideal shape is at least a convex set, and there is some tendency for nations to be more satisfied if they have regularly round or rectangular outlines. Thus the detachment of East Prussia from the body of Germany by the Treaty of Versailles was an important factor in creating the fanatical discontent of the Nazis.

2. *Hostility vs. Friendliness*

A second important dimension of the national image is that of hostility or friendliness. At any one time a particular national image includes a rough scale of the friendliness or hostility of, or toward, other nations. The relationship is not necessarily either consistent or reciprocal —in nation A the prevailing image may be that B is friendly, whereas in nation B itself the prevailing image may be one of hostility toward A; or again in both nations there may be an image of friendliness of A toward B but of hostility of B toward A. On the whole, however, there is a tendency toward both consistency and reciprocation—if a nation A pictures itself as hostile toward B, it usually also pictures B as hostile toward it, and the image is likely to be repeated in B. One exception to this rule seems to be observable: most nations seem to feel that their enemies are more hostile toward them than they are toward their enemies. This is a typical paranoid reaction; the nation visualizes itself as surrounded by hostile nations toward which it has only the nicest and friendliest of intentions.

An important subdimension of the hostility-friendliness image is that of the stability or security of the relationship. A friendly relationship is frequently formalized as an alliance. Alliances, however, are shifting; some friendly relations are fairly permanent, others change as the world kaleidoscope changes, as new enemies arise, or as governments change. Thus a bare fifteen or twenty years ago most people in the United States visualized Germany and Japan, even before the outbreak of the war, as enemies, and after Hitler's invasion of Russia, Russia was for a while regarded as a valuable friend and ally. Today the picture is quite changed: Germany and Japan are valuable friends and allies; Russia is the great enemy. We can roughly classify the reciprocal relations of nations along some scale of friendliness-hostility. At one extreme we have stable friendliness, such as between Britain and Portugal or between Britain and the Commonwealth countries. At the other extreme we have stable hostility—the "traditional enemies" such as France and Germany. Between these extremes we have a great many pairs characterized by shifting alliances. On the whole, stable friendly relations seem to exist mainly between strong nations and weaker nations which they have an interest in preserving and stable hostile relations between adjacent nations each of which has played a large part in the formation of the other.

3. *Strength vs. Weakness*

Another important dimension both of the image and of the "reality" of the nation-state is its strength or weakness. This is, in turn a structure made up of many elements—economic resources and productivity, political organization and tradition, willingness to incur sacrifice and inflict cruelties, and so on. It, still makes some kind of sense to assess nations on a strength-weakness scale at any one time. Strength is frequently thought of in military terms as the ability to hurt an opponent or to prevent one's self from being hurt by him. There are also more subtle elements in terms of symbolic loyalties and affections which are hard to assess but which must be included in any complete picture. Many arrays of bristling armaments have been brought low by the sheer inability of their wielders to attract any lasting respect or affection. No social organization can survive indefinitely unless it can command the support of its members, and a continuing sense of the significance of the organization or group as such is much more durable a source of support than is the fleeting booty of war or monopoly. The Jews have outlasted an impressive succession of conquerors. These questions regarding the ultimate sources of continuing strength or weakness are difficult, and we shall neglect them in this paper.

The Image Matrix

In order to bring together the variables associated with each nation or pair of nations into an international system, we must resort to the device of a matrix, as in Figure 29.1.

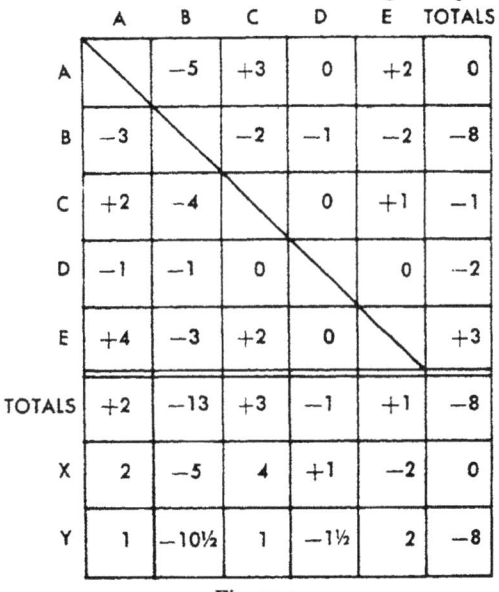

	A	B	C	D	E	TOTALS
A		−5	+3	0	+2	0
B	−3		−2	−1	−2	−8
C	+2	−4		0	+1	−1
D	−1	−1	0		0	−2
E	+4	−3	+2	0		+3
TOTALS	+2	−13	+3	−1	+1	−8
X	2	−5	4	+1	−2	0
Y	1	−10½	1	−1½	2	−8

Fig. 29.1

Here the hostility-friendliness variable is used as an example. Each cell, a_{ij}, indicates the degree of hostility or friendliness of nation I (of the row) toward nation J (of the column). For purposes of illustration, arbitrary figures have been inserted on a scale from 5 to −5, −5 meaning very hostile, 5 very friendly, and 0 neutral. A matrix of this kind has many interesting properties, not all of which can be worked out here but which depend on the kind of restraints that we impose on it. If we suppose, for instance, that the relations of nations are reciprocal, so that I's attitude toward J is the same as J's toward I, the matrix becomes symmetrical about its major diagonal—that is, the lower left-hand triangle is a mirror image of the upper right-hand triangle. This is a very severe restriction and is certainly violated in fact: there are unrequited loves and hates among the nations as there are among individuals. We can recognize a *tendency*, however, for the matrix to become symmetrical. There is a certain instability about an unrequited feeling. If I loves J and J hates I, then either J's constant rebuff of I's affections will turn I's love to hate or I's persistant wooing will break down J's distaste and transform it into affection. Unfortunately for the history of human relations, the former seems to be the more frequent pattern, but the latter is by no means unknown.

The sum totals of the rows represent the over-all friendliness or hostility of the nation at the head of the row; the sum totals of the columns represent the degree of hostility or friendliness *toward* the nation at the head of the column. The sum of either of these sums (which must be equal, as each represents a way of adding up all the figures of the matrix) is a measure of the over-all friendliness or hostility of the system. In the example of Figure 1, B is evidently a "paranoid" nation, feeling hostile toward everyone and receiving hostility in return; D is a "neutral" nation, with low values for either hostility or friendliness; E is a "friendly" nation, reciprocating B's general hostility but otherwise having positive relations with everyone. In this figure it is evident that A, C, and E are likely to be allied against B, and D is likely to be uncommitted.

In the matrix of Figure 29.1 no account is taken of the relative size or power of the different nations. This dimension of the system can easily be accommodated, however. All that is necessary is to take the power of the smallest nation as a convenient unit and express the power of the others in multiples of this unit. Then in the matrix we simply give each nation a number of places along the axes equal to the measure of its power. Thus in Figure 29.2 we suppose a system of three nations, where B is twice as powerful as C and A is three times as powerful as C; A is then

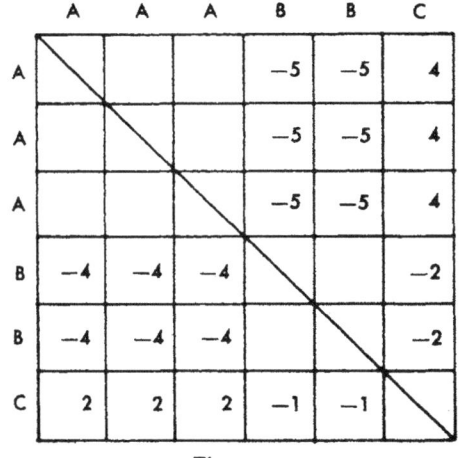

	A	A	A	B	B	C
A				−5	−5	4
A				−5	−5	4
A				−5	−5	4
B	−4	−4	−4			−2
B	−4	−4	−4			−2
C	2	2	2	−1	−1	

Fig. 29.2

allotted three spaces along the axes, B two, and C one. The analysis of the matrix proceeds as before, with the additional constraint that all the figures in the larger boxes bounded by the lines which divide the nations should be the same, as in the figure.

The difference between the sum of a nation's column, representing the general degree of support or affection it *receives*, and the sum of a nation's row, representing the sum of support or affection it *gives*, might be called its *affectional* balance. This is shown in the row X in Figure 29.1. It is a necessary property of a matrix of this kind that the sum of all these balances shall be zero. They measure the relative position of each nation in regard to the degree of support it can expect from the international system as a whole. Thus in Figure 29.1 it is clear that B is in the worst position, and C in the best position, vis-à-vis the system as a whole. Another figure of some interest might be called the *affectional contribution*, shown in the line Y. This is the mean of the column and row totals for each nation. The total affectional contribution is equal to the total of all the figures of the matrix, which measures the general hostility or friendliness of the whole system. The affectional contribution is then a rough measure of how much each nation contributes to the general level of hostility of the whole system. Thus in the example of Figure 29.1 we see that nation B (the paranoid) actually contributes more than 100 per cent to the total hostility of the system, its extreme hostility being offset to some extent by other nations' friendliness.

Dynamics of the Image Matrix

One critical problem of an international system, then, is that of the *dynamics* of the hostility matrix. We can conceive of a succession of such matrices at successive points of time. If there is a system with a solution, we should be able to predict the matrix at t_1 from the knowledge we have of the matrix at t_0 or at various earlier times. The matrix itself will not, in general, carry enough information to make such predictions possible, even though it is easy to specify theoretical models in which a determinate dynamic system can be derived from the information in the matrix alone.

The difficulty with "simple" systems of this nature is that they are very much more simple than the reality which they symbolize. This is because, in reality, the variables of the system consist of the innumerable dimensions of the images of large numbers of people, and the dynamics of the image are much more complex than the dynamics of mechanical systems. This is because of the structural nature of the image; it cannot be represented simply by a set of quantities or variables. Because of this structural nature, it is capable occasionally of very dramatic changes as a message hits some vital part of the structure and the whole image reorganizes itself. Certain events—like the German invasion of Belgium in 1914, the Japanese attack on Pearl Harbor in 1941, the American use of the atom bomb at Hiroshima and Nagasaki, the merciless destruction of Dresden, and the Russian success with Sputnik I—have profound effects and possibly long-run effects on reorganizing the various national images. The "reorganizing" events are hard both to specify and to predict; they introduce, however, a marked element of uncertainty into any dynamic international system which does not exist, for instance, in the solar system!

In spite of this difficulty, which, oddly enough, is particularly acute in short-term prediction, one gets the impression from the observation of history that we are in the presence of a true system with a real dynamics of its own. We do observe, for instance, cumulative processes of hostility. If we had some measures of the hostility matrix, however crude, it would be possible to identify these processes in more detail, especially the "turning points." There is an analogy here with the business cycle, which also represents a system of cumulative stochastic processes subject to occasional "reorganizations" of its basic equations. Just as we can trace cumulative upward and downward movements in national income, the downward movements often (though not always) culminating in financial crisis and the upward movements often leading to inflation and a subsequent downturn, so we can trace cumulative movements in the hostility matrix. We have "prewar" periods corresponding to downswings, in which things go from bad to worse and hostility constantly increases. The total of all the hostility figures (e.g., -8 on Fig. 29.1) is a striking analogue of the national-income concept. It might be called the "international temperature." Just as there is a certain critical point in a deflation at which a financial crisis is likely to ensue because of the growing insolvency of heavily indebted businesses, so there is a critical point in the rise of hostility at which war breaks out. This critical point itself depends on a number of different factors and may not be constant. Some nations may be more tolerant of hostility than others; as the cost of war increases, the tolerance of hostility also increases, as we see today in the remarkable persistence of the "cold war." A deflation or downturn, however, *may* reverse itself without a crisis, and a "prewar" period may turn into a "postwar" period without a war. Indeed, in the period since 1945 we might identify almost as many small international cycles as there have been business cycles! The "upturn" may be a result of a change of government, the death of certain prominent individuals, or even a change of heart (or image!) on the part of existing rulers. The catharsis of a war usually produces the typical "postwar" period following, though this is often tragically short, as it was after the end of World War II, when a "downturn" began after the revolution in Czechoslovakia. The downturn is often the result of the reassertion of a persistent, long-run character of the system after a brief interlude of increasing friendliness. There seems to be a certain long-run tendency of an international system toward hostility, perhaps because of certain inescapable flaws in the very concept of a national image, just as there also seems to be a long-run tendency of an unregulated and undisturbed market economy toward deflation.

In considering the dynamics of an international system, the essential properties of the image matrix might be summed up in a broad concept of "compatibility." If the change in the system makes for greater compatibility the system may move to an equilibrium. The "balance-of-power" theory postulates the existence of an equilibrium of this nature. The record of history, however, suggests that, in the past at least, international systems have usually been unstable. The incompatibility of various national images has led to changes in the system which have created still greater incompatibility, and the system has moved to less and less stable situations until some crisis, such as war, is reached, which represents a discontinuity in the system. After a war the system is reorganized; some national units may disappear, others change their character, and the system starts off again. The incompatibility may be of many kinds, and it is a virtue of this kind of rather loose model that the historian can fill in the endlessly various details in the special situations which he studies. The model is a mere dress form on which the historian swathes the infinite variations of fashion and fact.

In the model we can distinguish two very different kinds of incompatibility of images. The first might be called "real" incompatibility, where we have two images of the future in which realization of one would prevent the realization of the other. Thus two nations may both claim a certain piece of territory, and each may feel dissatisfied unless the territory is incorporated into it. (One thinks of the innumerable irredenta which have stained the pages of history with so much blood!) Or two nations may both wish to feel stronger than, or superior to, each other. It is possible for two nations to be in a position where each is stronger than the other *at home*, provided that they are far enough apart and that the "loss of power gradient" (which measures the loss of power of each as we remove the point of application farther and farther from the home base) is large enough. It is rarely possible, however, for two nations each to dominate the other, except in the happy situation where each suffers from delusions of grandeur.

The other form of incompatibility might be called "illusory" incompatibility, in which there exists a condition of compatibility which would satisfy the "real" interests of the two parties but in which the dynamics of the situation or the illusions of the parties create a situation of perverse dynamics and misunderstandings, with increasing hostility simply as a result of the reactions of the parties to each other, not as a result of any basic differences of interest. We must be careful about this distinction: even "real" incompatibilities are functions of the national images rather than of physical fact and are therefore subject to change and control. It is hard for an ardent patriot to realize that his country is a mental, rather than a physical, phenomenon, but such indeed is the truth! It is not unreasonable to suppose, however, that "real" incompatibilities are more intractable and less subject to "therapy" than illusory ones.

Image Sophistication

One final point of interest concerns what might be called the impact of "sophistication" or "self-consciousness" on national images and the international system. The process of sophistication in the image is a very general one, and we cannot follow all its ramifications here. It occurs in every person in greater or less degree as he grows into adult awareness of himself as part of a larger system. It is akin almost to a Copernican revolution: the unsophisticated image sees the world only from the viewpoint of the viewer; the sophisticated image sees the world from many imagined viewpoints, as a system in which the viewer is only a part. The child sees everything through his own eyes and refers everything to his own immediate comfort. The adult learns to see the world through the eyes of others; his horizon extends to other times, places, and cultures than his own; he learns to distinguish between those elements in his experience which are universal and those which are particular. Many grown people, of course, never become adults in this sense, and it is these who fill our mental hospitals with themselves and their children.

The scientific subculture is an important agency in the sophistication of images. In the physical world we no longer attribute physical phenomena to spirits analogous to our own. In the social sciences we have an agency whereby men reach self-consciousness about their own cultures and institutions and therefore no longer regard these as simply given to them by "nature". In economics, for instance, we have learned to see the system as a whole, to realize that many things which are true of individual behavior are not true of the system and that the system itself is not incapable of a modicum of control. We no longer, for instance, regard depressions as "acts of God" but as system-made phenomena capable of control through relatively minor system change.

The national image, however, is the last great stronghold of unsophistication. Not even the professional international relations experts have come very far toward seeing the system as a whole, and the ordinary citizen and the powerful statesman alike have naïve, self-centered, and unsophisticated images of the world in which their nation moves. Nations are divided into "good" and "bad"— the enemy is all bad, one's own nation is of spotless virtue. Wars are either acts of God or acts of the other nations, which always catch us completely by surprise. To a student of international systems the national image even of respectable, intellectual, and powerful people seems naïve and untrue. The patriotism of the sophisticated cannot be a simple faith. There is, however, in the course of human history a powerful and probably irreversible movement toward sophistication. We can wise up, but we cannot wise down, except at enormous cost in the breakdown of civilizations, and not even a major breakdown results in much loss of knowledge. This movement must be taken into account in predicting the future of the international system. The present system as we have known it for the past hundreds or even thousands of years is based on the widespread acceptance of unsophisticated images, such as, for instance, that a nation can be made more secure *merely* by increasing its armaments. The growth of a systems-attitude toward international relations will have profound consequences for the dynamics of the system itself, just as the growth of a systems-attitude in economics has profound consequences for the dynamics of the economic system.

If, as I myself believe, we live in an international system so unstable that it threatens the very existence of life on earth, our main hope for change may lie in the rapid growth of sophistication, especially at the level of the images of the powerful. Sophistication, of course, has its dangers also. It is usually but a hair's-breadth removed from sophistry, and a false sophistication (of which Marxism in some respects is a good example) can be even more destructive to the stability of a system than a naïve image. Whichever way we move, however, there is danger. We have no secure place to stand where we are, and we live in a time when intellectual investment in developing more adequate international images and theories of international systems may bear an enormous rate of return in human welfare.

Decision Making

30

The West Indies Chooses a Capital

DAVID LOWENTHAL[*]

American geographers have neglected the location of capitals, perhaps because, Hartshorne suggests, the matter seems to them "unrelated to current practical problems."[1] Yet governmental seats are of fundamental significance in the structure of states. The character of a country's capitals reflects the attitudes of its citizens about the location and functions of cities. For example, reaction against centralization of power under British rule, together with admiration of rural virtues and suspicion of commercial influence in government, led Americans to choose relatively small places for federal and state capitals and even county seats, and the seclusion of government away from the main urban centers has in turn influenced other aspects of American life.[2]

Because the selection of a capital generates intense rivalry among aspirants, subjective and emotional considerations often prevail.

Reprinted by permission of the author and publisher from *Geographical Review*, XLVIII, July 1958.

[*] David Lowenthal (1923-) is a Research Associate of the American Geographical Society.

1. Richard Hartshorne: Political Geography, in *American Geography: Inventory & Prospect*, edited by P. E. James and C. F. Jones (Syracuse, 1954), pp. 167-225; reference on p. 215.

2. Derwent Whittlesey: *The Earth and the State: A Study of Political Geography* (New York, 1944), pp. 520-521 and 553-555; Merrill Jensen: *The New Nation: A History of the United States during the Confederation, 1781-1789* (New York, 1950), pp. 327-329; David Lowenthal: The Inferior Capital City: An American Phenomenon (MS.).

"Every choice," Leighly writes, "may have had in part an economic and hence half-rational motivation; but irrational, in a broad sense esthetic, motives always lurk behind ostensibly rational choices."[3] Such motives are apt to produce bitter and protracted struggles in federations; constituent territories, reluctant to give up sovereignty, consider the capital a symbol of both prestige and control. Conflicts of interest and outlook arise and reveal local motives and ambitions as well as images and attitudes about competing places. The nature and intensity of local self-consciousness are the heart of regional inquiry Systematic studies alone cannot bring to life the quintessential character of a territory. To understand what makes a place live, one must know not only its terrain and climate, economy and population, society and culture, but also what both its own inhabitants and outsiders think about it. Men behave in accordance with their own images of themselves, of others, and of their surroundings.

This article explores the geographical problems involved, and the images evoked, in the choice of a capital for the recent federation of The West Indies. It focuses mainly on portraits and self-portraits of the three major contenders, Jamaica, Trinidad, and Barbados, and especially on the last two, whose

3. John Leighly: Some Comments on Contemporary Geographic Method, *Annals of the Association of American Geographers*, Vol. 27, 1937, pp. 125-141; reference on p. 139.

"rivalry ... is as bitter as their scenery is contrasting"—perhaps the most spectacular example "of that exciting individualism that makes the West Indies what they are."[4]

. . . .

THE CAPITAL PROBLEM

If West Indian parochialism made federation difficult, physical insularity made it still harder to agree on the capital site, for the choice of any island would deprive all the others of direct contact with the seat of power. But besides the problem of communication, the spatial arrangement and character of the federating territories made each possible location seem unsatisfactory. The three most populous and politically most advanced units —Jamaica, Trinidad, and Barbados—lie at extremities of the federal arc, and each, moreover, has particular disadvantages. The smaller islands likewise present grave drawbacks. None of them has as many as 100,000 people, all are poor, most are difficult to reach, and their rugged interiors are traversed by few and inferior roads.

The federal histories of the Windwards and Leewards also augured badly for the selection of any of them as capital of an amalgamation. Dominica found "government by telegraph wire" from Antigua so crippling that it quit the Leewards; St. Kitts likewise resented Antigua's possession of colonial headquarters, and the Leeward Islands federation dissolved, to the satisfaction of most concerned, in 1956. Even the loose Windward confederation, an official noted in 1922, "excites opposition in St. Lucia and St. Vincent, owing to the fact that it is based upon Grenada."[5]

When West Indian delegates exchanged final federal vows in London in 1956, they failed to agree on a capital site. "This is rather like sending out invitations to your wedding," commented a Jamaican journalist, "before you have decided on your bride." In his opinion, the marriage would not endure anyhow, because "wherever you put the capital, it is going to be impossibly inconvenient."[6] The domestic simile is as pervasive as the pessimistic conclusion. As another observer wrote, the selection "has shown all the difficulties and intercolonial complications of a modern Judgment of Paris."[7] The best place for the capital, someone suggested, would be the sea floor.

Early feeling in the West Indies had seemed to favor a small-island bride. The Montego Bay Conference of 1947, at which the present federation was first seriously promoted, left the selection of a provisional captial to a committee, which in 1949 suggested Trinidad.[8] But when West Indian delegates met in London four years later to frame the federal constitution, opinion in the islands was generally anti-Trinidad. If some of the small islands were prepared to accept Port of Spain as the capital city, Jamaica and Barbados were unalterably opposed. Not that they demanded the capital for themselves. The Barbadians would accept a Windward or Leeward site, and the then Jamaican Chief Minister, W. A. Bustamante, cabled the conference that "the seat of the Federal Government must be in one of the small islands, preferably Antigua or Grenada, and there can be no compromise on this." "We must not want everything for the bigger islands."[9] A Jamaican paper explained that most federations had avoided major population centers in order "to screen [legislators] from the worst influences of urbanism" and to avoid accentuating jealousies among rivals. The West Indies should "take a new and picturesque site in Antigua or one of the other smaller islands, central in the chain, and start building from nothing a capital which could grow into a new and worthy city."[10]

After a prolonged deadlock, the delegates agreed on provisional headquarters in St. George's, Grenada, the picturesque, solidly built, red-brick capital (population 8000) of the nutmeg-and-cacao island north of Trini-

---

4. James Pope-Hennessy: *West Indian Summer: A Retrospect* (London, 1943), p. vii.
5. E. F. L. Wood: West Indies: Report by the Honourable E. F. L. Wood ... on His Visit to the West Indies and British Guiana, December, 1921–February, 1922, *Cmd. 1679*, London, 1922, p. 32.
6. Thomas Wright, Jamaica *Gleaner* [cited hereinafter as *Gleaner*], Feb. 29, 1956.
7. G. V. de Freitas: Wanted—A Federal Capital, *New Commonwealth*, Vol. 32, 1956, pp. 118–119.
8. Report of the British Standing Closer Association Committee 1948–1949, *Col[onial] No. 255*, London, 1950, p. 48.
9. Quoted in *Gleaner*, Apr. 22 and 27, 1953.
10. E. H. J. King: Choosing a Federal Capital, *Gleaner*, Apr. 23, 1953, and editorial, *ibid.*, Apr. 21, 1953.

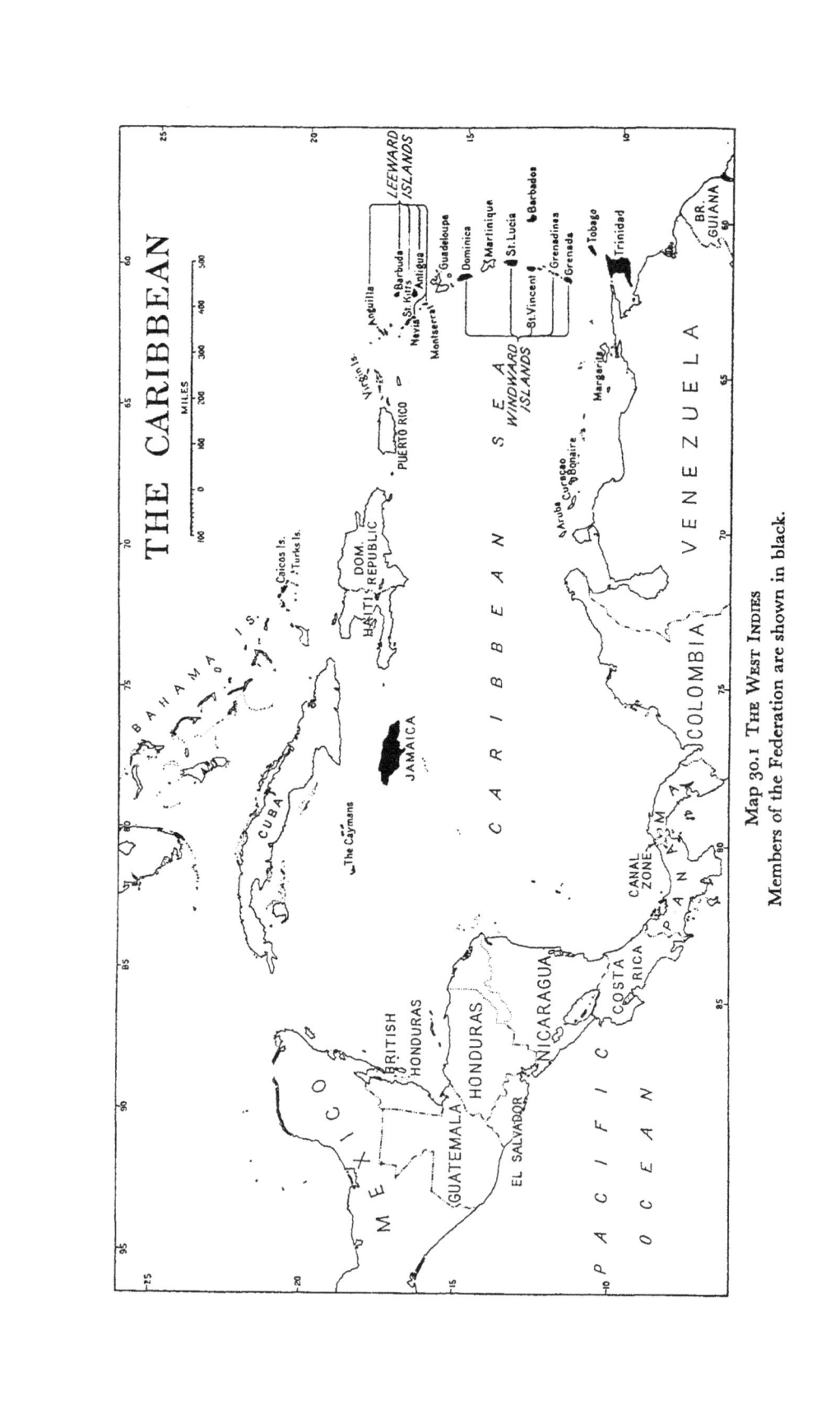

Map 30.1 THE WEST INDIES
Members of the Federation are shown in black.

dad.[11] Delighted Grenada regarded its election as a compliment to the island's charm and to T. A. Marryshow, a native son who was one of the West Indian "fathers" of federation. "A compliment is a kind of kiss, and they say that a kiss is as good as a promise," Grenada's Administrator told the Legislative Council, urging it "so to shape our policies" that the promise "may lead to a happy ending."[12]

But the other territories had led Grenada up the garden path. Barbadians warned against placing the capital on an "island which must be approached in a punt and where the drinking water for the federal legislators must be carried in barrels," and their Premier characterized the selection of Grenada as a "farcical suggestion . . . not seriously taken";[13] Trinidad likewise rejected the London decision. Particularly damaging to Grenada's chances was the 1955 report of the pre-federal Fiscal Commissioner, Sir Sydney Caine, who "found a widespread feeling that, for strictly practical reasons of convenience of communications and other facilities," the capital decision "ought to be reexamined." He warned that essential airfield and port installations could be constructed in Grenada only at prohibitive expense, and buildings and land alone would cost more than four times the £500,000 grant promised by Britain.[14]

Caine's somber report was fresh in the minds of the delegates when they met in London in February, 1956, this time with plenipotentiary powers, to hammer out constitutional details and choose the capital. Jamaica alone was not a serious contender. Trinidad relied on the 1949 report; Barbados had sought to strengthen its claim by passing a law outlawing racial discrimination in public places; Grenada depended on the 1953 compromise; Antigua, less attractive than Grenada but easier to reach and build on, had barely lost out in 1953; St. Lucia was centrally located, easily accessible by plane and ship, and, though Catholic and French-speaking, the most "West Indian," many thought, of all the territories.

In the bitter battle that followed the delegates again failed to agree on a capital. Instead they asked the Secretary of State for the Colonies to appoint a fact-finding commission "composed of three wholly impartial persons who have never resided in the West Indies" to spend not more than four months touring the area, and, on the basis of cost, convenience, communications, availability of land and facilities, and West Indian political and social sentiment, to recommend "the three most suitable sites in order of preference."[15] How strangers could study the social climate of all the islands in so short a time baffled a few people, but most felt that they "must accept the capital choice in good faith, even if placed on Sombrero"[16] (a barren dependency of St. Kitts, three miles long and half a mile wide, inhabited by a few lighthouse keepers).

The commissioners were appointed June 1, 1956, and promptly toured the islands, received depositions and offers of sites, made independent inquiries, and heard many "contradictory and peculiar stories."[17] In 66 days they saw every territory, including British Guiana, and devoted about a week to each of the serious contenders for the capital. Their visit was widely publicized everywhere, and although it aroused public interest in the capital site, it also exacerbated interisland jealousies.

THE CAPITAL COMMISSION REPORT

In federal states generally, Spate has shown, "the selection for the capital either of a completely new site or of a town of small importance in itself must be regarded as a normal . . . principle."[18] It was not followed in the

11. Report by the Conference on West Indian Federation Held in London in April, 1953, *Cmd. 8837*, London, 1953, p. 12.
12. Wallace Macmillan, Jan. 6, 1954, in "Minutes of the Legislative Council for the Half Year Ended 30th June, 1954" (Grenada, 1954), Appendix, p. 1.
13. *Barbados Advocate*, Apr. 25, 1953; Grantley Adams in the Barbados House of Assembly, Jan. 19, 1956, *Supplement to The Official Gazette*, Vol. 91, 1956, p. 1958.
14. The Plan for a British Caribbean Federation: Report of the Fiscal Commissioner, *Cmd. 9618*, London, 1955, pp. 5–10. Later in that year Grenada was badly damaged by Hurricane Janet.

15. Report by the Conference on British Caribbean Federation Held in London in February, 1956, *Cmd. 9733*, London, 1956, p. 14.
16. *Crusader*, St. Lucia, and *Workers' Voice*, Antigua, Feb. 24, 1956, in *Gleaner*, Feb. 29 and 28, 1956, respectively.
17. H. Myles Wright, personal communication, Sept. 5, 1957.
18. O. H. K. Spate: Factors in the Development of Capital Cities, *Geogr. Rev.*, Vol. 32, 1942, pp. 622–631; reference on p. 623.

West Indies. The guiding principle of the Capital Commission Report—completed in September but not released until January 3, 1957—was that the capital should be near one of the three largest existing cities. Since the London agreement of 1956 bound the West Indies to pick one of the three recommended sites, the report thus committed the federation to a large-island capital. ...

Opposed to remote sites, the commissioners also rejected existing cities. To represent all the islands, the capital must be autonomous. They recommended the creation of a federal district of 15 to 25 square miles, with a centrally located federal capital "not less than three and not much more than seven miles" from some established town of "size and standing" sufficient to serve as temporary capital. The new capital would eventually become a twin city to the base town. The twin-city formula eliminated the Leewards and Windwards. None of them, the commissioners decided, had a town with the requisite standard of services and living conditions for the temporary capital. Only the chief cities of the three largest territories—Bridgetown, Barbados; Port of Spain, Trinidad; Kingston, Jamaica—met the essential requirements.

. . . .

The commissioners ranked Trinidad lowest of the three on account of "the instability of that island's politics and the low standard accepted in its public life." Widespread accusations of Trinidadian corruption met, they found, with "almost universal belief in the other islands." Corruption might occur anywhere, but, commented the commissioners, "what is significant in the case of Trinidad ... is that these practices appear to be tolerated." Furthermore, Trinidad's large East Indian minority was widely alleged to "have ideals and loyalties differing from those to be found elsewhere in the Federation and they exercise a disruptive influence ... which would vitiate the social and political life of the capital." Neither accepting nor rejecting these allegations, the commissioners nevertheless believed that the racial cleavage "will make the growth of healthy political conditions in Trinidad even more difficult than it would otherwise have been." To locate the capital there would, they concluded, be "a very great risk."

The commissioners rejected Jamaica's claim to first place on two grounds. One was its "aloofness" from the eastern Caribbean. "'It is not so much that Jamaica is far away,'" one speaker told them, "'as that Jamaicans are.'" Even more serious, in their view, was Jamaica's size; "if it were chosen for the capital, ... the small islands would fear ... [that] their needs and aspirations" would be ignored. To place the capital in Jamaica would, the commissioners judged, "be a psychological mistake which would give the Federation a bad start."

This left Barbados. More crowded and less cosmopolitan than either Trinidad or Jamaica, Barbados had another, more serious, drawback—"accusations in the other islands" of "a prejudice against colour not found elsewhere." But the commissioners minimized the color bar. Barbados might have more "pockets of prejudice" than the other islands, but "changes occur more slowly in a stable society ... [and] we have no doubt that Barbados is changing like the rest." Among Barbados' advantages, the commissioners noted the availability of good sites near Bridgetown with "beauty and fine views ... [and] the benefit of the trade winds," a higher general level of education, and a keener "average intellectual atmosphere." They found—and shared—a widespread view that if either Jamaica or Trinidad got the capital it might dominate the federation. "But our main reason for preferring Barbados," they concluded, is that, "if possible, the capital should be on a small island."[19]

West Indian Reaction

"Capital Report Flayed," headlined the Jamaica *Gleaner* the day after publication; the next day it noted "Federal Storm Signals" and judged that the report had "inflamed latent animosities and insular prejudices and could possibly wreck the whole idea of federation." Everywhere except Barbados, the report was bitterly criticized. The commissioners were accused of glossing over Barbadian color prejudice, either through ignorance or because "Barbados would be a convenient funnel through which Colonial Office flavour-

19. Report of the British Caribbean Federal Capital Commission, *Colonial No. 328*, London, 1956, pp. 19-24.

ing could be dropped into the federal cake."[20] At the same time, West Indians denounced the "uncharitable unwarranted and libellous attack on the people of Trinidad," and the new Chief Minister, who had just won a sweeping victory on the issue of eradicating corruption, contended that "the report is not worth the paper it is written on with reference to what it says about Trinidad's political life.... It is a joke."[21] A prominent St. Lucian charged that the report "went out of its way to castigate ... this area." Were it "intended to dent the loyalty of West Indians ... [and] shake their faith in the Colonial Office then it could not have been better presented."[22]

Only a few remembered that the West Indians, "though clamouring to manage their own affairs," were responsible for the commission's character and terms of reference. "The crying baby politicians of the West Indies", commented the veteran Marryshow, "... asked to be spoon-fed by others in the choosing of a capital for them. They expected good cereal from the spoon, no doubt, but it has turned out to be castor oil."[23]

THE STANDING FEDERATION COMMITTEE MEETING

Less than three weeks after the report appeared, the West Indies acted on it. Delegates to the Standing Federation Committee —three each from Jamaica, Trinidad, and Barbados, and one from each of the seven other territories—met on January 22 at the Senate House of the University College of the West Indies in Jamaica but decided to postpone choosing the capital to the end of their conference, after the draft constitution and matters of federal establishment had been worked out. Some delegates later regretted this decision, partly because it resulted in more intense lobbying and put them under great public pressure, partly because such matters as salaries and cost-of-living allowances could not be properly determined beforehand. All sessions were secret, and as the days passed, public excitement grew and feelings about the capital were expressed with increasing vehemence.

"The one thing to be avoided in choosing the federal capital site," wrote a Jamaican columnist, "is an unseemly squabble."[24] But while amity generally prevailed in the conference room, the nature of the issue and of the report made squabbles unavoidable. On the second day of the conference, delegates read the front-page comment of a Jamaican planter-journalist traveling in the eastern Caribbean that Barbados did not "really belong to the West Indies at all in spirit" and should not even have been considered for the capital.[25] Tempers were again ignited when the Chief Minister of Trinidad publicly referred to Barbados as "a plantocracy ... entirely unsuitable to be the capital."[26] "It is bad enough," retorted the Premier of Barbados, "for people from one island to attack another," but an attack by a territorial leader endangered the spirit of federation.[27] The press magnified this rebuke into a threat that Barbados might leave the federation if it did not get the capital. A few Jamaican groups did threaten withdrawal, and in Trinidad too, some writers implied, possession of the capital was considered almost a *sine qua non* of federation. Delegates deprecated these reports and accused the press of fabrication. but feelings remained highly charged. All the recriminations, however, did not destroy the pervasive atmosphere of good feeling. Delegates from all the territories worked in harmony despite their different capital ambitions. Whatever anger or vexation they expressed was directed mainly toward the report or toward the press, not toward one another.

General condemnation of the report encouraged some small-islanders to hope again that they might get the capital for themselves. From the start of the conference, the St. Lucian delegate had urged total rejection of the report, and many in the Windwards and Leewards supported him. As an Antiguan

---

20. Thomas Wright, *Gleaner*, Jan. 9, 1957.
21. L. F. Seukeran and Eric Williams, quoted in *Gleaner*, Jan. 5 and 4, 1957, respectively.
22. Carl LaCorbiniere, speech at Standing Federation Committee [hereinafter cited as S.F.C.] meeting, Jamaica, Jan. 22, 1957, quoted in *Gleaner*, Jan. 23, 1957.
23. W. E. Julien, *West Indian*, Grenada, Jan. 10, 1957, T. A. Marryshow: Federation Facts and Fancies, *Gleaner*, Jan. 19 and Feb. 2, 1957.

24. F. S. Coon, *Gleaner*, Jan. 8, 1957.
25. Morris Cargill, quoted in *Gleaner*, Jan. 24, 1957.
26. Eric Williams: Some Historical Aspects of Federation, Feb. 5, 1957, quoted in *Gleaner*, Feb. 7, 1957.
27. Grantley Adams, quoted in *Public Opinion*, Kingston, Jamaica, Feb. 9, 1957.

journal put it, "The Commission said Jamaica is unsuitable, Trinidad is unsuitable, and the smaller islands unsuitable. Most of us think Barbados unsuitable. The only compromise is to shuffle the pack . . . and pull out a card . . . But are we big enough to ignore the report?"[28] Politically the small islands were bigger than they had ever been before or would be again. With less than 15 per cent of the federal population, they have 29 per cent of the votes in the federal House of Representatives; but on the Standing Federation Committee they had 7 out of 16 votes, or 45 per cent of the total—a commanding position.

But the Windwards and Leewards were not united enough to force the committee to scrap the capital report and compromise on a small-island site. They could, however, and did, use their strength to exact promises from the chief contenders. Most important were resolutions submitted by St. Vincent and St. Lucia to guarantee complete freedom of movement, without customs or immigration examination, to all federal citizens traveling to the capital; to stipulate that the territory chosen should donate at least 2000 acres to the federation without cost; and to make certain that workmen from all the islands would be employed in constructing the capital. Jamaica, Trinidad, and Barbados accepted all these conditions, and on February 11 the delegates cast secret ballots for the capital territory. On the first ballot Trinidad received seven votes, Barbados five, and Jamaica four. This eliminated Jamaica. The next ballot, taken without delay, gave the capital to Trinidad, eleven votes to five for Barbados.[29] Thus West Indians confirmed the initial proposal made eight years before.

THE MAJOR CONTENDERS

The rest of this paper explores the predominating and perhaps decisive images of each of the major contenders. Two disclaimers are needed. First, I do not attempt to describe the three territories as they really are, but rather to set forth widely held West Indian beliefs and attitudes about them. Second, although these attitudes affected the decisions, I do not know all the reasons or motivations that pre-

28. *Workers' Voice*, Antigua, reprinted in *Gleaner*, Jan. 25, 1957.
29. *Gleaner*, Feb. 5, 8, 9, and 12, 1957.

vailed with the 16 delegates when they cast their ballots. One may, however, as the Sprouts suggest, "reason from general assumptions as to how decision-makers operating in a given physical and social milieu are likely to act and react."[30]

JAMAICA

So obvious were Jamaica's advantages that at least one Jamaican was convinced that most of the delegates wanted the capital on his island and would have chosen it but for a southern Caribbean intrigue.[31] A friendly neutral, Jamaica might well have emerged as a compromise in the bitter rivalry between Barbados and Trinidad. Jamaica, its leaders pointed out, was the natural link between the Caribbean and the United States and Canada; "the economic future of the Federated territories is certain to be more closely related to North America than to the British Isles."[32] Finally, as host, Jamaica could show off its scenery, facilities, cosmopolitanism, and progress in many fields. But the guests saw more than the host intended. Small-island delegates were indeed impressed by many aspects of life in Kingston, but although they enjoyed Jamaican hospitality, not all of it was free, and prices appalled them. Most goods were more expensive in the Jamaican capital than in Port of Spain and Bridgetown, and a few delegates quit one of the foremost hotels because they could not afford the high "special" rates charged them as territorial ambassadors. "If there is one reason why Jamaica lost any chance it had," said Trinidad's Chief Minister afterward, "it was because of the fantastic cost of living."[33]

Jamaicans, on the other hand, view themselves as generous and kind-hearted. They feel imposed on by grasping, ungrateful neighbors, who "airily . . . dismiss us as if we were some avuncular relative with pockets as deep as Washington D.C. and endowed with a willingness to be kicked at every step."[34]

30. Harold and Margaret Sprout: *Man-Milieu Relationship Hypotheses in the Context of International Politics* (Princeton, 1956), p. 57.
31. "Capital: Why Trinidad Was Chosen," *Gleaner*, Feb. 17, 1957.
32. *Public Opinion*, Jan. 5, 1957.
33. Eric Williams in Trinidad Legislative Council, Mar. 1, 1957, reprinted in *Trinidad Guardian*, Mar. 2, 1957.
34. Political Reporter, *Gleaner*, Jan. 20, 1957.

But both small-island and home views are based on misapprehensions of Jamaica's wealth. Although Jamaica has considerable resources, the general level of living in the countryside is lower than in either Trinidad or Barbados, where people perhaps exaggerate Jamaican poverty. A Trinidadian has recently described Jamaica as "an unremittingly second-rate island hounded by Nature. Mountainous, its soil exhausted, it is subject to earthquakes and exposed to hurricanes [in contrast with Trinidad]. Jamaican sugar was never very good; Jamaican rum is not as good as Barbadian . . . ; Jamaican citrus is poor . . . ; Jamaican cigars are not as good as Cuban; in 1943 Canada refused to take any more Jamaican coffee; and people are beginning to complain about Jamaican bananas."[35] The Barbadian views Jamaica much as the Barbadian planter did a century ago: "When Jamaica is mentioned philanthropic compassion lights up his face, and he tells you how much he feels for the poor wretches there who call themselves planters. . . . 'Jamaica is a fine island, only utterly ruined.' "[36] Despite their present rapid progress in both agriculture and industry, Jamaicans are perhaps more conscious of impoverishment than Trinidadians and Barbadians.[37]

Rich or poor, Jamaica is much too big, small-islanders felt, to make a comfortable capital. Any of the Windwards or Leewards would be lost there; to give Jamaica the capital would be to invite their annihilation. Most Jamaicans, including some political leaders, had never even heard of many of the smaller islands and those who had heard seemed largely indifferent. By contrast, both Trinidad and Barbados had intimate and continuing contact with the Windwards and Leewards. Oriented towards a different world, Jamaica is as remote in location from the rest of the federation as it appeared to the small-islanders to be in spirit. Indeed, to reach Jamaica at all, most small-islanders have to change planes in Barbados or Trinidad.

Finally, despite their reputation for "always lookin' argument," Jamaicans simply did not care enough to fight hard: "there is no passion or overweening desire to have the federal capital sited in Jamaica."[38] At first aloof from the federation, Jamaica later— magnanimously or otherwise—favored a small-island capital in brief, as Chief Minister Norman Manley put it, "Jamaica entered the race too late."[39] Besides, Jamaica already had the University College, the most prestigeful and expensive federal institution, and was expected by many to provide the first leaders of the federal government. One Jamaican journal stated: "It would obviously be inadvisable for Jamaica to provide the Federation with its Capital, its Prime Minister and its Governor-General as well."[40]

BARBADOS

Barbados lost out chiefly because, to other West Indians, it stood for color prejudice and "slavish adherence to English customs and traditions."[41] Barbadians have traditionally been made fun of, but they have been respected and admired too. In the capital controversy, however, they were almost read out of the West Indies. If the Jamaica *Gleaner* thought "the Commission has done the West Indies a service by emphasising the progress which Barbados has made in overcoming its proud but anachronistic social dichotomy,"[42] most West Indians saw only special pleading in this section of the report. "The siting of the capital in Barbados," remarked an Antiguan journal, "would be like moving the United States capital to Dixieland to face the pressure of Jimcrowism."[43]

West Indian consciousness of Barbados' color line has been increased in recent years by some unfortunate episodes, such as the

---

35. V. S. Naipaul: Where the Rum Comes From, *New Statesman*, Vol. 55, 1958, pp. 20–21.
36. Anthony Trollope: *The West Indies and the Spanish Main* (London, 1859), pp. 208–209.
37. See M. G. Smith and G. J. Kruijer: *A Sociological Manual for Extension Workers in the Caribbean* (University College of the West Indies, The Extra-Mural Department [Mona, Jamaica], 1957), pp. 15–22; Yehudi Cohen: Character Formation and Social Structure in a Jamaican Community, *Psychiatry*, Vol. 18, 1955, pp. 275–296.

38. Editorial, *Gleaner*, Feb. 2, 1957.
39. On Radio Jamaica, Feb. 24, 1957, quoted in *Gleaner*, Feb. 26, 1957.
40. *Public Opinion*, Jan. 5, 1957. As things turned out, Jamaica provided none of the three. Its Governor, Sir Hugh Foot, became Governor of Cyprus; its Chief Minister decided not to run for federal office.
41. M. C. Alleyne, letter, *Gleaner*, Jan. 8, 1957.
42. Editorial, Jan. 3, 1957.
43. *Workers' Voice*, Antigua, quoted in *Gleaner*, Jan. 25, 1957.

refusal of service to an eminent colored British Guianese at a Bridgetown barbershop. Whites do constitute a much larger proportion of the population in Barbados—5 per cent—than in any of the other territories, and although discrimination in public places is nowhere official or legal, in social life the color bar is evident. The Barbadians themselves are well aware of all this, and the problem dominates many debates in the Assembly. "There is not the shadow of a doubt whatever," said the Premier, "that apart from social distinction, there are distinctions made on ground of race and colour by certain persons mainly in the hotel trade which not only causes irritations among Barbadians, but which often prevents visitors ... from having a good word to say about the Island."[44] Partly in order to publicize social progress, the Premier proposed and the legislature passed a law banning discrimination in public places.[45] But instead of acclaiming Barbadian progress, opponents interpreted this as evidence that "Barbados has found things so bad, so intolerable ... that they have had to rush this legislation on the Statute Book [but with] so many loopholes that it can be regarded as nothing more than a mere gesture." And rivals capitalized on statements by Barbadian antiadministration assemblymen that "there is no other colony in the British Caribbean in which colour prejudice is so rife as it is here" and "Barbados is not a very good society for men to live in."[46] Barbados was its own worst enemy.

However, it was less the existence of such conditions in Barbados than their whitewashing by the Capital Commission that provoked other West Indians to condemn and ridicule "Little England" as a "tropical Isle of Wight." Barbados became unacceptable for reasons that had never been thought of before, including the fact that it was "guilty of the crime of crimes, to have been English from 1625."[47] As the English choice, it could not be the West Indian. Still worse, Barbados seemed inferior even by English standards. The Jamaican press reprinted a comment by a recent English traveler that "Barbados reflects most faithfully the social and intellectual values and prejudices of a Golf Club in Outer London ... or of the married quarters of a barracks in Basutoland, which are not England's most interesting or precious contributions to world civilization."[48]

Although color bars are more apparent and more openly acknowledged in Barbados, they are hardly less prevalent on other West Indian islands. As one Barbadian pointed out, the main difference between Barbadian and Jamaican color prejudice was that in Jamaica there are "more kinds, since there are more colours," and a Jamaican found "less colour discrimination actually in Barbados than there is in Jamaica."[49] In Grenada and Dominica whites are few, though not insignificant, and racial discrimination is often reputed to be absent; in fact, however, family background and color gradations are of great importance. Whites still own most of Jamaica's major enterprises and many of Trinidad's, and on several of the small islands society is more rigidly stratified than in Barbados. Political leaders generally minimize these conditions, however, and so attempt to give the impression that colored West Indians control their own affairs and that racial distinctions no longer matter.

Barbados' supposed racial, social, and political drawbacks were linked by other West Indians to the sugar industry that dominates the island's economy. In the Caribbean, sugar has a bad press. Because the archetypal slave plantations grew sugar, the present-day West Indian dissociates himself from it. It stands for bondage under hard task masters, for political Bourbonism and imperial domination, for absentee ownership and peasant landlessness. Higher wages than for other agricultural work are needed to get men in Jamaica and Antigua to work on sugar plantations.[50] People were easily persuaded, therefore, that Barbados, where "the product itself has set the social and economic

---

44. Grantley Adams in the Barbados House of Assembly, Jan. 26, 1956, *Supplement to The Official Gazette*, Vol. 91, 1956, pp. 2028–2029.

45. Shops (Amendment) Act, 1956, Barbados *Official Gazette*, Vol. 91, No. 8, Jan. 26, 1956, pp. 1309–1310.

46. J. E. T. Brancker, W. A. Crawford, and F. L. Walcott in the Barbados House of Assembly, Jan. 26, 26, and 10, 1956, respectively, *Supplement to The Official Gazette*, Vol. 91, 1956, pp. 2033, 2030, and 1910.

47. C. N. Blackman, letter, *Gleaner*, Jan. 28, 1957.

48. P. L. Fermor: *The Traveller's Tree: A Journey through the Caribbean Islands* (New York [1950]), p. 140, quoted by Gordon Lewis, *Gleaner*, Jan. 7, 1957.

49. C. N. Blackman and Gloria Cumper, letters, *Gleaner*, Jan. 28, 1957, and Feb. 6, 1956, respectively.

50. Simon Rottenberg: Income and Leisure in an Underdeveloped Economy [Antigua], *Journ. of Polit. Econ.*, Vol. 60, 1952, pp. 95–101; reference on pp. 99–101.

tone of the island for centuries,"[51] was an "anachronism" in the modern Caribbean. "The mere selection of Barbados as one of the possible sites," remarked Trinidad's Chief Minister, "suggests a total ignorance of past West Indian history and a total lack of sympathy with the obvious West Indian aspirations for the future."[52]

Most of these stereotypes, however, no longer fit Barbados. The Labour party, in power since 1938, has not broken the economic hold of the sugar corporations, but it has brought workers notable gains in living standards and security. Peasants grow an increasing proportion of the cane, with estate and factory support not duplicated on the other islands. It is true that Barbados grows little besides sugar; but Jamaica and British Guiana grow more of it, and Trinidad as much, and plantations there and in St. Kitts are bigger, more highly centralized, and owned by wealthier men—many of them non-residents—than in Barbados, but these facts mattered little next to the dominant image of Barbados as a sugar plantocracy.

For its position as scapegoat, Barbados itself was partly responsible. "They display in their attitude towards and relations with sister colonies," a scholar wrote recently, "a national pride (or complacent insularity) . . . galling to their neighbors."[53] As a former governor put it, "Barbadians . . . consider that they and their institutions are perfect, and [are] indignant at criticisms from strangers."[54] The "imperturbable good humour and self-satisfaction" Froude noted there in 1887 were not new even then; a century ago Trollope found Barbados "a little self-glorious." "No people," he commented, "ever praised themselves so constantly; no set of men were ever so assured that they and their occupations are the main pegs on which the world hangs."[55]

Proud of their long history of self-government (Barbados has the third-oldest representative institution in the British Commonwealth) and of their educational attainments (Barbados has far fewer illiterates and more university graduates, proportionately, than any other Caribbean territory), Barbadians find it hard not to boast. Premier Grantley Adams could hardly be blamed for reminding other delegates that Barbados had the best constitution in the Caribbean and would gladly help the others attain higher standards; he was only "trying to be as modest as a Bajan can."[56]

One example of Barbadian self-importance, other delegates complained, was that Barbados claimed to fit both sides of the argument. It opposed Trinidad and Jamaica as too large, but in terms of votes at the meeting it was a "big" island itself. The capital commissioners' earlier acceptance of this ambiguity did not help Barbados with the "small' islanders. "Barbados cannot, when it suits her politicians, be permitted to claim as being a small territory, and at other times claim all the advantages of a large one," protested a Grenadan journal. "If this ain't bias what is it?" asked a St. Lucian editor. "When you call for large Barbados win, when you call for small you lose."[57]

To Trinidad and Jamaica, Barbados seemed very small indeed. "The Jamaican," wrote one of them, "is apt to get claustrophobia [there]." "Not only is it small in size, it *feels* small."[58] It was said that there was hardly room to die in Barbados, let alone to live; many delegates doubted whether a capital site of sufficient size could be found there. After all, 25 square miles (the recommended federal area) was more than one-seventh of Barbados! And even if room were found, how could federal representatives be fed? As a Trinidad calypso put it, "Let the Bajans say what they wish/The Capital can't live on flying fish." Barbados is indeed so densely populated that planned parenthood—little discussed so far in the other territories—

51. Robert Hallett: Barbados—Hub of the Caribbean? *Christian Science Monitor*, reprinted in *Gleaner*, Jan. 23, 1957.

52. Eric Williams: Some Historical Aspects of Federation, Feb. 5, 1957, quoted in *Gleaner*, Feb. 7, 1957.

53. Bruce Hamilton: *Barbados & the Confederation Question 1871-1885* (London, 1956), p. ix.

54. Sandford Freeling to Lord Carnarvon, Aug. 9, 1875, C. 1539, No. 14, p. 28, quoted in Hamilton, *op. cit.*, p. 1.

55. J. A. Froude: *The English in the West Indies; or The Bow of Ulysses* (New York, 1888), p. 43; Trollope, *op. cit.* [see footnote 36 above], pp. 203 and 208. See Fermor, *op. cit.* [see footnote 48 above], p. 133.

56. Grantley Adams, speech at Caribbean Federal Labour Party Conference, Feb. 3, 1957, and at S.F.C. meeting, Jamaica, Jan. 22, 1957, quoted in *Gleaner*, Feb. 4 and Jan. 23, 1957, respectively.

57. *The West Indian*, Grenada, Jan. 3, 1957, and Pierre Loti, *West Indian Crusader*, St. Lucia, quoted in *Gleaner*, Jan. 5 and 21, 1957.

58. Thomas Wright, *Gleaner*, Jan. 29 and 31, 1957.

has become government policy.[59] Overpopulation is relative, however: the capital would have provided work for many, so that its location in Barbados might have eased, not intensified, the population problem. But the delegates saw only the lack of space. And they considered the gentle, intensively cultivated Barbadian landscape monotonous and tame. Even nature was criticized as inadequate for the capital site. "Barbados has an extremely limited wildlife," wrote a University College staff member, "[a] limited variety of rocks and no evidence of aborigines."[60]

In the denigration of Barbados, the personality of its people was also attacked as "un-West Indian." The typical Barbadian was said to be stolid, cautious, smug, conservative, puritanical, and materialistic in the sense of being addicted to acquiring money; he lacked any flair for clothes, folk songs, poetry, dance.[61] The "typical" West Indian, by contrast, complained a defender of Barbados, "*must* be exuberant, he *must* wear his heart on his sleeve, he *must* 'jump-up' [Trinidad carnival street dancing], he *must* speak very loudly; he *must never* show any restraint."[62] Even political calm and stability were considered anti-West Indian because the commissioners had praised Barbados for possessing them. Most West Indians, a University College student commented, "do not regard the rigidity of the Sphinx or the immobility of the Alps as the pattern for our political and social life."[63]

TRINIDAD

In some respects the selection of Trinidad as the site of the capital appears more paradoxical than the rejection of Barbados. As the capital commissioners reported, criticism of Trinidadian corruption and fear of East Indian influence were widespread in the other territories, and what the commissioners wrote was mild compared with what the new Chief Minister had said about Trinidad's politics during his pre-election campaign: "We ... are the sick man of the Caribbean"—"The dishonesty and immorality of political life in Trinidad and Tobago are now a byword"—"The poison is seeping through the entire body politic"—"Graft and corruption... are now eating away our society"—"Discipline... is hardly known."[64] But Trinidadians felt that "while they are entitled to indulge in self-criticism they are not having it come from any 'upstart' Englishmen."[65] More remarkable, however, was that other West Indians joined them in denouncing the commissioners for the "slanders."

There was some substantive reason, to be sure, for the West Indian about-face. In September, 1956 (two months after the commissioners' visit), Trinidad had cleaned house by giving 13 of 24 elective seats in the Legislative Council to the tightly disciplined People's National Movement, started less than a year earlier by the dynamic and learned Dr. Eric Williams, one-time professor of history and formerly deputy secretary of the Caribbean Commission. In his political debut, Williams pledged himself to eliminate graft and corruption, to reduce official salaries and perquisites, to reform Trinidad's constitution, to rationalize territorial and local government, and, above all, to embark on large-scale economic development. Williams' astounding victory and his first acts as chief minister presaged a revolution in the Trinidadian character; under his guidance public life, formerly easygoing, fun-loving, spendthrift, tolerant of venality, plagued by violence and organized crime, was now to be austere, serious, and honest. "I stand here today," Williams stated in Jamaica, "as the symbol of political stability in Trinidad."[66] Observers wondered whether "even Dr. Eric Williams... [could] overnight banish a code of public conduct which has been developing for years."[67] But everyone

59. Report of the Joint Committee Appointed by the Two Houses of the Legislature to Examine the Question of Over-Population in Barbados and to Make Recommendations for Dealing with This Problem (Barbados, 1954); David Lowenthal: The Population of Barbados, *Social and Econ. Studies*, Vol. 6, 1957, pp. 445-501.
60. Garth Underwood, letter, *Gleaner*, Jan. 15, 1957.
61. C. L. Stanford, letter, *Gleaner*, Jan. 21, 1957.
62. John Figueroa: "Little England" Defended, *Public Opinion*, Feb. 2, 1957.
63. Letter, *Gleaner*, Jan. 5, 1957.

64. Eric Williams: The Case for Party Politics in Trinidad and Tobago, *Teachers Econ. and Cultural Assn., Ltd., Public Affairs Pamphlet No. 4*, Port of Spain [1955], pp. 1, 13, 15, and 17.
65. Thomas Wright, *Gleaner*, Jan. 14, 1957.
66. Statement before the S.F.C., Feb. 11, 1957, reprinted in *Gleaner*, Feb. 17, 1957.
67. Charles Archibald: Barbados—A Good Choice, *Gleaner*, Jan. 14, 1957. The defeat of the People's National Movement in the Trinidad federal elections of March, 1958, tends to confirm such doubts.

agreed that he had made a spectacular start. And he pledged that Trinidad would engage in no lobbying or bargaining to win the capital.

Yet no one made more promises, public and private, than the Trinidadians. Federation, they said, must mean development of *all* the islands. Trinidad's Minister of Industry, Commerce, and Tourism would shortly tour the Windwards and Leewards to assess their resource potentialities; and the federation's first task should be to raise funds for an integrated plan of economic development. That would be Trinidad's principal effort at the conference. This was not merely generosity: Trinidad would benefit if the small islands could export food and goods instead of laborers. Trinidad planned to develop its own island ward, Tobago (population 33,000), which could then serve as a guinea pig for rehabilitation of the Windwards and Leewards; "we can understand from our relationship with Tobago the problems of Federation as no other territory can."[68] Thus Trinidad made political capital out of its own "colony."

Trinidad also made capital out of being rich. Thanks to the oil industry, which furnishes two-thirds of the government's revenue, Trinidad today has the largest per capita income in the West Indies and contributes a disproportionate share of the cost of the federal budget. Trinidad, Williams emphasized, is wealthy, industrial, go-ahead. Should this atypical territory house the capital? Yes, because it mirrored West Indian aspirations; just as Barbados represented the past, so Trinidad stood for the future. Trinidad had the wherewithal, the interest, and the foresight to help the small islands to a place in the sun. The connection was clear; as Williams remarked, "We have capital; and we will *get* the Capital."[69]

It is not surprising, as a victory calypso put it, that "The people in the smaller territories/ Think that in Trinidad money grows on trees." Windward Islanders especially have long sought work and cash in Trinidad. But Williams' wooing of the small islands contrasted with the attitude of his predecessor, Albert Gomes, who had given the impression that Trinidad was doing them a favor by federating at all. "Where the Leewards and Windwards regarded . . . Gomes with suspicion, they regard Dr. Williams with awe and reverence, and as a sort of Messiah who will lead them out of their economic difficulties."[70] This image was not confined to small-islanders; Jamaicans, too, were won over by Williams' energetic idealism. Their own Chief Minister acclaimed him as "a man of mind and quality and heart" and rejoiced at the triumph in Trinidad of "honesty [and] intelligence."[71]

Trinidad's prosperity and high standard of living also impress Jamaicans. "The people are more advanced, on the whole, than they are in Jamaica," observed a reporter. He found there "little of the kind of dilapidation . . . [and] packing-case dreadfulness" that "one sees so much in Jamaica. . . . Indeed all of Trinidad (except for one bad slum) gives the impression of neatness and good order." Accustomed to "loud, vulgar talk" on streets at home, and to starved, mangy dogs, he remarked that in Trinidad "both dogs and people are well kept and disciplined." Furthermore, Trinidadians seemed punctual and businesslike. When he was told that they were often nearly half an hour late for appointments, he "had to explain . . . that in Jamaica, where people think nothing of missing an appointment by a day, or even by a week, this would be considered the height of precision." Finally, Trinidad "expresses to perfection . . . the new West Indian spirit."[72] Charming, gay, vivacious, Trinidadians seem tolerant and fun-loving in contrast with the more conservative Jamaicans.[73]

Barbadians feel somewhat ambivalent. "Trinidad is a nice place,"[74] they say, but they think it "unsafe" to live there. Assault, murder, and rape are always in the headlines, and there are many other "marks of degeneration." "Money in Trinidad has no value. At least there is not that value which the Barbadian at home and abroad attaches to his

---

68. Williams, Some Historical Aspects of Federation [author's transcript].
69. *Ibid.*
70. J. C. Proute: Trinidad's Eric Williams, *Public Opinion*, Feb. 23, 1957.
71. Norman Manley, speech at Caribbean Federal Labour Party Conference, Feb. 3, 1957, quoted in *Gleaner*, Feb. 4, 1957.
72. Thomas Wright, *Gleaner*, Jan. 21 and 31, 1957.
73. Aimee Webster: This Is Our Capital, *Gleaner*, Feb. 12, 1957.
74. George Lamming: *In the Castle of My Skin* (London, 1953), p. 272.

cash."[75] What particularly pains Barbadians is Trinidadian morality—"They think a man a hero the bigger thief he is."[76]

Unique economically in the British Caribbean, Trinidad claimed to be truly representative ethnically. Sparsely settled before its conquest by Britain in 1797, it became the West Indies melting pot; it grew chiefly by accretion from neighboring islands. In 1946, 12,384 Trinidadians were Barbadian-born—one for every 15 in Barbados—and 23,446 had come from Grenada, one-third of the population of that territory. Indeed, more than one Trinidad resident in ten is a legal immigrant from another British West Indian island, and most Creoles have a small-island parent or grandparent. Thus when the commissioners called Trinidad corrupt and irresponsible, "they were condemning the entire West Indian population," the best part of which, Williams maintained, had migrated to Trinidad.[77] This powerful argument was particularly effective on islands that hoped to resume emigration to relatively uncrowded Trinidad. For a number of years, on account of its prodigious population growth, Trinidad had restricted the entry of other West Indian laborers, but in 1955—as a prerequisite to federation—it agreed to yield eventual control over interterritorial movement (save on the ground of health or security) to the federal legislature and at the same time relaxed restrictions against non-Trinidadians in some 53 occupations.[78]

In line with Trinidad's quintessential West Indianism, its delegates maintained that Trinidad was more stanchly nationalistic than Barbados and Jamaica. Williams had recently announced that the Trinidad government would no longer favor "home" leaves for civil servants, who had been "treading on each other's heels as they journeyed across the Atlantic on public funds." This not only drained the exchequer; it encouraged the "colonial mentality, a dominant characteristic of which is to believe that life pretty nearly anywhere else is better than life in a colony." Huge sums would no longer be spent to hire English experts; Trinidad would seek advice and aid from Puerto Rico, the World Bank, or wherever they were available.[79] All this appealed to West Indian nationalism. At the same time, Trinidad's delegates promised to keep federal governmental costs at a minimum. In Trinidad, they suggested, the federal government would work in the same atmosphere of austerity and retrenchment as now animated the territorial government; thus all the islands would save money. And Trinidad's income-tax rate was the lowest in the British West Indies.

The absence of a major tourist industry in Trinidad was another point in its favor. To be sure, tourism is an important segment of Jamaican and Barbadian economy, but the presence of large numbers of Americans in luxury-hotel enclaves has fostered an unhealthful dichotomy. Tourists tend to intensify economic, social, and racial cleavages; they make some West Indians feel that their islands are not their own. Hence Williams' avowal that Trinidad would never attempt to duplicate Montego Bay was greeted with much applause.

Finally, Trinidad's East Indian population became an asset in the fight for the capital. Just two years earlier, the opposition of the East Indians had seemed likely to prevent Trinidad from federating at all, and their clannishness and separatism were bitterly criticized. Now all was changed. No group, Trinidadians asserted, was more loyal and progressive than the East Indians. Would the federation reject these 250,000 people—more than the entire population of Barbados? "You cannot take people and have them build up your society for one hundred years," said Williams, and then believe "three nit-wits . . . [who] say they are an alien society."[80] With an East Indian delegate, Trinidad appeared at the Standing Federation Committee meeting as a truly harmonious multiracial society. And delegates from the other territories all agreed that the

75. Mitchie Hewitt: Trinidad Revisited—3: Skyscrapers, But Still Shanty Town, *Barbados Advocate*, June 1, 1957.

76. Lamming, op. cit., p. 270.

77. Williams, Some Historical Aspects of Federation, and statement before S.F.C., Feb. 11, 1957. For population figures see West Indian Census 1946: Part A, General Report on the Census of Population 9th April, 1946 (Kingston, Jamaica, 1950), pp. 39–40 and 100.

78. Report of the Conference on Movement of Persons within a British Caribbean Federation (Trinidad, 1955). Eighty other occupations, however, are still closed to non-Trinidadians. See J. C. Proute: Freedom of Movement, *Public Opinion*, Feb. 2, 1957.

79. C. H. Archibald: Knocking It Out of the System, *Gleaner*, Dec. 14, 1956.

80. Some Historical Aspects of Federation [see footnote 52 above].

commissioners had been unfair to that minority.

This reversal of feeling has a variety of explanations. A few people used the East Indian question simply as a stick to beat the unpopular capital report and unmask its authors as bigots. Some small-islanders felt that if they made enough fuss about the "insult," the Standing Federation Committee might reject the whole report and give the small territories another chance. Still others thought that the selection of Trinidad might placate the Indians: "'getting' the Capital is necessary if the East Indian element is to be persuaded into accepting its present West Indian status and to cease looking on India as the Motherland."[81] Meanwhile, Trinidadians argued that the capital of a multiracial federation should be cosmopolitan. "Diversity of population," said Williams, "is a source of strength... We are a mixture... Look at the Trinidad delegation, look at it well. [In addition to the East Indian delegate, a legislative councilor, it included as advisers the Chinese colonial secretary, the white Barbadian attorney general, and the acting financial secretary, a Creole of French West Indian background.] Trinidad today, the West Indies tomorrow. That is what the West Indies of tomorrow is going to look like."[82] His party had "sought to bring all racial groups into its nationalist fold," and never before, he asserted, had "racial tension been of so little consequence."[83]

Trinidad has long been noted for the apparent ease with which its "startling and exotic amalgam" lives together. "A Trinidadian," according to a recent study, "feels no inconsistency in being a British citizen, a Negro in appearance, a Spaniard in name, a Roman Catholic at church, an obeah (magic) practitioner in private, a Hindu at lunch, a Chinese at dinner, a Portuguese at work, and a Colored at the polls. An orthodox Brahmin who has never eaten meat may still be the organizer of a Creole Carnival band representing Vikings or Scottish clansmen, or play the guitar at a Spanish-Venezuelan

81. Editorial, *Public Opinion*, Jan. 19, 1957.
82. Statement at S.F.C. plenary session, Feb. 11, 1957, quoted in *Gleaner*, Feb. 17, 1957.
83. Eric Williams: Race Relations in Caribbean Society, in *Caribbean Studies: A Symposium*, edited by Vera Rubin (Institute of Social and Economic Research, Kingston, Jamaica, 1957), pp. 54-60; reference on p. 59.

'cross wake.'"[84] East Indians have long preferred Trinidad to British Guiana and Jamaica,"[85] and Guianese today view Trinidadian integration as far more advanced: "In British Guiana we say we are Portuguese, Indian, Creole; in Trinidad everyone is a Trinidadian."[86] But beneath Trinidad's cosmopolitan and uninhibited atmosphere ethnic and color prejudice still exerts pressure in every walk of life. As Eric Williams himself remarked, "racial discrimination in employment... is... characteristic of our society."[87]

Another powerful motive for favoring Trinidad concerned "having our capital as a lure across the way from Demerara."[88] Two hundred miles down the coast from Port of Spain, British Guiana has an even larger proportion of East Indians—49 per cent—in its half-million population. Invited to join the federation, the mainland territory chose to stay out at the start and has postponed its final decision. Opposition to federation in British Guiana, as in Trinidad, has come chiefly from East Indians, who fear that their newly won and increasing local power will be lost to colored islanders. Guianese also fear that West Indian immigration will increase unemployment or that the islands will be "a millstone about the Guianese neck," and some of them look toward British Guiana's "continental destiny."[89]

Virtually all West Indians want British Guiana in the federation. They still view the mainland territory as the El Dorado that Raleigh sought near the Orinoco three and a half centuries ago, and they long to acquire that vast and mostly empty stretch of continent—about 83,000 square miles, 10 times their combined areas. But settlement of the

84. D. J. Crowley: Plural and Differential Acculturation in Trinidad, *Amer. Anthropologist*, Vol. 59, 1957, pp. 817-824; reference on p. 823. See also Gordon Lewis, *Gleaner*, Feb. 26, 1957.
85. J. D. Tyson: Report on the Conditions of Indians in Jamaica, British Guiana and Trinidad, 1938-39 (Simla, India, 1939), p. 24.
86. Conversations, March-April, 1957.
87. Williams, The Case for Party Politics in Trinidad and Tobago [see footnote 64 above], p. 19. For an excellent commentary on Trinidad's color problem, see Lloyd Braithwaite: Social Stratification in Trinidad, *Social and Econ. Studies*, Vol. 2, Nos. 2 and 3, 1953, pp. 5-175.
88. Editorial, *Gleaner*, Feb. 12, 1957.
89. Anthony McCowan: British Guiana and Federation, *Corona*, Vol. 9, 1957, pp. 85-88.

Guianese interior is a vain hope today. Access is difficult, soils are poor, and any large-scale development would require enormous capital investment. Few British Guianese think of the interior as the islanders do. Meanwhile, the narrow coastal strip is overpopulated. The abandoned estates and the bush on the frontlands must be cleared, drained, and irrigated before Guiana's own people can find adequate settlement and livelihoods. Nevertheless, West Indians persist in seeing British Guiana as a haven for migration and a land of opportunities; it is their frontier. "So far as Trinidad and Tobago go," stated Williams on the first day of the meeting, "economic development must include as a matter of course our continental neighbor." All the more necessary, therefore, to expunge the slur against East Indians, lest, as former Trinidad Governor Sir Hubert Rance warned, opposition to federation should stiffen in British Guiana. For British Guiana, Trinidad was obviously the best capital site, by virtue both of ethnic similarity and of proximity. British Guiana had no vote at the meeting, but its East Indian observer influenced many and has been described as Trinidad's most powerful supporter.

So Trinidad, "the most cosmopolitan, the liveliest and the most exciting of the territories," as the Jamaica *Gleaner* commented, became the capital site. This made the West Indies "a Protestant state with a Roman Catholic capital; a Christian majority surrounded by Moslem mosques and Hindu temples; . . . a staid, complacent people come to live and be led in the midst of the 'fete' and the calypso."[90] One critic has charged that the capital report "failed to assist the making of an intelligent choice between the three islands selected because its somewhat insensitive treatment of the social and political problems of the West Indies alienated the sympathies of local leaders."[91] But capital sites are generally chosen in spite of, rather than because of, expert advice; and emotional judgments may succeed better than rational ones. In one sense, the capital commissioners helped to unify the West Indies. Their supposed prejudice aroused anticolonial nationalist sentiment throughout the area. This made the selection of Trinidad more generally popular than any capital site might otherwise have been, for it came as a vindication of West Indian character and independence.[92] Perhaps the most cogent conclusion was that of Sir Hilary Blood:[93] "As an ex-governor of Barbados I regret profoundly that the capital is not to be in Barbados. As a perfectly truthful man I think Trinidad is the right place for it."

Postscript

Trinidad remained the federal capital throughout the brief existence (1958-1962) of the West Indies Federation. The Chaguaramas Bay area selected by the Standing Federation Committee as "by far the most suitable site" was, however, then an active American naval base. The Trinidad government finally persuaded the United States to yield the base, but too late to move the federal headquarters from the "provisional" capital, Port of Spain.

Federal-local conflicts in Port of Spain irritated both federal and territorial personnel, but the Federation dissolved mainly for reasons unrelated, though similar in tone, to capital site problems. Divergent views on the distribution of central and territorial powers; decisions of Jamaican and Trinidadian leaders not to stand for federal office; the election of a federal majority party dominated by men from the small islands; and complete ignorance at the grassroots level—especially in Jamaica—about the aims and problems of the Federation, were jointly responsible for the withdrawal, in turn, of Jamaica, Trinidad, and Barbados. Each has since achieved independence on its own.

The manner as well as the fact of federal demise intensified interisland suspicions. Left in the lurch by the larger territories, the Windwards and Leewards are wary about new overtures toward regional cooperation, such as the Caribbean Free Trade Association (CARIFTA). "Despite all the hoo-haa and flag-waving about closer Caribbean unity," warned a Dominican editor in 1967, "the big

---

90. Editorial, *Gleaner*, Feb. 12, 1957.
91. T. S. Simey: A New Capital for the British West Indies, *Town Planning Rev.*, Vol. 28, 1957, pp. 63-70; reference on p. 68.
92. Lloyd Braithwaite: Progress toward Federation, 1938-1956, *Social and Econ. Studies*, Vol. 6, 1957, pp. 133-184; reference on p. 162.
93. The West Indian Federation, *Journ. Royal Soc. of Arts*, Vol. 105, 1957, pp. 746-757; reference on p. 756.

four [Jamaica, Trinidad, and Tobago, Barbados, Guyana] are interested first, second, and last in themselves. What is left after that they will, with magnanimous condescension and pompousness, dole out to the 'small island boys.'"

The University of the West Indies, which antedates federation, is today the only significant federal survival, and is beset by sectionalism. Rivalries for personnel and services among the three campuses in Jamaica, Trinidad, and Barbados, and charges of neglect by the smaller units, recall the capital site controversy. Territories compete to have their nationals appointed to university positions, and threaten to withdraw financial support if new facilities are located elsewhere. The establishment of law and architectural faculties has been delayed for lack of agreement about where to site them. These conflicts figure in the continual jockeying among the Caribbean states for a wider range of prizes, including, as of mid-1968, the Vice-Chancellorship of the University, the disposition of British West Indian Airways, the headquarters of the Regional Development Bank, and the location of Caribbean Free Trade Area secretariat.

31

Toward a Geography of Urban Politics:
Chicago, a Case Study

ROGER E. KASPERSON*

Although the interest of the urban geographer has been channeled into diverse approaches to the city, one important dimension—the political geography of the city—has remained grossly neglected. Indeed, despite the incontestable importance of public decision-making for a wide variety of urban functions, a researcher is hard-pressed to unearth more than a handful of geographical studies upon this subject.[1] There are surely a number of reasons for this neglect, but one may well cite the association of urban geography with economic geography and the focus of political geography upon the national state as leading factors. The conviction that our understanding of urban problems would be greatly augmented by a fuller realization of their political attributes has generated the present research.

An inherited problem for any initial geographical interpretation of city politics, then, is the paucity of prior research. This underlines the constant need for drawing upon the findings of related disciplines. A "building-block" progression of research is necessary, not only to permit sound generalization but to provide a body of thought with which to interpret material gathered in the field. In the case of the geography of urban politics, this body of thought must be derived from the works of political scientists and sociologists.

It is beyond the scope and intent of this paper to summarize the findings of political scientists and sociologists upon urban politics, but several brief observations relevant to the present research are noteworthy. First, since the early 1950s, political scientists have become acutely aware of the shortcomings of viewing urban politics as the inefficiencies of city government and administration.[2] The inadequacies of a strictly formalistic approach to city politics are well illustrated by Chicago, which possesses a decentralized formal government, but whose politics are highly centralized in a powerful political machine.

Reprinted by permission of the author and publisher from *Economic Geography*, Vol. 41, 1965.
* Roger E. Kasperson is a co-editor of this volume.
1. H. J. Nelson: The Vernon Area, California: A Study of the Political Factor in Urban Geography, *Annals Assn. of Amer. Geogrs.*, Vol. 42, 1952, pp. 177–191; Malcolm J. Proudfoot: Chicago's Fragmented Political Structure, *Geogr. Rev.*, Vol. 47, 1957, pp. 106–117; Peirce F. Lewis: A Geography of the Politics of Flint (unpublished Ph.D. dissertation, University of Michigan, 1958).

2. See Lawrence J. R. Herson: The Lost World of Municipal Government, *Amer. Pol. Sci. Rev.*, Vol. 51, 1957, pp. 330–345; Allen Richards: Local Government Research: A Partial Evaluation, *Public Administration Review*, Vol. 14, 1954, pp. 271–277. A useful review of the literature can be found in Robert T. Daland: Political Science and the Study of Urbanism, A Bibliographical Essay, *Amer. Pol. Sci. Rev.*, Vol. 51, 1957, pp. 491–509.

Second, the elitist model formulated in the community power studies of sociologists has been criticized effectively by political scientists on both theoretical and methodological grounds. Political scientists have countered this view of a stable, ruling elite with a pluralist one of shifting, ephemeral coalitions of power. In the latter approach, the career public official participates more actively in the decision-making process. Although the pluralist interpretation is also subject to criticism, the writer would contend that it represents a more sophisticated understanding of the diffusion of power within the city.

Third, although no single interpretation of urban politics is complete in itself, useful guide posts for research can be found in classic statements on the governmental process and group and urban politics. Together with the geographical characteristics and the individual ethos of the city, these statements will form the foundation of any interpretation.

Problem

Within most American cities, there are certain areas in which political support and opposition are concentrated. The cores of these conflicting areas may be apparent, but their boundaries are blurred and in a constant state of flux. Indeed, the very flexibility of the zones plays an influential role in the politican's decision-making process. Moreover, since there is a constant struggle for political support in many of these areas, this competition has far-reaching implications for the politician's very existence in public life. To maintain or further his position, he must strive to maximize his political power at the expense of his opponents.

The way in which city issues are decided, then, operates within a spatial framework that is too often overlooked by the political scientist and the geographer. Can areas of conflict be determined and systematically arranged in a study of the geography of urban politics? What are the implications to the decision-making process of the existence of such areas?

Assumptions

Several factors are assumed in the following analysis. First, by politicians are meant those politicians who function on a city-wide base of power (i.e., a mayor or city treasurer), as opposed to those who operate on a more localized base of power (i.e., a ward alderman). The second assumption is that each politician, when faced with alternatives, chooses the one which he believes will return him the greatest benefits in terms of political advantage and the realization of certain goals. In actual situations, this choice will not always be conscious and such a rational maximizing of benefits and costs oversimplifies the decision-making process.[3] The assumption is necessary, however, for an initial assessment of the role of geographical differences in urban politics. Finally, when discussing the characteristics and political implications of the voting zones, it is assumed that zones are discrete and homogeneous units, though this is clearly not the case in reality.

Electoral Background and Zonal Delimitation

With its fifty wards (Map 31.1), Chicago typifies the "small-ward" American city, a characteristic which has important ramifications for Chicago politics. Chicago aldermen, elected from relatively small wards of 20,000–70,000 registered voters, have direct contact with a sizable number of their constituents. In addition, the coincidence of the location of wards with comparatively homogeneous ethnic and economic groups reinforces this link between the aldermen and the electorate.

In terms of formal governmental structure, Chicago's 50 aldermen comprise the ruling

---

3. Any such simple calculation would depend upon the extent of knowledge and the accuracy of perception of decision-makers. In municipal problems, such as urban renewal, the social background of the public official is an important factor in his perception. See Donald R. Mathews: *The Social Background of Political Decision-Makers* (Garden City, 1954). Many decision-makers probably do not "maximize" but "satisfice" by reducing alternative choices into broad classes of satisfactory outcomes. In urban decisions, considerable satisfaction is derived by merely playing the game of politics, and this modifies any rigid rational explanation. See Herbert Simon: Theories of Decision-Making in Economics and Behavioral Science, *Amer. Econ. Rev.*, Vol. 49, 1959, pp. 253–274. An interesting discussion of decision-making applied to natural resource management is available in Robert Kates: Hazard and Choice Perception in Flood Plain Management, *Univ. of Chicago, Dept. of Geogr., Research Paper No. 78*, 1962, pp. 12–28.

force in the city's politics.[4] Each is an independent representative of his own ward and is elected for a four-year term. Since he is elected from a localized base of power, his first duty is to the welfare of the population of his ward. City-wide issues are of secondary

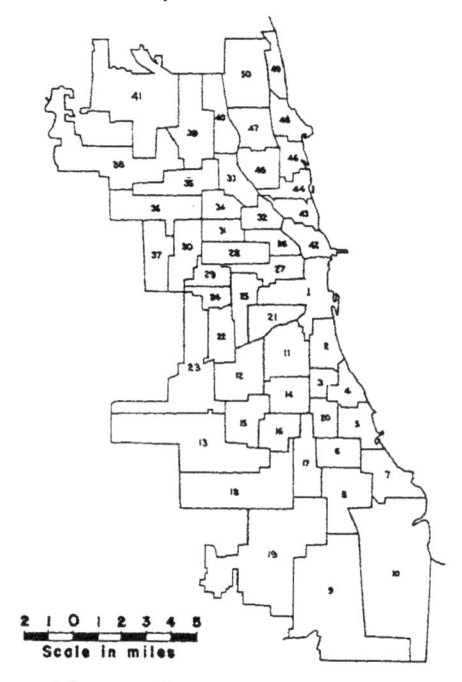

Map 31.1 CHICAGO IS TYPICAL OF THE "SMALL-WARD" AMERICAN CITY
Source: Board of Election Commissioners, City of Chicago.

importance to the alderman. This decentralized governmental structure doubtlessly would produce an ineffectual political system if informal controls were not present to centralize this dispersed power. Meyerson and Banfield recognize two chief sets of such informal control.[5] First a handful of powerful Democratic aldermen, usually working with the mayor, effectively control the City Council when key issues are at stake. This is accomplished largely by controlling committee assignments, especially those of the important Finance Committee. Second, the presence of the ward committeeman, the party leader in the ward, forces the alderman to toe the line. The ward committeeman decides who will run on the party's ticket in the ward, appoints and dismisses precinct captains, and distributes patronage.

By means of this informal integration, the Democratic machine has sustained itself in power since 1931. During the late 1940's, however, the machine under Mayor Kelly underwent heavy fire from a number of reform-demanding civic groups. Widespread scandals and corruption had convinced party leaders that some internal changes were mandatory. In 1947 Martin Kennelly, a Democratic businessman, was chosen to run for Mayor on the understanding that he would not become party leader. His subsequent election ushered in the politics of the 1950s.

To interpret the spatial aspects of the politics of this decade, voting returns have been mapped by wards and grouped into political zones based upon consistency of voting habits. Returns for the mayoral elections of 1951, 1955, and 1959 serve as data bases. Two principal considerations determined the choice of 1951 as the base year: (1) between the 1947 and 1951 elections, a major change was made in the distribution of wards, and (2) 1951 touched off a decade that has been characterized by urban politics as being of a nature different from that of the preceding two decades. The flagrantly corrupt administration of the traditional Chicago machine had become increasingly incompatible with the ethics of a modern American metropolis.

Based upon an analysis of area voting patterns for the three election years, Chicago can be divided into four political regions. The *core area* includes the wards in which the Democratic Party obtained over 80 per cent of the votes cast. The *inner zone* contains those wards in which 60–80 per cent of the electorate cast its vote for the Democratic Party. The *outer zone* consists of the wards in which the Republican Party received 60 per cent or more of the votes cast. The crucial area between the outer and inner zones is the frontier *zone of competition*, where no party received 60 per cent of the vote. The critical limits of these regions were chosen arbitrarily, but minor alterations would not seriously affect the over-all results of the study.

The voting patterns that led to the reelection of Mayor Kennelly in 1951 are shown on Map 31.2. The chief area of Democratic support was centered in the populous

4. Martin Meyerson and Edward C. Banfield: *Politics, Planning and the Public Interest: The Case of Public Housing in Chicago* (Glencoe, Ill., 1955), pp. 64 ff.
5. *Ibid.*

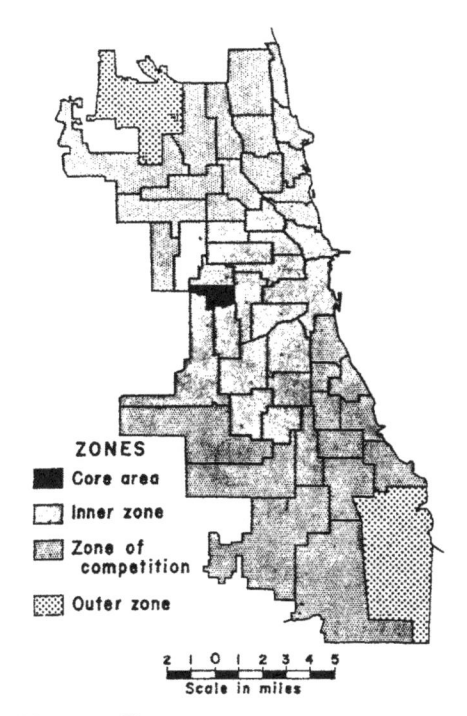

Map 31.2 ZONES ARE BASED ON THE MAYORAL ELECTION OF 1951
Source: Board of Election Commissioners, City of Chicago.

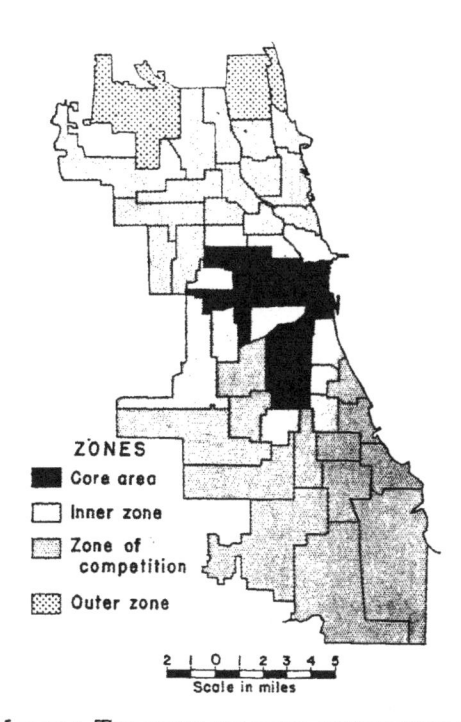

Map 31.3 THE ZONES ARE BASED ON THE MAYORAL ELECTION OF 1955
Source: Board of Election Commissioners, City of Chicago.

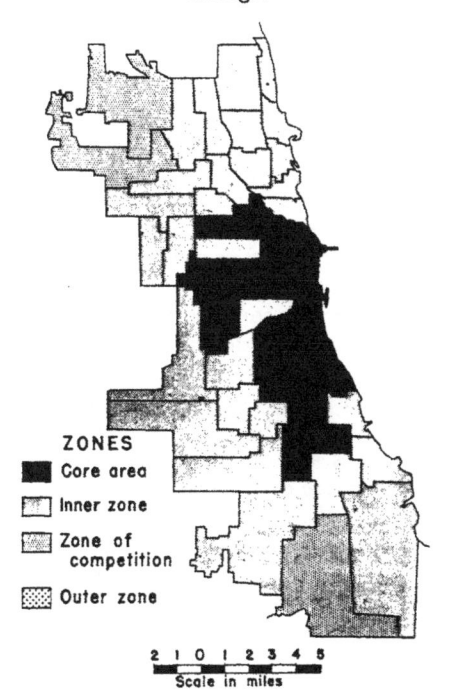

Map 31.4 BASED ON THE MAYORAL ELECTION RESULTS OF 1959
Source: Board of Election Commissioners, City of Chicago.

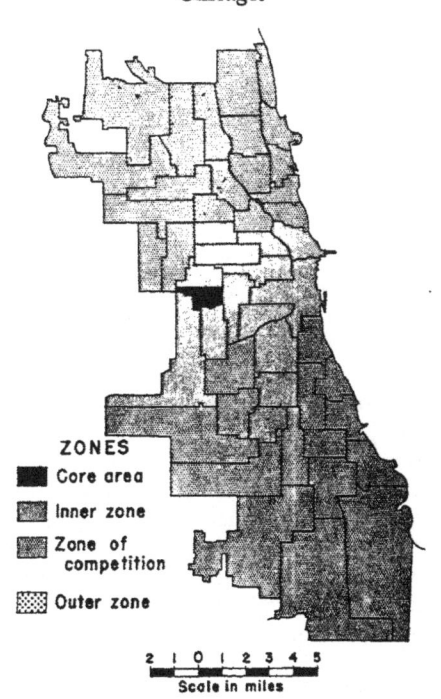

Map 31.5 THE COMPOSITE ZONES ARE BASED ON THE RESULTS OF THE MAYORAL ELECTIONS OF 1951, 1955, AND 1959

heart of the city with an important sub-center in the Calumet area. The frontier zone of competition was composed largely of the outlying wards north and south of the inner zone. Despite Kennelly's re-election, the Democratic machine increasingly came to regard him as a liability.[6] His drive to strengthen the civil service system had incurred a loss of important sources of patronage. In addition, Kennelly's role as a "ceremonial" mayor with weak leadership encouraged factional quarrels which threatened the internal coherence of the machine. With these and other grievances, 1955 ward leaders nominated Richard Daley as their mayoral candidate. Kennelly contested the primary with strong support from the newspapers and good-government groups, and Daley's victory shifted much of the Kennelly's former support to Robert Merriam, the Republican candidate. Nevertheless, receiving strong support from the key Democratic wards of the core area (Map 31.3), Mayor Daley won the election. The inner zone reveals the divisive effects of the election and the loss of the Calumet sub-center.

When Mayor Daley assumed office, there was a widely-held suspicion that Chicago was destined to return to the machine politics of Mayor Kelly. Daley, however, incorporated a number of reform programs into his administration and operated under the slogan "good government is good politics."[7] Public approval of this shotgun wedding may be inferred from Map 31.4. In the election of 1959, Mayor Daley faced weak opposition and garnered the support of newspapers, good-government groups, and prominent business and civic leaders. The core area expanded from seven to 19 wards, while all but three of the remaining 31 wards fell into the inner zone. The outer zone disappeared, for in no ward did the Republican candidate receive 60 per cent of the vote. The flexibility of the voting zones in these three elections is immediately apparent, and its significance will be examined later in the study.

For purposes of analysis, it was necessary to arrive at a composite set of regions from the three elections. The most satisfactory method of regionalization, though admittedly imperfect, was to delimit the wards of the core area and the inner and outer zones according to the aforementioned percentages for all three elections. For a ward to warrant inclusion in the core area, then, its electorate must have cast over 80 per cent of its votes for the Democratic Party in all three elections. The overlapping area which resulted was delegated to the frontier zone of competition, to which it more correctly belonged. The composite map (Map 31.5) thus constructed enabled the researcher to examine the social and economic characteristics of the zones and to evaluate them in relation to the urban politics of Chicago.

SOCIAL AND ECONOMIC CHARACTERISTICS

The concentric character of the voting zones is readily apparent in the electoral maps. The pattern immediately suggests a possible relationship to Burgess's concentric zone theory of land use.[8] In 1950, the beginning of the period in question, most of the core area and inner zone, corresponding roughly to Burgess's transition area and zone of independent workingmen's homes, had a median income per family of less than $3000, as compared with the city mean of $3956. These zones also contained large immigrant and Negro minorities. A low percentage of owner-occupied housing units and a high population density per dwelling unit are also characteristic of the inner zone. In contra-distinction to these characteristics are those of the frontier zone of competition and the outer zone, which generally correspond, respectively, to Burgess's zone of better residences and zone of commuting. Higher income per capita, lower population density per unit, better housing conditions, and a higher percentage of native-born whites all combine to distinguish these zones from the core area and the inner zone. This general pattern is confirmed by the census tract data for 1960.

A final significant zonal distinction revealed by a comparison of 1950 and 1960 census data is the character of population change within the city. Map 31.6 indicates community areas registering population in-

6. James Q. Wilson: Politics and Reform in American Cities (Reprint Series, Joint Center for Urban Studies of the Massachusetts Institute of Technology and Harvard University, 1962), pp. 44–45.
7. Ibid., p. 45.

8. Ernest W. Burgess: The Growth of the City, Robert E. Park, Ernest W. Burgess, and Roderick D. McKenzie, edits.: The City (Chicago, 1925), pp. 47–62.

creases and decreases between 1950 and 1960. Clearly, the core area and inner zone have experienced serious population declines, often in the order of 10–50 per cent of the total population of the community area. During the same period, community areas in the zone of competition and the outer zone revealed markedly smaller population losses, and many areas, particularly in the western portion of the city, experienced relative increases in population. These demographic changes hold far-reaching implications for Chicago politics.

The differing social and economic features of the voting zones are not to be interpreted as determinants of voting behavior. The spatial distinctions do contribute, however, to explanations of the varying types of appeals with which politicians court the zones, of the different interests in city issues, and of varied conceptions of the public interest on the part of the electorate of the zones. Finally, they provide an ecological setting against which the interplay of urban politics becomes more meaningful.

IMPLICATIONS FOR PUBLIC DECISION-MAKING

The relative importance of each zone is constantly changing. The population changes shown on Map 31.6 are increasingly forcing the politician to rely upon the zone of competition and the outer zone for support. The political efficacy of the core and inner zones, the traditional areas of Democratic support, is constantly being undermined by the population losses in these areas and by the rapid population increase in the outer areas of the zone of competition. These demographic changes find expression in the changes in voter registrations over the past decade (Map 31.7). The core area and inner zones showed

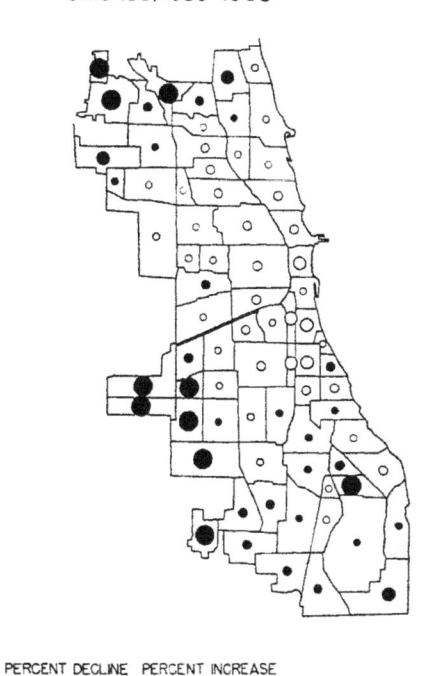

Map 31.6 POPULATION CHANGES ARE SHOWN BY COMMUNITY AREA
Source: Chicago Commission on Human Relations, as taken from Advance Table PH-1, *1960 Census of Population and Housing.*

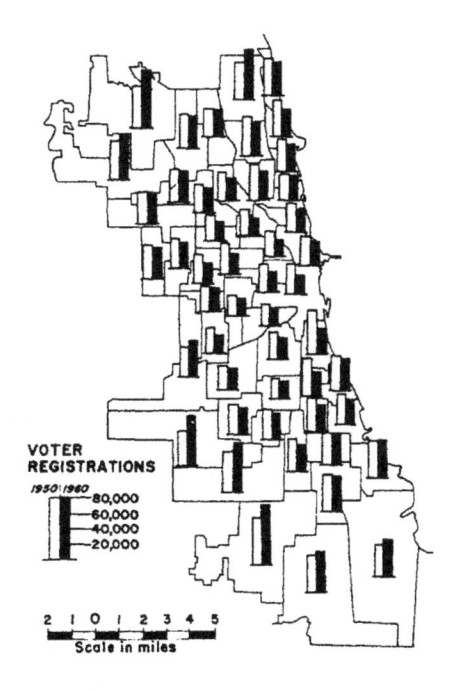

Map 31.7 CHANGES IN VOTER REGISTRATION SHOW A MARKED DECLINE IN THE CENTRAL PORTIONS OF THE CITY
Source: Board of Election Commissioners, City of Chicago.

TABLE 31.1 Changes in voter registrations, 1950–1960

Zone	1950	1952	1954	1956	1958	1960	Percentage change 1950–1960
Core area and inner zone	526,216	522,733	457,324	454,263	420,320	429,807	—13
Zone of competition	1,561,354	1,648,062	1,473,883	1,539,428	1,427,730	1,506,167	—4
Chicago total	2,087,570	2,170,795	1,931,207	1,993,691	1,848,050	1,935,974	—7

Source: Board of Election Commissioners, City of Chicago.

major declines between 1950 and 1960, whereas the chief increases occurred in the outer ring of wards encompassing the city. The vital statistics are summarized in Table 31.1. The entire city showed a decline of 7 per cent in voter registrations, but the losses did not occur uniformly in all sections of the city. The core area and inner zone showed a drop of 13 per cent, whereas the frontier zone of competition had only 4 per cent fewer registered voters in 1960 than in 1950. Because of these geographical changes in registrations, the Democratic politician is increasingly torn between his obligation to the core and inner zones and the need to capture votes in the zone of competition. This conflict is creating far-reaching changes in the character of Chicago politics.

With the increase of voting power in the frontier zone of competition, middle class ethics and values are becoming more influential in determining public policy. Here resides the politically conscious electorate which views government as a means of enacting general principles which should be of city-wide rather than of local neighborhood scope. Here the political process is conceived as necessitating farsighted planning rather than factional dispute and political bargaining. In short, this is the citadel of good government policy, urban planning, social welfare groups, and public reform. Because of such concerns, these areas are characterized by a responsiveness to the mass media. In fact, many of them have been dubbed, rather derisively, "newspaper wards" or "silk-stocking wards."[9] Professional politicians are acutely aware of the influence of the press in these areas and seek to maintain cordial relations with reporters and editors.

The inner zones, by contrast, shun many of the programs espoused by the outer zones and are less sensitive to the mass media. Here greater value is placed on neighborhood needs, material gifts and favors, and family and ethnic ties. In the past, politicians capitalized on the poverty-stricken and more transient population of this area to erect a political machine with its accompanying corruption.[10] Significantly enough, good government groups, such as the League of Women Voters, continue to post observers at polls in these wards in an attempt to eliminate possible electoral manipulations. Even with observers, however, it is noteworthy that most of the accusations of voting irregularities in the 1960 Presidential election were directed at these wards. Special objects of attention have been the so-called "river wards," located along the Chicago River in the core area and inner zone. A cultural antagonism exists between these zones which is more fundamental than voting data reveals.

The zonal differences in social and economic values have partially contributed to different methods of assembling political support in Chicago. To secure maximum support, the politician often varies his type of voter appeal to suit the value and interests of the particular ward. In the frontier zone of competition and in the outer zone, public support tends to rely more effectively on good government and reform programs than on patronage. This type of appeal can be termed

9. Meyerson and Banfield comment that in the newspaper wards "voters usually split the ticket in the way a newspaper advised. The alderman in the 'river wards' could afford to be contemptuous of the newspapers; in their wards editorials were words wasted." Meyerson and Banfield, op. cit., p. 75.

10. Harold F. Gosnell: Machine Politics: Chicago Model (Chicago, 1937). For a colorful and informative portrait of one such ward, see William Braden and Art Petacque: The Wayward First Ward, Chicago Sunday Sun-Times, February 10, 1963.

intangible as opposed to tangible.[11] Tangible appeals are more widely used in the core area and inner zone where the electorate has a low per-capita income and material benefits have real value. As the wife of one machine committeeman put it, "The system for becoming a leader is based on the number of favors a politician can do for the people in his ward. Needy people can't turn to their bank account, and they're appreciative of small things. In a silk-stocking ward, there's not much a politician can do except keep the streets clean. The people don't need small favors and so they have a different kind of politician."[12] Thus, political support in the inner zone is maintained by a system of carefully distributed city jobs and local favors. Even retribution of a tangible nature can be, and is, employed—fire inspections, police investigations (or lack thereof), and city ordinance enforcement.

The danger of adopting any one approach is that it may well boomerang on its originator. A politician's adoption of a particular appeal for one area may well create repercussions in other wards throughout the city. Consequently, the politician must weigh the relative areal benefits he will receive against the drawbacks incurred. In some situations, the methods of obtaining support in different zones are not irreconcilable. A particular appeal which generates nearly maximum support in one area may simultaneously appeal to a certain strata or segment in another. A controversial political issue recently resolved in Chicago exemplifies some of the spatial overtones of public decision-making.

Since the establishment of the Chicago Undergraduate Division of the University of Illinois in 1946, there has been considerable interest in establishing a Chicago campus.[13] The subsequent struggle over the location of the campus reveals the interplay of geography and politics in public decision-making. Miller Meadows, a county forest preserve in a western suburb, was one of the earliest sites under serious consideration. Strongly recommended by a real estate research organization which had been hired to recommend sites, its chief advantages were that it was inexpensive ($.29 per foot with a total cost of $3 million) and had reasonable accessibility (55.4 per cent of the potential students were only an hour away by public transportation). Furthermore, Miller Meadows boasted the added attraction of scenic beauty. On June 27, 1956, in the face of powerful opposition from the Advisory Committee of the Board of Forest Preserve Commissioners, the Board of Trustees of the University of Illinois selected Miller Meadows as the site for the new campus.

Legal difficulties and political opposition persistently hamstrung plans for this location, however, so that in early 1959 the Board of Trustees concluded that the adjacent Riverside Golf Club should be the site. At this juncture, Mayor Daley intervened. At a meeting of the Board of Trustees on February 23, 1959, he announced that the City of Chicago would defray any extraordinary cost arising out of the selection of alternative sites in Chicago as compared with the cost of the Riverside Golf Club location. In effect, this action allowed for a large number of alternative sites which were formerly economically unfeasible. A proposal to use Meigs Field was rejected because the city wanted to retain its services as an airport. When the Board of Trustees selected Garfield Park, Mayor Daley again countered with a successful proposal to locate the campus on Chicago's near west side.

In terms of political benefits, the near west side location possessed several important advantages. Strong support for this site was provided by local business interests, such as Sears-Roebuck Company, whose main plant was threatened by neighborhood deteriora-

---

11. This distinction is based upon the discussion of material and immaterial incentives in Chester I. Barnard: *The Functions of the Executive* (Cambridge 1956), pp. 142–160.

12. Mrs. Florence Pacelli, quoted in Braden and Petacque, *op. cit.* Another ward committeeman said, "What I look for in a prospective captain is a young person—man or woman—who is interested in getting some material return out of his political activity. I much prefer this type to the type that is enthused about the 'party cause' or all 'hot' on a particular issue. Enthusiasm for causes is short-lived, but the necessity of making a living is permanent." Meyerson and Banfield, *op. cit.*, pp. 70–71.

13. The following discussion is based upon Edward C. Banfield, *op. cit.*, pp. 159–189; Peter B. Clark: The Chicago Big Businessman as a Civic Leader (unpublished Ph.D. dissertation, Political Science Department, University of Chicago, 1959); pp. 254 ff.; *Chicago Daily Tribune*, February 11, 1961; *The University of Illinois at Congress Circle* (Chicago, 1961); Department of City Planning, City of Chicago: *Area Plan for West Central Community, Interim Report* (Chicago, 1961).

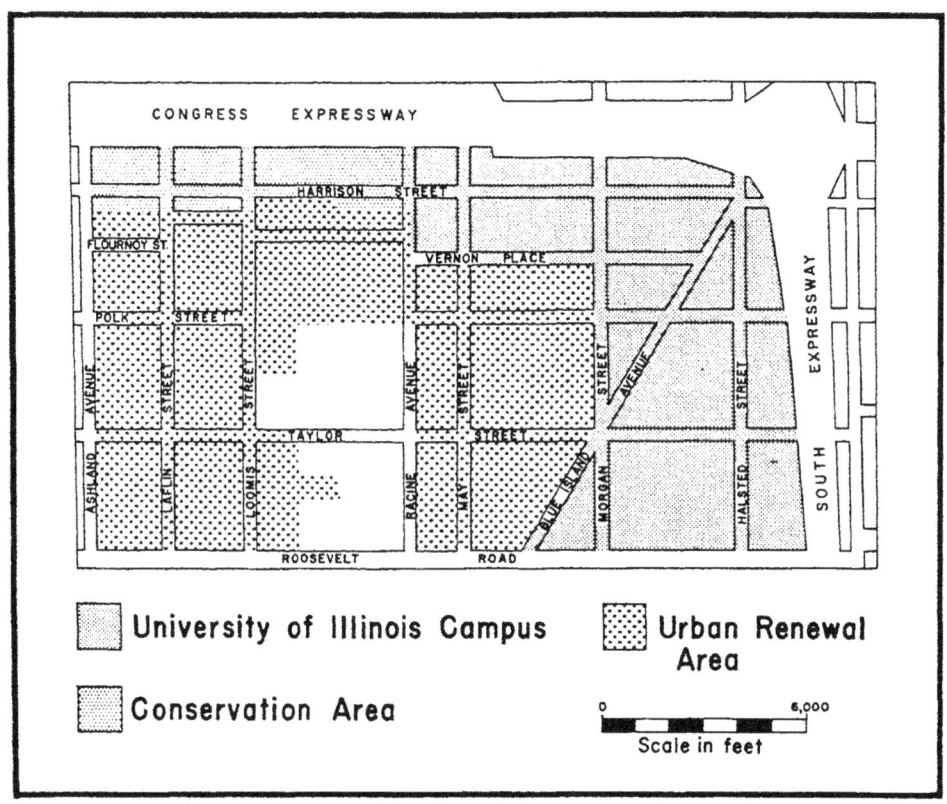

Map 31.8 THE FRONTAGE ALONG THE CONGRESS EXPRESSWAY REPRESENTS MORE THAN TWICE THE AMOUNT THAT WAS ORIGINALLY PLANNED
Source: Community Conservation Board, City of Chicago.

tion. Second, inhabitants of the core area and inner zone gained the advantage of a sizeable new source of employment and ease of accessibility for attending the University. Finally, the approved plan pleased many voters in the frontier zone of competition and the outer zone, because the plan included an extensive urban renewal and conservation plan which would eliminate the city's worst slum district and supplant it with an intellectual center. Moreover, two-thirds of the financing necessary for the project would be provided by federal sources.

Mayor Daley's adroit political maneuverings serve to illustrate the effectiveness of the politician's tools. To obtain a favorable decision on his proposal of the near west side site, his administration took the following actions. First, the city arranged for the University to secure more than twice the amount of frontage along the Congress Expressway than was originally planned (Map 31.8). In addition, elimination of a portion of the site originally proposed prevented the campus from being split by a major thoroughfare. Second, the city administration and the Chicago Land Clearance Commission pledged a new urban renewal program for the provision of new private apartment buildings in the area. Third, Mayor Daley guaranteed that city housing agencies would "push" a large community conservation program to the west of the campus. Finally, Mayor Daley's proposal conveniently received support when prominent business and civic groups announced that the city would contest the legality of the alternative area (Garfield Park). A visible grain of truth can be found in the angry remark of Sam K. Lenin, President of the Garfield Park Chamber of Commerce. "Our Garfield Park site has been overpowered by the downtown money interests and outmaneuvered by the Chicago politicians."[14]

While the politician is concerned with the

14. *Chicago Daily Tribune*, February 11, 1961.

potential voting capacity of a particular area, he must also consider its flexibility. If one ward is relatively inflexible, the politician can profitably risk alienating some of his support there in order to realize larger gains in another, more flexible ward. An examination by ward of zonal voting characteristics for all three elections affords some understanding of the variation among wards. It was found that the frontier zone of competition showed greater flexibility than the inner zone and core area.

The significance of this flexibility is illustrated in the 1959 election. Mayor Daley mobilized the Democratic machine to its fullest capacity and produced an overwhelming endorsement of his administration. In so doing, he gathered the support of the usually racalcitrant opposition press, voluntary associations, prominent business and civic leaders, and other typically Republican groups. It is not insignificant that his most impressive gains occurred in the zone of competition, not in the inner zone and core area (Map 31.4). In fact, some wards of the inner zone betrayed signs of a possible upper voting limit.

Another variation among voting zones may be related to the different types of appeals made. In the inner zone, rigid party control through patronage compels the ward alderman to toe the line. In the outer zones, however, the alderman is less dependent upon the political machine for patronage votes and more dependent upon his ability to appeal to mass media and local voters. Thus, there may well be a weakening of party loyalties in various areas which will confront the city-wide politician with labyrinthine problems. By garnering more total votes through intangible appeals, he is less and less likely to have a loyal and disciplined party of aldermen.

The spatial aspects of politics are implicit in a number of other city issues. For example, Mayor Daley is appointing more and more "blue-ribbon" candidates to public office, Police Superintendent Wilson being one the more recent of a large number of academic and professional figures. With every "blue-ribbon" appointment, one more patronage job, and perhaps indirectly more, is lost to the party. Another issue is the entire activity of urban planning and urban renewal. Urban planning receives much of its impetus, drive, and personnel from the frontier zone of competition and the outer zone, while the core area and inner zone often vehemently oppose it. The fact remains, however, that city politicians are increasingly recognizing the advantage of city planning in assembling and maintaining political support.[15] Doubtlessly, this is one important reason why the 1951-1961 decade has witnessed more political support for planning than have past decades, even though the cultural background of the politician himself may motivate him to oppose the general philosophy embodied in urban planning.

Conclusions

There are important spatial considerations influencing political decision-making and shaping public policy. The study set forth should be regarded properly as a series of hypotheses rather than an accumulation of well-established generalizations. Hopefully, however, this study presents a spatial framework within which to view voting habits and the political behavior of decision-makers. Certainly, further comparative investigation is required to test adequately the over-all results. Chicago represents but a single American city—a large city with a well-defined nucleus, a small-ward system, partisan politics, and a powerful political machine. Moreover, this study represents but one aspect of the political geography of the city. Other topics such as metropolitan political organization, the provision of urban functions, zoning, electoral geography, and urban renewal are all of potential value and should not be overlooked in a comprehensive study.

Nevertheless, geographers have long neglected the interplay of geography and politics in the city. There is evidence of an increase in attention to these problems, but research upon this subject cannot be delegated to the political geographer alone. Unless urban geographers assume the responsibility of viewing urban politics as something more than an obstacle to planning, a serious deficiency will continue to thwart our understanding of the geography of American cities.

15. See Norton Long: Planning and Politics in Urban Development, *Journ. of the Amer. Inst. of Planners*, Vol. 20, 1959, pp. 163-169.

32

Electoral Studies in Political Geography

J. R. V. PRESCOTT*

This essay modifies some of the earlier concepts about electoral geography[1] and introduces some new ones. Electoral geography has as its core the geographical analysis of elections at all levels of government in federal and unitary states. It has also come to include geographical analysis of referenda and plebiscites, which in the following discussion are considered with elections, and votes in national and international bodies which seem to have a regional significance, which must be considered separately. There are three aspects of elections which interest geographers; two are important while the third is much less significant. First, geographers must seek to understand what geographical reasons, if any, prompted or encouraged a government to select a particular electoral method, and, when the method requires the division of the state into constituencies, to select particular boundaries. Second, geographers must seek to discover what geographical factors, if any, have contributed to the resulting electoral pattern; and the extent to which that electoral pattern may be assumed to reflect the summation of political geographical variation throughout the state. Lastly, geographers should be aware that governments, sensitive to electoral patterns, may seek to alter them by actions which will increase the government's popularity and at the same time alter the economic geography of some constituencies.

GEOGRAPHICAL ANALYSIS OF ELECTORAL METHODS

The wide variety of electoral methods available has been adequately described by political scientists such as Van den Bergh[2] and Lakeman and Lambert.[3] The geographer's interest centres on the fact that different methods will present statistics in different forms which affect the technique and value of analysis.

A useful working classification of electoral methods distinguishes between those in which one person has to be elected and those in which more than one person has to be elected.

In the first group there are two main types. In the first type the person with the most votes is successful, while in the second type

---

* J. R. V. Prescott is Senior Lecturer in Geography at the University of Melbourne, Australia.

1. J. R. V. Prescott, "The Function and Methods of Electoral Geography," *Annals of the Association of American Geographers*, XL (Sept. 1959), 296–304.

2. G. Van den Bergh, *Unity in Diversity* (London: 1955).

3. E. Lakeman and J. D. Lambert, *Voting in Democracies: A Study of Majority and Proportional Electoral Systems* (London: 1959).

the elected candidate must obtain an absolute majority of the votes cast. Under the first method it is possible for the elected candidate to represent a minority of the voters. It would seem important to distinguish such marginal areas from those where the successful candidate represents a majority of the electors. In the second group, where more than one person has to be elected, there are again two main types: block vote and proportional representation. Both have several variations but it is sufficient here to outline their main characteristics. Under the block vote system each elector has as many votes as there are persons to be elected, and the required candidates with the highest number of votes are elected. This makes it possible for a majority however slight to gain all the representation, and such a system may mask important minorities. With proportional representation each voter has only one vote, making it possible for a minority to gain some representation. The government may graft various conditions on to any of these methods in order to produce a unique variety. The conditions will normally relate to the franchise or to the number of candidates of any type which may be elected. For example, under the 1961 and 1965 constitutions of Rhodesia, the electoral system was designed to lead gradually to majority African rule. The basic system consisted of a single-seat first-past-the-post method as in Britain, but the proposed advance in African representation was secured through the franchise system. There are two voting rolls called "A" and "B". "A" Roll voters elect fifty members while "B" Roll voters elect fifteen members. The two Rolls have common qualifications regarding citizenship, age, residence and language; the difference lies in the additional income and education qualifications. The practical effect of these additional qualifications is that most Europeans can qualify for the "A" Roll while there is a majority of Africans on the "B" Roll. Theoretically more and more Africans would satisfy the qualifications for the "A" Roll and they would be able to elect more and more members to parliament until they created an African majority. In Ceylon the Government abolished multimember constituencies because they were depriving minorities of representation. Single member electorates were introduced, and they were delimited to allow representation of minorities; as an additional safeguard, the Governor is allowed to appoint as many as six members to represent any important minority interests which failed to gain any representation. In the Lebanon, while candidates represent the whole nation rather than one part of it, the constitution stipulates that there must be six Christians elected for every five Moslems in the Chamber of Deputies.

Important qualifications may also be introduced for the conduct of referenda. For example, in the 1964 referendum to decide the future allegiance of the Ugandan counties of Buyaga and Bugangazzi, votes were restricted to those eligible to vote in the 1962 elections. This eliminated the votes of 20,000 ex-servicemen from Buganda who had settled in the area since 1962 and who would have probably voted as a bloc, in favour of continued union with Buganda. The referendum resulted in majorities of one thousand and seven thousand in Buyaga and Bugungazzi, respectively, in favor of union with Bungoro.

Just as the chances of one group can be improved by a preferential franchise, so electoral boundaries can be drawn to favor one party. The manipulation of electoral boundaries is known as gerrymandering and geographers such as Sauer[4] and Pounds[5] have contributed to the study of this phenomenon. There are two ways in which electoral boundaries may be gerrymandered. First, areas of equivalent population can be contained within curious and indefensible boundaries; Pounds[6] and Prescott[7] have described such cases in North America and Northern Ireland respectively. Second, constituencies of unequal population size can be defined. For example in many countries, including South Africa and Australia, the rural vote has a greater value than the urban vote. Supporters of this discrepancy justify it by the argument that if all electorates had equal populations the rural electorates would be too large. Hancock[8] has shown how the inflated value of the rural vote brought the National Party to power in South Africa in 1948, and more

4. Carl O. Sauer, "Geography and the Gerrymander," *American Political Science Review*, XII (1918), 403-426.
5. Norman J. G. Pounds, *Political Geography* (New York: McGraw-Hill, 1963).
6. *Ibid.*
7. Prescott, *loc. cit.*
8. W. K. Hancock, *Smuts 2: The Fields of Force* (Cambridge: Cambridge University Press, 1968).

recently the South Australian State election of 1968 saw the Labour Government defeated even though it won at least 52 per cent of the vote.

In many cases, of course, electoral boundaries are fixed by impartial tribunals who produce reports which allow geographers to understand the criteria employed. For example, in 1967 a report was issued on the delimitation of constituencies in Papua and New Guinea. It showed that the Commission was charged to create 69 open electorates, each with a population of about thirty thousand, and fifteen regional electorates. Both systems were to cover the whole area and it was stipulated that each regional electorate should be superimposed over the open electorates so that they coincided with District boundaries. The Commission discovered certain problems during their work. First the latest population figures of 2,183,036 gave an average population in each open electorate of 31,638. In fact no permissible deviations had been stated and eventually the largest electorate, Kainantu, contained 45,327 while the smallest electorate, Manus, contained 20,647. Second, the Commission discovered that eighteen Districts had two boundaries; the official gazetted boundary and the unofficial boundary of the area actually administered. Fifteen of the eighteen Districts administered areas outside their gazetted limits, usually because a group of people were separated from the *de jure* administrative centre by some major physical obstacle. The *de facto* administrative limits were selected as the boundaries to which the electoral limits should correspond. The Commission also considered the community of interest, local government boundaries, the planned movement of people into existing Districts, means of communications, physical features, census divisions, and existing electoral boundaries. When their first plan was outlined there were twenty objections within the allowed period. Nine of these were accepted and eleven were rejected on grounds that they would split local government areas or Districts, or because of tribal enmities, or because the complaint was based on personal grounds.

The 1965 Commission, appointed to delimit new electoral boundaries in Victoria, was instructed to give due consideration to four factors in determining the boundaries: the likelihood of changes in the number of electors in the foreseeable future, community or diversity of interest, means of communication, and physical features. In constructing the metropolitan areas, the Commissioners noted that they had used rivers and creeks and major thoroughfares as boundaries, so that people would be aware of the limits, and to reduce the inconvenience of having to cross such features to vote.

Even if the geographer is more interested in the influence of geographical factors on voting patterns he will have to begin by closely studying the electoral method, the franchise and the delimitation of constituencies. This study will indicate the level of reliance which can be placed upon the statistics. An examination of electoral systems throughout the world shows that in seventy-one cases the method allows profitable geographical analysis, although in some of these cases a restricted franchise or partial boundaries may qualify the value and results of analysis. By contrast in fifty-seven countries there is either no electoral system or the electoral system allows no expression of a choice. In such cases there seems to be no role for electoral geography to play.

	Number of countries where electoral method allows geographical analysis	Number of countries where electoral method prevents geographical analysis
Africa	10	29
Americas	22	3
Asia	12	9
Europe	20	11
Middle East	5	5
Oceania	2	—
Total	71	57

It must of course be undertood that while the system may theoretically allow a free choice, it may be operated in such a way that a free choice is prevented. This type of information will only be obtained by a detailed study of the political background to each election.

GEOGRAPHICAL ANALYSIS OF ELECTIONS

The earlier paper[9] expressed the view that the greatest contribution of electoral geography

9. Prescott, *loc. cit.*

concerned the regional geography of the state. While this view still seems sound it no longer seems valid to place greatest reliance on those elections which involve the *raison d'être* of the state, thus relegating elections which do not involve the *raison d'être* to the role of cross-checking regions based on other grounds. If it is accepted that the importance of electoral studies lies in the fact that they provide information about the areal variation of a complex of political views, it is just as useful to consider the pattern of voting, whether the issues concern the existence of the state, or the way in which the state should be organized. This means that in states where there is a uniform acceptance of the *raison d'être*, geographers will find it useful to study the areal variation of attitudes towards economic organization, internal administration, and foreign policy. Such political regions will be potentially less disruptive than those based on differences over the *raison d'être*, but they will still advance the understanding of the state's political geography.

Hartshorne[10] suggested that the concept of *raison d'être* offered one means of delimiting political regions within a state. The process involved the identification of the distinctive state-idea and the measurement of its varied territorial acceptance. The technique is not universally applicable, partly because in some states the *raison d'être* is uniformly accepted, partly because it is often difficult to identify the *raison d'être*, and partly because even if it can be identified its varied acceptance cannot be measured in precise terms. These difficulties disappear when accurate and unbiased returns are available for elections which involved the state-idea. This situation is likely to apply in certain states where the population includes militant groups which differ from each other in terms of race, nationality, tribe, religion or culture. The position is likely to be accentuated in those cases where intransigence on the part of one group is encouraged by another state. This situation has existed in Cyprus, where Greece and Turkey have clearly involved themselves in the politics of the island, and in Kenya and the Territory of the Afars and Isaas, where the Somali Government has expressed support for Somali groups.

The technique proved useful in a study of Northern Ireland and the Eastern Region of Nigeria. In Northern Ireland the *raison d'être* is loyalty to the British Crown and continued association with the United Kingdom. Elections since the partition of Ireland in 1920 have revealed a deep regional division over this concept. It is accepted in the lowlands associated with the lake-basin of Lough Neagh, and in the valleys of the Clogher, Erne and Foyle rivers. These areas, by virtue of their geological nature and glacial history, are the most fertile in Northern Ireland, and were selected for plantation or colonisation by English and Scots Protestants. Throughout these areas communications are good and all are economically and culturally oriented to Great Britain. The remaining areas, where the population rejects union with the United Kingdom, occupy hilly and infertile regions, including the Sperrin and Mourne mountains. The people of these areas are descended from the indigenous Irish stock and have preserved their Roman Catholic faith. They have closer cultural affinities with the people of Eire.

In 1957 elections for the regional parliament of Eastern Region in Nigeria centred on the continued unity of the area. The electoral pattern revealed two regions. In the core region, which occupied the western part of the state the pro-Government Party, in favor of continued unity, won every seat. This region was characterized by a high level of ethnic homogeneity, with more than ninety per cent of the population being Ibo, heavy population densities, and a higher level of productivity than neighboring regions. The peripheral region, in the eastern half of the state, returned only three pro-Government candidates compared with nineteen candidates from opposition parties in favor of the creation of another state. This peripheral region was characterized by a heterogeneous composition of tribes, low to medium population densities and a lower level of productivity than neighbouring areas of Nigeria. This distinct pattern was not maintained in the subsequent 1959 federal election and the 1961 regional election. In the 1959 federal election the issue was still related to the creation of more states, but the party opposed to further division extended its control eastwards and

---

10. Richard Hartshorne, "The Functional Approach in Political Geography," *Annals* of the Association of American Geographers, XL (1950), 95–130. This article appears in the Heritage section of the present volume.

the area returning opposition candidates contracted to the southeast region around Calabar. Before the 1961 election for the regional parliament, it had become clear that there was no chance of new states being formed. This produced a dual effect. First, the pro-Government party extended its area into the southeast around Calabar, further reducing the former peripheral area. Second, the reduced challenge removed the need for Ibo hegemony and a number of successful independents campaigned in the core region, producing a much less regular pattern.

While no other valid electoral evidence is available, it is worth recording, that during the fighting which followed the declaration of the independence of Eastern Region as the Republic of Biafra, federal troops seeking to restore federal authority made their most rapid advances in areas occupied by non-Ibo tribes, while the most stubborn resistance was encountered in the core region identified in 1957. The federal government's division of Nigeria into twelve states, which became effective in April 1968, designated the Ibo core region as one state, called the East Central State.

Turning to elections held in states where the *raison d'être* is not in dispute, it seems likely that the most definite analysis will be possible either when the electorate is offered two or more deeply contrasting policies covering a wide range of subjects, or where the election centres on one specific and clearly defined issue. The conflict between general policies will often concern economic issues, but may also involve administration and the conduct of international relations. But even if there are policy similarities between the main contesting parties, and if specific issues fail to emerge, the geographer should still feel challenged by the continual emergence of the same areas of party preponderance, at elections over a considerable period of time. Clearly, before an explanation of such regions can be attempted the geographer must collect detailed information on the issues of each election and the policies of the parties concerned.

Election statistics represent the most precise figures available to political geographers. It therefore follows that they should try to extract as much information from them as possible. Since the voting pattern is the result of a multitude of personal decisions made for a number of reasons, geographers are interested in statistical techniques, which uncover any basic pattern and order and eliminate the unimportant elements. For example Roberts and Rumage[11] analyzed the distribution of left-wing voting in England and Wales by means of a series of regression models, while Lewis and Skipworth[12] described the pattern of voting in the United Kingdom in terms of the standard deviation of the percentage votes for each party from the national mean. Cox[13] used factor analysis to throw light on the contrast between urban and suburban locations in respect to party preference and political participation in London.

Six points must be made about the statistical analysis of voting patterns. First, election returns differ enormously in the detail which they provide. In some cases, as in America, figures are available for very small areas; in other states, especially those using proportional representation, the figures may refer to very large areas which contain a wide variety of economic and social regions. The statistical method should always be appropriate to the level of detail available. Second, in many cases the units within which votes are recorded may not correspond to the units for which useful censal material is published. Lewis[14] has pointed out that in such cases the manipulation of censal and electoral statistics to make them match may be costly and may reduce the value of the original data. It is unfortunate that neither Rumage and Roberts nor Cox explained how they matched censal and electoral information in their studies of voting behavior in English urban areas. Butler, the noted electoral analyst, has frequently commented on this difficulty in studying British elections:

11. M. C. Roberts and K. W. Rumage, "The Spatial Variations in Urban Left-Wing Voting in England and Wales in 1951," *Annals* of the Association of American Geographers, LV (1965), 161-178.

12. P. W. Lewis and G. E. Skipworth, *Some Geographical and Statistical Aspects of the Distribution of Votes in Recent General Elections* (Hull, England: University of Hull, Dept. of Geography, 1966).

13. Kevin Cox, "Suburbia and Voting Behavior in the London Metropolitan Area," *Annals* of the Association of American Geographers, LVIII (March, 1968), 111-127.

14. Peirce F. Lewis, "Impact of Negro Migration on the Electoral Geography of Flint, Michigan, 1932-1962: A Cartographic Analysis," *Annals* of the Association of American Geographers, LV (March, 1965), 1-25 and reprinted in this volume.

In America Professor Merriam and Professor Gosnell in France M. Siegfried examined election returns in certain localities to see how far it was possible to discover the social composition of party support by comparing the voting figures district by district with known census data about the population. . . . they are techniques which can hardly be applied in Britain, because of the lack of sufficiently detailed data. Owing to the provisions of the Ballot Act, it is not possible to discover how any subdivision of a constituency voted. Only the total figures are available. The constituencies are too large and not clearly enough differentiated in social composition for any useful conclusions to be drawn by the methods used by Professor Merriam, Professor Gosnell and by M. Siegfried.[15]

If scholars present findings based on detailed statistical analysis they should set out not only their sources, but also the means by which they compared statistics for different territorial units. This will allow their work to be checked and compared with the findings of others. Lewis[16] has suggested detailed cartographic analysis in those cases where precise voting returns are available for small areas and where electoral and censal districts do not coincide. He used the technique very effectively in investigating the Negro vote in Flint, Michigan, and it is to be hoped that other geographers will follow his lead.

Third, it is essential that any analysis should be conducted at the smallest electoral level possible. There is no excuse for using constituency figures if returns are also shown for subdivisions of electorates, or for individual polling booths; the figures related to smaller areas will make it possible to draw the boundaries of voting regions with much greater precision.

Fourth, the only case where there may be problems about which figures to map concerns preferential voting. Under the preferential system the elected candidate must secure a majority of the votes cast, and voters are required to show the order in which the candidates are preferred. If after all the papers have been counted for the first time, no candidate has an absolute majority, the votes of the candidate with the smallest number of votes are distributed in accordance with the second preference of the voters. Candidates continue to be eliminated and their votes redistributed in this way, until one candidate receives more than half the votes. The decision to map the first preference votes or the final voting figures would vary with circumstances. For example, if only the final figures were mapped for the Australian State of Victoria, in either state or federal elections, the importance of the vote for the Democratic Labour Party would be masked. Although this party rarely gains any seats in the lower chambers, its vote of about 14–16 per cent is crucial in deciding which of the major parties wins particular seats. On the other hand the Democratic Labour Party is unimportant in New South Wales and a closer liaison between the two parties in the governing coalition, which means that they do not usually stand against each other, makes it realistic to use the final figures.

Fifth, it is important that conclusions should be based on the analysis of as many elections as possible. Reliance on a single election is dangerous because special issues or circumstances may produce an atypical voting pattern. Wright's warning is still valid:

Without the perspective that historical study should give, research in political geography can produce misleading results. If based too exclusively on a consideration of contemporary facts, however skilful the use may be of maps and statistics, political geography is a thing of shallow geometrical designs.[17]

Sixth, scholars should not be disappointed if complicated statistical techniques fail to throw new light on electoral patterns. In some cases the main contribution of their results will be to confirm what was already well-known. For example, the results of the investigation by Roberts and Rumage come as no surprise to anyone who has read Krebheil's pioneer paper of 1916. In some cases the statistical analysis will not reveal a significant relationship. For example, the conclusion by Cox that suburban characteristics are directly related to increased political participation, totally ignores the fact that turnout is vitally affected by the extent to which a seat is considered "safe" or "marginal."[18] In short, there is scope in electoral geography for both statistical analysis and commonsense, descriptive interpretation; in the best studies

15. D. E. Butler, *The British General Election of 1951* (London: 1952), pp. 7–8
16. Peirce F. Lewis, *loc. cit.*

17. J. K. Wright, "Training for Research in Political Geography," *Annals* of the Association of American Geographers, XXXIV (1944), 190–201.
18. Butler, *op. cit.*, p. 241.

these two approaches will complement each other.

Once the analysis is completed the geographer is faced with the problem of recording the information on maps. This should not present any problems but three persistent defects recur in many electoral maps. First, too many maps seem primarily concerned with showing which party won the election. Results are important and no political geographer would deny the importance of studying the relationships between geography and particular governments, but it is more important in electoral mapping to show clearly how the population voted in the smallest areas defined in the returns. If constituency figures are plotted, so that the winning party is obvious, electoral regions based on such figures will be tied to constituency boundaries and will lack the precision available by using more detailed figures. Second, too many maps employ choropleth shading which visually gives a disproportionate importance to sparsely-populated rural electorates. Since the important relationship is between the party and the people represented, rather than between the party and the land contained within the constituency, the choropleth method is unsuitable, except in a map of urban areas. Choropleth maps of rural and urban electorates would be slightly improved if the unpopulated rural areas were left unshaded; but the most satisfactory result would be obtained by using symbols. The symbols can be of two types. If the cartographer is anxious to show the winning party then the symbols must differ for each party, although they must be of equal sizes. The different symbols can be shaded according to the size of the majority. The earlier paper[19] showed this method for elections in Wales. Alternatively a uniform symbol, related to population size can be used and the symbol can be divided to show the proportion of votes won by each party. For example, Pounds[20] mapped the 1960 American presidential elections in this way.

Third, few maps have been constructed to show electoral trends on one map. This can only be done when constituency boundaries remain unchanged, but even when this condition is present too many results are simply presented as a series of maps for each election.

19. Prescott, *loc. cit.*
20. Pounds, *op. cit.*, p. 219.

For example, Adam[21] failed to devise a map which showed electoral trends in France during the period 1947–62 even though the electoral boundaries remained unchanged. Trends in the pattern of election results can be shown by a bar-graph for each unit, where each bar represents one election and its length is proportionate to the percentage of votes obtained by the successful candidate. Electoral results in Belfast during the period 1920–1957 have been mapped in this way.[22]

THE GEOGRAPHICAL INTERPRETATION OF VOTES IN NATIONAL AND INTERNATIONAL ASSEMBLIES

This subject has not attracted much attention. One of the earliest contributions was the publication in 1932, of maps showing how American Congressmen voted on major issues.[23] More recently, Smith and Hart[24] attempted a similar and more detailed exercise. Lastly, Friedheim,[25] a political scientist, analyzed the voting of nations on aspects of the law of the sea.

The analysis of votes in national assemblies is designed to show the attitude of different regions to important questions, and it is based on the assumption that the representative votes in accordance with the wishes of the majority of his constituents.

This is a dangerous belief on two grounds. First, it is possible for representatives, in some circumstances, to be elected by a minority of voters. Second, party discipline is usually too strong and constituency consultative machinery too weak to allow the representative always to be in harmony with his electors. This point was well made by Van den Bergh:

... the majority system with its representative of each constituency is based on the idea of local representation which has been out of date for a

21. G. Adam, *Atlas des élections sociales en France* (Paris: 1964).
22. Prescott, *loc. cit.*
23. C. O. Paullin, *Atlas of the Historical Geography of the U.S.* (Washington, D.C. and New York: Carnegie Institute and the American Geographical Society, 1932).
24. H. R. Smith and J. F. Hart, "The American Tariff Map," *Geographical Review*, XLV (1955), 327–346.
25. R. L. Friedheim, "Factor Analysis as a Tool in Studying the Law of the Sea," Chapter *in* Lewis M. Alexander (ed.), *The Law of the Sea* (Columbus: Ohio State University Press, 1967).

century ... it ... represents a clumsy attempt at building a 20th century political system on medieval foundations.[26]

The analysis of votes in international assemblies must also be approached cautiously. At a specific conference, such as that analyzed by Friedheim, when resolutions are likely to be implemented, the results may be very useful. However, it would be unwise to place too much reliance on voting within general international conferences, such as the United Nations' General Assembly. In this forum many states may vote in favor of certain resolutions for diplomatic reasons, in the full knowledge that they will never be implemented.

CONCLUSION

This discussion suggests five conclusions. First, political geographers should study elections which offer voters a real choice, and which are conducted under a system free from serious bias, in order to obtain insight into the regional political structure of the state. Second, descriptive, statistical, and cartographic techniques should be used in combination to extract as much detailed information as possible from the voting returns. Third, the presentation of election results in maps should be improved by reducing the reliance on choropleth shading and increasing the use of symbols. Fourth, comparative electoral geography will be difficult because elections are not held in every country, and because different electoral methods will present the returns at different levels of detail. There is some scope, however, for studying such aspects as the over-representation of rural interests in some countries, and the voting patterns of growing cities. Lastly, geographic analysis of votes in national and international assemblies needs more study before the value of this approach can be assessed.

26. Van den Bergh, *op. cit.*, p. 45.

33

Impact of Negro Migration on the Electoral Geography of Flint, Michigan, 1932-1962

A Cartographic Analysis

PEIRCE F. LEWIS*

The past three decades have seen a rapidly growing interest in the voting behavior of American Negroes. There have been excellent reasons for this interest, both among scholars and practicing politicians. In the first place, Negroes have earned a reputation for voting *en bloc*, perhaps more solidly than any other large minority group.[1] Secondly, there has been a rapid increase in the total numbers of Negroes voting, partly as a result of Negro population growth, but mainly because of increasing political consciousness among the nation's Negroes. Finally, and equally important, American Negroes have migrated to Northern cities in such numbers that they hold the key to political success in many urban areas. Since these same cities often hold the balance of votes in state and national elections, Negroes have come to enjoy a national political prominence disproportionate to their numbers, and wholly unknown thirty years ago. Indeed, this migration of Negroes to the North has produced an electoral revolution in the United States, and its battles are fought in the wards and precincts of Northern cities.

Although this revolution has produced nationwide repercussions, and although most Northern cities have participated in the revolution, political geographers have ignored it completely. For the most part, American electoral geography has been concerned with identifying and describing sizable political regions and has largely neglected the geographic results of bloc voting by racial

Reproduced by permission of the author and publisher from the *Annals* of the Association of American Geographers, Vol. 55, 1965.

* Peirce F. Lewis (1927-) is Professor of Geography at Pennsylvania State University.

1. L. Harris, for example, has termed Negroes "the most single-minded, determined group of voters in the entire electorate." *Is There a Republican Majority? Political Trends, 1952-1956* (New York: Harper and Brothers, 1954), p. 152. The same view is expounded in R. S. Sigel, "Race and Religion as Factors in the Kennedy Victory in Detroit, 1960," *Journal of Negro Education*, Vol. 31 (1962), p. 446; and in S. Lubell's *Revolt of the Moderates* (New York: Haper and Brothers, 1956), p. 245. It is only fair to note, however, that some authors have objected to the concept of "bloc voting," especially as applied to Negroes. See, for example, O. Glanz's excellent "The Negro Voter in Northern Industrial Cities," *The Western Political Quarterly*, Vol. 13 (1960), pp. 1006-07.

minorities. Neither has much attention been paid to the political geography of cities, much less their electoral geography, even with the political importance of urban areas, and even though precinct by precinct election returns are easily available for detailed investigation.

This study is designed to fill part of the gap by examining the impact of Negro voting on the electoral geography of Flint, Michigan, a Northern industrial city whose recent population growth has resulted in large part from Negro migration. Primary focus is on the time from 1932 to 1962, the period when most of this immigration occurred, and which simultaneously produced a nationwide upheaval in Negro political attitudes. Two basic questions are posed:

(1) In what way has Negro migration produced changes in Flint's population patterns and, in turn, in the composition and distribution of the city's electorate?

(2) To what extent and in what way has Flint's electoral geography been affected by these changes in Negro population, as well as by changes in Negro voting behavior?

Cartographic techniques are employed in answering these questions, and two general methodological arguments recur throughout the paper:

(1) That maps, heretofore largely neglected as tools in the study of urban elections, are economical and accurate devices for measuring the voting behavior of urban minority groups, providing that certain preconditions are satisfied.

(2) That detailed electoral maps can provide the geographer with a considerable fund of demographic information which cannot easily be obtained by other methods.

GROWTH OF NEGRO POPULATION IN FLINT

The growth of the Negro population in Flint, similar to many other Northern cities, was part of a more general population increase which resulted from the expansion of heavy industry (Fig. 33.1).[2] In Flint, the increase was both sudden and rapid, for it was almost entirely dependent on automobile manufacturing,[3] an industry which was almost un-

2. Information dealing with the demographic, economic, and political history of Flint has been drawn from a wide variety of sources. In addition to the obvious Census materials, primary sources were C. Crow, *The City of Flint Grows Up* (New York: Harper and Brothers, 1945); F. Rodolf, "An Industrial History of Flint" (unpublished MS. from the library of *The Flint Journal*, 1949 [?]); C. H. Clark, "Some Aspects of Voting Behavior in Flint, Michigan—A City with Nonpartisan Municipal Elections" (unpublished Ph.D. dissertation, Dept. of Political Science, University of Michigan, 1952); N. R. Heiden, "A Land Use Sequence Study of the Dort Highway Area, Flint, Michigan" (unpublished Ph.D. dissertation, Dept. of Geography, University of Michigan, 1949); H. Kraus, *The Many and the Few* (Los Angeles: The Plantin Press, 1947). The clip files of *The Flint Journal* also provided much useful information, as did numerous conversations with public officials and longtime residents of Flint. Mr. W. D. Chase, librarian of the *Journal*, deserves special thanks; without his help, collection of data for this study would have been immeasurably more difficult.

Information relating to the history of the Flint Negro community was largely provided by Messrs. Frank Corbett and Arthur Edmunds, both of the Flint Urban League. Both men were unsparing of their time, and their unfailing cooperation is deeply appreciated.

3. A. L. Rodgers, working with 1950 data, assigned Flint a "diversification index" of 934 on a scale where zero represented "perfect" industrial diversification, and 1,000 represented "maximum" specialization. Of the 126 American industrial areas which Rodgers analyzed, Flint was the least diversified—that is, most dependent on a single class of industry. "Some Aspects of Industrial Diversification in the United States," *Economic Geography*, Vol. 33 (1957), p. 20.

Not only is Flint a one-industry town, it is a company town as well. Without exception, the auto and auto-part factories are owned by the General Motors Corporation.

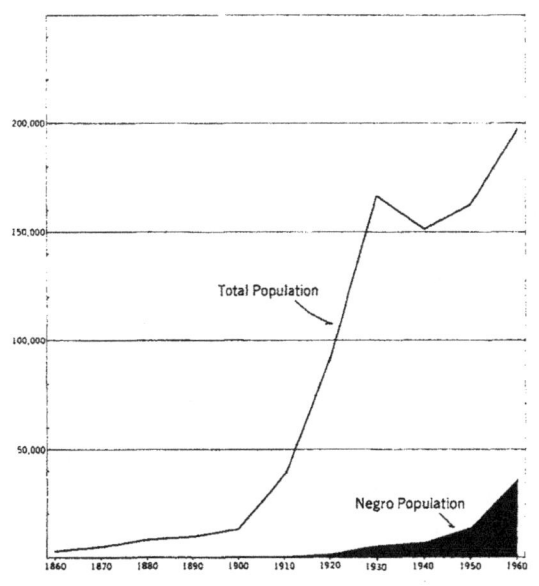

Fig. 33.1 GROWTH OF FLINT, MICHIGAN, 1860–1960

Map 33.1 Growth of Negro neighborhoods, Flint, Michigan

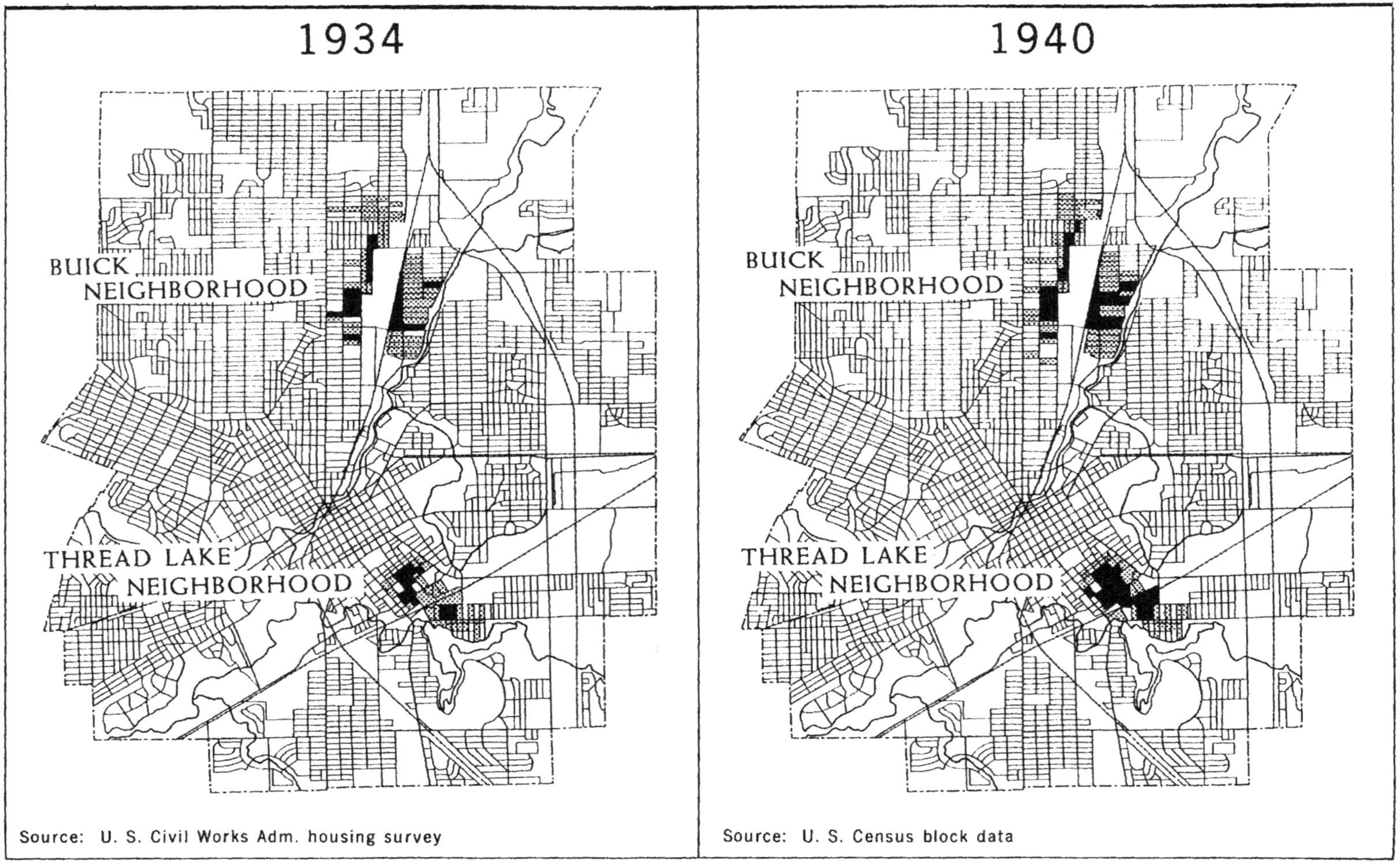

1934

BUICK NEIGHBORHOOD

THREAD LAKE NEIGHBORHOOD

Source: U. S. Civil Works Adm. housing survey

1940

BUICK NEIGHBORHOOD

THREAD LAKE NEIGHBORHOOD

Source: U. S. Census block data

1950

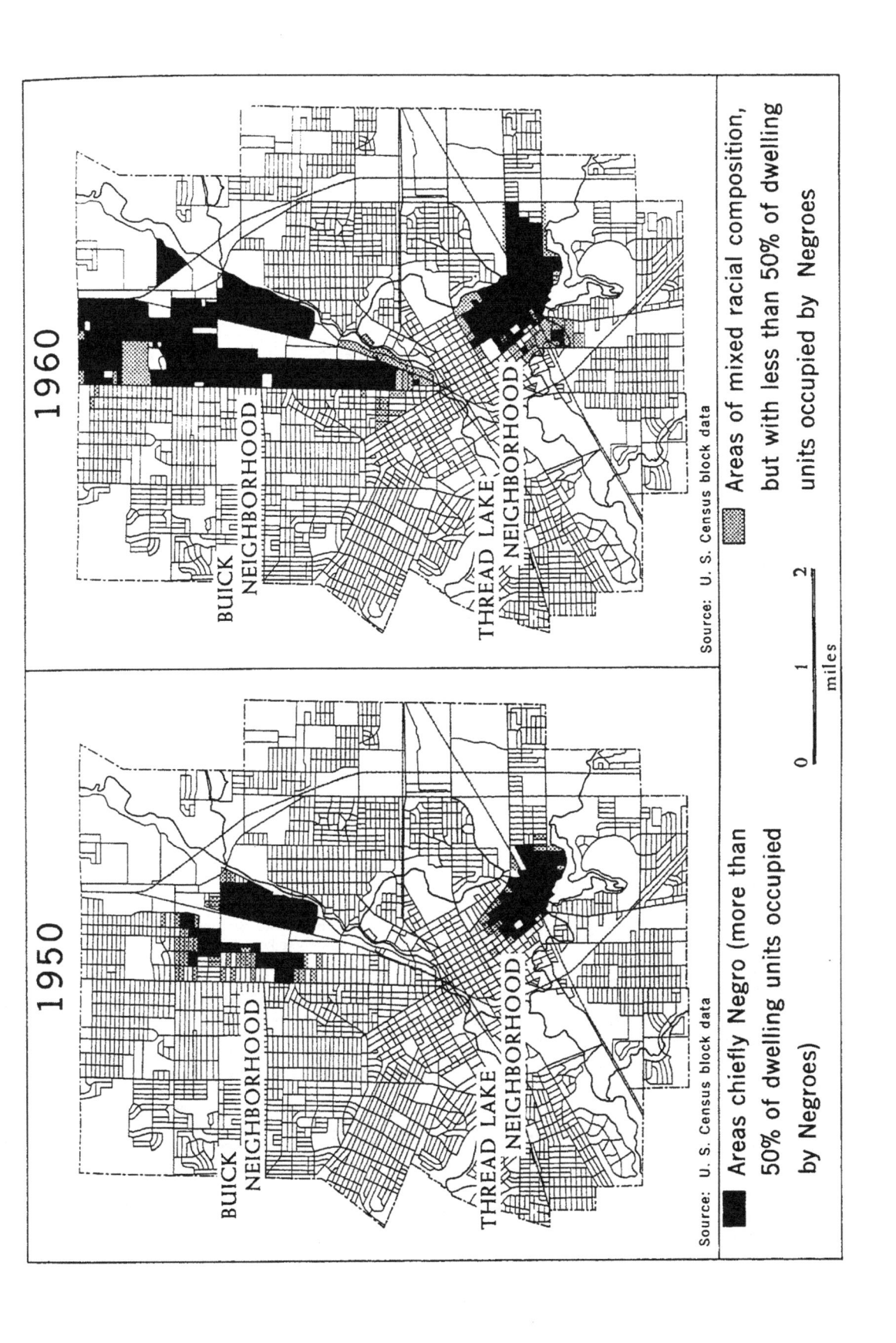

BUICK NEIGHBORHOOD

THREAD LAKE NEIGHBORHOOD

Source: U. S. Census block data

■ Areas chiefly Negro (more than 50% of dwelling units occupied by Negroes)

1960

BUICK NEIGHBORHOOD

THREAD LAKE NEIGHBORHOOD

Source: U. S. Census block data

▩ Areas of mixed racial composition, but with less than 50% of dwelling units occupied by Negroes

0   1   2
miles

known at the turn of the century, but which grew prodigiously once it had been established. In 1900, the year when the first automobile was built in Flint, the population of the city was slightly over 13,000. Ten years later, Flint was producing 30,000 cars per year, one-sixth of the nation's total output, and its population had nearly tripled. By 1920, it had more than doubled again, and in 1930, the Census counted more than 156,000 people in Flint, over twelve times as many as there had been at the beginning of the century.

This period of rapid growth also saw a sudden increase in the Negro population, albeit at different rates than the population at large. Like most other Michigan towns in the early 1900s, Flint had only a small colony of Negroes, numbering less than 300 people who were clustered in a small area near Thread Lake in the southeastern part of the city (Map 33.1). The first few years of the automobile boom brought no important changes in the Negro community, but by the second decade of the century, significant numbers of Negroes began arriving in the city. From 1910 to 1930, the Negro population of Flint increased by about 5,000 persons, reflecting a growth rate which was double that of the burgeoning white population.

The Depression marked a divide in Flint's demographic history, for its one-industry economy was struck an appalling blow. Thousands of workers left in search of jobs, and population declined for the first time since the city was founded. The economic catastrophe, moreover, accentuated the differences in rate of growth between the white and Negro populations, for the latter continued to increase throughout the 1930s, although much more slowly than before. In 1941, however, Negro population growth was again invigorated, partly owing to the war-time industrial boom, and partly because of a presidential order which discouraged racial discrimination in defense industries[4] and which opened assembly-line jobs to Flint Negroes for the first time. As a result, Negro population more than doubled during the 1940s and did so again during the 1950s. As before, this growth was relative as well as absolute, for although white population resumed its increase after the war, it did so slowly by contrast with the Negro population. Whereas in 1940 there was one Negro for every twenty-two whites in Flint, the ratio had risen to one in six by 1960. By that year, over 35,000 Negroes had made their homes in the city, more than a 100-fold increase in numbers since the turn of the century.[5]

Such rates of increase, of course, would have been impossible without a considerable influx of Negro migrants. Although data are not available for calculating the precise number of immigrants before the 1940s, it is possible to make a crude approximation of Negro migration by subtracting estimated natural increase from known total increase. Even if we assume a natural increase of four per cent per year (a figure which approaches the limits of biological possibility, and which is several times higher than the national Negro average), migration could have accounted for no less than eighty-five per cent of the Flint Negro population growth between 1910 and 1920, and eighty per cent between 1920 and 1930.[6] Although the depression produced a sharp decline in Negro migration, the lapse was only temporary. Bogue's data for the 1940s show that migrants constituted eighty-two per cent of Flint's Negro population growth during that decade,[7] and although the proportion

---

4. Franklin Roosevelt's now famous Executive Order 8802 of June 25, 1941. The text of this order is reproduced in the appendix to R. W. Logan, *Negro in the United States* (Princeton, N.J.: Van Nostrand, 1957).

5. These population figures are based only on the city of Flint, and do not take fringe areas into account. Since practically all of the Negroes in the Flint metropolitan area live within the city limits, however, the addition of fringe population would make little difference in the absolute figures cited above.

6. The estimate of a 4 per cent natural increase annually is so high as to be almost ludicrous, but was chosen deliberately to keep the final migration estimate as conservative as possible. More reasonable figures, perhaps, would be the nationwide annual increase for the Negro population: 0.6 per cent for 1910–1920 and 1.3 per cent for 1920–1930. Substitution of these numbers, however, leads to the staggering conclusion that during the 1910s in Flint, migrants constituted 98 per cent of the total Negro increase, and 94 per cent for the 1920s. Most likely, the latter percentages are too high, just as those cited above are certainly too low. Whichever figures are used, however, the conclusion is inescapable that migration produced the vast bulk of Negro population increase in Flint between 1910 and 1930.

7. D. J. Bogue, "Components of Population Change, 1940–50," *Studies in Population Distribution*, No. 12, Scripps Foundation for Research in Population Problems, Miami University, and the Population Research and Training Center, University of Chicago (Oxford, Ohio: Scripps Foundation, 1957), p. 124.

dropped somewhat during the 1950s it still stood at an impressive sixty-one per cent.[8]

Not surprisingly, the increase in numbers produced major economic and social changes in Flint's Negro population, and these changes quickly resulted in splitting the Negro community in two. The Negroes of preindustrial Flint, although relatively poor by comparison with the white population, were by no means indigent. This was not so, however, with those who came in the early days of the automobile boom. Many of the incoming Negroes were Southern farmers, who arrived in Flint with little more than the clothes on their backs. Working in Flint, moreover, did little to better their economic lot, since discriminatory policies in the auto plants restricted Negroes to menial and poorly paying jobs, usually as part-time janitors and sweepers. Living quarters in the established Negro neighborhood near Thread Lake, however inexpensive, were often beyond their means, and many took up residence in squalid slums along the fringes of the sprawling Buick factory in the northern part of Flint (Map 33.1). If, one day, the income of a newcomer grew large enough, he might move from the Buick to the Thread Lake neighborhood. The difference in distance between the two areas was about three miles, but socially and economically, it was a difference between two worlds. As time passed, and as both neighborhoods expanded into heretofore white areas, the economic differences grew less acute. Nevertheless, the physical distance still represented a considerable social barrier, with Thread Lake Negroes continuing to look on themselves as the custodians of Negro tradition in Flint, and in all ways superior to the upstart newcomers of the Buick neighborhood.

The growth of Negro population, of course, led to a substantial increase in the size of the Negro neighborhoods (Map 33.1). The general outlines of both the Buick and Thread Lake areas had been fixed at the beginning of the Depression, and up to 1950, their geographic extent changed only slightly. During that time, however, density of Negro population became greater and greater, and shortly after 1950, population pressures burst beyond the limits of the old neighborhoods. Most of the new expansion took the form of two wedges, projecting northward and eastward from the downtown area toward the city limits, but confined between the walls of jealously guarded white neighborhoods. Although, as all four of the maps demonstrate, areas of mixed populations can be found in any given year, such areas merely represent zones in rapid transition from white to Negro occupance. Just as in most American cities, truly interracial neighborhoods are extremely rare in Flint. This racial dichotomy, as we shall shortly see, has made a profound impression on the city's electoral geography.

Voting Behavior in Flint Before 1932

Surprisingly, politics in Flint has shown no immediate response to the economic and demographic upheaval which occurred during the first three decades of the twentieth century. Before 1900, Flint had mirrored the political character of many other small Northern towns by delivering heavy Republican majorities in election after election, and it continued to do so until 1930, despite the radical change in numbers and composition of population. Since major economic and social changes commonly produce corresponding political changes, it may seem strange that the swarms of migrants had so trivial an effect on the city's voting. A sizable number of the newcomers, after all, were white Southerners, to many of whom the Republican Party was anathema. Then too, many found Flint's living and working conditions less attractive than they had hoped, and might have been expected to vent their displeasure through votes against the established order which the G.O.P. represented. Unfortunately for the Democrats, however, the migrants had little voice in political affairs. Too often they were poorly educated and uninterested in politics at any level. Many, furthermore, were unable to vote in Flint because they returned home during the auto plants' summer layoffs and hence failed to satisfy the Michigan six-month residence requirements for November elections. Thus, voting in Flint remained largely the concern of longtime residents, who perpetuated the Republican tradition

---

8. For the 1950s, data are derived from annual volumes of *Vital Statistics of the United States;* natural increase was computed by subtracting deaths from births, and this total was then subtracted from the gross Negro population increase; the remainder was taken as the number of in-migrants.

long after the city's population had begun its meteoric increase. By the 1920s, Democratic prospects had grown so dismal that a party convention was called to consider whether the local Democratic organization should not be abandoned completely.[9]

During those same three decades, many of the eligible Negroes of Flint probably did not bother to cast ballots, but of those who did, it is likely that most were Republicans, just as most Northern Negroes had been Republicans ever since the Civil War. It is difficult to be precise about the degree of Negro allegiance to the G.O.P. since none of the city's precincts had yet become dominantly Negro in population, and it is therefore impossible to separate Negro from white election returns. In the most heavily Negro precinct, however, Republicans carried eighty-five per cent of the presidential vote in the 1928 election, which was far in excess of the city average. As a leading Negro Flint citizen (a devoted Democrat) put it sourly, "Negroes in this town were still voting for Abraham Lincoln."

The Depression, however, marked a major turning point in the political history of Flint, for it put an abrupt end to the long-standing Republican tradition, just as it did throughout much of the urban North. The city which had given Herbert Hoover seventy per cent of its votes in 1928 produced a clear majority for Franklin Roosevelt only four years later. By the mid-thirties, Flint had become a Democratic stronghold.

Curiously, Flint's Negroes were relatively untouched by the political upheaval of 1932. Although the most solidly Negro precinct showed an increase in Democratic voting over the 1928 election, the precinct still voted twenty percentage points more Republican than the average for the metropolitan area, and gave Roosevelt only a third of its total vote. However, 1932 was the last election in which Republicans could count on Negro support in Flint. The next two years saw a major swing in the voting of certain Negro districts and, in 1934, a largely Negro precinct gave the Democrats fifty-eight per cent of its vote. By 1936, the same precinct had returned a Democratic landslide of eighty-one per cent.

Thus, the 1932 election marks the end of an era, and the beginning of a fundamental change in the political behavior of Flint's Negro electorate. This election, therefore, serves as a yardstick against which subsequent political changes can be measured, and provides a logical starting point for analyzing the impact of Negro voting on the electoral geography of Flint—the second major problem posed in this paper.[10]

METHODOLOGY

The second problem, however, cannot be solved without first considering a methodological question inherent to any electoral study: How can election returns of a given population group be separated from those of other groups for purposes of comparative study? This paper will argue that, if certain preconditions are met, it is possible to use simple overlay maps to effect this separation of Negro and white votes in Flint and, furthermore, that a series of such overlays simultaneously provides a clear and reliable description of changes in the electoral geography through time. In addition, the paper will argue that such electoral maps yield important information about the changing distribution of Flint's Negro population, and that such maps can, therefore, be of considerable value to human geographers in general.

The Use of Maps in Electoral Analysis

For the most part, students of American voting behavior have employed statistical

9. *The Flint Journal*, Nov. 9, 1932, p. 1. There was good reason for Democratic despair. In the elections of 1920, 1924, and 1928, Republican presidential candidates carried the Flint metropolitan area by 75 per cent, 84 per cent, and 79 per cent, respectively.

10. In addition, there are two technical reasons which make it undesirable to extend a detailed analysis much before 1932. In the first place, 1934 is the first year for which an accurate map of Negro population can be made, and extrapolation is necessary for any previous years. For 1932 such extrapolation is safe enough, since the Depression had brought immigration to a halt, and had frozen the basic population patterns. Generalizations for the late 1920s are dangerous, however, and for the early 1920s impossible. Secondly, Flint's precincts during the 1920s were relatively large, and no precinct had a dominantly Negro population. Just before the 1932 election, however, precincts were subdivided and reduced in size. Thus, 1932 is the first time it is possible to speak of a "largely Negro precinct" in Flint.

methods for correlating election returns and population characteristics. These methods have proved extremely fruitful, but they involve difficulties in an urban area where Census data are used as measures of population characteristics. The chief problem stems from the fact that votes are counted by precincts, whereas urban Census data are enumerated by tracts or blocks. Seldom, however, are blocks or tracts coterminal with precincts, and direct statistical correlation is therefore impossible without preliminary manipulation of data. At best, such manipulation is costly of time and money. At worst, it may reduce considerably the utility of available data.

Several methods have been used to solve the problem, but each presents peculiar difficulties. Litchfield, for example, in a study of Detroit voting behavior took block data from the Census and recompiled them on a precinct basis so that they could be correlated with election returns, but he found the task to be both tedious and costly.[11] Another common method is to bypass the Census completely and make a special survey of population characteristics, tailoring the data to conform with precinct boundaries. Special surveys, however, are expensive and time-consuming, and may be redundant if Census data already exist. Then, too, since a survey can hardly be made retroactive, historical studies are impossible. Finally, as Glanz has done in a study of recent presidential elections in several Northern cities, it is possible to examine election returns from sample precincts which lie entirely within the bounds of Census tracts with known demographic characteristics.[12] In the study of large cities this method has considerable merit, as Glanz's excellent paper clearly demonstrates, but it runs the risk in cities the size of Flint of providing a sample population which is dangerously small.

Cartographic comparison, of course, provides yet another method of approaching this same problem, with maps of population characteristics related directly to maps of election returns. In using this simple and economical method, it makes little difference whether votes are enumerated by precincts, while population characteristics are counted by blocks, Census tracts, or some other type of enumeration district. It matters only that a clear and valid pattern emerges from each map, admitting direct comparisons between them.

To geographers, map comparison is such a familiar and obvious way of comparing dissimilar data that it comes as a surprise to learn that the technique has been completely neglected in studies of urban elections in the United States. To this author's knowledge, however, the political scientists and sociologists who have done most of the work with American election returns have never attempted to derive conclusions by cartographic comparison. Where they have used maps in their studies of voting behavior, such maps have served chiefly as incidental places to file information, or as devices to illustrate conclusions already established by statistical means. To be sure, both American and French studies in electoral geography have made liberal use of cartographic comparison, and the technique has met with conspicuous success.[13] This author, however, knows of no instance where this technique has been used in an American city, where the difficulties of comparing data from dissimilar enumeration districts are most acute. One purpose of the present study, therefore, is to test this traditional geographic technique in Flint, where exactly these difficulties arise.

The Use of Overlays

The derivation of generalizations from a comparison of maps, however, involves one

---

11. F. H. Litchfield, *Voting Behavior in a Metropolitan Area*, Michigan Governmental Studies No. 7, Bureau of Government, University of Michigan (Ann Arbor: University of Michigan Press, 1941), p. v.

12. Glanz, *op. cit.*, footnote 2, p. 1002.

13. A. Siegfried's monumental *Tableau politique de la France de l'ouest sous la troisième république* (Paris: Librarie Armand Colin, 1913) is the prototype of studies using maps to relate population characteristics with electoral behavior, and his methods have been adapted by other French scholars; see, for example, F. Goguel, *Géographie des élections françaises de 1870 a 1951*, Cahiers de la Fondation Nationale des Sciences Politiques, No. 27 (Paris: Librarie Armand Colin, 1951). Also, R. Arambourou, "La Gavacherie de Monségur au temps de la IIIe république," and Auguste Chauchat's "Géographie électorale de l'arrondissement d'Issoire (Puy-de-Dôme)," both in *Nouvelles études de sociologie électorale*, F. Goguel (Ed.) (Paris: Librarie Armand Colin, 1954). Many other similar studies, British, American, and Canadian as well as French, are cited by Prescott, *op. cit.*, footnote 7, pp. 296–97.

392 Peirce F. Lewis

HIGH INCOME AREAS FLINT, MICHIGAN 1950

Blocks with average value of 'owner-occupied... one-dwelling-unit structures' of $10,000 and more

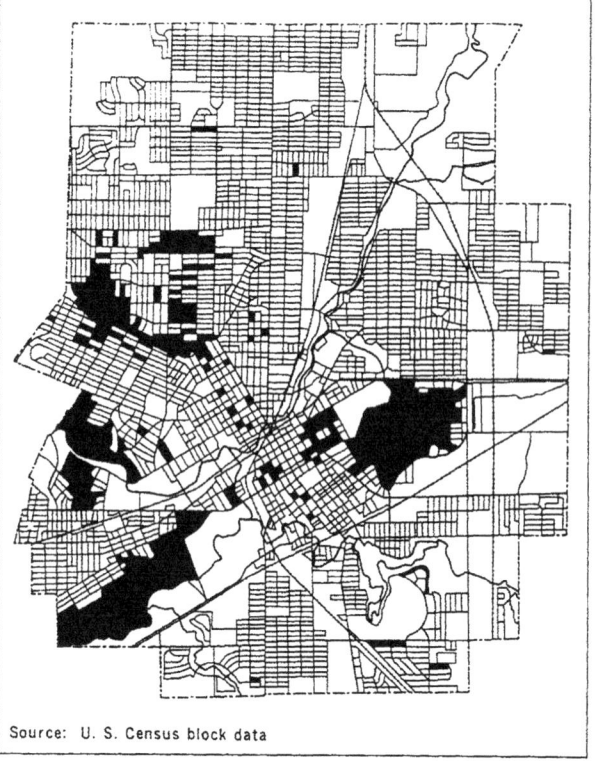

Source: U. S. Census block data

Map 33.2 HIGH-INCOME AREAS, FLINT, MICHIGAN, 1950

REPUBLICAN STRENGTH FLINT, MICHIGAN - 1950

Republican vote, as percentage of total precinct vote:

- 71 - 84
- 56 - 70
- 41 - 55
- 26 - 40
- 11 - 25

Percent Republican vote in individual precincts

Republican vote in Flint metropolitan area: 47%

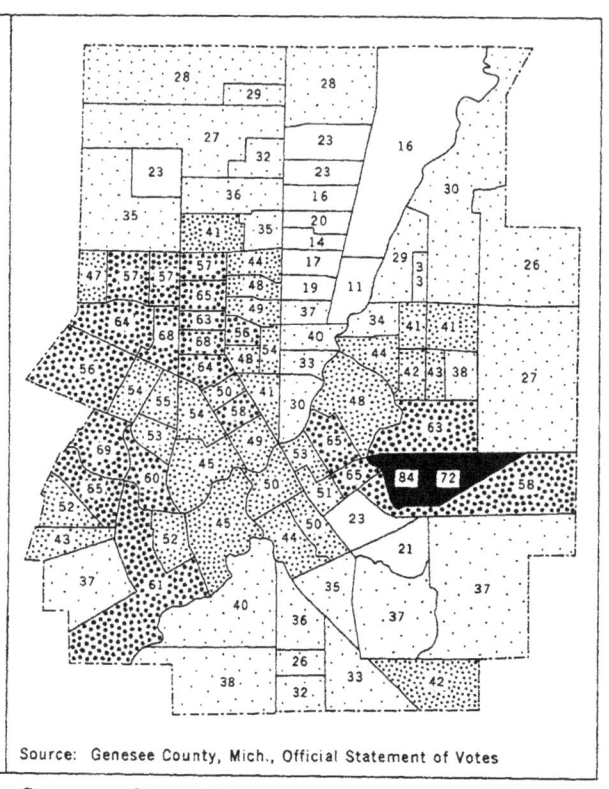

Source: Genesee County, Mich., Official Statement of Votes

Map 33.3 REPUBLICAN STRENGTH, FLINT, MICHIGAN, 1950

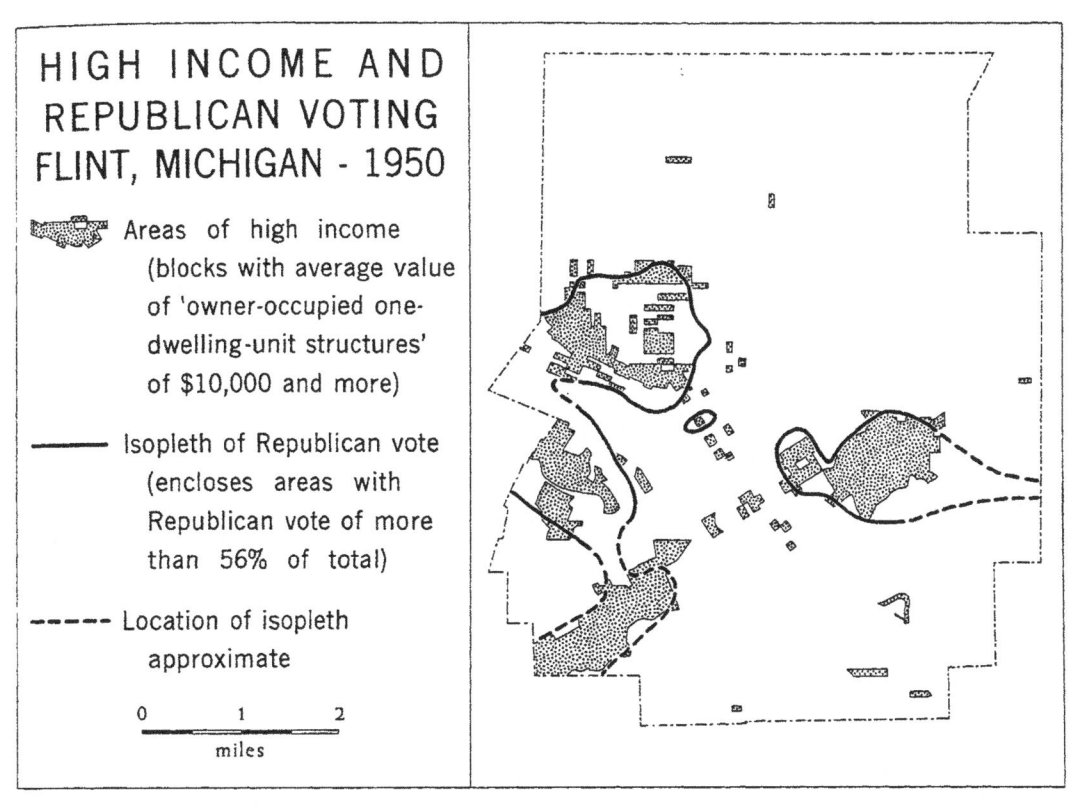

Map 33.4 HIGH-INCOME AREAS AND REPUBLICAN VOTING, FLINT, MICHIGAN, 1950

serious problem, namely, that any visual comparison is likely to be highly subjective, and hence undependable.[14] This problem is especially difficult when two choroplethic maps are compared, since the differing shapes of statistical units often introduce visual distractions which make dependable judgments almost impossible.[15] A more satisfactory procedure is to combine choroplethic and isoplethic devices on a single overlay, so as to eliminate such distractions and so as to make the comparison as explicit as possible. A familiar example, drawn from a recent Flint election, shows how such overlays can be made and what they mean, as well as pointing up some of the limitations of an overlay technique in analyzing electoral data.

To make the illustration as clear as possible, the example is a simple one, based on the truism of American politics that the Republican Party in the North has traditionally received its greatest support from high-income areas. A map of the high-income areas of Flint based on block data from the Census,[16] therefore, should correspond closely with a

14. Robinson and others have devoted considerable attention to the problem of correlating data from two or more disparate maps. For example, see A. H. Robinson, "Mapping the Correspondence of Isarithmic Maps," *Annals*, Association of American Geographers, Vol. 52 (1962), pp. 414-425, and the literature cited in the same paper. See also H. H. McCarty and N. E. Salisbury, *Visual Comparison of Isopleth Maps as a Means of Determining Correlations between Spatially Distributed Phenomena* (Iowa City, Iowa: Monograph, No. 3, Department of Geography, State University of Iowa, 1961).

15. McCarty and Salisbury, *op. cit.*, p. 78.

16. Strictly speaking, it is impossible to make a block map of income levels in Flint, since such data are published only by Census tracts. The use of house values as a measure of income, however, is a standard device in the literature of electoral analysis. Litchfield, for example, used this device in his massive study of Detroit elections on grounds that "shelter expenditure ... (constitutes) ... one of the largest and most consistent items in the budgets of all income classes." Litchfield, *op. cit.*, p. 76.

map of Republican strength,[17] and the comparison of Maps 33.2 and 33.3 suggests the possibility of such a correspondence. Not only do the darker tones on the two maps occupy approximately the same areas, but a closer examination shows that the high-income neighborhoods generally yielded Republican percentages in the high fifties and above. The correspondence between two maps, however, is far from convincing. In the first place, the disparity in pattern between the two maps makes it difficult for the reader to find the same area on both maps and to relate them with certainty. Secondly, there is such an abundance of data, especially on the electoral map, that there is no easy way to separate relevant from irrelevant information as the eye moves back and forth from one map to the other.

By constructing an overlay (Map 33.4), however, these difficulties can be largely eliminated. The high-income areas in Flint were reproduced without change from Map 33.2, but the extraneous street pattern was eliminated. The confusing welter of data on the electoral map was reduced to a single isopleth of Republican strength which encloses the city's Republican strongholds. The isoplethic value of fifty-six per cent was chosen by trial and error, and is merely the value which produces a line which most closely bounds the margins of the high-income neighborhoods. The particular percentage, of course, is not important, since it depends on an arbitrary definition of high income, and a change in that definition would presumably require a new choice of isoplethic value. Rather, the important question is how closely the boundaries of the city's Republican strongholds correspond with the boundaries of high-income areas. Since Map 33.4 shows most of the shaded areas to fall within the bounds of the isopleth, one may conclude, not surprisingly, that most of the wealthy Flint neighborhoods were producing a high proportion of Republican votes in the 1950 election.

Limitations of the Technique

The correlation on the overlay between high-income neighborhoods and areas of Republican strength, however, is by no means perfect. In part, at least, deviations may reflect the obvious fact that high income is not the sole gauge of Republican voting. Other aberrations, however, can be traced to limitations in the overlay technique.

Three classes of aberrations can be recognized. The first is illustrated in the northwestern part of the city, where sizable unshaded areas lie within the confines of the isopleth, thus suggesting, contrary to expectations, that areas of low income were producing a high Republican vote. A glance at Map 33.3, from which the isopleth was drawn, nevertheless shows that these unshaded areas on the overlay actually voted within a point or two of the isoplethic value, in short, that the deviations are trivial and may well be expected in transitional areas along the fringes of a party stronghold.

A second type of aberration, similar to the first, is exemplified by the scattering of high-income areas which lie outside the isopleth, especially near the center of the city. Here, one is led to believe that high-income areas were voting less heavily Republican than expected. Again, however, these areas lie in precincts where the percentage of Republican voting is very close to the isoplethic value, and, furthermore, are so small that the Republican vote has presumably been diluted by Democratic pluralities in adjacent low-income neighborhoods. This second type of

---

17. There is no way, of course, to measure "Republican voting," but only voting for particular Republican candidates. The best way of getting at the elusive concept of party voting in any given election, presumably, would be to average the vote for all of a party's candidates, and take the result as the party vote for that year. In Flint, however, where typical ballots in recent general elections have listed eighteen partisan contests in each of about 125 precincts, it would require more than 2,000 calculations to make a single election map. To avoid this task, the vote for a single candidate was taken as representative of his party in a given election. To ensure that this candidate would be truly typical of his party, and not one whose personal qualities caused special reactions in the electorate, the votes for all of the party's candidates running for contested offices in the Flint metropolitan area were added together and the resulting figure used to calculate the party's percentage of all votes cast; the candidate whose percentage most closely approximated the party percentage was selected to represent his party in that year. For the 1950 election, the typical Republican was found to be the candidate for Representative in Congress, who received 47.01 per cent of the vote for that office, as opposed to an average vote for all Republican candidates of 47.61 per cent. Thus, although Map 33.3 is entitled "Republican Strength... 1950," the map actually portrays the vote for the Republican candidate for Congress in that year.

aberration, like the first, presents no serious problems of interpretation.

A third type, however, cannot be dismissed so easily, and requires that the overlay itself be modified. In the eastern and southwestern parts of Flint, for example, the isopleth deviates considerably from the bounds of the high-income neighborhoods. In these cases, the problem stems from peculiarities in size and shape of precincts. In Michigan (and in many other states) law requires that precinct boundaries be drawn to include a given population, neither so large as to cause the polls to be swamped on election days, nor so small as to be uneconomical. As a result, precincts tend to be large in relatively sparsely populated areas. (Compare, for example, Maps 33.2 and 33.3. Note that precincts are largest in areas where the street grid, and hence population, is least dense.) In addition, such precincts commonly tend to assume peculiar geographic patterns, commonly the result of *ad hoc* adjustments in precinct boundaries with increasing population. These sprawling and often strangely shaped precincts frequently include a wide variety of people and, consequently, a substantial range of political persuasions. In such areas, the drawing of an isopleth to delineate cores of partisan strength becomes both difficult and uncertain. On the overlay, therefore, the isopleth is rendered as a dashed line in areas where its location is only approximate.

Adaptations of the Overlay Technique in Analyzing Negro Vote

Although these deviations suggest the need for caution when overlays are used to compare demographic and electoral data, they do not detract from the basic utility of the overlay technique, which was extended to the analysis of changing Negro electoral patterns in Flint between 1932 and 1962 (Map 33.5). In general, the procedure is similar to that cited in the example above, with areas of Negro population related to areas of partisan electoral strength by the use of shaded patterns and isopleths, respectively. Certain peculiarities of Negro population and voting habits in Flint, however, required modifications in the way the overlays were drawn.

In the first place, the very considerable changes in distribution of Flint's Negro population over the span of thirty years necessitated interpolating the bounds of Negro areas for intercensal periods. Since such interpolation was certain to produce inaccuracies, especially during the mid-1950s when Negro neighborhoods were expanding very rapidly, zones of Negro population were generalized on all the maps for the sake of consistency. In addition, transitional zones of mixed racial composition were also included, to emphasize the indeterminacy of location of the Negro neighborhoods' boundaries.

Minor adaptations were also required in rendering the isopleths, owing to the characteristics of Negro voting behavior over the thirty-year period. First of all, the isopleths have been drawn on the basis of Democratic strength, rather than Republican, because Flint's Negroes have been affiliated chiefly with the Democratic Party in recent years. There is also a difference in the way the isoplethic values are chosen. For any given map, this value represents the highest percentage of Democratic strength which still keeps Negro neighborhoods on the Democratic side of the isopleth. Thus, in any given election year, the Democratic percentage in all-Negro precincts was at least one percentage point higher than the value of the isopleth. Putting the idea in slightly different terms, the isoplethic value represents the lower threshold of Democratic strength in Negro neighborhoods for a given election.

The Meaning of the Isopleths

Consider the 1962 overlays (Map 33.5, 1962) as an example of how the isopleths were drawn, and what they mean. In 1962, the least strongly Democratic precinct in Flint's Negro areas turned in a Democratic majority of seventy-nine per cent. Accordingly, the isopleth was drawn one percentage lower than that figure: at seventy-eight per cent, as the map shows. This isopleth, which obviously encloses all precincts which voted more than seventy-eight per cent Democratic in 1962, clearly encircles the Negro neighborhoods, with practically all areas of white population excluded. The same, quite obviously, is true of all the overlays from 1952 to 1960, with the isopleths of Democratic strength keeping pace with the expanding boundaries of the Negro neighborhoods. These last six

396 *Peirce F. Lewis*

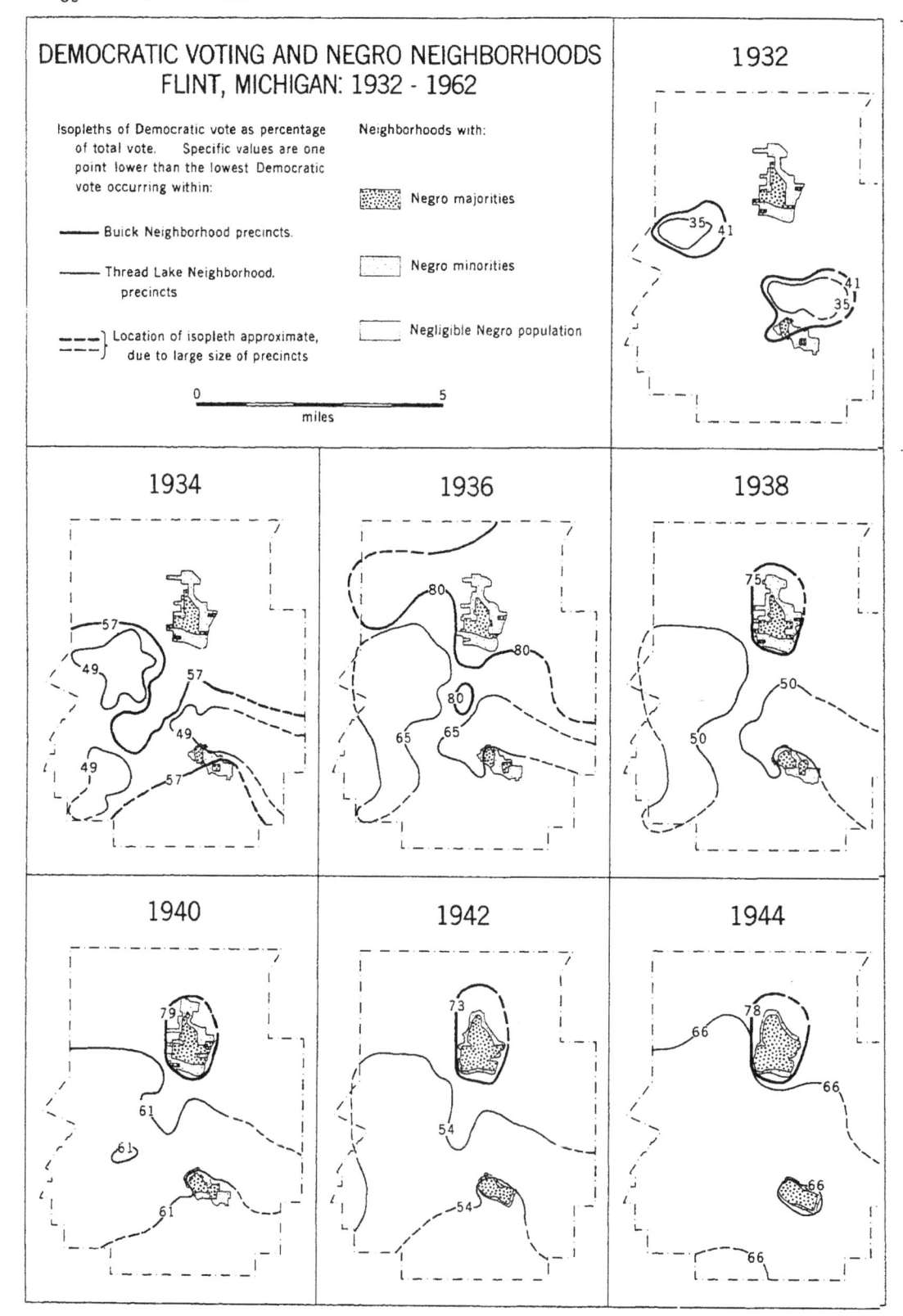

Map 33.5 Democratic voting and Negro neighborhoods, Flint, Michigan, 1932–1962

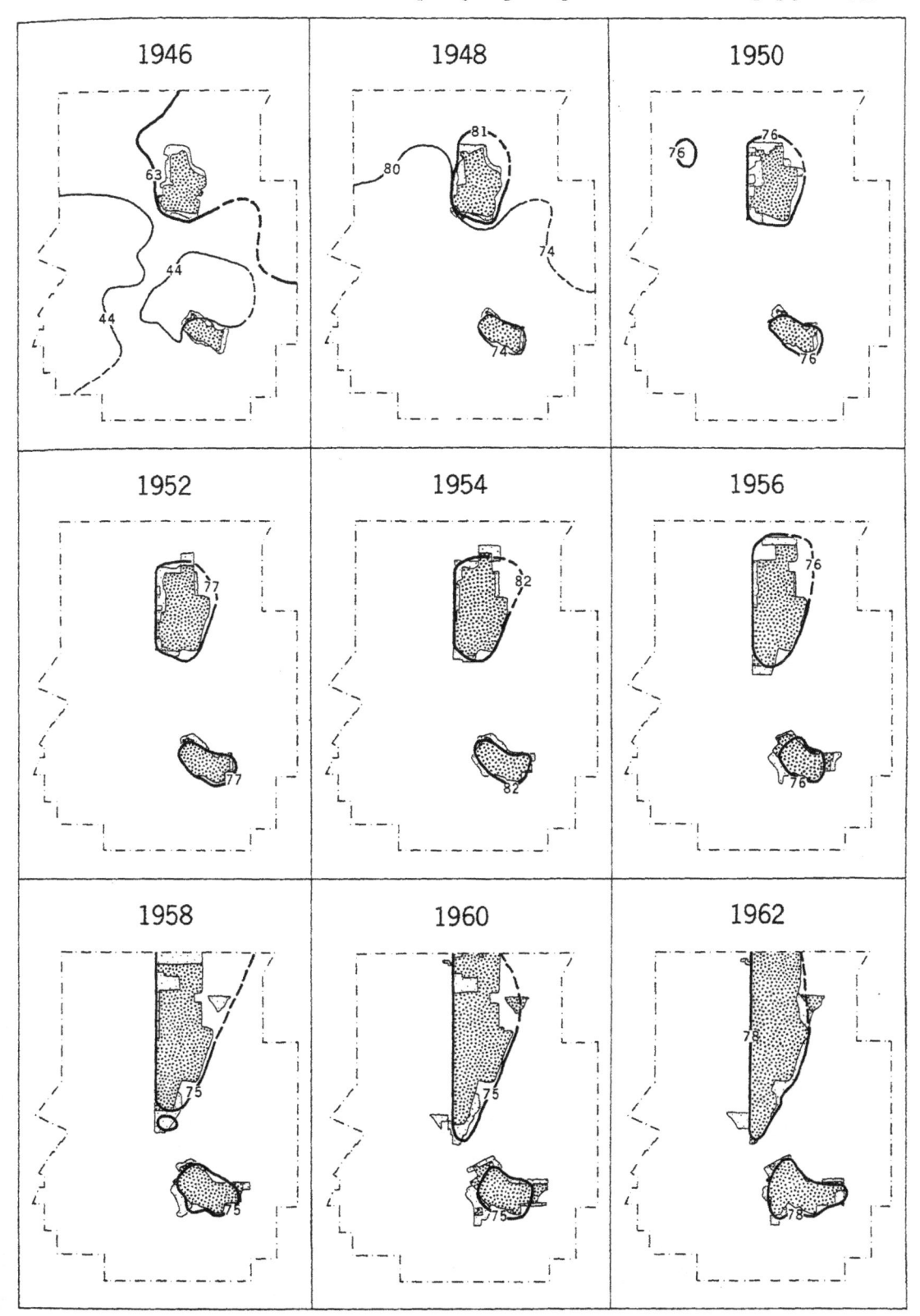

Impact of Negro Migration on Electoral Geography 397

maps obviously demand that two conclusions be drawn. The first is that Flint's Negro precincts constituted a bastion of Democratic strength during the 1950s and early 1960s, by majorities of four to one and above. The second conclusion is that this level of Democratic strength was not present in other parts of the city. In short, not only were the Negro neighborhoods strongly Democratic, but they were uniquely Democratic as well.

The overlays for the 1930s and 1940s, however, tell quite a different story, a story which has two separate aspects. In the first place, levels of Democratic strength in Negro neighborhoods were commonly lower in those earlier years. In 1932, for example, isoplethic values lie well below fifty per cent, making it obvious that Negroes were actually turning in Republican majorities in that year.[18] Indeed, only a small part of Flint was voting more heavily Republican than the Negro districts, a fact which is reflected by the limited area on the Republican side of the isopleths in 1932. Clearly, then, the period from 1932 to 1962 has seen not only a huge increase in the Negro population of Flint, but it has also seen a radical change in the voting habits of that population, from heavily Republican in 1932 to heavily Democratic in recent years.

The second story which the maps tell is that the Negro switch in party allegiance occurred in different places at different times. These differences are reflected in a marked disparity between the evolution of Buick and Thread Lake voting behavior, a disparity so great that it was necessary to use a separate isopleth for each of the two neighborhoods. Thus, the heavy line on the maps for the 1930s and 1940s represents the lower threshold of Democratic strength for the Buick neighborhood, whereas the lighter line represents that for Thread Lake. Until 1950, when the two isopleths finally merged, values for Thread Lake were consistently lower than those for Buick, reflecting the fact that the Buick neighborhood was returning a higher Democratic vote than the Thread Lake neighborhood.

One can see, by examining the 1946 overlay (Map 33.5, 1946), how extreme this difference was. The heavy isopleth stands at sixty-three per cent Democratic, and shows the Buick neighborhood to be almost unique in its degree of Democratic strength. By contrast, the isoplethic value for Thread Lake is only forty-seven per cent, nearly twenty percentage points less Democratic than that for Buick, and reflecting a narrow Republican majority. The shape of the Thread Lake isopleth is also revealing, for it corresponds very closely to the boundaries of Flint's high-income areas.[19] (Compare the isopleth on Map 33.5, 1946, with Map 33.2, and also with the isopleth on Map 33.4.) Indeed, the Thread Lake isopleth exhibits the same general shape for the whole period from 1932 to 1944; the chief change during that period is the tendency of the isopleth to delineate larger and larger areas, suggesting a gradual weakening of relative Republican proclivities among Thread Lake voters. By contrast, the Buick isopleth exhibits such a shape only in 1932 and 1934, and, by 1938, shows Buick area Negroes to be returning uniquely high majorities. It would appear, therefore, that up until 1946, ten years after the Buick area had become a bastion of Democratic strength, that the Thread Lake Negroes were among the most Republican voters in Flint, outdone in their devotion to the G.O.P. only by the wealthiest voters in the city. This is not to say, of course, that Thread Lake Negroes were returning Republican majorities. (See Map 33.5, 1936, 1940, 1942, and 1944, which shows the Democrats carrying Thread Lake by pluralities which ranged between fifty-four per cent and sixty-six per cent.) This high-income shape means only that the Thread Lake area was relatively more Republican than most of Flint's white neighborhoods.

Graphic Summary of Changing Isoplethic Values

On the basis of such interpretation of individual maps, one is likely to conclude that

---

18. Obvious, in view of the fact that Republican and Democratic votes usually total 100 per cent in Flint elections. Third-party candidates have seldom fared well with the city's voters. Even such a flamboyant candidate as Henry Wallace, who ran for President in 1948, drew only 2.3 per cent of the vote, and in contests for lesser offices, candidates outside the two major parties have seldom succeeded in garnering enough signatures on a candidacy petition even to qualify for a place on the ballot.

19. Although areas of Negro population expanded considerably during the thirty-year study period, Flint's high-income areas did not, remaining fairly static until the late 1950s. Thus, Map 33.2, the map of high-income areas for 1950, is a reasonably accurate representation of Flint's high-income areas for the whole period from 1932 to about 1955.

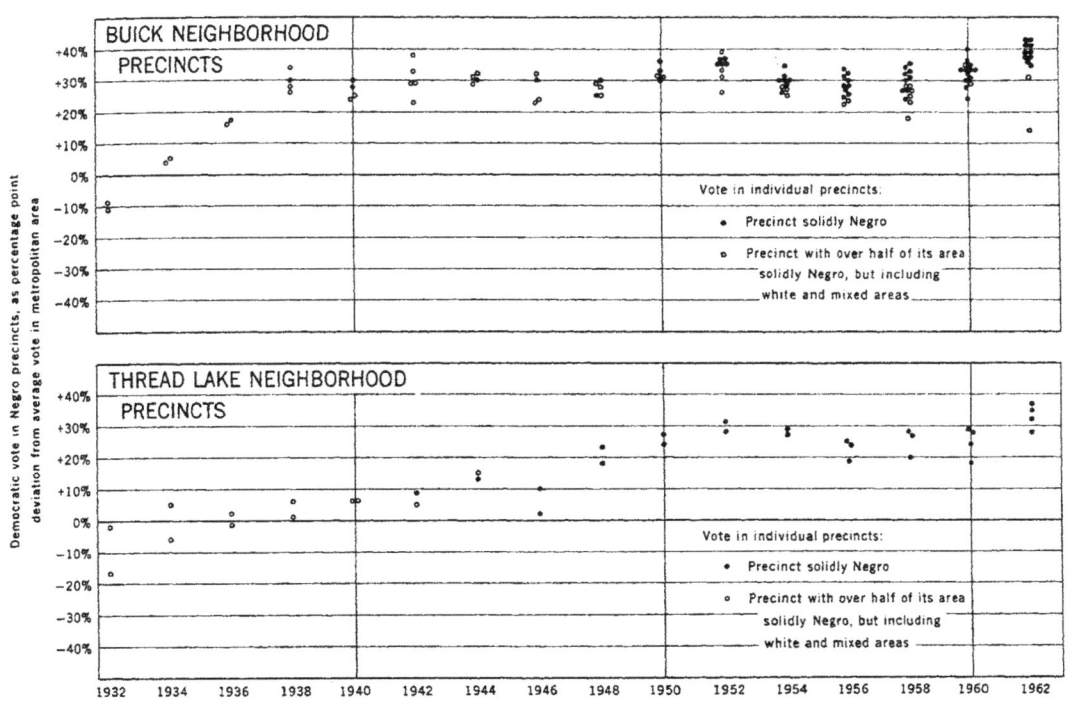

Fig. 33.2 CHANGES IN DEMOCRATIC VOTING OF NEGRO PRECINCTS, FLINT, MICHIGAN, 1932–1962

the evolution of Negro voting in Flint has been unstable and heterogeneous. By extracting information from electoral maps and summarizing the data on a series of graphs, however, it can be shown that Negro voting patterns in Flint have evolved in a sure and systematic way.

Figure 33.2 simply shows the percentage of Democratic vote in individual Negro precincts between 1932 and 1962, with one graph for the Buick neighborhood, and another for Thread Lake. Since the graphs are designed not to show which party won a given election, but rather how individual Negro precincts behaved in comparison with white areas, such precincts are plotted, not by their absolute Democratic percentages, but rather by the number of percentage points by which these precincts departed from the total Democratic vote for the metropolitan area. This technique largely eliminates the effect of year-to-year electoral vagaries, as in 1946, when Republicans carried both houses of Truman's Congress and made heavy inroads into all the

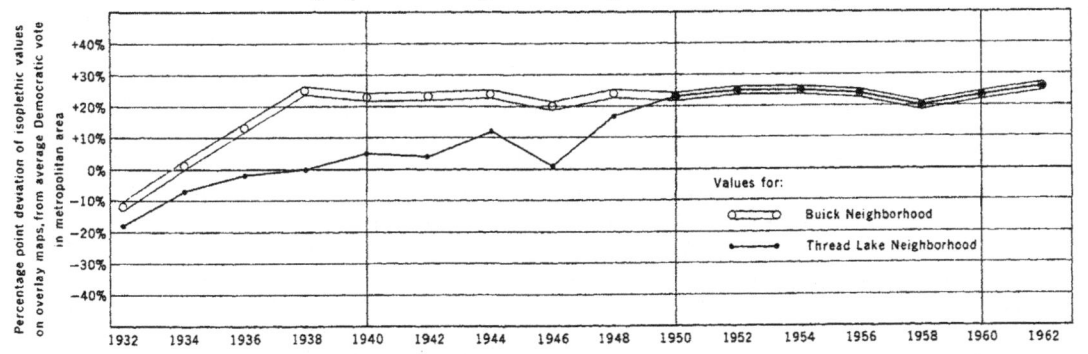

Fig. 33.3 CHANGES IN DEMOCRATIC VOTING IN NEGRO NEIGHBORHOODS, AS DERIVED FROM ISOPLETHS ON OVERLAY MAPS

Flint precincts; or as in 1936, year of the great Roosevelt landslide which saw an enormous increase in Democratic voting across the entire city. The horizontal axis of each graph, therefore, represents the total Democratic vote for the Flint metropolitan area. Points above the axis stand for precincts which are more Democratic than the average, whereas those below the axis are those less Democratic (i.e., more Republican) than the average.

Figure 33.3 shows the comparative Democratic strength of both Negro neighborhoods. Again, the horizontal axis represents the Flint metropolitan area's total Democratic vote. By contrast with Figure 33.2, however, which illustrates the relative voting behavior of individual precincts, Figure 33.3 portrays the percentage-point deviation of isoplethic values, taken directly from the overlays. This final graph, therefore, represents changes in the lower thresholds of Democratic strength in each of the Negro neighborhoods from election to election. Although minor differences can be detected, a close comparison of the three graphs will show that Figure 33.3 represents a simplified summary of the trends reflected in the more detailed graphs of Figure 33.2.

Characteristics of Negro Voting in Flint: 1932–1962

Four general conclusions emerge from these graphs and from the series of maps in Map 33.5.

(1) The isoplethic values in Map 33.5 show that both Flint Negro neighborhoods were Republican strongholds in 1932, but four years later had switched their allegiance to the Democrats. Only once since 1936 has a Negro precinct in Flint returned a Republican majority (see Map 33.5, 1946). By 1950, furthermore, both neighborhoods had reached a high plateau of Democratic strength, which was far in excess of the Democratic vote in the metropolitan area at large. Finally, as the location of the isopleths in Map 33.5 clearly demonstrates, 1950 is the last year in which any of Flint's white neighborhoods could match the Democratic majorities in the Negro precincts.

This switch in party allegiance, of course, was duplicated throughout the urban North, where the Republican Party, for seventy years associated with the Emancipation Proclamation, was replaced in Negro favor by the Democrats, who had been previously regarded as the party of Southern Bourbonism, but now, with Franklin Roosevelt and Harry Truman, the chief proponents of civil rights.[20] The rapid growth of the Flint Negro population during the 1940s and 1950s, furthermore, only deepened Negro disenchantment with the Republicans, who were blamed (deservedly or not) for conspiring with property owners and real estate dealers to confine the burgeoning Negro population to the least desirable sections of the city. Economics also militated against the G.O.P., which was associated with alleged anti-Negro hiring practices in the auto factories, and favored the Democrats who, according to a story widely circulated in the Flint Negro community, forced reluctant Republican plant owners to open assembly-line jobs to nonwhite workers.

(2) The first of Flint's Negroes to go enthusiastically Democratic were those living in the slums around the Buick plant (Figs. 33.2 and 33.3). There, Democratic strength gained rapidly during the early years of the New Deal, reached a peak by 1938, and has remained very strong ever since. This pattern is very different from that of the Thread Lake neighborhood, which continued its flirtation with the Republicans long after the Buick area had switched its allegiance. When I made this point to officials of the Flint Urban League several years ago, they speculated that the Buick neighborhood's sudden change was partly a result of highly effective political agitation by the Buick Local of the C.I.O., which had become one of the main supporters and chief spokesmen for the growing Democratic organization in Flint. The Local took no pains to conceal its distaste for the Republican Party, which was consistently denounced as a front for the General Motors Corporation. The Republicans, quite naturally, responded by tarring the Democrats with the brush of C.I.O. domination. This tactic may have helped the Republicans in

20. This trend was noted by Gosnell in a study of Negro voting in Chicago as early as 1941. Where Chicago's Negroes had previously voted Republican by four-to-one majorities, the proportion had declined to 50 per cent by 1940. H. F. Gosnell, "The Negro Vote in Northern Cities," *National Municipal Review*, Vol. 30 (May, 1941), p. 264.

some white areas, but it did them no good in Negro neighborhoods where the union was commonly held in high favor. In addition, it was asserted that Flint's Negro Republican leaders practically all lived in the Thread Lake neighborhood, and had little to do with their fellow Negroes who lived in the slums around the Buick factory.

(3) The Thread Lake neighborhood, perhaps because it was more prosperous and hence more conservative, abandoned the G.O.P. more slowly, but by 1944 was beginning to approach the levels of Democratic voting in the Buick area. The year 1946 represents an interruption in the trend for, although it was a bad year for Democrats across the nation, it was especially dismal in Flint's Negro precincts, where Democratic losses were even more drastic than in the white areas. In 1948, however, the Democratic surge was renewed, and by 1950 Thread Lake voting had matched the levels of the Buick neighborhood.

This delay in the change of Thread Lake voting patterns cannot be explained with certainty. It may be that fourteen years of continued New Deal and Fair Deal agitation for civil rights were necessary before the skeptical Thread Lake conservatives were convinced that their best hope of equal rights lay with the Democrats. It may be that the increasing number of migrants during the 1940s included enough new Democrats to swamp the handful of older Negroes who had maintained the Republican tradition, and who, at any rate, had been reduced in number by the attrition of time. It may be, according to a principle enunciated by Gosnell, that the relatively small proportion of factory workers in the Thread Lake neighborhood helped dampen Democratic enthusiasm.[21] Or, of course, the comparatively high economic level of the Thread Lake area, vis-à-vis Buick, may account for Thread Lake's reluctance to abandon the G.O.P. Whatever the reason, the Thread Lake neighborhood turned Democratic later and more slowly than did Buick, but when it did, the rejection of the Republican Party was no less complete.

(4) Although both neighborhoods have been voting heavily Democratic since 1950, it is possible to detect minor fluctuations in the high plateau of relative Democratic strength (Fig. 33.2). These fluctuations, furthermore, occur in both Negro neighborhoods simultaneously, suggesting that they are not random vagaries. A slight decline in Democratic voting followed Eisenhower's first victory in 1952, possibly the result of Negro hopes for support of civil rights by a new Republican administration. The latter half of the Eisenhower administration, however, saw a resurgence of relative Democratic strength, and this trend has continued through 1962. The 1962 election marked a record-breaking peak of Democratic voting in Flint's Negro areas, with certain precincts turning in Democratic majorities in excess of ten to one. Again, it is difficult to interpret these trends with certainty, but it is obvious that recent Republican appeals to Negro voters, in Flint at least, have fallen short of the mark.

Changes in Electoral Geography Resulting from Expansion of Negro Neighborhoods

Although the voting behavior of Flint Negroes has remained comparatively static for the past twelve years or so, the size of Negro neighborhoods has not, and the result has been a substantial change in the city's electoral geography. The nature of these changes is illustrated by Figure 33.4, which shows the political impact of Negro movement into previously white neighborhoods. By comparing maps of 1950 and 1960 Negro population distribution (Map 33.1, 1950 and 1960) with a map of the city's precincts during the same period (a map similar to the base on which Map 33.3 was drawn), it was possible to identify seven precincts whose white population was almost completely replaced by Negroes. The electoral behavior of each precinct was graphed as in Figures 33.2 and 33.3, with the Democratic vote recorded as a percentage-point deviation from the total Democratic percentage for the metropolitan area. Without exception the graphs show Negro occupance to be followed by an abrupt upsurge in relative Democratic strength. The most striking increase occurred in Precincts 50 and 52 on the margins of the Thread Lake neighborhood, where heavy Democratic voting by newly arrived Negroes contrasted sharply with the Republican

---

21. Gosnell (1941, *op. cit.*, p. 278) pointed out that during the late 1930s Negroes who were members of the industrial proletariat abandoned the Republican Party with greater alacrity than those who were not.

proclivities of a relatively high-income white population which had been displaced. In the Buick area, where precincts had previously been occupied by comparatively low income whites who had already been returning Democratic majorities in excess of the average, the change in voting behavior is less striking. Even so, the arrival of Negroes brought a perceptible increase in Democratic margins. For example, the wholly white population of Precinct 4 voted sixty-three per cent Democratic in 1950, compared with the metropolitan area's average of fifty-three per cent in that year. (The graph in Figure 33.4, therefore, records a 1950 Democratic deviation of +10 percentage points.) By 1962, after the precinct had become almost solidly Negro, it returned a top-heavy Democratic majority of eighty-seven per cent, thirty-six percentage points above the average for the metropolitan area, as the graph shows. In short, the Negro migration brought with it an absolute Democratic increase of twenty-four percentage points or twenty-six points if the figure is adjusted relative to the city total.

Electoral Maps as Reflections of Intercensal Population Changes

In some instances changes in voting were so abrupt that one can pinpoint the date of Negro occupance simply by comparing Democratic margins from one election to another. Census data show, for example, that the populated portions of Precincts 50 and 52 were occupied by Negroes at some time between 1950 and 1960.[22] Figure 33.4, however, strongly suggests that Negro migration into Precinct 52 did not begin until after the 1952 election and that the white population had been essentially replaced by 1956. In Precinct 50, by contrast, it seems probable that migration began shortly after 1954, but that subsequent Negro occupation proceeded more slowly and gradually than in Precinct 52.

The same reasoning can be applied to areas on the margins of the Buick neighborhoods, but the pattern of Negro occupance was apparently somewhat different than along the boundaries of the Thread Lake area. Although one might expect that southward expansion would have proceeded seriatim through Precincts 4, 3, and 2, respectively, the surge of Democratic strength is almost contemporaneous in all three, suggesting that this extension of the Buick neighborhood occurred by a simultaneous Negro occupation of the whole area, rather than as a block-by-block advance. Along the northern boundaries of the Buick neighborhood as well, the graphs for Precincts 96 and 10 also give evidence of simultaneous replacement of white population.

Suburbanization and Negro Voting

The maps reveal another aspect of Negro voting which bodes no good for the Flint Republican Party. Although, as has already been noted, there is a commonly recognized relationship between high-income levels and heavy Republican voting, this relationship apparently does not now hold in Flint's Negro areas, where even the wealthiest neighborhoods return huge Democratic pluralities. The relationship may have applied between 1934 and 1950, when the first Negroes were transferring their loyalties from the Republicans to the Democrats, but even during that period, the only effect of economic differences may have been to slow the transition in the relatively high-income Thread Lake neighborhood, and perhaps to hasten it in the area's slums.

Evidence for this idea is provided in recent events along the eastern fringe of the Thread Lake neighborhood where wealthy Negroes have moved into a relatively luxurious new subdivision, which, despite its location inside the city limits, has a typically suburban atmosphere.[23] If these Negroes had reacted politically in the same way that white minority groups have done in other parts of the nation —that is, if they had become more conservative as they moved to the green suburbs—

22. The phrase "populated portions" is important, especially in reference to Precinct 52. Most of this precinct is industrial, commercial, or vacant land; houses occupy only the extreme western part. Thus, although Negroes moved into a mere fraction of the precinct's total area they effectively supplanted most of the white residents.

23. The new subdivision was built in the late 1950s, and thus is not shown on the 1950 map of high-income neighborhoods (Map 33.2). It can be located, however, by comparing the maps of Negro population for 1950 and 1960 (Map 33.1), and noting the expanded Negro area on the eastern fringes of the Thread Lake neighborhood.

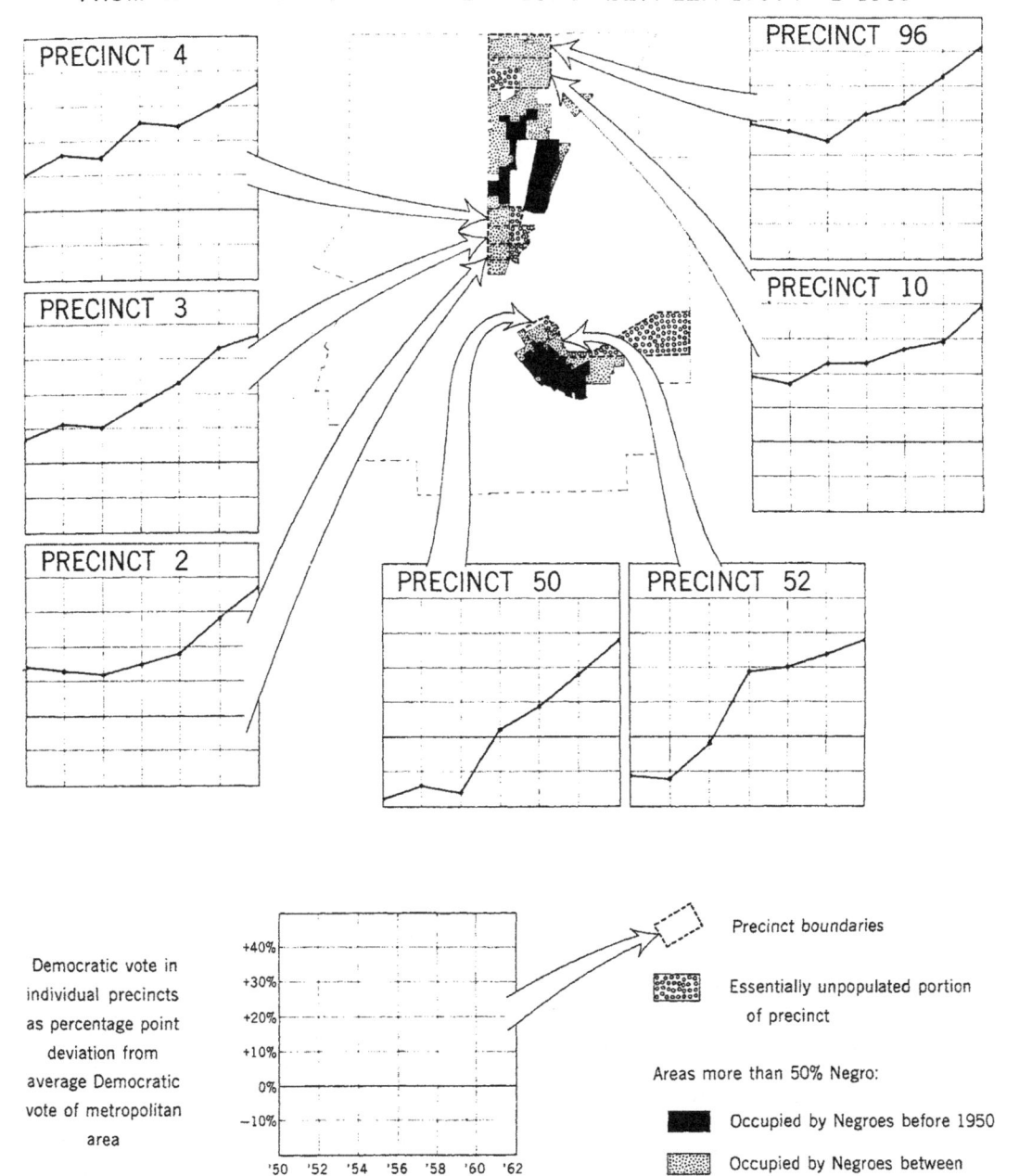

Impact of Negro Migration on Electoral Geography   403

Fig. 33.4 CHANGES IN DEMOCRATIC STRENGTH OF PRECINCTS WHOSE POPULATION CHANGED FROM CHIEFLY WHITE TO CHIEFLY NEGRO BETWEEN 1950 AND 1960

this new subdivision should have returned a Republican majority, or, at the very least, there should have been a sharp reduction in Democratic majorities in contrast to the balance of Flint's Negroes. In fact, no such thing happened. In the 1962 election (in previous years, the area was located in so large a precinct that analysis of its vote was impossible) the subdivision gave eighty-three per cent of its vote to the Democrats, a majority nearly as high as those produced by the poorest sections of the Buick neighborhood. In short, if this single instance is a reliable indicator, it would seem that racial consciousness among Flint Negroes has immunized them against Republican appeals which have long been successful among white minority groups in wealthy new suburban areas elsewhere.

A REVALUATION OF METHODOLOGY

This cartographic analysis of the relationship between Negro migration and the changing electoral geography of Flint permits the drawing of two general conclusions. The first concerns the virtues and limitations of the overlay technique as a method of electoral analysis, in short, as a tool for students of political behavior. The second deals with the utility of detailed electoral maps to the human geographer.

(1) The example of Flint suggests that map overlays can yield useful information about the voting behavior of minority groups in American cities, providing that certain preconditions are fulfilled. In the first place, the population whose voting is under study must occupy a well-defined geographic area, so that on a map the population can be clearly associated with that area and no other. The Negro populations of Northern American cities, which commonly occupy clearly bounded ghettos, obviously meet this criterion. Where neighborhood boundaries are ill-defined or gradational (e.g., the boundaries of Flint's high-income areas), map overlays are less satisfactory, and where a given minority group is assimilated with the general population, overlays probably would not work at all. It might be possible, for example, to use electoral overlays in studying the voting behavior of European immigrants in eastern cities in the early part of the century before they had become assimilated. In contrast, map overlays probably would be of no use in a study of the voting behavior of Baptists, for the simple reason that a peculiarly Baptist neighborhood probably does not exist in any American city.

A second precondition for the use of electoral overlays is that the population group under study must exhibit extremes of voting behavior, such as the Democratic vote of Flint Negroes, or the Republican vote of the city's wealthy population.[24] It was only this extremely partisan behavior, after all, that permitted the drawing of threshold isopleths which separated the uniquely high Democratic majorities of Flint's Negro areas from the more moderate voting behavior of white neighborhoods, and thus permitted the association of Negroes with the Democratic Party after the mid-1930's.

Such extremely partisan voting as that exhibited by Northern Negroes, however, is not common, as Harris has suggested,[25] and it might therefore appear that the utility of map overlays as tools of electoral analysis is limited to unusual situations. This limitation, however, is more apparent than real. When one considers the possibility of mathematical manipulation of election returns, beyond the calculation of simple percentages of votes cast, the possibilities for fruitful research with detailed electoral maps are considerably extended. One example of such research is a recent unpublished paper by Burton Witthuhn, a graduate student at The Pennsylvania State University, who mapped the residuals from a simple linear regression,[26] relating the degree of urbanization in each of Pennsylvania's sixty-seven counties with the percentage of Democratic votes cast in those same counties. Witthuhn found, not surprisingly, a fair degree of association between these two phenomena ($r^2 = 0.31$), but he also discovered that his map of residuals showed marked resemblance to a map of Pennsyl-

---

24. McCarty and Salisbury, *op. cit.*, make the same point when they note that "only in cases in which the degree of association is very high does the process (of visual comparison) produce results which approach the standards of accuracy generally demanded in present-day research and teaching."

25. *Supra*, footnote 1.

26. The method of mapping residuals from regression is illustrated in Robinson, *op. cit.*, pp. 414 ff. See especially Figure 1, p. 415.

vania's foreign-born population. Witthuhn's map of residuals, therefore, led him to undertake a multiple correlation, in which urbanization and foreign-born population were both treated as independent variables, and which produced a significantly higher coefficient of determination ($R^2 = 0.65$). A second map of residuals drawn from this multiple regression produced no immediately recognizable pattern, but it showed areas of strong negative and positive residuals which merit investigation. Witthuhn's procedure, in short, proves two things: first, that the extremes of political behavior which are needed for the making of useful electoral maps can be described in other ways than by simple percentages; secondly, that the mapping of intelligently manipulated electoral data can help the student of political behavior by pinpointing areas of profitable inquiry.

(2) The example of Flint also suggests the potential importance of precinct-by-precinct electoral maps as research tools for the social or population geographer, even though his interests lie neither in the field of voting behavior, nor even in electoral geography. An electoral map, after all, is simply a special kind of population map, which shows the distribution of people with given political attitudes. Where extreme political attitudes can be linked with certain population groups, it is obvious that maps of election returns can be used in lieu of (or in combination with) other maps to establish the distribution of those population groups—ethnic, religious, racial, and so on. Such electoral maps are especially useful where population data are scanty or otherwise unsatisfactory. It was exactly this line of reasoning, of course, which made possible the use of electoral maps in Flint to delineate the changing boundaries of Negro neighborhoods in intercensal periods when direct counts of Negro population were unavailable. Thus, the isopleths in Map 33.5 from 1952 to 1958 represent not merely certain levels of Democratic strength, but more importantly, they provide a convenient and accurate way to delineate Flint's growing Negro neighborhoods, a delineation impossible by the use of Census data alone.

The use of electoral maps to detect spatial differences in the composition of populations, of course, is not new to population geographers nor to students of electoral behavior. To cite only two examples, Zelinsky employed a combination of electoral, demographic, and economic maps in an attempt to establish regional boundaries for the American South,[27] and Lubell used a similar technique to describe a regional dichotomy between the people of "low country" and "upcountry" South Carolina.[28] More commonly, however, geographers have sought to explain such maps, rather than to use the maps themselves as a basis for further explanation. This paper does not argue that one way is better than the other; it does argue, however, that aside from their use in electoral geography *per se*, electoral maps have been neglected as tools of research in human geography.

There are two important reasons for regretting this neglect. In this first place, there is an enormous volume of electoral data waiting to be mapped and interpreted by population geographers. Every political unit in the United States holds an election at least every two years, and sometimes oftener. Secondly, the small size of electoral precincts offers an unequalled opportunity for detailed population study. Most precincts, for example, are no larger than minor civil divisions and, in areas of relatively dense population, these minor civil divisions are commonly broken into many smaller units for purposes of tabulating votes. It is unfortunate, therefore, that most published maps of American elections have been collated on the basis of states, counties, or congressional districts— gross units indeed when compared with the average precinct. This neglect of precinct data is partly understandable, in view of the fact that it is often difficult to determine the precise location of precinct boundaries. These boundaries are notoriously fluid, and precinct numbering systems are commonly erratic. Then too, the responsibility for drawing precinct boundaries is often delegated to local municipal or township officials, each of whom must be consulted individually before an accurate map can be made. To make matters worse, these officials seldom see any reason for keeping careful records of past changes in boundaries, and are even hazy at times about their contemporary locations. These problems, however, usually evaporate

27. W. Zelinsky, "Where the South Begins: The Northern Limit of the Cis-Appalachian South in Terms of Settlement Landscape," *Social Forces*, Vol. 30 (1951), pp. 174-77.
28. Lubell, *op. cit.*, pp. 200-201.

in an urban place, where records are usually more systematic, and where, at any rate, old precinct maps can be found in the clip files of the local newspaper. Even in rural areas, however, where it may be impossible to determine the location of precinct boundaries, the mapping of returns by minor civil divisions can reveal important geographic differences which a county map obscures completely.

This paper would suggest, therefore, that human geographers would do well to examine this abundance of American election returns as a basis for making highly detailed demographic maps. There are at least two lines of investigation wherein such maps might prove fruitful. The first is similar to the line pursued in this study of Flint, where the changes in location of a given population (Negroes in this instance) can be traced by changes in the distribution of partisan strongholds. The same line of reasoning might be used, for example, in mapping the expansion of Democratic strongholds in post-Civil War Boston as a reflection of Irish settlement in hitherto Brahman and Republican neighborhoods. In a rural setting, a township-by-township map which contrasted heavy Republican voting in the 1916 and 1918 congressional elections might help to delineate the distribution of German and Scandinavian populations in portions of the upper Lakes states, where antagonism to "Wilson's War" produced a mass exodus of these two groups from the Democratic Party.[29]

A second line of inquiry would utilize detailed electoral maps to identify areas of aberrant political behavior, and thus serve as devices by which to focus attention on areas of special demographic interest. In Flint, for example, heavy Democratic margins are not expected in high-income neighborhoods; but as noted above, just such margins were produced in an area at the east end of the Thread Lake neighborhood in the 1962 election, an area, as it turned out, which coincided with Flint's only upper-income Negro subdivision. This example is so simple as to require no further elaboration, but all such situations are not so obvious. In rural central Pennsylvania, for example, top-heavy Republican majorities are typical of township after township—majorities which are fairly predictable where the population is chiefly white, Protestant, and of Anglo-Saxon origin. Certain villages and townships, however, stand out prominently on electoral maps as bastions of Democratic strength. These areas, incidentally, are invisible on a county map of Pennsylvania election returns. This deviant electoral behavior, of course, strongly suggests the presence of demographic peculiarities in these townships and villages, and poses a problem in population geography which is, to the knowledge of this author, as yet unsolved.

SUMMARY

Although this investigation has sought to explain the changing electoral geography of a particular Midwestern city during a particular time in history, one of the chief purposes has been to illustrate the value of highly detailed electoral maps as tools of research. The example of Flint suggests the possibility of using such maps to help describe the nature of group voting behavior through time, especially in American cities where statistical analysis of voting often is difficult and cumbersome. In this role, electoral maps serve the purposes of political and other behavioral sciences. The same example, however, has shown that detailed maps of election returns can also provide useful information about the present and past distribution of human populations, and thus serve the needs of human geography. In the opinion of this author, the value of such maps can be great for geographers and other behavioral scientists—a value which seems limited only by the imagination of the scholars whose tools they should be.

29. See Chapter 7, "The Myth of Isolationism" in S. Lubell, *The Future of American Politics* (2nd ed. rev.; Garden City, N.Y.: Doubleday, 1956), p. 54, footnote 30.

34

Discovering Voting Groups in the United Nations

BRUCE M. RUSSETT*

The discussion of voting groups or blocs within the United Nations General Assembly has long been a popular pastime. It is, of course, merely a special case of a wider concern with groups and coalitions in all aspects of international politics. With the apparent loosening of the early postwar bipolarity it is increasingly important to discern the number, composition, and relative strength of whatever coalitions of nations may emerge from the present seemingly transitional period.

Voting groups in the General Assembly provide a relevant datum, though hardly the only one, for an effort to identify these groups. The United Nations gives no perfect image of broader international politics; due to the one-nation one-vote principle and to the fact that it is not a world government with authority to enforce its decisions, power relationships within the Assembly are not the same as in other arenas, such as functional or geographic ones. It might well be argued that because of the majority-rule principle the smaller and poorer states have an incentive to band together in the UN that they do not have elsewhere. Thus the discovery of a "bloc" of underdeveloped countries in the UN proves nothing about the cohesion of that "bloc" in other contexts. Yet votes in the General Assembly do provide a unique set of data where many national governments commit themselves simultaneously and publicly on a wide variety of major issues. The range of issues includes almost everything of major worldwide concern; even policy positions on parochial or regional questions (the intra-bloc relations of Communist states, for instance) can often be inferred from the nations' votes on other issues. However warped or distorted an image of general world politics the General Assembly may convey, it remains one of our best sources of replicable information policy positions for its 100-plus members.

An interest in voting groups may have a number of payoffs. From a frankly manipulative point of view, it may give information which can assist American policy-makers to increase their gains in the UN political process. Of more scientific interest, it can tell us about blocs and coalitions in ways that can be related to broader theories about parliamentary behavior. And finally it can indeed give some, admittedly imperfect, information about the nature—such as bipolar or

---

Reproduced by permission of the author and publisher from *The American Political Science Review*, Vol. LX, June 1966.

* Bruce M. Russett (1935–) is Associate Professor of Political Science at Yale University and Director of the Yale Political Data Program.

multipolar, etc.—of the emerging international system.

Thus no fully satisfactory method for the identification of voting groups has yet appeared in the international organization literature. What is required is a technique which is *inductive*, given to a means of presentation which is readily *interpretable*, which shows *gradations* in agreement among nations (not just whether or not they exceed a particular level of agreement), which reliably *identifies all the groupings*, and which can be applied either to a *selected* set of issues or to *all* roll-call votes of a Session.

I believe that factor analysis, and more specifically a particular application of factor analysis, the so-called "Q-technique," is such a method. Originally developed by psychologists, during the past several years factor analysis has been employed sufficiently widely by political scientists that it probably requires no detailed introduction or justification to most readers, though its application to the United Nations has so far been limited.[1] In the most common employment of factor analysis every variable is correlated with every other variable, using the product-moment correlation coefficient. Factor analysis is then a data-reduction technique, as those variables which show high correlations among themselves and very low correlation with other variables are interpreted as pointing to a single underlying dimension, or *factor*. The factors themselves are uncorrelated with each other. Thus in Alker's initial application of the technique to UN voting patterns it was found that certain roll-calls (e.g. in 1961 on South Africa, Angola, Rhodesia, Ruanda-Urundi, trade, and economic aid) had similar voting alignments that pointed to an underlying "self-determination" issue. These voting alignments were unrelated to those on such issues as Cuba, Hungary, Tibet, and disarmament, which were like each other and pointed to a different underlying issue (the cold war). In this application each roll-call vote was a variable, with each "actor" (country) serving as an item or observation.

The versatility of factor analysis, however, suggests an alternative use. It can just as readily be used to find similar *actors* (test takers, legislators, nations) as similar *variables* (questions on a psychological test, roll-call votes). If, for example, one began with a table (matrix) where each country was a row and each column a roll-call, one could simply turn the table 90 degrees so that, in effect, the countries became variables and the roll-calls became observations. When the matrix is then factor-analyzed in this fashion the correlations identify *countries* with similar voting patterns and the factors point to voting groups or blocs. This procedure is usually designated "Q-analysis" to distinguish it from the somewhat more common technique mentioned first (R-analysis). To repeat, the procedure is inductive in that it involves no prior specification of the groups to be looked for, nor is even the number of such groups specified in advance.

Cohesive Voting Groups:
A Q-Analysis of the 18th Session

We shall illustrate the technique with an analysis of roll-call votes in the 18th Session, beginning in the autumn of 1963, and in the process be able to make some useful substantive points about the nature of politics in the Assembly. Because of the United States vs. Russia and France controversy over dues there was only a single recorded vote in the 19th (1964) Session, so these are the most recent data available or likely to become so until the *Official Records* of the 20th (1965) Session are published sometime in 1967.

Our data consist of all 66 roll-call votes, both plenary and committee, except those which are virtually unanimous (defined here as more than 90 per cent of those voting taking one side—usually in favor). This restriction is necessary because the product-moment correlation coefficient is seriously distorted by a distribution more lopsided than 90–10. The omission might result in the hiding of any very small group that was consistently in the minority, but is not likely to be important because typically such very lopsided votes account for less than 10 per cent of all those in a session. In practice the only real possibility of a group whose cohesion and isolation might be understated is the handful of states (Portugal, Spain, South

---

[1]. Hayward R. Alker, Jr., "Dimensions of Conflict in the General Assembly," *American Political Science Review*, LVIII (1964), 642–657. Hayward R. Alker, Jr., and Bruce M. Russett, *World Politics in the General Assembly* (New Haven, Conn.: Yale University Press, 1965), ch. 12.

Africa, France, Belgium, sometimes the United Kingdom) which are so out of step with the Assembly majority on African colonial issues. As we shall see below Portugal and Spain do actually cluster together anyway, and South Africa is not even included in the analysis because of high absenteeism. This example, however, constitutes a warning against processing the data too mechanically without a careful inspection of the *Records*.

On every vote each state was coded either 2 (affirmative) 1 (abstain) or 0 (negative). Absenteeism is rather frequent in the Assembly, however, and posed something of a problem. In a few cases a country, though absent, later officially recorded its position. I listed it as if it had so voted. Also, in some cases an absence is clearly intended to demonstrate opposition to the resolution, or a conviction that the Assembly is overstepping the bounds of its authority in considering the issue. The United Kingdom found itself in such a position over several votes on Southern Rhodesia in the 18th Session. In those cases I recorded the absence as a negative vote. Both of these procedures are in conformity with the practice of earlier researches.

The remaining absences are in general concentrated on a few countries, often those with small delegations. While it would sometimes be possible to estimate an absent nation's voting position from the votes of other states in its geographical area or caucusing group, in our inductive search for voting groups such a procedure would prejudice the results and would not be admissible. Instead I chose to equate an absence with abstention. In many instances an absence does in fact mean abstention, but by no means always, and when it does not the result is to incorporate a degree of imprecision in the analysis. The average absenteeism for the Assembly is about 12 per cent, and for the vast majority of states less than 25 per cent. Since the equation of absence with abstention actually assigns a state to a middle position on our three-point scale, and since it is sometimes the correct interpretation anyway, this treatment of absences will not seriously distort the voting position of all countries with 25 per cent for fewer absences—their scores on the factors below are not affected by more than about 8 per cent. For those countries (11 in the 18th Session) with greater absenteeism the distortion is potentially more serious, and they are marked with a † symbol to indicate that their positions should be treated with some caution. Four other states (Dominican Republic, Honduras, Luxembourg, and South Africa) were absent more than 40 per cent of the time and so were excluded entirely from the analysis. Kenya and Zanzibar, admitted well after the Session was under way, were also omitted.

Table 34.1 presents the factor "loadings" of every country on each of the six meaningful factors which emerge from the analysis. Each factor identifies a group of countries whose voting patterns are very similar, and the loadings are product-moment correlation coefficients of a country's voting pattern with the underlying factor. The highest loadings or correlations identify those countries with the "purest" pattern, those whose voting is most fully described by the factor. Labelling the factors is always somewhat arbitrary, but in most cases the descriptive label should be appropriate. The percentages at the head of each column indicate the percentage of the total variation (variance) among all 107 countries that is explained (accounted for) by the factor. All loadings of .50 or greater have been underlined for emphasis, as loadings in the .40s are underscored with dashed lines. Squaring the correlation coefficient provides a means of discovering the amount of the country's total variance which is accounted for by the underlying factor. Thus it is reasonable largely to ignore correlations below .40 since the factor in question accounts for less than a sixth of the variance. The countries are listed in descending order of their loadings on the factor which best "explains" their voting pattern. Countries with no loading above .49 (and thus for whom no one factor "explains" as much as one-fourth of their voting variance) seemed best left "unclassifiable." In factor analytic terms the table presents the orthogonal solution, which means that the factors are uncorrelated with each other.

I have labelled the first factor "Western Community" in an attempt to indicate the predominance of European and European-settled states among those with high loadings. "Western Community" in this context must be interpreted as a cultural and not just a geographical phenomenon, including the white Commonwealth. This relationship is

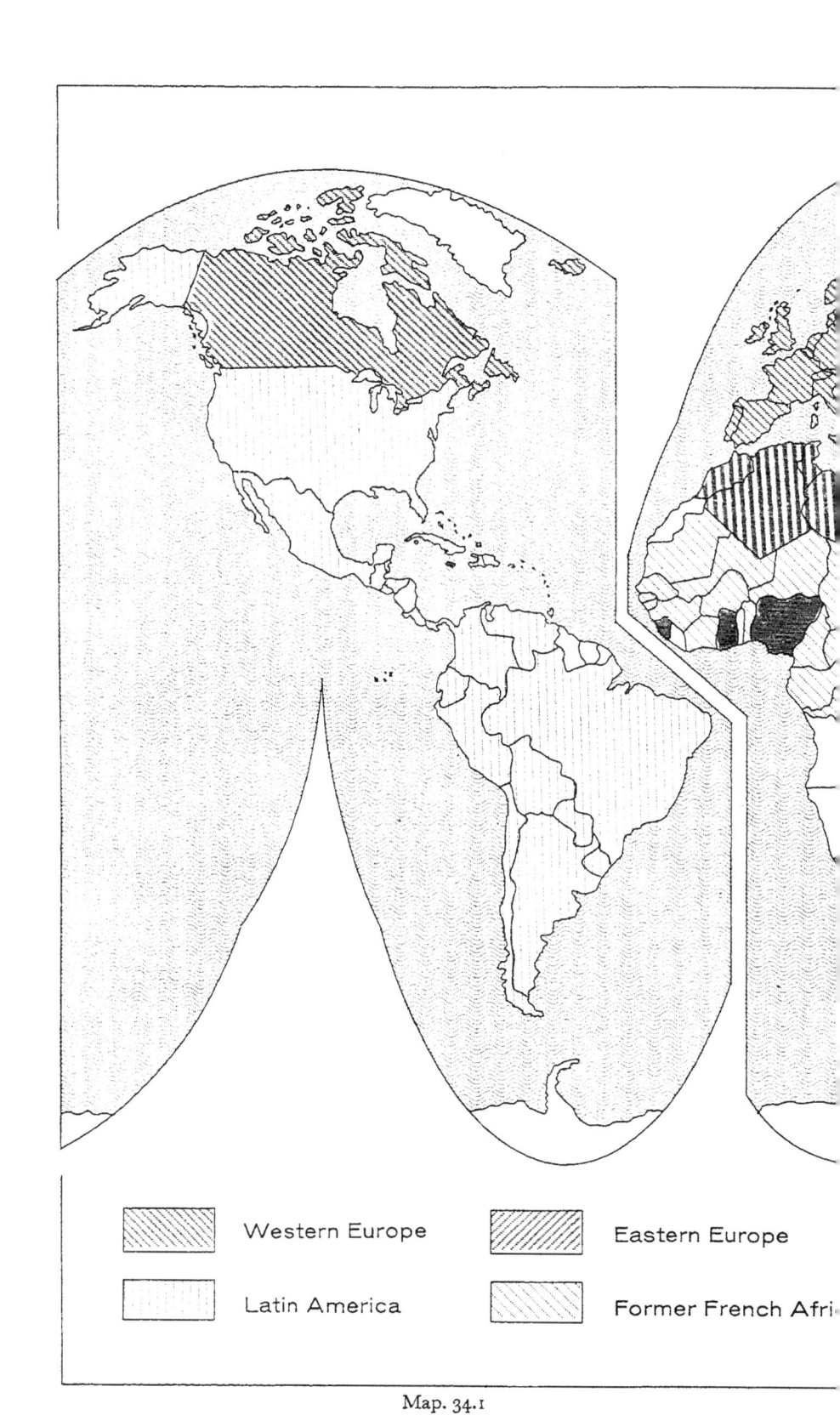

| | Western Europe | | Eastern Europe |
| | Latin America | | Former French Afri- |

Map. 34.1
Map reprinted from Bruce M. Russett, *International Regions and the
International System* (Chicago: Rand McNally, 1967), pp. 72–73.

| Former British Africa | Asia |
| Arabs |

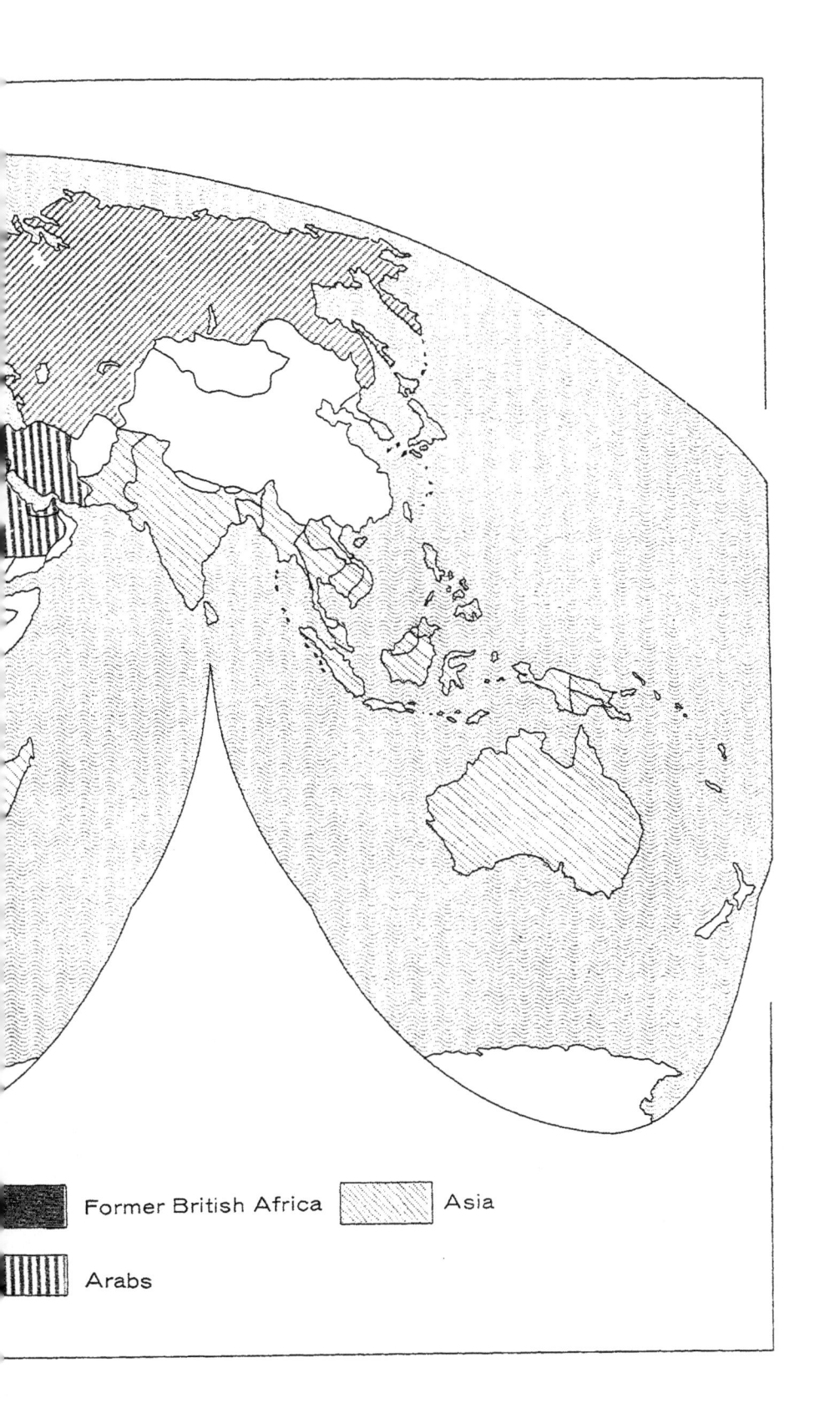

indicated by the fact that of 35 U.N. members either physically located in Europe or whose population is predominantly of European origin (Argentina, Australia, Canada, Costa Rica, Cyprus, New Zealand, Uruguay, and United States), 22 have loadings of .50 or greater on the second factor. This works out to a fairly low correlation coefficient of .35. Each of the top 15 loadings, however, is held by such a country.

Note also the high loadings of Japan and (nationalist) China on this factor. Japan's basic foreign policy has become quite well integrated with those of her North Atlantic associates in recent years, and is so perceived by Afro-Asian observers. Nationalist China is of course heavily dependent upon United States military and diplomatic support. This leads to another observation about the factor: among those with .50 or higher loadings are 33 of the 38 U.N. members who have a formal military alliance with the United States (including the United States itself and counting Iran). Such a close association produces a correlation of .79. France is by far the lowest of all NATO allies on this factor, with also a strong *negative* loading on the Afro-Asian factor (number three).

TABLE 34.1   United Nations groupings in 1963

Nation	Factor 1 "Western Community" 23%	Factor 2 "Brazzaville Africans" 17%	Factor 3 "Afro-Asians" 16%	Factor 4 "Communist Bloc" 11%	Factor 5 "Conservative Arabs" 4%	Factor 6 "Iberia" 2%
\multicolumn{7}{c}{"Western Community"}
Denmark	.90	.12	−.02	−.27	−.01	−.17
Norway	.89	.10	−.03	−.23	−.11	−.04
Sweden	.89	.09	−.03	−.25	−.12	−.09
Finland	.88	.06	.03	−.22	−.04	−.10
Austria	.87	.20	.00	−.17	−.10	−.01
Ireland	.86	.15	−.08	−.25	.16	−.03
Turkey	.83	.18	−.10	−.33	−.04	.23
Australia	.82	.10	−.15	−.38	.01	.10
Belgium	.82	.13	−.15	−.44	−.07	.15
New Zealand	.82	.17	−.14	−.27	.07	.05
Iceland	.82	.14	−.05	−.22	.14	−.20
United States	.81	.07	.23	−.27	.09	.23
Italy	.81	.12	−.12	−.37	.14	.11
Canada	.80	.09	−.15	−.44	−.02	.17
Netherlands	.80	.05	−.11	−.46	.03	.09
Japan	.76	.23	−.11	−.33	.31	.06
China	.75	.40	−.01	−.11	.07	.09
United Kingdom	.72	−.16	−.22	−.46	.07	.09
Greece	.71	.23	−.21	−.29	−.03	.15
*Venezuela	.70	.52	−.01	−.07	.13	−.02
*Argentina	.70	.49	−.04	−.10	.12	.09
*Guatemala	.65	.52	.07	−.17	.09	−.05
*Panama	.63	.51	.05	.08	.09	.05
*Colombia	.62	.52	.15	.08	.16	.09
*Ecuador	.62	.50	−.05	−.06	.32	.05
Iran	.61	.38	−.01	−.04	.33	−.04
*Costa Rica	.61	.61	.09	.11	.11	.05

* Moderately high loadings on Factors 1 and 2.

TABLE 34.1.—(Continued)

Nation	Factor 1 "Western Community" 23%	Factor 2 "Brazzaville Africans" 17%	Factor 3 "Afro-Asians" 16%	Factor 4 "Communist Bloc" 11%	Factor 5 "Conservative Arabs" 4%	Factor 6 "Iberia" 2%
*Mexico	.61	.52	.11	.01	.39	-.07
*Thailand	.60	.52	.05	-.02	.15	.14
*Jamaica	.59	.51	.03	.06	.32	-.19
†El Salvador	.59	.36	.00	-.29	.29	.34
France	.59	.01	-.48	-.02	-.23	.27
*Chile	.58	.52	.28	-.08	.18	.05
*Brazil	.56	.43	.01	-.04	.10	.05
*Peru	.56	.49	.03	.02	.17	.34
*Malaysia	.55	.55	.21	.06	.43	.03
†Nicaragua	.55	.38	.09	-.32	.02	.17
*Paraguay	.53	.47	.00	-.20	.19	.18
"Brazzaville Africans"						
Chad	.12	.87	.17	.01	-.03	.06
Cameroun	.20	.79	.29	-.08	-.08	-.06
†Gabon	.20	.79	.23	.08	.06	.04
Central African Rep.	.17	.78	.03	.01	-.09	.10
Niger	.02	.78	.34	-.03	.04	.14
Congo (B)	.07	.77	.28	.08	-.09	-.00
Rwanda	.23	.76	.16	-.09	.05	-.20
†Haiti	.16	.74	-.06	.00	.01	.10
Ivory Coast	.08	.73	.35	-.04	.27	-.04
Upper Volta	-.09	.73	.37	.05	-.12	-.06
Congo (L)	.22	.72	.22	.01	.01	-.17
*Cyprus	.52	.71	.04	-.06	.08	.01
Dahomey	.07	.70	.32	-.03	.05	-.11
†Bolivia	.37	.68	.10	-.15	.14	.01
Senegal	.12	.68	.26	.19	.19	.15
Uruguay	.35	.68	.11	.08	.23	.04
*Philippines	.49	.63	.09	-.05	.26	.03
Madagascar	.39	.62	.05	-.14	.32	-.09
Sierra Leone	.05	.62	.41	-.01	-.02	-.09
Liberia	.41	.62	.09	-.14	.32	-.17
Togo	.09	.62	.49	-.02	.23	-.01
*Israel	.43	.53	-.04	-.18	.04	-.31
*Pakistan	.50	.51	.21	.01	.09	-.09
"Afro-Asians"						
Ghana	-.09	.14	.88	.17	-.11	-.04
Afghanistan	.15	.15	.84	.23	-.00	.06
Indonesia	-.17	.08	.82	.13	-.19	.12
Egypt	-.09	.07	.82	.30	.06	.06

* Moderately high loadings on Factors 1 and 2.
† More than 25% absenteeism (but less than 40%); absent equated with abstain.

TABLE 34.1.—(Continued)

Nation	Factor 1 "Western Community" 23%	Factor 2 "Brazzaville Africans" 17%	Factor 3 "Afro-Asians" 16%	Factor 4 "Communist Bloc" 11%	Factor 5 "Conservative Arabs" 4%	Factor 6 "Iberia" 2%
Syria	−.05	.09	.82	.30	.04	.07
Ethiopia	−.02	.11	.82	.18	.00	−.14
Yugoslavia	−.18	.15	.80	.29	−.03	.02
India	.12	.19	.75	.02	.31	−.07
Algeria	−.22	.16	.74	.40	.09	.02
Nigeria	.01	.26	.74	−.13	.04	.25
Iraq	−.24	.15	.73	.30	.25	−.04
Tunisia	−.02	.25	.73	.13	−.01	−.07
†Burma	.05	.13	.72	.24	−.06	.08
Cambodia	−.13	.13	.72	.31	.03	−.03
Tanganyika	−.18	.33	.67	.22	.10	−.16
Guinea	−.13	.29	.67	.32	.09	.05
Mali	−.25	.09	.65	.42	.27	−.11
Ceylon	.02	.19	.65	.21	.05	−.02
Sudan	.00	.24	.60	.24	.05	−.09
Morocco	−.15	.13	.58	.35	.40	−.06
†Somalia	−.04	.22	.55	.11	.08	−.27
†Uganda	−.02	.32	.55	.27	.06	.03
†Yemen	−.02	.24	.53	.32	.04	−.13
"Communist Bloc"						
Czechoslovakia	−.42	−.04	.28	.85	−.02	−.02
U.S.S.R.	−.42	−.04	.28	.85	−.02	−.02
Bulgaria	−.41	−.05	.29	.85	−.03	−.02
Byelorussia	−.42	−.05	.29	.85	.07	−.06
Poland	−.42	−.05	.29	.85	.07	−.06
Cuba	−.36	.00	.28	.85	−.07	−.02
Romania	−.39	−.05	.32	.84	−.02	.02
Ukraine	−.45	−.02	.28	.83	−.04	−.03
Hungary	−.40	−.07	.27	.83	.16	−.08
Mongolia	−.42	−.06	.29	.82	.16	−.10
Albania	−.27	.01	−.49	.59	−.05	−.07
"Conservative Arabs"						
Lebanon	.09	.16	.46	.08	.66	.10
Jordan	.17	.34	.46	.25	.58	−.03
Libya	.21	.44	.45	.01	.54	−.05
Mauritania	.08	.53	.38	.18	.49	.00
Kuwait	.14	.29	.58	.24	.47	−.06
"Iberia"						
Portugal	.23	−.25	−.06	−.44	−.08	.68
Spain	.52	.13	−.11	−.26	.09	.66

† More than 25% absenteeism (but less than 40%); absent equated with abstain.

TABLE 34.1.—(Continued)

Nation	Factor 1 "Western Community" 23%	Factor 2 "Brazzaville Africans" 17%	Factor 3 "Afro-Asians" 16%	Factor 4 "Communist Bloc" 11%	Factor 5 "Conservative Arabs" 4%	Factor 6 "Iberia" 2%
			Unclassifiable			
Burundi	.14	.30	.48	.19	−.09	−.17
†Laos	.26	.19	.40	.07	.27	.04
Nepal	.14	.36	.47	−.06	.04	−.01
†Saudi Arabia	.22	.14	.39	.32	.18	.15
Trinidad & Tobago	.42	.41	.18	.06	.07	−.03

† More than 25% absenteeism (but less than 40%); absent equated with abstain.

The second factor is named "Brazzaville Africans," though the name is far from perfect and a number of non-African states also correlate with it. The six highest loadings, and 14 above .50 in all, are possessed by countries which were members of the former Brazzaville caucusing group, of whom all but the Congo (Leopoldville) were ex-French colonies. Both the Brazzaville and Casablanca groupings had been formally dissolved by the 18th (1963) Session, ostensibly in the interest of promoting African unity, but the essential differences in voting patterns seem still to persist. Note also the high loadings of Haiti (Negro, very under-developed) and of several Asian and Latin American states. Previous studies have noted that the Brazzaville states tend to be less anti-Western on cold war issues than the Afro-Asian "neutralists," but more so, and especially on colonial questions, than the typical Latin American state. This second factor then picks out, in addition to the Brazzaville Africans, both several of the more pro-Western Asians (Philippines and Pakistan, plus Israel) and a number of Latin Americans who are rather to the "east" of their caucusing group (Uruguay and Bolivia, for example). The first two factors together account for 40 per cent of the total roll-call variance, and indicate most of the states which can generally be expected to take the Western position on most cold war issues.

The third factor quite clearly picks out those Asians and Africans sometimes identified by the term Afro-Asian neutralists. More often than not they vote with the Soviet Union on both cold war and colonial questions. They include such long-time leaders of this group as Egypt, India, and Indonesia, most of the Arab countries, Yugoslavia, and a number of African states, especially (but not only) those with rather leftist governments which belonged to the former "Casablanca" caucusing group. And while these are (except for Yugoslavia) non-Communist governments, of 24 U.N. members outside of the Sino-Soviet bloc known to have received economic and/or military aid from China, the U.S.S.R., or Eastern Europe by mid-1962, 19 have loadings of at least .05 with this third factor. Using all 96 non-Soviet bloc governments in this table, and simple receipt or non-receipt of Sino-Soviet aid as the variable, this produces a correlation (r) of .72. All of the top nine countries on this factor received such aid.

Not surprisingly, the Soviet bloc accounts for the other major factor. Only Communist states load heavily on this factor—though Yugoslavia emphatically does not and belongs with Factor 3. Cuba and Mongolia are virtually indistinguishable from the European members of the bloc. But one important evidence of the crack in what had in previous years been a solid voting alignment is the behavior of Albania. Since the defection of Yugoslavia in 1948 this is the first time that any study of the United Nations has shown a noticeable deviation by a Communist nation. Albania's loading on the factor is a mere .59, and if we return to the original votes from which the factor analysis is derived, Albania's voting pattern correlates but .75 with those of other Soviet "bloc" states. That is, voting by the U.S.S.R. "accounts for" little more than half the variance in Albania's behavior in the Assembly.

Finally, there are two minor factors, each accounting for but four and two per cent of the total variance. Factor five has three countries loading highly on it: Lebanon, Jordan, and Libya. The name "Conservative Arabs" seems appropriate, for all are non-revolutionary regimes, in cold-war politics these states vote relatively often with the Western powers, and each has received substantial foreign aid from the United States. Factor six picks out Portugal and Spain only; the label "Iberia" is obvious.

Most commonly in a factor analysis of this sort the factors can with relative ease be used to identify "groups" of variables (in this case nations). This is true for four of our six factors, but not for two other. Many of the countries loading on Factors 1 or 2 (called "Western Community" and "Brazzaville Africans") actually show fairly high loadings on *both* factors, so that they cannot unequivocally be identified with either. The majority of states with loadings between .50 and .70 on either factor share this property. In such circumstances it is often useful to make a scattergram and plot the positions of the countries in question on the two competing factors. Figure 34.1 is a graph where the

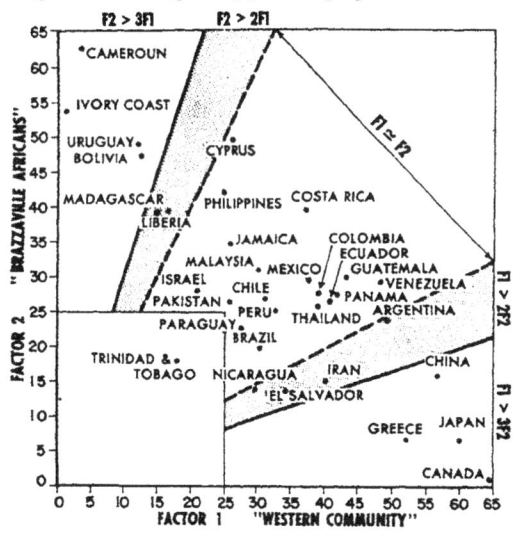

Fig. 34.1 "Latin American" grouping as identified by moderate loadings on Factors 1 and 2

vertical axis represents the percentage of variance (simply 100 times the factor loading squared) accounted for by Factor 2, and the horizontal axis the percentage explained by Factor 1. All countries with loadings of .40 or higher on *both* factors are represented, as well as a couple of others for reference.

In some instances one factor accounts for three or more times as much of a country's variance as does the other, and when this happens there is little question as to where the nation should be grouped. This applies, for example, to Uruguay and Bolivia, for whom Factor 2 accounts for almost 50 per cent of the variance and Factor 1 less than 15 per cent. Any country which occupies a position either between the vertical axis and the sloping solid line to its right, or between the horizontal axis and the sloping solid line above it, has this variance ratio of more than three to one. The sloping dashed lines to the right and above the solid ones respectively mark the gray area where the variance ratio is over two to one. Although the countries occupying this space are distinctly more marginal than one lying closer to the axes, it is probably not unreasonable still to assign them as weak members of the group whose factor accounts for more than twice as much variance as any other. Most clearly it seems appropriate to think of Liberia and Madagascar with the "Brazzaville" countries. And for any state which has less than 25 per cent of its variance accounted for by any factor (e.g. Trinidad & Tobago) we have little choice but to term it "unclassifiable." The square in the lower left marks out this area of the diagram.

But for the countries where the percentage of variance explained by the most powerful factor is less than twice that of the next most important factor, it may be misleading to label them as belonging with either of the groups for which the factor is named. This is especially so in the situation illustrated in the above figure, where no less than 18 states occupy the area between the two dashed lines. Here we must speak of yet another voting group, which we can label "Latin America." Twelve of these nations are physically located in the Western Hemisphere. With Honduras and the Dominican Republic excluded from our analysis for excessive absenteeism, only Haiti, Bolivia, Uruguay, Cuba, Trinidad & Tobago (in the lower left box) El Salvador, Argentina, and Nicaragua do not fall into this area. And the latter two are extremely marginal. Those 20 countries (including Argentina and Nicaragua) have been marked with an asterisk in Table 34.1 and should be considered as comprising a separate group. A number of pro-Western Asian states—Malaysia, Thailand,

Pakistan, Philippines and Israel—have quite similar voting patterns.

. . . .

Voting Groups and General Assembly Politics

In the Q-analysis we found that an inductive procedure identified six factors, and through them seven voting groups, in the Assembly. The six factors together accounted for 73 per cent of all the countries' variance. Thus the political process is relatively structured and subject to description by a small number of alignments. Yet the groups resembled only to a limited degree those which would be discovered from a list of geographical or caucusing groups alone. While geographical labels have sometimes been used they are very approximate and neither inclusive nor exclusive (e.g., "Brazzaville Africans"). Of our inductively-derived groups only the "Communists" closely resembled a caucusing group in terms both of who was included and who excluded.

In contrast to the mere evidence of caucusing groups the Q-analysis reveals other politically based groupings as follows.

1. The members of the Scandinavian caucusing group do indeed agree almost entirely among themselves in this Session, but Ireland and Austria differ from them in no significant way.

2. Analysis of the Latin American caucusing group would find a moderate element of cohesion, but entirely miss the very high similarity of Israel and several pro-Western Asians to the Latin voting pattern.

3. If the examination were based on caucusing groups extant in 1963 it would also not uncover the great consensus remaining within the officially disbanded Brazzaville and Casablanca groups.

4. The convergence of interest among the North Atlantic countries would not be found by examining any formal caucusing group.

The use of an inductive procedure also permits us to make some more general statements about politics in the Assembly. A simplified East-West-Neutral categorization which has characterized so much journalistic and even scholarly analysis of the world organization is utterly misleading. In terms of the states' behavior, five major groups (on four factors) emerge, in addition to two small groups and a few marginal countries. It should be emphasized that the identification of these groups depends upon their final behavior in the vote, not upon tacit or explicit bargaining among diverse log-rolling coalitions which may exchange promises of support before the vote. It might be supposed, for instance, that one set of countries might offer its support to another set on cold war issues, in response to the other's votes on a self-determination roll-call. While this kind of bargaining undoubtedly does occur, an analysis of voting patterns alone would not find it since both sets of countries would *vote* identically, whatever their reasons for doing so. But a number of groups in the General Assembly retain their distinctiveness in the actual balloting. Two or more groups must combine to make a majority, and majorities on each of the different super-issues are composed differently. Comparisons with politics within national parliamentary assemblies may provide many fruitful insights and hypotheses, but the multiparty pattern of shifting coalitions that was approximated in the French Third and Fourth Republic may provide a closer analogy than will the aggregation of multiple interests within two stable parties as in Britain or even the United States.

Finally, there is reason to believe that this multi-group phenomenon is not especially new. It existed both before the well-known conflicts within NATO and the communist countries became evident, and largely before the admission of most of the new states. I conducted a similar Q-analysis of voters in the 1952 and 1957 sessions, to be reported upon more fully elsewhere.[2] By the same criteria employed here the 1952 analysis found four groups, and the 1957 analysis uncovered eight, though four were quite small. Therefore the discovery of but five large groups and two small ones in 1963 comes as something of a surprise, especially since the 1952 and 1957 analyses were performed on only 57 and 81 countries respectively. The expansion of Assembly membership (to 107 for purposes of this analysis) has in fact outpaced the differentiation of new voting groups. Nor has their composition

2. Bruce M. Russett, *International Regions and the International System* (Chicago: Rand McNally, 1967).

altered radically. Except for the emergence of the "Brazzaville" group and a certain greater differentiation between most other Afro-Asians and a somewhat pro-Western minority, the changes over the three sessions have not been great. Recent discoveries of a complex pattern of relationships in the General Assembly not only identify new reality but also show some lag between reality and our perception of it.

Annotated Bibliography

ALMOND, GABRIEL A. and SIDNEY VERBA
The Civic Culture, (Boston: Little, Brown and Co., 1965).
    A thorough study contrasting political attitudes in five countries—Germany, Italy, Mexico, Great Britain, and the United States. The authors contrast knowledge and attitudes to participation (system inputs) and to governing (system outputs). Chapter 12 summarizes the theoretical contrasts in national political behavior.

BACKSTROM, CHARLES H. and GERALD D. HURSH
Survey Research, (Evanston: Northwestern University Press, 1963).
    Available in paperback, this is an excellent handbook for anyone engaging in survey research. The authors deal with such topics as research design, sampling, interview and questionnaire construction, field work, and data processing.

BANFIELD, EDWARD C.
The Moral Basis of a Backward Society (Glencoe: Free Press, 1958).
    A study of political behavior in a small village in southern Italy. The author describes the inhabitants as "amoral familists" who act according to the rule: maximize the material, short-run advantage of the nuclear family; assume that all others will do likewise. Seventeen rules of behavior are suggested which flow from the general rule.

BERELSON, BERNARD and GARY A. STEINER
Human Behavior: An Inventory of Scientific Findings (N.Y.: Harcourt, Brace and World, 1964).
    As the subtitle indicates, this volume is a summary of scientific knowledge about human behavior as of 1964. Definition and propositions are presented as well as full bibliographical citations to the literature.

BUCHANAN, WILLIAM and HADLEY CANTRIL
How Nations See Each Other (Urbana: University of Illinois Press, 1953).
    Based upon surveys in nine countries—Australia, Britain, France, Germany, Italy, Mexico, Netherlands, Norway, and the United States,—the authors compare international differences in class consciousness, personal security, friendliness and tensions, national stereotypes, and national character.

BUCKLEY, WALTER, ed.
Modern Systems Research for the Behavioral Scientist (Chicago: Aldine, 1968).
    A source book of materials from general systems research, cybernetics, and information and communications theory which provides a useful overview of basic theory and current interdisciplinary research. Examines the systemic nature of behavior on three levels—organismic and evolutionary, psychological, and sociocultural. An essential collection for those interested in relating behavior to general systems.

BURGHARDT, ANDREW F.
"The Bases of Support for Political Parties in Burgenland," *Annals of the Association of American Geographers*, LIV (September 1964), pp. 372-390.
    An analysis of geographical patterns of voting behavior, relating political support to demographic and economic characteristics of the population in a province of Austria. The author concludes that location and religion were the principal factors influencing voting.

CAMPBELL, ANGUS, *et al.*
The American Voter (N.Y.: John Wiley and Sons, 1960).
    The classic volume on American voting behavior which is indispensible to any student of electoral topics.

CONVERSE, PHILIP E., AAGE R. CLAUSEN, and WARREN E. MILLER
"Electoral Myth and Reality: The 1964 Election," *American Political Science Review*, LIX (June 1965), pp. 321-336.

Using data collected by the Survey Research Center, this study examines the gap between the perception and reality of what is known about the 1964 presidential election. Useful to geographers principally for its consideration of the role of perception in the formulation of spatial strategy in the campaign.

Cox, Kevin R.
"Suburbia and Voting Behavior in the London Metropolitan Area," *Annals of the Association of American Geographers*, LVIII (March 1968), pp. 111–127.

A study of the spatial contrasts in party preference and turnout between suburbs and the central city in the London metropolitan area. The author employs both factor and correlation techniques and attempts to develop a causal model.

Deutsch, Karl W.
The Nerves of Government (N.Y.: Free Press, 1966).

Part I, "The Search for Models of Society and Politics" is an excellent review of the general nature of theory and models, classic organic and mechanistic models, recent social science models, and game theory.

Girod, Roger
"Geography of the Swiss Party System," in Erik Allardt and Yrjo Littunen, eds., *Cleavages, Ideologies and Party Systems* (Helsinki: Westermarck Society, Transactions, Vol. X, 1964), pp. 132–161.

Utilizing such data as election returns, questionnaires, and historical archives, the author examines patterns of party support, competition, and cooperation. The study devotes attention to both the cantonal and communal levels of party organization.

Goguel, François
Géographie des élections françaises de 1870 à 1951 (Paris: Armand Colin, 1951).

A classic study in electoral geography which consists of a series of maps and commentaries followed by a brief interpretive essay which relates election results to socio-economic distributions.

Guetzkow, Harold
"A Use of Simulation in the Study of Inter-Nation Relations," *Behavioral Science*, IV (July 1959), pp. 183–191.

A description of the author's experiments with simulation in an international setting, which includes such activities as resource allocation decisions and spatial interaction. He suggests possible uses for simulation in model-building and training.

Hall, Edward T.
The Hidden Dimension (Garden City, N.Y.: Doubleday and Co., 1966).

An anthropologist's analysis of the role of proxemics in human behavior which may be one of the most valuable works for political geographers produced in spatial behavior. The cross-cultural comparisons of how people use space are particularly useful.

Herman, Theodore
"Group Values Toward the National Space: The Case of China," *Geographical Review*, XLIX (1959), pp. 164–182.

Based upon a review of the writings of China's literary and political elite, the author analyzes the values and attitudes of the dominant group toward the national space of China. Pride in an old culture, a strong defensiveness against inroads to China's areal control, and the demand for economic, political and social improvements are the key values.

Hoffman, Stanley
"Perceptions, Reality, and the Franco-American Conflict," *Journal of International Affairs*, XXI, No. 1 (1967), pp. 57–71.

An evaluation of the role that contrasting views of international affairs and inter-nation perception have played in the French-American conflict. The author devotes special attention to the repercussions of contrasting perception on the issues of Vietnam and Europe.

Kasperson, Roger E.
The Dodecanese: Diversity and Unity in Island Politics (Chicago: University of Chicago, Department of Geography Research Paper No. 108, 1966).

An examination of the effects of such experiences as sponge-fishing, emigration and depopulation, and changing political sovereignty upon spatial variations in political attitudes and behavior.

Kasperson, Roger E.
"Political Behavior and the Decision-Making Process in the Allocation of Water Resources Between Recreational and Municipal Use," *Natural Resources Journal*, VIII, No. 2 (1969).

An analysis of political behavior in a crisis situation involving resource allocations. The author deals with such variables as perception, knowledge, attitudes and participation. Both interviews and content analysis are employed in the research.

Kelman, Herbert C., ed.
International Behavior: A Social-Psychological Analysis (N.Y.: Holt, Rinehart, and Winston, 1966).

A collection of original essays dealing with the socio-psychological processes occurring when nationals and governments interact. Part I, "National and International Images," includes a number of studies analyzing the formation of images and several showing the relevance of such images to foreign policy and international conflict. Part II, "Processes of Interaction in International Relations," has contributions on bargaining, decision-making, and spatial interaction. Lengthy bibliographies are provided at the end of each essay.

KEY, V. O., Jr.
Southern Politics (N.Y.: Random House, 1940).
One of the monumental regional studies of American politics. Both the extensive use of maps and the analysis itself reflect an appreciation of the contribution of spatial analysis.

KOCH, HOWARD E., Jr., ROBERT D. NORTH, and DINA A. ZINNES
"Some Theoretical Notes on Geography and International Conflict," *Journal of Conflict Resolution*, IV (1960), pp. 4–14.
Although few will accept the definition of geography employed, the article is useful for its discussion of the interaction between "geographical elements" and patterns of international conflict. Readers will also find rewarding the treatment on concepts basic to a study of conflict.

LORENZ, KONRAD
On Aggression (N.Y.: Harcourt, Brace, and World, 1963).
A controversial study of aggression in animal species which attempts to draw parallels for human societies. Lorenz devotes special attention to the territorial structure of aggression.

MERRITT, RICHARD L.
"West Berlin: Center or Periphery?" in Richard L. Merritt and Stein Rokkan, eds., *Comparing Nations* (New Haven: Yale University Press, 1966). pp. 321–336.
Using public opinion survey results, the author examines the extent to which West Berlin lies at the center or periphery of West German life. He finds that it occupies a central role in the consciousness of West Germans but a peripheral role in day-to-day life.

MILBRATH, LESTER W.
Political Participation (Chicago: Rand McNally, 1965).
An excellent bibliographical and conceptual summary of research on this topic. Propositions of interest to political geographers are scattered throughout the volume.

PATTERSON, SAMUEL C.
"The Political Cultures of the American States," *Journal of Politics*, XXX (February 1968), pp. 187–209.
A discussion of patterns of political behavior in the United States which draws heavily upon concepts developed in *The Civic Culture*. Geographers will find the analysis of interstate variations (pp. 194–204) especially interesting.

POOL, Ithiel de Sola et al.
"The Influence of Foreign Travel on Political Attitudes of American Businessmen," *Public Opinion Quarterly*, XX (1965), pp. 161–195.
In a study of 903 heads of firms, the authors found that foreign travel broadened their range of awareness in economic and political matters. This change occurred not through liberalization but through a new framework of reference groups.

RICHARDSON, LEWIS F.
"The Problem of Contiguity: An Appendix to Statistics of Deadly Quarrels," *General Systems*, VI (1961), pp. 139–187.
A mathematical, empirical analysis of the role of geographical contiguity in the occurrence of wars within and between nations. The treatment is useful primarily for its methodological contributions, such as the discussion of topological theorems and the measurement of compactness and lengths of land and sea boundaries.

ROBERTS, MICHAEL C. and Kennerd W. RUMAGE
"The Spatial Variations in Urban Left-Wing Voting in England and Wales in 1951," *Annals* of the Association of American Geographers, LV (March 1965), pp. 161–178.
Useful primarily as an illustration of multiple regression analysis in voting behavior. Note especially the maps of regression residuals.

ROKKAN, STEIN and HENRY VALEN
"Regional Contrasts in Norwegian Politics," in Erik Allardt and Yrjo Littunen, eds., *Cleavages, Ideologies and Party Systems* (Helsinki: Westermarck Society, *Transactions*, Vol. X, 1964), pp. 162–238.
One of a series of studies by the authors growing out of the activities of the Michelsen Institute and the Institute for Social Research (Norway), this paper is certainly one of the important contributions to the geography of political behavior. Using election data for all local and national elections from 1945 to 1961 and census data for 1950 and 1960, the authors employ multivariate techniques to analyze regional differences in party strength and the sources of these variations. A particularly interesting portion of the paper deals with spatial conflicts over entry into the European Common Market.

RUMMEL, R. J.
:   "Dimensions of Conflict Behavior Within and Between Nations," *General Systems*, VIII (1963), pp. 1–50.

    Based upon data collected for twenty-two measures of conflict behavior for seventy-seven nations for the years 1955, 1956, and 1957, the study has three objectives: to find the dimensions of variation among nations in conflict behavior, to discover the variations among nations along these dimensions, and to ascertain relationship between foreign and domestic conflict. Appendix 2, a full list of conflict data for all the countries studied, will be highly useful to political geographers.

SIMON HERBERT A.
:   *Administrative Behavior*, 2nd ed. (N.Y.: Free Press, 1957).

    A classic study which contributed greatly to the growth of behavioralism. Chapters 4 and 5 are especially useful for their treatment of rationality and decision making. Also see the author's introduction to the second edition which updates his earlier findings.

SINGER, J. DAVID
:   "The Relevance of the Behavioral Sciences to the Study of International Relations," *Behavioral Science*, VI (October 1961), pp. 324–335.

    A statement of theories and methods developed in the behavioral sciences which have application to the study of international relations.

SMITH, DON D.
:   "Modal Attitude Clusters: A Supplement for the Study of National Character," *Social Forces*, XLIV (June 1966), pp. 526–533.

    After a discussion of the inadequacies of research on national character, the author proposes a method employing modal attitude clusters. He suggests a typology of appropriate psychological attributes and methods of data collection. Finally, he suggests that this method may be useful for both within and between nation groupings and may also provide a measure for intensity as well.

SNYDER, RICHARD C.
:   "A Decision-Making Approach to the Study of Political Phenomena," in Roland Young, ed., *Approaches to the Study of Politics* (Evanston: Northwestern University Press, 1958), pp. 3–38.

    A general discussion of the utility and methodological problems in the decision-making approach by one of its leading practitioners.

SOMMER, ROBERT
:   "The Ecology of Privacy," *Library Quarterly*, XXXVI (1966), pp. 234–248.

    An analysis of the role of spatial arrangements in regulating patterns of social interaction. The author relates territorial defense and privacy with optimal offensive and defensive positioning.

WILLIAMS, J. ALLEN
:   "Regional Differences in Authoritarianism," *Social Forces*, XLV (December 1966), pp. 273–277.

    Based upon data collected in 1953 in a national survey by the National Opinion Research Center, the study finds positive association between authoritarianism and prejudice both between and within regions.

WOLPERT, JULIAN
:   "The Decision Process in Spatial Context," *Annals* of the Association of American Geographers LIV (December 1964), pp. 537–558.

    Although dealing with economic behavior, this study is a valuable treatment of many of the variables, such as goal orientation, levels of knowledge, uncertainty, and the choice process, which enter into any behavioral analysis.

WRIGHT, QUINCY
:   "The Nature of Conflict" *Western Political Quarterly*, IV (June 1951), pp. 193–209.

    A theoretical analysis of conflict and its relation to inconsistency, tension, and competition. The author also examines the types and methods of conflict and their relationship to conflict resolution.

Part V: ENVIRONMENT

Introduction

The preceding sections have demonstrated the interdependence among structure, processes, and behavior in the study of political geography. The environment provides the context for the interaction among these elements; in fact, the environment obtains meaning only in its relations with that which it environs. Due to its position astride the social and natural sciences, geography enjoys a rich tradition in the analysis of these interrelationships. Because of geography's association with environmentalism in the United States, however, few political geographers now deal specifically with the environment except to refute the more blatant of environmental interpretations. We have banished our black sheep to some forgotten pasture.

Despite the geographer's comfort in this sheltered security, the growing concern over the quality of the environment is sufficiently serious to find expression in "television editorials," the sure sign that an issue has arrived. The New Frontier and the Great Society moved extensively to alleviate water pollution, to improve scenic beauty along our highways, and to provide wilderness parks for refreshing man's communion with nature. Not only has the private citizen confronted the "silent spring," but, since the Great Depression, he has seen the solution in large-scale public intervention in the management of the environment. The social and natural sciences will play a critical role in such thorny policy issues as air pollution abatement, the ensuring of adequate municipal water supplies, public provision of aesthetic beauty, and the mobilization of natural resources in economic development and modernization.

This section explores three major themes relating to the environment: the effect of the environment upon politics, the impress of politics upon the environment, and the public management of the environment. The discussion and selections all focus on long-standing questions and attempt to identify some of the conceptual problems, major theories, methodological difficulties, and future research needs which are implicit in political-environmental studies.

THE IMPRESS OF THE ENVIRONMENT UPON POLITICS

Environmental Writers

Interest in environmental questions dates back at least to Hippocrates who concluded in his *On Airs, Waters, Places*[1] that climate provided explanations for the physical and intellectual differences among people. Stressing the correspondence between the physical enviroment and national character, Aristotle (see his selection in Part I, Heritage) paid particular attention to the intermediary role of human occupations.[2] The common medieval view held that people inhabiting temperate climates were better suited to governing than were

1. Hippocrates, "On Airs, Waters, Places," in Emerson C. Kelly (comp.), *Medical Classics* (Baltimore: Williams and Wilkins, 1938), Vol. III, pp. 19–42.
2. Aristotle, *The Politics of Aristotle*, Ernest Barker, Trans. (New York: Oxford University Press, 1962), Book VII.

the "dullards" of the more northern zones or the "weak and cowardly" populations of the more tropical climes. The renowned writer of this period was the Arab philosopher Ibn-Khaldūn, who detailed the effects of climate upon diet, race, and pigmentation.[3] He conceived man's proper place in the universe as an integral part of the physical environment; an "overthrow" or "conquest" of nature only resulted in man's alienation from the moral order. Ibn-Khaldūn integrated this environmental theory with one of the first expositions of the life cycle of the state.[4]

Jean Bodin, who presented the first systematic treatment of the effects of climate upon man, influenced such successors as Milton, Montesquieu, and Burke.[5] Bodin tried to explain the diversity of human character in terms of environmental differences and even suggested that political systems should accommodate the variety of human character as molded by the environment. He went far in the direction of determinism by asserting that the environment not only limits our capacity to do certain things but even determines our will to do or not to do them.

By considering the interaction between environments and "human wants," and its results in variations in economies, manners of living, and legal systems, Montesquieu advanced environmental thinking a major stride forward.[6] It is unfortunate that most readers concentrate on his treatment of direct climatic effects, for it is in Montesquieu's discussion of soil, subsistence patterns, and political and legal organization, where he is at his best. Kriesel recently pointed out that Montesquieu is not a determinist or environmentalist at all but a possibilist.[7]

A writer all too often overlooked by geographers is the erudite English historian Henry Thomas Buckle, who, like Toynbee, searched for laws of history.[8] Unlike many of his predecessors, Buckle refused to separate the individual elements of the physical environment but rather considered the impact of environmental complexes upon man. He divided environmental effects into two major classes—those acting directly upon man via his economy, food supply, and accumulation of wealth, and those acting upon the intellect and psychology of man.

Most readers will be more familiar with modern geographers and historians who have employed environmental factors in their analyses. Both Friedrich Ratzel and Rudolf Kjellén (see Ratzel's selection and the discussion in the introduction to Part I, Heritage) gave the physical environment a prominent role in their organic analogue models, but neither was an out-and-out determinist. Ellen Church Semple, in her *Influences of Geographic Environment*, examined the direct effects of environmental factors on health, energy, and population density and the indirect effects upon crops, animals, economy and commerce.[9] Two prominent American historians—Walter Prescott Webb and Frederick Jackson Turner—stressed the interaction within regional settings between man and physical environment.

Perhaps the best known American environmental writer is Ellsworth Huntington, who explicitly avows his determinism and attempts to explain the broad sweep of mankind by environmental and biological foundations. Despite the impressive marshalling of factual data in such books as *Climate and Civilization* and *Mainsprings of Civilization*,[10] the deficiencies in his analysis of statistical aggregates, the errors in historical evidence, and the intrusion of personal values in his generalizations are well known. It should be recognized, on the other hand, that Huntington assigns to cultural factors a more prominent role than critics generally recognize. Like Buckle, Huntington will continue to be disapproved on methodological grounds rather than disproved in thesis because his treatment is so sweeping that it eludes testing by systematic and scientific means.

3. Ibn-Khaldūn, *The Muqaddimah*, Franz Rosenthal, trans. (New York: Pantheon Books, 1958).
4. *Ibid.*, Vol. I, pp. 253–254.
5. Jean Bodin, *Les six livres de la république* (S.: Gabriel Carter, 1608).
6. Charles Louis Montesquieu, *The Spirit of Laws*, Thomas Nugent, trans. (London: Nourse, 1766).
7. Karl Marcus Kriesel, "Montesquieu: Possibilistic Political Geographer," *Annals* of the Association of American Geographers, LVIII (September, 1968), pp. 557–574.
8. Henry Thomas Buckle, *History of Civilization in England* (New York: Hearst's International Library Co., 1913).
9. Ellen Church Semple, *Influences of Geographic Environment* (New York: Henry Holt and Co., 1911).
10. Ellsworth Huntington, *Climate and Civilization* (New Haven: Yale University Press, 1915); Ellsworth Huntington, *Mainsprings of Civilization* (New York: John Wiley and Sons, 1945).

Environment and Political Systems: Two Theories

For political geography, the two most influential theories, both included in this section, are those of Arnold Toynbee and Karl Wittfogel. In his "The Challenge of the Environment," Toynbee develops his famous challenge-response thesis, essentially a psychological proposition using civilizations as the major unit of analysis. He begins with the question: is the stimulus toward civilization stronger in proportion as the environment becomes more difficult? He uses two situations to answer this question. First, by examining selected pairs of "hard" and "easy" ground, he concludes that civilizations have developed in the more difficult environments. Second, he contends that if his thesis is valid it should be particularly apparent in cases where "new ground" must be broken, and he presents a number of examples which support his argument. The treatment of overseas migration is particularly interesting because it deals not only with the psychological response to the transition from a "stable" situation to one of "storm and stress" but also because Toynbee argues that the voyage results in a mutation of political organization from the former kinship structure to a new contract basis. In short, both cases illustrate Toynbee's thesis—the greater the stimulus, the greater the response.

The monumental *A Study of History*,[11] from which the selection is taken, is unquestionably one of the academic achievements of our time, a work almost overwhelming in its breadth, erudition, and style. Reference to the full work, and not the excellent Somervell abridgement, is necessary for a full appreciation of Toynbee's achievement. The thesis rests heavily upon geographical foundations, and one may criticize the firmness of these underpinnings. First, in considering variations in the physical environments and their relative difficulties, Toynbee holds constant that which is being environed, namely people in all their individual and cultural diversity. Yet human diversity would undoubtedly bear heavily upon the degree of stimulation experienced and the mode and intensity of response. In any event, as Pierre Gourou asks, "Comment une civilisation supérieure, qui est un ensemble complexe de faits humains, pourrait-elle être produit par un milieu naturel qui est un ensemble complexe des faits physiques?"[12] Second, Toynbee devotes little attention to location and links with other areas; yet these were vital factors in the emergence of Prussia and New England as areas of "positive response." Third, as O. H. K. Spate puts it, Toynbee "treads too confidently over ground which he has perhaps reconnoitered rather than surveyed."[13] There are weaknesses in the handling of concrete geographical facts—he is a better historian than a geographer. In his discussion of regional competition in North America, for example, he argues that "it is impossible to deny that the original colonial home of the New Englanders was the hardest country of all." Yet, comparison of climate, soils, and transport routes would show that Lower Canada was in every way more difficult. Fourth, in his selection of examples he tends to include those which support his arguments and to exclude those which conflict with them. In his discussions of sea-crossings, for example, he avoids discussion of vandals, one of the most obvious cases, which would have conflicted with his treatment. Finally, one can question the validity of his thesis since, carried to its ultimate conclusion, it suggests that civilizations should be concentrated in the most unfavorable environments—ice caps, tropical rainforests, and deserts. As a trenchant Toynbee critic has observed, a blow on the head may stimulate one to fisticuffs, but it may be so hard as to knock one out.[14] Is Toynbee really suggesting there is in the physical environment an optimal level of stimulation which is conducive to development? There is a body of psychological theory which can be brought to bear on this question.[15]

---

11. Arnold J. Toynbee, *A Study of History* (New York: Oxford University Press, 1951).

12. "How can a superior civilization, which is a complex ensemble of human facts, be produced by a natural milieu which is a complex ensemble of physical facts?" Pierre Gourou, "Civilisations et malchance géographique," *Annales, Économies, Sociétés, Civilisations*, IV (1949), pp. 445-446.

13. O. H. K. Spate, "Toynbee and Huntington: A Study in Determinism," *Geographical Journal*, CXVIII (December 1952), p. 409.

14. Pieter Geyl, "Toynbee's System of Civilizations," *Journal of the History of Ideas*, IX (1948), pp. 93-124.

15. See, for example, Joachim F. Wohlwill, "The Physical Environment: A Problem for a Psychology of Stimulation," *Journal of Social Issues*, XXII (October 1966), pp. 29-38.

The appearance of Karl Wittfogel's theory of the "hydraulic civilization" in his *Oriental Despotism*[16] in 1957 heralded a scholarly ovation accorded to few works produced in the social sciences: "This is a truly great book, one of the major contributions to the science of man in our time . . . and may conceivably even outrank (the importance) of the entire corpus of theoretical literature in political science."[17] Wittfogel employs an economic-political mode of analysis rather than Toynbee's psychological approach, although both look to history for documentation of their theories. Wittfogel begins by contending that water is the only element in the physical environment which can be accumulated in bulk. Whereas rainfall farming and hydroagriculture tend to produce small-scale enterprises and a multi-centered society, "hydraulic" societies, he argues, require large-scale effort, a single-centered society, and a government monopoly of political power. The state keeps private power weak and divided.

Wittfogel examines in detail preparatory operations, tillage, and labor investments which combine to produce the hydraulic and non-hydraulic states. He also devotes considerable attention to the spatial expansion and diffusion of the hydraulic state, which he sees as having spread far beyond the area of the hydraulic economy proper. He suggests that the efficiency and durability of the hydraulic form of political organization accounts for its success in many "marginal" areas. Finally, Wittfogel specifically considers values by contending that hydraulic or "Oriental" despotism was costly in human affairs; Aristotle's "society of free men" never emerged in hydraulic society.

Wittfogel's enthusiastic reception in the West is perhaps not unrelated to the fact that his theory supports a Madisonian conception of government and provides a solid framework for an assault on Marxist historical interpretations. Wittfogel's China and the Soviet Union, throwbacks to a common precapitalistic political organization, differ from older societies largely in their greater bureaucratic control and suppression of individual freedom. Such hydraulic societies are doomed to slow stagnation, but Western societies enjoy the more happy prospect for adaptive and progressive social change. In a review of *Oriental Despotism*, Arnold Toynbee dissented from the prevailing praise by holding that "this is a queer book by a fine scholar"[18] and arguing that it "is really a political book and not a scientific one,"[19] ". . . "something of an aberration and still more of a menace."[20] Wittfogel retorted "If my efforts help us to analyze and develop our great heritage of human freedom, and if they help us to understand and combat more effectively the total negation of freedom, then I will gladly bear Toynbee's wrath. He calls my book a 'menace'. A menace to what? To the worst form of total power? I hope it is."[21] In this context, Wittfogel is an ex-Marxist and Toynbee's implication was that, in the usual tradition of converts, he was going too far to be accurate.

Wittfogel's thesis does award to political institutions the decisive role in social change. Unlike hydraulic states, Western non-hydraulic societies possess powerful competing institutions such as the church, the guilds, and property interests, which restrain the power of the state over the individual. Predictably, this interpretation has come under fire by non-Western reviewers who emphasize instead the role of the passive stratum of producers located in virtually self-contained villages in the evolution of despotism.[22] In addition, they argue that pre-conceived values concerning the "sanctity" of private property and Western conceptions of private freedom permeate the theory of hydraulic civilizations.

In treating the physical environment, Wittfogel is considerably more sophisticated than Toynbee. Although Wittfogel's "natural setting" provided the potential for the emergence of hydraulic states, it must be "actualized" under certain conditions, thus allowing for human choice. ". . . I show the dependence of the latter on cultural conditions which

---

16. Karl Wittfogel, *Oriental Despotism: Comparative Study of Total Power* (New Haven: Yale University Press, 1957).
17. See George Peter Murdoch's review in the *American Anthropologist*, LIX (June 1957), p. 545.
18. *American Political Science Review*, LII (March, 1958), p. 195.
19. *Ibid.*, p. 196.
20. *Ibid.*, p. 198.
21. Karl Wittfogel, "Reply to Arnold Toynbee," *American Political Science Review*, LII (June 1958), p. 506.
22. See, for example, Theodore Shabad, "Non-Western Views of the 'Hydraulic Society'," *Annals of the Association of American Geographers*, XLIX (September 1959), pp. 324–325.

in open historical situations offer a variety of choices."[23] Societies in adjacent marginal areas, according to Wittfogel, choose to accept or reject this form of political society.

Though sounder in empirical data than Toynbee, Wittfogel has his share of omissions and errors. His analysis of India pays only scant attention to the monsoon season and the caste system. He overlooks Burma, Cambodia, and dry-zone Ceylon, yet all had hydraulic states for which reasonably detailed political history is available. Like Toynbee, Wittfogel chooses his documentation carefully; he avoids a number of examples of despotism in the West and autonomous and democratic states in the East. Also, by positing a spread of hydraulic societies to areas lacking the environment usually associated with hydraulic economies and by recognizing a class of "loose" hydraulic societies, Wittfogel can incorporate any deviations or negative evidence as variants of the ideal type. As a result, "loose" or "marginal" examples have cropped up all around the globe. Finally, O. H. K. Spate's conclusion that "the main argument appears incontrovertibly valid..." is debatable, for it is entirely possible that means more modest than irrigation on a grand scale or large-scale political control and administrative action could solve the environmental problems. As E. R. Leach demonstrates,[24] major hydraulic works may have arisen haphazardly as pieces of self-advertisement for individual leaders.

Conceptual Clarification Elsewhere the Sprouts have unraveled much of the conceptual snarl surrounding treatments of environmental impress upon politics.[25] They define the "milieu" as all the phenomena to which the unit's activity may be related and which includes the physical, social, and psychological environments. Further, they establish a typology—comprising environmental determinism, free-will environmentalism, possibilism, cognitive behavioralism, and environmental probabilism—which encompasses all discussions of man-milieu relationships. By carefully defining each category, the authors dissolve much of the confusion surrounding the assumptions and implications of a particular conceptual position. In particular, they distinguish possibilism, which refers to the results of a particular action in the "operational environment," from the other categories which relate to motives and decisions. They then proceed to a detailed analysis of cognitive behavioralism in foreign policy, emphasizing the salience of such factors as discrepancy among the psychological and operational environments, prediction, environmental knowledge, and the utilization of knowledge.

To be sure the Sprouts have managed to clear away much of the misconceptual underbrush. Yet, while they provide a definition of *milieu*, they understandably shrink from the task of distinguishing the limits between the physical and non-physical environments. Since the very term "environment" suggests an interactional domain, it is important to recognize that the "physical" or the "social" environment exists only as an ideal type. Such environments are by no means mutually exclusive.

Environmental impress upon politics also poses the problem of determining the unit of analysis. In political geography, this unit may be man himself or the political system of which he is a part. Most past research has centered upon man, and this unit merits reconsideration in the light of contemporary empirical evidence. Like Wittfogel and Toynbee, geographers may find in the interplay between political systems and their environments an increasingly fruitful subject for analysis. David Easton, in his influential theory of the political system,[26] conceives of the environment as all those aspects of society that fall outside the boundaries of the political system. He divides the environment into two major parts—intrasocietal and extrasocietal. The former comprises the environment lying beyond the boundaries of the political system but within the same society, whereas the latter refers to whatever lies beyond society's boundaries, usually the international ecological, social, and political systems. The dynamic properties of both the environment and the political system lead to exchange or flows of effects. A political system is "open" or "closed," depending upon the extent to

---

23. Wittfogel, "Reply to Arnold Toynbee," p. 504.
24. E. R. Leach, "Hydraulic Society in Ceylon," *Past and Present*, XV (April 1959), pp. 2–26.
25. Harold and Margaret Sprout, "Environmental Factors in the Study of International Politics," *Journal of Conflict Resolution*, I, No. 4 (1957), pp. 309–328.
26. For a discussion of this concept, see David Easton, *A Framework for Political Analysis* (Englewood Cliffs, N.J.: Prentice-Hall, 1965).

which it is exposed to environmental events.

Two empirical studies demonstrate the possibilities of the political system–environmental unit of analysis. A recent study analyzes the effects of a hurricane upon an urban election in New Orleans.[27] Despite lack of preparation, the incumbent mayor managed to transform a political threat into a political advantage. Kasperson, in a study included in this volume, examines drought within a framework of multiple environmental stresses acting upon a municipal political system. He develops a general model to explain how managers perceive, evaluate, and resolve the complex of stresses in a setting of scarce resources. Both studies use behavioral techniques to analyze the political effects of natural hazards, and the latter employs a general systems approach as well.

Unfortunately, researchers seldom distinguish carefully among the types of environmental effects. It is possible to propose three classes of effects. *Mechanical* effects refer to the biological stresses acting upon the organism from such environmental elements as temperature, noise, and irritating materials. *Psychological* effects are those emanating from the environment in its functions as a stimulus field. Man converts these stimuli into sets of symbols, and then reacts to the symbols as if they were the actual environmental stimuli. It is misleading, therefore, simply to link certain stimuli and particular responses, as past writers have usually done, for as Kates and Wohlwill note: man's response is "complex, multi-faceted, and a multi-layered affair."[28] Finally, *actual constraints* are those involved in the Sprouts' conception of possibilism; they refer to the limitations on the outcomes of particular choices in the "objective" or "operational" environment.

A final clarification concerns the processes of "adjustment" or "adaptation" either by man himself or, speaking metaphorically, by the political system. Most past writers have thought in terms of *adjustment*, defined here as a homeostatic response to environmental change. Assuming a static equilibrium relationship between man and his environment, adjustment may lead to dangerous conclusions concerning "imbalances" or "guidances" from nature. In the case of political system-environmental relations, the comparable equilibrium concept would be "system maintenance," which has the same static deficiencies. *Adaptation*, a more sophisticated notion, incorporates the possibility of reduced or increased sensitivity, thereby bypassing any assumption of equilibrium.[29] An environmental change may not elicit any response, therefore, because man over time may become less sensitive to the initial conditions or his values may change. Changing conceptions of privacy in the United States are a good example. In political systems, the hierarchy of goals and stresses fluctuates over time. In speaking of political adjustment, therefore, the concept of "system persistence" is useful for it recognizes these dynamic properties and allows for a changing matrix of policy priorities.[30] This notion raises interesting research possibilities concerning long-run exposures to certain environments, shifts in values over time, and variabilities in individual or political levels of tolerance.

THE IMPRESS OF POLITICS UPON THE ENVIRONMENT

In his selection "The Impress of Effective Central Authority Upon the Landscape," Derwent Whittlesey over three decades ago examined the various ways by which politics can modify the landscape. He divided his treatment into four major sections—expressions of security, special features of boundaries, expressions of government activity, and the effects of the legal system. His subsequent discussion suggests the wide scope of political impress on the environment.

In the case of political security, for example, he notes effects upon the distribution of settlement, the form of cities, and even the architecture of buildings. He envisions political boundaries as providing special features (such as military garrisons), special economic functions (here he anticipates Loesch), and

---

27. Glen F. Abney and Larry B. Hill, "Natural Disasters as a Political Variable: The Effects of a Hurricane on an Urban Election," *American Political Science Review*, LX (December 1966), pp. 974–981.

28. Robert W. Kates and Joachim F. Wohlwill, "Man's Response to the Physical Environment: Introduction," *Journal of Social Issues*, XXII (October 1966), p. 18.

29. See the discussion in Joseph Sonnenfeld, "Variable Values in Space and Landscape; An Inquiry into the Nature of Environmental Necessity," *Journal of Social Issues*, XXII (October 1966), pp. 71–82.

30. Easton, *op. cit.*, Chapter 6.

even levels of personal risk. He further delineates the broad range of governmental impact upon the landscape—postoffice architecture, land and street patterns, migrations, regional development, and the lavish development of capital cities. Finally, in his particularly stimulating discussion of laws and the landscape Whittlesey analyzes the role that tariffs, embargoes, and land laws play in various geographical distributions.

Whittlesey uncorks many fine wines, but in sampling the diversity one comes away with more of a headiness than an appreciation of vintages. Some deeper draughts from each bottle are necessary before we can assess the relative merits of aroma, bouquet, and body. To begin with, although the political impress may be conceived in man-land terms, we are dealing with a variety of spatial distributions, some of which are visible in the landscape and others which may be illuminated only very indirectly. It may be useful, therefore, to structure political impress on the environment into four major components—political goals, agents of impress, processes, and effects.

Political goals include such objectives as security, autarchy, spatial integration, status, and economic growth. Nearly all governments seek security, although its rank among other goals may vary in relation to perceived threat or hostility in the environment. The Cuban government of Fidel Castro has lived with a high degree of both perceived and actual hostility, and security has been a prime objective of the regime. Autarchy, an objective perhaps more prized at earlier periods of history than now, is still a strong consideration among nation-states. The Soviet-Union, especially in the years following 1928, made autarchy a keystone of its economic and foreign policy. The United States has sought to reduce its reliance upon external strategic minerals through stockpiling and technological innovation. A country's position along the autarchy-interdependence continuum may greatly affect its willingness to engage in inefficient resource exploitation.

The degree of spatial integration or segregation sought by a political system may vary widely. Urban political leaders may seek to segregate ghettoes from other residential areas or they may genuinely attempt integration. Nation-states such as Canada, the Congo, India, and the Soviet Union have taken strong measures to foster the spatial integration of culturally diverse and often widely separated areas. Status, often an important objective, takes such diverse forms as citation as an "all-American city," the presence of a national airline, the erection of a steel plant, or ordinances requiring one-acre minimum lot size. Rapid economic growth often provides an index of the efficacy of political leadership, and a government can rise or fall on this issue. The military regime in Greece, for example, justified its coup on this basis. In regard to the environment, such a goal may entail a particular stance concerning the degree of public intervention into the harnessing of natural resources for the national "good."

Agents of political impress are the vehicles or means by which political processes manifest themselves in the environment. The legal system, legislation, interest groups and voluntary associations, political partitions, and degrees of political security are all examples of such agents. The political partitioning of space, particularly that separating national political systems, is critical. Discussions of boundary impact really center upon the differential impact of divergent policies and degrees of centralized power.

The legal system, along with prevailing customs and mores, may regulate extensively the use and development of the physical environment. Regulations concerning property are basic to spatial patterns in any political unit. Alternative systems of land survey and tenure, inheritance, and dowry arrangements may produce such contrasting landscapes as the seigneural land patterns in French Canada, communal landholdings in Africa or pre-European North America, checkerboard land patterns in the contemporary Midwest, or the fragmented lands of Mediterranean Europe.

Legislation, one of the most direct means available for regulation or development of the physical environment, offers a wide range of ordinance types. At the community level in the United States, property and income taxation, building codes, subdivision ordinances, zoning, and planning all exemplify these measures. At higher levels in the political hierarchy, tariffs, embargoes, pricing systems, national domains, government quotas on production, and developmental projects can be utilized in political impress.

Finally, the degree of political security

prevalent in a particular area can leave its mark in a variety of ways. As Whittlesey shows, settlement patterns and architectural types reflect this variable. Mediterranean settlements often perch on hilltops in the protective shadow of churches, castles, or monasteries. As political security increased over time, maritime or land trade precipitated a downslope growth of settlement. The wide streets of Paris, constructed to ensure security against possible uprisings, present another example. The threat of nuclear war at present has given rise to efforts, not all of them successful, to disperse key industrial firms and military bases.

Only several *processes of political impress* will be noted here. *Symbolization* refers to political activities which create on the landscape symbols designed to signify certain values to indigenous inhabitants or to others. Mary McCarthy records a striking symbol of political defiance etched into the North Vietnamese landscape during the American bombing raids:

On a big billboard in the city center, the number of US planes shot down is revised forward almost daily in red paint—2818, they claimed when I left, and the number keeps growing. In villages the score is kept on a blackboard. Everything they build is dated, down to the family wells in a hamlet—a means of visibly recording progress, like penciling the heights of children, with the dates opposite, on a door. And each date has a clear significance in the story of resistance: 1965 or 1966, stamped on a mill, proclaims that it was built *in spite of* air pirates.[31]

In occupied territories and along hostile boundary lines, especially those separating competing ideological and political systems, "showcases" sometimes appear to symbolize the success of a particular political path. West Berlin has functioned in this role since World War II. Mussolini lavishly developed the city of Rhodes to signify Fascist glory and the benevolence of Il Duce. Landscape symbols may also have a calculated function, such as the political integration, independence from foreign powers, and developmental potentialities of the interior which the new capital cities of Brasilia (Brazil) and Islamabad (Pakistan) proudly proclaim.

Political symbolism in the landscape may assume a variety of styles. Chicago's lakefront is an homage to the city of the "master plan". The St. Louis arch not only represents the gateway to the West but a new "image" for a lack-luster city. "Resurrection City's" distasteful image to many whites in 1968 was entirely appropriate for the "Poor People's Campaign" which it symbolized and the functions for which it was designed. Every community expresses its values and aspirations in its monuments, restorations, public buildings, and architecture. Some national governments maintain boundary markers and supporting patterns to indicate past glories or disputed areas, whereas others go to great lengths to eradicate any suggestion of prior political sovereignty. The changing of names on gravestones in the South Tyrol represents an extreme measure of the latter type.

Redistribution constitutes another very basic process of political impress on the environment. Utilization of the environment often involves the collection of funds from diverse areas of a political system to finance projects in spatially-concentrated locales. The process, often a purposeful one, may have its roots in political goals, such as providing incentives in Canada or Australia for settlement and resources exploitation or supporting the Appalachia program in the United States. The spatial distribution of funds for developmental projects has been a serious bone of contention between East and West Pakistan. As the next subsection will show, this process is one of the most pervasive problems in the public management of the environment.

Spatial Competition and Conflict is a process closely related to and by no means mutually exclusive from redistribution. Within any political unit, local interests vie for the rewards of redistribution and developmental schemes. Success in competition not only brings tangible benefits for the local citizenry but strengthens the reservoir of support for politicians among their constituents. Again the issues are multifarious—government contracts, shipyard closings, NASA installations, hospitals, libraries, school sites, highways, etc. The archetype of this process is the annual "harbors and rivers" budget. This process illustrates the useful perspective provided by the spatial structure of a political economy. Actually, analysis of the entire process can take the form of a game in which players representing various geographical sections of

---

31. *The New York Review of Books*, X, No. 10 (May 23, 1968), p. 4.

the political system compete for the spatial allocation of public funds.[32]

Effects are the last analytical component of political impress on the environment. Some of these effects (e.g., land and street patterns) will be visible in the landscape, whereas others (e.g., prices, land values) will not. Geographers have at their disposal various techniques and concepts for analyzing these effects. Thus, after Peter Haggett,[33] analysis can focus on geometry: movement, networks, nodes, hierarchies, and surfaces. On the other hand, it is possible to discuss effects in terms of their structural-functional attributes, after Part II of this book. In that sense, barriers like the Berlin Wall take on a divergent function in regard to spatial-political integration.

The Berlin Wall can, in fact, serve to exemplify the interrelationship of these components of political impress. West Berlin posed a serious policy problem for East Germany during the 1950s. The outflow of migrants through West Berlin had become sufficiently grave as to jeopardize the economic and political security of the East German regime. With increased security as the objective, the government redistributed funds to erect a spatial barrier, the function of which was the interruption of a threatening form of spatial interaction. On the other hand, the decision-makers hoped for greater stability and integration in their political area. The resultant pattern in the landscape was linear, divergent, and possibly areally different. The wall symbolized determination on the part of East Germany to protect its security, but, from the Western viewpoint, it signified an admission of the regime's failure to achieve voluntary support from its inhabitants.

The other selection dealing with political impress on the environment also illustrates very well the conceptual structure outlined above. In his "Political Influence in Australian Geography," K. W. Robinson points out that development has been a widely espoused goal among the various political divisions. Because of political autonomy and differing developmental policies, Australia's territorial structure has been instrumental in spatial differentiation. Robinson also demonstrates that agents of political impress have included informal means, such as pressure groups and labor unrest, as well as formal governmental activity. He analyzes the processes of manipulation, natural resource development, and interstate competition for industry and migrants as well as the effects on spatial distributions. Competitive political demands have influenced the location of steel plants as well as contributing to a Federal protectionist policy. He also describes effects in terms of wheatbelt town-and-rail patterns in four states, distinguishing nodal, digital, diffuse, and marginal types.

A study not reprinted here provides a detailed analysis of how agents of political impress can produce a striking pattern of spatial differentiation in the urban landscape.[34] Nelson begins by noting the anomalous character of Vernon, California, in regional residential, commercial, industrial, transportational, and public land use patterns. Since the region is relatively homogeneous in physical geography and cultural evolution, he examines the use of agents of political impress. He finds that the city government had used its powers of incorporation—license, taxation, and local regulation—as well as annexations, hostility to residential development, and the provision of public facilities to accomplish its unstated objectives. Nelson's accompanying maps demonstrate vividly the results on spatial distributions.

Many of the problems and processes of political impress on the environment concern the larger question of the public management of natural resources. This topic deserves separate treatment.

THE PUBLIC MANAGEMENT OF THE ENVIRONMENT

Environmental management is a subject sufficiently broad as to merit the attention of both the physical and social sciences. Because of their bridge position between these major divisions of knowledge, geographers historic-

---

32. There are games which do exactly this. The game of *Section* in the High School Geography Project and Richard Duke's *Metropolis* are two such examples. For an extensive review of these games, see Roger E. Kasperson, "Games as Educational Media," *Journal of Geography*, LXVII (October 1968), 409–428.

33. Peter Haggett, *Locational Analysis in Human Geography* (New York: St. Martin's Press, 1966).

34. Howard J. Nelson, "The Vernon Area, California—A Study of the Political Factor in Urban Geography," *Annals* of the Association of American Geographers, XLII (June 1952), pp. 177–191.

ally have played a strong role in resource management studies. Harlan Barrows stimulated an early interest in conservation which has had a rich tradition at The University of Chicago. Dating from the Natural Resources Planning Board of the 1930s, Barrows, Charles Colby, and Gilbert F. White have had an important impact upon governmental policy. Curiously enough, however, political geographers have demonstrated very little interest in an area for which they are academically well-equipped and in which geography boasts a distinguished heritage. Despite recognition in *The Science of Geography* as one of the major problem areas in geography (see Part I, Heritage), environmental management seldom receives the attention it merits. While geography has certainly contributed extensively to policy and political issues surrounding natural resource use, the contributions have come from a group of geographers—such as White, Burton, Kates, Lucas and Sewell—who have had an unusually strong policy orientation. By comparison, research by scholars who consider themselves political geographers has been scanty at best. Young geographers might do well to explore the political dimensions of resource management.

Most geographical research has dealt with entrepreneurial activities. The focus of political geography, by contrast, is upon the role of public institutions and political conflict in the patterns and processes of environmental management. The present discussion recognizes three major themes—environmental policy and planning, resource allocation, and spatial linkages and area repercussion—of special interest to the political geographer. Individual selections illustrate the theoretical issues.

Environmental Policy and Planning

Not only can geographers provide much of the background analysis concerning the environment, but they can also contribute to the examination of underlying issues involved in a policy decision. The issues would include the public goals of particular actions, the assumptions upon which policy rests, the implications and probable results of particular decisions, the validity of evaluation methodologies, and policy conflicts and implementation difficulties.

The public interest is an issue which seldom receives more than lip-service in resource decisions. The growth of government's role as a resource manager, however, has accentuated the significance of this consideration. Decision-makers justify particular actions because they contribute to the "general welfare" or the "greatest good for the greatest number." This notion, seemingly desirable in theory, can be labyrinthine in practice. David Lowenthal has demonstrated the diversity in interpretations of scenic beauty,[35] and Robert Lucas has indicated the wide variations in wilderness preferences.[36] Traditionally, government has determined the public interest à la General Motors—through benefit-cost analysis and cost effectiveness.[37] Difficulties in measuring such benefits as recreation and aesthetics have thwarted strict adherence even to so limited a notion of the public interest, or at least provided considerable latitude for formula manipulation. For geographers, the question of scale is important—are cost and benefits calculated for the national, regional, or local level? Are benefits and costs spatially allocated in a way which achieves public objectives? In 1968, for example, the Corps of Engineers explicitly incorporated a political objective—the redistribution of national income—into their justification of a project which had not received a favorable ratio in prior evaluations. Public managers of the environment must recognize not only a *political* economy but also that the "public good" is a protean beast.

Public and professional values, attitudes, and information are involved in natural resource policy. There are often basic conflicts in values over what policy objectives should be. Urban renewal, for example, has been more the goal of middle-class urbanites

35. David Lowenthal, "Not Every Prospect Pleases—What is Our Criterion for Scenic Beauty?," *Landscape*, XII (Winter 1962–63), pp. 19–23.

36. Robert Lucas, "Wilderness Perception and Use: The Example of the Boundary Waters Canoe Area," *National Resources Journal*, III (1963), pp. 394–411. See also Robert Lucas, "The Contribution of Environmental Research to Wilderness Policy," *Journal of Social Issues*, XXII (October 1966), pp. 116–126.

37. For a critical discussion of benefit-cost decision-making, see Arthur Maass, "Benefit-Cost Analysis: Its Relevance to Public Investment Decisions," in Allen V. Kneese and Stephen C. Smith (eds.), *Water Research* (Baltimore: Resources For the Future, 1966), pp. 311–328.

than the inhabitants of the areas affected. Very often little is known about the attitudes of the grass-roots, or, if they conflict with those of professional planners or agency representatives, they are discounted as stemming from ignorance, cupidity, or irrationality.[38] Yet, as Irving Fox shows, differing values and attitudes can sometimes play a major role in patterns of natural resource exploitation.[39]

Whereas many experts have espoused an "economic rationality view" which sees water use for agriculture in western parts of the United States as a relatively low-value use, the widespread public value in arid and semi-arid areas for water development has influenced greatly the decisions of political leaders. In the East, while economists and engineers view waste disposal as a valuable use of water resources, many political officials and the public have preferred complete abatement as a public goal. Much public policy at the state and local levels seems to be an outgrowth of the latter preference.

Since environmental decisions are usually predicted on some desired future state of affairs, prediction is an important part of policy and planning. A correct evaluation of the range of choice and the correspondence between outcomes and anticipations depends upon the accuracy of prediction. The dire predictions of neo-Malthusians concerning world population and food supply, for example, teeters precariously upon prognostications of such complex factors as birth rates, leisure, technological innovations, wars, and economic growth. One need only review periodic warnings that United States oil reserves are on the verge of exhaustion to realize the margin of error possible. Despite methodological improvements in social prediction, there still is a lag in their diffusion to many natural resource consulting groups and a reluctance among technical experts to communicate uncertainty and probable error levels to political officials.

Conflicts in policy arise among private interests, public agencies, and governments themselves. The Corps of Engineers stressing flood control, and the Soil Conservation Service stressing land reclamation, have long been at odds concerning water resource developmental policy. The fragmented pattern of government responsibility not only facilitates major policy disagreements such as that between public health and recreation departments, but explains why a mysterious "Mister Z" proposes a Natural Resources Department at the Cabinet level to coordinate activity and eliminate conflicts and overlappings of responsibility.[40] The political partitioning of space may result in divergent policies centered on a shared resource or such local-national conflict as that between British Columbia and the Canadian federal government.[41]

Finally, the role of crisis in resource development deserves attention. Henry Hart has noted that innovations in resource developments tend to follow close on the heels of crisis.[42] Flood control measures, for example, tend to cluster over time in response to flood events. The study (included in this section) of drought in a municipal water system does substantiate Hart's thesis but it also suggests that crisis will not necessarily affect or alter the accuracy of prediction, the consideration of alternatives, or the decision itself.

Resource Allocations

Three types of natural resource allocation create political problems. *Structural allocation* refers to the distribution of resources, both in their quantity and quality, throughout the citizenry of a political community. From Aristotle to Marx and Wittfogel, this is a topic which has concerned philosophers and political theorists. Derwent Whittlesey's stimulating discussion of the "exploitable world,"[43] a

---

38. Robert W. Kates, "Variations in Flood Hazard Perception: Implications for Rational Flood Plain Use," *Spatial Organization of Land Uses: The Willamette Valley* (Corvallis: Oregon State University, 1964), pp. 97–112.

39. The following discussion is based upon Irving K. Fox, "Policy Problems in the Field of Water Resources," in Kneese and Smith, *op. cit.*, pp. 271–278.

40. Mister Z, "The Case for a Department of Natural Resources," *Natural Resources Journal*, I (November 1961), pp. 197–206.

41. W. R. Derrick Sewell, "The Columbia River Treaty: Some Lessons and Implications," *Canadian Geographer*, X (1966), pp. 145–156.

42. Henry C. Hart, "Crisis, Community and Consent in Water Politics," *Law and Contemporary Problems*, XXII (Summer 1957), pp. 510–537. See also William E. Leuchtenburg, *Flood Control Politics* (Cambridge: Harvard University Press, 1953).

43. Derwent S. Whittlesey, *The Earth and the State* (New York: Henry Holt and Company, 1939), pp. 78–85.

concept which bares the spatial and political relationships inherent in colonialism, demonstrates the global scale. Structural allocation is a major issue in Rhodesia and the Republic of South Africa where land distribution is very uneven. Bruce Russett has examined the relationship between land allocation and political instability.[44] As the pattern of looting in American cities suggests, urban violence may be, in large part, a conflict over structural allocation.

Functional allocation is the allotment of a resource among alternative uses. Ideally, a manager can develop a natural resource for "multiple use" without major conflicts in functions. In actuality, of course, this goal is often difficult to realize for many uses do conflict. Marion Marts and W. R. Derrick Sewell's analysis of the conflict between fish and power resources in the Pacific Northwest exemplifies the adverse repercussions that one use may have upon another.[45] Pollution abatement may conflict directly with a river's uses for municipal water supply, scenic beauty, and recreation. It often becomes necessary to choose among alternative uses, or at least to develop some uses to a greater degree than others. In such cases, accurate prediction and evaluation of alternatives are essential. Nevertheless, choice will almost always leave in its wake some gainers or losers so that group interests and political conflict are seldom absent.

Spatial allocation, as the term suggests, refers to the geographical allotment of the benefits and costs of a managerial decision, often among different political divisions. International river basin development is a good example. If a particular resource extends across hostile political boundaries, as in the Jordan River and Mekong River basins, coordination difficulties may take on formidable proportions. Another type of problem arises when the demand for a particular resource does not coincide with its location, for spatial movement of its benefits may enter the picture. It is interesting to note in this context that differing perceptions and values may influence resource exploitation. Spatial movement of iron ore seldom creates controversy but water generally does. Since water may be often politically immovable, electricity has to be transferred. In a recent study, Frank Quinn illustrates this point by showing that continued economic development of the West depends heavily upon regional and interregional transfers of water.[46] Yet, political resistances and conflicts are creating serious difficulties in instituting acceptable schemes for resource allocations. The concept of spatial allocation even embraces foreign aid which can be conceived as a form of reallocation where wealth from resource exploitation is moved spatially from one state to another.

Spatial Linkages and Area Repercussion

Closely related to the theme of resource allocation, these concepts relate to the lack of correspondence between the spatial extent and distribution of natural resources and the political partitioning of space. Resource development often links one area with another, and activities in one area may reverberate in another. Air pollution, for example, is a particularly thorny political problem because the sources of emission are frequently concentrated in one political unit (the central city) which enjoys whatever benefits accrue from the responsible activity while paying only a portion of the costs (noxious effects). Meanwhile, the other political units of the metropolitan area pay the costs while deriving only a small portion of the benefits (employment opportunities). The examples of shipwrecked oil tankers off the coasts of England and Puerto Rico in 1967 and 1968 provide striking demonstrations of area repercussion across territorial limits. Water withdrawals from the Great Lakes had spatial repercussions all along the shorelines and necessitated interstate and international agreements. Even the development of a public park or an urban renewal project will have profound effects upon land values in adjacent areas. Upstream-downstream conflicts are, of course, the classic example of spatial linkage and area repercussion.

---

44. Bruce M. Russett, "Inequality and Instability: The Relation of Land Tenure to Politics," *World Politics*, XVI (April 1964), pp. 442–454.

45. Marion Marts and W. R. Derrick Sewell, "Conflict Between Fish and Power Resources in the Pacific Northwest," *Annals of the Association of American Geographers*, L (1960), pp. 42–50.

46. Frank Quinn, "Water Transfers: Must the American West Be Won Again?," *Geographical Review*, LVIII (January 1968), pp. 108–132.

Introduction to the Selections

Julian Minghi's "The Conflict of Salmon Fishing Policies in the North Pacific" analyzes a natural resource dispute at the international level. The article illustrates such aspects of the preceding conceptual discussion as policy conflicts, problems in prediction, spatial allocation, and area repercussion. Minghi's analysis demonstrates effectively the role of conflicting values, for the Japanese do not share the philosophy on which the Convention regulating fishing rests. Depending upon maritime resources, Japan strongly supports freedom of the seas and a three mile limit to territorial waters. Moreover, the Russians have an entirely different set of game rules. Many Americans, on the other hand, assume that declining fishing yields are "area repercussion" from Japanese overfishing. Furthermore, the fishing industry tends to operate on the erroneous premise that the United States possesses property rights over the salmon and that an American policy of exclusive exploitation would be entirely proper.

Minghi's treatment shows very well the political complications which can arise from faulty natural resource information and predictions. Based upon scant scientific evidence concerning the movements of the salmon, the line determining spatial allocation has contributed to political conflict. The problem does concretely show the contribution which geographers can make to natural resource policy decisions.

Finally, the study demonstrates the intricacies involved in spatial linkages and area repercussion. Although many Americans have blamed Japanese fishing for the declining runs in Bristol Bay, the evidence is by no means unambiguous, especially given the recent increase in salmon runs indicated in the postcript. A change in spatial allocation would, in any case, have serious repercussions on the Japanese economy. Even if the parties possessed accurate information, it might still be difficult to reach a mutually satisfactory apportionment of exploitation rights.

Like the Minghi study, the selection by Kasperson on "Environmental Stress and the Municipal Political System: The Brockton Water Crisis of 1961–1966" deals with a number of issues in environmental management. In terms of their relationship with the political system, the author shows that disturbances in both the physical and social environments may be viewed as forms of stress which compete for scarce municipal resources. To analyze such stresses, Kasperson conceptualizes a managerial matrix, interrelating types and intensities of stresses, which is part of a more general model of stress management. Each stage of the model may be examined in terms of its behavioral and systemic properties. The author then applies the model to an actual drought situation to test its validity and usefulness. The subsequent discussion illustrates how environmental stresses arise, the importance of managerial goals, the role of reference groups, the interplay of competing stresses, and how the stress is eventually resolved.

Future Research Needs

Suggesting future research on the environment in political geography is a question of where to begin. The abundance of exciting problems is almost staggering, but the three major themes suggested in this section indicate some of the possibilities. Given a rich heritage in environmental research, geography is long overdue in conducting fresh investigations in the light of new empirical evidence and using contemporary social science theory and methods. The questions at stake strike to the very roots of political theory and the quality of man's existence. In view of the potential contribution, political geographers should not eschew a major commitment.

35

The Challenge of the Environment

ARNOLD J. TOYNBEE[*]

(1) THE STIMULUS OF HARD COUNTRIES

. . . .

Can we say that the stimulus towards civilization grows positively stronger in proportion as the environment grows more difficult? Let us review the evidence in favour of this proposition and then the evidence against it, and see what inference emerges. Evidence indicating that the difficulty and the stimulus of an environment are apt to increase *pari passu* is not hard to lay hands upon. Rather, we are likely to be embarrassed by the wealth of illustrations that leap to the mind. Most of these illustrations present themselves in the form of comparisons. Let us begin by sorting out our illustrations into two groups in which the points of comparison relate to the physical environment and the human environment respectively; and let us first consider the physical group. It subdivides itself into two categories: comparisons between the respective stimulating effects of physical environments which present different degrees of difficulty; and comparisons between the respective stimulating effects of old ground and new ground, apart from the intrinsic nature of the terrain.

From *A Study of History*, Volumes I–VI, by Arnold J. Toynbee, abridged by D. C. Somervell. Copyright 1946 by Oxford University Press. Reprinted by permission of the author and publisher.

[*] Arnold J. Toynbee (1889–   ) is a British historian and Professor Emiritus at the London School of Economics.

The Yellow River and the Yangtse

Let us, as a first example, consider the different degrees of difficulty presented by the lower valleys of the two great rivers of China. It seems that when man first took in hand the watery chaos of the lower valley of the Yellow River (Hwang Ho), the river was not navigable at any season; in the winter it was either frozen or choked with floating ice, and the melting of this ice every spring produced devastating floods which repeatedly changed the river's course by carving out new channels, while the old channels turned into jungle-covered swamps. Even to-day, when some three or four thousand years of human effort have drained the swamps and confined the river within embankments, the devastating action of the floods has not been eliminated. As recently as 1852 the channel of the Lower Hwang Ho was entirely changed and its outflow into the sea shifted from the southern to the northern side of the Shantung Peninsula, a distance of over a hundred miles. The Yangtse, on the other hand, must always have been navigable, and its floods, though they occasionally assume devastating proportions, are less frequent than those of the Yellow River. In the Yangtse Valley, moreover, the winters are less severe. Nevertheless, it was on the Yellow River and not on the Yangtse that the Sinic Civilization came to birth.

. . . .

Brandenburg and the Rhineland

As you travel through the unprepossessing country which formed the original domain of Frederick the Great—Brandenburg, Pomerania and East Prussia—with its starveling pine plantations and sandy fields, you might fancy you were traversing some outlying portion of the Eurasian Steppe. In whichever direction you travel out of it, to the pastures and beechwoods of Denmark, the black earth of Lithuania or the vineyards of the Rhineland, you pass into easier and pleasanter country. Yet the descendants of the medieval colonists who occupied these "bad lands" have played an exceptional part in the history of our Western Society. It is not only that in the nineteenth century they mastered Germany and in the twentieth led the Germans in a strenuous attempt to provide our society with its universal state. The Prussian also taught his neighbors how to make sand produce cereals by enriching it with artificial manures; how to raise a whole population to a standard of unprecedented social efficiency by a system of compulsory education and of unprecedented social security by a system of compulsory health and unemployment insurance. We may not like him but we cannot deny that we have learnt from him lessons of importance and value.

Scotland and England

There is no need to argue the point that Scotland is a "harder" land than England, nor to elaborate the notorious difference of temperament between the traditional Scotsman—solemn, parsimonious, precise, persistent, cautious, conscientious and well educated—and the traditional Englishman—frivolous, extravagant, vague, spasmodic, careless, free and easy and ill grounded in book-learning. The English may regard this traditional comparison as rather a joke; they regard most things as rather a joke; but the Scots do not. Johnson used to chaff Boswell with his apparently oft repeated *mot* that the finest prospect a Scotsman ever sees is the road to England; and before Johnson was born a wit of Queen Anne's day said that, if Cain had been a Scotsman, his punishment would have been reversed and, instead of being condemned to be a wanderer on the face of the Earth, he would have been sentenced to stay at home. The popular impression that the Scots have played a part disproportionate to their numbers in the making of the British Empire and in the occupancy of the high places of church and state is undoubtedly well founded. The classic parliamentary conflict of Victorian England was between a pure-bred Scot and a pure-bred Jew, and, of Gladstone's successors in the premiership of the United Kingdom down to this day, nearly half have been Scots.

The Struggle for North America

The classic illustration of our present theme in our own Western history is the outcome of the competition between half a dozen different groups of colonists for the mastery of North America. The victors in this contest were the New Englanders, and in the preceding chapter we have already taken note of the unusual difficulty of the local environment which first fell to the lot of the ultimate masters of the Continent. Let us now compare this New England environment, of which the site of Town Hill is a fair specimen, with the earliest American environments of the New Englanders' unsuccessful competitors: the Dutch, the French, the Spaniards and the other English colonists who settled along the southern section of the Atlantic seaboard, in and around Virginia.

In the middle of the seventeenth century, when all these groups had found their first footing on the fringes of the American mainland, it would have been easy to predict the coming conflict between them for the possession of the interior, but the most far-sighted observer then alive would not have been likely to hit the mark if he had been asked, in 1650, to pick the winner. He might have had the acumen to rule out the Spaniards in spite of their two obvious assets: their ownership of Mexico, the only North American region that had been broken in by a previous civilization, and the reputation then still enjoyed, but no longer deserved, by Spain among European Powers. He might have discounted Mexico in view of its outlying position, and discounted Spanish prestige in consideration of Spain's failures in the European war (the Thirty Years' War) just concluded. "France," he might have said, "will succeed to the military primacy of Spain in Europe, Holland and England to her naval and commercial primacy at sea. The competition for North America lies between Holland, France and England. On a short view Holland's chances might appear to be the most promising. She is superior to both England and France at sea, and in America she holds a splendid water-gate to the interior, the valley of the Hudson. But on a longer view France seems likely to be the winner. She holds a still finer water-gate, the St. Lawrence, and she has it in her power to exhaust and immobilize the Dutch by using against their homeland her overwhelming military superiority. But both the English groups," he might have added, "I can confidently rule out. Possibly the southern English colonists, with their relatively genial soil and climate, will survive as an enclave, cut off from the interior by the French or the Dutch—whichever of them wins the Mississippi Valley. One thing is certain, however: the little group of settlements in bleak and barren New England is bound to disappear, cut off, as they are, from their kinsfolk by the Dutch and the Hudson, while the French press in upon them from the St. Lawrence."

. . . .

Shall we endow our observer with superhuman length of life, in order that he may review the situation in the year 1803? If we preserve him alive till then, he will be forced to confess that his wits have not been worthy of his longevity. By the end of 1803 the French flag has disappeared off the political map of North America altogether. For forty years past Canada has been a possession of the British Crown, while Louisiana, after being ceded by France to Spain and retroceded again, has just been sold by Napoleon to the United States—the new Great Power that has emerged out of the thirteen British colonies.

In this year 1803 the United States have the Continent in their pockets and the scope of prophecy is reduced. It only remains to forecast which section of the United States is going to pocket the larger share of this vast estate. And surely this time there can be no mistake. The Southern States are the manifest masters of the Union. Look how they are leading in the final round of the competition in an inter-American race for the Winning of the West. It is the backwoodsmen of Virginia who have founded Kentucky—the first new State to be established west of those mountain ranges which have so long conspired with the French to keep the English settlers from penetrating the interior. Kentucky lies along the Ohio and the Ohio leads to the Mississippi. Meanwhile the new cotton-mills of Lancashire are offering these Southerners an ever-expanding market for the cotton crop which their soil and climate enable them to raise.

. . . .

In the year 1865 the situation is already transformed, out of all recognition, from what it was in 1807. In the Winning of the West the Southern planter has been outstripped and outflanked by his Northern rival. After almost winning his way to the Great Lakes through Indiana and getting the best of the bargain over Missouri (1821), he has been decisively defeated in Kansas (1854–60) and he has never reached the Pacific. The New Englanders are now masters of the Pacific coast all the way from Seattle to Los Angeles. The Southerner had counted on his Mississippi steam-boats to draw the whole of the West into a Southern system of economic and political relations. But "Yankee notions" have not ceased. The railway locomotive has succeeded the steam-boat, and has taken away from the Southerner more than the steam-boat ever gave him; for the potential value of the Hudson Valley and New York, as the main gateway from the Atlantic to the West, has been actualized at last in the Railway Age. Railway traffic from Chicago to New York is surpassing river traffic from St. Louis to New Orleans. The lines of communication within the Continent have been switched from the vertical direction to the horizontal. The North-West has been detached from the South and welded on to the North-East in interest and in sentiment.

Indeed the Easterner, who once presented the South with the river-steamer and the cotton-gin, has now won the heart of the North-Westerner with a double gift; he has come to him with a locomotive in one hand and a reaper-and-binder in the other, and so provided him with solutions for both his problems: transport and labor. By these two "Yankee notions" the allegiance of the North-West has been decided and the Civil War lost by the South before it has been fought. In taking up arms in the hope of redressing her economic reverses by a military counter-stroke, the South has merely consummated a *débâcle* that was already inevitable.

It may be said that all the different groups of colonists in North America had severe challenges to meet from their environments. In Canada the French had to encounter almost Arctic winters and in Louisiana the vagaries of a river almost as treacherous and devastating as the Yellow River of China, of which we took note in the first of the comparisons in this series. Still, taking all in all—soil, climate, transport facilities and the rest—it is impossible to deny that the original colonial home of the New Englanders was the hardest country of all. Thus North American history tells in favor of the proposition: the greater the difficulty, the greater the stimulus.

(2) THE STIMULUS OF NEW GROUND

So much for comparisons between the respective stimulating effects of physical environments which present different degrees of difficulty. Let us now approach the same question from a different angle by comparing the respective stimulating effects of old ground and new ground, apart from the intrinsic nature of the terrain.

Does the effect of breaking new ground act as a stimulus in itself? The question is answered in the affirmative in the myth of the Expulsion from Eden and in the myth of the Exodus from Egypt. In their removal out of the magic garden into the work-a-day world Adam and Eve transcend the food-gathering economy of primitive man and give birth to the founders of an agricultural and a pastoral civilization. In their exodus from Egypt the Children of Israel give birth to a generation which helps to lay the foundations of the Syriac Civilization. When we turn from myths to the history of religions we find these intuitions confirmed. We find, for example, that—to the consternation of those who ask "Can any good thing come out of Nazareth?"—the Messiah of Jewry does come out of that obscure village in "Galilee of the Gentiles," an outlying piece of new ground which had been conquered for Jewry by the Maccabees rather less than a century before the date of Jesus's birth. And when the indomitable growth of this Galilaean grain of mustard-seed turns the consternation of Jewry into active hostility, and this not only in Judaea itself but among the Jewish *diaspora*, the propagators of the new faith deliberately "turn to the Gentiles" and proceed to conquer new worlds for Christianity on ground far beyond the farthest limits of the Maccabaean kingdom. In the history of Buddhism it is the same story, for the decisive victories of this Indic faith are not won on the old ground of the Indic World. The Hīnayāna first finds an open road in Ceylon, which was a colonial annex of the Indic Civilization. And the Mahāyāna starts its long and round-about journey towards its future domain in the Far East by capturing the Syriacized and Hellenized Indic province of the Panjab. It is on the new ground of these alien worlds that the highest expressions of both the Syriac and the Indic religious genius eventually bear their fruit—in witness to the truth that "a prophet is not without honor save in his own country and in his own house."

. . . .

If it is true, as our evidence suggests, that new ground provides a greater stimulus to activity than old ground, one would expect to find such stimulus specially marked in cases where the new ground is separated from the old by a sea voyage. This special stimulus of transmarine colonization appears very clearly in the history of the Mediterranean during the first half of the last millennium (1000–500) B.C., when its western basin was being colonized competitively by maritime pioneers from three different civilizations in the Levant. It appears, for instance, in the degree to which the two greatest of these colonial foundations, Syriac Carthage and Hellenic Syracuse, outstripped their parent cities, Tyre and Corinth. The Achaean colonies in Magna Graecia (southern Italy and Sicily) became busy seats of commerce and brilliant centers of thought, while the parent Achaean communities along the northern coast of the Peloponnese remained in a backwater until after the Hellenic Civilization had passed its zenith. Similarly the Epizephyrian Locrians in Italy far surpassed the Locrians who remained in Greece.

The most striking case of all is that of the Etruscans, the third party competing with Phoenicians and Greeks in the colonization of the Western Mediterranean. The Etruscans who went west, unlike the Greeks and Phoenicians, were not content to remain within sight of the sea across which they had come. They pushed inland from the west coast of Italy across the Apennines and the Po to the foot of the Alps. The Etruscans who stayed at home, however, attained the very nadir of obscurity, for they are unknown to history and no record of the precise location of their homeland survives, though Egyptian records indicate that the original Etruscans took part with the Achaeans in the post-Minoan Völkerwanderung and had their base of operations somewhere on the Asiatic coast of the Levant.

The stimulating effect of a sea-crossing is perhaps greatest of all in a transmarine migration occurring in the course of a Völkerwanderung. Such occurrences seem to be uncommon. The only instances which the writer of this Study can call to mind are the migration, during the post-Minoan Völkerwanderung, of Teucrians, Aeolians, Ionians and Dorians across the Aegean to the west coast of Anatolia, and of Teucrians and Philistines to the coast of Syria; the migration of the Angles and Jutes to Britain during the post-Hellenic Völkerwanderung; the consequent migration of Britons across the Channel to what then came to be called Brittany; the contemporary migration of the Irish Scots to Argyll; and the migration of the Scandinavian Vikings in the Völkerwanderung which followed the abortive evocation of the ghost of the Roman Empire by the Carolingians: six instances in all. Of these, the Philistine migration proved comparatively unproductive, and the subsequent history of the Bretons was undistinguished, but the other four overseas migrations present certain striking phenomena which are not to be observed in the far more numerous instances of migration overland.

These overseas migrations have in common one and the same simple fact: in transmarine migration the social apparatus of the migrants has to be packed on board ship before it can leave the shores of the old country, and then be unpacked again at the end of the voyage. All kinds of apparatus—persons and property, techniques and institutions and ideas—are subject to this law. Anything that cannot stand the sea voyage at all has to be left behind, and many things—not only material objects—which the migrants do take with them, have to be taken to pieces, never perhaps to be reassembled in their original form. When unpacked, they are found to have suffered "a sea change into something rich and strange." When such a transmarine migration occurs in the course of a Völkerwanderung, the challenge is the more formidable and the stimulus the more intense because the society that is making the response is not one that is already socially progressive (like the Greek and Phoenician colonizers discussed above), but one that is still in that static condition which is the last state of primitive man. The transition, in a Völkerwanderung, from this passivity to a sudden paroxysm of storm and stress produces a dynamic effect on the life of any community, but this effect is naturally more intense when the migrants take ship than when they trek over solid ground, carrying with them much of the social apparatus which has to be discarded by the seafarer.

. . . .

The other positive creation that emerges from the ordeal of transmarine migration in the course of a Völkerwanderung is political. This new kind of polity is based not on kinship but on contract.

The most famous examples, perhaps, are the city states founded by the sea-faring Greek migrants on the coast of Anatolia in the districts subsequently known as Aeolis, Ionia and Doris, for the scanty records of Hellenic constitutional history seem to show that the principle of organization by law and locality instead of by custom and kinship asserted itself first in these Greek settlements overseas and was afterwards imitated in European Greece. In the oversea city states thus founded, the "cells" of the new political organization would be, not kindreds, but ships' companies. Having cooperated at sea as men do cooperate when they are "all in the same boat" amid the perils of the deep, they would continue to feel and act in the same way ashore when they had to hold a hardly won strip of coast against the menace of a hostile hinterland. On shore, as at sea, comradeship would count for more than kin, and the orders of a chosen and trusted leader would override the promptings of custom. In fact a collection of ships' companies joining forces to conquer a new home for themselves overseas would turn spontaneously into a city state articulated into local "tribes" and governed by an elective magistracy.

When we turn to the Scandinavian Völkerwanderung, we can discern the rudiments of a similar political development. If the abortive Scandinavian Civilization had come to birth instead of being swallowed up by that of Western Europe, the part once played by the city states of Aeolis and Ionia might have been played by the five city states of the Ostmen on the Irish coast or by the five boroughs (Lincoln, Stamford, Leicester, Derby and Nottingham) which were organized by the Danes to guard the landward frontier of their conquests in Mercia. But the finest flowering of an oversea Scandinavian polity was the Republic of Iceland, founded on the apparently unpromising soil of an Arctic island five hundred miles away from the nearest Scandinavian *point d'appui* in the Faroe Islands.

As for the political consequences of the transmarine migrations of the Angles and Jutes to Britain, it is perhaps something more than a coincidence that an island which was occupied at the dawn of Western history by immigrants who had shaken off the shackles of the primitive kin-group in crossing the sea should afterwards have been the country in which our Western Society achieved some of its most important steps in political progress. The Danish and Norman invaders who followed on the heels of the Angles, and who share the credit for subsequent English political achievements, enjoyed the same liberating experience. Such a combination of peoples offered an unusually favorable soil for political cultivation. It is not surprising that our Western Society should have succeeded, in England, in creating first "the King's Peace" and thereafter parliamentary government, while on the Continent our Western political development was retarded by the survival of the kin-group among the Franks and Lombards, who had not been relieved of that social incubus at the outset by the liberating transit of the sea.

. . . .

36

The Hydraulic Civilizations

KARL A. WITTFOGEL*

THE HYDRAULIC AND THE URBAN REVOLUTION

A great deal has recently been said about the "urban revolution"—a process of differentiation that split an originally village-centered agrarian society into an urban and a rural sector: town and village. The distinction between town and village considerably interested certain classical economists. Properly employed, it opens up important sociohistorical vistas.

However, those who use it today, either as part of a general developmental scheme or as a means for juxtaposing urban and rural ("folk") culture, tend to disregard two essential methodological precautions. Stress on the revolutionary character of the rise of the town one-sidedly accents what at the most is only one among several features of cultural change. For instance, Childe, who is eager to accustom his readers to the idea of revolution,[1] thus promotes historical views that are highly problematic. And his unqualified emphasis on urbanization as a developmental feature bulwarks the thesis of a general evolution in agrarian civilization that is manifestly false. This thesis, which culminates in the concept of a unilinear and necessarily progressive development of society, clearly contradicts the facts of history. It also contradicts the views of the classical economists, who with varying consistency recognized that the higher agrarian civilizations of the "Orient" and their urban and rural conditions followed a pattern of development decidedly unlike that of the West.

A juxtaposition of rural and urban institutions will promote our analysis of agrarian history to the extent to which we realize that there are at least two major types of rural-urban agrarian civilizations—hydraulic and non-hydraulic—and that the primitive farmers who started on an agrohydraulic course initiated a revolution that, structurally and for a whole epoch, split the higher civilizations into two different parts. Prior to the urban revolution and with extraordinary consequences, the fate of agricultural man was profoundly shaped by what may be suitably called the "hydraulic revolution."

MAJOR EFFECTS OF THE HYDRAULIC REVOLUTION

Hydraulic Agriculture

The peculiarities of agrohydraulic civilization become apparent as soon as we realize the

---

Reprinted from *Man's Role in Changing the Face of the Earth* by William R. Thomas (ed.) by permission of the author and The University of Chicago Press. © 1956 by The University of Chicago Press.

* Karl A. Wittfogel (1896–   ) is Director of the Chinese History Project and Professor of Chinese History at the University of Washington.

1. V. Gordon Childe, *Man Makes Himself* (New York: Mentor Books, 1952), p. 19.

role that the management of water has played in the subsistence economy of certain agrarian societies. To be sure, water is no more essential to agriculture than several other basic factors, such as temperature, the lay of the land, the fertility of the soil, and the character of the cultivable plants. But water is specific in that, among the manipulative essentials, it is the only element which tends to agglomerate in bulk. In its agriculturally most precious occurrence—as the water of rivers and large streams in arid or semiarid regions—it therefore defied the small-scale approach which, under preindustrial conditions, was so effective in the treatment of soil and plants. In order to bring fertility to large water-deficient areas by the management of substantial sources of water supply, man had to create large-scale enterprises that usually were operated by the government. The emergence of big productive water works (for irrigation) was frequently accompanied by the emergence of big protective water works (for flood control), and at times the latter even surpassed the former in magnitude and urgency. I suggest that this type of agrarian economy be called "hydraulic agriculture" to distinguish it from rainfall farming and hydroagriculture.

It is customary to apply the term "rainfall agriculture" to a situation in which a favorable climate permits cultivation on the basis of natural precipitation. The term "hydroagriculture" may be applied to a situation in which the members of a farming community resort to irrigation but, because of the scarcity and fragmentation of the available moisture, to irrigation on a small scale only. The term "hydraulic agriculture" may be applied to a situation in which the dimension of the available water supply leads to the creation of large productive and protective water works that are managed by the government.

Institutional Essence of Hydraulic Civilization

Irrigation was practiced in parts of Greece to compensate for the deficiencies of a semiarid climate and in Japan for the cultivation of an aquatic plant—rice. But in both countries a broken terrain permitted the growth of only small irrigation works, which could be handled without government direction. This fact has had far-reaching sociohistorical consequences. Japan established a simple variant of the same feudal society which, in a more complex form, emerged in medieval Europe. And Greece, prior to the Hellenistic period, developed aristocratic and democratic ways of life. In each case hydroagriculture encouraged the evolution of a multicentered society, an institutional conformation that assumed great significance in the rainfall-based civilizations of feudal Europe.

The contrast between this development and that of the agrohydraulic world is striking. Where agriculture required substantial and centralized works of water control, the representatives of the government monopolized political power and societal leadership, and they dominated their country's economy. By preventing the growth of strong competitive forces, such as a feudal knighthood, an autonomous church, or self-governing guild cities, they were able to make themselves the sole masters of their society. It is this combination of a hydraulic agriculture, a hydraulic government, and a single-centered society that constitutes the institutional essence of hydraulic civilization.

Differentiations

Within the orbit of hydraulic civilization immense cultural differences occur; but this essay cannot elaborate on them. An inquiry dealing with man's impact upon his natural environment may content itself with discussing certain subdivisions of the general institutional order that concern this man-nature relation.

Development in political structure is most consequential when the primitive governments of hydraulic tribes, managed largely by part-time functionaries, evolve into statelike organizations, managed by a body of full-time officials. The hydraulic state provides more comprehensive opportunities for imposing hydraulic installations upon the natural environment, but it also gives the men of the state apparatus the opportunity to neglect water works which will benefit the people, in order to build huge palaces and tombs and process precious organic and inorganic materials which will benefit the rulers.

Development in the patterns of property may lead from a predominance of state control over land and over professional handicraft and trade (simple hydraulic society) to a configuration in which mobile property in industry and trade is largely private, while land remains government controlled (semicomplex hydraulic society), or to a configuration in which private property in land is also widespread (complex hydraulic society). The rise of a semicomplex hydraulic order tends to differentiate the individual producer's interaction with nature; and it furthers the processes of locomotion which overcome difficulties of space and terrain. The rise of private property in land (tenancy as well as ownership) tends to stimulate careful agriculture. The intensive farmers of the ancient Near East were mainly tenants of public (state and temple) lands or of private estates. In China the transition to private landownership evoked the comment that the peasants worked less carefully on the public fields than on their own land.[2] Chinese peasant farming, which for over two thousand years has been based on private property of land, represents perhaps the most advanced form of intensive agriculture prior to the machine age.

Development in the spatial expansion of the hydraulic state is equally consequential. It is a historical fact that certain non-hydraulic *constructional* patterns and the major *organizational* and *acquisitive* patterns of hydraulic ("Oriental") despotism advanced far beyond the area of hydraulic economy proper. In "loose" hydraulic civilizations, such as China, India, and pre-Spanish Mexico, the monopolistic state apparatus controlled wide areas that had no comprehensive water works and in some cases not even small-scale irrigation.

This aspect was readily accepted by earlier analysts of "Asiatic" society, from the classical economists to Max Weber. But little effort has been made to explain the underlying mechanics of power. Still less analytic attention has been given to the fact that, either through a breakoff from a hydraulic regime proper (later Byzantium) or through institutional transfer (Mongol and post-Mongol Russia and probably Maya society), there may be governments which fulfil few or no agrohydraulic functions but which utilize the organizational methods of hydraulic despotism (such as record-keeping, censustaking, centralized armies, a state system of post and intelligence) as well as its acquisitive methods (such as general labor service, general and heavy taxation, and periodic confiscations) and its legal and political methods (such as fragmentative laws of inheritance and the suppression of independent political organizations) to keep private property weak and the nonbureaucratic forces of society politically impotent.

In fact, so strong were the devices of hydraulic statecraft and social control that they operated successfully in "marginal" areas without those large-scale water works which persisted in the hydraulic core areas and which apparently were an essential feature in the genesis of all historically relevant agrarian monopoly despotisms. From the standpoint of man's relation to man, the institutional periphery of the hydraulic world has been important in that it enormously widened the range of this despotic order. From the standpoint of man's relation to nature, it has been important in that, like the hydraulic core area, it frustrated the development of a big mechanized industry—the most profound recent change in man's attitude toward his natural environment.

MAN AND NATURE IN HYDRAULIC CIVILIZATION

Having considered the institutional setting of hydraulic civilization, we are now ready to contemplate more closely the specific relations between man and nature within it. These relations involve a peculiar system of mass labor in one segment of the economic order and a peculiar system of intensive work in another.

Government-directed Preparatory Operations: Division of Labor and Cooperation, Bureaucracy, Astronomical and Mathematical Sciences

Hydraulic civilization came into being not through a technological but through an organizational revolution. Its rise necessitated the establishment of a new system of division of labor and cooperation.

---

2. [Lü], *Lü-shih ch'un-ch'iu* ("Mr. Lü's Spring and Autumn Annals"), in *Ssŭpu Pei-yao*. Chung-hua ed. (Shanghai: 1936), Chapter 17.

Economic historians, when dealing with this matter, frequently assert that until recent times agriculture, in contrast to industry, involved little division of labor and no significant co-operation.[3] By and large, this view is justified with regard to the conditions of non-hydraulic farming. But it does not fit the operational pattern of hydraulic agriculture. A major separation between "preparatory labor"[4] and production proper is held to have occurred first in the industrial revolution. Actually, it took place much earlier and on an enormous scale in the hydraulic revolution.

Comprehensive preparatory activities were necessary to make cultivation either possible (in arid areas) or safe and rewarding (in semi-arid areas) or specific (in humid areas suitable for the growth of aquatic plants, such as rice and wet taro). The difference between this type of preparatory labor and the preparatory labor employed in modern industry is obvious. In industry preparatory labor provides the ultimate producer with raw material, with auxiliary material (e.g., coal for fuel and oil for lubrication), and also with special tools (machinery). In hydraulic economy preparatory labor consisted essentially in the gathering, conducting, and distributing of one auxiliary material—water. In modern industry the workers who engage in preparatory activities, such as mining, the making of machinery, etc., tend to work full time at their various jobs. In agrohydraulic economy division of labor proceeded differently. The great mass of the men who made and maintained the canals and dikes and who watched for floods did not do so full time and for the greater part of the year but part time and for as short a period as possible. In their overwhelming majority they were farmers, and the very authorities who mobilized them for hydraulic and other *corvée* duties were eager to have them return in good time to their villages to attend properly to the cultivation of their fields.

Thus, like modern industry, hydraulic agriculture involves significant division of labor; but, unlike modern industry, it involves no significant division of laborers. And while the organizers of preparatory work in industry endeavor to achieve their purpose with as small a labor force as possible, the organizers of the hydraulic *corvée* are interested in mobilizing as large a labor force as circumstances permit.

In hydraulic tribes, such as the Suk and Chagga of East Africa and the Pueblo Indians of New Mexico, all able-bodied males participated as a matter of course in the ditch work. In small, state-centered hydraulic civilizations, such as Bali and the early Mesopotamian and Indian city-states, the same mobilization pattern seems to have been customary.[5] A list of canal workers in ancient Lagash includes one corviable person from each commoner family.[6] In an irrigation conflict which, according to a pious legend, led to the Buddha's personal interference, the whole laboring population of the towns involved is said to have engaged in the hydraulic work.[7] Even clusters of territorial states may, at times, have gathered their combined populations to execute a big hydraulic task. This appears to have been the case in the Mexican federation prior to the arrival of the Spaniards. And it may have been a recurring trend in countries such as Egypt, where all villages depended on one huge source of irrigation water and where, therefore, their labor forces could be called up, either simultaneously or in shifts, to dig, dam, and watch for floods.

In larger hydraulic civilizations varying regional conditions suggested varying patterns of state-directed *corvée* labor, but its mass character remained unchanged. The underlying mobilization principle is drastically formulated by a historian of Mogul economy: "The King by his *firman* (order) could collect any number of men he liked. There was no

---

3. Edwin R. A. Seligman, *Principles of Economics* (New York: Longmans, Green & Co., 1914), p. 350; Werner Sombart, *Das Wirtschaftsleben im Zeitalter des Hochkapitalismus* (Munich: Duncker & Humblot, 1927), II, 825 ff.; Alfred Marshall, *Principles of Economics* (London: Macmillan, 1946), p. 290; for pioneer formulations see Adam Smith, *An Inquiry into the Nature and Causes of the Wealth of Nations* (New York: Modern Library, 1937), p. 6; and Karl Marx, *Das Kapital* (Hamburg: Meissner, 1919), I, 300, 322 ff.

4. For use of this term, see John S. Mill, *Principles of Political Economy* (London and New York: Longmans, Green and Co., 1909), p. 31.

5. Karl Wittfogel, *Oriental Despotism* (New Haven: Yale University Press, 1957), Chapter II.

6. Anna Scheider, *Die Anfänge der Kulturwirtschaft: Die sumerische Tempelstadt* (Essen: G. D. Baedeker, 1920), 108 ff.

7. Anonymous, *Jātakam: Das Buch der Erzählungen aus früheren Existenzen Buddhas*, Vol. V, Trans. by Julius Dutoit (Munich: Oskar Schloss, n.d.), p. 441.

limit to his massing of laborers, save the number of people in his Empire."[8] Pant was speaking of Mogul India, but his statement is valid for all analogous periods and countries. In hydraulic economy man extended his power over the arid, the semiarid, and certain humid parts of the globe through a government-directed division of labor and a mode of cooperation not practiced in agrarian civilizations of the non-hydraulic type.

The development of such a work pattern meant more than the agglomeration of large numbers of men. To have many persons cooperate periodically and effectively, there had to be planning, record-keeping, communication, and supervision. There had to be organization in depth. And above the tribal level this involved permanent offices and officials to man them—bureaucrats.

Of course, there were scribes in the city-states of ancient Greece and Rome and on the manorial estates, at the courts, and in the church centers of medieval Europe. But there was no national managerial network. In the great Oriental civilizations a hydraulic bureaucracy emerged together with the new type of organization in depth.

It was in these same Oriental (hydraulic) civilizations that man, in seeking a more rational approach to nature, laid the foundations for several sciences: astronomy, algebra, and geometry. Significantly, Greek mathematics and astronomy drew their early inspiration from the Oriental Near East, and they reached their climax under Euclid, Heron, and Ptolemy, not in Greece, but in one of the foremost centers of hydraulic culture—Egypt.

To be sure, neither the bureaucratic nor the scientific possibilities of hydraulic civilization were always exhausted. Some simpler hydraulic civilizations did not advance far. But the major hydraulic centers created elaborate administrations, and their astronomical and mathematical accomplishments were impressive. Thus any attempt to define hydraulic man's relation to nature must also consider the organizational (bureaucratic) and the scientific aspects of hydraulic economy.

[8.] D. Pant, *The Commercial Policy of the Moguls* (Bombay: D. B. Taraporevala Sons & Co., 1930), p. 70.

Irrigation Farming with Intensive Labor and Special Operations of Tillage

Government management of the great hydraulic works is supplemented by intensive farming based on irrigation. As stated above, irrigation farming also occurs in certain non-hydraulic societies, and to this extent the subsequent statements have validity beyond the borders of hydraulic civilization. But, while irrigation farming occurs occasionally in the non-hydraulic agricultural world, it is essential in the core areas of hydraulic civilization.

Irrigation demands a treatment of soil and water that is not customary in rainfall farming. The typical irrigation peasant has (1) to dig and re-dig ditches and furrows; (2) to terrace the land if it is uneven; (3) to raise the moisture if the level of the water supply is below the surface of the fields; and (4) to regulate the flow of the water from the source to the goal, directing its ultimate application to the crop. Tasks (1) and (4) are essential to all irrigation farming proper (inundation farming requires damming rather than ditching). Task (3) is also a frequent one, for, except at the time of high floods, the level of water tends to lie below that of the cultivated fields.

The type and amount of work involved in these operations become clear when we contrast the labor budget of an Oriental irrigation farmer with that of a rainfall farmer of medieval Europe. The medieval peasant usually plowed his field once or twice, then he sowed, and he harvested his crop at the end of the season. As a rule he spent no time watering.

The irrigation farmer, who, of course, plows, sows, and harvests, is in addition burdened with a number of other chores. In regions like Egypt, which depended mainly on inundation, these activities were insignificant, yet such regions were not very numerous. In others, such as ancient Mesopotamia, inundation was supplemented by canal irrigation. In this case a considerable amount of time was devoted to the watering of the fields. In modern India the husbandmen of a Punjab village spend much time irrigating their crops, wheat receiving three to four waterings in January, February, and March during more than twenty days. This work period is the most time-consuming item listed in the year's agricultural calendar. Sugar cane is an old Indian crop, requiring a great deal of water. In certain Deccan villages favoring its cultivation, the total cost of plowing, harrowing, planting, harvesting, and related operations is about 97 rupees as against 157 rupees for watering. In a South Gujarat village, studied by Mukhtyar,[9] watering is by far the heaviest expense item in the labor budget of the grower of sugar cane.

Concerning Chinese traditional irrigation economy, Buck has provided us with valuable numerical data. In 1923, 152 farms in Pinghsiang (in present Hopeh Province) grew wheat as their main crop. Of the time devoted to this crop, the peasant spent 10.2 per cent in plowing, 1.7 per cent in harrowing, 9.2 per cent in harvesting, or altogether 21.1 per cent, as against 58.5 per cent in irrigating.[10] In 1924 two groups of farmers in Kiangsu Province spent 21 and 25.1 per cent, respectively, in plowing, harrowing, and harvesting their main rice crop, as against 18.1 and 39.6 per cent in its irrigation.[11] As may be expected, the labor budgets show great variation in detail, but they all reveal that the amount of work involved in watering operations is commonly far in excess of the combined operations of a non-irrigation farmer.

Repeated preparatory tillage—plowing or hoeing—was also undertaken by the rainfall farmers of feudal Europe. But it was primarily on the manorial domain that the fields were "worked" three or four times, while the "poor peasants could often only work their land once to the detriment of the yield."[12]

Except for some cutting of thistles, intertillage was then, as now, technically impossible for grain crops, because, under conditions of rainfall farming, these "can be grown satisfactorily and most economically by planting them in solid stands so that they cover all the ground equally." As a rule, they are today "given no tillage while they are growing."[13]

Plants grown in rows are easily approached and easily cultivated. But the most important of these, corn and potatoes, appeared in Europe only after the discovery of America, and even after the sixteenth century their economic importance remained definitely secondary to that of the cereals. In the West the modern dry farmer still hesitates to cultivate grain crops in rows. After an early harrowing he frequently lets nature take its course.

Irrigation agriculture requires a rowlike arrangement of the seeds not only for crops such as corn and potatoes but also for cereals. Plants can be watered by ditches only if proper space for the distributing furrows is provided. The layout of the fields differs in accordance with economic experience, crops, and terrain, but all patterns aim at making the plants accessible to the irrigation farmer, who may work the soil and the crop as thoroughly as he wishes.

Intensive techniques are not limited to the period between sowing and harvesting. Frequently the soil is plowed or harrowed several times before the sowing. Nor are these techniques limited to the fields for which irrigation water is available. In semiarid areas (under conditions of full aridity cultivation ends where the water supply ends) the farmers are eager to grow not only crops which they can water but also crops which may mature without the benefit of irrigation.

Chinese farmers in the province of Kiangsu who had sufficient water for two main crops only, rice and vegetables, used to grow wheat and barley without irrigation. However, they treated the last two as intensively as the first two. Of all labor devoted to wheat, intertillage accounted for over 20 per cent; in the case of barley, it accounted for almost 33 per cent; and in the case of kaoliang, which in some parts of Hopeh is grown without irrigation, it accounted for more than 40 per cent.[14]

9. G. C. Mukhtyar, *Life and Labour in a South Gujarat Village*. Ed. C. N. Vakil (London and New York: Longmans, Green, 1930), p. 96.
10. John L. Buck, *Chinese Farm Economy* (Nanking: University of Nanking; Chicago: University of Chicago Press, 1930), p. 306.
11. *Ibid.*, p. 310.
12. Charles Parain, "The Evolution of Agricultural Technique," in J. H. Clapham and E. Power (eds.), *Cambridge Economic History*, Vol. I (Cambridge: Cambridge University Press, 1942), p. 141. *Cf.* Karl G. Lamprecht, *Deutsches Wirtschaftsleben im Mittelalter: Untersuchungen über die materielle Kultur des platten Landes auf Grund der Quellen zunächst des Mosellandes*, Vol. I, no. 1 (Leipzig: Alphons Dürr, 1886), p. 557.
13. John S. Cole & O. R. Mathews, "Tillage," in U.S. Dept. of Agriculture, *Soils and Men: Yearbook of Agriculture* (Washington, D.C.: Govt. Printing Office, 1938), p. 327.
14. Buck, *op. cit.*, p. 306.

In India certain Deccan villages grow their main cereal crop, *bajri*, also without irrigation. But, like the irrigated cereals, it is planted in rows and intensively cultivated. It gets one plowing and four harrowings before sowing and further treatment after sowing.

The good Aztec farmer made beds for his corn, pulverized the soil, and kept his crop free of weeds. He irrigated whenever this was possible, but he obviously was expected to farm intensively under any circumstances. The Mayan peasants of Yucatán, who did not water their crops, weeded them as carefully as did the inhabitants of the highland regions in which irrigation farming was customary.

Thus, as the political patterns of hydraulic civilization spread far beyond the areas of hydraulic economy, so the techniques or irrigation farming spread far beyond the irrigated fields. These techniques established an agronomical relation among man, soil, and plants that, in terms of a given amount of land, was much more rewarding than the agriculture of preindustrial Europe. Early in the twentieth century a European agronomist found the Indian peasants, who by and large followed their traditional pattern of cultivation, quite as good as the average modern British farmer and in some respects better. The father of organic chemistry, Justus von Liebig, in comparing nineteenth-century German agriculture with contemporary Chinese farming, viewed the former as the procedure of "a child compared to that of a mature and experienced man."[15]

. . . .

Dimensions of Hydraulic Civilization in Time, Space, and Manpower

According to conservative estimates hydraulic civilizations took shape in the ancient Near East not later than the fourth millennium B.C., and they persisted until very recent times. It may therefore be said safely that in this area hydraulic civilization endured for about five millenniums.

The great hydraulic civilizations of India and China maintained themselves for some three or four millenniums. And recent archeological finds suggest that in certain areas of the Western Hemisphere, such as Peru, hydraulic civilizations may have existed at least since the first millennium B.C., that is, for more than two millenniums prior to the arrival of the Spaniards.

Neither ancient Greece nor feudal Europe nor Japan can equal these figures. Greek agrarian civilization seems to have lasted for a millennium until Hellenistic despotism put an end to its non-Oriental pattern. The societies of feudal Europe and Japan had an even shorter duration.

The core areas and the margins of the hydraulic civilizations covered the greater part of western, southern, and eastern Asia. The Hellenistic regimes, the Orientalized Roman Empire, the Arab conquests of Spain and Sicily, and the Byzantine, Turkish, and Russian expansions imposed Orientally despotic regimes on large areas of Europe.

In Africa north of the Sahara, a hydraulic way of life prevailed for millenniums. A thousand years ago it seems to have spread temporarily from Lake Tanganyika and Kenya to Rhodesia. . . . In recent times it was observed among the Chagga and a few other tribes of central East Africa.

Hydraulic agriculture and government persisted in some major Pacific islands, such as Hawaii. In pre-Columbian America hydraulic developments spread beyond the Rio Grande in the north. In the Meso-American highlands and in the lowlands of Yucatán, clusters of loose and marginal hydraulic civilizations emerged. And in the south hydraulic expansion reached its maximum on the eve of the Spanish conquest. Early in the sixteenth century the Inca Empire stretched from Peru to Ecuador in the north and to Bolivia and Chile in the west and south. It coordinated practically all important centers of higher agrarian development in South America. Clearly, hydraulic civilizations covered a vastly larger proportion of the surface of the globe than all other significant agrarian civilizations taken together.

. . . According to our present information, it would seem that, prior to the commercial and industrial revolution, the majority of all human beings lived within the orbit of hydraulic civilization.

---

15. Justus von Liebig, *Chemische Briefe*, 6th ed. (Leipzig and Heidelberg: Carl Winters, 1878), p. 453.

Costs and Perspectives of Hydraulic Civilization

Manifestly, then, this civilization was an eminently successful "going concern." It stimulated organization in depth. It gave birth to certain sciences. And it refined farming and handicraft. Yet, in terms of human affairs, it was as costly as it was tenacious. While such scientific aids to counting and measuring as astronomy and mathematics emerged, these developments eventually stalled, and the experimental sciences never gained significance. Masses of men were coordinated for public works and warfare, but the patterns of integration were crude, and they improved little throughout the centuries. Farming techniques were subtle, but from the standpoint of the main protagonist, the peasant, their one-sidedly laborintensive development was frustrating. Hydraulic agriculture made the cultivator till his fields with a minimum of labor-saving tools and animals and with a maximum of human labor. Being politically without influence, the hydraulic farmer maintained a man-nature relation that involved unending drudgery on a socially and culturally depressing level.

Aristotle's vision of a society of free men based on the advance of the mechanical arts is increasingly being realized in the multicentered industrial societies of the West. It never materialized in hydraulic society. For reasons inherent in this institutional conformation, the masters of hydraulic civilization succeeded in perpetuating the economic and technological order which was the *raison d'être* for their existence.

The stationary character of the great Oriental civilizations was noted incisively in the eighteenth and nineteenth centuries, when the expanding commercial and industrial societies of the West began to loosen up what had previously seemed to be an indestructible societal edifice. The Western impact on man-nature relations in the countries of Oriental despotism was as varied as the forms in which it occurred. No fair-minded observer will deny its destructive aspects. But he will also point to the positive and non-totalitarian innovations that not infrequently accompanied it. And he will submit that, even in its most predatory and aggressive manifestations, Western colonialism, which today is subsiding, is more superficial than the new totalitarian colonialism, which is spreading so rapidly.

Hydraulic ("Oriental") civilization has been in transition for generations. It continues to change in a global situation dominated, on the one hand, by the forces of the totalitarian revolution and, on the other hand, by the forces of the multicentered Western world, in which the growth of an increasingly open society is enhanced by the democratic version of a second industrial revolution. The future of hydraulic civilization and of man's relation to nature and man everywhere ultimately depends on the relative strength of these two competing revolutions.

37

The Impress of Effective Central Authority upon the Landscape

DERWENT S. WHITTLESEY*

Political activities leave their impress upon the landscape, just as economic pursuits do. Many acts of government become apparent in the landscape only as phenomena of economic geography; others express themselves directly. Deep and widely ramified impress upon the landscape is stamped by the functioning of effective central authority.

By "central authority" is meant sovereignty over an area of marked diversity. To be "effective" the central government must exert more than nominal control over its area. Today "effective central authority" is a function of the national state.[1]

EXPRESSIONS OF SECURITY

Security is one of the most valued products of effective central authority—the guarantee against molestation within the state and the assurance of resistance to invasion from without.

In the state which feels itself secure habitations are disseminated wherever this mode of settlement suits the economic life. In new countries (by "new" is meant those which have been settled in the current age of central authority) farmsteads are dispersed in most types of agricultural occupance. Even where the agricultural mode favors clustering, as in irrigated districts and on plantations and market gardens, the farmsteads commonly line up as stringtowns along roads, so that each may be centrally located in the midst of its farm land. This is in marked contrast to the farm villages in similar agricultural units of old countries. There the houses may cluster in tight knots. A good many are perched on defensible hills or protected by water, and are therefore inconveniently remote from the farm land. A comparison of the settlement patterns of Southern California and Southern Italy illustrates this distinction. In countries which were settled in eras of insecurity, defense points have now been to some degree abandoned in favor of more convenient sites. Crowded hills are deserted for open plain, as at Les Baux in Provence. Or hill villages expand downhill, but retain their ancient centers on the defense point; Spain supplies numerous examples of this shifting. In extreme cases the crest is denuded of buildings and reclaimed for gardening (*e.g.*, Loudon, France). Sicilian villages which formerly hugged the coast and its protecting waters are

---

Reproduced from the *Annals* of the Association of American Geographers, Vol. XXV, 1935.

* Derwent S. Whittlesey (1890-1956) was Professor of Geography at Harvard University.

1. Unless capitalized, "state" is used throughout in its generic sense of "sovereign power."

pushing tentacles of farmsteads into the rolling, open uplands, now that the Mafia has been deprived of its threat to life and property. Where artificial defenses were formerly maintained, moated granges and villages free themselves for expansion by filling their encircling waters with their encircling walls. Where the agricultural system cogently favors scattered habitations, isolated farmsteads appear, concomitant with security.

Urban centers are precluded by their function from dispersing in the way farm villages may do, but they may and do spread out. Security not only permits them to occupy more space, but it stimulates both trade and manufacturing, their two chief reasons for existing. Flourishing economic life demands land for port facilities, rail and road terminals, and wide thorofares; space must be provided for retailing on a large scale and for wholesaling; professions and other services multiply; new largeness of ideas sets up new space requirements for residence and for recreation. All these call for acreage undreamed of in days of straitened insecurity.

Trade follows security, and trade has forced walled seaports to burst their bonds. All of La Rochelle but its port lies on land which was outside the walls in the 17th century; so also with San Juan, Puerto Rico. The easily defended *calanque* which has fixed the Rhône Valley seaport of Marseilles for at least 2800 years has been turned over to the fishing fleet, and a new commercial port filched from the open Mediterranean by jetties. London, Antwerp, Rotterdam, Hamburg, and many another estuary city has dug a new harbor in soft alluvium adjacent to but below the ancient constricted port. To obtain space for new business nearly every commercial city in continental Europe, and the larger ones in Japan, have converted their moated walls into boulevards. Paris and Vienna are the most famous examples, but Toulouse, Cologne, Seville, Milan, and hundreds of others, large and small, disclose the same history in their street pattern. Less spectacular, but more costly, is the widening and straightening of countless streets, and the substitution of modern buildings for medieval rookeries. Of all the square miles pierced only by ten- or fifteen-foot streets and still narrower culs-de-sac which made up fourteenth century Paris, only one small fragment survives today. The dead-end and zigzag alleys of Japanese cities are giving way to more regular plats of streets. Three centuries ago hardly a cathedral in Europe stood free from a parasitic congeries of habitations; today their plazas are open. The cluttered and congested urban landscape which expressed the day when political security lagged behind expanding business has all but disappeared. New functions, particularly large-scale manufacturing and the manifold business of rail terminals, have grown up outside the "ring" boulevards which mark ancient fortifications.

The spacious residential suburb is likewise the product of an age of security as well as an age of fast transport. It has nothing but location in common with its precursor, the medieval faubourg, which was a slum huddled for protection against the walls of a city. Residences in most European and Asiatic cities retain the walled-in character of their predecessors. In the new countries of British origin, and even in Great Britain itself, dwelling houses are likely to face the street across open lawn, with no barrier except rarely a fence of wood or wire, or at most a low wall. The spacious habit of building each town house detached and not walled-off from its neighbors, seems to be the ultimate landscape expression of generations of security, beginning in Europe and transplanted to the colonies. At any rate it is practiced almost exclusively in English-speaking new countries, and most prevalently in the newer parts of them. But even there some time has generally elapsed between the abandonment of the stockade and the adoption of the detached house. The residential streets of little cities along the Atlantic seaboard of North America, such as Portsmouth (N. H.) and Charleston (S. C.) as well as the older sections of all the large seaboard centers, present solid ranks of abutting façades. West of the Appalachians only the most congested sections of the largest cities are built in solid blocks; in small cities and in residential sections of large ones the detached dwelling reigns, even where it is built with the intention of housing two or three families in "flats."

SPECIAL FEATURES OF BOUNDARIES

Expansiveness does not everywhere accompany security. Along international boundaries the landscape may be strewn with features intended by central authority to maintain security. At the least a customhouse and immigration post (often housed in the officer's home) stands sentinel at every major route crossing. On some European borders a gate, usually a heavy balanced pole, stands ready to be lowered at night and for any emergency. On minor roads a single military official is in sole charge. On main thorofares several men are stationed, often both civilian and military authorities. Even the undefended border between the United States and Canada is studded with official buildings where a few men are kept on duty. Along boundaries where acute tension is felt, either because of smuggling, antipathy between political systems which face each other across the line, or recent boundary displacements, the soldier guard may mount to a military encampment, although only at crucial passways. At the exit of the Vall d'Arán in the Pyrenees, where the temptation to smuggle is powerful, the border is controlled by a small company of soldiers. On the Carso the 1934 frontier between Italy and Yugoslavia near the strategic Peartree Pass is marked by a made-to-order garrison city, regiments of soldiers, airplane landing fields, ammunition dumps along the railroad, and freshly made military roads—all in a karst region almost bare of vegetation and apparently devoid of human inhabitants other than the garrison and its entourage. Even the St. Gotthard Pass on the border of peaceable Switzerland was heavily fortified.[2]

At railroad crossings there are, in addition to the usual officials, terminal facilities for trains which technically do not cross the border. In practice the terminal is generally in the town nearest the boundary, and not on the line. Whether the gauge differs or not, the terminal exists, because only a few of the trains go through, and in any event the locomotives and crews are changed. Many boundaries are closed to aircraft, except along specified lanes, which are as definite routes as roads or rails, although they are invisible.

Definition of boundary lines, *i.e.* replacement of boundary zones by boundary lines,

follows upon the establishment of effective central authority. When central authority is weak, border districts, even if legally subordinate, are in practice at liberty to carry on their life pretty much as they please. They usually work out intimate economic reprocity with neighboring political units, which themselves may be independent or nominally subordinate to some other inclusive state. Inhabitants of such harmoniously functioning border regions feel foreign to the people of their respective distant capitals, but not to their neighbors across the political boundary. When power is concentrated in a central locus, border zones are subordinated. Whenever the local interests clash with interests of the state as a whole, the border interests suffer. Central authority, to be effective, must proclaim fixed linear boundaries which can be defended against military aggression and economic penetration. Where political borders coincide with population deserts, such as oceans or large lakes, expanses of dunes without oases, perpetual ice, or dense forests, local life is little or not at all affected by fixing a linear boundary. In new countries, where a linear boundary has been drawn antecedent to settlement, the economic life conforms to it without strain, although tariffs often induce branch factories in border towns, and thus modify the landscape. Where manufacturing plants are built beyond the line to take advantage of tariffs, workers commute from their established homes across the boundary, or if distance prevents this, they may move to new "line" towns on the frontier of their homeland. Rarely, a double town bestrides the line. In most regions the substitution of linear for zonal boundaries cuts off kinsmen from each other, parts business associates, and severs chorologic units. This is true even along mountains which are commonly thought of as barriers (*e.g.*, the Pyrenees), and populous plains such as Flanders, Lorraine, Posen, Silesia, have repeatedly seen towns lopped off from part of their upland, and have occasionally suffered the arbitrary dissection of cities.

Boundaries recently displaced are likely to mark zones of personal risk. On borders of the Polish Corridor and Upper Silesia transgression in the 1930s without the proper papers made one liable to arrest and confinement, even though the culprit had not left his own property. Since boundaries are often arbitrarily drawn cross-country through farms

---

2. For details of border phenomena, especially those along the Franco-German boundary, see Hassinger, H.: "Der Staat als Landschaftsgestalter," *Zeitschrift für Geopolitik* 9 (1932), 117–122, 182–187.

and even through towns, this surveillance annoys the individual and so adds increments of personal hatred to the general enmity.

To guard against aggression many boundaries are lined with defenses, e.g., the interwar Franco-German border. Such defenses were linked by strategic roads and railroads, such as the Stelvio Pass road, the high-level bridge across the Kiel Canal, and certain railroads in pre–World War I Poland. The land thus used was withdrawn from other occupance. Towns along the boundary were semi-military, being differentiated from ordinary commercial towns by barracks, fortifications, and a general air of being supported by government rather than by business.

Boundary displacements may be followed by political acts which directly or indirectly modify the landscape. Slight changes, such as the substitution of one language for another on public buildings and street signs, are common. Even stores and offices may be required by law to display only the official language. Perhaps the extreme case in 1934 was the Lower Vistula Valley. There an important railroad bridge across the river was first closed, and later moved to another site. A fishing hamlet among the dunes was elevated into a modern port by the construction of costly harbor works, and linked to the interior of Poland by new stretches of railroad. Indirect pressure, such as government contracts, was exerted to deflect goods and people into this new all-Polish channel of ingress and egress. As a result Danzig, the ancient port city of the Vistula Valley, had to share the trade with its politically fostered rival. By treaty Danzig had accepted the smaller share—45 per cent to Gydnia's 55 per cent.[3] Routes and other communication patterns are frequently altered after a boundary displacement; at first certain connections are closed or so restricted by inspections at the border that they fall into disuse; then new connecting links, suited to the new alignment of territory, are built. All this in the name of security.

Expressions of Governmental Activity

Central authority usually undertakes to act for the whole of its territory in specified matters. This tends to produce uniformity in cultural impress even where the natural landscape is diverse.

Public buildings of uniform function and form are commonplace examples. The post-offices in France, the army posts in all countries, the state capitols in the United States (these by imitation rather than prescription), are easily recognized types. In a very heterogeneous country, such as the United States, regionalism may be given recognition. Generally nowadays the federal government builds its post-offices in conformity to local tradition. In New England they are "colonial"; in California, Spanish; in the Middle West, either classical or modernistic.

In many new countries a uniform land survey, including routes, has been sketched upon the landscape antecedent to settlement. This is notably true of English-speaking North America, except for the colonial settlements and the Old South. It also applies, but much more locally, to parts of Latin America and other new countries, including settlements made centuries ago in eastern Germany, when it was "new." Perhaps the system of Roman roads, still conspicuous features of the route pattern in Romanized Europe, may be cited as an additional and still earlier example of a pattern of communication ordained by central authority.

In the Roman permanent "camps" of Western Europe, and in towns laid out by Germans as they pushed eastward after the tenth century, rectilinear street patterns within circular or elliptical walls are common, although blocks are likely to be unequal and streets not quite straight. Modern national governments began to sponsor fiat towns early in the seventeenth century. The gridiron pattern of streets was seized upon as convenient, since the new towns were generally laid out in plains and defense was not necessary.[4] Richelieu in western France, laid out by an officer of the Church, and Mannheim on the Rhine, laid out by a military officer of the state, are samples. The grid proved to be an equally handy pattern for mushroom towns in new countries. Nearly every municipality of the Pampa, except Buenos Aires, is an example. Philadelphia is

---

3. Other modifications of Germanic border regions since 1914 are discussed by Hassinger, *op. cit.*

4. As compared to a jig-saw pattern shot through with a few radial lines, the gridiron city is difficult to defend. Ambush, barricades, and central command are handicapped.

an early case (1682) in North America. The Dutch followed the scheme in Batavia. In these cases the orientation is rarely due north-south and east-west. Compass orientation of city streets fits naturally into the coarser grid of the rectilinear survey, adopted in many new countries. Melbourne is an example from the antipodes. Chicago is the outstanding case of the very large city oriented north-south and east-west, and monotonously and regularly extended. The almost featureless lacustrine plain on which it lies has neither compelled nor encouraged deviation from the ideal plan. The offsets which accommodate the straight-line survey to the spherical earth appear as jogs in the street pattern. Numerous new suburbs of old cities throughout the world have been similarly platted. Where no rectilinear survey exists, grids may have any conceivable orientation, *e.g.*, along streams, country roads, or railroads, or hinged to a stretch of fortification-turned-boulevard.

Most gridiron street plans have not been directly imposed by governments. The appeal of convenience, however, has been irresistible in an age when new cities and new suburbs of old cities have been multiplying on open plains, thanks to increased trade and manufacturing made possible by powerful government.

Governments often stimulate migration into newly acquired areas by offering landholdings larger than those current in regions from which settlers are drawn. This distinction tends to disappear in time unless it is reinforced by the natural environment. In the Pampa large holdings, originally stock ranches, persist because they carry social prestige, but much of the land is now under the plow, being tilled by tenants on short-term leases. Eastern Germany of the 1930s, wrested from Slavs, was blocked out by the invaders from the west in large, uninterrupted units, strikingly in contrast to the crazyquilt of both holdings and fields in parent Germany. These very large units persisted chiefly in rugged, marshy, sterile districts where small farmers could not make a living and horse raising afforded a genteel occupation.

As the United States approaches demographic maturity, the average size of landholdings has undergone progressive change toward harmony with the environment. In the Corn Belt the typical patent from the government granted 160 acres, a figure not far from the unit which in that region can most effectively be worked by a single farm family. Farther west, in the semi-arid and desert country, this unit early proved too small, and homestead allotments double and later quadruple this size came to be permitted by law. Where grazing or dry-farming dominates, even 640 acres was too small a unit, and holdings were merged to form adequate ranches. In the irrigable areas of "Mediterranean" California and "Egyptian" Arizona, on the contrary, the original large holdings, many of them stock ranches dating from Spanish times, were morselled into twenty-, ten-, and even five-acre lots.

The existence of effective central authority implies the power to collect taxes and distribute funds throughout the whole territory of the state. Notable modifications of the landscape have resulted from the habit governments have of distributing to backward and to pioneer sections money collected from prosperous districts. This is, in other terms, a transfer from regions favored by the natural environment to regions laboring under temporary or permanent environmental handicaps. The Tennessee Valley Authority is a spectacular example, but the principle has long been in operation in the United States, thanks to loose construction of the Constitution. Much of the irrigation of land in western States has been paid for from federal funds; the federal government provides aid in building roads, especially in sparsely populated regions; and many of the railroads in North America (and in every other continent) have been similarly aided, wherever they have been trajected through difficult or unpeopled territory. In North America and Australia, at least, the States and the Provinces have carried this redistribution of funds further. The southern half of Michigan, Wisconsin, Minnesota, and Ontario each supports schools and roads in the northern quarters; in like fashion the eastern part of each Great Plains State contributes to the maintenance of its western part, and humid Australia to the arid ends of the several States. Lowlands in mountainous middle latitude countries spend a part of their taxes for objects which make habitation of the highlands possible. Forests and recreational preserves in handicapped regions are likely to be maintained by central government. From this view-point the study of pioneer areas undertaken by the

American Geographical Society* resolved itself into these problems: first, how much government aid is needed; and second, how much it is socially wise to disburse in any given area.

A number of regions, prosperous enough to support themselves in local affairs, can benefit greatly if given aid from the central government on specific problems which transcend a single region. Flood prevention in the Mississippi Basin is too comprehensive a task to be dealt with effectively by any existing political unit smaller than the United States. Reclamation of the Zuyder Zee by the Netherlands, reforestation in Alpine Europe and elsewhere, the construction of *autostrade* by the Italian state, the Canadian policy of supporting intersectional railroads, hydro-electric installations in Ireland and Russia—all these are examples of comprehensive undertakings which only central authority can handle.

Public funds available for regional redistribution may be misdirected. Some unwise expenditure results from necessary experimentation, since governments have had relatively little experience in enterprises of this nature. Political favor and log-rolling cause other and lamentable leaks. The federal appropriation for "rivers and harbors" in the United States has been notorious for a century. Every country no doubt has counterparts of our pork barrel. An abuse hard to eliminate arises naturally, as useful institutions become antedated or cease to satisfy the needs of the community. Vested interest, often supported by law, prolongs customary expenditure for indefinite periods. Army posts in the United States Indian Country, the support of the established church in England, are cases in point.

Government lays hands in a special way upon its capitals. The focussing of roads, railroads, and canals upon the seat of government is partly the result of economic evolution, but it is often encouraged by political aid. Berlin, for instance, was not the center of Germany to the degree indicated by its hub of communication lines. The location of some capitals has been shifted in harmony with migrating political power. Nearly every one of the original United States moved its capital from the seaboard to the interior, as population increased in the back country. The reverse process occured when colonial powers imposed their rule upon settled communities. The seat of administration was then brought to the coast, as from Cuzco to Lima, from Kandy to Colombo, and from Delhi to Calcutta.

Once fixed, capitals become the pets of government. On them public money is frequently lavished beyond present needs, even beyond the natural desire of the people to dress up their capital city. Delhi, Peiping, Berlin, Rome (both ancient and modern), have been notable examples of generous expenditure. All these cities are splendid to look at, and each looks very different from the ordinary commercial city. Minor capitals have been garnished in proportion to their funds. Every German quondam state has an imitation Versailles, and the democratic United States of America have spent staggering sums to house their governments. Washington and Canberra, as purely political fiat towns, are the clearest beneficiaries of political favor, but even London, primarily a world port and the leading manufacturing city of Britain, is impressively the national capital. The spaciousness of modern capitals—"Washington, city of magnificent distances," Paris with its broad boulevards, Rome, roomy enough to accommodate both the modern capital and its exhumed predecessor of antiquity, are made possible by the security which central authority affords. Some governments which have spent overmuch on dressing up their capital cities have been overthrown not long after. Athens of Pericles and Versailles of the later Bourbons by their very splendor contributed to the undoing of their sponsors.

Outside the capital city the hand of government puts its stamp on many places. Universities may form the nuclei of small cities. Prisons strikingly modify the landscape and in places, as at Princetown on Dartmoor, dominate it. Experimental farms may occupy large acreage. All these are exceptional. Most government agencies are housed in buildings more or less lost in ordinary towns and cities —district courts and police registration

---

* [Editors' note: In 1925 the American Geographical Society undertook a long-range program of research involving the study of pioneer settlement in different parts of the world. Eventually, the Society published four volumes: Isaiah Bowman, *Pioneer Fringe* (1931); *Pioneer Settlement* (a symposium by 26 authors, 1932); A. Grenfell Price, *White Settlers in the Tropics* (1939); Karl J. Pelzer. *Pioneer Settlement in the Asiatic Tropics* (1945).]

bureaus, central banks, port headquarters, and the like. Yet they are likely to bear clear evidence of their official character. If built of costly materials in a massive or a pretentious style, as is commonly the case, they stand out among their neighbors. The site too is likely to enhance their distinction. It may be a conspicuous hill, a plaza, or a park, such as only government can afford. On the other hand it may be an out-of-the-way spot or an obscure block on a mean street which people would never search out but for government compulsion. A government building erected in a poor neighborhood improves surrounding values. Conversely, if the site happens to be in a retail shopping section, the government building, lacking show windows and shops, no matter how fine a piece of architecture, serves as a damper to trade, and surrounding land values are thereby lessened.

Laws Resulting in Landscape Modifications

Tariffs imposed by central authority set their mark on widely separated regions. The incidence of tariffs is determined largely by economic geography. Those which fence out foreign manufactured goods have led to the creation of new manufactural districts, as in Montreal, Toronto, Hamilton, and Windsor, in Canada. Budapest and Ljubljana created factory districts to supply peoples once served by Vienna. Tariffs or subsidies applying to agricultural produce favor agricultural systems different from those which would exist with free trade. Examples: the large acreage of wheat in France, a cool, moist land; the intensive spots of tobacco and sugar beets in nearly every country of Western Europe; sugar-cane in Hawaii, Puerto Rico, the Philippines, and Louisiana.

Embargoes of other sorts alter the location of items in the landscape. The refusal of the State of Maine to permit the exportation of its water power led to the building of a large pulp-mill on the Lower Penobscot to use Kennebec power and imported pulpwood. Power developed in New Hampshire on the Upper Connecticut was once shipped to populous Boston and vicinity for miscellaneous manufacturing and lighting. Dissatisfaction with Mexican participation in an irrigation canal which crossed the international boundary in the Imperial Valley spurred on the construction of an all-American canal on less advantageous terrain.

Laws affect both the tempo and the direction of settlement in all new countries, although in the process the law itself is much modified, or where it conflicts too stridently with its new-found environment, abrogated.

The early European settlements in the New World, made in the fifteenth century, were launched under franchise from European governments; in many cases the present political subdivisions are bounded by the terms of those franchises. Sea-to-sea grants in British North America account for the east-west boundaries of several States on the Atlantic seaboard and in the Middle West, boundaries which run counter to the grain of the country. The Papal Line of Demarcation of 1493-4 accounts for Portugese Brazil in Spanish America and for four centuries of Spanish rule in the Philippines.

As settlement progressed inland from toeholds on harbors, it was protected or hampered or deflected by the aegis of the law. At the outset the seigneurial system dominant throughout Europe was transplanted to the new continents. It suited the plantation system of agriculture and has never been much modified where that mode of land use still prevails. For centuries it suited the Pampa, a remote grassland where livestock ranching paid better than any other agricultural system. With increasing demand for grain, all the more humid Pampa became potential wheat or mixed farming country. The social prestige of immense estates, fortified by the law, retarded their subdivision, although land was often tilled under a wasteful system of tenantry. In contrast to the Pampa stand Canada and the United States. In New England particularly, the seigneurial system never took root; elsewhere, except in the plantation South, it was abandoned because the small farm better fitted the environmental conditions. As settlement swept inland from the humid seaboard into the humid Middle West, homestead laws fixed the size of individual's claims to unappropriated public land at a figure which had proved satisfactory in the parent States. In sub-humid regions, where tillage has to be extensive, and still more in regions so dry that only grazing can prosper without irrigation, application of these laws predestined homesteaders to hopelessly inadequate holdings. The common practice of alloting alternate sections of the land to railroad companies as an inducement to extend the rails, further complicated the pattern of land holdings. Successive laws increased the acreage allowed, but they came too late to benefit most of the stock raising country. It has been found difficult, often impossible, to piece together from abandoned claims and the rigid checkerboard of railroad holdings, enough land with the proper balance between winter and summer pasture and with suitably spaced waterholes, to make a successful stock ranch. As a result some land is overgrazed while other land is not used to its capacity, or is occupied without legal right.

The general progression of settlement in new countries of British origin has been from humid to arid. The English Common Law did not require much modification to serve for the humid parts of the United States and the British Dominions, but when it began to be applied indiscriminately to dry regions some sections of the code were found to run so sharply counter to local needs that they had to be abrogated. To cite a notable example: riparian rights if adhered to would have prevented the installation of irrigation works, without serving any useful purpose in regions devoid of navigable streams. Conversely, laws had to be drafted to safeguard the rights of irrigation farming, since the Common Law, a native of the humid English climate, incorporated no such rules. In the San Joaquin Valley of California litigation between landholders who wished to maintain riparian rights and those who desired to divert water for irrigation, retarded the evolution of "Mediterranean" agriculture for decades. In 1934, not all the irrigable land was under ditch, and in each irrigated district the crops grown were dominantly those which promised profit at the time when legal controversies happened to be settled.

Laws affecting the use of land and natural resources are not confined to new countries. Every considerable social revolution produces its crop of laws affecting land holdings. Generally such laws are calculated to break up or to prevent the rise of large estates, to restrict holdings to small acreage, and to limit the agricultural occupance to those modes in which small holdings pay. In Rumania, Russia, Ireland, and other parts of Europe where estates have been subdivided during and since World War I, subsistence farming has generally replaced commercial farming, crude tools replaced machinery, fields were reduced in size, the percentages of crops grown and stock reared changed, and in places soil fertility decreased. In general small holdings in Europe favor stockraising at the expense of grain production, since the small proprietor can pay careful attention to his animals, whereas he may not be able to afford the machinery needed for economical grain growing on a commercial scale.

In the Philippines plantations large enough to attract foreign capital may not be owned by outsiders. In Java laws once imposed by the Dutch had the effect of maintaining a fixed ratio in the acreage of the major crops. This restricted unbridled planting of commercial crops and reserved adequate acreage for the food crops on which the natives subsisted. In Cuba and Brazil laws forbade or limited new plantations of certain cash crops produced in excess of the market demand.

GOVERNMENT AND REGIONAL GEOGRAPHY

Examples of cultural impress of effective central authority upon the landscape can be multiplied indefinitely. The cases cited suffice, however, to point to a group of geographic phenomena often overlooked. Each deserves more detailed study, particularly in its regional setting. Phenomena engendered by political forces should have a recognized place as elements in the geographic structure of every region.

38

Political Influence in Australian Geography

K. W. ROBINSON*

Most observers would agree that the political influence, in its broadest sense, can profoundly affect the distribution of geographical phenomena; yet few attempts have been made to measure the magnitude of the influence, or to assess the character of the effects. Many areas would provide a rewarding field for such an investigation; but perhaps countries of the New World lend themselves more readily to this type of analysis because of their comparatively uncomplicated histories. Australia is one such country. Here the federal system of government, which had its roots in certain basic areal characteristics, has itself acted as a geographical agent, influencing the regional distribution of activities, forming the framework for policy making and helping to strengthen the individuality of the various States.

The *political influence* as understood here is exerted both by the organized actions of governments and governmental institutions and by individuals or groups working in the interests of a particular cause, or idea. It follows that the appraisal of this influence as related to geography involves a variety of factors, which can be resolved into three major categories: (1) *The geographical character of political areas*, in which attention is directed to the relationship between governmental organization, history and environment on the one hand, and factors of the contemporary geographical scene (such as the location of manufacturing, settlement patterns and the regulation of transport) on the other. (2) *The influence of partisan activity*, as represented by trade unions, industrial cartels, religious factions and similar pressure groups, on the character and distribution patterns of human geography. (3) *The influence which the physical environment exerts on political action;* in Australia, for example, the environment poses problems of aridity, soil deficiencies and distance which no level of political activity can afford to ignore. The present discussion is concerned more with the first of these groups than with the second and third.

POLITICS AND REGIONAL CHARACTER

Australians have been compelled to gear their lives to a society in which dual political institutions have a direct and constant influence. In this society there are three levels where regional interests can influence decisions—Local, State and Federal—so that

---

Reprinted by permission of the author and publisher from *Pacific Viewpoint*, Vol. III, 1962.

* K. W. Robinson is Senior Lecturer in Geography at Newcastle University College, The University of New South Wales, Australia.

their contribution to existing geographical patterns has undoubtedly been important. The States themselves have acquired a sufficiently distinctive character for them to be considered as geographical units, while at the same time the status of Australia as a nation has reached the stage where it is no longer regarded, either internally or externally, as an outpost of empire.[1]

No general account of Australian geography should therefore overlook the federal framework of its governmental structure, both as a recognition of certain differences apparent at the time of Federation and as an instrument of subsequent development. A federation of this kind can take shape only where the primary patriotism of the people is for the larger, rather than the smaller area, so that a single nation-state, with subordinate parts, emerges. If the reverse had been the case in Australia, the result would have been a number of individual nation-states, eschewing the idea of federation as did New Zealand and as some former colonial territories in Africa have done more recently. Therefore the unifying, nation-oriented aspect of the Federation can be regarded as paramount where matters of national interest are concerned, welding the continent into a single whole. One important corollary of this is a complete freedom from international boundary problems; such problems are present to a greater or lesser degree in all other continents.

It is clear that the Act of Federation consolidated existing patterns which were the result of definite historical processes—processes of human action which were influenced by the environment, but which were also instrumental in changing the environment to produce the cultural landscape. Thus today's political divisions, which in many respects are primary agents of geographical change, owe much of their character to the colonial period of history. They have to a marked degree outgrown colonial attitudes, but not the separatism which accompanied those attitudes.

This separatism was of a kind more suited to the federal than to the unificationist machinery. The situation in the pre-Federation period was much in accordance with the arrangement of forces suggested by Wheare,[2] favoring federal rather than unitary government. The main points of this arrangement as far as Australia is concerned were: (1) The previous existence of a number of areas as distinct colonies; (2) a divergence of economic interests, resulting from separate historical development and leading to a desire to remain independent for some economic purposes; (3) factors of physical geography, particularly distance, isolation and the distribution of resources; and (4) the example of other areas, notably the United States. Economic interests were especially strong in border regions which stood to gain from the removal of customs barriers. The boundaries of influence of such interests were not coterminous with Colonial boundaries; but, as Parker has stated,[3] these interests were determined to retain as much local control over economic policy as they could, and this required the survival of the local parliaments which, in any case, had no intention of liquidating themselves.

Whatever the thinking behind the Federation movement, formation of the Commonwealth provided a mosaic of geographical patterns deep-rooted in past development. The States as regional entities within fixed boundary lines; patterns of crop agriculture, ranging from sugar in Queensland to berry fruits in Tasmania; local railway networks with different gauges; the emergent metropolitan centers: these are all examples of features which the Federation consolidated and, if anything, intensified. Whether different patterns would have resulted if Deakin, Parkes and Barton had argued on unificationist lines as Smuts, Merriman and de Villiers did so successfully in South Africa is doubtful. South African conditions were the outcome of vastly different historical, environmental and sociological conditions from those of Australia, even though most of the separatist prerequisites were there also.

. . . .

The core of the matter rests on the fact that the States are primarily political units, and it

---

1. K. W. Robinson, "Sixty Years of Federation in Australia," *The Geographical Review*, LI (January 1961), 20.

2. K. C. Wheare, *Federal Government* (London: 1956), pp. 35–54.

3. R. S. Parker, "Australian Federation: The Influence of Economic Interests and Political Pressures," *Historical Studies in Australia and New Zealand*, IV, 13, Melbourne, 1949, pp. 1–24.

is this political consciousness which is helping to mould regional character within State boundaries. Partridge has written[4] that "the States no longer correspond with distinct interests or attitudes... it is the political divisions themselves which are the important thing. The States seem now to be almost entirely political units, not coherent social and economic groups.... Without political separateness there could be nothing on which such a feeling (of separate community) could feed." What is happening is that the States, through their activities as developmental agencies, are *creating* the very kind of local attitudes and patterns which Partridge claims are no longer prevalent to justify their continued existence. In other words, the States are agents of geographical change, perpetuating themselves through the continuous process of development along divergent lines of interest in a varied environment.

The boundaries themselves, which began as arbitrary lines in little-used areas, are now less flexible, not so much because of the increased complexity of the machinery of government as because of the expressed conservatism of the people in matters of constitutional change. More significantly, the boundaries have crystallized through the activities of State governments within them. However, because of the size of the States and their relatively small populations, it is not everywhere along the border that differences between States are apparent to the eye. They *can* be noticed, for example, on either side of the Murray River, between northwestern Victoria and southwestern New South Wales (a contrast between cropped and grazing land); and on the boundary between Queensland and New South Wales.[5] Nevertheless, the boundaries generally are politically weak and the patterns which evolve on either side of them are the result less of the presence of the line than of the differential manipulation and development of resources in the contained area by the State concerned. The particular point of emphasis here is that some geographical phenomena within State regions of this kind cannot be understood without recourse to political explanations, or historical explanations within the political context.

An Example: Wheat Belt Town-and-Rail Patterns in Four States

A simple illustration of differential development comes from a comparison of four Wheat Belt areas in different States. Over the past 70 or 80 years, a characteristic livestock and crop combination has developed in each area, but with significant differences in the size and distribution of service towns and their accompanying rail network. Admittedly, such differences are related in part to variations in productivity and the degree of diversity of farming activity; but they are also due to political and historical circumstances associated with their development.

A *nodal* pattern characterizes the Central Slopes and Plains of New South Wales, where the towns of Parkes and Dubbo occupy pivotal positions, from each of which railway lines radiate in wheel formation, with smaller towns located along the "spokes." By contrast, the largest centers of Victoria's Wimmera-Mallee division occur in the extreme south of the belt, initiating a *digital* arrangement of five parallel lines running northwards into the wheat districts. Lesser towns, located along the railway routes, are fewer and smaller than those in New South Wales. Yet another grouping is provided by the South Australian districts, where a *diffuse* pattern is built on a more intensive network of moderately-sized towns than in any of the other regions. Finally, the fourth example from Western Australia shows a distinctly *marginal* relationship between towns and service area. All the large towns remain on the extreme humid margin of the belt, actually outside the main wheat-producing zone, but economically tied to it as well as to the mixed farming region further west.

Such differences cannot be attributed entirely to physical factors. In South Australia there was an early and intensive development of small areas, each with a central node linked to the major outlet at Adelaide, so that a pattern quickly stabilized in which at least one town was laid out in every "hundred."[6]

---

4. P. H. Partridge, "The Politics of Federation," in Geoffrey Sawer (ed.), *Federation: An Australian Jubilee Study* (Melbourne: 1952), p. 195.

5. A. J. Rose, "The Border between Queensland and New South Wales," *The Australian Geographer*, VI (January 1955), p. 13.

6. Donald W. Meinig, "Colonisation of Wheatlands: Some Australian and American Comparisons," *The Australian Geographer*, VII (August 1959), 211.

The Wimmera district of Victoria shows the influence of a northward push from the earlier-settled Midlands, as land hunger following the gold rushes was appeased by the opening of agricultural blocks. Towns were welded to the railways, which were constructed so that the major producing areas were readily accessible to silos and sidings with trade centers spaced on an average twenty miles apart.[7] This pattern became set at about the same time as the Flinders and Yorke areas of South Australia—in the 1870s and 1880s.

In Central New South Wales, where development came later, the growth of service centers seems to have been more spontaneous, and to have influenced the pattern of railway development to some extent; this is suggested by the nodal position of Parkes and Dubbo, almost equidistant between the eastern and western margins of the belt. Expansion into the extensive wheat areas of Western Australia occurred later still, and the line of western marginal towns obviously reflects the stabilization of an earlier frontier before the outward push began. Whereas in the eastern States a substantial part of the network was completed before 1900, in Western Australia only the two trunk lines were built at that date, much of the later mileage coming between 1911 and 1930. Such expansion did little to encourage town growth, both because of the relatively low wheat yields and because it came at a time when rural depopulation was already marked.[8]

State Individualism

Clearly the individuality of the States owes much to their histories as distinct political units, to the necessity for their developmental programmes to be conducted within fixed boundaries. The evolution of definite characteristics within such fixed boundaries bears a special relationship to three basic ideas: (1) The idea of *autonomy*, involving the right of an institution or area to self-government; to make its own laws and administer its own affairs; (2) The idea of *development*, which

7. A. J. and J. J. McIntyre, *The Country Towns of Victoria* (Melbourne: 1944), p. 9.
8. For maps of railway growth see S. Wadham, R. K. Wilson, and Joyce Wood, *Land Utilization in Australia* (Melbourne: 1957), pp. 18–20.

implies both the bringing out of latent capabilities and a gradual advancement to an objective through progressive stages; and (3) the idea of *competition*, which connotes the striving of two or more for the same object.

The Commonwealth Constitution gives the States autonomy in all matters not specifically allocated to the general government, although such autonomy is severely curtailed by the centralized control of finance. Particularly, this autonomy has continued to operate in the developmental sphere, to produce some well-known patterns in agriculture, transport, manufacturing and education. To what extent these patterns differ from each other as the result of such autonomous development, and not merely as a result of environmental differences, is admittedly a difficult matter to resolve. But we may compare, for example, the decentralization of railways in Queensland with their extreme centralization in New South Wales; or the disproportionately large numbers of dairy factories in Victoria and of pastoral leases in Queensland with those of other States. State legislation and State policy have obviously influenced these and many other divergent trends of development.

Added to this is the fact of competition between the States, which goes on unabated and has been responsible for many of the distinctive State traits. The inducements offered by the governments of South Australia and Victoria to encourage industrialists and migrants provide an excellent illustration of this idea in operation, particularly as opposed to New South Wales. Industries which might have been established in the latter State have been enticed away to States where labor costs are not so high, land is more plentiful and the overall planning policy more dynamic. State legislation in New South Wales, which has aimed at protecting the rights of the "working man" by providing for increases in wage payments and reductions in working time, has at the same time increased the cost of his labor and reduced his opportunities of employment. It is not by chance, therefore, that the State of New South Wales increased its population by only 1.94 per cent a year between the censuses of 1954 and 1961, whereas the rates for South Australia and Victoria were 2.83 per cent and 2.58 per cent respectively. The emergent geographical character of these two States is being born out of competition on the one

Commonwealth and States: The Struggle for Power

. . . .

State Expansion and State Rivalry

Despite tendencies towards uniformity, however, and notwithstanding a popular Australian belief that the power to tax involves the power to destroy, the authority of the Commonwealth has not been exercised for ends inconsistent with the separate existence of the States. It is true that the opportunities for independent expansion within each State are limited by finance, because there are serious revenue shortages. But if we recognize the States as being "pensioners of the Commonwealth" in a financial sense, we must admit that the "pension" (i.e. the annual allocation from federal revenue) together with additional grants for roads, universities, mental institutions, dairy and agricultural assistance and so on, is less niggardly than some State premiers would claim. Nor is the spending, even of special grants, as much under Federal control as might appear. Rather, the States, by being free to spend a great part of their reserves as they wish, have retained an important prerogative, which is basic to State character.

Federation is inspired by separatism, and in turn promotes it. At the same time it has encouraged centralization, both in terms of the general government and within the separate units themselves, because of the necessity for the cumbersome dual administration to work from central places. In each of the States there is a high concentration of population in capital cities, ranging from 65 per cent in Victoria to 33 per cent in Tasmania, and the identification of State control with capital city interests has led to considerable dissatisfaction. Any general correlation between population distribution and the distribution of natural resources has been distorted by the political division of the continent. It is probable that a unitary system of government would have favored greater decentralization because of the need for regional devolution of functions using smaller units than the present States; and the pattern would have been much different had there been independent nations.

. . . .

Pressure Groups and Organizational Conformity

. . . .

The most critical aspect of the political influence on geography concerns the power of pressure groups or interest groups in their relationship to the more important patterns of activity. Unfortunately, this is a field of investigation in which little has yet been attempted; but it is patent that the States themselves can act in this capacity, in order to correct the ill-balanced distribution of resources. The Australian steel industry, for example, which is based in New South Wales, has had to spread its operations widely in other States in order to meet demands for industrial growth as a concomitant of access to raw materials (iron ore particularly). The steel plant at Kwinana in Western Australia and the one under construction at Whyalla in South Australia, are the result of extra-State pressures rather than inherent locational advantages. The play of State attributes against each other in practically every field of manufacturing and service endeavor has produced patterns which are only partly explainable in economic terms: the location of oil refineries, branches of the motor industry and chemicals, to mention only a few, have all been influenced by political forces. The whole recent development of the Latrobe Valley brown coal deposits, on which Victoria's electricity grid is based, was stimulated by the breakdown of black coal supplies from New South Wales through labor unrest, shipping shortages and other factors. Who can say what the trend might have been had production in New South Wales been constant and reliable?[9] The very

---

9. Constructional work on briquetting factories in the Latrobe Valley has lagged, because at a critical time in the development programme, the State's allocation of loan funds was greatly reduced as a result of the deteriorating economic situation (1951–54). In subsequent years, the introduction of competitive fuel oil from new refineries again changed the whole power picture.

stature of manufacturing in Australia as a whole is the result of a Federal protectionist policy which has been abetted by the States (through Chambers of Commerce and similar organizations) in the interests of their own internal development.

In these various ways, the Australian scene has much to offer in the field of geographical causation. While the political influence might not be predominant, it is at least one of the forces to be reckoned with and to be considered as a counter to determinist philosophies of complete environmental control. The national capital, Canberra, located between the rival State-cities of Sydney and Melbourne, stands as a monument to inter-State jealousies and to the satisfaction of a new want emerging from the federal principle. It is the clearest expression of the political influence, and its current rapid growth testimony to its dynamism. It emphasizes at once the dichotomous nature of the society which created it, the national character of Australia and, in its present rate of multiplication, the ever-increasing powers of the general government.

Clearly there is an argument for recognizing the continued individuality of the States, and just as clearly there is a need to study the interplay of feeling, or awareness of each other, which exists between the States; for it is evident that the *apparent* advantages which one State possesses over another constitute a prime reason for inter-State migration. On the other hand, there is also the possibility that the world of the "Organization Man" has proceeded so far that all Australian environments are tending to become the same, in order to fit in with his needs. There are signs of an increasing cultural uniformity, of the "package suburb" style, resulting from the ramifications of big business enterprises with their requirements for a continually moving stream of employees over a wide area. The recent frequency of large take-over bids supports this view, well expressed by Whyte[10] in respect of American business enterprises as follows:

"By deliberately exposing a man to a succession of environments, they best obtain that necessity of the large organisation—the man who can fit in anywhere. . . . And is not this the whole drift of our society? We are not interchangeable in the sense of being people without differences, but in the externals of existence we are united by a culture increasingly national. And this is part of the momentum of mobility. The more people move about the more similar the environments become, and the more similar they become, the easier it is to move about."

Parts of Australia—the large cities particularly—have come under this organizational spell; and, if the cities *are* virtually the States, then the prospects of increasing cultural uniformity are very real, and the dangers of States losing their individuality thereby increased. Such organizational uniformity is of a kind altogether different from that implied in the word "nation," and not to be confused with it. The essence of the nation springs from a healthy diversity between its component parts, and if this is weakened, then the national character will be adversely affected. At present such diversity is still a key to the geographical and political personality of Australia, and therefore deserves the closest scrutiny.

10. William F. Whyte, *The Organization Man* (New York: 1956), p. 305.

The Conflict of Salmon Fishing Policies in the North Pacific

JULIAN V. MINGHI[*]

INTRODUCTION

The North Pacific Salmon Fisheries issue is one of true international proportions, involving Japan, the United States, the Soviet Union, and, to a lesser extent, Canada.

The political geographer is interested in the effects of the competing interests of nations and the differences these interests produce upon the use of natural resources. The salmon are a highly, but not completely mobile natural resource which range across existing political boundaries into areas where unambiguous spatial sovereignty is difficult to maintain. The problem this condition creates is considered in this study both from a legal and a geographical point of view. Conflicts between national salmon fishing policies have been traditionally adjusted by legal means by international treaties, generally according to the wishes of the dominant power. The aim of this paper is to present a survey of the forms, origin and background of the current salmon fishing policies and legal position of the United States and Japan. Also considered is the compatibility of existing and proposed legal arrangements with the ecological realities of the salmon cycle and with the economics of salmon fishing in the North Pacific.

Traditionally, marine resources on the high seas can be utilized by all mankind, and become private property only when caught. However, the problem is more than just the conflict over the exploitation of a valuable marine resource of the North Pacific. The peculiar nature of the salmon complicates the problem further. The salmon spawns and hatches in fresh water streams. By beginning and finishing its life cycle within the boundaries of national domains it comes within the full jurisdiction of the coastal state, that is, while it is not on the high seas. Hence, for the coastal state, even the usual basic premise in disputes involving fishing outside territorial waters, that the living resources of the high seas are common to all mankind is overshadowed by property claims. This leaves even less common ground than usual among the contestants. In the dispute in question, the United States occupies the position of the coastal state, while Japan which fishes on the high seas, holds to the traditional philosophy of the freedom of the seas. The policy emanating from the United States position is clouded by conflicts among different private interests and government agencies, such as those between the United States Department of the Interior and the State Department, the former giving

Reprinted by permission from *Pacific Viewpoint*, Vol. II, 1961.
[*] Julian V. Minghi is a co-editor of this volume.

paramount importance to a policy of conservation, and the latter primarily interested in international relations.

The salmon of the North Pacific present such a complicated resource problem that the value of this study lies in the summaries and generalizations attempted which are based on the evaluation of the many factors and points of view involved. The urgency of the problem requires generalizations in the political and economic fields even if other scientific researchers cannot yet fully sanction these generalizations on the evidence presently available.

Salmon involved in the dispute in the North Pacific Ocean are spawned and hatched in Asian and American waters. The Asian-spawned salmon are mainly from Soviet Siberian streams, while the American-spawned are mainly from Alaskan streams, specifically those flowing into Bristol Bay. Because of their strong homing instinct the salmon, after three to five years on the high seas, return to their parent stream. Salmon in climbing upstream to reach the spawning grounds deteriorate in their physical state. Hence, they are of greater commercial value as they enter fresh water from salt water than at any other time thereafter. The necessary concentration of the salmon as they run towards their parent streams from the open sea renders commercial exploitations easiest at the mouths of these streams.

Commercial exploitation of salmon in Siberia and Alaska began, therefore, at river mouths along the coasts. The seasonality of the salmon runs, the remoteness of these areas from markets, the high unit-weight value and the severity of the climate in winter, have given this form of economic activity some peculiar characteristics. The salmon catch, a highly perishable commodity, must be conserved to reach the market in an acceptable condition. This has led to a heavy capital investment in a large canning industry in these remote areas. The salmon run only in the summer months. Since there are few or no off-season employment opportunities, labor in the fishing and canning industries in these isolated areas migrates seasonally. Commercial salmon fishing has continued in this fashion in Bristol Bay under the direction of United States labor and industrial interests and by the Japanese, under a lot-renting system from the Russians, along the Siberian coast. Japan began high-seas fishing for salmon off Siberian waters in the early 1930s. Later in the decade, Japan entered Bristol Bay with experimental and survey vessels with alleged intent to extend large-scale salmon fishing activity to these waters in the future. After protests from the United States Government, Japan announced that she would not fish in Bristol Bay in the future and withdrew. However, the problem of the conflict between the coastal state and the highseas maritime nation over the exploitation of salmon had been raised for the first time in the North Pacific.

After the War, measures were taken by the United States to exclude Japan from fisheries where salmon spawned in Bristol Bay streams occur. By the terms of the Treaty of Peace, Japan was committed to enter into negotiations with other countries, and hence joined Canada and the United States as a party to the International North Pacific Fisheries Convention (I.N.P.F.C.) in 1953. In the early 1950s the only Pacific nations with active interests in commercial salmon fishing were Canada, the United States, Japan, and the U.S.S.R. Although the Soviet Union had been actively fishing salmon on an increasing scale since the 1930s, her activity was confined to coastal fishing along the Siberian coast. Added to this was the fact that the Soviet Union shared little common political interest with the other three nations. Hence, it was possible for Canada, the United States and Japan to agree on measures covering most of the North Pacific that would apply to themselves, and would theoretically exclude "newcomers" from catching salmon in convention waters. The area of the North Pacific covered by the terms of the I.N.P.F.C. is 3.2 million square miles, and contains approximately one-third of the world's fish resources.

The I.N.P.F.C. members agreed that, under certain conditions, they would abstain from catching salmon, and also halibut and herring. Hence a "piecemeal" approach to the fishery problem was adopted. The Japanese agreed not to catch salmon of North American origin, and asked if a line might be established in the North Pacific which would facilitate their complying with the agreement. Thus, on the scientific evidence available at the time, a line at 175 degrees West was established to divide the Asian and American salmon by origin, east of which the Japanese would not fish. This set up a zone contiguous to the American coast within which no parties of the Convention could fish for salmon. It has since become known as the "zone of abstention." At the time, this line was thought to divide satisfactorily American-spawned salmon from Asian-spawned. In international law there is a lack of acceptable procedures and principles for delimiting any contiguous off-shore zone of a coastal state in order to carry out an intended conservation policy. Hence, such a zone as this can only be established by mutual consent between interested parties, and can only be changed under the same terms. The view of the American fishery interests is that the "doctrine of abstention" is an outgrowth of the concept of "historic rights," which in turn is based on the notion that, by virtue of the location of the spawning grounds and the history of sole exploitation, the salmon are an American resource, and hence American property. There is no way for fishermen to recognize the distinction between Asian and American-spawned salmon, and only lately have biologists been able to differentiate. However, the official United States view, which is that of the State Department, is that the abstention doctrine is valid: (1) when the resource is being fully utilized and there is no waste; (2) when the resource's continued productive state is due to the research and regulations enacted by the countries exploiting the stock; and (3) when all countries presently participating in the fishery are allowed to continue to do so.

Ironically, the present conflict arises as a result of protests by the United States, the architect of the convention's measures, against the activities of Japan in assigned waters. Japan's high-seas fishing catch has been increasing and the runs in Bristol Bay have been falling. The Fish and Wildlife Service of the United States Department of the Interior has adopted a conservation policy which demands that there be a minimum escapement allowed upstream to ensure propagation of the salmon at a sustained yield level. Hence, partly due to Congressional legislation based on inadequate scientific research, catches have fallen more rapidly in Bristol Bay than they would have done, even taking into consideration the diminishing runs of salmon. The explanation of the over-all depleted stocks of salmon has yet to be found. American fishery interests think over-fishing by Japanese fishermen is largely to blame for the depletion in 1957 and 1958, in the belief that the 175 degree West line is, after all, misplaced, and does not satisfactorily divide Alaska-spawned stocks from Asian-spawned. For the explanation of the drop in the total run, however, one must go back considerably earlier. That catching of these salmon, *even* west of the abstention zone, is held to be contrary to the "spirit and intent" of the treaty. Consequently, the United States now urges that the abstention line be moved westward. The Japanese argue that the line can only be moved if conclusive scientific evidence can be produced to show that the line does not conform to the convention's intentions.

The convention obligates the signatory powers to carry out scientific research into all aspects concerned with salmon and their movements on the high seas. The results so far show that there exists a broad zone of intermingling of Asian and American-spawned salmon. There is also great variation in the size and movements of stocks of these salmon from one year to another and annually of different species of salmon. Thus, Japan argues that there is no conclusive evidence as yet, and that there will possibly never be a basis for moving the line within the terms of the convention. Obviously a time will come when two lines could be drawn based on biological evidence. One would mark the absolute eastern limit of Asian-spawned salmon, and the other the westernmost limit of American-spawned salmon. If future evidence follows the trends of the findings so far, these two lines would be extremely wide apart, and would contain a number of intermingling salmon. The United States of course, would support the westernmost line, and in fact, has proposed a move westwards of 15 degrees, to 170 degrees East. Japan would use the argument for the eastward line as a counter to the United States proposal, and also as justification for not moving the line from its present position.

From the above reasoning several points arise. The inherent difficulties behind establishing a line running North and South across an ocean to divide salmon by origin can now be seen. The 175 degree West line was meant to be provisional, an administrative procedure to solve an immediate spatial fishery problem. Although this practical solution was meant as a temporary compromise at a certain point in time, inertia set in, as with any provisional line where vested interests are vitally involved on land or on water. The selection of the 175 degree West line in 1952 for the division by origin shows the fallacy of founding legislation on scant scientific evidence, rather than determining if a certain type of legislation would be effective scientifically, and if so, establishing measures accordingly. Lines of absolute limit of one origin or another could eventually be drawn, but any line in between would merely cut through the zone of intermingling. In the case under consideration it seems that in the immediate future no *one* line can be drawn on a scientific basis, whether all parties agree to the principle of equitability by origin or to one of equitability by some quantitative measure involving different species of salmon. Any such line would have to be based on many years of data collection. As with other problems in the natural sciences, there has existed a need for many years of intensive research if prediction techniques are to be developed to such a degree that a movable line, or several lines for several species, can be delimited annually. Under presently-known techniques, although there have been considerable improvements, such delimitation would be impossible.

The basic difference of opinion is not one of a scientific nature but one of attitude. Although the United States and Japan are parties to the same convention, Japan does not share the philosophy upon which the convention is based, a philosophy of abstention and equitability by origin. Japan herself, however, is in no position to counter American claims with arguments using the same philosophy because the bulk of the Asian-spawned salmon, and by far the greater part of the Japanese catch on the high seas in the post-war period, is of Russian origin. Ever since the 1930s Japan has been progressively constricted in Siberian coastal regions. High-seas fishing temporarily solved this problem, although it has raised others with the United States. Now Russia is evidently also beginning to indulge in high-seas fishing for salmon,[1] further complicating the issue, for although she is fishing largely for salmon of her own origin, she will be competing with Japan, and antagonizing the United States. She is not a member of the I.N.P.F.C. and will presumably fish exclusively under her own regulations. One thing is certain. In the words of Milton E. Brooding, spokesman for the United States National Section at the 1958 I.N.P.F.C. meeting, "Bristol Bay sockeye runs can be exterminated if both of these intensive fisheries—the Japanese high-seas fishery and the United States inshore fishery—are not adequately regulated."[2]

The Japanese Case

Background

Although salmon is not of great relative importance in the total Japanese fishery economy, the great expansion of the export market is largely due to increased exportation of canned salmon to the United States, to which 45 per cent of Japan's total value of salmon exports is sent. European demand for Japanese canned salmon has also risen in the last few years.

In the period since 1930 the great feature in salmon fishing has been the increased efficiency of the mother-ship system. Catch per vessel increased tenfold during the period 1930 to 1935. Over the same period the number of catcher-ships increased at the same rate, although through technical advances the number of mother-ships needed to handle this increased productivity has merely doubled. About 90 per cent of Japan's total salmon catch comes under the realm of the mother-ship system. The vessels are equipped with such modern devices as ultra short-wave radio which allows a working radius of 35 miles from the mother-ship, fish detectors, echo-sounders, direction finders, gyro-compasses, radar and even aqua-television. The mother-ship programmes the orderly arrival and discharge of her catchers, to avoid loss of time and confusion. Ever since the resumption of this type of salmon fishing soon after the war, there has been a progressive increase in productivity due to the increase in the efficiency of effort, and to a larger North Pacific population of salmon in the immediate post-war years.

---

1. So far there is evidence only of research fishing. Under Soviet regulations only traps and seines are permitted. Gill nets are outlawed as injurious.

2. International North Pacific Fisheries Commission, *Proceedings* of the Fifth Annual Meeting, Tokyo, Japan, November 4–10, 1958 (Vancouver, B.C.: I.N.P.F.C., 1959), p. 53.

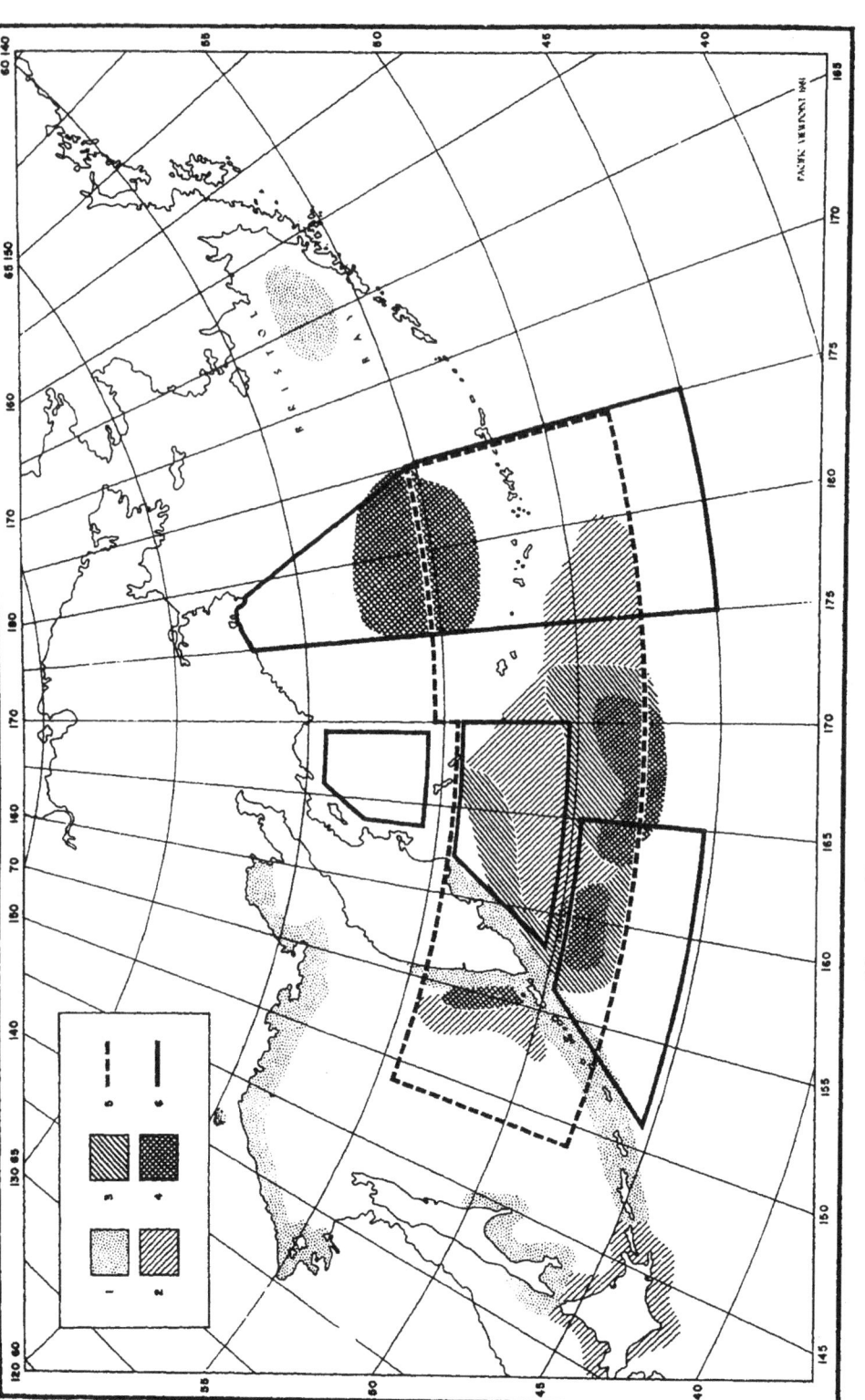

Map 39.1 THE HISTORY OF JAPANESE SALMON FISHERIES
Key: 1. Pre-War areas, 2. Post-War light catch, 3. Post-War medium catch, 4. Post-War dense catch, 5. Japanese Govt. authorized fishing area, 1954, 6. Soviet proposed fishing areas, March, 1959.

The post-war scene has been characterized by the limitation of Japanese activity in salmon fisheries under various agreements with the U.S.S.R., and under the terms of the I.N.P.F.C. (Map 39.1 and Fig. 39.1). The former agreements are flexible in terms of quotas, season and location of fishing, and vary annually. By a Russo-Japanese fisheries agreement for the 1958 salmon season, Japan cut her fleet in the Okhotsk Sea by 50 per cent from the previous year, and reduced her quota from 120,000 metric tons to 110,000. On the other hand, by its very terms, the I.N.P.F.C. has been inflexible and has led to a *status quo* which has been a distinct disadvantage to the United States, the original formulator of the I.N.P.F.C. The Japanese-Soviet Fishery Convention, signed in 1956,

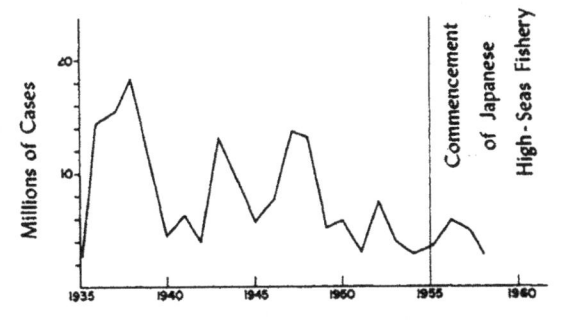

Fig. 39.1 BRISTOL BAY RED SALMON PACKS

gave the Soviet Union a good bargaining position by which to limit Japanese fishing activity still further. The Soviets were in a position to take action on unilateral decisions, whereas, by the terms of the I.N.P.F.C., the United States is not. The Soviets have cut quotas on presumption of depletion through overfishing, and as a result there has been much Japanese irritation over Soviet policy. The Fishery Convention settles no problems on a long-term basis, but resolves itself into a yearly battle in which scientific research is of little or no consideration.

In the present decade, deep-sea fishing has been a basic issue. The 1956 Fisheries Pact between Japan and the U.S.S.R. places restrictions on size of catch in the Northwest Pacific. Questions, however, were settled politically, and not scientifically. Agreements were made on scanty scientific evidence. The Soviets argued for conservation against indiscriminate fishing, and the Japanese maintained that statistical data did not support the thesis that stocks of salmon were diminishing. At a conference in Tokyo in March, 1959, the U.S.S.R. made staggering curtailment proposals for the 1959 salmon fishing season to Japan. After more than a month of discussion, the original Soviet proposal of a quota figure totalling 50,000 tons had expanded, and the Japanese demand for 160,000 tons had contracted to reach an agreed compromise quota of 94,000 tons for the 1959 season.[3]

Although these latest Soviet proposals would place severe limitations on Japanese salmon fishing, they do recognize the right, or necessity, of the Japanese high-seas operation to catch salmon which are mainly of Russian origin. There is, so far, no attempt to prohibit absolutely the catching of Russian-spawned salmon by the Japanese. In this respect the Russians differ in attitude from the Americans. The difference is basically an historic one. The Japanese were largely responsible for developing the Siberian fishery, whereas they have no historic rights whatsoever over the North American salmon. Another point raised is the possible conflict between the two treaties, the I.N.P.F.C. and the Russo-Japanese Agreement, over potentially the same waters and resource therein, and involving a member of both treaties, i.e., Japan. This possible conflict of regulations would seem to illustrate as unwise the conclusion of different treaties over waters which essentially form one unit in terms of high-seas fishery regulations. Of course, it can be argued that, although the high seas form a legal unity in the North Pacific, there is a division of stocks based on origin. The intermingling of these stocks during the migration period and the Japanese high-seas fishing activity in the intermingling area, serves to blur this distinction based on origin-division. As Senator Magnuson of Washington has said, if the purpose of the I.N.P.F.C. is to conserve and perpetuate salmon resources, it "must include all four nations substantially utilizing that resource."[4]

In a way these latest Russian proposals are a continuation of the annual discussions which occur between Japan and Russia before every fishing season over salmon fishing regulations in the Northwest Pacific. However, the 1959 proposals are unique. For the first time they have considered waters up to the I.N.P.F.C.

3. *Pacific Fisherman*, LVII (January 1959), 1.
4. *Pacific Fisherman*, LVII (May 1959), 29.

Abstention line to be "treaty" waters, and have placed limitations on them accordingly. In doing this, the U.S.S.R. has adopted the same arguments of "conservation" and "special rights" of the coastal state, as the United States had adopted to protect its interest, although the abstention philosophy of the two powers is considerably different.

The history of the I.N.P.F.C. has been equally turbulent. At the annual meetings of the convention, national policies are aired, and supported as best as possible by scientific evidence prepared by each country's research group during the previous year. Increasing catches by Japanese fleets in assigned waters have contrasted with a steady decline in the Bristol Bay runs. At the last two meetings the United States has demanded that the line of abstention be moved westwards. On the other hand, Japan has seemingly made several concessions. During the 1958 season Japan agreed to restrict operations near the 175 degree West line, and also agreed to a quota. In fact the Japanese fleet did not fish east of the 170 degree East line. These promises were extracted from Japan at the threat of possible economic sanctions instigated by American industrial and labour interests. If the Pelly Bill[5] or several other similar bills were made law and enforced, the Japanese salmon canning industry would suffer a great loss of market. It is of course an open question whether the Japanese fleet stood by her promises purely as a friendly gesture, or because of the absence of fish in the vicinity.

Early in 1959, following the announcement of the closure of Bristol Bay to salmon fishing for the 1959 season, American antagonism against the Japanese developed to a degree reminiscent of the 1930s. The United States Secretary of State has been petitioned by Pacific Northwest and Alaskan senators to bring the State Department directly into the issue, just as Cordell Hull had been petitioned over 20 years before. Threats to pass legislation which would ban the importation of Japanese salmon were renewed. On the other hand, the Japanese allege widespread misunderstanding of the causes of the depletion of Bristol Bay salmon, and deny that their high-seas fishing activity is responsible.

5. A bill before Congress that would ban the importation into the United States of canned salmon caught under circumstances illegal to American fishermen i.e., all Japanese canned salmon.

International Law Standing

In general terms the Japanese case rests on the traditional international law concept of the freedom of the seas. Japan is one of the staunchest supporters of the three-mile limit rule. Japan's case is centered on her attitude toward the control of the exploitation of the riches of the sea, and to the doctrines of the contiguous zone, and the coastal state.

Japan maintains that the coastal state is not allowed to claim the exclusive exploitation of natural resources under any other institution than that of the territorial sea. The Japanese distinguish between the problem of marine resources, especially the conservation of biological resources, and the problem of the contiguous zone. The doctrine of the contiguous zone cannot be interpreted to justify a monopoly of fisheries outside territorial limits, since a monopoly can be asserted only as an exercise of the right of sovereignty within an area subject to sovereignty. The maritime states, with ability and improved techniques for fishing on the high seas, will never renounce the rights of exploitation established thereon.

The area between the three-mile limit off the Alaska coast and the 175 degree West line of abstention is certainly in the "contiguous zone" class. The monopolistic connotations of abstention zones declared unilaterally by a foreign state are obvious. The suspicion and fear entertained by Japan over these declarations have been well grounded in the Kamchatka Sea, where, in 1956, a monopoly of high-class salmon fishing was set up by the unilateral action of the Soviet Union. Japan supports the traditional principle that the freedom of the seas cannot be violated by any unilateral declaration or by any new theory. Japan recognizes the need for conservation, but with regulations set up by conventions between interested parties.

One of the notes, discussing the place of the coastal state in a fishery conservation programme, in the Report of the Rome Conference in 1955 states that no conservation measures should be taken by the coastal state on the high seas without international agreement. The reasoning behind this is that conservation measures are based on scientific and technical evidence, and the coastal state has not necessarily got the best, let alone a monopoly of such evidence. Hence, all users should have equal rights to supply information and to formulate measures. Consequently, Japan argues that there is no reason to elevate the coastal state to a superior position. Geographical position alone is not evidence of interest or scientific knowledge about conservation. Mr. Tsuruoka, a member of the Japanese delegation at Geneva in 1958, declared: "As the concept of conservation is primarily scientific, and not political or economic in nature, the coastal state should have no unilateral rights to regulate fisheries by virtue of its geographical position."[6] The argument that the coastal state is in a "special position" based on social and economic reasons is considered untenable. Such an idea could lead to abuse of foreign fishermen, and also to under-fishing. The very purpose of a non-coastal state's fishing so far afield is explained by the lack of adequate resources available near home to sustain its population. To cut off non-coastal states from these distant resources would deprive a large section of the population of their present standard of living.

According to the Japanese point of view the abstention theory, which forms the basis of the I.N.P.F.C., is held invalid because it lacks a scientific base, and hence has nothing to do with conservation.[7] The main seed of controversy in the dispute hinges on the line of abstention and the "zone of intermingling." The possibility of Asian and American salmon intermingling was realized in 1951, and the 175 degree West lines was meant to be a temporary measure. To move it, three process stages are provided under the convention: (1) scientific investigation up to a point when conclusive evidence of a discrepancy between the line, and the location and movement of salmon of different origin is available to support a shift; (2) political and diplomatic approval; *and if this fails*, (3) an impartially decided scientific line. The convention is still concerned with stage one. From the American point of view there has been some success because the Japanese have been kept west of the abstention line and away from Japan's alleged just claim of up to the three-mile limit. Japan, who has opposed the abstention principle that she feels the convention forced on her in 1951, is obviously in no mood for further concessions. Japan contends that arguments to move the line westward are arbitrary, and based on extremely insufficient scientific data, and that to move the line *now* would be to scrap the convention. She also contends that proof is insufficient that there are large proportions of American-spawned salmon among the different species in the intermingling zone.

The freedom of the seas concept is the cornerstone of the Japanese case. In the past Japan has used this concept aggressively, but now she is using it to defend her position against further loss. As a signatory to the convention she has prejudiced her position somewhat. Japan, however, has since taken a very strong position against any further extension of the abstention doctrine and the coastal state concept. She has to be very careful not to set precedents in policy in the convention, which would be detrimental to her position in other fishing disputes with other states.

At present, Japan's population has been increasing by 700,000 annually. To offset the threat of economic chaos the standard of living must be maintained and improved, and the greatest possible resource base must be sought in order that technical and organizational innovations may be fully utilized. In her effort to expand her fisheries, Japan has had to vary her policy to reach compromises in different situations. A programme suggested in 1949 for the future of Japanese fisheries proposed such measures as reorientation and improvements of fishery methods, improvement in collection and computation for production statistics, reappraisal of legislation, improved handling and transportation of fish, exchange of fishery products on the foreign market, and expansion of fishery areas.[8] Since then, under national guidance, all these measures have been carried out, but the expansion of the fishing industry has met with international complications, and Japan has only submitted to limitations on this policy when conclusive scientific evidence has shown that the fishery in question is becoming seriously depleted due to over-fishing. The high-seas salmon fishery operates under such adverse conditions as foul weather (about one-third of the days during the season are impossible for fishing) and conservation

---

6. United Nations, Conference on the Law of the Sea, Volume V, *High Seas*, A/CONF. 13/31, 1958 (Geneva, 1958), p. 7.

7. *Ibid.*, p. 41.

8. Ada Espenshade, "A Program for Japanese Fisheries," *Geographical Review*, XXXIX (January 1949), 82.

measures. There are restrictions on the length of nets, the size of mesh, as well as the distance between nets. Quantity of catch is regulated by quotas, and all fishing is prohibited after 10 August. Even given continuous good weather, the nets are down in water for a maximum of 42 hours a week. The great economic potential, flexibility, a real mobility, and high order of technological efficiency, has given the mother-ship system the greatest possibility of success. With this fact of economic success and that of heavy capitalization in the industry, the other arguments for the Japanese case, those of dependence upon exports on this high-value, low-bulk product, of protein, diet and occupational dependence are reinforced.

The United States Case

Background

Salmon fishing is of only local and regional significance in the United States. It has lost much of its pre-war importance in terms of labor, taxes rendered and installed capital.

The salmon-fishing industry has formed an integral part of the regional economy of the Alaskan coast, and salmon fishing is still the most important fishing activity there in terms of value. Diminishing runs of salmon, domestic conservation legislation and foreign competition have rendered the industry unable to keep pace with the steady growth of domestic and foreign markets. Imports, principally from Japan, are annually more able to compete in the domestic market. Imports of canned salmon for 1958 showed a 25 per cent increase on those of 1957. Japan accounted for 73 per cent of the total canned salmon imports of United States. During the years of increasing catches up to the mid-1930s, the industry was characterized by the domination of a half-dozen large firms which forced the smaller firms out by their ability to lead in the pricing field and by virtue of the economies of scale and vertical integration they enjoyed. Decreasing runs of salmon have led to diseconomies of scale, to the failure to reach threshold requirements, to lower productivity and, consequently, to a finished good at rising cost. Despite this drop in economic importance the industrial and labor interests concerned continue to have a strong political voice. All the companies together have maintained for some 30 years a negotiating body, The Alaska Salmon Industry Inc., while the Alaska Fishermen's Union represents the labor interests of the seasonal workers in the salmon industry. Because of the seasonality of employment, the industry has some extra-regional importance. A large proportion of workers come from the Puget Sound area. There are few opportunities for work in the off-season. The isolation of the industry along the Alaskan coast means that the organisation centre is on Puget Sound. In fact, the capital investment and profit sharing involves many Pacific Northwest interests.

The basis and growth of the Alaskan economy has depended upon the exploitation of minerals and fish. Mining is a "robber" economy and its raw material is irreplaceable. In fishing, however, a policy designed to maintain an optimum level for exploitation is thought possible. Alaskan Statehood will doubtless lead to a decrease in dependence on Federal funds, and a growing increase in the responsibility of the new state to balance its own budget. Taxes on fisheries have for some time been the chief source of Alaskan revenue, and the fisheries produce an export surplus in the balance of trade. Moreover, in terms of total value over the long run, salmon have contributed more to the economy of Alaska than all the gold mined there.

Historical Context of Salmon Fishing

The development of the industry in Alaska has been basically conditioned by the character and location of its raw material supply. As mentioned above, the peculiar characteristics of the salmon are such that the ideal time and place to catch them is at the river mouths where they run in large schools near the surface before ascending the freshwater streams to spawn and die. Before technical advances made mass-exploitation possible on the high seas, it was most convenient and profitable to begin salmon fishing, as the Japanese had begun in Siberia, in waters close to the shore and at river mouths. It is still sounder economics to fish for salmon at the river mouths, but for obvious political reasons this is no longer possible for the Japanese.

Because of its marginal geographical situation, Bristol Bay did not come under intensive salmon fishing activity until the early years of this century. Due to its physical excellence in terms of factors controlling quality and quantity of salmon runs, it was exploited successfully with increasing returns until the late 1930s. As a result of bitter lessons learned in the past along the entire Pacific Coast, a conservation policy was adopted even in the early days of salmon fishing activity in Bristol Bay. Since early Congressional legislation in 1906 proved not particularly effective, the White Act was passed in 1924. Under the White Act the Bureau of Fisheries was given full power over all fishing in Alaska. The act provided for at least a 50 per cent escapement of all salmon entering the rivers to spawn. It was recognized that the number allowed up the river to spawn, known as the "escapement," was related to the size of the run a few years hence, and that conservation based on a "minimum escapement" policy would render a direct return in the area applied, thus initiating a principle of optimum sustained yield. This would make for a very close spatial relationship between sacrifices made, and benefits reaped.

Up to World War II, the Alaska salmon pack led the world in output. In 1935 Freeman wrote, "so far the Asiatic output has not seriously disturbed our markets."[9] Within the last decade the picture has changed considerably. Salmon runs have been steadily falling since 1935 despite the minimum escapement policy strictly adhered to by the United States Fish and Wildlife Service (F.W.S.). Catches have dropped accordingly. Techniques developed in recent years have been prohibited by law in the interests of conservation. Decisions about areas and times allowed for salmon fishing are often made during the season by the F.W.S. Federal Law forbids United States citizens taking salmon by nets on the high seas. The fish trap which, in economic terms, is the best method of catching salmon is also forbidden. Quality is a prime requisite for success in the salmon canning industry; hence the time between death and canning must be as short as possible. Fish traps are ideal for minimizing this critical period because the supply to the cannery can be stabilized by leaving the salmon alive in the traps, and removing the mat such times and in such a number as the cannery might require. The F.W.S. has chosen to legislate in this way to avoid any sudden drastic dislocation in the industry. However, a satisfactory sustained yield has not been realized, and growing inefficiency, despite some organizational changes, has been characteristic of the industry since the War.

In 1957 the situation became critical. Overfishing by the Japanese was blamed for the drop in the Bristol Bay runs. During the 1958 season the Japanese complied with an American request to fish only a given number of salmon and, if possible, to catch them all west of 170 degrees East. Again this was not an official agreement as the Japanese were much afraid of prejudicing their chances of a satisfactory agreement with the Russians, by openly agreeing to limitation with the United States. After preliminary warnings in December, 1958, the F.W.S. decided in March 1959, that, to ensure sufficient escapement to maintain the resource, Bristol Bay would be closed to fishing for the 1959 season, although, in late May 1959 after the Japanese had agreed to reduce fishing intensity for the 1959 season, the Bureau of Commercial Fisheries announced that a limited red salmon catch would be allowed in Bristol Bay. The relationship of escapement to runs has been reasonably good, except for 1957, when the Japanese high-seas fishery for the first time operated north of the Aleutians, catching some 20 million salmon, including about 70 per cent of all red salmon taken in the North Pacific that season. The non-materialization of the predicted run is circumstantial evidence that Japanese fishing affected the Bristol Bay run in that particular year. On the assumption that the situation is due entirely to Japanese fishing of Alaska-spawned salmon in water assigned to them under the I.N.P.F.C., both industry and labor have tried by various means to force Japan to agree on a westerly move of the present abstention line. Proposed legislation would also ban imports of Japanese salmon. For the last two years imported Japanese canned salmon had exceeded the total production from Bristol Bay. Further proposals would ban *all* fish imports from Japan, Such proposals have been justified as "conservation measures."[10]

9. Otis W. Freeman, "Salmon Industry of the Pacific Coast," *Economic Geography*, XI (April 1935), 129.

10. *Seattle Times*, 3 April, 1959.

The recent appearance of deep-sea Soviet fishing trawlers in the convention waters has further complicated the issue. Subject to no treaty agreements the Russians feel free to fish salmon outside the territorial limits of Alaska. However, a trawler does not normally fish for salmon, and there is no proof that Russian vessels in the eastern Bering Sea are, or will be fishing salmon. Japanese trawlers have been trawling for bottom fish for several years in the areas where the Russian trawlers have been currently located.

International Law Standing

There are divergent opinions as to exactly what the United States' case is based upon. The views of the fishery interests on this point can hardly be accepted despite the wide support they have been given. The State Department is, after all, the spokesman for the United States in international law. The United States' case is based upon the philosophy and practice of a sound conservation policy, especially in this case where there is a real danger of extinction of the resource. These conservation procedures have been approved and recognised by most nations in both the Rome Conference on Conservation in 1955, and the Law of the Sea Conference at Geneva in 1958. There is also the special interest of the coastal state in a fishery conservation programme. The peculiar nature of the salmon gives the United States presumed grounds for the opportunity of claiming a property right over salmon which are spawned, hatched, have their early development, and return to die in national and territorial waters. Added to these two factors of "special interest" and "property" claims, the United States has also claimed a historic right for exclusive exploitation of this resource. The fishermen of the United States and Canada are held to be solely responsible for the maximum development of fisheries, and have enjoyed almost exclusive rights in them.

The first official statement of policy by the United States came in November, 1937, from the then Secretary of State Cordell Hull, after the Japanese high-seas fishing fleet had spent a season researching and catching some salmon commercially in Bristol Bay. In a note to the Japanese Government he argued that both the United States Government and private interests had developed the salmon resource to its present state. A law of Congress protected the salmon and put strict control on fishing activity. All this the Japanese had ignored. In the light of the annual investment of the United States in conservation, the hardship of the industry and steady decrease in total pack, the United States claimed a superior interest in Alaskan salmon, and suggested that it was to be regarded as an American resource. Such doctrines as "prior occupation", "prescription" and "usage" were used to bolster the United States' case. As a matter of policy the United States could not abandon its control in this case without some domestic hostility and public disgrace. The pre-war question was one of conservation and competing national interests, for this affair came at a time when there was growing friction between the United States and Japan on policy in the Pacific area.

Since the War, the United States' case has little changed. In 1943, Tomasevich thought that, in terms of power of protection, fishery conservation should have the same standing as revenue laws or defense of a neutral coastal state against belligerent activities.[11] Even Japan voted for the "coastal state" measures at Geneva in the hope that the extension of exclusive fishing rights would not be pressed by other countries. On the presumption that the production of most fisheries can be maintained at a near-maximum with conservation policies, the United States argues that, with increased activity in fishing, the most important aspect of the international law of fisheries is the promotion of effective conservation. The doctrine of freedom of the seas has never been absolute, and extra-territorial rights for various functions have always existed. Allen has stated: "There is a definite distinction between the right of sovereignty and the right to exercise protective or preventive jurisdiction over an area outside the national domain."[12]

There seems to be some conflict within the terms of the 1956 International Law Com-

11. Jozo Tomasevich, *International Agreements on Conservation of Marine Resources, With Special Reference to the North Pacific* (Stanford: Food Research Institute, Stanford University, 1943), p. 35.

12. Edward W. Allen, "The American View" *in* American Society of International Law, Marginal Seas and Pacific Fisheries, *Proceedings of Regional Meeting; Its Bulletin* XII pt. 2 (June 1956); Seattle: 1956, p. 22.

mission articles.[13] The regulations do not "limit or restrict the freedom of the seas" and yet they include provisions for compulsory arbitration of disputes over fisheries conservation. This would seem to rule against the absolutist doctrine of the freedom of the seas as a premise, as it would deny the necessity of achieving a balance of competing claims. There was however, an accepted qualification to the freedom of the seas by which abstention would be practised under sound conservation measures.

On the grounds that any salmon caught before they begin to run from salt water to fresh water are immature, the Washington State Director of Fisheries, Milo Moore, claims that salmon "should rightfully remain unmolested on the high seas."[14] It is further held that the scale and manner of the Japanese operation "violates the law of nature," and that if such an operation continues, salmon fishing in the North Pacific will no longer be an economic undertaking in four to ten years' time.

It is not so much the problem of moving or not moving the abstention line that is the question. It is rather the validity of the philosophy supporting the line that is debatable. The United States has used many arguments to strengthen its position. Perhaps the one that has won most international recognition has been that of the "special interest" of the coastal state in fishery conservation policy. The two concepts of abstention, and special interest of the coastal state, are, however, not strictly connected. Even if the arguments for the validity of the "American property" claim are accepted, the demands for the 15 degree shift westwards of the abstention line are founded on assertions that have limited support from scientific data. The crux of the matter lies in the interpretation of the protocol of the convention.

In 1940, Gregory observed that "allowing extra-territorial exploitation of the North Pacific reserves was distasteful not only to capital and labour interests but to the whole country."[15] Behind this is the concept that the Alaska-spawned salmon are distinctly a domestic resource, a concept which forms the basis of the American fishery interests' view in the dispute.

The second part of the Truman Proclamation of 1945 declared an extension of United States' interests over the contiguous coastal seas for the purpose of, among other things, effecting fishery conservation policy, on an agreement basis with other countries if necessary. On the presupposition that salmon do not migrate westwards outside the continental shelf, they could, for all practical purposes, be called an American resource. However, research shows that the salmon migrate far beyond the limits of the immediate coastal zone.

After the Japanese "scare" in the 1930s, effective assertion of exclusive United States and Canadian rights and effective instruments to carry them out were called for as an assurance to the fishing and conservation interests. The I.N.P.F.C. was to have been the effective instrument. It was to ensure the reciprocity or the equitability between Asian and American interests determined by origin of the resource as well as to stop "the invasion of the other fellow's *natural* fishing grounds."[16]

Two main lines of policy are being pursued at the moment, one direct and the other indirect. Within the terms of the I.N.P.F.C. the Japanese are being asked to suspend fishing in the area of intermingling where North American salmon occur in significant proportions. Indirectly the vested interests are attempting to force legislation through Congress that would bring pressure to bear on Japanese fishing activities through economic sanctions, such as banning imports from Japan of canned fish. There are also attempts to use organized labor to take action such as refusing to unload goods from Japan at the port of entry into the United States.

The United States Government agencies can adopt various policies. The F.W.S. is legally bound to reduce fishing activity by United States citizens in accordance with its commitment to its conservation policy. The United States Department of State can only present such facts as depletion and economic hardship to the Japanese, for the Japanese Government has exclusive power over her vessels on the high seas. At first glance it is

---

13. *American Journal of International Law*, 1957, Supplement, Official Documents LI, United Nations Report of the International Law Commission, Part II, High Seas; p. 223 *et seq*.

14. K. McLeod (ed.), *Fisheries* (Olympia, Washington: State Department of Fisheries, 1958), p. 134.

15. Homer E. Gregory, "Salmon Industry of the Pacific Coast," *Economic Geography*, XVI (October 1940), 412.

16. Edward W. Allen, "Fishery Geography of the North Pacific Ocean," *Geographical Review*, XLIII (October 1953), 560.

difficult to see what the exact United States policy is, because there is considerable internal conflict between interested parties. The government policy is clear, but that of other interested parties is not. The salmon-fishing industry has stated that it "will not make any more sacrifices for the benefit of the Japanese."[17] It believes that the F.W.S. must provide not only minimum escapement, but also benefits to United States fishermen.

In 1938 Bingham wrote, "The future peace and security of the United States is our policy. It is the protection of our interests in our coastal fisheries off the Pacific coast damaging invasion and foreign use."[18] In 21 years this point of view has not changed.

The Relative Standing of the Two Cases

The reports of the various sub-committees to the Committee on Biology and Research on the Progress of Research on the Problems raised by Protocol of the I.N.P.F.C. contain the best statement on current expert opinion of all parties to the convention. The Committee's report to the 1958 Meeting of the I.N.P.F.C. in Tokyo provides the latest statement.[19]

The proposed fields of study agreed upon at the first meeting of the I.N.P.F.C. in 1954 were: (1) the distribution of salmon on the high seas; (2) the use of various techniques to distinguish origin; (3) the tagging of salmon to obtain direct evidence of movement; and (4) oceanographic background study for this salmon distribution and movement data. At the 1957 meeting, the zone of intermingling was delimited as spreading over about 30 degrees of longitude between 170 degrees East and 160 degrees West. In this large area there is considerable difficulty in observing the distribution of salmon by their origin. The evidence shows that each stock may vary from year to year in distribution and size. The present research programme leaves many gaps, and it is impossible to describe the high seas distribution of all the important races quantitatively and qualitatively. Although the distribution of salmon in 1956 and 1957 prove the year to year variation, they do not contradict some over-all general conclusions which can be made.

Tagged red salmon of American origin have been found to predominate over Asian-spawned salmon as far as 175 degrees East and to exist as far as 170 degrees East; yet, Asian parasite characteristics have been found as far east as 170 degrees West. Within the intermingling zone there is a definite north-south apportionment, with American-spawned salmon predominating in the Bering Sea, and Asian south of the Aleutians. However, "the dynamic rather than the static nature of the distribution of red salmon is emphasized." So far any quantitative conclusions on pink salmon are impossible. Marked intra- and inter-seasonal fluctuations exist in number and distribution. No research work on chum salmon had been carried out prior to 1954. After three years of intensive research by tagging and scale analysis, a conclusion that the centre of the intermingling zone falls about 175 degrees West, with a 15 degree spread on either side, can be made. However, measurement of intermingling within the zone in terms of assessed proportions is still quite vague.

Riesenfeld wrote that "in the Law of the Sea national egotism, rash generalisations, insufficient consideration of basic questions have caused more conflicts and uncertainties than in any other aspect of International Law.[20] The present conflict over salmon exploitation in the North Pacific is well illustrated by this statement. Both sides have pursued increasingly incompatible policies. The motives behind these policies have often been influenced by chauvinism and local self-interest, and by political considerations not directly related to the problem in question, rather than by notions of equity.

At the extreme, the fishery interests interpret the United States' case as founded on the premise that she has property rights over the salmon, and relate this to a policy of exclusive exploitation based on origin. Japan, of course, does not recognize this in practice. Hence many arguments are not founded on common ground. By municipal law involving conser-

17. *Pacific Fisherman*, LVII (January 1959), 7.
18. Joseph Walter Bingham, *Report on the International Law of the Pacific* (Stanford, California: 1938).
19. International North Pacific Fisheries Commission, *op. cit.*

20. Stephan A. Riesenfeld, *Protection of Coastal Fisheries Under International Law* (Washington, D.C.: Carnegie Endowment for International Peace, Division of International Law, 1942), p. ix.

vation measures, and by such policy as the terms of the I.N.P.F.C., the United States has passed legislation in an attempt to achieve her goal of exclusive rights to exploitation. However, municipal legislation has been flexible, whereas the terms of the I.N.P.F.C. have not. The United States has thus tried to find scientific evidence to substantiate its legislative measures.

More logically, legislation and exploitation should be in the light of scientific evidence because the mass-exploitation has a scientific base. In all fairness, however, it must be pointed out that the present illogicality of the line 175 degrees West, although due to the lack of proper scientific evidence at the time, cannot really be blamed on its creators as it was supposed to be a temporary measure to meet immediate demands. Rash generalizations on both sides have led to serious misconceptions. The Japanese claim that there is no conclusive scientific evidence which related the drop in runs of Bristol Bay salmon to Japanese fishing of salmon on the high seas (Fig. 39.1) and that, moreover, there is no evidence that the Japanese are catching immature salmon or that the small mesh nets used by the Japanese kill or injure young salmon. The Japanese maintain that the need for the stringent conservation measures in Bristol Bay is a result of the coincidence of a cyclical low with an unusual limited escapement (Fig. 39.2) in the two main years, 1954

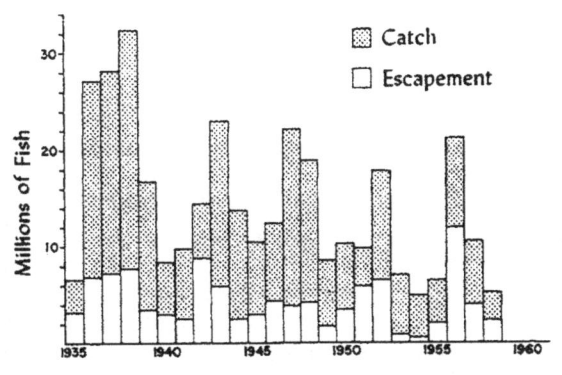

Fig. 39.2 RED SALMON RUN IN BRISTOL BAY

and 1955, in which the 1959 run was spawned. However, it has been found that about one per cent of the salmon running in Bristol Bay in 1958 had gill-net marks. Even so, the questions remain: how many injured salmon die before reaching Bristol Bay, and how many of the injured salmon that died, would die anyway due to other agents contributing to the "natural mortality" rate?

Professor M. Uda, of the Tokyo University of Fisheries, said in the spring of 1959: "It has been prematurely supposed by some that the main cause (of the decline of Alaska-spawned salmon) was over-fishing by the Japanese high-seas salmon fisheries. However, the declining trend began before Japanese high-seas fishing. The peaks in the sockeye pack in Bristol Bay were in the decade from 1930 to 1940. The fluctuation in natural environmental conditions as the falling of water levels and freezing of spawning beds due to climatic change, together with deforestation, water pollution, dam obstructions, effect of natural enemies, predators, etc., and changes in survival, or mortality rates due to changes in ocean climate, may be mainly responsible for such a broad change in sub-Arctic waters."[21] Fisheries experts in the United States are in general agreement with Professor Uda's statement. Dr. William F. Thompson, one-time Director of the University of Washington's Fisheries Research Institute, has stated, "... the (United States fishing) industry must not make the mistake of trying to remedy by law something that is a natural occurrence."[22] Obviously a distinction must be made between two trends. There is a definite over-all reduction in salmon runs for which the Japanese cannot be held responsible. However, a yearly fluctuation can also be observed.

The Japanese operate their high-seas salmon fishing industry in a manner similar to the way in which they operate several other industries producing goods deemed essential by the Japanese Government to the country's economy. It is an administered non-competitive industry entered within the hands of several large corporations. The industry, beset by political complications in the international field in which the government participates, receives government support. It is at the same time efficient and inefficient from the economic standpoint. In terms of scale of operation and utilization of available techniques, the Japanese industry is more

21. M. Uda, "The Salmon Fisheries," *Fisheries Seminars*, 3, March–May 1959 (Nanaimo, British Columbia: Fisheries Research Board of Canada, 1959), pp. 8–9.

22. *University of Washington Daily*, 8 April 1954.

efficient than the Bristol Bay salmon fishery. However, it is hardly efficient when certain considerations are examined. Such considerations would include its short-term policy of a high rate of discount to the future, the increased input necessitated by substituting transport and search costs for the natural concentration found at river mouths, and the failure to allow the salmon to reach full maturity, and hence highest quality which they attain as they begin to run upstream from the open sea. Return per unit effort, if measured by number of salmon per unit of gear fished, is far lower on the high seas where salmon are scattered, than in Bristol Bay where they are schooled. On the high seas twenty-five men and a large boat must fish six to eight miles of net to equal the daily catch of two men in an open skiff using 150 fathoms of net. These questions of technical efficiency and high returns must be considered in the light of short-term exploitation and sacrifice of quality.

The United States' industry, on the other hand, has not been able to use optimum methods of exploitation because conservation legislation has been against this. Fishing techniques have become anachronistic. In 1939, when restrictions were not as severe as now, Deloach stated that ". . . such restrictions . . . serve to reduce the available supply for market purposes as well as to forestall wasteful use of the resource."[23] Up to the early 1950s, regulations were still severe in terms of legislation against more efficient techniques. The tendency has been for the F.W.S. to maintain a technical *status quo* in this manner. There have been various pressures behind such a policy. Ostensibly the desire for the conservation of the resource is fundamental. However, there are other factors, such as the vested interests of the boat owners, and the aspect of the asserted social benefit to the Alaskan native. Some type of benefit/cost analysis would be needed to gauge the validity of the last mentioned factor. There has been heavy investment in the industry to offset the lack of economies brought about by these inefficiencies. However, for the last 20 years, runs of salmon have been diminishing, hence productivity has further dropped. The great feature of salmon fishing is the lack of reliable prediction in terms of quantity, quality and time of species. Obviously, despite the factor of concentration, for the immobile site of the Alaskan industry this unpredictability is going to have a greater effect than for the mobile high-seas operation of the Japanese. This uncertainty means great risk. Up to the early 1920s the small cannery, typical of a risk industry, accounted for the major part of the pack. However, the tendency since then has been towards economies of scale by vertical integration, as the smaller canneries began to suffer competition from under-pricing by the bigger companies. As long as the runs did not deteriorate appreciably this was sound economics, and productivity increased. However, with progressive decreases in runs the catch dropped quickly below threshold requirements. The unit cost of the salmon has thus increased, giving the more cheaply produced Japanese article a comparative advantage and a strong competitive position in the American market. In fact, despite the low productivity per worker (or per capita unit in gear), caused by the need for search and large area covered by nets, the Japanese can put a lower cost per unit commodity on the American market due to other relative costs of factor inputs in the production process. Primarily lower wages per worker in the Japanese industry enable it to achieve comparable labor costs to the American industry even though the Japanese use more men per salmon catch per unit of time. Secondly the Japanese government subsidises the industry in technical improvement as compared to government restraint in the United States' policy. These two factors would seem to explain the superior competitive position of the Japanese despite the natural advantage of concentration the Alaskan industry enjoys. Logically, then, it would seem that if the United States' policy toward Bristol Bay salmon fishing were changed to one of government subsidies for technical improvement plus restricted entry into the market, the present industry would lower costs of salmon catch, and consequently lower prices of the commodity. This restriction would essentially mean the adoption of a monopoly operation of the industry after the Japanese style. The United States monopoly would never get out of hand as long as Japanese salmon were not restricted from the American market. There is one other important factor which must be considered. Because of the present nature of

23. Daniel B. DeLoach, *The Salmon Canning Industry* (Corvallis, Oregon, 1939), p. 39.

the resource, its availability rather than the volume of the market might ultimately set the limit.

The pressure for a solution to this international problem is essentially desired from the use or value both parties see in the resource. Therefore a solution to the economics of the salmon business in each country is fundamental in perpetuating the resource.

At the Law of the Sea Conference in Geneva 1958, the United States' case probably gained a little on the Japanese policy in terms of world opinion. The abstention principle found support, conservation was declared the duty of all nations, and the special interests of the coastal state were recognized. The convention must be ratified, and this will be binding only on the states accepting the obligations. Hence, regional and special organisations must continue to tackle conservation problems.

There is need for a permanent solution to the problem, a solution which must come through diplomacy and international law. However, there are many problems to be overcome before arriving at any agreement. Under the terms of the I.N.P.F.C., if any disagreements should arise in connection with the conclusions of research work, an independent committee is to decide on the recommendations to be made.[24] As Japan has never recognized the United States property claim, there is a question of the "spirit and intent" of the two disputants. Not only are there differences over the interpretation of the protocol of the I.N.P.F.C. but there are also varying opinions regarding the statistical inference of the data collected in salmon research. The accumulated scientific evidence since 1954 shows that disagreements will increase as the data mount. Complications and intricacies, unimagined in 1952, are becoming more evident as the sum of Canadian, American and Japanese data is brought out annually at the I.N.P.F.C. meetings. At the same time, any independent committee would be faced with so many alternatives that an objective solution based solely on scientific data will probably be impossible. Diplomatic compromise would then probably be necessary to settle the issue. Unilateral action can be ruled out as a solution, for it can scarcely be the basis of a fundamental and equitable solution of the fisheries problem. The United States realises that any policy of extending territorial jurisdiction can be a two-edged sword. Salmon fisheries are not the only important fisheries of the United States. The tuna-fishing industry of California finds the United States in the role of the high-seas state, and there is regional pressure from California against any national policy which would adversely affect the vested interests of the Californian high-seas tuna fleet.

The Canadians act as independent observers at the I.N.P.F.C. meetings. As they are satisfied that no salmon spawned in Canadian streams cross the 175 degree West line at any time, the Canadians can afford to be neutral. The Canadians state that it is not just a case of picking up the abstention line and moving it a little westwards, as the United States demands. They suggest that several new lines must be drawn to divide the stocks of salmon by species determined by an equal-ration proportion in terms of numbers of each species. These lines would have to vary from season to season. If such a solution were to be founded on scientific evidence in the terms that the I.N.P.F.C. demands, then it could only take place when and if sound and conclusive means of predicting salmon movement are developed. So far there is a lack of sufficient evidence for conclusive statements of any fundamental nature. Interpretation of data presently available varies, and allows for no conclusive proof of determinant factors. A mutually satisfactory line based on averages of migration extents seems a long way.

Japanese and American policies are at opposite poles. Even with some flexibility of either policy, there seems little possibility of a solution coming through the efforts of the contending national and sectional parties. There is a legal deadlock at the international level and disagreement on the interpretation of scientific data. However, diplomacy may yet find a way.

From this study of the conflict over the utilisation of the natural resource several features come to light: (1) the limitations and possible dangers of an exclusive fishery pact covering large areas of the high seas; (2) the economic need of Japan to maintain this valuable export at its present level; (3) the basic difference between the economics of the

---

24. United Nations, "Report of the International Technical Conference on The Conservation of the Living Resources of the Sea, Rome," *Objectives of Fishery Conservation*, A/CONF. 10/6 (New York: 1955).

Japanese and American salmon fishing organisations; (4) the basic contrasts in attitudes between Japan on one side, and the two principal "coastal" states, the United States and the Soviet Union, on the other, over the depletion and exploitation of salmon stocks; and (5) the confused state of international law relating to the freedom of the high seas and fishing rights.

Postscript

During the decade since this paper first appeared, there have been few basic changes in the nature of the policy conflict. Until 1966, the Bristol Bay salmon runs continued to decline, and the United States continued, unsuccessfully, to press for a shift in the 175 degrees West meridian eastwards to limit the spatial extent of Japanese high-seas salmon fishing in the North Pacific. The United States in 1965 threatened severe restrictions on the importation of Japanese fishery products in reaction to continued Japanese fishing and declining salmon runs.

Despite the tremendous improvements in the techniques of biological research, fishery experts have deplored the lack of scientific knowledge upon which the I.N.P.F.C. and other similar treaties are based, and to question the direction which research is taking in its narrow devotion to determining legal lines as part of a static system of ownership of North Pacific salmon.[25]

By the late 1960s, however, salmon runs at Bristol Bay had increased substantially, and, despite Japanese fishing, the 1969 run was expected to exceed that of any year since Japan started her high-seas salmon fishing activity in the North Pacific.

25. W. F. Thompson, "Fishing Treaties and Salmon in the North Pacific," *Science*, Vol. 150, No. 3705 (December 31, 1965), pp. 1786–1789.

40

Environmental Stress and the Municipal Political System

ROGER E. KASPERSON*

On August 18 and 19, 1955, Hurricane Diane struck the eastern seaboard of the United States and left 176 dead and damage estimated at $3.75 billions. In its wake, national and local governmental agencies launched widespread hurricane and flood control projects. On September 9, 1965, Hurricane Betsey caused widespread damages in southeastern Louisiana. Alleging that the incumbent administration had left New Orleans inadequately prepared, the local political opposition attempted to capitalize on the disaster in order to defeat Mayor Victor Shiro in the forthcoming election. Yet, the Mayor, using his extensive resources and political acumen, was able to weather the crisis.[1] Environmental disturbances and changes often create stresses, and sometimes crises, in political systems and test whether governments and managers can accomodate these stresses through innovation or whether they will fail and be replaced by competitors.[2] In the case of natural resource management debate has centered upon the implications of periodic environmental crises for optimal resource management and planning.[3]

The city of Brockton, located in southeastern Massachusetts, had in 1965 a population of approximately 83,500; city leaders faced a deteriorating water use/safe yield (WU/SY) ratio which, if drought occurred, threatened to deplete rapidly the municipal water supply. In fact, by 1957 water consumption had already reached 5.4 mgd for Brockton's chief reservoir (Silver Lake) and 1.5 mgd of low quality emergency supply in

---

* Roger E. Kasperson is a co-editor of this volume.

1. F. Glen Abney and Larry B. Hill, "Natural Disasters as a Political Variable; The Effect of a Hurricane on an Urban Election," *American Political Science Review*, LX (December 1966), pp. 974–981.

2. Political scientists have noted that dictatorships usually arise during periods of crisis. See, for example, J. O. Hertzler, "Crisis and Dictatorship," *American Sociological Review*, V (1940), pp. 157–169. Other relevant studies include the following: Amitai Etzioni and William R. Taher, "Scope, Pervasiveness, and Tension Management in Complex Organizations," *Social Research*, XXX (Summer 1963), pp. 220–238; E. Feit, "Political Groups under Severe Pressure: A Comparative Study Based on the Communication Control Model," *General Systems*, IX (1964), pp. 245–281.

3. Henry C. Hart, "Crisis, Community and Consent in Water Politics," *Law and Contemporary Problems*, XXII (Summer 1957), pp. 510–537; William E. Leuchtenburg, *Flood Control Politics* (Cambridge: Harvard University Press, 1953).

Avon Reservoir. When the drought did occur during 1961–1966, a major crisis—and one which proved extremely difficult to resolve—confronted city officials.

The purpose of this research is to examine the process by which drought became a major political issue and was eventually resolved. The study will devote particular attention to the ways by which actors in the municipal political system perceived and managed this form of environmental stress. Ultimately, of course, there is an attempt to generalize beyond the limits of a single case-study.

Data Sources

A number of sources provided data for the research. First, lengthy interviews with the two Brockton mayors whose respective terms of office spanned the drought period, the city water superintendent, and members of the bureaucracy provided detailed information on the perception of the drought problem, the views of the community, and the political issues which arose. Second, interviews with members of the engineering firm of Camp, Dresser, and McKee, the technical consultants to Brockton, and correspondence with representatives of governmental agencies contributed useful information in assessing their roles in solving the drought problem. Finally, a collection of editorials and newspaper accounts of the drought in the *Brockton Daily Enterprise* and the *Silver Lake News* constituted a third source of data.

The Brockton Water Supply Problem

Constructed in 1880, Avon Reservoir, with its safe yield of 1.5 mgd, was the original municipal supply (Map 40.1). In 1897, however, increases in water consumption led the city Board of Water Commissioners to recommend the acquisition of Silver Lake, located within the political limits of nearby communities. The Brockton Water District, established at this time, included the city of Brockton and the small adjacent communities of Whitman, East Bridgewater, Pembroke, Halifax, the village of South Easton, and a portion of Hanson.

This supply sufficed until 1950 when the Board of Water Commissioners, concerned over the increase of water use to an average of 4.8 mgd, engaged the engineering firm of Camp, Dresser, and McKee to prepare a thorough evaluation of Brockton's water supply and to make recommendations for future planning. After a lengthy study, the consultants concluded that the present supply was inadequate to meet future demand and that new water sources were needed. After weighing alternatives, they recommended three ponds (Furnace, Oldham, and Monponsett) and two streams located close to Silver Lake (Map 40.1). By diverting these sources to Silver Lake, the engineers saw a new safe yield of 10.2 mgd, sufficient in their view to the year 2000.

According to Massachusetts law, however, the ponds were "great" ponds and consequently state property. Great ponds may be used for water supply by a municipality with approval of the state legislature. Efforts to secure approval in 1952, 1957, and 1963 all failed because of intense political opposition in the Silver Lake area where the ponds served recreational purposes. In 1957, for example, 1,800 angry people, including summer residents from all over eastern Massachusetts, stormed into a public hearing in Boston to protest the proposed legislation. Although Brockton presented a modified bill to divert only winter overflow waters—and thereby not to interfere with local recreational rights—in 1963, Silver Lake area residents scoffed at the guarantees and the result was the same.[4]

Meanwhile water consumption continued to increase. By 1957, average annual consumption was 5.4 mgd, a WU/SY of high quality water of 1.17 and of all water supply of .89. By 1962, the comparable ratios had risen respectively to 1.70 and 1.28. During the latter 1950s, the supply remained adequate because of the fortunate coincidence of a rainfall average 20 per cent above normal. Beginning in 1961, however, the advent of drought quickly brought the already unfavorable WU/SY ratio to a point of crisis. Given this situation, how did the managers of the political system perceive and deal with the drought? To analyze this

---

4. For a detailed analysis of the intercommunity conflict see Roger E. Kasperson, "Political Behavior and the Decision-Making Process in the Allocation of Water Resources Between Recreational and Municipal Use," *Natural Resources Journal*, IX (April 1969).

Map 40.1

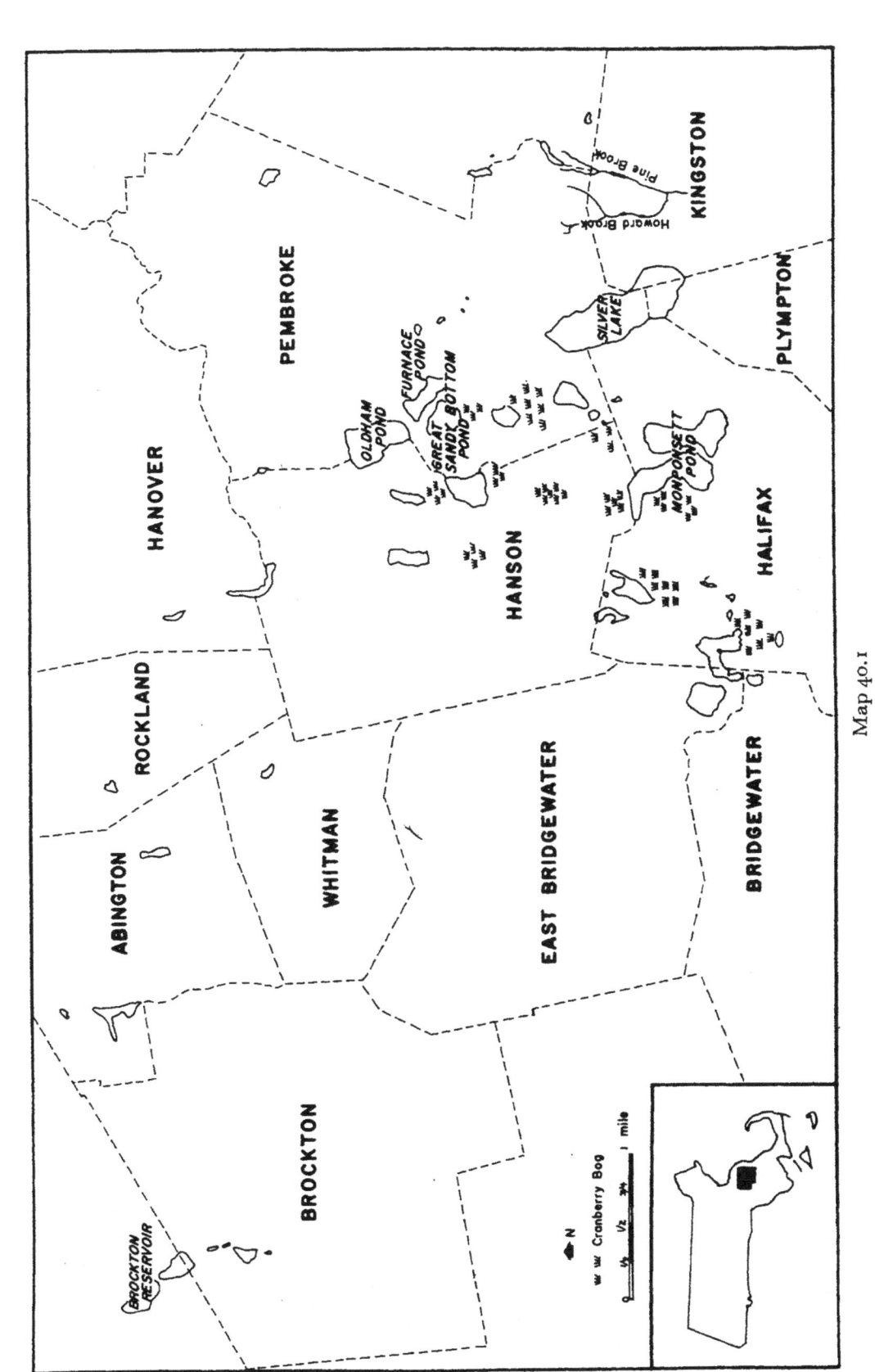

The Brockton – Silver Lake Area

process, it may be useful to present a model of stress management within the municipal political system.

A General Model of Municipal Stress Management

One method of evaluating the management of natural resources is to formulate normative theory given some assumed objectives and constraints, and then to compare the empirical case with the referent model. Such a research methodology, however, may have objectionable properties arising from the isolation of the unit of analysis. In fact, the process of natural resource management is only one subsystem operating within the confines of the larger political system. The sub-system does not operate in isolation for the maximization of any optimal pattern of resource management, but rather the various sub-systems, in order to reduce stresses, compete with one another for the allocation of scarce resources. The managers of the political system cope with the diverse stresses according to goals and objectives which they bring to office and in order to play the game of politics within the rules and constraints of their particular roles. This analysis, then, views drought within the context of other stresses acting upon the city and the differing, shifting objectives of actors in the municipal political system.

The model presented here is simply a way of ordering the process by which the managers of a municipal political system evaluate and attempt to solve the stresses acting upon a city. By "stress" is meant "noxious or potentially noxious environmental forces upon the individual."[5] "Strain," in turn, refers to the individual's perception, evaluation, and reaction to the stimulus. In an urban setting, stress may arise as a result of gradual accumulation or by a precipitous change in the environmental framework in which the municipal political system operates. It may also be internal as well as external to the system. Stress, via strain, will become a "crisis" when the managers of the system view themselves or the system as being in a hazardous situation.[6] In all cases strain involves the notion of threat either to the actor or the political system as a whole.[7]

The model, influenced by prior theories of Gilbert F. White and David Easton,[8] is shown in Figure 40.1. To begin with, the dynamic nature of the physical and social environment will periodically, if not continually, create stresses upon the political system. These stresses may arise from an extreme event in the environment, such as a tornado, fire, or riot, or they may constitute the cumulative period of gradual change, such as school inadequacy or housing deterioration. The stresses will then be articulated to the managers of the system, and the articulation vehicle may heavily influence the manager's perception and evaluation of the stress. Stress articulated by a major urban newspaper or a racial interest group, for example, may exert more strain than stress communicated within the administrative framework since the former is much more capable of inducing threat into the political environment of the decision-maker.

The manager will perceive and evaluate both the stress stimulus and the vehicle of articulation, and build a cognitive model of the stress situation. His adaptations will then be "rational" to this model of reality.[9]

---

5. There is considerable debate as to the appropriate definition of stress; the range is presented in F. E. Horvath, "Psychological Stress: A Review of Definitions and Experimental Research," *General Systems Yearbook*, IV (1959), pp. 203–230. For some theoretical considerations, with particular applicability to disasters, see Irving L. Janis, "Problems of Theory in the Analysis of Stress Behavior," *Journal of Social Issues*, X (1954), pp. 12–25. The definition used here is that of Wolpert; see Julian Wolpert, "Migration as an Adjustment to Environmental Stress," *Journal of Social Issues*, XXII (October 1966), p. 93.

6. See Kent Miller, "The Concept of Crisis: Current Status and Mental Health Implications," *Human Organization*, XXII (Fall 1963), pp. 195–201.

7. See the searching discussion of stress and political systems in David Easton, *A Framework for Political Analysis* (Englewood Cliffs, N.J.: Prentice-Hall, 1965), pp. 90–135.

8. Gilbert F. White, *Choice of Adjustment to Floods*, The University of Chicago, Department of Geography Research Paper No. 93 (Chicago: 1964); David Easton, "An Approach to the Analysis of Political Systems," *World Politics*, IX (April 1957), pp. 383–400; David Easton, *A Systems Analysis of Political Life* (N.Y.: John Wiley and Sons, 1965). Normative theory relevant to the following analysis is contained in Arthur Maass, "System Design and the Political Process: A General Statement," in Arthur Maass et al., *Design of Water Resource Systems* (Cambridge: Harvard University Press, 1962), pp. 565–604.

9. This is the concept of "intended" or "bounded" rationality as presented in Herbert A. Simon, *Models of Man* (N.Y.: John Wiley and Sons, 1957), p. 198.

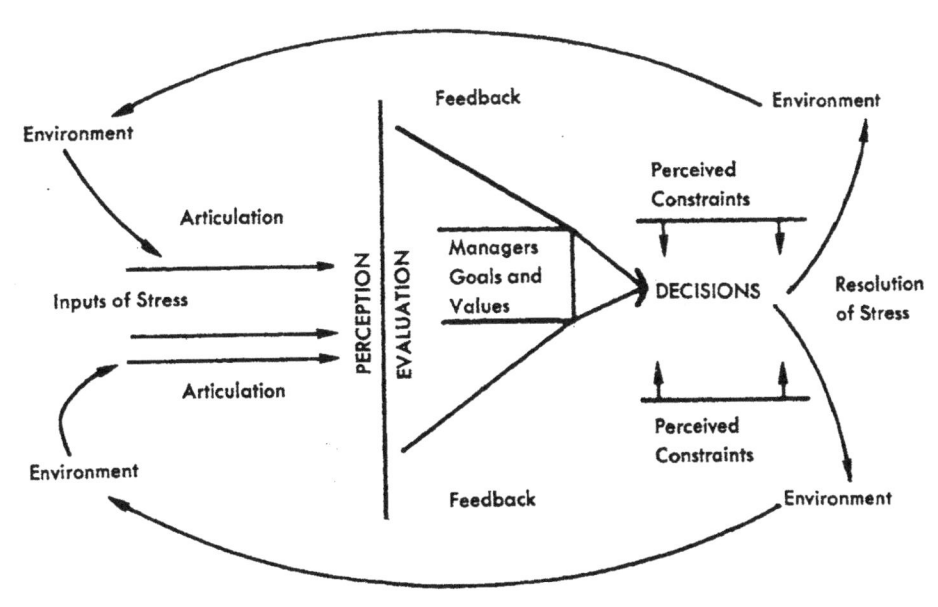

Fig. 40.1 A General Model of Municipal Stress Management

TYPE OF STRESS

		Housing	Schools	Water	Civil Rights	Sewage
PERCEIVED INTENSITY OF STRESS	Low	x		x	x	
	Medium					x
	High		x			

Fig. 40.2 The Managerial Matrix

Moreover, he will evaluate the stress within the context of the various other stresses acting upon the political system. The evaluation will involve gathering of information and consultation with members of the actor's reference groups. The view of city problems from the policy-making bridge may be conceived as a managerial matrix in which the various stresses are located along one axis and the perceived intensity of stress along the other. Figure 40.2 shows a simplified hypothetical example.

The manager will then incorporate this matrix into the goals and values that he brings to office and into the role that he plays within the political game. Within this game there will be, as Norton Long notes, "a well-established set of goals whose achievement indicates success or failure for the participants, a set of socialized roles making participant behavior highly predictable, a set of strategies and tactics handed down through experience and occasionally subject to improvement and change, an elite public whose approbation is appreciated, and, finally, a general public which has some appreciation for the standing of the players."[10] Given his goals, his role and his particular personality, the manager will then search for choice alternatives and will eventually allocate resources among the various stresses in the managerial matrix in an attempt to resolve or reduce their pressure on political system.[11] Throughout, he will seek to broaden his "decision environment" and to reduce the uncertainty attached to the range of choice and the probable outcomes of particular decisions.[12]

The decision process occurs within the constraints that a manager sees restricting his alternatives for choice and relates to the actor's cognitive model of the managerial matrix. Many decisions will be incremental over time while others will involve "satisficing rather than optimizing strategies." In short we are dealing with "administrative," not "economic" man.[13] As Wolpert notes, in stress situations "an excitation is present in the environment which may take the form of time pressure to reach the decision, insufficient information or ambiguity about alternatives or an overabundance of information that cannot be assimilated or cues from the environment which indicate that one's energy and ability are insufficient to deal with the problem at hand or other stressors."[14] Most elected officials, for example, see a minimal level of support maintenance as an important constraint. Alienation of certain interest groups, a particular elite public, or the mass media may be unacceptable. In most municipalities, the City Council, particularly by virtue of its control over public expenditures, functions as a constraint on alternative executive policies. It is noteworthy, however, that a manager may well be able to incur short-run losses of support or public failure by means of "reservoirs of support" which he has accumulated in the system over time.[15]

Finally, there will be some resolution of or reduction in the combination of stresses acting upon the political system. The system is capable of accepting and processing the full set of stresses generated by a dynamic environment. Feedback will occur in the form of changes in the environment and in information concerning the process of stress input and stress resolution. The system is thereby capable of responding and learning.[16] Also, the decisions may well have altered the constraints on the system and the relative level of support in storage.

APPLICATION OF THE MODEL TO THE BROCKTON WATER CRISIS

The Context of Stresses

During the period 1961–1966, drought was by no means the only problem facing the city of Brockton. In the primary election of 1963, the League of Women Voters asked each candidate what they viewed as the major problem facing the city. Only one candidate cited drought as *the* major problem, and he subsequently suffered defeat in the primary. Both of the successful candidates, by contrast, gave priority to the school problem and included water shortages with sewage, traffic, and urban renewal as other important problems.[17] This illustrates a simple political fact-of-life about a declining municipal water supply system—it does not generate as much public concern as do many other municipal problems. Until the supply becomes so depleted as to necessitate rigid use restrictions or to impair seriously quality of water, an unfavorable WU/SY ratio is a worrywart for bored engineers and unoccupied water superintendents.

10. Norton E. Long, "The Local Community as an Ecology of Games," in Ronald L. Warren, ed., *Perspectives on the American Community* (Chicago: Rand McNally, 1966), p. 56.

11. Richard C. Snyder, "A Decision-Making Approach to the Study of Political Phenomena" in Roland Young, ed., *Approaches to the Study of Politics* (Evanston: Northwestern University Press, 1958), pp. 24–36.

12. Wolpert notes, for example, that Swedish farmers attempted to reduce uncertainty by arranging "negotiated environments." See Julian Wolpert, "The Decision Process in Spatial Context," *Annals* of the Association of American Geographers, LIV (December 1964), pp. 548–552, 557–558.

13. Herbert A. Simon, *Administrative Behavior: A Study of Decision-Making Processes in Administrative Organization*, 2nd ed. (N.Y.: Free Press, 1957), pp. XXV–XXVI.

14. Julian Wolpert, "Departures from the Usual Environment in Locational Analysis" (Paper prepared for Delivery at the Center for Regional Studies, University of Kansas, October 31, 1967), p. 4.

15. Easton, "An Approach to the Analysis of Political Systems," p. 396.

16. For a full discussion of feedback in social systems, see Karl W. Deutsch, *The Nerves of Government* (N.Y.: Free Press, 1966), pp. 88–91, 182–199.

17. *Brockton Enterprise*, October 4, 1963.

The school problem, by contrast, was a pressing issue for most residents of Brockton. The city had built no elementary schools since 1916, all schools were overcrowded, and several were wooden structures which the school board wanted to close. A school building program, launched in 1949, produced four new junior high schools but by 1963 rapid population growth (the city's population increased from 63,000 in 1950 to 78,000 in 1960) had overtaken these facilities. Beginning in 1962, three elementary schools and the one antiquated municipal high school were forced to go on double session and the others were all badly overcrowded. As the Superintendent of Schools noted: "Nothing was done over a long period of time. We have had plans for new schools since 1956 but we could not get anything done."[18] Members of the public felt this stress keenly since it entered daily with an immediate urgency into the lives of their children, and also caused difficulties in personnel recruitment for city industries.

Sewage was also a major problem during the drought years. The city had built its sewage treatment plant more than 50 years before, and its capacity was no longer adequate for the increased population. As a result, the city was forced to divert untreated sewage into a nearby stream, thereby creating a major health hazard. Mayor F. Milton McGrath (1962–1963) considered this danger his most pressing problem and noted that "first things must come first."[19] The widespread deterioration of housing in the central sections of Brockton was another problem the city had neglected almost entirely. In the central business district, for example, 37 per cent of all buildings were classified as deteriorated or dilapidated.[20] Nevertheless, the city did not as yet even have a redevelopment program. Within the context of city problems, then, drought was certainly a major issue—but only one of several.

Stress Articulation

The engineering firm of Camp, Dresser, and McKee served as the major agent of articulation for the drought problem. First engaged for a full-scale study in 1950, the firm made periodic reports on the water supply situation to the city administration. In the basic 1951 report, the engineers estimated future water consumption by use of population projections and by assuming that per-capita water consumption would be somewhat higher than a simple extension of the relatively constant rate of increase between 1900 and 1950.[21] Working from their assumptions, they predicted an interim demand for 1975 of between 6.0 and 8.0 mgd. The fact that use had already reached 7.8 mgd by 1962 indicates the extent to which they underestimated demand.

Camp, Dresser, and McKee evaluated the safe yield of the municipal water system at about 6.1 mgd, 4.6 mgd in Silver Lake and 1.5 mgd in the poor-quality, emergency supply of Avon Reservoir. Obviously, the city needed new, additional supplies. For alternative sources, the consultants considered three possibilities. First, they labelled existing ground water supplies inadequate because of the probability of high iron and manganese content.[22] Second, they weighed the possibility of a connection with the distant Boston Metropolitan District Commission but rejected this alternative because of the higher costs involved in pumping, connecting pipelines, and the higher water rates in the District.

The firm gave preference, therefore, to the ponds and streams (Furnace, Oldham, and Monponsett ponds and Howard and Pine brooks) in the southeastern portion of the state (Map 40.1). The engineers estimated that these five sources would produce a safe yield of 10.2 mgd (revised in 1966 to 12.0 mgd). In 1951 the consultants clearly envisioned only single-purpose use for the proposed sources, although under heavy political pressure in 1957 they altered this proposal to include

18. Personal interview, August 6, 1967.
19. Personal interview, July 19, 1967.
20. Brockton Redevelopment Authority, *Brockton: Community Renewal Program* (Brockton: 1966), p. 30.
21. The following is from the unpublished report by Camp, Dresser, and McKee prepared for the City of Brockton. See the Board of Water Commissioners, "Report on Water Work Improvement for the City of Brockton" (Boston: November 2, 1951). In fact, per-capita water consumption skyrocketed between 1951 and 1957.
22. This was also the considered opinion on the Massachusetts Water Resources Commission and the United States Geological Survey. Detailed analysis is available in a joint report of these two agencies *Massachusetts Basic Data Report No. 5, Groundwater Series, Brockton-Pembroke Area.*

only the use of overflow waters during October to May, a change which would allow summer recreational use.

In an effort to publicize their report, the engineers communicated their recommendations and warnings to the *Brockton Daily Enterprise* as well as to the political officials. Both the Mayor and Water Superintendent, for reasons of political support and professionalism, were very sensitive to the effect upon public opinion. Several other less important sources were involved in articulation. The Water Department, of course, kept careful records of water consumption and supply and formulated plans to anticipate future needs. Several times during the early part of the drought, distributional inadequacies created problems in a few limited parts of the city. Also self-appointed guardians of the municipal supply and hopeful businessmen at intervals issued public statements. In 1963, for example, a local well-drilling firm, perhaps in a bid to be considered for contract, described Brockton as "one of the greatest water-producing areas for rock wells in New England."[23]

The Managers

The Mayor, the Water Superintendent, the Board of Water Commissioners, and, to a lesser extent, the City Council were the primary actors involved in the management of the municipal water system. Of these managers, the Mayor both because of his command over the varied resources of the political system and the limitations on the Water Department, was unquestionably the major source of innovation.

A comparison of the two drought mayors provides an interesting contrast in conceptions of the drought, political goals, and leadership during the period of drought stress. Mayor F. Milton McGrath (1962–1963), a veteran of 20 years in local politics, exemplifies the traditional leadership found in many small and medium-sized American cities. A graduate of the City Business College, he had worked his way up in the ranks as school committee member, city councillor, and two terms as City Council president. Mayor Alvin Jack Sims (1964–1967), by contrast, represents the dynamic, youthful element in politics. Only 38 years old during his campaign for the mayorship, he had held several minor political offices. A graduate of Boston University Law School, he exemplified his political style in a campaign speech:

With a population growth among the greatest of any Massachusetts city, we are still living with sewage and water systems, schools, building codes, zoning regulations, traffic flow, and police and fire protection—and worst of all a municipal administration—geared to the horse and buggy era.[24]

In spite of their radically different professional backgrounds, experience, and political styles, it is striking that these mayors tended to see their role in much the same manner. In an interview, Mayor McGrath described his role:

Brockton is the city I live in; I was born here. I take great pride in the city. I call three-fourths of the people by their first name. As mayor, I strived to keep Brockton growing and to deal with its major problems. Of course, I dealt with the most pressing items first—sewage, schools, and water. You know, being mayor is the hardest and most thankless job in the world. People pressure you for what they want, but when you need help they are never there.[25]

Both saw their job as dealing with the managerial matrix to the best of their ability. Both saw their range for innovation as tightly constrained by a variety of limitations. Finally, a common component of their professionalism is the view of an ill-informed, self-centered public and City Council, unappreciative of the complexity and range of a mayor's problems.

Superintendent Paul F. Kingman of the Brockton Water Department was, like Mayor McGrath, a creature of the city and its traditions, and shared many of the same referents. He had inherited his position from his father and had served in the office for over three decades. Lacking any special professional training for the post, he was heavily reliant upon his extensive practical experience and the advice of outside technical experts from consulting engineering firms and governmental agencies.

The Board of Water Commissioners was an

---

23. *Brockton Daily Enterprise*, March 20, 1963.
24. *Brockton Daily Enterprise*, September 30, 1963.
25. Personal interview, July 19, 1967.

actor of considerable power and independence in the management of the city water supply. A three-man elected group, the Board established general policy, determined priorities for future developments, set the budget which was submitted to the Mayor, and exercised complete authority over restrictions on water use. Board members' longer terms and frequent reelections often permitted them to outlive the Mayor's administration, and to acquire a degree of permanence in their positions. Each of the three members was a local businessman and each lacked any professional water supply training.

Finally, the City Council played a role as managerial agent, largely through its control of purse strings, its function as a sounding board for public opinion, and through recommendations to the executive branch of the government. It had a Jekyll and Hyde character, however, because it functioned as an important constraint on the decisions of other managers.

The Brockton Managerial Matrix

The management of drought depended heavily upon how the political actors evaluated its impact on the municipal water supply. The evidence suggests that Mayor McGrath never perceived the deteriorating WU/SY ratio to be as serious as some of the other stresses acting upon the city. During the summer of 1962, when Silver Lake reservoir dropped $33\frac{1}{4}$ inches below normal, the Mayor issued statements reassuring the public that the water supply was adequate, that the lake had "always been able to come back in the past," and that the only problem was one of "efficient distribution." He apparently genuinely confused the problems of distribution and supply. On several occasions in 1962 he indicated that once the city solved its distributional difficulties, the water supply problem would pass. Even at the conclusion of the drought, he still did not understand the random nature of drought occurrence:

Droughts occur once in a hundred years. 1880 was the last one. They are always six-year droughts, which can end or you can have another six years. They occur when there are mild winters with very little snow. This is because our water comes from New Hampshire and Vermont. Drought probably cannot happen in the next decade or two.[26]

The Mayor also indicated that he had doubts about the validity of the Camp, Dresser, and McKee reports and that he also wanted the opinions of others. The Mayor betrayed both a noticeable tendency to distrust these "outside" experts and an inclination to give equal weight to the opinions of old friends and associates. Disagreement concerning the financial obligation of the city to the engineering consultants further complicated this relationship. In searching for alternative water sources to enlarge the municipal supply, Mayor McGrath gave serious consideration to the advice offered by local citizens—a priest who offered to make seismographic tests and the well-drilling firm (R. E. Chapman), which expressed its optimism concerning ground water supplies. The Mayor's reliance upon trusted community referents is most apparent in the case of the "Stig Rosenburg swamps." The Mayor described Stig Rosenburg as a man who "loved the city and tried to be real helpful" by offering the swamps in back of his house as a possible source of supply. Mayor McGrath mused both personally and publicly about the feasibility of solving the need (of a magnitude of about 4–5 mgd) through this suggestion.

Mayor McGrath's key associate in drought management, Water Superintendent Paul F. Kingman, had a rather similar perception of the drought and the municipal supply. In 1962, at a time when the annual average WU/SY had reached 1.28 and Silver Lake stood at a record low of 62 inches below normal, Superintendent Kingman informed reporters that "distribution remains the key problem here. The average depth of the lake is 26 feet and in some places there is more than 100 feet of water. Even if use continues at the present rate, the supply will remain adequate".[27] This evaluation was possible even in the face of such stress, because he too evidently did not conceive of drought as a random event. He assumed, for example, a

---

26. Personal interview, July 17, 1967. The Mayor's comments perhaps reflect a common myth in the Brockton area that local water supplies came from a "giant underground river" which flowed from New Hampshire and Vermont, through Brockton, and eventually out to sea. See Kasperson, *op. cit.*

27. *Brockton Daily Enterprise*, August 7, 1962.

predictable pattern of water supply in his 1963 statement that "heavy rains in the near future will help alleviate the situation (i.e., drought) but the traditional spring moisture has been lacking this year."[28] His assertion in 1966 that "God ain't gonna let us go without water" may indicate a metaphysical stance which influenced policy decisions.[29]

With the hope that future rains might restore the municipal water supply situation to "normal," a suspicion that the engineers might have unduly exaggerated the present hazard, and a feeling (perhaps not unfounded!) that the state would not, in the final analysis, allow the town to "go dry," the sewage and school problems appeared to be the more pressing to the McGrath administration. Moreover, schools especially carried more of a political "payoff" than did public resources expended on the water supply. Ultimately, both political considerations and stress accumulation provided the impetus for system innovation.

Political Constraints

Before analyzing managerial behavior, it may be useful to note what managers viewed as the constraints on their actions. The two mayors provide an interesting contrast in perceived constraints.

Both mayors saw the City Council as a serious constraint upon their opportunity for innovation. In fact, however, it was much more of a limitation upon Mayor Sims, since he was a Republican and the City Council overwhelmingly Democrat. Mayor McGrath, as leader of the local Democratic Party, was in a far better position to enact legislation. More basically, the City Council was a serious constraint upon Mayor Sims because he was attempting to change extensively the urban situation, whereas Mayor McGrath only wanted minor modifications in the status quo. As Mayor Sims observed of the City Council: "I try to deal with problems as best as I can; yet to accomplish things it is necessary to back councillors to the wall so that they cannot squirm out. This is time-consuming and wasteful, and worthwhile projects are delayed".[30] This concern led Mayor Sims to include during his campaign for reelection an appeal for a "responsible City Council" that would permit him to enact numerous projects, such as a new high school and a water filtration plant.

A minimal level of political support was obviously a second important constraint upon both mayors. Despite a 1965 breakdown of registered voters of 18,627 Democrats, 9,399 Republicans, and 8,910 Independents, the Democrat McGrath worried about support maintenance and his subsequent loss to Mayor Sims in 1963 justified his concern. As a Mayor with deep historical roots in Brockton, he feared the "Do-Gooders" and the "Cliff-Hangers" (reformers out on "Cloud 9"). The large number of new residents who pressed for a wide variety of better municipal facilities was, according to Mayor McGrath, his biggest problem.[31] He also resisted any major increases in the city tax rate. As one of his departmental supervisors, who requested anonymity, noted: "We have had great difficulty putting our plans into effect because mayors like to keep the tax rate down".[32]

Mayor Sims, committed to extensive reforms, berated the inertia of an inherited administration which mired his pet projects in delay and resistance. Describing this constraint, he noted: "My biggest problem as Mayor is that, by virtue of the political situation, I am unable to appoint qualified people. This hampers me in solving problems".[33] Although he was concerned about assembling and maintaining support in a city dominated by the opposition party, his strategy was the opposite of that of Mayor McGrath. Sims sought, by extensive reforms and imaginative development programs, to capture most of the Independents and to make serious inroads in Democratic strongholds. His electoral sweep of one heavily Democratic ward, a section containing many new residents and an area where the candidate Sims campaigned vigorously for new schools and a better water supply, attests to the soundness of his tactics.

A final constraint which deserves mention lies in the limitations of the municipal budget. Only a small proportion—perhaps 10 per cent—of the budget can be subject to much manipulation. Most of the budget consists of

---

28. *Brockton Daily Enterprise*, April 18, 1963.
29. Personal communication from David Arey.
30. Personal interview, July 21, 1967.
31. Personal interview, July 21, 1967.
32. Personal interview, July 21, 1967.
33. Personal interview, July 21, 1967.

expenditures which are more or less fixed. Mayor Sims was able to penetrate much of this constraint by obtaining federal funds and by gaining approval for issuing municipal bonds, the device by which most large-scale capital improvements are obtained.

Decision Making

During his term in office, Mayor McGrath pursued a policy directed at attempts to enlarge the municipal water supply. With an updated report from Camp, Dresser, and McKee, he resubmitted a bill aimed at diverting surplus overflow waters from October to May. The proposed legislation guaranteed all recreational rights and uses of the ponds for flooding cranberry bogs and established minimum water units below which diversions could not take place.

Yet in guiding the bill through its legislative struggle, Mayor McGrath adopted an essentially apolitical strategy—a strategy which might be termed the "faith in science" approach. It rested upon the assumption that the merits of the case would determine the outcome of the legislative bid. In accordance with this strategy, Brockton leaders relied heavily upon expert testimony from the consulting engineers and representatives from government agencies.

City leaders did not attempt during the legislative effort to mobilize public opinion and participation in the Brockton Water District. Given the simultaneous effort of Mayor McGrath and Water Superintendent Kingman to reassure the local citizenry that the water situation was fully under control, it would have been difficult to break through apathy, disinterest, and lack of knowledge. The purposeful lulling of public concern over the water supply is clearly apparent in McGrath's candid public statement at a State legislative hearing: "We could scare our people by telling them the truth of our water problem, but we do not want hysteria." [34]

The reasons for such a conflicting and inconsistent managerial policy are twofold. First, city officials, in Mayor McGrath's term, despite long discussions with and detailed memoranda from consulting engineers and State water resource agencies, never really understood the scope or ramifications of the dwindling supply balance or the feasible alternatives for enlarging the supply to meet increases in consumption. Both the public statements of these officials on the supply problem and the Mayor's evaluation of plans from laymen and experts alike provide evidence for this interpretation. Second, the city mayor not only must deal with the various stresses in the managerial matrix, but he has political considerations as well.

In early 1963, Mayor McGrath announced that he would run for reelection. He needed, therefore, to convince voters that he was effectively handling the multitude of problems facing Brockton. This political need prompted one of the few managerial innovations, shown in the longitudinal profile of the city water system (Fig. 40.3), of his administration. Under fire from other candidates who charged that he had done nothing to solve the water supply problem, Mayor McGrath requested funds from the City Council to conduct a search for underground water in the Brockton area, despite the fact that Camp, Dresser, and McKee, the Massachusetts Water Resources Commission, and the United States Geological Survey all agreed that ground water in sufficient quantity did not exist.

Mayor McGrath's failure to solve the water supply problem undoubtedly contributed to his failure to be reelected. In fact, Mayor-elect Sims credited his upset victory to "public dissatisfaction with the lack of progress in building new schools and finding a solution to the city water problem." [35] Mayor Sims brought a very different conception of drought and political strategy to the city administration. Even before he took office, he met with the consulting engineers for briefing on the drought prospect and the status of the water supply. In any event, campaign promises committed him to an early solution of the problem.

An extreme personal antagonism between Silver Lake area residents and Mayor McGrath and his City Solicitor Pasquale J. Piscitelli presented a major obstacle to compromise in the dispute. There had been almost no direct communication between the Mayor and political leaders in the Silver Lake area. Capitalizing on the stalemate over the proposed legislation, Mayor Sims initiated quiet talks with Silver Lake area officials who were

34. *Silver Lake News*, January 31, 1963.

35. *Brockton Daily Enterprise*, November 6, 1963.

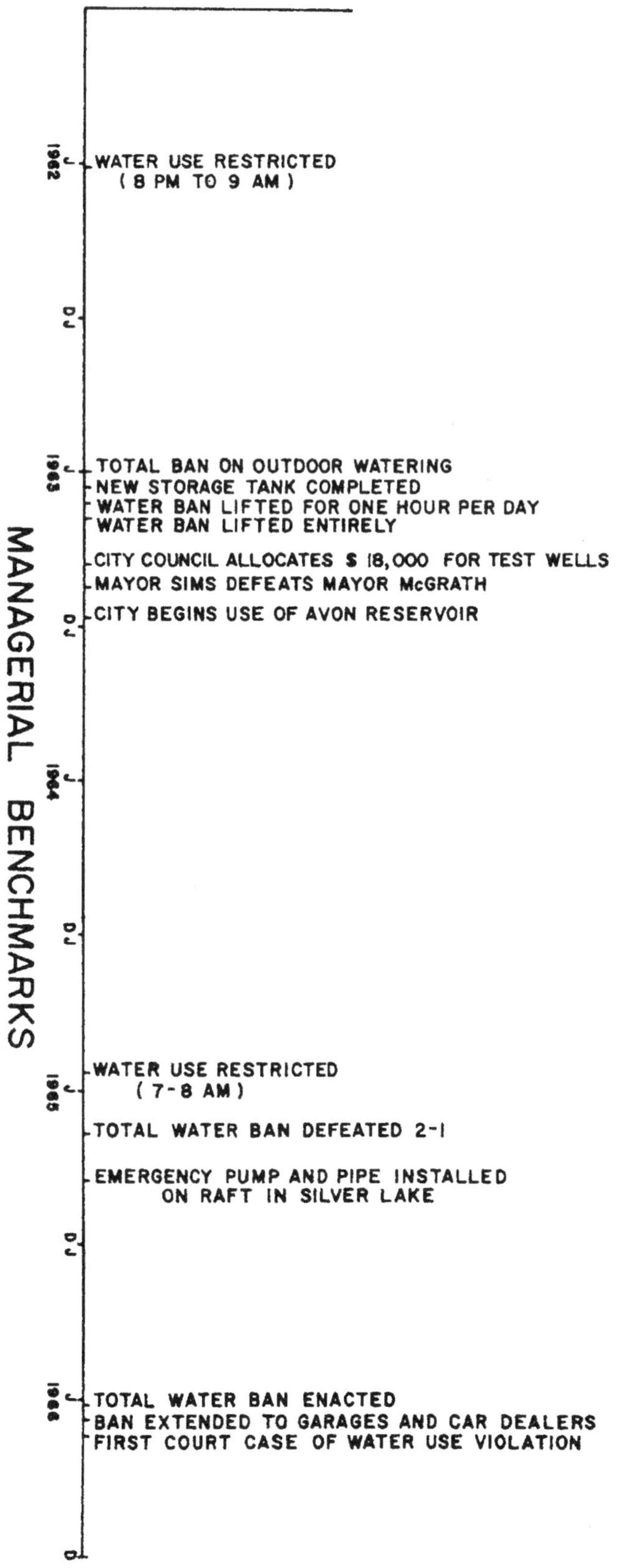

MANAGERIAL BENCHMARKS

1962
- WATER USE RESTRICTED (8 PM TO 9 AM)

1963
- TOTAL BAN ON OUTDOOR WATERING
- NEW STORAGE TANK COMPLETED
- WATER BAN LIFTED FOR ONE HOUR PER DAY
- WATER BAN LIFTED ENTIRELY
- CITY COUNCIL ALLOCATES $18,000 FOR TEST WELLS
- MAYOR SIMS DEFEATS MAYOR McGRATH
- CITY BEGINS USE OF AVON RESERVOIR

1964

1965
- WATER USE RESTRICTED (7-8 AM)
- TOTAL WATER BAN DEFEATED 2-1
- EMERGENCY PUMP AND PIPE INSTALLED ON RAFT IN SILVER LAKE

1966
- TOTAL WATER BAN ENACTED
- BAN EXTENDED TO GARAGES AND CAR DEALERS
- FIRST COURT CASE OF WATER USE VIOLATION

Fig. 40·3
Longitudinal Profile of the Brockton Water Supply System (1962–1966)

Fig. 40.3—continued

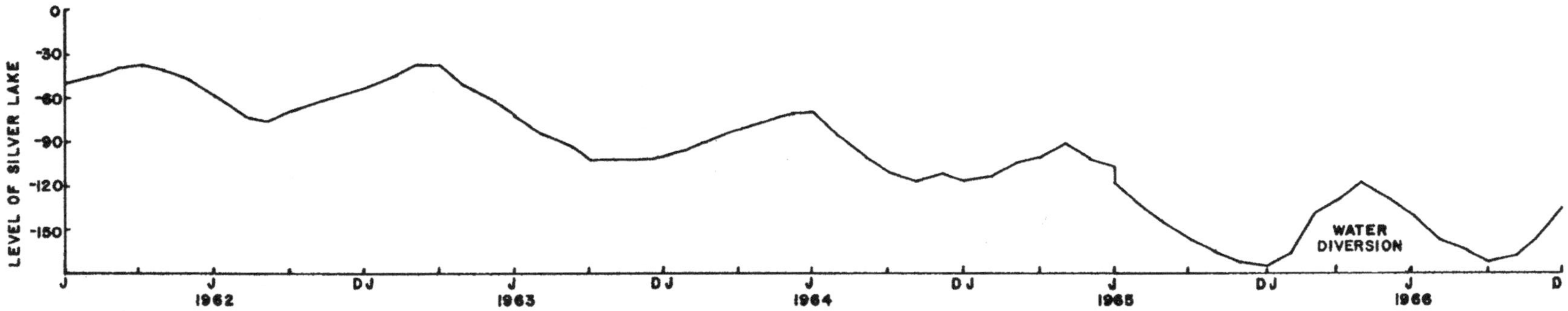

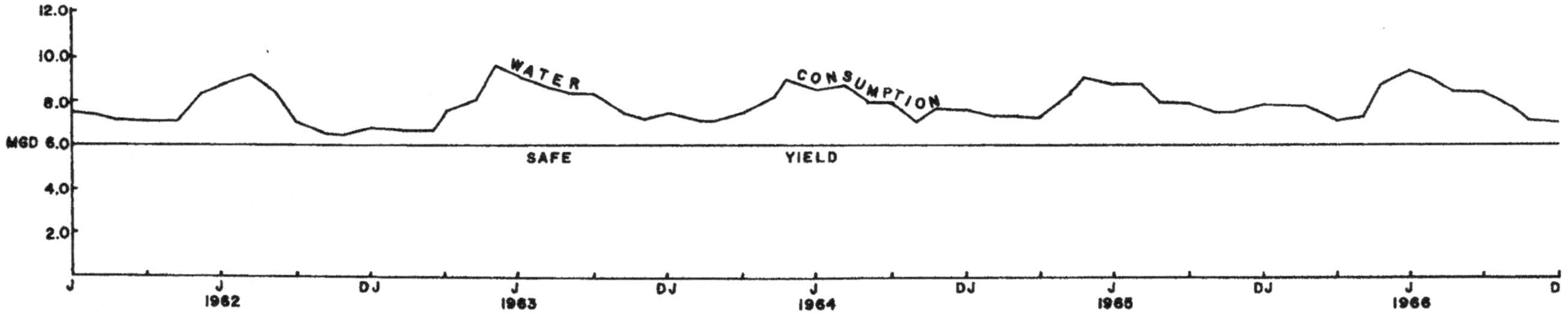

members of a State Study Commission on the problem. He worked hard on all members who were on the fence concerning the issue. In addition, drawing upon federal funds available 'for municipal water supply improvement, he was able "to keep the possibility of a filtration plant up my sleeve."[36] A filtration plant on Silver Lake would not only guarantee permanent recreation on the new supply sources but could also possibly open Silver Lake for recreation, a move which would provide dramatic recreational opportunities and benefit local businessmen and community tax rates. Playing this ace card, Mayor Sims converted the adverse 10-3 majority to a favorable 12-0 (with one abstention) vote in the Study Commission at the time of the report. The State Legislature, where three previous attempts had met ignoble deaths, still loomed as a formidable obstacle.

Unlike Mayor McGrath, Mayor Sims recognized the Legislature in Boston as a political arena, and tailored his strategy accordingly. He contacted representatives from throughout the state, assembling support both by virtue of the Brockton case and by political logrolling. At the Legislative hearings, in addition to utilizing the same experts for testimony, he convinced local groups to donate busses and filled them with "golden agers" who were happy to go anywhere. He also arranged to have these supporters arrive early to fill all the available seats, so that Silver Lake area opponents had to stand at the rear of the room. By the time the lengthy Brockton case finished at 4:30 in the afternoon, many disgruntled critics had already left and many others were impatient to go home. And so the State approved the Brockton bill.

The Board of Water Commissioners also proved to be a critical component in the municipal management of water supply. This group acted quite independently of the Mayor who had little control over its decisions, and illustrates vividly the problems and frustrations which can accompany the splintering of policy-making functions. The Mayor's opportunities for managerial innovation were confined to supply alternatives because the Board of Water Commissioners had complete authority over restrictions on water consumption. Moreover, group members had no special professional competence in water resource management and, as longtime Brockton businessmen, were very susceptible to public pressures. The sum effect of the Board's decisions on consumption restrictions was to contribute to the hazard presented by the drought and to reinforce the public confusion arising from the conflicting policy statements on water supply adequacy by Mayor McGrath and Water Superintendent Kingman.

A longitudinal analysis of policy on consumption restrictions during the drought will document the foregoing contention (Fig. 40.3) and illustrate maladaptive response to stress by a political system. In the summer of 1962, when the WU/SY ratio stood at 1.28 and Silver Lake was 62 inches below normal, Brockton—unlike four surrounding towns—did not enact a water ban. Instead, the Board restricted outdoor watering to between 8:00 p.m. to 9:00 a.m. As the stress mounted during 1963 and the need for a consistent water policy became more urgent, the conflicts and inconsistencies became more pronounced.

On June 1, 1963, the Board enacted a total ban on outdoor watering. By the end of the month, the Massachusetts Department of Public Health deemed the situation sufficiently grave to warrant the declaration of a state of emergency. Yet, when a heavy rain temporarily restored Avon Reservoir, the limited emergency supply, to its normal level, the Board lifted the ban on outdoor watering for one hour per day. Daily water consumption immediately jumped from 8 mg to 10.49 mg. On August 21, in the face of this heavy summer consumption, more rainfall, and the completion of a new storage tank, the Board lifted entirely the outdoor watering ban. A short 18 days later, Silver Lake reached its all time low of 81 inches below normal.

Water Superintendent Kingman stated in the fall that he had no plans to seek a ban, partial or complete, on the use of water for outside purposes. This attitude evidently arose from his expectation of winters rains and an anticipated drop in daily water consumption. He noted in the same interview that consumption had dropped by 600,000 in one day, and that "cooler weather which began today will help considerably for fewer gallons will be pumped from the water

---

36. Personal interview, July 21, 1967.

fractions. Nevertheless, the initial drop in use to 8.4 mgd returned to an average of 10.5 mgd within a few days. The Water Department responded angrily by threatening to shut off water to any violator, and the Board extended the ban for the first time to garages and car dealers (but not to car-wash establishments).

At this point, Mayor Sims intervened with a plea for more effective restrictions on water consumption. He called for a more comprehensive and rigidly enforced water ban and an increase in water rates. Despite his appeal, the City Council President could note that "people shrug their shoulders and do not face the fact that there is a serious problem."[37] The fact that the first court case on a violation of the ban did not occur until August 2, 1966, however, suggests that laxity in enforcement may have contributed to this public apathy. Finally, heavy rains during winter and spring of 1966-67 brought the drought to an end, and on April 25, 1967, under the recommendation of Camp, Dresser, and McKee, the Board reduced the ban to modest use restrictions.

The City Council was a final actor in the management of the water system. Its functions were largely restricted, however, to making policy recommendations to the executive branch. A good example of Council activity occurred at its special meeting on the water problem on December 8, 1965. At this session, councillors suggested such innovations as a public information campaign through the schools and press, the publication of a pamphlet to be entitled "The Ten Commandments for Water Conservation," and a possible quota on public car washes.[38] These recommendations led to no new changes. The City Council's other managerial contributions consisted of passing fund requests from Mayors McGrath and Sims and resolutions designed to influence the Board of Water Commission's policy on use restrictions.

Stress Resolution and Feedback

The success of Mayor Sims' administration in gaining State approval of the Brockton bill and thereby enlarging the municipal supply solved the city water problem for the short-run. This solution is only one of many innovations distributed through time in any municipal water system. The ephemeral nature of the enlargement of supply stems from the fact that the predictions upon which the plans rested were grossly faulty from the start. While the consulting engineers had predicted that the legislation would meet demand until the year 2000 (when they projected demand at a minimum of 7.3 mgd and a maximum of 11.2 mgd), in fact Brockton even with the new additions had an average annual 1966 demand of 8.16 mgd and a safe yield of 10.2 mgd, a WU/SY ratio of .80. In the near future, the city will undoubtedly have to find additional sources. In 1966, the engineers themselves predicted that the new supply would suffice only to 1980.[39]

Finally in the process of solving the water supply problem informational and political feedback was taking place. The major actors became more cognizant of the technical and political problems implicit in municipal water supply management, political leaders learned the efficacy of a change in political strategy, and Mayor Sims built a reservoir of "reserve support" in the political system which better enabled him to deal with other stresses or sustain short-term failures or defeats.

CONCLUSIONS

Innovations in the Brockton water system were the product of both myriad forces operating within the political system and the accumulating stress of the deteriorating municipal water supply. Growth and development in the water system depended heavily upon the complex of stresses acting upon the political system, and the managers' evaluations and searches for alternative solutions. The division of functions among a number of policy-making actors—especially the Mayor, Water Superintendent, and Board of Water Commissioners—raised obstacles to coordinated management schemes and a clear public understanding of the water supply problem. Yet, perhaps the most striking conclusions

---

37. *Brockton Daily Enterprise*, October 28, 1963.
38. *Brockton Daily Enterprise*, December 8, 1965.
39. See the report prepared by Camp, Dresser, and McKee for the city of Brockton entitled "Report on Improvements to the Water Distribution and Transmission Systems" (June 1966).

which arise from the study relate both to the properties of the municipal political system and to the behavioral characteristics of the actors. In regard to the former, it is clear that an understanding of policy decision necessitates a recognition of the sub-system status of the municipal water supply. Inaction or maladaption leading to an accumulation of stress on the political system may well alter the reservoirs of political support and even produce changes in managers. Crisis in itself does not necessarily appear to lead to hasty consideration of alternatives, maladaptive behavior, or inefficient choice, since all administrative departments are continually planning for projected future situations. Rather, crisis alters priorities in the managerial matrix, strengthens the ability of certain sub-systems in competing for scarce resources in the municipal political system, and may pave the way for consensus in the elite and general public.

In regard to the behavior of the managers several variables stand out. The goals, values and perceived role that each actor brought to office patterned substantially the decision process. The Brockton drought indicated the importance of referent sources and the sets of strategies and tactics developed through past experience in the mayors' evaluations of and adaptations to stresses. An understanding of the perceived managerial matrices of decision-makers will undoubtedly contribute much to analyzing the distribution of innovations through time within any municipal sub-system. Finally, the personality and political style of the actors also merit considerable attention for, in large part, the resolution of the Brockton water crisis was a tale of two mayors.

Annotated Bibliography

ABNEY, F. GLEN and LARRY B. HILL
"Natural Disasters as a Political Variable: The Effects of a Hurricane on an Urban Election," *American Political Science Review*, LX (December 1966), pp. 974-981.
    Based upon interview results immediately after the hurricane in "dry" and flooded precincts, the authors examine the political and material capability of the government to deal with a natural disaster. They argue that the electoral effect also depended upon the extent to which responsibility for dealing with the disaster was specific and understood, the citizens' perceptions of government, and the extent to which citizens considered the hurricane as a legitimate political variable.

BREWER, MICHAEL F.
"Local Government Assessment: Its Impact on Land and Water Use," *Land Economics*, XXXVII (August 1961), pp. 207-217.
    An examination of the public water district's use of assessment as an integral part of the pricing device by which water use is allocated. The author discusses the assessment components: assessment base, spatial extent of district, and rate of levy.

BROWN, HARRISON
The Challenge of Man's Future (N.Y.: Viking Press, 1954).
    Although somewhat dated, this remains one of the best general treatments of the world population–natural resource balance. Chapter 7, "Patterns of the Future" is especially useful because of its exploration of the study's implications for birth control and foreign policy.

COOLEY, RICHARD A.
Politics and Conservation: The Decline of the Alaska Salmon (N.Y.: Harper and Row, 1963).
    A controversial examination of federal policies designed to protect the Alaskan salmon. The author presents a critical account of political ineffectiveness and the often sordid role of private interests. Particularly useful for its illustration of the problems which functional allocation can pose to public policy.

DUBOS, RENE
Man Adapting, (New Haven: Yale University Press, 1965).
    A searching, comprehensive analysis of environmental influences and man's adaptation in the light of modern biological, medical, genetic, and psychological research. A must item for anyone interested in environmental research. An exhaustive bibliography is included.

EASTON, DAVID
"The Environment of a Political System," Chapter 5 in *A Framework for Political Analysis* (Englewood Cliffs: Prentice-Hall, 1965), pp. 59-75.
    Although difficult to appreciate fully except within the context of Easton's general theory, the chapter provides a useful treatment of the interaction between the total environment and the political system. The physical environment itself receives relatively little attention.

EWALD, WILLIAM R. Jr., ed.
Environment for Man: The Next Fifty Years (Bloomington, Indiana: The University of Indiana Press, 1967).
    The published papers of a conference dealing with the theme "Optimum Environment with Man as the Measure." Particular attention is given to the future urban environment, especially the physiological, psychological, and sociological impact of the physical environment.

FIELDING, GORDON J.
"The Los Angeles Milkshed: A Study of the Political Factor in Agriculture," *Geographical Review*, LIV (January 1964), pp. 1-12.

An analysis of the impact of state legislation controlling the production and pricing of milk and local land-zoning on dairying areas about Los Angeles. Political programs have outlined their original purposes and assured the preeminence of the southern producing area.

Foss, PHILLIP O.
Politics and Grass (Seattle: University of Washington Press, 1960).

After outlining the history of the public domain, the author examines the formation and administration of public policy for the control and regulation of the federal range under the Taylor Grazing Act. The study is particularly useful for its detailed discussion of policy-formulation and the conflicts between the public and private interests.

Fox, IRVING K.
"Policy Problems in the Field of Water Resources," in Allen V. Kneese and Stephen C. Smith, eds., *Water Research* (Baltimore: Resources for the Future, 1966), pp. 271-289.

A stimulating discussion of three major policy problems: (a) How to achieve a rational public understanding of water resource use problems and opportunities, (b) How to achieve a reasonable approximation of a social optimum through public decision-making process, and (c) How to change policy to accord with the changing environment within which water resources activities are undertaken.

GINSBURG, NORTON S.
"Natural Resources and Economic Development," *Annals* of the Association of American Geographers, XLVII, No. 3 (1957), pp. 197-212.

A discussion of the role of natural resources in economic development which deals with such problems as the measurement of development, comparing natural resource endowment with per-capita product, the relation of natural resources to other factors in economic development, and the distribution of underdevelopment. Brief case studies of Japan, Malaya, China and India are included. See a more recent discussion by Ginsburg in "On Geography and Economic Development," in Saul B. Cohen, ed., *Problems and Trends in American Geography* (New York: Basic Books, 1968).

HAAR, CHARLES M., ed.
Law and Land (Cambridge: Harvard University Press, 1964).

A collection of articles constituting a comparative study of the legal control of land use in England and the United States. Special attention is devoted to the evaluation of alternative approaches to land use and resource allocation planning. Major topics include land planning and ownership, developmental plans, the machinery of planning, and the regulation and taking of property under planning laws.

HAUSER, PHILIP M.
"Demographic Dimensions of World Politics," *Science*, CXXXI, No. 3414 (June 3, 1960), pp. 1641-1647.

A discussion of the ways in which findings in demography illuminate the world political scene. The relationships between population growth and "lebensraum," the distribution of energy sources, urbanization, and regions of political instability are explored. The author suggests alternatives to present trends. From the standpoint of the political geographer, the division of the globe into the "Communist Bloc" and the "Free World" is an unfortunate geographical framework.

HAUSER, PHILIP M.
Population and World Politics (Glencoe: Free Press, 1958).

Part III, "Population Policy and Politics," includes essays on population politics in the Communist and non-Communist world, the relation of population to political instability in underdeveloped areas, and population considerations in American foreign policy.

KASPERSON, ROGER E.
"Political Behavior and the Decision-Making Process in the Allocation of Water Resources Between Recreational and Municipal Use," *Natural Resources Journal*, VIII, No. 2 (April 1969).

Dealing with a regional conflict among local political communities, the author utilizes interviewing, content analysis, planning studies, newspaper accounts, and legislative actions to analyze problems of spatial and functional allocation of water resources. Particular attention is given to the emergence of conflicts, the conflict-resolution process, myths and misinformation, political participation, and conflicting community goals.

KATES, ROBERT W. and JOACHIM F. WOHLWILL, eds.
"Man's Response to the Physical Environment," *Journal of Social Issues*, XXII (October 1966).

A symposium of geographical and psychological contributions dealing with the impress of the environment upon man. The collection of articles illustrates the variety of topics and problem currently under research, and shows the possibilities of environmental research using empirical theory and data.

KONIGSBERG, CHARLES
"Climate and Society: A Review of the Literature," *Journal of Conflict Resolution*, IV, No. 1 (March 1960), pp. 67-82.

A detailed review of the voluminous literature on this subject. The author supports many of the arguments of Huntington, and presents research findings demonstrating the effects and manipulative possibilities of climates.

LARGE, DAVID C.
"Cotton in the San Joaquin Valley: A Study of Government in Agriculture, *Geographical Review*, XLVII (July 1957), pp. 365–380.

An illustration of the impact of government quotas on cotton farms and competition among alternative land uses in California. Effects upon yields, mechanization, and types of cotton are all explored.

LOGAN, W. A.
"The Changing Landscape Significance of the Victoria–South Australia Boundary," *Annals* of the Association of American Geographers, LVIII (March 1968), pp. 128–154.

A discussion of various historical stages in the political impact of a boundary upon the landscape. The author shows that in recent times the chief significance of the boundary has been in its division between differing administrative policies. A striking aerial photograph (Figure 15, p. 147) illustrates this last thesis.

LOWENTHAL, DAVID, ed.
Environmental Perception and Behavior, The University of Chicago, Department of Geography Research Paper No. 109 (Chicago: 1967).

A symposium of papers presented at the 1965 annual meetings of the Association of American Geographers. In toto, the collection provides an excellent introduction to concepts and approaches dealing with man's perception, experience, and interaction with the environment. Papers explore such topics as attitudes toward the environment, the theory of spatial meaning, environmental perception and adaptation level in the Arctic, perception of storm hazard, and images of the city.

LYDEN, FREMONT J. and GEORGE A. SHIPMAN
"Public Policy Issues Raised by Weather Modification: Possible Alternative Strategies for Government Action," in W. R. Derrick Sewell, ed., *Human Dimensions of Weather Modification*, The University of Chicago, Department of Geography Research Paper No. 105 (Chicago: 1966), pp. 289–303.

An analysis of the public policy issues in weather modification which gives particular attention to the forms of possible governmental actions. The forms distinguished are self-help, coercive-determinative and non-determinative, and non-coercive. The author then relates varying actions to different public policy settings.

MANN, DEAN E.
The Politics of Water in Arizona (Tucson: University of Arizona Press, 1963).

A critical examination of public policies and institutions for state water resource management. Particular attention is given to the conflict of interests in public policy and the use of public machinery in resource decision-making.

MCKINLEY, CHARLES
Uncle Sam in the Pacific Northwest (Berkeley: University of California Press, 1952).

A thorough study of the pattern of federal administrative structure and activity involved in resource management in the Columbia Valley. Particularly useful for its critical analysis of interagency competition, overlap, and conflict. The author examines alternative organizational arrangements to those existing in the present situation.

NELSON, HOWARD J.
"The Vernon Area, California—A study of the Political Factor in Urban Geography," *Annals* of the Association of American Geographers, XLII (June 1952), pp. 177–191.

A striking study of the spatial differentiation in an urban landscape produced by political factors. The author shows how a previously homogeneous area becomes an anomaly within the region. The series of accompanying maps are particularly interesting.

PATTISON, WILLIAM D.
The Beginnings of the American Rectangular Land Survey System, 1784–1800, The University of Chicago, Department of Geography Research Paper No. 50 (Chicago: 1957).

An excellent example of political impress upon land and settlement patterns. The study is divided into three parts—the original plan for national rectangular surveying, an analysis of public land surveying under the ordinance, and an account of continued rectangular surveying through the Land Act of 1796 and the early years of federal surveying.

QUINN, FRANK
"Water Transfers: Must the American West Be Won Again?," *Geographical Review*, LVIII (January 1968), pp. 108–132.

Problems in the spatial and functional allocation of water resources are related to the development of the West. The author identifies three stages in the evolution of competitive demands for water rights and discusses various plans for regional and interregional transfers. The political partitioning of space creates serious problems in efficient water allocation. Finally, the author concludes that the concern for protecting the individual against change expressed in state water codes constitutes the greatest obstacle to legislative reform.

RUSSETT, BRUCE M.
"Inequality and Instability: The Relation of Land Tenure to Politics," *World Politics*, XVI (April 1964), pp. 442–454.

A very useful study both because of its findings concerning structural allocation and the indices used to measure land inequality and political instability. Use of Lorenz curves of land distribution and correlation analysis leads the author to conclude that while land tenure considerations alone cannot explain variance in political instability, it is nevertheless probably safe to say that no state can long maintain a democratic form of government if the major sources of economic gain are divided very unequally among its citizens.

SEWELL, W. R. DERRICK

"The Columbia River Treaty: Some Lessons and Implications," *Canadian Geographer*, X (1966), pp. 145–156.

An analysis of the problems of federal-provincial relations in the development of international rivers and the difficulties of implementing comprehensive planning concepts. The treaty emphasizes two serious shortcomings: (1) the emphasis on inventory and the neglect of economic and social aspects, and (2) the need to weigh the value of one water use against others.

SEWELL, W. R. DERRICK, ROBERT W. KATES and LEE E. PHILLIPS

"Human Response to Weather and Climate: Geography Contributions," *Geographical Review*, LVIII (April 1968), pp. 262–280.

After noting the geographer's decline of interest in the study of environmentalism (see especially the diagram on published articles), the authors illustrate the need for such knowledge in future attempts at weather modification. In the light of current evidence, they examine what is known about the effects of weather and climate on agriculture, transportation, industry, tertiary activities, and decision-making processes. The article is also especially valuable for its extensive bibliographical coverage.

SMITH, C. G.

"The Disputed Waters of the Jordan," *Institute of British Geographers, Transactions*, XL (December 1966), pp. 111–128.

An examination of the problems involved in the diversion of waters from the Jordan River for irrigation. Reviews the major developmental schemes and concludes that the principal problem is political not technical. The author suggests that limited diversions may lead to a *de facto* sharing of water.

SPROUT, HAROLD, and MARGARET SPROUT

"Environmental Factors in the Study of International Politics," *Journal of Conflict Resolution*, I, No. 4 (1957), pp. 309–328.

A detailed examination of how environmental factors relate to political phenomena and what forms of speech are most fruitful in expressing these relationships. The authors classify relationships into environmental determinism, free-will environmentalism, possibilism, cognitive behavioralism, and environmental probabilism, and carefully analyze the meaning and implication of each term. A useful starting point for the study of environmental impress upon politics. See also a more thorough discussion of these issues in Harold and Margaret Sprout, *The Ecological Perspective on Human Affairs* (Princeton: Princeton University Press, 1965).

WAGNER, PHILIP, *The Human Use of the Earth* (Glencoe: Free Press, 1960).

A thoughtful general treatment which is both geographical and ecological. The author analyzes how different human cultures and social arrangements express themselves in artificial features of landscape, and how these man-made installations affect the life conditions of human individuals and the natural features of the earth.

WENGERT, NORMAN

Natural Resources and the Political Struggle (Garden City, N.Y.: Doubleday & Co., 1955).

An excellent overview of the interaction between natural resources and the political processes. Especially useful are the chapters on resource policy, intergovernmental relations, and the public interest.

WENGERT, NORMAN

"Resource Development and the Public Interest: A Challenge for Research," *Natural Resources Journal*, I (November 1961), pp. 207–223.

Pointing out that the notion of the "public interest" is often uncritical or a rationalization for particular policies, the author reviews criteria which can be used in evaluation. Suggestions are made for an operational definition and methodology in determinations of the public interest.

Appendix

Aids to Research in Political Geography

JEANNE X. KASPERSON

If the present volume is indeed the stuff of political geography, then clearly an interdisciplinary wind is blowing. Political geographers find it increasingly necessary to draw upon research findings in other disciplines. Non-geographers—economists, anthropologists, sociologists, political scientists, psychologists, and other social scientists—are writing political geography or something closely akin to political geography. Hence the serious political geographer, in order to keep abreast of pertinent research in related fields, requires a working knowledge of reference tools in the social sciences. Given the current information explosion, this is no easy task.

Let it be clear at the outset, then, that the present appendix is by no means an exhaustive bibliographic discourse, an undertaking which could easily bulge a fat volume. The aim is rather to suggest some of the more useful—and those less likely to be familiar to the student of political geography—sources of information. The discussion is for the most part descriptive rather than critical. English-language titles predominate, partly because of a realistic awareness that few readers of the present volume would scurry to foreign-language sources. Should there appear to be a U.S. bias—and this is particularly likely in the discussion of statistical sources and data archives—it is for the same types of reasons. In deference to the Now Generation, there is perhaps a perceptible leaning toward current rather than retrospective bibliography. Dozens of useful titles make no appearance in the succeeding paragraphs. Hopefully, however, the sources—guides, encyclopedias, bibliographies, indexes, abstracting services, and statistical and data archives—cited therein will prove relevant to research in political geography.

There is no comprehensive up-to-date guide to geographical literature. *Aids to Geographical Research* by John K. Wright and Elizabeth T. Platt[1] is now more than twenty years old, but this is not to deny its usefulness as far as it goes. This annotated listing of 1174 reference materials in various languages falls into three categories: (*a*) General aids (*b*) Topical aids (*c*) Regional aids and general geographical periodicals. Author, subject, and title indexes direct the user to the annotations, for the most part descriptive, of specific items. Although international in scope, *Aids* . . . does betray an American-British bias. Consequently, Elia Migliorini's *Guida bibliografica allo studio della geografia*,[2] which contains 938 selected titles on the countries of Europe,

---

1. John K. Wright and Elizabeth J. Platt, *Aids to Geographical Research* (2d. ed.; New York: Published for the American Geographical Society by Columbia University Press, 1947).
2. Elia Migliorini; *Guida bibliografica allo studio della geografia* (Naples: Pironti, 1949).

serves as something of a supplement to Wright and Platt.

A more legitimate supplement, and one which merits wider distribution than its mimeographed format encourages, is Chauncy Harris's *Bibliographies and References for Research in Geography*.[3] Designed for a beginning graduate course at The University of Chicago, the bibliography falls into two sections: General Guides and Reference Works of Value in Geographic Research (328 entries) and Geographic Bibliographies and Reference Works (291 entries). Annotations where they occur are brief, no doubt because class discussions and trips to the library are part of the course. Yet all major reference tools, both general and geographical, appear in the bibliography. Taken with Wright and Platt, Harris is a bibliographic treasure map. A fully annotated version, one which would pinpoint the specific research value of each title, would seem a worthwhile publication venture for the Association of American Geographers. Such a compilation could well reduce much of the present discussion to a footnote.

A new tool has appeared, but since *Geography: A Reference Handbook*[4] was unavailable for firsthand scrutiny, the following comments are dependent on impressions garnered from a few sample pages. International in scope but with an avowed British bias, the alphabetical listing of 467 entries and cross-references describes significant works and outstanding scholars in geography. The biographical entries, which exclude living geographers, stress academic achievement and scholarly publications rather than personal details. Entries for prominent organizations include brief histories and lists of publications. The compiler has plans for a future publication which will maintain a balanced coverage both regionally and thematically.

Obviously, geographers can tap the bibliographic guides of other social science disciplines. From political science comes a recent source which gives to geography—indeed, to political geography—its due as an "auxiliary area" of political science. Indeed, geography holds its own in L. R. Wynar's *Guide to Reference Materials in Political Science: A Selective Bibliography*.[5] The first volume stresses the interdisciplinary nature of political science and includes brief, descriptive entries for important reference sources in social sciences in general and in each of the fields of history, anthopology, economics, psychology, *geography*, education, law, and sociology—and, of course, political science itself. Volume 2 contains separate chapters on specific topics, some of which—political behavior, for instance—would surely interest a political geographer.

For some reason geography does not always occupy so respectable a niche. *Sources of Information in the Social Sciences*[6] makes only passing references to geography and citations to geographical sources appear, almost as afterthoughts, in the history section. The book, incidentally, is still useful for the political geographer in that it contains a wealth of information on the literature of the other social sciences, each of which boasts a separate chapter.

Part IV (Behavior) of the present volume notwithstanding, political geography does not always seem to qualify as a full-fledged behavioral science. *A Current Appraisal of the Behavioral Sciences*[7] overlooks geography, but the book is still valuable to geographers of the behavioral persuasion who are seeking information and pertinent bibliography on related fields.

An excellent starting-place for the uninitiated is *A Reader's Guide to the Social Sciences*,[8] a collection of bibliographic essays on the fields of anthropology, economics, history, political science, psychology, sociology, and—lo and behold, geography. Each essay is the contribution of an expert in the field. Norton Ginsburg has written the section on geography.[9] The Hoselitz volume also boasts a superb introductory essay on the social sciences as a whole.

---

3. Chauncy Harris, *Bibliographies and References for Research in Geography* (rev. ed.; Chicago: Department of Geography, The University of Chicago, 1967).

4. C. B. Muriel Lock, *Geography: A Reference Handbook* (Hamden, Connecticut: Archon Books and Clive Bingley, 1968).

5. Lubomyr R. Wynar, *Guide to Reference Materials in Political Science: A Selective Bibliography*, Vols. 1–2 (Denver: Colorado Bibliographic Institute, 1966–1968).

6. Carl M. White, *Sources of Information in the Social Sciences* (Totowa, New Jersey: Bedminster Press, 1964).

7. Rollo Handy and Paul Kurtz, *A Current Appraisal of the Behavioral Sciences* (Great Barrington, Mass.: Behavioral Sciences Research Council, 1964).

8. Bert F. Hoselitz ed., *A Reader's Guide to the Social Sciences* (Glencoe, Illinois: Free Press, 1959).

9. *Ibid.*, pp. 70–88.

For additional background material on any of the social sciences, the encyclopedia is a respectable source. The scholarly *International Encyclopedia of the Social Sciences*[10] includes a separate article on political geography, complete with a bibliography (not annotated) of some 90 selected items, by Harold Sprout. The same article directs the reader to related headings: Ecology, International Politics, Enclaves and Exclaves, and International Relations. In the index volume, Boundaries, Territoriality, Natural resources (political and social aspects), and Political behavior (with a mass of sub-classifications) are only a few topics of interest to the student of political geography. Biographical articles on prominent geographers also appear in the encyclopedia, which contains for example an article on Friedrich Ratzel by Marvin Mikesell. Signed scholarly articles on all aspects of the social sciences and an outstanding index with numerous cross-references demonstrate the interrelationships among the various social sciences.

Another encyclopedia provides condensed, factual data on each country of the world. *The Worldmark Encyclopedia of Nations*[11]—"a practical guide to the geographic, historical, political, social, and economic status of all nations, and the United Nations system"—includes bibliographies following the data on each country.

For a fuller treatment of a particular area, it is well to check the titles in Van Nostrand's Searchlight series, edited by G. Etzel Pearcy and George Hoffman. Written by geographers and area specialists, these regional monographs are rich in information and in the application of concepts in political geography. Some titles—e.g., *The Russo-Chinese Borderlands: Zone of Peaceful Contact or Potential Conflict*[12] and *Transportation and Politics*[13]—focus on special topics in political geography.

Also deserving of special mention are the *International Boundary Studies*[14] issued by the Office of the Geographer, U.S. Dept. of State. Each study generally includes the boundary brief, geographical background (including landscape, climate, political geography, and ethnography), an analysis of boundary alignment, an account of treaties, and an overall summary of a specific boundary issue. The series is particularly useful for those students concerned with the boundary subsection in Part II (Structure) of the present volume.

It is impossible to mention here the hundreds of other encyclopedias, handbooks, regional studies, etc. which can aid the political geographer. Moreover, such sources simply cannot supply all of the bibliographic information sought by most researchers. Bibliographies, indexes, and abstracts better serve that function.

The social sciences abound with bibliographic sources, many of which have particular relevance for the student of political geography. A fifteen-volume photoreproduction of the research catalog of the American Geographical Society[15] lists, both systematically and regionally, the books, pamphlets, periodical articles, and government documents in the Society's collection. The Society also issues *Current Geographical Publications*,[16] a monthly list of additions to the research catalog. Each issue of *Current Geographical Publications* lists approximately 600 titles arranged by general subject and regions. Annual author, subject, and regional indexes enhance its usefulness. Unfortunately, however, bibliographical annotations are brief and entirely descriptive.

Longer and sometimes critical annotations accompany most of the entries in the selective *Bibliographie géographique internationale*.[17] An annual compilation by area and topic, the bibliography covers all aspects of geography. Political geography (*géographie politique*) is a regular if not always lengthy subsection in the *Géographie humaine* section. An added feature is specific reference to reviews of books cited in the bibliography.

10. *International Encyclopedia of the Social Sciences*, ed. by David L. Sills (New York: Macmillan and Free Press, 1968), seventeen volumes.
11. *Worldmark Encyclopedia of the Nations* (New York: World Press, Harper, 1963), five volumes.
12. W. A. Douglas Jackson, *Russo-Chinese Borderlands—Zone of Peaceful Contact or Potential Conflict?* (Princeton, New Jersey: Van Nostrand, 1962).
13. Roy I. Wolfe, *Transportation and Politics* (Princeton, New Jersey: Van Nostrand, 1963).
14. U.S. State Department. Office of the Geographer, *International Boundary Study*, No. 1—, 1961—.

15. American Geographical Society. Library, *Research Catalogue* (Boston: G. K. Hall, 1962), fifteen vols. and map supplement.
16. American Geographical Society of New York, *Current Geographical Publications* (New York: The Society, 1938—). Monthly, except July and August.
17. *Bibliographie géographique internationale* (Paris: Colin, 1894—). Annual. Title varies: vols. 1–24 appeared with *Annales de géographie*.

Unfortunately, the German *Geographischer Jahrbuch*,[18] an outstanding source for critical overviews of specific geographic fields (e.g. political geography) has not appeared since 1956. Some of the back volumes are nevertheless valuable for the political geographer who reads German.

Students of political geography might want to seek out the pertinent literature of other social sciences. Articles in the *International Encyclopedia of the Social Sciences* and the Handy and Hoselitz volumes (all three cited above)[19] are only a few representative sources of summaries which include significant bibliographic references. Dozens of publications exist for specific fields. Certain issues of the *Biennial Review of Anthropology* contain special bibliographic essays on political anthropology.[20] UNESCO's *Current Sociology*[21] keeps abreast of trends in special aspects of sociology, e.g. political sociology.

Another UNESCO venture, the "International Bibliography of the Social Sciences" series, published annually in four parts (Sociology, Political Science, Economics, and Social and Cultural Anthropology)[22] is in its aim to include all publications of "scientific value" perhaps the most comprehensive. The extensive bibliographies, which list books, pamphlets, articles, and government publications from all over the world, contain subject and author indexes in both French and English. The Political Science section alone boasts some 4–5,000 entries annually. It is significant to note that beginning in 1955 the *International Bibliography of Political Science* cites abstract numbers for those titles analyzed in a sister publication, *International Political Science Abstracts* (discussed below). Both publications are likely to contain in their subject indexes a reasonable number of references under political geography, electoral behavior, boundaries, etc. The anthropology, economics, and political science volumes should yield additional related titles.

Obviously, these mammoth bibliographies are a boon to researchers, an encouragement to prospective thesis writers. Perhaps less so, and yet worth mentioning here as a logical starting-place, is a more general reference tool, *The Bibliographic Index*.[23] This cumulative index lists alphabetically by subject bibliographies published separately or included in books, chapters of books, or periodical articles. The thesis writer can save valuable steps by employing this index; there is simply no point in starting from scratch, so to speak, if someone has already compiled a respectable bibliography, say, on political integration. Another similar tool[24] has the advantage of a comprehensive cumulation but lists only separately published bibliographies. In any case, however, one cannot overemphasize the economy of beginning a research project or a term paper on a particular topic by ascertaining first what bibliographies already exist.

Many other indexes can serve the student of political geography. The *Social Sciences and Humanities Index*[25] indexes approximately 180 British and American periodicals, including the major geographical journals. Public Affairs Information Service issues a bulletin, known as *P.A.I.S.*,[26] a subject index to current English-language literature in the broad field of public affairs—including political science, government, legislation, economics, and sociology. *P.A.I.S.* is particularly useful in locating elusive pamphlets, reports of various public and private agencies, and government publications, and, in many cases indicates sources for obtaining such materials, gratis or otherwise. Of course, for publications of the United States Government, the Government Printing Office issues a monthly catalog.[27] Political geographers ought to make more use

18. *Geographisches Jahrbuch* (Gotha: Perthes, 1866—).
19. *Supra*, Notes 10, 7, and 8, respectively.
20. E.g. David Easton, "Political Anthropology," in B. J. Siegel, ed., *Biennial Review of Anthropology* (Stanford, California: Stanford University Press, 1959).
21. *Current Sociology* (Paris: UNESCO, 1952–1957; London: Blackwell, 1958—). Quarterly.
22. *International Bibliography of Sociology*. 1951— (Chicago: Aldine, 1952—); *International Bibliography of Political Science*. 1953— (Chicago: Aldine, 1952—); *International Bibliography of Economics*. 1952—(Chicago: Aldine, 1955—); and *International Bibliography of Social and Cultural Anthropology*. 1958—(Chicago: Aldine, 1958—). All four are annual publications. Publisher varies.

23. *Bibliographic Index*, 1937— (New York: Wilson, 1938—).
24. Theodore Besterman, *A World Bibliography of Bibliographies* (4th ed. rev. and enl.; Geneva: Societas Bibliografica, 1965–1966), five volumes. Geography Vol. II, 2436–2457.
25. *Social Sciences and Humanities Index:* Formerly *International Index* (New York: Wilson, 1916—).
26. Public Affairs Information Service. *Bulletin.* (New York: Author, 1915—).
27. U.S. Superintendent of Documents. *United States Government Publications: Monthly Catalog* (Washington: Government Printing Office, 1895—).

of the *Monthly Catalog*, e.g., its listing of bills and committee hearings on natural resource projects such as the national seashores or the proposed redwoods park in California. The index provides invaluable firsthand data on issues and conflicts.

Nearly every country in the world has its counterparts to one or more of these indexes, but it is impossible to indulge in full bibliographic citations here. In view of the current information crisis in the social sciences, however, it seems reasonable to assume the superior utility of abstracting, as opposed to indexing, media. Surely abstracts reveal more in the way of content and methodology than do brief, unannotated entries in index bibliographies. How often has a harried researcher pursued a promising title only to confront a red herring!

Geographical Abstracts appears six times per year in four parts[28] and contains brief signed abstracts on a host of geographical topics. Most useful for the political geographer is Part D (Social Geography) which includes in its classified arrangement a separate subsection, often rather sparse, on political geography.

Fortunately, the political geographer, "wayward" as he is, can employ abstracting services of other disciplines. *International Political Science Abstracts*[29] contains annually some 1400–1500 abstracts (in English or French) of books and articles from a wide range of periodicals, including some geography journals. *Sociological Abstracts*[30] analyzes a considerable number of articles from the major sociological journals of twelve countries. Given a current concern with perception and behavioralism, *Psychological Abstracts*[31] (9–12,000 abstracts annually) is worth consulting. For those inspired by Part IV (Behavior) of the present volume, the *ABS Guide to Recent Publications of the Behavioral Sciences*[32] is particularly useful. The "New Studies" (also published separately) section of *The American Behavioral Scientist* updates the guide. Brief abstracts pinpoint the significant behavioral literature emanating from a number of social sciences.

One of the most ambitious bibliographical ventures of the sixties is the interdisciplinary *Universal Reference System (U.R.S.)*.[33] Designed "for political and behavioral scientists," this conglomerate index-bibliography-abstracting service aims "to provide subject awareness at all times and also to furnish a working tool for research." The Political Science, Government, and Public Policy Series, first step in a projected plan to cover all of the social sciences, now covers ten fields of political science, ranging from International Affairs to Legislative Process, Representation and Decision-Making to Comparative Government and Cultures. Concise abstracts are "retrievable" in some cases from as many as *eighteen* places in the detailed index. For each field, a biennial Codex will update selectively the annual sub-codex and the quarterly tabloids. Each Codex comprises a catalogue of annotated titles and an extensive "in-depth" index, arranged according to subject, concept, or methodology references—all of which correspond to a specially developed classification scheme, à la Alfred de Grazia. Each Codex, as plans now stand, will contain a maximum of 5000 items. Although Codex volumes are in fact easy to use, it is advisable to read the prefatory material very carefully.

Thanks to the computer, *U.R.S.* is beginning to provide for the social sciences the kind of so-called "awareness insurance" characterizing retrieval systems in the physical sciences. Some articles appear in *U.R.S.* as soon as a week after their original publication. It is becoming possible for a student to keep abreast of interdisciplinary aspects of a current subject.

By 1969, the Institute of Scientific Information will have issued *Current Contents: Behavioral, Social, and Management Sciences*. The weekly publication will contain the contents pages of a selected number of journals, an author index, and even an address directory. A tear-sheet service will entitle subscribers to purchase original pages of articles they wish to obtain. Of course, the more enterprising student will use the address directory to

---

28. *Geographical Abstracts* (London: London School of Economics, 1966—). Four series, each issued six times annually: A. Geomorphology; B. Biogeography, Climatology, and Cartography; C. Economic Geography; D. Social Geography.

29. *International Political Science Abstracts, 1951*—(London: Blackwell, 1952—). Quarterly. Publisher varies.

30. *Sociological Abstracts* (New York: Title, 1952—), nine times annually.

31. *Psychological Abstracts*, 1927—(Lancaster, Pennsylvania: American Psychological Association, 1927—).

32. The American Behavioral Scientist, *The ABS Guide to Recent Publications in the Social and Behavioral Sciences* (New York: Author, 1965; Supplements, 1966 and 1967).

33. *Universal Reference System* (Princeton, New Jersey: Metron, Inc., 1966—).

locate the author and request a free copy.

Theoretically at least, a Ph.D. dissertation requires original research on a new subject or an unexplored aspect of an old subject. The graduate student ought to be aware of *Dissertation Abstracts*,[34] the closest the United States comes to a national bibliography of dissertations. *Dissertation Abstracts* is a compilation of abstracts of doctoral dissertations submitted to University Microfilms by some 140 cooperating institutions.[35] The service is extremely valuable, not only in helping to prevent needless duplication, but in making available (in microfilm or xerox form) unpublished research.

Most countries maintain their own versions, in some instances more exhaustive ones, of *Dissertation Abstracts*. Also, many universities, both in the United States and abroad, publish their own lists or abstracts of dissertations completed and/or in progress. Some professional journals perform this function on a continuing basis. The *Professional Geographer*, for example, publishes each November a list of "Recent Geography Theses Completed and in Preparation".[36] "Doctoral Dissertations in Political Science in American Universities" was, until recently, a regular two-part (dissertations in progress and dissertations completed) feature of the *American Political Science Review*.[37] The July issue of the *American Journal of Sociology* does the same for that field. Obviously, these listings are only representative of a kind of valuable information too often overlooked or forgotten by readers of scholarly journals.

The serious student cannot afford to forego a regular scanning of professional journals. Presumably, present readers are familiar with the *Annals* of the Association of American Geographers, *The Geographical Review*, *The Professional Geographer*, *The Canadian Geographer*, *Geography*, *The Journal of Geography*, *Regional Science*, and the new *Geographical Analysis*. With the exception of the *Annals*, all these journals contain book reviews, though some of the reviews lag far behind the original publication date.

Geographers, especially political geographers, need also to cultivate an inter-disciplinary awareness of the pertinent literature of other professions. Even occasional scanning of articles and book reviews in such journals as the *American Political Science Review*, *American Anthropologist*, *American Behavioral Scientist* (*A.B.S.*), *American Sociological Review*, *The Journal of Conflict Resolution*, *The Journal of Politics*, *The Natural Resources Journal*, *Public Opinion Quarterly*, *World Politics*, and the *Annals* of the American Academy of Political and Social Science will bring home the close relationships among various social science fields. There are numerous sources offering capsule descriptions of periodicals, but nothing is more instructive than a firsthand look at the journals themselves.

The *Annals* of The American Academy of Political and Social Science deserve special consideration. An extensive Book Department contains signed critical reviews of important new publications. More important, each issue (bi-monthly) is a symposium on a selected topic, often one particularly relevant to political geography.[38] Generally, established scholars from various branches of the social sciences treat different aspects of the subject in question. An author and subject index accompanies each symposium issue.

Such symposia can eliminate hours of research, for each article—in addition to its own informational value—usually contains bibliographical references helpful for anyone wishing to delve more deeply into a particular subject. Students would do well to investigate the possibility of a symposium or a "special issue"—usually indexed in one or more of the media—devoted to a particular subject. To cite a single example, a special issue of *Social Research* (Volume XXV, Spring 1968) entitled "Focus—Trends and Issues in American Political Science" is worth seeking out, especially for those concerned with Part IV (Behavior) of the present volume.

In this heyday of the quantifiers, it is

---

34. *Dissertation Abstracts* (Ann Arbor, Michigan: University Microfilms, Vol. 12—, 1952—). Continues *Microfilm Abstracts*, Vols. 1–11, 1935–1951.

35. It is worth noting that some universities, notably e.g., The University of Chicago and Harvard (both of which maintain their own services) do not participate.

36. For specific references to published lists of dissertations in geography, see Table II in Chancy Harris, *op. cit.*, Appendix 4, p. 3. Note, too, that lists in *The Professional Geographer*, subject to the sometimes lapses of departmental chairmen, are not always complete.

37. As of 1960, the list includes dissertations from Canadian universities. Note that beginning in 1968 the list appears in the summer issue of *P.S.*, the newsletter of the American Political Science Association.

38. See, e.g. March, 1967: "National Character in the Perspective of the Social Sciences."

mandatory that a researcher have some cognizance of the statistical sources and data archives at his disposal. There is little virtue in collecting firsthand that data already available from reliable sources. Moreover, there is a distinct advantage—and one which political geographers have been particularly slow in seizing—to making judicious use of existing data. The introduction to the present volume indicates a growing concern with empirical testing of hypotheses and with comparative analysis. Given such aspirations, it would seem advisable to know what types of data are available from various national, international, and educational agencies.

The political geographer for one can ill afford to ignore data which are revealing man's political environment and behavior. Much information is obtainable from such reputable sources as the U.S. Bureau of the Census and the United Nations, UNESCO, and a number of affiliated agencies.

The U.S. Bureau of the Census is a valuable source of aggregate data, much of which bears upon political geography research. *The Statistical Abstract of the United States*[39] is an annual compilation of social, political and economic data, chiefly on a national scale. Two supplements—*County and City Data Book*[40] and *Congressional Districts Data Book*[41]—contain detailed information for smaller areas. Then, too, *Historical Statistics of the United States*[42] offers comparative statistics, for the most part on an annual basis, for the period 1610–1957. All these sources have obvious utility for the student attempting to discern patterns of political regionalism, electoral geography, reapportionment, gerrymandering, or changes in the political hierarchy.

Those political geographers concerned with electoral geography *à la française* or in the manner of J. R. V. Prescott or Peirce Lewis (both represented in this volume) may need recourse to official voting statistics. *America Votes*[43] is a biennial compilation, ordered alphabetically by state, of the voting results from the presidential, gubernatorial, senatorial, and congressional elections beginning with 1956.[44] The handbook contains also: the voting statistics by county and ward for the most recent presidential, gubernatorial, and senatorial elections; electoral maps of each state, some large cities, congressional districts, etc.

Again, most countries of the world issue comparable publications, but it is impossible to cite them all here. UNESCO has undertaken to produce an *International Guide to Electoral Statistics*[45] as part of a projected series (International Guides to Data for Comparative Research) which will attempt to coordinate data of various countries in order to facilitate cross-national research. UNESCO and other U.N. subsidiaries issue a staggering array of reliable statistical compendia, many of which are useful to the political geographer. *The Statistical Yearbook of the United Nations*,[46] which provides numerous tables (usually covering a twenty-year span) covering a variety of social, demographic, and economic statistics, is only one example of a tool valuable for comparative research.

The editors of the present collection note several times that progress in political geography will depend to some degree on an increased use of comparative analysis. This should come as a matter of course to anyone passing as a geographer. Comparative research in the social sciences has elicited a number of landmark studies which deserve to enjoy more attention from political geographers.

---

39. U.S. Bureau of the Census, *Statistical Abstract of the United States*, V. 1—, 1878—(Washington: Government Printing Office, 1879—)

40. U.S. Bureau of the Census, *County and City Data Book 1956*—(Washington: Government Printing Office 1957—). Irregular.

41. U.S. Bureau of the Census, *Congressional Districts Data Book* (Washington: Government Printing Office, 1961).

42. U.S. Bureau of the Census, *Historical Statistics of the United States, Colonial Times to 1957* (Washington: Government Printing Office, 1960).

43. *America Votes*. V. 1.—,1956—(New York: Published for Governmental Affairs Institute by Macmillan, 1956—).

44. For earlier years, see Edgar E. Robinson, *The Presidential Vote, 1896-1932* (Stanford, California: Stanford University Press, 1947) and *They Voted for Roosevelt; The Presidential Vote, 1932-1944* (Stanford, California: Stanford University Press, 1947); W. Dean Burnham, *Presidential Ballots, 1836-1892* (Baltimore: Johns Hopkins, 1955). Also, note that the Inter-University Consortium for Political Research (I.C.P.R.) is computerizing much of this data.

45. UNESCO, *International Guide to Electoral Statistics* (Paris: International Committee for Social Sciences Documentation in cooperation with the International Social Science Council, 1967—).

46. United Nations. Statistical Office. *Statistical Yearbook*, no. 1—(New York: 1948—). Continues *Statistical Yearbook of the League of Nations* (Geneva: 1927-1945).

The Human Relations Area File (H.R.A.F.) represents an early attempt to gather into a single system all existing ethnographic data (published and unpublished) on a sample of cultures throughout the world. HRAF offers equivalent descriptive coverage, retrievable via a specially-devised code,[47] on all aspects of social life and human behavior of some 400 cultures. *Political behavior* and *territorial organization* are only two examples of categories relevant to political geography. Obviously, such a massive compilation has both advantages and disadvantages, but space limitations prevent detailed evaluation here.[48] Suffice it to say that H.R.A.F. is an aggregate data bank available in printed form at some 18 universities and on microform at a number of other institutions. Used judiciously, much of the information could generate or supplement some types of research in political geography. Given an unfortunate lack of attention by political geographers to non-western polities, however, few have tapped the resources of H.R.A.F. Perhaps the definite anthropological slant has been a deterrent, although the file does contain a considerable amount of explicity-political data.

A relatively recent publication—*A Cross-Polity Survey (C.P.S.)*[49]—purports to deal exclusively with political phenomena. *C.P.S.*, which employs an H.R.A.F.-type approach, contains in the form of computer-printout equivalent political data for 115 polities. The intent is to aid and abet cross-national research by indicating "what class of polities co-occur with what other classes." The compilers of *C.P.S.* make no attempt to explain *why* the co-occurrence, but this is not to discount the research value of the data themselves.

Complementing *C.P.S.* are two companion pieces in a series entitled "Tools and Methods of Comparative Research." *The World Handbook of Political and Social Indicators*[50] makes broad cross-national comparisons employing data gathered under the auspices of the Yale Political Data Program (discussed below). The volume is in two sections: Part A contains distribution profiles on 75 variables for 133 polities; Part B offers a preliminary analysis of the data and suggests a variety of research applications. *Comparing Nations*,[51] a compilation of 25 papers presented at the International Conference on the Use of Quantitative Political, Social, and Cultural Data in Cross-National Comparison,[52] includes expert critical analysis of the types of issues generated by the use of quantitative data. The book also contains some articles on various social science data banks.

Numerous agencies collect, analyze, verify, and organize aggregate and/or survey data and make it available in various forms—punched card decks, tapes, distribution profiles, etc.—to the academic community. Since it is impossible to discuss each data bank individually, what follows is a discussion of a few sample types.

The Yale Political Data Program (Y.P.D.P.),[53] in addition to publishing the *World Handbook* . . . , issues periodically data sheets, profile charts, graphs, and surveys of aggregate political data gathered under its direction. The academic community, for a nominal fee, has access to the data. Yale's Political Science Research Library houses the machine-readable Y.P.D.P. data along with other aggregate data and much of the survey data collected by other agencies such as Roper and the Inter-University Consortium for Political Research (see below).

Both Y.P.D.P. and *C.P.S.*, although presently limited to aggregate data, purport to be amenable to a combination of aggregate and survey data. The political geographer should be aware of both kinds of data, their advan-

---

47. For a key to H.R.A.F., see George P. Murdock *et al.*, *Outline of Cultural Materials* (4th rev. ed.; New Haven: Yale, 1961).

48. For a fuller description of H.R.A.F., see Gladys W. White, "The Human Relations Area Files," *College and Research Libraries*, XIX (March 1958), 111–117. For a discussion of merits and disadvantages, see Robert Marsh, *Comparative Sociology* (New York: Harcourt, Brace and World, 1967), pp. 261–270.

49. Arthur S. Banks and Robert B. Textor, *A Cross-Polity Survey* (Cambridge, Mass.: M. I. T. Press, 1963). For reviews, see *American Sociological Review*, XXIX (August, 1964), 635–636; *World Politics*, XIX (October, 1966), 106.

50. Bruce Russett *et al.*, *World Handbook of Political and Social Indicators* (New Haven: Yale University Press, 1964. A review appears in *World Politics*, XIX (October 1966), 106.

51. Richard Merritt and Stein Rokkan, eds., *Comparing Nations* (New Haven: Yale University Press, 1966).

52. Held at Yale University, September 10–20, 1963.

53. For fuller discussions, see Karl W. Deutsch *et al*, "The Yale Political Data Program" in Merritt and Rokkan, *op. cit.*, pp. 81–94; Bruce Russett. "The Yale Political Data Program: Experiences and Prospects," *Ibid.*, pp. 95–107.

tages and limitations.[54] H.R.A.F., C.P.S., and Y.P.D.P. (including the *World Handbook*) represent three voluminous aggregate data banks useful to students of global structure, electoral geography, political integration, etc.

Yet the pages of the *Annals* of the Association of American Geographers are surprisingly bare of such applications. This is not to suggest that political geographers are using survey data, for that has enjoyed even less attention. As the introduction to the Behavior section indicates, most research has concentrated on voting behavior and even there has tended to employ aggregate data. As behavioralism takes hold in political geography, however, increased use of survey data is mandatory. A major breakthrough may well occur when some bright graduate student taps extensive data banks to examine the spatial characteristics of public opinion in the United States.

The Roper Public Opinion Research Center (Williamstown, Massachusetts) is only one of a number of social science data archives. As a major polling agency, the Center has amassed over time a great fund of data from various areas of the United States and abroad. It aims "to have in its files as much of the survey and poll data collected by commercial, academic, and governmental organizations throughout the world as possible."[55] Accredited scholars—and this includes Ph.D. candidates—may for a nominal fee use the archives at Williamstown, borrow duplicate sets of punched card decks, or request frequency tables, marginal distributions, etc. The M.I.T. Center for International Studies has recoded and reprocessed much of the data and returned it to Roper for diffusion. Thus potential users have recourse to at least two sources.[56]

The Inter-University Consortium for Political Research (I.C.P.R.)[57] is working toward an integrated collection of survey, aggregate, and other data relating to political phenomena. Although originally restricted to survey data, I.C.P.R. has begun to compile machine-readable data by county—in effect, to computerize *America Votes* and its predecessors and the U.S. Census information (1824–present). The Consortium represents an ambitious attempt to house in machine-readable format "all social sciences information which political scientists, political sociologists, and historians deem relevant for the study of political matters."[58] Members have noted fairly frequently that no one has yet concentrated specifically on the spatial attributes of the data. Yet the data is quite accessible to political geographers, for I.C.P.R. entails a cooperative arrangement between The University of Michigan Survey Research Center and a number of major universities (including, incidentally, most institutions with graduate programs in geography).

Indeed, most data archives are easily available to members of the academic community, and usually at reasonable cost—in some instances, for the price of a postage stamp. A researcher cannot hope to collect his own data on a scale comparable to that of existing data banks. Comprehensive efforts in political geography will more and more have to rely on data collected by others. Hence the existence of such tools—and data banks are *only tools*—ought to be apparent to the student, perhaps especially to the prospective thesis-writer. Space permitting, one could proceed indefinitely listing various data archives and their services, citing their usefulness for political geography.[59]

Exhaustive inventory, however, is not the purpose of the present appendix. At best, the foregoing paragraphs are only suggestive, no more than an economy tour of the kinds of research aids available to the student of political geography. Of each kind, there are literally dozens more, both geographical and general. Hopefully, the variety of sources cited will bring home the interdisciplinary nature—so evident in the choice of selections in the present volume—of political geography. Perhaps too one can hope for a reduction, if not an elimination, of some of the wasteful duplication of research all too rampant in the social sciences.

---

54. Geographers may find it helpful to consult Otis Dudley Duncan, *Statistical Geography* (Glencoe, Illinois: Free Press, 1958); many of the articles in Merritt and Rokkan, *op. cit.*; and most issues of *Social Sciences Information*.

55. Ralph L. Bisco, "Social Science Data Archives: A Review of Developments," *American Political Science Review*, LX (March 1966), 93–109.

56. Moreover, according to Bisco, *Ibid.*: "A principal benefit is that the data reprocessed by the M.I.T. Center are more amenable to computer analysis than is the original information."

57. Institute for Social Research, University of Michigan, Ann Arbor.

58. Bisco, *op. cit.*, 98.

59. For a list of data archives, their services and publications, refer to Council of Social Science Data Archives, *Social Science Data Archives in the United States, 1967* (New York: Author, 1967).

Name Index

Abelson, Robert, 314f
Abney, Glen F., 428f, 481f, 497
Ackerman, Edward W., 61, 64, 233f
Ad Hoc Committee on Geography, xi, 8f, 57–65, 195
Adam, G., 382, 382f
Ake, Claude, 198, 293
Alexander, Lewis M., 60, 82, 150, 155–6, 187, 205f
Alker, Hayward R., 408, 408f
Allen, Edward W., 475f
Allport, Gordon W., 306f
Almond, Gabriel A., 69f, 187, 293, 419
Ancel, J., 142f
Arambourou, R., 313f, 391f
Ardrey, Robert, 81, 308, 309, 309f, 310, 319–322
Aristotle, 1–4, 13–16, 423, 426, 433, 449
Ashby, W. Ross, 231f
Augelli, John P., 80f

Bachrach, Peter, 303f
Backstrom, Charles H., 419
Badgely, John, 338f
Bailyn, Bernard, 250
Baker, Robert, 306f
Ball, George, 187
Ball, Sue Simmons, 75
Banfield, Edward C., 293, 310, 310f, 368f, 372f, 373f, 419
Banks, Arthur S., 85f, 86, 508f
Baratz, Morton S., 303f
Barnard, Chester I., 373f
Barrows, Harlan, 61, 432

Beard, Charles A., 215f
Beloff, Max, 187, 222f
Benedict, Burton, 187
Benedict, Ruth, 216
Bendix, Reinhard, 206f
Benton, Thomas J., 136, 137, 138
Berelson, Bernard R., 314f, 419
Bergh, G. Van den, 376, 376f, 382, 383f
Berns, Walter, 304f
Bernstein, Robert A., 187–8
Berry, Brian J. L., 82, 207
Billet, H., 313f
Bisco, Ralph L., 303f, 509f
Blackwood, G., 63
Blair, Patricia Wohlgemuth, 188
Blumer, Herbert, 300f
Bodin, Jean, 4, 424, 424f
Boggs, S. W., 60, 142, 143, 144, 145, 146, 155, 156
Bogue, D. J., 388, 388f
Bolin, Ronald L., ix, 6, 17–28
Boorman, H. L., 331f
Boulding, Kenneth, 198, 308, 309f, 312, 341–349, 342f
Bowman, Isaiah, 10, 66, 455f
Brams, Steven J., 199, 209f, 235f, 237f, 241f, 293
Brecher, Michael, 293
Brewer, Michael F., 497
Brigham, Albert Perry, 142
Brodbeck, May, 301f
Broek, Jan, 144
Brown, Harrison, 85, 497
Brown, Robert H., 71, 310f
Bruner, Jerome S., 305f
Brunton, Douglas, 119f

Bryson, L., 212f
Buchanan, Keith, 188
Buchanan, William, 311, 311f, 419
Buckle, Henry Thomas, 424, 424f
Buckley, Walter, 419
Bunge, William, 303f
Burgess, E. W., 332, 332f, 370f
Burghardt, Andrew, 72f, 152, 316f, 419
Burton, Ian, 432
Butler, David E., 380, 381f

Calhoun, John B., 132, 136, 309f
Campbell, Angus, 308f, 314f, 315, 315f, 316f, 419
Cancian, Frank, 307f
Cantril, Hadley, 311, 311f, 419
Carpenter, C. R., 309f
Carroll, Lewis, 215
Chapin, F. Stuart, 313, 313f
Chauchat, Auguste, 391f
Cherry, Colin, 231f
Childe, V. Gordon, 442, 442f
Clark, Peter B., 373f
Clawson, M. B., 63
Clifford, E. H. M., 152f
Clubb, O. E., 330f, 337f
Cohen, Saul B., 66, 84, 85, 88, 178–183
Colby, Charles C., 44f, 61, 66, 147f, 148f, 432
Coleman, James S., 69f
Combs, Arthur W., 305f
Commager, Henry Steele, 251
Conant, James M., 292f
Converse, Philip, 315f, 419

Name Index

Cooley, Richard A., 497
Cornish, Vaughan, 74
Coser, Lewis, 318, 318f
Cox, Kevin R., 316f, 380, 380f, 420
Cree, D., 153
Cressey, George B., 337f
Crisler, Robert, 316, 316f
Curry, Leslie, 302, 302f
Cutright, Phillip, 293

Dacey, M. F., 238f
Dahl, Robert A., 299, 299f
Daland, Robert T., 366f
Dale, Edmund H., 72f, 86f, 188, 200f, 201, 294
Darling, Frank Fraser, 319, 319f
Dauzat, A., 264f
Davies, James C., 304f, 305f
Davis, John W., 151f
Dean, Vera K., 316, 316f
de Blij, Harm J., 71f, 74, 195, 205f
Debray, Régis, 76, 77
De Gaulle, Charles, 86
de Grazia, Alfred, 299f, 505
de Lapradelle, Paul, 127f, 142f
De Seversky, Alexander P. (see Seversky)
Denton, Frank H., 318f
de Sola Pool, Ithiel, 314f, 421
Deutsch, Karl W., 12, 52–53, 62, 154, 197, 198, 199, 208, 211–220, 225, 227, 228, 232, 234, 252f, 281f, 283f, 306f, 420, 486f, 508f
Dickenson, John, 254
Dobyns, Henry F., 326, 326f
Dodge, Stanley, 152
Dominian, Leon, 9
Downs, Anthony, 210, 286–292, 307
Dray, William, 302f
Dubos, Rene, 497
Duke, Richard, 431f
Dunn, Frederick S., 55f
Dutt, V. P., 338f
Dybowski, 23
Dye, Thomas R., 200, 210f, 294

East, W. Gordon, 72f, 147, 155f, 188
Easton, David, 232f, 427, 427f, 428f, 484, 484f, 486f, 497, 504f
Eibl-Eibesfeldt, I., 309f

Espenshade, Ada, 471f
Eto, Shinkichi, 337f
Etzioni, Amitai, 74, 196–7, 198f, 200, 202, 208, 221–230, 294, 481f
Ewald, William R., Jr., 497

Fair, T. J. D., 238f
Fairbank, John K., 330f, 332f, 334f
Fairgrieve, James, 184
Fawcett, Charles B., 141–2
Feit, E., 481f
Fesler, James W., 51
Fielding, Gordon J., 497
Fifield, Russell H., 8f, 66
Fischer, Eric, 52, 54, 146
Fisher, Charles A., 188, 200f, 294, 340f
Fitzgerald, C. P., 330f, 332f
Flanigan, William, 69–70
Fleming, Douglas K., 294
Fogelman, Edwin, 69–70
Foltz, William J., 209–10, 252f, 281–5
Foss, Philip O., 498
Fox, Irving, 433, 433f, 498
Franklin, Benjamin, 252
Freeman, Otis W., 473
Friedheim, R. L., 382, 382f
Frings, Theodor, 213f
Furniss, Edgar S., 188

Galloway, Joseph, 255, 256
Garrison, William L., 151f, 238f
Gaurnier, C., 264f
Geyl, Pieter, 425f
Giap, Vo Nguyen, 76
Gilbert, E. W., 158
Gilchrist, J. C., 305f
Ginsburg, Norton, 58f, 61, 308, 311–312, 330–340, 498, 502
Girod, Roger, 420
Glanz, O., 384f, 391, 391f
Glaser, William, 224f
Goguel, François, 313, 313f, 391f, 420
Golledge, R. G., 306f
Goodman, C. C., 305f
Goodman, L. A., 235f
Gosnell, Harold, 314, 314f, 372f, 400f, 401f
Gottmann, Jean, 12, 50–51, 53–54, 59, 70, 154, 188–9, 196, 199
Gould, Peter, 206f, 302f
Gourou, Pierre, 425, 425f

Gregg, Phillip M., 85f, 86, 189
Gregory, Homer E., 475f
Griffith, W. E., 337f
Guetzkow, Harold, 420
Guevara, Ernesto (Ché), 76, 86
Guichonnet, Paul, 313f
Gurin, Gerald, 314f
Gyorgy, Andrew, 62

Haar, Charles M., 498
Haas, Ernst B., 189, 196, 228–9
Haddon, John, 311f
Hägerstrand, T., 238f
Haggett, Peter, 431, 431f
Hall, Arthur R., 84f, 189
Hall, Edward T., 304, 304f, 305f, 311, 311f, 324, 420
Halle, Louis J., 312f
Hamdan, G., 75, 189
Hamelin, Jean, 313f
Hamelin, Marcel, 313f
Hance, William A., 237f
Handy, Rollo, 502f
Harary, Frank, 189
Haring, Lloyd H., 316f
Harris, Chauncy, 502, 502f, 506f
Harris, Louis, 384f, 404f
Hart, Henry C., 433, 433f, 481f
Hart, John Fraser, 316, 316f, 382, 382f
Hartshorne, Richard, xi, 1, 9f, 11–12, 34–49, 50–51, 53–54, 56, 59, 60ff, 66–7, 70, 72, 79, 127f, 142, 144, 147–8, 149, 154, 157, 189, 195, 196, 197, 199, 202, 231f, 258f, 349f, 379
Hassert, Kurt, 6f
Hassinger, Hugo, 39, 452f, 453f
Hauser, Philip M., 498
Haushofer, Karl, 2, 8–9, 39f, 130, 142f, 170
Hazlewood, Arthur, 295
Hediger, H., 309f
Held, Colbert C., 63, 148
Hemper, Carl G., 302f
Henderson, A. M., 206f
Herman, Theodore, 75, 330f, 331f, 332f, 337f, 420
Herson, Lawrence J. R., 366f
Hertzler, J. O., 481f
Herz, John H., 73, 189

Name Index

Heslinga, M. W., 189, 203f
Hill, Larry B., 428f, 481f, 497
Hill, Norman, 149f
Hippocrates, 3, 13, 423
Hoffman, George, 503
Hoffman, Stanley, 420
Holdich, Thomas H., 141
Holt, Robert T., 69f
Horvath, F. E., 484f
Hoselitz, Bert F., 502f
House, J. W., 150-51, 206, 209, 258-272
Howard, H. E., 309, 309f
Hugonnier, S., 313f
Hull, Clark L., 300f
Hunker, Henry L., 295, 231f
Hursh, Gerald D., 419

Ibn-Khaldūn, 3-4, 195, 424
Inglehart, Ronald, 199
Insko, Chester A., 306f
Isaacs, Harold R., 311f
Isard, Walter, 234f

Jackson, W. A. Douglas, xi, 67, 84f, 189-90, 503f
Jacob, Philip E., 197, 198, 200f, 209f, 232f, 295
Jacobson, C., 69f
Jaffa, Henry V., 304f
Janis, Irving L., 484f
Jefferson, Mark, 93
Jefferson, Thomas, 138
Jennings, M. Kent, 305f
Jensen, Merrill, 349f
Johnson, Chalmers, 76f
Johnson, Douglas W., 103, 141
Johnson, James H., 203f, 295
Johnson, John, 284f
Jones, Stephen B., 1, 11-12, 50-56, 58, 59, 60, 63, 70, 83f, 84f, 128f, 140f, 145-6, 147, 152, 157, 158, 190, 196, 208

Kant, Immanuel, 6f
Kapil, Ravi, 78f, 205
Kaplan, Abraham, 54
Kaplan, Morton A., 200f, 295
Karan, P. P., 156, 203f
Kasperson, Jeanne X., 501-509
Kasperson, Roger E., 308, 312-313, 316f, 366-375, 420, 428, 431f, 435, 481-496, 482f, 489f, 498
Kates, Robert W., 302, 302f, 306f, 307, 367f, 428, 428f, 432, 433f, 498, 500
Kelman, Herbert C., 420
Kennan, George, 181-2
Key, V. O., Jr., 315, 315f, 316, 316f, 421
Kim, K. W., 303f
Kirk, William, 62, 308, 308f
Kjellén, Rudolf, 8-10, 39f, 424
Klein, Donald W., 331f
Klieman, Aaron S., 202-3
Klineberg, Otto, 311f
Koch, Howard E., Jr., 421
Koch, J., 62ff
Konigsberg, Charles, 498
Kostbade, J. Trenton, 316f
Krebhiel, Edward, 313, 313f, 381
Kriesel, Karl Marcus, 4f, 5, 67, 424
Kristof, Ladis K. D., 67, 82, 87, 126-131, 146-7, 190
Kuhn, Philip, 332f
Kurtz, Paul, 502f

Laboree, Leonard W., 250f, 251
La Feber, Walter, 312f
Lakeman, E., 376, 376f
Lamar, 136
Lambert, J. O., 376, 376f
Lambert, Wallace E., 311f
Langfeldt, M., 8
Large, David C., 499
Lasswell, Harold D., 54
Lattimore, Owen, 127f, 190, 335
Lazarsfeld, Paul F., 223f, 314f
Lazarus, R., 306f
Leach, E. R., 190, 427, 427f
Leighly, John, 349, 349f
Lenin, V. I., 76
Lerner, Daniel, 295
Leroy-Beaulieu, 18f
Letarte, Jacques, 313f
Leuchtenburg, William E., 481f
Levi, Marion, 69
Lévy-Strauss, C., 69f
Lewin, Kurt, 308, 308f
Lewis, P. W., 380f
Lewis, Peirce, 61, 309, 316f, 317, 366f, 380, 380f, 381, 381f, 384-406, 507
Leys, Colin, 237f
Lichtheim, George, 230f
Lippmann, Walter, 311, 311f
Lin Piao, 76, 85, 86, 190-1, 339

Livingston, William S., 96
Lock, C. B. Muriel, 502f
Loef (See Löf)
Loesch, August (See Lösch)
Löf, 61, 64
Logan, W. A., 499
London, Ivan, 304, 304f
Long, Norton, 290f, 375f, 485, 486f
Lorenz, Konrad, 310, 310f, 318, 421
Lösch, August, 142-3, 144, 151, 428
Lowenthal, David, ix, 201, 308, 312, 349, 349f, 350-365, 360f, 432, 432f, 499
Lubasz, Heinz, 295
Lubell, Samuel, 384f, 406f
Lucas, Robert, 432, 432f
Lyde, Lionel William, 128f, 141, 143, 146, 147
Lyden, Fremont J., 499

Maass, Arthur, 73f, 191, 432f, 484f
McCarty, H. H., 393f, 404f
McColl, Robert W., 76-77, 191
McCune, Shannon, 203f
McGee, T. G., 208f, 295-6
Mackay, J. Ross, 60, 80, 154, 158-9, 160, 234f, 238f
Mack, Raymond W., 318f
Mackenzie, W. J. M., 231f
Mackinder, Halford J., 2, 9, 62, 83-4, 85, 86, 88, 162-169, 170, 171, 174-5, 176, 177, 181, 191, 196, 213f, 335
McKinley, Charles, 499
McNulty, M. L., 81-2
McPhee, William N., 314f
Madison, James, 138
Mahan, A. T., 83, 166
Malof, Peter, 198f
Mann, Dean E., 499
Mao Tsetung, 76, 330
Marco Polo, 121
Marinelli, O., 264f
Marlele, D. F., 238f
Marshall, Charles Burton, 225f
Martin, Roscoe, 76f
Martindale, Don, 69, 70ff, 191
Marts, Marion E., 151f, 434
Marx, Karl, 38, 125, 183, 426, 433, 445f
Masseport, Jean, 313f

Name Index

Mathews, Donald R., 367f
Maull, Otto, 39, 142f
Meier, Richard L., 232, 233f, 289
Meinig, Donald W., 84f, 191, 460f
Melamid, Alexander, 203f, 204, 296, 311f
Menzel, Herbert, 223f
Merriam, Charles M., 314f
Merritt, Richard L., 197, 198, 202, 209, 243-257, 296, 421, 508f, 509f
Merton, Robert, 69f
Meyerson, Martin, 368f, 372f
Michel, Aloys A., 203f, 296
Migliorini, Elia, 501
Mikesell, Marvin W., 191, 503
Milbrath, Lester, 302, 302f, 421
Miles, Edward J., 316f
Miller, J. G., 231f, 232f
Miller, Kent, 484f
Miller, Warren E., 300f, 314f, 315f, 419
Minghi, Julian V., 60, 72f, 80, 88, 140-160, 191, 203f, 204, 304f, 435, 464-480
Mommsen, 20, 23
Montesquieu, Charles Baron de, 4-5, 10, 424
Moodie, A. E., 146, 149, 150, 155, 258f, 296
Morgan, Lewis, 20
Morgenstern, Oscar, 215f
Morison, Samuel E., 251, 253f, 254f, 255f
Morriss, Margaret Shove, 250
Moule, A. C., 121f
Murdoch, George Peter, 69f, 426
Murphey, Rhoads, 85, 87, 117-125, 191, 338f

Nachtigal, 23, 24
Nadler, Josef, 213f
Nasser, Gamal Abdul, 86, 192
N'Diaye, J. P., 283f
Nelson, Howard J., 159, 366f, 431, 499
Niemi, Richard G., 305f
Nkrumah, Kwame, 277
North, Robert D., 63, 421
Nye, J. S., 235f
Nystrom, J. Warren, 198f
Nystuen, John D., 80, 238f

Ogata, Sadako, 338f
Ogburn, William F., 314f
Olivesi, Antoine, 313f
Osgood, Charles E., 299f
Osmond, Humphrey, 310, 310f
Otis, James, 253-4

Packenham, Robert A., 207, 296
Padelford, Norman, 224f
Parker, R. S., 459f
Parr, A. E., 326, 326f
Parsons, Talcott, 69, 206f, 227f
Paton, Alan, 218f
Patten, Simon N., 142
Patterson, Samuel C., 421
Pattison, William D., 499
Paullin, C. O., 313, 313f, 383f
Peake, E. R. L., 152-3
Pearcy, G. Etzel, 8f, 60, 66, 78f, 155, 156, 503
Peattie, Roderick, 145
Pedreschi, L., 154
Pelliot, Paul, 121f
Pelzer, Karl J., 53f, 455f
Pennington, D. H., 119f
Perloff, H., 63
Pitts, Forrest R., 192, 203f
Pizzigallo, V., 270f
Platt, Elizabeth J., 501, 502
Platt, Robert S., 44f, 148f
Poltoratzky, Nikolai, 304, 304f
Popper, Karl R., 301, 301f
Posselt, H., 258f
Postman, L., 305f
Pounds, Norman J. G., 74, 75, 152, 155f, 192, 203f, 204, 205f, 377, 382f
Pred, Allan, 302f
Prescott, J. R. V., ix, 82, 159, 192, 204, 297, 308, 315-317, 376-383, 377, 382f, 391f, 507
Price, A. Grenfell, 455f
Proudfoot, Malcolm J., 366f
Pye, Lucian W., 206f, 207, 284f, 297

Quinn, Frank, 434, 434f, 499

Radcliffe-Brown, A. R., 69f, 192
Randall, Richard, 148
Ranney, Austin, 300f
Rapoport, Anatol, 302f, 341f
Ratzel, Friedrich, ix, 1-2, 6-10, 17-28, 35, 39, 62, 64, 67, 141, 142, 206, 424, 503

Reitzel, William, 53, 57f
Reynolds, David R., 81-2
Rice, Stuart, 313, 313f
Richards, Allen, 366f
Richards, Cara B., 326, 326f
Richardson, Lewis F., 341, 341f, 421
Riesenfeld, Stephan A., 476, 476f
Riggs, Fred W., 297
Ritter, Karl, 5-6, 8, 62
Roberts, Michael C., 380, 380f, 381, 421
Robinson, Arthur H., 393f, 404f
Robinson, G. W. S., 72f, 153-4, 192
Robinson, K. W., 86f, 192, 200f, 431, 458-463, 459f
Robinson, W. S., 300, 300f
Robson, Peter, 237f
Rodgers, A. L., 385, 385f
Rokkan, Stein, 318, 318f, 421, 508f, 509f
Roncayolo, Marcel, 313f
Rose, A. J., 192, 460f
Rosenau, James N., 197f, 202f, 297
Rosenthal, Franz, 3f
Rostow, W. W., 228f
Rothchild, Donald S., 297
Rovere, Richard H., 312f
Rumage, K. W., 380, 380f, 381, 421
Rummel, R. J., 318f, 422
Russett, Bruce M., 78f, 84, 86, 192-3, 197, 198, 199, 309, 317, 407-418, 408f, 410f, 417f, 434, 499, 508f

Sabbagh, M. Ernest, 297
Salisbury, N. S., 393f, 404f
Sauer, Carl O., xi, 301f, 377, 377f
Savage, I. R., 234
Schaffer, B. B., 205
Schoeller, Peter (See Schöller)
Schoepf, B. C. (trans.), 69f
Schöller, Peter, 147, 154, 297
Schramm, Wilbur, 238f
Schroeder, Klaus, 154
Schumpeter, Joseph, 216
Schweinfurth, 19
Schwind, M., 258f
Secord, P. F., 305f
Semple, Ellen Churchill, 7, 140-41, 424

Name Index

Seversky, Alexander P. de, 84, 188, 196
Sewell, W. R. Derrick, 432, 433f, 434, 434f, 500
Shabad, Theodore, 426f
Shannon, Claude, 231f
Shalowitz, Aaron, 155
Shaudys, Vincent K., 81f, 205, 297
Shen-yu, Dai, 332f, 335f
Sherif, Carolyn W., 306f
Shipman, George A., 499
Shirer, William L., 9f
Siegfried, André, 60, 313, 313f, 391f
Sigel, R. S., 384f
Simon, Herbert A., 306, 306f, 307, 307f, 311, 367f, 422, 484f
Singer, J. David, 62, 78f, 422
Skinner, B. F., 299, 299f
Skipworth, G. E., 380f
Smailes, A. E., 54
Smelser, Neil, 69f
Smith, C. G., 500
Smith, Don D., 422
Smith, Howard R., 316, 316f, 382, 382f
Smith, M. B., 306f
Snyder, Richard C., 307f, 318f, 422, 486f
Snygg, Donald, 305f
Soja, Edward W., 198, 199f, 208, 231–242
Sölch, J., 258f
Sommer, Robert, 310, 310f, 324, 422
Sonnenfeld, Joseph, 428f
Soustrelle, Jacques, 193
Spate, O. H. K., 54, 73, 74–5, 193, 203f, 204, 298, 353, 425, 427
Spotswood, Governor of Virginia 1717, 135
Sprout, Harold, 62, 67, 193, 300, 356, 427, 500, 503
Sprout, Margaret, 62, 193, 300, 356, 427, 500
Spykman, Nicholas, 2, 84, 86, 88, 130f, 145, 170–177, 193, 196
Stea, David, 71, 308, 310, 310f, 323–327
Steidle, Carolyn Ann, 316f

Stephenson, Glenn V., 193
Stokes, Donald E., 314f, 315f
Stolpler, Wolfgang, 142f
Strabo, 3

Tarlton, Charles D., 86, 94–98, 201
Tawney, R. H., 124
Tayyeb, A., 203f, 298
Teune, Henry, 197, 198, 209f
Textor, Robert B., 508f
Thermaenius, Edward, 8, 67
Thomas, Benjamin E., 52, 158
Thompson, W. F., 480f
Thrasher, Fred M., 309f
Tibbits, Clark, 314f
Tondel, L. M., Jr., 330f
Toscano, James V., 197f, 198f, 200f, 232f, 233f, 295
Toynbee, Arnold, 55, 206, 424, 425, 425f, 426, 427, 436–441
Turner, Frederick Jackson, 82, 83, 87–8, 127, 129f, 132–139, 424

Ullman, Edward L., 60, 157–8

Valen, Henry, 318, 318f, 421
Van den Bergh, G. (See Bergh)
Van Duzer, Edward F., 316f
Van Valkenburg, Samuel, 195
Vance, James E., Jr., 193, 200
Verba, Sidney, 419
Vernon, Raymond, 286f, 287f
Vogel, William, 306f
Von Bertalanffy, L., 231f
Von Neumann, John, 215f
Von Vorys, Karl, 298

Wagner, Philip, 86, 89–93, 500
Wallerstein, Immanuel, 206, 209, 273–280, 298
Wang, Yi-Tong, 338f
Wanklyn, Harriet, 6f
Warkentin, John, 72f
Warren, General, 24f
Washington, George, 136, 138
Watson, John B., 299, 299f
Weaver, Warren, 231f

Weber, Max, 206, 444
Webb, Walter Prescott, 424
Weigend, Guido G., 150, 298
Weigert, Hans W., 67, 146, 311f
Weiner, Norbert, 231f
Wengert, Norman, 500
Wheare, K. C., 225f, 459, 459f
Wheaton, William L. C., 200
White, Carl M., 502f
White, Gilbert F., 61, 432, 484, 484f
Whitney, Joseph B. R., 332f
Whittlesey, Derwent S., 1, 10–11, 29–33, 36, 50, 52, 59, 61, 67–8, 70, 75, 86–7, 93, 99–116, 127f, 153, 195, 213f, 258f, 349f, 428–429, 433, 450–457
Wilkenson, H. R., 148, 258f
Wilkinson, Spenser, 166
Williams, Eric, 355f, 356f, 359f, 360f, 361f, 362f, 363f
Willis, Richard H., 311f
Wilson, James Q., 254, 370f
Witthuhn, Burton, 404
Wings, L., 63
Wittfogel, Karl A., 87, 122, 123f, 426, 427, 442–449, 445f
Woglom, William B., 142f
Wohlwill, Joachim, 425f, 428, 428f, 498
Wolfe, Roy I., 208f, 298, 503f
Wolpert, Julian, 302, 302f, 307, 307f, 308, 308f, 422, 484f, 486, 486f
Wood, Robert, 76f, 193, 289f
Wright, John K., 60, 68, 313, 313f, 381, 381f, 501, 501f
Wright, Quincy, 422
Wynar, Lubomyr R., 502, 502f
Wynne-Edwards, V. C., 309f

Yi, Chen, 340, 340f
Yilvisaker, Paul, 73f

Zaidi, Iqtidar H., 193
Zelinsky, Wilbur, 405, 405f
Zinnes, Dina A., 63, 421

Subject Index

Action space, 308
Adaptation, 428
Adjustment, 428
Administrative man, 486
Affectional balance, 347
Afro-Asians, 412-418
Aggression, 310, 323, 421, 453
Alice in Wonderland, 215
American Geographical Society, 10, 455, 503
American Revolution (See Revolution)
Animal territoriality, 89-90, 309-310, 319-322
Annexation, 7, 99, 157, 200
Arab Union, 35
Area repercussion, 434-435
Areal voting data, 316, 381-382, 390
Ashanti, 274
Assembly voting, 317, 382-383, 407-418
Association of American Geographers, 11, 39, 147
Attitudes, 37, 306, 311, 329, 356, 419, 420, 421, 422
  map, 311, 329
Autarchy, 2, 429
Autonomy, 461
  neighborhood, 289-291
Azimuth error, 152

Babylon, 27, 166
Balance-of-power, 348
Balfour Declaration, 52
Bedouins, 3
Behavior, 81-82, 299-422, 481-496, 508
  aggregate, 300
  cognitive, 427, 500
  conflict, 318, 367, 421, 422, 433
  definition, 300
  individual, 300
  role, 488-489
  satisficing, 307, 367, 486
  in space, 301, 313, 318
  spatial, 300-301, 309-311, 318
  territorial, 3, 8, 57, 71-73, 86, 198, 208, 301, 318-327, 344-345
  voting, 62, 65, 303, 313-317, 368-370, 376-419, 507
    objectives, 316-317, 383, 404-406, 407-408
    (See also Areal voting data, Assembly voting, Elections, Normal vote)
Behavioral environment, 308
Behavioralism, 299, 303-304, 502
  vs. behaviorism, 299
  characteristics, 303
  limitations, 303-304
Behaviorism, 62, 299
  vs. behavioralism, 299
Bibliographic aids, 501-509
Biological nation, 309
Bloc vote (See Elections, systems; Behavior, voting)
Bobbs-Merrill Reprints, ix
Borderlands, 60, 72, 78-79, 115, 127, 141ff, 149, 151ff, 155, 452
  landscape, 78-79
Boston "tea party," 255
Boundaries, xii, 3, 44, 54-55, 70-71, 77-82, 114, 116, 140-160 (esp. 140-147), 150, 206, 209, 235, 258-272, 274, 289, 319-322, 332-340, 344, 378, 428, 451-453, 460, 464-480, 503
  antecedent, 142, 152
  change, 75, 115, 145, 149-151, 160, 184, 204-206, 209, 258-272
  classification, 79ff, 88, 130, 142ff
  concepts, 344
  delimitation and demarcation, 151, 152-153, 378
    (See also Gerrymandering, Redistricting)
  evolution, 58, 151-152, 160
  form, 78-79, 115
  function, 7-8, 23-24, 44-45, 60, 79-81, 127, 140
  historical, 146
  impact, 80-81, 143, 145, 160, 238, 460
  interaction hypothesis, 158ff, 160
  internal, 58, 146, 157-160, 378
  International Boundary Studies, 503
  interruptive factor, 143, 146, 158ff
  intrenchment factor, 143ff
  maritime, 60, 155-156, 160, 464-480,
    classification, 155
  misleading notions, 78
  nature, 30, 77-78, 87, 126-131 (esp. 127), 141
  perception and behavior, 81-82
  relict, 152
  watershed, 153
Brahmanism, 165
Brazzaville group, 85, 317, 412-418

Subject Index

British Broadcasting Corporation, 158
British East India Company, 119
British Empire, 19ff, 170, 174ff, 179, 281ff
British Imperial System, 169, 209
British-Russian Entente, 175
Buddhism, 165, 174
Buffer states, 145, 184ff
Buffer zones, 70, 111–114, 174
Bürolandschaft, 325–327

Canada-United States border, 60, 72, 141, 155
Canadian Broadcasting Corporation, 72
Canadian National Railways, 45
Canadian Pacific Railway, 44
Capitals, 2–3, 10–11, 30, 54–55, 70, 73, 74–75, 208, 213, 312, 350–365, 455, 463
Castle-and-border thesis, 319–322
Central African Federation, 201, 279
Central authority, 428, 450–457
Centrality, 11, 73–77, 86–87, 198
Centrifugal forces, 11, 36–38, 50, 87, 128, 148, 154, 196
Centripetal forces, 11, 38–39, 50, 87, 127ff, 154, 196
Certainty-uncertainty continuum, 307–308
Challenge-response thesis, 425, 436
Chinese Communist Party, 125
Chinese Empire, 170
Chinese Treaty Pacts, 120ff
Christianity, 129, 165
Circulation, 50ff, 140, 146, 151, 154, 157, 158ff, 327
Circulatory system, 157
Cities, 54–55, 93
  centers of change, 117–125
City states, 15ff
Civil War, U.S., 136
Claimant state, 148ff
Climate, 488, 500
Coastland complex, 156
Colonial world, 153
Common Market, 65, 198, 208, 223, 271–272, 421

Commonwealth of Nations, 35, 47, 248
Communications
  impact upon political integration, 198ff, 208, 231–242
  networks, 157, 208, 212, 213–214
  overloads, 198, 227
  theory, 199
Communism, 53, 124, 125, 181
  communist bloc, 183, 185, 224, 412–418
  communist world, 179, 181
Competition, 461
Conflict (See Behavior, conflict)
Conservative Arabs, 414–418
Constitution, U.S., 139, 226
Content analysis, 198, 209, 420, 482, 482ff
Contiguity, 149, 154, 181, 205, 225, 421
  (See also Noncontiguity)
Continental Congress, 254ff
Core areas, 10, 30, 41–43, 71, 73–74, 75–76, 87, 208, 212–213, 332, 368–372, 380, 448
Cost-benefit analysis, 63, 197, 367, 432
Crisis, 433, 481, 484
Crush zone, 184
Cultivated land of the world (map), 173
Cybernetics, 231ff, 306
Cycle theory of state growth (See States, life-cycles)

Dark Ages, 4
Data archives, 507–509
Decision, 62–63, 197ff, 210, 227, 306–308, 312–313, 342, 371–375, 481–496, 505
  constraints, 490–491
  definition, 306, 342
  environment, 308, 486
  locus, 306–307
  objectives, 306–307
  point, 307
  stress, 308, 326, 481–496
  uncertainty, 307, 422, 486
Declaration of Independence, U.S., 256
Defederation, 201, 203
  (See also Disintegration, Federalism, Federation)
Delaware River Basin Commission, 62

Development (See Growth and Development)
Diarchy period, 205
Diffuse patterns (See Patterns, diffuse)
Digital pattern (See Patterns, digital)
Discontiguity (See Noncontiguity)
Disintegration, 196, 201–204, 209, 243–257, 364–365
  (See also Defederation)
Disputed areas, 147–149, 151
Domino theory, 85, 338
Downstream state, 156
Drang nach Osten, 9
Dutch Empire, 179

East African Economic Community (EAEC), 239ff
Economic rationality view, 433
Ecumene, 30, 93, 181, 183, 332, 334, 335
Egyptian army, 225
Elections, 314–316, 376–377
  plebiscites, 115, 148, 265
  statistics, 507
  systems, 376–377
  turnout, 315
  types, 314–316
  (See also Behavior, voting)
Electoral geography (See Behavior, voting; Elections)
Empires, dissolution of, 201, 202, 203
Enclaves and exclaves, 63, 72, 147, 153–155, 160, 503
  quasi-exclave, 153
Encyclopedias, 503
Environment, xii, 2–9, 12, 62, 70, 77, 134, 153, 157, 195, 209, 224ff, 308, 423–500
  behavioral, 308
  cues, 309
  designed, 323–327
  determinism (See Environmental determinism)
  effects, 428
  extrasocietal, 427–428
  impress upon politics, 1–6, 12, 423–428, 436–449
  agents, 429–430, 451–457
  effects, 431, 453–457
  political goals, 429, 450–451
  processes, 430–431, 450–457

Subject Index

intrasocietal, 427-428
modified by politics, 428-431, 450-463, 499
operational, 427, 428
optimal, 497
policy and planning, 432-433, 491-496, 498
public management, 431-434, 464-496
stress *(See* Environmental stress; *See also* Managerial matrix)*
variability, 326-327
Environmental cues, 309
Environmental determinism, 2, 3-10, 423-424, 500
Environmental probabilism, 427, 500
Environmental stress, 481-496
Erie Canal, 134
Ethnic awareness, 212, 217-218
European states system, 75, 243ff
Exchange economics, 212
Exclaves *(See* Enclaves and exclaves)
Explanation, 301-302
  causal, 301
  rational, 302
  statistical, 301, 380-382
Exploitable world, 433-434

Factor analysis, 314, 317, 382, 408-418
Fascism, 150
Federalism, 34, 86, 94-98, 201, 350-365, 458-463
  symmetry and asymmetry, 86, 94-98, 201
  (See also Defederation, Disintegration, Federation)
Federation, 128, 200ff, 238ff, 240, 248, 278-280
Field theory, 11-12, 50-56, 58, 70, 325
  (See also Unified field theory)
Fishing conflicts, 464-480
Flemish corridor, 113
Flemish region, 112
Forty-ninth parallel, 141, 152
Fragmentation, political, 4-5, 156, 159, 184ff, 204, 209, 288-289
Franco-Belgian boundary, 118
Franco-German boundary, 44, 114ff
Franco-Italian boundary, 150ff, 206, 209, 258-272

French Empire, 170, 179, 281ff
French Revolution, 38, 101ff
Frontiers, xii, 70-71, 77, 82-83, 87-88, 126-129, 140, 146ff, 151, 258, 269-272
  natural, 144
Frontiers (Turner), 132-139
  checks and regulations, 138-139
  influences, 135-137
  national tendencies, 137-138
  stages of advances, 133-134
  succession, 135
  West, 134
Fulbe states, 23ff
Functional allocation, 434, 464-497
Functional interests, 198
Functionalism, 10-11, 34-49, 196
Funnel of causality, 315

Game theory, 63
Geography, electoral *(See* Behavior, voting; Elections)
Geography, political *(See* Political geography)
Geopolitical equilibrium, 60, 63
Geopolitical forces, 31-32
Geopolitical regions, 84-85, 88, 178-186
Geopolitics, xi, 1, 6-9 (esp. 8-9), 32-33
Geopolitics and Trade (map), 182
Geostrategic regions, 84-85, 88, 178-186
  map, 180
German Customs Union, 22ff
German Empire, 17ff, 37, 110
German-Polish boundary, 44, 149
Gerrymandering, 377-378, 507
Ghetto, 290, 429
Global strategic views, 178ff
Global structure, 2, 4, 5-6, 12, 71, 83-86, 88, 161-186, 196
Grid pattern, 453-454
Growth and Development, 196, 204-207, 209-210, 281-292, 458-463
  (See also States, lifecycles)

Growth of nations, 211-220
Guerrilla warfare, 76-77, 86

Hamites, 26
Hansa, 28, 118
Heartland, 2, 9, 83ff, 170-177 (esp. 171-174), 178ff, 181, 309
Heterogeneity, 223-224, 453
Hierarchy, 3, 57ff, 71-73, 78, 86, 197ff, 208
High seas, 59, 155ff
  (See also Fishing conflicts)
Hohenstaufens, empire of, 19, 38
Holy Roman Empire, 23, 243
Homogeneity, 202
Hostility, 341-342, 345, 349
Hudson's Bay Company, 146, 155
Huguenots, 108
Human Relations Area File, 508
Huns, 164
Hydroagriculture, 426-427, 442-449
Hydraulic civilization, 426-427, 442-449

Iberia, 412-418
Iconography, 50ff, 154, 199
Idea-area chain *(See* Unified field theory)
Ideal state (Aristotle), 2-3, 13-16
Ile de France, 105-107, 213
Image, 312, 341-349, 421
  compatability, 348
  definition, 342
  derogatory, 329
  elite, 342-343
  folk, 342-343
  formation, 342-344
  historical, 343
  matrix, 346-349
  residual, 206
  sophistication, 349
Imperial system, disintegration of (map), 257
  transition (map), 253
Inca empire, 20ff
Incorporation, 200
Independence, 63-64, 81, 198, 204, 205-206 (esp. 205), 209, 273-280
Indexes, 504-506
Industrial revolution, 113, 216
Information theory, 231ff, 306, 342
Inner crescent, 170ff (map)

Subject Index

Instability, political *(See* Political instability)
Institute for Geopolitics (Munich), 8
Integration
  political, 2, 11, 199ff, 208, 277ff
    (See also Political unification)
  behavioral, 199
  communications theory, 199
  structural, 199
  systemic, 200
  territorial, 91, 196-201, 208, 231-242
Integration and Disintegration, 211-257
Interaction fields, 154
Interaction Hypothesis, 154, 158-159, 160
International conflict, 62, 464-480
International law, 128, 155ff, 474-476
  (See also Law of the sea; Legal systems)
International rivers, 156
Inter-university Consortium for Political Research, 509
Inventory approach, 10
Iron curtain, 55, 65
Iroquois, 133
Irredentism, 42, 282, 337-340
Irrigation, 446-448
Islam, 217
Islamic states, 28
Italo-Yugoslav boundary, 149ff

Jacqueries, 120, 124
Japanese empire, 170
Jews, 129, 345
Jim Crowism, 37
Julian March, 149
Junker, 19ff

Kaffir boundary, 24
Kinetic fields, 55ff

Labor, 444-446
Land holdings, 454
Land power, 168ff, 175ff, 178ff, 184
Land survey, 453, 599
Land tenure, 434
  (See also Primogeniture)
Landscape, 10-11, 30-31, 140, 203, 456-457, 459, 499
  (See also Bürolandschaft)
  impact of laws, 10-11, 30-31, 456-457
Law of the sea, 83, 474-476
Lebensraum, 9
Legal systems, 429, 456-457, 498
  (See also International law)
  impact upon landscape, 456-457
Life cycle theory (of state growth), 3ff, 12, 195ff, 206ff
Life space, 308
Lift-pump effect, 212, 214-215
Linear boundary, 152
Locarno, treaty of, 44
Locational conflict
  capital site, 350-365
  in the city, 371-375
Loss-of-power gradient, 348
Lunda empire, 26

Mackinder dictum, 176
  (See also Heartland)
Malaysian federation, 201
Managerial matrix, 308, 435, 481-496
Map analysis, 382, 390-406, 421
Marginal relationships, 460
Maritime boundaries *(See* Boundaries, maritime)
Maritime law, 83, 474-476
Maritime power *(See* Sea power)
Marshall Plan, 226
Median line, 155
Mental map, 325, 328, 344-345
Mercantile Imperial System (map), 245
Mercantilism, 209, 244ff
Mesopotamia, 26, 40, 165
Metropolitan growth, 81, 200, 286-292
  neighborhood autonomy, 289-291
  political fragmentation, 58, 159, 200, 210, 288-289
Middle ages, 158, 166, 260
Migration, 439-441, 454
Milieu *(See* Environment)
Minimum circulation, Zone of, 157
Minority groups, 65, 147ff, 210, 291
  (See also Negroes)
Models, 420, 424, 428, 484-496

Molotov plan, 226
Mongol empire, 129
Monroe doctrine, 169
Mont Blanc tunnels, 266
Montezume, empire, 20
Motivation, 305-306, 350
  induced, 305-306
  intrinsic, 305
Movement factor *(See* Circulation)
Mutual knowledge, 198

Nation
  concept, 40-41, 211ff, 275, 343
  friendly, 346
  growth, 211-220
  paranoid, 346
Nation-building, 206ff, 209ff, 212ff, 274ff, 281-285
  long-run problems, 284-285
  short-run strategies, 281-284
Nation state, 202, 207, 211, 217-218, 277
National character, 4, 422, 506
National hero, 209, 273-278, 284ff
National power, 54, 62, 345
National Socialism, 9, 55
National symbols, 212, 217-218
Nationalism, 145, 147, 153, 209, 211, 219
National frontiers, 144
Natural resources, 59, 61-62, 64-65, 156, 157, 160, 433-434, 464-496, 503
  allocations, 420, 433-434, 464-496
  functional, 434
  spatial, 434
  structural, 433-434
Naziism (National Socialism), 9, 55
Negroes, 21ff, 278, 290ff, 357-359, 384-406
Neighborhood autonomy, 289-291
Neo-colonialism, 282
New states, 75, 198, 209ff, 273-285
Newspaper wards, 372
Nodality, 2-3, 11, 71, 73-77, 86-87, 157, 208, 460
Noncontiguity, 202, 209, 224-225
  (See also Contiguity)
Nonevents, 303

Subject Index

Nordic Association, 208
Normal vote, 314-315
Normans, 27, 107ff
North Atlantic Treaty Organization (NATO), 47, 57, 224
North Atlantic Union, 35
Noyau, 81, 309-310, 319-322

Oceanic sovereignty, 156-157
Ocean Trade-Dependent group, 181ff
Ocean Trade-Oriented group, 181ff
Organic state, 1, 5, 6-9, 12, 195ff
Ottoman Empire, 202, 243
Outer crescent (map), 167

Pan-Africanism, 210, 278-280
Pan American Highway, 224
Panregions (Haushofer), 2
Pan-slavism, 21
Papal states, 38
Participation
  spatial parameters, 318, 420
  (See also Elections, turnout)
Partition, 12, 36, 91-93, 141, 156-157, 202, 202-204, 262, 265, 269
  definition, 202
Patterns
  diffuse, 460
  digital, 460
  nodal, 2-3, 11, 71, 73-77, 86-87, 157, 208, 460
Perception, 81-82, 305, 311-312, 328-350, 419-420, 489-490
  definition, 305
  spatial, 250-255, 311-312, 318, 328-350
Persian empire, 18ff
Phoenicans, 25ff
Pioneer areas, 454-455
Pivot area (Mackinder), 9, 83, 88, 168ff
Plebiscites (See Elections, plebiscites)
Polish corridor, 36, 60, 147ff, 225
Political access, 287ff
Political area, 29-30
Political community, 62, 196ff, 254
Political fragmentation, 4-5, 156, 159, 184ff, 204, 209, 288-289

Political Geography
  behavior, xii, 12, 60, 70, 210, 299-422
  bibliographic aids, 501-509
  definition, xi-xii, 33, 58, 195
  earmarks, 17, 29-33
  environment, 423-500
  evolutionary, 87
  functional approach, 34-49, 70, 196
  heritage, xii, 1-68 (esp. 1-12), 195ff
  historical approach, 10-11, 59-60
  interdisciplinary nature of, ix, 62-63, 64, 70, 501ff
  morphological approach, 10-11
  process, xii, 57-58, 70, 195-298 (esp. 195-210)
  structure, xii, 12, 69-193 (esp. 69-88), 195
  textbooks, 146
Political hierarchy (See Hierarchy)
Political identification, 196
Political influence, 458
Political instability, 434, 499-500
Political integration (See Integration)
Political security, 429-431, 450-451
Political system, 5, 57, 198, 202, 208, 427-428, 481-496
  closed, 427-428
  maintenance, 428
  open, 427-428
  persistence, 428
  (See also Systems analysis)
Political unification, 200, 208, 221-230
  take-off stage, 228-229
  termination state, 208, 222, 229-230
Population, 2, 13-15, 37, 73, 498
Portuguese empire, 179
Possibilism, 427, 500
Power, 167, 226-227, 342
  classification, 226-227
  natural seats of (map), 167
Power potential, 145, 171, 175
Power structure, 145, 366-367
Prediction, 433
Pressure groups, 462-463
Pre-unification state, 221, 222-226

Primogeniture, 150 (See also Land tenure)
Privacy and space, 422
Probabilism, environmental (See Environmental probabilism)
Proportional representation (See Elections, systems)
Proxemics, 311
Proximity hypothesis, 197
Psychology, topological, 325
Public domain, 136-137
Public interest, 432, 500
Pyrrhic Wars, 23

Quaglio-Bidault agreement, 267
Quasi-exclave, 153

Raison d'être, 379-380, 449
  (See also State-idea)
Range of choice (See Decisions)
Rationality, 307, 350, 422, 484
  bounded, 307
  intended, 307
Redistribution, 430
Redistricting, 62, 405-406
  (See also Gerrymandering)
Reformation, 108, 120
Regionalism, 145, 158, 178-186, 277
  in city politics, 369-375
  in United Nations voting, 407-418
Regions, geopolitical, 84-85, 88, 178-186
Regions, geostrategic, 84-85, 88, 178-186
  map, 180
Relative Acceptance index, 237ff
Relative location, 72-73
Research aids, 501-509
Resource access, 287-288
Revolution
  American Revolution, 134, 254
  Revolutionary War, 76-77, 85
  Revolutionary rural base areas, 76-77
Rhode Island-Massachusetts boundary, 60, 157-158
Rimland (Spykman), 2, 84ff, 88, 170-178 (esp. 174)
Rimland dictum, 176
Risk, 307-308, 375, 452

Subject Index

Risk cartograms, 308
Roman Empire, 3, 19ff, 53, 87, 126, 170
Roman law, 125
Roper Public Opinion Research Center, 509
Roya-Bévéra system, 259ff
Royal Geographical Society, 83, 150
Russian boundary, 17, 503
Russian empire, 168ff, 170, 175
Russo-Persian treaties, 17

Salience, 199, 233ff
Sardinian Kingdom, 262ff
Satisficing *(See* Behavior, satisficing)
Saxon-Bohemian border, 25
Sea boundaries *(See* Boundaries, maritime)
Sea power, 83ff, 168ff, 174ff, 178ff
Security, political, 429–431, 450–451
Segregation, 429
Seigneural system, 456
Self-interest, concept of, 212, 215–217
Semites, 26, 166
Sense of efficacy, 308
Sensitization, 305
Shatterbelts, 84, 85, 184–185
Silk-stocking wards, 372
Simulation, 420
Single-party system, 209ff, 276ff, 283ff
Sino-Soviet alliance, 183
Slavs, 168
Social communication, 198ff, 208, 219
Social complementarity, 62
Sovereignty, 81, 127, 149, 156ff, 198
  oceanic, 156–157
  transfer, 81, 196, 201, 204–206, 209, 258–280, 420
Soviet heartland, 183ff
Space, 310, 323–325
  collective, 325
  individual, 325
  personal, 324
  sociofugal, 310
  sociopetal, 310
Space-polity, 311–312, 334
Spanish empire, 179
Spatial allocation, 434, 464–496

Spatial linkages, 434–435, 599
Spatial perception, 250–255, 311–312, 318, 328–350
State-idea, 11–12, 39–40, 42–43, 50ff, 74, 199, 201, 379
  (See also Raison d'être)
States
  claimant, 148ff
  economic relations, 45–46
  external relations, 14–15, 26–27, 43–48, 59
  federal *(See* Federalism)
  growth, 12
  (See also Growth and development)
  hydraulic, 442–449
  ideal, 2–3, 13–16
  internal structure, 15–16, 35–43
  laws of spatial growth, 6–9, 17–28, 195, 206
  life-cycles, 3, 12, 195, 206, 424
  political relations, 47–48
  sedentary and nomadic, 3–4
  strategic relations, 48
  successor, 201
  territorial relations, 43–45
  unitary, 86
  upstream, 156
Statistics *(See* Data archives)
Stress *(See* Decision, stress; Environmental stress)
Structural allocation, 433–434
Structural-functional analysis, 69–71
Surge and decline *(See* Election turnout)
Survey research, 419
Symbolization, 74, 198, 430
System maintenance, 428
System persistence, 428
Systems analysis, 231ff, 419, 481–496
  (See also Political system)

Take-off stage *(See* Political unification, take-off stage)
Telephone traffic (long distance), 158–159, 208ff, 235ff
Television in border regions, 72
Termination state *(See* Political unification, termination state)
Territorial claims, 146

Territorial cluster, 324–327
Territorial complex, 324–327
Territorial sea, 155ff
Territorial unit, 324–327
Territoriality *(See* Behavior, territorial; Animal territoriality)
Territory, 309–311, 323–327, 344, 508
  aggression, 310
  functions, 309
  size and shape, 2, 14, 36, 72, 89–93, 224–225, 345
Theory, 302–303
Time, 304–305
  phenomenal, 304–305
  physical, 304
Topological psychology, 325
Trade-Dependent Maritime World, 84, 85, 179ff
Transaction flow, 198ff, 208ff, 231–242
Transfer of sovereignty *(See* Sovereignty)
Trans-Siberian Railway, 168
Truman doctrine, 53

Uncertainty *(See* Decision, uncertainty)
Unification *(See* Political unification)
Unified field theory, 11–12, 50–56, 58, 70
  (See also Field theory)
United Nations, 48, 57ff, 65, 85, 341, 407–418
United States constitution, 71
United States Department of State, 60, 145
United States-Mexican boundary, 143
Upstream-downstream conflicts *(See* Spatial linkages; Area repercussion)
Upstream state, 156
Urban planning and politics, 375
Urban renewal, 432–433
Utrecht, Treaty of, 262

Values, 304–305, 420, 428, 432–433
  toward national space, 420
Versailles Peace Treaty, 142, 176
Viet Minh, 183
Völkerwanderung, 440–441
Volstead Act, 51–52
Voting *(See* Behavior, voting)

Watershed boundary, 153
Weather modification, 499
Western community, 409, 412–418
Western European Federation, 35

Western hemisphere, 84–85
Whiskey rebellion, 120
World island, 83ff, 176

Yale political data program, 508

Yugoslav-Hungarian boundary, 153

Zone of minimum circulation, 157
Zulu, 23ff